W9-CTW-421

Contemporary Literary Criticism

Guide to Gale Literary Criticism Series

For criticism on	You need these Gale series
Authors now living or who died after December 31, 1959	*CONTEMPORARY LITERARY CRITICISM (CLC)*
Authors who died between 1900 and 1959	*TWENTIETH-CENTURY LITERARY CRITICISM (TCLC)*
Authors who died between 1800 and 1899	*NINETEENTH-CENTURY LITERATURE CRITICISM (NCLC)*
Authors who died between 1400 and 1799	*LITERATURE CRITICISM FROM 1400 TO 1800 (LC)* *SHAKESPEAREAN CRITICISM (SC)*
Authors who died before 1400	*CLASSICAL AND MEDIEVAL LITERATURE CRITICISM (CMLC)*
Authors of books for children and young adults	*CHILDREN'S LITERATURE REVIEW (CLR)*
Black writers of the past two hundred years	*BLACK LITERATURE CRITICISM (BLC)*
Short story writers	*SHORT STORY CRITICISM (SSC)*
Poets	*POETRY CRITICISM (PC)*
Dramatists	*DRAMA CRITICISM (DC)*
Major authors from the Renaissance to the present	*WORLD LITERATURE CRITICISM, 1500 TO THE PRESENT (WLC)*

For criticism on visual artists since 1850, see

MODERN ARTS CRITICISM (MAC)

ISSN 0091-3421

R

Volume 78

Contemporary Literary Criticism

Excerpts from Criticism of the Works
of Today's Novelists, Poets, Playwrights,
Short Story Writers, Scriptwriters, and
Other Creative Writers

James P. Draper
EDITOR

Jennifer Brostrom
Jeffery Chapman
Jennifer Gariepy
Christopher Giroux
Drew Kalasky
Thomas Ligotti
Kyung-Sun Lim
Brigham Narins
Sean René Pollock
Janet Witalec
ASSOCIATE EDITORS

 *Gale Research Inc.* • *DETROIT* • *WASHINGTON, D.C.* • *LONDON*

Ref
PN
771
C 59
V. 78

Library of Congress Catalog Card Number 76-38938
ISBN 0-8103-4986-8
ISSN 0091-3421

Printed in the United States of America
Published simultaneously in the United Kingdom
by Gale Research International Limited
(An affiliated company of Gale Research Inc.)
10 9 8 7 6 5 4 3 2 1

I(T)P™

The trademark **ITP** is used under license.

Contents

Preface vii

Acknowledgments xi

Preface

A Comprehensive Information Source
on Contemporary Literature

Named "one of the twenty-five most distinguished reference titles published during the past twenty-five years" by *Reference Quarterly*, the *Contemporary Literary Criticism (CLC)* series provides readers with critical commentary and general information on more than 2,000 authors now living or who died after December 31, 1959. Previous to the publication of the first volume of *CLC* in 1973, there was no ongoing digest monitoring scholarly and popular sources of critical opinion and explication of modern literature. *CLC*, therefore, has fulfilled an essential need, particularly since the complexity and variety of contemporary literature makes the function of criticism especially important to today's reader.

Scope of the Series

CLC presents significant passages from published criticism of works by creative writers. Since many of the authors covered by *CLC* inspire continual critical commentary, writers are often represented in more than one volume. There is, of course, no duplication of reprinted criticism.

Authors are selected for inclusion for a variety of reasons, among them the publication or dramatic production of a critically acclaimed new work, the reception of a major literary award, revival of interest in past writings, or the adaptation of a literary work to film or television.

Attention is also given to several other groups of writers—authors of considerable public interest—about whose work criticism is often difficult to locate. These include mystery and science fiction writers, literary and social critics, foreign writers, and authors who represent particular ethnic groups within the United States.

Format of the Book

Each *CLC* volume contains about 500 individual excerpts taken from hundreds of book review periodicals, general magazines, scholarly journals, monographs, and books. Entries include critical evaluations spanning from the beginning of an author's career to the most current commentary. Interviews, feature articles, and other published writings that offer insight into the author's works are also presented. Students, teachers, librarians, and researchers will find that the generous excerpts and supplementary material in *CLC* provide them with vital information required to write a term paper, analyze a poem, or lead a book discussion group. In addition, complete bibliographical citations note the original source and all of the information necessary for a term paper footnote or bibliography.

Features

A *CLC* author entry consists of the following elements:

- The **Author Heading** cites the author's name in the form under which the author has most commonly published, followed by birth date, and death date when applicable. Uncertainty as to a birth or death date is indicated by a question mark.

- A **Portrait** of the author is included when available.

- A brief **Biographical and Critical Introduction** to the author and his or her work precedes the excerpted criticism. The first line of the introduction provides the author's full name, pseudonyms (if applicable), nationality, and a listing of genres in which the author has written. Previous volumes of *CLC* in which the author has been featured are also listed in the introduction.

- A list of **Principal Works** notes the most important works by the author.

- The **Excerpted Criticism** represents various kinds of critical writing, ranging in form from the brief review to the scholarly exegesis. Essays are selected by the editors to reflect the spectrum of opinion about a specific work or about an author's literary career in general. The excerpts are presented chronologically, adding a useful perspective to the entry. All titles by the author featured in the entry are printed in boldface type, which enables the reader to easily identify the works being discussed. Publication information (such as publisher names and book prices) and parenthetical numerical references (such as footnotes or page and line references to specific editions of a work) have been deleted at the editor's discretion to provide smoother reading of the text.

- Critical essays are prefaced by **Explanatory Notes** as an additional aid to readers. These notes may provide several types of valuable information, including: the reputation of the critic, the importance of the work of criticism, the commentator's approach to the author's work, the purpose of the criticism, and changes in critical trends regarding the author.

- A complete **Bibliographical Citation** designed to help the user find the original essay or book follows each excerpt.

- A concise **Further Reading** section appears at the end of entries on authors for whom a significant amount of criticism exists in addition to the pieces reprinted in *CLC*. Cross-references to other useful sources published by Gale Research in which the author has appeared are also included: *Children's Literature Review, Contemporary Authors, Something about the Author, Dictionary of Literary Biography, Drama Criticism, Poetry Criticism, Short Story Criticism, Contemporary Authors Autobiography Series,* and *Something about the Author Autobiography Series*.

Other Features

CLC also includes the following features:

- An **Acknowledgments** section lists the copyright holders who have granted permission to reprint material in this volume of *CLC*. It does not, however, list every book or periodical reprinted or consulted during the preparation of the volume.

- A **Cumulative Author Index** lists all the authors who have appeared in the various literary criticism series published by Gale Research, with cross-references to Gale's biographical and autobiographical series. A full listing of the series referenced there appears on the first page of the indexes of this volume. Readers will welcome this cumulated author index as a useful tool for locating an author within the various series. The index, which lists birth and death dates when available, will be particularly valuable for those authors who are identified with a certain period but whose death dates cause them to be placed in another, or for those authors whose careers span two periods. For example, Ernest Hemingway is found in *CLC*, yet a writer often associated with him, F. Scott Fitzgerald, is found in *Twentieth-Century Literary Criticism.*

- A **Cumulative Nationality Index** alphabetically lists all authors featured in *CLC* by nationality, followed by numbers corresponding to the volumes in which the authors appear.

- A **Title Index** alphabetically lists all titles reviewed in the current volume of *CLC*. Listings are followed by the author's name and the corresponding page numbers where the titles are discussed. English translations of foreign titles and variations of titles are cross-referenced to the title under which a work was originally published. Titles of novels, novellas, dramas, films, record albums, and poetry, short story, and essay collections are printed in italics, while all individual poems, short stories, essays, and songs are printed in roman type within quotation marks; when published separately (e.g., T. S. Eliot's poem *The Waste Land*), the titles of long poems are printed in italics.

- In response to numerous suggestions from librarians, Gale has also produced a **Special Paperbound Edition** of the *CLC* title index. This annual cumulation, which alphabetically lists all titles reviewed in the series, is available to all customers and is published with the first volume of *CLC* issued in each calendar year. Additional copies of the index are available upon request. Librarians and patrons will welcome this separate index: it saves shelf space, is easy to use, and is recyclable upon receipt of the following year's cumulation.

Citing *Contemporary Literary Criticism*

When writing papers, students who quote directly from any volume in the Literary Criticism Series may use the following general forms to footnote reprinted criticism. The first example pertains to material drawn from periodicals, the second to material reprinted in books:

[1]Anne Tyler, "Manic Monologue," *The New Republic* 200 (April 17, 1989), 44-6; excerpted and reprinted in *Contemporary Literary Criticism,* Vol. 58, ed. Roger Matuz (Detroit: Gale Research Inc., 1990), p. 325.

[2]Patrick Reilly, *The Literature of Guilt: From 'Gulliver' to Golding* (University of Iowa Press, 1988); excerpted and reprinted in *Contemporary Literary Criticism,* Vol. 58, ed. Roger Matuz (Detroit: Gale Research Inc., 1990), pp. 206-12.

Suggestions Are Welcome

The editor hopes that readers will find *CLC* a useful reference tool and welcomes comments about the work. Send comments and suggestions to: Editor, *Contemporary Literary Criticism,* Gale Research Inc., Penobscot Building, Detroit, MI 48226-4094.

Acknowledgments

The editors wish to thank the copyright holders of the excerpted criticism included in this volume, the permissions managers of many book and magazine publishing companies for assisting us in securing reprint rights, and Anthony Bogucki for assistance with copyright research. We are also grateful to the staffs of the Detroit Public Library, the Library of Congress, the University of Detroit Library, Wayne State University Purdy/Kresge Library Complex, and the University of Michigan Libraries for making their resources available to us. Following is a list of the copyright holders who have granted us permission to reprint material in this volume of *CLC*. Every effort has been made to trace copyright, but if omissions have been made, please let us know.

COPYRIGHTED EXCERPTS IN *CLC*, VOLUME 78, WERE REPRINTED FROM THE FOLLOWING PERIODICALS:

The Advocate, April 7, 1992 for an interview with Dorothy Allison by Bo Huston. Reprinted by permission of Dorothy Allison and the Literary Estate of Bo Huston.—*The American Poetry Review,* v. 12, November-December, 1983 for "The Contradictions of Frank O'Hara" by James Breslin; v. 19, July-August, 1990 for "Comment: The Feel of a Century" by Marianne Boruch. Copyright © 1983, 1990 by World Poetry, Inc. Both reprinted by permission of the respective authors.—*The Antigonish Review,* n. 47, Autumn, 1981 for "Roch Carrier's Bicycle" by Alexandre L. Amprimoz. Copyright 1981 by the author. Reprinted by permission of the publisher and the author.—*Book World—The Washington Post,* October 1, 1989; October 6, 1991, May 3, 1992. © 1989, 1991, 1992, *The Washington Post.* All reprinted with permission of the publisher.—*Booklist,* v. 86, August, 1990. Copyright © 1990 by The American Library Association.—*Books in Canada,* v. 15, May, 1986./ v. 8, November, 1979 for "Budding Breasts, Brooding Beasts" by Wayne Grady; v. 11, February, 1982 for "Je me souviens" by Wayne Grady; v. XX, November, 1991 for "Innocence and Experience" by Wayne Grady; v. XXI, April, 1992 for "A Celebration of Difference" by Janice Kulyk Keefer. All reprinted by permission of the respective authors.—*boundary 2,* vs. VI & VII, Spring & Fall, 1978. Copyright © *boundary 2,* 1978. Reprinted by permission of the publisher.—*The Canadian Forum,* v. LXI, February, 1982./ v. L. September, 1970 for "La Guerre, Yes Sir!" by Mark Levene; v. IV, July, 1971 for "Floralie, Where Are You?" by Mark Levene; v. LIV, May-June, 1974 for "They Won't Demolish Me" by Barbara Godard; v. LIX, September, 1979 for "Lunar Gems" by Michael Benazon; v. LIX, March, 1980 for "Petites, Tragedies, pour Adultes" by Jon Kertzer; v. LXVII, December, 1987 for "Carrier's Road" by Jeannette Urbas. All reprinted by permission of the respective authors.—*Canadian Literature,* n. 50, Autumn, 1971 for "Uses of the Grotesque" by Ronald Sutherland; n. 80, Spring, 1979 for "Carrier's Fiction" by David J. Bond; n. 104, Spring, 1985 for "Reading Carrier's 'The Nun Who Returned to Ireland'" by Michael Darling; n. 109, Summer, 1986 for "Silence into Sound: The Riddle of Concentric Worlds in 'Obasan'" by Erika Gottlieb; ns. 122-23, Autumn-Winter, 1989 for "Roads & Arteries" by John Lennox; n. 127, Winter, 1990 for "Broken Generations in 'Obasan'" by Mason Harris. All reprinted by permission of the respective authors.—*Chicago Tribune—Books,* September 9, 1990 for "Failure to Connect" by Diane Cole. © copyright 1990, Chicago Tribune Company. All rights reserved. Reprinted by permission of the author.—*College English,* v. 26, November, 1964 for "Arthur Miller's 'The Crucible'" by Henry Popkin. Copyright © 1964, renewed 1992 by the National Council of Teachers of English. Renewed 1992. Reprinted by permission of the publisher and the author.—*Commentary,* v. 24, July, 1957 for "Fantasist of the Ordinary" by Alfred Kazin. Copyright © 1957 by the American Jewish Committee. Renewed 1985. All rights reserved. Reprinted by permission of the publisher and the author.—*Concerning Poetry,* v. 16, Spring, 1983. Copyright © 1983, Bureau for Faculty Research, Western Washington University. Reprinted by permission of the publisher.—*Contemporary Literature,* v. XXIII, Winter 1982; v. XXXII, Summer, 1991. © 1982, 1991 by the Regents of the University of Wisconsin System. Reprinted by permission of The University of Wisconsin Press.—*Faith and Reason,* v. VII, Winter, 1981. © Christendon Educational Corporation 1981. Reprinted by permission of the publisher.—*Fantasy Review,* v. 8, March, 1985. Copyright © 1985 by Carol Sherr Hand./ v. 10, January-February, 1987 for "The Suspense Novel as Oriental Food" by Bill Collins. Copyright © 1987 by the author. Reprinted by permission of the author.—*The French Review,* v.

Dorothy Allison

1949-

American novelist, short story writer, poet, and essayist.

This entry provides an overview of Allison's career through 1993.

INTRODUCTION

Allison is best known for *Bastard Out of Carolina,* a novel about a young girl growing up in rural South Carolina during the 1960s. As with her other works, particularly *The Women Who Hate Me* and *Trash, Bastard Out of Carolina* has garnered widespread praise for its realism, vivid characterization, and laconic prose.

Allison was born in Greenville County, South Carolina. A self-labeled "lesbian-feminist" and incest survivor, Allison incorporates events from her life into her work. In 1983 she published a collection of poems, *The Women Who Hate Me,* which was well-received, despite objections to its graphic depictions of lesbian sex. *Trash,* Allison's next work, comprises fourteen interrelated short stories that describe a woman's attempts to escape painful childhood memories. In "River of Names," for example, the narrator recalls episodes of sexual abuse and domestic violence as well as suicides of family members. A few of the stories from this collection, including an expanded "River of Names," appear in the novel *Bastard Out of Carolina.*

Bastard Out of Carolina centers on Ruth Anne Boatwright, nicknamed Bone by her family. She grows up surrounded by a close-knit extended family, among them Granny, the rough-talking family matriarch; Aunt Raylene, a strong and independent lesbian; and Uncles Earle, Beau, and Nevil, hard-drinking, violent men whom Bone adores. Central to the novel is Bone's relationship with her mother Anney and stepfather Daddy Glen. When Bone first meets Daddy Glen, he is gentle and loving towards her and her sister Reese. After he marries Anney, however, he becomes violent and begins sexually molesting Bone. Scared and ashamed to tell her mother, Bone endures Daddy Glen's cruel beatings and repeated rapes for the next five years. When Bone is thirteen years old, Anney discovers her husband raping Bone and becomes enraged. Moved by Daddy Glen's pleas of forgiveness, however, Anney decides to remain with him, leaving Bone in the care of Aunt Raylene.

Critics have lauded *Bastard Out of Carolina* for its realistic characters and sensitive depiction of incest and family violence. Allison's descriptions of Bone's sexual abuse and feelings of betrayal have garnered the most attention. Vince Aletti observed: "Allison casts a savage, unblinking eye, . . . describing the terrible knot of violence and eroticism without ever slipping into soft-core voyeurism or shocked prudery. . . . 'I made my life, the same way it

looks like you're gonna make yours—out of pride and stubbornness and too much anger,' Aunt Raylene tells Bone. It's that volatile combination that saves Bone and gives *Bastard* an extraordinary pent-up power."

PRINCIPAL WORKS

The Women Who Hate Me (poetry) 1983; also published as *The Women Who Hate Me: Poetry, 1980-1990* [revised edition], 1991
Trash (short stories) 1988
Bastard Out of Carolina (novel) 1992
Skin (essays) 1993

CRITICISM

Kirkus Reviews　(review date 15 October 1988)

[*In the following review, the critic describes* Trash *as "uneven, sometimes shocking fiction."*]

To quote from the author's preface, [*Trash* is] about a girl who grew up in a white southern milieu of poverty and brutality and "became the one who got away" is "not biography and yet not lies . . . [but] condensed and reinvented experience of a . . . working-class lesbian, addicted to violence, language and hope."

At college, on scholarship, Allison "met the people I had always read about: girls whose fathers loved them—innocently; boys who drove cars they had not stolen." Her strongest stories, including the wrenchingly painful **"River of Names,"** explore the intersection of her two worlds and show a narrator haunted by childhood memories of sudden death, unremitting yet casual violence, and bitter contained rage; she hides much of this past from her lovers, but it emerges in the form of lies, funny southern stories, an inability to love, a resort to wild sex (sometimes graphically described), alcohol and physical fights as distraction and escape. The result is an intimate glimpse into the tormented heart of a survivor. There's almost enough power here to make one want to overlook the weaknesses: most of the stories go on too long; the author, who has previously published poetry, sometimes chooses moments and ideas too small to satisfy as fiction; the slice-of-life stories that provide realistic portrayals of contemporary lesbian-feminist society are workmanlike but not compelling.

Uneven, sometimes shocking fiction, then, from a writer of promise, beginning to claim her history and her voice.

A review of "Trash," in Kirkus Reviews, *Vol. LVI, No. 20, October 15, 1988, p. 1484.*

Publishers Weekly　(review date 18 November 1988)

[*In the review below, the critic briefly assesses* Trash.]

In 14 gritty, intimate stories, Allison's fictional persona exposes with poetic frankness the complexities of being "a cross-eyed working-class lesbian, addicted to violence, language, and hope," rebelling against the Southern "poor white trash" roots that inevitably define her. Bridging the bedrooms, bars and kitchens of its narrator's adult world, and the dirt yards and diners of her '50s South Carolina childhood, this magnetic collection [*Trash*] charts a fascinating woman's struggle for self-realization and acceptance through a sensual, often horrific tapestry of the lives of women to whom she is connected. In the mythically resonant early pieces, the conflicts of her foremothers, like Great-grandmother Shirley, "the meanest woman that ever left Tennessee," embody a grim legacy of drudgery that presages the seeds of her own rage and cavernous hunger, later finely played out through various love affairs. With a keen feel for the languid rhythms of Southern speech, Allison (*The Women Who Hate Me*) masterfully suspends the reader between voyeurism and empathy, breathing life into a vast body of symbolic feminine imagery.

A review of "Trash," in Publishers Weekly, *Vol. 234, No. 21, November 18, 1988, p. 74.*

Allison's ability as a craftswoman of short fiction is exceptional. Rarely have I read such unsparing narrative, dense and gritty with realism, crackling with anger, pulsing with uncompromised sexuality.

**—*Patricia Roth Schwartz, in a review of* Trash *in* Belles Lettres, *Spring 1989.*

Liz Galst　(review date July 1989)

[*In the following excerpt, Galst favorably reviews* Trash, *praising in particular the work's emotional power.*]

Of all the tales of women's survival I've read recently, Dorothy Allison's *Trash* is by far the most riveting. Hers is the kind of fiction that doubles as autobiography, or vice versa. But her work is so honest that it doesn't really matter which genre it falls into. *Trash* is a collection of stories about a poor white Southern woman's decision to confront the violence, poverty and pain of her existence, and in the face of all of it to embrace her class, her culture, her lesbian sexuality. I sometimes found Allison's style clunky, but her stories cut to the core. Don't be misled by the title. This is no pulp romance; it's an analysis of what it means to be expendable in this country, and what it takes to pick yourself off the junk heap.

Get ready for a rough ride. The introduction, **"Preface: Deciding to Live,"** and the first story, **"River of Names,"** laid me out for a week. Allison says in **"Preface"**:

> After my childhood, after all that long terrible struggle to simply survive, to escape my stepfather, uncles, speeding Pontiacs, broken glass and rotten floorboards, or that inevitable death by misadventure that claimed so many of my cousins; after watching so many die around me, I had not imagined that I would ever need to make . . . a choice. I had imagined the hunger for life in me was insatiable, endless, unshakable . . .
>
> Like many others who had gone before me, I began to dream longingly of my own death.
>
> I began to court it.

"River of Names" is a litany, a recitation of the violence that pervaded the lives of the narrator and her flock of cousins. "My cousin, Tommy, eight years old as I was, swung in the sunlight with his face as black as his shoes—the rope around his neck pulled up into the sunlit heights of the barn . . . " "Lucille climbed out the front window of Aunt Raylene's house and jumped. They said she jumped. No one said why." "Almost always, we were raped, my cousins and I. That was some kind of joke, too. *What's a South Carolina virgin? 'At's a ten-year-old can run fast.''*

In that story the narrator is unable to admit her own pain to anyone but herself; but others of Allison's characters learn, finally, to shout theirs out loud. In **"Don't Tell Me You Don't Know,"** the narrator is confronted by her Aunt Alma, her mother's oldest sister, who shows up on her Northern doorstep. As a younger woman, Alma somehow managed to sustain her sister and her niece through the most difficult of times, and it's the narrator's belief in the power of these women that has kept her alive all the succeeding years.

But this belief is also what's kept them apart. As they play pool together in the living room, Alma, acting as proxy for her sister, begins to hound her niece. Why hasn't she had children? After exploding at her aunt as her aunt has exploded at her, the narrator explains at last:

> Some people never do have babies, you know. Some people get raped at eleven by a stepfather their mama half-hates, but can't afford to leave. Some people then have to lie and hide it 'cause it would make so much trouble. So nobody will know, not the law and not the rest of the family. Nobody but the women supposed to be the ones who take care of everything, who know what to do and how to do it, the women who make children who believe in them and trust in them, and sometimes die for it. Some people never go to a doctor and don't find out for ten years that the son of a bitch gave them some goddamned disease.

Through this confrontation she comes to see that even the combined strength of her mother and her aunts was not enough to protect her. Then and only then is she able to reconnect with their powerful, sustaining love.

I was deeply touched by nearly every story in *Trash.* Whether she's writing about family, lovers, or the violence of poverty, Allison's emotions come sailing through her work. That's not always easy for me as a reader. There were times her anger and disdain frightened me; times when her narrator's lost sense of self and all-consuming pain were too much like my own. And times, too, when I thought I might drown in sentimentality. But *Trash,* honest and gripping, is a challenge to readers and writers everywhere. (p. 15)

> *Liz Galst, "The Uses of Adversity," in* The Women's Review of Books, *Vol. VI, Nos. 10 & 11, July, 1989, pp. 14-15.*

Publishers Weekly (review date 22 March 1991)

[*In the excerpt below, the critic offers a mixed review of* The Women Who Hate Me, *briefly touching on Allison's thematic concerns and writing style.*]

[Allison] writes poems that brim with emotion, sometimes focused and tender, but more often confused and enraged. The subject in this expanded edition of her collection of poems [*The Women Who Hate Me*] is Allison's lesbian-ism. Although she mentions the freedoms denied her and her "sisters," the poet ultimately seems to care little for furthering people's acceptance of lesbianism. Indeed, she goes so far as to proclaim: "I do not believe anymore in the natural superiority / of the lesbian." The poet realizes, bitterly, that she has been unable to escape her past. Abused as a child, she seeks dominant lovers who like to play rough: "I have never been able to resist" a woman who "talks mean" and "makes shell-puckered hickey-bite marks." As a child, the poet's family was "despised," her mother called *"no-count, low down, disgusting"* for her affairs with various "uncles." Allison acknowledges that she is her "mama's daughter," with "at least as much lust / in [her] life as pain." The poet's imagery is explicit and jarring but her wordplay unpolished. Except for a couple of sentimental love poems, what takes precedence here is a sense of vengeance against all who "hate" her.

> *A review of "The Women Who Hate Me: Poetry, 1980-1990," in* Publishers Weekly, *Vol. 238, No. 14, March 22, 1991, p. 77.*

Dorothy Allison with Bo Huston (interview date 7 April 1992)

[*In the following excerpt, Allison parallels events in her own life with those described in* Bastard Out of Carolina *and discusses how her experiences have defined her sexual orientation and identity.*]

[*Huston*]: *What is trash?*

[Allison]: That's me. I'm many generations trash. Trash is those people who keep their cars up on blocks and don't work for a living. We're the caricatures of the society—the laundry workers and whores of America. I come from bigoted, violent people; shotguns, beer, and pickup trucks. I was born in Greenville, S. C. The word *poor* doesn't describe it enough. I feel like I came out of a world nobody knows about, that maybe doesn't exist anymore.

You must have rather complex feelings about moving away from that home, escaping and surviving it.

God, yes. It's an amazing knot of shame, pride, and rage. Guilt too. That's the thing I tried to put in [*Bastard Out of Carolina*]. I love my family, but I'm terrified of them. It's a complicated love.

Do you find people get confused about what you're constructing as fiction and what is the truth of your own life?

People assume that fiction's real life—if you do it well. Good storytelling is convincing. Then it gets tricky about how explicit to be about your own experience. Particularly because so much of my story—and the story in my novel—is about incest and poverty.

I'm past 40 now, and it's taken me my entire life to figure out what happened to me as a kid. Because the things that you have to do to survive with some kind of sense of yourself, the emotional maneuverings, really obstruct accurate memory. So I'm not ever going to be convinced about the distinctions between fiction and reality anyway.

In terms of this book, there are a few things that are true

about my life. The first chapter, the story of how I was born and how I was named, is accurate. I was born in a car accident. My mother was unconscious for the first three days of my life, and my aunts named me and took care of me. I was registered a bastard in the state of South Carolina because the aunts didn't get the facts straight with the hospital. So that's how I learned storytelling; this was my aunts and my grandmother's favorite story to tell me. It had passion, excitement, nobility, and all that Southern pathos.

And it is true that I had a painful, difficult relationship with my stepfather, that he was physically violent, and that he raped me as a child. But the book is not autobiography. Rather, it is telling my emotional truth.

What is your relationship with your stepfather like now?

I've tried to maintain a matter-of-fact bluntness about the past. That's healthy for me. I mean, the greatest pain of my life has been that my mother stayed with my stepfather. She left him twice, but she went back.

But she knew he was abusing you?

She knew. My mother tried to control it, to contain it. And I cooperated with him in hiding it from her. When I finally moved away, I refused for years to go back and visit. When my stepfather started acting out violently outside the home, they put him on psychotropic drugs. They pay more attention when you're beating up some man in a parking lot than when you're beating up children at home. So he's been on medication for some time. But still, I can't be near him. Our relationship . . . it's been a lifelong blackmail.

You are very public as a leather S/M lesbian. How is the violent sexual abuse you endured in childhood related to your sexuality today?

I think that most of what everyone says about S/M is a product of their own obsessions and fears. I don't trust any theorists about it. I think sex is individual. For me, sexual power is about struggle and resistance. My sexual icons tend to be martyrs—people who grit their teeth and struggle to the end, you know? Like Joan of Arc. When I was in my 20s, I tried to renounce sex and be good, because it seemed to me that my sexuality was inherently sick and twisted, evil. The very things I needed in order to come were so horrifying to me, connected to the brutality of my childhood.

Then one day I just decided this is fucked. I thought, *I am not getting what I want. I am miserable. I am working myself to death. I'm sleeping with people who treat me terrible. What the fuck am I afraid of?* So I just threw up my hands and said, "OK, I *am* that evil person. I *am* that sick, twisted person they talk about, and I'm going to find out what that means." I discovered I loved bondage and started to make an effort to be healthy in my own mind about it.

I felt like a spy. During the daytime I was a nice, clean lesbian-feminist, living in a collective; at night I was a subterranean slut. That was the only way I could survive. This was 1975 or so, and nobody even used the term *S/M*. I was

dating older butch women who had no problem at all with the fact that I wanted to be tied down and fucked.

Did you feel conflicted: ideology versus desire?

For me, sex and bondage is safe—and powerful. But there was a lot of sexual ignorance among the lesbian-feminists [of the time]. And there was still a prejudice against sluts. I mean, nonmonogamy was officially part of the theory, but if you carried it to the extent of *enjoying* it . . .

Listen, I was into anonymous sex. I did not want a lover. I didn't want all the lesbian buy-a-house shit. I just wanted to fuck around. I believed that the best way to get to know a woman was to go to bed with her. The second best way was to take her by the throat and see what she did. So pretty much everywhere I've lived I've had a real bad reputation. But it has gotten me a lot of interesting dates.

Do you sense an expectation, based upon your book, that you will be some kind of spokesperson about incest or child abuse or lesbian sexuality?

Sexual honesty is an ethic in my life. But sexual revelation isn't necessarily important for other people. And I'll tell you right now, it's pretty damn tiresome having to explain what you do in bed all the time. The thing that makes me angry is the assumption that queers know more about sex than anybody else. We're supposed to be sexual experts just because we fuck around and are honest about it.

Well, as a pervert, I get that doubled. I get this constant labeling that because I'm open about being a pervert, I must have a secret knowledge about human sexuality. But all I really know is my own stuff. I don't have any theory of how incest shapes human life or a theory about sexuality. And my life's work is not sexual research. Personally, I need to know myself, *that's* life's work, figuring myself out. But I can't explain anybody else's life.

There has been a lot of excitement about **Bastard Out of Carolina.** *Was receiving such a large advance a source of pressure for you?*

It scared the living piss out of me. When the book was sold, it was only half finished. Basically, I had been telling this story, in short stories, for a long time. I wanted to write a book about a girl in a working-class environment who loves her family and is smart and powerful. Not the stereotypical damaged-victim kid. I wanted a strong, fascinating kid. And I wanted to be honest about what happens when that girl is subject to physical and sexual abuse.

I hate victim portraits. And I hate the pornography of victimization. Half of the incest books or family-violence books sell on sexual voyeurism. That's what I was afraid of when I got that much money—that they would try to push me to make it more sexy. It's very hard not to titillate when you're working with this kind of material, because American culture is consumed with it. That's one strength of queer literature, even when it's not successful: We're acknowledging sexuality, exploring it—not mystifying it. Let's face it, most of the published lesbian erotic literature is neither erotic nor good writing.

You've had a problematic alliance with the women's movement. Why?

In New York I was one of the organizers of the Lesbian Sex Mafia, which was specifically for perverse women. I was fascinated with anyone who had the courage to think of herself as perverse. I was part of quite a few groups— basically consciousness-raising groups for sluts. We'd get together and talk about dirty books, fantasies, fears. It was self-discovery. Also, I got a lot of good trade.

But that meant that I became visible and to some extent a target. The antiporn people saw our groups as collaborators with the pornographic empire. In 1982 I was presenting a paper at Barnard College and got picketed; they said I was an enemy of the people. The worst accusation, though, was that I was guilty of child sexual abuse because of the writing I was doing. That horrified me. Always there is this terror incest survivors have: that by telling your experience, you will betray or hurt someone else. That [feeling] is deep.

Your lover of the past four years, Alix Layman, is pregnant. What's that going to mean to your work and relationship?

Well, straight people have been doing it forever. They manage, so I figure why the hell not! (pp. 70-2)

> *Dorothy Allison and Bo Huston, in an interview in* The Advocate, *April 7, 1992, pp. 70-2.*

A lot of [*Bastard Out of Carolina*] is based on real experience, but not the entire thing. The characters are modeled on members of my family and on stories I heard when I was growing up. But I made her, Bone, a stronger child than I was, and—more important—I gave her a way out. If the book had been autobiographical, it would have been a lot meaner.

—Dorothy Allison, in an interview with Lynn Karpen in The New York Times Book Review, 5 July 1992.

Jean Hanff Korelitz   (review date 3 May 1992)

[*In the review below, Korelitz offers a mixed review of* Bastard Out of Carolina.]

Dorothy Allison, the winner of two Lambda Literary Awards for her short story collection, *Trash,* sets her first novel, *Bastard out of Carolina,* in Greenville, S. C., "the most beautiful place in the world." The bastard in question is Ruth Ann Boatwright, whose birth certificate must, by state decree and despite the determined campaigning of her mother Anney, bear the stamp "illegitimate." Ruth Ann, known as "Bone," is an observant and keen narrator, in love with her landscape no less than with the trouble and mess and wisdom of her wide family. Still, it is to the women in her family, particularly her many aunts, that Bone is drawn: "I liked being one of the women with my

aunts, liked feeling a part of something nasty and strong and separate from my big rough boy-cousins and the whole world of spitting, growling, overbearing males."

But Bone's circle of women must alter to admit the man her mother marries. Daddy-Glen is the ne'er-do-well son of a wealthy family who takes out his anger not on the wife he adores but on Bone, whom he alternately molests and beats. Throughout her childhood, she scrambles for self-respect where she can find it, even as Anney returns to Daddy-Glen over and over again.

Bone's relationship with her stepfather forms the core of the novel, but *Bastard out of Carolina* has a tendency to bog down in its own heat, speech and atmosphere. Allison has a superb ear for the specific dialogue of her characters, and Bone is a spunky and memorable heroine, but the book seems more often to meander than to move, lending its conclusion an air of inconclusiveness. Allison, abundantly gifted, will certainly go on to write better novels, and *Bastard out of Carolina* will just as certainly alert readers to her promise.

> *Jean Hanff Korelitz, in a review of "Bastard Out of Carolina," in* Book World—The Washington Post, *May 3, 1992, p. 11.*

Vince Aletti   (review date June 1992)

[*In the following summary of* Bastard out of Carolina, *Aletti praises Allison's clear and concise prose.*]

The bound galleys of Dorothy Allison's debut novel came with a two-page author's letter that begins like this: "There are many books a writer can choose to write, only one or two a writer has to write. *Bastard out of Carolina* is the book I had to write. It is not a lesbian coming-of-age story, not a charming portrait of growing up poor in the South of the fifties and sixties. Rather it is a frankly harrowing account of family violence and incest."

But forget you ever read that. The Dorothy Allison who wrote that letter—peppered with stiff, stumbling phrases like "the possibilities inherent in our chosen families"—is simply not the same woman who wrote *Bastard out of Carolina.* Neither Allison is exactly an elegant stylist, but the novelist is a hell of a writer—tough and loose, clear and passionate, incapable, certainly, of such awkward book-jacket jargon. And *Bastard* is far from artless: Allison's construction, especially her balance of light and dark material, is deft, often witty; there's a no-nonsense assurance here that never once suggests first-novel bravado. Trimming the book of writerly fat and burning off all excess description, Allison's left not with fashionable minimalism but with the sinewy, measured drawl of a Southern storyteller.

Told from the point of view of Ruth Anne Boatwright, a scrappy, illegitimate preteen in Greenville County, South Carolina, *Bastard out of Carolina* is about a dazzling constellation of extended family with Ruth Anne's troubled household spinning out of control at its core. The Boatwright clan—a snuff-spitting Granny, three rowdy uncles, four independent aunts, countless cousins—both toughens

There are many books a writer can choose to write, only one or two a writer has to write. *Bastard out of Carolina* is the book I had to write. It is not a lesbian coming-of-age story, not a charming portrait of growing up poor in the South of the fifties and sixties. Rather it is a frankly harrowing account of family violence and incest.

—Dorothy Allison

and protects Ruth Anne, whom they all call Bone (because baby Ruth, said her uncle Earle, was "no bigger than a knucklebone"). Their voices act like a down-home Greek chorus, and their stories, repeated or witnessed by Bone, buffer both narrator and reader against the sudden, unpredictable brutality that erupts within her small family.

Bone's mother Anney has married a man who is crazy in love but ominously opaque. When his first (and only) child with Anney dies at birth, he begins, in Uncle Nevil's words, to "turn like whiskey in a bad barrel." Daddy Glen, as Bone calls her stepfather, doesn't wait for disappointment to set him off, however; it's as if he anticipates disaster, embraces defeat, and sets out to poison his little world. His assaults on Bone begin in the hospital parking lot the night Anney goes into labor, in the front seat of the family car. Bone's description has a painful, understated clarity:

> Glen put his hand on my neck, and the stars seemed to wink at me. I wasn't used to him touching me, so I hugged my blanket and held still. He slid out from behind the steering wheel a little and pulled me up on his lap. He started humming to the music, shifting me a little on his thighs. . . . He pushed my skirt to the side and slid his left hand down between my legs, up against my cotton panties. He began to rock me then, between his stomach and his wrist, his fingers fumbling at his britches.

The attacks that follow are more vicious—disciplinary beatings that boil over into hugs and fumblings that Bone, at 10, can't find words for: "It wasn't sex, not like a man and woman pushing their naked bodies into each other, but then, it was something like sex, something powerful and frightening that he wanted badly and I did not understand at all." Though echoes of these scenes reverberate in Bone's masturbatory fantasies, they're tangled up with shame and internalized contempt. "I was evil. Of course I was. I admitted it to myself, locked my fingers into fists, and shut my eyes to everything I did not understand."

Allison casts a savage, unblinking eye on these moments, describing the terrible knot of violence and eroticism without ever slipping into soft-core voyeurism or shocked prudery. She makes it clear that Daddy Glen's assaults are only intimate manifestations of the casual violence that

flares up all around. And because she embeds them so deeply within Bone's experience of her wider family—especially her vivid, flinty aunts—we understand exactly how the battered girl manages to survive.

Allison's already used some of this material in her short-story collection, *Trash* (1988), and she's been remarkably frank about its intensely personal nature. The writer grew up in Greenville, South Carolina, in the heart of a large, poor, haphazardly supportive family and left, she writes in *Trash*'s preface, to "escape my stepfather, uncles, speeding Pontiacs, broken glass and rotten floorboards, or that inevitable death by misadventure that claimed so many of my cousins."

But if *Bastard out of Carolina* is rooted in autobiography, it never takes on the obsessive tone of a confessional or the crusading fervor of an exposé. Allison has turned the rage she describes so brilliantly—"I was boiling inside. I was cooking away"—into a compressed, exacting language that need never raise its voice to grab our attention. "I made my life, the same way it looks like you're gonna make yours—out of pride and stubbornness and too much anger," Aunt Raylene tells Bone. It's that volatile combination that saves Bone and gives *Bastard* an extraordinary pent-up power.

> *Vince Aletti, in a review of "Bastard Out of Carolina," in VLS, No. 106, June, 1992, p. 7.*

Amber Hollibaugh   (review date July 1992)

[*In the following review of* Bastard Out of Carolina, *Hollibaugh examines Allison's narrative style and complex portrayal of family life in the South.*]

Dorothy Allison knows who she is. A white woman who's lived too much of this novel's poverty, her book gives the lie to the myth that there's no class system in this country, and no white people who live hungry. ***Bastard Out of Carolina*** defies our terrible amnesia and confusion about poverty, gender and race. In a society where a white jury can decide that Rodney King's videotaped beating by the police was "justified" and where we're told that poor people are just "folks who don't want to work very hard," this book is bitter testimony to the opposite.

Allison's images force the reader to understand how being poor settles into the skin and backbone of a life and shapes every living hour. "Hunger makes you restless," Bone, her main character, says.

> You dream about food—not just any food, but perfect food, the best food, magical meals, famous and awe-inspiring, the one piece of meat, the exact taste of buttery corn, tomatoes so ripe they split and sweeten the air, beans so crisp they snap between the teeth, gravy like mother's milk singing in your bloodstream. When I got hungry, my hands would not stay still. . . . I'd chew my fingernails or suck on toothpicks and read anything I hadn't read more than twice already. But when Reese got hungry and there was nothing to eat, she would just sob, shiny fat tears running down her pink cheeks. Nothing would distract her.

This is Bone's story, and the novel travels from her illegitimate birth as Ruth Anne Boatwright in Greenville, South Carolina, through her estrangement as a twelve-year-old from her mother, Anney, at the novel's end. Allison leads us into the deepest locations of a family's secret life, into its caring and its terrible betrayals, especially of the girl-children by their mothers. The novel's foundation is the love that Bone and her mother share for each other; its action is fueled by incest and the violence of a stepfather's hand and shiny, cool leather belt; it details the simple leverage of hunger and the weight of working too many hours for too many years with no hope left for yourself and almost none for your children. This is, as Allison says, "a very hard book to read." It is a book you long to put down even as you can't resist it. But those of us who loved Dorothy Allison's short story collection *Trash* and her earlier book of poetry, *The Women Who Hate Me,* have gotten nothing less than what we expected and hoped for.

This is a book I had dreamed of reading since I first discovered Allison's writing in *Conditions* in the late seventies. Long before I met her or we had become friends, she had written short stories which captured the life of a "cross-eyed working-class lesbian" and of the people she came from. She had created people I knew like the back of my hand, my own flesh and blood; people who had raised me, and who knew all about being laughed at and humiliated for being "poor white trash." My own stories took place in the growing valleys of California, but it didn't matter. I knew how we sounded no matter what state we happened to be born in, and I'd longed to hear these women's stories in the multiplying fiction of the women's movement of the late seventies and early eighties.

But until Allison was published, I could find only Tillie Olsen and Toni Morrison who captured a corner of the story I had lived out. It was a lonely time to be a white-trash girl, and it spoke more of who had joined the women's movement, of who could, than of the actual breadth and variety of women's lives and experiences.

> . . . Mama hated to be called trash, hated the memory of every day she'd ever spent bent over other people's peanuts and strawberry plants while they stood tall and looked at her like she was a rock on the ground. . . . She'd work her hands to claws, her back to a shovel shape, her mouth to a bent and awkward smile—anything to deny what Greenville County wanted to name her. Now a soft-talking black-eyed man had done it for them—set a mark on her and hers. It was all she could do to pull herself up eight days after I was born and go back to work waiting tables with a tight mouth and swollen eyes.

It is here that the story Dorothy Allison intends to tell begins, a story she has obviously been writing inside her own head since childhood—a chronicle, she said in a reading in New York City this March, which she vowed she'd stay alive long enough to tell. It is the tragedy her family could find no way to escape, together with the sharp-edged beauty of the writing, which shapes this novel's unique perspective. As storyteller, Allison is finally in control of this rendition of the fable, and she insists on bringing the Boatwright family's deep love for each other, their fierce family

pride and loyalty, together with the hopelessness and waste of life that are the legacy of being poor and without voice.

> Family is family, but even love can't keep people from eating at each other. Mama's pride, Granny's resentment that there should even be anything to consider shameful, my aunts' fear and bitter humor, my uncles' hard-mouthed contempt for anything that could not be handled with a shotgun or a two-by-four—all combined to grow my mama up fast and painfully.

It is when the slowly constructed story of Bone's stepfather's violence begins to build that the book's inner heart is exposed. Bone, oldest and best-loved of Anney's two daughters, becomes the devil's bookmark for Daddy Glen's unrelenting sexual rage.

> He never said "Don't tell your mama." He never had to say it. I did not know how to tell anyone what I felt, what scared me and shamed me and still made me stand, unmoving and desperate, while he rubbed against me and ground his face into my neck. I could not tell Mama. I would not have known how to explain why I stood there and let him touch me. It wasn't sex, not like a man and a woman pushing their naked bodies into each other, but then, it was something like sex, something powerful and frightening that he wanted badly and I did not understand at all. Worse, when Daddy Glen held me that way, it was the only time his hands were gentle, and when he let me go, I would rock on uncertain feet.

Here Allison does something I've never seen executed so powerfully in any other book. Refusing to repeat, page to page, the variations in the ways Daddy Glen beats and abuses Bone, she goes instead inside Bone's head, assembling in minute detail the identity the child is forced to accept as the truth about herself.

". . . I knew there was nothing I had done that made him beat me. It was just me, the fact of my life, who I was in his eyes and mine. I was evil. Of course I was. I admitted it to myself, locked my fingers into fists, and shut my eyes to everything I did not understand." That is incest's cruelest irony, that a child begins to believe that what is happening to her is her own fault, that there is something intrinsic to her very being which is so vile that she has brought it on herself; a girl-child poisoned at the root. Each of us who has survived this is stalked by that nameless terror, worse even than the original violence.

But the gravest challenge, the deepest inquiry, that Allison takes up, harder even than the story of incest and violence by Daddy Glen, is the tale of betrayal among the women, between Bone and her mother Anney, between Anney and her sisters, between the sisters and each and every one of their passionately loved daughters. This, rather than the more painfully predictable story of women's betrayal by men whom they try to love, is the bitter kernel of grief that propels the novel to its resolution.

To take this on at all, Allison must write women characters whose strength, humor, wisdom and commitment to other women is undoubted, complex and unequivocal. The lush writing is set on fire by her love of the women whose stories she's telling. These are women who fight for each other's survival, who tell each other the truth when it's the hardest to hear and who would kill any man who tried to get between them; but they are also women who believe in suffering, believe that women are meant to abide and grieve and endure, that we are meant to live through this hell as a natural part of being female. This leaves them unable to imagine a radically different world, a world so altered that to betray other women and themselves would be impossible to conceive of.

Allison makes it clear that the treacheries that rip through her pages began long before anybody in this book started drinking heavily, having kids or sleeping around. The novel works because she dares to take her readers home: she invites you into that hastily rented house with its broken-down yard, a place too many people have gawked at as they've driven past but never stopped to go inside. *You know what I mean*—that old beat-up house with cars rusting in the front and countless babies in dirty diapers running through the ancient nails and broken glass that make up a yard . . . you know, y'all? *That yard.*

But not this time. This time she writes you through the door and into the front room. She moves you on to the kitchen and invites you to sit down for what there is on that table. Then she puts on some gospel music, turns the volume up good and loud, and makes you stay till the very end. As you sit at that table she brings the whole family over for you to meet. The lesbian aunts and sweet-faced boy cousins, the self-righteous relations who turn their nose up when they have to come for Sunday dinner and Granny who is tougher than any of her own children and tells them so. For 309 pages she takes you into that house so totally that you believe you'll never be able to leave it, never escape—and maybe, since she makes you fall in love with her people, never really want to. But at the same time she never lets you forget that inside that house, while you're sitting at that table listening to these stories, your life is perishing and so is everyone's you've come to love.

Allison drives the book ruthlessly to its final confrontation. "We do terrible things to the ones we love sometimes," says Aunt Raylene. "We can't explain it. We can't excuse it. It eats us up, but we do it just the same." All the strategies and silences that have been used to keep the family together begin to unravel relentlessly. It makes harsh, beautiful reading, the way an honest sentence is after too much hot air.

Allison doesn't let up, doesn't create heroines but gambles instead that her readers need truth more than pretty pictures and paper Goliaths. She goes back to the traditions forged in the earliest days of the women's movement and "speaks bitterness," letting the weight of what her readers already know come together with the power of her vision. She is right to say that her novel isn't easy to read, but neither are our lives. This is a book as consequential as our own stories: a novel that could save a life.

> Amber Hollibaugh, *"In the House of Childhood," in* The Women's Review of Books, *Vol. IX, Nos. 10-11, July, 1992, p. 15.*

Dorothy Allison with Amber Hollibaugh (interview date July 1992)

[In the following interview, Allison discusses her sexual abuse and the difficulty she had writing Bastard Out of Carolina.*]*

[Hollibaugh]: When you open your readings of **Bastard Out of Carolina**, *your first words to your audience are: I warn you this is a hard book to read. Why? Why do you warn them?*

[Allison]: I worried a lot about saying that, actually. 'Cause I didn't want to scare people off from the book, but I didn't want them to come to it with any illusions. The book is not about growing up queer successfully, and I got the real strong impression from talking to people was, what they hoped I would write would be the lesbian biography in which we grow up, we discover we're queer and everything is solved by being a lesbian and coming out and finding the right girlfriend and the community and everything is happy.

An updated Rubyfruit Jungle.

You got it. With a sense of humor, and it's Southern! But that's not what I've ever been interested in writing. And I wouldn't know how. 'Cause that's not what happened to me in my life. And I've had a real problem because I hate also to look people in the eye and say: this is a book about incest. Saying that is so reductive of what I tried to accomplish. It's not a book about incest. It's a book about a young girl in a working-class family in the South, in a family that in many ways provides her with a model for how to survive, but at the same time cannot save her from what she experiences, which is physical violence, incest and emotional abuse, and eventually the loss of her mother.

That's hard material. It's a mean story. So to a large extent what I try to do is say to people: this is a mean story, get ready. Do not expect that you are just going to hear lots of slap and tickle and easy answers.

I remember when Daughters' Press published the first few books, when Blanche Boyd's book came out, *Riverfinger Woman* came out, Rita Mae Brown's book . . . I remember reading those books and thinking: This is worth it. This is worth taking a vow of poverty for. None of them were slap and tickle books. They were not easy, upbeat, they weren't mysteries, they weren't genre fiction. They were complicated, deeply risky novels. No happy endings. Real explorations of what most of us have had to survive in order to become the lesbians we are.

With the demise of most of those early lesbian feminist presses, what we have had is a great many books that are disposable fiction. Some of them have really good moments. You'll get one scene or one strong character. You'll get a little piece of what you need. But it's not meat for the soul. Mostly where I've found it has been in lesbian short stories. Elly Bulkin used to have a theory that the reason we had so many good short stories and so few good novels, really strong inspirational novels, was because none of our writers got the time to write novels. That basically we were writing short stories because it was a limited form that you fit between your day job and your night-time meetings.

So what did it take you to get to write this book?

It took a fucking miracle. The largest thing that I had to overcome was the simple fact that I hate being poor. I've done it. I know what it's like. I know that it's the death of the soul in many ways. And it is an absolute fact that being a lesbian writer at this point in history is about being poor.

I do not make enough money to survive. I don't have health insurance. I can't get it. I can't even figure out a way to hustle it and I'm a good hustler. I finished *Trash* on my savings from having worked seven, eight years, and having left my lover and sold the house that we'd bought together. I used everything I had to finish that book, and when I finished it and it was published, I had nothing. I had no savings, no job, no income. I had to start all over again, and I was sick. Too many years of not enough sleep and not enough good health care.

When I was writing *Trash* and living on my savings, I expected that when I finished the book I would die, because I couldn't see past it and I knew how long the money was going to run. I knew where I would wind up and I expected to die.

When I signed the contract for *Bastard* and got that check, I only saw to the end of *Bastard,* and then I expected to die. Right now I am surprised that I am still alive. I've never gotten a grant as a writer in my entire life. I've never had that time provided. I've had to steal it. Mostly I've stolen it from my health.

I was raised to think nobody helps you, so I find it really difficult to accept help. And needing it, needing it is so painful. I just can't get over my sense that I should die first.

Let's go back to where you learned that. There's often an assumption that white trash is a fiction, or that it existed in the South but nowhere else.

It's a lie: I find us everywhere. I can always find us. I find these girls—you can always spot 'em, they generally have bad skin, bad teeth, shadows under their eyes and their heads are down. And if you look at them for longer than a minute you can see that there's other things that they want to be doing. And that they're not doing them partly because they don't have the resources, but also because they do not believe that they deserve them. The hardest thing for a lot of the students that I hunt out—because I really hunt for working-class kids to teach—is convincing them that yeah, you not only have the right to be a writer, you have an absolute responsibility. And that's the only way I can hook 'em. Because working-class kids, especially those of us who've managed any kind of escape—if you are not working in the mill or still living at home, you do not believe you deserve anything. You have this enormous shame and this conviction that you're not working as hard as your momma.

Now I've seen girls tell me how easy they have it. I've got a young woman I've worked with who's a wonderful story-teller working as a fucking dishwasher in Oakland. Will not quit the job. Working a day job, working as a dishwasher at night, she does not believe that she has the right to quit that dishwashing job because, after all, her momma worked three jobs and raised eight children. She ain't got eight children so she's got it easy. And when she says it to me I can hear myself say it—I've said it the last few weeks when I've been traveling around the country doing readings and I'm so tired I can barely talk to people, and I keep saying: this is nothing compared to doing what my momma did. You want to see tired? You shoulda seen my momma after she come home.

It gives us an enormous strength to come out of that family, but at the same time it's like having a bear-trap on your ankle. I feel sometimes like I had to chew my ankle off to get out of it. To get out of the shame. I don't want out of my family. I had to fight really hard to claim them, and cling to them. I want them desperately. But I had to get out of some of the patterns of shame, self-hatred and dis-entitlement that I learned in my family.

What did you have to go through to decide to tell the truth about family, when families have always been ashamed for exactly the things you had to write about?

I had to pull the same trick on myself that I pull on my students. I had to convince myself that I *had* to write this book. That it was my debt, my responsibility, to do it and do it right. To tell the truth and to pay homage to the people who helped to make me the person I've become.

I show you my aunts in their drunken rages, my uncles in their meanness. And that's exactly who we are said to be. That's what white trash is all about. We're all supposed to be drunks standing in our yards with our broken-down cars and our dirty babies. Some of that stuff is true. But to write about it I had to find a way to pull the reader in and show you those people as larger than that contempt-ible myth. And show you why those men drink, why those women hate themselves and get old and can't protect themselves or their children. Show you human beings in-stead of fold-up, mean, cardboard figures.

But in order to write Bone, the character I created, and to write her mother and to write those people, I had to for-give them, and I had to forgive myself, which is the hard thing. I had to forgive my mother, really forgive her in order to show a child who couldn't forgive her. And I don't think it would have happened the way it happened if she hadn't died while I was writing it.

What do you mean?

Writing is not as simple as just telling a story. Even if you know the story you're gonna tell, and I knew the story I was going tell, you go in and you live the characters and you dream them. The woman that I made Bone's mother, Anney, was so much of my own mother, the easy parts to write in some ways were the lyrical parts in which Bone just loves her. The hard parts were the places where Anney fails her daughters. I couldn't do it until I looked at what my mother had done with me as a child.

Then when she got really sick and I went home, I wound up having these conversations with her in which the fact that I was still angry at her didn't matter. But I had not expected her to die and I had not expected her to die so fast. And I spent a good six months with a real need to rewrite the book and make Anney a heroine. I needed a way to vindicate her. I needed a way to vindicate my mother.

I wrote an ending in which Anney and Bone together killed Daddy Glen. I'm not a damn fool. I wrote an ending in which it was ambiguous, there was a whole question of who intended what, and of course there was an enormous amount of guilt. And even writing it I realized that that act would have destroyed both of them. There was just no way that that child could survive it. I don't believe in easy answers. You can't just kill the mother-fuckers. Even though sometimes that's all you really want to do.

So what did it mean to try to write a book where the betrayal that women practice on each other is the story in the story?

Pretending that we do not do these things, pretending that our mothers do not fail us, pretending that our mothers do not literally betray us, just puts a gloss over this gaping wound which allows it to lie there and fester the rest of your life. You'll never get out of it, you'll never get over it.

When my mother was dying and we talked, the undercurrent of everything we said to each other was the fact that she had never forgiven herself and couldn't. My mother could never look at what had happened because she could not talk about it. She could not say the words—incest, violence, betrayal. She couldn't say: I knew he was fucking you. She could only say: I never meant for those things to happen. She'd say "those things." And she'd say: I know you'll never be able to forgive me. And no matter how many times I told her that wasn't the question, she didn't believe me because she couldn't forgive herself.

I do not know what will finally change things. But it's a simple fact that in this culture we teach our girls to keep silent and to suffer and that that's the lot of women. Even in this book with these strong women they all believe that suffering is what they are supposed to do. And they pass it on to their children.

You kill a man, somebody goes to jail. I lived my whole childhood being told if we do anything they'll step in, you'll be in juvenile hall, I'll never see you again. My mother told me this. My aunts told me this. You cannot fight back because they'll destroy the family and all we have is each other.

I am still confused about how we fix that. We've set up an impossible situation, because the social institutions that we have created that are supposed to help children do not help them. Look at any child who was a victim of incest or family violence that has ever been taken out of the family and track what happens to them.

My mother was cold about it. Said: Maybe we won't go to jail, but you'll never go to college, and the only way you're going to go to college is if we get you a scholarship. My mother bribed me the last two years that I was at home not to kill my stepfather and not to kill myself. And she did it very deliberately. She said: You stay alive 'til summer, I'll send you to stay with your aunt. We got one more year and you're going to college.

I saw what happened to the other girls who flipped out, I know little girls who knifed their fathers and left. I know girls who trashed the family car and left. They went on the streets, or they went into juvenile hall. There is no institution in this society that really rescues working-class kids.

We do more damage to those kids in some ways than breaking their bones does when they're getting slapped around. We make them believe that they are unilaterally ruined, that they have no way out, that they have no other options, that they are for the rest of their lives gonna be that fucked creature. It shaped a lot of how I wrote the book, because I deliberately tried to avoid giving you any detail of how Daddy Glenn fucks Bone. I did not want that to be the core. I wanted you to know that kid's rage, shame and confusion, but I didn't even want you to know how he put his dick in.

What were your goals when you were writing the book?

I wanted to make those people real. I wanted people to understand the situation that I was portraying. The bottom line was, I wanted them to fall in love with those people. I did not want anyone to ever be able to use the words "white trash" again without thinking about all my characters. I wanted them to remember Raylene. I wanted them to know that there were dykes in the south, working-class dykes who survived, who lived in their families, and their families knew who they were.

As a writer who is from the South, how do you see yourself within the context of Southern writing?

I see myself in the tradition of Tennessee Williams, Flannery O'Connor, Carson McCullers and James Baldwin. Now James Baldwin's from Harlem, honey. But he was the first writer I ever fell in love with, because he wrote a language that I absolutely understood and he dealt with people I believed in and could see all around me. The fact that he wrote about Black people was just a gift to me because I lived in the South at a time in which my access to Black people was really limited. I was a kid in the fifties, when the civil rights movement was just beginning, and I watched it on TV and was awed and excited about it because it looked like it was a possibility for freedom for all of us.

But when I grew up, I started looking around and realizing, you're white, you're from the South, and everybody's going to make these assumptions for the rest of your life—and they do. You want to write? Every time you ever write, the first thing they're gonna talk about is the tradition of the grotesque in Southern literature.

Now I happen to like the tradition of the grotesque in Southern literature. I read Flannery O'Connor, I appreciate what she's doing, her Catholicism does not get in the way for me. But I hated the fact that when *Publishers Weekly* reviewed the book the first two words that they sprung out at me were "grotesque" and "slatternly." Which I think if you read this book there ain't nobody grotesque in it. So the women in my family lost their teeth—where I come from that's normal. I think it's normal up

North too. I've met quite a few people with false teeth up North.

But at the same time Southern literature gives me some categories and it gives me some possibilities I wouldn't have otherwise. It gives me a tradition of language that's enormously valuable. Southern writing is like gospel music. A lot of the really fine Southern writers that I read over and over again—Flannery O'Connor, Carson Mc-Cullers—they take you through an enormous amount of pain in order to bring you to a sense of vindication and meaning.

To get to healing you have to break your heart first. You have to crack the scar. That's what good writing is about. That's what good music is about. You have to purge all of that lying shame. And that's a Southern tradition. But it's pure bullshit to think that it's only Southern. I can take you to Agnes Smedley. The girl was not Southern, but she was damn good. She was a Northern working-class writer. Go read Muriel Rukeyser, go read any working-class writer. It's the same. It doesn't matter if we're in the South or not. The only thing I see that differs is the language.

Talk to me about what it means to have written **Bastard** *as a lesbian writer.*

I do not think that my purpose in life is to explain, particularly to explain to straight people, what lesbian lives are like. My purpose in life is to write books in which lesbians live. I don't like these didactic books. And I don't like these romantic solution books. It's like: I found god in myself and I loved her fiercely. Well, the lesbian stereotype is: I found god in my lover and I loved her fiercely and everything was fine from then on.

I don't believe that story, so I can't write it and it seems to me to be a very small thing to do with a book. My concept of writing a book is that you look for a large canvas. You look for real people, and you watch them interact and you see what happens and you make people believe in those characters and in their lives and what happens to them.

Toni Morrison said when someone asked how she felt about being a woman and an African American—did she feel reduced by those? And she said: Why should I feel reduced by the places that give me voice?

Absolutely. I'll tell you the damn sure truth. If I wasn't queer, I wouldn't be a writer. I'd live in a trailer park. Probably in Greenville, South Carolina. I would probably have six kids. I would probably beat them. I would probably drink. I would probably be dead. I'm forty-three. In my family that's a long time to live. I think that being a lesbian gave me the possibility to see my life in different terms. (pp. 16-17)

> *Dorothy Allison and Amber Hollibaugh, in an interview in* The Women's Review of Books, *Vol. IX, Nos. 10-11, July, 1992, pp. 16-17.*

George Garrett   (review date 5 July 1992)

[*In the following review of* Bastard Out of Carolina,

Garrett applauds Allison's skills as a writer, focusing on her lyrical language and rich characterization.]

"All the Boatwrights told stories, it was one of the things we were known for, and what one cousin swore was gospel, another swore was an unqualified lie," says Ruth Anne Boatwright, more often called Bone by her kinfolk and a few close friends. Bone is the narrator of the larger story of *Bastard Out of Carolina,* itself as richly various, with its stories and memories and dreams, as a well-made quilt. It is not surprising that this first novel is so abundantly anecdotal; Dorothy Allison has published stories in magazines and anthologies for some time, and her first book, *Trash,* was a critically praised collection of stories.

What is surprising, however, is that the relentless narrative of this powerful novel in no way seems to be a patchwork of short stories linked together. Everything, each part, belongs only to the novel. Indeed, the technical skill in both large things and details, so gracefully executed as to be always at the service of the story and its characters and thus almost invisible, is simply stunning, about as close to flawless as any reader could ask for and any writer, at any age or stage, could hope for and aspire to.

When I finished *Bastard Out of Carolina* I wanted to blow a bugle to alert the reading public that a wonderful work of fiction by a major new talent has arrived on the scene. It is one of those once-in-a-blue-moon occasions when the jacket copy seems inadequate and all the blurbs are examples of rhetorical understatement. Please reserve a seat of honor at the high table of the art of fiction for Dorothy Allison.

In a manner as authentic as that of any credible autobiographer, Bone, the bastard of the title and the daughter of the beautifully realized Anney Boatwright, tells us the story of her life and her world up to the age of 13 when, as a result of a terrible trauma, she imagines that her life is over and done with. (That she has gone on to tell this story to us later belies that grim conclusion.) Beginning in the deftly evoked 1950's, in and around Greenville, S. C., it is a story with a host of characters, each distinct and memorable, each a recognizable physical presence. There is Reese, Bone's younger sister, and Granny, the sharp-tongued Boatwright matriarch. There are cousins beyond counting; Bone's ne'er-do-well Boatwright uncles, Earle and Beau and Nevil; her aunts Ruth, Alma and (of special importance to Bone) Raylene, a proud, independent woman who once worked for a carnival and who had another woman as her lover. And there is the menacing Glen Waddell, called Daddy Glen, Bone's stepfather, who abuses and violates her in every possible way.

These people are what some would call white trash, rednecks, crackers (words not used in this book). They are members of the white working poor. Family matters most, all the network and history of it. The men are proud, loving, violent and spoiled. The strong Boatwright women keep them that way. Men and women alike are complex people who manage to transcend their own disguises and society's stereotypes of them.

Bone spends a lot of her youthful energy "looking for something special in me, something magical." On the other hand, she has plenty of evidence for what kind of future awaits her: "Growing up was like falling into a hole. The boys would quit school and sooner or later go to jail for something silly. I might not quit school, not while Mama had any say in the matter, but what difference would that make? What was I going to do in five years? Work in the textile mill? Join Mama at the diner? It all looked bleak to me. No wonder people got crazy as they grew up."

These people all work hard (at hopeless jobs), play hard and are often poor enough to be ragged and hungry. The recited details of poverty are precise and exact. Bone is typical of the family in her love of gospel and country music. Boatwright kin swap stories continually, listen to the radio and watch a little television, though not as much as you might think. The men drink and fight and find trouble in various shapes and forms. Bone reads a lot, un-self-consciously. Near the end of the novel she has been able to sneak *The Group* out of the local library. All kinds of things, adventures and misadventures, happen to Bone and to her extended family. There are births and deaths, plenty of accidents (one horrible to consider), sicknesses and sorrows; and there is life and the humming energy of it on every page.

The literary territory that Dorothy Allison has set out to explore is dangerous turf, a minefield strewn with booby traps where the least false step could lead to disaster. It is a great pleasure to see her succeed, blithe and graceful as Baryshnikov in performance. What dangers? Well, there is the whole Southern thing. Terminal cuteness is the dread disease of too much new Southern writing, especially first-person stories about eccentric families, a contagion compounded by the fact that too many people, reviewers as well as readers, are unable to distinguish the authentic from the spurious. The author, like her narrator, is often funny, never cute.

But Ms. Allison has more serious threats to overcome, more important than purely literary matters. Anybody who wants to write truly and well about poor people has to contend with the temptation to turn characters into case studies. Too many readers and reviewers are relieved by that abstraction from the pain of felt experience. Similarly, sentimentality, with all its inherent denigration of intelligence and the human spirit, has become an acceptable mode in this sentimental age of ours. Dorothy Allison can be deeply moving, yet she is never sentimental.

What saves her from all the possible pitfalls is the living language she has created for Bone. It is as exact and innovative as the language of *To Kill A Mockingbird* and *The Catcher in the Rye*. The special qualities of her style include a perfect ear for speech and its natural rhythms; an unassertive, cumulative lyricism; an intensely imagined and presented sensory world, with all five senses working together; and, above all, again and again a language for the direct articulation of deep and complex feelings.

Throughout the book Bone dreams of being a gospel singer, but she lacks the voice for it. With the grace and magic

---

An excerpt from *Bastard Out of Carolina*

Shannon threw another handful of flowers at me. "I'm crazy? Me? What do you think you are? You and your mama and your whole family. Everybody knows you're all a bunch of drunks and thieves and bastards. Everybody knows you just come round so you can eat off my mama's table and beg scraps we don't want no more. Everybody knows who you are . . . "

I was moving before I could stop myself, my hands flying up to slap together right in front of her face—a last-minute attempt not to hit her. "You bitch, you white-assed bitch." I wrung my hands, trying to keep myself from slapping her pasty face. "Don't you never hit anybody in the face," Mama always said.

"You little shit, you fuck off." I put the words out as slick and fast as any of my uncles. Shannon's mouth fell open. "You just fuck off!" I kicked red dirt up onto her gingham skirt.

Shannon's face twisted. "You an't never gonna go to another gospel show with us again! I'm gonna tell my mama what you called me, and she an't ever gonna let you come near me again."

"Your mama, your mama. You'd piss in a Pepsi bottle if your mama told you to."

"Listen to you. You . . . you trash. You nothing but trash. Your mama's trash, and your grandma, and your whole dirty family . . . "

I swung at her then with my hand wide open, right at her face, but I was too angry. I was crazy angry and I tripped, falling onto the red dirt on my spread hands. My right hand came down on a broken clay pot, hurting me so bad I could barely see Shannon's dripping, flushed cheeks.

"Oh . . . shit. You . . . shit." If I could have jumped up and caught her, I would have ripped out handfuls of that cotton-candy hair.

Shannon stood still and watched as I pushed myself up and grabbed my right hand with my left. I was crying, I realized, the tears running down my face while behind us the choir had never stopped singing. That woman's voice still rolled over the cottonwoods. *Was blind but now I see . . .*

"You're ugly." I swallowed my tears and made myself speak very quietly. "You're God's own ugly child and you're gonna be an ugly woman. A lonely, ugly old woman."

Shannon's lips started to tremble, poking out of her face so that she was uglier than I'd ever seen her, a doll carved out of cold grease melting in the heat.

"You ugly thing," I went on. "You monster, you greasy cross-eyed stinking sweaty-faced ugly thing!" I pointed all my fingers at her and spit at her patent-leather shoes. "You so ugly your own mama don't even love you." Shannon backed off, turned around, and started running.

"Mamaaaaa!" she wailed as she ran. I kept yelling after her, more to keep myself from crying now than to hurt her.

"Ugly . . . ugly . . . ugly."

Dorothy Allison, in her Bastard Out of Carolina, *Dutton, 1992.*

of art, the author has transformed Bone's words and stories into something close to Bone's vision: "Their voices rose smoothly, but Mrs. Pearl's moan went on and on, rising into the close sweaty air, a song with no meter, no rhythm—but gospel, the purest gospel, a song of absolute hopeless grief."

George Garrett, " 'No Wonder People Got Crazy as They Grew Up'," in The New York Times Book Review, *July 5, 1992, p. 3.*

Mary Hawthorne   (review date 14 August 1992)

[*In the essay below, Hawthorne considers Allison's thematic concerns in* Bastard Out of Carolina.]

[In ***Bastard Out of Carolina***] Bone's inauspicious entry into the world—"no bigger than a knucklebone", her boozy, philandering Uncle Earle quips—is precipitated by a head-on car crash, in which her fifteen-year-old mother, Anney, eight months pregnant, is hurtled through the windshield of a car driven by Bone's drunken Uncle Travis. Nevertheless, Anney escapes with mere cuts and bruises, and Bone seems, if destined for the school of hard knocks, then softened at least by the comforts of a proud, affectionate and eccentric clan: uncles with broken teeth who regularly serve time at the county farm; aunts who rinse their hair in baby piss to keep it blond during pregnancy; cousins game to burgle the local Woolworth's. At seventeen, Anney marries a sweet man who pumps gas at the Texaco station and changes tires at the stock-car races on Sundays while she waits tables at the local diner. When he's killed in a freak highway accident, she finds herself succumbing to the patient, timorous advances of Glen Waddell, the black sheep of a family of dairy owners, lawyers and dentists. "Daddy Glen", Bone and her younger sister, Reese, call him. The night Anney gives birth to their stillborn child, Daddy Glen sexually abuses Bone in the hospital parking lot; two years later, by the time Bone is ten, he begins beating her up as well. From that point, his appearances in the book are few, but he stalks the pages and the reader lives in the fear and certainty of meeting him. The novel shifts to the interior life of Bone—to the insidious rage that takes hold of her, to her longing for power and escape, and to the birth of her complicated sexuality, a simultaneous fascination with and morbid shame of her own sickening torture.

> Oiled, smooth and supple . . . those belts hung behind the door of his closet where I could see them and smell them when I helped Mama put away his clothes. I would reach up and touch the leather, feel it warm under my palms. Sometimes I would make myself go in that closet and wrap

my fingers around those belts as if they were something animal that could be tamed. . . . There was no heroism possible in the real beatings. There was just being beaten until I was covered with snot and misery.

The complexity of cruelty is Allison's subject, and, not surprisingly, the forces of poverty, social inequity and the psychosis of the family are at work. (Daddy Glen is not a wholly convincing character, but Allison does give us an idea of the sources of his abusiveness.) But will and transcendence—what goes into making the sometimes unspeakably difficult decision simply to live—are also her subjects, and she is careful to temper her grim tale by evoking the equally complex force of love. Bone and Anney's relationship is tenderly drawn, as is the network of their extended family (whose wisecracking bonhomie can, however, seem relentless). One sometimes hears the clunk of fiction not sufficiently dissembled, and an indulgent meandering of plot into subplots that lead nowhere (one of her earlier stories, is reproduced, virtually unchanged, here) diminishes the book's potency. But the voice that reaches us is coming from the heart.

Mary Hawthorne, "Born of Ignorance," in The Times Literary Supplement, *No. 4663, August 14, 1992, p. 18.*

FURTHER READING

Drabelle, Dennis. "No Friends of Dorothy." *The Advocate* (9 March 1992): 67.

> Discusses the controversy surrounding Allison's visit to Oklahoma, which was ultimately cancelled because the Oklahoma Center for the Book allegedly found Allison's open lesbianism and *Bastard Out of Carolina* offensive.

Goodrich, Chris. Review of *Bastard Out of Carolina,* by Dorothy Allison. *Los Angeles Times Book Review* (16 August 1992): 6.

> Briefly reviews *Bastard Out of Carolina,* praising Allison's narrative style and evocation of "white-trash lives."

Osen, Ray. Review of *Trash,* by Dorothy Allison. *Booklist* 85, No. 6 (15 November 1988): 537.

> Favorably reviews *Trash,* noting that the stories are "written in a steady, authoritative prose that admits neither sentiment nor sensation."

Review of *Bastard Out of Carolina,* by Dorothy Allison. *Publishers Weekly* 239, No. 6 (27 January 1992): 88.

Briefly examines the characters in *Bastard Out of Carolina,* concluding: "[Allison] doesn't condescend to her 'white trash' characters; she portrays them with understanding and love."

Additional coverage of Allison's life and career is contained in the following source published by Gale Research: *Contemporary Authors,* **Vol. 140.**

Charles Baxter

1947-

(Full name Charles Morley Baxter) American short story writer, novelist, and poet.

The following entry provides criticism on Baxter's career through 1993. For further information on his life and works, see *CLC,* Volume 45.

INTRODUCTION

In his novels and short stories Baxter utilizes minimalistic language and imagery to depict ordinary people who strive to achieve order and harmony in their lives but whose good intentions are undermined by the pervading tensions of contemporary life. His characters subsequently wrestle with feelings of futility, disillusionment, and alienation. Baxter frequently underscores his protagonists' angst by setting his works in his native Midwest, which, he states, "in its nondescript landscape has a tendency to turn people inward. We don't have the wild verbalisms of the South, the spectacular vistas of the West or the urban culture of the East. There's a sense of learning to make do with limitations. I once described it as being married to a woman who will not kiss you back. It's my spiritual enterprise to write about this." Although Baxter's writings emphasize limitations, disappointment, and emotional isolation, critics note that the compassion and honesty with which Baxter presents his characters instill his works with a sense of hope and optimism.

Baxter is generally regarded as a master of the short story, and his work in the genre has been favorably compared to that of Raymond Carver and William Trevor. His short stories often focus on individuals who, for a variety of reasons, are unable to take control of their lives. In the acclaimed title story of *Harmony of the World,* for example, a competent but uninspired pianist is consistently frustrated in his artistic ambitions, failing to recognize the discordant qualities evident in both his life and music. While critics have claimed that *Through the Safety Net* is occasionally weakened by Baxter's self-conscious narration, this collection, like *Harmony of the World,* has been praised for its sensitive treatment of persons confronting loss, isolation, and a growing sense of self-awareness. *A Relative Stranger, and Other Stories* similarly details average individuals who are unable to alleviate their fears and feelings of alienation. "Shelter" recounts one man's attempts to help the homeless and the anxiety and resentment his actions provoke in his family. Another story, "Westland," details a social worker's concern for a troubled teenage girl and his subsequent feelings of futility concerning the state of society. In assessing Baxter's work in the genre, Greg Johnson commented: "Almost without exception, Baxter's best stories are traditional narratives which establish a bond of compassionate identification be-

tween the writer and the characters, an empathy with their pain and fragility, which Baxter's precise, artful prose enables the reader to share."

Baxter's novels, *First Light* and *Shadow Play,* are both set in the fictional city of Five Oaks, Michigan, and examine the complexity of interpersonal relationships and the moral implications of an individual's actions. *First Light* delineates the relationship between Hugh, a car salesman, and his sister Dorsey, an astrophysicist. Basing the novel on Danish philosopher Søren Kierkegaard's belief that "life can only be understood backwards; but it must be lived forward," Baxter uses an antichronological approach to document Hugh and Dorsey's upbringing, the disparate nature of their lives, and their growing disenchantment and ambivalence. Critics have disagreed about the effectiveness of Baxter's manipulation of time in *First Light*—the book opens when Dorsey and Hugh are adults and closes with Dorsey's birth. While some have claimed that the work's narrative structure lessens the intensity of the tale, others agree with Michiko Kakutani, who observed that "by orchestrating tiny details of observation and larger emotional patterns, Mr. Baxter makes us understand both the shifting balance of power that has occurred between Dorsey and Hugh over the years, and the bonds of affection and shared experience that unite them. The result is a remarkably supple novel that gleams with the smoky chiaroscuro of familial love recalled through time."

Shadow Play, which employs more conventional narrative strategies, centers on Wyatt Palmer, who, after his father's death and his mother's confinement to an insane asylum, is raised by an aunt whose life's goal is to rewrite the Bible from an existentialist perspective. In his desire for normalcy and acceptance, Wyatt strives to become a model citizen and is instrumental in bringing WaldChem, a plastics plant owned by an old classmate, to the economically depressed Five Oaks. Wyatt never reports the company's numerous environmental violations to state authorities, and when the town's cancer rate rises, he grapples with his guilt. Although such topical issues as environmental pollution and assisted suicide are central to the plot, Baxter emphasizes that *Shadow Play* was intended as an examination of humanity's need for spiritual redemption and self-awareness in an increasingly complex and morally ambiguous world. Baxter has stated: "I didn't want the book to be a social-problem novel. . . . I was trying to balance issues I thought were of concern and interest socially with matters of the soul and the heart—to make them reflect each other."

PRINCIPAL WORKS

Chameleon (poetry) 1970
The South Dakota Guidebook (poetry) 1974
Harmony of the World (short stories) 1984
Through the Safety Net (short stories) 1985
First Light (novel) 1987
Imaginary Paintings, and Other Poems (poetry) 1989
A Relative Stranger, and Other Stories (short stories) 1990
Shadow Play (novel) 1993

CRITICISM

Greg Johnson (review date Summer 1986)

[*In the essay below, Johnson discusses the predominant themes of* Harmony of the World *and* Through the Safety Net.]

Charles Baxter has made an auspicious debut as a writer of short fiction. His first two collections, published only a year apart, show him as a writer dedicated to the wondrous variety of the story form as practiced in America today. Unlike certain of his contemporaries—Frederick

Barthelme, say, or Ann Beattie—he has not focused upon recurring character types who share the same backgrounds, relationships and neuroses. Instead, Baxter's stories range impressively across a broad spectrum of American experience and show a similar range in adapting fictional technique to specific material, rather than vice versa. The experienced Baxter reader (unlike the reader of Barthelme or Beattie) does not know what to expect when encountering a new story; Baxter's ability to vary his effects and his willingness to explore unfamiliar territory are among his best virtues as a writer. He can portray the contemporary disillusionment that is such a popular theme with today's younger writers, but a story of his is just as likely to center on a five-year-old boy confronting death for the first time, or on a woman in her seventies coping with the effects of age on herself and her husband, or on a middle-aged American capitalist who has grown tired of making money.

The stories in both [*Harmony of the World* and *Through the Safety Net*] are linked, though loosely, by the theme of dislocation, of emotional crisis and its aftermath. Like his later volume, whose title explicitly suggests this theme, *Harmony of the World* (whose title is ironic) shows a variety of people in disharmonious relationships with the surrounding culture and with their own lives. In two of the stories, for instance, musical ambition and aesthetic ideals clash painfully with low self-esteem, making either inner or outer harmony seem unattainable. The volume's title story narrates a romance between two mediocre musicians, allowing Baxter to explore not only the collapsed artistic ambitions of these intelligent, wounded people but also the cultural disharmony between genuine art and an audience which prefers the mediocre, wanting to sustain a spurious faith in the harmony of the world. The hapless Kate, protagonist of **"Gershwin's Second Prelude,"** continues doggedly with her music lessons even as she pursues a degrading relationship and doubts her musical talent. When her loutish boyfriend finally abandons her, Kate's sense of aloneness becomes nearly unbearable:

> Kate had turned thirty that month. With Wiley gone, she thought of her past, of the music scholarships, the lost jobs, the men, the empty bank accounts. She thought of her parents. They didn't like her to call because she just gave them bad news.

Kate's story is resolved in a surprising encounter with her music teacher—the aged, eccentric, Polish-born Madame Gutowski—in which Kate's brutal self-assessment ("I'm a nitwit") is tempered by the older woman's breadth of experience and compassion.

Youthful disillusionment is also the subject of **"Xavier Speaking,"** a witty and ingeniously constructed tale of the Sixties and its aftermath, and of **"A Short Course in Nietzschean Ethics,"** in which two college roommates take the opposing paths of conformity and rebellion. Perhaps the most impressive story in this group, however, and the one most pertinent to the past decade of American culture, is **"Weights,"** in which a young man's lack of employment and general dissatisfaction with his life bring him to the point of breakdown. Although Tobias becomes obsessed with body-building—literally lifting "weights" as though to defend against mounting psychological pressures—his single-mindedness allows him to ignore his deteriorating relationships and leads ultimately to an act of casual violence, a gesture of hopelessness that Tobias himself can scarcely recognize as such. A subtle, powerful story of alienation and psychological turmoil, **"Weights"** gains in power from Baxter's restrained, carefully modulated prose. Consider this paragraph, whose brief declarative sentences adroitly convey a moment of both literal and psychological violence:

> The boy lay out in the snow after Tobias hit him. Some bystander grabbed Tobias's elbow, and Tobias hit him, too. Six months of continual weight training gave Tobias enough strength to deck another man who was interfering: it required only one blow. The faces moved back. Boris was barking. Tobias held his fists up into the air and noticed that at night snow looks more gray than white. The moon was a smile without a face, pasted into the winter sky. He felt like hitting someone else, but no one else was against him.

Other remarkable stories in this volume include **"Horace and Margaret's Fifty-second,"** a heartrending story of an aged couple's decline, and **"The Model,"** the amusing and entirely convincing account of Carter, a beautiful, narcissistic man—an artist's model—who inspires adoration in others but feels almost nothing himself. Torn between an established homosexual relationship and a confused affair with a female art student, Carter hurts both his partners and finally gets his just deserts—but not before Baxter brings this "model," sympathetically, to the brink of becoming human.

Like its predecessor, *Through the Safety Net* displays a remarkable versatility as Baxter's characters cope with various traumas that have destroyed the normal stability and security of their lives. Almost without exception, Baxter is hard on his characters; his concern with extreme pain and loss seems nearly obsessive. In **"Surprised by Joy,"** which is almost too painful to read, a couple endures debilitating grief and remorse after the accidental death of their young daughter. The story adroitly captures the moment when one parent begins to show signs of recovery, leaving the other in an intensified state of alienation and continued anguish. **"Talk Show,"** an extremely effective story, also deals with a death in the family—this time as perceived by a small boy. The boy's evasions, his glimmers of understanding, and his gradual introduction into the adult world of grief help make this a story of great emotional power.

As in *Harmony of the World,* a number of stories dramatize crucial moments of disillusionment. **"Stained Glass"** begins as the story of an ordinary romantic break-up but turns into a tale of obsessive love that's by turns funny and horrifying. In **"Cataract,"** a successful businessman suddenly decides to retire and take up painting, achieving in the process a painful self-knowledge that he'd successfully avoided in the past. As in the earlier story **"Weights,"** Baxter's younger characters feel burdened by a sense of failure, of having disappointed parents, lovers, and society at large. The protagonist of **"Media Event,"** the son of affluent parents who has begun doing hospital janitorial work, is an extreme example:

> Here's what happened: George Eliot Christianson, Jr., took a slight psychotic tumble. He fell into a bit of depression about himself and his ultimate human prospects here in this, our, America. He got depressed, and so did the economy. It's a free country if you have a million dollars, but if you don't and you're a little discouraged about things, you take what they give you. At Mt. Hope they were passing out mops. He took one.

Though thematically linked to Baxter's other stories, **"Media Event"** is not among his best: he shows a tendency here, and in other stories in both volumes—**"Winter Journey," "The Crank"**—to adopt a heavily ironic, tongue-in-cheek approach which allows for momentary cleverness but leads away from the emotional impact of his finest work. In creating such over-familiar character types as the would-be criminal celebrity *à la* John Hinckley or Squeaky Fromme (**"Media Event"**), or the grubby, anxiety-ridden graduate student (**"Winter Journey"**), Baxter distances both himself and the reader from his material. In general, Baxter's attempts at experimental writing—such as **"The Cliff,"** an awkward and self-conscious allegorical tale—have the same effect. Likewise he has an unfortunate tendency in some stories to adopt a self-consciously academic tone, often through explicit literary allusion or interpolated quotations from such disparate figures as Nietzsche, Chekhov, Delmore Schwartz, and the composer Paul Hindemith. This occurs even in his better stories, and serves only to stop the action cold and to disrupt, sometimes near-fatally, what John Gardner called the "vivid continuous dream" that any fiction must maintain to keep its imaginative hold on the reader. One hopes that in his future work Baxter will avoid faddish experimentation and especially the kind of allusive, self-referential, "post-modernist" fictional modes that can serve only to ossify the dynamic psychological realism which is his true *métier.*

Almost without exception, Baxter's best stories are traditional narratives which establish a bond of compassionate identification between the writer and his characters, and empathy with their pain and fragility which Baxter's precise, artful prose enables the reader to share. His recurring impulse to give a compassionate rendering of his characters is perhaps best exemplified by **"A Late Sunday Afternoon by the Huron,"** the final story of *Through the Safety Net.* Here Baxter does not focus upon a particular character, however, but ranges over a cross-section of the population—a University professor, a pair of young lovers, a carload of eighteen-year-old boys, several families complete with children, dogs, and grandmothers—who have all come to a park situated beside the Huron River. The story alludes, of course, to George Seurat's [painting] *Sunday Afternoon on the Island of La Grande Jatte,* and indeed might have been titled "Sunday in the Park With Charles," since the author himself makes several appearances:

> As I doze off, I think about all the people here,

the beautiful random motion of everyone taking the day off, and for an instant I think of fitting them into some kind of story. But it's impossible. There is no story here.

There *is* a story, however, and it's quite an impressive one. Deliberately laconic as its focus moves among the various individuals and groups, the fragmented narrative presents facts and description with a painterly eye for detail. The story is packed with seemingly random, trivial events: the professor becomes irate over the loud music being played by the teenagers, and asks them to turn it down; a man walks by with a pet raccoon, exciting momentary attention. But mostly these people are absorbed in their own leisure-time activities: a young boy fishes idly in the river; the young couple, Lincoln and Evie, makes love; one of the families barbecues a chicken. But the story is much more than a detached glimpse of a few disparate individuals. Slowly this cluster of tiny stories gains in power until it becomes one story; deftly combining the spontaneity and particularity of this handful of people with the omnipresent, gently intrusive presence of the artist, Baxter welds the scene into a breathtaking unity. Although he strains, perhaps, for too broad a perspective—content not only with presenting the characters but also offering detailed weather reports as the day passes, and the precise latitude and longitude of the park—his effort to compose a timeless moment, a fully rendered particular setting which represents the universal, is wholly successful, and the result is a moving, incontestably genuine portrait of American life in a moment of repose.

Baxter's artistic intentions are stated baldly in the paragraph marking his own final appearance in the story, yet given the rhetorical detachment and unlimited scope of the narrative, this paragraph is not an intrusion but a climactic moment of longing:

> For an instant I glance at all the other people here and try to fix them into a scene of stationary, luminous repose, as if under glass, in which they would be given an instant of formal visual precision, without reference to who they are as people. Even now, with the light changing, the sun moving more rapidly toward the horizon and the light gradually acquiring that slightly unnatural peach tint it has before twilight when the shadows are grotesquely elongated, I cannot do it. These people keep moving out and away from the neat visual pattern I am hoping for.

The key phrase here describes the artist's wish to present his characters *without reference to who they are as people;* this does not imply a cold, impersonal detachment, however, but a desire to honor these particular individuals as representative members of the human family. As the story's last line suggests, Sunday is a day of repose but also a "day of forgiveness." Perceiving his characters with a clear eye, the artist nonetheless refuses to impose judgment. This substitution of compassionate acceptance for moral judgment characterizes Baxter's stories as a whole.

In its unusual form, **"A Late Sunday Afternoon by the Huron"** is anomalous in Baxter's work thus far; ordinarily he focuses upon a single, tautly dramatic situation and cuts quickly to the emotional core of his people. This story

resembles others in both volumes, however, in describing human fragility and sorrow but also a saving strength, humor and resilience. Likewise, the story could be seen to represent the distinctive qualities of his work as a whole: its impressive scope, its careful observation, and its life-affirming compassion. (pp. 616-21)

Greg Johnson, "Charles Baxter and the Art of Forgiveness," in Michigan Quarterly Review, *Vol. XXV, No. 3, Summer, 1986, pp. 616-21.*

James Brock (review date Fall 1986)

[In the following essay, Brock praises the compassion and characterization in Through the Safety Net.]*

Although *Through the Safety Net* is only his second collection of stories and he has yet to publish in the large circulation "name" magazines, Charles Baxter must be counted among one of our best short fiction writers. The author of these eleven stories is a mature, accomplished writer, as evident in **"Winter Journey"** and **"Surprised by Joy."** The suggestive title of the collection unites the stories and has many referents, including the title story and the Reaganomic notion that beneath society stretches a safety net, really. The most telling referent, however, appears in **"A Late Sunday Afternoon at the Huron,"** which features these lines from a Delmore Schwartz poem:

> The sunlight, the soaring trees and the Seine
> Are as a great net in which Seurat seeks to seize and hold
> All living being in a parade and promenade of mild, calm
> happiness.

Baxter's characters, though falling through a spiritual abyss, have known a mild happiness. As they fall, they can still remember a happiness, or at least they can conjure one. Some even land safely.

Baxter celebrates in his falling characters that ability to acknowledge the life in those who still balance upon the tightrope. In **"The Eleventh Floor,"** an alcoholic commercial writer, Mr. Bradbury, is shrouded in a cynical indifference to the world, and not until Mr. Bradbury recognizes the deep, sexual love between his son and his son's lover does life affect him:

> From far down on the other side of the hallway, he heard Darlene's loud laugh. He started to slip in under the covers, thought better of it, and went to his window to part the curtains. Getting back into bed, he switched off the bulb; then, with his head on the pillow, he gazed at the city skyline, half-consciously counting the few apartments in the highrise across the street that still had all their lights burning.

Having spent the latter part of his life in an alcoholic blur, blindly falling, Mr. Bradbury may not be redeemed by his understanding, for he has merely drawn open his own frailty. Yet for someone who is falling, parting the curtains to see the world is a worthy act. Baxter does not gratuitously play with his subjects. Rather, he proffers the hope and possibility that another net will gather beneath the falling, provided that those who fall are humane enough to recognize their own vulnerability.

Through the Safety Net is not a collection of Carverean stories of good, inarticulate people living bad lives; neither do these stories wallow in modern malaise; neither are they simple regional tales. Baxter's Michigan is inhabited by cars, half-employed workers, burned-out graduate students, half-sane school teachers, would-be painters, dogs, young boys, and angels—a Michigan meriting forgiveness and blessing. Life is affirmed, even when living is grievous or bitter. In a time in which many short stories are written either as thinly veiled autobiography or as *l'art pour l'art* exercises, these stories are profound in how Baxter brings back authority to the teller of the tale. In short, he has something to say *for* us, and he takes on that moral responsibility with humor, wisdom, and compassion. (pp. 459-60)

James Brock, in a review of "Through the Safety Net," in Studies in Short Fiction, *Vol. 23, No. 4, Fall, 1986, pp. 459-60.*

Michiko Kakutani   (review date 24 August 1987)

[*In the essay below, Kakutani praises Baxter's depiction of familial relationships in* First Light.]

"Life can only be understood backwards," Kierkegaard once observed, "but it must be lived forwards." Backward into memory and childhood—that is the direction taken by Charles Baxter's highly accomplished first novel [***First Light***]. Like the Broadway shows *Merrily We Roll Along* and *Betrayal*, ***First Light*** consists of a series of episodes that recede further and further into the past, and with each backward step, the reader is granted further insight into the characters' lives. The process is not unlike the one used by psychiatrists: as ancient family history is sifted, clues are yielded that shed new light on the present. In one's beginnings are found seeds of what is yet to come.

As he has already demonstrated in two impressive collections of short stories, ***Harmony of the World*** and ***Through the Safety Net,*** Mr. Baxter possesses an intuitive understanding of the hazards and rewards of domestic life—especially as practiced by survivors of the 60's. In ***First Light,*** he trains his gifts of sympathy and observation on a single family, the Welches of Five Oaks, Mich. More specifically, his focus is on Hugh Welch, a Buick salesman, and his brilliant sister, Dorsey, who left home to become a famous astrophysicist.

When we first meet Dorsey, she's just returned for a Fourth of July visit to her hometown, with her new husband and her deaf son, Noah, in tow. Hugh, it seems, has been dreading the visit for days: though he's spent his life "watching over" his kid sister, he's recently begun to doubt that she needs his help at all. To make matters worse, he's already taken a decided dislike to her husband, Simon, a glib, self-conscious actor who seems to be constantly putting him down. Indeed, the initial impressions that Simon and Dorsey make on the reader is less than positive: Dorsey comes across as a snobbish academic who patronizes her working-class brother, and Simon strikes

us as a self-absorbed fool, a small-town cad who not only cheats on Dorsey all the time but also likes to boast about it.

"All I ever wanted," Hugh tells Dorsey, "was to make sure . . . that you were all right. You know: safe."

"That's sweet," she replies, echoing a sentiment expressed by many of the characters in ***Through the Safety Net.*** "But it won't ever work. Not for me. It hasn't ever worked. Besides, there's no safety in safety. So I might as well live with Simon. You and I, Hugh—we've been divorced, haven't we? Can brothers and sisters get divorces from each other? I think they can, and I think we got one."

From this nervous, nearly adversarial exchange, Mr. Baxter slowly draws us into Dorsey's and Hugh's past; we begin to understand just how this "divorce" has occurred. Over the years, after all, Dorsey and Hugh have drifted into different worlds. As their paths have diverged, their memories of each other have become uncomfortable reminders of what they once were—and might have been.

Having elected to stay in Five Oaks and marry a girl he dated in school, Hugh now leads a simple, tactile life: though his marriage has devolved into a passionless routine, punctuated with occasional motel room liaisons, he still derives a blunt, unaccommodated pleasure from selling Buicks, and he enjoys renovating the house he inherited from his parents. "To record the passage of time through his life," writes Mr. Baxter, "Hugh alters his house room by room. He surrounds himself with the work of his hands."

Dorsey, in contrast, has gone on to study the cold, starry skies. She has made a life for herself in the cerebral spheres of academia, fulfilling all the brave, high expectations of her parents and teachers. She has worked for her doctorate, had a disturbing affair with her mentor, a brooding physicist named Carlo Pavorese, and borne his child, Noah. In the wake of those events, she has abruptly married Simon, a willful, self-absorbed man, in whose adolescent pranks she delights.

The men in Dorsey's life are drawn, by Mr. Baxter, in uncharacteristically broad strokes; they tend to feel more like generic types than individuals. Carlo is a caricature of the mad genius—tormented, brilliant and domineering—while Simon seems like a shallow alter ego of Hugh. Where Hugh is adept with his hands, Simon is inept; where Hugh is earnest and sincere, Simon is posturing and phony, etc.

Happily enough, the two-dimensionality of these fellows doesn't really bother us, so wrapped up are we in the story of Dorsey and Hugh. As the novel progresses, the retreat into their past accelerates; we see their youth and childhoods revealed, like rapidly turned pages in a snapshot album. Dorsey's appeal to Hugh for help, as she lies alone in a hospital room with her newborn baby; Dorsey's delivery of the valedictory speech at the Five Oaks high school; Hugh's growing reputation as a ladies' man in Five Oaks; Dorsey's difficulty finding a date for the school dance, her sense of being a social outcast; Hugh's dazzling performance as a hockey player, in front of his adoring sister's

eyes; Dorsey's fascination, as a child, with the stars and planets of the nighttime sky.

In reading of these events, we see why Dorsey and Hugh each made the choices that they did, how their childhood dreams were translated into adult decisions. We see how Hugh looked for Dorsey in his wife, Laurie; how Dorsey's hero worship of her brother led her to pick men so different in temperament and talents. In fact, by orchestrating tiny details of observation and larger emotional patterns, Mr. Baxter makes us understand both the shifting balance of power that has occurred between Dorsey and Hugh over the years, and the bonds of affection and shared experience that unite them. The result is a remarkably supple novel that gleams with the smoky chiaroscuro of familial love recalled through time.

> *Michiko Kakutani, in a review of "First Light," in* The New York Times, *August 24, 1987, p. C13.*

Margot Mifflin   (review date 4 October 1987)

[*In the essay below, Mifflin provides a mixed assessment of* First Light.]

[*First Light*] is a first novel that moves backward in time, from a day in the adult lives of two siblings struggling to bridge a gap that geography and education have wedged between them, to the first morning of their lives together. The story unfolds like a mystery: every step backward explains another piece in the puzzle of their relationship, and a puzzling relationship it is.

Hugh is a Buick salesman who never left his hometown. Dorsey, his younger sister, is an astrophysicist who got all the brains in the family, an advantage she, Hugh and the author treat as proof that she's a better person than her brother. While Dorsey is openly contemptuous of Hugh's suburban life style and passionless marriage, he carries a torch of fraternal devotion to her, inspired by his late parents' urgings to take care of her.

For all her supercilious conduct, Dorsey is hardly in control of her own life. She spends much of her marriage to Simon, a self-infatuated, philandering actor, in deference to him. She has a son, Noah (the result of an affair with her physics teacher, Carlo, in graduate school), a deaf child, who serves as a reminder of her one true heartthrob; she justifies her marriage by showing that though Simon is a repugnant creep, he's a great father to her stepson.

How do you respond to a novel in which the only sympathetic character becomes so by default? Hugh isn't imaginative or articulate, but he's spared the flaw that plagues his fellow characters: a smug intellectualism. He offers the only glimmer of sensitivity in a book where ideas eclipse emotions, and where much of the drama involves people humbling each other with glib put-downs. Hugh has dropped everything to bail Dorsey out of various crises since high school, but when she visits him in their Michigan hometown she thwarts his brotherly inquiries about her happiness by saying: "You and I, Hugh—we've been divorced, haven't we? Can brothers and sisters get divorces from each other? I think they can, and I think we got one." And Hugh, not Dorsey, is the one who suffers in this paralyzed relationship.

There are lots of interesting ideas running through *First Light*—the possibility that siblings can in essence be "married," and that their marriages really can't be annulled; Dorsey's perceptions as an astrophysicist and the analogies she makes between the universe and her own life; and the use of a backward structure. Charles Baxter sets up a dramatic overlap between two chapters in which the same scene—Hugh's visit to Dorsey in the maternity ward—is described from complementary perspectives, showing their unbalanced perceptions of each other. But the coldness of these characters makes it difficult to understand their motivations (no matter how far back we look into their childhood) and harder yet to identify with them. If only *someone* in these pages would stop straining for a clever turn of phrase and communicate honestly. Dorsey's love for Carlo is confused with her respect for his intellect; she can't stand him physically, she tires of his broken-down monologues about Robert Oppenheimer, but she's stuck on him and keeps his baby for unexplained reasons. Her marriage to Simon is arranged on their first date, when she, four months pregnant, remarks, "You'd be an odd husband, but a person could do worse." And a major hole in the plot doesn't help matters: Mr. Baxter doesn't clarify when and why Dorsey stops seeing Hugh as a heroic big brother and starts treating him as a mentally deficient errand boy. But in a book so mannered that spaghetti sauce can have "subtle ambitions" and young men are said to acknowledge "the common sexual decencies," there comes a point at which the reader ceases to care.

Margot Mifflin, "Siblings Divorced," in The New York Times Book Review, *October 4, 1987, p. 18.*

Elizabeth Tallent   (review date 6 December 1987)

[*Tallent is an American short story writer, novelist, and critic. In the following essay, she examines the narrative structure of* First Light.]

First Light, intent on its gently resonant, subtly compounding complications, unfolds in a queer way: backward. Charles Baxter's serenely unflashy first novel comes dressed with a promissory epigraph from Kierkegaard: "Life can only be understood backwards; but it must be lived forwards." In a kind of reverse *Bildungsroman,* then, ***First Light*** begins with adult characters and gradually, chapter by chapter, setting up a rich system of echoes and connections, reduces them to children. "Reduces" is probably the wrong word: The reader experiences an avid interest in these children, having known them as grown-ups. There is the kind of interest an elderly woman acquaintance demonstrates when she claims, "I knew you when you were a *child,*" thus declaring her special stake in you, and yours in her—she knew the original you; possibly you will catch some reflection of that long-vanished self in her eyes. If she's sly, she exploits this. The possibility renders her current, slightly critical gaze (How have you changed?) bearable. This novel takes that kind of inquisitive, proprietary, utterly natural interest and turns it inside out.

The novel begins, and therefore ends, with backyard fireworks on the Fourth of July in Five Oaks, Mich. Metaphorically, at least, fireworks represent brilliant sudden illumination of a kind that ***First Light*** otherwise avoids; the Fourth symbolizes jubilant release, while the novel has taken for its quiet subject the insistent claims of siblinghood as they exist between a brilliant astrophysicist, Dorsey Welch—"a beauty without innocence . . . because of her eyes. Insomniac attentiveness has darkened them"— and her older brother Hugh, a Buick salesman whose existence has been altogether more modest and fettered. One of his chief fetters has always been to his sister: "My father once told me to watch after her, to take care of her. So I tried. . . . It's not like being married. It's this other kind of love. There's no name for it. Sometimes I think I've spent my life watching her, watching over her."

The novel's first paragraph consists of a qualification, by Dorsey, of something Hugh has just said. He's referred to fireworks as explosives, and she fastidiously corrects him: They are toys. Explosions, the author seems to imply, though they occur elsewhere, have seldom rocked these lives; and when, in the backyard, a toy airport constructed by Dorsey's husband, Simon, is blown apart, Simon's ir-

reverence infuriates Hugh, who has already, within 20 pages, settled into the novel's emblem of soberly vigilant love.

> "A revolution is a revolution!" Simon shouts, lighting the cherry bomb. . . . Hugh raises his head, closes his eyes as the bomb explodes, tearing apart both the car and the Athens airport next to it, and blowing out several cardboard people inside the airport onto the grass. Hugh looks up and sees a flock of sparrows. He wants to see them form into a pattern, an arrow or a letter, but flocks of sparrows never make formations, he reminds himself; they go where they want to.

Hugh's recognition—"flocks of sparrows never make formations"—underscores Baxter's respect for the vagueness and untidiness of perception, and its refusal to fall neatly into compact fictional shapes. This respect, one imagines, underlies this novel's unorthodox narrative form. The novel harbors a number of striking images that comment on its own backward-seeking structure, as in a scene of Hugh, Dorsey, and their parents viewing an eclipse through photographic negatives. Hugh sees " . . . all of the separate images piled on top of one another, one large distinct collection of the past, and, in the middle of it, the darkening sun, now shaped like a burning three-quarter moon, shining through them."

This novel's time, in not going forward, seems curiously deep and still. My impression that this was a really long novel persisted, though, in fact, it's 286 pages—solid but not massive. The characters' childhoods are treated with great psychological naturalism: What is enigmatic in those scenes is what would be enigmatic in a child's eyes, and the reader, who has by then been drawn in very close to Hugh and Dorsey, is confronted with a world mysterious, duplicitous, baffling. Baxter is the author of two previous books, both collections of stories, ***Harmony of the World*** and ***Through the Safety Net.*** A story in ***Through the Safety Net,*** **"Talk Show,"** is written in simple, short paragraphs, each isolated from the rest of the story by white space, representing the choppy but intense segments of a young boy's attention and dealing with his fascinated incomprehension of his grandmother's slow death. It is compelling in the way that the childhood chapters of ***First Light*** are compelling: The measure of darkness is taken by clear but uncomprehending eyes.

Despite its affection for discontinuity, this novel's loose ends have a way of sliding together into memorably firm knots. Hugh's wife and daughters remain shadowy, and Hugh and Dorsey's parents never quite emerge as individuals, so there is a slightness where the reader could have wished for greater depth, in figures so close to Hugh. In the ending, however, a single gesture is packed with meaning distilled from the previous 285 pages; a crucial instant, frozen in time, concludes this intricately reflective, simply beautiful book.

Elizabeth Tallent, "Live Forward, Understand Backward," in Los Angeles Times Book Review, *December 6, 1987, p. 3.*

Bret Lott (review date Summer 1988)

[*Lott is an American novelist, short story writer, critic, and educator. In the following excerpt, he praises Baxter's use of time as a method of character development in* First Light.]

Sometimes, the distance between reader and story disappears, and when a reviewer reads a book of such luminous transparence, sheer delight takes over: that's why we read, isn't it? To move elsewhere, discover something new about other people, and, by extension, ourselves? Reading Charles Baxter's first novel, *First Light,* has been one of these experiences. When I am drawn as fully into the lives of other people as I have been with *First Light,* I regret I *am* reviewing the book. But that is the surest sign of a fine work: that you give up your own sense of time and history to be swept up into the lives before you.

Which is precisely what this book is about: the *lives* of two people, Hugh and Dorsey Welch, brother and sister. Baxter, the author of two story collections, *Through the Safety Net* and *Harmony of the World,* begins his novel with its final scene; that is, the book progresses antichronologically, the action in each chapter occurring before the chapter it follows, so that in the first chapter we have a Fourth of July gathering and fireworks display at Hugh's house in their hometown of Five Oaks, Michigan, while the second chapter chronicles Dorsey and her actor husband Simon's drive to Hugh's house along backroad Ohio a couple of days before, their deaf son Noah in the backseat, asleep.

The device is deceptively simple, the subtle shift in time and story so small at first as to seem *only* a device. But then, once we start heading deeper and deeper into their lives, finding out the secrets both hold, the secrets they both share with one another and keep from one another, the cumulative effect is one of increasing enchantment and ambiguity. The pieces of action do not lead to any sort of climax, any denouement; there will be no rising action or falling action; those ordinary concerns of fiction seem petty now in the face of the entire lives we have before us. The reader keeps searching his memory for what happened in the first chapter that was of utmost importance, a revelation in advance of its determinants, until he comes to understand there neither *was* nor is a single event in that

or any chapter that will signal what information to keep and what to throw away. Hugh, while helping to drive Simon and Dorsey and baby Noah across the country to Buffalo and her first job after graduate school—she is an astrophysicist with a Ph.D. from Berkeley—begins to tell Simon about his father's life, and starts with how he died at the breakfast table one Sunday morning, to which Simon retorts: " 'Why is it . . . when you ask people about somebody's life, they tell you how the person died?' 'You start with the last things first, ass-backwards, if you're me,' Hugh says, sure of that. 'You start with the period instead of the capital letter. That way you're always sure how everything ends.' " We *are* certain how things will end—we have only to reread the first chapter to find that out—and yet the beauty of this novel is how with each turn of the page we are drawn closer and closer to a satisfying and inevitable end: when Hugh, just a toddler, meets his newborn sister for the very first time in the hospital only a day after she is born, and touches her with a sense of destiny we, not he, fully appreciate.

Between the end of the story and its beginning are events that seem, as time moves backward, to move toward less complexity, toward more black and white choices and situations, and thereby back (or forward) to the innocence of youth. The adult Dorsey has an affair with Carlo Pavorese, an aged faculty member at Berkeley whose claim to fame was his work with Oppenheimer in New Mexico; he is everything her scientific, astrophysicist-astronomer's mind has wanted all her life, but she finds no rationale for making love to him: "She wished she had had more wine: she could not remember ever being touched by a man toward whom she felt physical curiosity rather than attraction." We readily accept her giving herself to him, even though the affair only twists her toward some inevitable chaos, her career heading "off the main track onto a spur line where the rails are hardly visible for the multitude of weeds growing between them." And it's not until later in the novel—and earlier in her life—that we see the groundwork that sets up her surrender to Pavorese when, as a teenager waiting for the phone she has herself installed in her room, no boys call: "With the telephone on her desk, Dorsey expects things to change, more calls, more invitations. But usually when her phone buzzes, it's for her mother or father. When it's for Dorsey, it's nearly always from someone who needs help on a math problem."

Matters for Hugh, too, move from complex to simple, just as they do in all of our lives if we look back on what worried us when we were growing up and what worries us today. Hugh, never the one for high marks in school, has only car sales to lead him through life now. But cars are what he loves, and standing in the showroom at the Buick dealership he works for, he takes pleasure in his domain:

> As usual, the cars give him a huge sense of their own appropriateness. They are antidotes to life as it is. Hugh loves Buicks. He loves them almost as much as he loves his own family, almost as much as he loves women. A person can't stay with women all day, however. Hugh thinks of his attraction to women, his love for them, as a character flaw. . . . Absentmindedly, he pats the dark gray Skylark on the fender above the

left front wheel. The steel and wax do not feel like skin but an approximation of it, a powerfully erotic metallic sheath.

This sensuous regard for cars shines through succeeding chapters like some warning beacon for Hugh, whose grades plunge ever lower, whose ice hockey scholarship is lost because he can't seem to push himself for the grades, back and farther back. Parking their Nash two spaces away from all the other cars in the hospital parking lot the morning they are to see Dorsey for the first time, Hugh's father says, "You do this . . . and they don't bang their doors against you when they open them." And little Hugh "doesn't know what his father is talking about."

But most important is the winding back to the beginning points; how brother and sister love each other, hate each other, accommodate themselves to each other. When Dorsey has her baby, the baby we already know will be deaf though at the present moment neither Dorsey nor Hugh has a clue that Noah is anything but perfectly normal, Hugh leaves Michigan for California almost as soon as he hangs up the phone, this is a result, we see later in the book, of Hugh's mother's words after the boy complains of all the attention his baby sister receives:

> "Now listen to me," she says. "This is important. . . . Your sister is younger than you are. She is always going to be younger than you are. She will never be older. That means something. What it means is that you will have to take care of her. Your father and I may not always be around. You are Dorsey's older brother. That is a responsibility. Are you listening to me?" Hugh nods, hopelessly. "I want you to make me a promise," she says. "I want you to promise that you will be a brother to Dorsey, and look after her, and watch out for her, always and forever." She stares at him, pounding her gaze into his heart. "Do you promise? Raise your right hand and promise." The hand goes up. He nods, says "I promise," and begins to cry.

The mother has spoken the truth: they in fact die, Dorsey in fact needs her brother's help from time to time during their lives, and Hugh always remains the older brother, the one who must be there when he is needed, no matter what. And he is always ready, even from the moment, when just before he meets his sister, Hugh's father stops to tell him something in the hospital corridor:

> His father squats down and faces Hugh. He's going to tell Hugh how to act. What not to say. But no: in a voice dropped so low that Hugh can hardly hear it, his father tells Hugh that he loves him, he will always love him, that he is a wonderful boy and he has a sister now, and he'll have to love her and take care of her. And Hugh, behind his surgical mask, says, "Daddy, what did I do?" "You didn't do anything," his father says. "Let's go in."

This is perhaps the most poignant moment in the book because it is now, we realize, that Hugh will begin what will be the rest of a life spent accommodating himself to the presence of his sister, the moment when the competition—for love, for grades, for everything—begins, the moment

which precipitates in the first chapter Hugh's words to his sister in the midnight kitchen of the house he inherited when their mother died: " 'All I ever wanted,' he says, suddenly afraid of his own generalization, 'was to make sure . . . that you were all right. You know: safe.' "

The sorrow felt here and throughout the book, though, isn't that of observing tragic lives, because both these characters possess the resilience and *amor fati* of survivors. Like the origins of the universe, an indeterminable problem that fascinates Dorsey, their deepest secrets elude our full comprehension, though we gather plenty of information from the discrete scenes flashed across our eyes. Baxter is suggesting that the novelist, no less than the physicist or psychoanalyst, has no business meddling with the omega of our lives, only with the alpha points of birth, childhood, adolescence, and every age short of death, each marking an end as well as a beginning, perpetually. It is only the Oppenheimers who insist on making and knowing the end of the human story, unsatisfied with the ordinary act of living, the creaturely pleasures and disappointments that Baxter records with such compelling sympathy. Reading lives backward, then, becomes an act of prophecy in the sense of knowing what is commonly hidden from sight.

Baxter's technique is nothing short of brilliant. Nowhere in this book is there any faltering of voice, of imagery, of observation. The sad truth Baxter gives us that we are alone, all of us, and have only our own histories to guide us. "They raised us," Dorsey says to Hugh while in the car on the way to Buffalo, "and then they left us alone by ourselves to manage any way we could. . . . The way parents do. They died, and there we were, out in the world. Hell, everyone's an orphan sooner or later." One puts this book down looking to find one's own children somewhere in the house, wonder what they are up to, who they will become as a result of our scoldings, our praise, our love or our indifference; and one thinks of one's own parents, what they did and what we did to make us who we are. (pp. 520-24)

> *Bret Lott, "Believing the Story: Three Recent Novels," in* Michigan Quarterly Review, *Vol. XXVII, No. 3, Summer, 1988, pp. 516-24.*

Gary Davenport   (review date Summer 1989)

[*In the excerpt below, Davenport concludes that Baxter's antichronological approach in* First Light *provides a series of kaleidoscopic images rather than definitive character portraits.*]

There is no denying that historical amnesia can be joyously liberating, at least temporarily. In a shorter view than Santayana's those of us who can't or won't remember the past are *free* to relive it, and almost every sphere of contemporary life has known the delights of this emancipation. Examples could be adduced from such diverse areas as art, technology, economics, international relations—and literary criticism, which, despite its current sense of itself as brilliantly radical, commonly offers as a breakthrough what no responsible reader ever doubted. We like to think of ourselves as living in a jaded, demystified, post-everything world, but at least half of our energy goes into the daily reinvention of the wheel.

Although contemporary fiction is itself not always free of this convenient amnesia, I think the best of it can be seen primarily as a reaction to the age's historical naiveté rather than a symptom of it. I see everywhere in recent fiction a scrutiny of the present in terms of the way it remembers, mishandles, and forgets the past, both personal and historical. That may seem a sloppy way of defining the past, but the best of today's novelists, in the tradition of Pound, Eliot, Joyce, Bergson, R. G. Collingwood, and many other modern artists and thinkers, tend to see the past not as objective, linear, and disjunctive but as subjective and simultaneous. (This is one important way, incidentally, in which postmodernism seems not to have gone beyond modernism: if anything, it represents a dilution of this central modernist concept.) Sharp lines of demarcation do not always exist between what happened to a character last week and what happened in the days of Rousseau, King Edwin of Northumbria, and the Big Bang (all of which figure into the novels under consideration here).

To put the very first things first: in Charles Baxter's first novel *First Light* the monstrous explosion that is alleged to have created the universe is the research topic of a physicist named Dorsey Welch, who is thus professionally committed to an understanding of the ultimate past. Her brother Hugh, the novel's other main character, appears at first to be just the opposite—a Buick salesman who lives a normal and unreflective life in the small Michigan town where they grew up. When Dorsey asks her brother to "imagine going back to the first second of the Big Bang," and to "imagine time reversed," he replies curtly: "No. You think about it. I don't have to—I live here." He is of course not this simple: his resistance to Dorsey is more personal than anything else, and he is perfectly capable of visualizing, while waiting for a stoplight, "Bacon Drug to his right, the Quik-'n'-Ezy to his left, buried under the water left behind by the melting glaciers," and "huge Pleistocene fish swimming down the main street."

Hugh's problems with Dorsey stem from his frustrated role as her big brother and protector: he cannot come to terms with the fact that his kid sister lives in a larger and more important world than his. Their past is still valid for him—more valid than the present. Hence the chief structural device of the novel: its chapters move back through the lives of these protagonists to end at the point when Hugh touches his newborn sister's hand for the first time. (Of course a theme of this nature can be and often is successfully explored in chronologically straightforward fiction—and could have been, I think, in *First Light*.) The author quotes Kierkegaard at the beginning of the book— "Life can only be understood backwards; but it must be lived forwards"—and that observation might well stand as an epigraph for any number of contemporary fictional characters: the only meaning they can hope to give their lives is retrospective.

Fictional lives can and should have meaning for readers at least, but despite its self-conscious study of the problem of making sense of life, *First Light* is not very satisfying in this regard. We know that Hugh is hungry for affection,

that he fears and hates a life of multiplicity, relativity, and contingency, and that he and his sister's deaf son have a strange bond; we know that Dorsey has had a brief affair with a prominent physicist who now won't leave her alone; we know that her actor husband Simon is a chameleonic "original" whose predictable eccentricity is apparently fascinating to the author but tiresome to Hugh (and to at least one reader of the novel). Despite the aura of significance that hovers over the events, none of this ever adds up. For instance, when Hugh and Dorsey are children, their father gets the family out at dawn one morning to watch a solar eclipse. For protection they watch this display of first light through a stack of old photographic negatives—family pictures: "Hugh sees Ruby superimposed on his big granny, and himself as a baby over the two of them, and his grandfather on his tractor superimposed on top of himself holding hands with his sister, all of the separate images piled on top of one another, one large distinct collection of the past, and, in the middle of it, the darkening sun, now shaped like a burning three-quarter moon, shining through them." This seems to be a carefully devised symbol that cries out for an exegesis— indeed, was apparently designed for exegesis—but I am unable to provide one.

Although Baxter's novel is deftly written and contains much accurate observation and characterization, it seems to me to pretend to a significance that it doesn't have: even after we follow the author's prescription and view life in reverse, we still have only a stack of negatives rather than a single picture. (pp. 468-70)

> *Gary Davenport, "Making Virtue of Necessity," in* The Sewanee Review, *Vol. XCVII, No. 3, Summer, 1989, pp. 468-74.*

Penny Kaganoff   (review date 2 March 1990)

[In the following essay, Kaganoff praises the originality of Imaginary Paintings.]

The poems in [*Imaginary Paintings*] evoke the artistry of Edward Hopper as fiction writer Baxter (*Through the Safety Net*) plays with images of light, hopelessness and the loss of American innocence and creativity. The poet fashions a vista of shopping malls, factories and highways in order to rail—often heavy-handedly—against complacency and naïveté: "Say that it's hollow and they'll just laugh / . . . which is why if you tilt American heads backwards / American eyes, like dolls' eyes, snap shut suddenly." The way out of this "sleep," Baxter convincingly argues, is via the imagination—the "current" that will "pass through deadened arms, / until all the stories will be original again." In poems that celebrate art, music and literature, "life is proved / to be, not a still life, but otherwise." Despite some awkward imagery ("his favorite word flung in your face / like a blood clot"), and a sometimes blatant didacticism meant to implicate the reader, this volume is redeemed by its inventiveness and originality of form, content and spirit.

> *Penny Kaganoff, in a review of "Imaginary Paintings," in* Publishers Weekly, *Vol. 237, No. 9, March 2, 1990, p. 78.*

> I don't want to sound conservative or
> fusty, but I want to watch how people
> behave. . . . You know, people who want
> to lead good lives and who are failing and
> succeeding at it. It's much more
> interesting than people eagerly and
> constantly misbehaving.
>
> —*Charles Baxter, in an interview with
> Neely Tucker in the* Detroit Free Press,
> *23 December 1992.*

Jim Elledge   (review date August 1990)

[*Elledge is an American poet, editor, critic, and educator. In the following review, he states that the poems in* Imaginary Paintings *focus on contemporary American society.*]

[*Imaginary Paintings, and Other Poems,* Baxter's first poetry collection in over a decade and a half,] is a vivid slice of Americana, a deftly conducted tour across the nation's landscape, punctuated by sometimes frightening but always gripping stopovers. In **"Country Road H,"** the poet admits, "We are driving a gray road at night, / no signs, far from friends," and it is such isolation—the narrator's from his companion and the rest of humanity—that underscores one of Baxter's recurring themes, that alienation is a chief characteristic of our lives. "There must be happiness. I will force happiness / into a package wrapped in waxed paper" begins **"Fighting Depression, I Take My Family on a Picnic,"** but the gap between the speaker's life and his family's is not bridged. Yet, as he claims in **"Harvest Home,"** "American optimism triumphs." Indeed, in many of these graceful, powerfully written poems, Baxter's claim is at least inferred if not proven.

> *Jim Elledge, in a review of "Imaginary Paintings, and Other Poems," in* Booklist, *Vol. 86, No. 22, August, 1990, p. 2149.*

Michiko Kakutani   (review date 4 September 1990)

[*In the review below, Kakutani examines how the tales in* A Relative Stranger, *like Baxter's other works, reflect "a view of the world as a highly precarious place."*]

In Charles Baxter's wonderful new collection of stories, [*A Relative Stranger*], people are constantly having odd encounters with strangers that disrupt their quiet, humdrum lives and send them skidding in unexpected new directions.

In **"Westland,"** a social worker befriends a teen-age girl who says she plans to shoot one of the lions at the zoo, and he is drawn into a lazy spiral of events that ends with his firing the same gun at a nuclear reactor. In **"A Relative Stranger,"** a checkout clerk with a bad marriage and no ambition receives a phone call from his long-lost brother (the two were adopted by different parents in infancy) and finds himself forced to admit this pushy new acquaintance into his bleak, hermetic life. And in **"The Disappeared,"** a Swedish tourist picks up a pretty young woman in Detroit and discovers that his fantasy of an amusing one-night stand has turned into a hellish, existential adventure.

As readers of Mr. Baxter's earlier books (*Through the Safety Net, First Light, Harmony of the World*) are aware, such events are not merely isolated epiphanies. Rather, they underscore a view of the world as a highly precarious place, where the arc of a life may be suddenly and irrevocably altered by a random occurrence, where happiness and domestic calm are highly provisional—subject to accidents, bad luck, unexpected passions and unforeseen twists of fate.

An idealistic man befriends a crazed, homeless man, then realizes that his act of good will has awakened fears and resentments in his wife and son (**"Shelter"**). A 12-year-old boy accompanies his older brother and his girlfriend to a lake where a car has fallen through the ice, and he has a glimpse of the perils and uncertainties of the grown-up world that awaits him (**"Snow"**). A woman who realizes that she loves her husband's best friend develops an irrational fear of prowlers that keeps her awake at night.

"Look at these houses you and your neighbors live in," the friend says to the husband. "Little rectangular temples of light. Nothing here but families and fireplaces and Duraflame logs and children of God. Not the sort of place where a married woman ought to be worried about prowlers."

Perhaps because they worry so much about domestic and emotional safety, Mr. Baxter's characters also seem preoccupied with the more abstract questions of goodness, happiness and justice—questions that give them a way of trying to quantify the world, explain its mysterious and random motions. A publicity writer named Fenstad, who longs to be "a good person," teaches a composition class at night "because he enjoyed the sense of hope that classrooms held for him." A baker is haunted by his encounter with a homeless person and starts doing volunteer work at a shelter.

In another story, a teacher named Saul, who feels unable to live easily "in the real," starts evaluating the happiness of everyone around him. "Now he believed," writes Mr. Baxter,

> that compared to others he was actually and truly unhappy, especially since his mind insisted on thinking about the problem, pouring over it, ragging him on and on. It was like the discontent of adolescence, the discontent with situations, but this was larger, the discontent with being itself, a psychic itch with nowhere to scratch.

The events in this story, which eventually bring Saul his own version of happiness, include a car accident, a disturbing encounter with a former student, a desultory Scrabble game with his wife, an offer of wisdom found on a matchbook cover, and a glimpse of an albino deer—events that are at once completely ordinary and unexpected, startling yet familiar.

Indeed, all the stories in this collection attest to Mr. Baxter's ability to orchestrate the details of mundane day-to-day reality into surprising patterns of grace and revelation, his gentle but persuasive knack for finding and describing the fleeting moments that indelibly define a life.

Whether he's writing about an overly self-conscious intellectual or an inarticulate street person, Mr. Baxter is able to map out their emotions persuasively and delineate the shape of their spiritual confusion. If his men tend to be adolescent idealists, ineffectual and doubting, his women emerge as strong, centered individuals, sure of what they want and more than willing to humor their wayward spouses. One woman consoles her dying husband with fanciful and highly fictionalized accounts of their long-ago adventures together (**"Scheherazade"**). Another woman, who predicts that her boyfriend wants her to behave unpredictably, affectionately complies with his wishes (**"Lake Stephen"**).

Though each story in this volume stands serenely on its own (many first appeared in such small magazines as *The Georgia Review, The Iowa Review, Michigan Quarterly Review* and *Denver Quarterly*), the final tale, **"Saul and Patsy Are Pregnant,"** brings together many of the characters we've previously met. We learn that they all live in or around the small Michigan town of Five Oaks, that their paths have unwittingly intersected; and we finish the book with the satisfaction of having been immersed in a beautifully rendered and fully imagined world.

> *Michiko Kakutani, "Encounters Odd and Normal at Once," in* The New York Times, *September 4, 1990, p. C15.*

Diane Cole   (review date 9 September 1990)

[*An American editor and critic, Cole is best known for her self-help books. In the excerpt below, she examines the themes, tone, and dialogue in* A Relative Stranger.]

If novels bring us the news, then short stories deliver the headlines. Charles Baxter, an underrated master of the genre, and David Leavitt, a gifted but inconsistent writer, illustrate the varied art of storytelling in two new collections that struggle to interpret a world that is increasingly puzzling and alien.

Characters in [Baxter's *A Relative Stranger*, and Leavitt's *A Place I've Never Been*] seek to discover ways to "connect" with each other, their families or their communities, and most of all to wrest some meaning from the muddle of their vaguely discontented lives. A lucky few find answers; most do not.

Charles Baxter has written three other short story collections and a novel, *First Light*, yet he has not won the reputation he deserves. *A Relative Stranger*, his newest work, confirms his talent and his vision.

Baxter's strength as a writer derives from his mysterious, haunting tone, his razorsharp imagery and the slightly surreal quality to his characters' conversation. Throughout his work, small, slightly absurd gestures come to stand for larger conflicts that will never be resolved: In **"Snow,"**

for instance, a teenage girl stands barefoot on an ice-covered lake in order to impress a cold-hearted suitor. In **"Scissors,"** thousands of coupons, dumped from a hot air balloon, waft through a deserted street as a barber gives his ex-lover's little boy his first haircut.

Baxter's dialogue alone can make you pause and smile with nervous recognition. In **"Fenstad's Mother,"** the collection's arresting opening tale, an irascible old woman, fighting to hide her vulnerability and hold on to her identity, becomes the star pupil of her distant, middle-aged son's writing class. "What I hate about being my age is how nice everyone tries to be," she laments. "I was never nice, but now everybody is pelting me with sugar cubes."

Well-intentioned do-gooders figure prominently in Baxter's tales. But in the disoriented and disorienting world that Baxter describes, even the most ordinary acts of decency can backfire. In **"Shelter,"** a baker who volunteers at a shelter for the homeless shocks his family by bringing a homeless man to their house; instead of teaching his son charity, however, the visit plants fear. Similarly, in **"Westland,"** the attempt to help a troubled teenager forces a social worker to confront his inability to effect even the smallest, most symbolic change.

These and other stories pose troubling questions in a vivid way: What does it mean to do or be "good" in a society so fearful that decent citizens are taught to ignore the homeless? Is it righteous, or only foolish, to risk your own well-being to help a stranger? And even if you dare, will it make any difference at all?

Baxter's characters go in search of something that will reach beyond their ordered, ordinary lives. In story after story, they hope beyond hope that they will discover a sense of attachment or connection to another person, or a reason to have faith in the universe. Baxter portrays these quests as both peculiar and noble, even when they fail or yield inconclusive results. (p. 6)

> *Diane Cole, "Failures to Connect," in* Chicago Tribune—Books, *September 9, 1990, pp. 6-7.*

William Ferguson   (review date 21 October 1990)

[*Ferguson is an American poet, short story writer, editor, and educator. In the following essay, he offers a thematic analysis of* A Relative Stranger.]

The 13 stories in *A Relative Stranger*, all quietly accomplished, suggest a mysterious yet fundamental marriage of despair and joy. Though in one way or another each story ends in disillusionment, the road that leads us to that dismal state is so richly peopled, so finely drawn, that the effect is oddly reassuring.

The much-praised author, Charles Baxter, has published a novel, *First Light*, as well as two previous collections of stories *Harmony of the World* and *Through the Safety Net*.

Many of the male protagonists in this new collection are confused and timid souls in search of something to believe in; they are all intelligent and sensitive, yet somehow unexceptional. By contrast, the women around them tend to be strong and colorful people who accept life easily—and whose impatience with the men is manifest.

In **"Prowlers,"** Pastor Robinson manages to tolerate a visit by his wife Angie's lover, an abrasive person named Benjamin; when the visit is over, Angie muses to her husband that she and Benjamin know all each other's secrets. Robinson gently protests: "You know my secrets." Angie: "Sweetheart, you don't have any secrets. You've never wanted a single bad thing in your life."

Characters like Robinson have the fatal transparency of goodness, a passive blamelessness that may in itself be a tragic flaw. This hapless virtue has a parallel in Cooper, the hero of a story called **"Shelter."** Cooper is a generous soul who becomes so involved with the homeless—entirely out of brotherly love, a quality he refuses to recognize in himself—that he puts the autonomy of his own family in danger.

Anders, a Swedish businessman in **"The Disappeared,"** finds his childish expectations of America are crippled by his relationship with a stranger in Detroit. Fenstad is a teacher whose pallid devotion to logic is no match for his mother's irrational vitalities (significantly, the story's title is not "Fenstad" but **"Fenstad's Mother"**). Warren, in **"Westland,"** is hanging around the zoo one day when he meets a teen-age girl who announces that she wants to shoot a lion. She doesn't do it, but in a bizarre echo of the girl's words, Warren later fires shots at the local nuclear reactor to protest the fouling of the environment. It's another portrait of impulsive, undirected goodness, and again its medium is a heartbreaking ineffectuality.

One story that stands out from all the others, in both style and theme, is **"The Old Fascist in Retirement,"** an elegant fictional imagination of Ezra Pound's latter days in Italy. The bitterness of the title contrasts with the rather sympathetic portrait the story contains; the underlying message (so familiar) may be that Pound was not really evil, only deeply confused. If so, then the old poet begins to look like a version—augmented, to be sure, by his peculiar genius— of Fenstad or Cooper or Robinson: a good, articulate man who tragically failed to understand something fundamental about the social contract.

In the powerful title story, **"A Relative Stranger,"** a man discovers late in life that he has a brother. Both men, as infants, were given up for adoption. It appears that two lost souls are headed for a joyful reunion. Yet fraternity turns out to be a burden, another of nature's unpardonable hoaxes; the two brothers are wholly incompatible. One of the brothers says: "I was always homesick for the rest of the world. My brother does not understand that. He thinks home is where he is now."

Few of the protagonists in this collection would make the brother's mistake (if it is one). They are the temperamentally homeless, the ones who look on in amazement as other people accept the conditions of the everyday world without even the murmur of an existential question. If these stories have a common theme, it may be this abiding failure, in leading characters, to imagine what is most real. By contrast, Charles Baxter's chronicling of such human

debilities represents a continuing triumph of the imaginative will.

William Ferguson, "The Timid Life," in The New York Times Book Review, *October 21, 1990, p. 18.*

Baxter on the American Midwest:

You can feel like a mole here, under these skies. . . . It's a sense of enclosure. There's no ocean to solve anything. No mountains. Just . . . gray. And perhaps it's not a coincidence that in the rural Midwest, there's an odd sense of privacy, of things unsaid. You don't run across it in LA or New York, and you certainly don't in the rural South.

Charles Baxter, in an interview with Neely Tucker in the Detroit Free Press, *23 December 1992.*

Perry Glasser   (review date December 1990)

[*Glasser is an American short story writer, novelist, and educator. In the following excerpt, he provides an overview of* A Relative Stranger *and praises Baxter's unassuming style.*]

[You'd] hurt nothing at all by introducing yourself to Charles Baxter's *A Relative Stranger.* Straight out, let's announce this reviewer is a fan, and in these pages reviewed an earlier work, *Harmony of the World.* Baxter just gets better. Where Rick Hillis dazzles the eye and Daniel Stern makes mind play, Charles Baxter writes straight for the heart. His style is unassuming. Metaphors are rare. There are no pyrotechnical displays of language. All proceeds via understatement, a style that leaves unadorned sadness and passion in stark relief against the page. This prose is glass.

In **"Westland,"** in circumstances that have nothing to do with his job, when a social worker becomes involved with a dysfunctional family he gains possession of a small pistol. He fires it four times at the blank wall of a nuclear reactor. Driving home he finds himself behind a car with a green bumpersticker that reads: "CAUTION: THIS VEHICLE EXPLODES UPON IMPACT!" and the social worker thinks, "That's me. . . . I am that vehicle." Many lesser writers, having achieved such a moment, would have quit, but Baxter always works his material completely, squeezing every final nuance from his characters and plot. At the invitation of the dysfunctional family's father, Earl, the social worker brings his own family to a televised Westland Labor Day Picnic organized to raise money for Jerry's Kids. It is raining. They wager on Earl, who is entered in a foot race to be run by grown men dressed as clowns. The charitable LOVE NETWORK announcer fires the starting gun, and the social worker sees Earl's daughter watching:

> . . . She had her eyes fixed on her father. By God, she looked affectionate. If he wanted his daughter's love, he had it. I watched her clench her fists and start to jump up and down, cheering him on. . . .

I looked around the parking lot and thought: everyone here understands what's going on better than I do. But then I remembered that I had fired shots at a nuclear reactor . . . And I remembered my mother's first sentence to me when we arrived in New York harbor when I was ten years old. She pointed down from the ship at the pier, at the crowds, and she said, "Warren, look at all those Americans." I felt then that if I looked at that crowd for too long, something inside my body would explode . . . And it came back to me in that shopping center parking lot, full of those LOVE NETWORK people, that feeling of pressure of American crowds and exuberance.

"The Disappeared" is the story of a Swedish engineer, Anders, summoned to Detroit by General Motors to discuss his work in metal alloys. He is fascinated by America, "especially its colorful disorderliness." His ambition is "to sleep with an American woman in an American bed," and once his business is completed, he has three days in "a wide-open American city, not quite in the wild West, but close enough to suit him." Now, most American readers will know that Anders would have been safer in Wichita, Dodge City, or even Tombstone in 1880 than on the streets of contemporary Detroit. Doormen and cab drivers give him warning, but Anders's ignorance makes him fearless. He meets a woman, of course, and being unsure of racial identifications he is mystified by what race she may be. She is one of the Last Ones, a member of the Church of the Millenium, "where they preach the Gospel of Last Things."

> "What is that?" he asked.
> "We don't make plans," she
> said. "No big plans at all."
>
> "That is not so unusual," he said, trying to normalize what she was saying. "Many people don't like to make—"
>
> "It's not liking," she said. "It doesn't have anything to do with liking or not liking. It's a faith."

Detroit eventually turns on him, of course. Anders comes to feel "that he must get home to Sweden quickly, before he becomes a very different person, unrecognizeable even to himself," and he steps out of a building into air "which smelled as it always had, of powerful combustible materials and their traces, fire and ash." A very American landscape.

As an author, Charles Baxter is a rare representative of an endangered species—the American writer obsessed with defining the American character. That's a theme that to many seems so presumptuous, so vast and overdone, that they have retreated to neo-regionalism, taking refuge from the the Whitmanesque impulses that have shaped so much of our literature, hiding in the more manageable landscape of a specific time and place. But Charles Baxter returns to the bigger theme again and again, and thank goodness. As we change, we need new voices that will redefine us anew.

In other stories, Baxter exquisitely explores relationships between two people, relationships that are always uneven.

In the title story, a man who was an adopted child meets another man who informs him they are brothers. **"Fenstad's Mother"** describes an elderly woman who is, because of her humanistic Old Left Politics, more dynamic, more at ease, more compassionate, and more alive than her son, a teacher, can ever hope to be. And each of **"Three Parabolic Tales"** explores how men and women need and abuse each other. The first story is about a young couple, the second about middle age, the third about an older man and wife. The stories make a lovely trio.

A Relative Stranger is a rich display of Charles Baxter's talents. The intelligence behind the prose is so quiet and so muted, that the reader is never aware of the contrivance of Art. The stories just seem to *be,* sprung fully grown and fully armored, just as they are, and imagining alternatives—that they might have once been something else that the writer judged, revised and refinished—seems impossible.

Introduce yourself to Charles Baxter if you don't already know him. You can never tell what might come of it. Give yourself a reward. (pp. 63-4)

Perry Glasser, "Making Introductions," in The North American Review, *Vol. 275, No. 4, December, 1990, pp. 60-4.*

Jonathan Holden   (review date Spring 1991)

[*An American poet, critic, and educator, Holden has commented that "the 'poem' is a blatantly artificial convention [and that] poetry evolves to serve specialized uses that cannot be as efficiently served by other means, uses which are not merely academic and exegetical." In the following excerpt, he examines Baxter's use of narrative voice in* Imaginary Paintings.]

Most of the poems in Charles Baxter's *Imaginary Paintings* are written from an Olympian, omniscient third-person perspective. They are ruthless in their refusal of sentiment. They have the clarity and the objectivity of Flaubert. They have the look of discarded "scenes," out-takes from Baxter's prose fiction enterprises. This "scenic" quality in the poems is further emphasized by the way in which many of them are framed by their titles: **"The Lady With the Dog," "Diptych: Jesus and the Stone," "Beggar in the Snow," "Fleetwood Cafe,"** etc. : . . . He knows where to break lines, and he has an unerring sense of rhetorical closure. Indeed, as the very title *Imaginary Paintings* might suggest, Baxter's poems appear to be grounded in a closely reasoned aesthetic. He is conducting experiments similar to those of Louis Simpson. As Simpson put it in "The Character of the Poet":

> . . . how is one to find poetry in an office where secretaries sit typing or the aisle of a supermarket? Yet it is imperative for poetry to deal with such material—it is all around us. Not only urban scenes but the minds of people need to be represented . . . I mean poetry about the people you actually meet and the ideas they have, including the banal, foolish ones.
>
> This is the step that has to be taken, and some poets have already taken it. . . .

Simpson's position is that poems should be, like realistic prose fiction or cinema, so caught up in their human subject matter that the reader loses consciousness of the medium of the poem's language altogether and simply experiences the human drama which a poem is picturing. The language of a good poem must be "transparent," like the language which Valéry ascribes to "prose" (as opposed to "poetry")—a means to an end rather than an end in itself. One of the better poems in Baxter's book—**"The Passionate Shopping Mall"**—suggests the trade-offs involved in Simpson's/Baxter's novelistic aesthetic:

> There was a scream and a cry
> and the sound of shoes running on cleaned
> marble, and there was a woman
> with straight gray hair held back
> with a braid wandering toward the fountain
>
> where she washed her hands again and again,
> and there was a child named Lonnie
> who bought an airplane and whose mother beat
>   him
> in the aisle, and there was light
> from nowhere that fell over everything.
>
> You could tell how serious the mall was
> by the way the people got lost there,
> wondering where the light had come from
> and what they had driven there to do,
> and you could tell that the teenagers kissing
>
> each other didn't exactly want to, but went on
> because someone told them. Maybe it was
> the shoes. Maybe people came to see
> the clothes and the colors and felt bad
> about themselves and decided not to have
>
> affairs but to spend money instead. Maybe
> the mall said, "People are ugly
> fundamentally." Anyway, there's still
> the little girl pushing the plastic
> seal on wheels, and an old woman who won't
>
> stop mumbling and sixteen TV sets
> tuned to the same channel. Maybe the mall
> owns the colors and just won't sell them.
> It is a world of pianos and barbells
> and dust going home in bags in a fury.

In this poem, the trade-offs between novelistic virtues and lyric virtues more or less speak for themselves: cool hauteur instead of the potentially mawkish compassion and earnestness of [D. H.] Fenza's authorial voice, photographic realism instead of the visionary quality of [Edward] Hirsch's "Skywriting," mature resignation in place of the sexual/epistemological desire of "In Your Own Sweet Time," formal elegance in place of heuristic discovery. The best poems in *Imaginary Paintings* are those in which the author tentatively admits his own presence, for example **"The Slow Classroom,"** which begins:

> You could see windstorms and a piece of floating
>   string
> making their way to the school
> for hours—you could watch the sun,
> and the teacher agreed. She had
> no ideas either. Everything that happened
> took a week in that air, in that frame
> of bulletin boards and tiny fluorescent lights,

> but when you found a pencil at least
> that's what you had, a pencil. They planned the
>   day
> for some hours but usually they just said "Be
>   here."
>
> A plant grew quietly on the windowsill, and ev-
>   erybody
> knew it was a good soldier and they nodded
>   hello
> if they were standing there and thought it was
>   trying
> hard. Where was Hawaii, or any worldly place?

The poem continues in this offhanded style—realism balancing on the edge of the surreal, of the comic but not quite comic, not quite satire. The underlying motive force of the poem is a supreme, justifiable disdain. (pp. 362-64)

> *Jonathan Holden, " 'Over and Over': Seven Books of Contemporary Poetry," in* Michigan Quarterly Review, *Vol. XXX, No. 2, Spring, 1991, pp. 354-66.*

Terry Caesar   (review date Summer 1991)

[*In the following excerpt, Caesar identifies what he considers the best stories in* A Relative Stranger.]

One of Baxter's strongest stories [in *A Relative Stranger*], **"Shelter,"** is about a baker, Cooper, whose insistent concern for homeless people eventually leads him to one young man, Billy Bell, whose self-proclaimed, aimless "saintliness" mocks Cooper's own. Cooper takes the man home. A dog appears—then a child, a wife, and there is a baseball game on television. Billy Bell is moved. He gives a speech as inspired as anything in all these volumes, and it deserves to be quoted at some length:

> Here's what I'd like to do. I want to be *just like all of you.* I'd put on a chef's hat and stand outside in my apron like one of those assholes you see in the Sunday magazine section with a spatula in his hand and, like, I'll be flipping hamburgers and telling my kids to keep their hands out of the chive dip and go run in the sprinkler or do some shit like that. I'll belong to do-good groups like Save the Rainforests, and I'll ask my wife how she likes her meat, rare or well-done, and she'll say well-done with that pretty smile she has, and that's how I'll do it. A wonderful fucking barbecue, this is, with folding aluminum chairs and paper plates and ketchup all over the goddamn place. Oceans of vodka and floods of beer. Oh, and we've sprayed the yard with that big spray that kills anything that moves, and all the mosquitoes and bunnies are dead at our feet. Talk about the good life. That has got to be it.

Cooper and his wife are appalled. Cooper drives Billy Bell away. Two days later the bakery is broken into. The story ends with Cooper and his wife in bed. "Shelter me," he says. "Which way this time? Which way?" she asks. Baxter is very good, very implacable about such moments. Although there are public spaces in his stories—classrooms, malls—most of them are located around a house which is threatened by something outside, which the story steadily clarifies as a function of some fear already inside, or some force, as in **"Shelter,"** which would effectively turn the inside out. What to do?

In another story a Swedish businessman arrives in Detroit. Business done, and still excited about being in America, he asks the doorman at his downtown hotel where he would recommend a walk. "You want my recommendation? Don't walk anywhere. I would not recommend a walk. Sit in the bar and watch the soaps." The third sentence here is typical of how finely Baxter catches spoken idioms—he has page after page of small, sharp pleasures such as these—as if the doorman, here, has suddenly warmed to the role of being a doorman, whose function is to preside over a wholly safe, already represented world.

The businessman, Anders, takes possession of his own role of European visitor less warily. He goes jogging in a park. He meets a woman who quickly embodies for him the sexual lure of the country. She professes odd religious beliefs: "We do what everyone else does. We work and we go home and have dinner and go to bed. There is only one thing that we do that is special. . . . We don't make plans. No big plans at all." Anders doesn't understand her. She understands him. ("Did they tell you we were all soulless here? Did they say that?") They sleep together. Anders is almost shattered by her indifference about seeing him again. She lives with her grandmother, who warns him: "You can't invest in her. You can't do that at all. She won't let you."

In other words, the woman is at ease with her life, whose essence is, in a sense, that she has disappeared from it. The story, entitled **"The Disappeared,"** is, to my mind, the most compelling in *A Relative Stranger* in part because it is the longest; Baxter, who has a novel as well as two other volumes of short stories, at times deals with his themes too knowingly, almost schematically (**"Prowlers"** is an example of this) and works best when he allows himself room to let details infiltrate a settled structure and gradually reveal it to be fragile, confounded, and precious. Another reason **"The Disappeared"**—a wonderful inversion of the Jamesian International Theme—is so powerful is because Anders, who is mugged by the end when he goes to try to find the woman's church, comes to realize that he has fallen into a country whose energies are based on vacancies that are simply alien to him. He's got too much identity. These Americans are people who have too little and are proud of it. It is as if something that could be called "the good life" is so obvious that one option which is available is casually to abandon it.

And when the good life is occupied? Baxter's concluding story is entitled, **"Saul and Patsy Are Pregnant,"** a continuation of the delightful **"Saul and Patsy Are Getting Comfortable in Michigan"** from his previous volume. Saul is still a harried Jewish intellectual. After a minor auto accident he and his far more happily equanimous wife chance upon the home of a former student of his. "Not a single ironic sentence had ever been spoken here, everything in the room was sincere, everything except himself. In the midst of all this Midwestern earnestness, he was the one thing wrong. What was he doing here? What was he doing anywhere? He was accustomed to asking himself such

questions." The last sentence is beautifully telling. The fact that the former student has not even begun to ask such questions is, exactly, "relative" to the former teacher. The good life, we might say, is always exposed to the vacancy of somebody else.

Indeed, life itself is. One of Baxter's strongest stories, **"The Old Fascist in Retirement,"** is about Ezra Pound. At first glance this seems a surprising subject for Baxter. But not when we attend to how his Pound is all grim irony and deprived of "purifying light" as well as a home. (In a way he is an elderly, pitiless Saul, without either Michigan or Patsy.) Toward the conclusion, the Old Fascist heads out in a gondola over a Venetian canal, imagines a paradise without any people at all, and then there is an instant where he wishes "in the innermost core cell of his heart for the obliteration of all human life." Much of Baxter's own imagination, I think, aspires to be answerable to such a wish—the sort of evacuated humanity in which it becomes possible, or the sort of rooted humanity that might defeat it.

Baxter is a rarely *decent* writer. People in his stories care about things, and not just why they care about things. (Most of them are men, often the kind that women are accustomed to call "sensitive." "Patriarchy, carnage, rape, pleasurable bloodletting and bloodsport," thinks Saul, who "would admit to a gender responsibility for all of these, if anyone asked him, though no one ever did.") If they're happy, they want to be held accountable for their happiness. It is not Fenstead, of **"Fenstead's Mother,"** one of the two or three best stories in the volume, who asks: "What was the price one paid for loving one's own life?" It may as well be. Fenstead is the sort of man who likes to skate because "he was impressed with the way skates improved human character." His own price is that he feels too exclusively himself. He can't even go skating without assessing it in ethical terms, and not only because he feels inadequate to a far more vivid mother who is not so complacent in her progressive politics that she cannot befriend a young black man in her son's night school class and invite him over to listen to his jazz records. "What glimpses," Fenstead's mother listens carefully and concludes. Her new friend's music has made life good, and strange, all over again. She doesn't care if it improves her character. (pp. 508-11)

Terry Caesar, "Glimpses, Surfaces, Ecstasies: Three Books of Short Fiction," in Michigan Quarterly Review, *Vol. XXX, No. 3, Summer, 1991, pp. 506-18.*

Sybil Steinberg (review date 19 October 1992)

[*In the following essay, Steinberg praises the language, characterization, and moral clarity in* Shadow Play.]

The remarkably talented Baxter (the novel *First Light* and three short story collections) should earn the wide audience he deserves with this triumph of a novel [*Shadow Play*]. Quirky, playful, poetic—and dead serious in its moral vision—the narrative focuses on a man who feels remote and unsubstantial, unengaged with life. Wyatt Palmer has attempted to make up for the chaos of his child-

Baxter is well on his way to becoming the next master of the short story and, like Trevor and Carver, has the special gift of capturing the shadow of genuine significance as it flits across the face of the ordinary.

—*Ted Solotaroff, in* The Nation, *30 December 1991.*

hood—his father died young and his depressive mother retreated into spacey lassitude and a mental asylum—by creating an orderly, circumscribed existence for himself, his supportive wife and their two children. He keeps his inner life in shadow, going through the motions of connecting; on the surface he is cheerful, but he hides a self-destructive streak. A safe if unfulfilling job as assistant city manager of his native Five Oaks, an economically depressed small town in the Midwest, seems to have Wyatt securely anchored to the conventional middle class. But he is caught in a moral dilemma when former high school classmate Jerry Schwartzwalder asks him to bend the rules so that he can establish a chemical company in Five Oaks. Wyatt cooperates; as a reward, Schwartzwalder hires his feckless foster brother, Cyril. Then Cyril comes down with a fatal disease caused by toxic wastes, and Wyatt becomes acutely aware of his responsibility. Filled with "purifying rage," he determines to take revenge and to change his life.

Baxter tells his tale in language so carefully honed it sings; his metaphors and apercus are striking and luminous, and several scenes—notably Wyatt and Cyril's final bonding—are unforgettable. Baxter's take on 20th-century angst, delivered through Wyatt's aunt Ellen ("God doesn't love us; He is merely curious about what happens to our lives . . . we're on our own down here") is provocative. His often eccentric characters blossom under his empathy for their emotional bewilderment, and his ability to render the shadings of their personalities makes them enormously appealing. Though the lack of a conventional resolution may disappoint some readers, this lyrical, witty, dramatic and moving story has the clarity of sunshine, the haunting suggestion of shadow play.

Sybil Steinberg, in a review of "Shadow Play," in Publishers Weekly, *Vol. 239, No. 46, October 19, 1992, p. 57.*

Richard Locke   (review date 5 February 1993)

[*In the following essay, Locke places* Shadow Play *in the tradition of American moral realism.*]

Perhaps because our literature got off to such a shaky and self-conscious start, with boastful calls for literary independence and anxious lists of all the things that made America so difficult for writers, for many years it was the fashion to think of American literature as divided into rival camps: rough vs. smooth, lowbrow vs. highbrow, frontier crudeness vs. drawing-room formality, or, as one critic put it in less ethnically enlightened times, "redskin" vs. "paleface." All this suggests some archetypical face-off between Walt Whitman and Henry James.

But like a lot of brawling and bawling in the woods, such dichotomies tend toward sentimental simplifications. Whitman's work is anything but crude and artless, James's career resembles the labors of Hercules, and no strong artist ever drops a stitch of style, be it homespun or silk or blue ironic polyester. All kinds of writers share our national taste for big themes: intimations of immortality, the echoes of collapsing religious certainties, life on some frontier or on the edge. And even today the most well-mannered, socially observant, realistic domestic fiction may in truth—deep in its dramatic structure, psychology and pattern of imagery—be hunting a white whale or lighting out for new territory.

I'm suggesting, of course, that Charles Baxter's novel **Shadow Play** is deceptively modest; it turns out to be a lot more than the story of a Middle American family or a study of provincial manners and morals. Mr. Baxter's second novel and fifth work of fiction in nine years (his first novel was the moving and much admired **First Light** in 1987), **Shadow Play** is altogether impressive: emotionally, intellectually, technically. It's both original and thoroughly a part of our deceptively complex native tradition.

It begins with a crow calling from a rainy wood to an eight-year-old boy running away from his gentle drunk father, a small-town architect doing carpentry in the basement, and his dreamy, distant mother stirring "one of her gloomy stews" in the kitchen. The boy runs into the woods with his teddy bear, his Scottie-dog night light and some carefully folded clothes. He hopes to live there or with his Aunt Ellen. In time we learn she is working on an alternative Bible about a God who doesn't love us (that God went away) but who is endlessly curious about his creation (like an author). The novel ends some 20 years later with a crow dropping down from a tree to snatch a seed from the palm of that same Aunt Ellen in a last moment of winter light.

In between lies the story of the runaway boy, Wyatt Palmer, who almost drowns at the age of six, whose father dies when he is eight, whose mother drifts into madness, who is brought up by his theological aunt, and whose life is shadowed by his beloved, self-destructive li'l devil of a cousin. In college, Wyatt marries a ponytailed expert on the balance beam, who does magic tricks with coins and rabbits, adores his watchfulness and is supremely sensitive, a counterweight, to his shadowy side: "She resisted sadness, to exactly the degree that he invited it."

Wyatt seeks refuge in the Midwestern ordinary. His mother, who makes up nutty "word-heaps," calls him "corilineal," "so normal it's strange." He becomes assistant to the city manager (the book is set in Five Oaks, Michigan, the town Mr. Baxter has been writing about for nearly a decade). He helps support his mother and his rowdy cousin; he becomes the father of two children. He's drawn into helping a cheesy entrepreneur build a biotech factory that brings in much needed money and new jobs. There's even, in gratitude, a job for his cousin. The risks are palpable: "Are you guys [in the city government] going to start whining and wringing your hands if we spill a little hoo-hah on the floor?" asks the entrepreneur. But you can't make an omelette without breaking eggs, so Wyatt goes along with this little industrial revolution.

The narrative approaches melodrama without missing a beat. His cousin gets sick and Wyatt starts to cross the line from bored good citizen, husband and father to half-mad prowler, accessory to crime, bent on revenge, plunging into shadow. The psychology and religious issues become darker and grander. The patterns of incidents and characters and images become clearer: not only Wyatt and his cousin and their paired wives, or the crazy mother and eccentric aunt, but sunshine and shadow, drowning and floating, and an interplay of earth, air, fire and water.

All this is going on in the midst of a realistic novel of extraordinarily precise and suggestive diction. For example, on the way to deep trouble, Wyatt notices the high grass "slithered and hissed against the side of the car." His sick cousin jokes, "I'm half angel already." A tattoo is "a shadow nailed to [a character's] upper arm." A fairground version of "La Cucaracha" suggests "tinfoil instruments played by scorpions."

After a decade of so much play-it-safe fiction of photo-realistic gloom, it's a pleasure to encounter a novel in the great tradition of American moral realism touched by shards of gnostic faith and glints of transcendental light.

> Richard Locke, "The Intricate Patterns of a Young Man's Life," in The Wall Street Journal, February 5, 1993, p. A11.

Lorrie Moore (review date 14 February 1993)

[*Moore is an American short story writer and novelist. In the following essay, she lauds Baxter's insightful discussion of contemporary issues and their impact on the individual in* Shadow Play.]

Often when short-story writers go to write novels they get jaunty. They take deep breaths and become brazen—the way shy people do on wine. Donald Barthelme becomes mythic and parodic, Alice Munro boldly seamsterly (stitching novels from stories). Andre Dubus asks us to reconsider the novella (as an equivalent form). Perhaps Grace Paley has shown the greatest bravado of all in simply not bothering.

Charles Baxter, whose three brilliant collections of short stories (**Harmony of the World, Through the Safety Net** and **A Relative Stranger**) may place him in the same rank as the above writers, constructed his first novel in reverse chronology. **First Light** (1987), the hauntingly detailed story of a brother and sister from Five Oaks, Mich., is an intricate unknotting, a narrative progression backward in time toward the moment when the boy, Hugh, first touches his infant sister's hand. It is a strategy intended, no doubt, to make the form Mr. Baxter's own, as well as to show the inextricability of sibling ties. Now, in his second novel, **Shadow Play** the novel is no longer a form to be seized and remade, but a capacious place in which to move

around. Mr. Baxter is looser, less strict. The narrative has not been trained; Mr. Baxter indulges it, affectionately musses its hair, lets it go where it may. The result is, paradoxically, both a more conventionally constructed novel and a more surprising and suspenseful book.

Shadow Play is primarily the story of Wyatt Palmer, a fiercely bright and artistic boy who grows up to find himself stuck in the most pedestrian of existences: by day a bored government bureaucrat, by night a tired husband, father and homeowner. When a chemical company called WaldChem sets itself up in town and pressures the city management (for the sake of the local economy, of course) to look the other way as health regulations are violated, Wyatt is suddenly and precariously placed at the center of a drama involving ethical behavior in "postethical" times.

In a contracting economy, too many citizens of Five Oaks appear willing to make a devil's pact: health for cash; lives for jobs. As assistant city manager, Wyatt would like to "notify the state that the on-site waste management guidelines and regulations and licensing restrictions are being violated."

But the head of WaldChem is a high school buddy; Wyatt plays golf with him; he has given Wyatt's wayward foster brother, Cyril, a job in the plant. And, as the city manager tells Wyatt, "the times are against you." By remaining quiet and polite and helpful to those around him, Wyatt strikes a most unholy bargain—with himself as well as with the world. He is no longer his troubled brother's keeper; he is a member of the audience. As Mr. Baxter wrote in **First Light**, "No one knows how to do that in this country, how to be a brother."

Not unlike Shirley Jackson's story "The Lottery," Mr. Baxter's **Shadow Play** takes large themes of good and evil and primitive deal making, and situates them in municipal terms and local ritual. He is interested in those shadowy corners of civilization in which barbarity manages to nestle and thrive. The America of this book has become a kind of hell. "The houses gave off a dingy little light, the light of I'm-not-sorry-for-anything, the light of Listen-to-me. . . . That way you didn't even need eternal fire."

Shadow Play is also an examination of how the Midwestern values of niceness, passivity, helpfulness and just-going-along can contribute to the rot and demise of a community. When Wyatt's foster brother develops lung cancer while holding down his custodial job at the plant, Wyatt is impassive. "They didn't have to make Wald-Chem so dangerous, those bastards," rages the dying Cyril. "They could have made it safer."

"You smoked, Cyril," Wyatt replies quietly. "You smoked cigarettes all your life." It is a response so wicked in its neutrality that later "he stood in his own living room, repressing the impulse to scream." "The verdict on him, he now knew, was that he was obliging and careless, an accessory." When Wyatt agrees to help Cyril commit suicide (one is reminded here of a fellow Michigander, Dr. Jack Kevorkian) he has not only enacted the central metaphor of the book but effectively set himself up for a nervous breakdown, one replete with tattoo, adultery, arson and a move to Brooklyn!

This last is no amusing little fillip; in the geographical paradigm of Mr. Baxter's book, New York City is Eden as anti-Eden. Here the fruit of the tree of knowledge is not rotting in anyone's driveway. There are no driveways; the trees were cut down years ago. The good fight has long since been waged and lost, and here one can live in something akin to aftermath if not to peace. As a boy Wyatt had memorized a map of the New York subway system, and as a young man he lived there as an artist, a painter of shadow portraits; now, in New York with his family, he can resume where he left off before the heart- and hinterland so rudely interrupted him. He can attempt something *un*-Midwestern, something unthwarted, adventurous, something like a coda, a twilight sequel; in unecological times, an ecology of hope and loss.

One of Mr. Baxter's great strengths as a writer has always been his ability to capture the stranded inner lives of the Middle West's repressed eccentrics. And here, in his second novel, he is at full throttle. The character of Wyatt's mother is a figure of alleged madness, but (whether it speaks to Mr. Baxter's talent or should be cause for this reader's concern) the passages that give voice to her insanity are lucid, lovely, sympathetic: "She knew that birds sometimes agreed or disagreed with their names but she kept that information to herself." "Angels," she thinks, "were so vain, so pretty. They wore coral earrings and distressfully unassembled hats." When Wyatt brings his mother to New York, and she finds the life of a bag lady a congenial one, Mr. Baxter treats this with a certain heartening dignity rather than a forlorn condescension.

He also gives much of the book over to the voice and point of view of Wyatt's bright, quirky Aunt Ellen, who functions as a sapient observer of the world of the novel. She believes not in a benevolent God but in a God of pure curiosity; moreover, she believes she is writing the Bible of that God. "There is absolutely no love coming to us from that realm," she says of the more traditional deity. "None at all. You might as well pray to a telephone pole."

Aunt Ellen, even more than Wyatt, is the moral center of the book—hers is the most trenchant of the solitudes fashioned and recorded here. That Mr. Baxter can traverse gender and offer such a deep and authentic rendition of a woman's voice and thoughts should not in itself be remarkable in contemporary fiction, yet still it is.

Because his work doesn't offer itself up in gaudy ways for popular consumption or intellectual play (theorists and critics have failed to descend en masse with their scissors and forks), Mr. Baxter has acquired the reputation of being that rare and pleasurable thing: a writer's writer. He has steadily taken beautiful and precise language and gone into the ordinary and secret places of people—their moral and emotional quandaries, their typically American circumstances, their burning intelligence, their negotiations with what is trapped, stunted, violent, sustaining, decent or miraculous in their lives. In writing about ordinary people he derives narrative authority from having imagined farther and more profoundly than we have, making his lit-

erary presence a necessary and important one, and making *Shadow Play* a novel that is big, moving, rich with life and story—something so much more than a writer's anxious vacation from shorter forms. (pp. 7-8)

> *Lorrie Moore, "God Does Not Love Aunt Ellen," in* The New York Times Book Review, *February 14, 1993, pp. 7-8.*

Winston Groom   (review date 21 March 1993)

[*Groom is an American novelist and journalist. In the following mixed review, he provides a thematic analysis of* Shadow Play.]

Charles Baxter is a clever writer whose purpose in [**Shadow Play**] is to caricature the humdrum lives of middle-class Americans and provide a cautionary tale of the evils of industrial immorality.

Wyatt Palmer is the assistant city manager of a small Michigan town, the flavor of which is summed up by the following sentence: "His classmates from Five Oaks High had either disappeared out of town or gone down various drains or were working intermittent dumb jobs." Into this unappealing setting, Wyatt returns—after having run away some time earlier—with a wife named Susan whose specialty is performing magic tricks such as pulling coins from behind people's ears, walking on her hands and other entertaining things.

We get to meet his family—the crazy mother and dull father, the eccentric aunt Ellen, who is writing a new bible that embraces the existential philosophy of an absurd universe where God is merely a curious onlooker of human folly, and cousin Cyril who, when he is released from jail, rents an apartment above a beauty parlor and begins a life as a scavenger.

Wyatt and Susan have children, and he takes the job in the city manager's office with a sort of faint hope of improving the way things are. His main accomplishment is assisting Jerry Schwartzwalder—an old high school chum who has defied convention by making it big—in bringing to town a company that manufactures plastics for artificial body parts. As a bonus, Wyatt gets his screwy cousin Cyril-the-scavenger a job at the plant.

Meanwhile, we are treated to large doses of the meager *Sturm und Drang* of life in Five Oaks. Aunt Ellen is working furiously on her scriptures and jots down truths as they come to her: "Everything written about God is wrong. . . . The world exists because God is curious about it," she says, at the same time dispensing advice based on her philosophy: "Have some adventures! . . . Avoid irony! . . . Share beautiful things! . . . Take responsibility!"

Not only that, but Wyatt's own slightly nutty mother has emerged as something of a linguistic inventor, devising new words like *zark-like, nutomberized, bremuss* and *descorbitant*. In fact, practically everybody in this Dullsville, USA, is cramped by artsy allusions to Strindberg, Grant Wood, Montaigne, Don Quixote, Matisse, John Stuart Mill, Frank Lloyd Wright, Simone Weil, Robert Louis

Stevenson, Chopin, Schumann, Shakespeare, Vermeer, Bonnard, Kant, William Blake, Macaulay, Swedenborg and so on.

Furthermore, I guess to balance things off toward the folksy, the reader is treated from the beginning to a litany of brand names that almost constitutes an advertising campaign for entities such as Cheerios, Macy's, Jack Daniel's, S.S. Kresge, Woolworth's, Budweiser, Oldsmobile, Dr. Pepper, Jeep, AlumaCraft, Hersey, IGA, Xerox, Dodge, Saf-T-Seat, McDonald's, Styrofoam, Coke, Rainbird, Dairy Queen, Chevy, M & M's, Reese's Peanut Butter Cups, Kleenex and Ivory Soap.

About midway through the book, things start to heat up when old friend Jerry Swartzwalder's chemical plant, WaldChem, is found to be environmentally unsafe. In fact, the air inside the plant is anywhere from a pink to a yellow to a blue fog; illegal discharges are discovered and barrels of toxic waste are being sent to Mexico for disposal. Workers inside the plant are sick and dying, including Wyatt's cousin Cyril, but, "they aren't saying much, on account of their wages are good. And you know how it is with these whistle blowers . . . people get their houses bombed, their cars pushed off the road and all that other fine American stuff."

Of course, this puts Wyatt in a quandary; after all, he was responsible for WalChem coming to Five Oaks in the first place, and he has to decide whether he's made a Faustian bargain with Schwartzwalder or is he going to blow the whistle himself ? When Cyril finally commits suicide in lieu of the lingering death in store for him, Aunt Ellen uses the occasion to take her soapbox public, and frame for the citizens of Five Oaks the credo on which this story turns—which, in her own words, is this:

> You might as well pray to a telephone pole. I mean, if God loved us, we would know it, wouldn't we? . . . This God just does not care beyond being curious about how every event works out. . . . This God does not love us. . . . We have to save the world if we want to live in it, because God won't.

Naturally, Wyatt must now take a stand; which one must be left for the reader to divine. Baxter has created a scenario in which alienation and anxiety are the norm, a kind of dubious universe where people are neither good nor evil but instead are driven by 20th-Century pragmatism into a twilight zone of utter practicality. There are many delightful side stories in this book, but it is for readers other than myself to find satisfaction in its themes.

> Winston Groom, "Marching to a Different Humdrum," in Los Angeles Times Book Review, *March 21, 1993, p. 5.*

FURTHER READING

Busch, Frederick. "Contemporary American Short Fiction." *The Southern Review* 27, No. 2 (April 1991): 465-71.

> Positive assessment of *A Relative Stranger* in which Busch states that the characters in this collection "are made of clean, unpretentious, yet always-remarkable prose."

Gray, Paul. "Regressions." *Time* 130, No. 10 (7 September 1987): 81, 83.

> Praises the narrative structure of *First Light.*

Oliver, Bill. "Rick DeMarinas, Charles Baxter, and the Art of Surprise." *New England Review* 14, No. 3 (Summer 1992): 234-41.

> Comparative analysis of Baxter's *A Relative Stranger* and Rick DeMarinas's *The Coming Triumph of the Free World* and *The Voice of America.*

Phillips, Robert. "Fiction Chronicle." *The Hudson Review* XLIV, No. 1 (Spring 1991): 133-41.

> Compares the stories in *A Relative Stranger* to those of Raymond Carver.

Sheppard, R. Z. "Where God Is Curious." *Time* 141, No. 4 (25 January 1993): 7.

> Praises Baxter's depiction of the boredom and isolation associated with small-town America. Sheppard maintains: "*Shadow Play* could have turned into another clever existential dead end. But Baxter fills the void with a hundred human touches, a style as intimate as chamber music."

Additional coverage of Baxter's life and career is contained in the following sources published by Gale Research: *Contemporary Authors,* Vols. 57-60; *Contemporary Authors New Revision Series,* Vol. 40; *Contemporary Literary Criticism,* Vol. 45; and *Dictionary of Literary Biography,* Vol. 130.

Roch Carrier

1937-

French-Canadian novelist, short story writer, playwright, poet, scriptwriter, and author of children's books.

The following entry provides an overview of Carrier's career. For additional information on Carrier's life and works, see *CLC,* Volume 13.

INTRODUCTION

Carrier is widely recognized as one of Quebec's most prolific and successful writers. In his poetry and prose he dramatizes the political and social concerns that have defined Quebecois history, particularly the problems of cultural assimilation and colonization. The differences in values and beliefs between Quebec's rural and urban communities are also prominent in Carrier's writings. His best-known works are frequently praised for their autobiographical content, insightful critique of Quebec's bicultural heritage, and realistic depictions of violence, chaos, and oppression.

Carrier was born in Sainte-Justine-de-Dorchester, Quebec, and much of his fiction incorporates memories of his upbringing in this small rural community. The only student in his class to pursue an advanced degree, Carrier attended college in New Brunswick and Montreal, where he studied French literature. He traveled to France and in 1964, after completing graduate work at the University of Paris, returned to Quebec where he began teaching. His first collection of short stories, *Jolis deuils, petites tragédies pour adultes,* was awarded the Prix Littéraire de la Province de Québec that same year. He has since won the Grand Prix Littéraire de la Ville de Montréal. Carrier has also been active in Canadian theater; between 1970 and 1975 he served as secretary-general of the Théâtre du Nouveau Monde.

Carrier's best-known works, collectively known as *La trilogie de l'âge sombre,* include *La guerre, Yes Sir!; Floralie, où es-tu? (Floralie, Where Are You?);* and *Il est par là, le soleil (Is It the Sun, Philibert?).* According to Carrier, these anecdotal novels delineate the "three dark ages of Quebec history" and emphasize the Quebec people's struggle for survival and dignity in an environment characterized by fear, violence, prejudice, and oppression. The first two works in the trilogy are set in rural Quebec and examine the contradictory moral tenets and religious superstitions of the Quebecois. *La guerre, Yes Sir!* focuses on the conscription crisis of World War II when numerous French Canadians were drafted to serve in what they considered the "accursed English war." A series of vignettes, this work sketches the villagers' reaction to the war after Corriveau, a local youth, is killed while serving in Europe: one character chops off his hand to avoid the draft; mourners ignorantly mumble blasphemous prayers at Corriveau's wake and funeral; and the villagers ultimately riot and attack the English soldiers who have escorted the coffin home. *Floralie, Where Are You?,* the next novel in the series, is set in the nineteenth century and addresses the Quebecois' strict, though frequently hypocritical, values. The novel begins with the wedding night of Corriveau's parents, Anthyme and Floralie. After consummating their marriage, Anthyme leaves Floralie when he discovers that she was not a virgin. The community's religious superstitions and values are further revealed when Floralie performs the role of the Virgin Mary in a morality play. The allegorical novel concludes with the bride and groom waking at their wedding reception, unsure whether their shared experiences were a dream. With *Is It the Sun, Philibert?,* set in Montreal during the 1950s, Carrier's emphasis shifts from the rural to the urban landscape. Focusing on a character introduced in *La guerre, Yes Sir!,* Carrier dramatizes the discrimination encountered by the naive but eternally optimistic Philibert, who is politically disenfranchised and socially ostracized due to his inability to speak English. The works comprising *La trilogie de l'âge sombre* have been praised for their realistic portraits of individuals who are defined by their violent behavior, cultural alienation, and obsession with death and spiritual damnation.

The social and political arena of contemporary Quebec is similarly discussed in many of Carrier's later novels. *Le deux-millième étage* (*They Won't Demolish Me!*) is set in a 1950s Montreal apartment complex scheduled for demolition and delineates the conflicts that capitalism and urban renewal posed for Quebecois trying to preserve the past. *Il n'y a pas de pays sans grand-père* (*No Country without Grandfathers*), often described as Carrier's most anti-English work, dramatizes the conflicts that arise between generations, cultures, and the French- and English-speaking people of Quebec. In this work the elderly Vieux-Thomas reminisces about the Quebec of his youth as he attempts to free his grandson Jean-Thomas, who has been imprisoned for criticizing England's queen. Set in the 1950s when Maurice Duplessis was the premier of Quebec, *De l'amour dans la ferraille* (*Heartbreaks along the Road*) satirizes the Canadian government's attempts to manipulate voters in the fictional city of Saint-Toussaint-des-Saints by creating jobs and covertly appealing to their religious beliefs and laws.

While central to all of his fiction, Carrier's use of fantasy and dreams, stream-of-consciousness narration, and interior monologue is considered most effective in the drama *La céleste bicyclette* (*The Celestial Bicycle*) and the short story collection *Jolis deuils, petites tragédies pour adultes.* In *The Celestial Bicycle* the protagonist, who has allegedly journeyed into space on his bike, is confined to an insane asylum where he is continually questioned and analyzed by doctors. Lauding Carrier's use of monologue and surrealism, critics have praised *The Celestial Bicycle* as an irreverent satire on madness, the psychiatric profession, and humanity's desire to objectify reality. *Jolis deuils, petites tragédies pour adultes* also incorporates elements of fantasy and is often placed within the tradition of the tightly structured and often highly unrealistic French *conte,* or short adventure tale. In the critically acclaimed "L'encre," for example, two generals from rival nations attempt to ratify a peace treaty. As they discuss the terms of the pact, ink from a leaky fountain pen spills and covers the document, the table on which it rests, the room, and eventually the world. This leads to another declaration of war, and the story concludes as the generals begin to negotiate a new treaty with another leaky pen.

Carrier's more recent short fiction collections are highly autobiographical and return to the themes and settings of his earlier novels. The short story collection *Les enfants du bonhomme dans la lune* (*The Hockey Sweater, and Other Stories*) documents a Canadian boy's upbringing, education, and growing sense of cultural alienation from his community. In "La religieuse qui retourna en Irlande" ("The Nun Who Returned to Ireland") Carrier parallels the alienation experienced by a French boy who learns to read French with an English accent with that of his teacher, an elderly English-speaking nun who longs to return to her native Ireland. *Prières d'un enfant très très sage* (*Prayers of a Very Wise Child*) relates a seven-year-old Quebec boy's attempts to rationalize the existence of war, death, and injustice in a world ruled by a benevolent su-

preme being. The collection, in which the child offers prayers of thanksgiving for the beauty of his surroundings and his developing knowledge of sex, evokes the naivete, innocence, and enchantment associated with youth.

Carrier is additionally known for his children's books, his screenplays, and several stage adaptations of his novels, which similarly focus on his Quebecois heritage. Recognizing the political and regional concerns of Carrier's work, Michael Benazon observed that "Carrier is essentially the mythmaker of Quebec rural life, a regional writer and a prose elegist like Thomas Hardy or William Faulkner." Such critics as Philip Stratford, however, have argued that Carrier's aims are more diverse and universal: "[Roch Carrier] thinks of himself as a popular writer and maintains that his style and way of seeing things do not come from literature but from life and in particular from the life of his native village. . . . His books, after all, have celebrated such antinomies: violence and laughter; gusto and defeat; man's potential grandeur and his faltering potential; life, or as Carrier would prefer to put it, love and death."

PRINCIPAL WORKS

Les jeux incompris (poetry) 1956

Cherche tes mots, cherche tes pas (short stories) 1958

Jolis deuils, petites tragédies pour adultes (short stories) 1964

**La guerre, Yes Sir!* (novel) 1968
  [*La guerre, Yes Sir!,* 1970]

Contes pour mille oreilles (short stories) 1969; published in journal *Ecrits du Canada français*

**Floralie, où es-tu?* (novel) 1969
  [*Floralie, Where Are You?,* 1971]

La guerre, Yes Sir!: Pièce en quatre parties (drama) 1970

**Il est par là, le soleil* (novel) 1970
  [*Is It the Sun, Philibert?,* 1972]

Le martien de noël (screenplay) 1970

L'aube d'acier (poetry) 1971

The Ungrateful Land (screenplay) 1972

Le deux-millième étage (novel) 1973
  [*They Won't Demolish Me!,* 1973]

Floralie (drama) 1974

Le jardin des délices (novel) 1975
  [*The Garden of Delights,* 1978]

†*Il n'y a pas de pays sans grand-père* (novel) 1977
  [*No Country without Grandfathers,* 1981]

‡*La céleste bicyclette* (drama) 1979
  [*The Celestial Bicycle,* 1982]

Les enfants du bonhomme dans la lune (short stories) 1979
  [*The Hockey Sweater, and Other Stories,* 1979]

Les fleurs vivent-elles ailleurs que sur la terre? (novel) 1980

The Hockey Sweater (screenplay) 1980

Les voyageurs de l'arc-en-ciel (juvenilia) 1980

La dame qui avait des chaînes aux chevilles (novel) 1981
  [*Lady with Chains,* 1984]

De l'amour dans la ferraille (novel) 1984
  [*Heartbreaks along the Road,* 1987]
Ne faites pas mal à l'avenir (juvenilia) 1984
Prières d'un enfant très très sage (short stories) 1988
  [*Prayers of a Very Wise Child,* 1991]

*These works are collectively known as *La trilogie de l'âge sombre.*

†This work was adapted for the stage in 1978.

‡This work was published as a novel in 1980.

CRITICISM

Andy Wainwright   (review date May 1970)

[*In the following review, Wainwright discusses war as both a predominant theme and metaphor in* La guerre, Yes Sir!]

> . . . Joseph spread the five fingers of his left hand on the log . . . his other fingers, his other hand, seized the axe. It crashed down between the wrist and the hand, which leapt into the snow and was slowly drowned in his blood.

Roch Carrier doesn't pull any punches in **La Guerre, Yes Sir!** Joseph cuts off his hand because he doesn't want to fight in the *maudit Anglais'* war; Henri, who has fought, comes home on leave and decides that he cannot go back; Bérubé, who cleaned latrines along with the Poles, Italians, Hungarians, and Greeks at Gander, Newfoundland, has come home with his newly-acquired English wife (and former prostitute), Molly. Around the subsequent moral dilemmas of these three men Carrier constructs a black comedy of devastating effect. Joseph has become a cripple, but he laughs with joy; Henri must share his home and wife, Amélie, with Arthur, a neighbour who refused to serve and who has fathered two sets of twins by Amélie while Henri has been away: Bérubé hates *les Anglais,* but first and foremost he is a soldier and the word "attention" from the mouth of an English sergeant turns him into an English fighting machine.

These characters, along with the others in the small Quebec village, are brought together at the homecoming of a village boy, Corriveau; but the homecoming is really a wake, for Corriveau has been killed in the *Anglais'* war. To celebrate properly the death of a hero, Father Corriveau digs up his treasured cider and Mother Corriveau cooks an entire pig, and the villagers come to the Corriveau home to drink, eat and pray, in that order.

The plot and language of **La Guerre** are deceptively simple, for while the villagers pray that young Corriveau's body not remain too long in purgatory, Carrier transforms the village itself into a kind of absurd purgatory where Corriveau becomes a Christ figure around whom the villagers congregate and seek salvation. The path through this purgatory is strewn with humour, bitter irony, and a subtle prophetic indication that salvation is not all roses. The unifying feature is the war, and, as Henri says, "Ever since this goddamn war started, there's been no justice."

It is the war, the Second World War, that has brought the villagers together, and it is the war that divides them. Seven English soldiers have brought the body of Corriveau home; they are on duty throughout the night of the wake and cannot accept food or drink. The French Canadians resent not only the impoliteness of their intrusion but also their silence, for the English can neither understand nor speak French. A villager, Arsène, begins to mock the role of the Quebecker who serves in an English war and is savagely beaten by Bérubé. When the English throw the villagers out of the house a fight begins and Bérubé is brought to the English side by the single word "attention." The book is brought to a close with the burial of Corriveau, and Carrier tells the reader, but not the villagers, that his death was very far from being that of a hero.

Carrier's use of a particular and general war as metaphor delves deeply into the substance of French-Canadian rural life. It is a life of obeisance to Church ritual, but only the sexual act brings certain of the villagers close to escaping the tight village structure into a wider realm: "Bérubé rolled onto Molly. It was a death that they stabbed at, violently." Amélie's taking of two husbands is simply a double affirmation of living in the face of continual hardship: "Hurry up," she said, "I'm cold. Hear the wind. It's sad, a winter wind. Come on, hurry up." It is ironic that Corriveau's sister, Esmalda, who has become a nun, is called a saint by the villagers. A saint is someone outside the all-important *norm* of living in the village: Esmalda is not the very real Molly who appears naked in front of Corriveau's coffin, nor does she have the real reactions to living of Joseph's wife, whose major concern is Joseph's ability in bed now that he has only one hand. There is a continual balancing act between the necessities of life and religion. The kids play hockey with Joseph's hand as a puck, but Joseph is forgiven because the Gospels say, "Tear out thy hand or throw it on the fire," and Amélie is forgiven her adultery because she is a "good woman" who prays for Corriveau's salvation.

Through the tobacco smoke and smell of pork at the wake float the religious phrases: "Pour nous pauvres pêcheurs," and "salut pleine et grasse;" through Henri's guilt-ridden mind floats the vision of an entire world passing into Corriveau's coffin; and through the minds of the villagers float the words of their priest assuring them that Corriveau has died for their sins. It is this latter fact that overcomes religion itself, Henri's prophetic vision, and the war—it is the balancing act that will allow village life to continue as usual. The great war in Europe is simply a continuation of the war of 1759 and the conflicts brought out in the Corriveau household are part of a hatred and misunderstanding that has existed for two hundred years between French and English in Canada. It is true, as Carrier says, that "the war had dirtied the snow;" but more snow will fall on rural Quebec villages and the celebration of life will continue for many more winters before the *real* war can be resolved. (pp. 42-3)

Andy Wainwright, "War as Metaphor," in

Saturday Night, *Vol. 85, No. 5, May, 1970, pp. 42-3.*

Mark Levene (review date September 1970)

[In the essay below, Levene argues that in La guerre, Yes Sir! *Carrier incorporates political and social themes and attempts to depict the world as a hostile place.]*

With pride, guilt, and anger Canadian readers will continue to celebrate the publication by Anansi of Roch Carrier's ***La Guerre, Yes Sir!:*** pride because Carrier, a French Canadian novelist displays a fine, demanding talent in his stark telling of the winter funeral of a village youth, guilt and anger because of the continuation of what his narrator calls "the little war" between French Canadians during the Second World War. These reactions are inevitable, but the novel is too good and despite lapses into political predictability too wide in scope to be obscured by them.

Corriveau's coffin, brought to the unnamed village by English soldiers, is the center of ***La Guerre.*** With a brilliant sense of narrative pace, Carrier rapidly details three symbolic responses to its arrival, to the war of the "big guys" it represents, an English war. To evade the manipulations of the *maudits* Anglais, Joseph chops off a hand. The thought of Corriveau makes Arthur relinquish his turn in Amélie's bed to her husband, Henri, who by deserting has also refused the fate of the young soldier. Ironically, only Philibert who helps his father dig graves and slaughter pigs for wakes has a vision of murderous heroism.

The culmination of the novel's political emphasis is the soldier's expulsion of the guests from the Corriveau home. The villagers attack because they will not accept this insult and ultimate claim of the Anglais on the body of one of their own. But ***La Guerre*** is not a predominantly political novel. Carrier attempts to balance the historical dimensions of his story with the challenge to life which the coffin instills in the villagers. The little war occurs only after we are shown the intensely personal feelings of the characters: the grasping for love by the young and the old, the nightmares of a deserter and a young girl, the questioning of life's purpose by Corriveau's parents, the echo of Joseph's laughter in his neighbours' voices, a sound of mingled pain and joy like sex a spitting at death.

The balance is the coffin from the war and the arrival of another soldier, Bérubé, and his English wife, Molly. While the prayers, eating, drinking, and fighting reflect the villagers' thankfulness that at least they are still alive, while the soldiers stand transfixed by duty, the couple sleep and make love upstairs in the dead man's old room. But their stabbing at death is interrupted by Bérubé's hatred of the war and his mad need to show the gravedigger the dehumanization he had been joking about.

Carrier is not completely successful in formulating the claims of both life and history. We see the English soldiers from too great a distance; their thoughts come to us through a veil which tempts but reveals little. They are automatons conditioned to obey and to thinking of French Canadians as pigs, but Carrier's creation of them is equally automatic. He has given Bérubé so magnificent an ener-gy and spontaneity that the soldier's abrupt coming to attention shows us nothing but the author. At the end Carrier allows another momentary blurring of his focus by using his pointer again. We briefly see Corriveau with a Negro soldier; the political connection is neatly made, but feels prefabricated.

More startling than the violence of Joseph's action or the horror of the gravedigger's military education is the ease with which Carrier moves between the comic and the grotesque, between the realistic and the nightmarish. The foolishness of Father Corriveau gives way to the appearance at the window of his daughter, Esmalda, a nun whose smile and decayed teeth are more daemonic than saintly. "She's a saint!" exclaimed Mother Corriveau. "Let's shut that window fast," said Anthyme. To the villagers Molly, an ex-whore, exhibits the real saintliness of life in all its temptations and beauty.

Like Esmalda's face, the nightmares are heightened extensions of the gathering intensity of the highly realistic wake. Henri imagines that the coffin absorbs all earthly life, even opposing armies. "On the whole earth, only Corriveau's coffin under the Anglais flag still existed." We meet Mireille, a young girl only once, in the novel's most horrifying vision. Unable to move she watches Corriveau light her wax toes and then return to his coffin which has supplanted her brother's bed. It is in these episodes that the English war and the war against time emerges.

The novel closes with Philibert leaving home for the war. And in her wedding dress, dirtied by the war like the snow, Molly accompanies another coffin through the whiteness. Any kind of war makes the angel of death and the angel of life indistinguishable.

Mark Levene, in a review of "La guerre, Yes Sir!" in The Canadian Forum, *Vol. L, No. 597, September, 1970, p. 220.*

Mark Levene (review date July 1971)

[In the following essay, Levene offers a mixed assessment of Floralie, Where Are You?]

Floralie, Where Are You? is the second part of Roch Carrier's trilogy about rural Quebec, but the opening pages confront us with differences precisely calculated to set it apart from the first novel in both mood and approach. ***La Guerre, Yes Sir!*** concerned the winter wake held by the aging Corriveau parents for their boy killed in the "English" war against Hitler. ***Floralie, Where Are You?*** retreats in time to their May wedding and bizarre honeymoon in the night forests of Quebec and in the darkness of the spirit. In fact, this novel has a greater kinship with Carrier's haunting, parabolical stories recently published in *Ellipse*, particularly with one called **"The Wedding."** Despite the considerable power of the early sections, however, ***Floralie, Where Are You?*** possesses little of the overall control and intensity which mark his other work. Instead of responding to the novel directly, one watches Carrier revealing it at a vast distance. Often what he reveals is a confusion of formal and ethical purposes.

In its exploration of Anthyme's masculine expectations

and Floralie's desire for life, the first third of the book displays the stark brilliance of style which is Carrier's distinctive talent. Floralie wants to express her love, but because her mother has made her wear black for the journey through the forest, all she can say is "I'm scared." Anthyme meets her fear with silence and clumsy fingers. When he needs to hear her love, the sound is boredom and indifference. These gaps of understanding and response, in part the result of culturally determined roles for men and women, but also a fact of simply being human, become concentrated in the pathetic comedy of Anthyme's effort to decide whether or not Floralie was a virgin: "I'm going to go and see the priest. He'll know if women have a wall or a curtain . . . " Because Anthyme is not conditioned to recognize intangible, emotional barriers, the anguish and isolation of the night ensue.

Since he is compelled to fulfil the idea of manhood with which he grew up, Anthyme damns Floralie; she is a fallen woman and doomed to hell. The novel's most remarkable passage details Floralie's reactions to his curse. "Floralie was damned, but she was alive. She was young, beautiful. She was damned, but she was smiling." Love for the smell of the earth and sun, for the memory of her first lover, battles against the the growing convictions of her sin and damnation. Life—inevitably we feel—gives way to crippling doctrine, and in her mind the lover, a joyful railway worker, becomes a terrible demon.

Ironically, the triumph of death and fear leads to a steady reduction in the novel's immediacy. The alternation between each one's tortured thoughts about betrayal, sin, or God's indifference is increasingly mechanical and distant. There are similarities in the couple's dilemmas, potential bonds of fear: each sees the night as a predatory animal, for both the past is consumed by the darkness. But Carrier merely notes these contacts and leaps to more elaborate visions. His normally tight, economical prose virtually disappears and is replaced by an irritating indulgence in metaphor.

Floralie, Where Are You? is shaped like a mediaeval dream fable, but the brutality of the human spirit creates visions of hell, not heaven. The insistence on fantasy and its fluid link with definable experience is far heavier than in *La Guerre, Yes Sir!,* but the nightmarish force of the stories is rarely achieved. We are shown neither a clear differentiation between illusion and reality nor a consistent exploration of the way the mind can exclude such precise boundaries.

Separately, Anthyme and Floralie meet Néron, an Indian mountebank with a carriage full of chanting children and sacred mice. The open question of Néron's reality temporarily intensifies our sense of the couple's guilt and suffering. But in a sudden and unjustified transition Carrier moves from their visions of the grotesque seer to show us Néron's own consciousness at work. He wants to go to the United States where chimney smoke falls to the ground in a rain of gold. "He would have liked Floralie to come too, but she refused to go to the United States with him." The political direction is gratuitous; the change in viewpoint destroys almost all the ambiguity of the part Néron plays in the couple's dreams. Subsequent encounters with the

Seven Deadly Sins and God-weary Father Nombrillet present similar problems of perspective. When Floralie leaves Néron's carriage, she is pelted with mice which crawl all over her. Again we just watch.

Sheila Fischman, Carrier's able translator, claims a comparison between the novel and Bergman's films. Canadian culture may need a Bergman, but there is a greater urgency for a Roch Carrier writing at his best.

> *Mark Levene, in a review of "Floralie, Where Are You?" in* The Canadian Forum, *Vol. IV, No. 605, July, 1971, p. 36.*

Ronald Sutherland   (review date Autumn 1971)

[*Sutherland is a Canadian novelist, critic, educator, and journalist. In the following essay, he discusses Carrier's use of grotesque in* Il est par là, le soleil, *which the critic translates as* It's Over There, The Sun.]

Roch Carrier has now proven that the language fireworks, the scenic brilliance and the comic diabolics of *La Guerre, yes sir!* were not a one-night stand. With *Il est par là le soleil (It's over there, the sun)* he completes the trilogy which began with *La Guerre* and continued with *Floralie, où es-tu.* The expression "trilogy", however, is used loosely by Carrier. Certain of the fascinating characters introduced in *La Guerre* reappear in the two other novels; the protagonist of *Il est par là* is Philibert, son of the grave-digger Arsène. But the third novel, like the second, is quite different in spirit from *La Guerre,* though it has a lot more in common with the powerful first novel than with the somewhat disappointing *Floralie.*

For one thing, in *Il est par là* Carrier exhibits again the extraordinary capacity for fantastical realism (as opposed to pure fantasy) which characterized *La Guerre.* Here again he uses depiction of the unusual and the grotesque not simply for the sake of shock value and absurdity, but with purpose, often charged with bitter irony. The procession of the Laliberté family through the village streets, for instance, is stunning and unforgettable. Behind the priest and the mother and father, the Laliberté children are being pushed in wheelbarrows, twenty-one outsized heads and helpless blobs of flesh! They must be wheeled with great care; otherwise "les corps de chair liquide s'écouleraient par terre comme une eau sale." Meanwhile, Jonas Laliberté and his wife murmur prayers as they march along: they are thanking God because "ils ont été élus pour être les protecteurs des vingt-et-un petits anges que Dieu a choisis dans son ciel pour les envoyer représenter sur terre sa justice et sa bonté." One is reminded of Gabrielle Roy's Rosanna and the perverse "résignation chrétienne". But Carrier with his skill at exploiting the grotesque strikes the imagination far more effectively than Roy has ever done in all her books.

Il est par là, it must be said, is inferior to *La Guerre* in organic unity and artistic structure, but there is compensation in terms of variety and depth of social insight. It is a picaresque novel, held together by Philibert's journey from his small Quebec village to the metropolis of Montreal. The adventures of Philibert include running on to the ice of the Montreal Forum to throw a punch at a Toronto Maple Leafs defenceman who had just tripped Maurice Rocket Richard. The picaresque technique allows Carrier to explore a cross-section of society and to create a number of ironic situations. Philibert, whose English is limited to "yes sir", eventually finds himself in an English-speaking city district (Westmount?) after hitchhiking from home. Hungry, he finds a shovel and clears the snow from several walks in the hope of earning some money. Finally a woman opens her door: "Poor boy," she says. "You don't speak English. . . . Are you an Italian?" The woman goes on to speculate: "What a pity! These immigrants ought to learn the language of the country before they set out for Canada."

The climactic irony of the book is Philibert being named the heir of "La Neuvième Merveille du Monde", a giant who had made his living by performances where people paid to pummel him with their fists. For a time Philibert was the impresario for this man, "Donato Ambrosio, alias Louis Durand, alias Agadad Aglagayan, alias Jean-Baptiste Turcotte, alias Boris Rataploffsky". The giant, of course, is ironically symbolic of the little man in modern society, and in particular of "les petits Canadiens français". And when this embodiment of immense human power decides that he has been punched enough, the results are dramatic and the implications sinister.

Il est par là, le soleil is filled with typical Carrier humour, a highly amusing novel with a sensitivity for language and life. Compared to much of the soul-searching, *engagé*, tormented writing produced in Quebec over the past ten years or so, it is a gust of fresh air. (pp. 87-8)

> Ronald Sutherland, "Uses of the Grotesque," in Canadian Literature, No. 50, Autumn, 1971, pp. 87-8.

Sheila Fischman   (essay date 1971)

[*Fischman has translated many of Carrier's works into English. In the following excerpt, taken from her translator's foreword to* Floralie, Where Are You?, *she briefly compares the work to* La guerre, Yes Sir! *and discusses the stylistic, thematic, and religious elements of Carrier's fiction.*]

Roch Carrier's second novel, *Floralie, Where Are You?* is technically a sequel to *La Guerre, Yes Sir!* but it is possible that readers of *La Guerre* may not recognize in Anthyme Corriveau and his young bride Floralie the elderly couple whose dead son, his coffin draped in the British flag and carried by English soldiers, provided the occasion for an ironic confrontation with death during the long winter night of *La Guerre.* For the sequel takes us back some thirty years; the season is spring, not winter; and the occasion is a wedding night, not a wake. But just as death may ask what it is that joins us together, love may ask what it is that divides. Night again sets the scene for much of the action. It is the time when our inner life reveals itself best in dream or nightmare. So the night here separates and tests and discovers the characters, to themselves and to the reader. The result is a kind of medieval comedy dramatizing conflicts characteristic not only of the experience of

Quebeckers of a generation past but of that perennial mixture of dream and reality we call life.

Floralie, Where Are You? indicates, perhaps more clearly than *La Guerre, Yes Sir!* that Roch Carrier is no sociologist. He is not a realist except in the sense that the classic folk tale, in its primitive and sometimes ribald action and in its delineation of essential types, is realistic. And he writes in a style that has something of the classic purity and simplicity of the tale. Thus, though some English-language reviewers have spoken of Carrier's use of "joual" in *La Guerre, Yes Sir!* they are mistaken. Some writers, like the poet Gérald Godin and the novelist Jacques Renaud, may employ "joual," partly to make a political statement. Carrier does not. He sees "joual" as a degradation of his language and, although his characters may *speak* that way, he leaves it to the reader to *hear* the accent and the mispronunciation. A real-life Anthyme may call his horse (cheval) a "joual," but that's not Roch Carrier's doing. (If he were writing in English he probably wouldn't write "hoss" either.)

> Roch Carrier is no sociologist. He is not a realist except in the sense that the classic folk tale, in its primitive and sometimes ribald action and in its delineation of essential types, is realistic. And he writes in a style that has something of the classic purity and simplicity of the tale.
>
> —*Sheila Fischman*

The young Anthyme has not yet developed into the virtuoso blasphemer of *La Guerre, Yes Sir!* He directs a remarkable variation on a biblical harangue to an unresponsive deity, but his cursing is mostly limited to "hostie," the sacred host. . . . (pp. v-vi)

The kind of Catholicism that was until not too long ago one of the strongest forces in Québec is very evident here. The name of the priest, Father Nombrillet, is significant. "Nombril" means navel, and the name might suggest the rather narrow range of much clerical contemplation of the time. Some readers will be troubled by what may seem to be an exaggerated preoccupation with images of hell and damnation, but to the Roman Catholic Québécois these are very real, an important part of their spiritual or, if you will, "folkloric" formation.

Ingmar Bergman is another artist who deals with specific religious concerns and uses his own northern landscape to make statements with universal relevance and appeal. Just as his films are not exclusively Swedish, so Carrier is not *exclusively* a Québec writer. Still it is Québec that gives to his work its particular flair. In any human society there will be those who see in change, the coming of the railway, a threat to the moral order, the work of the devil and of foreigners. But they will not all be like the local politician who unwittingly sees his fellow citizens as cows, stampeded by the train, and sees in the train the diabolical designs of the "maudits Anglais." It is the ironic incarnation of the type, the play of the novel and the conventional, in which the reader delights. And in this instance, perhaps no reader more than the *maudit Anglais* himself. (pp. vi-vii)

Sheila Fischman, "Translator's Foreword," in Floralie, Where Are You? *by Roch Carrier, translated by Sheila Fischman, Anansi, 1971, pp. v-vii.*

Nancy I. Bailey (essay date Summer 1972)

[*In the essay below, Bailey provides a thematic analysis of* La guerre, Yes Sir! *and discusses the novel's universal appeal.*]

In 1968, when *La Guerre, Yes Sir!* was published, Roch Carrier was hailed as the potential French-Canadian Faulkner. Since then, *La Guerre* in its dramatic version has played successfully in many countries of Europe and is scheduled for the Canadian Stratford this summer (1972). Now, five years after its publication, a closer look at this novel suggests that its wide appeal may come less from a regional social realism than from the universal themes around which Carrier builds his fable, themes as true for Europeans and Americans as for Canadians. Carrier dedicates the novel (which he says he has "dreamed") "to those who have perhaps lived it." The vividness of his treatment of the lives of his Quebec villagers during World War II often resembles the grotesque, slightly enlarged scenes of dream and nightmare. But his themes, though mirrored in the concreteness of the French Canadian village, are concerned with the issues of our time: the hatred of war and the impossibility of being isolated from it; the failure of the Church to deal with problems of faith, or morality, and of alienation; the difficulty of relating to other cultures in the global village; and above all, the strange, stimulating presence of death as a means to authentic existence in life itself. These are not trivial themes, nor are they of concern only to French Canadians.

Each of Carrier's themes is centered on a group of two or three characters. The hatred of war, its dehumanizing effect, and the impossibility of evading its influence are best seen in Joseph, Bérubé and the English soldiers. The failure of the Church is clearest in its representatives, the nun and the priest. The breakdown of conventional morality and the need to grope towards something else is presented to us in the polyandrous relationship of Amélie with Henri and Arthur. The problem of the two cultures is seen in Molly and the elder Corriveaus. Running through the episodic structure of the novel and connecting these various groups is the thematic conflict between the instincts of life and death which divides the characters into two groups, those associated with the on-going force of life, and those who are numbered among the living dead.

The book opens with a gruesome incident; Joseph, to dodge the draft, lays his left hand on a log and lops it off with his right hand. Later, the villagers connect this self-mutilation with the gospel-saying, "If thy right hand scandalize thee, lop it off; it is better to enter the kingdom of heaven with one hand than with two hands to be cast into the hell of fire." To Joseph, war is hell on earth; it is better to lop off one of your hands than to be thrown into that inferno. The priest, in his sermon at the end of the book, endorses this demythologizing of hell when he says, "Perhaps the war, at this moment, is a little like the fires of hell that God is pouring over the old countries."

Joseph is no coward. He has courageously chosen what he believes to be the lesser of two evils. The incident reveals an important fact of human existence which preachers and moralists rarely admit; that, the world being as it is, sometimes, and indeed often, the best we can choose is the lesser of two evils. Joseph cannot evade the influence of the war. Will he choose to cut off his right hand and retain his inner autonomy, or will he allow himself to be dehumanized like Bérubé or even "made into jam" like Corriveau who sat on a land mine? Joseph chooses a limited life under his own auspices rather than the dehumanized existence of a soldier, living or dead, under the British flag. And his pragmatic choice is to lose his left hand, as a less grievous evil than his right hand with which he works. However, his hand-lopping does not win him access to a demythologized heaven on earth. The nearest thing to heaven in this French Canadian village is the warm bed of a shapely woman. Joseph, by his self-mutilation, becomes sexually repulsive to his own wife. She does not fancy the embrace of an arm that ends with a stump: "You're not a man. I wonder what I'm sleeping with," she says. But Joseph has the last word: "Is Corriveau a man?" (Later, he proves his manhood. It is "Joseph-with-the-hand-cut-off" who becomes the leader of the assault on the English soldiers.) Better to make love and fight the battles of life with one hand than lie in a coffin with two hands and a face that is smashed in like a crushed strawberry.

Shortly after the hand-chopping incident, we see a group of seven English soldiers bring the coffin of Corriveau, the French Canadian soldier, back to his native village. The men are close to breaking point as they stagger on through the snow under the weight of the coffin. They are the dead burying the dead, for their humanity has been crushed out of them by their military training. Throughout the wake, since they are "on duty," they will not eat or drink or relax with the villagers. The language barrier too cuts them off from the mourners. And when violence breaks out among the mourners, they fling them out into the street. Again in this incident Carrier presents a contrast which points up the division between the living and the living dead. Despite their grief, Corriveau's parents respond with charity to their uninvited soldier guests.

> Mother Corriveau, without saying another word, indicated to the Anglais that they should sit down at the table where she served them generous portions of *tourtière* swimming in fragrant sauce.

> Father Anthyme didn't want his cider drunk by these Anglais who had kicked out the people who had come to pray for his son. But he went down to his cellar and dug up some more bottles. "We know how to live," he said to the soldiers,

who smiled because they didn't understand a word.

The soldiers make no attempt to explain their ritual celebration of death. The cultural barrier is only a symbol of a deeper barrier, the chasm between life and death. The seven soldiers fit into the medieval, allegorical framework which Carrier has suggested for his trilogy; but instead of being particularized as the seven deadly sins, they seem to portray more closely Dante's view that the source of all seven sins is imperfect love. The sloth, lust and gluttony of the villagers comes from excess of the love of life and can be redeemed, but the soldiers are doomed to return as they came, escorting the dead.

Nevertheless, the *Anglais* are presented with sympathy and even with compassion. What can the ordinary man do when everyone whom he trusts—parents, priests, teachers, government—tells him that it is his duty to join the army and defend his country? This again is part of the sadness of our human condition: that a man trusts his well-meaning teachers, and finds out very slowly, at great cost to himself and others, that they were wrong.

The most vivid and shocking example of the dehumanizing effect of war is Bérubé, the soldier who is home on leave. He expresses his intuitive understanding of the horror of the war the only way he can, in physical violence. Though he beats up his fellow-villager Arsène to demonstrate the reality of war to him, this fight ends in reconciliation and with the victim laughing. But twice when Bérubé is on the point of following his own personal emotions and impulses, the sergeant has only to yell "Atten-shun!" and he is transformed into an automation to act or not to act according to the will of his military superior, who, in the second instance, commands him to kill his own people. The natural violence of life in the village is here contrasted to that other violence which can be instilled into men to make them act like Pavlov's dogs.

All three boys whom the village has sent to the war return bearing its contaminating marks. As Henri's tormenting dream makes clear, war has followed him to the village; he becomes a murderer. Bérubé is destroyed. Corriveau returns dead, with an escort of English soldiers. The explosion of violence in the village, forshadowed by Joseph's initial action, is not occasioned, as [Ronald Sutherland has suggested in *Canadian Literature* (1969)], from within, from internal inhibitions or frustrations, but is more like the response of a healthy living body rejecting a foreign element. Unlike the war of the big guys against the little ones in which "the big guys get bigger and the little ones go bust," the wake, despite its violence, draws the villagers together and becomes a celebration of life. The mixture of praying and eating, laughter and tears, women, and men, drinking and fighting portrays the natural, honest and spontaneous embrace the villagers give to life in its totality, with all its terror and its joy. This is the war to which one can say "Yes sir!"

Throughout the novel we are kept aware of the villagers' religion—a popular form of Catholicism, to which the older people cling for comfort. The younger people are more inclined to use its sacred terms—*hostie, calice, tabernacle, cruicifice,* etc.—in their blasphemies. The theological implications of prayers for the dead rise to the surface now and them: Corriveau was not bad enough to be burned in hellfire for ever, but he was bad enough to be burned in purgatory for quite a while, and God, who put him in the milder flames for his purification, will take him out sooner if they all keep repeating their garbled, nonsensical prayers. No wonder they need frequent draughts of cider to keep them at it. In the end, even old Corriveau cannot stand any more of it; his wife asks him to pray again, and he says he will go to the barn to curse.

Old Corriveau's daughter has become a nun. In the middle of the Wake she returns home to pray for her brother, but her holy rule will not allow her to enter her father's house. Instead, she forces him, much against his will, to remove a window. The result is that the mourners inside are practically frozen. It never occurs to the nun that in order to keep her holy rule she is breaking the rule of charity which should overrule all lesser rules. There is a touch of caricature in this portrait of the nun of the '40s but not much. When one looks back, it is almost incredible what fatuous, pharisaical nonsense was perpetrated in the name of "religious obedience." The religious order and its religious obedience alienate Sister Esmeralda from her people no less effectively than the army and its military obedience alientate Bérubé. Both become dehumanized but the deformation of the nun is the more shocking because it is all done in the name of Christian charity. Moreover, Bérubé has some idea of what has happened to him but the sister has not.

The priest is another alienated, isolated figure. He is noticably absent from the Wake. He feels no compassion for the dead man. In his funeral sermon, he glorifies war in one breath, and his priesthood in the next. He seems quite unaware that the picture of God which he presents in his sermon is barbaric, incredible, and in its own way blasphemous:

> I, your priest, to whom God has given the privilege of knowing, through holy confession, the most intimate secrets of your consciences, I know, God permits me to know that there are several among you, blasphemers, immodest, fornicators, violators of God's sixth commandment which forbids sins of the flesh, drunkards, and you, women, who refuse the children that God would give you, women who are not happy with the ten children God has entrusted to you, and who refuse to have others, women who threaten by your weakness the future of our Catholic faith on this continent; I know that without Christ, who dies every day on the altar when I celebrate the holy mass, I know that you would be damned.

Again it is a caricature, but not greatly overdrawn. The priest is repeating, to the best of his ability, what he thinks he was taught. He is not speaking his own thoughts. One might pity him, if he did not seem so proud of his priestly dignity. In his alienation he reminds one of Father McKenzie "writing the words of a sermon that no one will hear . . . darning his socks in the night when there's nobody there." But John Lennon has greater compassion for the isolated priest than has Carrier. Both of them see the irony of the phenomenon: the priest who should be a creator of community is himself among the loneliest of men.

The many parallels Carrier establishes between the war and the Church convey his criticism of this the dominant institution of the village. Through images too he links the Church to the life-diminishing forces of the community. The holy water freezes as the priest sprinkles Corriveau's grave. In the warped mind of Henri the Church and death are so closely associated that Corriveau's coffin becomes the ark into which the whole world enters. The nun with her thin smile and sharp teeth appears like a vulture peering in through the open window from the dark cold winter night on to the mourners, "whose sweat turned to ice on their backs." Her question echoes Joseph's: "Who is dead? Who is alive?" But her conclusion, "Perhaps the dead man is alive; perhaps the living are dead," is a part of her own isolation from the villagers who *are* living, though each is responding in his own way to the death of Corriveau. This response unites the community and includes Amélie while it cannot reach Esmeralda. The village conclusion is that

> despite her impure life Amélie was a good woman. Occasions like this evening were fortunate, people would say: you have to have deaths and burials from time to time to remember the goodness of people.

Though the institution of the Church has failed to rectify the dilemmas created by war for Henri, Bérubé and Joseph, the villagers have assimilated something from it which gives them a certain sense of security and a support for their dedication to life. There is consolation for Madame Joseph, acceptance for Amélie and Molly, and a freedom from the guilt of original sin. By the standards of the official Church, their beliefs may be ignorant and misinformed, but their faith as their language is their own. It strengthens the social group and allows life forces to dominate despite the everpresent threat of death as symbolised in the snow and the "sad winter wind" that Amélie fears.

Amélie is introduced early in the novel. She has given refuge in her attic to a deserter named Arthur, taken him into her bed, and born him two pairs of twins. Then her husband Henri comes home like another Agamemnon—with less military glory, but to the same kind of situation at home. Amélie does not fell him with a chopper in the bath; there is an evening of bickering, kicking and punching, but "when they were worn out they made peace." Amélie dictates the terms: the two men can sleep with her on alternate nights. Naturally, this leads to more bickerings as to which night is whose, especially as Amélie finds every now and then that she must have a man during the daytime. She will be cooking meat on the stove when she goes off and gets one of her two men, telling him to hurry up or the meat will burn. She reminds one of the girl in Shakespeare who was married of an afternoon while she went into the garden to gather parsley.

The triangular marriage is unheroic and even comic, but it also provides food for serious reflection. War creates situations in which conventional, peacetime morality places an almost intolerable strain on human nature. To preserve the normal pattern of one-man-one-woman, Amélie might have killed Arthur or Henri, or either of these might have

killed the other; whereupon doubtless the police would have played Orestes. Amélie finds a solution, shocking to conventional morality, and gravely sinful, even worthy of hellfire, in the eyes of the Church, but perhaps again, the lesser of two evils. If one cannot imagine Clytemnestra sleeping alternate nights with Aegisthus and Agamemnon, it is because they were proud, arrogant pagans; these Quebeckers have more practical common sense and more of the Lawrencian life force.

With the Church threatening hell fire in the background, these people of the forties look at their situation and do what their conscience tells them is the best thing in their wretched circumstances. The ecclesiastics had to learn, through their own blunders in the fifties and sixties, that maybe the people were right. Men and women are not to be bludgeoned with rules formulated by celibate theologians in the quiet of rural seminaries. Situation Ethics is common sense made theologically respectable.

In the passage quoted above from the funeral sermon the priest bullies the women of the parish who have ten children and refuse to have more: their "weakness" is a threat to the Catholic faith! Carrier exaggerates a little, but within living memory priests did talk that way. Looking back, we must feel compassion for both priests and people, and more for the priests than for the people—who have shown a marvelous instinct for phasing out what conflicts with common sense. In the novel, the one thing that mother Corriveau hears in the sermon is that her son is saved.

Throughout the book one is conscious of the problem of the two cultures. A French Canadian soldier has died in not-very-glorious circumstances but on active duty (he went behind a hedge to relieve himself and trod or sat on a land mine). The authorities tactlessly send an escort of seven non-Francophone soldiers to bring home the corpse to the village. Being unable to participate in the wake, unable to understand what is said to them, and unable to relax when on duty, they are forced into a posture of aloofness, almost as if their charge were to keep the unruly natives in order. A fight starts among the French Canadians; the soldiers decide to intervene; the French are insulted; and a local war breaks out between French and English in which an English soldier is shot dead. This chain of incidents is a paradigm of so many situations today. The village could be in Northern Ireland. Everyone is right, everyone is wrong, no solution will satisfy half the parties involved, and the poor British serviceman finds himself in impossible situations which he cannot understand, let alone control.

There are several characters in the novel who do something to bridge the cultural gap. There are the Corriveau parents who rely on traditional hospitality. There is the warped character Bérubé who has joined the army and submitted to British military discipline. And there is English Molly, the prostitute from Newfoundland whom Bérubé marries. Molly, in her earthy way, has loved both French and English, and she alone speaks both English and French. In her there might seem to be a spark of hope for a solution of the bicultural problem, but her marriage is not based on cultural idealism. Bérubé has been conditioned by the ecclesiastical drill-sergeant to believe that if he has her before marrying her, he will fall into hell fire. He marries her to satisfy the flames of his lust without falling into the flames of hell. She is the remedy for his concupiscence, as the Thomists would say. There is no marriage of idealistic minds. The damage that the combined forces of the war and the Church have done to Bérubé is indicated when he flings Molly into the snow as they enter the village.

For Molly is not, as she may first appear, the symbol of the English seducing Bérubé away from the spontaneous vitality of the village to his death as he escorts the dead English soldier away from the village. Carrier establishes many parallels between Molly and Amélie, and contrasts her with Esmeralda. It is significant that as the cortege of the English soldier leaves the village and Bérubé who carried Molly from the station carries the dead body out, it is Molly to whom Carrier draws attention. It is she, in her white wedding gown, who fades first into the overall whiteness of the snow-covered earth. Molly like Amélie is the representative of the principle of life which alone can bridge any two cultures. But the life-enhancing sensuality cannot win out over the *thanatos* of the impersonal, ritualized killing of modern war.

The book is founded on a paradox and itself participates in the paradox which it discovers to us, namely, that it is death which teaches us to appreciate life, just as hunger makes us appreciate food, and absence makes the heart grow fonder. Carrier has observed that the villagers are never so enamoured of life as when they are celebrating a wake. He therefore makes his novel the story of a wake. But paradoxically, the book, like the wake, turns out to be a celebration of life. The characters, who may at first sight appear to be a bunch of warped individuals, full of frustrations and inhibitions, turn out, on better acquaintance, to have a healthy love of live—and more common sense than the Church.

The bilingual title of the novel reflects the division between Canadian cultures but also the more essential thematic conflict between the negative force of death and the positive affirmation of life. Through Carrier's mastery of the technique of the modern fable, the war of the title takes on the implications of the war of life itself, with its division between man and woman, man and his God, man and himself, father and son. But the pessimism of the novel does not stem from the recognition that this is a condition of life. The blackness of *La Guerre, Yes Sir!* arises from the inexorable advance of what man seeks most to avoid, namely death, through the very agencies which man has created, Church and State, agencies which he may hate but cannot entirely avoid. The village puts up a good resistance, but, as Carrier concludes, "the war had dirtied the snow."

It is the same dirty snow that greets Philibert, the *La Guerre* gravedigger's son, when he runs away to Montreal to seek his freedom and a new life. In Montreal where the people "were bushy, living overcoats . . . the snow tasted of mud." In this last novel of Carrier's trilogy, *Is it the sun, Philibert?* there are many echoes of *La Guerre.* Molly, who faded against the snow, reappears in Philibert's nameless love, the English matron who gives him

happiness along with food and sex, but whose home disappears as "streets . . . stretched out, crossed one another, made knots, formed letters that could only be deciphered from the sky . . . " and Philibert feels "the immense hand of the city . . . closing up." Now instead of thinking the city should have been called Bonheur, he fears "he would be crushed between these streets that looked so much alike," for "he had no idea where to find the house of the woman who had changed his life."

The graves Arsène digs in the village become the endless trench Philibert is digging in the "dead city earth" under Sainte Catherine Street, and his conclusion that "the good Lord is like the boss—you don't get to see him too often," parallels the attitude of big guys versus the little ones in *La Guerre.*

The echoes make all the more striking the contrasts between the two novels. Gone is the warmth and vitality of the gatherings in *La Guerre,* which mitigated the claustrophobic atmosphere of the Corriveau home and the loneliness of the winter night. The movement of Henri and Arthur from the dark cold attic to the warmth of Amélie's bed while the roast is cooking is much different from Philibert's abortive trip to "Heaven," out of the dark, lightless cellar where he peels potatoes, into the bed in the cellar with Papatakos's wife, guided there by the husband. Philibert returns to his potato job hungry and sad because "when the woman was in his arms he had wept because he felt so little joy." In *Is it the sun, Philibert?* the gatherings in restaurants and fairs, not in homes, celebrate the unnatural. Violence for its own sake motivates the people who pay to assault the Ninth Wonder of the World, the Man with the Face of Steel, who will not hit back. Food, a major metaphor in *La Guerre,* is replaced by hunger in the city-world where in Philibert's room even "the water pipes rumbled like a hungry belly," while his memory of life in the village is like "the fragrance of fresh bread," and Philibert becomes "so drunk that he forgets his whole life." The joyful wake of *La Guerre* becomes the perverted veneration by Philibert's landlord and his wife of the skeleton of their dead child who they insist "lives."

The same themes of life and death unite the novels and their essential difference does not stem from the social realism, the dominance of the English so evident in *Is it the sun, Philibert?* but from the fact that in the society of the latter novel *thanatos* dominates. Death has become a way of life not just for those contaminated as in *La Guerre* by the war or the Church but for all the urban dwellers. Montreal is "like a funeral wreath placed on the ground" and Philibert's instinct for life, inherited from the village, cannot overcome the antagonist in this hostile urban environment. As the Ninth Wonder of the World recognizes, Philibert is "a good boy," but he is totally isolated in the Hell of the City which he continues mistakenly to view as freedom, even as he continues to reject it.

Philibert never becomes completely corrupted by this world of death, because he still has the desire to love, the *eros* that is man's last defense against *thanatos.* His last thought before his accident is of the woman whose "woman's heart would know that (he) was capable of love." Carrier reinforces this theme by ending the section immediately before the car overturns with the repetition, "Ah! To love . . . to love . . . to love. . . . " But in a world where no one is living no one can love.

From his upside-down position in the overturned car whose spinning wheel is gradually coming to a halt, Philibert hails the coming of death with the question, "Is that the sun?" It is significant though that the title (in translation) of this novel is not the affirmative of **La Guerre, Yes Sir!** but the question which "Philibert thought he said" and appears directed to him by the omniscient author. Philibert has been mistaken in thinking that in Montreal he is free. And while he is right in affirming that "God doesn't exist, but me, I exist; you haven't been born till you've said those words . . . ," he is wrong in thinking these words must be said "in the middle of the night, crossing Sainte Catherine Street, weaving through the cars that whistle past your nose like scythes."

In contrast to **La Guerre,** only Philibert fights the encroachment of death in his novel, and only he lives. The rest are automatons. But *thanatos* has triumphed not through inhibitions, poverty and fear that Philibert associates with the village, but through materialism and the technological society.

The daylight settings of the third novel are much darker than the nocturnal ones of the preceeding two. The village world of the past contained all of life including death. The sun that Carrier sees rising over the modern world is that of death, replacing the procreative and life-enhancing though often violent instincts and filling the vacuum left by the disappearance of warmth, kindness and love. Without these instincts there is no healthy struggle against death which then becomes the victor in the war that is life itself. (pp. 43-7)

> *Nancy I. Bailey, "The Corriveau Wake: Carrier's Celebration of Life," in* Journal of Canadian Fiction, *Vol. I, No. 3, Summer, 1972, pp. 43-7.*

Philip Stratford on Carrier:

Roch Carrier is an instinctive writer. He claims to write not so much to display as to discover what he knows. He has continued to experiment, not following any school but in an individualistic way, from book to book, capitalizing on new techniques without ever betraying the distinctive voice and vision which have marked all his work. In the long run, he insists that his interest in form is secondary to the more pressing need he feels to invent stories that reveal Quebec to itself. He thinks of himself as a popular writer and maintains that his style and way of seeing things do not come from literature but from life and in particular from the life of his native village.

> *Philip Stratford, in* Dictionary of Literary Biography, *Vol. 53, Gale Research Company, 1986.*

Roch Carrier with Silver Donald Cameron (interview date 1973)

[*Cameron is a Canadian novelist, short story writer, critic, and author of children's books. In the interview below, Carrier discusses his fiction and dramas, his identity as a French Canadian, and his aims and experiences as a writer.*]

[*Cameron*]: *Your novels are often terrifying and frightening, but they're also very funny. They're like folk tales, in a way.*

[Carrier]: Yes, because the comedy in my novels does not come from reading, or from literary tradition: it comes from something which was lived. In my family or in my village, people there have a kind of sense of seeing things and people more big and more funny and more brave than they are. It's in that living tradition that I learned to build up a character, to build up an action, and not in a literary way. A novel like **La Guerre, Yes Sir!** is not a novel which takes place in a tradition, because to write that novel I really had to forget everything I had learned in books and in La Sorbonne, everything. I tried to find in myself everything in that book. Everything which was in myself was from my village, from people I know. That's why it's very difficult to situate that novel in a literary tradition. I tried to find something which was instinctive.

But the village in the book is not exactly St. Justin de Dorchester. How did you build that village in the book out of the village in south Québec?

That book was not made the way people think. When I came back from Europe in '64, after five years away, the *révolution tranquille* was just taking place in Québec; people were concerned about new political problems. The change was almost unbelievable for someone who was not in Québec. I met friends on my return: many of them were separatists, and I could not understand what was happening. I told myself that maybe by writing I could really live what people had lived before, some years before. I thought that taking a little village, which is a microcosm, would be a good place for me to let live all those forces which were in the French Canadian. I did not want to understand the situation in an intellectual way, because when you are intellectual you always go in a system, and I did not want to have any system. So I told myself, if I can let free those forces in a French Canadian, I will look at what will happen. Believing that, I began to write **La Guerre.**

Did you feel at the end of it that you did understand a lot more than you had?

Yes, I think so, I think so. When the book was published, many people in Québec thought it's a novel of old times, but I heard also it's a prophetic novel. During the October events, I heard, many times: You prophet!

Did the novel change you yourself? Do you feel differently about being Québécois?

When **La Guerre** was finished, I had the deep feeling that I had to continue to try to understand, and I found that if the events of **La Guerre** were happening like they happened in **La Guerre,** there were other causes. That's why I wrote **Floralie,** to understand what was in a French Canadian other than a political feeling, other than that aggressiveness against English Canada. The book *Floralie* is about Catholic conscience. I think that Catholic conscience has a great influence on the way we live now, on the way we look at problems and try to give them solutions. Many people became involved in politics in the same way that they were involved in religion some years ago, with the same severeness, the same aggressiveness.

Catholicism also seems to have left a very rich folk imagination that you explore in **Floralie.**

It's not imaginative: I think everything is real. It's a realistic novel. What a young French-Canadian girl thinks about in the night, that's what I tell in the novel.

Yes, but it's internal reality. Presumably even in Québec you didn't have Néron chugging through the woods with his car full of children.

Yes, yes, why not? I thought of it, so it's true.

Well, I won't argue. What sort of thing are you doing now?

I don't know where I'm going exactly. I am working now on another novel. It's quite different from what I've written, but it's quite similar at the same time. I am not a formal writer, I don't really experiment with form. Why, I don't know. In France now there are a lot of very interesting formal experiments in the novel, but all those experiments were done against a tradition, and here in Québec we have no tradition of novels. So I told myself, let's write things as I see them, the most efficient way; and after that we'll build novels, if we have time, which are beautiful in form. It's not very high as a philosophy, but I think we have to clear the way. After that our children will do another thing. I write something, and I look at it, and I say, No, ça marche pas, it's no good. Then I try something else—that's the way I write.

You've tried a lot of things, in your short stories especially.

When I wrote the short stories in *Jolis Deuils,* like those translated in *Ellipse,* I was in France and I was very poor, but it was the free life and among all my reading I had a little time to write. So I used to write two or three short stories a day, because I was discovering the world. Everything was new for me, just everything in Europe. I saw a statue with a pigeon on his head, and it was a subject of a short story. I had a kind of sensibility that made me able to feel something deep in everything. Reality was like a wall, and I had to find something on the other side of the wall. I remember one day it was very cold in my apartment and I wrote a short story, which is the first in *Ellipse,* about that winter in which everybody's cold, all the city is frozen. I had to go on the other side of the mirror, if you want. Why, I don't know—but it was a kind of venture to go, d'aller plus loin, si vous voulez, to go further. And those characteristics suit my way of feeling things very well. We can find them in my novels. In *Floralie* or in *La Guerre,* or *Il Est Par Là, Le Soleil,* the third novel, we had something of those short stories. I need to go a little bit further than the reality.

Could you do a whole novel just dealing with the behind-the-mirror thing that you get in the short stories?

I think I will succeed in doing that. You see, I am learning everything: I am learning life, I am learning a way of writing. Far, very far, I see a kind of big book in which everything I learn will be found, and every novel, every short story I write, prepares me to do that kind of book. In that book there will be formal experiments, but it will be a great disorder, if you want, like life. I will be myself in the book, and it will be interesting to be in, but I have so much to learn—!

Do you feel very young at the moment?

Yes.

Is that new, or were you always like that?

I was always the same. I never feel old, I never feel really tired, except maybe intellectually. But it's not tiredness in approaching life. Everything is great, everything is to be discovered, every person is to be more known. Yes, I think I feel young, and I feel young because I know the very tiny importance of one man. I read the papers and I see friends who say I am the biggest one, the greatest one. It's funny but it's not very serious for me, because a man is always learning, he's always trying to understand better, and that's my kind of involvement.

Is that why you left teaching to become a dramaturge?

Yes, I left university to live the adventure of the theatre, and it's great, I am learning a lot. Maybe in two or three years it will be too small, and I will have to find something else.

The first work you ever did for the theatre was the adaptation of **La Guerre,** *wasn't it?*

Yes. One day, it was a spring day, I had a phone call asking me if I wanted to write an adaptation for the theatre from my novel *La Guerre, Yes Sir!* and without thinking I said Yes. And I did it. I had a big chance, and it was a good success in Montréal. After that the Théâtre du Nouveau Monde needed a play to go on a European tour; they asked for my play and I said Yes. Everything went well in Europe, too. The play was done in Paris and in Rennes. In Belgium we did the play in five or six towns, including Brussels. In Switzerland we played in Lausanne; in Luxembourg, we played in Luxembourg, and in Czechoslovakia we played in Prague and two other cities.

How did the European audiences react to it? Did they find it strange and exotic?

I was invited as a writer by the Canada Council to do the tour, to learn about different audiences. I made two main discoveries. First, the French my people spoke, which is not *joual* but is Québécois dialect, could be understood everywhere in France and Switzerland. The most important discovery was that the only way of being international is to be very national. The main theme of my play is the reaction of a minority in front of a majority, and when we were in France they understood very well. When we were in Switzerland people there understood very well; they saw themselves in front of the Germans. When we were in Brussels it was the same thing, the French people there feel as a minority in front of the Flamands. In Prague the Czechoslovakians feel as a minority in front of the Russians and in every review that was mentioned: that the play was Québécois, but it was also Belgian, or Swiss, or Czechoslovakian.

That must give you a tremendous feeling of confidence.

I am really not confident. It's a marvellous experience, that success, but it doesn't make me self-confident. On the contrary, I was unable to write for the theatre afterwards. The Théâtre du Nouveau Monde asked me to write a play, but I was really unable during the winter to write it, and I worked on a novel instead of writing a play. I lived that adventure, the theatre, for a year very deeply, and it's really too much for a man to feel. I had to sit down and to think of another thing, to forget about that, because when I was at my work table, within myself I was preparing another *La Guerre.* If such a play worked one time, if it was efficient one time, instinctively you want to repeat it. That's very very very bad. So this year I have to forget about that.

When you came to work in the theatre, did you find it difficult really to think as a dramatist rather than a fiction writer?

It was not very hard, but there were many problems. When you write a novel the way I write them, you're God. You create the temperature, you create the space, you can do everything. On the stage you have to accept some limits. Look at the stage here; it's ninety feet wide. In my novel *La Guerre,* I had some dialogue between Bérubé and Molly in bed, and when I wrote the adaptation I automatically saw a bed on the stage. But let's try to put the bed on a ninety-foot-wide stage. That makes no sense at all, so I had to change that. And it's true you can be helped by the lights and the music, but everything, I think, is in the dialogue. The dialogue has to be very strong, much stronger than normal, to reach people. One has to find what is the most theatrical. The play *La Guerre* was not really theatrical, I must say, because it was a novel done on the stage. I could answer you better in some months, because when I am ready I will write something, a real creation written directly for the stage.

I was going to ask if that wouldn't be what you'd want to do now.

Yeah. It was good to have the security of a novel behind me, but I think that a man who writes for the theatre has to write for the theatre, to find a theatrical way. And at Théâtre du Nouveau Monde we are looking for a popular public, we have to find a popular way to be understood by that public. That's very difficult.

What kind of an audience did you get for **La Guerre***? Mostly middle-class people, or did you get some working people?*

We noticed from the inquiries that a lot of people who did not usually come to the theatre came for *La Guerre.* I was very glad of that, but there was a kind of misunderstanding: they were coming to see a funny play about a wake.

And did they enjoy it?

Oh yes, yes. Somebody kept the time, and we had forty-five minutes of laughing during the play, so they laughed a lot. But there was a misunderstanding. The director, Albert Millaire, and I thought it was a tragedy. Both of us were in the back, watching the first words and the first reactions, and two seconds after the beginning there was a big laugh. We were almost crying, because of the misunderstanding there. I don't complain about it, though. It's better that the people come here even through a misunderstanding.

When you say **La Guerre** *was intended to be a tragedy, do you feel the same way about the novel?*

Yes.

Can you tell me why?

It's very sad for me. Every character is sad because he's condemned to failure. The only people who do not fail are père et mère Corriveau. They are simple; I think that they love themselves, and they are the only ones that are not failing their lives. But Philibert will fail, Bérubé will fail, Molly is failing—everybody is failing, and everybody maybe had many possibilities. They were reasonably intelligent, but life did not give them the opportunity of exploiting that intelligence, that force they had, so everybody is really condemned to be nothing and to live nothing. That's sad. Another thing which is sad is that inevitable war between the French and the English. For me it's really a conviction, that, which I found in writing my novel, that it was impossible not to collide. In the novel, I put all those contrary forces and I let them free, and ils se sont frappés.

You think that will happen in reality.

Yes, it will come. When I hear the news from Ireland, it's so near Québec. We will have another October event, maybe in December this time, and the army will come back, and there will be little smashes, but—

—eventually you see a big smash?

Yes. Let's say, in a cold way, you don't accept that somebody takes what's yours. I think that for an English Canadian Québec is his property. Ontario is not the property of a Québécois but I think that Ontarians feel that Québec is their property because it's part of the country, and nobody wants to lose what belongs to him. Québec will leave Confederation under new legislation maybe, but it's not possible to imagine Québec leaving smoothly. That's what I discovered by writing that book too: the villagers have nothing against the soldiers, the soldiers have nothing against the villagers, they are doing their job. But things go on, and the machine is running. They have to smash. I don't want that smash, and I remember a sentence by [Mordecai] Richler one year ago in a magazine: he was saying that Québec was going through the same sterility as Ireland. And I was quite surprised to read what I was thinking myself. I don't want that sterility, I don't want that smash. So I decided to work, to do something in Québec, to continue to participate in the building of a literature, participate more and more in what I know, the cultural life, and maybe to try to have friends outside the frontier. I try to know a little bit more what's happening there. Maybe it will be possible to have a kind of collaboration. Naturally I prefer to try to find something we have in common; that's better than an opposition. So that's

The front and back covers of Carrier's La guerre, Yes Sir!

what I'm working on. The Québécois is very much frustrated because he doesn't feel he has his real part in Canada. I think we have to go outside, we have to take part.

Something like touring the country with the English version of La Guerre *might be tremendously useful.*

I think it would be, because the first task we have is to tell the truth. You have to take some risk to tell the truth.

Is that how you see the writer's job? To tell the truth?

It's the most honourable one, the most honourable task, I think. If we were a free country, and a rich country, if everybody around the world were well-nourished, writers could write perfect and formal novels, but instead we have to work in the street, in the garden. I think to tell the truth is the best way to live now.

I think everybody, in any kind of work, asks himself these days, Is this the most useful thing to be doing now?

Two years ago I was asking myself that question, and I had an answer. I thought it was important to give a lecture on [André] Malraux, it was important to give a lecture on Corneille; it was *really* important, and I was trusting myself saying that. But at a certain time I was unable to trust

myself, and I thought, It's time now to get out. I was speaking about telling the truth: my third novel, the sequel of *La Guerre,* tells the story of a young Québécois trying to live in Montréal. It's not an experience I lived myself, exactly, because I was much better prepared than my character, but it was the story of many many many Québécois who come to Montréal. The work here was English, and they were French paysans; the work here was technical, and they were badly prepared for it. It was a drama for them which has an influence on what is happening now. I did not live that experience but I think as a writer I had the task—le devoir, the duty—to speak in place of those who don't know how to speak. This experience has to be told. It's important that we know our past; it helps us to understand the present.

How do you manage to see things from the point of view of, say, Floralie? She's a woman thirty or forty years your senior, living in a village, an unquestioning Catholic and so on.

I don't know, exactly. I think I take myself as I am and I go in the reverse direction from what I live; and following that reverse logic, I can reach a woman like Floralie. Because without the chances I had, I could have been a man like Floralie. I don't know how these things happen, though; it's a mysterious chemistry. Flaubert described the work of a writer. He kept his diary about Madame Bovary and in one page he wrote, Today I was a horse, I was a leaf in autumn, I was a man, I was a woman, I was a lover. A writer is everything and everybody. At least he tries to be.

When it's really going well and you're working on a novel like **Floralie,** *do you forget Roch Carrier?*

Yes. There is a horse in the novel, and I became a horse. One day I was in St. Tropez and I was writing a short story about hockey. I was in my house and I was walking like this—and my wife asked, What are you doing? I said, I'm playing hockey—and it was true. I said that without thinking I was writing, but just trying to keep the feeling in my wrists.

Does the work stay with you all the time, or can you just throw it off when you go out to teach or work at the theatre?

I think of what I'm writing all the time—too much, I'm very preoccupied. But to write I sit down at my table. It's difficult to begin to put something on the paper, but after several minutes I become, like *hot.* And there, it's true, I *am* my character. It continues like that maybe for fifteen minutes at the most, and I am really what I have to be. After that there is a phone call or something, I don't know. I think I am very tired. Afterwards I continue to write, but not very long. But in the intense moment, I can write very very speedily. I spend one hour a day at my worktable, not more than that. But *every* day, *every* day.

At a special time?

No, when I am free. It's not very long, but if I write one hour a day I can do a lot of writing during a year.

How long does it take you to do a novel?

La Guerre was written very fast. It took me twelve days.

Twelve days?

Yes. It was very intense. For many many years I had thought about something like **La Guerre,** so I was ready for it; it was not new material. **Floralie** is more well-written than **La Guerre,** more formal, and it took me almost one year to write this book. The third one, **Il Est Par Là, Le Soleil,** took me a whole year.

How would a character like old Corriveau come to you?

Corriveau is the type of the old French-Canadian man, a strong man, married to weak little Floralie. Floralie was very much Catholic, so they made love by the hole in the night jacket; Father Corriveau was strong, and would like a woman, would like to drink, but Floralie was always there saying No, no, you have to be a good Catholic. So Father Corriveau is very frustrated, and at the wake we see his frustration, but at the same time the chance he took to liberate himself. He's the type of the old French-Canadian paysan. But I am Father Corriveau every time my wife finds I come home too late at night. It's something a man feels every day, not to be able to do what he wants to do, to fail.

How did you get into the third novel?

When **La Guerre** was finished, I had the feeling I had to go before that to understand other causes of the problem, so I wrote **Floralie.** But when **Floralie** was finished, everything was not told; I had to go after **La Guerre,** to see what would happen to young Philibert, the child who left the village at the end of **La Guerre.** Those three books were one book, finally. The novel I am now writing is different. The place is Montréal, and it will be a novel of the city. For many years I have wanted to tell the story of a building—the main character of my novel is a building. How that came about I don't know. Things come and they take importance, and I have to fight with them.

Are you following the life of the building itself?

I would prefer not to speak about what is not exactly finished. The building will be built, but it is a story of people involved in that building.

Many novelists say that when they're working on a novel they can't discuss it. Do you feel the same way about it?

Yes and no. I think I could speak about what is written now and what I intend to do, but I want to preserve a kind of freedom, you see. If I say to somebody, This thing will happen, instinctively I will have the feeling that I should write what I said, or do the contrary of what I said. When we write we have choices to make. I think the choice of something, the choice of a road, the choice of a word, the choice of an action, must come when the pencil is on the paper, at that point when everything is hot.

In that big book you see far off, you told me you would really be yourself. Do you feel you haven't been, so far?

No, not exactly. When I read the proofs of **La Guerre** I was almost shocked, because that book was so different from what I am and what I was. It was something strange, mysterious. And the same for **Floralie,** and the same for Philibert. Those books permitted me to discover a part of myself which was unknown to me. When I say those books are strangers, they are not really strangers, because it is impossible for a writer to invent what is actually unknown to him. I had not lived directly those things, but I had had repercussions on me of those lives lived by other people. It's so difficult for me to try to be intelligent in English, and it's also difficult because all the things we are speaking about are difficult even in French. I explain things very badly.

No, you make more sense in your second language than most of us do in our first. You said over lunch that this was a very exciting time to be an artist in Québec. What is it like?

It's quite simple. During lunch I compared the time we live in in Québec with the time a man becomes a man. Québec is growing and maturing, and we feel that we have a lot of things to do. It's fun to do them; everybody is really involved in a different experience. I speak about the writers: before 1960 writers did one book, or two, or three, and then they found a job and their literary work was finished because they had no good reason to continue; but here and now in Québec the young writers have the feeling that we are building the French-Canadian Québécois literature. It's an important time to do it. In doing it, we have the feeling of saving things from the past, and we have also the feeling of preparing what is coming. There are readers who wait for our books, who wait for our plays, with great interest. People read less and less French literature from France, and the main interest is in what is happening here in Québec. Even in France they know that their foreign literature is important; they become interested in it too. So writers feel that they are necessary, they are as useful as anybody, they are not outside of the society but they are in the society and they are an important part. In the schools the young students are very much interested in the past literature of Québec, that old literature that we don't know because of religious and political censorship; they discover those old authors with great pleasure, great interest, but they wait for the new authors. Often they buy books which are not yet published, they wait—and that's great! Writers here are people, we are workers, and we have a job to do which interests many people.

You're taking charge of the direction of Québec for yourselves intellectually and artistically as well.

No, I don't think we are taking charge, exactly. Other men have charge of Québec, stupid, incompetent men who love power. They have all the possibilities, the police and the army. I am trying to understand, to know what happened to our people. To know our people better, that is my job.

Do you get letters from your readers? Do people stop you in the street?

I have letters, but people don't stop a writer in the street: we have policemen to do that. I say that because of October 1970—but I have a kind of friendship with my readers. Very often I am invited to go to universities or go to schools and I have good discussions there, good conversations.

Do you think of yourself as an ambitious writer?

In life I have not very much ambition; I take things like they come. But literary ambition, yes.

You'd like to write the best damn novel of the century.

Yes. It's crazy, but that's the truth.

No, surely it's the only reason to write.

I am not that kind of guy who will meet important people to help him, that's not my kind of ambition. My kind of ambition is to do good books. The white page, that's where I want to be good. It's crazy.

It takes a long time. Do you brood about death? You often write of death.

I don't want to be anguished about that closing of the door. As long as the door is open, it's okay: let's go! If the door is smashed on my nose, what can I do? It's finished. In my novels, I speak many times about death, but that's not really myself; I speak about death because in our religious culture death was more important than life. Man was created, according to our religion, not to live but to die. The most important thing was death and the life after death, and that's why I speak so often of death, because

for all the French Canadians death was the main thing, life after death. So they did not care about life during life. But my personal options are not concerned by that.

Is that why the comedy in your work is often macabre?

It's a way for me to mock at what we've learned. But it's comic yes and no. At the end of my third novel there is Philibert, who dies—maybe, maybe, I'm not sure, and the reader is not sure either. He dies in a car accident and dying—if he dies—he sees himself hurt. After that he sees himself in hell, and then a big snake comes and gets him in his mouth, and he goes down and gets out the back again. It's macabre, sure; it's maybe comic, because it's really too much; but at the same time it's quite anguishing, because I remember when I was a child and I know that that story's true. For every French Canadian the presence of the snake has menace, and is terrifying and horrible. We saw him in our dreams. It was the punishment against bad actions. It's macabre because our education showed us macabre things. We have to tell the truth about that, too. (pp. 14-28)

Roch Carrier and Silver Donald Cameron, in an interview in Conversations with Canadian Novelists *by Donald Cameron, Macmillan of Canada, 1973, pp. 13-29.*

Words are not actual reality: thinking of a trout isn't holding it slippery and quivering in his hand, but words create a magic which revives dead things and brings to life what isn't yet alive. Words give life.

—*Roch Carrier, in his* No Country without Grandfathers, *1979.*

Barbara Godard   **(review date May-June 1974)**

[*In the following review of* They Won't Demolish Me!, *Godard examines Carrier's "tragi-comic" portrait of the Quebec people's resistance to change and urban renewal.*]

By the time you read this, the translation of Carrier's latest novel [*They Won't Demolish Me!*] will be available. I have been reading the typescript and am consequently tempted to offer suggestions for revision. None are required in the novel itself; as usual, [translator] Sheila Fischman has admirably captured the deceptively simple style of Carrier's fable with its many subtle ironies. These are lost though in the new English title which draws attention to the sentimental theme of the valiant efforts of one landlord, Dorval, to resist attempts to demolish his home for high rise apartments. I would have kept the original title, "the two thousandth floor", underlining the frequency of the compromising dream of upward mobility among these same combattants.

Anyone who has seen Denys Arcand's *Rejeanne Padovanni* knows what a serious and sometimes violent issue urban renewal now is in Montreal as its inhabitants prepare to see the last old districts destroyed in preparation for the Olympics. Carrier's depiction of the opposition movement is a tragi-comic one. While he celebrates the resistance of Dorval's lodgers in a series of extremely comic battle scenes, his conclusion is as pessimistic as Arcand's: the city divides people and makes organized resistance impossible. As they try to better their lives, all the tenants become involved in the destruction of their home. Their ironic motto is derived from the anticipated height of the building.

They Won't Demolish Me! echoes the earlier *There is the Sun Philibert* in following the difficult lives of those who fail to adopt the bigger-and-newer-is-better philosophy. Cowboy, the singing poet, leaves the house to explore the world, discovers his songs are not liked in the city and returns to a now empty house to hang himself. Like the artist, the socialist is not able to withstand urban pressures. The self-declared communist, Dorval, contrasts his increasingly futile efforts to hold his tenants together with the solidarity of the French resistants he had encountered during the war, people who had taught him the meaning of communism. In the last pages he faces Barnabé and Hildegarde, his former tenants, with their twelve children, come to bulldoze his house, and Dupont-la-France, planting plastic flowers around the high rise from whose two-thousandth floor Mignonne Fleury waves. The tenants, along with the Laterreur brothers, wrestling for tremendous sums in South America, have joined the capitalists.

Their efforts to enter these ranks provide some of the comic episodes in the book, which like *La Guerre, Yes Sir* is developed through a series of loosely linked scenes involving a tightly knit community. We witness the continuing struggles of Barnabé with the machine on his kitchen table, delivered as part of a correspondence course which will, as his goading wife Hildegarde reminds him, remove him from the ranks of the unemployed should he master it. The noise of their domestic battles resounds in the arena where they join the other tenants to watch the Laterreur brothers be beaten to a pulp in a fixed fight against the Gorgeous Glassgo Brothers from English Canada. These cries reecho in the funny vignettes in which all of the tenants seek vengeance on the English capitalists deemed responsible for the demolition of their home. In the various street battles is revealed the collective impotence of the group: the Laterreur brothers beat up a Chinaman, La Vieille attacks a priest quoting Latin, Barnabé and Hildegarde accidentally knock each other out, while Dorval discovers that the English prostitute is none other than Mignonne Fleury. After this futile effort, the house is abandoned as they seek individual solutions.

While this battle of comic misconceptions reveals Carrier's Molière-like dramatic powers, the turning point in the novel—when Mignonne comes back to the house to convert it into a brothel—illustrates once again the grotesque fantasy which permeates *Jolis Deuils* and the earlier fiction. La Vieille leaves the old-folks home to return to the house in one last attempt to find love. As the sheet-covered phantom in Room 9 she becomes the most requested woman until she suddenly dies. Comforting the distraught client, Mignonne quickly substitutes a regular prostitute under the sheet and continues to make the fortune which allows her to rent a penthouse in the new building. With the death of La Vieille all love leaves the house, and the brothel, which had seemed a gesture of solidarity with the striking workers, the epitome of resistance, becomes a temple to the capitalist ambitions of Mignonne. The house and its owner are both lost, Dorval realizes, as he chases Mignonne the "vendue" up to the top of the building and down, in a movement contrasted to his parachute descent into France, from the height of "the two thousandth floor", into the arms of Jeanne-the-Virgin, the girl of his dreams, who was "married to her country". The Québécois, we infer, are not going to save themselves from the enemy as the French did: there are too many collaborators among them and too few socialists—the political implications here are more obvious than in any of Carrier's other fiction.

Carrier has written another novel with the comic verve of *La Guerre, Yes Sir* which with the relevant theme of resisting urban renewal will undoubtedly transcend its nationalist implications to become popular throughout Canada. I prefer the earlier fiction though, particularly *Floralie Where Are You?* in which Carrier has probed the difficulties of the human quest for liberty with greater psychological depth of symbolic reference.

Barbara Godard, in a review of "They Won't Demolish Me," in The Canadian Forum, *Vol. LIV, Nos. 640-641, May-June, 1974, p. 26.*

Margot Northey (essay date 1976)

[*In the following excerpt, Northey examines Carrier's use of the grotesque in* La guerre, Yes Sir!]

In the middle of *La Guerre, Yes Sir!* the young nun Esmalda returns to her home in the village to pay homage to her dead brother, the soldier Corriveau. Obeying her religious order's strictures against entering the house, she views the mourners around the coffin through an opened window and asks: 'Who is dead? Who is alive? Perhaps the dead man is alive. Perhaps the living are dead.' Despite the unthinking, almost mechanical quality of her speaking, the question is important, underlining the complex and problematic issue of death in the novel. In *La Guerre, Yes Sir!* the coffin sits in the centre of the house as it remains in the centre of the characters' consciousness, and it is the symbolic focus of the story's meaning.

Roch Carrier has referred to his writing as 'a funny adventure,' and we can readily see the humour in his first novel. Varieties of humour can be found in almost every section, from the farcical fairness of Amelie's every-other-night policy with her two husbands, to the sexual jokes unconsciously contained in the prayers of the villagers, to the satirical bite in the depiction of Bérubé's first sexual encounter and in the priest's eulogy. Using Ruskin's terminology, it can be said that the novel moves away from the terrible towards the sportive grotesque. In other words, in Carrier's grotesqueness play or jest is more dominant than, for example, in Marie-Claire Blais's grotesque writing.

However, it is also clear that fearfulness is always present in the playing and that Carrier's mockery carries with it an almost constant undercurrent of horror. The bizarre and amusing actions of the characters have much in common with the type of black comedy found in *Le Chercheur de trésors,* a novel which Carrier admits he was much influenced by and whose motifs he obviously borrowed from. Moreover, as in so many other gothic and grotesque works, in *La Guerre, Yes Sir!* images of death are a primary source of the fearful or horrifying aspect.

The sense of death on a personal, physical level is of primary concern to the characters, a reality brought home to them by the returned body of one of their own villagers. He is treated as a hero, although we learn that he has been ingloriously killed in action while relieving himself behind a hedge in the army camp. Mother Corriveau questions the purpose of a life which leads inevitably to the grave:

> What was the use of having been a child with blue eyes, of having learned about life, its names, its colours, its laws, painfully as though it was against nature. What was the use of having been a child so unlucky in life . . . Everything was as useless as tears.

Where Mother Corriveau weeps in response to death, her husband Anthyme rages; where she attempts prayer, he can only swear.

The menacing fact of individual physical death is a metaphor for other kinds of death and dying which spread in widening circles of implication through the story. The unconscious blasphemies of the mourners' prayers emphasize the spiritually moribund condition of a people for whom their religious teaching is ironically itself a kind of death force. The priest tells his parishioners that life is unimportant except as a prelude to death and final judgment, 'that we live to die and we die to live.' His Jansenist sermon portrays a vengeful God, and warns of the torments of Hell awaiting mankind with its 'Sinful, voluptuous nature,' and especially awaiting those people who stray from the prescribed devotions. The narrow emptiness of his message is a bitter satire upon the whole Church, with its glorification of war and admonition to overburdened women to produce more children—the latter a grotesque and deadening distortion of the life force. The nun mouths the platitude, 'How sweet it is to come back among one's own people,' while remaining apart in the cold outdoors. The decayed teeth in her wan, thin face suggest that submission to the Church's dictates results in a withering of humanity.

The characters in *La Guerre, Yes Sir!* also face a cultural death; their sense of identity as individuals and as a community is being increasingly repressed. The villagers are powerless against the authority and force of the English-speaking soldiers, and in the end are thrown out of their own house by these strangers. The uncomprehending sergeant disdainfully views the 'pigs' who do not even speak a civilized language, and whose behaviour throughout the night is proof of the truth of his old history lesson on French-Canadian animality. Bérubé, who attempts to bridge both French and English cultures, is caught in the middle. At the conclusion he faces the prospect of his dismal future; considered by both sides to be a traitor, he is condemned to be a perpetual outsider. Thus the novel repeats the pattern of fear found in *Wacousta* and *For My Country* in which the notion of cultural annihilation is a primary anxiety; it reinforces the idea that collective social menace as much as individual menace is a recurring motif in Canadian gothic fiction. Yet there is a difference between Tardivel's nineteenth-century, French-Canadian version and Carrier's contemporary novel. In *For My Country,* the enemy is clearly defined as the non-Catholic, notably the Freemason and English-Canadian Protestant, while the French-Canadian ideological fortress of religion and *patrie* is still intact. In *La Guerre, Yes Sir!,* by contrast, the garrison has all but fallen, having been undermined from within as well as from without.

The enemy is also more nebulous, wearing many faces besides that of the *maudit anglais.* Despite the dominance of the soldiers and the subsequent resentment of them by the villagers, the awareness of menacing, cultural annihilation is more than the threat of English masters overriding French-Canadian victims. Margaret Atwood takes too limited a view of the menace in her analysis of *La Guerre, Yes Sir!,* when she emphasizes the two opposing cultures. The threat is also a matter of modern technological society stamping out indigenous cultural mores and desires, of massive, impersonal forces acting against the villagers' feebler human particularities and peculiarities. As the railway station employee observes, 'It's a war of the big guys against the little ones. Corriveau's dead. The little guys are dying. The big guys last forever.'

There is a gradually surfacing fear that even the big guys are on a path to destruction, that humanity as a whole will march to a mechanical doom. In Henri's nightmare, Corriveau's coffin enlarges and all the people in the world march into it 'just as they entered Church, bent over, submissive.' Significantly, the last to disappear are the armies of soldiers, as 'mechanically disciplined' as the group around Corriveau's bier. The latter stand like automatons, rigid and impassive, and even the girls notice 'it wasn't human for them to stay fixed there all night, stiff and motionless. It's not a position for the living.' Thus there is a warning that technological society with its will to power will not only turn man into a desensitized, impersonal robot, but will eventually draw him, ordered and submissive, to his doom. The train, roaring through the snowy wastes into the little village with its mechanized soldiers, is a technological engine of death not unlike the train which intrudes into the woods in Faulkner's 'The Bear.'

The horror of technological society, with its reduction of the spontaneously human to the automatic, is one more version of the gothic-grotesque motif of mechanism first discussed in the analysis of *Wacousta.* Carrier's soldiers, who seem to function without feeling and to move without motive, other than obedience to orders or the fulfilment of a mindless drill, represent the ultimate in dehumanization. In this, as in other modern grotesque works, technological automation suggests something demonic beyond the logical implications of a powerful system. It invokes fear of a world which is actively menacing as well as incomprehensible. In Henri's nightmare, the soldiers are like mechanical toys drawn by a central control in a little box, which marches them back into its depths and shuts the lid on them.

Despite the importance of death as a symbolic focus, Carrier's novel is not simply a tale about death, but as Nancy Bailey points out [in "The Corriveau Wake: Carrier's Celebration of Life" in *Journal of Canadian Fiction* III (Summer 1972)], it presents a battle between life and death in which the two forces are often surprisingly confused. This confusion and the resulting sense of both death-in-life and life-in-death is a key to much of the grotesqueness in the book. The nun's question reveals her uncertainty as to who is really alive, despite the Church's teaching that life after death is the only valid life. Henri senses that life on earth has become a living death, that 'man is unhappy wherever he is,' but like the other villagers, he fears the truth of an afterlife in which the flames of Hell and purgatory torment all sinners.

Despite the forces of death which threaten to squash their humanity, the villagers have an irrepressible desire for life:

> The villagers were alive, they were praying to remind themselves, to remember that they were not with Corriveau, that their life was not over; and all the time thinking they were praying for Corriveau's salvation, it was their own joy in being alive that they proclaimed in their sad prayers.

Corriveau underlines their life-in-death desire when he complains that if life must 'stop at a coffin, it was not fair for people to have an obvious love of life.'

Many of the activities of the villagers are a mixture of life and death forces. Although the eating and drinking bouts lead to a brawling, destructive conclusion, they are in themselves a defiant display of sensuousness. Mother Corriveau's cooking becomes an almost savage attack on death in which she sweatily beats at the pie dough, sensing that the perfume of the golden, baked tortière is the essence of living; she explains that 'when there is a dead man in the house, the house shouldn't smell of death.' In this role she becomes a kind of earth mother, a characterization which Carrier explores more fully in the second novel of the trilogy, *Floralie, Where are You?*.

Sex is both an instrument of death and of life. On the one hand, the Germans are described as killing women by raping them, and, to the sleeping Molly, the attacks of her loveless husband cause dreams of a knife tearing her stomach open. On the other hand Molly, a prostitute, represents the happiness of living to all the young soldiers who used to come to her. For Bérubé, the initial thought of sex outside a Church-blessed marriage leads to visions of damnation; yet with Molly in bed with him as his wife, 'it was death that they stabbed at violently.'

The pervasive violence also represents a confusion of life and death forces. In the story we find father beating up son, husband against wife, neighbour against neighbour, English against French, and the omnipresent spectre of the world war itself. The war beyond the village acts only as a catalyst for the war within. The violence is an expression of the villagers' intellectual and spiritual isolation from each other, of the decline of commonly held cultural values and the resultant profound ignorance and misunderstanding of each other. The violence is destructive, but it is also a positive response to repression. It is a sign 'of vitality badly used,' of an upsurge of life in a society where there is no common language of meaning but body language.

The recurring images of blood and snow suggest the dual implications of violence. At various points in the book, blood spills on the winter snow, whether it is the blood of the amputated hand or the beaten-up faces of the villagers in their battles with each other and with the soldiers. Snow is a traditional image of purity and innocence. In French-Canadian literature, it is also an image of isolation and the inward-looking naïveté or sterility it produces. Maria Chapdelaine comes to mind, as do the words of the familiar song by Gilles Vignault: 'Mon pays, ce n'est pas un pays, c'est l'hiver.' The French-Canadian garrison is built of snow and ice as much as it is reinforced by religious and nationalist principles. The bloody brawls are obviously disfiguring, cruel, and destructive. At the same time the blood that spills on the snow as well as on Molly's virginal, white wedding dress may suggest a human sensuous response which overrides traditional 'bloodless' ideals. Carrier's concluding statement in the novel—'the war had dirtied the snow'—has ironic rather than tragic overtones.

Whether violent or not, many of the activities and actions in the story relate to a selfhood not fully realized, and to a society where it is increasingly difficult to feel at home. At the beginning of the book Arthur tries to persuade Henri to accept the war and his soldier's role as a defence of traditional social values: 'Soldiers have a duty to protect farmers who are fathers of families, and the children and the cattle of the country.' Yet increasingly, Henri realizes his true position: 'his wife no longer belonged to him, nor his animals, nor even his children.' The characters' bizarre actions reflect their estrangement, their inarticulated anxieties about an alienated life.

Sherwood Anderson has related the quality of grotesqueness in people to a single-minded pursuit of partial truths. [In a review of *La Guerre, Yes Sir!* appearing in *Canadian Literature* (1969)] Ronald Sutherland has also suggested that Carrier's characters are grotesques because they cling to outworn truths. Thus Mother Corriveau's desperate observance of religious practices becomes grotesque in its distortion, and Bérubé's reflex-life response to the values implicit in the soldiers' way of life makes a grotesque of him, as when we see his frenzied and inhuman attempt to make a good soldier of Arsène. At the same time the characters may reflect D. W. Robertson's definition that the grotesque 'is a monster because of unresolved conflicts in his makeup' [*A Preface to Chaucer: Studies in Medieval Perspectives* (1969)]; sometimes 'the grotesque pretends to be one thing but is actually something else,' as is the case with Esmalda in particular. The unresolved conflicts often have to do with spiritual values or social attitudes which the character has ostensibly accepted, and another reality which he actually practises. The source of humour as well as of fearful meaninglessness or absurdity partially comes from his divided response.

In a more formal way, the grotesque quality of Carrier's writing relates to a constant juxtaposition of extreme incongruities. Repeatedly he combines the extreme poles of the sacred and profane in Quebec life, a characteristic similar to that found in the late gothic phase of medieval art, and which Charles Muscatine associates with a loss of purposeful direction in the culture.

> Its religion is incongruously stretched between new ecstasies of mysticism and a profane, almost tactile familiarity with sacred matters. Its sense of fact is often spiritless or actually morbid. For all its boisterous play, the age is profoundly pessimistic; it is preoccupied with irretrievable passage of time, with disorder, sickness, decay and death.

In *La Guerre, Yes Sir!* we find that the twin 'spiritual' values of patriotism and religion are incongruously yoked with the mundane practicalities of everyday living: the flag is a table cloth; the image of Christ on the cross merges with that of a stuffed pig; Mother Corriveau's prayer becomes an unconscious blasphemy when her Hail Mary invokes a picture of the pregnant Virgin. Similarly in Mireille's dream her toes become transformed into waxen votive candles. Sometimes the grotesque incongruity is achieved by yoking something tragic or horrible with something comical. Thus Joseph's amputation of his own hand to avoid going to war is horrifying, but it becomes grotesque when the hand is casually substituted for the frozen turd and used as a hockey puck, that commonplace of Canadian life. Disruption or confusion of our usual single response (the comic laugh with the tragic cry and the gothic gasp) reinforces our awareness of the confusion of the traditional world views and values.

There is a literary resonance in this latter image of the amputated hand which Carrier seems to be playing upon. As Madame Joseph snatches the hand from the child and tucks it under her coat before going on her way, one immediately recalls that other grotesque occasion in *Le Chercheur de trésors* when Charles Amand snatches the *main-de-gloire* from under the noses of the medical students. The act of dismemberment is yet another variation on that recurring motif of bodily disfiguration in French-Canadian literature. Joseph's self-mutilation may be seen as a parody of the motif by a kind of *reductio ad absurdum;* Carrier may also be extending the gothic death motif by a symbolic suggestion of cultural masochism or suicide.

In other ways *La Guerre, Yes Sir!* plays with or disturbs our literary expectancies, further providing a sense of strangeness or estrangement. The view from the window in which a captive being (usually a woman) looks out from her 'prison' is a repeated motif in gothic literature, but also has a special place in Quebec literature, where the captive spirit often symbolically represents the isolated containment of French-Canadian society, cut off from participation in the larger outside world. One remembers Elisabeth Rolland in *Kamouraska,* and the image of Maria Chapde-laine looking out both longingly and in fear upon the forest and its avenues of escape, from the confinement of her backwoods house. In the opening scene of *La Guerre, Yes Sir!* Joseph found, after cutting off his hand, that 'the cloudy window separating him from life gradually became very clear, transparent.' He had a brief moment of lucidity, in contrast to the image of Isobelle-Marie in *Mad Shadows'* opening scene, where she presses her face against the train window but soon sees nothing outside it. In nearly all cases there is a sense of a claustrophobic confinement behind the window. In *La Guerre, Yes Sir!,* it is a nun standing outside in the cold who is cut off and who is left to gaze through an open window at the bustle of activity within. In this image Carrier does not seem to imply a reversal of customary meaning, that is, he does not seem to suggest that the inner group rather than the outer world is the source of vitality. After all, there is death inside the room as well as without, in the coffin as well as in the decayed teeth of the nun. The nun's puzzling question as to who is alive and who is dead would rather suggest that Carrier means simply to disrupt or disturb the customary image and its cluster of associations.

Taken as a whole, the effect of *La Guerre, Yes Sir!*'s striking images is to startle the reader's thoughtful response rather than direct it; despite the visual clarity and dramatic impact, the images are most often ambiguous and paradoxical in their symbolic implications, unlike Carrier's later *Floralie, Where are You?,* in which the allegorical push is stronger and more insistent. Thus in this first novel in the trilogy, the grotesque alliance of horror and humour is essentially disruptive. Yet despite the sense of estrangement or absurdity which the disruptive grotesque usually expresses, *La Guerre, Yes Sir!* does not project a vision of annihilation but of cultural alteration.

Critics such as Ronald Sutherland have been quick to point out the similarity between Faulkner's *As I Lay Dying* and *La Guerre, Yes Sir!.* Both stories revolve around a coffin, and describe the grotesque behaviour and attitudes of rural characters in response to the death of one of their own. The American's novels, like Carrier's, reflect what he regards as the moral confusion and social decay of his society, and, as Malcolm Cowley remarks [in an introduction to *The Portable Faulkner* (1967)], Faulkner is 'continually seeking in them for violent images to convey his sense of outrage.' Faulkner's characters, like Carrier's, have a double meaning besides their place in the story, also serving as symbols or metaphors with a general application. In both novels, the incidents in the story represent forces and elements in society, although neither *As I Lay Dying* nor *La Guerre, Yes Sir!* can be explained as a connected, totally logical, allegory.

However, I think there is a fundamental difference in emphasis between *As I Lay Dying* and *La Guerre, Yes Sir!.* In the former novel, the smell of putrefaction, both literal and symbolic, hangs heavier in the air. Although some of the characters occasionally show signs of Faulkner's later statement that 'man will not merely endure; he will prevail,' survival seems an individual achievement in the face of a general social decay. In *La Guerre, Yes Sir!,* by comparison, the collective assertion of life is as pronounced as the smell of Mother Corriveau's cooking. What one senses in the grotesque distortions and inversions of dying values is the presence of change as much as of destruction; it is less a story of death than of metamorphosis. The general sense of confusion—in the characters' attitudes, in the symbolic values which issue from the story, and in the response of the reader—are signals of this process. Old shapes and images shift; patterns dissolve and the disparate elements come together in startling new associations.

Carrier's reference to his trilogy as a depiction of 'the Middle Ages of Quebec' reinforces this notion of change rather than doom as his central theme. In Carrier's reference, the Middle Ages stretches from a period before the Second World War to the middle sixties, and encompasses the end of the parochial period, the discovery of the outer industrial world and the passage from country to city life. The medieval analogy is apt, since the twentieth-century decades in Quebec, like those of earlier times, present an inward looking, church-dominated world, in which the old ways are no longer life-giving forces. It marks a time in which the gap between ideal and real, seen by many critics as the essence of late medieval 'decadent' gothicism, becomes an abyss in which the traditional beliefs and social values are to tumble. Yet society did not collapse at the end of the Middle Ages, but was infused with a new life; the Renaissance was a transformation of the old into new modes of activity and awareness.

In *La Guerre, Yes Sir!* the Renaissance is not yet accomplished, but the process of change has begun. The novel is disruptively grotesque, not because of any overriding feeling of futility, but because there is no specific moral or philosophic framework against which the grotesque distortions may be judged. Carrier gives no real hint of the shape of things to come, but the undying energy of his characters and the constant upsurge of humour against horror, precludes a vision of total despair. In *La Guerre, Yes Sir!,* as in the later *Floralie, Where are You?,* the process of metamorphosis is one in which the old grotesque encasements of society must be broken through, or overturned and discarded, before a new, freer being will emerge. In this sense, then, the wooden box carrying the body of Corriveau and by implication the whole of Quebec society is less a coffin than a cocoon.

To point out the element of optimism underlying Carrier's vision is not to undercut the emphasis on fear or horror. The individual characters themselves obviously live in a world of increasing uncertainty or absurdity, and it is clear that a man like Bérubé faces a personally meaningless and menacing future. Nor can the resurgent humour and playfulness in Carrier's depiction of French-Canadian society be considered frivolous. In discussing the sportive grotesque, Ruskin distinguishes between its noble and ignoble forms:

> For the master of the noble grotesque knows the depth of all at which he seems to mock, and would feel it at another time, or feels it in a certain undercurrent of thought even while he jests with it; but the workman of the ignoble grotesque can feel and understand nothing, and mocks at all things with the laughter of the idiot

and the cretin [John Ruskin, *The Stones of Venice*].

La Guerre, Yes Sir! both mocks and distorts in its depiction of French-Canadian life, but the disruptive vision of confusion and change does not reflect a lightheaded abandon. Rather Carrier fills Ruskin's prescription of thoughtful feeling; his sportive grotesque alliance of humour and horror is the play of a serious mind. (pp. 79-87)

> *Margot Northey, "Sportive Grotesque: 'La Guerre, Yes Sir!'," in her* The Haunted Wilderness: The Gothic and Grotesque in Canadian Fiction, *University of Toronto Press, 1976, pp. 79-87.*

David J. Bond   (essay date Spring 1979)

[*In the following essay, Bond provides a thematic and stylistic analysis of Carrier's fiction.*]

Roch Carrier is a born story-teller, a *raconteur* whose verve immediately grips the reader. As critics have been quick to point out, he uses all the techniques of the *raconteur:* grotesque exaggeration, caricature and a wild imagination which still leaves room for a kind of fantastic realism. Some critics have compared his work to Brueghel's, while others have commented on its epic and folklore qualities. Add to this a variety of dream-like sequences mingled with a great deal of violence and cruelty, and it can be seen that Carrier's work is a rich mixture of techniques designed to seize the reader's attention.

Carrier himself would seem to agree with those who emphasize the grotesque and exaggerated side of his work, for he has said: "Mes romans aiment l'invraisemblance; j'aime la démesure, j'aime la force, j'aime l'épopée." But another statement of Carrier's should warn us against seeing his work as *just* one of imagination and entertainment. Imagination, he says, is not opposed to real life and real life problems: "Quand je dis imaginaire, je n'oppose pas ce monde à celui que l'on nomme le monde réel; par imaginaire, je veux dire le monde réel perçu plus globalement avec toutes ses possibilités et ses significations par le roman." Carrier's techniques are, of course, used with the intention of entertaining, but they are also used as a means of conveying a view of the world, and of commenting on it. He says that, in *La Guerre, yes sir!* "J'ai essayé de trouver une certaine verité de vie." The same is true of his other fiction.

Beneath the grotesque adventures of Carrier's characters is another "truth." This is supported by his statement that his interest in literature, and, in a sense, his career as a writer, date from the time when he first read *Candide*. Voltaire's novel recounts the fantastic adventures of grotesque characters, but through the incredible events described, through the parody of the adventure novel and the caricature of human types, Voltaire was attacking certain explanations of reality current at his time, and commenting on a human situation he found intolerable. Like *Candide*, Carrier's novels exist on more than one level. They exist on three distinct yet closely integrated levels behind the literal one, for his fiction is a commentary on the situation of Quebec, on the problems of living in modern capitalist society, and on what Malraux calls "la condition humaine."

On the first of these levels, Carrier's novels correspond closely to *Candide*. He writes that, when he read *Candide*, "je découvrais avec Voltaire tout ce qui empoisonnait la vie au Québec. Mon pays m'apparaissait comme un pays du XVIIIᵉ siècle et Voltaire était le grand frère m'indiquant la voie à suivre." Carrier's novels are a protest against all the forces that have enslaved Quebec and prevented her from freely fulfilling her destiny. It is in the context of this protest that one must understand his attack on a particular type of religion once practised in Quebec. It is not so much the Church itself which Carrier attacks as a symbolic representation of all the forces of darkness, superstition and fear which would hamper the development of a people. It is all "official" explanations and justifications of Quebec's misfortunes which Carrier pillories, just as, in *Candide*, Voltaire attacked an over-optimistic and almost "official" explanation of reality.

In Carrier's fiction, the Church presents a view of man which denies his full humanity. He is seen as a plaything of his appetites, almost an animal, and in *Floralie, où es-tu?* his appetites are symbolized by Anthyme's horse. Riding off with his bride, Anthyme whips his horse into a frenzied gallop, while Floralie, frightened by the speed of the horse and apprehensive of Anthyme's sexual passions, thinks of the times horses have run wild in her village, causing havoc. The beat of Anthyme's heart is compared to a galloping horse, and Anthyme brutally consummates the marriage as the horse drags the buggy through the forest. These passions are seen by the Church as a potential cause of damnation, and are directly linked to Hell. Hence Floralie's fear of them, and hence the reaction of Bérubé in *La Guerre, yes sir!* when he contemplates the naked Molly and suddenly seems to hear a clock from Hell ticking and saying "Toujours, jamais." The act he was about to perform seems to him a prelude to damnation, and he trembles in terror. Molly herself, who represents sex and the enjoyment of sex, appears in the midst of the villagers "comme une autre incarnation du diable."

The religion of Carrier's characters represents the world as the battleground of God and the Devil. This view is neatly summed up in *Floralie, où es-tu?* by the mediaeval-style scenery used by the travelling actors, which depicts, on one side, smiling angels, and on the other, demons stoking the flames of Hell. According to the Church, man is only too inclined to gravitate towards the demons' side of the scene. The priest informs Anthyme: "Tu es un homme, et tout homme est un pécheur," and tells Floralie that "l'homme corrompt tout ce qu'il touche." The priest in *La Guerre, yes sir!* tells the villagers that many of them are on the road to Hell, and talks of "ces flammes auxquelles vous serez soumis à cause de votre nature pécheresse et voluptueuse." But the priest struggles against the Devil for the souls of men and this struggle is represented symbolically in *Floralie, où es-tu?* when Père Nombrillet chases away the actors playing the Seven Deadly Sins, and drives off Néron, the travelling seller of medicines which cure by the help of the Devil.

Any view of life which inhibits the individual's (and a people's) expression of life and strength is bound to have disastrous effects. It produces a childhood like Philibert's, full of images of death. Philibert, as a child, spends much of his time helping his father dig graves (symbols of death), and playing in the graveyard, where he imagines he is sounding the trumpet of the Last Judgment, and expecting the dead to rise from their graves. It makes him lie awake at night imagining the ducks caught in the ice of the river, their heads severed by a hunter. It produces in Floralie all kinds of nightmares as she runs through the forest looking for Anthyme, convinced she is a "fille damnée" and imagining Hell gaping beneath her feet. It produces in Anthyme similar fears as he wanders through the night, thinking his horse has been stolen by the Devil and imagining it riding across the sky. Significantly, it is while making love (i.e., expressing these life forces) that Carrier's characters often find themselves thinking of death. When Arthur is about to make love to Amélie in *La Guerre, yes sir!*, he finds the thought of the dead Corriveau obsessing him. Bérubé, as we have seen, is assailed by thoughts of Hell in the same situation.

While Carrier's novels have a message for Quebec, and an unmistakably Quebec setting, his message applies to all men. It is Carrier's genius to have combined successfully a meditation on the destiny of a community, on the role of the individual in modern society, and on the fate of man in general.

—David J. Bond

This religion also stifles the life forces by its attitude to marriage. Sexual relations are allowed only when sanctified by the Church, which is why Bérubé asks Molly the prostitute to marry him before he has relations with her. It is also why Anthyme is filled with dismay and anger when he discovers his bride is not a virgin. He condemns her as "fille damnée," and symbolically loses his virility, for it is at this point that his horse disappears and passes (together with Floralie) into the hands of Néron. "Un homme qui ne sait pas se faire aimer d'un cheval n'est pas un homme," he concludes when he thinks his horse has bolted, implying at the same time that a man who has not received a pure wife is no man either. But if Anthyme's attitude to his own virility is distorted, his attitude to his wife is worse. He has been taught to see women as temptresses, except after marriage, when they are to be taken brutally. The wife's task, he believes (as does Floralie herself) is to obey, for "marier un homme, c'était le suivre pour lui obéir." Such a relationship between men and women stifles love, and Floralie finds herself unable to tell Anthyme she loves him. Instead, all she can say is: "J'ai peur, Anthyme." It is through this forest of misunderstandings, misconceptions and superstition, represented by the real forest in which they wander, that Anthyme and Floralie have to find one another.

The forces which separate Anthyme and Floralie divide the whole community. Religion comes between the men, who barely accept its restrictions, and the women, who seek their consolation in it. It comes between father and son, causing Arsène to beat and kick Philibert because he has blasphemed. It comes between parents and daughter, preventing Esmalda from entering her parents' house because it is against the rules of the religious order to which she belongs. It divides men within themselves, causing them to deny their own instincts. It separates English from French, causing the latter to marvel that the English can even pray before Corriveau's coffin, but never allowing them to doubt that the English God is a false one, and that "Eux, les Anglais protestants sont damnés."

The constant strife within the French-Canadian community is symbolized by war, which lurks in the background of *Il est par là, le soleil,* still lives in the memories of Dorval in *Le Deux-millième étage,* and is the very subject of *La Guerre, yes sir!.* Even before the war comes to the villagers in *La Guerre, yes sir!,* they are at war with themselves. As Carrier puts it: "Mes personnages ne se sentent pas concernés par cette guerre, au tout début, ils vivent en marge, mais ils sont en état de guerre permanente en eux-mêmes, contre les autres, ils vivent au niveau de l'instinct."

But if war represents the strife within the French-Canadian community, it even more obviously represents strife between French-Canadians and English. The English are depicted as another force oppressing the French-Canadian, and the war they foist on French-Canadians is exploitation at its most cruel. The characters in the novels make it clear that for them, the war is waged by "les gros," and, although one of them condemns Germans, English, French, Russians, Chinese and Japanese as all being "gros," it is obvious that they hold the English mainly responsible. They cannot understand why their sons are sent to fight for a land which, one of them says, is "au bout du monde." They know nothing of that country, and Corriveau's mother does not even realise that the Union Jack on her son's coffin is also "her" flag. Even those who seem to go to war willingly have no choice, since, for the likes of Corriveau and Philibert, the army is their only means of escape from a community which stifles and inhibits them.

The war clearly demonstrates a relationship already established between the two communities: that of master and servant. The attitude of the French-Canadians to their "masters" seems at first one of servility, represented by the villager who welcomes the English soldiers bringing back Corriveau's body by saying: "I understand English, boys. You may speak English, I learned it when I was in the Navy . . . Royal Navy." But the real feelings of this man are revealed when he curses the soldiers (albeit when they are out of hearing) for leaving the door open. He assumes that the English must use French-Canadians in the Army to close their doors, and, of course, he is right. Even in the Army, the French-Canadian is used to perform menial tasks. His position is summed up by Bérubé's task, which is to clean the Air Force latrines at Gander (together with a motley crowd of Polish, Italians, Hungarians and Greeks). As for Corriveau, when his body arrives at the station, it is treated as part of the English soldiers' baggage. This does not mean, of course, that the Army is not willing to make a national hero out of Corriveau for the encouragement of the French-Canadians. In reality, Corriveau's death was not so glorious: he was blown to pieces while relieving himself behind a bush.

The effect of war is often to dehumanize, and this is seen in the soldiers in *La Guerre, yes sir!,* who are depicted as robots. As one character puts it, "Un soldat ne fait rien, ne pète même pas sans un ordre." The English soldiers are disciplined to the point where they are expressionless, and only able to give vent to their feelings when ordered to do so. As for the villagers, they are all mutilated in some way by the war, mutilated mentally and spiritually. Joseph, who cuts off his hand to escape being drafted, is symbolic of them all. The war can even turn men against themselves, as is the case of Henri, who hates himself for fearing the war. It turns them against one another, as when Bérubé, unable to turn on the sergeant who issues orders to him, vents his hatred by humiliating Arsène. It is, in fact, Bérubé who best represents the mutilation and humiliation of the French-Canadian. As a soldier, he obeys the sergeant's orders and fights beside the English soldiers in the brawl with the villagers. When he later attempts to pray beside Corriveau's coffin, the villagers naturally reject him, but when he turns to pray beside the English soldier killed in the brawl, the English reject him too. This scene sums up succinctly the situation of the French-Canadian fighting for the English: he has no place in either community.

Carrier depicts French-Canadians as outsiders in their own land. This is conveyed in the scene where the English soldiers, tired of the unseemly conduct of the villagers at the "veillée du corps," eject them from the Corriveau house. It is also suggested in *Il est par là, le soleil* when Philibert, newly arrived in Montreal, finds himself in an English-speaking district where nobody understands him, but where everybody assumes (presumably because he speaks French) that he is a beggar. When one lady does take pity on him, she decides he must be an Italian, and is shocked that Italians are arriving in Canada without even bothering to learn the language of the country.

French-Canadians in Carrier's works are villagers, farmers or proletarians. They are the exploited section of the population, and the exploiters are English. "Elle parle quelle langue, la voix du capitalisme," asks Dorval, and answers: "It speaks English." It is because he is French-Canadian that Philibert is reduced to a series of degrading ways of earning a living, and it is also why he cannot understand the financial pages of the newspaper, even when they are in French. Carrier protests against this state of affairs, but at the same time he is protesting against the exploitation of masses of people in any modern industrial society, and against the fate of all individuals in modern cities. The "little man" in modern society is represented by Boris Rataploffsky, who allows himself to have blows rained upon him by anybody who will pay him. Boris is an ironic embodiment of the "little man," for he is, in fact, a giant with great strength, but it is a purely passive strength, which allows him to endure ill-treatment rather than impelling him to rebel.

Carrier protests against a system in which heartless employers, like the one in **"L'Ouvrier modèle,"** wear out a man in their service, then dismiss him. More often, the exploiters are distant and anonymous, like the ones who use the immigrant worker in **"Le Pair."** The cities where these workers live are also anonymous and inhuman, and a man can waste his life away in them, like the character in **"Le Métro,"** who grows old as he travels to work. In these cities, despite the teeming masses around him, the individual is condemned to solitude. Dorval meditates on the absurdity of men who build cities in order not to be alone, but who then surround themselves with walls. The machine dominates these cities, and the ease with which men can become its slaves is demonstrated in **"Le Réveillematin,"** where a man's life is taken over by an over-zealous alarm clock which will not let him do anything of which it disapproves, or in **"L'Invention,"** where a man builds a machine which, once started, cannot be stopped. The best symbol of the machine's power is the brute, senseless and inhuman bulldozer which comes to demolish Dorval's house, "cette masse de fer sans intelligence qui, au commandement, chargerait et saccagerait sans jamais savoir pourquoi." Dorval's purely human solution of pouring beer into its fuel tank has no effect, for the machine is not susceptible to human solutions.

The life of individuals in modern cities is the subject of *Le Deux-millième étage,* which tells how a remote city authority decides to destroy Dorval's home to make way for "progress"—an immense block of apartments. As one minor official puts it: "L'avenir est dans la déconstruction." The authorities, unable to appreciate the vitality of life in districts such as Dorval's, only bother to send delegates to explain their actions, and these delegates meet with delegates of the unions, delegates of the police, delegates of the bank, delegates of the political parties, delegates of the American Consulate, and so on.

There are, in this novel, various reactions to the threat of demolition, and to the problem of life in the city. Marchessault, for example, is the man of peasant origins who accepts the need for progress and repeats parrot-fashion all the mindless clichés about scientific and technological advancement. He even says, and here he hits on the truth: "Un homme à notre époque c'est pas un homme, mais un esclave s'il sait pas dominer la machine." So he sets to work and tries to learn, by correspondence course, how to handle machines. Unfortunately, when he tries to drive a bulldozer, he has no idea of how to make it work. He is beaten by the machine, and it is as though his very manhood is destroyed, for his wife turns on him, taunting him as "impuissant."

Marchessault tries to come to terms with progress; Dupont La France rejects it. His is the utopian dream of destroying the city, returning to nature, and living off apples (an ironic response from a character from France, presented as the representative of a sophisticated and highly developed civilization). His answer is no more ef-

fective than Marchessault's, for when Dorval and his tenants decide to cultivate the land, the best they can do is scratch around the demolished buildings with knives, forks, nails, screwdrivers and broom handles, and then to urinate on the seeds they plant.

Mignonne Fleury's response is to seek an outlet in sex, but it is just commercialized sex, for she is nothing but a prostitute, and, at one point, turns Dorval's house into a brothel for the construction workers. It is presumably because of her commercial view of sex that she refuses the advances of Dorval, who sees sex in an entirely different light. Cowboy looks for an answer in song, but songs too are commercialized, even songs of protest. The Old Woman spends her time thinking of death, while the Negro gets by through simply ignoring all around him.

Dorval's response is the most active one, as befits a Communist. His communism is, however, of a rather simplistic variety, and it never seems to occur to him that it is incongrous for a Communist to be a property-owner and a landlord. It is clear that, in any case, the Revolution he preaches will change nothing, and, as one character says: "Après la Révolution, mes maudites pommes vont encore pourrir!" Yet Dorval does at least fight the authorities, and at first, he even has some success. He chases away those who come to evict him, but, unfortunately, these are only the humblest representatives of the system, and the real heads are too distant for him to reach. He has to admit: "Mais les gros Boss, les Big Boss, on dirait qu'i'ont pas de face. On les a jamais vus." His fight begins to flag, and he can only revive it by such grotesque schemes of caricatural vengeance as sending out his tenants on a "chasse aux Anglais," promising a reward for every pair of English ears brought back. He relies more and more on beer to keep up his spirits and to encourage his tenants. He drifts frequently into memories of the past, when he fought with the French Resistance, a real resistance movement which makes his own seem puny.

Destruction continues to advance on Dorval's house, senseless, absurd, seemingly impelled by a momentum of its own. He meditates: "Ça marche parce que ça marche, ça marche pour marcher. Ça pète de certitude tandis que notre vie d'homme boite, piétine, hésite, avec les jours, les nuits, les maladies, les nuits blanches, les colères, la fatigue, le rêve, les rêves." But the worst blow comes when Dorval has to recognize how easily the capitalist system recuperates the exploited and uses them against one another. The construction workers go on strike, not against the absurd conditions of work, but for more pay. They are about to smash up the building they have been making when the union tells them they have won a victory, and sends them back to the same senseless jobs. Dorval's lodgers desert him one by one, Mignonne Fleury even moving into the new apartment block. Then Marchessault reappears, having passed his examinations at last, driving a bulldozer he is going to use to demolish Dorval's house. Even Dupont La France is glimpsed cleaning the plastic flowers outside the new apartments. Dorval sums up the situation: "Dans chaque culotte de maudit pauvre . . . y a un cul de capitaliste qui se cache."

The Laterreur Brothers and Mignonne Fleury are the best

examples of how the system uses people. The Laterreur Brothers canalize the discontent of the exploited (and especially of French Canadians) into harmless demonstrations of anger when they lose their wrestling matches to English and foreign opponents. They have prostituted themselves and earn a fortune by regularly allowing themselves to be beaten. Mignonne Fleury even more obviously prostitutes herself. It is significant that, when at last she does offer herself to Dorval in the gaudy luxury of her new apartment, he refuses to take off his dirty shoes, refuses to compromise with her surroundings, and refuses her.

Yet, for all his defiance, Dorval's struggle is hopeless, and it seems that he will finally capitulate, for the novel ends as he walks out of his house, which Marchessault's bulldozer is about to demolish, trying to remember the words of Cowboy's last song. The words, which indicate the need to capitulate and accept, are:

> Dans les airs
> Sur la terre
> Il faut se taire
> Et l'on se terre
> Dessous la terre.

Philibert's plight is just as hopeless as Dorval's. He is doomed to failure by his education, which has, as he himself points out, taught him how to get to Heaven, but not how to get to the bank. In one important scene, he reads a newspaper article which explains how young men from certain social backgrounds seem to be fascinated by failure, and spend their lives preparing for it. Philibert is, of course, one of these. He is forced to take the sort of employment nobody else wants, and spends much of his time working in pits: digging holes in the road, working in the grease pit of a garage, peeling potatoes in a dark basement. He is here repeating his early training, which was done helping his father dig graves. These pits are, of course, symbolic of the hopeless, absurd situation in which he finds himself, and Carrier comments: "Philibert creuse sa propre fosse."

At one point, Philibert works in a factory making boots, and he has a dream which sums up the absurdity of his life. He has become so dehumanized by work in the factory that, in his dream, he turns into a boot. One day, he rebels and kicks the foreman. At that moment, he says, he felt that, "J'étais plus une bottine, mais un homme." Clearly, only by rebelling against an absurd situation can he become a man again, so he abandons his employment in the factory.

There are two symbols of hope in Philibert's life: the sun and girls. He soon learns that attractive young girls are not for him. The bank clerk he assumes will fall into his arms drives off in a beautiful new car, while Philibert gives chase in a taxi, until he has to give up through lack of money for the fare. The only type of woman available to him is the restaurant owner's wife, whom he pays for a cold and joyless coupling. As for the sun, although he glimpses it, he rarely sees it from the pits where he works. As he lies dying, he imagines he sees the sun, but: "Il est par là, le soleil . . . ," in other words, out of reach.

Philibert has no hope of changing things, and feels so politically powerless that he does not bother to vote. When he inherits some money, he dreams of going into politics, but death cuts short that dream. Death is, in fact, the only way out. A Portuguese worker on Philibert's construction site deliberately blows himself up. Philibert approves this act, saying it is the only form of protest the man has left, and it is less ridiculous than digging holes in the road.

The absurdity of life in the modern city, and the fate of men like Philibert, are also an image of the absurdity of life in general, for Carrier's work also exists on a third level, where, like *Candide,* it is a commentary on and a protest against the incomprehensible absurdity and cruelty of man's lot. Sometimes this metaphysical level is intimately connected with the commentary on life in the modern city, and Philibert's dream of being a boot, for example, can be seen both as an image of his life in the factory, or as an image of man ground underfoot by powers over which he has no control. Other times, only the metaphysical level seems appropriate. The strange things which happen to characters in Carrier's short stories, where apples spill out peculiar destructive forces (**"Les Pommes,"** *Jolis deuils*), characters suddenly grow old (**"Le Métro"**) and men are faced with inexplicable changes in their life (**"Les Cartes postales"** and **"La Chambre,"** *Contes pour mille oreilles*), are probably best seen on a metaphysical level as allegories of man in a world where he is subject to inhuman and cruel forces, such as death and the passing of time.

Carrier rejects as cruel and despotic, not only the God foisted on his characters by a particular type of religion, but any God who would impose such forces on man. It is no coincidence that, having watched the procession of twenty-one little monsters in their wheel-barrows, followed by an assortment of lame and halt, Philibert starts pulling the legs off grasshoppers: he is merely imitating a God who allows, or practises, the mutilation of men. Such a God would never listen to man, and never helped Anthyme when, as a child, he lay awake at night, terrified of the dark. Now that he wanders alone in the forest, Anthyme realizes that it is no use seeking God's help, for: "Dieu n'aurait jamais allumé le soleil pour un homme comme Anthyme."

Since he permits the existence of the social system which crushes Philibert, God must presumably be responsible for that too. As one character tells Philibert: "Le responsable . . . c'est le bon Dieu, qui a fait le monde comme il l'a voulu avec des riches et des pauvres, des petits comme nous et des gros." By the same logic, God must be responsible for the war and, if war and the social system are forced on men by "les gros," God must be, as one character says, "plus gros que les gros." Philibert says: "Le bon Dieu, il est comme le patron, on le voit pas souvent. Il fréquente pas notre genre de monde, le bon Dieu." It is significant that, in *Floralie, où es-tu?,* God's representative, the priest, is depicted as fat, that is, literally "gros." God and his priests oppress mankind, and it is no wonder that Philibert says, when praying, in a truly Freudian slip of the tongue: "Au fond, tu m'abîmes, Seigneur, Seigneur."

The veritable litanies of blasphemy which flow from the

lips of Carrier's characters can be seen as a revolt both against the kind of God their religion forces on them, and against any God. The women tend to accept injustice, and Corriveau's mother, standing before his coffin, seeks consolation in prayer. The men usually rebel, which is why Corriveau's father prefers to retire to the barn and blaspheme. In Carrier's work it is a sign that a boy has grown up when he blasphemes. Philibert, as a child, sits before the severed head of the pig his father has slaughtered, imagines it is blaspheming, and longs for the time when he is old enough to do the same. In *La Guerre, yes sir!* that time arrives, and his father tells him: "Maintenant tu es un homme. Tu sais parler comme un homme."

Philibert learns later that this is not so. Blasphemy implies belief in God, or else it is meaningless; revolt implies revolt against something or someone whose existence one does not doubt. Men only become men in all senses of the word when they reject the very idea of God, as Anthyme does when he climbs a tree, challenges God to come down and settle matters like a man, and, when nothing happens, realizes God is afraid of men who do not fear him. Philibert himself says: "Un jour, je me suis aperçu qu'il y avait pas plus de bon Dieu dans le ciel que de serpent à sonnette électrique au Québec." He concludes that, since God does not exist, he, Philibert, does. Rejection of God is seen, then, as the step which liberates man, and makes him assume his own freedom and identity. The frequent blaspheming by Carrier's characters is only the first step towards this freedom, and it is in this sense that one must understand Carrier's statement that blasphemy is "la première affirmation d'une conscience individuelle."

By his own example, and by the example of his characters, Carrier urges the need for Quebec to accept itself, to free itself from its fears, and to live. His is a literature of liberation.

—David J. Bond

Yet, even free from the burden of belief in God, Carrier's characters still inhabit a cruel, oppressive world where they have no power over their fate. The short stories, for example, frequently have unpleasant endings, and *Jolis deuils* is subtitled "Petites Tragédies pour adultes." From the very beginning of *Floralie, où es-tu?* we are made aware that trouble is in store for the main characters: Floralie is made to wear a black dress; she is warned: "La route sera dure"; and she is terrified by a grass snake, which she thinks is really the Devil. But nowhere is the dark fatality hanging over men conveyed so well as in **"La Main,"** where Carrier describes a giant hand descending from the sky, hanging over a city, pressing down on it, and then dying.

Carrier's characters are very conscious of the futility of life, and are nearly all, at one time or another, sickened by the thought of it. "La vie d'un homme ne vaut pas un pet," says Dorval; Philibert's grandmother asks: "A quoi ça sert de vivre?" while Philibert himself complains: "On m'a donné la vie sans que je la demande, comme un coup de pied au derrière."

But, if life is absurd, death is even more so. Henri in *La Guerre, yes sir!* has a dream in which he sees the whole village, followed by many other people, the sea, and troops of marching men, all enter Bérubé's coffin. The message is obvious: death is the fate of all men. What is the point, Corriveau's parents wonder, in rearing children, caring for them and bringing them to adulthood, if they end up, like their son, in a coffin? Death is ever-present in Carrier's novels: in the violent end of Philibert and Corriveau, or in the symbolic form of the graves Philibert digs, the pits he works in, and the huge holes excavated around Dorval's house. Yet, mingled with images of death, are symbols of hope and life. The sun is one such symbol, and, although it shines mainly on others, Philibert does at least glimpse it. Then there are the girls in the short stories: the one who walks naked through the streets, so that everyone drops what he or she is doing to follow her in a joyous procession (**"La Jeune fille"**), and the one whose footsteps a man follows in the snow (**"Les Pas"**). In both these stories, the girl flies away, symbolizing hope, and, although one of them is shot down by a policeman, hope is kept alive, symbolized this time by the bird which flies from the policeman's severed head and perches on the guillotine.

There is hope for the individual if he will affirm himself and the life forces within him, just as there is hope for the community which will not let its life be smothered by forces representing death. Carrier's characters instinctively affirm life in the face of death, as, for example, in the famous "fête sauvage" around Corriveau's coffin. As the villagers pray, then slip off to eat, drink, blaspheme, eye the women and tell salacious stories, they are affirming life. Even their prayers are a kind of rejoicing that it is not they in the coffin. The English soldiers, with their silent, straight faces, their refusal of food and drink, and their contempt for the villagers, represent death. They are death because they wage war, but also the threat of death to the community because, as well as being soldiers, they are *English* soldiers. It is against these men too that the villagers affirm themselves, and when they are ejected by the soldiers from the Corriveau house, the old man still insists: "Nous savons vivre."

It is in the act of love, however, that Carrier's characters most obviously affirm the forces of life. It is true that the thought of death sometimes interrupts their love-making, but at other times the love-making is presented as a revolt against death. As Molly and Bérubé make love, "C'est la mort qu'ils poignardèrent violemment." Molly herself represents the forces of life as she suddenly appears half-naked amidst the villagers, a kind of antidote to Esmalda's dramatic appearance at the window and her morbid talk of death and damnation. In the midst of the ruins and destruction Dorval discovers a young couple making love, and the boy informs him: "Nous, on cherche un sens à la vie." Even the Old Woman in *Le Deux-millième étage* finds consolation in sex, and is working in Mignonne Fleury's brothel when she dies. Dorval, although he dismisses romantic love as "du vent," cannot deny the forces of life which push him towards Mignonne Fleury. Indeed, his very communism is the result of his love for a woman Communist he knew in France.

Carrier's message is that men must cling to the earth and to life. Both Floralie and Anthyme learn during their nightmare experiences in the forest that they must turn their back on visions of death and Hell, and must cling to life. Floralie, when she regrets not having been "martyred" in the fire which destroys Père Nombrillet's chapel, is told by an old man: "Crois-moi, petite jeunesse, il vaut mieux être une fille en chair et en os qu'un saint en cendre et fumée." Anthyme, assailed by visions of Hell, grasps the earth and pulls up a handful of grass, which tastes sweet in his mouth. He realizes that "Le salut ne viendrait pas du ciel, et il posa les yeux sur la terre." When Floralie and Anthyme finally find each other, they fall asleep on the ground, to be discovered next morning by the delighted villagers, who pour beer on them, a libation to the earth and a baptism into a new life. In *La Guerre, yes sir!* the earth is represented by old Corriveau's cider, which fills the villagers with joy, and which contains the "forces merveilleuses de la terre." Dorval too loves the earth, cries out: "Moi, j'aime la terre," and symbolically revolts against death by urinating in the pit dug by the demolishers.

Characters such as these are individuals finding their own destiny, but they are also representatives of a community. Just as the individual must cling to life, must throw off the forces of death and affirm himself, so, Carrier implies, must Quebec. He says that, when he became a writer, he had to reject the influence of the culture of France, although he greatly admired it, and cling to his own culture. He had to affirm himself as a representative of that culture, and affirm his culture as a living thing. Writing of *La Guerre, yes sir!,* he says: "Écrivant mon roman, je ne me situe pas dans un univers de culture romanesque, je prends place parmi un Québec qui a été dépossédé de sa culture et qui, petit à petit, avec acharnement s'applique à se donner une âme."

By his own example, and by the example of his characters, Carrier urges the need for Quebec to accept itself, to free itself from its fears, and to live. His is a literature of liberation. Yet, while his novels have a message for Quebec, and an unmistakably Quebec setting, his message applies to all men. It is Carrier's genius to have combined successfully a meditation on the destiny of a community, on the role of the individual in modern society, and on the fate of man in general. (pp. 120-30)

David J. Bond, "Carrier's Fiction," in Canadian Literature, No. 80, Spring, 1979, pp. 120-31.

Paula Gilbert Lewis (review date April 1979)

[*In the following positive assessment of* Il n'y a pas de pays sans grand-père, *Lewis lauds Carrier's ability to successfully combine social and political commentary with philosophical debate.*]

Previously well known in Quebec for his novels, *La Guerre, yes sir!, Floralie, où es-tu?,* and *Il est par là, le soleil* . . . , and for his theatrical adaptations of the first two, Roch Carrier published in May 1977 his latest novel, *Il n'y a pas de pays sans grand-père.* In March 1978 Carrier saw, for the third time, his own theatrical adaptation presented in Montreal.

The novel is in the form of a long, intense reflection on life by Vieux-Thomas, an old man condemned by his family to await death while sitting in the rocking chair that he had built as a young man. The movement of the rocker, of his thoughts, and of the novel itself, with no chapters and few paragraphs, is stressed at the outset: "Attendre . . . 'Cher bon Dieu, combien de temps? Aller et venir, au même endroit, toujours, dans la même chaise berceuse, et regarder les jours tomber autour de soi comme des feuilles d'automne, de fin d'automne . . . Se bercer et attendre la fin. . . . ' " Like the rocker, Vieux-Thomas's thoughts and the novel will oscillate back and forth, between the present and the past.

The present consists of solitude, silence, a sense of uselessness, and a fear of total dependency upon his surrounding family, "Les Autres," whom he dislikes. It is a constant reminder of the cruelty and laziness of the younger generation, his grandchildren, who make fun of him and, in his mind, anxiously await his death so that they can inherit his rocker. In this pitiful present, Vieux-Thomas can speak honestly only to God.

He can also freely reminisce. Much of the novel relates nostalgic anecdotes from Vieux-Thomas's past: the construction of his rocker and his home, his winters as an employee of an English-Canadian company, his one winter on a ship, his love of hunting, and the like. These interesting excursions into the past help alleviate present anxieties, further aggravated by a letter from the government.

In Vieux-Thomas's present, he feels love for only one person, Jean-Thomas, the only grandchild whose name he can remember, and who, after having participated in a demonstration against the Queen, has been incarcerated. The news of his arrest precipitates in the old man a flood of thoughts about the current Quebec political situation which he tries to understand, the differences between his generation of silent resignation and his grandson's generation of revolt, and, especially, his personal hatred of the English and the historical facts about the French and English presence in Quebec, facts that Jean-Thomas had often related to him.

Il n'y a pas de pays sans grand-père, as of this point, becomes a deeply political and social novel. Vieux-Thomas recalls the sense of alienation that he has always felt as a *Québécois,* exploited by a wealthy, English-speaking, Protestant minority that has conquered his country and has tried to force on the inhabitants an allegiance to the British crown. He links his own experiences to those of Jean-Thomas and anxiously awaits his return: "Nous marcherons sur la terre où ton père a marché, avant qu'i' soit terrassé par le désespoir, où mon père a marché, et son père avant lui, et son grand-père . . . nous savons, toé et moé, que le bon Dieu a créé cette terre pour nous et nos enfants . . . " Vieux-Thomas and Jean-Thomas will become one, the symbol of the *Québécois* who is "d'une race qui ne sait pas mourir," as Jean-Thomas had once quoted to him from *Maria Chapdelaine.*

But first the old man must try to release his grandson: he must imitate the plane hijackers whom he has seen so often on television. In his glorious moment of renewed youth and courage, Vieux-Thomas hijacks a bus but is caught by the police and sent to an old age home. "Les Autres" have undoubtedly taken his rocker, and Vieux-Thomas can only hope for the arrival of his grandson who will release him so that he can return to his rocker to die.

Vieux-Thomas's rocker, like the Quebec that it can symbolize, must be defended to the end by two generations, united in fierce social protest. The novel itself, although at times somewhat exaggerated and tedious in its political and social criticism, is indeed effective both as this biting social commentary and as a meditation on youth, old age, and life. Roch Carrier has created a work well worth reading. (pp. 789-90)

> *Paula Gilbert Lewis, in a review of "Il n'y a pas de pays sans grand-père," in* The French Review, *Vol. LII, No. 5, April, 1979, pp. 789-90.*

Michael Benazon   (review date September 1979)

[*In the excerpt below, Benazon praises* Les enfants du bonhomme dans la lune, *calling Carrier "the myth-maker of Quebec rural life, a regional writer and prose elegist like Thomas Hardy or William Faulkner."*]

Les Enfants du bonhomme dans la lune (The Children of the Man in the Moon) is a gem of a book. It is Roch Carrier at his best, his most personal work of prose fiction thus far, and a gently ironic account of Quebec village life written by a man whose imagination has been largely shaped by his upbringing in Ste-Justine de Dorchester, the Quebec village described in the book.

Les Enfants appears to be a collection of short tales, but it rapidly becomes obvious that the book is unified by the setting, the recurring characters, the first person central consciousness and, most importantly, by the gradual development of the sensitive narrator from a child of seven to the mature writer, Carrier himself, who returns to the villaige in the last story to assist in the NFB filming of the characters and scenes which shape his fiction. The book is therefore a *bildungsroman,* the apprenticeship novel so congenial to Canadian writers in English and French. It is similar in form to Gabrielle Roy's collections—*Street of Riches, The Road Past Altamont* and lately, *Children of My Heart*—fictions which are as much an attempt to discover the essence of a particular region of Canada as they are an authorial quest for self-discovery. But where Gabrielle Roy works mainly within a tradition of realism, Carrier usually seeks out the odd, the bizarre, the fantastic. Despite his forays into the city in **Is It the Sun Philibert?** and **They Won't Demolish Me!,** Carrier is essentially the mythmaker of Quebec rural life, a regional writer and a prose elegist like Thomas Hardy or William Faulkner. Though not a polemicist or ideologist, Carrier is con-

cerned with the economic, political and social issues which divide English- and French-speaking Canadians.

Carrier cherishes the old ways of life and this perhaps explains the nostalgic, elegiac tone in which he laments the slow disappearance of, whatever its imperfections, a warm, vital and authentic existence.

—Michael Benazon

In **Les Enfants du bonhomme dans la lune,** as elsewhere in his fiction, Carrier draws on the myth of the integrated, fulfilled, almost Edenic existence lived in a small Quebec village which, in the eyes of its inhabitants at least, seems constantly threatened by outside forces—the English, the Communists, the Americans, the Protestants, the black man, the Jewish merchant, in short *l'etranger,* in whatever form he might appear. These fears and prejudices are subtly called in question by the childish narrator who initially looks up to the surrounding adults. As the story unfolds, young Carrier becomes increasingly conscious of the imperfections in the narrow world of the village, and gradually sheds his own illusions and misconceptions. Like Hardy who left the village of his birth yet remained close to it, Carrier cherishes the old ways of life and this perhaps explains the nostalgic, elegiac tone in which he laments the slow disappearance of, whatever its imperfections, a warm, vital and authentic existence:

> La vie était là, tout autour de nous, et au-dessus de nous, vibrante, lumineuse, remplie d'arbres; elle offrait des champs pleins de marguerites et menait á des collines où se cachaient de grands mysteres.

The book is beautifully written. Carrier gives free rein to his flair for concrete description and for light, clear, apparently naive prose. The symbolic and occasionally allegorical passages are distinctly poetic. Yet despite the nostalgic tone, Carrier never lapses into sentiment. His pervasive humour and irony maintain an essential balance:

> Un soir, des hommes du village étaient assis avec mon père, sur la galerie de bois. Avec la fumeé de leurs pipes montaient des paroles aussi sombres que la nuit approchante. Ils racontaient comment la vie allait mal dans le monde. Mais ils s'avouaient heureux d'avoir un chef comme Duplessis pour protéger le Québec. Enfant parmi eux, j'écoutais, fasciné par tout le savoir de ces hommes.

> *Michael Benazon, "Lunar Gems," in* The Canadian Forum, *Vol. LIX, No. 692, September, 1979, p. 30.*

Wayne Grady (review date November 1979)

[*In the following positive review, Grady identifies elements of autobiography and the French* conte *in* The Hockey Sweater, and Other Stories.]

Like many writers caught early in a multiplicity of cultural influences, Roch Carrier has ended up writing like none of them. His work is neither typically *québécois* nor mimetically English, has only distant echoes of France, and is decidedly un-American. Sheila Fischman quite rightly mentions Ingmar Bergman in a preface to her translation of Carrier's early novel, *Floralie, Where Are You?* And some of Carrier's early stories are reminiscent of such diverse internationalists as Borges and Jules Supervielle, the French writer who spent much of his time in Uruguay.

The timeless and placeless quality is superimposed quite deftly over a highly developed sense of time and place. The 20 stories in [*The Hockey Sweater, and Other Stories*] (none of them longer than four pages) are set in the small village of Ste-Justine, about 60 miles south-east of Quebec City and a stone's throw from the Maine border. They concern the boyhood and adolescence of the narrator as well as the daily comings and goings of the other villagers. Many of them take place during the war (Carrier was born in 1937), but such irrelevant details as conscription, taxation, and Duplessis are mere asides to the more burning conversational fervour over the size of Pierette's budding breasts and the visit of a small, country circus. Homely stuff, to be sure, but Carrier weaves his stories into a sort of charmed circle, a garden of delights, using everything at his disposal—autobiography, history, folklore, local mythology (including Catholicism: every Good Friday the bells of Ste-Justine fly off to Rome and return on Sunday blessed by the Pope)—to create his own record, both personal and traditional, of life.

A word must be said about the form of these stories. There is no French equivalent of "short story." French writers write *récits, contes,* or *nouvelles,* the latter corresponding most closely to the English short story. Carrier writes *contes*—amusing, light-hearted fables that often end, and sometimes begin, with an explanatory summation, in case any of his hearers miss the point. The *conte* is not a careful delineation of character or even of situation, but rather a graceful blend of parable and prose poem designed simply to make people smile and feel a little closer to one another. Its aim is social rather than individual. It's a difficult genre for the English ear to adapt to, which may explain why Carrier's first two collections of them—*Jolis deuils, petites tragédies pour adultes,* and *Contes pour milles oreilles*—remain untranslated.

> *Wayne Grady, "Budding Breasts, Brooding Beasts," in* Books in Canada, *Vol. 8, No. 9, November, 1979, p. 10.*

Emile J. Talbot (review date Winter 1980)

[*In the following essay, Talbot offers praise for Carrier's semiautobiographical* Les enfants du bonhomme de la lune.]

Roch Carrier's first published prose fiction was a collection of short stories, *Jolis deuils* (1964), and it is to the short tale that Carrier returns in *Les enfants du bonhomme dans la lune.* Like Faulkner's, most of Carrier's fiction has a geographical center. In Carrier, it is the small town in rural Québec, and all the stories in this collection take place in the forties in Carrier's own hometown of Sainte-Justine. The link between them is the young boy (much of the material appears to be autobiographical) through whose fresh and naïve perspective the tales are told.

Two of the stories ("Il se pourrait bien que les arbres voyagent" and "Grand-père n'avait peur de rien ni de personne") are repetitive of material in Carrier's last novel, *Il n'y a pas de pays sans grand-père,* but the remaining eighteen are new renditions of some of Carrier's favorite themes such as French-Canadian national pride (as in the boy's utter humiliation at having to wear a Toronto Maple Leafs jersey), fear of the English (which takes an unusual twist in "La machine à détecter tout ce qui est américain") and the humorous results of the English-French language barrier. Religious practices, village superstitions and small-town rivalries are presented as more silly than dangerous, and Carrier treats them with indulgence, as he does anti-communism, anti-Semitism and racism, which he mocks but which are seen to stem more from ignorance than from deep-seated hostilities.

Some of the stories reveal the author's admiration for his father, a wheeler-dealer who gets involved in some amusing business deals, but who represents somehow the life of this town for which Carrier obviously has a great deal of affection. In the last story, "Le secret perdu dans l'eau," the boy has become a man and returns to his native village to shoot a film. While there, he is reminded of his father's gift for finding water with an alder branch, a technique which he himself had once learned. But now, over a well that his father had discovered, he finds that the branch will no longer move under his grip. The world of his father and of his village is gone and cannot be brought back to life—except, the reader will conclude, through fiction such as this.

There is in this book none of the violence which marked much of Carrier's previous writing of rural life, and the irony is sufficiently detached to provoke a low-keyed humor throughout. The result is a light, pleasurable narrative by one of Québec's most gifted storytellers.

> *Emile J. Talbot, in a review of "Les enfants du bonhomme dans la lune," in* World Literature Today, *Vol. 54, No. 1, Winter, 1980, p. 67.*

Jon Kertzer (review date March 1980)

[*Kertzer is a Canadian critic and educator. In the following essay, he praises Carrier's use of folklore, irony and sympathy, and child and adult perspectives in* The Hockey Sweater, and Other Stories.]

The subtitle of Roch Carrier's first collection of stories, *Jolis Deuils,* is "petites tragédies pour adultes," an unusual combination of terms that sums up nicely the style and vision that Carrier has refined throughout his career. In all his books he works on a small scale, presenting anecdotes and incidents about the ordinary folk of rural Quebec, simple people whose lives consist of basic routines, minor events and familiar prejudices. If their lives are limited, however, their passions are great: they are intensely Catholic, intensely traditional, intensely joyful or rebellious or despairing. They are capable of great suffering, and consequently the small tragedies which they inevitably encounter are unexpectedly poignant. Even when there is humour in their stories, the comedy is bitter-sweet.

Carrier's first subtitle applies just as well to his latest collection, *The Hockey Sweater and other stories* (the sixth volume translated by Sheila Fischman), which consists of twenty tales of only six to eight pages each. These stories were originally read on radio and television, and in them Carrier recalls events from his boyhood in the town of Sainte-Justine in the 1940s. He fuses perfectly the autobiographical and the fictional, as well as the small, tragic and adult features characteristic of his work, by adopting a child's point of view. The world of children is small, but from their own perspective it seems vast and amazing. Because they are wonderfully ignorant, their stories are simple in their ignorance, but wonderful in their simplicity. This is the style at which Carrier excels. From his childish point of view, ordinary facts take on a mysterious aura: "Life was there all around us, vibrant and luminous, filled with trees; it offered us fields of daisies and it led to hills that concealed great mysteries." The young Carrier eagerly examines the wonderful world of adults, considering such tragic issues as World War Two, Hiroshima, Communism, sex and death; and such comic ones as Americans, hockey, taxes, sex and death. Because childish and adult views are necessarily at odds, the stories always have an ironic bite: Carrier mocks himself for his ingenuousness. For example, his parents watch in amusement when their son piously expects to be carried to Rome by the ringing of the church bells on Good Friday. But the son has the last laugh, because he builds a double irony into his tales. A few days later they receive a postcard in their son's handwriting decorated with a magnificent stamp from Rome. Has he indeed been transported there through the fervour of his ludicrous but intense piety?

The double irony arises because Carrier presents himself as a child confronting a world of child-like men. The adults are peasants: naive in their wisdom, credulous in their scepticism.

His characters have no real parallel in English-Canadian literature. They are not like the inhabitants of Leacock's Mariposa, who are more sophisticated and modern, less coarse and far less vulnerable than Carrier's *habitants*. Perhaps the latter are closer to some of the figures in Isaac Bashevis Singer's tales—an unexpected but illuminating comparison. Carrier's colourful characters, like Singer's, are little men with great desires. They live in the real world and suffer continually from its hardships, its oppression, its small tragedies; but it is a world whose superstitious boundaries extend into the realm of the fantastic: "I remember hearing the story of a man who had gone to the place where the sky meets the earth: he'd had to bend down so he wouldn't bump his head against the sky." It is a world endowed with magical properties and presided over by deities like Rocket Richard and Maurice Duples-

sis. Both authors present characters who are devoted to a highly traditional, religious past, of which they are nevertheless sceptical. They admire yet resent the intrusions of modern life. Both authors delight in the peculiar twist of mind by which their heroes argue their lives into an eccentric but meaningful disorder.

The French title of this volume, *Les enfants du bonhomme dans la lune* (*The children of the man in the moon*), suggests that we might regard these stories—again like Singer's—as folktales or as fables designed to illustrate some moral or truth about human nature. In part, this is true: in each tale, Carrier learns a lesson about the world and about his own precarious place in it. But because of the multiple ironies which the author elaborates, the lessons tend to be devious, following the logical illogic of their subjects. Each story is based on a conflict of forces that at first appear to be in clear opposition: child and adult, French and English, virtue and sin, strength and weakness, tradition and novelty, and so on. But the young Carrier, through his effort to maintain this balance and keep the issues straight, manages only to entangle them absurdly, usually with tragi-comic effect. His encounter with the supernatural causes him to reverse the usual attitude, as he finally asks: "Do ghosts no longer believe in the living?" His grandfather is proud of his strength, until he reveals a secret fear of Protestants. The cynical Monsieur Veilleux disputes the reasonableness of religion, only to replace it with a lively superstition of his own. Monsieur Juste, the blacksmith, invents an absurd device to prevent cows from twitching when being milked (to promote it, he gives it an English name: "Anti-Cow-Kicks"), only to find himself ruined by success when he is overwhelmed by an order for 2,500 dozen of them. Carrier and his friend Lapin, who have been taught to beware of Communists and Jews, go to spy on a Jewish merchant, expecting him to be "the enemy of the entire world," but they emerge from his store bewildered, having bought a suit at half price.

Many of the anecdotes depend on unexpected twists of this kind, which surprise not only the reader, but the characters themselves, who thought they could make sense of their world by following their traditions, their instincts, or the instructions published regularly in *L'Action Catholique*. Especially subtle in this regard is the treatment of French-English relations, a familiar theme in Carrier's work. The young boy has never met English-Canadians, whom he regards as alien beings. When his teacher, an Irish nun named Sister Brigitte, teaches him to read French, he quite naturally follows her example, and his parents are amazed to hear him speaking French with an English accent: "But as far as knowing whether Sister Brigitte had an English accent, how could I? I'd never heard a single word of English." This irony grows complex and pathetic, however, when the sick and aging nun wanders barefoot in a snow storm, and when she is rescued explains in English that she was returning to Ireland. Unstated, but powerfully suggested in this episode, is the recognition that the woman has a village, language and traditions of her own, which are as rich and compelling as the French-Canadian ways, and to which she wishes to return in order to die at home. In stories like this, it is above all the sympathy promoted by Carrier's style and vision that makes his small tragi-comedies for adults so moving. (pp. 36-7)

Jon Kertzer, *"Petites Tragedies pour Adultes,"* in The Canadian Forum, *Vol. LIX, No. 697, March, 1980, pp. 36-7.*

Alexandre L. Amprimoz   (essay date Autumn 1981)

[*Amprimoz is an Italian-born poet, translator, and critic. In the following excerpt, he discusses Carrier's portrait of madness in* La céleste bicyclette, *which he characterizes as "a type of fantasy closely related to magic realism" and a satire of the medical community.*]

Montreal, December 5, 1979, *Place des Arts, Le Café de la Place.* One of Quebec's best actors, Albert Millaire, begins an hour-long monologue specially created for him by Roch Carrier.

A few months later the play *La Céleste Bicyclette* becomes the book *La Céleste Bicyclette.* (p. 91)

Carrier began as a young poet with two collections: *Misunderstood Games* (*Les Jeux incompris,* 1956) and *Look for your Words, Look for your Steps* (*Cherche tes mots, cherche tes pas,* 1958). In 1965, he received the Prize of the Province of Quebec for his collection of stories *Pretty Mournings, Small Tragedies* (*Jolis Deuils, petites tragédies*). Carrier's two most recent novels confirm the fact that he can be both an excellent narrator and prose poet: *The Garden of Delights* (*Le Jardin des délices,* 1975) was followed by *No Country Without a Grandfather* (*Il n'y a pas de pays sans grand-père,* 1977).

To the English reader, Roch Carrier's novels appear to be a clever combination of humour, fantasy, violence, sex and even a little conventional realism. But Quebec critics, like Jacques Allard, have stressed that such novels as *No Country Without a Grandfather* are very sophisticated attempts to define the consciousness of a race and the image of a future nation.

Before *La Céleste Bicyclette* (*The Celestial Bicycle*), Carrier wrote a collection of twenty short stories: *Les Enfants du bonhomme dans la lune.* The title, *The Children of the Man in the Moon,* leaves no doubt as to the literary genre.

Like the previous book, *The Celestial Bicycle* can be seen as the type of fantasy closely related to magic realism. What we have here is the wise monologue of an actor apparently gone mad. From his cell he tells the story of his life to an invisible visitor—the spectator, the reader. Essentially, one fine evening the actor, while riding his bicycle, goes up into the sky and, on the way down, breaks his leg because he doesn't pay attention to the road. At the hospital the doctors take good care of his leg, but, because they do not believe his story, he is confined to a mental institution.

Right from the beginning the tone of the actor is vaguely reminiscent of some of Molière's best comedies:

> When the doctors officially declared that I had flies in my idea box, I told myself that I would soon be alone. Well, I was wrong. All day long, doctors stand in line to see my show. Those who

can't get in, they look through the keyhole. Not to mention the nurses . . . Thanks for coming. Yes, I've been granted my idiot's diploma, an official diploma, the only diploma I'll be able to hang on my wall while I wait for customers. According to the diploma signed by the doctors— some of those guys are able to write—I am an official idiot, a competent one.

This type of irony is not reserved for the medical profession. Language itself is the source of humour when the actor speaks, for instance, of his small collection of "orthographs" (spellings) on his cast while obviously meaning "autographs". It is also through language that Carrier questions the condition of the mentally ill in our modern societies:

> But who should be locked up? Is that the great question? All things considered, they decided to apply simply the law of profit. I am more profitable to society here, locked up, than out there: I provide employment for doctors, nurses, union labourers, bureaucrats, medicine salesmen, administrators . . .

The actor also speaks, in indirect but colorful terms, of the need for a rational society to put an analyst between the mentally ill and itself. We find here the notion of rational screen elaborated by French philosopher Michel Foucault.

One aspect of insanity runs through the narrative structure. Several times the actor promises to give the invisible audience an account of how he broke his leg, but then proceeds towards some other topic. The technique is similar to the one used by Denis Diderot in *Jacques Le Fataliste:* the reader is always expecting to find out how Jacques lost his virginity.

Below the surface, the humour reveals a deep understanding of the present impasse of psychiatry. The actor's madness consists, for one thing, of refusing to enter the insanity of psychiatry:

> My cast hadn't dried yet when in came a man who seemed to have been a cross between a cop and a pastor, to which a dash of undertaker might have been added: he must have been a psychiatrist.

With this kind of remark the actor expresses opinions that echo, through a Breton connection, the recognized existence of madness within psychiatric methods. Often the madness of the traditional analyst is stressed by contrasting it with the assumed notion of common sense. The result is, of course, rather humorous:

> The shrink came to question me several times: "Have you ever felt like sleeping with your mother? . . . With your sister? . . . Have you ever felt like sleeping with your father? . . .

> Once I answered his questions this way:

> "I'll tell you the truth, doctor, the whole truth: with my father, my mother, my sister, and my grandfather, I would have liked to have a small party all together! Knowing that my grandmoth-

er, wearing leather boots, would be spying on us through the keyhole!"

The shrink then asked very seriously:

"How many times a week?"

So I answered:

"What interests you more: your questions or my answers?"

The long monologue allows the actor to ridicule not only the medical profession but also the typical marital relationship and the world of politics. Certain details are quite amusing. A conversation between Millaire and the Quebec Premier ends with the latter saying: "You and I are both actors. But you, you know the play while I have to improvise every day."

In the end, the reader is left with the echo of the many poetic passages evoking man's old dream to fly. Then madness appears as the courage to believe in a better universe:

> I don't know what attracts me, I don't know who attracts me, but I know that my true country is up there in that unknown space. It's up there in that distant and unknown homeland that I have my true roots. It's from there that the sap that gives me life comes. I'm growing on earth only for the instant of a smile. When the curtain falls, when my smile hardens in my final mask, I will only be dead on earth. Life will continue to stir to the depths of unknown space in these invisible roots that dive god knows where and that make us eternal. Believe me, distinguished doctors and nurses, you will never be able to stop me from jumping onto my bicycle and fleeing from this earth which is not too cute to see, where men busy themselves by locking each other up. There's a place up there for the man who refuses to distinguish between dream and reality.

It is reassuring to see that, after VanGough, Artaud, Nietzsche and Nelligan, Roch Carrier renews—in all sanity—the power and the glory of madness by pointing out that, in the end, the analyst must be tried by the patient. Indeed, if the former is a tool in the hands of power, the latter, being an artist, has the permanence of his created monuments testifying for him. (pp. 91-4)

> *Alexandre L. Amprimoz, "Roch Carrier's Bicycle," in* The Antigonish Review, *No. 47, Autumn, 1981, pp. 91-4.*

Wayne Grady (review date February 1982)

[*In the essay below, Grady lauds Carrier's call for political resistance in* No Country without Grandfathers *and argues that the novel is as "specifically anti-English as Carrier has ever been."*]

[*No Country without Grandfathers*], originally called *Il n'y a pas de pays sans grand-père* and published in 1979, was inspired by a trip Roch Carrier made to his own grandfather's farm in southeastern Quebec during the making of the film *The Ungrateful Land.* (This trip also inspired some of the stories included in *The Hockey Sweater.*) It takes the form of a single, long soliloquy by a 73-year-old man known as Vieux-Thomas, or Pépére, over the course of about 24 hours. Confined for the most part to his rocking chair by his family, which he refers to simply as "the Others," he feels he has been "nailed to his rocking chair like Jesus on his cross." To keep his mind alive he rehearses to himself the story of his life.

He remembers his Late Wife (though he can't quite recall her name), the winters he spent in the bush cutting down trees for the *Anglais,* killing deer with his bare hands and a hunting knife, building his own house, and raising his large family. His thoughts are periodically invaded by the Others, whose ways are more foreign to him than those of the *Anglais.* "The Others have enough poison in their mouths to infect a poisonous snake," he thinks. When he reads a newspaper his eyes fall on the obituary page: "Do you see your name there, Pépére?" his grandchildren ask. When a letter arrives from the Government, Pépére tries to read it, but he has forgotten so many words: "You'll have to go back to school, Pépére," says one of the Others. "It'll be handy, Pépére," adds another; "the school's right next to the graveyard."

Because Vieux-Thomas can't or won't speak to the Others, no one guesses how deeply he is affected by the news in the Government letter that his favourite grandson, Jean-Thomas, has been imprisoned for demonstrating against the Queen of England "and of Canada." The Others are ashamed that their honour in the village has been stained, and even Vieux-Thomas is confused at first: "In Vieux-Thomas's day," he muses, "people had learned to be silent the way Jesus Christ suffered on his cross, without a word: to suffer in silence to atone for the sin of being born."

Gradually Vieux-Thomas realizes that Jean-Thomas's anger and resistance are not only justified, but have been inherited, passed down from father to son since the initial resistance on the Plains of Abraham. Jean-Thomas's father (Vieux-Thomas's son), Dieu-donné, had rebelled against his English bosses by dumping a load of logs on the lawn of the paper company's president, and had done nothing since but smoke cigarettes and read books. Vieux-Thomas, when he worked as a logger, had been "young himself in those days and scatterbrained like all young people; a young man didn't have blood in his veins back then, he had fire." When he left his home for the lumber camp the first time he had walked for days through the bush, alone, unsure of his way, and when he had arrived at the camp he had heard English spoken for the first time. Terrified, he had turned and fled. But still, the resistance of this new generation leaves him cold: their very language is foreign to him. "If we analyze history," he overhears them saying, "the aspirations of the people of the Land of Quebec have always been censured by the dominant power."

"Words aren't the true reality," Vieux-Thomas has told himself earlier on. "But words make a kind of magic that revives dead things and brings to life other things not yet alive. Words bestow life." For Vieux-Thomas, words also threaten life: the Others' words cut straight into his heart, and Jean-Thomas has been thrown into prison for shouting words at the Queen. Throughout the entire soliloquy Vieux-Thomas does not audibly utter a single word, though he is often told to keep quiet by the Others. He occasionally addresses a silent question to his God: "And how much longer, dear Lord, will you let me keep the gift of standing on my own two feet?" In the end, as Jean-Thomas has taught him, it is actions that count, however fruitless and life-denying those actions might be.

As Vieux-Thomas's narrative progresses the tone becomes more and more anti-English—perhaps as specifically anti-English as Carrier has ever been—and the old man's memories become correspondingly darker and more eloquent. There is, for example, Carrier's version of the "Rose Latulip" story, in which a beautiful village girl dances with a handsome stranger who turns out to be the Devil. In Carrier's version the handsome stranger is a well-dressed *Anglais* from the city, who is physically beaten by a village lad and sent packing back to his office. There is also the very powerful story of Vieux-Thomas's winter spent shovelling coal in the bottom of an old steamship run by an English captain. Vieux-Thomas—who at that time might very well have been called Jean-Thomas—worked side-by-side with a black man whose moans of sorrow and pain became a new but, unlike English, entirely understandable language to Vieux-Thomas.

The end of the novel is a long, passionate, and eloquent appeal for the return of Jean-Thomas, in which the young man assumes mythic proportions as the Saviour of Quebec. Vieux-Thomas represents the *idea* of Quebec that Jean-Thomas is trying to protect—it is not an intangible idea, like freedom, but a very real and specific idea, like the land, like the rocks and trees and rivers that make up the Country of Quebec and were stolen by the English. And without which, indeed, there would be no Country at all. (pp. 9-10)

> Wayne Grady, "Je me souviens," in Books in Canada, Vol. 11, No. 2, February, 1982, pp. 9-10.

David J. Bond   (essay date Fall 1982)

[*In the essay below, Bond examines the importance of death in Carrier's works.*]

In the space of fifteen years, Roch Carrier has established a reputation as one of the finest writers of fiction in Quebec. His first work, **Jolis Deuils** (1964), is a collection of short stories, some of which are only a couple of pages long, and which relate a series of tragic events in a highly poetic style. This collection was followed by a trilogy of novels depicting the lives of various characters from the same Quebec village. The first of the three, **La Guerre, Yes Sir!** (1968), examines the impact of the Second World War on this village. Carrier shows how, suddenly, the reality of war is brought home to the villagers when the body of Corriveau, one of their number who has been killed in action, is returned for burial. The same day that Corriveau's body arrives, accompanied by a group of English soldiers, Bérubé, another villager who has joined the army, returns with his bride Molly, a prostitute whom he met in Newfoundland. The next novel in the trilogy,

Floralie, où es-tu? (1969), goes farther into the past and describes the marriage of Corriveau's parents, Floralie and Anthyme. The couple are separated in the forest as Anthyme takes his wife home from the wedding, and, after a night of wandering and nightmare, they are reunited in Anthyme's village. *Il est par là, le soleil* (1970), the third volume in the trilogy, follows the misfortunes of Philibert, the son of the gravedigger in the first novel, as he leaves home and moves to the city. He goes from one menial and pointless task to another, until, finally on the brink of success, he dies in a car accident. While writing this trilogy, Carrier also published a group of short stories [in *Ecrits du Canada français* 25] called **Contes pour mille oreilles** (1969), which have themes similar to those in his first volume of short fiction.

Other novels were to follow. In 1973, came **Le deuxmillième étage,** the story of a man who owns an old apartment building in a poor district of a city (probably Montreal), and who refuses to allow it to be demolished for a new building project. **Le Jardin des délices** (1975) is set in the same village as Carrier's first two novels, and it tells of how a confidence man persuades the villagers that there is gold on their land and sells them shares in a fictitious mining company. Interwoven with this story is that of the local lawyer, who, because he wanted to return to earth after his death, was buried with most of his worldly wealth. The most recent of Carrier's novels, **Il n'y a pas de pays sans grand-père** (1977), is narrated by an old man, confined to his rocking-chair, who laments the softness and decadence of modern Québécois. The only person with whom he can communicate is his grandson, and, when the latter is arrested at a demonstration against the Queen's visit to Quebec, the old man decides to rescue him. Brandishing his hunting knife, he hijacks a bus and sets off to Quebec City. Finally, he is overpowered, put in a straight jacket and sent to a mental institution. In 1979, Carrier published **Les Enfants du bonhomme dans la lune,** a collection of short stories inspired by his childhood.

Summaries such as these cannot convey how Carrier's fiction grips the reader. He is a *raconteur* who uses an amazing combination of caricature, exaggeration and the grotesque to create a very special world. He himself has admitted: "My novels revel in the unlikely; I love exaggeration, I love force, I love the epic." But he is also careful to point out that a writer's flights of imagination do not necessarily divorce him from reality. While admitting the importance of imagination in his works, he adds: "When I say imaginary, I do not create a distinction between the imaginary world and the one we call the real world; by imaginary, I mean the real world perceived more globally by the novel, with all its possibilities and its meanings." Interestingly enough, Carrier dates his vocation as a novelist from the time when, at the age of twelve, he read *Candide*. It need hardly be added that, in this work, Voltaire used the grotesque and the exaggerated to say some very serious things about the nature of life. Carrier, too, through his use of what one critic has called "fantastical realism," is an equally serious writer. His work in one of its most important aspects, is an examination of the very forces of life, and of the forces of death which oppose them.

Roch Carrier

LA CÉLESTE BICYCLETTE

Stanké

Cover of Carrier's La céleste bicyclette.

The presence of death as a theme in these works should be no surprise, for, as Margaret Atwood puts it [in her *Survival: A Thematic Guide to Canadian Literature* (1972)], "the general Canadian predilection for coffins" is, in Quebec literature, "intensified almost to a mania." And, indeed, in *La Guerre, Yes Sir!,* the coffin containing Corriveau's body is at the center of the most important scene: a wake held in his memory. The arrival of the coffin represents the intrusion of death into the lives of the villagers, and, from the moment Corriveau's body arrives, death is foremost in every character's consciousness. In certain of the short stories, death is equally important. **"La Main"** describes a huge dead hand which descends over a town, blocking out all warmth and light. The hero of **"Les Lunettes"** acquires a pair of spectacles which change his view of the world: his secretary appears as a skeleton, his car becomes a hearse pulled by skeletal horses, the city streets look desolate and ruined, and when he enters what he believes is his home, he discovers that it is his coffin. In **"La Chambre nuptiale,"** a newly-married couple discover that they have become aged and corpse-like.

Frequently death has a symbolic presence. Many of Carrier's works are set in winter, for example, and the cold and snow can be seen as symbols of death (as Margaret At-

wood points out, winter often plays this role in Canadian novels). The whole of *La Guerre, Yes Sir!* takes place in winter, as does much of *Le Jardin des délices.* In the latter, the approach of winter is linked explicitly to death through references to dead moose carried off by hunters, the "dry bones" of the trees, and the long nights. Obviously, night, too, is symbolic of death, and nearly all of *Floralie, où es-tu?* takes place at night, while the wake in *La Guerre, Yes Sir!* and several scenes of *Le Jardin des délices* are set at night.

Sometimes it is the dull routine of life in the city which Carrier equates with death. In **"Le Téléphone,"** a man wears himself out by repeating the same formula every time the telephone rings in the office of a large company. After his death, his wife takes over the task, until she, too, dies. **"Le métro"** tells of a man traveling to work in the subway, who suddenly realizes that he and all the other passengers have grown old, worn away by the routine of existence in the city. But it is in the life of Philibert from *Il est par là, le soleil* that death and the city are most closely linked. From his earliest childhood, Philibert is haunted by death, for his father is both the village butcher and its gravedigger. The opening pages of the novel are full of the images which obsess the child's mind: a hunter who decapitates ducks caught in a frozen lake, slaughtered pigs hanging up while being gutted, times spent helping his father dig graves. When Philibert goes to the city, he finds himself repeating these experiences of death, since he is forced to work in places which strongly resemble the grave. He works at digging up roads, peeling potatoes in a dark restaurant basement, scrubbing floors under restaurant tables and repairing cars in the grease pit of a garage. Even his sexual urges—the very affirmation of life—are not allowed free expression. He does not have the money to court the beautiful bank clerk who catches his eye, so he pays the restaurant owner for a joyless coupling with his wife.

In *Le deux-millième étage,* the impersonal destructive force of city living is centered on the machines which are sent to destroy Dorval's apartments. One of Dorval's tenants, Barnabé, illustrates particularly well the effect of such machines. Barnabé is determined to become a mechanic, because, he says: "A man in our times is not a man, but a slave if he cannot dominate the machine." Unfortunately, he fails all his correspondence course examinations and seems to be robbed even of his virility. When he tries to work a bulldozer, he is totally baffled by it, and his wife shouts "Impotent!" at him. Meanwhile, the machines advance inexorably upon the apartments, destroying them and filling the air with the smell of rotten wood, old plaster and brick dust. The mindless destruction is represented principally by the bulldozer, which remains impervious to the characters' feelings. When Dorval pours beer in its fuel tank, this ridiculously human gesture has no effect.

Dorval's solution to the problems posed by modern capitalist society is a simplistic form of communism (he does not even realize that, as a property owner, he, too, is part of the system). But Carrier's point is that, whatever changes are made to society, the fundamental problems of life remain. As one character says: "After the Revolution, my damned apples will still go rotten!" No revolution can hide the pointlessness of a life in which men must die. "A man's life isn't worth a fart," to quote Barnabé. Behind the social concerns of novels like *Le deux-millième étage* lurk more fundamental problems. Corriveau's mother, in front of her son's coffin, wonders what use it is spending one's life producing and rearing children when they must all die. In *La Guerre, Yes Sir!* Henri has a dream which conveys the fate of all mankind: he sees a huge coffin into which the inhabitants of the village march, followed by those from neighbouring villages and by crowds from all over the world.

This is not an optimistic view of life, but Roch Carrier's characters do not lead happy lives. They die in wars, they are exploited by employers and they barely manage to scratch a living from the soil. "Life is a curse," Philibert comments, and, when one of the workers on the construction site deliberately blows himself up, Philibert approves of the act, seeing it as less stupid than docile acceptance of a life of misery. But this sombre view of existence is lightened by Carrier's obvious pity for his characters and for mankind. He does not revel in the dismal picture he paints, but shows great warmth for a humanity which must suffer and die. This feeling is best expressed in the scene in *Le Jardin des délices* where two drunken villagers dig up the lawyer's grave to get at his wealth. Although terrified by the dark graveyard, they are still able to show their pity when they see the lawyer's body. They burst into tears, and one of them exclaims: "Damn it, death is sad!" "Damn it, life is sad," replies the other.

It has always been the task of religion to deal with problems such as these, but, in Carrier's works, religion is itself depicted as a morbid force, even as a form of death worship. The priests in his novels constantly warn the faithful that death stalks them and that they must always bear that in mind. "My brothers," says the priest in *La Guerre, Yes Sir!,* "never forget that we live to die and that we die to live." In *Il est par là, le soleil,* the couple with whom Philibert lodges introduces him one day into a dark room lit only by a candle. In the middle is a coffin containing the remains of their dead child, before whom they come to pray. When Philibert asks what is in the coffin, they murmur: "It is life."

Associated with this exaltation of death is an attempt by the Church to frighten men. Carrier sees religion, not as a liberating force, but as one which imprisons through fear of sin. During Corriveau's funeral, the priest gives a lurid description of the torments of hell, and tells his listeners: "Because you are men and women, because the flesh is weak, you are condemned to perish in the flames of Hell, to perish without end unless God in His infinite goodness forgives your sins." The priests in *Floralie, où es-tu?* and *Le Jardin des délices* preach essentially the same message, and its effect is to replace enjoyment of life with fear of death. The children in **"Les Fantômes du temps des feuilles mortes"** are terrified of ghosts; Henri in *La Guerre, Yes Sir!* fears that the dead Corriveau is wandering around the house; Anthyme's childhood is marred by nights of terror spent cowering under his bed; Floralie sees

Hell and demons everywhere. These characters are all taught to see life as a battle between God and the Devil. The traveling actors in *Floralie, où es-tu?* sum up this view of existence when they perform a mystery play. "We are the Seven Deadly Sins," announces one of them. "We are the kings of the earth, we reign over the world."

This kind of religion destroys life, and nowhere is this better illustrated than in the scene from *La Guerre, Yes Sir!* in which Corriveau's sister appears at the wake. Esmalda is a nun who has not seen her family for many years. She knocks on the window at a time when the villagers, warmed by Anthyme's cider and Floralie's baking, are beginning to forget that they are in the presence of death. The noise reduces them to terrified silence, and, when the window is opened, a blast of cold air chills them. Esmalda immediately delivers dire warnings of death and damnation, her smile revealing decayed teeth which symbolize her role as the representative of death.

The Church is also equated with death because, by associating sex with sin, it suppresses one of the life forces. Hence, Bérubé is about to go to bed with Molly when he hears a clock ticking in Hell. It seems to say: "Always, never," and he sees in his mind's eye the souls of the damned tormented by flames and serpents. Naturally, his sexual urge dies, and he can revive it only by making it legitimate in the eyes of the Church: he asks Molly to marry him. Anthyme in *Floralie, où es-tu?* has lived a life of abstinence and frustration through fear of sin, and, when he realizes that Floralie is not a virgin, he concludes that she must be damned. "I am not even a man," he decides when he knows that Floralie has had a lover before him. His loss of virility is confirmed when Floralie and his horse (which symbolizes his "animal" instincts) pass into the hands of Néron, a traveling medicine man who happens by when the couple are separated in the forest.

[By writing] I take my place in a Quebec which has been dispossessed of its culture and which, little by little, is trying tenaciously to create a soul for itself.

—*Roch Carrier*

The religion which these characters practise is so unnatural that they scarcely understand its rituals. Their prayers are a hilarious muddle of misunderstood words, and the Hail Mary becomes: "Je vous salue, Marie, pleine et grasse" ("Hail Mary, pregnant and fat"). Sometimes, however, a garbled prayer hits on the truth, as when one character prays: "Au fond, tu m'abimes, Seigneur, Seigneur" ("In the depths, You destroy me, O Lord, O Lord"). And the God they worship is indeed destructive. He is also unjust, and one question which is posed in *La Guerre, Yes Sir!* is why He permits innocent young men to die in wars. Philibert wonders how his father can illtreat him in the name of God, and when he finds no justice in life, he comments: "I've been given life without asking for it, like a kick in the behind." Yet the Church tells people that they must thank God for His kindness. The most bitterly ironic scene in Carrier's work is one in *Il est par là, le soleil* which describes a procession of sick and halt making its way to the church. They are led by the Laliberté family and their twenty-one hydrocephalic children pushed in wheelbarrows. They are going to give thanks for the twenty-one angels with whom their union has been blessed. As Philibert watches them, he pulls the legs off a grasshopper, thus unconsciously imitating the casual cruelty of God.

It is important to remember, however, that the religion and the God depicted in Carrier's novels are presented as belonging to a particular community. His characters, as well as being individuals, are French-Canadians, and their religion is the kind of medieval Catholicism practised until quite recently in Quebec. The nightmares and religious fears of people like Anthyme, Floralie, Bérubé and Philibert are those of a whole people, and their sad lives are those of many Québécois. In Carrier's opinion, the people of Quebec have always led an unhappy existence, and, writing of the work of another Quebec novelist, he says something which applies to any one of his own novels: "Quebec is as sad as this book." The background of his novels, while clearly Quebec, is kept vague in order to make it representative of the whole province. For this reason, the village where most of the works take place is never named, and the apartment building in *Le deux-millième étage* is any such building in a poor district of Montreal.

As a community, Carrier's French-Canadians are threatened primarily by the English-speaking world. Corriveau is killed in a war forced on him by the English, and, in this respect, he represents all French-Canadians, for whom the English are death. The English soldiers who bring back Corriveau's body typify this threat. They incarnate death because they are English and because they are soldiers. They are trained to be robots who obey the sergeant's orders without question and who are impervious to the warmth of the French-Canadians. Indeed, they despise the villagers as "turbulent, undisciplined and crazy pigs." In the army they treat French-Canadians no better. Henri sweeps the barracks floors and Bérubé (together with Italians, Greeks, Poles, Hungarians and other "foreigners") cleans the latrines.

Carrier's characters never really understand why they are involved in a war, and Floralie does not even realize that the Union Jack on her son's coffin is "her" flag. Joseph tries to escape the war by cutting off his hand, a symbolic castration and loss of the life forces. His wife asks: "What will my Joseph do in my bed with his stump of an arm?" and to her husband she says: "A man who hasn't the courage to go to war to protect his country isn't a man." Other characters are mutilated mentally and spiritually. Bérubé, for example, is turned into an automaton who mechanically obeys the sergeant's orders to help expel the French-Canadians from the wake. He tries later to pray beside Corriveau's coffin, but the villagers turn him away. When he joins the soldiers to pray in English, they, too, reject him. He now belongs to neither community.

Québécois face death as a people because the English have dispossessed them in their own land. In *Il n'y a pas de pays sans grand-père* Vieux-Thomas still remembers being prevented from fishing in a lake because it belonged to English-Canadians. When Philibert arrives in the city and tries to earn money by sweeping sidewalks in an English district, one lady is amazed that he cannot speak English. She concludes that he must be an Italian immigrant, and she laments that such people are allowed into the country without learning its language. In *La Guerre, Yes Sir!* the dispossession of French-Canadians is summed up in the scene in which the English soldiers, unable to bear the disgusting manners of the French-Canadians, eject them from Corriveau's house.

Even the forces of capitalism which exploit characters like Philibert are seen as English, or, at least, Anglo-American. Giving his tenants a lesson on capitalism, Dorval asks: "What language does the voice of capitalism speak?" and then answers his own question: "It speaks English." Vieux-Thomas, in his youth, worked for an English company, and was insulted and ordered about in English. Philibert, when he inherits some money, decides to set up a business, but first he must learn English, for, "If you don't know English, you can't even go for a piss when you want to." His failure is due largely to the fact that he is a French-Canadian in an English capitalist system. This is made clear when he reads a newspaper article explaining that French-Canadians suffer from a fascination with failure. The Laterreur brothers in *Le deux-millième étage* turn this fascination into a kind of success. They are wrestlers who make money by deliberately losing their fights, and thereby ensure that the frustration and anger of the spectators is turned harmlessly against the winners of the fights rather than against their real exploiters.

Yet all is not death and failure in Carrier's work, for he deals with life as well. The characters affirm their will to live in the face of death; they gather to drink, laugh and dance in the tavern in *Le Jardin des délices* despite the winter forces outside; they gather at Corriveau's wake in *La Guerre, Yes Sir!* to express their relief at being alive themselves. The latter gathering especially turns into a Rabelaisian celebration of life as the villagers eat, drink and exchange salacious stories. This is done as a reaction against the presence of death symbolized by the coffin, but also against the English soldiers, to whom Anthyme says: "We know how to live." Dorval echoes these words as he cries to the demolishers: "*I* am alive." For him, the symbol of life is the beer with which he fortifies himself and his tenants, as it is in *Le Jardin des délices,* in which the villagers drink it in large quantities in the tavern, and in *Floralie, où es-tu?,* where it is poured over the sleeping couple when they are discovered in the morning. The cider that Anthyme offers the mourners is another such symbol, for it is described as full of "the marvelous forces of the earth."

Several of Carrier's characters prefer life as it is now, with all its suffering and misery, to a hypothetical afterlife. The women usually cling to the religion of death, but the men often reject this religion, question the justice of God and even deny His existence. One of the men at the wake says:

"It's not my boy who's in the coffin, but I wonder: if there is a God, why does he insist on sending back children in those boxes?" Anthyme tends to agree and is far less willing than his wife to see the hand of God in events. After Esmalda leaves, Floralie exclaims: "She's a saint!," but Anthyme's only comment is: "Let's close that window quick!" He and the other men display their rejection of God in the litanies of blasphemy which pour from their lips. It is taken as a sign that a boy has become a man when he blasphemes. Hence, when Philibert begins to swear, his father tells him: "Now you're a man. You can speak like a man."

But blasphemy is not total rejection of God, for, to take His name in vain implies belief in His existence. Anthyme's revolt is more fundamental than this, and its origin is seen in *Floralie, où es-tu?* During his night of wandering in the forest, Anthyme learns to overcome his religious nightmares and to cling to the earth—a decision symbolized by his act of pulling up a handful of grass to suck, and finding that "In his mouth, it was fresh and good." He questions the justice of God, wondering why he, who has always tried to observe God's laws, should be punished. Then he climbs a tree and issues a challenge: "God, I say You're not just. . . . If You think I'm lying, come down and get me: we'll settle this business like men." When there is no answer, Anthyme realizes that God is powerless against him. "I've understood Your game," he says. "You're afraid of a man who's not afraid of You." When Anthyme walks off after this discovery, "his feet are set down solidly and without hesitation."

Philibert comes to the same conclusions as Anthyme. He says: "One day I realized there was no more a God in Heaven than electric rattlesnakes in Quebec." This means that only life here and now counts, or as Philibert says: "God doesn't exist, but *I* exist." Dorval too rejects God, for he believes that man needs no God to be happy; he merely has to fulfil his basic needs. "If a man sleeps well, eats well, and if his intestines want to empty themselves at least once a day, I proclaim him a happy man." He argues that man must keep his feet firmly on the ground and avoid seeking happiness in Heaven. Relating how, during the war, he parachuted into France, he describes his terror at no longer having his feet on solid ground. "I love the Earth," he explains. "I was made with earth and, when I'm unmade, I'll become earth again." The lawyer in *Le Jardin des délices* loves the earth so much that he is determined to come back to it after his death. What he and the villagers who seek gold on their land dimly realize is that they must look earthwards for the only real wealth. There may not literally be gold in the earth, but the earth itself is the only gold necessary.

Characters like these learn the lesson which Carrier describes in **"Les Médailles flottent-elles sur la mer?"** Here he tells how, when he was a child, he wore dozens of holy medals around his neck. One day, he realized that they were too heavy, so he threw them away. His characters learn that all prophets are charlatans, like Néron the quack doctor in *Floralie, où es-tu?*; that all prophets lie, like J. J. Bourdage with his promises of gold. They discover, like Carrier himself in **"Le jour où je devins un apostat,"** that the "miracles" of religion are just fables.

Besides this conscious rejection of religion, there is also, however, an instinctive rejection of death. Carrier's characters react to death by expressing their sexual urges. As Dorval puts it: "Wanting to make love is a sign of life: the dead don't have that kind of urge." Even Philibert longs for love, and his last thoughts before he dies are of the beautiful bank clerk. Amidst death and destruction, people go on asserting their will to live through sex. In the ruins of the demolished buildings, Dorval discovers two adolescents making love, and they tell him: "We're taking advantage of life before it makes us too unhappy." It is worth noting that even Dorval's communism is inspired by his love for a girl communist whom he met in the French Resistance.

In *Le Jardin des délices,* the two men who dig up the lawyer's grave keep their fears at bay by thinking of the pictures of naked women they have seen on calendars. When Henri and his wife in *La Guerre, Yes Sir!* see Corriveau's coffin taken past their house, their reaction is to go to bed and make love. As Molly and Bérubé make love in the room above the coffin, "It was death which they violently stabbed." Molly, in fact, incarnates sex and life, and her presence at the wake counteracts Esmalda's. The two women stand in direct contrast: Esmalda with her talk of death, her decayed teeth and her insistence on letting the cold into the room; Molly with her voluptuous body, her warmth and her ability to console. Miss Catéchime, the catechism teacher in *Le Jardin des délices,* plays a role similar to Molly's, for she reveals the pleasures of sex to the priest. Even the old woman who lives in one of Dorval's apartments discovers sex and becomes the most popular worker in Mignonne Fleury's brothel.

The role of sex in Carrier's fiction is conveyed humorously in *Le Jardin des délices* in the incident of the "zizis japonais"—tiny wax models of penises which suddenly appear in the village. The places where they are found are particularly important. Often they appear in the snow, which is symbolic of death. One of them is found in the Church tabernacle, the very center of the institution from which emanates the religion of death. The first one is seen by Miss Catéchime, whose task as catechism teacher, we are told, is to reveal the secrets of life. (Something she does very proficiently for the priest.) We finally learn that these wax models were made by a teacher who molded them on his pupils' naked bodies. Of course, the priest interprets them as a plague sent by God to punish the villagers.

This incident is important because of its humor, for humor is another way used by both Carrier and his characters to face death. The rich vein of grotesque comedy running through Carrier's work lifts it above the gloom into which it would otherwise sink. His characters transcend the absurd cruelty of death by laughing at it and making it more bearable. The two men who dig up the lawyer's body, for example, keep their spirits up and their fears at bay by joking about the man and his death. During the wake in *La Guerre, Yes Sir!* the mourners show the same sense of humor in the presence of death.

As well as affirming their will to live as individuals, the characters in Carrier's novels have the will to survive as a group. They live in a harsh land and a cruel climate, but they struggle against them and endure. "We are not the race of those who give up," says the lawyer [in *Le Jardin des délices*]. One character tells his fellow villagers that they should leave the land and seek an easier life, but another replies: "You can calmly say that as you smoke, but we never do it." Against all odds, against a hostile environment and against a stronger culture, French-Canadians have survived and have maintained their own language and culture. In *Il n'y a pas de pays sans grand-père,* the old man's grandson reads him a passage from Louis Hémon's *Maria Chapdelaine* which expresses this will to survive: "We came here three hundred years ago and we stayed. . . . We have drawn a map of the new continent, from the Gaspé to Montreal, from Saint-Jean-d'Iberville to the Ungava, saying: here everything we have brought with us, our religion, our language, our virtues and even our weaknesses become sacred, untouchable things, which must remain to the end."

When they remember this past, this history of endurance, Vieux-Thomas and his grandson achieve a kind of victory over death by bringing the past alive. Carrier himself obviously loves Quebec and cherishes memories of his childhood there. *Les Enfants du bonhomme dans la lune* is essentially an attempt to revive that childhood and memories of the Quebec which formed him. For a culture to survive, it is important that the past not be forgotten, and the older characters in Carrier's works often possess a knowledge gleaned from the past which the younger ones lack. In **"Le Secret perdu dans l'eau"** Carrier tells how his father once taught him the art of water divining, but he soon forgot it. Later, as an adult, he met an old man who talked of his father's skill as a water diviner, and Carrier was filled with sadness at having forgotten the art. "Along the roads I had taken since the village of my childhood, I had forgotten somewhere my father's knowledge," he says.

Worse even than such forgetfulness is the defilement of the past experienced by Philibert's grandparents. Philibert loves this old couple, their stories of the past and the house which symbolizes their past. But, when the couple sell their house to provide their children with an inheritance, the children turn it into a pigsty and force them to live with the pigs. Vieux-Thomas in *Il n'y a pas de pays sans grand-père* is treated with similar disrespect: he is confined to his rocking chair by his daughter-in-law, has his pipe and hunting knife taken from him and is continually mocked by the children of the house. He, in turn, despises the young and equates them with death and weakness. He views with horror the weapons of destruction and the wars which he sees every day on the television. People now, he believes, are obsessed with death, and are consequently unable to create. He dreams of his own youth when he built his home and his furniture. The young today are incapable of this, and they are not even interested in producing children. "When people don't make children any more, it's because people don't want to live any more," he says. Their animals are no better, for they have to be artificially inseminated with semen bought from the Government. "Soon," he concludes, "people, instead of making their own dung, will prefer to buy it in plastic bags."

The one exception to Vieux-Thomas's scorn is his grandson, Jean-Thomas. The latter's willingness to listen to Vieux-Thomas makes the old man rethink his past and listen to the younger man. As Jean-Thomas reads to him about Quebec's history, Vieux-Thomas remembers injustices he has suffered at the hands of the English. When his grandson is arrested, the old man begins to question why the Queen should come to Quebec. He puts aside his old fears, and, when he commandeers the bus, he rides through the English village which, at one time, he would never enter. But what is equally important is that Jean-Thomas learns from his grandfather and applies the old man's personal knowledge of the past to the present situation. Carrier writes: "Jean-Thomas needs the old men's remembrances. In Jean-Thomas's mouth, the old men's remembrances become the dreams of young men. His voice unites the past as it is told in old books with Vieux-Thomas's past; Jean-Thomas vows to make the future out of this past."

By talking of the past, Vieux-Thomas recaptures his youth. "Vieux-Thomas will tell the tale and, as usual, while he tells it, he will come alive again as if telling the tale of his youth brought back his youth." The telling of stories is a reaction against death and oblivion, and this is why the characters in **Le Jardin des délices** gather in the depth of winter to tell stories and to talk of the past. By doing so, they seem to hold the cold at bay. "In the midst of winter," Carrier writes, "words maintain the warmth of life. The breath of words tries to chase away the breath of the wind." While people remember the past it is not dead, just as Jean-Thomas is not abandoned in his prison as long as Vieux-Thomas thinks of him.

To write is to agree to play the great game of life, of love and of death where the soul is condemned to lose at the end of the game, and the novelist is he who never really accepts this role.

—Roch Carrier

In this process of resisting death by talking of the past, the listener is as important as the story-teller. Somebody must, like Jean-Thomas, listen to the old man's tales or they will be lost. Obviously, one way of bringing the past to the attention of others is to write it down, and this is exactly what Carrier does. In bringing before us these characters who incarnate the spirit of Quebec, he attempts to ensure his own survival and that of the French-Canadians of whom he writes. He makes them come alive, and he passes on to us the story of their indomitable spirit. He is doing the same as Louis Hémon, whom he quotes in **Il n'y a pas de pays sans grand-père.** He is doing what Jean-Thomas does: "As long as he hears himself speaking, he will not be dead. Words are not actual reality: thinking of a trout isn't holding it slippery and quivering in his hand, but words create a magic which revives dead things and brings to life what isn't yet alive. Words give life."

By writing of the past, Carrier can make Québécois aware of their heritage and help them prepare for the future. Talking of his decision to depict a certain Quebec of the past in *La Guerre, Yes Sir!*, he says: "My Québécois brothers, do not see in this a return to the past or an evasion of the present, see rather a will to go towards the future." He believes that, with his novels, he is assuming his role among many other Quebec writers who are preparing the future of their people. "By writing my novel," he says, "I take my place in a Quebec which has been dispossessed of its culture and which, little by little, is trying tenaciously to create a soul for itself."

It may be objected that Vieux-Thomas, with all his memories of the past, achieves nothing, since he is unable to liberate Jean-Thomas. This is true, but, at the end of the novel, although Vieux-Thomas and Jean-Thomas are both locked safely away, the reader remains. He has lived the lives of these two, and of the many characters in the other novels. He is the real listener who accepts Carrier's message and who realizes that, as individuals and as French-Canadians, Carrier's characters represent life in the midst of death. Nobody, having read these novels, can remain impervious to the message that men in general, and Québécois as a race, reject the forces of death. Man can never overcome death, but he will always go on resisting it, and novelists like Roch Carrier will celebrate this struggle. As Carrier himself says: "To write is to agree to play the great game of life, of love and of death where the soul is condemned to lose at the end of the game, and the novelist is he who never really accepts this role." (pp. 59-72)

> *David J. Bond, "The Forces of Life and Death in Roch Carrier's Fiction," in* Studies in Twentieth Century Literature, *Vol. 7, No. 1, Fall, 1982, pp. 59-76.*

Sherie Posesorski   (review date March 1985)

[*In the following review, Posesorski praises Carrier's psychological and realistic depiction of the protagonist of* Lady with Chains.]

Powerless and submissive in the face of arbitrary parental authority, children can accumulate enough ferocity to annihilate the oblivious parent. Staring with the intensity of a laser beam out of Roch Carrier's latest novel, *Lady With Chains,* is Virginie. Treated like a child all her life by her parents, the church, and her husband Victor, Virginie attains the responsibilities and stature of adulthood only in one relationship—with her son. When her husband inadvertently causes the death of the son, she withdraws into the autistic silence of her mind, her only arena of omnipotence. Her dreams and plans centre on one thought: retribution by murder.

In Virginie, Carrier has created a character of terrifying single-mindedness. He locks the reader inside Virginie's mind as the circle of her thoughts grows tighter and smaller until she reaches the vortex of the night when her child died. The tension and suspense created by sharing Virginie's obsessive thoughts is periodically relieved by the black comedy of her husband's garrulous monologues. Her burning stare and silence force Victor to fill in her blankness with endless nervous chatter filled with self-rationalizations and naïve plans for the future.

Lady With Chains is simultaneously a fable and a novel of acute psychological realism. In his poem "Meru," Yeats wrote, "Man's life is thought . . . Ravening, raging and uprooting that he may come / Into the desolation of reality." Carrier's book envelops and engages the reader as he journeys with Virginie to the core of her desolation.

> *Sherie Posesorski, in a review of "Lady with Chains," in* Quill and Quire, *Vol. 51, No. 3, March, 1985, p. 72.*

Michael Darling   (essay date Spring 1985)

[*In the essay below, Darling examines how Carrier's use of double voices and parallel plots in the short story "The Nun Who Returned to Ireland" contributes to the work's themes of innocence, experience, and cultural dissimilation.*]

Roch Carrier's **"The Nun Who Returned to Ireland" ("La Religieuse qui retourna en Irlande")** concerns a young French boy learning to read with an English accent. His school learning, signified by his newly-acquired English accent, is opposed to his absorbed knowledge, the speech he shares with his family and friends, and it is these conflicting codes of knowledge that initiate and sustain the discourse of the text. As Jonathan Culler observes [in his *The Pursuit of Signs: Semiotics, Literature, Deconstruction* (1981)], "it is the nature of codes to be always already in existence, to have lost origins." The codes we have absorbed are never recognized *as codes* until we have allowed them to be supplanted by others, until we have been required to unlearn them. It is the fate of the teacher in this story to demand the very process of unlearning, of cultural dissimilation which she herself has undergone in order to become a teacher. And it is the fate of the boy to repeat as an adult the painful awakening he has prompted in his teacher.

The text offers an enigma in its opening lines:

> After my first day of school I ran back to the house, holding out my reader. 'Mama, I learned how to read!' I announced.

We know that boys who have just learned to read are incapable of writing about it, and we therefore infer an older narrator, setting up a familiar antithesis: innocent I/experienced I, the doubling of narrative voice well-known to Canadian readers in the short stories of Clark Blaise, Margaret Laurence, and Alice Munro. And this doubled voice also announces a corresponding theme (innocence/experience) developed through an action or series of actions in which the young narrator takes part. That these actions constitute rites of passage in the life of the narrator is one of the expectations aroused in the mind of the reader by his identification of the generic tradition to which the story belongs. In the course of our analysis, we shall see whether the text does indeed fulfil these expectations.

That this is an important day to both the child and his parents is only mildly undercut by the father's little joke— " 'Pretty soon, son, you'll be able to do like me—read the newspaper upside down in your sleep!' " The image of the father snoring on the couch with a newspaper over his face does not suggest a social milieu in which reading is in itself a particularly valued activity. Furthermore, the rendering of the father's speech, his *parole,* reinforces our view of him as an unsophisticated, uneducated man (" 'Betôt, mon garçon, tu vas pouvoir faire comme moé, lire le journal à l'envers en dormant!' ").

Ignoring the jests of his father, the boy demands to be heard:

> And I read the sentence I'd learned in school that day, from Sister Brigitte. But instead of picking me up and lifting me in his arms, my father looked at my mother and my mother didn't come and kiss her little boy who'd learned to read so quickly.

Wherever the antithesis of young narrator/old narrator, innocence/experience, naiveté/sophistication is manifested, we may expect the presence of irony. Irony presupposes conflicting interpretations and thus conflicting codes for, as Robert Scholes points out [in *Semiotics and Interpretation* (1982)], "irony, of all figures, is the one that must always take us out of the text and into codes, contexts, and situations." When the narrator employs the phrase "her little boy who'd learned to read so quickly," referring to himself in the third person, we apprehend directly what we had already inferred from the opening sentence: that is, the separation of actor and narrator, of the boy he was and the adult he has become, and as the "little boy who'd learned to read so quickly," he is mocked by his adult self. The excitement of learning is undermined, for what the boy has learned is perceived by his parents as error. Worse, what he has learned has involved the unlearning of his cultural code, the learning that is osmotic, absorbed from his milieu. His newly-acquired accent is identifiably alien:

> 'You're reading with an English accent!' my mother exclaimed.
>
> 'I'm reading the way Sister Brigitte taught me.'
>
> 'Don't tell me he's learning his own mother tongue in English,' my father protested.

The learning process that the reader has expected from his identification of the generic tradition of the story is thus ironically inverted. To paraphrase the father, the boy has learned to read French in English, and this learning can only divide him from his parents, his friends, and his village. Nevertheless, there is something comically extreme in the father's choice of words (" 'Dis-moé pas qu'i' va apprendre sa langue maternelle en anglais' ") that undercuts the seriousness of the situation, just as his previous remark about reading the newspaper upside down in his sleep served to undermine the importance of learning to read in his culture.

The boy has his own explanation of his teacher's strange accent:

> I had noticed that Sister Brigitte didn't speak the way we did, but that was quite natural because we all knew that nuns don't do anything the way other people do. . . .

The phrase "we all knew" ("nous le savions") implies its opposite. What we all know (certainly what children know) about any particular group of people is usually a stereotype or a myth, never more than partially true. Though nuns may not dress like everybody else, may not get married nor have children, and may live in seclusion ("toujours cachées"), no other differences need apply. The ironic humour of the boy's assertion only reinforces his naiveté, and we feel behind this admission the less than covert manipulation of the adult narrator indulging himself in self-mockery. And as the ironic statements of the father revealed his cultural code, here the boy's statement links him to his father in its disclosure of a shared code.

After all, the boy has ample reason not to feel guilty about his adoption of an English accent:

> But as far as knowing whether Sister Brigitte had an English accent, how could I? I'd never heard a single word of English.

The boy's failure to recognize English is an indicator of the isolation of the family from the cosmopolitan world, an isolation emphasized in the paragraph that follows:

> Over the next few days I learned that she hadn't been born in our village; it seemed very strange that someone could live in the village without being born there, because everyone else in the village had been born in the village.

To be a villager then is to be born one and to remain one. The nun will always be an outsider because she was born elsewhere. The importance of birthplace as a qualification for citizenship, for belonging to the community, is confirmed with the mention of Monsieur Cassidy, the undertaker, who is Irish like Sister Brigitte but who has been born in the village and is therefore accepted by the community. The "whispers" ("chuchotements") of the parents on the subject of Sister Brigitte suggest all those unpleasant connotations of the small, isolated, inward-looking community: narrow-mindedness, prejudice, distrust of strangers. This is the dark side of the cultural isolation or deprivation we have identified with the father. It is appropriate then that the boy, desiring knowledge, should turn to the more sympathetic mother:

> 'Where's Ireland?' I asked my mother.
>
> 'It's a very small, very green little country in the ocean, far, far away.'

In other words, Ireland is very like the community of which she herself is a member: small and isolated, with the implication that distance reinforces alienation and difference. To be Irish then is strangely to be something like French-Canadian, though the difference between the two is as great as the distance that separates their two worlds, the difference of language.

Why does the boy wish to learn from Sister Brigitte, since to learn from her is to forget his own osmotic knowledge? "I was so impatient to read the books my uncles brought back from their far-off colleges." Not surprisingly, the boy equates the strangeness of his teacher's accent with the exotic splendour of his uncles' books, brought from far-away places. The "far-off colleges" ("des collèges lointains") signify not only knowledge but also sophistication, and yet apparently nothing is lost in the gaining of such knowledge for it is not necessary for the boy to go away, to leave the safety of home. It is enough that the family has been represented in strange places by the uncles, who have safely confined the threat of alien sophistication to the printed page. But we know already that something *is* lost, that the learning of the alien code involves the unlearning of the native one. And the lessening of the native influence is seen in a corresponding lessening of the authority of the home. The boy turns to his teacher with the same question he has posed to his mother:

> 'Sister Brigitte, where's Ireland?'

Why was the mother's answer unsatisfactory? Did the boy suspect that her answer was wrong or merely in need of supplementation? The repetition of the question forces us to compare the two responses. Here is the nun's:

> 'Ireland is the country where my parents were born, and my grandparents and my great-grandparents. And I was born in Ireland too. I was a little girl in Ireland. When I was a child like you I lived in Ireland. We had horses and sheep.'

Is this speech to be representative of the exotic alien sophistication that the boy desires? In style it is childlike, tautological, more primitive than sophisticated in its incantatory repetition. In this initial speech of the nun we are suddenly brought home to the truth of the mother's answer and our identification of village with Ireland. In a sense, the mother, though she has failed to satisfy the boy's curiosity, has given a truer answer than the Irish woman has, for the nun does not attempt to describe *where* Ireland is, but rather *what* it is to *her*. Her mentality is not cosmopolitan at all, and in its unworldliness suggests kinship with the villagers who are so suspicious of her.

When the teacher goes on to say that " 'the Lord asked me to become his servant,' " the boy is especially puzzled:

> 'What does that mean?'
>
> 'The Lord asked me if I wanted to become a nun. I said yes. So then I left my family and I forgot Ireland and my village.'
>
> 'Forgot your village?'
>
> I could see in her eyes that she didn't want to answer my question.

In the cultural code that we have identified with the boy and his milieu, it is clear that the sense of belonging to the place one is born in is the key to identity. It is equally clear that the nun herself has at one time adhered to this same code. But she has transgressed this code to follow another. In order to learn Christian obedience and self-denial she has had to unlearn the same fidelity to home, culture, language, family, and place that characterizes the village she lives in. She is doubly exiled then, having voluntarily abandoned one community never to be accepted by the other. " 'Forgot your village?' " It is not necessary to add " 'How could you?' " The nun avoids this question as she avoided the question about Ireland because she knows that a reaffirmation of her loyalty to Ireland would be a denial of her Christian faith. How can these separate codes be reconciled?

The irony of the nun's situation is that in doing her duty to God she must not only reject her own personal ties to home and family but must also force her pupils to do the same. And the irony is deepened by the fact that it is her own pupil who reminds her of this.

The boy relentlessly pursues his inquiry:

> Sister Brigitte's face, surrounded by her starched coif, had no age; I learned that she was old, very old, because she had been a teacher to grandparents.
>
> 'Have you ever gone back to Ireland?'
>
> 'God didn't want to send me back.'
>
> 'You must miss your country.'
>
> 'God asked me to teach little children to read and write so every child could read the great book of life.'

The nun's attempts to deflect the boy's questions have the quality of responses learned by rote. Our expectations of the fulfillment of the innocence/experience genre are increasingly frustrated by the nun's failure to assume the teaching role we have assigned to her. Now we see the nun playing the role in which we have previously cast the young narrator—the innocent and unquestioning student—a role that the boy has already begun to abandon in his quest for the source and meaning of Ireland.

His knowledge of the nun's age leads the boy to his final question:

> 'Sister Brigitte, you're older than our grandparents! Will you go back to Ireland before you die?'
>
> The old nun must have known from my expression that death was so remote for me I could speak of it quite innocently, as I would speak of the grass or the sky. She said simply:
>
> 'Let's go on with our reading. School children in Ireland aren't as disorderly as you.'

The title of the story anticipates the boy's question. The title lies behind and beyond the conflicting codes, promising a resolution that the nun's answer would seem merely to temporarily postpone: " 'Let's go on with our reading.' " But re-reading the story with the ending in mind we can see a far more sinister implication in this indirect reply. We can also see the planting of the seed that will produce a possible resolution of the enigma posed by the boy, the unanswered question: " 'Where's Ireland?' "

In the narrator's comment on death we hear the voice of his mature self, the self that is now conscious of its mortality, and therefore able to reflect ironically on his youthful

The cover of the English-language version of Carrier's Les enfants du bonhomme dans la lune.

naiveté. But the nun's response is also interpreted for us by the mature narrator's choice of words: "The old nun *must have known* from my expression that death was so remote for me . . . " ("La vieille religieuse *dut comprendre* dans mon regard que la mort était pour moi si lointaine . . . "). From his experienced point of view he allows us to understand what he himself never realized at the time—that Sister Brigitte knows her death is imminent. As Ireland is "loin, loin" for the mother, and the colleges attended by the uncles are "lointains," so for the boy death is "lointaine." But for the nun, whom we know is old—some of her former pupils are now grandparents—death cannot be far away. And though she has made a conscious choice to leave her home, she has not succeeded in forgetting it; she has merely allowed her religious code to suppress her cultural code.

It is this suppressed code that re-emerges with a vengeance as her end approaches:

> All that autumn we applied ourselves to our reading; by December we could read the brief texts Sister Brigitte wrote on the blackboard herself, in a pious script we tried awkwardly to imitate; in every text the word Ireland always ap-peared. It was by writing the word Ireland that I learned to form a capital I.

Imitation is again the basis of the learning process, but what is being imitated now is not merely an aberration in form (the wrong accent) but a distortion of content (Ireland as subject). The "pious script" ("une calligraphie pieuse") that the class attempts to imitate might properly be associated with the nun's position as a religious teacher, but we should not ignore the suggested cross-linkage of piety with or towards Irishness. Since the conflicting demands of the nun's life are already manifested in the idea of teaching Irishness—an almost oxymoronic concept involving the juxtaposition of Christian duty and that which Christian duty has supplanted—it is not surprising to find that the formal aspect of the nun's behaviour (her piety) can be transferred from one code to the other. But in paying heed to both competing codes at the same time, the nun is threatened with the loss of the clear Christian path of her life. For the boy, to gain the skills of reading and writing involves a loss of cultural memory; for the nun, a corresponding regaining of cultural memory involves a loss of conscious memory. The boy, however, has a simpler explanation:

From our parents' whispers we learned that Sister Brigitte had lost her memory. We weren't surprised. We knew that old people always lose their memories and Sister Brigitte was an old person because she had been a teacher to grandparents.

The same kind of clichéd assertion made about Sister Brigitte as *nun* is here applied to her as *old person:* the boy's osmotic learning always leads to *a priori* reasoning. There can be no other explanation than age for the loss of memory. That this is possibly true in no way subtracts from the ironic implications of the statement. All unquestioned assertions of the innocent narrator are subject to ironic exposure. In this, at least, the text fulfills the expectations it arouses.

The story ends with the apparent death of Sister Brigitte, a death which is also, in some ways, a "homecoming":

> Late in January, the nuns in the convent discovered that Sister Brigitte had left her room. They looked everywhere for her, in all the rooms and all the classrooms. Outside, a storm was blowing gusts of snow and wind; you couldn't see Heaven or earth, as they said. Sister Brigitte, who had spent the last few weeks in her bed, had fled into the storm. Some men from the village spotted her black form in the blizzard: beneath her vast mantle she was barefoot. When the men asked her where she was going, Sister Brigitte replied in English that she was going home, to Ireland.

The storm is a symbol of the confusion in the nun's mind. The narrator's colloquialism ("comme l'on disait, on ne voyait ni ciel ni terre") is, like the other ideas and sayings prompted by his cultural code, a true remark couched in a hyperbolic platitude: Sister Brigitte, at least, cannot see Heaven or earth because she knows not whether to heed the code of Heaven or the code of earth or home. In seeking home, she is destroyed by an act of God, perhaps a suitable punishment for having fled the convent. Her "black form" seen against the white blizzard ("la poudrerie") is an appropriate symbolic antithesis, but less suggestive than the contrast of her bare feet with her "vast mantle." To go barefoot in the snow has traditional religious connotations of self-denial, even masochistically saint-like humility, but bare feet and black clothing are also signs of the corpse prepared for burial, the body on its last earthly journey, the journey that immediately precedes the soul's homecoming.

Does the nun return to Ireland? The title implies that she did ("retourna"—past definite); the last sentence suggests only that she was making the attempt ("elle s'en retournait chez elle, en Irlande.") Common sense dictates that she could never have made it, being old, sick, and barefoot in the storm.

Now one of the goals of any interpretation is the resolution of whatever enigmas are posed by the hermeneutic code of the text. In fact, we expect the text itself to provide answers to the questions it raises. But this text has not always justified the expectations we have had of it. We expected the boy to *learn* something, for why else would the mature narrator have told the story? What has he learnt?

We expected the nun to return to Ireland, for the title informed us that she did. Has she returned to Ireland? We might also have expected an answer to the reiterated question, "Where's Ireland?"

Let us examine some possible answers to these interlocking questions. Ireland is a sign both of foreignness and of home, just as the village is. Therefore to ask "Where's Ireland?" is to ask "Where's home?" or "Where is the source of your identity?" But our exploration of the code of home has revealed a web of connotations: home is language, family, superstition, custom, all part of the cultural code absorbed from birth. This code can be suppressed—indeed, all knowledge acquired in school suppresses it—but it can never be destroyed. In the story, the initial action that raises the question of difference is the conflict of English and French pronunciation. The nun has suppressed her language, but she has not been able to assimilate the correct pronunciation of her adopted tongue. Therefore, when she abandons the imposed code of Christian duty to start on her journey home, she begins, once again, to speak in English, her native tongue. This is the triumph of osmotic knowledge over rote learning. In a sense, to speak English is already to be back in Ireland, to be home, and therefore the tense of the verb in the title is finally justifiable. But is this what the narrator learns? That we carry our home with us wherever we go, embodied in the cultural code we have assimilated from birth? Or is it a darker truth that he learns: "You can't go home again"?

To accept one conclusion—that the nun "goes home" in spirit—is also to acknowledge its corollary—that she does not go home in body. Indeed, one might go further and suggest that only by dying can she "go home": the gain is offset by the greatest loss of all. Another factor intrudes at this point: the nun has sacrificed her calling, has abnegated her sworn duty, to make her journey home. Of what use is it to gain the world and lose one's soul in the process? There are no clear choices, no gains without losses. Is this the lesson the narrator has learned? Is this the theme of the story?

Before answering these questions, we might consider another story from the same collection that throws some light on the present text. In *The Hockey Sweater and Other Stories,* the voice is consistently that of the doubled narrator, simultaneously child and adult, except in the last story, **"A Secret Lost in the Water,"** in which an event of the recent past (when the narrator is an adult) is compared to an event of the distant past (when he was a boy). It is in this story that the narrator is most closely identified with Carrier himself:

> Years passed; I went to other schools, saw other countries, I had children, I wrote some books and my poor father is lying in the earth where so many times he had found fresh water.
>
> One day someone began to make a film about my village and its inhabitants, from whom I've stolen so many of the stories that I tell.

This statement admits the autobiographical while simultaneously denying it, saying in effect, yes, this is the village where I was born, the father described was my father, and the little boy was me, but the stories were not stories about me—they have been appropriated from others and are not to be taken as a record of my life. This story, however, for all its difference from the other stories in the collection, is also the summation of the other narratives, the thread that weaves the disparate pieces of cloth into a recognizable whole. In **"A Secret Lost in the Water,"** we are told that, as a boy, the narrator could, like his father, find water by divination. But, as an adult, he has lost the power to do so. Here is the way the story, and the collection, ends:

> The alder stayed motionless in my hands and the water beneath the earth refused to sing.
>
> Somewhere along the roads I'd taken since the village of my childhood I had forgotten my father's knowledge.
>
> 'Don't feel sorry,' said the man, thinking no doubt of his farm and his childhood; 'nowadays fathers can't pass on anything to the next generation.'
>
> And he took the alder branch from my hands.

The emphasis in the text is on loss, not gain: maturity, education, sophistication are poor replacements for magic and belief. The old man cannot hand anything down to the young; the alder branch is withheld. But even as the text mourns this loss, it also celebrates the worth of what has been lost, in effect immortalizing it. This is the paradigm that we have learned to recognize in the immortalizing convention of the Elizabethan love sonnet, and this is the paradox that informs all stories of innocence and experience, not least the story with which we began. What does the story of innocence and experience suggest? That to gain experience (which is valuable because it is learning) is to lose innocence (which is valuable because it is uncorrupted). But as long as the story can be told, and told in the doubled narrative voice, that innocence is never lost, that experience is not yet gained. To go home to innocence is to abandon adulthood, but wanting to go home is in itself an assertion of adulthood, of experience, since no innocent ever wants to remain in that state. This is the double bind of the doubled narrator, whose story denies what his narration of it would affirm—that his present self co-exists with the child he was. The value of innocence is never perceived until it is gone, is never present until it is absent. The code goes unrecognized until it has been replaced by another. The real value of experience, the replacement code, the gain, the discovery of selfhood, is to remind us of what has been suppressed, lost, undiscovered. But such contrary states of the human psyche cannot co-exist. Thus the paradox of the nun who returned to Ireland can now be reformulated: for her to return home, to innocence, and to unlearn the learned, is to be what she is not, to cease to be. This is the real meaning of "you can't go home again."

We can now see the significance of the author's formulation of his theme in the context of reading. Self-awareness is a recognition not only of one's difference from others but also of one's difference from the self/selves one has

abandoned. For the narrator of **"The Nun Who Returned to Ireland,"** this self-awareness begins with reading. For the reader of the story, awareness begins in the same way. It is in this sense that the story is "already read," for we cannot read it without becoming aware that it is our story too. (pp. 24-33)

> Michael Darling, "Reading Carrier's 'The Nun Who Returned to Ireland'," in Canadian Literature, No. 104, Spring, 1985, pp. 24-33.

Philip Stratford on Carrier's *La trilogie de l'âge sombre*:

It is not so much plot or character that are memorable in Carrier's [*La trilogie de l'âge sombre*] as it is a series of original, kaleidoscopic images, made virtually indelible by their explosive violence, shot through with grim humor, and set against the little, downtrodden man's faith, against all odds, that life should be beautiful and that "the good Lord" must have some hidden plan for his long-suffering, doggedly cheerful creatures.

> *Philip Stratford, in* Dictionary of Literary Biography, *Vol. 53, Gale Research Company, 1986.*

Mark Abley   (essay date October 1987)

[*Abley is an English-born editor, essayist, poet, and travel writer. In the following essay, he discusses Carrier's life and career and the significance of* Heartbreaks along the Road, *which he claims is Carrier's masterpiece.*]

As a boy in the 1940s, looking out of his bedroom window in the remote village of Sainte-Justine-de-Dorchester, Roch Carrier could see a forest stretching through the Beauce region of southeastern Quebec, broken only by a road. Leaning from the window, he could watch his father going down the road to pursue his career as a travelling salesman. At one house he might sell a headache medicine; at the next, a floor cleaner. He'd buy a cow at a little farm; he'd trade it at the next for a horse. And when he returned from his travels, he would tell the villagers all that he'd seen of the world. "My father was very important in my education," Carrier says, "because he was a storyteller. That made him a hero." One of his *father's* heroes was Maurice Duplessis, the premier of Quebec for nearly twenty years. Whenever an election approached, the local agents of Duplessis's party, the Union Nationale, would create make-work projects in return for votes. In Carrier's memory, his father never received one of these jobs; "for him, the Union Nationale was a kind of metaphysical experience. In his mind Duplessis was like Maurice Richard—a French Canadian who could stand up to *les anglais*." There were practical reasons too why Carrier's father revered the premier. For one thing, Duplessis brought electricity to the local farmers. For another, he built roads that didn't turn into quagmires each spring.

Roch Carrier was the only one of the thirty children in his class who went to college. Already he had the impulse to write. One day he left the Collège Saint-Louis in Edmundston, New Brunswick, and hitchhiked down the road to Montreal to sell his poems on the city streets. Later he returned to Montreal as a university student. Only then did he arrive at an understanding of the corruption and petty tyranny of Maurice Duplessis's regime. Only then did he learn that anybody hauling gravel to build a road in the province of Quebec might have to pay fifteen per cent of his fee to the "right" party—the Union Nationale.

Carrier's own road led him to become a storyteller, playwright, teacher, theatre administrator, and one of the finest novelists in Quebec. He's still best known for his first novel, *La Guerre, Yes Sir!,* a book he wrote in white heat in a single week. Set in rural Quebec during the Second World War, *La Guerre, Yes Sir!* reduced the world to the size of a village: "To imaginations steeped in pork fat and cider, the flames of hell were scarcely bigger than the candleflames on Corriveau's coffin." Eight novels later, in his 1984 book *De l'amour dans la ferraille*—newly translated by Sheila Fischman as *Heartbreaks Along the Road*—Carrier expanded his vision so that a single village seems as big as the world.

The novel centres on the building of a road during a summer-long election campaign. Le Chef—who represents Maurice Duplessis—tells his compliant ministers that "to harvest votes, you must sow roads. You're going to scatter strips of road all across this province." In a remote Beauce village that Carrier calls Saint-Toussaint-des-Saints (literally, St. All Saints of the Saints), the priest and mayor are delighted to collaborate with the Right Party. They know that such collaboration will get them a new road. The head of construction is an Italian immigrant, Nino Verrochio, who built important highways across the province until he made the error of donating a small sum to the opposition as well as the Right Party. Only the intervention of his wife, who submits to the sexual desires of the Minister of Roads and Bridges, prevents Verrochio's total ruin and allows him to build the little road near Saint-Toussaint-des-Saints.

At 529 pages *Heartbreaks Along the Road* is Carrier's longest and most ambitious novel. What unifies its farrago of incident and character is the recurrent image of a road. There are the physical roads that lead to Quebec City or the wilderness or the United States. There are the spiritual roads to God, or death, or rebirth. There are the psychological roads that lead to joy or despair. There is, above all, the great road to nowhere that the Right Party is building for Quebec. In the novel's most astonishing chapter, "What Is Life But a Procession?", the entire population of the region gathers for a parade to bless the new road and to thank God for the miracle He performed in healing a brain-damaged child called Opportun. When the child promptly drowns in a vat of boiling oil—the oil was being used to cook French fries—the Local Riding Minister names the road Chemin Opportun. It is a monument, indeed, to opportunism.

Opportun's fate is typical of the lavish torments Carrier devises for his characters. Though he tells most of the tales with a light touch, *Heartbreaks Along the Road* is packed full of suicide, murder, rape, incest, and accidental death.

One of the few people to escape this Gothic devastation is a young poet called Jeannot Tremblay, who is picked up by a beautiful woman, driven to the sea, and initiated into the mysteries of love. Jeannot writes to a friend: "The sea has no direction, it does not follow a path. . . . The sea is made of roads that erase one another." But the friend is deeply implicated in the Right Party's corruption, and within a few pages is dead.

The Right Party rules the province partly through its complicity with the people, its cynical understanding of their insecurities and dreams. In a despairing manifesto, "J'Accuse!", a journalist called Sautereau (literally, Leapwater) charges the government with "blackmail, abduction, cooking the books, lying, favoritism, threats, slander, influence-peddling and bargaining in human flesh." Then he kills himself by jumping off a bridge into the St. Lawrence. Le Chef reads "J'Accuse!" and thinks: "If you knew some other way to govern, Sautereau, why didn't you tell me before you jumped?" The insidious power of such corruption, Carrier implies, lies in its normality—the way people come to accept as right and proper an intolerable state of affairs.

It is, furthermore, a state of affairs explained and justified by wordsmiths: the politicians, the conniving journalists, the priests. When the *curé* in Saint-Toussaint-des-Saints instructs his parishioners to follow both "the path of God and the road of the Right Party," Carrier tells us that "his words sounded like a divine command." His novel makes abundant use of speeches, monologues, newspaper articles, a sermon, a long poem, and other forms of heightened discourse. The effect is to suggest that the Right Party has bought Quebec's soul by appropriating its language.

In many ways *Heartbreaks Along the Road* sums up Roch Carrier's fiction, developing themes and plot ideas that were only hinted at in earlier novels. The fantastic action in *Floralie, Where Are You?* took place on or beside a road carved through the wilderness; *The Garden of Delights* featured a fatal religious miracle; *Is It the Sun, Philibert?* contained a bridge, built by the government, "in a flat pasture where there was neither a river nor a stream. There was no road leading to the bridge; there wasn't even a road to the pasture." In the new novel the sense of futility is even greater. In its final chapter the Local Riding Minister tells the assembled villagers: "Not only has the Right Party built you a new road, now it's going to take it apart. . . . Thanks to the Right Party and its Chef, workers will be able to work on the deconstruction of the new road."

Carrier is a sly and witty writer. Professional critics will interpret this "deconstruction" as a reference to the school of literary criticism founded by the French theorist Jacques Derrida. Carrier's particular skill as a novelist, perhaps, is the way his literary sophistication buttresses a confident intimacy with ancient traditions of storytelling. Like the Acadian novelist Antonine Maillet, he's the product of an oral culture in which people had to create their own entertainment.

"In Sainte-Justine," he admits, "we were living as though in the Middle Ages." For an aspiring writer, this was not necessarily a handicap. The medieval tone of "What Is Life But a Procession?" arises naturally from the material, but it also emerges from Carrier's knowledge of medieval literature; he is perhaps the only novelist in Canada, in either language, who shows the influence of Chaucer's *Canterbury Tales.*

The two great influences on Carrier, however, are French: Rabelais and Voltaire. In the early 1960s, when he was studying for his doctorate in Paris, Carrier went to a class on Rabelais, the great storyteller of sixteenth-century France—"and I discovered I was the only one there who could understand his language. It was the language of my grandmother, even my mother. That link just wasn't there for the French students." Carrier's own style combines the classical poise of Voltaire with the burly gusto of Rabelais; he stylizes and heightens the speech of rural Quebec. By contrast, he shows little interest in working with the urban *joual* used by such Quebec writers as Michel Tremblay and Gérald Godin. "Both Rabelais and Voltaire were revolutionaries," Carrier observes. "Voltaire wanted to transform a sick society, and Rabelais was a doctor who tried to cure his patients by laughter."

But surely Carrier isn't a revolutionary? "A laugh," he says, "is always revolutionary."

In all probability, *Heartbreaks Along the Road* is Carrier's best novel and one of the most important Canadian books of our time. Despite its unevenness and its not entirely justified length, it evokes comparison with such modern classics as Salman Rushdie's *Midnight's Children* and Gabriel García Márquez's *One Hundred Years of Solitude,* novels that transform and illuminate a fragment of the visible world with the grace and force of myth. Just as the fiction of Márquez made a Colombian backwater magically real to readers everywhere, Carrier's novels have exaggerated, distilled, and ultimately defined the rural Quebec of the past. Like almost all writers in Quebec, he needs a regular job to survive, and the writing of *Heartbreaks Along the Road*—in moments snatched during the weekends and vacations of his teaching job at the Collège Militaire Royal de Saint-Jean—took him four years. It exhausted him; its reception by literary critics in Quebec profoundly disappointed him.

Carrier's reputation within Quebec has rarely been commensurate with his renown in English Canada; he may be the only Quebec writer for whom this has ever been true. Some of his books, it's true, have been praised at home—his fellow novelist André Major described *No Country Without Grandfathers* as "a disturbing and magnificently written novel that bears witness to a literary maturity we badly need"—but none of them has even made it as far as the short list for the governor general's award. Unlike many of his fellow writers, Carrier never campaigned for Quebec independence and he has never gone out of his way to flatter critics. *Heartbreaks Along the Road* received only a few warm reviews when it first appeared in French. "It's not a book that gives a good P.R. image," Carrier admits. "It looks back to the past." The power of Parisian attitudes and prejudices in Quebec's critical circles may also help to account for the novel's relative neglect. As the author coolly observes, "A novel like this one

has never been written in France, so some of the critics felt it couldn't be very interesting."

Carrier is normally a prolific author, but in the three and a half years since he completed *Heartbreaks Along the Road* he has written no novels or plays. He has, however, produced a pair of brief travel books (about Australia and Jordan) as well as some articles and short stories. On a recent trip to Copenhagen he was wryly amused to discover that many Danish children learn English by reading Sheila Fischman's rugged, loving translations of his work. For three years he has served as the chairman of Montreal's annual Salon du Livre, and he has contemplated entering federal politics. Worthy activities, to be sure, but not quite what one expects from a major novelist at the height of his powers. Carrier is now fifty, and it seems clear that with *Heartbreaks Along the Road* he wrote himself dry. "But," he insists with a smile, "I haven't finished my career as a novelist!"

The jaunty defiance of that remark is typical of the man. "Perhaps I'm a naive optimist," he adds. "But when the good God created the world, He was a naive optimist too." For all the bitterness and anger in *Heartbreaks Along the Road,* Carrier still conveys an affection for his battered characters and a joy in their ravaged lives. Many artists and writers in the province remain dubious about the future of their culture, yet Carrier finds reasons for hope.

Earlier this year, he spoke at a French-language school in Montreal containing children of fifty-four nationalities. "That's Quebec's future," he says, "and I find it marvellous—a metaphor for the world's future." The paths of lines below his eyes uncrease when he tells a story. "None of those fifty-four nationalities felt despised or excluded. You know, maybe one day I'll write the opposite of *Two Solitudes.* I'd call it 'No Solitudes.'" (pp. 59-62)

> Mark Abley, "Heartbreak Road," in Saturday Night, *Vol. 102, No. 10, October, 1987, pp. 59-62.*

Jeannette Urbas   (review date December 1987)

[*In the essay below, Urbas discusses the historical aspects of* Heartbreaks along the Road.]

With the publication of *La Guerre, Yes Sir!* in 1970 Roch Carrier began to build a considerable following among English-Canadian readers. They were intrigued by his particular brand of robust, dark humour in a tale about misunderstandings between Canada's two founding groups. This first novel also cast a critical eye on the narrowness and limitations of Quebec village life.

Heartbreaks Along the Road, the ninth Carrier title in English, returns to the theme of backwoods village life, this time in the Duplessis era. The fictional village of Saint-Toussaint-des-Saints is a microcosm of Quebec under the domination of Maurice Duplessis and his Union Nationale Party. In the novel the premier is known only by Duplessis' own popular designation *Le Chef,*—not the cook, but the boss. His party, the Right Party, faces a summer-long election campaign which it intends to win by hook or by crook.

Sheila Fischman's translation aptly reflects the dash and verve of the original French work. Her long association with Carrier's writing has made her responsive to the nuances of his style and familiar with the colloquialisms of the speech of rural Quebec.

The Duplessis regime has become synonymous with despotic rule and a cynical subversion of the democratic process. Bribery and corruption were systematically used to garner votes and maintain power. Fear and the dread accusation of communism were manipulated to stifle any opposition. Carrier's story creates a wide range of characters to exemplify the (im)moral ramifications of this approach to government. But, as Carrier pointed out in an interview in Quebec broadcast by CKRL-FM in December 1984, it is not a historical novel. It goes beyond a historical reconstitution of the premier and his party. Carrier was fascinated by the way in which Duplessis' name was consistently identified with the idea of power in the minds of the Quebecois.

In *Is It the Sun, Philibert?,* published in 1972, Carrier dealt satirically with some aspects of the Duplessis period. These aspects are now amplified. A grotesque religious procession has its counterpart in chapter XVI of *Heartbreaks Along the Road:* "What is life but a procession?" The building of a bridge in the midst of nowhere, without a river or a stream, presages the equally unnecessary Opportun Road, which also goes nowhere and exists only to buy votes and provide badly needed jobs. In both novels blackmail effectively demolishes political opposition.

Heartbreaks Along the Road is a long, sprawling and digressive novel. It contains a multitude of secondary and peripheral characters, who are loosely held together by the building of the road. The book's length is one of its weaknesses. It is difficult for the author to sustain interest uniformly over 529 pages. The result is unevenness in the writing and a tendency to be repetitious in some sections. This is offset by the successful creation of a panoramic fresco of the Quebec rural scene.

Carrier, who grew up in a small village, has a sharp eye for the foibles and venalities of the local population. He depicts their willingness to connive with and profit from the unscrupulous actions of the government ministers. He also shows the strength of the alliance with the Catholic Church, which was one of the mainstays of Duplessis' power.

The spiritual leader of Saint-Toussaint-des-Saints is the Curé Fourré, whose highly descriptive name can mean "filled," like chocolate creams or cream puffs, or more vulgarly, "to screw." As the faithful of the village prepare for the procession, the priest and the local politician, a cabinet minister, vie with one another for prestige, each trying to eclipse the other. Through quick thinking the minister succeeds in naming the new road Chemin Opportun in honour of the new saint who has just perished in a vat of boiling french-fry oil. The Curé Fourré, not to be outdone, hides the minister from view by lifting the broad sleeves of his splendid alb. He reminds the minister and the con-

gregation that only the Church, of which he is a humble apostle, has the power to baptize the new road.

Some events exhibit a bizarre circular pattern. The little saint, Opportun Lachance, suffered brain damage during the previous election when he was hit by a car driven by Domitius Vacher who was rushing to be the first one to get a job on the then new road. He was saved from death by falling on a heap of hay in Malice Blanchette's wagon. The accident is repeated, same place, same people, four years later, only this time Opportun's brain damage is miraculously cured.

History also repeats itself in the sequences devoted to the subversion of the press. Sautereau, the editor of the *Provincial Sun,* starts off as a young and idealistic journalist but is corrupted by the Right Party. The same fate awaits his successor, Achille Bédard. When each man in turn attempts to rebel, he is blackmailed by compromising photographs taken in a brothel.

Some of the episodes have a darker side: there is the pathetic child, Homélie Plante, who knows what men are like because she has just been raped by her father. And the deranged Charlemagne Saint-Ours who is wise enough to want to limit the suffering and destruction caused by war but cannot get anyone to listen to him. There is also Pommette Rossignol, the only woman working on the road, who knows she is worth as much as a man and resists her husband's efforts to give her an 18th child by threatening to cut off his "shiggy!"

The road becomes the concentration of all the ambitions, affronts, calculations and desires of the characters. It is also a metaphorical road, assuming many forms: it can lead to heaven, power, manhood, and above all, death. In fact, death is everywhere, especially in the surreal, bizarre ending.

The circular pattern surfaces again in the final chapter. Because the Americans, who control Quebec financially, disapprove of the location of the road, it is declared open and doomed to demolition in the same breath. A new new road is scheduled to be built where the Americans want it. The concluding sentence states: "Everything was about to begin." (pp. 41-2)

> *Jeannette Urbas, "Carrier's Road," in* The Canadian Forum, *Vol. LXVII, No. 774, December, 1987, pp. 41-2.*

John Lennox   (review date Autumn-Winter 1989)

[*In the following review of* Heartbreaks along the Road, *Lennox discusses the novel's thematic and stylistic elements.*]

"Honorable ministers, he who would harvest first must sow; to harvest votes, you must sow roads. . . . Every rural part of this Province has to have its strip of road, because roads are the arteries of a country—and politics are its life." So begins the election campaign which provides the narrative thread of Roch Carrier's latest novel whose 500-plus pages are alive with farce and tragedy. Structurally *Heartbreaks Along the Road* is Carrier's most ambitious piece of fiction so far and many of the characteristics we have come to associate with his work are present: satire, burlesque, abundant and ribald sensuality, episodic structure, and a pervasive darkness that seems to lie at the heart of all Carrier's fiction. They reiterate what is a fundamental tension in his work, a love of the living balanced by a despair at life. In the cultural and religious context about which he writes, he is confronting two sins: those of the flesh and the sin against the Holy Ghost. Against such a background, nobody wins.

In its pace and detail, this is what might be called a "sprawling" novel full of incident, digression, and often hilarious incongruity. The Province of Quebec is governed by the "Right Party" whose "Chef" decides to call an election; the novel traces the course of the campaign primarily in terms of its effect on a rural Appalachian village, Saint-Toussaint-des-Saints, where the road-building, traditionally associated with provincial elections, promises employment to the inhabitants of the hamlet. In the course of the campaign the young recipient of a miracle is immolated in french-fry oil and becomes a candidate for sainthood, a student expelled from college obliterates himself with dynamite, two editors of the Quebec City newspaper in the pay of the Right Party commit suicide, and the inauguration of the new highway at Saint-Toussaint-des-Saints spawns a wreckum race that ends in bloody carnage reminiscent of the conclusion to *Le jardin des délices.* The interdependence of the governing party and the church, the domination of "Le Chef," and the widespread corruption described in the novel have unmistakable affinities with the Duplessis era in Quebec. The village priest, Curé Fourré, preaches the goodness of God and the Right Party, the Chef dispenses power and largesse as he wishes, and the province remains enslaved by the Right Party's ability to slake appetites and blackmail critics. Such a monolith is ripe for satire and Carrier makes the most of it. In so doing, he enlarges the imaginative picture of the two decades between 1940 and 1960 which he has treated in his earlier novels. Carrier also makes us aware of the extent to which he is indebted to Roger Lemelin whose *Au pied de la pente douce* (1944), published in the Duplessis era, used many of the same satiric and comic techniques.

While *Heartbreaks* makes occasional reference to literary figures like Rimbaud and Melville, Carrier's religious parody and his emphasis on the body link him to the anticlerical satire and scatological humour of Rabelais. Innocent Loiseau, the expelled student, is given "enough to feed Gargantua" while an angry newspaper editor, in imitation of Émile Zola's "J'accuse," addresses the Chef whom the editor wishes to provoke to the point where "your fundament, to use Rabelais' fine word, bursts." The appetites—physical and political—are central to *Heartbreaks* and essential to its vitality. The world to which Carrier returns in this novel borders on the Famine River, a hungry country, where self-interest and greed operate at a primitive, instinctive level and are as enduring as the country itself. Technological innovation—electrification and highway building—are offered as sops to temporarily satisfy the appetites which reemerge as rampant and heedless as ever.

As dominant image and metaphor of the novel, the road provides most of the drama of *Heartbreaks.* Its associations with life and pilgrimages reach a Rabelaisian apogee in the epic village procession in honour of the miracle at Saint-Toussaint-des-Saints. Feudal in its occasion and order, the procession's components are described in high-spirited detail with numerous digressions about the foibles of various members of the procession. The event terminates with carnivalesque laughter and a storm of rotten eggs from the opponents of the Right Party: "All that was still alive in the night, in the very great procession, the greatest ever organized in the Appalachians, was Ligouri Lafleur's joke, which was repeated, heard, laughed at, repeated and laughed at again and again, because it was so inexhaustibly comical." The comic sensuality is also reflected in the magnificent cavalcade of names that seems to be Carrier's forte and a particular source of pleasure: Opportun Lachance, Curé Fouré, Mozusse Chabotte, Uguzon Dubois, Poutine Lachance, Charlemagne Saint-Ours, Cytriste Tanguay, Montcalm O. Labranche, Azellus Loiseau, Téton Lachapelle. The action of each is appropriate to his or her name and among the most absurdly appropriate is "shiggy," a unique variation of Sigmund, which the villagers use as a term for the phallus.

For all its satire and burlesque, however, this is a disturbing novel. The recurrence of gratuitous death and suicide, the graphic reference to child abuse, and the inevitable corruption of the young are symptomatic of the underside of Carrier's recurrent, dark vision. The Rabelaisian part of him lampoons and celebrates, while the twentieth century in which he lives imposes despair. Unlike the route followed by the returning Acadians in Antonine Maillet's *Pélagie-la-charrette,* another fiction of the road which celebrates in Rabelaisian style the restoration and rebirth of a culture, the completed road in *Heartbreaks* leads nowhere and will be "deconstructed" in order to be rerouted toward the cottage of the friend of an influential American governor—"Something about free trade with the United States" as one character remarks.

From *La Guerre, Yes Sir!* to the present, Carrier's satiric impulse has been consistently directed at repressive dogma and excessive power. As he has persisted in doing so, however, Carrier's novels have grown in size largely, I think, because of his interest in the human comedy. He is a student not so much of individuals as of human behaviour and the big, representative canvas reminiscent of Brueghel and Bosch that we glimpse in his earlier work emerges full-blown in this latest novel. As his books have become longer, they have lost the tension created by the brevity of *La Guerre* and *Floralie, où es-tu?* or the seasonal structure of *Le jardin des délices.* In *Heartbreaks* the road is the event, the setting, and the symbol linking different stories together not as a unified whole, but as parts of a heterogeneity to which unity is incidental. Some readers may regret the lack of unity and find the episodic structure spun out to stunning excess. Others will be content to follow the curves and digressions in Carrier's road. In either case, the tension between comedy and despair is unmistakable and always troubling. As much as we might want to emphasize the vitality of Carrier's people, we also have to recognize the abyss that swallows them whole. (pp. 209-11)

John Lennox, "Roads & Arteries," in Canadi-an Literature, Nos. 122-23, Autumn-Winter, 1989, pp. 209-11.

Wayne Grady   (review date November 1991)

[*In the following essay, Grady offers a positive assess-ment of* Prayers of a Very Wise Child.]

In *La Guerre, Yes Sir!,* Roch Carrier's 1968 novel about the effects of the Second World War on the people in a small Quebec village, one of the central characters says, "I don't like the war because in a war little children are killed; I don't want little children to be killed." Twenty-three years later, in *Prayers of a Very Wise Child,* Carrier is still asking the same questions: "God, why didn't You stop the war?" his *"enfant très très sage"* asks in one of his prayers; "What good does it do to have children suffer? Does it make You more perfect? Does it make the universe You created a finer place?"

These days, however, Carrier is asking the question with a difference. In the earlier novel, the person asking the question is a grown man, a deserter, talking to the children of the woman who is hiding him; in *Prayers of a Very Wise Child* the questioner is a seven-year-old boy talking to God. It's a big difference. It's the difference between Blake's Innocence and Experience. *La Guerre, Yes Sir!,* as the title implies, is as much an examination of the two solitudes as it is of the role of evil in the world—the war, after all, was an English affair. Carrier's new book, deliv-ered by means of 16 stories or "prayers," told by a child to a God who may or may not be listening, is really about the hardheadedness of innocence. The questions he asks are penetrating, reasonable, and completely unanswer-able: "The other day it said in the newspaper: 'War to end in thirty-five days.' Why do You have to wait for so many days?"

This particular seven-year-old was born, like Carrier, in a small Quebec village in the 1930s: "A world war broke out shortly after his birth," Carrier writes in the introduc-tion. "It wasn't his fault." Not all the stories are about war and suffering; some are little more than amusing anec-dotes—as in most of Carrier's books, the poignant and the hilarious are mixed in truly "primitive" (as in, say, a Ku-relek painting) tradition. **"Bum Prayer,"** for example, is an account of a "bum-showing party" held in a large tun-nel dug into a snowbank; in **"Titties Prayer,"** the boy tells God about catching a glimpse of a young girl's breasts as she steps down from a wagon: "Thank you, God, for mak-ing titties appear to me. Now I understand one mystery in Your Creation."

But sex is about the only mystery the boy is let in on. In **"Funeral Prayer,"** Carrier quickly plunges us back into the unfathomable; "Why Ginette?" asks the boy. "Her parents have hardly any children: four or five. Why didn't you pluck a child from a family with sixteen or seven-teen?" And: "Killing someone is a sin. God, why did You kill Ginette?" And by implication: if the Germans were

monsters because they kill children, what does that make God? In fact, God comes out as a fairly dubious benefac-tor in most of the mysteries explored by Carrier's inquisi-tive child. In **"The Hanged Man's Prayer,"** in which a man is found hanging from the rafters of a burned barn where his wife and children have died, the boy asks the question that has tormented humanity since Job: "God, why do You send such sad things to Earth?" Saint Augus-tine, who also asked that question, finally interpreted God's silence as a measure of his own ignorance; Carrier's child is too young and innocent to be afraid to draw con-clusions. "Is our religion the best, God," he asks, "because it's the one where you suffer the most?"

"Writing," Carrier has his wise child say, "is the best thing to do in the world after looking out the window." And later: "Praying and writing are a little bit the same." But praying to an indifferent or absentee God for a more rational, more compassionate world hasn't helped to make such a world become reality: perhaps writing for one, as Carrier has been doing for the past three decades, will prove more effective in the long run.

Wayne Grady, "Innocence and Experience," in Books in Canada, Vol. XX, No. 8, Novem-ber, 1991, p. 48.

[Carrier's novels celebrate] violence and laughter; gusto and defeat; man's potential grandeur and his faltering performance; life, or as Carrier would prefer to put it, love and death.

—*Philip Stratford, in* Dictionary of Literary Biography, *Vol. 53, 1986.*

Paula K. Kamenish   (essay date 1992-1993)

[*In the excerpt below, Kamenish examines Carrier's use of violence in* La guerre, Yes Sir!]

Carrier's *Trilogie de l'âge sombre* records three genera-tions of Québécois revolt by focusing on selected episodes in the lives of the members of a small isolated community. *La Guerre, Yes Sir!,* the first section of the work to be published, appeared in 1968 and was adapted shortly thereafter for both stage and screen. *La Guerre,* the cen-tral panel of what Carrier refers to as his triptych of Love, Death and Work, is a modern fable set in the 1940s. It re-lates a series of bloody events that occur in a rural commu-nity when seven English soldiers return the body of An-thyme Corriveau's son to its French-Canadian home. Chronologically speaking, the epic begins in *Floralie, Où es-tu?* the allegorical tale of the wedding night of An-thyme and his tainted bride, Floralie. The tenebrous for-ests of Quebec become a place of refuge and revelation for Floralie and the husband who beats and then hunts her through the night. In the third novel, *Il est là, le soleil,* Carrier records the failure of Philibert, the abused son of the village butcher and gravedigger, to survive Montreal's urban dangers. He revolts against the tyranny of his father, but finds no redemption in his escape to freedom.

The conjunctive theme of violence is traceable throughout the trilogy, from the beating and verbal abuse of Floralie to the life-long physical suffering of Philibert. Carrier's trilogy, however, is not infested with violence for violence's sake. In all three novels violent acts and abusive language fulfill essential roles in the creation of plot, character and theme. In each novel, acts of violence become the outward manifestations of a character's revolt against oppression.

Nowhere is this theme so systematically explored as in *La Guerre, Yes Sir!* where one witnesses the very ritualization of violence as a temporarily satisfying means of revolt. By uncovering various displays of violence imbedded in the narration and in the language of the characters, one can begin to understand the passion and fury of the French Canadians whose cultural existence is threatened by the powerful "Anglais" who surround them.

René Girard's *Violence and the Sacred* provides a fascinating point of departure for the study of violence in *La Guerre.* Girard's work is an anthropologically based study of violence as it is ritualized to restore order through sacrifice. The sacrificial victim serves the all-important role of diverting a society's violence into proper channels so as to avoid the venting of violent impulses on its own members.

Literature is one means of ritualizing violence, in that it takes the form of ritual and redirects the violent impulse. The written text distances the violent act from the reader, but, at the same time, allows participation and the resulting catharsis that only the witnessing of a blood sacrifice can offer to the human animal. This is because, as Robert Penn Warren explains in the *American Scholar* Symposium on "Violence in Literature," when one puts violence into words, it becomes an object, it becomes ritualized because it is outside the event. The author of a violent scene is "indulging his appetite for violence through ritualization, and indulging yours through the use of ritualization too. It's a way of knowing—and in the right context, of absolving." Ritual absolves. Writing violence and reading violence quells the urge because the text serves as a surrogate victim.

This is not to imply that Carrier's motivation for writing *La Guerre* is to find an outlet for his impulses toward violence. In René Dionne's study of *La Guerre* [appearing in *Relations* (October 1968)] the novelist is described as "un homme doux" who confesses: "Maintenant que ce livre est fait, je m'étonne de l'avoir fait. Parce qu'il contient une violence dans le langage et dans l'action que je n'ai pas moi-même, mais qui nous appartient." The unspecified "nous" leaves one to wonder if Carrier is defining a Québécois trait or a general human characteristic. Carrier's following justification of his abundant use of the language of violence suggests an answer: "Le sacré, par exemple, dont personnellement je n'use pas, que je n'ai jamais entendu dans ma famille, j'en fais grand usage dans le livre, parce qu'il m'apparaît comme la première affirmation d'une conscience individuelle. La structure syntaxique du blas-

phème raconte bien notre histoire, le flou de notre expression, le piétinement de la pensée et de la vie. . . . " The novelist associates the violent language of abuse and blasphemy with the French-Canadian consciousness. In some ways, the syntactic mishandling of language in *La Guerre, Yes Sir!* is a form of revolt against the mother tongue, the language of the colonists' first oppressors. But, ironically, the French language is also a linguistic fact that unites them against the more recent Anglophone aggression. In this respect, it serves as a "protective value," but proves to be a dangerous suit of armour that imprisons as it protects.

Carrier's novel suggests that linguistic expressions of violence loosen the restraints imposed by those protective values represented by the French language. Judging from specific examples, the language of violence in Carrier's *La Guerre* would shake the very foundations of the Academie Française. From the mouths of the villagers it is the language of blasphemy in a Roman Catholic community. Sometimes humourous and playful, sometimes abusive, they never tire of their litanies of "ce baptême-là," "cette tabernacle de guerre," "calice d'hostie," "hostie de mule," "vieille pipe de Christ," ou "merde de Christ." *La Guerre, Yes Sir!* is likewise punctuated with violent threats reinforced by aggressive behaviour. The narration reveals what at first glance appears to be a world of spiteful cruelty, of the verbal and physical abuse of the weak by the powerful. But this neat division between oppressor and oppressed does not account for the complexity of the violence witnessed.

The first reference to violence in the novel is provided by the title, *La Guerre, Yes Sir!* Carrier originally entitled his text *La Nuit blanche,* but he was persuaded by Jacques Hébert to invent a more stirring title. After numerous efforts he appropriately chose to emphasize the two most influential elements in his text, namely the English and their war. "Yes Sir!" confirms the English domination, while it hammers out a reminder of military submission by the cadence of its one-syllable sharpness.

Ironically, "Yes Sir!" is not the exclamatory affirmation that it would appear. Carrier's French Canadians exhibit very strong feelings of opposition to the European war. In their view it is the war of the "big guys." An unnamed employee at the train station sums up this opinion:

> Ils sont tous semblables: les Allemands, les Anglais, les Français, les Russes, les Chinois, les Japons; ils se ressemblent tellement qu'ils doivent porter des costumes différents pour se distinguer avant de se lancer les grenades. Ils sont des gros qui veulent rester gros. . . . C'est pourquoi je pense que cette guerre, c'est la guerre des gros contre les petits. Corriveau est mort. Les petits meurent. Les gros sont éternels.

The employee has unknowingly identified the colonial imperialists, who as "les gros," form one homologous mass of menace.

The British, the most immediate oppressors of the community, are held responsible for sending French-Canadian boys to die. Arthur, who takes refuge in Amélie's bed while her husband fights in Europe, refuses to obey his conscription notice: "Je ne veux pas me faire déchirer la figure dans leur maudite guerre. Est-ce qu'ils nous ont demandé si nous la voulions, cette maudite guerre? Non. Mais quand ils ont besoin de bras pour la faire, cette maudite guerre, alors là, ils nous aiment bien." When Bérubé complains that his new wife, the anglophone prostitute Molly, sleeps too much, he echoes Arthur's observation: "Ces crucifix d'Anglais dorment tout le temps. C'est pour ça qu'ils ont des petites familles. Et quand les Anglais font une guerre, ils viennent chercher les Canadiens français."

The Corriveau home, isolated from the world by fields of snow, becomes a microcosm of the Province of Quebec. Under the watchful eyes of Corriveau's English escorts, it becomes the perfect setting for a confrontation of two eternal enemies. The close quarters of a small house surrounded by snow allow for a heightened sense of the potential fatality in the opposition of the oppressor and the oppressed. The wake draws the community together, concentrating and distilling the tensions that will eventually explode in violent behaviour. During the course of the night-long vigil the reader discovers that all the villagers have been mutilated by the war in some way, if not physically, then mentally or spiritually. Unable to rid themselves of the tyranny under which they must suffer, they turn against one another. Or, as in the case of Joseph and Henri, they mutilate themselves. Finally, they join forces and channel their aggression to attack the company of English soldiers guarding Corriveau's coffin.

The most moving portrayal of violence against one's brother takes place in the beating and humiliation of Arsène by the French-Canadian soldier Bérubé. Bérubé, who serves as a latrine cleaner in the English army, already exhibits his violent nature when he beats, bites and abandons his bride in the snow on their way from the train station. Bérubé's aggressive behaviour can be explained by the frustrations and humiliations he suffers at the hands of others. Unable to turn on his military leaders who degrade him, powerless against the Church that has instilled in him a fear of hell so strong that he must ask Molly to marry him before he can make love to her, he displaces his aggressive feeling to a convenient victim. Girard documents this phenomenon: "When unappeased, violence seeks and always finds a surrogate victim. The creature that excited its fury is abruptly replaced by another, chosen only because it is vulnerable and close at hand." [Albert] Memmi offers another motivation for this behaviour in "Are the French Canadians Colonized?" in which he professes that "any community seeking independence must also *wage war on itself*" [in his *Dominated Man: Notes toward a Portrait* (1968)]. The colonized must denounce "the structure of their own institutions, their families and their scale of values" because these native values and traditions "become limiting and have to be discarded." But, surprisingly, Bérubé incorporates what might be interpreted as deep-seated cultural traditions in his attack on his Québécois victim.

The scene in question begins and ends in bloodshed. Arsène accidently breaks a glass and, in doing so, he cuts Arthur's cheek. The villagers encircle Arthur like flies, fascinated by the sight of so much blood from such a small wound. The blood inspires Arsène to go to war:

> Il me semble qu'avoir à ses pieds un Allemand qui perd tout son sang de maudit Allemand, cela doit satisfaire un homme. Mais il paraît que nos soldats ne voient pas les Allemands quand ils perdent leur sang. Nos soldats lancent des petits coups de fusil, puis ils se cachent aussitôt, pissant dans leurs culottes de peur d'avoir attrapé un Allemand. . . .

A threatening voice answers from upstairs: "Fermez vos grandes gueules." Bérubé descends and grabs Arsène with such force that he rips his shirt. He repeatedly slaps his victim while he threatens: "Calice de ciboire d'hostie! Christ en bicyclette sur son Calvaire! Tu trouves qu'on s'amuse à la guerre? Gros tas de merde debout! La guerre est drôle? Je vais te faire comprendre ce qu'est la guerre. Tu vas rire."

With kicks and well-aimed punches Bérubé brutally forces Arsène to don layers of coats and to dance with the scantily dressed Molly on his shoulders. The sweat pours down Arsène's body as he marches and sways to the rhythm of his tormentor's commands and flinches at each impact. No one can stop the prolonged, humiliating torture of the victim. When a bystander tries to intervene he is silenced by a fist in his face. More blood flows. The villagers, no longer having the courage to interfere, become accomplices: "Pour ne pas se sentir lâches, ils essayaient de s'amuser et réussissaient à rire comme jamais ils n'avaient ri dans leur vie." Through its nervous laughter the entire community participates in the sacrifice, combining humour with violence. The scene takes on a festive, party-like air, suggesting a village carnival. With the complicity of the onlookers, Bérubé continues to hit his little soldier, spits in his face, boxes his ears, punches him in the stomach. The ritual fills thirteen pages of the text. Finally, at the point at which the reader's sensibilities are numbed by the proliferation of violence, Arsène is stripped naked and thrown into the snow. The ritual beating thus ends with Arsène's christening in the purity of the regenerative snow, a frozen sacramental water. Arsène undergoes a naked rebirth into the community, for he reunites with his tormentors in the subsequent snow battle with the English.

The ritualized violence of this scene exhibits some of the characteristics of what Girard describes as the "festival." In most societies the festival allows the deliberate violation of laws, such as those governing social hierarchy and sexuality. Julia Kristeva concurs [in *The Kristeva Reader* (1986)], noting that "the carnival challenges God, authority and social law; in so far as it is dialogical, it is rebellious." Furthermore, Mikhail Bakhtin's research reveals that as part of both French and Spanish *Corpus Cristi* religious processions, certain sacrilegious aspects became consecrated by tradition. For example, there were "extremely free, grotesque images of the body," including a monster combining cosmic, animal, and human features, with "the Babylonian harlot astride the monster" [*Rabelais and His World* (1968)]. Arsène personifies the substitute king or "king of fools" in a forced dance, complete with the chanting of abusive language and crowned with

Front cover of De L'amour dans la ferraille.

the erotic English prostitute. The "king of fools" is nothing more than a victim to be sacrificed at the end of the ceremony.

Bakhtin, in his study of carnivalesque elements in Rabelais, points out that thrashing and abuse are not necessarily personal chastisement, but can be symbolic actions directed at something on a higher level, at "the king," "the oppressor":

> In such a system the king is the clown. He is elected by all the people and is mocked by all the people. He is abused and beaten when the time of his reign is over, just as the carnival dummy of winter or the dying year is mocked, beaten, torn to pieces, burned, or drowned even in our time. They are "gay monsters." The clown was first disguised as a king, but once his reign had come to an end his costume was changed, "travestied," to turn him once more into a clown. The abuse and thrashing are equivalent to a change of costume, to a metamorphosis. Abuse reveals the other, true face of the abused, it tears off his disguise and mask. It is the king's uncrowning. . . . But in this system death is followed by regeneration, by the new year, new youth, and a new spring.

Arsène is dressed in layers of coats, the robes of the king. Mockery and thrashing lead to his uncrowning, his disrobing, being stripped of coats.

Arsène receives the beating that Bérubé would like to give to the sergeant, or to the entire English army. The sacrificial substitution of Arsène for the intended victims implies a degree of unconscious confusion, yet the tormentor must seem to conceal the fact of this displacement of aggression without losing sight of the original object of violence. Girard points out that without that underlying awareness, the sacrifice loses all efficacy. Fortunately, at the conclusion of the sacrifice, the appearance of the English soldiers reminds the crowd of the true object of their violence. This, however, only muddles Bérubé, whose urge to violence is not allowed to be satisfied. When he finally gets his chance to show "à ces Anglais ce qu'un Canadien français portait au bout du poing," he is transformed into an obedient soldier with the sergeant's "Atten . . . tion!" Again, instead of venting his frustrations on the true object of his hatred, he is commanded to attack his fellow villagers, once more serving as mere substitute victims in his revolt. According to Girard, this is one of the qualities that lends violence its particular terror, "the strange propensity to seize upon the surrogate victims, to actually conspire with the enemy and at the right moment toss him a morsel. . . . " As a result of his obedient acquiescence, the French-Canadian community rejects Bérubé. His keen penchant for violence makes him a man of confused loyalties. The French Canadians consider him a traitor, the English refuse to mix with his kind.

Moreover, Bérubé is the key to the novel's oppressor-victim schema of displaced aggression which describes the English-French relationship and its effect on the members of the Québécois community. The pattern of subjugation takes the following form: the sergeant rules Bérubé, who in turn attacks Molly and Arsène. Arsène repeatedly abuses his son, Philibert. Thus, the English overpowers the French soldier, the male subjugates the female, the military overcomes the civilian and the parent beats the child. It is noteworthy that in the role of the male ruling the female, Bérubé also acts out his dream of the Québécois vanquishing the English, for Molly is his "English" bride. On the other hand, when Bérubé attacks Arsène, the aggressor ironically defends the (English) Canadian army, whose reputation as a valiant fighting corps is questioned by the French-Canadian gravedigger. Soon thereafter, Bérubé essentially joins forces with the English, rejecting his heritage in his assault on his kinsmen. This rejection of his heritage, however, is not the type of denunciation called for by Memmi, for the goal is not the same. Bérubé does not revolt against the values of his community with an eye to strengthening the position of his fellow colonized and overcoming their colonizers. Such ideals do not preoccupy Bérubé. His Pavlovian response to the sergeant's command is a trained reflex, an instinctual concern for his own survival.

Carrier proves that violence is contagious. It spreads and colors all it touches as does its most obvious manifestation, blood. The very fluidity of blood signals its ability to spill easily and diffuse the fascination and attraction that the human animal finds in an act of violence.

The interminable sequence of violence in **La Guerre** begins in the opening lines of the novel with Joseph's drastic attempt to escape the war. In order to avoid being blown to bits and "made into jam" as was young Corriveau, Joseph's fear leads him to chop off his left hand with an axe. His self-mutilation is the first blood sacrifice the reader witnesses. The first page of Carrier's novel presents the cold and determined severing of the farmer's hand in descriptive detail. As the blood drowns his hand where it falls on the snow, Joseph breaks into a fit of laughter at having finally freed himself from the fear that has haunted him for months.

A later vignette which continues the story of Joseph, describes an enthusiastic game of hockey played by a group of youngsters. Madame Joseph strolls by and remarks to herself how the children fight over the object they use as a puck, "probablement un crottin de cheval gelé." Gradually, the identity of the object is revealed to her and she sets off swinging fists and sticks to beat the children away so as to retrieve her husband's hand. As soon as the reader has begun to recover from the horror of the scene, Madame Joseph returns home to scold her husband. She insists that Joseph thank her for saving his hand because the children might have broken it. To her nagging, her husband finally answers: "Que veux-tu faire de ma main? De la soupe?" Even with this touch of macabre humour the violence does not end. Madame Joseph, in turn, whistles to call the dog who comes running to the door. She tosses the hand into the snow and the reader watches as the hungry animal leaps upon its supper with satisfaction. The dog concludes the ritual of the sacrifice by devouring the sacrificial victim, or rather a part of him.

Joseph's bloody act of revolt perhaps prevents him from having to serve in a foreign war, but, according to his wife, he pays for his freedom with his masculinity. She cannot accept a cowardly husband who cuts off his own hand. In her mind, the act is equated with emasculation. She laments to her friends: "Vous mariez un homme et vous vous apercevez que vous couchez avec un infirme. Dans mon lit qu'est-ce que mon Joseph fera avec son moignon?" The sexual imagery is reinforced with Joseph's declaration: "Qu'ils viennent me prendre, maintenant, pour faire leur Christ de guerre! Je leur couperai le zizoui, s'ils en ont un. Je leur couperai comme j'ai coupé ma main."

Henri likewise undergoes a type of emasculation when he returns home as a deserter and agrees to take up residence in the attic. Arthur the draft-dodger has usurped Henri's role as husband to Amélie, fathering two sets of twins with another child on the way. Henri, a cowardly Agamemnon, is permitted to sleep in his wife's bed on alternate nights. He agrees to the arrangement, knowing that Amélie prefers her new "husband" Arthur. Henri's submission is a form of self-mutilation. He accepts his humiliation without a whimper. Nevertheless, as he hovers above the passionate couple, freezing in his icy attic, he nurses a powerful self-hatred, an emotion that can only lead to violence. Later, at the novel's climax, the mild-mannered Henri commits murder. Surprisingly, neither his wife nor her

lover is the victim; instead, he kills one of the English soldiers, the metaphorically "proper" victim and true cause of his frustration.

While the rest of the villagers participate in the wake, Henri's nightmares lead him to believe that the coffin of Corriveau joins him in his lonely attic and an invisible hand pushes him to enter. Henri does not take up his rifle with thoughts of vengeance, but out of self-defense. In a fit of madness he rushes to the wake to escape his haunted isolation.

Meanwhile the English soldiers have just managed to empty the Corriveau home. Disgusted by the drunkenness, belching and farting of the French Canadians, the soldiers collect coats and hats and toss them onto the snow. After gathering its clothing, the crowd, led by Joseph waving his bloody stump, retaliates by attacking the soldiers with kicks and punches, a sequential reversal of the Bérubé-Arsène scene. When the women start grabbing the genitals of the soldiers, the sergeant commands: "Let's go, boys! Let's kill' em." An intense fray ensues, comparable in magnitude to the carnivalesque beating that precedes it, but different in its clear division of the traditional enemy camps.

As an English soldier rushes toward him, Henri fires. The shooting ends the violent clash of disciplined English and rowdy French Canadians, a battle that bloodies the snow. The dead soldier becomes yet another blood sacrifice in the novel. He is the scapegoat who satisfies the villagers' underlying need for a victim to revenge the death of one of their sons. This familial characteristic of the community is explained by Corriveau's mother: "Tous les gens qui étaient ici étaient un peu ses parents et les jeunes étaient ses frères ou ses soeurs. . . . Même quand il arrive un malheur dans le village, nous aimons nous retrouver ensemble, nous nous partageons le malheur. . . . " With the surrogate victim's death all hostility ends. According to Girard's theory, the community requires a sacrifice in order to quell violence. He describes the phenomenon thus: "If left unappeased, violence will accumulate until it overflows its confines and floods the surrounding area. The role of sacrifice is to stem this rising tide of indiscriminate substitutions and redirect violence into 'proper' channels."

The proper victim for the Québécois is not his vulnerable neighbor, but the ruling English. The soldiers represent a pair of threatening enemies against which the French-Canadian characters believe themselves to be powerless: "les Anglais" et "la maudite guerre." Girard remarks that all victims "bear a certain *resemblance* to the object they replace." The young man dressed in the uniform of an English soldier represents all men of his nationality and profession. Carrier uses the character as a synecdoche, signifying all "maudits Anglais," and thus, by implication, all the "gros" who wage war and force the subjugated French Canadians to serve and die for a cause that is not theirs.

In portraying the two diverse cultures and their irreconcilable separation, Carrier foregrounds the obvious differences of religion and language that have been at the root of a Euro-based xenophobia for nearly five centuries.

When the battles of the Old World are transplanted to a new hemisphere, the cultural racism of European nationalism takes on new meaning. It is no longer a struggle between two parallel and equal forces who clash over the ideologies of class, religion, politics and national boundaries. Instead, within the imperialist paradigm of the New World, the colonized must take up (sometimes enthusiastically, sometimes reluctantly) the banner of the mother country, if not to defend her politics, then at least to show support in those areas that have been exported and adapted to the new society, namely in the realm of culture, language and religion.

The English Protestants are puzzled and insulted by the pig-like conduct of the Canadian Catholics at the ceremonious vigil: "Ils avaient regardé d'un oeil impassible cette fête sauvage noyée de rires épais, de cidre et de lourdes tourtières mais le dégoût leur serrait les lèvres. Quelle sorte d'animaux étaient donc ces French Canadians?" The English Protestants find the carnival-like atmosphere of the wake incongruous and repulsive within the confines of their own value and belief system. They draw the conclusion that the French have the manners of pigs in a pigpen: " . . . ils étaient de vrais porcs, ces French Canadians dont la civilisation consistait à boire, manger, péter, roter." Anthyme attempts to justify the generous consumption of alcohol as he offers more bottles to his guests: "—Nous savons vivre, dit-il aux soldats qui sourirent parce qu'ils ne comprenaient pas." Polite smiles mask the potentially dangerous fact that the soldiers will never comprehend the simplest explanations of French-Canadian customs.

Language becomes a second barrier between the two cultures. Effective communication is not possible and misunderstandings abound. When the soldiers deliver Corriveau's coffin to his home, his mother requests that they place it on the kitchen table. The soldiers do not understand. The parents restate their wishes. The soldiers do not move. Clearly, "les soldats Anglais ne comprenaient pas ce langage que les vieux parlaient. Ils savaient que c'était du French, mais ils en avaient rarement entendu." The père Corriveau becomes frustrated and shakes his fist at the sergeant "qui se demandait pourquoi tout le monde ne parlait pas English comme lui." This episode well illustrates the cultural phenomenon of linguistic deficiency. That is, from the point of view of the colonizers, the colonized people are devalued by their inability to converse in the official working language of the ruling class, the language of urban affairs. Memmi reveals the all-pervasive consequences of the problem: "So linguistic deficiency . . . is not only an ideological or purely cultural problem. A kind of circular movement is set up: economic and political domination gives rise to a cultural subordination, and this cultural subordination in its turn maintains the economic and political subdomination" (*Dominated Man*). Difference is automatically labelled deficiency within in the ruling system.

Ironically, there are rare moments when the villagers realize the porous nature of the border that separates them from their enemy. In some ways the English guards are not unlike themselves. When praying at the coffin of their fallen countryman, the English soldiers surprise Anthyme: "Vieille pipe de Christ, . . . ces maudits protestants savent prier aussi bien que les Canadiens français." Arsène simplifies the comparison for Philibert who has never before seen an Anglais: "Les Anglais, mon fils, sont des gens comme tout le monde: les hommes pissent debout et les femmes assises." Especially when reduced to such straightforward and primitive images, it is clear that the villagers bear resemblance to the hated objects they represent. Consequently, it is not surprising that they mistakenly turn their anger and violence toward themselves and their neighbors as accessible substitute victims.

Although Arsène proves that men are physiologically similar the world over, cultural and linguistic differences, aggravated by the oppression of colonization, can become nevertheless adequate justification for aggressive acts. Violence can often be a way of revolting against what is in actuality too powerful to defeat (English rule), or what is beyond one's control (the English war), or beyond one's comprehension (the death of a young man). Unbridled violence is often the only recourse when fighting against omnipresent and omnipotent powers.

According to Franz Fanon "decolonization is always a violent phenomenon" [*The Wretched of the Earth* (1982)], and *La Guerre, Yes Sir!* is essentially a novel of decolonization. Carrier exposes the dangerous "protective values" of commitment to the land and to the Church, the fallacies of tradition by which the French-Canadian people have been subordinated and dominated. The novel's attempt to reject the debilitating view of a peaceful, idyllic rural life, as portrayed in *Maria Chapdelaine,* successfully brings to light the violence, both linguistic and behavioural, that characterizes a colonial revolt. Beneath the enticing humour of the characters, Carrier imbeds a sense of shame. Seeing such a portrait of one's past causes the colonized to feel ashamed of their weaknesses and their submission. Marx said that shame is a revolutionary sentiment. Feeling this shame, all the Josephs, Henris, Bérubés, Corriveaus and Arsènes of modern Quebec seek to reject the role of the colonized, a role of acquiescence and complicity.

The fictional characters in Carrier's novel feel unable to overcome the social, religious, sexual, political and economic realities that frustrate them. The French Canadians' unending combat against these forces unites them as a culturally homologous community. But their struggle also ties them to their oppressors. Memmi remarks that "the violence of the oppressed is a mere reflection of the violence of the oppressor. . . . [F]rom the bond between oppressor and oppressed there is no escape." The colonizer owes the fact of his existence as a species to the subservient existence of the colonized. Without his subjects, the ruler has no kingdom, and thus no function. Colonizers and colonized live in a mutually dependent relationship. The Québécois are inextricably linked to "les maudits Anglais," geographically, politically and socially. Even metaphysically, the two groups are united by their human mortality. The war, that figures so prominently in Carrier's title, does not distinguish between English and French Canadians when choosing victims. As Estelle Dansereau points out [in her "Le Fantastique chez Roch Carrier et Jacques Benoit" in *Canadian Literature* 88 (Spring 1981)]: "le cercueil de Corriveau, dans lequel Henri voit tout son village pénétrer, devient symbole de la mort, de cette mort qui, un jour, unifiera les québécois et les soldats anglais." Carrier appropriately labelled this episode of his trilogy "Death," for it is death that ultimately dissolves the differences by treating equally all men. Like it or not, the contrastive cultures in **La Guerre, Yes Sir!** have been, to borrow from Samuel Johnson, yoked by violence together. (pp. 94-107)

Paula K. Kamenish, "Carrier's French and English: 'Yoked by Violence Together'," in Studies in Canadian Literature, *Vol. 17, No. 2, 1992-93, pp. 92-108.*

FURTHER READING

Mills, John. "The Road Most Travelled." *Essays on Canadian Writing,* No. 40 (Spring 1990): 32-9.
> Praises the episodic *Heartbreaks along the Road* as a caricature of the political and social situation in Quebec under the Duplessis government of the 1950s.

Sutherland, Ronald. "Faulknerian Quebec." *Canadian Literature,* No. 40 (Spring 1967): 86-7.
> Positive assessment of *La guerre, Yes Sir!,* in which Sutherland compares Carrier's storytelling abilities to those of William Faulkner.

———. "The Calvinist-Jansenist Pantomime." In his *Second Image: Comparative Studies in Québec/Canadian Literature,* pp. 60-87. Toronto: New Press, 1971.
> Places *La guerre, Yes Sir!* in the Calvinist-Jansenist religious tradition of Canadian literature. Sutherland states: "*La guerre, Yes Sir!* includes a good example of the terror sermon, delivered by a parish priest at the burial service for [a] dead soldier. It is typical that this sermon should contain several threatening allusions to sins of the flesh, for undoubtedly sex relations have been more greatly distorted by the Puritan ethos than has any other area of human activity."

Fred Chappell

1936-

(Full name Fred Davis Chappell) American poet, novelist, and short story writer.

The following entry provides an overview of Chappell's career through 1991. For further discussion of Chappell's works, see *CLC,* Volume 40.

INTRODUCTION

Known for his gentle humor and superb storytelling, Chappell uses the Appalachian region where he was born and raised as the setting for both his poetry and fiction. He is praised for his erudition and mastery of poetic forms, as well as for the vital sense of community and Southern values found in his work.

Chappell was born and raised in a small town in western North Carolina. He graduated from Duke University in 1961 with a bachelor's degree in fiction writing. After earning a master's degree from Duke in 1964, Chappell became an instructor of writing at the University of North Carolina in Greensboro, where he has taught for more than twenty-five years.

Chappell's early works are dark, psychological novels characterized by violence and madness. James Christopher, the protagonist of Chappell's first novel, *It Is Time, Lord,* is a disillusioned man whose life lacks meaning and purpose. Alternating between past and present, this novel juxtaposes images from Christopher's childhood with present-day scenes of idleness, drunkenness, and infidelity. *Dagon* centers on a minister who, after moving to a small town with his wife, becomes obsessed with the fascinating and violent daughter of a tenant farmer. Chappell's more recent work, most notably the novels *I Am One of You Forever* and *Brighten the Corner Where You Are,* are praised for their humor and vivid imagery. These two novels follow the exploits of Joe Robert Kirkman and the coming-of-age of his son Jess in a small town in North Carolina. Chappell's 1991 collection of short stories, *More Shapes Than One,* humorously incorporates supernatural, historical, and Southern elements.

While Chappell first attracted critical attention as a novelist, he considers himself primarily a poet. *Midquest,* his most highly acclaimed work, comprises four previously published volumes—*River, Bloodfire, Wind Mountain,* and *Earthsleep.* Each focuses on the reminiscences and experiences of the author on his thirty-fifth birthday, which he identifies as the midpoint of his life. Incorporating a variety of verse forms such as terza rima, rhymed couplets, and syllabics, *Midquest* features a conglomeration of perspectives and poetic voices, blending past and present, narration, meditation, and dialogue. In *First and Last Words* Chappell writes about distinguished authors and

literary texts throughout history and his reaction to them. As John Lang maintains, the range of philosophical meditation in the poems "reveals the error of any attempt to view Chappell as simply a 'regional' writer."

PRINCIPAL WORKS

It Is Time, Lord (novel) 1963
The Inkling (novel) 1965
Dagon (novel) 1968
The World between the Eyes (poetry) 1971
The Gaudy Place (novel) 1973
River (poetry) 1975
The Man Twice Married to Fire (poetry) 1977
Bloodfire (poetry) 1978
Awakening to Music (poetry) 1979
Wind Mountain (poetry) 1979
Earthsleep (poetry) 1980
Moments of Light (short stories) 1980
Driftlake: A Lieder Cycle (poetry) 1981

CRITICISM

Alan Nadel (essay date Winter 1983)

[*In the following essay, Nadel analyzes themes and poetic forms in* Midquest.]

In **"My Father Burns Washington,"** the seventh poem of the second volume in his tetralogy, *Midquest,* Fred Chappell describes his father's starting to burn a dollar bill during the time of "Hoover's deep / Depression":

> He got a match.
> We listened, frozen in time,
> To the ugly inarticulate scratch
> And watched the tender blooming of the flame.
> "I never figured on getting rich."
> *Revenge was sweet with doom.*

Like the listeners and watchers within the narrative, this moment—the one before "He lit the single"—is frozen in time. By recording the animation of the poet's memory and imagination, and thus turning it into an inanimate record, the poem itself freezes that moment. The formality of the verse emphasizes this activity, this description being a complete stanza, one of 18 6-line stanzas, each containing two rhymes repeated three times. In each stanza, furthermore, the first line contains two stresses, the second three, the third four, the fourth five, the fifth four and the sixth three; all but one of the stanzas end in a full stop. Since the prosody helps freeze that moment, it also helps diminish the difference between the active father and the passive family by making them both seem more passive or, some might suggest, more eternal.

The situation too is in deadlock: The father's actions to end his enslavement to money will only increase his dependence as will the awestruck family's inaction. Action and inaction counterbalance each other, leading to the same futile end, an end ironic as is the *blooming flame* which *freezes them in time.* In many ways then the conflict between freeze and flame, action and inertia, desire and impotence paralyzes the stanza, which reduces to the italicized oxymoron that identifies the shared fate of revenger and victim. The title of the poem, however, identifies that victim not as Hoover, the Depression or money itself, but as the father of our country and / or the capital: father ver-

sus patriarch and fatherland in a burning deathlock, *sweet with doom.*

Midquest is full of such moments, involving the poet's persona, "Fred," or Fred's family and friends. In **"Dead Soldiers,"** Virgil Campbell, the town drunk, fires a rifle into the flood waters which are destroying his store. **"Burning the Frankenstein Monster; Elegiac Letter to Richard Dillard"** closes with the insight that "The courageous monsters perish / Always alone, yet always in the final light / Glorious and stark. As the hilltop mill is always burning, / Raising its arms of clean blaze against the stars." And in **"The Autumn Bleat of the Weathervane Trombone,"** Fred perches himself on the barn roof to practice trombone, follows the flow of music over the landscape of the imagination and back to the blower surveying the doomed fall of his wind on the valley of cows:

> So I'll straddle the barn and lip the exercises,
> Improve my embouchure and wiggle my slide
> Till I get a somewhat humaner-looking lover
> Than those bored Guernseys. Girls! girls!
> Where are you? Don't you hear Fred's lonesome
>   trombone
> Mating call from the highest point in the valley?
> You wouldn't let the music of this world die?
>
> Would you?

The governing futility of the whole tetralogy, of course, the endeavor most sweet with doom, is Chappell's attempt to freeze the day of his 35th birthday. To this end he creates four eleven-poem volumes, each eleven thematically linked by imagery relating to one of the four elements: *River, Bloodfire, Wind Mountain,* and *Earthsleep.* The conflict in each independently, and even moreso as a group, is between the ingenuity of a temporal man and the power of the eternal elements which doom that ingenuity. But instead of asserting that he will in some form—e.g. through his immortal soul or the immortality of his verse—transcend his doom, Chappell attempts to forestall that doom by iterating and reiterating the primacy of that moment long before, the frozen mid-point in his alleged three score and ten. By embracing his temporality, he tries to make time stand still, the frozen moment contain the fluid, burning, windy, earthy stories of the lives of his life.

In her book *Lyric Time,* Sharon Cameron says lyric poetry attempts to eternalize the moment by arresting our sense of time. As she demonstrates with Dickinson's poetry, "grown sufficiently disparate, the maneuvers of speech can stop time dead." In the sense of Cameron's definition, then, Chappell's tetralogy is lyric, but if so it is, I would contend, "epic lyric." This is not a contradiction in terms but rather describes a common American form of the long poem, and the only form available, I believe, for an epic attempted in the first-person personal voice, a voice, that is, in which the poet's persona occupies a realm distinctly similar to the poet's own environs. Although in the introduction Chappell compares his persona to Dante's, I think it is more akin to Whitman's or Williams's and still very much that of an epic hero.

The epic hero, as G. M. Cuthbertson points out in his book *Political Myth and Epic,* is an archetype of virtue standing at

the center of a configuration of social values . . .
Through a queer political synecdoche the hero
comes to represent the entire community. The
individual members participate emphatically in
his exploits, in his tests. The hero becomes su-
perorganic. His search projects the wish fulfill-
ments of a nation. . . . Often the hero is
plagued by a very human sense of loss; he must
search; he must suffer. Frequently he is searching for his weird, his *alter ego.* In a political context, he searches for security, for power, for legitimacy, for knowledge.

To Cuthbertson's definition, I would add that if heroes differ from gods in that they are mortal, they differ from ordinary humans in that they have the power to live their lives
to the end instead of dying, as average people do, in the
midst of their frustrations, anxieties, unfulfilled dreams.
Unlike the common throng, heroes work their motivating
passion through, expel their wrath, find their way home.
This trait particularly, I think, enables epic heroes to work
that "queer political synecdoche"; they represent the potential resolution of dreams that normally end frustrated.

Revealing this completeness to the course of a life requires
a perspective impossible to someone in the midst of it.
Hence when Walt Whitman wants to sing of himself who
is also the nation, or when William Carlos Williams wants
to sing of Paterson city who is also himself, they must
avoid the chronological format of traditional epics lest the
story seem incomplete. Put most simply, one can say with
much more credibility, "*They* lived happily ever after"
than "*I* lived happily ever after." When any poet, therefore, tries to write a first-person personal epic, he is I think
attempting the impossible task of narrating the end from
the midpoint.

Chappell's title suggests an awareness of this problem, for
it identifies an unspecified quest only to focus our attention
on its extended hiatus. Extending that hiatus, paradoxically, is the goal of Chappell's quest, and the end, by generic
convention unknowable, is defined as *nothing*: In **"My
Grandfather Dishes the Dirt,"** Fred's grandfather states
from the grave, "The dead I'm here to say have nothing
to say." And in **"Second Wind,"** Fred's grandmother recalls the day of his grandfather's burial:

> What was I thinking? Nothing nothing nothing.
> Nothing I could nicely put a name to.
> There's a point in feeling bad that we come to
> Where everything is hard as flint: breathing,
> Walking, crying even. It's a heathen
> Sorrow over us. Whatever we do,
> It's nothing nothing nothing. We want to die,
> And that's the bitter end of all our loving.

Not the *nothingness* at the end, but the *somethingness* at
the middle is Chappell's goal. As Fred says to himself in
the doggerel couplets that parody birthday card verse, in
"Birthday 35: Diary Entry," "But *everything* means *something,* that's my faith; / Despair begins when I stop my
mouth." Especially given the italicizing, we cannot know
whether Fred is saying that all things have some significance or that, almost to the contrary, the word that signifies *all* only means *some.* Fred's faith is thus ambiguous,
and on the next page he says:

> I'd sleep in the eiderdown of the True Believer
> And never nightmare about Either / Or

> If I had a different person in my head.
> But this gnawing worm shows that I'm not dead.

> Therefore: either I live with doubt
> Or get out.

Midquest is a manifestation of a faith (flirting with bravu-
ra) in the somethingness of everything, with Fred's something found in the center of his Southern family, friends
and wife, Susan, the bedmate to whom he wakes and with
whom he makes love on this central morning of this central day of his midlife. With a moment of love at its center,
the quest becomes the desire to sustain that moment, in
all its lyric intensity, against the encroachment of chronology, of time.

Perhaps one way to look at *Midquest,* then, is from the
center out. At the center of the tetralogy is the last poem
of *Bloodfire,* **"Bloodfire in the Garden,"** which ends returning to the bed Fred shares with Susan:

> In this garden our bed we have burned
> down again to the ghost of us,
> green Aprils collide
> in our blood.

> Burnt-off, we are being prepared.
> The seeds of fresh rain advance,
> wind bearing from the south,
> out of the green isles
> of Eden.

The burning down yields ghost not ash, and hence memory is not stirred with the dull desire of cruel April but rather the collision of green Aprils. Rather than end with dry
seed, the fire sermon of *Bloodfire* ends with renewal and
the seeds of fresh rain. Instead of a waste land, a Garden
of Eden borders this bed, a garden as Chappell renders
it—with recycled spirits and timeless fertility—not unlike
Spenser's Garden of Adonis. Entering this bed and the
center of his life and his poem and his Susan, then, is as
close to entering paradise as Fred comes.

Each volume begins with Fred's awakening to a sense of
birth and closes with intimations of mortality. The penul-
timate poem of the last volume, *Earthsleep,* **"Stillpoint
Hill That Other Shore,"** tells us:

> We beaten creatures cannot evermore
> bear. Too long
> we have thrashed in earthfire,
> our limbs quiver,
> exhaustion of stale guilt.

This poem, which almost concludes the tetralogy, goes on
to modify that sense of doom, making it sweeter: "*Sleeping
we are harmless at last. / Through silence moves a cloudless
peace.*" If sleeping modifies death on one hand, the poem
itself modifies the Edenic assertions found at its midpoint
by reminding us that, despite its assertiveness and expanse, *Midquest* is still just a poem, a personal poem of
someone still very much a part of his own unfolding narrative. Chappell makes us aware with the phrase "shall I tell
you" that the "*cloudless peace*" is only a personal fabrica-

tion, more valid as an offer of comfort than an assertion of cosmic verity:

> The peace that shall seize us
> in sleepgrip,
> that peace shall I tell you
> be all the black frenzies of our flesh
> in one green cuddle,
> let us descend to our house
> our bed
> and invite the mornings,
> which reach out to touch us
> with the hands of one another.

So too, against the doom, he offers again their bed, no longer covered by the winds of Eden or the infinite mornings of rebirth, but rather by the act of inviting the infinite, so that the poem ends with an invitation to immortality sealed by the clasp of two very mortal hands.

If this poem modifies the earlier assertions, it is in turn modified by the last poem of the tetralogy, **"Earthsleep,"** which seems to return to the voice of assertion, changing again our sense of that sleep:

> It is the bottomless swoon of never forgetting.
>
> It is the foul well of salvation.
>
> It is the skin of eternity like a coverlet.
>
> It is a tree of fire with tongues of wind.
>
> It is the grandfather lying in the earth and the father digging.
>
> The mother aloft in the air, the grandmother singing.
>
> It is the fire that eats the tree of life.
>
> It is Susan in the hand of sleep a new creature.

These assertions, however, shift by the end of the poem to a final focus on Susan and metaphors for the act of loving her, so that she becomes both the temporal and eternal center against which the end is weighed.

In the constant refocusing impelled by comparing parallel sections of this work, we find one form of modification. The poem has many others, and we might even say that its mode of development is modification rather than narration. Such a mode of developments suits the intention of *Midquest* well because, being revisionary, it forces us to look back rather than forward and hence moves us away from the chronological toward the timeless. To this end, Chappell uses a very wide variety of verse forms to focus on a small group of people—Fred's mother, father, grandmother, grandfather, and Virgil Campbell, returning at the beginning, end and center of each volume to that central figure, Susan. Each of these figures thus confronts not only the elements of nature but also the elements of poetry, and each return to the figures at the center of Fred's life modifies our sense of those figures by telling us something new, making us see them in a different element and, finally, making us see them through the conventions of a different verse form. Each modification thus reminds us of the impossibility of the quest—a quest for forms which

will capture everything, prevent loss in the temporal human motion from somethingness to nothingness.

To that contest with nothingness, Chappell brings two weapons. The first is his pure poetic skill. He not only chooses a wide range of forms but employs them with deftness and authority. Although his subject matter is often the anecdotal tales of a rural Southern family, the poetry is never bathetic because, without denying the foibles of those who made his midquest possible, Chappell never suggests they are inappropriate subjects for elevated verse. This balance requires the kind of skill evident in the following stanza from **"Rimbaud Fire Letter to Jim Applewhite"**:

> Those were the days! . . .—But they went on
>   and on.
> The failure I saw myself grew darker and darker.
> And hearing the hard new myths from Bob Mi-
>   randon,
> I got Rimbaud confused with Charlie Parker.
> It was a mess, mon vieux. Finally
> They kicked me out, and back to the hills I went.
> But not before they'd taught me how to see
> Myself as halfway halved and halfway blent.

In the rich allusiveness, the not-uncritical nostalgia, the rhyming of proper names, the mixture of literary and musical figures, and the sentimental lapse into a foreign language, this piece might pass as the Southern version of something by perhaps our most polished contemporary poet, James Merrill. The poem, like many of Merrill's, deals with the influence of the arts, and especially of a specific poet, on the self-as-naif. Loss of innocence, in such a poem, means a growing literary sophistication in which the love of a style matures warily into love of style itself. "Form's what affirms" Merrill says in one poem, in good-natured mockery of his poet-as-pedant voice. One senses that Merrill finds the statement not so much untrue as limited. Form affirms only experience already felt, Merrill suggests, and Chappell brings to his quest that second vital weapon—a strong awareness of the sensual world, the world worth retaining. Thus again, in the logic of his work, just as Chappell pursues his quest by not moving, so he collects material for eternalizing from his deciduous surroundings, material constantly being buried, or washing, burning, blowing away.

In many ways *Midquest* resembles most closely, of contemporary works, Merrill's first-person personal epic trilogy, recently published in one volume under the title *The Changing Light at Sandover*. Significantly, both Merrill and Chappell see the need for organizing structures which violate chronology. The numbers, words and letters of the Ouija board provide Merrill's structure as the four elements do Chappell's. Although important in both works, time is subordinated in both to that structure, which blurs distinctions between past and present, life and death. That quality, found in Spenser's Garden of Adonis, which typifies Fred's bed at the end of his second volume also informs Merrill's work. Merrill in fact quotes Spenser's Garden of Adonis passage near the end of his first volume.

This tribute is not surprising because the story of Venus and Adonis focuses the issue of permanence and change central to the first-person personal epic. The Garden of Adonis is the privileged place which permits the wedding of Venus—a goddess, by definition unchanging—and Adonis—a mortal, by definition mutable. The story of Venus and Adonis thus represents the dual, paradoxical demands we make of art: that it be mimetic, mirror the vicissitudes of decay endemic to the human condition; and that it defy or transcend that condition by providing something that will endure unchanged.

If Spenser's Garden of Adonis suggests a place where such dual demands—of mortality and immortality—can be met, we must remember that Spenser sets his Garden outside human time. (It is a prelapsarian garden, we know, because Amoret, the infant who leads us there, was born without giving her mother, Chrysogone, pain.) Only in this prelapsarian state, for Spenser, does it seem possible to meet the dual demands of narrative and lyric, but in the post-Renaissance world the requisite belief in such a state grows harder and harder to posit.

Wordsworth locates his prelapsarian world in childhood. The child thus becomes the father of the man, and emotion recollected in tranquility—a lyric endeavor—often produces stories of childhood—a narrative result. Wordsworth's long first-person personal poem therefore fails, despite its insistent effort, to become epic for the same reason that Whitman's and Williams's succeed: the need for the author to establish a perspective free from the limitations of his own life's timeframe. Chappell and Merrill create such a perspective through the structures of their epics, and by thinking of Chappell in connection with Merrill's already much-discussed trilogy, we can see that *Midquest* is in the tradition of those poems trying to meet the near-impossible demands put by the modern age on the epic genre.

If Wordsworth's privileged world of childhood was more narrow and limited than Spenser's Garden, it was perhaps only slightly less sacrosanct. It still implied faith in a transcendent state which allowed the mortal to have intimations of immortality. In the modern age, faith is harder to find, and in the twentieth century Wallace Stevens posed the question, in "Sunday Morning," for which the Garden of Adonis no longer provided an adequate answer: "Is there no change of death in paradise? / Does ripe fruit never fall?" One response, I have suggested, is an epic lyric like *Midquest.* (pp. 323-31)

> Alan Nadel, "Quest and Midquest: Fred Chappell and the First-Person Personal Epic," in New England Review and Bread Loaf Quarterly, *Vol. VI, No. 2, Winter, 1983, pp. 323-31.*

Dabney Stuart   (essay date 1987)

[*Stuart is an American poet, short story writer, and educator. In the following essay, he provides an overview of Chappell's fiction and poetry.*]

In *Poison Pen,* his recent compendium of cultural and literary satire, novelist and poet George Garrett, faintly disguised, calls Fred Chappell the John-Boy Walton of American poetry. It's a facetious remark, of course, but

Cover for the paperback edition of Chappell's "poetic autobiography."

there's enough truth in it to afford an unexpected entrance to Fred Chappell's work. Chappell was born May 28, 1936, and grew up on a farm in Canton, near Asheville, North Carolina, but his family poems in *Midquest* give a tougher, less whimsical access to the kind of hardscrabble farm life popularized in Earl Hamner's television series.

Midquest's narrator, "Ole Fred"—composed of Chappell's attitudes, memories, and experiences, but not identical with the author—celebrates his thirty-fifth birthday in four groups of poems, one series each for the elements once believed to have been the components of all matter—earth, air, fire, and water. He begins the second poem of the volume by quoting Dante—"Midway in this life I came to a darksome wood"—establishing another classical basis for what follows. I will come back to this, but the focus for now is Ole Fred's family, which populates the volume via monologue and dialogue (with Fred as a boy), centering its down-home humor, grit, and independence.

His grandparents and parents are the principals, sharply individualized, economically rendered, living at harmonious odds with each other in hard times, honoring each other's idiosyncrasies, complementing strength with weakness, weakness with strength. The mother's account of her unique courtship—J.T., who taught at the same schoolhouse, borrowed her slip to use in his class experiments with electricity, flying it past her window like Ben Franklin's kite—acts as a screen memory that helps her not dwell too closely on how difficult life actually was. Her real code word is "hard." Fred's father, for whom money is scarce and a burden simultaneously ("Thinking of nothing but money makes me sick") burns a dollar bill to assert his freedom, and in another instance makes up for his son a beguiling tale in which he itemizes the contents of the layers of a hurricane. For the grandmother it's the disintegration of the family that is worrisome. Noting Fred's "bookishness," she fears he'll grow up to be a lawyer, becoming "second-generation-respectable." She also believes he can never cut loose from his roots altogether; she says to him,

> "Not all the money in this world can wash true-
>   poor
> True rich. Fatback just won't change to arti-
>   chokes."
>
> "What's artichokes?"
>
>   "Pray Jesus you'll never know.
> For if you do it'll be a sign you've grown
> Away from what you are. . . . ."

Another central character, though not family, is Virgil Campbell, who runs a general store and generally keeps the community from hunkering too morosely on its problems. His first name echoes his literary predecessor, but one of the pitfalls Chappell successfully skirts is solemnity, and his guide through the difficulties of daily life navigates by means of humor. "Campbell," he writes in the introduction to *Midquest,* "is supposed to give to the whole its specifically regional, its Appalachian, context." In **"Dead Soldiers,"** instead of recalling disaster and loss, the focus is on Campbell's shooting his emptied jars of whiskey as they float from the basement of his store on floodwater. Eventually the bridge just upriver starts to sway and groan, so he takes a shot at it as it falls, becoming known as the man who killed the bridge.

There is, of course, more to such procedures than fun. Humor's relationship to survival and sanity is a matter for celebration on any account. To this Chappell adds, as a premise on which his "character" poems rest, the understanding of the psyche's way of turning its attention aside from events of disaster and grief to scenes and activities obliquely attached to them. Too direct a memory numbs; the indirect route makes us able to continue the trip. It's a compromise struck between facing reality head on and trying to evade it altogether, and is one reason this aspect of Chappell's work, though affectionate and open, is bracingly unsentimental (which helps, incidentally, to distinguish him further as a storyteller from John-Boy Walton).

The focus on rural character and situation I have approached through *Midquest* extends, unsurprisingly, into Chappell's prose as well. A cluster of four stories in *Moments of Light* could be considered as stages in the declension of the life of Mark Vance from the coherencies of rural experience to the debilitation of the city. Though he is not uniformly happy as a boy on the farm—indeed, one observes in his inattention and lack of will the seeds of

later problems—he is nonetheless in an environment that requires certain contributions from him necessary to survival. If he doesn't get water to his father at work in the long sun, for instance, the man's labor will be more tortuous; if he's not responsible with his ignorance about items such as blasting caps, his life is at risk. He is also surrounded by people who care about him, and who seek to help him grow into a productive place among the family and its traditions.

In the university town where we later see him, however, he is cut off from such people and the land with which they share a covenant of nurture and increase. The result is a harrowing rootlessness. To feel how sharply Chappell suggests the disparity of the two environments one could compare the good-humored, brightly surprising introduction to sex Rosemary gives Mark (in **"The Weather"**) with the dissolute, hollow visit he has with Norma in **"The Thousand Ways."**

One of the few black characters in Chappell's fiction, Stovebolt Johnson in **"Blue Dive,"** acts as a central instance of civility, decorum, and balanced regard for both himself and other people. The dramatic structure again involves the paradigmatic polarization of rural and urban. This time, however, Chappell puts the big city dude—Locklear Hawkins, who runs the dive where Johnson seeks a job as a guitarist—in farm country, an inversion that enables him to have Johnson play with the homefield advantage. His ability to restrain his anger under considerable pressure is in part due to his being surrounded by people whose pace and habits he is familiar with and can therefore draw succor and support from. Chappell's phrase for a central quality of farmers is "inspired patience," an attribute that Johnson, though not a farmer, embodies.

Although over half of *Moments of Light* deals with other subjects, Chappell sets all of *I Am One of You Forever* on a farm. It is a series of stories, too, but they are loosely connected through form and characters to approximate a novel. Chappell's use of humorous exaggeration in many of the chapters is an obvious indication of the book's genial tone. *I Am One of You Forever* is also his most extensive dramatization of the values of a farm family's cohesion and support, which foster the mutual independence and growth of its members.

The various eccentric uncles who visit young Jess and his parents become involved in situations whose familiar American hyperbole (à la Paul Bunyan, Epaminondas, and Mark Twain) is, first of all, entertaining. It is also, I think, suggestive of one of the necessities in a kind of life whose intimacy and death-defying routine are always simmering tensions that might eventually erupt in strife and disharmony. That necessity is the acceptance of idiosyncrasy and outright craziness. A farm family has to make room for its loonies, much as certain tribes of native Americans once did. Again, the issue is survival, and comic inventiveness plays a basic role.

One of the uncles out—Don Juans his namesake until his life is bogusly threatened; another's beard grows to incredible lengths; another, when he comes to visit, brings his coffin and sleeps in it. The pleasure of observing young Jess watch these men includes seeing him become alternately curious about and afraid of them, and, eventually, with his father's help, learning to incorporate them into his sense of life and its possibilities. Chappell complicates those possibilities by interpolating other considerations through occasional non-uncle chapters. The audience he desires, whatever else it may be, is not naive. Humor isn't escape, but accommodation; Chappell romanticizes neither it nor country life. Jess must confront, among other things, the loss of a close friend, the challenge of competition with other men, and the eternal need on a farm to rebuild what nature destroys and will destroy again. The following paragraph concludes **"Overspill,"** a story about just such a destruction. Jess's mother has come home to find that the bridge built for her has been brought to nothing by a flood.

> The tear on my mother's cheek got larger and larger. It detached from her face and became a shiny globe, widening outward like an inflating balloon. At first the tear floated in air between them, but as it expanded it took my mother and father into itself. I saw them suspended, separate but beginning to drift slowly toward one another. Then my mother looked past my father's shoulder, looked through the bright skin of the tear, at me. The tear enlarged until at last it took me in too. It was warm and salt. As soon as I got used to the strange light inside the tear, I began to swim clumsily toward my parents.

Jess's vision here reveals better than any commentary the complex centrality of family life as I have been discussing it in Fred Chappell's work. But if he was born and raised in rural western North Carolina, he went east to a fancy college, "deserting," he says, "manual for intellectual labor," and has made his living as a teacher of literature and writing for twenty-two years. It would be a shock similar to encountering a black hole in space if his fiction and poetry didn't reflect the part humane letters has played in his life, too.

Chappell has been around long enough, in fact, for apocryphal rumors to have sprouted. He is alleged to have started writing before he could talk, and in his early teens to have printed reams of science fiction stories under an undivulged pseudonym. Fortunately, more dependable information is available about him as a poet in high school, and later during his checkered undergraduate career at Duke University. His **"Rimbaud Fire Letter to Jim Applewhite"** (in the *Bloodfire* section of *Midquest*) reveals, from an affectionately amused adult perspective, something of the intensity with which he immersed himself in his image of the feverish young *auteur.*

> Four things I knew: Rimbaud was genius pure;
> The colors of the vowels and verb tenses;
> That civilization was going up in fire;
> And how to derange every last one of my senses:
> Kind of a handbook on how to be weird and
>   silly.

I don't want to veer toward biography here so much as to point at the fierce allegiance, however adolescent, to literature the poem recounts. It is one of three such letters in *Midquest,* written to other authors, that focus this allegiance, as well as a few of its particular objects: Rimbaud, Dante, and science fiction authors, especially Poe, H. P. Lovecraft, and H. G. Wells.

A cursory skimming of *Midquest* will show how pervasive Dante is, for instance. The conception of the book, as well as much of its overall structure, derives from *The Divine Comedy.* I've already mentioned the "darksome wood" beginnings of both poems, and Virgil Campbell's kinship to the Roman epic poet who guides Dante through hell to heaven. That *Midquest* lacks the inclusive theological system of Dante's trilogy is part of its meaning. It is, after all, written three-quarters of the way through an exhaustingly secular century, determined, it sometimes appears, to exceed past human horrors without the hope the church afforded in previous times. Chappell's poem, however, is no less serious in its scope and intention than *The Divine Comedy;* God and the Bible suffuse it. There are descents into hell (**"Cleaning the Well"**), rebirths (**"Bloodfire," "Fire Now Wakening on the River"**), frequent ponderings on flesh and spirit (**"Firewood"**), and no embarrassment accompanies the evocation of the spirits of the dead.

From this perspective even the discussion of literature in the playlet **"Hallowind"** (whose title, too, has religious implications) assumes an added spiritual dimension. Note this exchange between Ole Fred, Reynolds Price, and the personified rain:

> FRED.   The most symbolic line there is,
>   And fullest of hard realities,
>   Is Shakespearean: "Exeunt omnes."
>
> REYNOLDS. Your poet's a foe to love and
>   laughter.
>   Here's the line one gives one's life
>   for:
>   "They all lived happily ever
>   after."
>
> THE RAIN. What say we work us up some brio
>   And drown this silly wayward
>   trio?
>   My favorite line is "Ex Nihilo."

From **"Ex Nihilo,"** with its suggestion of the creation, to "exeunt omnes" covers much of the ground human beings travel. When the narrator prays at the close of the opening poem in *Earthsleep,* "Hello Destiny, I'm harmless Fred, / Treat me sweet Please," he isn't asking for a favorable literary reputation.

The Divine Comedy is to *Midquest* as Vergil to Dante, I think. This is the most important antecedent evident in the poem, though Chaucer's *Canterbury Tales,* Byron's two comic epics, Browning's monologists, and Chekhov's tender, clear-eyed stories exert their acknowledged influences as well. Chappell cites others in his preface, adding that "some of the grand idols of my admiration—Baudelaire, Rimbaud, Rilke, Pound—did not show up, or appeared only in order to be made fun of."

It is in Chappell's early novels that those grand idols exert their power without the filter of distance and humor, more by their example of intoxicated, romantic sacrifice of everything for literature ("Be drunk with something," Baudelaire urged) than by any specific borrowing Chappell does. Thomas Mann and William Faulkner are among the more accessible pantries he raids for particular goodies, using shifting time perspectives and narration within narration in *It Is Time, Lord,* and, in *The Inkling* and *Dagon,* a sweaty determinism reminiscent of *The Sound and the Fury. The Gaudy Place,* a sprightlier, less hermetic book, has the multiple narrators of *As I Lay Dying,* as well as something of its mordant humor.

Still, taken together, Chappell's first four novels are very much his own; they receive a fine extended discussion by R. H. W. Dillard in *The Hollins Critic.* From the wider perspective of his later work, the first three of them constitute a little package of experiment and exorcism, a descent into the maelstrom it appears now to have been necessary to hazard and survive. They honor, as does all Chappell's output, the darker, inarticulate regions of human nature, the ineffable dreamwork done in those depths and the actual dreams that issue from them. They embody, however, as the work that follows them does not, the horrible possibility that the animal in us might indeed be severed from the articulation of mind and soul, and that human life might be reduced again to the mute, destructive servitude of the will. In these books the vision is unremittingly demonic, lacking the modest openness and broad curiosity, and the resulting humor, of the poetry and fiction that have followed them.

I began this focus on education and influence by using the phrase "humane letters" instead of "literature" because Chappell's reading includes an abundance of stuff from a variety of areas. Beyond Vergil, whose *Georgies* are relevant to a farm boy turned author, his classical interests include Lucretius, Horace, Pliny, and Ovid. His historical fiction, much of it uncollected, reveals more than a nodding acquaintance with an astronomer, Sir William Herschel, a botanist, Carl Linnaeus, a vain geographer, Maupertuis, and composers such as Haydn, Offenbach, and Mozart. Apparently minor figures from American cultural and theological history turn up, too, as witness Thomas Morton, whose experiences with his Merrymounters underpin the Puritan explorations (kin also to Hawthorne) in *Dagon.*

This is a partial list, indicative of the breadth of Chappell's interests, but not of the ease with which he carries his erudition. It is not paraded, but subsumed into appropriate situation, event, and character, alluded to quietly enough to alert an informed reader without putting off a less informed one. *Castle Tzingal* and *Source,* his two most recent collections of poems, are further cases in point.

In the former, a verse novel in voices—almost, indeed, a play without stage directions—Chappell plies together, amidst a diversity of forms similar to *Midquest,* a number of allusive threads. The context and plot are medieval, as is enough of the vocabulary ("grutch," "frore") to suggest the period: a deranged king murders and decapitates a traveling minstrel whose isolated head continues to sing, haunting the surviving members of the court. The consequent societal- and self-destruction is Biblical in its visitation of sin upon the sinner, and assumes that humankind has an operative conscience despite the modern overlays

of this or that theoretical utopian salve. A background twine is the legend of Orpheus, to which Chappell gives a science-fiction twist. Instead of being borne down the river Hebrus, the singer's "comely head," hidden in "a grotesque undercellar," is "suspended in fluids beside a gurgling retort."

Source shows Chappell moving through various image clusters in the book's earlier sections to a culminating vision that is atomic, explicitly based in Lucretius' depiction of the universe in *De Rerum Natura.* Chappell's use of Lucretius' atomism ranges from the minute—frost seen as "emery," a fog dissolving solid objects "into spirit"—to the intergalactic: the stars, in a representative instance, are a "bright fishnet lifting from darkness those broken / many heroes we read the mind with." Between these extremes the volume's individual poems show the illusorily solid human species carrying out its daily heroism, its sweet music, its longing for rest, as well as its potentially sudden joining up with the eternal smithereens.

Though from the outset of his career Chappell has published poems in which he observes particular details in nature, he has not, to my mind, ever been a "Nature" poet. The poems in *Source* offer a fresh illustration of this point. They refer consistently to such items as Queen Anne's lace, the milking of cows, the slow spread of evening, and much else we associate with the term *nature.* All these details, however, are perceived as parts of an inclusive vision of human experience, current and historical. Of all theories of matter, atomism by definition dwells most insistently on the discrete, but it also views its particulars from a unifying perspective. (pp. xi-xix)

Fred Chappell the author who thinks is Fred Chappell the farm boy grown up, and what he thinks about is partly unified by that process. His grandmother's warning that he might grow away from himself wasn't an old woman's ignorant fear, but it appears equally true that Ole Fred has grown toward himself as well, as any plant grows away from its necessary root to flower. The fifty years this has taken (so far) is misleading if one conceives of it spatially—a "long" time. It is more helpful to say it is *one* time. Fred Chappell is one person, though unfinished; in *Midquest* Ole Fred refers to himself as "halfway halved and halfway blent." Similarly, his thought is rooted in that gaping child, who, as we all do, took everything in without thought. Chappell's tireless, wide-ranging intellectual curiosity, and the poetry and fiction that issue from it, are the attempt to understand wholly that "ulterior motive," however complex, that comes with consciousness. Intellect is vapid if it doesn't proceed from feeling; the feeling intellect in search of ecstasy keeps the twin hopes of recovery and synthesis alive, the future positive.

Finally, Fred Chappell concludes a recent essay about Vergil's idealized vision of the farmer in his bucolic poetry with a paragraph that could as well be, and I suspect is, about himself.

> Most poets would make better lutenists than farmers. But even the most inept of us still feel close kinship with the man in the fields, with his life of ordered observation and inspired patience. That is the one life besides poetry and natural

philosophy that still touches an essential harmony of things, and when a civilization discards that way of life, it breaks the most fundamental covenant mankind can remember.

(p. xx)

Dabney Stuart, " 'What's Artichokes?': An Introduction to the Work of Fred Chappell," in The Fred Chappell Reader, *St. Martin's Press, 1987, pp. xi-xx.*

Chappell's characters are especially interesting because they find fulfillment not by denying tragedy, but by consciously defying it through a heightened sensitivity to everyday events.

—Alex Raksin, in the Los Angeles Times Book Review, *1987*.

Publisher's Weekly (review date 23 December 1988)

[*In the following review, the critic discusses Chappell's use of language in* First and Last Words.]

Erudition and stylistic refinement mark [*First and Last Words*], in which critical interpretation joins hands with poetic invention: most of the poems reconsider literary or artistic works (Virgil's *Georgics,* Aaron Copland's *Appalachian Spring,* Vermeer's *The Astronomer*). A third of the book tells of the poet's own life and times ("The house is changed where death has come, / as the rose is changed / by the visit of the bee"). Ranging far and wide, Chappell's (*Source*) intellectual poetry is at times abstruse, with words and lines carefully positioned within the constraints of a larger design. Yet, in the down-to-earth **"Dipperful,"** a young man accepts a drink of water from an old-timer and lends an ear to his rambling chat, delightfully rendered. Vernacular appeals to some ears, critical discussion to others; it is the rare poet who, like Chappell, speaks both languages.

A review of "First and Last Words," in Publishers Weekly, *Vol. 234, No. 26, December 23, 1988, p. 78.*

Amy Tipton Gray (essay date 1988)

[*In the following essay, Gray determines the influence of H.P. Lovecraft's horror stories on* Dagon.]

Throughout most of his career Fred Chappell has suffered the fate of the prophet who stays in and in his case, writes about his own land. While his early novels in particular have enjoyed success overseas, and have earned him such honors as the 1971 Prix de Meilleurs des Lettres Etrangeres (awarded for *Dagon*) recognition in his own country has been slow in coming. In fact, only his most recent novel, *I Am One Of You Forever,* published over

twenty years after his first, has received any sort of general critical acclaim. The same is not true of his poetry, which has attracted a wider and more appreciative audience and for which he has been the recipient of many awards, including the 1985 Bollinger Prize. It would be easy to assume, then, that Chappell's success as a poet names him a failure as a novelist. This is most emphatically not the case. For it is in Chappell's first three novels that themes of his poetry are first explored, and many of the problems in his early writing (prose as well as poetry) are worked out. Moreover, *Dagon* is clearly the pivotal work in Chappell's early corpus. It embodies both the culmination and resolution of Chappell's early difficulties, and points the way to the superior work that will follow. But in addition to suffering from Chappell's characteristic experiments with theme and style, *Dagon* has consistently been either dismissed or misinterpreted because of the writer's use of names and incantations taken from the Cthulhu mythos invented by H. P. Lovecraft. Such misapprehension must be cleared up before the novel can be appreciated for what it is: something more significant than just one more story about the reappearance of Lovecraft's mythical continent R'Lyeh, couched in this case in just one more of Chappell's difficult and unappealing first novels.

It is easy to discern the reasons for the unpopularity of Chappell's early work, especially *Dagon.* For Chappell "is an experimental novelist, a designation he himself has acknowledged" [David Paul Ragan, "Fred Chappell" in *Dictionary of Literary Biography,* Vol. 6]. To use his own term, he is "a writer of the arabesque." Quillen quotes Chappell's definition of such a writer as one who "is less concerned with delivering basic narrative materials than with manipulating these materials in an idiosyncratic manner" [Rita S. Quillen, "Looking for Native Ground: The Appalachian Poetry of Fred Chappell and Wayne Miller," *Appalachian Heritage,* 1980]. A writer of the arabesque provides "a satisfactory narrative outline" and "then manipulates the elements so that the train of his narrative becomes of secondary importance" (Quillen). Most readers who are not interested in post-modernist theory and who buy books precisely because what they want is a good ride on that narrative train, find little in this technique to recommend. And when combined with unsympathetic and unappealing characters, abstruse symbolism and obscure allegory, and an unrelenting exposition of the dark side of human nature, the novel of the arabesque is practically a sure-fire failure. Which critically, of course, Chappell's first three novels were.

Dagon was called by one critic "another horse from the dilapidated stable of the Southern Gothic novel." Another wrote, "There is nothing here to commend it to libraries." It was accused of being both a gothic retread and an unprofitable reworking of the Lovecraftian vein. A summary of the plot quickly demonstrates why *Dagon* has suffered these epithets. The novel opens with a quotation that proves indecipherable to anyone who is not familiar with the work of Lovecraft: "Ph'nglui mglw' nafh Cthulhu R'lyeh wgah'nagl fhtagn" A prolonged scarch will eventually lead to "The Call of Cthulhu," which yields this unhelpful translation: "In his house at R'lyeh dead Cthulhu waits dreaming." After passing that arcane beginning, the reader pushes on to learn that, true to Chappell's then favorite form, the basic plot of the novel is simple to outline—once it has been unearthed.

Peter Leland, a minister, inherits an old house and decides to take a leave of absence from his ministry to write a book titled *Remnant Pagan Forces In American Puritanism*, a topic inspired by William Bradford's account of the Merry Mount (Mount Dagon) incident. Once he and his wife Sheila have moved in, Peter discovers a horde of old documents stored in the house, documents that are filled with words such as "Shoggoth," "Pnakotic," "Nyarlath," and "Nephreu" (which, as the only word not found in Lovecraft's stories, may well be Chappell's own contribution to the pantheon). He also discovers his neighbor Mina Morgan, with whom he immediately becomes erotically obsessed. As Peter falls more and more under the spell of both Mina and the old papers, he begins to personify one of the major themes of Chappell's early work, the struggle between will and appetite. Eventually, appetite is victorious. Peter, angered by Sheila's insistence that he kill a snake (what else?), kills his wife instead and moves in with Mina, who ensures the triumph of appetite by drugging him with sex and moonshine until he becomes devoid of will, both literally and figuratively impotent.

At this point the Lovecraftian elements of the story take on a new twist. Mina finds a new man to serve as an acolyte of sorts; they pour Peter into his car and take him to the seaport town of Gordon (perhaps Chappell's pun on the famous frozen fish company). There she hires two whores, and the four will them proceed to tattoo Peter's entire body while simultaneously reducing him to a childlike state. When the tattooing is finished, Mina has Peter taken to an altar where he is sacrificed before a maimed and truncated fertility deity Dagon. But Peter maintains his identity throughout the encounter, welcomes his sacrificial death instead of fighting it, and after dying gains a profound and detached understanding of the universe. He is transformed into Leviathan, the cosmic fish (perhaps the only aquatic being to escape Lovecraft), and settles into eternity: "joyfully bellowing, he wallowed and sported upon the rich darkness that flows between the stars."

In the face of such evidence. it is easy to see why many have believed that **Dagon** should as a matter of course be subsumed into the Lovecraftian genre, especially since Lovecraft himself "encouraged other writers to write stories in his framework" [L. Sprague deCamp, in *Lovecraft: A Biography*]. However, although Chappell and Lovecraft employed the same set of entities, both the purpose to which each put these creatures and the effect each was trying to achieve were widely disparate. Furthermore, while it can be said that critics such as S. T. Joshi (whose area of expertise is Lovecraft criticism) are correct in stating that "Chappell's **Dagon** . . . [strives] not to imitate slavishly Lovecraft's own plots," it cannot be asserted, as Joshi goes on to do, that Chappell sought "to elaborate on [Lovecraft's] ideas."

Lovecraft, an admirer of Poe and the eighteenth century, sought to revitalize horror fiction and bring it out of the disreputable corner of American letters in which it had so long sat. While he did not accomplish this goal, he did suc-

ceed in both redefining the genre and influencing the generation of writers who succeeded him (which included Robert E Howard and Stephen King). Lovecraft's genius was two-fold. First, he "firmly attached the emotion of spectral dread to such concepts as outer space . . . and alien beings," transferring "the focus of supernatural" anxiety "from man and his little world and his gods, to the stars and the black and unplumbed gulfs of . . . space" [Fritz Lieber, "A Literary Copernicus," in *Something About Cats,* August Derleth, ed.]. Second, he created a pantheon of monsters who, unlike any found in any horror story written up to that time, were absolutely indifferent to mankind. These powerful fish-beings had fallen to earth from somewhere in space to rule the planet from R'lyeh, the continent that sank beneath the sea upon their eventual overthrow. All but oblivious to the existence of that pitiful animal man, they were concerned only with using the priests and priestesses of their ancient cult to regain their former kingdom.

The invention of these viscoid creatures marks a major development in the world of science fiction. Before Lovecraft, even monsters from outer space had deliberate, personal reasons for wreaking havoc on the earth. Lovecraft, however, understood that true horror lies in the meaningless, pointless attack, in the fear peculiar to the twentieth century: the fear of being destroyed by something that cannot even be said to be uncaring, something that does not know or even think it is important to know who its victim is.

But the monsters of the mythos served another purpose in Lovecraft's fiction. Lovecraft believed that "the cosmos" was neither "basically inimicable" nor "beneficial to man" [Dirk W. Mosig, "H. P. Lovecraft: Myth-Maker." In *H. P. Lovecraft: Four Decades of Literary Criticism,* S. J. Joshi, editor.]. To this end he employed his creatures as metaphors for a dispassionate universe. Lovecraft, "a mechanistic materialist," saw man as merely another tiny accident in a universe full of tiny accidents, perpetually the victim of forces he neither understands nor controls. From this belief comes "the source of terror in Lovecraft's tales" [S. J. Joshi, in *H. P. Lovecraft: Four Decades of Literary Criticism*]. The grotesque eings of the mythos highlight what their creator perceives to be man's insignificance in a "universe revealed by materialistic science" to be a "purposeless soulless place" (Leiber). That most men would go mad if they were forced to face the true nature of reality is a matter of no great concern to Lovecraft. One should simply accept the fact that philosophy is an illusion, that human action is unimportant, and carry on.

Most critics, either knowing little or nothing of Lovecraft's philosophy or being unwilling to accept it, have focused on the creatures themselves rather than on the function they were designed to serve. Some critics have even gone so far as to impose their own religious beliefs, specifically traditional Christian doctrine, on a fictional system that patently did not support such interpretation. There is no redemption, not even existential, in the ethos upon which Lovecraft based his work.

Furthermore, Lovecraft's style, which even his devotees sometimes have difficulty admiring, has also contributed to the misinterpretation of his work. His admiration for Poe and the eighteenth century (which has been well documented) gave him his literary voice, a voice that does not speak in accents pleasing to the twentieth century ear. Unlike Chappell, he was no experimenter; he found nothing in the new to be recommended. Instead he strove to reproduce in his works a "style . . . in vogue in the Romantic era much used by Poe and his Gothic predecessors" [Kenneth W. Faig, Jr., in *H. P. Lovecraft: Four Decades of Literary Criticism*]. In this he succeeded; so much so that in many ways his work provides an almost faultless reproduction of the gothic style. His writing is verbose, difficult, inflated, and full of lurid, polychrome adjectives. His stories are set in mysterious old houses (the American version of the crumbling castle) by the sea; his plots overflow with violence and terror. His characters are flat. All motivation is exterior. And the plot invariably builds to a "terminal climax" by means of "confirmation rather than revelation" (Lieber).

Chappell, on the other hand, consistently has been praised for the clarity of his prose and the beauty of his descriptions. The motivation of his characters is interior; it is the war man fights against himself that fascinates Chappell. While he too has a fondness for old houses, his settings usually serve an allegorical purpose, unlike the mansions of Lovecraft, which function only as dilapidated props. Moreover, it is ironic that the difficulties in Chappell's works have come about because of his enthusiasm for experiment, while Lovecraft's stories suffer from that author's attempts to recreate the style of an age long past.

Thus it is neither archaic diction, nor a slavish adherence to the gothic, that has caused *Dagon*'s troubles. For in addition to suffering from the troubles that typically hound experimental novels, the book has consistently resisted classification. Despite its setting, it certainly could not be called an Appalachian novel, for its characters not to mention its plot do not fall into the patterns outlined by Cratis Williams, Isabel D. Harris and others. In addition, Chappell, by choosing a fictional mythos upon which to pin his narrative, effectively cut off his novel from a group of its contemporaries to which it could have easily belonged. Gardner's *Grendel,* Updike's *Centaur,* Barth's *Chimera* and even Mailer's *Ancient Evenings,* to name a few, all are based on reinterpretation of traditional mythologies. The key word, of course, is traditional; because of Cthulhu and company, *Dagon* was labeled, understandably science fiction. And with equal immediacy, it was dismissed as not being worthy of serious study.

The original idea for *Dagon* came not from Lovecraft, however, but from William Bradford. As Chappell puts it, "I discovered a literal event in Bradford's *History of the Plymouth Colony* which seemed to me to be metaphorically true of our own times. To drag Bradford's reported event into the present I posited a secret religious cult which had survived unseen for two centuries" [in his "Six Propositions about Literature and History," in *New Literary History,* 1970]. And the cult of Cthulhu, of which Dagon is a deity, is the cult that for better or worse came to Chappell's mind.

But Chappell used Lovecraft's mythos not because he

sought to write a horror story, but because he saw it as a powerful metaphor for man's interior struggle against evil (will against appetite), a struggle that must be manifested in the material world. Balanced between Calvin and Camus, Chappell believes that each individual is responsible for making sense of original sin (defined as a set of conditions existing before the characters come on the scene) in his own terms. Darkness triumphs only when man refuses to recognize the limitations with which he has no choice but to live, and refuses to work within those limitations. Unlike Lovecraft, Chappell does not believe philosophy is a comforting illusion maintained in the teeth of a meaningless existence. For this reason, Chappell went against all advice and refused to remove the final scene, in which Peter becomes Leviathan, from the novel. He could not, he said, "accept the triumph of evil that way in the world," and could not end *Dagon* without an attempt "to alleviate the agony of it" (Ragan).

The final evidence that Chappell is neither thrashing out another southern gothic nor reworking Lovecraft lies in the definition of the romance as set out by Richard Chase in *The American Novel and Its Tradition.* Chase states that the characters in a romance "will on the whole be shown in ideal relation. . . . they will share emotions only after they have become abstract or symbolic." When such characters do "become profoundly involved in some way," as Peter Leland does with Mina, they can only experience "a deep, narrow, and obsessive involvement." All moves towards abstraction and idealism. And as it is "less committed to the immediate rendition of reality" than other types of works, "the romance will more freely veer toward mythic allegorical and symbolistic forms." What better description can be found of *Dagon,* or indeed, of Chappell's early work as a whole?

It is clear that Chappell's *Dagon* should not be catalogued with the works of H. P. Lovecraft. While Chappell employs the names and incantations invented by Lovecraft in the rituals performed for the god Dagon, he does so with a purpose that goes far beyond Lovecraft's original intent. Chappell, unconcerned with intensifying the horror factor, imbues these figures with a symbolic power not found in the original stories for which they were created. In doing so Chappell dislodges his readers from their comfortable assumptions about reality and forces them to face what is darkest in themselves. From Lovecraft's perspective, man was merely a minuscule victim of forces beyond his cognizance; self-knowledge was of no help in deflecting the violence perpetuated by an amoral cosmos. To this end he used the characters from the Cthulhu mythos to give a new form to the horror story, for in his work, the terror comes from outside man's experience from external, indifferent beings rather than from within man's own being.

This is not true of Chappell, who believes that man, torn between will and appetite, can only resolve that struggle through self-knowledge; this is also the only means by which he can come to a resolution about the nature of the world and his place in it. In Chappell's cosmos conflict arises from each person's inner struggle to balance the opposing forces that beset us all. In Lovecraft's world, these forces are unimportant; one man's inner conflict means nothing when placed beside the devastation that can be on humanity by ancient forces, manifested in weird creatures beyond its ken. In short, Lovecraft's lexicon does not include the concept of hope; there is no escape from Cthulhu.

But Chappell, through Peter and Leviathan, has shown us the way out of R'lyeh. (pp. 73-8)

> *Amy Tipton Gray, "R'lyeh in Appalachia: Lovecraft's Influence on Fred Chappell's Dagon," in* Remembrance, Reunion and Revival: Celebrating a Decade of Appalachian Studies: Proceedings of the Tenth Annual Appalachian Studies Conference, *edited by Helen Roseberry, Appalachian Consortium Press, 1988, pp. 73-9.*

Harry Middleton   (review date 17 September 1989)

[*In the following review, Middleton discusses* Brighten the Corner Where You Are.]

His name is Joe Robert Kirkman. He is a science teacher at the Tipton high school in the mountains of North Carolina and he is in big trouble.

Kirkman is a man who likes to push life, feel it completely, live it fully. He delights in risks and challenge, in all that life is—its great joys, its telling tragedies, its promise and potential. Admirable characteristics, you would think, especially for a high school science teacher, but Kirkman's exuberance for life has gotten him, at last, into more trouble than he can handle. Perhaps.

In this deeply felt, warm, and funny novel [***Brighten the Corner Where You Are***] Fred Chappell, one of the South's and indeed the country's finest writers, introduces us to a character whose passion for life, for the hardness of truth, changes not only his life, but the lives of those around him.

Chappell's narrative, told by young Jess, Kirkman's son (Chappell readers will remember Jess from the novel *I Am One of You Forever*), probes close to bone and nerve, giving us a telling portrait not only of Joe Robert Kirkman, but of life in the small mountain town of Tipton just at the end of World War II.

As this single day in the life of Kirkman unravels so does the life of Tipton, in all its darkness and promise. Chappell, a master storyteller, weaves a wonderful tale, one full of wild humor and honest humanity, all of it surfacing in but a single day in a man's life.

It is, however, no ordinary day, but then Kirkman is no ordinary science teacher. Besides being a teacher, Kirkman is a farmer, an outdoorsman, something of a philosopher, and a most inventive and imaginative dreamer. In a place "so lacking in spice," he is a man of "derring-do." Tipton, N.C., is a town in need of a jolt of passion and Kirkman is just the man to deliver the blow. Kirkman can feel it's time to make his mark on life: "His glory days were coming. He could feel the bright glow of them on his face like a rising dawn."

Kirkman's less than traditional teaching methods, espe-cially concerning his handling of Darwin and the theory of evolution, have landed him in hot water with the local school board which has called a special session. Kirkman is to appear before them, explain himself. But things aren't going well for Kirkman. His day and his life seem starstruck. The day begins with Kirkman in the deep mountain night up a tree battling what he calls a devil-opossum (a bobcat) and getting the worst of the encounter; saving a drowning child in Trivet Creek and ruining his only suit in the process; meeting a ghost in the school's basement, and trying to coax a philosophical goat off the high school's roof and losing. And so on. By the time of his meeting with the school board, it seems Joe Robert Kirkman is indeed doomed.

But sometimes things work out, even if it takes a little magic, and it does here, but Chappell, a novelist and poet of great range and talent, handles it with great humor and grace, making it magic of the best sort: not just possible, but believable.

> *Harry Middleton, "Derring-do in a Land without Spice," in* Los Angeles Times Book Review, *September 17, 1989, p. 13.*

Michael Malone   (review date 1 October 1989)

[*Malone is an American novelist, playwright, and critic. In the following review, he examines the characters in* Brighten The Corner Where You Are.]

Chappell lives and teaches in North Carolina, whose modern literary landscape he has, with much wise humor and lyric grace, helped to define. The stylistic range of this "immensely gifted, exuberant, versatile writer" (William Styron's words) is evident from the opening pages of ***Brighten the Corner Where You Are.*** A Southern tall tale set in 1946, the novel leads us with a sure hand and a merry heart through one eventful May day in the life of Joe Robert Kirkman, a good-looking Appalachian schoolteacher, family man, farmer and visionary, as that day is imagined by his son Jess (from Chappell's last novel *I Am One of You Forever*).

The book opens with Jeff's fantasy about how his father steals the moon one night (it's gotten so large, you have to duck under it), hides it in a milk can; where it turns to cool creamy cheese, and then later climbs a ladder in order to return the moon to a sky that's blackly tanged with stars "unsteady and restless as fireflies." Joe Robert just laughs and says, well, he had to try it. The story is a perfect introduction to this quixotic hero, who sees himself as the local champion of reason and science, but who lies like a poet (or, as he puts it, like Jesus with his parables), and who looks to others "mounted backwards" on his steed, with his "shining armor clattering eerily about him like a tinware peddler's cart." (Rather like Alice's White Knight).

Throughout his comically catastrophic day, Joe Robert keeps climbing after the moon. Trapped into the exploit by his exaggerations to his "hunting" companions (the Crazy Creek Wildlife Appreciation Committee, a group of loafers worthy of Twain, who never actually hunt, just drink whiskey and listen to their hounds run), Joe Robert finds himself atop a poplar tree, inches from a huge angry bobcat. Next, determined to make an upright impression on the school board—scheduled to interrogate him that afternoon about complaints from fundamentalist parents that he's teaching their son irreligious Darwinism—Joe Robert instead ruins his good suit by jumping in a creek to save a drowning child. Already looking like a clownish bumpkin, and covered with bruises and plaster dust, he gets butted into a sooty chimney by a goat he's chased onto the schoolhouse roof.

But mostly Joe Robert talks, in a joyful excess of language. He talks to the goat Bacchus about philosophy, until the creature proves himself a decadent aesthete with a pederastic bent. He talks to his general science class about Kepler and Wegener and "oppugnant sobriquet[s]" and teaches them songs about the diluvial geologist William Burklund. In his world history class on the "death of Socrates," (both his great hero and a "windy old crank whose idea of a good time was just to get on people's nerves"), he stages a dialogue about his Darwin troubles with a student playing the Greek philosopher. He's a very good teacher, and we can see that on the page. Though he (and his creator) are occasionally a bit too boyishly coy, too sentimentally innocent about the seductive earth-mother wisdom of his pretty prize student (who proves to be married and pregnant), Joe Robert Kirkman is undeniably as charming as everybody thinks he is. If Scopes had had this man's personality, he wouldn't have needed Clarence Darrow.

And Joe Robert is destined for greatness, as he always suspected. Even his abrupt resignation to the school board backfires: " *'Look here,'* my father shouted. *"You can't fire me. I quit."* Then he backed out of the room, slammed the door, and was gone." Bewildered, the school board members ask each other "What in the world was that?" Did he say, "You can't hire me not to quit," or "Sugar, you Campfire girls are sweet" or something else altogether obscene?

Told with the fine control and the easy tone of Faulkner's *Reivers,* this novel is a whimsical love song to living, and to language. It is comic in a serious sense of that term— never ignoring the sorrow and evil of a "soul-harrowing" human "history steeped in blood and reveling in it," but never silenced by despair over that history. The book is filled with laughter, and with images of light—from the fire color of red foxes in the sun, to the arrival of electrical power to the North Carolina mountains "where such light had never been heard of before." May Chappell's wry, compassionate vision continue to brighten the corner of our fiction where he lives.

Michael Malone, "Pilgrim at Crazy Creek," in Book World—The Washington Post, *October 1, 1989, p. 7.*

Kate M. Cooper   **(essay date 1990)**

[*In the following excerpt, Cooper assesses the influence of the Southern literary tradition on* Castle Tzingal.]

Similar to [Chappell's] acclaimed *Midquest* tetralogy and

his more recent poetic collection *Source, Castle Tzingal* is a formally structured verse work in which the four classical elements—earth, water, wind, and fire—play highly symbolic roles. But instead of the southern rural landscapes that serve as backdrop in so much of Chappell's poetry, the setting of *Castle Tzingal* is the mythical court of a deranged king, a mad monarch whose obsessive attempts to insure total control over his subjects lead to the dissolution of his own kingdom.

Chappell's achievement in *Castle Tzingal* consists in part of his customary mastery of innumerable verse forms and traditions, combined with the ever-startling novelty of his own style. The overriding singularity of *Castle Tzingal,* however, resides in the insights it lends to a range of crucial issues. The intricate series of articulations that this text establishes between nature and culture, language and desire, poetry and power, point not only to the problematics of its own writing but also to the questions of production inherent to every literary undertaking. And if *Castle Tzingal* may be read as a clue to the understanding of southern culture and literature, it also speaks with uncanny explicitness to the issues of contemporary French theory.

The poem is a series of monologues, ballades, dramatic dialogues, and epistles that tell a devastating story of political decay, moral corruption, and loss. The tale relates the search for a poet/harpist named Marco whose prolonged absence has disturbed King Tzingal's court (especially the King's wife, Queen Frynna) and the neighboring realm of the mad King's half brother, King Reynal. Knowledge of Marco's whereabouts and of the circumstances of his disappearance is the goal of a quest that King Reynal has delegated to his emissary and first cousin, Petrus. Petrus's mission leads him within the walls of Castle Tzingal to various encounters with the depraved King's grotesque subjects, encounters which he then resumes in report form for King Reynal. Inside the dank walls of the castle, however, Marco's absence is the disturbing evocation of a melodic, disembodied voice (see Chappell's comment at the beginning of this discussion) that haunts the sleep of King Tzingal's subjects and troubles the depths of their memory. The perturbing lyrics of the disembodied voice conjure madness in those who hear them, and finally impel Queen Frynna and Tzingal's old, pensioned Admiral to their deaths.

Causally, then, Marco's mysterious disappearance and his spectral reemergence in song are the pretext of all speech and activity in the textual world of *Castle Tzingal.* Though the mad King's castle is the site of the entire poem, the effects of Marco's absence upon the respective kingdoms of Reynal and Tzingal give rise to two separate understandings of political rule, social order, and genealogical filiation in the text.

In Reynal's realm, effective political rule and genealogical linking are coterminous. Petrus's relation to the king signals this overlay of royal and familial orders since the emissary is at the same time a titled member of the court and the monarch's first cousin. In this "other" kingdom, Marco's protracted absence represents not only dismem-

> **Chappell's achievement in *Castle Tzingal* consists in part of his customary mastery of innumerable verse forms and traditions, combined with the ever-startling novelty of his own style.**
>
> **—*Kate M. Cooper***

berment of the body politic but also an excision from the royal family tree. Petrus's first letter from Castle Tzingal to his regent comments on this genealogical relation between King Reynal and the poet:

> Of your nephew Marco, whose silent disappear-
> ance
> I've come here to trace,—not much.
> I have unveiled some puzzling hints
> And know that he stopped here indeed
> Last year, received the gracious encouragements
> Of Queen Frynna.

Further, under Reynal the solid bonds of polity and kinship are only enhanced by the affective ties that the kingdom's members profess for each other and for their lost poet. In his first report to Reynal, Petrus comments on the infected atmosphere of Castle Tzingal and its unsuitability for a youth of Marco's constitution:

> A lad devoted to sport in open fields, to song
> And skillful love-converse, as Marco was,
> Would have but villeyn company in this place
> And much dour argument.
>
> . . . . .
>
> Marco's affections would not be for this place
> Or for these folk. And I do admit
> Neither is the liking of your close and faithful
> envoy.

The concurrence of filial, affective, and political ties linking King Reynal and his subjects suggests that his reign has been one approaching holism, one in which the structures of kinship, authority, and desire have achieved a viable balance. If there is an equilibrium implied by the cohesiveness of these public and private structures, it is only reinforced by the solidity of the genealogical relations between the kingdom's members. As first cousins, Reynal and Petrus share a linear tie to the same ancestors; as uncle and nephew, Reynal and Marco are descended in different degrees from the same parents. All three genealogical links (between the King and his emissary, between Petrus and the poet Marco, between Marco and the King) imply marital or sibling alliances—lateral bonds—that remain absent in the language of the text. Bound in relations of both affinity and consanguinity, the members of this poem's "other" kingdom are allied in multidimensional terms.

But such is not the case inside the walls of Castle Tzingal. The mad king's rule is one of strict linearity, a governance that seeks to control even the erratic supervention of de-

sire. In order to maintain his preeminent authority, Tzingal threatens his subjects with knowledge of their innermost fears and dreams, with the awareness of their own perverse humanity. In repeated attempts to assert his own supereminence, the obsessive King invokes either the illicit sexual conduct of his court members or their static purposelessness as mere functionaries in his realm. After one particularly brutal evening meal, the court's Astrologer reports the vitriolic tirade launched by Tzingal against the old Admiral:

> "Tell us," he told the Admiral, "how you took
> Zomara, and what you said when they struck
> Their colors. What joy
> That victory must have been! Or were you—
> As I have heard—below, buggering the pretty
> cabin boy?"
> The Admiral stared unseeing into his plate.
> "I know," the King continued, "of field commis-
> sions in battle.
> But to raise a lad from lackey to First Mate?
> I fear you take no prize for being subtle."

But neither is the Astrologer himself immune to King Tzingal's invective:

> "For you, Astrologer,"
> He said, "all energies of life have lost their savor.
> You are sick and cowardly and have betrayed
> Some best part of yourself. Do you recall
> The earnest scholar once you were and have
> since unmade?"

Thus, desire and its vagaries constitute the target of Tzingal's barbarous threats. In the case of the old Admiral, the alleged secret of desire and ensuing act of sodomy make for a faulty and humiliating infraction under Tzingal's law. Perhaps most interesting is the fact that the wretched King views that infraction in terms of a hierarchical displacement ("But to raise a lad from lackey to First Mate?"). On the other hand, the Astrologer is accused by his regent of a lack of desire itself, a stagnation of the vital forces which had formerly infused his work. In either case, in the furtive expression of sexual desire or in the demonstration of its loss, King Tzingal's subjects are called wanton because they want.

The King takes pains to exempt himself from the circuits of desire that he mentions to recriminate his court members. Tzingal's marriage to Queen Frynna, though a plausible locus for the licit expression of sexual desire, is a purely formal and barren relation overridden by the harsh imposition of the monarch's order. The Queen views her own plight as the grotesque inversion of her childhood:

> In Castle Tzingal I sigh long sighs
> And wish I were a silly child again,
> Nestled beneath my father's stout roof
> And never stolen away to be the wife
> Of an iron and fruitless man.
>
> . . . . .
>
> I am not suited for the intricate gloom
> And thorny intrigue of a blackguard time.
> There is a child, a sunny child
> Who dances within my breast and combs
> Her sunny hair and coddles a painted mammet.

In these bleak years I am defiled
By the drunken ambitions, the nightmare de-
   signs
Of a petty Mahomet.

The painted mammet of Queen Frynna's youth, the doll she embraced during childhood play, is now transformed into a false deity who alienates and repugns her with his possessive schemes. The royal couple's alliance is perhaps this poem's clearest expression of the sterilizing effects of an absolute, imposed order, a rule that alienates desire by seeking to appropriate it.

It is of course clear in the poem that Tzingal's consuming ardor in the poem is tantamount to poetic desire itself: the desire for total knowledge, truth, and the union of these two in an absolute expression. The fulminating regent seeks to fulfill this desire through the creation of the Homunculus, a miniature man made to order by the court Astrologer. Properly named Flyting but called Tweak throughout the poem, the Homunculus is the monarch's eyes and ears, a creature small enough to inhabit the undetected recesses of the castle walls and to accumulate the secrets of its denizens. Moreover, the tiny spy's loyalty to King Tzingal is unswerving:

—Ah no, I can't be bribed to speak. Whatever
Could you bribe me with?
The things I dream of are forever
Beyond my reach, sunk deep in earth
Or at a human height.

King Tzingal thus maintains control of his gloomy kingdom through the invasive scrutiny of his subjects' desires. To this end, Tweak is his most perfectly accomplished agent: in accordance with the King's command, the Homunculus spies upon the castle inhabitants, then reports the politics and gossip gleaned through his undetected surveillance. In the text, Tweak is a pure sign of the economy of knowledge—knowledge construed here in terms of plans for political rupture or as the secrets of personal desire. As the poem suggests, Tweak is tightly bound to the King in a relation of profound specularity: this "minim" man (and it is noteworthy that the adjective reads the same forward and backward) owes the debt of his existence to the King and thus reports the findings of his wily espionage only to the mad monarch:

I'm silent in a dusty nook
But in the Council Chamber I speak
My mind straight out and am respected.
No one can trust me but the King
Who caused me to be made.
That's my safety from the murderous boot
And poison marmalade.

The Homunculus serves all the deranged King's possessive designs: the order, agent, and reflection of political scheming and secret desire, Tweak stands within the poem as the perfectly efficient instrument of King Tzingal's complete dominion. By transmitting information to the King, he furnishes his sovereign's desire for absolute rule with the substance of knowledge.

But perhaps Tweak's most startling feature is his avowed immunity to the seduction of being loved:

I have no love of being loved; a minim man
Prefers to flourish by means of fear,
To cast beyond his stature giant shade.

What insures the miniature man's perfect efficacity in this role is his *lack* of affective need, and consequently, his insouciance regarding recognition for his services. Much as his name suggests, Tweak inhabits the elusive wrinkles of the text, and within them, gathers, witholds, and betrays all secrets. His omniscience is implied not only in the economy of his function in the poem but also in the circumstances of his creation. "Conceived with purpose" and "drawn up to plan," this minuscule model of a man represents the final achievement of the magic arts, the result of an elaborate alchemical rite:

My father was a mage, my mother a pour
Of mystery chemicals. I was born
On a table bright with flame and glassware,
And had no childhood except an ignorance
Of politics and gossip.

Tweak's omniscience in the poem may be allied to his fleeting omnipresence. Unlike the other figures in the realm who have distinctly ascribed private chambers in the castle, the little spy's only abode is a bottle through which he has perceptual access to all of the castle's hidden places—its nooks and crannies, cracks and crevices:

I'm hardly the first man to live in a bottle
And see the world through a different size.
I'm the King's most privy counselor,
And know the secrets lisped at midnight
By love-performing ministers
And cunning courtesans. I spy the spies
Who never seek beneath their beds
Or in the arras-folds hard by the banisters
Of the shadowed gallery.

Omniscient and omnipresent, exempt from the desire for personal recognition and betraying no human or tangible need, Tweak symbolizes the infallible alliance of knowledge and power. He stands in the text as the King's agent of authority, secure in his allegiance because of his unconcern for otherness or material gratification.

Yet there is something in the poem that ultimately overturns this rigid economy in which all knowledge is submitted to King Tzingal's glowering, intransigent rule. In the introductory stanzas of the poem, Tweak explains his own origins and privileged status in the castle to a strangely silent interlocutor. Much in the same way that he stirs anxiety and suspicion among the other figures in the text, the dwarf "tweaks" us as readers with a curious innuendo at the end of the first monologue:

I was conceived with purpose, drawn up to plan
And have a surer measure than a man.
It's s [*sic*] rarefied temptation
Could smudge my honesty,
And as for what *you* offer . . .
               Well, we'll see.

Who is this "you" in the passage? Is the miniature man suggesting that his unwavering loyalty to the King might be swayed? If so, what possibly could decide this "minim man"—along with all the absolute inferences of his poetic form and function—to switch allegiance? And to what place or political group would his newfound allegiance be directed?

As the poem progresses, we are gradually led to assimilate this mysterious "you" in Tweak's introductory monologue with Petrus, King Reynal's Master Envoy. Paradoxically, Petrus's mission is similar to Tweak's because he has been engaged to discover the whereabouts of the poem's emblem of desire, the poet/harpist Marco. But unlike Tweak, for whom the royal command to gather information (especially the knowledge of hidden desire) has no purpose or compensatory value beyond the fulfillment of the task, Petrus is both personally and politically implicated in his fictional quest. What Petrus seeks is knowledge with a view toward restitution of desire's lost object; what the Homunculus seeks is knowledge of desire with a view toward its submission to Tzingal's absolute control. Marco's absence represents in both courts the pretext of all speech and activity; knowledge of his whereabouts is thus the subject and object of all quests in the poem.

Petrus's inquiry leads him into dialogue with several of the poem's characters, one of which is the Astrologer's Page, Pollio. Prior to Petrus's interview with the Astrologer, the Page introduces himself to the emissary and seizes the opportunity to engage in private conversation. He questions Petrus about the outside world, and finally recommends that the emissary purchase his debenture. To embellish the proposal Pollio enumerates some of the qualities that make him worthy as a servant:

> —Oh no, sir, I'm not unhappy here,
> But adventurous to roam the wider world:
> It's the youth blood in me, and curiosity.
> But I'm no featherwit, as soon you'd see,
> Were you my master. For I have a clever
> Way with secrets, how to weasel them out
> And noise them all abroad,
> Or how to keep them quiet as a shroud
>
> . . . . .
>
> You'd find me, Master-Envoy, quicksilver-deft
> At any use or task, in bedchamber or in foyer.
>
> For there are matters, both of word and deed,
> That here have taken shape and would have
>   value,
> If ever they be known outside these walls
> To rival principates; and all you
> Could ever desire to know is in my head.

Like Tzingal's "minim man," the Page claims to withold the quiet power of knowledge as well as the awareness of how and when to use that knowledge. Again like Tweak, Pollio's secrets and abilities are not limited to any one particular cognitive area: his services useful "in bedchamber or in foyer," the Page hints that his knowledge spans the official arena of politics as well as the private sphere of desire. But unlike the Homunculus, Pollio announces that his competence and loyalty may be had for the mere price of his debenture.

The successive interviews between Petrus, Tweak, and the Page not only lead to the eclipse of King Tzingal's mad designs, but also imply the dilemmas inherent to any attempt at poetic writing. If the poetic enterprise is the search for a totalizing linguistic form, for the perfect expression of man's experience and condition, then the three figures named above play major roles in demonstrating the seduction and pitfalls of that undertaking.

As go-betweens or intermediaries, these three figures occupy a privileged status in the poetic circuits of knowledge and desire; because of their access to both inner and outer worlds, they enjoy a certain immunity to the authorities whom they encounter or serve. Tweak, for example, operates in a circuit between King Tzingal and the deranged monarch's underlings or foes; through him, secrets and knowledge of the other are transformed into an armament of absolute control. Yet, the miniature man has no titular role or defined place in the oppressive government that he so effectively reinforces. Omnipresent, evanescent, and omniscient, combining in his poetic presence the inferences of authority, the fundamental elements of nature, and the highest achievement of the magic arts, Tweak informs and supersedes the hierarchy that he serves. As the mirror of the mad King's realm, he dwells in the fissures of the castle walls, ferreting out the frenzied desires of Tzingal's subjects. His rigorous economy and function within the text remain secure because of his imperviousness to the desires he detects and because of his professed resistance to the lure of recompense.

Pollio, too, is a liminal figure in the poem since he serves both the official and erotic interests of the court's Astrologer. Unlike Tweak, however, the Page is initially subservient to the bloodless lust and dead erudition of his master. The young servant claims to withold a "nether history / Of Castle Tzingal" but will divulge his information to Petrus if the emissary assumes his debenture. Knowing how to dislodge and retain the secrets of their poetic world, Tweak and the Page suggest similar cognitive acuities. But their knowledge can be had only at a price, a price which for each reflects the specificity of his function and desire in the poem. Pollio's desire, openly claimed in the text, is for the experience of otherness or difference, for change from the withering stagnation and servitude that he lives with the Astrologer. Upon taking leave from his master, the Page decries the Astrologer's interpretive practices, strategies that wholly submit the signs of nature to the transient political ploys of men:

> How often have the stars said right
> As you interpret them?
> I have no fear to grapple whatever fate
> You foretell mine. I go to seek a saner home,
> Petrus my mentor and I no catamite.
> I hear no stars speak politics at night.

Despite Tweak's claim that his services cannot be bought, Petrus finally comes up with the offer that causes the tiny spy to reveal the circumstances of Marco's disappearance. But what sort of leverage can be used with this minim man who symbolically combines the forces of nature, culture, knowledge, and art and who seems to lack nothing? What sort of promise could be made to Tweak that would cause him to divulge the required information and switch allegiance? Though the dilemma permits no facile solutions, King Reynal's Master-Envoy strikes an imaginative bargain that buys the information he's seeking:

Do you bear a more imaginative bribe
Than that you offered me when
You first approached me? I hope
You've racked your brain for— . . .
                                    You say
That under King Reynal I'd have a duchy?
There's a thought might cause my fealty to slip.

Thus, this miniature man, this inscription of omniscience
and omnipotence, will reveal his secrets in exchange for
property—for the legitimacy implicit to the status of landowner in King Reynal's realm. Unlike the Page, who seeks
a way out of the conditions of his servitude, Tweak is
swayed by the prospect of having a place within a hierarchical structure.

Though accurate, the knowledge that Petrus's offer pro-
cures from Tweak comprises no glad tidings. The Homunculus tells Reynal's emissary that:

> King Tzingal conceived a jealousy of the poet;
> Gave orders for his murder
> And then with his own hand chopped off his
>   head.
> He ordered my father Astrologer to do it
> With a burning poison, but reserved the harder
> Pleasure for his own royal sword.
> He fancied you see that Marco and the
>   Queen . . .
> Well, you need no pictures drawn.
> And there was no truth in it, not the least,
> But King Tzingal never inquires for proof.

Nevertheless, the mission that King Reynal delegated to
Petrus has been carried out, since the emissary was in-
structed to discover either Marco's whereabouts or the circumstances of his absence. With the news of the
poet/harpist's decapitation at the hands of King Reynal,
Petrus hastens to recommend retaliatory measures to his
own regent.

Before scrutinizing the consequences of Petrus's retaliatory decision, let us examine a bit further this remarkable
interlude between the Master-Envoy and King Tzingal's
tiny spy. This scene between two of the poem's middle
men is a pivotal interval in the text because it assembles
the poem's major themes; moreover, this passage speaks
with outstanding clarity to the wider-ranging questions of
poetic production outlined in the beginning pages of this
essay. Of the numerous clues to reading contained in this
scene, three features are especially noteworthy.

The first of these concerns Petrus's formal status in the
poem. Like Tweak and the Page, Petrus is a go-between,
a messenger whose quest leads him to cross the boundary
between distinct but neighboring orders. Unlike these two
figures, however, Petrus maintains a balanced or harmonious relation to the titular authority he serves. Tweak ultimately controls and overrules King Tzingal through a
canny manipulation of the mad monarch's desires.
Though Tzingal may use the secrets that Tweak confides
to enforce obedience and terror among his subjects, the
King himself is not humanly immune to the effects of the
miniature man's information. Apprised of the Queen's
fancy for Marco, Tzingal conceives a jealousy so overwhelming that he breaks his own rule by murdering the
poet. The King's secret infraction then places him in an

ambiguous relation to Tweak, because Tweak's knowledge
of the murder carries a potential threat to the royal order.
On the other hand, Pollio's persona suggests the subjugation of vital desire to a statically imposed order. Conform-
able with Tzingal's allegations, the master Astrologer has
lost desire's creative impulse, and has reduced his magic
art to a sterile formula of signs. The knowledge he imposes
upon Pollio, along with the domestic and erotic services
he exacts from the Page, betrays a disregard for the vitality
apparent in the servant's competence and desire for
knowledge.

By now it is evident that the order of authority examined
here and represented in *Castle Tzingal* by various mon-
archs, magicians, and middle men is in a more extended
sense a synonym for poetic language in its quest for universal signification. Considering that the poetic project is
an attempt to express the pure note of meaning, the articulation of ultimate truth, we must recognize the profound
ambivalence of that enterprise. How can one express that
which is eternal, universal, and absolute through writing—a form of representation that has its own force, form,
laws, and hierarchy? How can the poet express universal
oneness through a medium that establishes and enforces
difference? If Tweak and Pollio's verse performances in relation to their own masters remind us of the unstable and
ultimately failed relation between language (hierarchy,
order) and the expression of human desire, then Petrus's
presence in the text ingeniously hypothesizes the possibility of that relation.

As the representative of this text's "other" kingdom, a
realm in which political organization, family structure,
and the forces of desire have apparently achieved a functional balance, Petrus stands forth in the poem as the missing link between Tzingal's dark, fractured regency and a
nearly idyllic peace. Implied in his figure is the equilibrium of social hierarchy, kinship, and desire that is so sorely
wanting inside Tzingal's court. But this balance, this
strength that Petrus symbolizes is strangely conveyed in
the language of the poem by his absence from all direct
modes of speech. Petrus exists in the poem only as the silent interlocutor of a dialogue or as the origin of the various letters addressed to King Reynal. Always implied but
never explicit, Petrus's agency in Tzingal's land is a silent
one. This is the first significant feature of the dialogue between Petrus and Tweak.

Second, this passage is of foremost importance because of
its place in the overall organization of the poem. Like most
of Chappell's poetry, *Castle Tzingal* has a classically precise organization; a careful look at the dialogue between
Petrus and Tweak shows us that it is the twelfth of twenty-
three poetic segments. This versified conversation between
two middle men thus constitutes, in the most literal and
graphic sense, the absolute middle of the poem.

Finally, this dialogue is notable for the multiple ways that
it alludes to absence as a vehicle of meaning. Through this
dialogue, we will remember, Petrus learns of Marco's
death at the hands of King Tzingal. Much like an attempt
to enforce and control desire itself, the deranged monarch's act in killing the poet is similar to one of the aspects
of poetic writing. By decapitating Marco, the monarch im-

poses the absence of ruptured loss and death upon his kingdom, thereby stirring the very frenzy of desire that he had hoped to deflect or quell. The song that then haunts the castle and points to Marco's absence mirrors the King's murderous act because it rends the continuity of sleep and evokes the schismatic pain of memory. The tale that Tweak tells is one of a tearing and murderous difference, a void signifying exclusion, dismemberment, loss, separation, and death. But Petrus's absence from all forms of direct speech in this passage (and throughout the poem) is an absence of a completely different nature. Petrus's exclusion from all direct forms of speech in the poem is a silence that unifies instead of one that divides and destroys. The knowledge he acquires from Tweak represents fulfillment and loss at the same time: fulfillment because in gathering the news of Marco's death, Petrus accomplishes the mission delegated to him, and loss because the news of Marco's death signifies a dolorous blow for all of King Reynal's realm. This dual signification of life and death implicit to Petrus's silence is repeated in the strategies he employs to gain Tweak's allegiance. By promising Tweak a place and property in Reynal's kingdom, Petrus manages to break the spy's ties of loyalty to Tzingal and to establish a new bond to Reynal. Though the nearly idyllic unity of Reynal's kingdom has been destroyed by the news of Marco's death, a reformulated, though slightly less pure, unity is hinted in the triple alliance of Petrus, Tweak, and the Page.

If I have dwelled at length on the roles of Petrus, Tweak, and the Page, it is because these are the only three figures of the poem to escape the murderous touch of Tzingal and the destruction of his kingdom by any means other than death. Tzingal's Admiral seeks the peace of death by hanging himself in his bedchamber, whereas Queen Frynna, more and more haunted by the ghostly melody that she hears during sleep, drinks a potion that induces death's slumber. Finally, at Petrus's behest, Tweak serves the King a blood-searing elixir that brings on the monarch's own demise. Before he draws his final breath, Tzingal sees Tweak put a torch to his chamber's tapestries:

> I take the flambeau here
> And flame the curtain, and now the tapestry
> That celebrates your coronation we see flare
> Like the glory of holy martyrs.

Thus, in a highly symbolic gesture, Tweak burns the tapestry depicting Tzingal's coronation before the dying King's eyes. In much the same way that Tzingal's murder of Marco placed the monarch at the mercy of the dwarf's whim, the image of Tzingal's coronation is here submitted to the consuming flames. The only remaining words of the poem are those of the Song for a Disembodied Voice.

The image of a burning edifice is a prominent motif in some of Chappell's other poetry, and is often accompanied by a chaotic dispersion of voices. But if fire is a dominant motif in Chappell's writing, it is still only one of many elements that he uses to dramatize his largest concern: the ontological implications of poetry. In his poem **"A Prayer for Truth,"** Chappell's hope is that his verse "find the solid places," that it not be abandoned to the more savage and unstable regions of earth. Is this not the foremost allusion of *Castle Tzingal* as well?

I have pointed out that Tweak, Petrus, and the Page are the only ones to escape unscathed from Tzingal's murderous rule and the ultimate devastation of his castle. But what remains to be emphasized is the very inviting relation between these three figures' names or titles and the components—material and cognitive—of poetic writing. As his name suggests, Tweak is that pinch of consciousness representative of the omniscience, skill, and perceptual infallibility necessary for the supreme articulation. The Page, on the other hand, is the one begging exposure to otherness and desire, similar to the blank page of writing that beckons to the poet's inscription. And finally, Petrus as a figure in the poem comes to signify the balance and solidity implied by the phonic and etymological resonances of his name. The name "Petrus" is phonically and graphically similar to the term "petrous," which as an adjective means "stony, hard, solid." As a noun, however, the petrous is a bone behind the temple that supports the inner ear, which is the physiological site of hearing and equilibrium. Both as an adjective and as a noun, the term derives from the Greek *petra,* "a rock." So with a little onomastic liberty, we may see in the threesome who are freed from Castle Tzingal's walls allegories of poetic creation: Tweak and Pollio, symbolizing omniscience, skill, desire, and the locus of writing, find a place with Petrus, the solid figure who assures their solidarity in another land. The scheme seems nearly perfect.

I say "nearly perfect" because, after the gloomy sojourn through Castle Tzingal, the prospect of renewed solidarity suggested by the silent withdrawal of Petrus, Tweak, and the Page must remain conjectural and slightly impure. As the Song for a Disembodied Voice so poignantly reminds us, "The happy season of the world has left no mark." In fact, if the possibility of restored unity obtains in the survivors' departure to the "other" place, that possibility is transmitted to the reader only by or as an absence. The text of *Castle Tzingal* emerges from an instance of originary loss or fractured perfection; throughout the text, the poem's writing consistently echoes that loss and postpones all possible restitution. The spectre of ruptured perfection revealed in Marco's disappearance and death will always taint the possibility of paradise regained. The decapitation of the poet/harpist is thus a nearly paradigmatic illustration of writing's ambivalence as invoked by Blanchot: in the language of *Castle Tzingal,* the perfection of truth is implied only by the graphic figures of its destruction or deferral.

Paradoxically, it is perhaps through these figures of loss or absence that we may best consider *Castle Tzingal* (or any of Chappell's poetry) exemplary of a southern literary tradition. In what may be termed a bifurcated concept of community, many writers of the American South since Faulkner have posited that the region's identity is rooted in a loss of faith in the redemptive potential of history and in a profoundly isolated view of the individual in society. Robert Penn Warren's novel *Flood,* for example, shows us a protagonist, Brad Tolliver, returning to his native town in Tennessee in an attempt to discover the connections between his adulthood and a more general, locatable notion of culture. Accompanied by a friend who will direct the movie of his script in the making, Brad visits a cemetery where he hopes to find the grave of a figure alive in his childhood memories. Recalling the impressive individuality of the deceased character, Brad turns his own memory into a larger reflection upon the South: "Hell, no Southerner believes that there is any South. He just believes that if he keeps on saying the word he will lose some of the angry lonesomeness." Further along, Brad remarks that southerners do not believe in God, but pray because they believe in "the black hole in the sky God left when He went away." [In his *Dispossessed Garden*] Lewis Simpson's discussion of this and other works of southern literature after the First World War suggests that the sense of place so clearly discernible in much contemporary southern writing is a place of mourning and dream instead of a strictly mimetic representation.

On both internal and external levels, *Castle Tzingal* stands as a sparkling demonstration of this premise: forever seeking restoration of its own lost wholeness, the writing of the text constitutes that differential interval between the moment of solidarity's failure and the fervent, but silent intimation of its renewed possibility. (pp. 92-107)

> Kate M. Cooper, "Reading between the Lines: Fred Chappell's 'Castle Tzingal'," in Southern Literature and Literary Theory, *edited by Jefferson Humphries, The University of Georgia Press, 1990, pp. 88-108.*

Chappell on being a poet:

I think, in some respects, the poet is more primitive than other folks. That is, there's something babyish about someone who likes to play with his mouth all the time, play with words. The poet who is worth his salt is the one who has the visions of a truly civilized society, a truly civilized world—whether he thinks it should be tribal or whether he thinks it should be modeled after the family, or if he thinks it should be a technological Utopia. Whatever his ideas are, he's the one who holds to the dreams of civilization.

> *Fred Chappel, in an interview with Irv Broughton in* The Writer's Mind: Interviews with American Authors, *1990.*

Fred Chappell with Irv Broughton   (interview date 1990)

[*In the following excerpt from an interview, Chappell discusses his life and literary career.*]

[*Broughton*]: *Do you have any favorite folk tale or anything that used to be told to you over and over?*

[Chappell]: No. There were a lot of stories that were told on one another, but they were generally family stories. They weren't exactly folk tales. I guess they would change to folk tales, over a period of time. The family stories often just bored me, because I didn't know who they were talking about. I didn't know those members of the family. Our family was scattered all over a couple of counties, and, also, parents and grandparents tend to talk about people who died long before you were born. So some of the stories weren't interesting merely because terms didn't mean that much to me. They were always nineteenth-century terms, in some cases experiences that were obsolescent. So those words don't remain with me. Just the sound of their voices talking, and the way the stories were put together, just the general outline, the form, sticks with me. But not the stories themselves. I don't remember them.

Was there anything distinctive about the forms? Specifically distinctive, or was it just storytelling?

It was oral storytelling which has its own almost ritualistic form. It's extremely formal and can be analyzed without any trouble. And these stories as I remember adhered to that outline. But what those specific stories were, I don't remember. But you know I wouldn't tell you anyway, I'd save them to write. (*Laughs.*)

Do you remember anything about the nineteenth-century terms—any classic terms?

The terms you hear in common language, which struck me as being very nineteenth century and being extremely literary at the same time, are those you'd find in nineteenth-century hymns—Baptist hymns. Nothing strikes me right at the moment, but you would recognize it in a minute. Charles Portis, who wrote *True Grit*, leaned very heavily on this. That was the speech that I heard spoken.

What do you owe your puritanism?

A boatload of useless guilt, I expect. The absolute conviction that the past is going to catch up with you, even if it was relatively mild, and probably also the fear of whatever happens after death. I owe puritanism a whole lot of that. Also, I suspect a fair amount of personal prissiness in manners of morality—a smallness of outlook that's truly bothersome. There are some good things about it. You learn the Bible, you learn the book fairly well. And it stays with you forever. You learn a sense of community, which sometimes you outgrow. You find it stifling, but nevertheless you have a sense of community, and you never forget that you have a place to belong. I can always go back to the mountains if I get a chance, and I will feel at home there. I'm not sure that a lot of people have that.

How important are your roots to you now?

Well, more and more important all the time. For some reason I'm not really clear about, my past has become the material I'm writing about these days. It was Graham Greene who said that "childhood is the writer's capital," and I've been spending mine for a long time. I don't know why they say that, but it seems to be a more striking experience than my later experiences, and also because everyone tends to remember the earlier experiences more vividly than later experiences.

Do you have a photographic memory?

No.

The "rap" on you is that this guy has got this tremendous intelligence.

That's very sweet, but I certainly don't have a photographic memory. Nobody who has drunk as long as I have has a photographic memory. I have a very blurred memory a great deal of the time. But the things that interest me and the things people tell me and the things I read stick with me. When they stick at all, they stick with me—for a long time. They become important to me.

What were your grandparents like? You were raised by them, weren't you?

They were very sweet, stern mountain people—not poor, but not wealthy. But insofar as there was a middle class in the mountains, they belonged to it. They were farmers day and night and my grandfather and father, and sometimes my mother and grandmother, had other jobs so you could make some cash money, because you can't make a livin' on a farm. My grandfather was a carpenter; my parents were schoolteachers. My grandmother was a schoolteacher and they did other jobs too. My father even worked in a factory for a while.

Any real background history of family and how they ended up in the mountains?

No, I've heard lots of things. And I have an uncle who can tell you everything. But I find this irrelevant and boring. Somewhere in our ancestry is Buffalo Bill Cody.

At what age did you decide to be a writer?

I think probably around twelve or thirteen. I was writing at twelve or thirteen, and I think I decided at that time that's what I wanted to do. That's not the same as deciding to be a writer; that's deciding to want to be a writer. I think the final decision was when I was about nineteen. I had moved from the mountains to Duke University, and I met a lot of people who were also interested in writing and who did not think it was *outré* or an impossible thing to try to be. They certainly recognized that it was not easy but they also thought it was possible. And the sense of having a lot of writers around me gave me some reassurance. The writers were Jim Applewhite, Reynolds Price, Wallace Kaufman, and Anne Tyler.

Any great advice you received from Reynolds Price?

No, but he was a wonderful namedropper. He would mention lots and lots and lots of modern writers, modern artists, and minor ones that I'd never heard of—like Herbert Read, for example, or William Empson, William Plomer, William Sansome—he would know writers like that. I would know Thomas Mann, James Joyce, but I wouldn't know the whole litter of smaller rabbits.

The transition to college life wasn't easy?

It was a shock, to tell you the truth, because I'd expected hot stuff things from college. I thought college was going to be an entirely intellectual community, and we would just sit around and talk about intellectual ideas. But, of course, all colleges are a bunch of fraternity boys, trying to get drunk. And I was good at that, so that part didn't bother me. But I was a little disappointed that it wasn't

a little more intellectually attuned type of place. That's being naive—so I was naive. The hardest part was adjusting to the freedom I had, being away from a very strict household and not being under the purview of my grandparents and my parents. Having two sets of parents got kind of stifling after a while. And I really didn't know how to handle living on my own, so that took awhile.

What did you have to learn?

Oh, I just had to learn to calm down, to not be quite so hysterical—get some sort of order into life.

Was the headline in the paper, "The Wildman from Canton Hits Campus," about you?

That's about it. You got it. (*Laughs.*)

What about manners? Did you feel out of place at all?

Well, out of place to a certain extent. So many of the students at Duke were wealthy—they came from wealthy families. But I expected that, and it didn't bother me too much. One thing I had some trouble adjusting to was that so many of them were from down east in North Carolina, which is very much like the deep South. And, anyway, we had a lot of folks from the deep South. And I, at that time, simply did not know anything about the deep South. Appalachia is not like the South at all. It's different in a great many aspects—background, culture—everybody knows the differences. And it took me awhile to get used to that.

Any arts orientation in your family?

My parents were schoolteachers, which gave me a jump because there were books in our house. They had encyclopedias and the middle-class editions of writers you could get in the thirties. And I read lots and lots. That's when I was very young.

How young is very young?

Oh, from about age six on to about age eleven, twelve, or thirteen. Then, at that age, I got interested in science fiction, which was the only modern literature I knew for a long time—until I was about sixteen years old. And I read a great deal of that, and was fascinated by it, because I could buy the books myself by skipping lunch, by taking my lunch money and buying a pulp magazine or paperbacks and reading my own books.

It seems like you see some of that science fiction influence in your work—mice crawling out of a person's mouth in **The Inkling.**

I think everyone's attracted as a child to the supernatural, fairy tales, that sort of thing. As a kid my favorite Shakespeare play was *A Midsummer Night's Dream*. I must have read it six or seven times between ages eight and twelve. It still remains one of my favorite plays.

Why?

I like the transition or almost a lack of transition between the supernatural and the realistic elements of the play—the bridge of comedy Shakespeare uses there which loosens the mind and opens it up, then leads right into the fairytale element. The element of the fairies seems to me masterful.

Do you use those kinds of transitions?

I'm interested in getting rid of the division between what is wished for, what is imagined, and what is generally thought to be realistic or recognized as factual.

What was the hardest transition of that type you've ever had to make in your writing?

In **Dagon. Dagon** was the hardest book to write for any number of reasons. But there the difficult thing was in getting the reader to accept a sudden violent event, the murder of the wife, which opened the doorway to the supernatural, which culminated in the supernatural events in the book. That was very difficult. I didn't know how to work it out. Finally, I had to do it twice, once as a dream and once as reality and that blurred the distinction enough so that I was about to go on. But for a long time I couldn't find any way out of that.

Is there anything you had to unlearn from science fiction?

Oh, yes, most of it. Like most literature, popular or unpopular, it is junk. Ninety-five percent of it is pure junk. This judgment is called Sturgeon's Law.

And a lot of things you have to unlearn from science fiction?

You've got to learn to characterize people. You've got to learn a very practical use of visual, aural, sensual detail that science fiction often overlooks, and you have to learn not to swallow improbabilities so easily. You have to learn to prepare for them more logically than science fiction is used to doing. You have to learn to slow down the pace of a story so that readers absorb the different elements and don't just read it like a comic book, so that it's memorable and makes a meaningful design. You have to write English prose style, which most science fiction writers never learned.

You actually wrote science fiction, didn't you?

Oh yes, I wrote a whole bunch of it when I was in high school. It was published mostly in amateur magazines.

What did you write about?

Oh, the same as everybody else—spaceships flying around, traveling into outer space. Robert Silverberg, Harlan Ellison—people like that—published magazines, and I wrote for their magazines.

What was the best story you ever wrote?

I'm guessing. I wrote scores of these things, and I remember hardly any of them. I do remember one that Bob Silverberg published, called **"The Tin Can."** Somebody actually wrote a letter to me about it five years ago because they'd come across an old magazine.

What was that about?

It seems to me it was about some guy in a spaceship who was going wacko. Oh, I remember how it started. I was corresponding with a feller who is now a psychologist, a guy named Charles Catania. He lived in New York, and we used to dare each other to write stories about ideas and give each other challenges to write stories about. He drew a little cartoon of the rings of Saturn and a tin can floating among the rings and challenged me to write a story about it. When I wrote the story and he saw it, he said I cheated because I made the guy hallucinate the tin can. And I think he's right—I did not play fair. (*Laughs.*)

What if you hadn't escaped the mountains? What would you be doing there?

Well, I might have been running the family business as they wanted me to do, tried to get me to do for a long period of time. My father also had a retail furniture business besides the family farm. So I probably would have been doing that, or I would have gone on and written science fiction. Sometimes I wish I had done that. I certainly would have made a lot more money than I'm making now because I was pretty good at it. But there was no way to get support for myself in the early days—if I'd done that. It would have been impossible.

Did you have to conceal your intellect up there?

I would try to. I'm not really all that intelligent, Irv.

Well, let's just say you're above average.

I think I thought of myself as being some kind of hot stuff intelligence, and I soon learned to keep my mouth shut. The trouble was, I was so excitable I couldn't keep my mouth shut, and I always wound up getting beat on or kicked around or embarrassed or something in some physical fashion or another. I learned to live with that, but for a long time it bothered me when I was eleven or twelve or thirteen. After that, it was just part of the weather. I didn't pay it much mind.

If you could have lived in any age, what age would you live in?

This one. This is the worst and the best of ages in history—this is the one to live in. From now on it's downhill and getting up here was downhill, too. This is the safest age to live in as far as accidents and disease, as far as medical attention goes. But it is also the one that's going to destroy the planet.

If you had to live in another age?

Well, either the Renaissance or the eighteenth century sound good to me. In the Renaissance if you were fairly well off and had enough sense to pick up a little classical learning, a little mathematics, there was opportunity for you. You could do things—you had some freedom in the world that you didn't have for a long time. In the eighteenth century, there was the freedom to be a writer. It's the first time we had professional writers, and also I admire the thought and impulse of the eighteenth century. Rationalism seems to me to be a tenable way of thought. Everybody says that the enlightenment failed—I think it was never actually tried. So that was the best of the them. That was the clearest period of human thought—the most detailed, the most involved, sometimes the most despairing. But it gave us, besides all the eighteenth-century literature we usually think of, it gave us our American Constitution.

Who is your favorite eighteenth-century thinker?

Samuel Johnson. I like a man who knows his own mind.

I don't like these wishy-washy guys who pussyfoot around with their statements. I like somebody who says something definite. I like all *The Lives of the Poets.* The judgments sometimes seem to us right on and sometimes they seem to us scatterbrained these days. Nevertheless, the authority of the prose, the ability to handle abstractions in such a way that they don't seem abstract in the least but have the conviction of concrete statements, the ability to read and perceive the inner outlines, the inner structure of work, that seems to me to be very rare; and the ability to put things in definite form with seeming ease, even in conversation—I have to admire somebody like that.

You mentioned "scatterbrained." An example?

His one judgment that everyone knows sticks in my mind—he said of *Paradise Lost,* "No one ever wished it longer." I kind of disagree. I wish *Paradise Lost* was a little longer. (*Laughs.*)

If you had to be another person in all history, who would you be?

An anonymous person, someone you'd never heard of. Perhaps just a farmer who lived modestly and pursued his own ideas and lived and died quietly in an age of peace, if possible. Otherwise, if it had to be somebody we'd heard of, I'd be the poet Horace.

Why Horace?

For the same reason I chose my gentleman farmer, because the life he lived seems to come very close to the kind of ideals he celebrates in his poetry for the most part. And I like a poet who shows his whole humanity in his poems, his faults as well as his virtues. I like the calming influence of Horace's poetry—as well as the wit.

If you had to say three commandments of poetry, what would they be?

First, learn how to write poetry. Learn all the possible technique you can muster. Second, forget how to write poetry. Forget all the techniques that you've learned. And third, write less poetry than you would like to.

Midquest: A Poem *is really a sort of Divine Comedy.*

Yes, that was my model for the time structure as well as for a lot of allusive material in it, and for the whole idea generally: a man taking stock of his life during the middle of it.

Can you talk about the process and the stages of **Midquest?**

It started not as a conception at all. It started as a poem I'd written—the first poem of the first volume. I think it's called **"The River Awakening in the Sea."** At the first it wasn't even a poem. It was just notes lying around that I didn't do anything with. Then a magazine called *The Monmouth Review* wrote and asked me for a poem. I'm not quite sure why they did that, but I gathered these fragments up and made a kind of poem out of it. (pp. 95-106)

Anyway, I sent it off and forgot about it. In about a year and a half the *Monmouth Review* came out, and I'd forgotten that I'd ever given them this poem, and there was this poem. I read it and as soon as I read it, I realized that this poem was incomplete, that there were all kinds of things—that this poem should go somewhere and that it was part of something much larger. I was sitting there thinking, and the plan for the first book came into my mind, the plan for **River,** and so I started to gather material for some poems that were companion poems, to finish out the volume, and the plan of the whole thing after I'd written a third poem of a four-volume series popped into my mind. As it turned out, I didn't have to change a line I'd written. I think the plan was already in my head and I just didn't know it.

How long has that plan been in your head?

I can date it from my days at Duke. I wrote a longish poem called **"Familiar Poem"** around 1961-62 and it was published in the student magazine. And after **Midquest** was complete, I realized the germ of that was contained in that earlier student poem that I'd written.

Which of the elements in the poem—earth, fire, water, air—interests you the most as an idea, as a concept?

That kept changing as I worked on the poems. The one that gave me the most problem was air because it's so disordered and there just doesn't seem to be enough substance to it. (*Laughs.*) But once I linked it to music, it became a lot easier for me because music probably stands in my poems most of the time for exaltation, exalted spirits, ecstatic visionary knowledge. After I got that, that poem opened up a lot for me.

What was the easiest?

The one I found easiest was **Bloodfire,** because the imagery of fire is easily adapted to all kinds of symbolism. The one I'm really interested in the most is the last one, **Earthsleep.** It's the saddest one for me because it's about the deaths of all the people who comfort one through one's early life. But, even so, of the bunch I felt that was the most genuinely felt volume.

Is it hard getting yourself out of some effort that long and that precise?

I just kept working on it. I always write different things at the same time. I wrote some fiction, some journalism, and some criticism during those years, but mostly I just worked on that poem. That was my major project, and there were times I was working on it so intensely I would begin to think in poetry. I would wake up in the morning thinking of poetry, and at different parts of the day, when I was shopping or whatever, I'd begin thinking in meter and in rhyme and stuff. And that's not very good for me. Something affects your mind there in a way that at least in our time is not very healthy, and you become a little schizophrenic about the way you think and the way you talk, even. So I wouldn't recommend for people to do that, unless they have ways of protecting themselves. That is, if you don't have to earn a living and do ordinary things, I think you'll do fine with it. But, if you have to go out to teach or do other kinds of work it's going to bother you.

Did it ever get you in actual trouble?

Probably it did in minor ways I don't remember now—

inattentiveness, for example. I think it's dangerous to drive like that. Otherwise, no.

What technically gave you a challenge with **Midquest?**

My plan with it was to write as many different kinds of forms and meters as I possibly could because what I had in mind, considering the rural homespun nature of the material, was to make it like a sampler. Each of the poetic forms would stand for a different stitch. After a while—unless you invent forms like Thomas Hardy—you run out of the different forms of English poetry, and you have to go to forms of foreign languages—especially to the forms of classical poetry which was what would fit in the nineteenth century and the eighteenth century, in a sample. And some of those I found I couldn't do. I could not do Sapphics. I must have tried a hundred times to do Sapphics, and they just don't work for me. I have a poem in elegiacs there, that classical meter, and that took me forever.

That's the poem to Richard Dillard.

Yes. That took me forever because it is very difficult for me to transliterate classical meter into an accentual verse. I've been doing it so long now I'm getting used to it, but it really was difficult. The long poem about Susan bathing is an adaptation of classical hexameters, for example, but you wouldn't really know it because I couldn't get it that close. (*Laughs.*)

What do you owe Erskine Caldwell?

I owe him perhaps the germ or one of the germs for the idea of **Dagon.** When I thought of the idea of **Dagon,** it was, of course, first inspired by the story of Samson in the Bible. I tried to imagine myself drawing a large, heroic figure like Samson—but I don't believe we have those in our context now. Then I was wondering if I could write a whole book about some jerk who was a victim from page one, almost, to the end of the book and still make an interesting book out of it. I came across a small obscure novel by Caldwell—it was privately published, he paid for its publication before he got to be well known—called *Poor Fool,* about a broken-down boxer who falls in with some weird people who just victimize him completely, and that gave me the idea that it could be done. There was something very strange and surrealistic about that book. It's not well written, but even so it had a kind of power and vision that I wanted to get on my own.

You like a lot of popular writers, don't you? What favorite popular writer have you most completely outgrown?

I think Ray Bradbury's the one. For thousands of adolescent kids in the forties and fifties, he seemed a wonderful and fresh, even a poetic writer. Now he seems a little flat to me, and a little hysterical at the same time. He's kind of overwrought. Don't get me wrong. I still admire his work, and I think it's a terrific achievement, but only for a certain time of life, perhaps, in the way that Jack Kerouac is, another writer I outgrew in a very short time, and perhaps in a way Thomas Wolfe is. I don't know that one outgrows these writers—that's insulting to the writer. What one does is pursue another different predilection that these writers aroused in the first place.

As a young man, what was your greatest writer discovery?

That's easy. Thomas Mann and his book *Doctor Faustus.* That's the single novel I've read more than others, except for *Huckleberry Finn.* I would say I've read that at least ten times.

Is the poet, by nature, a kind of primitive?

I think most people are primitives. I think, in some respects, the poet is more primitive than other folks. That is, there's something babyish about someone who likes to play with his mouth all the time, play with words. The poet who is worth his salt is the one who has the visions of a truly civilized society, a truly civilized world—whether he thinks it should be tribal or whether he thinks it should be modeled after the family, or if he thinks it should be a technological Utopia. Whatever his ideas are, he's the one who holds to the dreams of civilization.

When you began at Greensboro, Randall Jarrell taught there didn't he?

I took over Randall's courses after he died. I took a course he taught called "Approach to Narrative" and also his "Modern Poetry." He was teaching a third course called "Russian Literature," and I didn't feel equipped to handle that one—though it was offered. I taught both of those courses for six or seven years after Randall's death, and the poetry course for maybe ten years after his death. People were still, in their papers and exams, comparing the

Chappell in 1978.

way I taught the course with the way Randall taught the course—he was that famous a teacher and his teaching methods were that well known. That is amazing, it seems to me, that you'd have that kind of a legendary quality about a teacher for so many years. Randall himself I remember as witty, sometimes very sarcastic, and a little manic. People have told me that I didn't really know him since I only knew him the last five years of his life—that he had changed. He suffered from depression, and one of the treatments in those days was drugs, especially lithium, which was widely used. He was on lithium, and I don't think the side effects of it were well known. There are some people in whom it causes a schizophrenic side effect. Anyway, I hold the drug treatments of Randall responsible for his death.

You knew Peter Taylor.

(*Laughs.*) I never think of Peter Taylor without smiling. He's one of the most charming, witty, funny, and knowledgeable persons about literature that I've ever known. We are, for the most part, very consonant in our tastes. We like the same writers: Faulkner, Colette, Trollope, Allen Tate—those kind of writers. He disapproved in a joking way with my fascination with some popular writers like Caldwell and Simenon. But he could never tell if I was joking or serious so he let it go. The only writer we really fell out over, not violently, was Edgar Allan Poe. I love Poe. Peter Taylor thinks Poe sucks, more or less.

When did you meet Taylor?

I was at Duke. I was an undergraduate and I was working on my first novel, though I didn't know it then. Peter came down as a visiting writer. We had a panel and they talked about it. Dr. Blackburn was convinced that I was a hotstuff writer and I needed a powerful friend like Peter Taylor to help me along—that's the way Dr. Blackburn felt about all his students—he was a very fine gentleman. At that time Peter had some property over in Hillsboro, and he flew down to Duke and didn't have any way to look at his houses. So Dr. Blackburn very kindly suggested that I would drive Peter over to Hillsboro. We'd look at his houses. We'd get to be great friends, and when I got a chance I'd send Peter a short story and he would suggest it to the *New Yorker* editor and I would be launched. Well, we drove to Hillsboro, swapped stories, likes and dislikes, had dinner at the inn there—just had a wonderful time. I didn't ever send him a story. That seemed to me to be very bad manners. But I admired his willingness to put up with a very young man. In fact, he seemed to enjoy the whole idea. I was on pins and needles—it was asking too much of a visitor to do this sort of thing. I didn't tell him until about ten years later, I guess it was, that I didn't have a driving license in those days.

It's easy to be on pins and needles when you're around greats.

Yes. Once I was sitting in a little coffee shop next to the college. There were three of us, William Pitt Root, the poet, and myself and Allen Tate, just sort of idling away the morning, when in comes a very nice woman. Allen Tate, of course, was very famous, had his name all over the newspaper, and she knew him anyway from years past.

So she ran up to the table, greeted him, talked, and, as she was leaving, said, "I hope you boys know how lucky you are to be sitting here talking to Allen Tate." She trotted away and was gone out the door. Allen said, "Who in the world was that?" because he didn't recognize her. The door flung open, and she came back to the table and said, "And, of course, he's lucky to be talking to you, too."

How important are dreams?

They used to be extremely important. I used to keep a little journal of dreams. I used to try to borrow ideas and imageries, and especially transition passages from dreams, which interest me—how you get from one place to another in a dream. But now I don't do that much any more. I don't care much for dreams in literature, except as an obvious literary device that has nothing to do with dreams. I think it's a weakness in my early books, the use of dreams, because I think the story should tell itself with events and not with dreams. What takes place in the story should be real and that's how the story should play itself out.

Any recurring dream?

I don't recall my dreams at all now. I know I dream because Susan says I laugh like a lunatic in my sleep. Most of my dreams must be very pleasant—I tend to laugh a lot in dreams. My dreams used to be and still are, I suppose, full of puns and jokes—the wit at unconscious play.

Do they call you an unconscious wit?

They call me "unconscious" a lot of times.

In **Moments of Light** *the stories range a lot in time. There aren't many writers who are able to juggle time in that way.*

I got interested in writing the historical short story, which is a difficult form because you have to get in so much detail and you have to keep it in short story form, too. I was teaching a course in American literature, and we got to Benjamin Franklin. My students knew who Franklin was, but they could not form any opinion of him, any conception of him as a living person, any notion of what he was like. It seemed they are not able to imagine a time other than their own, and as far as they're concerned Franklin is just another guy who lived a long time ago before people knew how to boogie down. So I decided to write a short story about Benjamin Franklin centered on his wife's family in order that my students could try to understand this person as a living human being. I would read it to them and they would get some feeling for him, some feeling for the eighteenth century, and we'd go on. So I did that, and I actually read the story to my class, the year following, and they resented it because it was another piece of material that was not going to appear on the exam, so why did they have to hear that? So just doing that one story got me interested in the idea of writing historical short stories and drawing familiar characters in a fictional way and dealing with actual events. Almost all the short stories have things that actually took place. In the Handel story, a lot of those events actually do take place. I've written others that you haven't seen yet. So it became a challenge to draw the character, to use the actual event and to make it interesting fiction and not just a history lecture.

Which was the hardest story to write?

A little sketch called **"Judas"** was the hardest for me to write because I could never quite match up the bureaucratic language of the present time with the situations there. That's what I wanted to do—to show him not as an evil person, but somebody who is not an actively evil person, but a passively evil person—somebody who gave in to the demands of the bureaucracies of a police state, which Rome is imagined as being in that story. But I never had enough opportunity to use modern bureaucratic jargon in order to make my point in that story, so the story is a little unsatisfactory. The other hard one was **"Ladies from Lapland,"** a story about an eighteenth-century polar explorer which you haven't seen yet. That was simply because there was so much material I had to cover—Newton, the explorer himself and his assistants, and the Laplanders.

Tell me about writing I Am One of You Forever. *One gets a feeling from the book of a kind of "magic realism"—sort of like García Márquez. Was he an influence?*

No, I read one book by him a long time ago called *No One Writes to the Colonel,* and it's no influence on me that I can discern. I have read a lot of magic realism, I guess. Borges was an important writer at one point or another. All I did in *I Am One of Your Forever* is simply take folk stories and use them as literal story. Nothing in there that you can't find in Mark Twain, whom I've never heard referred to as a "magic realist."

Let's talk about writing about the past—are there certain things that are becoming clearer?

Oh, partly that, I guess. I've never really covered duration much in literature, even when I wrote about the past. I've only covered a very short period of time and done it with very immediate means. The reason I'm working on this tetralogy of novels now is to give myself a chance to work with some duration, with a work that takes place over twenty years. That gives me a chance to work on something with time having passed and things having changed, characters changing, landscape changing, and history changing. And that's a fascinating challenge to me. That's supposed to be what fiction is all about, but I've never really attempted it before. The reason it's a tetralogy, though, is that I find that I'm not able, because of my writing schedule, to do this in a single volume, so I had to find a form to break it up so I could do it in smaller books. If I had to sit down and write an eight-hundred-page novel or close to that I couldn't do it. I would just have to give up because there's no way I can ever get a thousand-page novel done. I can get shorter novels done, but with the pressures of teaching and schoolwork there's no way to write a long novel and ever get anything else done.

But I understood that you like the short novel form.

I used to like it very much but now it's just a matter of convenience and necessity to me. I've learned not to like the short novel form so much anymore. I guess I've changed my mind on that.

How do you build a character?

The hardest character I've ever had to draw was the protagonist of **Dagon,** Peter Leland, because he was so bleeding passive. All he did was sit there, and I stuck pins into him, and it was very difficult to give him any character at all. I started out by making him a scholar—a research scholar going up to his homestead—but that gave him no character. So I made him into a minister which at least gave him some strand of character. After that I could point him up a little more by having his wife in particular make fun of his earnestness—and that helped a little bit. But I was never able to make him more than a sad puppet. That's because the events of the novel were so crushing that he could never get out from under it. That was the hardest character—I never resolved it.

Balzac said we need order in our personal life so we can go crazy in our writing.

Bill Styron's been saying that lately. I think order in your personal life is a marvelous thing. If you can get it, good luck to you. Most writers are not able to get it, simply because we don't live in a very orderly world. I suppose no one ever did, but it's gotten worse if you ask me. Balzac is not one to talk about order in his life.

Could you be a good actor?

I tried it once or twice, and it seemed to me I was awkward and clumsy on stage. My impulse was always to change the script as I went along, as new ideas about the character kept occurring to me. I played in *The Iceman Cometh* one time in college. The raw material O'Neill gave me seemed to be an interesting take-off, and I would like to write stories about it. But even without wanting to, I kept changing the lines. I'm embarrassed by public attention—it bothers me a great deal and it seems to me if you're an actor you have to live with it.

Is the mental process different for writing poetry as opposed to fiction?

Yes, it's miles apart. All I can tell you is that it's extremely different and that it's extremely difficult for me to go from one medium to another—one discipline to another. I have to have some sort of transition period, usually, because there's a real physical difference: your metabolism is different when you're writing fiction than when you're writing poetry. Poetry is a slower and graver, and I think, nobler sort of art. It's the difference between walking and riding a bicycle, between writing poetry and writing fiction. In poetry you learn to deliberate, you learn to bear down on things nobody else in the world is supposed to notice, so that the total effect is an accumulation of unnoticeable detail. With fiction you have to write with a certain amount of speed to ever get it finished—that is, if you don't write so many words a day when you're writing fiction, you're never going to come to the end of it. In poetry canceling two lines is a good day's work.

Has your writing of poetry helped with your writing of dialogue?

Maybe. I think often of the rhythm of dialogue. One of the harder things I've learned to do, and one I take some pride in, is the use of dialogue in poetry. There's lots and lots of dialogue in the poems of **Midquest**—people in the mountains talking to one another. The real challenge is to make it poetry and make it realistic dialogue at the same time. That's what Shakespeare's all about. I don't know if I solved it or not, but there are certain passages in there that seem to me to work pretty well. There's a long poem called **"My Grandmother's Dream of Plowing"** which actually is a rhymed poem in which nobody notices the rhyme, but it's in a kind of straightforward blank verse and yet has a kind of looseness and extempore quality that I like in dialogue. It has to seem spontaneous or it doesn't sound like dialogue. On the other hand, dialogue in poetry is not spontaneous—it just has to seem that way. Here's an example from the poem:

> Bent my head down
> But I couldn't hear, no more than you hear the
> dark.
> "It's not my baby, and just never you mind,"
> I said to Frank. "This baby I've found will bring
> Us luck," I said, "because it turned from gold
> To flesh. That means—it has to mean—
> something
> To us, something to help us when we're old."
> "We're old," Frank said, "we're old already,
> Anne.
> And, see, the baby's changed to something else.
> It's turned into an ugly little man."
> I looked, and felt the beating of my pulse
> Grow harder in my throat, knowing it was true.

John Ciardi wrote a piece entitled "An Ulcer, Gentlemen, Is an Unwritten Poem."

That's an interesting idea. And you know who's responsible for that idea—it's a gentleman called John Lane, at the turn of the century, who traced all our diseases to internal desires. This became a very important idea for W. H. Auden who got it from Allen Upward. The liar has quinsy because he can't stop stammering and stuttering because he's telling lies. Cancer is caused by a blocked creative impulse.

What is the impact of alcohol on your life and writing? You've put that behind you, haven't you?

No one ever does. No one ever puts it behind him. It's been, for the most part, deleterious—as you can expect. It hasn't been entirely deleterious. Alcohol has been an escape from the pressures of writing when I had no money to go anywhere else—so it's good and bad. Also, I have used it in order to heighten some of the effects of poetry—in order to accomplish an exalted state. You can't write when you're drinking, of course, but you can kind of recapture the memory of certain states and write from that. So it hasn't been entirely horrible—it hasn't been good, but it hasn't been entirely horrible.

But you don't advise it for a person, do you?

No, I certainly do not. Not in any shape or form. No drugs whatsoever is the deal.

If you could have only one single work of art in your life, what would it be?

I guess it would probably have to be one of the plays of Shakespeare—I don't know. I'd hate to settle on which one. Maybe a comedy. I can tell you what, I'll go ahead and take *The Canterbury Tales.* I read it again last summer. It's still what it is.

Writing what book was the most cathartic process?

The one I was happiest with when I finished, besides **Midquest,** was *I Am One of You Forever* because as soon as I got it right, after the rewrites, I knew I had done almost exactly what I wanted to do with the book. I feel now that it should be about thirty pages longer and that it should have two more stories. But I wasn't able to think of any good enough, so it's a little shorter than I'd like. The book took about ten years from the first sentence to the last, but I did not work on it continuously. About a third of it was written while I was working on **Midquest,** and some of it had been written long before that. That one kind of collected like a snowball over the years.

Didn't you get lost once going to a reading at Hollins?

Oh, that was a hoax. I was coming up with a friend named George Moore, and I said, "George, let's stop here." We were about fifty miles out of Roanoke. I said, "Let's call Richard Dillard and tell him we're lost and we'll get there as soon as we can." So I called Richard, got him, and told him we were lost in a place called Eat, Virginia. That's all the sign we could see, just a big sign that said "Eat." And he said, "Oh Lord, I know where that place is. You know what will happen if you don't arrive here?" And I said, "No, what?" And he said, "They're gonna make me read." And I said, "Hell, I'd just as soon hear Richard read—maybe we'll come in late." But we showed up on time, and I was teasing Richard about the hoax, and he made me feel like three cents. He said, "Well, you duped the world's most gullible person." (*Laughs.*)

In what ways is Fred Chappell most misunderstood?

I don't know that I am.

I'm saying you are.

(*Laughs.*) Oh, really. I think sometimes my attempts at humor are misunderstood, that people think I'm making snotty jokes at their expense when I'm really not. I'm just babbling along, trying to make some kind of pun or something. That happens—that's carelessness, sloppiness on my part. I am not a misunderstood person. What you see is what you get.

Joyce said that at some point in his life as things became easier he had a decision on which way to go.

Writing has not become easy for me. When I get to do it regularly, it becomes more fun than just doing it occasionally—that is, if you can get up every day and write some fiction, it's more fun than having to start back fresh writing fiction after a long let-up. The same is true with poetry to a certain extent. But finding the right word in the right sentence is still just as hard as it was twenty years ago for me, I think. At least I don't seem to be writing at any faster rate.

And then there's the juggling of your schedule, time constraints.

Sometimes for me it's a problem because I have to choose a project I know I can get done by a certain date because

I have other projects coming up. That's kind of tedious. If I'm going to write a short story, I have to calculate even before I start how many pages it's going to take, how many days it's going to take, because at the end of that period I have to go off writing for a while, and I won't be able to pick up easily when I come back. Also, I just like to do things in a certain time. I don't like to have things hanging. I can't stand to owe money, for example. I like to go straight ahead to the end. (pp. 108-22)

> Fred Chappell and Irv Broughton, in an interview in The Writer's Mind: Interviews with American Authors, Vol. III, edited by Irv Broughton, The University of Arkansas Press, 1990, pp. 91-122.

Michael Dirda (review date 6 October 1991)

[In the following review of More Shapes Than One, Dirda praises Chappell's talents as a storyteller.]

Long a problem for schools, grade inflation has become a vexation for book reviewers. The least reservation, the teeniest gripe, sometimes even measured, rather than full-blown, enthusiasm, can sink a novel or collection of stories, dropping it from the category of "Must buy right now" down to that of "Might read in paperback." Make the book sound too offbeat and it immediately joins the serried ranks of those titles that we half-heartedly intend to "keep an eye out for at the library."

Given all this, Fred Chappell's **More Shapes Than One** should be welcomed with fanfare and fireworks just to make sure that it finds at least a few good readers. As it happens, though, these terrifically enjoyable stories are more the kind one associates with, say, Tennessee sipping whisky than with high-octane hoopla: Here are low-keyed tales of ghosts and strange beings, historical imaginings (about the biologist Linnaeus, the explorer-scientist Maupertuis, the mathematician Feuerbach), a comic gem about a symbolist poem blocking a small country road. Fantasy? Magical realism? Either will do for a category but an even-better one is the old-fashioned, after-dinner story, the kind told when the fire burns low and the one stranger in the company leans forward to whisper, "This reminds me of a rather odd thing that once happened to a friend of mine." And what follows is very odd indeed.

"Weird Tales," for instance, starts out this way: "The visionary poet Hart Crane and the equally visionary horror-story writer H. P. Lovecraft met four times"—an irresistible narrative hook—and then neatly segues into a homage to those palpitatingly overwrought chillers by Lovecraft about the god Cthulhu, fungi from Yoggoth or the accursed Necronomicon. In its turn **"The Adder"** relates, with tongue-in-cheek horror, what happens when a copy of the Necronomicon comes into the possession of a second-hand bookdealer. Later **"The Somewhere Doors"** portrays a withdrawn young man who composes wistful, poetic science fiction (e.g. "The Marooned Aldebaran") that calls to mind the brocaded fancies of Lovecraft's contemporary, Clark Ashton Smith. (By contrast, **"Alma"** projects a brutal world—in the deep past or the distant future isn't clear—where women are herded together and sold like animals.) Even Chappell's best-known novel, **Dagon,** inscribes a Faulknerian tale of depravity and degradation within a Lovecraftian frame.

The stories of **More Shapes Than One** can be divided into three main sorts. The first are these updated, often slyly humorous supernatural fantasies. A second are the stylish historical jeux d'esprit, in which Linnaeus glimpses the actual realm of the goddess Flora or the composer Offenbach encounters his double on the streets of Vienna. The third loose category contains tales of Southern types: The prim Miss Prue, who entertains the ghost of her longtime gentleman caller and tells him that their relationship "positively swilled nuance"; the man who shot the faithless Phoebe Redd and runs from the law, only to meet his destiny on spooky Ember mountain; the good ole boy who reveals a special gift when he sings at the funeral of his best friend; and best of all the down-home sheriff and his aw-shucks deputies who discover a poet in their midst. (Kipling fans will enjoy this last story as a kind of regional variant of "Wireless.")

Chappell's prose always moves swiftly and cleanly, with a tale-spinner's ease. A story set in the early 18th century possesses an appropriately Augustan hauteur. "Once fired, passion for the philosophy of Isaac Newton proved unquenchable in Europe." Another tale grounded in hard-scrabble country can toss off just the right homely observation: "And then the silence let up a little and I could hear the hood of the truck ticking as the motor cooled . . . " With such an ear, Chappell can parody with the best of them, in one case Donald Barthelme. A prissy scientist sent from the State Office analyzes the all too substantial dream blocking a rural highway: " 'I hate to tell you,' Dr. Litmouse said, 'but I believe it's a symbolist poem. I'd stake my professional reputation that it's a symbolist poem.' " Later he adds, after falling into a swoon from tasting the dream, "I remember no details. I have only impressions. I would say that the poem is informed by tenuous allusion, strong synesthesia, and a wide array of hermetic symbols. But it was quite confusing, and I could gather no details, no specifics." Ultimately, to get rid of this lyric road block the sheriff announces a poetry contest, with a $50 first prize. Symbolism preferred.

Fred Chappell has earned the Bollingen Prize for his poetry, been honored for **Dagon** by the French Academy (best foreign novel) and seen a selection of his work published as **The Fred Chappell Reader.** I still don't think he's well enough known or sufficiently read. I also think his stories sometimes trail off a little vaguely, but I'm making this mild criticism here at the end in the hope that potential purchasers of **More Shapes Than One** will miss it. These entrancing pages deserve all the readers they can get.

> Michael Dirda, "Strange Tales from the Hills," in Book World—The Washington Post, October 6, 1991, p. 5.

Bill Christophersen (review date 6 October 1991)

[In the following review, Christophersen offers a mixed appraisal of More Shapes Than One.]

The North Carolina poet and fiction writer Fred Chappell, as his second collection of short stories [*More Shapes Than One*], demonstrates, is a sly *farceur* with a pliant voice. If the narrator of one tale—about a world in which practicing science is a crime—sounds like James Stewart waxing urbanely ironic ("I'm a dangerous bad man, Bert. You'd better put me away. I'm out to destroy civilization"), the narrator of another sounds like Huck Finn grown crusty in the territories ("It was the plumb sorriest string of women ever I laid eyes on. Most of them wouldn't make good buzzard bait"). Still more various are Mr. Chappell's antic plots. **"The Adder,"** for example, concerns a book dealer who acquires an ancient text that drains substance from any book placed next to it. And in the tallest tale of the lot, **"Mankind Journeys Through Forests of Symbols,"** an enormous dream obstructs a highway. Sometimes lyrical, often burlesque, Mr. Chappell's wit is a skipping stone. He asks too much, though, when he bids that wit to change course in midflight. **"Alma,"** a hoax about a drover who rustles women, jackknifes in trying to become a love story. **"The Somewhere Doors,"** in which a science fiction writer is visited by a mystery woman and a gumshoe who says the woman is a spy, seems at first to be a spoof of pop genres, but ends as a trite fable whose moral is something akin to "Be here, now." The waggish Fred Chappell, as *More Shapes Than One* makes plain, is much better at being anyplace else.

> *Bill Christophersen, in a review of "More Shapes Than One," in* The New York Times Book Review, *October 6, 1991, p. 20.*

FURTHER READING

Criticism

Cherry, Kelly. "A Writer's Harmonious World." *Parnassus* 9, No. 2 (Fall-Winter 1981): 115-29.
  Examines the "idea of odyssey" in *Midquest,* concluding that the work "affirms the resurrection-power of art."

Ellis, Normandi. "Swarpin." *American Book Review* 10, No. 2 (May-June 1988): 15, 18.
  Explores Chappell's depiction of Southern life and themes in *I Am One of You Forever.*

Mississippi Quarterly: The Journal of Southern Culture, Special Issue: The Work of Fred Chappell XXXVII, No. 1 (Winter 1983-84): 3-88.
  Issue devoted to various aspects of Chappell's work. Also includes a primary bibliography through 1983.

Stuart, Dabney. "Spiritual Matter in Fred Chappell's Poetry: A Prologue." *The Southern Review* 27, No. 1 (Winter 1991): 200-20.
  Discusses themes and structures in *Midquest* and *Source.*

Interview

Ruffin, Paul. "Interview with Fred Chappell." *Pembroke Magazine* 17 (1985): 131-5.
  Chappell comments on *Midquest* and the Southern literary tradition.

Additional coverage of Chappell's life and career is contained in the following sources published by Gale Research: *Contemporary Authors,* **Vols. 5-8 rev. ed.;** *Contemporary Authors Autobiography Series,* **Vol. 4;** *Contemporary Authors New Revision Series,* **Vols. 8, 33;** *Contemporary Literary Criticism,* **Vol. 40; and** *Dictionary of Literary Biography,* **Vols. 6, 105.**

Robert Creeley

1926-

(Full name Robert White Creeley) American poet, novelist, short story writer, essayist, and editor.

The following entry provides a general overview of Creeley's career. For further information on his life and works, see *CLC*, Volumes 1, 2, 4, 8, 11, 15, and 36.

INTRODUCTION

Along with American poets Charles Olson, Robert Duncan, and Denise Levertov, Creeley is credited with establishing what came to be known as the "Black Mountain" school of poetry. Drawing upon the work of modernist poets Ezra Pound and William Carlos Williams, these individuals developed the theory of "projective verse," a form of free verse that makes use of natural speech rhythms to achieve a spontaneous presentation of the poet's emotional and intellectual state. Creeley's frequently quoted belief that "form is never more than an extension of content" derives from his conviction that the inevitable self-discovery resulting from the creative process—the act of writing—is more important than the work itself.

Creeley published several volumes of poetry during the 1950s while teaching at Black Mountain College in North Carolina and editing the school's literary journal, the *Black Mountain Review*. He did not receive widespread recognition, however, until the 1962 publication of *For Love: Poems 1950-1960,* which presents many of his characteristic concerns, including language and human relationships. Critics attribute the precise imagery, arresting rhythms, and unusual syntax, punctuation, and grammar in Creeley's poetry to the strong influence of jazz and contemporary visual art, especially Abstract Expressionism. With his 1968 collection *Pieces,* Creeley's poetry became more austere and experimental, with some compositions consisting of only a few words.

In his more recent poems Creeley moves toward a less compressed, more articulate verse and addresses such themes as aging, death, sexuality, and memory. While some critics have faulted *Mirrors* and *Memory Gardens* for being banal and narrowly personal, others have praised *Windows* for subtle wit and originality. *The Collected Essays of Robert Creeley* chronicles Creeley's history with the Black Mountain and Beat Poets, his evolution as a theorist, and his conviction that the act of writing is paramount to a poet's existence. With the release of his 1991 *Selected Poems,* a compilation of over forty years of work, most critics acknowledged Creeley as a major influence on younger writers and an influential voice in American literature. In a review of *Selected Poems,* Carol Muske Dukes characterizes Creeley as "a quintessentially American

poet, democratic in his idiom, funny and street-wise in his diction and tone, a maverick of passion and sagacity."

PRINCIPAL WORKS

The Immoral Proposition (poetry) 1953
The Gold Diggers (short stories) 1954; also published as *The Gold Diggers, and Other Stories* [enlarged edition], 1965
All That Is Lovely in Men (poetry) 1955
A Form of Women (poetry) 1959
For Love: Poems 1950-1960 (poetry) 1962
The Island (novel) 1963
Distance (poetry) 1964
Words (poetry) 1965; also published as *Words* [enlarged edition], 1967
About Women (poetry) 1966
Pieces (poetry) 1968; also published as *Pieces* [enlarged edition], 1969
Hero (poetry) 1969

Mazatlan: Sea (poetry) 1969

Change (poetry) 1972

A Day Book (prose) 1972

In London (poetry) 1972

Hello (poetry) 1976; also published as *Hello: A Journal, February 29–May 3, 1976* [enlarged edition], 1978

*Mabel: A Story, and Other Prose (poetry and short stories) 1976

Presences (poetry) 1976

Selected Poems (poetry) 1976

Later (poetry) 1978; also published as *Later* [enlarged edition], 1979

The Collected Poems of Robert Creeley, 1945-1975 (poetry) 1982

Echoes (poetry) 1982

Mirrors (poetry) 1983

Collected Prose (prose) 1984; also published as *Collected Prose* [corrected edition], 1987

Memories (poetry) 1984

Memory Gardens (poetry) 1986

The Collected Essays of Robert Creeley (essays) 1989

Windows (poetry) 1990

Selected Poems (poetry) 1991

*This volume contains the prose and poetry collections *A Day Book* and *Presences.*

CRITICISM

Robert Kern　(essay date Spring-Fall 1978)

[*In the following essay, Kern traces Creeley's development as critic, poet, and theorist.*]

Virtually from the beginning of his career in the late 1940's, Robert Creeley's development as a poet (and as a writer of fiction as well) has been accompanied by a steady stream of critical and theoretical commentary, often personal or autobiographical in nature, in the form of prefaces, notes, reviews, essays, letters, lectures, and, somewhat later, interviews, a body of statement which adds up to an influential source of poetic information (and perhaps also a *poetics in formation*) about the period during which it evolves. This is, of course, the period which witnesses what is now widely regarded as a significant changeover from the values and presuppositions of modernism in the arts to a new or radically revised set of possibilities designated as "postmodern" by literary commentators and historians who use the term in ways ranging from the merely descriptive to the zealously ideological. Instead of pursuing in any detail the main features of this changeover, however, my purpose here will be the more limited one of investigating Creeley's work as critic or theorist, rather than strictly as practitioner, of the poem in the context of that aspect of postmodern literary theory that Charles Olson has called "projective verse" and that might be

more broadly and inclusively referred to as the poetics of open form. While widely accepted and at least nominally practiced by contemporary poets, this is a poetics which, to be sure, is hardly the same thing for all of them, though in its general outlines it does illuminate much of what they hold in common as writers working within a postmodern or simply contemporary context. My assumption, of course, is that Creeley's work in this area affords us an especially useful means of access not only to his own important body of poetry but to a significant part of the general literary landscape in its evolution over the last several decades.

"I'm *given* to write poems" [*A Quick Graph*], Creeley says in one of the most comprehensive of his statements on poetics, and any investigation of his work as critic or theorist properly begins with the recognition that his primary sense of the poetic act is that he is its object, the humble witness rather than the organizing manipulator of the poem's occasion. This distinction in itself—that between humble witness and organizing manipulator—might serve as a fruitful point of departure, since open form poetics is often predicated upon the conviction that it is the order and value *out there,* in the external world, that is important, as opposed to what immediately issues from the poet's private creative imagination, the poem itself regarded as the locus of value. Of course this conviction depends upon a prior one—the assumption that there is in fact an immanent order and value in external reality, or at least that there are forces outside the poet that ultimately control and indeed *permit* the act of composition—forces which the poet must recognize in order to write at all.

The emphasis here falls on the notion of the poet as medium more than as maker, an emphasis that is clear in Denise Levertov's statement, "I believe poets are instruments on which the power of poetry plays." Although she goes on immediately to qualify this remark by saying that poets are "also *makers,* craftsmen," whose responsibility it is to communicate what they see, the act of making seems temporally distinct in her definition from the act of recognition, or seeing, which is primary, prior to any making, and without which making would be impossible or trivial. Thinking of the poet as both medium and maker, in any event, does not prevent Levertov from defining her own mode of "organic" poetry as a method "of recognizing what we perceive" that is based, in turn, on "an intuition of an order, a form beyond forms, in which forms partake" [*The Poet in the World*], where the important point is clearly that there is an order in experience which not only transcends but provides a ground for the conventional forms of poetic tradition, and which it is the poet's fundamental task to disclose.

Creeley's articulation of similar intuitions puts even greater stress on the humility demanded by the act of composition regarded as a process of recognition:

> I have used all the intelligence that I can muster to follow the possibilities that the poem "under hand," as Olson would say, is declaring, but I cannot anticipate the necessary conclusions of the activity, nor can I judge in any sense, in moments of writing, the significance of that writing more than to recognize that it is being *permitted*

to continue, I'm trying to say that, in writing, at least as I have experienced it, one is *in* the activity. . . . [*A Quick Graph*]

Seemingly more radical than Levertov, Creeley is implying that he does not know where he is going until he gets there, a notion of the creative process that brings to mind his frequent use of the example of driving a car as an analogy for writing, where it is the external road that determines the driver's decisions from moment to moment and that he must strictly attend to if he is to maintain himself in not only a unified relationship with his experience but literally a safe one. Consider the friend's reply to the speaker in Creeley's well-known poem **"I Know a Man"**:

> As I sd to my
> friend, because I am
> always talking,—John, I
>
> sd, which was not his
> name, the darkness sur-
> rounds us, what
>
> can we do against
> it, or else, shall we &
> why not, buy a goddamn big car,
>
> drive, he sd, for
> christ's sake, look
> out where yr going.

In remarking on the poetic process in an interview with Charles Tomlinson—remarks that lead to yet another use of the driving metaphor—Creeley observes that his conception of writing is "an awfully precarious situation to be in, because you can obliterate everything in one instant. You've got to be utterly awake to recognize what is happening, and to be responsible for all the things you must do before you can even recognize what their full significance is" [*Contexts of Poetry*]. In the poem, the friend is attempting to bring the speaker back into immediate relationship with the experience at hand by breaking into the speaker's self-distracting and potentially self-destructive rhetoric of metaphysical despair and escapist fantasy.

Creeley's position, then, is one which allows no temporal gap between writing and experience—or what Levertov calls making and seeing—no separation between *poesis* and *mimesis,* so to speak. What a poem is *about* is literally its own making or unfolding. The poet, in such a conception, is *inside* the act of composition, which is entirely self-limiting, a record of the circumstances of its own occasion. If for Levertov it is the contemplation of experience that leads to the first words of the poem, for Creeley the poem is in some sense always already there (as the road is for the driver), declaring its own possibilities—possibilities which he cannot anticipate but which he must nevertheless follow if he is to be true to his "experience"—which is, at the level most important to him, always experience of the act of writing itself. As Creeley puts it in a brief note called **"Poems Are a Complex"**:

> I think I first felt a poem to be what might exist in words as primarily the fact of its own activity. Later, of course, I did see that poems might comment on many things, and reveal many attitudes and qualifications. Still, it was never what

they said *about* things that interested me. I wanted the poem itself to exist and that could never be possible as long as some subject significantly elsewhere was involved.

In the "Introduction" to the anthology *The New Writing in the USA* (1965), Creeley extends this personal feeling about the poem into a generalization about recent literary history when he observes that the traditional idea of " 'subject' as a conceptual focus or order has given place to the literal activity of the writing itself," an awareness of a displacement that suggests the emphasis in structuralism (specifically in the work of Roland Barthes) on the idea that modern writing is primarily constituted by its own intransitive activity, and not by the intentions of an author anterior to the work. There is, moreover, an interesting corollary to Creeley's position here. If the act of writing is not a generalized experience for him, but always a unique and specific one, conditioned by its own circumstances, then one cannot, so to speak, enter the same poem twice. If each act of composition, that is to say, is unique, then revision is impossible; one cannot go back and rewrite a poem so as to improve it. At least the result of such an effort, from Creeley's perspective, will not be a better or improved poem, but simply a different one.

Differences between writers as artistically close and compatible as Levertov and Creeley are no doubt easy to exaggerate, and it is perhaps more important to focus on what they share in their approaches to open form—that sense, for example, as Levertov speaks of it, that the poet is being led "through the world of the poem, its unique inscape revealing itself as he goes." In equally proposing the possibility of an open or "organic" poetry in intimate relation with the experience from which it comes, and in understanding that experience to have form in itself, to be immanently *informed* by an order from which the conventional orderings of poetic tradition are irrelevant distractions, both writers are in essential agreement about the basic ingredients of such a poetry.

The extent to which a poetry of open form seems to depend on a sense of immanent order in experience, or indeed in the universe, is made clear by another writer close to both Creeley and Levertov, Robert Duncan, when he subordinates "the order man may contrive or impose upon the things about him or upon his own language" to "the divine order or natural order he may discover in them." In his essay "Towards an Open Universe" [in *The Poetics of the New American Poetry*], Duncan insists, against the emphasis in modernism that all value and meaning have their source in the human imagination, or in what man creates, that

> We do not make things meaningful, but in our making we work towards an awareness of meaning; poetry reveals itself to us as we obey the orders that appear in our work. In writing I do not organize words but follow my consciousness of—but it is also a desire that goes towards—orders in the play of forms and meanings toward poetic form.

It is tempting to regard the emergence of such attitudes, more or less collectively expressed as they are (even by such a small but influential group as that comprised of Olson, Creeley, Levertov, and Duncan), as a primary factor in the development of a postmodern literary imagination—or at least as strong evidence for a break with the presuppositions and values of modernism by a significant part of a later generation of poets. The antipathy toward the New Criticism and what he calls "an *idea* of form extrinsic to the given instance" that runs through Creeley's essays, as well as his recollections of the 1940's as a "hostile time" for himself and like-minded writers in terms of achieving publication, are but a few symptoms. Even more important, the notion of open form or "composition by field," and the closely allied idea of the world itself as the locus of order and value, run directly counter to some of the most cherished notions of modernism—particularly its insistence upon the creative primacy of the poet as craftsman and its strong sense of the poem as the locus of value in opposition to a world of chaotic flux.

In terms of the largest and most obvious generalizations, to be sure, the idea of an authentic postmodernism certainly seems to be confirmed. In its most typical formulations, for example, modernist poetics stresses the way in which the poem is a closed, self-sufficient object whose unity depends on the formal relationships of its parts. Postmodern writing, on the other hand, seeks a greater openness for the poem, an openness to the world and to experience which culminates in the ideal of the text not as a utopian structure immune to the contradictions and confusions of immediate experience but as continuous with or an extension of such experience, the here and now of ordinary reality. In Heideggerian terms, if we can arbitrarily split apart the phrases of the equation which bespeaks the very essence of language for Heidegger [in his *On the Way to Language*], we might say that modernists are concerned with "the being of language," its independent, systematic character, while postmodernists pursue "the language of being," the language that discloses reality. In accord with such aims, postmodernists seek a poetry that will embody the presence of living speech, Heidegger's "Saying" or the *parole* of the structuralists, intent on avoiding the mere textuality, or *écriture,* of the written or printed text, what Olson [in his *Selected Writings*] has called "that verse which print bred." For Heidegger, "Saying" means "to show, to let appear, to let be seen and heard," and "Saying as Showing" is "The essential being of language," whose "showing character is not based on signs of any kind," the idea of language as merely a means of signification, but on its ability or function to disclose being, to be the language of being through which or in which the world comes into presence. Creeley himself makes a similar distinction when he contrasts "poets of 'content,' " who use the poem "as a means to recognition, a signboard as it were," with poets like Olson, for whom the poem is "a structure of 'recognition' or—better—cognition itself."

The rejection of conventional, pre-established literary forms in Creeley's poetics (as well as in Olson's) is based in large part on the conviction that such forms preclude the achievement of continuity between writing and experience, prevent a use of language as a truly Heideggerian "Saying." What is rejected, however, is not form *per se,* but the pre-determined form that is viewed as prior, and therefore possibly irrelevant, to the experience at hand. As Creeley insists, "The point is that no form can exist as a possibility apart from that which informs it, the content of which it is the issue." Like this statement, Creeley's famous axiom, that form is never more than an extension of content, clearly gives the priority to content, to what is happening, and sees form as emerging from it, the shape of what has happened, which can only be known or perceived after the event.

In this and similar contexts, Creeley often invokes Olson's remarkably Heideggerian distinction between "language as the act of the instant and language as the act of thought about the instant." The distinction comes from Olson's essay "Human Universe," in which he begins by addressing himself to "the present condition of language," by which he means "language exactly in its double sense of discrimination (logos) and of shout (tongue)." He continues:

> We have lived long in a generalizing time, at least since 450 B. C. And it has had its effects on the best of men, on the best of things. Logos, or discourse, for example, has, in that time, so worked its abstractions into our concept and use of language that language's other function, speech, seems so in need of restoration that several of us go back to hieroglyphs or to ideograms to right the balance.

Olson's complaint here is against the abstractions of discourse by which we become separated from the world and from our own actions. Like Heidegger, who protests against the use of language as a system of significations essentially removed from what they signify, Olson emphasizes that aspect of language which is the prereflective "act of the instant"—Heidegger's language of being based on an original unity between word and thing. Both valorize language as what Heidegger calls "the primordial poetry in which a people speaks being," language not as a reflective medium but as a direct manifestation of the being or activity of the world—language, that is to say—and this is particularly the case in Olson's view—as action. In order to recover such a language, both also prescribe a return to origins—Olson to hieroglyphs and ideograms, and Heidegger, especially in his *Introduction to Metaphysics,* to the pre-Socratic philosophers, for whom *Logos,* as he argues, was not rational discourse but originally an act of "gathering," which he interprets as "opening, making manifest." As an act of disclosure, Gerald L. Bruns suggests [in his *Modern Poetry and the Idea of Language*], this gathering is essentially a poetic act, so that *Logos* for Heidegger is not reason but poetry, which is, again, the primordial unity of word and thing.

Creeley's version of this unity, of the poet whose speech is an act manifesting being, is clearly based on Olson's distinction between discourse and speech "as the act of the instant." It leads not only to a conception of art that (again quoting Olson) "does not seek to describe but to enact," but to "a kind of writing that is never more, nor less, than 'what it has to say,' " and to a sense of involvement in creative activity from which "at no moment may one step aside—to think *about* the world, rather than *in* it or *of* it or *as* it." It returns poetry to what Creeley calls "its relation with *physiological* condition."

In a variety of ways and contexts, then, Creeley is constantly being led back to the same points. His continual insistence on "the poem in its *full impact of speech,*" his antipathy toward poetry as a descriptive act, by which he means "any act which leaves the attention outside the poem," and his fondness for Jackson Pollock's statement about the relation of the artist to his activity, a statement which he finds accurate to his own sense of such relation—

> When I am in my painting, I'm not aware of what I'm doing. It is only after a sort of "get acquainted" period that I see what I have been about. I have no fears about making changes, destroying the image, etc., because the painting has a life of its own. I try to let it come through. It is only when I lose contact with the painting that the result is a mess. Otherwise there is pure harmony, an easy give and take, and the painting comes out well.

—all are instances of Creeley's fundamental conviction that writing is an activity limited only by its own nature in the time and place at which it occurs. The implications of this conviction emerge most clearly in Creeley's response to an interviewer who asked him [in *Paris Review* (1968)] if he has some "point" to make as a writer. Creeley replied, "The point I wish to make is that I am writing. Writing is my primary articulation. So when I write, that's what I'm at work with—an articulation of what confronts me, which I can't really realize or anticipate prior to the writing." We can recognize here, once again, the humility of the writer before the world of his experience, and his use of writing as a means of discovering the nature of that experience. The apparent formalist insistence on the being of language in Creeley's work, or on what he calls the poem as "the fact of its own activity," seems to lead easily to the language of being, the articulation or realization "of what confronts me."

Yet we must also recognize that this formalism in Creeley, this vestige of modernist thinking about the poem (for that is what it seems to be in part), not only persists in his writing but becomes particularly prominent whenever he offers his characterization of the ideal text as an activity or talks about such poetic heroes of his as William Carlos Williams and Louis Zukofsky, writers who always seem to arouse Creeley's interest in language *as language,* independent of meaning—or in a use of language in poetry that suspends the process of signification, even more than is usually the case, to focus attention on itself. Indeed, in describing this aspect of Creeley's poetics, it is quite possible to employ the terms of so extreme a formalist as Roland Barthes, for whom modern, as opposed to "classical," writing is best characterized as a passive, intransitive mode of discourse, a non-intentional act which can be defined, as Gerald L. Bruns points out [in *Modern Poetry and the Idea of Language*] much more accurately in terms of its self-limiting nature as an activity than in terms of any product or outcome of that activity. In this sense, it becomes difficult to regard Creeley's explicit statements on poetics as fully or definitively postmodern. Any attempt to do so, in fact, must sooner or later confront two

serious, and related, qualifications. One is precisely the nagging persistence in Creeley's writing of the modernist or at least formalist notion of the poem as autotelic object, the made or crafted thing that preserves its own reasons for being, and the other is the fact that there are clearly versions of open form theory in contemporary writing that do not depend on assumptions about an immanent order in experience, or that regard such assumptions with greater skepticism or pessimism than the essentially positive version that we have been examining in Creeley, Levertov, and Duncan.

Such writers as William Bronk and Gilbert Sorrentino, for example, must be regarded as reluctant or skeptical or even negative open formalists, in the sense that they see no alternative in the contemporary context to openness of form, viewing the use of inherited, conventional forms, like most of their contemporaries, as a meaningless act of repetition by which nothing new can be discovered. On the other hand, it is possible that nothing new can be discovered anyway, since for these writers the idea of the poet as witness or medium, standing in privileged relation to the immanent order of experience, seems unacceptable. Bronk's poetry in particular communicates a radical sense of epistemological instability. At the risk of oversimplifying his position, we might say that he continues to express a sense of reality whose most powerful source in modern poetry is Wallace Stevens' lyric "The Snow Man"—reality as "Nothing that is not there and the nothing that is." Bronk's starting-point [in his *The World, The Worldless*] is the knowledge that "One is nothing with no world." Like the modernists, he recognizes that such a world must be made, "that one needs to make / a world for survival." But at the same time, he is continually led by his own logic to the conclusion that there is "Not / for us ever any familiar and definite world," that "There is Ignorant Silence in the Center of Things," and that our made worlds will never correspond to any reality. We need a world, a sense or idea of order, by which to live, but such conceptions are inevitably fictions, ideas that are "always wrong," and that in any case are never confirmed by anything beyond us. Life for Bronk is thus a slow spectacle of change in which "heavens and styles collide meaninglessly," in which our ideas are constantly being undermined by a reality that is nevertheless unknowable and inaccessible, a reality whose "Huge factors stand ready to leap in / to alter or destroy a world we defend alone."

The situation that Bronk's poetry is based on seems to be one in which the modernist fear or suspicion that human creations are ultimately fictions, without ontological validity, predominates. But that fear is unmitigated for Bronk by any of the modernist strategies for its resolution, which most often take the form of defining art as a separate and unique reality whose relation to the world is deliberately unintended and unintentional. For Stevens, who ultimately posits the notion of the poem as the supreme fiction, the "exquisite truth" is to "believe in a fiction, which you know to be a fiction, there being nothing else." Even in Frost's well-known definition of the poem as "a momentary stay against confusion," one of the most convenient and revealing of modernist formulas, the assumption seems to be that "confusion" is the truth of reality, a truth that the poem can only temporarily avoid by following its inherently fictive directions. But these are directions which Bronk refuses to take, a refusal which leaves him at the end of speech, at the undefinable "heart of things. / This nothing. This full silence. To not know." In this sense, his poetry calls itself radically into question and precipitates personal as well as literary crisis, for the mind without ideas "has freedom to be / nothing, worldless—not to exist at all."

[In *The Perfect Fiction*] Gilbert Sorrentino writes in a situation of difficulty or crisis that is similar to Bronk's, and that, in its particular terms, contrasts tellingly with Creeley's. Describing himself as a depressing man who writes depressing poems, and defining the world or reality as what he calls "the perfect fiction," Sorrentino's speaker (in the book-length sequence of that title) reduces himself as a poet to the production of imperfect fictions, *fictional* fictions, let us say—patterns or structures that, in their disharmony with the pattern of the world, leave him with a bitter sense of alienation or solipsism:

> What is to be understood:
> the world, one's place
> in it. The meaning of
>
> it, the meaning of
> any part of any of
> it, this desk, from
>
> wood, of wood. Quiet
> forests underneath the
> sky. A blue sky, a black
>
> sky, endless. There is
> a pattern, not what we choose
> to make, the humiliated artist.

Rather than the artist as humble witness, Sorrentino's poet becomes the humiliated artist, humiliated by the natural or divine perfection of a pattern in the world which exceeds that of the poem and with which he cannot make his own aesthetic choices and patternings correspond. The world may be a fiction for Sorrentino, but it is a perfect one, and his self-confessed inability to bring his poems into harmony with it suggests his own redoubled distance from the world, an intensified isolation in fictions of his own making.

From the perspective of the difficulties suffered by poets like Bronk and Sorrentino, Creeley's retention of a formalist or modernist notion of the poem as a self-limiting, self-sustaining activity becomes understandable. It is a way for writing to escape the status of fiction, to be a substantial reality, in and of itself, in the world. As Creeley puts it, "I've never felt that writing was fiction, that it was something made up about something. I've felt that it was direct evidence of the writer's engagement with his own feelings and with the possibilities that words offered him." Creeley's formalism, moreover, precisely to the extent that it is linked to his assumptions about form as an extension of content, must ultimately be regarded as distinct from modernism's countermimesis, its antagonistic recoil from the world into its own textuality. Creeley's ideal text does not flee from confusion, erecting a momentary stay against it, but seeks to disclose the reality of feeling that the writer

is directly engaged with in the act of composition, in addition to the possibilities offered by words themselves. At the same time that he insists on the being of language, or, to put it another way, on the poem as an object—emphasizing its independence, its formal ability to constitute an order of discourse that is real in its own terms, without reference to anything outside it—he also wants the poem to be a process, an embodiment of the language of being that is not merely the extension but the revelation of its content, an energy or activity that directly manifests what Heidegger calls man's "being-in-the-world."

Creeley's poetics thus encompasses both aspects of poetic speech as Gerald L. Bruns has defined them in his valuable study, *Modern Poetry and the Idea of Language.* Using the terms "hermetic" and "Orphic" for these two aspects or modes of literary expression, Bruns describes them, respectively, as the speech of language and the speech of the world. Although he speaks of them at first as broadly antithetical concepts, he comes ultimately to regard them as constituting the necessary "doubleness of language," the "two essential movements" of which any poetic act consists: "a withdrawal from the world into a universe of language, which is a movement whose immediate end is to celebrate the transcendence of language, its being as such; and a return . . . to earth, which is a movement that brings word and world together. . . . " This insistence on the doubleness of language, by which both its hermetic and Orphic dimensions are contained in a dialectical unity, is useful here because it provides us with a way of accounting for the apparently contradictory movements in Creeley's writings between a formalist poetics and a poetics of action, and it also allows us to avoid the merely chronological contradictions between modernism and postmodernism, blending the historical differences that a theorist of either period would want to emphasize and attempting to mediate between them with a theory of the poem as both object and utterance, structure and act. It seems clear, at any rate, that when Creeley speaks, in the same essay, of poetry as a separate reality, as "a very distinct and definite *place,* that poetry not only creates but itself issues from," and also of poetry as "an agency or fact" through which one can "experience oneself as *in* the world," he is regarding poetry from the perspective of both linguistic or expressive possibilities that Bruns describes.

If one should still insist on the difference between modernism and postmodernism, however, there is yet another way to understand Creeley's formalism as distinct from modernist formalism, and that is to recognize that it derives, more than anything else, from William Carlos Williams' way of talking about the poem as an object made of words that are also objects, and about the poem as "a field of action." Williams, of course, who provided Creeley with what he calls his "largest example" as a poetic influence, was one of the first poets in the modern tradition to break away from the idea of the poem as an isolated preserve of peace and to come to regard it instead as "a field of action," not separate from the rest of the world but an extension of it, with all its swarming possibilities intact. In such a conception, it is formal pattern that must be avoided, for formal patterns "represent arrests of the truth in some particular phase of its mutations, and immediately thereafter, unless they change, become mutilations." What is suggested here is an idea that would be developed more elaborately in Olson's action-oriented theory of projective verse, an idea of the poem not as an arrest of the truth but as an embodiment of its energies or dynamics, a poem whose form is the effect, and not the cause, of its action. Clearly important as a link between Williams and the poets who follow him, this idea also suggests that easy assumptions about any total rupture of continuity between modernism and postmodernism need to be qualified. Is Williams a late modernist, or an early postmodernist?

In any event, what is even more important than Williams' direct anticipation of later developments is his particular sense of poetry, which for Creeley is to be located primarily in the preface to Williams' 1944 collection, *The Wedge*:

> When a man makes a poem, makes it, mind you, he takes words as he finds them interrelated about him and composes them—without distortion which would mar their exact significances—into an intense expression of his perceptions and ardors that they may constitute a revelation in the speech that he uses. It isn't what he *says* that counts as a work of art, it's what he makes, with such intensity of perception that it lives with an intrinsic movement of its own to verify its authenticity.

Very much a statement that looks both backwards and forwards, recalling, for example, modernist conceptions of impersonality, and even MacLeish's slogan about the poem that "must not mean / But be," its significance for Creeley lies in its stress on *making,* but a making that constitutes a "revelation." In its insistence on the reality of the text as a thing made, Williams' preface provides a way of avoiding the fictive and ephemeral nature of the poem as mere statement, and emphasizes the substantial qualities of language as "the fact of its own activity." In this sense, it is especially significant that Williams should speak of the poet as one who "takes words as he finds them interrelated about him," as though words were so many objects in the environment, and then builds them into a structure of speech that authenticates its reality by its own "intrinsic movement." As Creeley sees it, in so far as a poem possesses this "intrinsic movement of its own," it need not be "simply a wish on the part of the writer (or not simply a communication, saying "I'm telling you this'), but has within it all that it needs to survive in its own statement."

Despite the fact, however, that Creeley, as it should now be clear, speaks everywhere in his statements on poetics of the poem as a self-determining activity, of the poem that realizes itself in the poet's literal act of writing, it should also be clear that this is an ideal characterization of the text and of the creative process, and as such not often or at least not immediately accurate to what Creeley achieves in his actual poetic practice. Denise Levertov provides a crucial distinction that suggests as much when she points out, in a review of the volume *Pieces* (1969), that Creeley's early poem **"The Door"** "was, more than any other poem of his up to that time, not an examination of what happens but an immersion in what happens," and goes on to observe that Creeley's writing had in fact been more often

"conclusive" than exploratory, a sealing off rather than a pursuit of its own possibilities. What is suggested here, of course, is not merely that Creeley's early poems lag behind his theoretical presuppositions, but that his emotional relationship to his writing was one that made it impossible for him to meet the demands of open form poetics or composition as recognition. There is, to be sure, a strong sense in which Creeley's early work, up to and including *For Love* (1962), is very much a search for security and stability, both in the world and the poem, and not an abandonment of the self to the act of writing. In many ways, that volume seems dominated by Creeley's tormented figure of "The unsure egoist" (in the poem **"The Immoral Proposition"**), the person whose solipsistic sense of self and world *could* satisfy him if it were not for the fact that it is constantly being put in question by an opposing sense that there is something else, that being "spared the tragedy of human relation- / ships," for example, is also a deprivation and precisely what keeps the egoist "unsure." Thus, he is a figure who "is not / good for himself," denied the stability or certainty of his egoism by the doubt that continually qualifies it and makes him long for some alternative.

One could go so far as to say that in his early work, Creeley might very well have been satisfied, emotionally if not theoretically, by the idea of the poem as a stay against confusion. As Charles Altieri implies in a detailed and comprehensive account of Creeley's poetic development ["The Unsure Egoist: Robert Creeley and the Theme of Nothingness," *Contemporary Literature* (1972)], the quest that he undertakes and more or less accomplishes in *For Love* involves the pursuit of "a permanent peace outside the flux of time," a peace that Creeley identifies with love and the domestic conditions in which it both becomes possible and flourishes. The beautiful lyrics at the end of the book are grateful celebrations of "the company of love" and of the sense of being "brought now home" that it introduces into the poet's life. At long last, he feels himself to be beyond alienation and solipsism:

> Love comes quietly,
> finally, drops
> about me, on me,
> in the old ways.
>
> What did I know
> thinking myself
> able to go
> alone all the way.

Yet, as Altieri also points out, the resolution achieved in *For Love* is finally inadequate, and Creeley himself was soon to realize that "real peace must be found within, not beyond, the flux," a realization important not only for Creeley's development in terms of epistemological and emotional difficulties, but crucial also to his specific growth as a writer anxious to follow the imperatives of composition as recognition. What is clear, at any rate, even more in interviews and autobiographical statements than in the poetry, is the fact that Creeley first became interested in writing basically as a way of counteracting a strong sense of isolation:

> The insistent preoccupation with words did

begin for me early, just that I did want so much to know what people were saying, and what, more precisely, they meant by it. . . . I used books as a very real *place* to be. Not merely an escape from the world—the difficulty was how to get *into* it, not away—books proved a place very deeply open to me, at moments of reading, in a sense few others were ever to be.

At the same time that Creeley was trying to get *into* the world, however, his sense of "the reality experienced in writing" or, equally, the sense of *place* that books provided for him would become an object of insistent pursuit, not to be seriously questioned or modified until after the publication of *For Love* and the writing of his novel, *The Island* (1963). In the preface to this novel (with its revealing title), Creeley writes:

> People try with an increasing despair to live, and to come to something, some place, or person. They want an island in which the world will be at least a place circumscribed by visible horizons. They want to love free of a continuity of roads, and other places. This island is, finally, not real, however tangible it once seemed to me. I have found that time, even if it will not offer much more than a place to die in, nonetheless carries one on, away from this or any other island.

As Creeley abandons the ideal of an island, of "a place circumscribed by visible horizons" and therefore secure, he also abandons, we might say, in terms of his movement toward more open forms, the ideal of the poem as a "conclusive" structure, a separate, stable *place* beyond the flux of experience. The goal is no longer "to fit experience to possible orders of language," but to return language "to its place *in* experience," and in the volume *Words* (1967), Creeley consciously attempts to actualize this goal, writing, as he puts it, "for the immediacy of the pleasure and without having to pay attention to some final code of significance." It is not until *Words,* that is to say, that Creeley's poetic practice catches up with his explicit poetics, that aesthetic choice ceases to be an "act of will" for him and becomes instead an "act of recognition."

I want to conclude with just one example of this ultimate coincidence between theory and practice in Creeley. It is, appropriately enough, "For W. C. W.," a poem which mediates, I think in a helpful way, on the very issue of open and closed form, and which also demonstrates the differences between fitting experience to possible orders of language and returning language to its place in experience, so that language becomes the direct expression of experience:

> The rhyme is after
> all the repeated
> insistence.
>
> There, you say, and
> there, and there,
> and *and* becomes
>
> just so. And
> what one wants is
> what one wants,

> yet complexly
> as you
> say.
>
> Let's
> let it go.
> I want—
>
> Then there is—
> and,
> I want.

The poem is somewhat confusing at first because it uses language both discursively and demonstratively or substantively, giving small, often unnoticed words like "and" and "there" a double role to play as both functional elements within a propositional discourse, forwarding the syntax, and meaningful significations in themselves ("and *and* becomes"), standing for ideas or states of being. This is especially the case at the end of the poem, where whole phrases are used as a kind of shorthand for large, abstract concepts. Thus, what the speaker literally wants at the end is the state, so to speak, of "Then there is" and the state of "I want," where the first is the notion of an autonomous external reality, independent of the speaker, and the second is the idea of the equally independent and autonomous desiring self.

In so far as the poem arrives at a recognition of the self and the world as separate, independent realities, it points to the inadequacy of rhyme, or at least conventional rhyme, which is, as Charles Altieri observes in his suggestive reading of this poem, "an attempt to impose a fictive order on the world" in which subject and object, desire and result, coincide. In the poem's own language, rhyme is, after all, "the repeated / insistence," a recurring gesture within a closed system of discourse, without reference to anything outside it. Within such a system, governed by arbitrary rule rather than by experience, "what one wants is / what one wants"—that is, one is free to fashion one's own world, making it "just so," so that it corresponds exactly to the desires of the self. Such a conception, however, not only ignores the inescapable gap between self and world but amounts to a regressive return, from the perspective of Creeley's development, to the ideal of the poem as an island or *place,* "free of a continuity" with other realities and places. It is this conception to which Creeley bids farewell in the poem—"Let's / let it go"—recognizing instead that one is always carried on by time to new senses of the world forever separate from the self's desires.

If the poem rejects conventional rhyme, however, it also defines a different kind of rhyme—or possibility of relationship between self and world—that Creeley speaks of elsewhere as an "experience of 'order' far more various and intensive than habituated and programmed limits of its subtleties can recognize." This kind of rhyme is not "the repeated / insistence" that the prose sense of the poem's first stanza defines, but rather, if we pay strict attention to the scoring of Creeley's line-breaks, it is what comes *after* the repeated insistence, what is left after the repeated insistence is exhausted. What the poem suggests, then, is that when we have let conventional rhyming, and all that it implies, go, or ceased to try and fit experience to possible orders of language, then we are left once again with the existential realities of self and world, beyond the distortions and deprivations of solipsism or mere acts of will. But we are also left with a larger and liberating experience of order, as well as the possibility of registering it in an open form of speech that is not only responsible to experience and flux but that takes its place within their greater form. (pp. 211-27)

> Robert Kern, "Composition as Recognition: Robert Creeley and Postmodern Poetics," in boundary 2, *Vols. VI & VII, Nos. 3 & 1, Spring & Fall, 1978, pp. 211-30.*

Creeley on writing poetry:

I think I first felt a poem to be what might exist in words as primarily the fact of its own activity. Later, of course, I did see that poems might comment on many things, and reveal many attitudes and qualifications. Still, it was never what they said *about* things that interested me. I wanted the poem itself to exist and that could never be possible as long as some subject significantly elsewhere was involved.

Robert Creeley, in his A Quick Graph, *1970.*

Michael Davidson   (essay date Spring-Fall 1978)

[*Davidson is an American poet and educator. In the following essay, he notes the differences between Creeley's treatment of morality in his early poetry and that of his more recent prose.*]

In a well-known poem from *For Love,* Robert Creeley presents a dilemma that occurs throughout his work:

"The Immoral Proposition"

> If you never do anything for anyone else
> you are spared the tragedy of human relation-
>
> ships. If quietly and like another time
> there is the passage of an unexpected thing:
>
> to look at it is more
> than it was. God knows
>
> nothing is competent nothing is
> all there is. The unsure
>
> egoist is not
> good for himself.

What is immoral about the "immoral proposition" is the idea that one can avoid the "tragedy of human relation-// ships," by detaching oneself from the world. Obviously the "passage of an unexpected thing" shatters the self-protective frame in which the egoist hopes to barricade himself. However, "to look at it is more / than it was"; that is, to pay even the merest attention is to become implicated in its existence, a fact which occasions the recognition of the poem's closing couplet. To do more than "look at it" is to ascribe a value and thereby initiate a discourse.

The issue of this poem is not prescriptive morality but rather the terms by which moral propositions are made.

A proposition, as [Alfred North Whitehead notes in his *Process and Reality: A Cosmology*], is a "lure for feeling," a potentiality whose locus exists in an actual world of events and persons. It is not, in short, a judgment. Its elaboration resembles that of [René] Descartes, who, in the *Discourse on Method,* refuses to set an example for others and proceeds to show how he arrived at his own:

> So I offer this work as no more than a tale (*une histoire*) or a fable, if you prefer, in which you may find several examples you can imitate and others, perhaps, you may have no reason to follow, and I hope it will be useful to some, offensive to none, and that all will take pleasure in my openness.

If a moral proposition is variable, what then gives it its ethical character? This is a question that has interested Creeley for some years. In his preface to **The Gold Diggers,** he provides the beginnings of an answer:

> Had I lived some years ago, I think I would have been a moralist, i.e., one who lays down, so to speak, rules of behavior with no small amount of self-satisfaction. But the writer isn't allowed that function anymore, or no man can take the job on very happily, being aware (as he must be) of what precisely that will make him.
>
> So there is left this other area, still the short story or really the tale, and all that can be made of it. Whereas the novel is a continuum, of necessity, chapter to chapter, the story can escape some of that obligation, and function exactly in terms of whatever emotion best can serve it.

Between the two paragraphs lies a curious syllogism: if not a moralist, then a writer of tales. But what is a moralist for Creeley, and how does the tale provide a substitute for the moral function? The stories in **The Gold Diggers** are not moral fabliaux but instances which exemplify particular moral and ethical choices. "As the man responsible," he continues in his preface, "I wanted to say what I thought was true, and make that the fact." That is, truth is the condition under which an event becomes problematic; it is not to be confused with virtue, lawfulness or efficacy (as [Friedrich] Nietzsche points out in *The Genealogy of Morals*). In **"Mr. Blue,"** a circus dwarf's stare opens up the vulnerability of a marriage; in **"The Party,"** a man's confused attempts to silence crying children parallels a sense of failure in a relationship; in **"The Dress,"** a bizarre underground cavern is created to embody the self-protective needs of the male protagonist. In these and other stories, "nothing" happens, at least in the usual narrative sense. What occurs instead are momentary snapshots of a psychological condition in a moment of heightened tension.

Creeley's early writing, in its investigation of moral propositions, is often based around a double-bind. On the one hand, he wants to locate a center or focus which will provide a comprehensive statement of things as they are. On the other hand, this center exists in a dialectical relation to the language which proposes it, and so he must endlessly rephrase and reformulate its existence. In the poetry of *For Love,* this situation manifests itself as a dialogue between the romantic-idealist and the existential skeptic:

"The Way"

My love's manners in bed
are not to be discussed by me,
as mine by her
I would not credit comment upon gracefully.

Yet I ride by the margin of that lake in
the wood, the castle,
and the excitement of strongholds;
and have a small boy's notion of doing good.

Oh well, I will say here,
knowing each man,
let you find a good wife too,
and love her as hard as you can.

The middle stanza here provides, as it often does in the early poems, a kind of dialectical turn where the idealisms of the first stanza lead into the more worldly recognitions of the third. The "margin of that lake" which the poet-hero rides is one separating the romantic vision of the woman as sanctuary and the literal, day-to-day experience of her. The casual "Oh well" and the more grandiose claim, "knowing each man," are highly suspect; they are evasive tactics which indicate why **"The Way"** is not easy. The poet has, by these asides, indicated a kind of resignation to an incomplete vision, one for which he is ultimately responsible. But this resignation is an active context of awareness compared to the cavalier assumptions of the courtier poet:

Running to the door, I ran down
as a clock runs down. Walked backwards,
stumbled, sat down
hard on the floor near the wall.

Where were You.
How absurd, how vicious.
There is nothing to do but get up.
My knees were iron, I rusted in worship, of You.

For that one sings, one
writes the spring poem, one goes on walking.
The Lady has always moved to the next town
and you stumble on after Her.

This dialogue between courtier and "unsure egoist" cannot be reconciled in one direction or the other but exists in a state of constant tension. At the same time that the poet attempts to secure some permanence (usually in terms of wife or woman), he recognizes that the idea of permanence is predicated on a lack ("For that one sings . . . "). The primary function of the poem is to interrogate the boundary separating opposing terms. No "objective correlative" will provide a sufficient form since the terms are discovered in the activity of writing.

Until the publication of **Pieces** in 1969, Creeley's poetry and prose was inscribed within the crisis of the double-bind. With **Pieces** he enters into a new period in which the frame of self-analysis is broken down and a new permission is granted the poem to note the literal condition of things without stepping quite so far back for a reflective look:

So that I felt the kind of writing I'd been doing . . . was nevertheless partial to a limited emotional agency and therefore I wanted to find

means to include a far more various kind of statement through a sense of writing I got from [Charles] Olson and [Robert] Duncan . . . **Pieces** really became a kind of open writing in the sense that it was composed in a journal as daily writing.

Pieces significantly changes the nature of Creeley's moral-ethical quandary from one dealing with possible choices among alternatives to one in which choice *per se* is the central value:

The choice is simply,
I will—as mind is a finger,
pointing, as wonder,
a place to be.

Time ceases to function as a teleological structure but emerges as a dimension of subjective apprehension. "Here" and "there" cease to be mutually exclusive poles in a dialectic of presence and absence; both are merged into a single present—but a present that refuses to stay in one place:

Where it is
was and
will be never
only here.

Creeley's desire for a state of immediacy, of pure presence, is more closely realized in these new poems by allowing the shape of his conjecture free rein, but as Charles Altieri points out [in his "The Unsure Egoist: Robert Creeley and the Theme of Nothingness," *Contemporary Literature*, Spring 1972], this "quest for a secure place" remains to be satisfied:

As Creeley reconciled himself in **Words** with one form of nothingness, in **Pieces** he must admit another kind of void or absence—one not so much in the rhythm of one's life as in the actual condition or absent system which defines the terms of that rhythm. In the most simple terms, "here" requires a whole system of language for its meaning, especially its opposite term "there," just as the person needs to reconcile himself to the social and psychological forms which define his own particular apprehension of place.

Creeley's interrogation of the limits of expression (and of his own language) in **Pieces** represents a fundamental change from the psychologically charged lyrics of earlier work. The transition from "present" to "presence," the idea of time as a visitation or revelation, is part of this interrogation:

A period
at the end of a sentence
which

began *it was*
into a present,
a presence

saying
something
as it goes.

The "presence" of the "present" is that condition in which acts of pointing, locating, placing and establishing release experience from its non-reflective condition in time. The new moral proposition is made in each gesture towards significance, in each attempt to bring language into the foreground. The signifying act is a way of being, not simply a function. Time obtains value and dimension only when it intersects with human concern:

> This point of so-called
> consciousness is forever
> a word making up
> this world of more
> or less than it is.

This new *logos* projects a temporal field in which each moment is potentially revelatory. Where before the poem maintained a tension between transcendence and objectivity, between the ideal lady of courtier lyric and the literal companion, the new writing collapses these alternating poles into a single gesture of recognition. "I feel such trust in life," he says of the new direction proposed in *Pieces;* "once I stop all that previous qualification—just that I know I'm alive, and witness it with such pleasure in others, 'we are here'—I'm happy, in the most simplistic of senses."

This openness to immediate experience can be observed in a number of recent prose works published after *Pieces. A Day Book, Presences* and *Mabel: A Story* investigate moments in which ordinary activity resonates. Much of this prose is transcribed from notebooks and journals, and Creeley uses this open format to maintain the immediacy of the occasion. Unlike the prose of *The Gold Diggers* or *The Island,* the new work provides no narrative frame except that of Creeley's wandering, curious eye. The journal quality is reinforced by the poet's contact with a new group of poets during the late sixties, including Tom Clark, Joanne Kyger and Ted Berrigan, whose works take the present occasion as sufficient material for the poem. In the work of these poets there are no privileged moments or places; words, as Creeley says of Berrigan's poems, are returned "to an almost primal circumstance by a technique that makes use of feedback . . . where words are curiously returned to an almost objective state of presence so that *they* speak rather than someone speaking with them."

A Day Book, published while the poet was living in Bolinas, California, reflects this "objective" quality of language by a prose both meditational and notational. The cover, designed by Robert Indiana, reproduces the pages of a desk calendar, its large block letters and numerals indicating the initial and terminal dates of the writing contained: November 19, 1968, and June 11, 1971. These dates are no more important than any others, but Creeley, by framing them, indicates the primacy of daily writing and the way in which it gives value to the present. The prose meditates upon events, readings, senses of obligation, quotes and conversations, motivated only by the "fact of reality and the pressure" (as he had spoken of the stories in *The Gold Diggers*). The book opens with a moment of doubt encountered upon waking:

> He is waking to two particulars. One, that he is
> to make, before sending it, a copy of the letter,
> and then realizes the letter has been mailed. And

two, that all the assumptions involved in what has happened to himself and his wife, in their so-called fantasy, are literal assumptions. They are neither right or wrong. How is the intersection possible?

The "intersection" of what? The occasion of the letter and the fact of assumptions? Rightness or wrongness? Assumptions? Does "They" refer only to "assumptions" or are husband and wife also included? The ambiguity of the "intersection" leads to further discussion as though Creeley wishes to answer his final query by describing all possible antecedents and cases:

> The letter leads only to further complications.
> He will pay the money if required to. The man
> for whom it is committed is in jail in Mexico. He
> has never met nor seen him. There is only a
> somewhat vast emptiness of sentimental assumption to make reason. He had been told of
> the circumstance weeks ago, slightly, perhaps altogether, drunk, sitting at a table with two younger men who had come to see him, one to interview him for a small local radio station. His so-called, his actual, ego swelled. He saw his head
> again magnified as the penis now huge he thinks
> is taken in the hand, then mouth, is sucked in a
> wetly rhythmic insistence until he feels it, or
> something in him gathered to a locus, explode,
> implode, into her face.

The transformation of swelled ego into swelled penis begins to explain the nature of the waking figure's guilt. His confused sense of political obligation, apparently motivated by personal demands, gives way to sexual fantasy which offers a more immediate but no more satisfying resolution. The language, instead of producing a sensual accompaniment to the sexual, is alternately analytical ("wetly rhythmic insistence") and violent ("explode, implode . . . "). Neither gesture, the sending of a letter or the fantasy, is complete in itself. Each intersects in the poet's waking anxiety as he attempts to settle the morality of "assumptions" in his marriage. "They are not right or wrong," he attempts to convince himself, but what these assumptions are is never made clear. We never learn the exact terms for his crisis; instead, we are allowed to observe the process of thinking that makes it a crisis in the first place, and we are given the language equivalent to his actual anger and guilt. We are shown a series of baffles, frames, wrong turns and justifications which mediate the experience. The fragmentation of this event causes Creeley to affirm his own form-giving powers in a Beckett-like monologue of assurances:

> I know the condition of those around me, or
> rather think I do. One wants to say, *these days.*
> There is a tacit paranoia I have begun to enter
> into all such accounting. Again, I do not know
> if it is an age, my own, biological, or something
> so patently the case that no one moves apart
> from it.

Much of the book deals with this solipsistic self-assurance while, at the same time, the prose points diacritically at the limitations of its own activity—particularly where the writing deals with sexuality. The writing act parallels the sexual fantasy, and Creeley seems conscious of the dangers implicit in following one by means of the other. At one point a letter from Keats to his brother and sister (March 19, 1819) is introduced to this end:

> Even here though I myself am pursuing the same instinctive course as the veriest human animal you can think of—I am however young [old] writing at random—straining at particles of light in the midst of a great darkness—without knowing the bearing of any one assertion of any one opinion. Yet may I not be in this free from sin?

Although Creeley is quoting Keats, the concern is his own: the danger of following an "instinctive course." He wants a form that will be spontaneous and immediate to each occasion—a form, that is, which carries the same sexual charge as fantasy. He realizes, however, that such immediacy may result in empty speculation and unfulfilled longing. Like Keats, Creeley strains "at particles of light in the midst of a great darkness" without knowing the "bearing of one assertion of any one opinion." The test of the moral dimension comes not by rationalizing opposing poles but through the "energies displayed" in their conflict.

> Though a quarrel in the streets is a thing to be hated, the energies displayed in it are fine; the commonest man shows a grace in his quarrel. By a superior being our reasonings may take the same tone—though erroneous they may be fine. This is the very thing in which consists poetry; and if so it is not so fine a thing as philosophy— for the same reason that an eagle is not so fine a thing as truth. Give me credit. Do you not think I strive—to know myself?

The final question is rhetorical. Creeley's (and Keats's) process of self-discovery must include those moments in which experience will not come into focus—the points at which language itself offers a barrier. At this point of contention, the "moral proposition" is set into high relief; its terms are those which, as Creeley will often remind us, are given rather than anticipated. A proposition gains its ethical character through the intensity with which its opposite asserts itself. This wandering, interrogative prose allows for moments in which even mistakes and false leads are incorporated:

> Whether errors, as meaning to write *Echoes* becomes *Whether,* as the finger meant to strike the E key, hits the W—and the thought moves to include it, to use it in the thought, and so on.

The intended object of his discourse disintegrates before his difficulty in transcribing it. A typing mistake discovers a hidden relationship between "errors" and "echoes," leading to an almost totally abstract patterning of phrases. Once the pattern is begun, other echoes emerge:

> Echoes. And, ands. Possible possibilities. . . . Syntax making articulate, i.e., coming literally to sound in the context, fact of fatigue and distraction. The machine talking too, as one fumbles in use of it. Barking doors. Crying tables. Split lights. All that clutter. . . .

In this kind of improvisatory phrasing, words obtain that objective quality which Creeley admires in Berrigan's work. At the same time that they are decontextualized, the words in their phrasal groupings accurately map the desultory quality of his attentions ("the fact of fatigue and distraction"). Syntax becomes active; the typewriter, rather than passively recording the poet's intentions, creates new directions. Words which obey this scattered but intensive notation refuse to reflect any discrete experience but point to a complex activity of assimilation.

In its larger implications, this tracking or tracing of fragmentary perceptions undermines the idea of containment and limit. While on the one hand *A Day Book* proposes to record autobiographically, on the other it exposes the impossibility of "getting it all down." Each investigation opens others; writing becomes discovery, inquiry and variation—qualities that Creeley admires in poets like [William Carlos] Williams and Olson and in painters like [Jackson] Pollock and [Franz Joseph] Kline. The major component in this aesthetic is the ability to respond and to hear what the language is suggesting, even at a point where its referential function breaks down. As I have said, such responsiveness is more than a stylistic feature for Creeley; it emerges as a form of honesty. The typographical mistake and the dangerous confession are linked as mutual facets of a single impulse. The act of writing (and its attendant blockages) is as much an element in the recording of the sexual fantasy as is the fantasy itself.

Much of the book deals with sexual fantasy, as I have said, as though Creeley wishes once and for all to break down certain qualities of reserve and discretion that marked his earlier work. Combined with the theme of sexual fantasy is that of age and the aging process. The meditation on age is made dramatic by reference to the deaths of his Aunt Bernice and his friend, the painter John Altoon. Sexual fantasy and reflection on age come together in a section in which Creeley recognizes his own daughter's womanhood—one of the book's most poignant moments. He begins with the literal occasion of writing and the special difficulties in beginning:

> Even to begin to say this takes extraordinary care, i.e., the paper gets jammed, the wrong key gets punched, and what literally *is* to be said gets as adamant as the timetable for an eastern railroad, or the seating arrangements at some unimaginable ball.

He then describes states of mind (inertia, frustration, paranoia, anger) which occur throughout a day of various activities: going to the airport, teaching, driving and finally arriving to pick up his daughters at the dentist's office. His appearance at the latter involves "instant displacement and paranoia," brought on, to some extent, by the presence of a disagreeable woman in the waiting room who " 'checks out,' as the expression is, any *late* arrival to her own environs. . . . " His displacement is briefly relieved by the sight of a "young woman, pleasant in appearance, sitting to the left, with legs crossed, attractive, and a lovely fall of brown hair, absorbed, as they say, in a magazine." These details serve to frame the recognition which concludes the section—namely, that the attractive young woman is, in fact, his own daughter:

What *is* to say, is, this day, I give testament to my daughter's having entered that opaque state, for me, god knows male, of whatever it is, is womanhood. I did not recognize her, but saw, instead, a young woman of viable and attractive form—and liked her, and wanted therefore to know more of her. In short, a momentous day— to be swept clean of idiot distractions, persons, the dead student, the vicious elder woman, the timetable, the clutter—to be clearly, Sarah, age eleven, *is* a woman.

The paragraph achieves much of its strength from being set against the background of other random events and their emotive responses—what Creeley calls a "tribunal of impossibilities." His revelation is not without its problematic aspect since the continuing sexual concerns of the book now extend to his own daughter. He calls his description a "testament," not solely of his daughter's age but equally of his own culpability in recognizing it.

Compared to his earlier poetry, this "testament" lacks the invariable modifications and qualifications, even though it is framed by its surrounding circumstances. The materials are charged, but the confession is free from his previous "uptight" reflectiveness. Much of the candor is linked to his desire to understand something about his age— biological and historical—which is spent largely in the company of youth. The late sixties and the context of so-called "youth culture" provide a lively and charged backdrop for more "adult" preoccupations:

> I've been trying to know what it is to be specifically myself in this point of age, almost asking people how they are feeling in it, as one would fellow travelers in some situation, shipwreck or great happiness, possibly. Such confoundings of myself, in the past, are seemingly now absent. Fears, ways of stating oneself, and so on, do seem truly to have taken themselves off.

What has indeed been stripped from his new work is the rhetoric of evasion which produced poems like **"The Whip"** and **"The Door"** and certain stories in *The Gold Diggers.* The distinctly sexual passages of *A Day Book* are attempts to "give evidence," to throw off reticence and begin to move in a freer ambience of recognitions. Of course, to declare that Creeley has liberated himself from past habits of self-reflection would be to overstate the point; he never loses the halting, interrogative tone but seems to have discovered a permission, through prose, to present the charged occasion on its own terms.

The prose of *A Day Book,* like the short poems in *Pieces,* is an inquiry into the limits of statement. The value of any statement is not dependent on how much it contains or how well it expresses a given condition but, rather, how accurate it is to the emotional nexus. This continues Creeley's long-standing belief in Pound's statement that "nothing counts save the quality of the emotion." In those moments when he seems to be doing little more than spinning his wheels—framing and shaping what amounts to a syntactic environment lacking any concrete image—he is registering the most characteristic emotion for him: the anxiety of beginning to speak.

Creeley's most recent book, *Presences,* also consists of meditative prose fragments. It interrogates what gives dimension to things, what creates difference and opposition, what renders value. As in *A Day Book,* the prose focuses on incidents that, in the process of being articulated, attain new importance. The book's title provides a double-edged term for this prose: "presence" as a temporal field as well as a spirit of place. What arrests attention generates temporal and spatial relations and, beyond them, values and modes of thought. When the "present" becomes charged with significance, it becomes a "presence," a spirit larger than the moment. Meaning derives from these heightened moments which call attention not to an absent or desired situation but which insist on themselves. An art based on presence is, according to Donald Sutherland's epigraph to the book, classical: "It does not consider that it has come or that it will go away; it merely proposes to be there where it is."

Creeley's use of this quotation could be seen as an attempt to distance himself from previous forms of romantic longing and anxiety and to develop an aesthetic responsive to a work like *Pieces,* but despite Sutherland's quotation, the prose in *Presences* continues to focus on distance and desire. This writing could hardly be termed classical by this or any other definition, but in *Presences,* more than anywhere else, Creeley incurs the limits that mediate experience. By pointing endlessly to size and scale, to boundary and limit, he investigates a continually shifting perspective which attempts at each moment to establish a realm of value for that instant. Perhaps the most important single word in the book is "scale" since it appropriates ideas of big and small, density and opacity, background and foreground into the world of human concern:

> There is a top, and a bottom. From the one to the other may be a distance. Equally it may be so dense, or vaporous, so tangential to touch, that an inextricable time passes in the simplest way.

> It was in memory that this scale of things shifting was particularly interesting to him. He knew of those constructed rooms used for purposes of psychiatric analysis in which perspectives may be altered to accommodate the patient's experience of the spatial relationships of substances on an apparently fixed plane of reference.

Creeley thinks of this attempt to register the boundaries of a field of concern as "autobiography," which he describes elsewhere as "life tracking itself." Unlike the more conventional view of autobiography as chronological sequence, Creeley's self-tracking begins at the moment of attention: "You begin at any point, and move from that point forward or backward, up or down—or in a direction you yourself choose." *Presences* provides a vivid instance of this desultory tracking, moving from a recognition or memory inward to its felt implications.

The book accompanies full-page photographs of sculptures by Marisol, whose hieratic wooden figures stare impassively out of two-dimensional expressions. Faces and body parts are superimposed on large, wooden blocks so that anatomical features are somehow detached from their surfaces and exist in a life of their own. Marisol's sculpture detaches expressions from faces and faces from bodies, juxtaposing volumes and weights and thereby confusing conventional dichotomies like big/small, open/closed, young/old. In **"Inside Out,"** Creeley speaks approvingly of Marisol's ability to use herself "over and over in her work," and quotes her as saying, "When I show myself as I am I return to reality," a remark which he transforms in his own text:

> I began to make self-portraits because working at night I had no other model. Thinks that the world is little. Weather walking, in rain. I used myself over and over again. Sees green. Passing people, goes forward, goes green, goes white. I would learn about myself. . . .
>
> I put things where they belong. I return to reality. People should think of themselves. . . .

Self-portraiture, in Marisol's terms, and autobiography, in Creeley's, involve a continual testing of inherited, pre-established modes. Marisol's large, blocklike sculptures with their vacant stares and stiff postures, refuse the naturalistic ordering of features and volumes. She, like Creeley, creates "presences" of lived experience—authority, family, sexuality, childhood—through grotesque and at times visionary exaggerations of human form. The isolation of bodily parts, the separation of them from their natural positions, illustrates, in another way, a problem of scale.

Individual sections of the book alternately reflect and avoid the accompanying Marisol sculptures. At times, Creeley seems to illustrate a particular photograph, as in the prose facing *Women Sitting on a Mirror:*

> In case the terrible sun of the tropics shines for an instant, she wears sun glasses, a profound night of the eyes.

Marisol's female figure fits the description, but Creeley's prose extends the figure into a landscape of his own making:

> This is the woman to the left of the driver, hooded figure, they now discern, with long talonlike fingers holding the wheel. The night prepares to fly from these depths of quiet objects.

The prose provides a variation on certain visual details, reading images in terms of their darker implications. The woman in sun glasses, by Creeley's transformation, becomes a sorceress or witch; her glasses reveal "a profound night of the eyes." Marisol's flat, cutout faces, blank stares and rigid, columnar bodies bespeak ritualized poses waiting to be animated. Creeley's prose provides that linkage, touching on and varying the visual.

This give and take between sculpture and writing finds an important extension in the opening movement to section four, in which a painting by Poussin is described. At first, only a landscape is visible:

> It is a scene with some distance so that a lake, or sky, floats in the far perspective. Immediately to the left, at the front, is a woman with upper torso clothed in a light hazy autumn brown colored tunic with lower half swathed in an apparent sheet. . . .

Soon we are informed that the landscape is part of a painting, *L'Inspiration du Poète* by [Nicholas] Poussin; the scene becomes animated by a new frame. The poet in the painting is inspired by "a man or more accurately, a god," who stands to the poet's right and to the right of whom stands a woman who

> the more she is observed, seems to be waiting for the god, as if he were shortly to be finished and they might go somewhere else together. Or else she waits for the poet?

The "reading" of the painting by Creeley is complicated by the revelation that the painting comes as a postcard with "a postmark which includes a section of the god's head, and then a sequence of horizontal wavy lines to the right of it. . . ." The nature of the poet's inspiration has, obviously, been grounded in a literal message: "I send greetings with this card and the wish for a sustained and sustaining inspiration." This offers a third frame, and a fourth is added when a voice (perhaps from a television ad) from another room interrupts: "Check it out. I'd like to tell you about something truly exciting. . . . It's a soft little cup which adapts to you individually." At this point, the frames which separate poet from inspirational source are collapsed into the most banal acknowledgment of the prophylactic; yet Creeley sustains all four frames—painting, postcard, TV ad and his own prose—in a single, agglutinant form. The density of this "inspiration" is made all the more complex by a fifth frame: that of Marisol's depiction of *The Dealers* on the facing pages. Her subject is not the inspiration of the poet but rather art dealers, those figures whose entrepreneurial role in the work of art has performed another kind of framing. The prose provides a complex contextualizing of the poet's position in relation to the idea of inspirational source. The various layers, by remaining unresolved, point all the more strongly to the gap separating metonymic terms: man and god, poet and inspiration, secular message and sacred command. The final lines of the section establish the amalgamation of these frames in terms of the background of Poussin's painting—that landscape with which the prose began:

> The sun sets and all disperse, leaving the three trees they had chosen to sit by, for the accomplishment of their severally appointed ends.

The conclusion returns to the beginning, "a landscape with some distance," but the distance mentioned has gone through important qualifications. The poet's inspiration is literal, no further away than today's postcard; that is, it comes "always from lovely nowhere," that point of mutually intersecting attentions in time which raises the present into a "presence." "It is as if Poussin had anticipated these possibilities and it is a lovely thought."

The distance separating Creeley from Poussin or poet from inspiration is both temporal and spatial. A recurrent theme throughout *Presences* is the need to secure some sense of location, in terms of both physical place and person. Place, for Creeley, has always been "where the heart finds rest" (Robert Duncan). The desire for this point of satisfaction is accompanied by a meditation on size since to recognize one's distance from desired place is to recognize one's physical presence in another. To recognize something as being "too large" or "too small" is to establish a ratio of size relations to oneself. In Creeley's early story **"Mr. Blue,"** a circus midget embodies the main character's disaffection with his wife by means of a silent but piercing look. The midget's smallness articulates the husband's sense of powerlessness, even though he is large—"in fact one of the largest in town." The variation in size between midget and husband becomes a concrete image of the husband's distance and estrangement.

This equation of distance and size takes many forms in *Presences,* but in each case, the theme involves some form of isolation:

> He recalls now many things, many people. He thinks of a beach in Truro, in Deya, in Gloucester, in San Diego. He puts people on it, many men and many women, and many children. Dogs run past. Divers things are dropped, lost in the sand. The water comes upon the beach, goes back on the beach, with the tides. Why should *size* be so insistent a center. Is it simply that a toy car won't hurt you and a real one will? He couldn't accept the isolation of condition implicit in that logic. The big man wants to help you, the little one hasn't the strength?

The "isolation of condition" whereby smallness is safe, largeness is dangerous finds its equivalence in the isolation that the poet feels from those beaches locked in the memory. He inverts the logic to discover its opposite case: "The big man wants to help you, the little one hasn't the strength?" Such oscillation between propositions interrogates their usefulness and exposes the assumptions on which they are based. His desire to penetrate, contain, locate and position these places and people reverses direction, and he sees himself in "the ridiculous posture of renewal" (as he called it in **"The Door"**):

> But how could he reach her, then. Way off she was somewhere, truly somewhere else. He could take an actual map and with a pin make precise her location, but here she was not. He crawled into the core of the telephone wires and pushed with all his strength to make a way. Foolish. He wrapped himself with paper, scrunched down into the ink, licked, then patted, and sealed it all over him, then stamped it. All the same, impossible. He was always too big, too small, it didn't really matter.

Again, to be "too small" is to register one's sense of distance, inadequacy and frustration. Size has no absolute condition, only a variable context:

> As soon as you're born, they make you feel small.

> You are very big, you think. You were small, a speck merely, a twinkle in the universe.

> She picked him up and threw him into another place. His little seersucker coat tightly hugged the space under his arms, his armpits and his di-

minutive body became rumpled with the impact of being elsewhere.

Marisol's accompanying sculptures add to the theme with their juxtapositions of gigantic blocks and flat planes, at times resembling huge baby dolls holding miniscule "adult" dolls. Such confusions of size and age disturb any comfortable vantage.

These investigations of scale in Creeley's work are manifestations of the larger theme of value as I have stated it earlier. Each recognition of size and distance presupposes a limit which, in turn, emerges out of an intense human relationship. The limit is discovered in the act of transgressing it—by going "too far" or coming "too close," thereby establishing a scale for that particular situation. Creeley continues to "ride by the margin of that lake in / the wood" on the one side of which is present danger and on the other his "small boy's notion of doing good." To maintain the margin is to constantly step beyond it if only to know that the limit is there. Michel Foucault, following Nietzsche, speaks of the inextricable bond that links limit and transgression:

> Transgression does not seek to oppose one thing to another, nor does it achieve its purpose through mockery or by upsetting the solidity of foundations; it does not transform the other side of the mirror, beyond an invisible and uncrossable line, into a glittering expanse. Transgression is neither violence in a divided world (in an ethical world) nor a victory over limits (in a dialectical or revolutionary world): and exactly for this reason, its role is to measure the excessive distance that it opens at the heart of the limit and to trace the flashing line that causes the limit to arise. Transgression contains nothing negative, but affirms limited being—affirms the limitlessness into which it leaps as it opens this zone to existence for the first time.

In *Presences* this interplay of limit and transgression can be seen most vividly in Creeley's descriptions of those inaugural moments in which a moral condition is established. The prevailing theme of boyhood, for example, presents those first occasions of transgression when a limit is overstepped and thus seen *as a limit.* In section three, Creeley recounts early memories of athletic contests, figures of authority, boyhood pranks, fights, classmates and games—not as nostalgic snapshots but as first experiences of anger, guilt, sympathy and honor: "Myself is what one comes to think of then, letting the well fill up, things happen." Boyhood is obviously a period in which the question of scale is continually at stake, in which one's size determines a literal distance from the world which reappears in adult life in psychological terms.

This "distance" is figured variously throughout the book but most intensely in section four with its description of time spent at an historic Italian villa where the writer and his wife are vacationing. The marital bickering which provides the foreground for the section is set against a panorama of European history as reflected in the various personages who have visited there (members of the Sforza family, Leonardo, the Kennedys, Stendhal, Flaubert, Mussolini) and a host of equally august current visitors (a famous journalist, a historian, a militarist). The angry exchanges between husband and wife appear ludicrous against "the *oldness* of Europe" (Creeley's emphasis), causing the writer to feel like "an upstart" among the various vacationers at the villa. What salvages these feelings of "tortured sensibility," as he calls such situations, is the "intrusion of factual needs upon affairs of conjecture and assumption." The distance felt between husband and wife, between the present and history, between the American cultural experience and the European, becomes the "experience of the world entirely." The writer sits in an isolated *caseta* (a latter-day "Lime Tree Bower"?) and recognizes the almost salvific importance of momentary attentions which reduce both historical panorama and existential crisis to a single field:

> He could hear the sound of a small outboard motor on a boat below him, voices talking, laughing. Best that one's needs be simple because there seemed no true alternative to that condition. No one of those previously to have been here, not the farmer nor soldier nor monk nor artist nor writer, nor dictator nor anyone at all, were more actual, after all. It came and then went. "Birds singing / measure distance, / intervals between / echo silence."

Creeley does not, by this, exonerate himself from the situation; he cannot simply separate himself from responsibilities but must incur these relationships as they happen. The poem that results from this meditation and which is quoted above contains a distillation of everything that has preceded it; "Birds singing" *do* "measure distance," articulating what before had been an empty and abstract void. In this context, Creeley's poetry and poetics are firmly locked into the Romantic tradition.

What distresses critics of Creeley's work is his relentless self-interrogation and indulgence in personal matters. He broods over what seem to be insignificant details of human relationships and raises them to the level of existential crisis. He does not provide any "objective correlative" for his anxiety (as the Confessional poets do) nor has he developed any avant-gardist "art stance" toward his problems. In a period of radically disjunctive operations at the level of meaning, he continues to worry about ethical choices and self-delusion. His critics fail to recognize the reflexive nature of his position; by not providing an "adequate" frame—stylistic, thematic, rhetorical or otherwise—for his doubts and anxieties, he addresses the double-bind in its own terms. Its terms are encountered suddenly, in daily circumstance, in casual talk, and its implications for the moral dimension of human life are profound.

In *A Day Book* and *Presences,* the notebook entries, meditations, reflections and verbal freeplay evidence a new investigation of the moral proposition. This recent prose by its sheer openness provides him with the opportunity to present a variety of individual situations and extend them into their problematic interrelationships. Like his earlier prose, the new work investigates the conditions under which moral decisions are made; "to look at it is more / than it was" remains a crucial index of ethical choice. But in his recent work, Creeley embodies the ethical choice in his form; the open-ended, exploratory style with its lack

Ann and Robert Creeley, Mallorca, 1953.

of closure and its awareness of contextual frames becomes a kind of moral condition in itself. "One path only is left for us to speak of," he says; "namely, that *It is.*" However little assurance this may give us, for Creeley it is the permission necessary to create. "In this path are very many tokens that what is is uncreated and indestructible; for it is complete, immoveable, and without end. Nor was it ever, nor will it be; for now *it is,* all at once, a continuous one." (pp. 545-63)

> *Michael Davidson, "The Presence of the Present: Morality and the Problem of Value in Robert Creeley's Recent Prose," in* boundary 2, *Vols. VI & VII, Nos. 3 & 1, Spring & Fall, 1978, pp. 545-64.*

Ross Feld (essay date 1984)

[Feld is an American poet and novelist. In the following essay, he traces the evolution of Creeley's poetry.]

Creeley was a Fifties knight. His stringbean candor struggled and gangled in its thin suit of mail: "Ultimate: no man shall go unattended. / No man shall be an idiot for purely exterior reasons." (**"The Rites."**) Fifties recognizably, too, because so much of the time the subject was monogamous sexual vexation—either courtly ("My love's manners in bed / are not to be discussed by me, / as mine by her / I would not credit comment upon gracefully" [**"The Way"**]) or passively gored:

> I spent a night turning in bed,

my love was a feather, a flat

sleeping thing. She was
very white

and quiet, and above us on
the roof, there was another woman I

also loved, had
addressed myself to in

a fit she
returned. That

encompasses it. But now I was
lonely, I yelled,

but what is that? Ugh,
she said, beside me, she put

her hand on
my back, for which act

I think to say this
wrongly.

                                        ("The Whip")

Some striking mid-century valences are echoed in Creeley:
the lyrically discordant, hypenated tact of a Thelonious
Monk; [Ezra] Pound's Provence fantasies coming out of
the mouth of a New England Petrarchan; a nervous focus
on what is subtlest, glossiest, and most omnivorous in the
other sex, *à la* DeKooning's *Women.* They all seemed to
sluice into Creeley's sweet new style, its courtesy and
humor and frustrated postponements:

I called her across the room,
could see that what she stood on
held her up, and now she came
as if she moved in time.

In time to what she moved,
her hands, her hair, her eyes, all things
by which I took her to be there
did come along.

It was not right or wrong
but signally despair, to be about
to speak to her
as if her substance shouted.

                                        ("The Woman")

He is one of those artists who enters upon his scene exactly
at the moment he ought to. His lodestars—[William Car-
los] Williams, [Louis] Zukofsky, [Charles] Olson—
seemed to be leaving him with the very short, pinched-off
poem as an inheritance while they went off in pursuit of
larger constellations. Pre-*For Love,* Creeley's first major
collection, he works at getting comfortable with the legacy, with being what Williams (in *Paterson* I) called "the
radiant gist that resists crystallization," but it takes a little
doing. The angles frequently go awry, like this histrionic
Olsonian swatch:

Hélas! Or Christus fails.
The day is the indefinite. The shapes of light
have surrounded the senses,
but will not take them to hand (as would an axe-
    edge
take to its stone. . . .)

                                        ("Hélas")

—or they go mushy, not withdrawn in time from sentiment's warm coils (which even in later Creeley is an occasional problem, especially at the conclusion of poems: a
flattened piety that, like a punctured tire, slaps across the
last few yards anyway):

Time we all went home,
or back,
to where it all was,
where it all was.

This limply ends a poem, **"The Picnic,"** that began with
all the quick sleek smartness that negative space plus
combed metrics plus ordinary language ideally would result in:

Ducks in the pond,
icecream & beer,
all remind me
of West Acton, Mass—

where I lived when young
in a large old house
with 14 rooms
and woods out back.

Yet by the time of the poems of *For Love,* without real fear
of argument, Creeley was able to announce of what alloys
his shining medallions demonstrably were cast:

For love—I would
split open your head and put
a candle in
behind the eyes.

Love is dead in us
if we forget
the virtues of an amulet
and quick surprise.

                                        ("The Warning")

Here the alloys are eccentric rhymes, an aggressively (in
fact a gory) sexual image, and a pocket agenda for pocket
poems. The triad proves to be charmingly sturdy, and
must be: it supports a wobbler. The Fifties knight is one
of boyishly eternal discomfort, as in a poem like **"The
Lover":**

What should the young
man say, because he is buying
Modess? Should he

blush or not? Or
turn coyly, his head, to
one side, as if in

the exactitude of his emotion he
were not offended? Were
proud? Of what? To buy

a thing like that.

A latter-day Wyatt: the resignation also means to be the
gift. Better than anyone of his generation, Creeley *is* the
poet of the winsome flinch:

I did not expect you
to stay married to
one man all your life
no matter you were his wife.

I thought the pain was endless—

but the form existent,
as it is form,
and as such I loved it.

I loved you as well
even as you might tell,
giving evidence
as to how much was penitence.

(**"The Letter"**)

It's interesting to set this next to lines from
W. D. Snodgrass' "Heart's Needle," a poem roughly con-
temporaneous and motored by the same spark:

> I walk among the growths,
> by gangrenous tissue, goitre, cysts,
>   by fistulas and cancers,
> where the malignancy man loathes
> is held suspended and persists.
>   And I don't know the answers.
>
> The window's turning white.
> The world moves like a diseased heart
>   packed with ice and snow.
> Three months now we have been apart
> less than a mile. I cannot fight
>   or let you go.

The knurled trope and the more distributed rhymes sit like
so many stage-scenery boulders while the word Snodgrass
requires above all others does its work: "among" is a dilat-
ing tool, a speculum that sanctions a small poetical stroll
until it's recalled by the whispery, disingenuous-feeling "I
don't know the answers." Apart from feeling (for whatever it's worth) more "honest" in their awkwardness and
suspension, the Creeley lines significantly replace Snodgrass' other device—the metaphor of the window, looking
out open an evermore dispiriting situation—with a reus-
able inner porthole, a category: "I thought the pain was
endless— / but the form existent, / as it is form, / and as
such I loved it." Snodgrass loves the form of the agony
too—what poet doesn't?—but he uses it up in performance. Creeley's clunky final rhyme instead ties the poem
off with a slight late windiness, as letters will—hinting that
a complex more is yet to be said, maybe said better. And
there will be more: "Being unsure, there is the fate / of
doing nothing right" (**"For The New Year"**). It's almost
a nominative self-portrait of this knight: the Being Unsure.

Unsureness has its public as well as private side. Creeley's
best-known poem is a good example of how postwar
French existentialist doubt became transposed into American Beat fear; how the closed café turned into the semi-
enclosed, more vulnerable automobile.

> As I sd to my
> friend, because I am
> always talking,—John, I
>
> sd, which was not his
> name, the darkness sur-
> rounds us, what
>
> Can we do against
> it, or else, shall we &
> why not, buy a goddamn big car,
>
> drive, he sd, for

> christ's sake, look
> out where yr going.

(**"I Know a Man"**)

A classic era-poem: the shambling comedy, the neat-as-a-
drunk rhythms, even the Coleridgean/organicist aesthetic
of *proceeding not preceding* it can be milked of. Maybe as
illuminating is its context within *For Love.* Whenever a
poem addresses another man, Creeley has a tendency to
turn hipster. This can be read as macho swagger, but it's
more a specific stage of literary bohemianism. The French
have always been able to nurture a romance of male amity
([Alexandre] Dumas' musketeers, [Henri] Murger's gar-
ret-mates, conceivably even [Jack] Kerouac's mobile
bindlestiffs); in English, though, with [Ernest] Hemingway, modern nonconformity as a subject becomes inextricably wound-up with female complication. Lawrence is an
even better example—and in this respect *For Love* happens to be a tight corollary to the poems of *Look! We Have
Come Through!* (Creeley employs a fragment of "Hymn
to Priapus" as the epigraph to the **Collected Poems**:
"Grief, grief I suppose and sufficient / Grief makes us free
/ To be faithless and faithful together / As we have to
be.") There is the same not-quite-highborn rhyming, and
identical stages of domestic love: fatigue, merciful and
quick recuperation, the grateful termination of aggressive
personality (male). Both poets are keen to ratify the initial
botch in order to get down to the inevitable joy. [D. H.]
Lawrence's "First Morning":

> The night was a failure
>   but why not ———?

Creeley's **"The First Time"**:

> You likewise
> with me must be
> testament
> to pain's indifference.
>
> We are only careful
> for such a memory, more
> careful, I think,
> than we ever thought to be.

Lawrence's "Valentine Night":

> You shadow and flame,
> You interchange,
> You death in the game!
>
> Now I gather you up,
> Now I put you back
> Like a poppy in its cup.

Creeley's **"Fire"**:

> Clear smoke,
> a fire in the far off
> haze of summer,
> burning somewhere.
>
> What is
> a lonely heart for
> if not
> for itself alone.
>
> Do the questions
> answer themselves,
> all wonder

brought to a reckoning?

When you are done,
I am done,
then it seems that
one by one
we can leave it all,
to go on.

An unseen woman's tidal, pendant weight is what rounds off both poetries, though much more famously distorting Lawrence—"New phase in the germ of you; / New sunny streams of blood / Washing you through. / / You are born again of me. / I, Adam, from the veins of me / The Eve that is to be." ("Birth Night")—than it does the less transubstantive Creeley: "Nothing for a dirty man / but soap in his bathtub, a / / greasy hand, lover's / nuts / / perhaps. Or else / / something like sand / with which to scour him / / for all / that is lovely in women." (**"All That Is Lovely in Men"**).

Monogamy is eye-crossingly private: it attracts abstractionists. Creeley is one, unmistakably. At his most anecdotal, the figures upon his ground still seem mosaical:

> Light eyes would have been more fortunate.
> They have cares like store windows.
> All the water was shut off,
> and winter settled in the house.
>
> The first week they wrote a letter.
> He wrote it.
> She thought about it.
> Peace was in the house like a broken staircase.
>
> I was neat about it, she later wrote
> to a relative in Spokane.
> She spoke in accents low
> as she told me.
>
>   **("The Interview")**

Louis Zukofsky's lines, from "A" 2, are useful: "There is space to step to the central heart . . . / . . . The leaves never topple from each other, / Each leaf a buttress flung for the others." Mutually-flung buttresses fly and knit in Creeley, making for mini-dialogues and inner conversations between man and woman, emotion and emotion, even space and space:

> My embarrassment at his nakedness,
> at the pool's edge,
> and my wife, with his,
> standing, watching—
>
> this was a freedom
> not given me who am
> more naked,
> less contained
>
> by my own white flesh
> and the ability
> to take quietly
> what comes to me.
>
> The sense of myself
> separate, grew
> a white mirror
> in the quiet water
>
> he breaks with his hands

and feet, kicking,
pulls up to land
on the edge by the feet

of these women
who must know
that for each
man is a speech

describes him, makes
the day grow white
and sure, a quietness of water
in the mind,

let hang, descriptive
as a risk, something
for which he cannot find
a means or time.

                    ("The Pool")

The poem is itself a series of feeds, of strokes. One eye stays upon the speaker's shrivelling heart, the other on a virile approaching swimmer who with every gaining yard marks off one more station of the other man's cross: embarrassment, comparison, self-reproach, alienation (the cataract of "a white mirror"). The pool of the speaker's ego ("the ability to take quietly / what comes to me") is badly moiled; and tensed he stands there, waiting with the knowing women, to see the newly landed man's penis, that which disrupts "a quietness of water / in the mind" and instead is "let hang, descriptive / as a risk." One of the longer poems of *For Love,* it could be the book's lanyard: the sexual edginess in braid with homiletic theory: "for each man / is a speech / / describes him, makes / the day grow white / and sure, a quietness of water / in the mind." Speech is the penis, the eccentric medallion; whereas the poem has been striving for the whole quiet of water (a nice specimen, this, of what Mandelstam calls the "Hericlitean metaphor" found so much in Dante, which "emphasizes the fluidity of the phenomenon and cancels it out with such a flourish, that direct contemplation, after the metaphor has completed its work, is essentially left with nothing to sustain it."). At play here too (because Creeley takes its dialectic seriously) is Zukofsky's notion (in his Midrashic essay concerning Charles Reznikoff, "Sincerity and Objectification") of the artistic equivalent to unearned and irresistible Grace: "Presented with sincerity, the mind even tends to supply . . . the totality not always found in sincerity and necessary only for perfect rest, complete appreciation." Like Zukofsky, Creeley repeatedly will use rhyme in an outrageous test of sincerity's limitations . . . and the guaranty objectification provides. Zukofsky's rhymes are largely pre-lapsarian: the mind is encouraged by them to see "love bear the semblance / of things, related is equated" ("A"). Creeley's probably should be called post-: the doggerel or nursery rhymes describe a nursery that's in fact a garden—Eden; the fumbles-turned-disasters of normative marriage; snafu'd children in the bodies of backed-to-the-wall adults.

Creeley's peculiar version of objectification can be puzzled out of **"The Pool."** His poems's "perfect rest, complete appreciation" turns out to be a kind of paralysis. A game of "freeze." Feelings and words attached to them start out as morphemes of sincerity. Then they cake. Another poem therefore has to be begun, out of another short whole block. Another mistake has to be made. The gist has crystallized, how could it not? but the crystals are kept small, singular.

Under the very rules that foster it, then, Creeley's amulet was bound to modify. In *For Love*'s successor, *Words* (1967), the lean is more ideational, noticeable in a poem such as **"Water"**:

> The sun's
> sky in
> form of
> blue sky
> that
>
> water will
> never make
> even
> in
> reflection.
>
> Sing, song,
> mind's form
> *feeling*
> if mistaken,
>
> shaken,
> broken water's
> forms, love's
> error
> in water.

The swimmer, the watcher, and the two women of **"The Pool"** are removed; felt embarrassment is gone too, leaving only its category. Feeling, italicized, is only as good at reflecting what we truly are as water sky. The poem shimmers with incapacity. "A song / inflated to fifty pounds pressure" (Williams) is what Creeley increasingly resembles now.

> Position is where you
> put it, where it is,
> did you, for example, that
>
> large tank there, silvered,
> with the white church along-
> side, lift
>
> all that, to what
> purpose . . .
>   **("The Window")**

This poem finishes: "It / all drops into / place. My / / face is heavy / with the sight. I can / feel my eye breaking."— and you believe it. You also notice how the speech elisions and asides, so sharply lost and funny in **"I Know A Man,"** now have an integral part in the snagging, unitary voice; in a long poem like **"Anger,"** with its Pinteresque megrims, there's a hint as well of a ventriloquial chorus.

Though Creeley at times can seem an unnecessarily filial poet (the way that John Updike, another Fifties knight, sometimes seems a disturbingly filial novelist: extraordinary effort to the poise, with a sense that it very much wants one specific and approving audience), his inherited lessons don't always survive the actual poem. The taking of inventory, for example, while the store still is open:

> The rhyme is after
> all the repeated

insistence.

> There, you say, and
> there, and there,
> and *and* becomes
>
> just so. And
> what one wants is
> what one wants,
>
> yet complexly
> as you
> say.
>
> Let's
> let it go.
> I want—
>
> Then there is—
> and,
> I want.
>   **("For W. C. W.")**

The knight will never wholly be made a priest: this anti-apostolic poem is clear on that. Against the fixity of naming and placing there will still have to be more—and potentially wrong—words. The situation, a poet and his words, is exactly a marriage's: greed fighting shame. "And" is the term for desire, "there" the one for reality. Yet, though ashamed (an echo of [Williams's] *The Desert Music*'s memorable lines: "I am a poet! I / am. I am. I am a poet, I reaffirmed, ashamed."): "Then, there is— / and, / I want." Much as some of *Words* wants to dryly curb and self-correct the "long habit of much delaying thought / to savor terms of the impression" (**"A Tally"**), what thought at its own speed best savors is its unchangingness:

> I propose to you
> a body bleached, a body
> which would be dead
> were it not alive.
>
> We will stand it up
> in the garden, which
> we have taken such pains
> to water. All the flowers
>
> will grow at its feet,
> and evenings it will
> soften there as the darkness
> comes down from such space.
>
> Perhaps small sounds
> will come from it, perhaps
> the wind only, but its
> mouth, could one see it,
>
> will flutter. There will be
> a day it walks just before
> we come to look at it, but by then
> it will have returned to its place.
>   **("The Statue")**

Creeley's avid conceptualism does finally assert itself fully, however. The first shoots of it, in *Words,* look merely, greenly willful:

> One and
> one, two,
> three.

Not so overt, but also revealing, is how in less demonstrative and more capacious poems multi-syllabics seem to have to claw for purchase now, especially at the ends of lines. A word like "interesting" may hold on by virtue of its indeterminancy; "indulgence" or "accumulation" seem antiquely rhetorical, destined for the scrap heap.

By 1969 and *Pieces* the modal concept that is Creeley's planted flag was very sparsely shared by his poet peers. It was much more on the minds of visual artists of the Sixties. Consider the giant toothbrushes, the wooden Indians, the Sunoco signs, the exploded comic strip panels, the flags and the ale cans, the free-floating bathrobes, the Brillo boxes: they all not only set charges under the sociological middle-distance on which much of abstract art depends; they also pushed a single, unitary object—a monad—to the fore, whether or not it seemed to merit the promotion.

> The first
> time is
> the first
> time. The
> second
> time think
> again.
>
> •
>
> There you
> were,
> all
> the time.
>
> •
>
> I can
> not give
> it back.
>
> •
>
> *Your* was there
> here in any
> way you
> were.

The typographical device of the bullet-ornament that segments the amazing terseness nearly is unlawful; the small word-barnacles it leaves huddling above and below dangle in a dizzying "present, / a presence / / saying / something / as it goes." "Sequences / / of words that are not to be understood / but somehow given to a world," semiotic knots to be taken "as mind is a finger, / pointing"—they lost Creeley many readers; it's from *Pieces* on that he's had less than full attention trained upon him. Tension looked like it had turned entirely technical. Dipped into an acid-bath of unstressedness, the aesthetic of complaisance that was partly *For Love*'s came out shrivelled and nuggetted:

> Back where things were
> sweeter, water falls
> and thinks again.
>
> •
>
> Here, there,
> every-
> where.

> •
>
> Never write
> to say more
> than saying
> something.

> _____
>
> Words
> are
> pleasure.
> All
> words.

Creeley can now meander nosingly (and with the same occasionally perverse epicurianism as his Modernist forefathers) in so neat a privacy that he thinks nothing of pausing a moment to re-tuck and recall, memo-style: "Want to get the sense of 'I' into Zukofsky's 'eye'—a locus / of experience, not a presumption of expected value." Zukofsky is the model on *Pieces'* mind and is the book's dedicatee. Something like this Zukofsky splendidness—the opening of "So That Even A Lover":

> Little wrists,
> Is your content
> My sight or hold,
> Or your small air
> That lights and trysts?
>
> Red Alder berry
> Will singly break;
> But you—how slight—do:
> So that even
> A lover exists.

Creeley will not attempt to duplicate in diaphaneity the darning-needle flight of the rhyme. He will labor instead to re-animate the process of location-through-syntax that Zukofsky's lyric—beneath (or above) its fragile music—most basically is about:

> The car
> moving
> the hill
> down
>
> which yellow
> leaves
> light forms
> declare.

It requires a parsing minute. The car, clearly, is the subject of the poem. Syntactical probability says so. But subjects have qualities as well as actions: the car has (and is) a vantage-point. However obviously, then, that it's moving down the hill, the car also seems (as the poet in the driver's seat well knows) to *move* the hill, to be moving it down. The visual illusion of plowing, of forward propulsion as well as impulsion, needs in addition a background, a contrast against which it will stand out. Here it's the yellow leaves. Or is it . . . *Are* the leaves yellow? Where *do* the disappeared commas go in this second, recessed stanza? Is the hill scattered with yellow leaves, autumnal light? Or could *leaves* be a verb?: *which, [being] yellow, leaves light, forms declare.* A vast undertaking in two four-lined stanzas of six words each: to bring a subject into action, broaden it against a scrim, and then fit it within an abstraction (that is itself activated, declaring) which turns out ultimately to have been the genuine subject all along.

Received any more grossly, a minim like this simply evaporates, ceases to be. Creeley is no "ordinary language" philosopher, no Wittgenstein or Austin or Cavell; but **Pieces** does ask legitimately for a sedulous reading—and when it gets one, it yields up a surprise. It turns out to resemble less the innovations of early Williams or Zukofsky's pan-adhesive music than it does a book like *My Sister Life*. Nothing at first blush could seem further from Pasternak's busy, funneling, full-sponge imagism than **Pieces'** grains of sand. But there are few other modern books of poetry as serious in their complementary investigation of the categorical.

Pasternak, who as a young man went to Marburg to study philosophy under the neo-Kantian, Hermann Cohen, writes in *Safe Conduct:*

> Focused upon a reality that has been displaced by feeling, art is a record of this displacement. It copies from nature. How then does nature become displaced? Details gain in sharpness, each losing its independent meaning. Each one of them could be replaced by another. Any one of them is precious. Any one, chosen at random, will serve as evidence of the state which envelops the whole of transposed reality. When the signs of this condition are transferred onto paper, the characteristics of life become the characteristics of creation. The latter stand out more sharply than the former.

and:

> We cease to recognize reality. It presents itself in some new category. This category seems to us to be its, not our, condition. Except for this condition everything in the world has been named. It alone is unnamed and new. We try to name it. The result is art.

Specifically this kind of art—the famous "Oars At Rest" from *My Sister Life:*

> A boat throbs in the sleeping breast.
> Willows overhung, kiss collarbones,
> Elbows and rowlocks—O, wait,
> After all, this could happen to anyone!
>
> For everyone is amused by this in a song.
> For this implies—the ash of a lilac,
> Largesse of chopped camomile in dew
> Lips and lips got in trade for stars.
>
> For this implies—embracing the sky,
> Entwining huge Hercules in your arms,
> For this implies—for ages on end
> Squandering nights on the trilling of warblers!
>   (trans. by Dale L. Plank)

It's a poem displaced by itself, fueled by transition, sensuous yet full of cool "trades." Categories discover themselves; feelingful intuition overshoots realities to discover (and become) forms. Creeley's procedure is analogous:

> When they were
> first made, all the
> earth must have

> been their reflected
> bodies, for a moment—
> a flood of seeming
> bent for a moment back
> to the water's glimmering—
> how lovely they came
>
> What you wanted
> I felt, or felt I felt.
> This was more than one.
>
> This point of so-called
> consciousness is forever
> a word making up
> this world of more
> or less than it is.
>
> Don't leave me.
> Love me. One by one
> As if to sit
> by me were another
> who did. So
>
> to make you
> mine, in the mind,
> to know you.
>   **("Two")**

Isn't this what Creeley's reiterated symbols of water and mirror have been all about: "this world of more / or less than it is"? The above is one of the set-piece sections of "Numbers"—one to zero, a conventional opportunity to improvise upon the properties of the integers. Very *uncon*-ventionally, the poems (as in **"Two"**'s Adam and Eve, its ontology myth) lodge repeatedly under an overhang, with a meaning in the margin that Pasternak would have recognized instantly. Creeley's "being unsure," always available to error, enfranchises a world that is more than a voice, a choice, a poet:

> Somehow the game
> where a nutshell covers
> the one object, a
>
> stone or coin, and
> the hand is
> quicker than the eye—
>
> how is that *nine,*
> and not *three*
> chances, except that
>
> three imaginations of it
> might be, and there are
> two who play—
>
> making six, but
> the world is real also,
> in itself.
>   **("Nine")**

Both poets have the quickest, most feathery of touches when pressing down on individual words or images; they reserve their muscle for ordering. In **Pieces** Creeley writes: "My plan is / these little boxes / make sequences." Roman Jakobson, writing about Pasternak during the Thirties, found him not a metaphorist but a maker of metonymies: "Anything sequent is a simile." In "the world of more / or less than it is," of "transposed reality," the more usual metaphorical position finds itself overheavy, laden. Creeley and Pasternak do completely without its frontal weight. Rigorous yet underplayed, they stay determined innocents; not by accident are *My Sister Life* and *Pieces* both diaries, cognitive diaries—one saturated, the other intensely skimmed.

Creeley in *Pieces* is at his freest. His special glide—the comic straight into the stranded—is pervasive:

> Sure,
> Herbert—
> Take a bite—
>
> The crowd
> milling on the bridge, the
> night forms in
>
> the air. So
> much has gone
> away.
>
> ("Ice Cream")

And being free of the metaphorical was something of no small value in the Sixties, when a statement lurked around every corner, when Fifties Beat fear had stylized itself (synecdoche'd itself) into "political" paranoia (the Allen Ginsberg trap):

> What could
> they give me I
> hadn't myself
> discovered—
>
> The *world,*—that
> I'd fallen upon
> in some
> distracted drunkenness—
>
> Or that the rules
> were *wrong,* an
> observation they
> as well as I
> knew now—
>
> *They* were imagination
> also. If they
> would be as the
> mind could see *them,*
>
> then it all was
> true and the
> mind followed and
> *I* also.
>
> ("They")

A categorical or metynomic poetry isn't very impressed by "hot" italics and weighted vogue words. *World, wrong, they, them, I*—they're utterly equal.

It can be argued that the Seventies was the first truly and wholly mingy decade for American poetry since the century set out, and that Creeley did not escape the pallor. Whether or not the misreading (or unreading) of *Pieces* had something to do with it, he appears to have both personally and artistically endured the period—and little more: "The so-called poet of love / is not so much silent as absorbed." Certainly the world comes off decisively *less* than it is.

> A sudden
> loss of hope,

> flutters, the
> loss of something
> known too well.
>
> ("Echoes")

Songs occasionally are maudlin:

> We will laugh, smile, on provocation.
> No hysterics shall obtain. We will
>
> love perhaps in other modes but the
> yearning, at least my own, will not
>
> grow less, and as I sit now writing this,
> a sense of time passing surely,
>
> but with nothing of itself to say,
> opaque as the night, dense, always there.
>
> ("A Testament")

Favorite Creeley words, like "dear" and "care" ("Oh love, oh rocks, / of time, oh ashes I / left in the bucket,— / care, care, care, care.") are strewn however humorously like gravel for want of firmer pavement. A recognizable Creeleyan dilemma shapes up:

> Taking walks, swimming,
> drinking, I am always afraid
> of having more. Hence a true
>
> Puritan, I shall never rest from my labors
> until all rest with me, until I am
> driven by that density home.
>
> ("On Vacation")

yet the avoirdupois of the unit-poem *Pieces*-style grows perversely lighter, a set of needy signs:

> The boy
> with the
> finger in
> the hole
> of the
> dike in
> Holland.
>
> A true story.
>
> •
>
> Here—
>
> •
>
> This is
> it.
>
> ("Hero")

The two larger collections of the period, *In London* (1972, with its epigraph " 'But what to do? and What to do next?' " from Williams' *A Voyage to Pagany*) and *Hello: A Journal, February 29–May 3, 1976* (1978—its subtitle as calibrated as a jail sentence) significantly are both books of transplant and journey, the latter especially cloven by a traveller's sterilely precise notations ("cars / like toys pass, / / below, fourteen stories / down / / on those streets. / In park / kids wade / / in a pool.") and the periodic writhings of retrospection that unfamiliarity can set off (". . . you / never went anywhere. / / I did—and here / in the world, looking back / / on so-called life / with its impeccable / / talk and legs and breasts, / I loved you / / but not as some / gross habit, please.") It's confessional poetry, but of a different order than Berryman's or Sexton's (defeat by self-mythology): it confesses banality and repetitiveness, it seems to have lost its ego like a piece of luggage that didn't get unloaded:

> If it's New Zealand
> where it ends,
> that makes a weird sense
> too. I'd never have guessed it.
>
> Say that all the ways
> are one—*consumatum est*—
> like some soup
> I'd love to eat with you.
>
> ("**Soup**")

Broken fairly hard by these feckless and banal Seventies books is Creeley's lavaliere-poem; the voice was never before so much the untethered incarnated verb. But a pendant gravity does survive—and two admissions are noteworthy: "I wanted to find something / worthy of respect—like / my family, any one knows" (**"Pacing . . ."**). And: "My middle / aged hippy number / is more words . . . / I think of things, / I'm loyal. Narcissist, I want." (**"Dear Dorothy"**)

Fortune had it that age would present Creeley the poet with everything he seems to have asked of love and of words: a world more and less than itself, an ultimate category. In *Pieces,* speculative abstraction still obtained:

> Counting age as form
> I feel the mark of one
> who has been born and grown
> to a little past return.
>
> The body will not go
> apart from itself to be
> another possibility.
> It loves where it finds home.
>
> Thinking to alter all
> I looked first to myself,
> but have learned the foolishness
> that wants an altered form.
>
> Here now I am at best,
> or what I think I am
> must follow as the rest
> and live the best it can.

"Being grown / to a little past return," however, has more dramatic palpability by the time **"Box"** appears in *Mirrors,* one of the two extraordinarily reconstitutive books Creeley has most recently published. **"Home"** now is self-evident—Creeley is *in* his fifties, no longer *of* them. The "altered form" is simply a matter of settling upon the most comfortable position in which to greet the Great Paradox of open-ended enclosure:

> Say it,
> you're afraid
> but of what
> you can't locate.
>
> You love yet
> distracted fear
>
> the body's change,
> yourself inside it.

Candor has new use—"He is a very interesting man, / this intensively sensitive person, / but he has to die somehow" (**"Flaubert's Early Prose"**)—and its seed is wide-tossed both in *Later* (1979) and *Mirrors* (1983). Meters, as in the startling and Fellini-like **"Erotica"** (*Later*), have renewed, a springing tone:

> On the path
> down here, to the sea,
> there are bits.
>
> of pages
> from a magazine, scattered,
> the *big tits*
>
> of my adolescence
> caught on bushes,
> stepped on, faces
>
> of the women, naked,
> still smiling out at me
> from the grass. . . .

A master, after *Pieces,* of tessellation, his stripped delicacy catches breath:

> When the light leaves
> and sky's black,
> no nothing
> to look at,
>
> day's done.
> That's it.
>
> ("**Night Time**")

(The visual pun of the sinking sun and shrinking light could be itself a microfilmed anthology of the Objectivist penchant for valediction.) Nor before has he been so moving a message-passer, with a give-and-go artlessness that marks most major poetry in maturity:

> I see you, Aunt Bernice—
> and your smile anticipating reality.
> I don't care any longer that you're older.
> There are times all the time the same.
>
> I'm a young old man here on earth,
> sticks, dust, rain, trees, people.
> Your cat killing rats in Florida was incredible—
> *Pete*—weird, sweet presence. Strong.
>
> You were good to me. You had *wit*—
> value beyond all other human possibility.
> You could smile at the kids, the old cars.
> Your house in N.H. was lovely.
>
> ("**I Love You**")

The language of the books has the slick and the slide of an abacus—that utilitarian. Consolation may polish some of the pain, as in the Hardyesque ending of **"To Say It"** from *Mirrors:*

> If, as in a bottle, the message
> has been placed, if air, water
> and earth try to say so with
> human agency, no matter the imperfect,
>
> useless gesture, all that is lost,
> or mistaken, the arrogance
> of trying to, the light comes again,
> comes here, after brief darkness is still here.

—though the active concepts are still what they've been continually: the placement of mind (memory as experience); words as *regretted* things, most to be understood and felt *after* the instant of aim and release; the redemptiveness of mistake; the ever-patient, waiting categories; the world always more or less than itself.

Pasternak, in *Doctor Zhivago,* writes of how "Language, the home and receptacle of beauty and meaning, itself begins to think and speak for man and turns wholly into music, not in terms of sonority but in terms of the impetuousness and power of its inward flow." Under its guise of thinness, of Sir Giacometti, Creeley's impetuous and powerful inner flow has been constant. Few flows seem as particular, though: passive, transitional, reversing. From *Mirrors:*

> The words will one day come
> back to you, birds returning,
> the movie run backward.
>
> Nothing so strange in its talk,
> just words. The people
> who wrote them are the dead ones.
>
> This here paper talks like anything
> but is only one thing,
> "birds returning."
>
> You can "run the movie
> backward" but "the movie run
> backward." The movie run backward.
>
> **("The Movie Run Backward")**

Since we still step around Pasternak at his most intentional and valuable, I can't see how Creeley will quickly accrue more than the imprecise and approximate respect he's gotten and gets. The long habit of metaphor—its compounding interest—is entrenched; the additional and subtractional actions of metonymy remain unfamiliar. Convention finds Pasternak's music over-upholstered, Creeley's too wizened. But at core they're the same, both singing marginally not at the world but of and within the beleagured categories that develop the world. Both acknowledge that no word or series of words is also so exquisite that it can't not usually miss those categories altogether, lodging elsewhere, requiring a further word. One day a concordance will tell us exactly how many times Creeley uses the word "in." But we already know. The poet of true error cannot ever be *outside* anything:

> Water all around me
> the front of sky ahead
> sand off to the edges
> light dazzle wind
>
> way of where waves of
> pleasure it can be here
> am I dead or alive
> in which is it.
>
> **("Question")**
> (pp. 95-122)

Ross Feld, "The Fate of Doing Nothing Right," in Parnassus: Poetry in Review, *Vol. 12, No. 1, 1984, pp. 95-122.*

Albert Cook (essay date 1985)

[*Cook is an American poet and critic. In the following excerpt, he compares Creeley's poetics to those of other poets, both historical and contemporary*].

Creeley remained fairly classical in principle: form as an extension of content was already a maxim of [Paul] Valéry's before [William Carlos] Williams took it over. Creeley's poems usually eschew juxtaposition of image in favor of keenly syncopated rythmic juxtaposition, "of rhythm is image." Taken as rhetorical statements, Creeley's poems exhibit a coherence that would have pleased John Crowe Ransom (who in fact was the first major editor to publish Creeley). It is in what the angles of the lines reveal of the stance and ratiocinative energies of the speaker that the purification of image, the "construct," lies. Creeley has leaped a step in Olson's definition series; he exemplifies "of rhythm . . . is knowing":

> **"Blue Skies Motel"**
>
> Look at
> that mother-fucking smoke-stack
>
> pointing
> straight up.
>
> See those clouds
> old time fleecy pillows,
>
> like they say, whites and greys,
> float by.
>
> There's cars
> on the street,
>
> there's a swimming pool
> out front—
>
> and the trees
> go yellow
>
> now
> it's the fall.

Written at a time in the late seventies when Photographic Realists dominated a whole sector of painting, this poem could be taken as an ekphrastic description of such a painting. Certainly the subject is one that has no parallel in Creeley's earlier work. While following Williams' lead in the acceptance of what the eye takes in, Creeley allows his speaker reactions of a greater miscellany. He also keeps them below the threshold of Williams' often very philosophical reflections.

The speaker begins in the first two lines to register the familiar reaction of the vacationer: he has not left the industrial city behind. The priority of what is noticed, and the single tired colloquial compound taking up half the line (*mother-fucking*), assimilate his reaction to a Freudian undertone that slows into obsession in the more deliberate lines three and four. In the next lines the speaker turns away, still confined to tired comparison (*pillows*) and tired qualification (*like they say*), along with the visual catalogue (*whites and greys*) that relaxes still further into the last four couplets of the poem, ending in a perfectly routine memory of why it is the leaves would be yellow. The only feature not routine in this poem is the rhythmic disposition of its three sentences evenly into eight couplets arranged 2-2-4, while unevenly into varied line-lengths and into modulations that the relative shortness of the lines tends to magnify. Between the evenness and the unevenness, the sound of the poem comes into being. This is true of all poetry, but Creeley has purified the principle and made it serve delineation. "Of rhythm is image." A single process of visual perception distributes its elements in a structure that rises to an abstractness allowing, without allegory, an assimilation to the more than visual. [Piet] Mondrian is, so to speak, re-rendered as a Photo-Realist. The post-Surrealism of Marisol, which Creeley approaches in a gingerly prose, has been bypassed through further depersonalization.

In another poem from the same collection, the visual remains the focus, and the play of three simple colors reminds one of Williams' practice in this regard. But the occasion has abjured Williams' intellectual content; it is a "shaggy dog" image, an image that presents itself as lacking point:

"Morning"

Light's bright glimmer
through green bottle

on shelf
above. Light's white

fair air,
shimmer,

blue summer's
come.

The modulation increases as the intellectual energy declines. The whole poem confines itself to the process of inferring from two visual details of light, connected to green and to white respectively, that something else is present of a third color, *blue summer*. "Of knowing there is a construct." Turning this realization, which would usually be subliminal, of how summer light may be identified, into a sequence of common, modulated words, abstracts a relation between the visual and the subliminal.

The goal of the painter has been brought over into words. Proprioception has taken place, through means very different from Olson's. "Of image is knowing." (pp. 153-55)

Creeley is to Williams as [Stéphane] Mallarmé is to [Charles-Pierre] Baudelaire. His abstractness, too, develops increasingly the big jump between early (*For Love,* 1962) and middle (*Words,* 1967). Intellection is triggered by an abruptness in the conjunction of word and line.

The adolescent Creeley announced himself publicly as a prospective Latin teacher—and subsequently spent a spell as one. This fact finds its embodiment in the hard-bitten words lodged into place over a fleeting sentiment or, indifferently, a minimally characterized image (as the vague poetic purpose was concealed under the intention to teach a dead language). The dead words take on new life by being treated as inert; their overtones are released for double play by being arrested into an ordonnance that the opted "natural" voice is made to seem easily to govern. Qualification of image becomes implicit in rhythm. One

near analogy for the rhythms of Creeley may thus be the *Odes* of Horace, except Horace's poems are far more bound than Creeley's, and his consistent abstractness pares down his poems. Williams releases Creeley from Horace, and releases him to use that for which Horace stands while bypassing entirely the Mallarmean tradition he recapitulates roundabout.

Creeley's phrasal suspension, his near hyperbaton, also may be taken as a version of Mallarmé's—it can be found so markedly in neither Williams nor Olson. It takes the visual for granted as only the work of a successor to Mallarmé and Williams could. The movement is mild enough not to rise to stern abstraction, its strategy for self-possession being the sound of a hesitant, nascently apologetic voice, which directs visual perceptions to psychological use.

These are preconscious poems in which all the functions of the *I* and the *it* take place. Under a Diogenes self-light. Their shadow includes conscious and precludes unconscious, by the act of eschewing special structures while concentrating on the sort of urban feature highlighted in photographs like those of Aaron Siskind and paintings like those of [Jean] Dubuffet:

"The Cracks"

Don't step
so lightly, Break
your back, missed
the step. Don't go

away mad, lady in
the nightmare. You
are central,
even necessary.

I will attempt to describe you.
I will be completely without
face, a lost
chance, nothing at all left.

"Well," he said
as he was leaving,
"blood
tells."

But you remembered quickly
other times, other faces
and I slipped between the good
intentions, breathlessly.

What a good boy am I who
want to. Will you,
mother, come quickly,
won't you. Why not

go quietly, be left
with a memory
of an insinuation or two
of cracks in a pavement.

The movement here operates under the aegis of a Freudian interpretation of crack. But it does not close the gap with such an interpretation. Like someone hopping the cracks in the pavement, it at once avoids and evokes such associations, minimizing and gliding past, while focusing on, the child's superstition as it shades into a common area with the "lady" traditionally addressed in poems from Dante to the T. S. Eliot and the Robert Graves of Creeley's youth. The poem remains focused, from beginning to end, on the cracks. They at once permit it to stray far and haunt an act of straying with psychic significance. The voice hesitates before the largeness of experience that it will bring off an act of suggesting. "Attention a whip of surmise."

In such poems the "something evermore about to be" of Wordsworth is flattened out into visual traces. His rhythmic modulation gives Creeley, deservedly, a classic air. "It is all a rhythm" (**"The Rhythm,"** *Words*); and this is often put to visual use:

> no sun
> but sun

This is an entire strophe, two words repeated and one like pattern repeated, arguably four pitch levels and even four stress levels, paradox caught and transcended in the exactness and delicate modulation of the voice. A central doctrine of Wallace Stevens' is pared even below the Williams threshold for conversational use. It is minimalist. The style achieves a balance between the fluid and the sculpturesque—almost a visual impression as the reader assimilates the lightly freighted short lines and slips through the frequent enjambements on to the next. Creeley is poised, so to speak, between the soft fluency of late Merwin and the "powerful frozen moments" of Gary Snyder.

There is another minimalism, of Ponge, say, fixed on an inspected object; or of "deep image," given over to feelings of mystery aroused by object. Creeley is also cryptically an anti-Surrealist, coming around behind post-Surrealism in the prolonged meditation on Marisol. He does not dwell on images, much as he hinges on presenting them. In **"The Flower"** the particularity of the arbitrary image, repeated, escapes into deadly anecdote. "Pain is a flower like that one, / like that one, / like this one" (*For Love*).

> My voice is
> a foot. My
> head is
>
> a foot. I
> club
> people in
>
> my mind, I
> push them this
> way, that
>
> way . . .

Here what begins as something like [René] Magritte's Surrealist lexicon of arbitrary significations quickly moves itself, in its elementary economy, back into the stream of simple personal interchange, "the damn function of simile always a displacement of what *is* happening" (*Pieces*). The soft equivalences are not meant to cancel each other out. They would, if the earnestness of this voice is fully credited. Hence the hesitancy.

On the farm, we imagine, Creeley acted out, and acted beyond, as a chicken farmer, "the white chickens" of Williams' famous *so much depends*. Clucking and pecking, ducking to pick up grain by grain, *singulatim,* the singularity of the chickens escapes their fixed image.

"She Went to Stay"

> Trying to chop mother down is like
> hunting deer inside Russia
> with phalangists for hat-pins.
> I couldn't.

> (*For Love*)

This is the overblown, arbitrary simile and image complex as a final hesitancy. The mind going through the poem is made to move around such possibilities. To joke about them in necessary transit.

A displaced and self-displacing pseudoepigrammatic shot at "defining" an intangible moral stance makes it so elusive as to be revelatory—so elusive no image will do, only the fragment of a tale. The image of Williams is redone and abstracted as an action of small actions in process:

"The Rocks"

> Trying to think of
> some way out, the
> rocks of thought
>
> which displace,
> dropped in
> the water,
>
> much else.

The convolutions of an inexplicably folding world stand also ready, increasingly so in Creeley's prose. In his prose work of most commanding presence, ***Presences,*** the hesitancies expand their habitat and relax before small humiliations and the shadow of horrors, taking their distant cue from visual artifacts, the sculptures of Marisol. Even such an entity as the Rockefeller villa at Bellagio dissolves into vignettes of a mordant hesitancy. At the same time the voice counts on acceptance. In *Presences* real people from a remembered past do not suffer the dimness of ***The Island*** or the paleness of ***The Gold Diggers.***

The intermultiplying numbers of these sections do not shrink to the somewhat willed definitions of ***Numbers***: they play off against each other as distantly as Creeley's vignettes play off against Marisol's sculptures.

We are gradually made aware that he touches these artifacts with a mobile ten-foot pole. The distance between Marisol's sculptured objects and the random personal associations of the poet's prose is maintained adroitly, and the terms of possible connection are adroitly varied at the same time. This distance may be equaled to that between her ikons, slapped into place with terrible jauntiness, and the laminations in the unconscious that they evidence; or to the distance between the deep subject of a Creeley poem and its offered *momenta* of intermittent, resolutely abstract, and minimal visualization:

> Go forth, go forth
> saith the grandmother, the fire
> of that old form, and turns
> away from the form.
>
> And the forest is dark,
> mist hides it, trees
> are dim, but I turn
> to my father in the dark.

> (*For Love*)

Creeley's father is persistent but absent; Olson's is present but intricately struggling with history. Constructing the image helps both poets to say so. (pp. 161-66)

> *Albert Cook, "Maximizing Minimalism: The Construct of Image in Olson and Creeley," in his* Figural Choice in Poetry and Art, *University Press of New England, 1985, pp. 149-66.*

Creeley on reading:

I'm what the contemporary expression might be, I'm "torqued up." I feel an emotional tension in the words in reading them. They require it of me, at least as I read them, so that the rhythms and the apparent texture of the poems insist upon emotional intensity. The tension both excites and becomes useful, like a violin string or a drum head. I really require that. I know that when I was younger reading oftentimes people would presume that I was in some awful existentially nervous state. It really wasn't that. It appeared that way, very obviously, but it wasn't something I couldn't relax from. It takes time to quiet down afterwards.

Robert Creeley, in an interview with Emily Keller in The American Poetry Review, *1983.*

Stephen Fredman (essay date Fall 1987)

[*In the following essay, Fredman examines the issues of personal and national identity in Creeley's poetry.*]

> Americans . . . feel that they, perhaps more than any other group of people upon the earth at this moment, have had both to imagine and thereby to *make* that reality which they are then given to live in. It is as though they had to *realize* the world anew.
>
> [*A Quick Graph*]

In the statement above, Robert Creeley enunciates an essential issue for the understanding of his own poetry, of the movement of projectivist poetry, and of the direction of American poetry in general. The present essay will examine how this issue, with its ramifications at the various levels I have mentioned, functions in some of Creeley's later poetry.

But first we must consider more closely what is implied when Creeley states that Americans have had to create their own reality. Primarily, this creation is necessary because there is no established reality given by a unified tradition. "It may well be that in the absence of such allusive society as European literature, in its own condition, has necessarily developed, that the American in contrast must so realize each specific thing of his own." In this statement, Creeley both points to the profound vacuum at the base of American culture in our lack of a coherent tradition and also offers one of the characteristic solutions by which our poets have sought to redress this lack—through a powerful coupling of things and individual experience to "*realize* the world anew."

It may at first seem absurd to speak of a lack of coherent tradition within American culture, when this culture is fabricated mainly from longstanding elements of European culture. What differentiates our situation, however, is the missing factor of coherence in our sense of tradition. A unified tradition is so important because it provides a secure foundation upon which cultural constructions may be erected. With our Reformation heritage of dissent and revolution, Americans always have had an ambivalent relationship toward this deepest sort of tradition—desiring on the one hand to establish a grounding for a new culture that would derive from our own values, while on the other hand maintaining an innate suspicion toward any established doctrines or institutions. As a result, American culture, though it has contributed substantially to the world culture of our age, has never been able to accept or establish for itself a commonly held tradition that would provide an unquestioned grounding for its manifold productions.

Without the benefit of a ground, many sorts of cultural endeavors—particularly the most self-conscious, such as the arts—are presented with a crucial problem right at the outset of their creation. In the field of poetry, for example, the primary question facing our poets is not the obvious one before poets whose cultural situation includes a grounding tradition, namely, which of the tradition's values to represent and which to oppose; rather, the underlying question of whether an American poetry is possible at all has generally, from the nineteenth century on, exercised a tremendous influence over American poetic production.

American poetry has an irregular or unbalanced quality to it that one rarely finds in cultural contexts where a longstanding tradition holds sway. At the deepest level, this awkwardness manifests the foundational anxiety beneath our poetry. All of the major American poets show conspicuous signs of grappling with this question. In Poe, for example, we find a poet so self-conscious of British formal excellence that he overcultivates the formal qualities of his own verse and insists so stridently upon formal issues in his criticism; clearly, this is in part an attempt to overcome the fear of writing within a groundless context. In the case of Emerson, a major poetic talent confesses to the inability to write verse of the stature that matches his conceptions and instead begs for the poetic qualities of his prose. Whitman, on the other hand, feels the necessity to construct single-handedly a massive prophetic platform on which to ground his poetic activity. Dickinson is so plagued by doubts about the place of poetry in America that she never publishes her astonishing oeuvre. And in the twentieth century, Pound, Eliot, and Williams, among many others, also show the battle scars of this struggle in numerous facets of their work. Pound, for instance, feels he has to adopt, reform, and become the spokesman for European tradition in order to be allowed to speak as an American poet. Eliot, in "Tradition and the Individual Talent," betrays his severe anxiety in the face of the void when he insists upon the requirement of a writer *earning* his or her tradition; since a grounding tradition is given a priori, Eliot can only be asserting that it is possible for an American to make his or her way into that sacred ground. Of these three Moderns, Williams is probably the most constantly and acutely aware of this question; the title of his late book of reflections upon his career, *I Wanted to Write a Poem,* gives this away, as does the wrenching climax of his great later poem, "The Desert Music," in which he cries out, "I *am* a poet! I / am. I am."

In daily life, Americans somehow manage to get by without reflecting upon the fundamentally disorienting lack of a stable ground beneath their feet. Our writers, however, cannot choose to ignore this radical instability, for the writer must be "authorized" in order to write, and authorization normally comes to writers from one or both of two sources: God and tradition. Unable fully to claim either source of legitimacy within America, our poets have had to constitute an alternative ground for themselves. What I consider the most vital strain in American poetry—that arising from Emerson and continuing in the Transcendentalists, the Modernists, the Objectivists, and the Projectivists—has always confronted this issue squarely. In so doing, these poets have discovered and continue to discover a number of powerful substitutes for an enabling tradition. Briefly stated, the attempts at providing an alternative grounding for poetry consist in devices such as the following: (1) the initiatory cult, which gives a social power and permission to the poet who places him or herself within a communal, though exclusive, enterprise; (2) the idiosyncratic endeavor of building a tradition of one's own, which involves the construction of an authorizing lineage from the vast lumberyard of world literature; (3) the curiously American typological invention of the notion of "picture-writing"—an attempt to yoke nature and language together as a substitute for tradition; (4) the choice of a *place* as a multidimensional ground for writing, which includes geography, history, politics, etc.; and (5) the use of prose of all kinds (discursive, polemical, poetic, autobiographical and fictional) to construct ideological and philosophical bases for poetry.

As a major figure within this Emersonian lineage, Creeley has always been acutely aware of the need for establishing a ground for his writing. When he calls on the American poet to "realize each specific thing of his own," Creeley is speaking of the third alternative mentioned above, this hermeneutic activity in which nature and experience are linked together through the "hieroglyphic," or picture-writing. In America, picture-writing takes the place of a writing arising from tradition, and words themselves are called on to function as hieroglyphs, capable, through interpretation, of illuminating both the internal and the external worlds and the connections between the two. Walt Whitman states this viewpoint succinctly in "Song of Myself": "To me the converging objects of the universe perpetually flow, / All are written to me, and I must get what the writing means." In addition to Creeley's deep concern with reading self, world, and word as primary texts, he also participates in the first and fifth alternatives listed above through the initiatory cult of the Black Mountain or projectivist poets and the use of many kinds of prose as part of his poetic activity.

Beyond these fruitful substitutes that Creeley, like many another American poet, adopts to secure an alternative

grounding, his writing is also notable for its direct confrontation with the notion of the ground. One way to view his writing as a whole is to see it as a constant attempt at grounding, in which the fundamental question of whether it is possible to write at all becomes the question of whether there is a *place* from which one can write. Clearly, this is a metaphysical as well as a practical concern; Creeley is aware to such an extent of the metaphysical nature of approaching the ground in writing that the act of composing a poem takes on a kind of religious sanctity. Because there is no authoritative tradition, and thus in Creeley's eyes no ground for poetry outside of the moment itself, that moment and its action, in their intensities, are in his estimation the true gifts an American poet has to offer.

This emphasis upon the moment of composition itself as an ontological situation is a hallmark of projective poetry. Although it has been generally acknowledged that this elevates "process" in the poem to a primary role above any separable "subject matter," it has not been easy to define more clearly what the process is. In "Projective Verse," Charles Olson states that the process is theoretically unmediated by any restrictive notions of form ("Form is never more than an extension of content.") and that it is instantaneous ("One perception must immediately and directly lead to a further perception"). These dicta are so general and vague that it would be impossible to define a particular poetic technique based upon them.

In the same discussion, however, Olson speaks more helpfully of the poet having to engage in "a whole series of new recognitions" at every level of composition. The term "recognition" is a useful one for exploring what actually occurs in projective composition. When Olson appropriates Edward Dahlberg's command that "One perception must immediately and directly lead to a further perception," he seems to mean more precisely that one *recognition* must immediately follow another. The projective verse of poets like Olson, Creeley, Robert Duncan, Denise Levertov, and Edward Dorn does not strike one primarily as a sketchbook of momentary perceptions. Rather, the poetry reads like a series of recognitions in which each recognition opens up to the next without any intervening development or discussion.

Recognition in itself is not by any means an activity confined to projectivist poetry. However, there is something unique about constructing a poem so that it represents the process of recognition. According to Hans-Georg Gadamer in *Truth and Method,* a work of art *is,* in an ontological sense, that which it represents. What the work of art *does* is provoke our recognition of what it represents. Speaking of the origins of this essential artistic activity in childhood play, Gadamer says, "The child does not want at any cost to be discovered behind his disguise. He intends that what he represents should exist, and if something is to be guessed, then this is it. What it 'is' should be recognized." Recognition is a basic process of consciousness, and Gadamer contends that it has a central role in art; in fact, it renders art more true than reality because art always involves a recognition of the essence of what is represented, while in life we are often to a large extent incognizant. Eschewing the forms of tradition and the designs of social manipulation, projectivist poetry uniquely dedicates itself to representing the activity of recognition. In other words, where all poetry must involve recognition, projectivist poetry insists upon the recognition of recognition; it represents less any given situation, perception, or idea than it does the process of recognition itself.

Why is recognition important? Because, Olson might answer, employing his touchstone quote from Heraclitus, "Man is estranged from that with which he is most familiar." The poetry of Olson and Creeley is largely an attempt to bring us into greater awareness of the whole universe that inheres in the very place and moment where we are. In line with the projectivist insistence that "Form is never more than an extension of content," Gadamer also emphasizes the primacy of recognition:

> One does not, as with a circus performer, admire the art with which something is done. This has only secondary interest. What one experiences in a work of art and what one is directed towards is rather how true it is, i.e., to what extent one knows and recognizes something and oneself.

> But we do not understand what recognition is in its profoundest nature, if we only see that something that we know already is known again, i.e., that what is familiar is recognized again. The joy of recognition is rather that more becomes known than is already known. In recognition what we know emerges, as if through an illumination, from all the chance and variable circumstances that condition it and is grasped in its essence. It is known as something.

When it occurs, recognition has the quality of swiftness or instantaneousness, of direct perception, which is why Olson speaks of it as instantaneous perception. Recognition is not merely perception, though, for it involves a sudden expansion, a sudden sense of fittingness. When we continue to dwell in the state of recognition, one expansion opens into the next directly, without any intervening rumination or explanation. The feeling of things *fitting* grows stronger and stronger as recognition opens into recognition. Followed far enough, this process of expansion produces a sense of oneness, which is an experience of the ground, of that which underlies everything.

Phenomenologically speaking, what we call truth is at base the sensation of recognition: "Aha! Now I see it! This really does fit with that! What I have always heard or felt really does apply to this actual event." From a wider perspective, all acts of interpretation involve recognition, although they may also consist of many other operations as well. The truth, however, is the experience of recognition itself; as the recognition becomes incorporated into an interpretive scheme, it strays further and further from the truth. This is why Olson and the other projectivists insist upon the movement from one recognition to the next, without stopping for a mental consolidation of gains. Also, this makes clear why the patterns Olson and Duncan characteristically develop in poems, lectures, and essays for explaining how everything fits together do not themselves coalesce into a stable system: they are meant to be the representation of acts of recognition and not a

series of static symbols for the mind to manipulate authoritatively. As Los says in Blake's *Jerusalem,* "I must Create a System, or be enslav'd by another Man's." The secret, however, to resisting such "mind-forg'd manacles" is, as both Blake and Olson realize, to create a constantly evolving, open system that resists formulation and codification while retaining its primary function of enhancing individual experience (and, through that, communal experience) by providing a ground for instantaneous recognitions.

The projectivists propose a state of attentive passivity as the most effective way to achieve recognitions and to resist interpretive rigidity. In **"A Sense of Measure,"** Creeley in particular offers a clear formulation of this attitude:

> I am more interested, at present, in what is *given* to me to write apart from what I might intend. I have never explicitly known—before writing— what it was that I would say. For myself, articulation is the intelligent ability to recognize the experience of what is so given, in words. I do not feel that such a sense of writing is "mindless" or "automatic" in a perjorative way.

The continuing fidelity to and refinement of this approach to writing defines the direction of Creeley's poetry over the years. Through cultivating the process of recognition, which is the central tenant of projectivism, his poetry has become more and more actively an exploration of the ground.

Certain admirers of his early writing profess puzzlement at the direction he has taken in the last fifteen years, as this exploration has progressed. Dating from the breakthrough book *Pieces* (1969), Creeley's poetry and prose have undergone a transformation from the tight, compact, tortured expression of a lyric or narrative moment in *For Love* (1962) and *The Gold Diggers* (1965) to a more relaxed and open-ended poetry and prose. In the baldest terms, one could say that Creeley's focus shifts dramatically from the expression of a wounded ego, with its pain, anger, and supplication prominent, to an exploration of the ground of experience in which the self finds itself. In adopting this more expanded focus Creeley works against our ingrained habits of attention, which may account for why he finds some readers inattentive. We are so used to forming *gestalts* in the mind, composed of a figure set against a ground, that a work of art calling our attention primarily to the ground can seem odd and even pointless.

What remains unchanged in this shift of focus is Creeley's characteristic intensity. Readers note that the dramatic effect produced by searing rage or aching self-doubt in the early writing has nearly disappeared in books like *Hello* (1978) or *Presences* (1976). What replaces the earlier emotional intensity, however, is a correspondingly powerful concentration on two more pervasive aspects of writing and experience: appearance and language. Instead of using a poem to lift a lyric moment out of the flux and make it timeless, as poets have classically done, Creeley returns us patiently to the ground of the mundane world of appearances in which our lives are actually being led. Likewise, instead of creating brilliant images that encapsulate particular emotions or states of mind, Creeley often gives us the language overheard—whether from songs, the radio, conversation, other writers, or from the voice inside one's head—that provides the mental context in which we all live. By framing this language and these mundane appearances into a poem, Creeley asks us to stop ignoring them and to recognize them as the ground of our experience.

In Creeley's world, there is one major purpose in attending to the ground: to increase our ability to be present. Fundamentally, the present is made up of ground, of context; within this ground, the isolate figure to which we narrowly attend is a siren seducing us to get "lost in thought." Again and again, Creeley assigns a poem to retrieve the present by recognizing and foregrounding the context from which his errant thought has wandered. Look, for example, at a poem from the collection *Later* (1979):

"This World"

If night's the harder,
closer time, days
come. The morning
opens with light

at the window.
Then, as now, sun
climbs in blue sky.
At noon

on the beach
I could watch
these glittering
waves forever,

follow their sound
deep into mind
and echoes—
let light

as air
be relief.
The wind
pulls at face

and hands,
grows cold. What
can one think—
the beach

is myriad stone.
Clouds pass,
grey undersides,
white clusters

of air, all
air. Water
moves at the edges,
blue, green,

white twists
of foam.
What then
will be lost,

recovered.
What
matters as one
in this world?

This poem begins with thought about the differences between night and day. At night the ground seems to recede,

leaving us, if we are awake, framed in the bright, harsh light of our attention. In the daytime we can relax this self-absorption and surrender to what the day brings (the word "come" always carries for Creeley the connotation of surrender). "The morning / opens with light," bringing us another light to live by than our intellectual lamp; and this light, if we allow it to, "opens" us, making apparent to us the "window" of awareness that connects the inside with the outside. Still thinking about how often the day provides a welcome relief from the night's preoccupations, the poet remembers a "then" in which this has occurred before and which he compares to the "now" in which it is happening again.

Once we reach the word "now," however, the poem shifts location from that of the self-enclosed mind engaged in reflection to that of the present world now being revealed. The sun, ruler of the temporal world, claims its place in the sky and carries the poet with it into the fully lighted world, the world of "noon." It is worth commenting, parenthetically, upon the subtle modulations of sound Creeley works with the simplest words. In lines three through eight, in which the sun comes to dominate the poem, Creeley orchestrates the pleasant hum of the "n" and the shadings of "o" and "u." There is a complex rhyming of the words "morning," "open," "window," "then," "now," "sun," and "noon" that reinforces the gentle but inexorable power of the sun as light of the world. Returning, though, to the question of context, we find that when the sun reaches full power at "noon," the poem itself fully enters a present moment, one in which the ground is allowed to speak with full force.

We are located on the beach, in that open, relaxed posture in which the empty mind takes interest in what is happening around it. "I could watch / these glittering / waves forever": the sense of self is freely and fully given to the sun and the reiterative context it illumines. There is nothing of "interest" for the restless mind here, only a place to be. Attending more insistently to the unfixable waves, one feels them surround the senses and in their rhythmic penetrations take over the mind—controlling not only its present focus but also arranging its latent contents through a progression of "echoes." Once this transformation of consciousness is effected by the waves as ground, then one can attend to the even more subtle principle that illumines the ground itself: one can "let light // as air / be relief," and in the insistent alliteration and assonance of those lines find oneself at one with the sun itself.

As the poem continues, there is an alternation between this absorption in the ground and the questioning done by the mind. The questions are suggested by the words and appearances that occur, while answers come in the form of a return to the actual context. For instance, after the "relief" of feeling "light // as air," the air takes motion as wind and begins to "pull at face / and hands," to awaken the expressive and manipulative parts of the body, causing one to shrink and feel cold. At this point the mind returns to action, asking its own foundational question: "What / can one think." Instead of responding with personal preoccupations, such as were likely predominant in the "harder, / closer" night, Creeley looks back to the ground for an answer: "the beach," he finds, "is myriad stone." This "myriad stone" may seem a cold, mute reply to the inquiring mind, but its very resistance and unassimilability are oddly comforting to one who trusts the ground. It calls to mind Whitman's similar faith expressed in one of the finest lines of "Song of Myself": "My foothold is tenon'd and mortis'd in granite." In the next three stanzas the poet staunchly witnesses the streaming context—clouds, air, water—and is content with whatever it produces, such as "white twists / of foam."

At the end of the poem the pondering mind comes back for three final questions:

> What then
> will be lost,
>
> recovered.
> What
> matters as one
> in this world?

These three questions Creeley is coming to ask more and more frequently in his later poetry and prose where the issue of identity is paramount. The aging man, aware of the passage of time, asks who he is and to what extent he can be said to live in his body, in his memories, in his actions. What does it mean, though, to proffer these nagging questions in the present context? Having assigned such primacy to the ground in reading the poem thus far, I hear the repetition of these questions at the end of the poem (when only the ground can return with its tacit answer) as an ultimate gesture of surrender, a giving up of the claims of identity in favor of another kind of self. This self would be constituted solely as a witness, whether of thoughts, of language or of the world. Such a view of the self hinges upon an understanding of that most basic word in Creeley's vocabulary: "one." "One" is Creeley's ultimate pun because it unites in English both the number and the grammatical person. To be a one is to be both a self and a unity, i.e., the ground. "What / matters" is to attain the detached, witnessing perspective that allows one to see, finally, that the questioning mind, the communal language, and the sun in the sky are all equally "in this world." In other words, these questions do not provoke a discrete answer but instead lead to a recognition that ultimately everything is ground: "one and one and one," as Creeley so often puts it.

If the poem is used to dissolve personal identity, then why doesn't the poem itself dissolve? What can hold together such intense moments of expansion and openness? The ability to do this is central to projectivist writing. When Olson talks about "composition by field" in "Projective Verse," he is proposing that the poet him or herself creates a context, just as the sun does in **"This World."** To create a context takes a strenuous concentration as well as a sense of freedom and openness. In a context, everything fits, but the sense of fit can only be recognized, not imposed by ideation. For instance, in life the most seemingly disparate and unrelated events can occur on the beach, and yet one can still see them fitting easily into the context of "an afternoon at the beach." So in projectivist writing one creates a context as vivid and coherent as "an afternoon at the beach" by scrupulously engaging in the process of recognition. Projectivist writing is so different from, say, Romanticism or Surrealism because of the strict limits the context (what is "there") imposes. In projectivist writing, a sunny day at the beach does not become a snowy night in the woods. In other words, there is a kind of concentration and containment in the context-building of projectivist writing that offsets its evident freedom and limitlessness and that keeps an ever-widening context of recognitions, such as Creeley arrives at in **"This World,"** from dissolving the poetry.

Though it is apparent at all levels of structuring in Creeley's later writing, this concentration is most easily seen at the level of the word. Following Pound, Williams, and Zukofsky, Creeley regards his words, the palpable atoms of his text, as living objects in the world. The words are simple, predominantly monosyllabic (80% in **"This World"**), each one lit so brilliantly that a reader is often surprised, unaccustomed to the glare reflecting back from so plain a word as "air" or "what."

This relationship to words is a characteristically American one. In America one finds **Words** (the title of a 1967 volume of Creeley's poetry) rather than The Word. In European culture the Greco-Christian Logos *is* tradition and authority. In America, where tradition and authority are uncertain, our relationship to words is identifiably different. Since words do not speak to them with the absolute authority of divinity or tradition, American writers have used them to provide an alternative source of grounding; the proposition is that words, instead of revealing God's truth to us, reveal the truths and interconnection of nature and experience. The focus of truth shifts from The Word to each word. In classic European culture, symbols control words, so that by following the graded levels of interpretation (such as the four Dante codified) one can use the symbol to reach an experience of the Logos. In America, words are not so tightly governed by symbols; instead, they are seen to have a numinous quality of their own, which illumines the inner and outer realms of experience and nature.

The most general term for this American use of words is picture-writing. Thinking about this issue, insightful critics and writers themselves have demonstrated the importance of picture-writing—using terms such as typology, hieroglyph, ideogram, etc.—in virtually every period of American literature. One could begin to map out this pervasive alternative mode of grounding by stringing together Sacvan Bercovitch's *Puritan Origins of the American Self,* (1975), which chronicles the ways early American writers adapted biblical typology to their own attempts at self-definition through nature and contemporary history, John Irwin's *American Hieroglyphics* (1980), which analyzes the fascination of American Renaissance writers with the hieroglyph as a model of literary activity, and Laszlo Gefin's *Ideogram,* (1982), which traces the influence of Pound's Ideogrammic Method upon his own and subsequent American poetry. This insistent concern with picture-writing is something different from an interest in semiotics or grammatology. It is a primary attempt to write a new scripture in images that would allow us to read

Robert Creeley, Cambridge, Massachusetts, 1985.

truth in nature and in our own experience, rather than in the texts bequeathed by European tradition.

The locus classicus for this view of language is Emerson, particularly the "Language" chapter of *Nature* and the essay "The Poet." To the poet, Emerson feels, "Nature offers all her creatures . . . as a picture-language. Being used as a type [of human experience], a second wonderful value appears in the object, far better than its old value." Moreover, words themselves carry inherently this metaphorical connection between the outer world and the inner world. The correct use of words, then, can ground the poet through a direct experience of the conjunction of inner and outer. For the Twentieth Century, Ezra Pound effects a major continuation of this theme through the movement of Imagism. In one definition, an image is simply an enactment of the metamorphic moment in which something external darts across the threshold of recognition to become internal. Building upon this notion of the image, Williams and the Objectivists create a poetry in which there is an insistence that each word stand as a kind of hieroglyph, acting both to present a verbal image and to declare its own meaningfulness as a participant in language.

This orientation toward words has had a profound effect upon Creeley's writing. Creeley goes farther than any poet before him (with the possible exception of Louis Zukofsky) in treating words as objects with a right to stand on their own. Characteristically, Creeley will investigate a particular word by presenting it in different contexts, by setting it as a pun, or by letting it stand alone to gather its own context about it. In the opening stanzas of another poem from *Later,* "Corn Close," an affectionate homage to Basil Bunting, Creeley ponders particular words and the power of words in general:

> Words again, rehearsal
> "Are we going to
> get up *into*
>
> heaven after all?"
> What's
> the sound of *that,*
>
> who, where—
> and how.
> *One wonder,*
>
> one wonders, sees
> the world—
> specifically, this one.

With quotation marks and italics drawing attention to the words *as* words, Creeley constantly ponders *how* something is said while in the midst of saying it. This produces the uncanny sensation in a reader that the words are speaking the poet, rather than vice versa. As Creeley says later on in the poem,

> —Oh, I think
> the words come from
> the world and go
>
> "I know
> not
> where . . . "

Becoming aware of the power of particular words to create the reality in which one lives is a remarkably forceful act of recognition. In that recognition lies the understanding that every word is the picture-writing of the world, and that the world is co-extensive with one's awareness. Creeley celebrates the achievement of such a grounding in the final lines of **"Corn Close"**:

> What wonder
> more than
>
> to be where you are,
> and to know it?
> All's here.

> (*Later*)
>   (pp. 89-101)

Stephen Fredman, "Robert Creeley on the Ground," in North Dakota Quarterly, Vol. 55, No. 4, Fall, 1987, pp. 89-102.

Fred Moramarco   (essay date 1987)

[*Moramarco is an American educator and critic. In the following essay, originally delivered as a lecture at the 1984 MLA convention in slightly different form, he places Creeley within the projectivist movement and explores themes of aging and memory in the poet's later work.*]

One of the most consistent characteristics of Robert Creeley's earlier poetry—and I use the word "earlier" to describe the work done through the mid-seventies—has been its grounding in the immediacy of a present moment. His has been an empirical poetry of attention concentrated on an unfolding experience. Characteristically, the reader is plunged into the middle of an ongoing event, offered a snatch of conversation or a bit of internal monologue, which recreates the feeling of a fleeting moment, a sudden awareness, or a traumatic episode. Creeley was a leader in the generational shift that veered away from memory, history, and tradition as primary poetic sources and gave new importance to the ongoing experiences of an individual's life. Along with Ginsberg, Ferlinghetti, O'Hara, Blackburn, Snyder, and other poets whose work became prominent in the fifties and sixties, he developed a new poetics of experience and awakened a sense of new rhythmical possibilities for the spoken word. The unforgettable sound of his voice reading poetry typified Olson's famous dictum that poetry needed to put into itself "the breathing of the man who writes."

Creeley sharpened and developed his style throughout the sixties and seventies in a series of books that seemed almost designed to exemplify the principles of projective verse. These principles insisted that contemporary poetry divert its attention from the traditional tools of the poet—standard forms, metaphors, poetic diction, imagery, and so on—and concentrate instead on the outward structure of poetic movement, the self-generating form of the poem that took shape as the process of creating it was under way. Attention to experience on the one hand and attention to composition on the other were the twin poles of his poetry. He writes, in a poem called **"Waiting,"** of how the poet "pushes behind the words" struggling to bring poems into being, giving his emotions and experiences the formal contours that embody their meaning. Without the transformative aspects of poetry—its ability to distill and crystallize the flux of experience—life seems "a dull / space of hanging actions."

For Creeley poetry has always been both useful and necessary. By discovering appropriate forms for the transitory emotional states he needs to write about, he has always used poetry to take measure of both the world around him and the state of his being at any particular moment. *Measure* in Creeley's lexicon means much more than poetic meter and rhythm; it is a standard of valuation and judgment. To develop a sense of measure is to develop a sense of worth. "Measure . . . is my testament," he wrote in 1964. "What uses me is what I use and in that complex measure is the issue. I cannot cut down trees with my bare hand, which is measure of both tree and hand. In that way I feel that poetry, in the very subtlety of its relation to image and rhythm, offers an intensely various record of such facts. It is equally one of them." This sense of measure, which includes taking stock, assessing value, and discovering those things one values most, is what links Creeley's earlier and later work.

In his two . . . collections, **Later** (1979) and **Mirrors,** (1983), the poetry seems to shift into a new phase characterized by a greater emphasis on memory, a new sense of life's discrete phases, and an intense preoccupation with aging. As Creeley approaches age sixty these seem appropriate enough concerns, but some readers have felt disoriented by the sense of pastness that emerges in these poems as an alternative to the "here and now" attentiveness of the earlier work. The poems in **Later,** as the title unflinchingly announces, face directly the fact that the later phase of Creeley's life and career has arrived. He realizes that

> I'll not write again
> things a young man
> thinks, not the words
> of that feeling

Creeley remains attuned to the present in these poems, but the words that convey present feelings both incorporate and reflect upon the past. These words continue to measure a life. Although memory is the source of many of the poems in both books, Creeley, following his mentor William Carlos Williams, is after the thing itself, not merely a current memory of the thing. He seems intent on recovering those "pieces" (a favorite Creeley word) of a past and ongoing life that can provide us with a representative image of that life. Each poem offers us a small piece of Creeley's reflective mirror of words. In poem after poem there are echoes of Pound's "dove sta memora" ("where is memory"), that major theme of the Pisan Cantos, which Pound wrote at age sixty, determined to perpetuate the memories of those things that meant most to him. "What thou lov'st well remains," he wrote in Canto 81's most famous lines,

> the rest is dross
> What thou lov'st well shall not be reft from thee
> What thou lov'st well is thy true heritage. . . .

And

> Pull down thy vanity, it is not man
> Made courage, or made order, or made grace,
> Pull down thy vanity, I say pull down

Creeley concludes a poem called **"Song"** in *Mirrors* with strikingly similar sentiments:

> . . . All vanity, all mind flies
> but love remains, love, nor dies
> even without me. Never dies.

These are the poems of a man taking leave of vanity and searching for his true heritage.

Certainly a major part of that heritage is the excitement and energy of the Black Mountain-Beat Generation days when poetry seemed much more central to American life and culture than it does today. Compared to the "oldtime density" he evokes in a poem called **"Place,"** the contemporary literary landscape often appears empty and alien. "I feel faint here," he writes,

> too far off, too
> enclosed in myself,
> can't make love a way out.
>
> I need the oldtime density,
> the dirt, the cold,
> the noise through the floor—
> my love in company.

The surety of purpose reflected in the poetry of the earlier period has given way to a sense of limits and uncertainty. **"Myself,"** the first poem in *Later,* announces this theme:

> What, younger, felt
> was possible, now knows
> is not—but still
> not changed enough—
>
> . . . . .
>
> I want, if older,
> still to know
> why, human, men
> and women are
>
> so torn, so lost,
> why hopes cannot
> find better world
> than this.

This futile but deeply human quest captures the spirit of Creeley's later work. It embodies a commonly shared realization: one becomes older but still knows very little about essential aspects of life, particularly the mysteries and complexities of human relationships. As Alan Williamson has noticed about the quality of many of the poems in *Later,* "In general, the stronger the note of elegiac bafflement and rage (the past utterly gone, the compensating wisdom not forthcoming), the better the writing." This is a brave theme for a mature poet to embrace because it leaves him vulnerable to the charge of having learned little from his experience. Creeley's candid admission that maturity has not always brought wisdom, and that he is sometimes less, not more certain of what he believes and values, is the subject of one of the best poems in *Later,* **"Prayer to Hermes."** Here he evokes the weakness that accompanies a loss of confident assurance in one's beliefs:

> What I understand
> of this life,
> what was right
> in it, what was wrong,
>
> I have forgotten
> in these days
> of physical change.
> I see the ways
>
> of knowing, of
> securing, life grow
> ridiculous. A weakness,
> a tormenting, relieving weakness
>
> comes to me.

But even in this confession of weakness, Creeley demonstrates his strength as a poet, his mastery of subtle vocal and linguistic patterns. In the first stanza, the assonance of "I," "life," "right," and the soft alliteration of "what," "what was," and "what was wrong" underscore the weariness the lines convey; in the second stanza the linking of "these days" and "see the ways" separated by the intrusive presence of "physical change" upsets the rhythmical pattern of the poem in the same way that actual physical change upsets the comfortable assumptions of youth; and in the third stanza the linking of end and internal rhymes ("knowing," "grow") and the repetition of the word "weakness" as the stanza grows weak with caesurae and unstressed end syllables—all demonstrate the Creeley style at its apex.

In *Mirrors* the commitment to identifying and reconstructing those past events that have shaped the fullness of his present life deepens. The epigraph to the collection is a quotation from Francis Bacon: "In Mirrours, there is the like Angle of Incidence, from the Object to the Glasse, and from the Glasse to the Eye." Poetry in this sense is the word mirror that deflects the experience of the past into our awareness in the present. For Creeley's later work it is the verbal space where past and present intersect.

A poem called **"Memory, 1930"** illustrates this conjunction. Creeley reaches into his store of semiconscious early childhood memories to illuminate the moment he became aware his father was dying. Since he experienced this trauma at age four, he was obviously too young to comprehend the impact it would have on his entire life. Here he presents it as a major fissure in his early life viewed from an angle of incidence over fifty years later. "My sister's / recollection of what happened won't / serve me," he writes, and then creates a picture of himself as a child, witnessing what appears as a nearly surreal scene:

> I sit, intent, fat,
>
> the youngest of the suddenly
> disjunct family, whose father is
>
> being then driven in an ambulance
> across the lawn, in the snow, to die.

The slowness of the final line with its two caesurae causes the image of the departing ambulance to disappear as if in slow motion. It is as if Creeley, who has written about the death of his father more obliquely in earlier work, can now bring that momentous event clearly into focus to observe the impact it had on his young self, who sits intently observing its occurrence. On some deep level the youngster registers the image, then buries it, to be exhumed a half-century later. The older Creeley watches the young Creeley watching his father being driven away in an ambulance to die.

This poem and others in *Mirrors* reveal how integral a part of ourselves our memories become with each passing year. As we age, we accumulate more experience and thus more memory, becoming more complex personalities. Sometimes we take on the mannerisms of those close to us and reexperience the situations of our pasts. In **"Mother's Voice,"** Creeley not only still hears his mother's voice after her death, but realizes that its very timbre and rhythms have become a part of his own voice:

> In these few years
> since her death I hear
> mother's voice say
> under my own, I won't
>
> want any more of that.
> My cheekbones resonate
> with her emphasis.

This theme of the present incorporating the past is developed figuratively and symbolically in **"Prospect,"** one of the most memorable and resonant poems in *Mirrors.* It is a completely atypical Creeley poem, and because it utilizes conventional elements of poetry—symbolism, metaphor, and imagery—in a surprisingly typical manner, it is not likely to be looked upon with favor by admirers of the earlier work, who sometimes prefer deconstructing such qualities into their component phonemes. It is, of all things, a nature poem, and conveys something of its author's psychological state. I think it takes no deep looking into the poem to see the landscape as emblematic of the state of Creeley's life at the time he wrote it, recently invigorated by a new marriage and the birth of a new child:

> Green's the predominant color here,
> but in tones so various, and muted
>
> by the flatness of sky and water,
> the oak trunks, the undershade back of the
>   lawns,
>
> it seems a subtle echo of itself.
> It is the color of life itself,
>
> it used to be. Not blood red,
> or sun yellow—but this green,

> echoing hills, echoing meadows,
> childhood summer's blowsiness, a youngness
>
> one remembers hopefully forever.

There is a nice ambiguity in that "hopefully." One remembers such a landscape as charged with hope, and one will hopefully continue to remember it. It is, in its current manifestation, a landscape filled with echoes and repetitions. Green, traditionally the color of life and vitality, dominates, but in various and muted tones that make it seem "a subtle echo of itself." This is not the "oldtime density" of actual youth, because it lacks the passion and energy of that stage of life ("not blood red, / or sun yellow"), but is instead the reflective, contemplative landscape of maturity:

> It is thoughtful, provokes here
>
> quiet reflections, settles the self
> down to waiting now apart
>
> from time, which is done,
> this green space, faintly painful.

That final phrase surprises, coming at the end of an otherwise tranquil and nearly celebratory poem. It implies that although embarking on a new life creates the illusion that we can exist in an Edenic landscape apart from time, in reality we carry our pasts into whatever new present we inhabit. "Fáintlў páinfŭl," with its echoing first syllable rhyme, is exactly right to convey the contrary feelings of relief and regret the poem ultimately leaves us with—relief that such transitions are not more painful, regret that there is any pain at all.

But pain, in its various manifestations, has been one of the most constant elements in Creeley's work, and this late poetry continues to search for words to express it with sensitivity and exactness, and without the sometimes maudlin excesses of "confessional verse." Though these poems are more rooted in memory than the earlier work, they remain committed to taking measure of a life—to getting things exactly right. Measure continues to be Creeley's testament, and as we look into the mirror of his later poems we see not only his aging, but our own. (pp. 335-43)

Fred Moramarco, "Pieces of a Mirror: Robert Creeley's Later Poetry," in Robert Creeley's Life and Work: A Sense of Increment, *edited by John Wilson, The University of Michigan Press, 1987, pp. 335-43.*

Brad Leithauser   (review date 19-25 February 1988)

[*Leithauser is an American poet and novelist. In the following excerpt, he offers an unfavorable review of* Memory Gardens.]

In **Memory Gardens,** his newest collection of poetry, Robert Creeley seems to have let his subject-matter get the better of him. Creeley's world has always been deliberately, spiritedly raffish—a place where the jostlings and the voices of the street are transplanted into verse with all of their happy vulgarity intact. In the past, the effect has been bracing. Although his name is often linked to the Black Mountain School, the figure Creeley (on his good days) most strongly evokes is E. E. Cummings—though Creeley in his prudently tight-lipped way rarely yields to the overblown whimsy that mars so much of Cummings's work. The final stanza of Creeley's new poem **"Earth"**, for example, has some of that mix of quirkiness and grandeur which characterizes Cummings at his best: "be only here as and forever / each and every thing is".

Although his name is often linked to the Black Mountain School, the figure Creeley (on his good days) most strongly evokes is E. E. Cummings—though Creeley in his prudently tight-lipped way rarely yields to the overblown whimsy that mars so much of Cummings's work.

—Brad Leithauser

Unfortunately, one finds few such pleasures in the byways of **Memory Gardens,** where something has gone wrong with the poet's voice. Both its pervasive disillusion and its moments of nostalgic tenderness sound weary. The result, inevitably, is that the banalities which Creeley likes to manipulate finally overwhelm him. A sadly representative stanza is the first in **"Wall"**:

> I've looked at this wall
> for months, bricks
> faded, chipped. . . .

If one takes these lines seriously—as Creeley's accomplishment and reputation insist we do—they must be deemed highly ambitious. They are, after all, so pointedly, so determinedly boring that the reader at once stands notified that the poem's eventual salvaging will require some rather spectacular fireworks. But no fireworks ensue. The final lines are nearly as dull as the initial ones: "Clouds overhead, patch of / shifting blue sky. Faint sun."

Creeley announces in **"Hotel"** that "the tv looks like a faded hailstorm". The reader ransacks the cramped corridors of **"Hotel"** for some sign that this cliché is being inverted or subverted—is being played with in some way. But the reader searches in vain. Such searching would be more fruitfully conducted in the Creeley volumes that have preceded this one—or, one hopes, in those that will follow.

> Brad Leithauser, "The Strictest Line," in The Times Literary Supplement, *No. 4,429, February 19-25, 1988, p. 180.*

Robert Creeley with David L. Elliott   (interview date April 1988)

[*In the following excerpt from an interview conducted in April 1988, Creeley discusses the relationship between his poetry and the rhythms of jazz music.*]

[*Elliott*]: *I'd like to start by talking with you about your re-lationship to jazz. You have sometimes referred to the influences of both jazz and abstract expressionist art on your poetry. Where do those two intersect for you?*

[Creeley]: I think in the sense of improvisation. Also the emphasis on feeling as a lead or a conductor, or a context in which to respond—how to articulate feeling. And then in either case the procedures, or what you did to have this possibility, were usually remarkably sophisticated. It never seemed to me that they were either crude or makeshift. I remember back in Black Mountain days that Stefan Wolpe, for example, felt that both Miles Davis and Charlie Parker were great musicians, and he was wanting to do a concerto or some such thing, for Charlie Parker in particular. He may have even done one. But he was fascinated by their authority as musicians. Very unlike Wynton Marsalis presently. That wasn't what he was talking about. That kind of pleasant popular rapport with the general public is certainly interesting, but it wasn't what he was meaning at all. These people were obviously geniuses.

I've been curious about one of your poems for years. Is "They" about free jazz?

Not specifically. As I look at it quickly, I think of Ed Dorn. There's a poem of his, when he's living in Santa Fe; it's in *The New American Poetry*. There's music in courts up the valley, and he hears this music. It's a sense of everyone has moved on. It's a classic nostalgic feeling of the late '50s, early '60s, that the people of one's heart are out there but the time has moved, the place and time have gone away, and "I wondered what had / happened to the chords." By the time I get through with this poem, its "they" becomes the sense of all other people. You could think of "love, love, love" or something. It's like the Beatles, the '60s. But first the feeling to me is that nostalgia, what had happened to them, what happened to that place where other people were. I'm really responding to Ed's poem. (pp. 45-6)

I've been wondering about your relationship to jazz as it developed from the late '50s into the '60s, because it has always seemed to me that in certain ways the music of Coltrane in the mid-'60s and Coleman and Cecil Taylor and others had some parallels with much of the post WWII poetry you would align yourself with. When you get into the '60s, a rhythmic step beyond Elvin Jones occurs. Elvin Jones reached a point where he really couldn't play with Coltrane any more, or chose not to, and a new drummer took over. It was a freeing of jazz from the rigidity of the bar line in addition to freeing it from the chords. It seems to me, despite the influence of Parker and bebop on people like yourself, that jazz had been in a sense lagging behind what poets like you were doing rhythmically. And it wasn't until the '60s that in certain respects jazz became as free as poetry had been.

I remember Bob Callahan, who's a poet and publisher on the West Coast. One time I had a reading at St. Mark's, and afterwards he came out and said hello, and I realized the fellow with him was Cecil Taylor, who seemed to have liked it. That was fascinating. I found a really useful rapport with musicians of this particular music. It had nothing to do with content. That wasn't what they were hearing, and that's what I found was interesting. Way back, the people whom I'd really be picked up on by—that is, people in the usual audience, the ones who could, quote, "get it," who didn't see any problems, so to speak—were almost without exception musicians. Mathematicians never had any problems, or dancers—anyone who had either to do with duration or ways of measure, any system of measure that didn't have a necessary content that had to be "I love my mother" or "I'm a good person." They didn't want to hear aggressive violent statements necessarily, but they certainly didn't worry about what was being said. They were fascinated by the system of the statement and how it worked as an effective system. I know Sheila Jordan, for instance, came generously to a reading not long ago and said, "It's like jazz," and I was very flattered.

I was fascinated by the agencies of stress and duration. That's what fascinated me with Parker initially, especially the numbers he played on the systems of time. I remember I had to share a place with a guy named Joe Laconi, who was going to the New England Conservatory of Music, and I was going to try to get myself to Harvard, so we shared this place on Tremont Street just around the corner from the Club Savoy and the Hi-Hat, where Serge Chaloff would be playing. Jackie Byard was the house piano for a long, long time.

Anyhow, we were there and Joe played trombone and I was supposed to learn bass and start playing with the group. But I remember playing records for Joe. Think of it—he was functionally a jazz musician with a sophistication in training, but I remember playing to him things like "Chasin' the Bird," and he said, "They can't do that." I said, "What do you mean, they can't do that? You've got two periods and at the same time two figures. What's the problem?" He said, "No, no, that's not jazz; that's not the way to conceive of this activity; the time is wrong; there's no congruence." But to me . . . I mean it wasn't that I was brighter. In fact I was probably less trained, so there was no problem. But something as simple as that was confusing to him. Or when Charlie Parker, for example, would almost reverse time, turn around the beat and play it backwards. That's before you could do that on a tape recorder, so to speak. That was probably the first time I had ever heard of that sound. He would just play incredibly funny numbers on time. He was utterly witful of what he was doing. (pp. 48-50)

In John Wilson's preface to the collection of essays about your work that he edited [Robert Creeley's Life and Work: A Sense of Increment] *he stressed something that I had thought about your poetry too, that of all the modern jazz musicians Monk seems to be the one that is somehow most in affinity with what you're doing rhythmically—that sort of fragmentation and delaying of accents.*

There's a sweet man in Boston, from Belmont, Pancho Savery, who wrote a piece, a very charming parallel between Thelonious Monk and my interests as a poet where he's making kind of a playful comparison—hats, for example, things of that kind.

You mentioned Sheila Jordan. Down Beat *gave a Blindfold Test to her a few years ago. As you probably know, what they usually do is if they have a vocalist as the subject they'll play vocalists for her to identify; if they have a trombonist they'll play trombonists and so on. So they were playing vocalists and she was commenting about people like Ella Fitzgerald. Then they threw her a poem by you. She had never heard you read, and she said, "Oh, that must be Robert Creeley." This was after she'd done the album with Steve Swallow* [Home: Music by Steve Swallow to Poems by Robert Creeley].

That's really great. She's an extremely dear person.

What was your reaction to Swallow's record?

I was dazzled and pleased. When we lived in Bolinas, Steve Swallow and his wife and children were living just at the head of the road we lived on, Terrace Avenue. It was a short road, and it was dramatically called "the edge of the sea." We lived about two-thirds of the way up, and Steve rented a house just at the head of the street. He was good friends with Ebbe Borregaard. His wife was a very interesting, pleasant woman. She was working as a nurse in Point Reyes, particularly involved with the clinic there that was interested to emphasize the communal, and practicality, and the human pleasure of home births—you know, go back to midwifery. At that time the whole imagination of the town was to do it yourself, the communal support. So she was working very much in that interest.

And Steve, whom I knew of but not really well, was described to me as this really incredible jazz bassist who chose to live out there. He's not shy, but he goes about his own business, quiet, and so Ebbe, I think, was the only friend that ever saw much of him. Ebbe later told me it was fascinating talking to him about music and ways you might hear things, try this, try that. I always felt friendly toward him. We would see each other, wave and say hello as neighbors. But I never had the chance to talk to him. So he would pick up jobs as groups came into San Francisco wanting an active bass player, and they'd always get him. And then I guess he decided it was getting too restrictive, because he couldn't just hang out and he never really had enough decision about whom he worked with.

So they determined to go back to the East Coast. They got a place in Connecticut, Guilford, and then I didn't hear from him for a while. He'd gone back working in New York, and then I got out of the blue a letter from him saying he'd done settings, as he put it, or compositions for some ten poems of mine, and there was now a chance to record them and would I mind, would I feel that was agreeable. And I thought, "Wow, terrific!" He was immensely fair. He meticulously set it up, got me enrolled in B.M.I., etc. He handled that whole business with impeccable clarity, so that for the first couple of years of the album's publication you certainly got a substantial feedback from it, payment of royalties on it, and very fairly dealt with. So I was fascinated. We were living in New Mexico when I actually heard the first track taped. And it took me a while to get located. I mean bebop is not Steve's favorite music. To him it would be like New Orleans to someone who was interested in bebop. It's like, "Come on, give us a break, we've heard that stuff until it's coming out our ears." He gets very bored with it as a structure, so he wasn't interested much in that at all.

So when Steve told me about the first recording session, he said it went absolutely great. They did just one take and everybody agreed it was just terrific and that was it. So they went home with this great elation and he gets home and there's a letter from his wife saying, "I'm leaving you." Wouldn't you know it, after a day of recording Robert Creeley you'd have a note like that. It sort of figured. [Laughing]

Then the other record, the Steve Lacy [*Futurities*]—that was very curious how that happened. I'd known of Steve Lacy I think with Cecil Taylor. The record of his I first really heard was the one that has "Easy to Love" on it. It was his first group, mid to late '50s, and he was beginning to play Thelonious Monk.

Then I sort of lost track of him [Lacy]. Occasionally friends would show me records. I knew he was living in France, but some couple of years ago, three or four at least, thanks to an editor of a magazine called *Entre Tien* that did a number on Williams, and a number on Beat writers or Projectivists, I got a reading in Paris, two very excellent readings, one at the Pompidou Center and the other at the museum, so these were very auspicious and active readings, with a great bunch of translators and what not. This editor also had a spot on Radio France called "The Wings of the Albatross." He asked me if I would mind doing an interview. I said terrific. Then low and behold, when I arrived in Paris there was Pierre Joris, a poet who had a magazine called *Six Pack* that did a beautiful sort of elegy issue for Paul Blackburn when he sadly died, and I knew his poetry and we had many friends in common. This other fellow, the editor, wanted to have it be a casual interview, so they'd been talking in the car, sort of *cinema verité* mode, lots of traffic noises, talking. They got talking about my poetry to the extent that they made me wait 20 minutes while they continued their conversation. But anyhow, as we were coming into the city, they said they knew my interest in jazz and therefore they were trying to find some situation or contact locally that could make a decor for that interest, make a context for it. So Pierre said, "Well, we thought of Steve Lacy." I said "Steve Lacy?" And he said, "Yes, he's a friend who lives just around here. He'd be pleased to say hello." I said I'd be pleased to say hello to him.

So up we went and I liked him on the instant and also Irene Aebi. She was great. It turned out Irene was the classic Swiss kid. She had had a great ambition in her youth to get to San Francisco and hang out with the Beats. So she got there, but she got there too late. She connected with Jack Spicer and that whole scene, so she had this remarkable lore. I mean she knew all of my friends from that particular world, and she's an incredibly literate and bright, good natured person. And then Steve—I had always imagined Steve (again, white man's burden) as some really swinging black man. No way, he's a Russian Jew. So I had had the wrong ethnic identity entirely. It turns out he was close friends of Larry Fagin. He knew Anne Waldman. There was a lot of interrelation.

And so he came to the reading that night. He did some improvising back of me that was kind of good-natured patience for the radio interest. The talking was very fine and good. I felt very at home with him. So he came that night and Brion Gysin, who was still alive and who was a friend of his, he came. Julian Beck was there. It was an incredible evening. As we were leaving we talked a bit about keeping in touch, and he said, "Would you mind if I tried a setting of that poem you read, 'The Rhythm'? If you could get me a text of that I'd be fascinated to try to do something." I said, "Yeah!" I was glad there was an interest. I sent him a book or two and I got back home, and again all was quiet, and that's fine.

Then suddenly comes this incredible notebook. I don't know if you've ever seen his final scores. They're incredible. He puts in little pictures and dedicates each piece to a particular artist or a hero of imagination, like Leonardo DaVinci or whomever; it's just very very funny and terrific. So then the whole project got more and more vast. I mean first he was going to do one poem. Now he's done twenty poems and he's imagining a whole musical, and it has two dancers—Douglas Dunn, this extraordinary dancer from New York, and also an African woman, Elsa Wolliaston. So they are the dancers, not opposed but quite different. She's a big hefty woman and he's a very lithe and slender man. So it was a very curious complement. They did the whole dance thing. And then Steve had a backdrop with a Ken Noland, a big Ken Noland triangle. They put it on in France, Italy, Switzerland, and England. I bleakly never got a chance to see it. I was trying to contrive to get over there. It came out in that two record set you probably know. It isn't Steve's responsibility or fault, but I've gotten one copy of the record I think that he sent me and that's about it.

To my ear, Sheila Jordan's voice seemed more compatible with . . .

Irene Aebi did it as a classic like *Sprechstimme.*

Somewhat strident.

Yes, strident and deliberate. But I think that Steve Lacy's take on it is very both legitimate and canny. The thing that really gets to me in Steve Swallow's, in Sheila Jordan's singing, is the extraordinary accuracy of the hearing. I mean the way she sings, for example, "Nowhere one / goes will / one ever / be away / enough from / wherever one was." The way she sings through that and hears the pattern of the sound is just . . . I mean how Steve wrote it. So that's delicious to have someone hear it that specifically. The other record is very different, although that **"Mind's Heart,"** that particular take, is really extraordinary. They certainly got that one. The music on it I enjoy.

I have a lot of respect for Lacy's music. He's a wonderful original.

I do too. He's really tough. He stays put.

I'm interested in what you said about the Steve Swallow song. One thing associated with your way of reading your poetry is the pause at the end of each line. Neither of the Steves nor of the vocalists does that.

Except for Sheila in that one, but mostly not.

Mostly not in others. I was wondering if you felt it was a valid approach, even though you wouldn't score it that way if you were reading it.

Steve Swallow said, after it was all done, that what he wanted was to let the poem, either at the beginning or the end of the activity, set and/or reflect on or qualify—be the sponsoring agency of—what either followed or preceded, so that it would set a thing in mind or a context. So I figured that's the case. No, I can't dictate the terms of how it's read more than the typography permits. If the typography doesn't do it then I don't know what will. "I wondered what had / happened to the chords. / There was a music, // they were following / a pattern. It was / an intention perhaps." [Reading a portion of **"They"**] I can hear that easily. I mean I can hear that as a pattern without any problems. I think probably Steve Swallow heard the rhythmic patterns more sensitively. He just heard my sense of them more particularly than did Steve Lacy. Steve Lacy was using them almost like kind of dramas, using them in a more melodramatic way. He's more interested in the subjects really. I don't think Steve Swallow was. He was, but not really.

The selection of poems reflected that difference.

Exactly.

I thought much of the success of Swallow's record was because of Sheila Jordan. She really seemed to me to get the tone of your poetry well. I also thought that on Swallow's record the melodic intervals and so on seemed very compatible with your poetry. I mean, if he wasn't getting the exact rhythmic feel that you get out of reading, the melodic contours were very compatible.

Absolutely, and the feeling he certainly gets incredibly. He sure knows what I'm talking about, and he knows what's important to me to get located. I wish selfishly I had more contact with him, but I really don't. I mean I know where he is, but he's on the road.

On the subject of the way you read, in an essay by Bob Hass . . .

An old colleague from Buffalo.

He talks about how someone has reported that you just assumed William Carlos Williams read his poetry with pauses at the line breaks, apparently because of how it looked on the page, without having . . .

That's true, because I was pretty displaced when I realized that neither he nor Zukofsky, those two poets who are crucial to me, seems to make a distinct . . . Louis reads right through line endings. I don't think I rarely if ever recall anything where they are crucial as a pivot. Williams was ambivalent, because there's a poem of his that I remember well from an early record published by the National Council of Teachers of English. It had on it, for example, the poem "The Wind Increases": "The harried / earth is swept / . . . / the tulip's bright / tips / sidle and / toss—" etc. etc. In that poem at least, if one takes the reading and puts it in context together with the text, there seems to be a pretty solid congruence of pacing according to the line endings and all, so the whole mode of the poem is explosive and emphatic. You know, "The Wind Increases"! Exclamation point! "The harried / earth is swept / . . . / the tulip's bright / tips / sidle and / toss . . . " I was fascinated by the way the breaks there seem to give it information. And then there's another poem of his, a very simple one: "Liquor and love / when the mind is dull / focus the wit / on a world of form . . . " ["The World Narrowed to a Point"]. In the second verse (there are only three verses, quatrains) there's the phrase, "inflections / ride the quick ear." I was fascinated by the way the word "inflections" and the rhythm of that word play on the base of the rhythm and shift the whole sense of duration. But as I say, I was disappointed that Williams, at least in my understanding, didn't seem to employ the line endings in quite the way I had anticipated.

Despite all the intensive writing on senses of measure and metric, I think the most articulate piece by Williams I know is still that very early one. I want to say the late teens maybe. I can't recall the title of the piece, but it has particularly to do with rhythm, and it's a very clear sense of cadence or how one measures in relation to rhythm and time. Otherwise, there is a letter to Eberhart where he's talking about the base of the prosody, what he's calling the variable foot, and that's sort of interesting. It isn't that his metric is hard. I mean you can feel it and get hold of it quite simply, but trying to spell it out for friends or students is awful because it doesn't have any reality for them. It's all so arbitrary they think.

Hass speculates that Williams's line endings were more for speed and to keep it going.

Yes. Mine are pivots. They give me a way to ground and/or to locate a rhythmic base.

One of the things that is sometimes said about metrical verse, in which you can see an analogy to music, is that the way a phrase goes over from one line to the next is sort of like a musician's phrasing over the bar line.

Yes, right.

In a sense you subvert that.

Yes, I hear you.

The syntax of a sentence goes over the pauses, but the pauses are creating, again, more Monk-like rhythmic units.

It almost becomes a parody of the metronome. I mean the beat is paradoxically more determining than the syntax, and that's what I love, the fact that the rhythm becomes an expressiveness equal to that of the statement.

I remember Robert Duncan . . . I had been reading quite a bit publicly, and I was complaining that I was really getting bored of my own writings. I was having to mouth it over and over. And then he said, "Well, why don't you read for a different action? Read it one night for the thing you are saying, but then read it just for the rhythms. Forget what else. . . . " And it was immensely useful. I realized I could read it a long time just as rhythmic structure, and whether people cried or laughed, I didn't really care or listen.

I'd like to move on to another area. The title of your most recent book is **Memory Gardens,** *but you have passages in earlier poems and essays that are speaking against memory, so to speak, and now there's so much of that in the recent poetry, the last three books really.*

Well, it's age obviously. I think of memory as kind of an accomplishment, a renewal, so that I don't feel in some agony of displacement that I could not have anticipated the prospect or fact of age as it proves to be. It's a new place, so the ways I felt about the world and myself in it in the, say, ages middle or late twenties through forties, are much changed at present. I think that's true. Memory becomes a mind function that is very, if not freaky, then curiously phenomenal in age, for many reasons. I mean the brain function begins to shift or to alter. Memory is not really dependable. It isn't something as dramatically displacing as Alzheimer's, gratefully, but it's a very funny circumstance to realize that memory is now constituting almost an equal time with reality, and that memory is now beginning to prove not a unifying disposition of world but a paradoxically isolating one. Take a song like "I Remember You." That's the classic human address to memory. I remember all the people who put me in this place. It's curious to realize you're remembering things that no one else remembers and you're not sure that you remember them either. It's a very funny human place to be. Nostalgia is very destructive, as with sentimentality. I like those two emotions, but I've never known how to propose them as public value without getting booed off the stage. I mean everyone seemingly has them.

The poets I find now probably as most active company to my own states of mind are Robert Duncan and John Ashbery. Really despite Robert's having died in February, he still stays immensely close to my heart, but also to my ways of thinking. For a long long time in our lives he's been very useful precedence for human life and real body. He was about seven years older, so he would always be just a phase ahead of me, so I could actually ask him what's it like and get an accurate and clear answer. Those poems in the last two books are incredibly articulate about senses of how death is humanly. I think they're incredible poems of that experience.

And the other poet I feel very close to in terms of what's in mind is John Ashbery. Really I must say he's getting to be closer and closer. I mean I had a time when I respected his poetry and even thought I liked it, but I didn't really hang out with it very much. Then I went back to the book that's really crucial for me, his *Three Poems.* I remember Bill Berkson, who was a neighbor in Bolinas, had "The New Spirit." He had the manuscript, much of the book, from John, and I remember he gave me "The New Spirit" to look through, and I thought it was kind of interesting, but I came to like it very much, and then I read the *Self Portrait in a Convex Mirror* that got happily such public approval. That was good natured and easy and bright, and that sort of sent me back to other stuff. I liked very much his recent book, *April Galleons.* He's involved with a work that's very parallel to the one I'm interested in. What does one know of memory until there's an adamant need or occasion for it? Otherwise memory's a bore. I remember, for example, I used *Three Poems* in teaching. I had to realize that here I was with a group of people, age 20-25, to whom that poem was a vast and insistent bore. You know, what does he mean he doesn't know who he is, or he's momently some place but what he presumes to be there is now dissipated? Forget it! How could he even remember where he parked the car? I thought how it's a very peculiar feeling, but this man is making it extremely articulate. But, sadly, for the social needs there's little interest in knowing about that.

I read a review of **Mirrors . . .**

I liked **Mirrors** a lot.

Yes, I do too, but this reviewer almost felt as if you had betrayed your earlier principles. But it seems to me that the point of intersection with your early work, or rather the reason why there is no divergence, is because it's not so much memory per se but attention to the mind in the act of memory.

Yes, thank you, because that would be my defense, that what one's trying to do is to stay in the attention that the mind permits. Tracking the mind is really where it's at, if you can track the mind with the mind, which seems a contradiction in possibility. That's what's interesting to me. I'd go anywhere it takes me, because I don't see where else would I go. I mean there are attitudes and commitments I hope to feel forever.

Penelope, my wife, says, "Watch out for the graveyard shift." The way the whole prospect of statement or address becomes just the sense that everything's going. I think that takes care of itself. I've been working more recently in different guises and ways.

I would like to become almost more clichéd, not in the sense of popular, but in the sense of becoming accessible. I've always loved clichés. I think that's what is interesting in Ashbery's writing. He is the master of cliché—a genius, and very funny. Clichés are endlessly droll and productive and interesting, so I would like to write a poetry that became less singularly invested and more commonly stated. By "common" I mean simply a diction common to usual understanding and use. But again, that's something I can't dictate entirely at all.

I thought at one time two things that I'd love to do would be to write a sequence of poems which were based on what I could remember of interesting poems I have or haven't read in the past, not as jokes but just an attempt to make a poem of my own memory of these virtues of the poem that I . . . I realized for years I misquoted poems of Hart Crane's. My quote was, "Square sheets they saw the marble into there at the island quarry." I looked at the poem ["Island Quarry"] in the last year or so and I realized there are at least two more syllables in that line, at least, and I've compacted it. Or I remember once way back in school days when I was asked to memorize a poem and write it down for the class—you know, that old fashioned scene. I must have been a junior in high school, and I memorized Emily Dickinson's "Inebriate of air am I." So I came in and wrote it down, and I remember the teacher, a pleasant man, said, "How in the name of heaven could you misquote that line?" And I thought, "What have I done?" "Instead of saying, 'Inebriate of air am I,' you say, 'I am an inebriate of air.' " It just shifts the whole modality and the rhythms again. Why is it those rhythms so change when you say it that way? That's fascinating. I couldn't say, "Inebriate of air am I." No one in my world said things like that. I just didn't feel the confidence to say it that way.

And then I'd like to translate. I did once in **Presences**. There's a section of the one on the Dane and the castle. It's approximate translations of material coming from a catalog on Marisol's work that was published in Venezuela, so I would just grab what looked to be melodramatic phrases, like "sunglasses" or something. They're describing the pieces and talking about the effects of the physical appearances of these images, but I frankly don't know Spanish. I don't have any Spanish dictionary and I'm sort of winging it. When I don't know a word I just put something in. It seems immensely irresponsible, but it's a lot of fun. It's a source, a source for doing something.

I came across an interview where you were telling someone (this was back in the early '70s, I guess, maybe just after **In London** *or around that time) that you were going through a period where poetry didn't seem very productive for you.*

Yes, well, I think Charles Bernstein said something yesterday that really had a lot of resonance. He said that he had happily met Carl Rakosi in the last couple weeks. He was amazed that this man now in his 80's was so articulate. It was a very pleasant meeting. In talking he had to realize that Carl Rakosi had a lot of questions about Louis Zukofsky's work, which I think is Charles Bernstein's interest in the same way that it is for me. He thinks a lot of it. He also thinks a lot of Rakosi and Oppen and Reznikoff, the whole cluster. But I think Louis is the most intellectually provocative to him as a writer. But in any case, Carl was saying he found it questionable that Zukofsky had seemingly these intensive ellipses in his writing that were very awkward for the reader because he/she was suddenly stuck with a gap. To which Charles replied (no aggression): "Well, think of it. You're writing and something thus can't be brought together in a way that makes an accessible continuity, and ellipsis is all you've got as an agency." He said he found if one were thinking of ellipses, to him the much more dramatic instance would be the fact that neither Rakosi nor Oppen was able to write for about 20 or 30 years on the basis of political/social preoccupation. Now that is a very big blank for the reader, so that Zukofsky's determination to be able to continue writing, with or without the coherences that Carl might think requisite, is finally more interesting than saying nothing for 20 years. I wonder what Carl says of that. It was a very curious point.

The thing is that if one is not so much committed to writing as though taking a pledge, but if writing is one's delight and means of doing something, should I say, then truly one wants as much provocation of its activity as one can get. I remember it's like Ted Berrigan used to say— "There's no such thing as a bad book." He loved to read, and he was in some respects indifferent to what was given

him to read. He was one of those readers who would literally finish one book, put it down, and pick up another. Anything that had a narrative, anything that went on he would read. I think that's really true. Anything that permitted him to read he would read. And the parallel, for example, is the great story about, I think, Trollope, who would, let's say, finish a novel at eleven in the morning and start another by three in the afternoon. My kind of writer! I mean, I was fascinated to be a writer of that order. I've had respect for people who are intensive journalists, who weren't writing for more than the effect of the day—a day's experience is what could be said. To me in poetry I'm certainly engaged and interested deeply by that which permits me to do this.

I think one factor of aging is that the expectable stimuli during, say, times of one's youth and/or middle age— emotional shifts, states, and so on—no longer become the intensive provocation that they had been, so they don't frankly serve as the, quote, "impulse" quite so either dependably or in fact. Now emotion is more complex, not so much one's to be wary of it. It's more complex in its relationship. One wants to be tied into the communal as much as possible because that's something that tends to dry up. I think children and old folks need community, not just to help them across the street but because it's a situation that they really need. Whereas adults can possibly live in deserts or tops of mountains and otherwise and get on for a while. I think age and childhood really require the species—you know, collectivity—rather than some isolated determinant. I think in one sense the provocations for an art come largely from that. Either that or a comfortable obsession, like Turner's, or Yeats's possibly, or Williams's. Williams was obviously absolutely intent upon getting something together, which was frustrating. It seems to have given him a base for writing right up to the end. Robert had a kind of grand design, as did Pound and Louis have a grand design. Louis had a project for each decade of his life. Remember, he finishes *A,* and then the next project in the '60s is the sequence involving flowers, but then trees would have been the next decade's prospect. He began them and then died in '72 or '73. So I think that would be immensely useful. I think one gets over the drama of one's own life as a singular value. Like I see ourselves more and more as I used to see chickens—terrific, but, you know, expectable.

Getting back to music for a minute . . . During all the phases of your career, the thing that holds everything together for me in terms of my interest is ultimately the rhythm.

Yes—"It is all a rhythm." I sure think so. I was thinking yesterday: in this undergraduate class I teach we've come pretty much to the end of the reading I'd thought to do. There's one more book, but it's a collection of critical articles, basically a vocabulary rather than a content I wanted to consider. So I'm trying to think of things that I can use as material to keep the center, and I was just walking . . . Buffalo, the campus, is very, very awkward. It's a sprawling campus, very decentralized. Because of the weather there are these long walkways between buildings, second floor tunnel-like walkways. And so I walk to the building that is the English department's location through at least three or possibly four other of these buildings, then through this long tunnel which is a communal walkway. I thought of taking a tape recorder and just hearing the rhythm of people saying things as I go along. It's terrific! I don't want to get too cozy or too cutsie about it, but just walking over it could really be interesting to hear what you hear. Try to think is there any point to it. I mean, people talking about lunch or I'll see you later or the world's ending. It's the rhythm, as you say, that's really interesting. (pp. 51-65)

Robert Creeley and David L. Elliott, in an interview in Sagetrieb, *Vol. 10, Nos. 1 & 2, Spring & Fall, 1991, pp. 45-65.*

Marianne Boruch   (review date July-August 1990)

[*In the following excerpt, Boruch comments on the sense of nostalgia manifest in Creeley's* Collected Essays.]

With ten years to go, it is probably presumptuous and uncomfortably romantic to be inviting the slow end of things—a whole century's gradual diminishing—into poems. Even *reading* it there, that certain odd aerial slant on things, might well be invention. Yet taking up Robert Creeley's **Collected Essays** gives permission; it is, in some sweet dark way, taking up a world we're slowly losing. In these essays that span nearly forty years, we meet Williams and Pound again and again, and their electrifying message of the immediate and the ordinary, the poem itself the *made* thing, not at all a matter of mere cleverness, pretty description, or high-handed allusion. With able, unquestioning affection, Creeley bears witness to other **"Heroes/Elders"**—Hart Crane, Zukofsky, Gertrude Stein among them—but it is to Pound and Williams that he returns most reverently, and to what he, as one of its surviving members, calls **"The Company,"** a celebrated, largely male assembly (Denise Levertov the great exception) that includes Charles Olson, Robert Duncan, Allen Ginsberg, Ed Dorn, and others. Less the original thinker, more the village explainer, Creeley nevertheless brings two villages back whole: the homeland that is Williams and Pound (and lurking beyond them, the tough and tender Whitman), and the homeland at Black Mountain, cut with crucial sidetrips into the San Francisco and New York of the fifties and the sixties, a world that for a seemingly jubilant time united many of the arts—poetry, music, and painting.

What survives the not-so-simple nostalgia in these essays—itself poignant and interesting enough—is that sense of "readiness," as Creeley quotes Duncan, demanded of both poem and poet, the power of "the work underhand," as Olson calls it. The sudden, unpredicted demands of the work itself *as it is being written* is that point of vital burning in the poem, not the generalized meaning which only follows the making, nor the initiating experience which might be the handy blur of an answer for the question "what is your poem about?" This readiness, Creeley seems to suggest, is of one sudden piece, a gift of the century's first half to its second: Pound by way of Williams by way of Olson.

Marianne Boruch, "Comment: The Feel of a Century," in The American Poetry Review, *Vol. 19, No. 4, July-August, 1990, p. 17.*

Michael Leddy   (review date Autumn 1990)

[*In the favorable review below, Leddy discusses thematic and structural aspects of* Windows, *calling Creeley "a poet of singular originality."*]

Windows, Robert Creeley's first collection since **Memory Gardens** (1986), presents ninety-one poems in six sections: "The Company," "Window," "Seven," "Dreams," "Eight Plus," and "Helsinki Window." At times it is difficult to account for a poem's presence in one section and not another, for the poems of **Windows** read like fragments of a mind's single ongoing work, and their echoing interrelations make Creeley's short, spare lines rich in suggestion. The poems are often about the windows of the volume's title, as frames for perception and as barriers between inner and outer worlds, here and there, self and other. Other oppositions emerge as Creeley dwells upon past and last things (or "the next thing," as he calls death in one poem); numerous poems, for instance, take up the words *echo* and *edge,* often in relation to a nearly inaccessible past and an ominous future. In the work of a less accomplished poet such repetition would soon become excruciating, but Creeley's acute sense of word and line enables him again and again to make new what we already know, as in the final stanza of **"After Pasternak"**: "Oh dull edge of prospect— / weary window on the past— / whatever is here now / cannot last."

Creeley's understated craft is evident, for instance, in his ironic use of *Oh:* it begins a line whose phrasing at first sounds "poetic," vaguely Shakespearean, but in the context of the three lines that follow, *Oh* turns back into the tired exclamation of contemporary speech, thus deflating the momentary apostrophizing. A similar wit informs the stanza's final line, which both fulfills and violates expectation, its rhyme granting a sense of closure and its shorter length pulling the reader up short—a combination of the expected and unexpected remarkably suggestive of the prospect that the poem concerns, that of death (certain to come, later or sooner). By placing the words *cannot last* on a separate line, moreover, Creeley gives both *now* and *-not* a sounded emphasis that they would lack as parts of a single longer line. Such purposeful choices put to shame the arbitrary lineation of so much contemporary poetry, and they are evident, as one might expect, throughout the volume.

Evident too, unexpectedly so, is an interest in Robert Frost, a poet not typically associated with Creeley. Frost's name does not appear in the index to Creeley's **Collected Essays** (1989); in *Robert Creeley: The Poet's Workshop* (1984) [edited by Carroll Terrell] Creeley makes one reference to Frost, calling his disparagement of free verse "relatively dumb." Elsewhere in that volume a student recalls Creeley admitting to an early dislike of Frost and playing a tape of Frost to a class—a sign, perhaps, of "greater tolerance." **Windows** reveals more than tolerance. In **"After Frost"** and **"What"** Creeley alludes to "The Road Not

Taken," considering in the latter the possibility of "walking off / by oneself down // that path in the / classic woods" and taking time "to think // of it all again." He quotes "Stopping by Woods on a Snowy Evening" and makes unmistakable references to "Desert Places": "Flakes falling / out window make / no place, no place— / no faces, traces" (**"Sparks Street Echo"**), "this loneliness of human spaces" (**"Echoes"**). In a more general way, poems in which Creeley observes trees from a window recall Frost's "Tree at My Window." Such affinities, though initially surprising, may not be so surprising after all: Frost and Creeley, for all their formal dissimilarity, are both resolute explorers of what Frost in "Tree at My Window" calls "inner weather." **Windows** records the recent explorations of a poet of singular originality.

> *Michael Leddy, in a review of "Windows," in* World Literature Today, *Vol. 64, No. 4, Autumn, 1990, p. 640.*

Carol Muske Dukes   (review date 23 June 1991)

[*In the following favorable review of* Selected Poems, *Dukes characterizes Creeley as a uniquely American poet.*]

In the brief but moving introduction to his **Selected Poems,** Robert Creeley notes that poet-critic Robert Graves once characterized him as a "domestic poet." This cheerful condescension of Graves' hit an unwitting backhanded critical bull's eye. As Creeley says, "With Robert Duncan I am committed to the hearth and love the echoes of that word. The fire is the center."

Fire is indeed the center of this collection of poems, and the conflagrations are domestic and wild. Selected by Creeley from his 13 previous volumes, the homeyness here has a back-bedroom, eccentric flavor and his epigrammatic, refrigerator-note style recalls no one so much as William Carlos Williams, that other anarchistic, domestic genius, whose imprimatur Creeley early received. Yet the paradox in these poems, as Creeley himself points out, is that he has "moved endlessly" within his imagination and only now can "find a place to return to."

Somehow this alchemical blend of transience and steadfastness produces the syllable-by-syllable blaze for which Creeley is so famous.

> I didn't go
> anywhere and
> I haven't
>   come back!
>
>   **"Eight Plus"**

Or, as in his most famous, hipster-manifesto 1950s poem about smoking dope and reordering aesthetic priorities, **"A Wicker Basket,"** we witness firsthand Creeley staking out his freaky home territory:

>   . . . and while certainly
> they are laughing at me, and
>   all around is racket
> of these cats not making it,
>   I make it
> in my wicker basket.
>
>   **"A Wicker Basket"**

Notice that the poem is called **"A Wicker Basket"** not *"The* Wicker Basket." The choice of article is not random. (Diction and punctuation choices in Creeley, as in all poetry, are profoundly significant, but for him the visual, topographical appearance of the poem on the page approximates Gertrude's Stein's syntax-paintings or Cézanne's obsession for every inch of the canvas, what Stein called "acute particularity.")

So he says it is *one* wicker basket, just one, maybe even *mine*: not the collective, monolithic, poetified "the." This is Creeley's religion here; it is the job of the poet to be specific, to fracture (or discover anew) "context," to avoid easy conclusions, familiar rhetoric. He tries to say exactly what he means, which produces a simplicity that is gnarled, inquiring, complex.

As with all genius, there can be, finally, no imitation: Nobody writes like Creeley, few have gone so stubbornly against the grain and left such fiery graffiti ("Creeley was here") within it.

—*Carol Muske Dukes*

The "cats not making it" are as much the amorous feline fence-sitting contingent as certain other poets, critics—the whole yowling Establishment of over-sayers, whom Creeley has sent up ever since he slipped a pea under the royal mattress of American poetry:

> One and
> one, two,
> three.
>
>   **"A Piece"**

I remember a teacher of mine considering this poem in a graduate school workshop at San Francisco State in 1970: What was it? How did it work? Was it a sham? No, it turned out, it was an articulation of a universal rhythm, it was cryptic, nutty but precise. It worked.

So this cat has been making it, on his own terms, for some time—it is hard to fathom this *enfant terrible* nearing 70! Never mind that some critics find that he is occasionally hyper-oblique, self-consciously cute, and, for all his brevity, overwrought. (Critic John Simon once said, "There are two things to be said about Creeley's poems: They are short; they are not short enough.")

Still, it is hard to imagine any reader, confronted with this body of nearly a life's work, *not* succumbing to the enchantment of these crooked litanies. Creeley's notorious music, his odd and meditative "patterning," grows, haunts, is pure inspiration as the poems accumulate. There is also the realization, turning pages, that Creeley was and is such an originator, a source of casual and startling innovation, influencing schools of imitators. Yet, as with all genius, there can be, finally, no imitation: Nobody writes like Creeley, few have gone so stubbornly against the grain and left such fiery graffiti ("Creeley was here") within it.

That he was himself (like all serious-minded poets) an imitator is evident here. Yet he quickly transformed what he took in. His roots in "projectivist verse," as practiced by his mentor, Charles Olson, and the Black Mountain school of poets, along with his absorption of the founder-poetics of Ezra Pound and William Carlos Williams, set him on a course of nonconformity, with a powerful reverence for the integrity of the poem itself. ("I love it that these words, 'made solely of air' as Williams said, have no owner finally to determine them.")

> It is all a rhythm,
> from the shutting
> door, to the window
> opening,
>
> the seasons, the sun's
> light, the moon,
> the oceans, the
> growing of things,
>
> the mind in men
> personal, recurring
> in them again,
> thinking the end
>
> is not the end, the
> time returning,
> themselves dead but
> someone else coming.
>
>   **"The Rhythm"**

Notice that it is the **"The Rhythm,"** the great poem that continues to live, as "men" come and go. Even our sense of immortality is the product of this rhythm—our sense of "return." Such gentle irony in the service of such formidable speculation is his signature.

Perhaps because of this underlying vision, his poems have changed stylistically very little from early to more recent books. **"The Charm"** and **"For Love"** present the same jazzy, deadpan, Catullian voice, marble-cake phrasing and zigzag shifts in tone that mark the more "mature" poems of *Memory Gardens* and *Windows.*

> Thinking to alter all
> I looked first to myself,
> but I have learned the
>   foolishness
> that wants an altered form.
>
>   **"Mazatlán Sea"**

With a kind of effortless hesitancy, a step and then another step, he's somehow airborne. When you think he's cold, he turns hot suddenly; where you expect flippancy, you get sudden, pure lyricism:

> Now then in wonder at evening, at
> the last small entrance of night,
> my mother calls it, and I
> call it *my father.*
>
> With angry face, with no
> rights, with impetuosity and
> sterile vision—and a great
> wind we ride.

"A Gift of Great Value"

Words, he says, depend on us for their very existence, "fail as our usage derides or excludes them." What a notion: one that contemporary linguistics has turned round on itself and made reductionist—unlimited language, limited author. Creeley's version of this theory is generous, pro-human—words depend on us for life, depend on us for honor equal to the triumphant experience of utterance.

In his poems, the poet is an active medium, moving in the light of that wild hearth-fire, allowing language to pass through the body like an invoked spirit.

> Locate I
> *love you* some—
> where in
> teeth and
> eyes, bite
> it but
> take care not
> to hurt, you
> want so
>
> much so
> little. Words
> say everything.
>
>   **"The Language"**

We live in a time when the accolade "poet" is bandied about unmercifully. All the stand-up artists, performance hacks, *faux-naïfs* (in particular celebrities ego-dumping into microphones and calling it poetry), all the "cats not making it" could do worse than attend to (that is to say, *read*) the tough, uncompromising, odd-elegant and wise poetry of Robert Creeley. For he is, perhaps, what they aspire to be: a quintessentially *American* poet, democratic in his idiom, funny and street-wise in his diction and tone, a maverick of passion and sagacity.

> In testament
> to a willingness
>
> to *live,* I,
> Robert Creeley,
>
> being of sound body
> and mind, admit
>
> to other preoccupations—
> with the future, with
>
> the past. But now—
> *but now* the wonder of life is
>
> that *it is* at all.
>
>   **"Later"**

The wonder of this poet is that he is, at all. Outrageous, uncontainable, domestic but never domesticated, standing by *and* just passing through, tending that hip Promethean fire, he's the best and only Creeley there is.

> *Carol Muske Dukes, "Straight from the Hearth," in* Los Angeles Times Book Review, *June 23, 1991, p. 8.*

FURTHER READING

Bibliography

Fox, Willard, III. "Robert Creeley." In his *Robert Creeley, Edward Dorn, and Robert Duncan: A Reference Guide.* Boston: G. K. Hall, 1989, 170 p.

Catalogs works by and about Creeley.

Criticism

Ashley, Paul. Review of *Memory Gardens,* by Robert Creeley. *Another Chicago Magazine* 17 (1987): 191-97.

Explores the theme of memory in Creeley's *Memory Gardens.*

Butterick, George F. "Robert Creeley and the Tradition." *Sagetrieb* 1, No. 3 (Winter 1982): 119-34.

Discusses the significance of Creeley's occasional use of traditional meter and poetic forms.

Ford, Arthur L. *Robert Creeley.* Boston: Twayne Publishers, 1978, 159 p.

Biographical and critical survey of Creeley's life and career.

Jarman, Mark. "The Curse of Discursiveness." *The Hudson Review* XLV, No. 1 (Spring 1992): 158-66.

Review of *Selected Poems* and other poetry collections. Jarman concludes that Creeley's earlier poetry is less indulgent and self-involved than his later work.

Kaufman, Robert F. "The Poetry of Robert Creeley." *Thoth* 11, No. 2 (Winter 1971): 28-36.

Analyzes the philosophical basis of Creeley's poetry in *For Love, Words,* and *Pieces.*

Keller, Lynn. "Lessons from William Carlos Williams: Robert Creeley's Early Poetry." *Modern Language Quarterly* 43, No. 4 (December 1982): 369-94.

Explores the influence of the work of William Carlos Williams on the poetry of Creeley.

Kirby, David. "Home and Hut." *The New York Times Book Review* (3 November 1991): 14.

Compares Creeley's 1991 *Selected Poems* to Diane Ackerman's recent poetry collection *Jaguar of Sweet Laughter.*

McGuire, Jerry. "No Boundaries: Robert Creeley as Post-Modern Man." *Sagetrieb* 1, No. 3 (Winter 1982): 97-118.

Examines the theoretical implications of Creeley's poetics for poststructuralist critics.

Mesch, Harold. "Robert Creeley's Epistemopathic Path." *Sagetrieb* 1, No. 3 (Winter 1982): 57-85.

Considers epistemological aspects of Creeley's poetry.

Paul, Sherman. "Robert Creeley." In his *The Lost America of Love: Rereading Robert Creeley, Edward Dorn, and Robert Duncan,* pp. 1-74. Baton Rouge: Louisiana State University Press, 1981.

Analyzes thematic and structural elements of Creeley's poetry.

Review of *Windows,* by Robert Creeley. *Publishers Weekly* 237, No. 15 (13 April 1990): 59.

Positive assessment of *Windows.*

Smith, Leverett T., Jr. "Robert Creeley: 'A So-Called Larger View.' " *Sagetrieb* 7, No. 2 (Fall 1988): 53-68.

Examines critical perspectives on Creeley's work.

Terrell, Carroll, ed. *Robert Creeley: The Poet's Workshop.* Orono, Maine: The National Poetry Foundation, 1984, 383 p.

Collection of essays that explores various aspects of Creeley's life and career. A bibliography of Creeley's work is included.

Wagner, Linda Welshimer. "The Poet as Novelist: Creeley's Novel." *Critique* VII, No. 1 (Spring 1964): 119-22.

Favorable review of Creeley's first novel *The Island.*

Interviews

Creeley, Robert, and Sheppard, Robert. "Stories: Being an Information; An Interview." *Sagetrieb* 1, No. 3 (Winter 1982): 35-56.

Interview in which Creeley describes his friendships with other American poets and his experiences as a teacher.

Keller, Emily. "An Interview by Emily Keller." *The American Poetry Review* 12, No. 3 (May-June 1983): 24-8.

Creeley discusses the autobiographical elements in his work, his philosophy of poetry, and the contemporary poetry scene.

Spanos, William V. "Talking with Robert Creeley." *boundary 2* VI & VII, Nos. 3 & 1 (Spring-Fall 1978): 11-74.

Creeley presents his views on the American poetic tradition and the relationship between his "open poetry" and the anti-metaphysical philosophy of Martin Heidegger.

Additional coverage of Creeley's life and career is contained in the following sources published by Gale Research: *Contemporary Authors,* Vols. 1-4, rev. ed.; *Contemporary Authors Autobiography Series,* Vol. 10; *Contemporary Authors New Revision Series,* Vol. 23; *Contemporary Literary Criticism,* Vols. 1, 2, 4, 8, 11, 15, 36; *Dictionary of Literary Biography,* Vols. 5, 16; and *Major 20th-Century Writers.*

Joy Kogawa

1935-

(Full name Joy Nozomi Kogawa) Canadian poet and novelist.

The following entry provides an overview of Kogawa's career through 1992.

INTRODUCTION

Best known for *Obasan*, a semi-autobiographical novel about the internment of Japanese Canadians during World War II, Kogawa addresses issues of racial and cultural diversity, persecution, and self-identity in her fiction and poetry. Critics have praised her concise, poetic language and, as Edward M. White has noted, her "magical ability to convey suffering and privation, inhumanity and racial prejudice, without losing in any way joy in life and in the poetic imagination."

Kogawa was born in Vancouver, British Columbia, and like the protagonist of *Obasan*, underwent internment in the Canadian interior during World War II. She published her first book of poetry, *The Splintered Moon*, in 1967 and subsequent collections, *A Choice of Dreams* and *Jericho Road*, in 1974 and 1977 respectively. From 1974 to 1976 she worked as a staff writer in the Office of the Prime Minister and was a writer in residence for one year at the University of Ottawa in 1978. Following the 1981 publication of *Obasan*, the first novel in the history of Canadian fiction to deal with the internment of Japanese Canadians, Kogawa garnered widespread critical attention, receiving the *Books in Canada* First Novel Award and the Canadian Authors' Association Book of the Year Award. She has since written a children's version of *Obasan* entitled *Naomi's Road*, the poetry collection *Woman in the Woods*, and the novel *Itsuka*.

Although Kogawa's poetry has received favorable reviews, most critics have focused on her novels, *Obasan* and *Itsuka*, which concern the development of a third-generation Japanese-Canadian named Naomi Nakane. *Obasan* delineates the effects of internment on Naomi, her family, and the Japanese-Canadian community, and describes the efforts of Japanese Canadians to secure compensation from the Canadian government. In addition to coming to terms with her painful memories of the camps and the death of her mother, Naomi must also confront her estrangement from mainstream Canadian society, her family, and traditional Japanese culture. Critics have praised Kogawa's rendering of the contrasts between Western and Japanese culture as well as the conflicts among the different generations of Japanese immigrants—the Issei, those born in Japan, and the Nisei, those born in Canada—as each group responds differently to the problems posed by living in Western society. Kogawa communicates such conflicts, which are closely tied to the protagonist's search for a female role model, through a

comparison of her aunts: Obasan, an Issei, and Aunt Emily, a Nisei. Obasan, who raised Naomi, confronts internment and its memories through silence and repression, believing that the ideal Japanese woman is quiet, accepting, and subservient. Emily, a political activist, responds to the injustices she suffered with letters, articles, and speeches in an attempt to obtain reparations for internment victims. Naomi does not consider either aunt's example fulfilling and only achieves a sense of wholeness after developing a perspective that reconciles their opposing outlooks.

Itsuka, a continuation of Naomi's story, deals with her involvement in an activist movement that hopes to attain redress for the victims of internment. Although commentators have criticized the novel for lacking the poetic language of *Obasan*, Janice Kulyk Keefer has argued that with *Itsuka*, Kogawa has moved "into a different kind of imaginative territory, exposing the politics of a multiculturalism that has in many ways abetted rather than eradicated the racism that she presents as an institutionalized aspect of Canadian life."

164

PRINCIPAL WORKS

The Splintered Moon   (poetry)   1967
A Choice of Dreams   (poetry)   1974
Jericho Road   (poetry)   1977
Obasan   (novel)   1981
Woman in the Woods   (poetry)   1985
Naomi's Road   (juvenilia)   1986
Itsuka   (novel)   1992

CRITICISM

Suanne Kelman   (review date February 1982)

[*In the following review, Kelman positively assesses* Obasan, *praising Kogawa's use of language and her ability to impart an understanding of experience in a manner that transcends autobiography and journalism.*]

Joy Kogawa's *Obasan* is a novel that seems to hover on the edge of pure autobiography. The effect is the result of finely honed craft. Ms. Kogawa has chosen to turn the story of Canada's interment of its own Japanese citizens into fiction. She could simply have drawn from her own life and from the actual letters and documents that she uses in the book. But her novel gives the experience of persecution a shape that imposes understanding where factual reporting would fail.

Obasan begins elusively. The narrator, Naomi Nakane, is a colourless, rather passive school teacher, apparently unable to communicate with anyone, even her immediate family. That family, Uncle and his wife, the title's Obasan, lives in almost total silence. They speak in a mixture of Japanese and English, mostly in two or three word sentences. Much of their speech is evasive, sliding away from questions.

The opening chapters are therefore reminiscent of other Japanese work, fiction as well as film. Ms. Kogawa writes in nuance—little is stated directly, but her characters are not cryptic by nature or choice. Naomi Nakane remembers a richer, more open childhood, warmed by her perfect attachment to her mother. The family's life had a Japanese flavour, not simply in its details, but in a pervasive reticence and respect for the individual's private world. But the context is obviously Canadian.

The family has become more foreign with time. It has also been destroyed.

The source of the destruction is of course the dispersal of the family during World War II. Uncle, Obasan and the children are exiled to a raw frontier town. Later, like so many others, they end up hacking sugar beets out of the earth on the Prairies. Naomi's father is shipped to a forced labour camp. Her beloved mother is trapped by a visit home to Japan.

This story is told from a multiple perspective. Naomi has her childhood memories, the half-responses of her aunt and uncle, and a sea of documents, letters and journals passed on by her militant Aunt Emily. This last material is clearly genuine; the quality of writing is very obviously inferior to Ms. Kogawa's own style.

But *Obasan* is much more than a political tract. The novel's greatest strength is hidden in what initially seems a weakness. The attenuation of the characters in the early chapters—their silence, evasiveness, passivity—communicates the final result of their purposeless suffering. The reader must share the growth of the characters themselves, as they try to recover feeling after years of numbing blows.

What *Obasan* makes concrete is the most horrible of all human paradoxes. Injustice provokes more guilt in its victims than in its perpetrators. Being punished makes innocent people feel ashamed. Like the survivors of concentration camps, or like battered children, *Obasan*'s characters are paralyzed by their humiliating inability to protect themselves and those they love.

The role of the family in *Obasan* comes eerily close to some of Jacobo Timerman's stories about Argentine prisons. The characters can no longer meet one another's eyes, because of the shame of the knowledge of suffering. Their defence is to try to spare one another. ("For the sake of the children" is an echoing refrain in the novel.) It becomes a paralyzing force in the family's life, since so much of that life is trapped in painful secrets. I think that Ms. Kogawa makes one major error here, in giving the family a final, special secret of hair-raising drama. She did not have to reach so far—the common story was good enough.

But *Obasan* can afford a few errors. It is not dependent on the tact and probability of its plot. The language alone is almost a sufficient reward. Joy Kogawa writes in a wholly unique voice that makes the novel into an extended poem:

> I notice these days, from time to time, how the present disappears in her mind. The past hungers for her. Feasts on her. And when its feasting is complete? She will dance and angle in the dark, like small insect bones, a fearful calligraphy—a dry reminder that once there was life flitting about in the weather.

Beyond that, *Obasan* offers an evocation of a vanished life—the sweet, false pre-War security, the misery and confusion of the war years. Kogawa establishes not only that the Canadian government pursued a course based not on security needs, but on greed and racism, but also that it is not possible for the victims to forgive and forget. With Naomi Nakane, the reader is forced to mourn the fragile beauty of a community and its delicate web of attachments, now never to be restored. (pp. 39-40)

Suanne Kelman, "Impossible to Forgive," in The Canadian Forum, *Vol. LXI, No. 715, February, 1982, pp. 39-40.*

Edward M. White   (review date 11 July 1982)

[*White is an American educator and critic. In the following review, he praises Kogawa's depictions of suffering, injustice, and survival within the context of specific historical events in* Obasan.]

"Nisei," we learn from this extraordinary first novel [*Obasan*], means "second generation," embracing the children of the Canadian and American first-generation immigrants from Japan. Everyone by now knows that the internment and theft of property suffered by Americans of Japanese descent during World War II represents a national disgrace second only to the massacres of Native Americans. It is a small comfort to realize that Canadian Nisei were treated at least as badly as the Americans, but the distance created by the Canadian setting perhaps will help make the pain this novel evokes more bearable for U.S. readers.

Joy Kogawa, a Canadian teacher and poet, has drawn upon her own experience as a displaced Canadian Nisei to write a unified story of a battered and broken family that endures under the worst conditions. The systematic outrages inflicted by the Canadian government on its own citizens echo the Nazi treatment of the Jews; the novel, in turn, shares some of the tone of *The Diary of Anne Frank* in its purity of vision under the stress of social outrage. This novel too has a magical ability to convey suffering and privation, inhumanity and racial prejudice, without losing in any way joy in life and in the poetic imagination.

The narrator is Naomi Nakane, now a 36-year-old teacher: "Marital status: Old maid. Health: Fine, I suppose. . . . Personality: Tense. Is that past or present tense? It's perpetual tense." Like her author, Naomi was torn at the age of 5 from a warm and loving family inside a secure Japanese-Canadian culture in Vancouver, British Columbia. Her mother is stranded in Japan, finally to encounter an atomic bomb, and her physician father's fragile health fails before the hardships of dispersal and brutal labor.

Naomi and her resentful brother Stephen (a musical prodigy) depend on their aunt, "Obasan," whose silence and strength form the solid center of the novel. The death of their uncle draws the family together, and draws Naomi's past into perspective as she reviews documents that expand her imperfect understanding of what has happened to her and her family. These documents include not only the diaries and notes collected by her irrepressible Aunt Emily, but a series of chilling nonfictional official papers and newspaper accounts.

Part of the strength of this novel is in its historical particularity, but another part is in its larger resonance: This is also an account of human barbarity wherever it occurs. This motif is made explicit early on in a description of Obasan:

> Squatting here with the putty knife in her hand, she is every old woman in every hamlet in the world. You see her on a street corner in southern France, in a black dress and black stockings. Or bent over stone steps in a Mexican mountain village. Everywhere the old woman stands as the true and rightful owner of the earth. She is the bearer of keys to unknown doorways and to a network of astonishing tunnels. She is the possessor of life's infinite personal details.

"Now old," Obasan repeats; "everything old." The rhythms of the prose, when under extreme pressure, expand into Biblical patterns:

> We are leaving the B.C. coast—rain, cloud, mist—an air overladen with weeping. Behind us lies a salty sea within which swim our drowning specks of memory—our small waterlogged eulogies. We are going down to the middle of the earth with pick-axe-eyes, tunneling by train to the Interior, carried along by the momentum of the expulsion into the waiting wilderness. . . . We are the silences that speak from stone. We are the despised rendered voiceless, stripped of car, radio, camera and every means of communication, a trainload of eyes covered with mud and spittle. We are the man in the Gospel of John, born into the world for the sake of the light.

The poetry remains quiet behind the prose, even as the universal theme radiates from the strong and driving plot. The story keeps unfolding, until its full sadness is complete. The next-to-last word is Nakane's:

> This body of grief is not fit for human habitation. Let there be flesh. The song of mourning is not a lifelong song. . . . The wild roses and the tiny wild flowers grow along the trickling stream. The perfume in the air is sweet and faint. If I hold my head a certain way, I can smell them from where I am.

The last word in the book is from the memorandum sent by the Co-operative Committee on Japanese Canadians to the House and the Senate of Canada in April, 1946. It points out that the orders-in-council for the deportation of Canadians of Japanese racial origin are "wrong and indefensible" and "are an adoption of the methods of Nazism." This protest was ignored by the government and by the world at large.

Kogawa's novel must be heard and admired; the art itself can claim the real last word, exposing the viciousness of the racist horror, embodying the beauty that somehow, wonderfully, survives.

> *Edward M. White, "The Silences That Speak from Stone," in* Los Angeles Times Book Review, *July 11, 1982, p. 3.*

Frank Manley   (review date May 1986)

[*Manley is an American educator and critic. In the following review, he offers a positive assessment of Kogawa's fourth poetry collection,* Woman in the Woods.]

Despite the imagery suggested by the title of [*Woman in the Woods*], the fourth book of poetry from Joy Kogawa, the poet's vision is obscured neither by forest nor trees: the insight found here is enlightening. Ostensibly about the "plight (and flight) of a woman and child," *Woman in the Woods* encompasses many aspects of life—it is poetry that reaches out.

The book begins with an axiom in **"Bird Song"**—"Flung from our nests / in the late spring / and ordered to fly / or die we are / weaned to the air"—and ends neatly with a hymn to faith in **"Water Song"**:

> who once on singing
> water walked
> on water still
> walks he
> in atmosphere
> so dense in miracle
> we here find fins
> for diving
> for flying

The poetry contained by these two poems is the elliptical journey of Kogawa's dramatic persona through experiences ranging from the epic to the whimsical.

Perhaps the most engaging virtue of this collection is the passion for life that Kogawa has, especially when much in the world offends the poet's sensibility. Take, for example, her satire in **"Last Day"**—"That day . . . in the elevator / no-one tried to be unusually friendly"—or in **"Experiment,"** where a researcher tortures animals to gain respectability: "He publishes his article / in *Psychology Today* / and makes an addition / to his curriculum vitae." In **"Give Us This Day"** (perhaps the best poem here) Kogawa finds in Shadrach—an opponent of Nebuchadnezzar, in the *Book of Daniel*—a symbol for faith in an age of alienation: "Shadrach's angel will find us / in the heart's fiery places." This motif is prominent in other poems such as **"Here We are a Point of Sanity"**: "Oh leap down leap down / to the thirst / to the flame." Kogawa often uses fire and colour (green) to suggest regeneration and hope.

Central to Kogawa's skill is her ability to say volumes with only a few words (a refreshing alternative to the verbosity of many of her contemporaries). In **"One Night's Standing,"** the lover departs "leaving her to journey / with one sense less / towards senselessness." Kogawa's careful diction binds the images together, giving each poem a reflexive mystique that encourages multiple readings. (pp. 43-4)

> *Frank Manley, in a review of "Woman in the Woods," in* Books in Canada, *Vol. 15, No. 4, May, 1986, pp. 43-4.*

Erika Gottlieb   (essay date Summer 1986)

[*Gottlieb received her Ph.D. in English literature at McGill University. Her books,* Lost Angels of a Ruined Paradise (Sunonis, 1981) *and* The Orwell Conundrum (Carleton University Press, 1992) *were awarded Publication Grants by the Canadian Federation for the Humanities. Her newest book,* Dystopia East and West, *is to be published by McGill-Queen's University Press. Her essays on British and Canadian literature have appeared in periodicals in Canada, the United States, Italy, Hungary, and India. In the following essay, she analyzes the characterization, imagery, language, and structure of* Obasan.]

Joy Kogawa's **Obasan** is an extremely quiet, slow moving book that yields its secret of exceptional power and intensity only gradually. It takes time to pick up the rich reverberations beneath the calm, controlled narrative voice, as we become aware that in returning to her past, the narrator, Naomi, undertakes a spiritual journey; she is urged by an inner need to find answers to a series of compelling questions: Is there a meaning to the persecution and suffering endured by the Japanese Canadians during and after World War II? Can the victim overcome the paralyzing effect of personal hurt and humiliation? Can a human being ever come to terms with the experience of evil on the psychological, the political, the universal level?

The novel sets up these multi-dimensional questions as puzzles arranged in a concentric pattern—container hidden within container within container—creating a sense of mystery and tension. The deliberate visibility of the concentric structure compels the reader to search for a central meaning at the core of the multi-layered texture of Naomi's narrative. To enter the psychological, political, and universal dimensions of Naomi's dilemma, the novel provides three openings, three distinct, yet interrelated landscapes. It is the first and shortest opening, the motto of the book, which introduces the widest, the universal dimension.

> To him that overcometh
> will I give to eat
> of the hidden manna
> and will give him
> a white stone
> and in the stone
> a new name written . . .

A quotation from the Book of Revelation, the motto introduces the cosmic-mythical symbols of renewal the narrator is in search of. Only by overcoming the trial of being lost in the desert of fear and hatred, only by overcoming the terrors of the Apocalypse, will one be led to the Tree of Life, to the hidden manna of spiritual nourishment.

The second opening is another piece of preliminary material, a description of the narrator's soul as a wasteland.

> There is a silence that cannot speak.
>
> There is a silence that will not speak.
>
> Beneath the grass the speaking dreams and beneath the dreams is a sensate sea. The speech that frees comes from the amniotic deep. To attend its voice, I can hear it say, is to embrace its absence. But I fail the task. The word is stone. I admit it.
>
> I hate the stillness. I hate the stone. I hate the sealed vault with its cold icon. I hate staring into the night, the questions thinning into space. The sky swallowing the echoes.
>
> Unless the stone bursts with telling, unless the seed flowers with speech, there is in my life no living word. The sound I hear is only sound. White sound. Words, when they fall, are pock marks on the earth. They are hailstones seeking an underground stream.
>
> If I could follow the stream down and down to the hidden voice, would I come at last to the

freeing word? I ask the night sky but the silence is steadfast. There is no reply.

The stillness of the landscape is the stillness of hopelessness, despair, the dead stillness of stone. To "overcome" her personal trial, Naomi must see the stone of death turn into the "white stone" with the "new name" on it. Before this could happen, however, she should trace the "hidden voice" to the "underground stream." The union between the stone and the living waters will produce the magic of life, and the seed shall flower with speech.

Not before the cosmic and internal landscapes reveal these symbolic-emotional signposts are we ready to enter the "real" Canadian landscape in the first chapter (the third opening). Here it becomes quickly apparent that elements of the two symbolic landscapes—stone, underground stream, seeds, flowers, and trees—will also figure in the realistic presentation of this specific scene carefully identified in time and space. Thus the natural setting in the first chapter is more than background: it represents the stillness and the tension in the cosmos and in the soul:

> 9.05 p.m. August 9, 1972.
>
> The coulee is so still right now that if a match were to be lit, the flame would not waver. The tall grasses stand without quivering, the tops flow this way and that. The whole dark sky is bright with stars and only the new moon moves . . .

The human characters in this landscape are Naomi, our Nisei, second generation Japanese Canadian narrator, and her old Uncle Isamu who have been making an annual pilgrimage to this site every August for the past eighteen years. In the first of many flashbacks the narrator returns to August 1954, the time of their first visit, and we begin to recognize the first sign of a mystery, and within it an intricate puzzle: Uncle's determination to observe this ritual is equal to his desire to keep its reason a secret. Here the question Naomi had been consumed by all her life takes a fairly simple form: "Why do we come here every year?" she asks. Not until the end of the novel will she find the answer.

Each of the opening landscapes contains a riddle: in the first, the hidden manna; in the second, the hidden voice; in the third, the hidden reason for the pilgrimages. To triumph over the stillness of death, we must find what is hidden, kept in secret. Adding to this suspense is our recognition that the relationship between the three landscapes is itself a riddle: each contains and is contained within the other. In this conundrum of container within container within container, the author also offers us a key to approach the puzzle at the heart of Naomi's quest for liberation and renewal. There will be only one solution to the three riddles, three questions. As if by magic, it will be the same answer that will resolve Naomi's dilemma in its personal, political, and universal dimensions.

There is suspense as we become immersed in **Obasan**'s allegorical language. A consistent nature symbolism emerges that challenges us to ask: What is the precise connection between the evocative language of the landscape and the unfolding of the human drama? The narrative framework will help answer the question: When in the second chapter Naomi learns about Uncle's death, she returns to comfort her Aunt Obasan and to prepare for the funeral. The rest of the novel takes shape as a mourner's meditation during a wake, a framework well suited to the novel's central metaphor of spiritual journey and its traditional nature symbolism. [In a footnote, Gottlieb refers to "Death and Disposal of the Dead (Japanese)," *Encyclopedia of Religion and Ethics,* Volume IV (1913) and states: "It is also significant for the framework of the narrative that all of Naomi's recollections (that is, the whole novel, except for the 'Prelude' of the first chapter) take place in the interval between Uncle's death and funeral, and in the ancient Buddhist tradition this 'interval between the encoffinment and the funeral is the most important period of the watching by the dead [a period now] generally passed in silence.' That Naomi's grappling with her accumulated silence takes place in the framework of a wake opens up another interesting dimension of her struggle: her trial is to take a journey through silence, in silence, ultimately to liberate herself from silence."] Waiting for Uncle's funeral, Naomi recollects her memories about all the dead in her past. Obasan and Uncle had been the mainstay of Naomi's traumatic childhood, since both she and her brother had been torn from their parents during the times of racist discrimination against Japanese Canadians between 1942 and 1951. By the end of her meditation about her family's tragic history, Naomi achieves a clarity and perception that comes from "emotion recollected in tranquillity" and she is finally allowed to hear the secret that had been withheld from her. With Obasan's permission, the Anglican clergyman, Sensei, who arrived to conduct the funeral, decides to read aloud the mysterious Japanese document, a letter on blue rice paper that had been in Obasan's possession for the past eighteen years. From the letter Naomi learns about her mother's suffering and death in Japan as a result of the atomic bomb dropped on Nagasaki. She finally understands the reason for the pilgrimages; Uncle observed the ritual to honour Mother's memory, although in respect of her wishes, he had to keep her death and its circumstances a secret from the children. In the last chapter, which deals with the morning after this revelation, Naomi reaches the end of her wake and her meditative journey back in time. She returns to the coulee, the site of her pilgrimage, and the previously dead landscape comes alive for her in the light of a new knowledge, a new understanding.

For the landscape to come alive, the dead stone had to turn into the "white stone"; the tree to bear fruit, the seed to flower, the stone had to join with the living waters. The final scene in the novel celebrates the breath of new life as the harmonious dance uniting trees, flowers, white stone, and water:

> Above the trees, the moon is pure white stone. The reflection is rippling in the river, water and stone dancing. Their joining together is the breath of life. It is a quiet ballet, soundless as breath.

The first and last chapters, then, are symmetrical like book ends. In the first chapter a question is asked, a puzzle set up. In the last chapter the question is answered, the puzzle resolved. In the first chapter the narrator embarks on her quest through the landscape: "Like the grass, I search the earth and the sky with a thin but persistent thirst." She thirsts for an answer for the unexplained, mysterious aspects of her childhood, the disappearing of her mother, the deportation of her people from British Columbia, the breaking-up of families, the confiscation of their property, the waves of war hysteria turned against the "treacherous yellow peril" of Japanese Canadians. Only through articulating the pain of the past will she find hope for liberation, healing, and renewal for herself and her people. In her search of the "freeing word," Naomi must overcome thirty years of paralyzing silence, hurt, humiliation; as a character in, and the narrator of the story, she must break the "stillness of the stone."

Obasan is a book about silence. The narrator is an extraordinarily quiet child whose relatives often wonder if she is in fact not mute. But this muteness is a deliberate withdrawal into silence. It is a child's resentful response to a world which has wounded her anonymously, impersonally, inexplicably.

—Erika Gottlieb

Obasan is a book about silence. The narrator is an extraordinarily quiet child whose relatives often wonder if she is in fact not mute. But this muteness is a deliberate withdrawal into silence. It is a child's resentful response to a world which has wounded her anonymously, impersonally, inexplicably. The most poignant contribution of this highly poetic book is the experience in which the little girl, who in the course of the novel has grown into a lonely and unhappy adult, is compelled to transform the silence of shame, hurt, and abandonment into words. Alerted by the symbolic landscapes, we witness an almost breathless quality as the narrative unfolds; silence on the verge of turning into sound. Silence speaks many tongues in this novel. For Obasan, silence is the language of service to the family, the language of her prayers. Uncle's silence is that of old Japanese Canadians who feel that the injustice and discrimination of a whole decade should be kept quiet. "In the world there is no better place . . . There is food. There is medicine. There is pension money. Gratitude. Gratitude."

Within the family is a conflict between the long oriental tradition of silence dictated by modesty, moderation, and stoicism, and Aunt Emily's "Western" compulsion to speak up and bring justice. [In a footnote, Gottlieb cites Michiko Lambertson's *"Obasan," Canadian Woman Studies* (1984). She writes: "According to Michiko Lambertson, 'In the absence of her mother Naomi uses Obasan and Aunt Emily as windows on the female adult world.'

I also feel, however, that the contrast between Obasan and Aunt Emily goes beyond the narrator's attitude to the female world; insights from this contrast are fundamental to her definition of her own identity in terms of Oriental and Western cultural, political, and psychological attitudes."] An active member of committees organizing inquests, petitions and conferences to combat discrimination, Aunt Emily is strident, angry, and dynamic. It is Aunt Emily who urges Naomi not to forget: "You are your history . . . If you cut it off, you're an amputee. Denial is gangrene." Her diagnosis is correct. For years Naomi's nightmares have been images of mutilation and death, and as she keeps going back and forth between her school in Cecil and Uncle's house in Granton, she is unable to go ahead in her own world, unable to stay with the old people in theirs.

Yet, Naomi is reluctant to take on the burden of commitment, and Aunt Emily's package of documents, diaries, and newspaper clippings lies abandoned and forgotten for years. Only when Obasan hands it to her before Uncle's funeral is Naomi finally compelled to read and respond to Aunt Emily's factual, angry, accusing testament. Naomi's response is distinctly different. She speaks in the first person singular; she describes only memories, a young child's experiences, set in the present. In spite of the strong political commitment that will, albeit reluctantly, emerge from the book, Naomi's narrative is both a child's recollection and the recollection of childhood. What she recaptures is the genuine feeling of childhood: unable to see what the next step may bring, unable to understand the causal connection between events, she is genuinely groping.

Tactile and auditory images are predominant. Visual images are sketchy, like line drawings, mere background to the far richer, more modulated sense of touch and sound. We learn for example that Naomi's mother was "yasashi," had a quality of softness, but this refers more to her inner being than to any quality we could visualize. Remarkably, the characters are almost faceless. The simplicity of their portrayal and lack of individual detail is reminiscent of folk and fairytales. We meet characters in their roles as grandfather, grandmother, uncle, aunt, teacher, clergyman, only to recognize that they all share one quality: the silent dignity of self-respect and duty towards the community. Regardless of how close they may be to the narrator, the characters are generalized, often allegorical. Even Obasan is more of an attitude, a presence:

> Squatting here with the putty knife in her hand, she is every old woman in every hamlet in the world . . . Everywhere the old woman stands as the true and rightful owner of the earth. She is the bearer of keys to unknown doorways and to a network of astonishing tunnels. She is the possessor of life's infinite personal details.

This method of distant, linear, and external characterization allows the author to develop a collective portraiture of human dignity in the face of aggression, of a tradition based on the profound regard for the vulnerabilities of the old, the young, and on mutual respect.

The scarcity of closeups, the lack of individual detail also allows for another effect. By the end of the novel Obasan emerges as every old woman who owns the earth: she becomes larger than life, holding the secret to mysteries, "the bearer of keys to unknown doorways." Another character who achieves such an allegorical presence is Naomi's mother. In the beginning she exists only as a photograph, associated with a colourful quilt, the tender music of nursery rhymes. Even at the end when we learn about her tragic fate in Nagasaki—the dramatic and symbolic centre of the book—we still have no individual portrait of her. Mother's role, or rather her absence, is nevertheless crucial in Naomi's characterization. After the paradise of childhood in which they are one, Mother suddenly leaves. It turns out to be their final separation; Naomi does not cry, but she does not smile or speak either.

The "rift" of separation and alienation remains unhealed even in the later years of relative peace and contentment. Twenty odd years after the traumatic experiences of her childhood, Naomi is a middle-aged, single, and rather frustrated schoolteacher, still blocked and benumbed by the experience. Doubtful about her own sexuality and ethnic identity, she is not attracted or attractive to the opposite sex, and in her own estimation she has "the social graces of a common housefly." She admits that "None of my friends today are Japanese Canadians"; yet she also feels resentment and suspicion of white Canadians. As a result of her dilemma, she withdraws into silence. What she says about her pupils describes her as well: "It is the children who say nothing who are in real trouble, more than the ones who complain."

Since the entire book is a document of silence turning into sound, we become intensely aware of the burden carried by language in this invocation of the consciousness of a silent people. To say that Joy Kogawa has a language of her own is not sufficient. Many good poets or writers do achieve that. But in Naomi's narration one often has the feeling that the writer is virtually reinventing language. Unmistakably, the style is the result of extensive linguistic experimentation, presenting us with the special flavour of Japanese Canadian speech patterns and their underlying sensibilities. [In a footnote, Gottlieb cites Edith Milton's "Unnecessary Precautions," *The New York Times Book Review* (1982). Gottlieb notes: "It has been observed, for example, that 'the syntax of her characters expresses fatalism.'"] The writer translates Japanese expressions, often including the Japanese turn of thought. Occasionally she mixes English words with Japanese: "Nothing changes me, I say."

Yet none of these devices can explain the suggestive cadences of the dialogue, for example, when Uncle is looking at the thirty-six-year-old Naomi: "Too young . . . Still too young." There are a lot of passive constructions: we cannot see, we cannot know the source of action. What is visible is only the subject acted upon. "Too much old man," he says and totters back . . . "Mo ikutsu? What is your age now?" And when the old people refuse to give answers to Naomi's repeated questions, their evasions sound like age old proverbs—"Everyone some day dies," or "Still young, too young. Some day."—that have to be decoded, solved like a riddle to get to the true meaning. The truncated sentences have their own slow movement:

"Burredo. Try. Good." Some sentences consist of nouns without verbs, or only of adjectives: "Now old," Obasan reports. "Everything old." Yet, in the hands of the skilful narrator-recorder this elliptical, barren language reminds the reader of the poetic quality of child's language, or of Shelley's definition of the language of the poet-Maker: it is vitally metaphorical.

The descriptions have a concrete, literal, imagistic quality. Yet, the poet-writer's strategies are also quite consistent in guiding our response to the world she presents. First she would carefully describe the natural phenomenon, creating an image in its "sensuous particularity." Then she proceeds to make further use of this image just created by relating it to the human world. By this method she assumes a fairly extensive control over our response. To look at one example: after Uncle's death, Obasan and Naomi go up to the attic to look for some old family documents, and they see a spider's web:

> As she pushes a box aside, she stretches the corner of a spider's web, exquisitely symmetrical, balanced between the box and the magazines. A round black blot, large as a cat's eye, suddenly sprouts legs and ambles across the web. Shaking it . . . I recoil, jerking my arm up, sending the beam of light over the ceiling and a whole cloudy scene of carnage. Ugh! What a sight! A graveyard and feasting ground combined . . . But we're trapped, Obasan and I, by our memories of the dead—all our dead—those who refuse to bury themselves. Like threads of old spider webs, still sticky and hovering, the past waits for us to submit, or depart. When I least expect it, a memory comes skittering out of the dark, spinning and netting the air, ready to snap me up and ensnare me in old and complex puzzles.

By now the conceit—the extended metaphor of man ensnared by the past as the poor insect is ensnared by the imperceptibly fast formation of the spider web—is taking shape in front of our eyes. It is an association the writer is testing out in its various aspects, but an association built on an image she had first created for us to see and touch—an earned association. And by weaving the metaphor with us, she also engages us in the puzzle, the central puzzle in Naomi's life:

> Just a glimpse of a worn-out patchwork of quilt and the old question comes thudding out of the night again like a giant moth. Why did my mother not return? After all these years, I find myself wondering, but with the dullness of expecting no response. "Please tell me about Mother," I would say as a child to Obasan. I was consumed by the question. Devoured alive.

The literal, down-to-earth associations behind the "complex puzzles" make it truly exciting that the narrator is "devoured alive." There is an imperceptible, sinister, extremely able spider working somewhere in the cosmos to set up these intriguing puzzles, and together with the narrator we are compelled to seek answers. "But Obasan gave me no answers. I did not have, I have never had, the key to the vault of her thoughts. Even now, I have no idea what urgency prompts her to explore this attic at midnight."

This, simply in terms of the naturalistic action, would be a very quiet, and not necessarily tense scene. And yet, in spite of the naturalistic quality of the everyday event, we become aware of a deeper, underlying significance, the tension of a barely named, yet fundamental anxiety: Is life meaningless, will death devour us as the spider's web devours its captives?

> I notice these days, from time to time, how the present disappears in her mind. The past hungers for her. Feasts on her. And when its feasting is complete? She will dance and dangle in the dark, like small insect bones, a fearful calligraphy—a dry reminder that once there was life flitting in the weather.

Death, old age, mutability—these are traditional themes for meditation, particularly appropriate within the framework of a wake for the dead. But here these traditional themes suddenly become vital in the context of the mourner's life. They become the centre of concern, of anxiety. The dancing and dangling of the small insect bones in the dark is a particularly painful definition of the cruelty and meaninglessness of life as seen through the eyes of a victim. Both the excitement of being "devoured alive" and of the past "feasting" on the old woman in death hint at the horror of existence with an intensity much stronger than that of any explicit explanation.

Kogawa's style is characterized by a controlled, concrete, non-subjective quality. The development of a theme begins with the keen impartial observation of natural phenomena as if observed by the objective gaze of a microscopic eye. No subjective, certainly no sentimental elements enter into the description; the voice is cold, almost clinical. Then, unexpectedly, this extremely concrete, specific image turns up, still in full closeup, to offer an analogy for the description of human motivation: suddenly it becomes internalized and humanized, yet loses none of its power through the process of generalization or abstraction. And as the insect caught in the spider's web is transformed to take on the characteristics of a human being, horror is seen in closeup through unflinching, open eyes. One of the most disturbing images in the book relates to Naomi's nightmare in which the Grand Inquisitor pries open her eyes. How different is this from traditional (Western or romantic) associations of evil with darkness. In this novel we are confronted with the mystery of evil in its most everyday manifestations and in forcibly full daylight.

On the political level the mystery of evil assumes the form of the following questions. Who is responsible? How can all this evil be explained? Why did all this have to happen to us, Japanese Canadians? Will it happen again to any minority in Canada? "Write the vision and make it plain [on tables]." It is ironic that the piece of paper with these words of the Old Testament prophet fell out of the documents Aunt Emily has prepared for Naomi. Moving as those documents are, it is through the silent Naomi's personal recollections that we ultimately get the impression of having heard the word of the prophet, the seer.

Aunt Emily's prose is expository: the voice is strident, angry, polemical. She feels that "the war was just an ex-cuse for the racism that was already there," and looking around she sees "Racism . . . the Nazis . . . everywhere." She registers shock and astonishment that Canada could have fallen into the trap: "Germany. That country is openly totalitarian. But Canada is supposed to be a democracy," and she cries out against "undemocratic racial antagonism—which is exactly what our democratic country is supposed to be fighting against." In writing to her sister, Naomi's mother, she also points out the bitter irony in the Japanese immigrants' situation: "We're the enemy. And what about you there? Have they arrested you because you are Canadian?" She is indignant, "What this country did to us, it did to itself." There is no doubt that her determination to bring justice often verges on the heroic:

> Out loud I said: "Why not leave the dead to bury the dead?" "Dead?" she asked. "I am not dead. You're not dead, Who's dead?" "But you can't fight a whole country." I said. "We are the country" she answered.

Yet, in spite of this passion and commitment worthy of the Old Testament prophet, Naomi finds that Aunt Emily's words "are not made flesh," and she sighs in frustration: "All my prayers disappear into space."

Aunt Emily's documents cannot help Naomi come to terms with her own bitterness and frustration: "Greed, selfishness and hatred remain as constant as the human condition, do they not? . . . Is there evidence for optimism?" Unlike Aunt Emily, Naomi feels that "time has solved few mysteries. War and rumours of war, racial hatreds and fears are with us still." As a result, she is slightly contemptuous of those who still "dance to the multicultural piper's tune." Her scepticism of the dream of a multicultural Canadian identity is dispelled only indirectly, and only in instances when she turns her attention to the Canadian landscape.

> 1942
>
> We are leaving the BC coast—rain, cloud, mist—an air overladen with weeping . . . We are going down to the middle of the earth . . . carried along by the momentum of the expulsion into the waiting wilderness . . . we are the man in the Gospel of John, born into the world for the sake of light. We are sent . . . to the sending that we may bring sight.

It is only in this sudden double exposure between the landscape and the people that she finds a ray of hope. In this perspective the human ordeal may assume Biblical significance, as the Japanese Canadians become the eyes for the Canadian community as a whole. Through their suffering they "bring sight," making sure that no minority is treated with injustice in the future.

Again and again it is less through the people than through the landscape that she approaches the troubled question of her Canadian identity.

> Where do any of us come from in this cold country? Oh, Canada. Whether it is admitted or not, we come from you, we come from you. From the same soil, from the cemeteries full of skeletons

with wild roses in their grinning teeth. We come from our untold tales that wait for their telling. We come from Canada, this land that is like every land, filled with the wise, the fearful, the compassionate, the corrupt.

It is more from Naomi's internal, private grief than from Aunt Emily's public statements that we understand the puzzle of political evil. Canada fell victim to the hysteria—fear, greed, the need for a scapegoat—it was fighting against. And it is through Naomi's private vision at the end that we approach the resolution of this political dilemma. When in the last scene it becomes clear to Naomi that this is the land where she wants to lay her dead ones to rest, she is no longer haunted by the "cemeteries full of skeletons with wild roses in their grinning teeth": In her new vision the entire landscape of "Uncle's spot" is permeated with the "sweet and faint" perfume of "the wild roses and the tiny wildflowers that grow along the trickling stream." The flowers of the Canadian soil are joining in the ritual of "water and stone dancing"—the Japanese ritual of the graceful dignified funerary flower dance finally becomes a ritual of acceptance and reconciliation. [In a footnote, Gottlieb cites *Encyclopedia of Religion and Ethics*, Volume IV (1913) and states: "Naomi's recurring references to the flower dance with the single long-stemmed rose should also alert us to a significant aspect of the ancient Buddhist ceremony in which 'a single branch of Shikimi' or a single flower with a long stem is offered before the coffin when the preparation for the funeral is complete. The interrupted ceremony of the flower dance referred to in the dreams and in other parts of the novel is completed in the last chapter in the 'wordless ballet' between 'water and stone dancing,' involving the 'seed which flowers with speech' and the 'wild roses and the tiny wildflowers that grow along the trickling stream.' Seeing the landscape come alive, also means that Naomi herself may be able to join in the ceremonial dance and assume the potential for spiritual renewal for herself, for her people, and for all the survivors of war and persecution."]

In her quest for enlightenment and spiritual liberation the narrator is aware that "Beneath the grass [is] the speaking dream and beneath the dream is the sensate sea." To reach the currents of the "living word," she has to reach down to the "underground stream," plumb the depth of memories, associations, dreams, the depth of the subconscious. Her dreams—each followed by her own interpretation and explication—play a significant role in delineating her journey in search of articulation and self-understanding: ultimately psychological liberation. The first dream demonstrates how easily and gracefully the author moves not only between the various timeplanes, but also between the naturalistic and the symbolic dimensions in the novel:

> Early in the still grey morning I can hear Obasan emptying her chamber pot in the toilet. I wait until she returns to her bed before I drift off again. Haze. Cloud. Again the descent.

On its surface the dream is ominous, but at this point not yet openly horrible. The dreamer sees a man and a woman in a landscape: "with a sickle she is harvesting the forest debris, gathering the branches into piles." He is a "British martinet. It is evident that he is in command. With his pruner's shears he is cutting the trees." At first the scene seems to be describing merely the endlessness of physical labour, obviously a memory from the work in Alberta in the late 1940's, the memory of weeding beets: "It is hard . . . with my hoe . . . and on the end of the long long row and the next and the next . . . weeding and weeding and weeding." And as the dream figures join in the dehumanizing, soundless labour "like an orchestra of fog," Naomi is once more reminded of her feeling that the whole family had turned into automatons: "We work together all day. At night we eat and sleep. We hardly talk any more."

Of course the personal recollection is merely the raw material of the dream which will yield its proper meaning only in the context of the dreamer's entire inscape. On the political level, the interpretation is fairly obvious: the man is a British martinet, indifferent to the destruction and the suffering he causes. He is in uniform and ready to kill, to obey orders unquestioningly. But beyond the political interpretation, the sickle and the endless movement should also alert us to another analogy, to the figure "with sharp sickle . . . [who was] gathering the vine of the earth, and cast it into the great vinepress of the wrath of God . . . and blood came out . . . " (Rev. 14. 14-20). The strange beast accompanying him—lion or dog or lion dog—is also familiar from the context: the landscape is that of the Book of Revelation, the vision preceding that of the Apocalypse. But the dream also adds its own interpretations to the archetypal manifestation of destruction: in Naomi's eyes evil becomes the result of an inhuman, mechanical obedience. The apocalyptic figure, the personification of destruction, is a martinet; his beast is a robot with a plastic mouth, and the woman is held together by metallic hinges—they manifest the destructiveness of evil as part of our unfeeling, indifferent, machine-like civilization.

At this point the dream scenery changes and the dreamer catches a glance of Uncle making a ceremonial bow: he has a rose with an endless stem in his mouth, acting out part of a ritual for the dead. The dreamer also catches sight of a figure behind him, but before she could discern the identity of this figure, it disappears and Naomi wakes up. To solve the personal-psychological dimensions of her puzzle Naomi should overcome the recurring threats of violation and be able to complete the peaceful, dignified measures of the funerary flower dance. Accordingly, the second nightmare picks up on both motives. To begin with, there is the threat again: soldiers in uniform, sickles turned into bayonets, paralyzing fear and nausea. The narrator has this dream after, and as it were in conjunction with, a painful recollection of a traumatic sexual experience as a five-year-old in Vancouver before the war:

> His name is Old Man Gower. He lives next door. I can see his house beyond the peach tree from my bedroom window. His belly is large and soft. His hair is thin and brown and the top of his head is a shiny skin cap. When he lifts me up in his arms, I do not wish him to lift me up but I do not know what is it to struggle. Every time he carries me away, he tells me I must not tell my mother. He asks me questions as he holds me but I do not answer.

Through their juxtaposition in the narrative, there is no

doubt that this long-buried accident from early child-hood—the experience of violation—is closely related to the recurring nightmare:

> Two weeks ago, the day of our first staff meeting at Cecil Consolidated, there was that dream again. The dream had a new and terrible ending. In earlier versions there was flight, terror and pursuit. The only way to be saved from harm was to become seductive. In this latest dream, three beautiful oriental woman lay naked in the muddy road, flat on their backs, their faces turned to the sky. They were lying straight as coffins, spaced several feet apart. They were lying perpendicular to the road like railway ties. Several soldiers stood or shuffled in front of them in the foreground. It appeared they were guarding these women who were probably pris-oners captured from a nearby village. The woman close by made a simpering coy gesture with her hands. She touched her hair and wig-gled her body slightly—seductively. An almost inaudible whimper or sob was drowned in her chest. She was trying to use the only weapon she had—her desirability. She lay on the edge of nausea, stretched between hatred and lust. The soldiers could not be won. Dread and a deathly loathing cut through the women.

The dream acts out the mutually corrupting relationship between victim and victimizer. The victim would like to win over the aggressor, to seduce him. The process is hu-miliating and self-destructive. The aggressor has a sadistic enjoyment of power—he has the bayonet, the uniform, while the victims are defenceless and naked. In the very process the victims experience the nausea of shame and self-loathing—the denial of their own humanity. This self-loathing is becoming a sense of paralysis, the inability to move.

The metaphor of rape and the victim's ensuing shame and paralysis works also on the level of the political allegory. In Naomi's dreams the sexual aggressors are always white soldiers in uniform. And when we come to young Ste-phen's response to the persecution of the Japanese Canadi-ans, we realize that rape is used as metaphor for any kind of violation or victimization:

> One day Stephen comes home from school, his glasses broken, black tear stains on his face.
>
> "What happened?" I whisper as Stephen comes up the stairs.
>
> He does not answer me. Is he ashamed, as I was in Old Man Gower's bathroom? Should I go away?

Although Stephen's experience does not display the sexual overtones of Naomi's nightmare, he also undergoes the typical symptoms of shame, paralysis, and self-loathing. As a child he develops a limp, has to wear a cast, and walk on crutches. As for his self-loathing, it is demonstrated by his lifelong difficulty in accepting his ethnic, family back-ground. Although he feels guilty about it, he is ill at ease with Uncle and Obasan and painfully avoids their compa-ny.

Yet, violation for Naomi has consequences even more seri-ous than for Stephen. In the course of her recollections she describes herself as suffering from a wound: "In my dreams a small child sits with a wound on her knees. The wound on her knees is on the back of her skull, large and moist. A double wound." The wound on the knee alludes to the sexual wound, to an incident with Old Man Gower: "One does not resist adults. But I know this is unnecessary for my knee. He is only pretending to fix my scratch." Just as important is the wound on the "back of her skull," the wound that comes from the victim's internalization of guilt of violation, the unhealing "seepage" of guilt and shame in her consciousness—the wound that Naomi shares with the rest of her people, possibly with most vic-tims of violation.

This is not the first time that the nightmare has acted out her traumatic experience with Old Man Gower: the night-mare is a recurring one. At this time, however, Naomi reaches a new stage of understanding when she asks: "Does Old Man Gower still walk through the hedges be-tween our houses in Vancouver, in Slocan, in Cecil?" Through this comment she acknowledges that she has been under the spell of, indeed haunted by this trauma throughout her childhood (Vancouver), her adolescence (Slocan), and her adult years (Cecil). The pain of the mem-ory and the recurring nightmares indicate to the adult Naomi that she is still paralyzed by the same shame, help-lessness, and self-loathing, feelings she has to overcome before she can finally liberate herself from the past.

The child Naomi's experience in Old Man Gower's hands is traumatic because it disrupts her natural childhood exis-tence, her oneness with Mother:

> I am clinging to my mother's leg, a flesh shaft that grows from the ground, a tree trunk of which I am the offshoot—a young branch at-tached by right of flesh and blood. Where she is rooted, I am rooted. If she walks, I will walk. Her blood is whispering through my veins. The shaft of her leg is the shaft of my body and I am her thoughts.
>
> . . . . .
>
> "Don't tell your mother", he whispers into my ear . . . Where in the darkness has my mother gone?"

Naomi describes her sense of loss and alienation in terms of a tormented landscape:

> But here in Mr. Gower's hands I become other—a parasite on her body, no longer of her mind . . . If I tell my mother about Mr. Gower, the alarm will send a tremor through our bodies and I will be torn from her. But the secret has already separated us. His hands are frightening and pleasureable. In the centre of my body is a rift . . . In my childhood dream the mountain yawns apart as the chasm spreads. My mother is on one side of the rift. I am on the other. We cannot reach each other. My legs are being sawn in half.

This rift, the chasm of separation, is a recurring motif in the book, especially since the incident with Mr. Gower was followed closely by the actual separation from Mother. "It is around this time that Mother disappears. I hardly dare to think, let alone ask why she has to leave." Naomi feels torn, amputated by her sexual experience. Tormented by guilt, she feels that her abandonment by Mother must be punishment for her unmentionable offence, her fall from innocence. Only at the end of the novel, when she receives the message of Mother's love, will she experience the healing of the rift in her cosmos. She understands then that it was not her guilt that brought about Mother's departure. Her Mother had to leave and stay away out of love. As a result, it becomes clear to the adult Naomi that she could not have been guilty, and, what is just as important, that she was always loved, that she can be loved, that she is lovable.

Of course nobody could convey this message to Naomi until she becomes ready to receive it, and it is the third dream that takes her to the final point in her journey, to understanding and receptivity. This final dream is that of the Grand Inquisitor, and once more it is a dream which begins with a vision of the threat of violation: "Always I dream of soldiers eager for murder, their weapons ready. We die again and again. In my dreams we are never safe enough." Yet, the dream also carries on the interrupted flower ceremony from the first dream, and by now the figure who then disappeared is ready to reveal herself to the dreamer:

> Mother stood in the centre. In her mouth she held a knotted string stem, like the twine and string of Obasan's ball which she keeps in the pantry. From the stem hung a red rose, red as a heart.

At this point, however, the dream reaches a different stage. Nevertheless, because of the peculiar patterns of dream-logic, both stages will prove instrumental in pointing the dreamer toward her resolution:

> Was it then that the nightmare began? The skin of the air became closer and denser, a formless hair vest. Up from the valley there rose a dark cloud—a great cape. It was the Grand Inquisitor descending over us, the top of his head a shiny skin cap. With his large hands he was prying open my mother's lips, prying open my eyes. I fell and cried out.

In Dostoyevski's story the Grand Inquisitor is sitting in judgement over Christ, prying, tormenting him with questions. In her dream Naomi has a vision of Mother's face torn and her own eyes being pried open. Interpreting this dream, she makes a sudden discovery about herself: "How the Grand Inquisitor gnaws at my bones," she cries out. She now comes to the realization that by her ceaseless questioning and prying she has been guilty of taking on the role of the Grand Inquisitor, of making judgement over her dead Mother. She makes a decision to give up her determined search, to have faith in Mother's love and to accept its silence. Only when willing to "admit" this silence, will it open itself to her. Paradoxically, Naomi cannot receive the message she so eagerly has searched for until she learns to give up the search; until she learns to affirm the

mystery that her Mother's love had been all pervasive although it had been silent.

Only after she has her last dream and succeeds in finding its interpretation will Naomi receive the detailed description of her mother's martyrdom and the long awaited proof of her silent love. The book culminates in Chapter 37 which describes Mother's horrible ordeal in Nagasaki, a vision that has been prepared by numerous allusions and Biblical images throughout. In the light of this vision all the accumulated puzzles of Naomi's life receive their solution, albeit a solution in the light of a tragic illumination:

> In the dark Slocan night, the bright light flares in my dreaming. I hear the screams and feel the mountain breaking. Your long black hair falls and falls into the chasm. My legs are sawn in half. The skin on your face bubbles like lava and melts from your bones. Mother, I see your face. Do not turn aside.

In the light of the Nagasaki conflagration, all the disasters in the life of the Japanese Canadian family pale in comparison. Yet, the disasters that befell Naomi and her family in Canada also had anticipated this disaster. In the same way all of Naomi's nightmares are pale in comparison to this ultimate nightmare vision of cosmic proportions—the total annihilation of the world as a result of the overpowering forces of evil—yet her dreams also anticipate, foreshadow this vision of the Last Judgement, the end of the world.

Once she is allowed to hear the content of the letter on the blue rice paper, Naomi's internal drama reaches its climax of recognition and reversal: she is able to understand the puzzle of the past and reach a resolution for a new life in the future. Offering a resolution to all of her previous puzzles, the climactic scene also puts Naomi's experience in a new perspective and opens up the cosmic, universal dimensions of the novel. What is it in this letter that allows Naomi to come to terms with her past, her sense of abandonment and separation? The letter describes Nasane, the beautiful Japanese woman rushing through the living hell of Nagasaki during the radiation, trying to protect her cousin's little daughter—a child who, we hear, also happens to bear a striking resemblance to Naomi. Harking back to the allegorical methods of communal portrait, it is quite likely that Naomi recognizes herself both in the child and in the mother at the moment. More important, it becomes clear that in spite of Mother's unspeakable suffering, she is still able to care for her cousin's child, and think of her own children. Not allowing Naomi and Stephen to know about her illness and her death, she wants to spare them of her own agony, putting considerations of their welfare before her own need for them, even in the most harrowing moments of her anguish.

Although Mother is a human figure in the family drama, through the author's allegorical methods of characterization and through the sensitive handling of the religious symbols, in her death she emerges as a witness, a martyr, the representative of the sacred. Reaffirming her bond with her Mother allows Naomi to understand the legacy of an absolute, even transcendental love in the cosmos, which gives new vitality to the deadly, desiccated landscape of her soul. The power of the mother's posthumous message is enormous. Before receiving this message Naomi sees herself rootless, wounded, amputated. Looking at her mother's faded photograph, she also sees her image as lifeless, distant, indifferent.

> The tree is a dead tree in the middle of the prairies. I sit on its roots still as a stone. In my dreams a small child sits with a wound . . . a double wound. The child is forever unable to speak. I apply the thick bandage but nothing can soak up the seepage. I beg that the woundedness may be healed and that the limbs may learn to dance. But you stay in the black and white photograph, smiling your yasashi smile.

Obsessed by her "double wound" Naomi withdraws into the hurt silence of woundedness. Benumbed, paralyzed by the past, she is unable to rejoice, to join in the celebratory dance of life.

Although the letter on the blue rice paper conveys a shocking, devastating message, it also brings about a healing change in Naomi: "The letters today are skeletons. Bones only. But the earth still stirs with dormant blooms. Love flows through the roots of the trees by our graves." Recognizing that the "living waters" nurture the roots of the trees at the graves allows Naomi to see that the flow of love has power to overcome death: now she is getting ready to join the dance of life by completing the funerary dance she had been preoccupied with in the previous dreams. Having heard the mother's message, Naomi has also come to accept her separation from her in the flesh and to understand oneness with her spiritually. As a result, the numbness of "woundedness" is over: the formerly "dead tree" has come alive, and so has the black and white photograph from her childhood. Addressing her mother with the fervour of a religious hymn, Naomi celebrates the power of regenerative love in her cosmos:

> You stand on the streetcorner in Vancouver in a straight silky dress and a light black coat . . . Your leg is a tree trunk and I am branch and butterfly. I am joined to your limbs by the right of birth; child of your flesh, leaf of your bough . . .

Experiencing the flow of love over the roots leads her to another affirmation: the organic unity or oneness of life. It is the affirmation of the oneness between the roots, the trunk, the bough, and the branches which allows the formerly dead tree to come alive. It has overcome the stone-like silence of paralysis and woundedness, ready to respond to the "new word" in the formerly dead landscape. But what is the significance of the "new word" in this context? Several direct quotations and numerous allusions to the Bible have prepared us to see the conflagration of Nagasaki as the doomsday vision of the Apocalypse, the destruction of the world by the powers of evil. But according to the Biblical scenario, this vision of the Apocalypse is precedent to the vision of a New Heaven and a New Earth. Does the "new word" sought by the narrator point toward a transcendental reality on the cosmic level? And in terms of the political conundrum, after their years of wandering in the desert of hatred, are the Nisei going to find the "hidden manna," or the fulfilment of their promised land in a multicultural Canadian democracy? Relating the same

question to the personal psychological dimensions, is Naomi being "reborn" to a new life emotionally, sexually, spiritually?

In spite of the rich and consistent texture of the Biblical imagery, the plot does not fulfil our expectation of the vision of a "New Heaven and New Earth." Or rather, the last stage of this drama is not translated into human action. Once Naomi has achieved her illumination, she simply returns to the natural landscape where we had first met her, back to the coulee in Southern Alberta. The exclusive focus on the natural landscape in this most dramatic moment should draw our attention to some of the unique characteristics of Joy Kogawa's universe. In spite of the indebtedness to the Judeo-Christian framework and the profusion of Biblical allusions, her world reveals profound connections with a fundamentally nature-centred, pantheistic tradition. The Buddhist tradition emphasizes the continuity between the dead and the living by affirming that death is also part of the nature cycle. Hence the finding of the physical location of the grave around the descendant's home in the community is a significant step in the ritual. There can be no new life, no creativity in the family until the repose of the dead has been assured, and the mourner cannot liberate himself from the "death taboo" before laying the dead in the earth with the proper ceremony to accompany this act. [In a footnote, Gottlieb cites *Japanese Religion: A Survey* (1972) and states: "When Naomi returns to Uncle's spot at the end, she is indeed old enough to understand the meaning of those annual visits. Harking back to the tradition of commemorating all the dead of the family at the same time, we may also assume that in the future she will include Uncle in her annual obsequies."] Therefore, the final scene in the novel in which Naomi affirms the location of the symbolic gravesite, the spot Uncle had chosen for the annual ritual to commemorate Mother's death, offers resolution to her own rootlessness and homelessness. As a matter of fact, this spot inevitably becomes the emotional, spiritual centre for Naomi's quest, and therefore the appropriate setting for its resolution.

Coincidence of Buddhist and Christian symbols in the quest often present the effect of superimposition or double exposure. Although the "new name" on the tablet and the vitality of the living waters that feed the Tree of Life have their particular consistency significant in the Biblical drama of Apocalypse and resurrection, the same images also have their consistency in the Buddhist tradition. Here the Tree of Life becomes the family tree, and the concept of resurrection evokes Naomi's affirmation of renewal through the nature cycle, that is, through the continuity between ancestor and mourner in the family line: "Father, Mother, my relatives, my ancestors, we have come to the forest tonight . . . we have turned and returned to your arms as you turn to earth and form the forest floor." As the wake for her dead becomes enriched by allusions to the Buddhist and the Biblical tradition, the images of tablets, water, stone, flower and fruit assume their multidimensional significance. The consistency of these archetypal symbols expresses beliefs shared by various ethnic and religious groups, as if to demonstrate that elusive ideal of multiculturalism that may offer the narrator hope for the political future. Harmony between these different contexts within the same narrative framework is also appropriate to Naomi's final resolution. Mixing the ashes of her dead with the Canadian soil allows her to claim Canada as not only her political, but also her spiritual home.

Yet, in spite of the consistency of a spiritual, even a mystical sensibility, the resolution in the landscape suggests that for the narrator resurrection and renewal are part of a human drama that has to be acted out exclusively in the here and now. In this soil, containing the bones of buffaloes, Indians, and early Canadian settlers Naomi has to lay her dead ones to "rest in [their] world of stone." It is here, in the coulee of Southern Alberta that she had to find the "living word" leading to a flowering, a fruition, a harmonious dance in her spiritual landscape.

There is no doubt that Kogawa's description of Naomi's spiritual journey comes alive through natural symbols, and that without these symbols we would be at a loss for the significance of the human drama. In terms of this drama, Aunt Emily's testament was the dead stone, containing a record of bitterness and anger against injustice. Mother's message from the past is the vital insight which allows Naomi to come alive emotionally, to accept the transcendental reality of love which flows through the roots at the very gravesides. Once she received this message, the seed will flower with speech, and Naomi's own testament will become the "white stone" with the "new name," the "living word." Ultimately, it is the message of love, which breaking the several seals of Aunt Emily's documents, will "overcome" the conflagration of the Apocalypse. [In a footnote, Gottlieb cites *Encyclopedia of Religion and Ethics,* Volume IV (1913) and states: "Although the context is undoubtedly Christian, several aspects of the sequence and a great deal of the spirit of Naomi's ritual of mourning are reminiscent of ancient Japanese tradition. There is no doubt that in the Biblical context of the universal drama 'the white stone with the new name' anticipates the apocalypse followed by resurrection. Yet, at the same time, the tablet with the 'new name' may also allude to ancient Buddhist or Japanese folk tradition in which it refers to the ritual drama in the family. In death the deceased receives a new name and will pass on his or her spirit to a newborn member of the family. To carry this reference even further, 'in some Buddhist families there is a large family ihai [a wooden tablet] in which the names of all the members are inscribed . . . some Buddhist sects . . . speak about two kinds of posthumous names . . . [and] the second one is a kind of new name "which no man knoweth saving the one that receiveth it." ' "] Once Naomi is able to "admit" this message in the innermost circle, the personal-psychological landscape, the currents of the vital emotion will inevitably overflow and bring to life the landscape in the second and third circles, that is, in the political and cosmic dimensions. The combination of the narrative devices—the three openings, the riddle in each, the interpenetration of the three landscapes, the task imposed on the reader to puzzle out nuances in the natural landscape as they become key elements in the human drama—results in a sophisticated game of hide and go seek, established at the start and resolved only at the end of the novel.

The author's mastery of her craft is also demonstrated by the fact that all these dimensions of the puzzle are held together by the unity of a circular, indeed a concentric structure. The reader is often reminded of the narrator's own image of the intricate weaving of the spider's web, as characters shuttle back and forth between the various locations and the various time planes. Starting in August 1972, we move back to August 1954 (Chapter 1). Then, we go back and forth between August and September 1972 (that is, between the narrator's last visit and Uncle's death). We also take several journeys in time between 1933 and 1941, then between 1941 and 1951, as we follow the various stages in the tribulations of the Japanese Canadian family on its journey from Vancouver to Slocan and Southern Alberta. Then, just before the climactic scene in Chapter 37, we take a big leap; from the present in 1972 we move back to 1954, the arrival of the letter on the blue rice paper with the tragic news. From here we go even further, back to the climactic scene in the novel, to Nagasaki in 1945. It is from this final and most significant leap in time and space that we have to return once more to the present, September 1972, the day of Uncle's funeral. We have come full circle.

Yet, side by side with these jumps back and forth in time, there is also narrative progress in a chronological, linear sequence. Advancing through the various stages in Naomi's life, we get closer and closer to its central mystery. Once this mystery has been revealed, however, the tight-knit spider's web might just as well dissolve. Her new understanding allows Naomi to extricate herself from the snare of her history. Central to the new message from the depth of the past is the revelation that at the hub of the wheel, at the centre of the web there is a force other than the meaningless destructiveness of evil.

In addition to and complementary to the spider's web is the ball of twine and string Obasan had collected from bits and pieces saved over the years. Powerful in her silence, Obasan is indeed in charge of "life's infinite details," as if the ball of string accumulated over the years would have somehow absorbed the wisdom and experience of those years themselves. As Naomi had anticipated, both the centerpiece and the end of the string—both the central secret and the key to its unravelling in the appropriate moment—have been in Obasan's hands all along. Struggling to overcome Obasan's silence, yet also inspired by its depth, Naomi has grappled with her task faithfully, unravelling her yarn in all its intricate patterns, yet also in full control of the tight-knit unity of its concentric, globe-within-globe-within-globe structure. And although it has taken Naomi less than three days between Uncle's death and the gathering of the family for the funeral to accomplish her elaborate journey back and forth in time, within this interval she succeeded in solving a lifetime of accumulated puzzles. She has also made the silence speak: *Obasan* is a testimony to that hard-won miracle of creativity which alone has the power to turn silence into sound. (pp. 34-52)

Erika Gottlieb, "Silence into Sound: The Riddle of Concentric Worlds in 'Obasan'," in Canadian Literature, No. 109, Summer, 1986, pp. 34-53.

An excerpt from *Obasan*

It isn't true, of course, that I never speak as a child. Inside the house in Vancouver there is confidence and laughter, music and meal times, games and storytelling. But outside, even in the backyard, there is an infinitely unpredictable, unknown, and often dangerous world. Speech hides within me, watchful and afraid.

One day, I am standing alone in the backyard. Beside the garage is a wire cage placed high above the ground, at about the level of a table. I can barely see the floor of the cage. A white hen struts in here, its head jerking as it scatters the hay looking for grain—claw scratch, claw scratch—jerking as it starts up in alarm, cocking its head sideways, its neck feathers fluffing in and out. Where its chin should be, a rubbery tongue flaps and jiggles. It seems constantly surprised, ready to utter its gurgles and squawks, its limited language of exclamation and alarm.

My mother and father have bought a dozen cotton-batten-soft yellow chicks, a light boxful of jostling fluff. Their feet are scratchy as twigs. If I stand on a stool, I can lift the wire gate. Carefully, I take the babies and put them into the cage one by one, the trembling bodies filling the palms of my hands.

In the corner of the cage where I place them, they are a clump of yellow puff balls, a piccolo orchestra. The white hen stops scratching and cocks her head at them. The chicks begin to leave the cluster, hopping, cheeping, their shiny round eyes black as apple seeds. One chick reaches the hen's feet. Without warning, the hen's sharp beak jabs down on the chick, up again and down, deliberate as the needle on the sewing-machine. A high trilling squeal and the chick spreads its short wings like a fan as it flops forward. Again and again the hen's beak strikes and the chick lies on its side on the floor, its neck twisted back, its wings, outstretched fingers. The hen lifts a scaly leg, the claws collapsing and clutching as it struts around the cage, bayoneting the chicks darting past her feet, their wings outspread.

I climb down from the stool and run up the back stairs into the house where my mother is sitting in the music room with Mrs. Sugimoto.

"Mama———"

Without a word and without alarm, she follows me quickly to the backyard. The arena is punctuated by short piercing trills as the hen keeps pecking and the chicks squeal and flutter, squeal and fall.

With swift deft fingers, Mother removes the live chicks first, placing them in her apron. All the while that she acts, there is calm efficiency in her face and she does not speak. Her eyes are steady and matter of fact—the eyes of Japanese motherhood. They do not invade and betray. They are eyes that protect, shielding what is hidden most deeply in the heart of the child. She makes safe the small stirrings underfoot and in the shadows. Physically, the sensation is not in the region of the heart, but in the belly. This that is in the belly is honoured when it is allowed to be, without fanfare, without reproach, without words. What is there is there. But even a glance, if it is not matter of fact, is a betrayal.

Joy Kogawa, in her Obasan, *David R. Godine, 1982.*

Gary Willis   (essay date 1987)

[In the following essay, Willis examines Kogawa's use of silence, speech, and insight in Obasan, *arguing that in this work Kogawa "wishes to define, in relation to each other, Japanese and Canadian ways of seeing, and even to combine these divergent perceptions in an integrated and distinctive vision."]*

In 1981 Joy Kogawa's ***Obasan*** appeared, the first novel on the internment of Canada's Japanese residents during the second world war. The political significance of the book's publication may be what strikes us first: the novel appeared at a time when the question of reparation to Japanese Canadians was beginning to receive exposure in the press; and since the newly elected Prime Minister Mulroney's promise of reparation in 1984, the issue has become "hard news" and receives continuing media attention. But ***Obasan's*** political significance alone does not explain why the novel won the 1981 *Books in Canada* First Novel Award and the Canadian Authors' Association 1982 Book of the Year Award. Nor does it explain why the novel was successful enough to be reprinted in paperback by Penguin Books in 1983. ***Obasan*** is a moving and original novel, expressive of a sensibility that wishes to define, in relation to each other, Japanese and Canadian ways of seeing, and even to combine these divergent perceptions in an integrated and distinctive vision.

Writing of carpentry, Kogawa makes a distinction between Japanese and Western techniques that can serve to elucidate a fundamental difference between Japanese and Canadian people. The central character, Naomi, reports:

> I can feel the outline of the plane with a wooden handle which he [Naomi's Grandfather Nakane] worked by pulling it towards him. There is a fundamental difference in Japanese workmanship— to pull with control rather than push with force.

Japanese are restrained; Canadians, forceful. In the novel, this contrast is seen strikingly in the difference between the Issei—Canadian residents born or raised in Japan—and the Nisei—people of Japanese extraction born and raised in Canada. Naomi has two aunts, one whom she calls "Obasan" or "Aya Obasan" and one whom she calls "Aunt Emily." "Obasan" is an Issei; "Aunt Emily," a Nisei. As the Japanese word for "aunt" is "obasan," each of the two may be termed an "obasan" of Naomi's. Each "obasan," in her own way, helps Naomi to survive the ordeal of internment; and, as the book's title intimates, the two "obasans" are, after Naomi, the most important characters in the novel.

Early in the novel, Kogawa draws a crucial distinction between her two aunts:

> How different my two aunts are. One lives in sound, the other in stone. Obasan's language remains deeply underground but Aunt Emily, BA, MA, is a word warrior. She's a crusader, a little old grey-haired Mighty Mouse, a Bachelor of

Advanced Activists and General Practitioner of Just Causes.

To "live in stone," Kogawa makes clear, is to live in silence—that is, to live without expressing in words one's deepest thoughts and feelings. When the persecution of Japanese Canadians begins in 1941, Obasan and her husband, Isamu or Uncle Sam, say nothing of it to Naomi, so that Naomi learns of the "danger" only through "whispers and frowns and too much gentleness." When Obasan and Sam finally, in 1954, learn the fate of Naomi's mother (who, disfigured by the nuclear blast at Nagasaki in 1945, survived for several years after), they refuse to tell the children, Naomi and Stephen. When Obasan's husband dies in 1972, "the language of her grief is silence." To Naomi, Obasan has become an icon of Japanese womanhood, "defined by her serving hands." She lives "in a silent territory"; she "has turned to stone."

To Naomi's Uncle Sam, Aunt Emily is "not like woman." Evidently she is more aggressive than a woman should be. When the persecution of Japanese Canadians begins in 1941, Aunt Emily, along with other Nisei men and women, protests vigorously; and she continues to do so throughout the remainder of her life. When Aunt Emily learns the fate of her sister, Naomi's mother, she tells Obasan and Sam, then urges them to tell Naomi and Stephen. After Naomi has grown up, Aunt Emily urges her to remember and to speak of the persecution she suffered:

> "You have to remember," Aunt Emily said. "You are your history. If you cut any of it off you're an amputee. Don't deny the past. Remember everything. If you're bitter, be bitter. Cry it out! Scream! Denial is gangrene."

Naomi's first response, however, is to take Obasan's stance against Aunt Emily: "Some memories, too, might better be forgotten. Didn't Obasan once say, 'It is better to forget'? . . . What is past recall is past pain."

Neither of Naomi's aunts provides her with a satisfactory model of womanly fulfilment. Entrusted with the care of two children by Naomi's mother (when she left for Japan, in September 1941, on a visit to her ailing grandmother), Obasan raises Naomi and Stephen with an unfailing tenderness that Naomi can never forget. But Obasan's marriage to Sam, though devoted, is empty of touch and tenderness. Obasan married Sam, she tells Naomi, to please her close friend, his mother; and, after conceiving two stillborn children, the couple evidently gave up sex. Though Naomi lived with them for years in a one-room shack, she has "never once seen them caressing." When Naomi, as a child, asks her uncle if he and Obasan are "in love," he replies: "In ruv? What that?" Aunt Emily's life, too, is devoid of romantic tenderness. Preoccupied with political activity, she has never married. Naomi has known her Aunt Emily only through infrequent visits from faraway Toronto. Obasan, on the other hand, she has known as a second mother; moreover, Obasan, like her mother (who was raised in Japan, though born in Canada), is an Issei, with values that remind Naomi of the mother whom Obasan replaced when Naomi was five. It is not surprising that, for a long time, Naomi rejects

Emily's values in favor of Obasan's. This rejection, however, is accompanied by its own emotional emptiness. When her uncle dies in 1972, Naomi is thirty-six years old, unmarried, uncomfortable with her life, unhappy. She is tired of silence, ready for change.

The haunting, lyrical passage that prefaces the novel distinguishes between two kinds of silence: "There is a silence that cannot speak. There is a silence that will not speak." In the first scenes of the novel, which take place in 1972, before and just after the death of Naomi's Uncle Sam, Naomi is clearly a victim of the "silence that will not speak." Looking at the package of documents on the internment sent her by Aunt Emily, she sees Aunt Emily's years of writing protest letters as enervating and futile: "Like Cupid, [Aunt Emily] aimed for the heart. But the heart was not there." But beneath Naomi's feeling that to speak of the past is futile lies a deeper feeling that to think of the past will be to drown in a "whirlpool": "If I linger in the longing [to remember her childhood], I am drawn into a whirlpool. I can only skirt the edges after all." The novel is presented as an autobiographical account by Naomi, the impetus for which comes from Naomi's conversion, after the death of her uncle, to Aunt Emily's view that silence is diseased and speech healthy. " 'It matters to get the facts straight,' Aunt Emily said last May. . . . 'What's right is right. What's wrong is wrong. Health starts somewhere.' " The assembling of written materials, ostensibly done by Naomi, is an enterprise whose first aim is therapeutic. Naomi is presented as a person lost in the nightmare created by her silence; only by expressing her feelings can she reach understanding and emotional health. The novel mimics the mental process by which the narrator, Naomi, achieves a deeper understanding of her life; also, the novel implies that it is the writing of the novel that constitutes the therapeutic process by which greater understanding is achieved.

If the novel is therapeutic for Naomi (and, presumably, for Naomi's creator, the author, Kogawa), it is also potentially therapeutic for the community of Japanese Canadians. By maintaining silence, the Japanese Canadians have allowed the lies about them to remain uncontradicted. This is a point made to Naomi by Aunt Emily.

> "None of us," [Aunt Emily] said, "escaped the naming. We were defined and identified by the way we were seen. A newspaper in B. C. headlined, 'They are a stench in the nostrils of the people of Canada.' "

From Aunt Emily, Naomi takes over the aim of contradicting the popular-press versions of the Japanese internment. For example, beside a newspaper account of how "grinning and happy" the Japanese beet workers in Alberta were, she places her own agonized account of squalor and exhaustion. " 'Grinning and happy' . . . ? That is one telling. It's not how it was." But the Japanese Canadians are a part of the Canadian society which deprived them of their Canadian rights; what was done to them has important implications for the health of Canada as a whole. "What this country did to us, it did to itself," Aunt Emily says to Naomi. The therapy proposed by the book is not just for Japanese Canadians, but for all Canadians, as Canada's future health as a democracy depends, at least in part, on its recognition of (and reparation for) its past failings.

Obasan is Issei or first-generation; Aunt Emily is Nisei or second-generation; Naomi is something quite different— Sansei or third-generation Japanese Canadian. Obasan is fifty years old when the persecution begins in 1941, Emily twenty-five; each is fully grown, her values fully formed. But Naomi is a child of five, not told what is happening, and too young to fully understand in any case: her perception of the persecution is bound to be quite different from that of either aunt. To say that Naomi converts from Obasan's view that silence is best to Aunt Emily's view that one has to speak out is, finally, to oversimplify. It is true that Naomi comes to an understanding that Aunt Emily's words of protest have not been futile: late in the novel she refers to them as "thin white wafers . . . symbols of communion." Aunt Emily has worked with the Co-operative Committee on Japanese Canadians, and it cannot be accidental that the book closes with an excerpt from the Memorandum by the Co-operative Committee that was instrumental in preventing the Government's planned deportation of all Japanese Canadians. But Naomi cannot speak in the same language as her Aunt Emily. To Aunt Emily, the persecution is "like a bad dream"; to Naomi it is like a nightmare from which there seems no waking, "a darkness that has crept into the house," a pervading silence. The aim of the narrator—and, presumably, of her creator, Kogawa—is to combine speech and silence, or to articulate the silence: "The speech that frees comes forth from the amniotic deep. To attend its voice, I can hear it say, is to embrace its absence." In the Buddhist tradition of Naomi's Grandfather Nakane, one "awakens" through apprehension of a something (or a nothing) that "cannot be put into words" [Alan W. Watts, *The Way of Zen* (1957)]; in the Western tradition, God is "the Word," and reality is apprehended through words. Naomi—like Kogawa—has roots in both traditions: the offspring of an Issei mother and a Nisei father, Naomi blends a Japanese attention to silence with a Western attention to words. Indeed, it is this blending that gives rise to the distinctive beauties and subtleties of *Obasan.*

Naomi's Aunt Emily seeks remedies for specific social evils: she looks in libraries and at conference agendas. Naomi seeks something much less easily defined, and her gaze is more wide-ranging. In one scene we see her as a fourteen-year-old sitting silently beside a swamp near her home in southern Alberta. "The longer I sit," she says, "the more I see." Through a passive receptiveness (what Wordsworth would call a wise passiveness), she gathers into her eyes a myriad of small swamp creatures, including a frog with a broken leg that she takes home and nurses back to health and freedom. When she returns home with the frog, she learns that her father has just died; and the slow organic healing of the frog's leg acts as a metonym for the slow and painful process by which Naomi recovers, first, from her grief over her father's death and, second, from the years-long ordeal of persecution (to which her father's early death may be partly attributed). "To pull with control rather than push with force," says Naomi, is the

Japanese way; and the healing of Naomi's spirit is, at first, not pushed by her will but pulled by powerful inner forces too deep to be named. The process is completed by an opposite and complementary urge, a change and activation of the will elicited by a "push" from her Aunt Emily.

Having willed herself to speak, Naomi wants to articulate something which her Aunt Emily only dimly perceives, the "silence that cannot speak." Such silence has many aspects; animals, being speechless, are locked in one kind of silence, and Naomi is intensely aware not only of animals, but of the kinship between their responses and ours. Describing chickens in the farmyard, Naomi seems, at the same time, to define the silent impulses that underlie the behaviour of the Japanese community when the persecution begins:

> If anything goes overhead—a cloud, an airplane . . .—they all seem to be connected to one another like a string of Christmas tree lights. Their orange eyes are in unison, and each head is crooked at an angle watching the overshadowing death.

One of the most important scenes in the novel again involves chickens. As a small child, Naomi puts some yellow chicks her parents have purchased into a cage with a white hen: to her horror, the hen starts pecking them to death. Such a scene can easily be allegorized: Canada is a sort of white "mother hen" that turned on some "yellow chicks," the Japanese residents who seemed to form a "Yellow Peril." But to see the scene as simply racial allegory is to miss its deeper significance: the hen's behaviour suggests that in all animals there exists, alongside an impulse to nurture, an opposite impulse, to destroy. The xenophobia of white Canadians after Pearl Harbor can be attacked by typewritten letters; but Naomi becomes aware that this xenophobia is part of a problem much larger and deeper: nature, the nature that all creatures share, seems mixed.

In *Obasan* the destructive behaviour of human beings far exceeds that of animals; and it appears not only in large events such as wars and political persecutions, but also in small, everyday events. After looking around the squalid hut in Slocan that his family will be forced to occupy during its internment, Naomi's brother, Stephen, walks outside and starts maiming butterflies with his crutch: " 'They're bad,' Stephen says. . . . 'They eat holes in your clothes.' " Words, by enabling us to understand experience, seem part of what makes us superior to other animals; but words can separate us from experience by hiding from us our real impulses. The butterflies, though victims of Stephen's anger, are not its real cause, any more than Japanese Canadians are the real cause of white Canadians' anger after Pearl Harbor. The deepest impulses underlying cruelty are, perhaps, as unarticulated in humans as they are in animals: to articulate them is, thus, to articulate silence.

The most shocking instance of human cruelty to animals in *Obasan* is a "small" event, but one that helps us gain some insight into the nature of human cruelty. On the way to school in Slocan, two "tough" Japanese boys slit a chicken's throat, and four other Japanese boys watch as the animal's blood slowly drips: " 'Got to make it suffer,' " says one of the two perpetrators. Stephen's slashing at the butterflies, like the white chicken's slashing at the yellow chicks, was a spontaneous effusion of rage; but the cruelty of the two "tough" boys is planned and deliberate. Stephen's act was beast-like; the two "tough" boys are all too human. We seem to see here the impulses that underlie the persecution of individuals and groups in human society; and the impulses seem to lie too deep to be eradicated by legislation. Like the boys in William Golding's *Lord of the Flies,* these two boys have plotted an unsophisticated sacrifice ritual. The ritual seems compensatory. By inflicting pain on the animal, the boys gain a sense of power and solidarity, and win momentary release from their own pain, inflicted by circumstance.

As this scene shows, words can be used to justify cruelty, but they can also be used to expose it: the power of words to mis-name does not cancel their power to name. A faith in the liberating power of words is something that Naomi comes to share with her Aunt Emily. Near the end of the book, after Stephen and Naomi have been told of how their mother was "broken" and disfigured by an atomic blast, the family's Anglican priest, Nakayama-sensei, says a prayer: " 'That there is brokenness,' he says quietly. 'That this world is brokenness. But within brokenness is the unbreakable name. How the whole earth groans till Love returns.' "

The "unbreakable name" is, of course, God, who in the Bible is identified with "the Word" and with Love. The novel implies that words springing from love lead to "the Word" and can share in its power to name experience accurately. But love is not merely a word and not merely Western. Naomi's central insight into the nature of love she gains not from reading the Bible, but from looking at the Japanese ideograph for "love," which contains "the root words 'heart' and 'hand' and 'action'—love as hands and heart in action together." Words are not enough by themselves; they must be "made flesh" by action.

Before Naomi learns this intellectually, she learns it experientially from a character who is neither "Western" nor "Eastern," but somewhere between or outside these two categories. His name is Rough Lock Bill, and he seems to be the sole survivor of an Amerindian tribe that once lived in [the] wilderness around Slocan, [British Columbia]. Rough Lock Bill is unlike any other character Naomi meets. Excluded from society more wholly than Naomi can ever be, he has a capacity to survive and thrive that is in itself exemplary. But he also teaches Naomi more specific lessons, in what he says and does. In June 1943, when Naomi meets Rough Lock Bill, she is a painfully quiet seven-year-old interned in Slocan. As she and a friend are playing by the lake, he walks up and not only speaks and writes his own name, but also demands that she speak and write hers. Naomi's Issei elders have conditioned her to feel a stare as "an invasion and a reproach"; and from white Canadians she has experienced many stares that were just that. But Rough Lock Bill's eyes, though they penetrate, do not invade or reproach. "Privacy" comes from the Latin *privare,* "to separate, deprive": Naomi's privacy is a state of deprivation, which Rough Lock Bill, by contrast to the white and the yellow people she has en-

countered, alters. He insists on communicating with her, which he does by telling her a story. But friendship entails more than words; and Rough Lock Bill confirms his friendship by deed when, a few minutes later, by disastrous chance, Naomi nearly drowns in the lake and Rough Lock Bill saves her. This physical rescue from death is a heroic enactment of the love for strangers that many people lack; but it is not his only rescue. Naomi has been "drowning" in her inner silences; and in "plunging" into her soul, Rough Lock has offered spiritual rescue in communion or fellowship.

Rough Lock's acts are equal and opposite to those of a white neighbor in Vancouver, Old Man Gower, who used to carry the four-year-old Naomi to a place of privacy and ask, "Would you like me to tell you a story?" What then transpired may be simply summarized as sexual abuse, but its effects on Naomi are not simple. The abuse makes Naomi feel abject, afraid, utterly helpless—but also desirous: she starts to seek out Old Man Gower herself, although the secret pleasure he gives her causes her to feel excruciatingly isolated from her mother. She used to feel that her mother was "a tree trunk of which I am an offshoot"; now she feels she is "a parasite on her [mother's] body, no longer of her [mother's] mind." Around this time her mother "disappears," and to Naomi "the stillness of waiting for her to return" comes to feel like "a shadow which grows and surrounds me like air." Describing the initial instance of sexual abuse, Naomi has written: "Is this where the terror begins?" The book implies that it is. At the centre of Naomi's silences is the unarticulated feeling that her mother's disappearance is a terrible punishment for Naomi's "betrayal" of her mother's love. Naomi knows that Old Man Gower is an enemy, his attentions a cruel parody of the way love acts; but she feels her own complicity in his invasion of her body and cannot forgive herself—indeed, cannot even do what must precede such forgiveness: she cannot revive the memory and subject it to mature scrutiny. Instead she tries to forget what she cannot forget and so perpetuates its tyranny over her. Sexual abuse of children is "taboo": to speak of this part of her past, Naomi must break the silence that we are conditioned to impose on the "taboo." The shock of her Uncle Sam's death stimulates her to revive the memory of Old Man Gower; and the shock soon after of learning her mother's fate further revives her feelings from their chronic numbness. The facts of what happened to her mother, though terrifying, disperse the mist of her imaginings; she comes to see herself and her mother as victims of a shared delusion—the delusion that silence heals. Naomi's mother and her grandmother, she learns, "were unable to talk of all the things that happened. The horror would surely die sooner, they felt, if they refused to speak." But Grandmother Sato breaks her silence to write to her husband in Toronto, while Naomi's mother "continued her vigil of silence." Naomi concludes that the silence intended to "protect" has maimed: "Gentle Mother, we were lost together in our silences. Our wordlessness was our mutal destruction."

One of the deepest of the silences "that cannot speak" is the silence of those absent or dead. Yet throughout her life Naomi has experienced moments of silent communion with her mother, expressed by Kogawa in passages of exquisite lyric beauty. In 1945, not long after the bombing of Nagasaki, Naomi woke suddenly to feel: "Something has touched me but I do not know what it is. . . . She is here. She is not here. She is reaching out to me with a touch deceptive as down." Now, in 1972, after learning the truth of her mother's fate, she hears "the sigh of your remembered breath, a wordless word." Once again she feels as if she is about to drown: "I sit on the raft begging for a tide to land me safely on the sand but you draw me to the white distance, skyward and away from this blood-drugged earth." The way to safety is speech, and the "speech that frees" is the word of the "wordless word" that is God. Remembering both the small sins committed by herself and her mother and the terrible sins perpetrated by nations, she invokes a prayer spoken by the priest Nakayama-sensei years ago at her Grandmother Nakane's funeral in Slocan: "We are abandoned yet we are not abandoned. You are present in every hell. Teach us to see Love's presence in our abandonment. Teach us to forgive."

Rough Lock Bill teaches Naomi through both what he does and what he says. What he says emphasizes the importance of words—he insists that both of them speak and write their names—and, in particular, of stories: "Never met a kid didn't like stories. Red skin, yellow skin, white skin, any skin." The particular story he tells is of his tribe's dying off till one brave finds a new place to live and leads the tribe there. " 'If you go slow,' [the brave] says [to the tribe], 'you can go. Slow can go. Slow can go'. . . . We call it Slocan now. Real name is Slow-can-go." Rough Lock's etymology may be facetious (many of the best tales are tall tales); but his faith in surviving adversity through "slow going" is adopted by Naomi, who, as she follows the bereaved Obasan to Obasan's attic in 1972, repeats, " 'Slow can go.' " Rough Lock's tale probably derives from a tribal folktale of the kind that Stith Thompson classifies [in *The Folktale* (1951)] as *Sage* or "local legend"; its basic movement, from identity to loss of identity to a renewal of identity, is one that Northrop Frye finds in all story. From Rough Lock Bill, Naomi learns the value of story: it can show a way to survive "brokenness"; it can unify experience by containing "brokenness" within a unified whole; it can unify a people by showing what all of them share. In writing the story of one woman's "brokenness" and her slow mending, Kogawa connects "heart to hand" and harnesses the power of narrative to enact love and faith—a power much greater than that of discursive argument.

Kogawa began as a poet, publishing three volumes of lyric verse before her novel; in the novel there is an accession of imaginative power that is connected with her adoption of narrative. Often the poems express feelings that emerge from a narrative context that is only partly defined. In a sequence called "Poems for My Enemies" in her third collection, *Jericho Road,* it is not clear who the woman's enemies may be or why, for example, she at one point imagines (in a striking surrealistic image) that her washing machine contains "buckets of mud":

> how can the wash get clean
> if the water is not clear

> if there are buckets of mud
> in the washing machine.

In *Obasan,* Naomi at one point finds a note on which her Aunt Emily has handwritten a quotation from the Book of Habakkuk in the Old Testament: "Write the vision and make it plain." Reading the note, Naomi thinks: "She's the one with the vision. . . . The truth for me is more murky, shadowy and grey." But in *Obasan* Kogawa has written the vision and made it plain: the book is an imaginative triumph over the forces that militate against expression of our inmost feelings. (pp. 239-49)

> *Gary Willis, "Speaking the Silence: Joy Kogawa's 'Obasan',"* in Studies in Canadian Literature, *Vol. 12, No. 2, 1987, pp. 239-49.*

Marilyn Russell Rose (essay date Spring 1988)

[*In the following essay, Rose examines Kogawa's use of narrative and rhetorical devices in* Obasan *and briefly analyzes the work's political and historical implications.*]

What is the relationship between literature and history, or literature and politics? *Can* art recreate historical "reality"? What is the effect of what Wayne C. Booth has called "the rhetoric of fiction" upon historical narratives? To what extent is fictionalized history more compelling, and indeed more "true," than the "factual" narratives of historians and journalists? Or is it true, as the deconstructionists would have it, that historical fiction is *never* true in any objective sense, and that novelists must inevitably subvert their own narratives, denying their status as "truth"— simply because authorized truth is itself an archaic fiction, and history itself [is] always altered by the lenses of present time and subjectivity through which it must be perceived?

These questions are significant, it seems to me, given the post-Saussurean critical climate in which we live and work. J. Hillis Miller, for example, refers to "the fiction of the referential, the illusion that the terms of [a] poem refer literally to something that exists" ["Stevens' Rock and Criticism as Cure," *Georgia Review* (1976)]. Yet historical fiction, like Joy Kogawa's *Obasan* (1981), would seem to deny the illusion of non-referentiality. In telling of the internment of Japanese-Canadians during World War II, *Obasan* stands at the intersection of history, politics and literature, and draws attention to the real historical experience which it seeks to portray. It is built upon the historical, journalistic and documentary accounts of the internment which preceded it. It assumes that ultimately language *can* convey actual human experience, whatever the complexity of the relationship between language and social context. Moreover, it is overtly rhetorical in its assumption that experiencing "real" human suffering, even indirectly, as when human experience is enacted in language, will radicalize the person who comes to know it, the reader.

To speak of rhetoric, of course, is to commit oneself to a kind of communications model in speaking of historical fiction. Rhetoric is "the art of persuasion" as Geoffrey

Hartman puts it [in *Criticism in the Wilderness: The Study of Literature Today* (1980)], in which language is used ideologically, shaping the reader's responses toward a subject of real-world relevance in prescriptive ways. When Booth speaks of the "rhetoric of fiction" [in *The Rhetoric of Fiction* (1961)], he assumes that there are "rhetorical resources" available to the writer of fiction, capacities inherent in fictional genres, which the writer can exploit, "consciously or unconsciously, to impose his fictional world upon the reader." Implicit in both Hartman's and Booth's comments is the assumption that a text is produced by an author for a reader and that it is written because the author has something to say about human experience.

Old-fashioned as that model may be, it seems appropriate for looking at historical fiction, and particularly at a novel like **Obasan** which is clearly political, taking an overtly ideological position on the historical episode which it portrays. Kogawa's achievement in **Obasan** is that she does so without, however, retreating into historical simple-mindedness: in fact, she is remarkably sophisticated about the complexities of writing (and reading) history and remarkably honest about the need to preserve a kind of humanistic faith in historical writing despite the ambivalences which surround the act.

What happened, in general, to Japanese-Canadians in Canada during World War II can be stated very simply and skeletally: "In February 1942 the federal cabinet ordered the expulsion of 22,000 Japanese Canadians residing within one hundred miles of the Pacific Coast. The order marked the beginning of a process that saw Canada's Japanese minority uprooted from their homes, confined in detention camps, stripped of their property and forcibly dispersed across Canada or shipped to a starving Japan" [Ann Gomer Sunahara, *The Politics of Racism: The Uprooting of Japanese-Canadians During the Second World War* (1981)].

By the time Kogawa began writing **Obasan** in the late 1970s, dozens of written accounts of the internment existed, both published and archival, virtually all of them "rhetorical" in protesting the injustice done to Japanese-Canadians during the war, and all of them assuming one of two forms, the historical narrative or the documentary, each type of discourse employing its own kind of rhetoric.

The historical account is typified by Ken Adachi's *The Enemy That Never Was,* which begins:

> There is something about the wartime evacuation and detention of nearly 21,000 people, three-quarters of whom were Canadian citizens, that had always disturbed me. It is something more complicated than a reaction to the suspect morality of the acts of a nation supposedly fighting to uphold democratic ideals but rounding up children, middle-aged men and women from their homes on the west coast of Canada, incarcerating them in detention and labour camps, confiscating and selling their property and then threatening to "deport" them unless they dispersed themselves across Canada. Those acts were rationalized on the need to maintain Canada's "national security" following Japan's attack on Pearl Harbour. But that excuse became rather threadbare when restrictive measures were maintained for almost four years after the end of World War II, denying the right of Japanese Canadians to live and work where they chose.

Adachi's language is restrained. Ironic understatement ("something . . . that had always disturbed me," "suspect morality," an "excuse . . . rather threadbare") is made to defuse his otherwise blunt accusations ("evacuations," "detention," "incarcerating," "confiscating," "threatening," "dispersed," "rationalized")—a rhetorical tactic which serves to "flag" his discursive stance as predominantly intellectual rather than predominantly emotional.

Ann Gomer Sunahara adopts a similarly moderate tone in her *Politics of Racism* (1981), another history of the internment: "this book is intended as a reminder that the tolerance we know is historically only a thin and recently applied veneer on Canadian society. [It expresses] the hope that the events discussed here will bring home a realization of how easy it is in our imperfect world for an ill-informed majority to wreak havoc on a blameless minority." She is outraged, as her language at times betrays ("thin . . . veneer," "ill-informed majority," "wreak havoc," "blameless minority"), but as a historian she must assume an objective stance through the inclusion of neutralizing words: her book is but a "reminder" of "our imperfect world" and a "hope" that readers will "realize" their capacity for social injustice.

In both cases, then, a historical rhetoric is employed which is a rhetoric of dispassion: emotional language is neutralized, a moderate tone is assumed despite the writing's being about rampant injustice, and the discourse is presented as reasonable above all else. Even the structure of historical accounts contributes to this rhetorical effect, as facts and details are marshaled and presented in orderly fashion, with emphasis on chronology and, within that, on causality. The effect is to persuade through intellect, to invite intellectual response to what has been presented as sequentially arranged objective fact. In consequence, there is a clinical quality to historical discourse, and it is clearly limited (deliberately so) in what might be called "readerly affect."

Documentary writing about the internment does not share this limitation, and it is in fact rhetorically opposite to historical narrative, as can be seen in Barry Broadfoot's "oral history" (as he calls it), *Years of Sorrow, Years of Shame* (1977). Describing his method and goals, Broadfoot writes: " . . . I have travelled around Canada with a tape recorder and a notebook collecting stories from persons who participated in [this] great event in Canadian history. I am putting the people back into history, and as far as I am concerned, the expulsion of the Japanese Canadians from B.C. is an event that deserves treatment." Broadfoot interviewed Japanese-Canadian survivors of the internment, some thirty years after their experience of it, then spliced together these ostensibly verbatim accounts, grouping them thematically, and thereby producing what might be called a "retro-documentary" on the subject.

The effect is powerfully rhetorical, as the voices of those who suffered "speak" with terrible directness and moving simplicity. Of the Hastings Park holding center, for example:

> It was awful. Where the horses were, that's where they put us. . . . Whole families in horse stalls. They put army blankets as partitions but what good were they? People used to come and visit us and they would say, "Say, how can you live like this? You're living where the animals were." I'd tell them to go talk to the soldiers about that, but they wouldn't because everybody was afraid. . . . The Livestock Building at the P.N.E. was the worst place I have ever been in. I never want to be in a place like that again. It was where they had the cattle and horses and oh, it was awful. . . . It was at the time that there was dysentery. Oh, that was terrible too. Everybody had it. . . . The smell was awful. You couldn't stand it but you had to.

Documentary writing, of course, attempts to (indeed purports to) render experience directly, without authorial/directorial intrusion. The voices of experience are foregrounded and authorial machinations concealed; the discourse thus takes on a testimonial quality which is utterly compelling—especially when that testimony is to the pain of victims of a historical injustice. It is as if reader and "speaker" meet within the illusion of shared, unmediated experience, and the effect on the reader can be intensely emotional. In fact, while the rhetoric of history is one mainly of intellect, the rhetoric of document is inherently emotional—neither, however, combining the two spheres (the thinking and the feeling) as effectively as can the rhetoric of fiction.

Obasan, the only fictional account of the historical experience of the Japanese-Canadians (except Kogawa's own *Naomi's Road,* a children's version of the Obasan story), attempts to *enact* historical experience, to bring the internment to life through imagined characters and invented story. Moreover, as with all fiction, there is a rhetorical impact in the *way* the story is told—that is, in its *constructs,* such as point of view, the structure of the narrative, the central metaphors which inform it and, ultimately, the presence or absence of closure within the narrative.

Obasan, the only fictional account of the historical experience of the Japanese-Canadians, attempts to *enact* historical experience, to bring the internment to life through imagined characters and invented story.

—Marilyn Russell Rose

Kogawa chooses to tell the story from the point of view of Naomi Nakane, a thirty-six-year-old spinster who had been a child of four when the dislocation began. Her family was not only dispersed but effectively destroyed: her mother permanently cut off by an ill-timed visit to aging

relatives in Japan; her father sent to work on a road gang; her mother's sister Emily fled to Toronto; and Naomi and her brother and aunt and uncle deployed to a ghost town, Slocan, in Alberta, and thence to the beet fields of Granton, near Lethbridge—where they will stay, rooted in its clay soil, apparently forever. By the time the war was over, Naomi and Stephen were orphans, wards of Aunt (Obasan) and Uncle, and the closest the fisherman uncle would ever get to the sea again would be the undulating grasslands of this wind-blistered corner of inland Canada.

Naomi is, at first glance, a strange choice as narrator, for she is, as the novel begins, a silent and silenced person. Even as a child she had been without speech (the most silent child Aunt Emily had ever seen), and now, as a painfully repressed adult, she recognizes the burden that her inability to speak aloud, to others, has imposed upon her. For Naomi is not without words. She is a poet, as the first words of the novel, its epigraph, assert:

> There is a silence that cannot speak.
>
> There is a silence that will not speak.
>
> Beneath the grass the speaking dreams and beneath the dreams is a sensate sea. The speech that frees comes forth, from that amniotic deep. To attend its voice, I can hear it say, is to embrace its absence.
> But I fail the task. The word is stone.
>
> I admit it.
>
> I hate the stillness. I hate the stone. I hate the sealed vault with its cold icon. I hate the staring into the night. The questions thinning into space. The sky swallowing the echoes.
>
> Unless the stone bursts with telling unless the seed flowers with speech, there is in my life no living word. . . .
>
> If I could follow the stream down and down to the hidden voice, would I come at last to the freeing word? I ask the night but the silence is steadfast. There is no reply.

Her problem is not with words *per se,* then, but with experience that is so frozen within her as the novel begins that it cannot be released into "freeing" language—spoken language, *recorded* words, public speech. Because that experience is past, moreover, and Naomi will have to return to the past to recover it, it is clear that the "freeing word" in *Obasan* is *historical* speech, that which recreates the past in and through the present. Because her own experience is representative of a communal, racially shared past, Naomi's words about it, when she is freed into speech, will be *bardic* in the sense of giving voice to the experience of an entire people as narrator of her "fiction."

Though that prospect terrifies Naomi ("Why not leave the dead to bury the dead?"), Kogawa makes it clear that Naomi Nakane has been *chosen* as ethnic historian, and that she is temperamentally suited to the task, whatever her level of resistance to it. In the first chapter of the novel, as she and Uncle make their annual pilgrimage to a coulee just outside Granton, Naomi is consumed with a single question which her uncle refuses to answer: "Uncle," she whispers, "why do we come here every year?" It is a historical question, and the alpha and omega of her quest. The date is 9 August 1972, the twenty-seventh anniversary of the bombing of Nagasaki, and in pursuing that single question Naomi will uncover the history not only of the Japanese-Canadian internment but of racial injustice in modern times on a truly apocalyptic scale.

A month later, when Uncle has died and Naomi has returned to Granton for his funeral, her status as historian is confirmed. When Obasan takes her up to the attic to locate a parcel left for her by Aunt Emily, Naomi reacts to the web-hung lumber room, to its spiders and flies and "carnage" and unburied dead, with horror:

> I would like to drop the lid of the trunk, go downstairs and back to bed. But we're trapped, Obasan and I, by our memories of the dead—all our dead—those who refuse to bury themselves. Like threads of old spider webs, still sticky and hovering, the past waits for us to submit, or depart. When I least expect it, a memory comes skittering out of the dark, spinning and netting the air, ready to snap me up and ensnare me in old and complex puzzles. Just a glimpse of a worn-out patchwork quilt and the old question comes thudding out of the night again like a giant moth. Why did my mother not return?

When Emily's parcel is placed in Naomi's hands, filled with documentation and bearing the "seven canonical words" from Habakkuk 2:2—"Write the vision and make it plain"—it is clear that Naomi will not be able to avoid her historical mission: the weight of the package, which is as heavy as a loaf of "stone bread," corresponds exactly to the weight of the stone which oppresses from within in the epigraph. It must be set free if Naomi is to be freed.

Naomi, however, is, Kogawa suggests, an ideal modern historian, because she *is* so voiceless, so unknowing and uncommitted, so historically virginal at the start. For prior to Naomi's there are two Japanese "voices" on the internment experience. One is the voice of silent suffering and resignation, Obasan's voice (the voice of the Issei), in which the past is denied validity by the profound and dignified passivity of its victims: as Naomi says of Obasan, "Over the years, silence within her small body has grown large and powerful." The other voice is the strident one of revisionist history and political compensation, the voice of the Nisei and Aunt Emily. Naomi stands in dialectical relation to both. A motherless child who has been "mothered" from the age of five by these two opposed aunts, she is clearly destined for synthesis. Thus, having been schooled in silence by Obasan and Uncle (*"kodomo ne tame"*—"for the sake of the children"), she must now listen to Emily, that "word warrior," that "crusader," that "little old grey-haired Mighty Mouse, a Bachelor of Advanced Activists and General Practitioner of Just Causes." The process will be painful. Indeed, as Emily's presence and documents assault her, and invade and alter her consciousness, Naomi will cry out: "Aunt Emily, are you a surgeon cutting at my scalp with your folders and your filing cards and your insistence on knowing all? . . . when will this operation be over Aunt Em?"

Having established her narrator, then, as a reluctant but exquisitely sensitive historian, whose task it is to unlock a painful, covert history, Kogawa structures Naomi's narrative in particularly evocative ways. The novel itself is shaped by Naomi's consciousness, as she stays with Obasan (in the present time of the novel) awaiting the uncle's burial. Zig-zagging back and forth in time, the narrative is structured associatively rather than chronologically by Naomi's experience during this period—by both her states of consciousness (her thought, memories and dreams) and her exposure to Emily's documents, which she reads during the three days of present narrative time.

When the narrative is sorted out chronologically in retrospect by the reader, however, it is clear that Kogawa has presented Naomi's family's experience as a journey—a journey compelled by faceless governmental edict—which takes the form of a descent into ever-deepening circles of hell. It begins in 1942, with uncertainty for Naomi and her family as they live in the shadow of Hastings Park where, they hear, detainees are "herded into the grounds and kept there like animals until they were shipped off" to road-work camps or "concentration camps." Frantically Emily struggles to spare the family the "noise," "confusion," "chaos," cramming and hysteria of Hastings Park, and at length manages it, so that the "inner family" of aunt, uncle and children, at least, avoids Hastings Park and is sent directly to one of the ghost towns, Slocan.

In Slocan, the second circle, hardship is a given. Their house is a rundown two-room wooden hut shared with strangers. Existence is marginal. Yet the children thrive, the community asserts itself, and in time gardens grow, crafts develop, stores open and life is tolerable again. Then, however, the war ends and, ironically, the third, the worst descent for the Nakane family begins after the cessation of hostilities, as the family is moved to Granton, to the Barker's sugarbeet farm, where exile becomes a virtual life of the damned.

In Granton, the very air is "angry," a "fist," and every plant is "deliberate and fierce." They live in a chicken coop uninsulated against winter cold and summer heat. The work is back-breaking, the sun "maddening," the field "an oven," and Naomi's "black head a sun-trap," her "tear glands [burned] out." In this "prison," they are "obedient as machines." Only Stephen, whose music is his way out, has recourse: Naomi sees him on his bike against the fuchsia, "like one of the Israelite children moving unharmed through the fiery furnace." What this image of Stephen suggests, of course, is that this exile to the "desert" of Granton is a racially-based diaspora like that of the Old Testament Jews.

Yet even Granton is not the worst, is not the final circle in this iconography of human cruelty. As horrible as it is, the beet farm is but a patch upon the greater horror which brings the novel to a close, that of Naomi's mother's end, for she was caught in the atomic holocaust of Nagasaki while on an errand of mercy with her own mother. Naomi paraphrases Grandmother Kato's words:

What she saw was incomprehensible. Almost all the buildings were flattened or in flames for as far as she could see. The landmarks were gone. Tall columns of fire rose through the haze and everywhere the dying and the wounded crawled, fled, stumbled like ghosts among the ruins. Voices screamed, calling the names of children, fathers, mothers, calling for help, calling for water.

Beneath some wreckage, she saw first the broken arm, then the writhing body of her niece, her head bent back, her hair singed, both her eye sockets blown out. In a weak and delirious voice, she was calling Tomio. Grandma Kato touched her niece's leg and the skin peeled off and stuck to the palm of her hand.

. . . . .

One evening, when she had given up the the search for the day, she sat down beside a naked woman she had seen earlier who was aimlessly chipping wood to make a pyre on which to cremate a dead baby. The woman was utterly disfigured. Her nose and one cheek were almost gone. Great wounds and pustules covered her entire face and body. She was completely bald. She sat in a cloud of flies and maggots wriggled among her wounds. As Grandma watched her, the woman gave her a vacant gaze, then let out a cry. It was my mother.

It is only after hearing this horrifying first-hand account of Nagasaki and the subsequent death of her mother—a truly apocalyptic knowledge—that Naomi is freed to feel, freed to speak, and the stone bursts forth into the flower that is the text of the novel.

Obasan, then, is an account of violation so horrible that a people (ironically, a community built upon service to and respect for others) is made to go through a succession of hells, and hells different "in degree only" from that inflicted upon Japan by American technology in the name of a just war. How, we wonder, and why, did these people suffer in silence, and for thirty years, Aunt Emily notwithstanding? The answer lies in the novel's central metaphor, which is perhaps Kogawa's most powerful rhetorical tool (because it most powerfully shapes our response to her discourse), the concept of rape—that crime in which the victim inevitably feels shame and suspects her own complicity, that she has indeed "invited" attack.

Early in the narrative, Naomi recounts her own sexual abuse by a neighbor, Old Man Gower, when she was four. He lures her to his house on the pretense of "fixing" a scraped knee, and touches her in ways that fill her with shame. For reasons that she cannot fathom, it happens again and again: "I do not wish him to lift me up, but I do not know what it is to struggle." It is the single thing which she cannot tell her mother, for she suspects that she enjoyed the subjegation. Nor was this an "isolated incident," she tells us, for later there was Percy in Slocan, who pushed her against a wall and warned her not to cry out. There was also an unshaven man, egged on by another in a restaurant, who propositioned her with a five-dollar bill when she was nine. Her adult dreams are filled with "Brit-

ish" soldiers who forever rape and maim anew. At one point she wonders, "Does Old Man Gower still walk through the hedges between our houses in Vancouver, in Slocan, in Granton and Cecil?" Even at thirty-six, Naomi's sense of violation is far from exorcised.

Indeed, the sexual violation of oriental women by white men is in *Obasan* a political act. Naomi herself makes this connection when Stephen is beaten up by white boys and he conceals it:

> "What happened?" I whisper as Stephen comes up the stairs.
>
> He doesn't answer me. Is he ashamed, as I was in Old Man Gower's bathroom? Should I go away?

What Kogawa suggests here is that the abuse of Japanese-Canadians by white Canada is a kind of sociopathic rape in response to which victims can only reel in silent shame.

This construct is underscored by the images of birds and chickens that recur throughout the novel. As a small child, Naomi was guilty of putting some yellow baby chicks in with a white hen who pecked as many to death as she could in the few minutes before Naomi's mother intervened. Chickens are "dim-witted pinbrains," Naomi tells us, timid and driven by a crude flock instinct: they "seem to be connected to one another like a string of Christmas tree lights"; necks crooked in unison, they look upward as if expecting death from the skies at any moment. No wonder they are so often victims, the natural victims of boys who torture and decapitate chickens on the way to school, the natural victims of kingbirds or chicken hawks, the naturally fearful "Chicken Littles" in any society.

Yet chickens and other birds are constantly connected in Naomi's imagination with Japanese-Canadians: Mother's hands were "quick as birds," as are Obasan's; Stephen, his cast removed, hops about "hesitant as a spring robin"; Nomura-Obasan is "like a plucked bird"; in Granton, the family members cling to the stove for warmth and "rotate like chickens on a spit"; an Order-in-Council at the end of the war is like a "giant hawk" sailing over a chicken yard, where there is much communal "flapping" and "squawking" and lunging for safety.

The implication is clear: some victims are naturals; they flock together, emphasizing their visibility, and invite death from the sky; they ask for it, silly creatures that they are, and hence *in their own eyes* have no right to complain. It is the same for chickens as for Japanese-Canadians as for victims of rape: when violation is somehow deserved, it is shameful to speak about it. Japanese-Canadians, says Kogawa, like Naomi at the start of the novel, blame themselves and therefore choose silence and invisibility, and thereby slow death.

Naomi, of course, must have "surgery" to prevent such spiritual death. The "stone" that she talks about in the epigraph, that "icon" in a "sealed vault," is a growth, in effect, placed there by her violation (by Mr. Gower, by all of white Canada) and by her own guilt and silence. Where there should be life, in the womb, there is stone/death.

Thus Aunt Emily, the political voice who confronts Naomi with history, is seen as a "surgeon" who forces Naomi to undergo an "operation" to remove that evil seed planted by that symbolic rape so many years ago. Naomi resists (". . . I cannot, I cannot bear the memory. There are some nightmares from which there is no waking. . . ."), but Emily's documentary invasion is relentless: "The memory drains down the sides of my face, but it isn't enough, is it? It's your hands in my abdomen, pulling the growth from the lining of my walls, but bring back the anaesthetist turn on the ether clamp down the gas mask bring on the chloroform when will this operation be over Aunt Em?" The sterile center, the false pregnancy, the stone, must be removed—by re-experiencing history—so that life may be restored.

In fact, life *is* restored through history in **Obasan.** In the last lines of the novel, when Naomi goes to the coulee alone on the day of her uncle's funeral and the day after she has learned of her mother's death, Kogawa makes it clear that the surgery has been successful: "I inch my way down the steep path that skirts the wild rose bushes, down slipping along the wet grass where the underground stream seeps through the earth. My shoes are mud-clogged again. At the very bottom, I come to the bank. Above the trees, the moon is a pure white stone. The reflection is rippling in the river—water and stone dancing. It's a quiet ballet, soundless as breath." The stone has been released into the sky, and Naomi's "thin but persistent thirst" is now assuaged as the stone, via reflection, unites and "dances" in a quiet ballet with the underground stream (water/life) that has finally surfaced in her.

Clearly Kogawa's rhetoric in **Obasan** includes closure, that "sense of an ending," to use Kermode's phrase, that consoles because it suggests that resolution is to some extent possible in temporal life. Indeed, it is worth scrutinizing her language here: the stone is released into water and sky as Naomi smells the wild roses that line the coulee—a detail that recalls another of Kogawa's motifs. Elsewhere Naomi has called her mother's story "a rose with a tangled stem" and reminded us that the Japanese ideograph for passionate love includes the symbols for "to tell" and "a long thread." Here the novel itself, Naomi's "fiction," is also a rose—a story of mother, aunts and a child which is at bottom a loving, healing history because it is, in experiential terms, a kind of release for both teller and reader.

This is not to say, however, that Kogawa sees writing history as an easy or direct task. Instead, she enunciates through Naomi some of the fundamental problems facing the modern historian. Naomi is profoundly skeptical at first about the nature of historical writing: Aunt Emily may see things clearly, she says, but "the truth for me is more murky, shadowy and grey." Besides, historical "facts" are altered in the telling, "changed in time, altered as much by the present as the present is shaped by the past"; and, as Emily herself knows, language itself cannot be trusted: "with language . . . you can disguise any crime," or anything else.

Ironically, that admission, and her constant reminders that "facts" are never equivalent to "truth"—insights which testify to historical limitation, to the *approximation*

of historical experience which "history" is—mark Naomi, and Kogawa, as "good" and convincing historians. In the end Naomi concedes that she does "need to be educated" through Emily's documents but, given her reservations about the objectivity of historical revision, she is thrown back upon the notion of responsible subjectivity: to speak of human experience, however fallibly, is our duty; we must be willing to be called, like Habakkuk, to the stand to bear witness as best we can, despite the limitations of language and sensibility which demarcate the human condition.

Kogawa would go even further. As a Christian humanist, she equates historical testimony—especially testimony to historical evil and the human suffering it engenders—with the sacrament of communion. In **Obasan,** Emily's documents are seen as "the thin white wafers in Sensei's [the minister's] silver box," a "holy nourishment" unfortunately received as less than holy by those unwilling to drink the "bitter wine" of recorded human suffering, but essential for redemption nonetheless. Certainly Naomi's own salvation, her release from constantly repressed pain, comes through experiencing a document, the blue letter from her grandmother about her mother's death. *Knowing* consoles her because, in Kogawa's view, history which provides contact with human suffering is redemptive, a means to transcendence.

The efficacy of Joy Kogawa as historian and rhetorician is, then, inarguable. In creating in Naomi a humble and tentative narrator, in reminding us of the multileveled hell through which her family and her people have been drawn, in characterizing their violation as a political and spiritual rape, in demonstrating the pain of movement into speech by a people so silenced, and in suggesting the possibility of transcendence through human suffering, her argument against this historically specific political injustice makes compelling art.

In fact, one test of the political effectiveness of Kogawa's novel is to read it against a piece of revisionist journalism written about the experience which she has so powerfully enacted. Historian J. L. Granatstein contends [in "The Enemy Within?" *Saturday Night* (1986)] that the internment of Japanese-Canadians was entirely justifiable given its political context: "the weight of historical evidence cautions against any hasty answers in the current redress debate. Military and intelligence concerns could indeed have justified the evacuation of Japanese Canadians from the Pacific coast. In retrospect, thanks to the evidence that is now available, it even appears that the arguments in favour of evacuation were stronger than they seemed in early 1942."

"Weight of historical evidence," "cautions," "justified," "in retrospect," "evidence," "stronger arguments"—here is a rhetoric of balanced and impartial judgment, much like the scholarly attitude so oblivious to human suffering found at the end of Margaret Atwood's *The Handmaid's Tale,* and just as inefficacious as that clinical speech when weighed against the rhetoric of human suffering that is **Obasan.** Are we not outraged against Granatstein after experiencing Kogawa's rhetoric? Is it not Aunt Emily's words that remain with us, and not Granatstein's? "You have to remember. You are your history. If you cut any of it off you're an amputee. Don't deny the past. Remember everything. If you're bitter, be bitter. Cry it out! Scream! Denial is gangrene." (pp. 215-25)

> Marilyn Russell Rose, "Politics into Art: Kogawa's 'Obasan' and the Rhetoric of Fiction," in Mosaic: A Journal for the Interdisciplinary Study of Literature, *Vol. XXI, Nos. 2-3, Spring, 1988, pp. 215-26.*

Mason Harris   (essay date Winter 1990)

[In the following essay, Harris provides a thematic analysis of Obasan, examining Kogawa's depiction of the historical and psychological effects of the Japanese-Canadian internment experience as they are illustrated and defined in the novel by mother-daughter relations, the conflicts that arise between generations, and the protagonist's attempts to reconcile herself to her past.]

The remarkable success of Joy Kogawa's documentary novel [*Obasan*] in weaving historical fact and subjective experience into a coherent whole is partly due to its ability to co-ordinate several layers of time around a single event: the internment and dispersal of the Japanese Canadians during and after the Second World War. The most obvious purpose of the novel is to reconstruct a suppressed chapter in Canadian history—this is Aunt Emily's special project. In counterpoint to Emily's facts and documents stands the intense personal history of Naomi's narrative, which reveals the damage inflicted on a child by the destruction of her community. As the narrative unfolds we become aware of another layer of history: that of the succeeding generations through which an immigrant community adjusts to a new culture, and the disruption of the relation between these generations by the dispersal of the Japanese Canadian community. Aunt Emily provides the essential facts, and Naomi's record of inner experience invites the reader to a strong emotional involvement in the narrative, but it is the history of the generations, as represented by the Kato and Nakane families, which binds together the various time-layers of the novel. Here I will stress the close connection between historical and psychological aspects of the novel by beginning with a discussion of the relation between generations, and then showing how this provides the basis for Naomi's relation to her two aunts and her absent mother, and also for some central imagery in which Naomi expresses both the fragmentation of her world and her final sense of resolution.

In all immigrant communities the first, second, and third generations represent crucial stages in adjustment to the adopted culture. The importance of these generations in the Japanese Canadian community is indicated by the fact that they are given special names: *Issei* (immigrants from Japan), *Nisei* (the first generation born in Canada), and *Sansei* (the children of the *Nisei*). In the novel, Obasan and Uncle Isamu represent the Issei, while Emily comes from the political side of the Nisei. Though Naomi is a Sansei by birth, the fact that she was raised by an immigrant aunt and uncle puts her more in the cultural situation of the Nisei, but without politics or community.

Emily and Naomi are drawn together by a mutual need to heal the breach the destruction of their community has opened between Nisei and Sansei generations. Emily pursues this goal actively over twenty years, with amazing persistence considering her niece's lack of response, while in the course of the novel Naomi gradually comes to recognize her need for the values her aunt conveys to her from the ideals of her own generation, so cruelly defeated by history. I will first consider Emily's pursuit of Naomi as an attempt to re-establish a relationship between the Nisei and Sansei generations, and then Naomi's resistance as the attitude of a damaged Sansei who has repressed her actual history while becoming fixated on an ideal past before the internment—an attitude which has much in common with the traditional generation represented by her aunt and uncle. In reconstructing her past under Emily's influence, she must confront her affinity to both generations as a route to accepting her own situation; her development involves the resolution of conflicting attitudes towards language, the outside world, and the traditional concept of woman.

In his comprehensive history of the Japanese Canadian community, Ken Adachi describes the conflicts between Issei and Nisei generations. These conflicts are characteristic of any immigrant culture, but made sharper for Japanese Canadians by the conservatism of the Issei community and its rejection of the *mores* of western culture. Like many first-generation immigrants, the Issei sought a dignified accommodation with the surrounding society, but without joining it or altering their way of life. They saw western society as an alien world with which they sought only a peaceful coexistence, bolstered by an idealized memory of their homeland. In contrast, the Nisei, the first generation born in Canada, eagerly sought to identify with the new country—an attitude reinforced by the Japanese emphasis on education, which induced the Canadian-born quickly to acquire English as their first language. Thus the Nisei found themselves in conflict both with their parents' generation and with the larger society with which they identified, but which responded to their enthusiasm with social rejection and exclusion from most of the professions for which their Canadian education qualified them.

One response to this situation—a response vigorously condemned by the Issei—was the formation of a group of young Nisei activists to agitate for full citizenship including the right to vote. In the late 1930s, politically-minded Nisei founded their own newspaper, *The New Canadian,* and sent delegations to Ottawa. Adachi observes [in *The Enemy That Never Was*] that their belief in the right to vote "grew into an exaggerated—and illusory—sense of the importance of political rights in a modern democracy. The growing sense of grievance and injustice . . . was still mitigated by the belief that a society which professed democratic ideals would ultimately practise them." If ineffectual and doomed to disillusionment, however, these activities provided the Nisei with a sense of western identity very different from the world-view of their parents. Under normal circumstances the activities of the progressive Nisei, however ineffectual in the short run, would have transmitted the new identity to the next generation, the Sansei, who could be expected to enter into full membership in Canadian society. The internment and dispersal which destroyed the progressive Nisei movement developing in Vancouver in the 1930s left Emily an activist without a political community and Naomi a deracinated, depressed, and apolitical Sansei with the psychological conflicts of the Nisei and no ethnic community to mediate between her sense of alienness and the WASP world of rural Alberta.

Emily's affiliation with the progressive Nisei of the 1930s is made clear in her diary, which also records her bitter disappointment as the justice and decency which she expected from Canadian society failed to appear. Emily does not, however, lose her confidence in what seems, for Naomi, a lost cause and a lost generation: "She believes in the Nisei, seeing them as networks and streamers of light dotting the country. For my part, I can only see a dark field with Aunt Emily beaming her flashlight to where the rest of us crouch and hide, our eyes downcast as we seek the safety of invisibility."

The frequency of Aunt Emily's visits to the family in Alberta and her persistent bombardment of Naomi with political reading and exhortation, indicate a profound need to rescue her niece from her frustrated solitude, and to hand on to her the zeal of her own generation—to find a political successor in her own family. Because of the loss of her own parents, however, Naomi has been raised by a very conventional though well-intentioned pair of Issei. She seems to side with her aunt and uncle in their disapproval of Emily's departure from female tradition— " 'Not like woman' " says Uncle, " 'Like that there can be no marriage' "—and of the "agitation" which she always introduces into the domestic circle. Naomi implicitly agrees with her uncle when he insists that " 'This country is the best. . . . Gratitude. Gratitude.' . . . He was right, I thought. If Aunt Emily with her billions of letters and articles and speeches . . . if all that couldn't bring contentment, what was the point?" This "contentment" which must exclude all "agitation" is a traditional Japanese ideal. Naomi's passive acceptance of the *status quo* indicates that she has no real sense of membership in Canadian society: " 'But you can't fight the whole country,' I said. 'We are the country,' [Emily] answered." Naomi seems to consider "the whole country" a hostile group to which she does not belong. Yet it is Emily's diary describing the effects of the deportation in Vancouver—the living heart of the bundle of documents Emily has sent to her niece—that will launch Naomi on her own reconstruction of the past.

Despite her emphasis on "contentment," Naomi reveals, in her "self-denigrating" self-presentation in chapter 2, an intense discontent with her way of life and personal appearance. A pun linking nervous tension with stoppage of time suggests a blocked sense of development: "Personality: Tense. Is that past or present tense? It's perpetual tense." A rather harsh observation from Emily provides objective confirmation of the sense of inner crippling which haunts Naomi through the narrative: " 'Look at you, Naomi, shuffling back and forth between Cecil and Granton, unable either to go or to stay in the world with even a semblance of grace or ease.' " Emily diagnoses

Naomi's psychic crippling as a case of repressed memory: " 'You have to remember. . . . You are your history. If you cut any of it off you're an amputee. . . . Cry it out! Scream! Denial is gangrene.' "

While this diagnosis is amply confirmed by the imagery in which Naomi thinks of herself, there is a certain injustice in Emily's exhortation to remember, for Naomi's experience of the war and post-war years was far more traumatic than hers. As the internment was taking place Emily had the luck to get permission to move to Toronto with her father, while Naomi went with her aunt and uncle first to internment in Slocan and then to a kind of slave labour in appalling conditions in Alberta. Most important, Emily is twenty years older than her niece; at the time of the internment she was twenty-five, and had already established an identity as political activist and non-traditional woman. Naomi, on the other hand, experiences internment, orphaning and, worst of all, six years living in an uninsulated one-room shack on a beet farm, between the ages of five and fifteen. For Emily remembering means re-establishing the facts of history; for Naomi, it forces the reliving of a damaged development—an exploration of the self in an area beyond Emily's experience and also beyond the limitations of her abstract, polemical discourse. Emily's speech is external and rhetorical because she is trying to maintain and persuade others of values she developed in the past. Naomi's narrative is subjective and connotative because she is trying to recover a past she experienced as a child, much of which, at the beginning of the novel, has been expelled from memory. In this exploration we encounter another aspect of Naomi's resistance to Emily—a memory of an ideal childhood provided by a very traditional mother.

Behind the strongly emphasized contrast between Naomi's two aunts—Emily and Obasan—lies a related contrast between Emily and Naomi's mother, pointed out by Naomi in her explanation of the family photograph: "Aunt Emily . . . definitely takes after Grandpa Kato— the round open face and the stocky build. . . . Not a beauty but, one might say, solid and intelligent-looking. Beside her, Mother is a fragile presence. Her face is oval as an egg and delicate." In this case, contrasting appearance also represents a difference in cultural values. Grandma Kato, a strong-minded but traditional woman, frequently returned to Japan and took her favourite daughter, Naomi's mother, with her, leaving Emily to stay with her father—eventually she would help him in his medical practice. Although born in Canada, Naomi's mother had a Japanese upbringing provided by Grandma Kato, while Emily's diary reveals her sense of closeness to her father.

Naomi's intense identification with her mother places her in a lineage of traditional women which includes Grandma Kato and Obassan. The leading characteristic of this concept of woman is defined by Obasan: "She has often spoken of my mother's 'yasashi kokoro', her tender, kind, and thoughtful heart." Naomi attributes the same quality to Obasan—she finds an "exquisite tenderness" in her expression in the family photograph. Naomi's intense memories of the perfect mother of her childhood make clear that for her this mother represents a feminine ideal:

"Mother's voice is yasashi, soft and tender. . . . She is altogether yasashi." In her own identification with the "yasashi kokoro" Naomi rejects Emily's brusque and angry discourse, but also finds it difficult to express or even acknowledge angry feelings of her own. (A use of the word "yasashi" by Emily implies an inability to survive outside the family circle. When the parents of Naomi's father are interned, Emily writes in her diary, "You know how yasashi Grandma is. This is too great a shock for her." Grandma Nakane is the first member of the family to die in exile.)

This ideal mother is the centre of a completely unified family life so perfect that it is painful to remember: "Every event was a warm-water wash, drawing us all closer till the fibre of our lives became an impenetrable mesh. . . . We were the original 'togetherness' people." This absolute "togetherness" makes possible the positive "silence" of Japanese family life, exemplified by an understanding of the child by the mother so complete that words would only be an intrusion. This intuitive understanding which does not require words is characteristic of a family group where, as exemplified in the oft-told story of Momotaro, "Simply by existing a child is delight." Family life is governed by a code of behaviour emphasizing self-restraint and consideration of others—a world of "sensitivity and appropriate gestures." One of its leading injunctions is that one must never burden others with distressful feelings of one's own. When Momotaro leaves home, his grandparents "are careful, as he goes, not to weight his pack with their sorrow." One must, like Momotaro, "behave with honour. . . . To do otherwise . . . brings dishonour to all." The ability of relatives to anticipate the needs of the child without words also provides the child with the best example of this code of behaviour: "To travel with confidence down this route the most reliable map I am given is the example of my mother's and Grandma's alert and accurate knowing. When I am hungry, and before I can ask, there is food . . . and if there is pain there is care simultaneously."

The loving "silence" of Naomi's childhood provides the basis for whatever sense of self-worth she retains despite the humiliation and dispersal of her community. Yet as an attitude towards life it is unable to provide an adequate response to this situation. To function, loving silence requires a community where everyone is perfectly known and from which no one feels alienated. A world where response is "simultaneous" and thus does not require words cannot deal with a drastic breach in continuity with the past. Without community, the loving silence of Naomi's childhood becomes the negative silence of Obasan—an inner "retreat" from which there is no return. Obasan's "silence that cannot speak" is a pathological response of the Issei world-view to permanent loss of community. She gives Naomi no direction into the outside world or the future.

The vulnerability of the language of silence lies in the dichotomy it fosters between an inner family world of complete togetherness and the hostile outer world of an alien society: "Inside the house in Vancouver there is confidence and laughter. . . . But outside . . . there is an infinitely unpredictable, unknown, and often dangerous world. Speech hides within me, watchful and afraid." The western world of eye-contact, so alarming to a child whose mother knows only the code of downcast eyes with which the traditional Japanese woman is obliged to greet the public world, also represents a larger world of possible relationships outside the family. Like her mother Naomi hides from threatening eyes, but she knows from the example of her Canadian-educated relatives that entrance into the outer world is possible: "Aunt Emily and Father, born and raised in Canada, are visually bilingual. I too learn the second language." Under the influence of her progressive Nisei relatives Naomi would have been able to make a natural transition from her supportive family life to the outside world, but the internment disrupts this process and separates her from those who would have provided the best guidance. While Naomi adapts externally to her life in exile, she, like the Issei, does not really trust the outer world or believe that it belongs to her. The political discourse which Emily brings from afar seems an alien language.

In Naomi's memory the language of silence represents the perfect childhood but its negative aspects are more evident from her point of view as adult narrator. The location of this language "in the belly" suggests a limitation as well as a childhood ideal. Circumscribed by a family womb, this language can deal neither with the relation between the self and the outside world, nor with conflicts within the self. The "language of eyes" is rejected not just because it represents an alien culture—even within the family the act of looking becomes suspect if it threatens to convey any consciousness which might be disturbing to family unity: "even a glance, if it is not matter of fact, is a betrayal." Hence the calmness and perfect trust of family life must depend partly on the suppression of undesirable knowledge. Naomi idealizes a childhood self inseparable from the mother when she asserts, "There is nothing about me that my mother does not know, nothing that is not safe to tell," but immediately contradicts this by telling of her seduction by Old Man Gower. Of course, a child would naturally be reluctant to talk about this experience, but for Naomi disclosure is inconceivable, and thus her secret experience results in a deep sense of self-division and separation from the mother, manifested in nightmares of dismemberment.

Later Obasan and Uncle deliberately suppress knowledge that might link a disturbing past to the present when, "for the sake of the children," they decide not to tell Naomi and Stephen why their mother has never communicated from Japan. Also, it appears that Naomi is never clearly informed of her father's death. The language "in the belly" is put in a negative context when, years later, she tries to mention her father's death in a matter-of-fact way and then collapses "with a sharp pain in my abdomen." Internalization of pain and anger that cannot be acknowledged finds expression in a particularly gruesome image when Naomi imagines Aunt Emily, with her "insistence on knowing all," as a surgeon cutting growths from her abdomen. The silence that seemed ideal in childhood becomes pathological for the adult.

In the disruptions of the internment, Naomi increasingly experiences as a burden the ethic behind the silent language, though she continues to identify with it. When their grandparents are taken away in Slocan the children must imitate the stoicism of Momotaro's grandparents: "We will make the way smooth by restraining emotion." The need to find verbal expression for the pain of separation is equated with selfishness: "To try to meet one's own needs in spite of the wishes of others is to be 'wagama-ma'—selfish and inconsiderate." Here Naomi does her best, but begins to find the traditional ethic less satisfactory as the world of the extended family breaks up: "It is such a tangle trying to decifer the needs and intents of others." Only in the present, nearing the conclusion of her narrative, does Naomi openly express a desire to rebel against the "decorum" required by the language of silence: "I want to break loose from the heavy identity. . . . I am tired of living between deaths and funerals, weighted with decorum, unable to shout or sing or dance, unable to scream or swear, unable to laugh, unable to breathe out loud." Here Naomi's sense of psychic crippling is related to a taboo against expressing anger, imposed by the family culture which is also her childhood ideal.

In addition to her anger at Canadian society and government, Naomi struggles with a hidden ambivalence towards the traditional values of the family life from which she seeks to draw a sense of identity. The peculiar intensity of this conflict is also the result of the internment. Disruption of her natural emergence into Canadian society has pushed her back towards the values of the Issei, which she now attempts to re-evaluate under Emily's provocation. Early in her narrative, when she is still siding with Uncle and Obasan against Emily, Naomi defends the ethic of self-restraint in a manner so ambiguous that her dissatisfaction with it is already evident. Accusing Emily of being one of those indecorous people "who talk a lot about their victimization" in order to "use their suffering as weapons or badges of some kind," Naomi concludes: "From my years of teaching I know it's the children who say nothing who are in trouble more than the ones who complain." Is this not an acknowledgement that talking is the cure, and that Naomi feels herself to be a child "in trouble"?

The dichotomy between an inner world of silent warmth and a cold, threatening outer world finds expression in a central contrast in the imagery of the novel: the opposition between protecting and fertile combinations of earth and water, and the empty, hostile sky. Naomi compares the Japanese Canadians to plants torn up or trees cut down. They are represented as seeking safety in undergrowth, tunnels, or "a door on the forest floor." The prairies are a dry land but may be rendered fertile by underground water, while Naomi associates her childhood with the rain forest and ocean of the west coast. A former fisherman, her uncle dreams of returning to the sea. Burrowing into the earth represents a regressive fixation on an ideal past as well as fear of the outer world. Naomi imagines her uncle's state of mind just before death: "Had the world turned upside down? Perhaps everything was reversing rapidly and he was tunnelling backwards top to bottom, his feet in an upstairs attic of humus and memory, his hands groping down . . . to the water, down to the underground sea."

Naomi adds a personal longing to the nostalgia of the Issei when she asks, in this fantasy, whether Uncle manages "to swim full circle back to that other shore and his mother's arms, her round moon face glowing down at her firstborn?" We hear nothing of Uncle's childhood—this "moon face" must belong to Naomi's ideally "yasashi" mother, lost forever in Japan. Again, nostalgia as well as exile is suggested when Naomi describes her people as plants uprooted and planted upside down, with their roots exposed to the prairie wind. The Issei aunt and uncle, and Naomi as well, bear the double burden of being immigrants in a strange land, and exiles from the community which might have provided a sense of home in that land.

Naomi's dislike for the open sky of the prairies could be taken simply as hostility towards her land of exile. Eventually the winter sky over the beet farm becomes associated with a sense of strangled development in the midst of her adolescence. The devastating physical hardship of Alberta, especially after years in the closed community of Slocan, constitutes the most damaging aspect of Naomi's experience, and the centre of her resistance to Emily's injunction to remember: "There are some nightmares from which there is no waking. . . . my late childhood growing-up days are sleepwalk years. . . . The sadness and absence are like a long winter storm. . . . Something dead is happening"—a sense of frozen process reflected in Naomi's present state of "perpetual tense."

The forced dispersal of the Japanese Canadian community after the war, which sent the family to forced labour in Alberta, was the most unjust and gratuitous aspect of the Canadian government's attack on Naomi's community. In addition to negative personal associations, the open sky of the prairies comes to stand for the public world of a country whose government is represented as a series of hawks hunting the Japanese Canadians: "one hawk after another circles overhead till the chickens are unable to come out of hiding. . . . The seasons pass and the leghorns no longer lay eggs. The nests are fouled and crawl with lice"—cultural continuity fails in an unhealthy enclosure imposed by fear of a hostile outer world.

Yet there is one benevolent influence in the sky—as a reward for her mastery of political discourse, Naomi consigns Aunt Emily to the upper air: "Love no doubt is in her. Love, like the coulee wind, rushing through her mind. . . . She never stays still long enough to hear the sound of her own voice." Just before she opens the diary, Naomi describes Emily as a pilot in a fog, looking in vain for a landing place on a "safe and sane strip of justice and reason. Not seeing these, she did not crash into the oblivion of either bitterness or futility but remained airborne." Since Naomi has little confidence that this airport will be found, the only cure for the dichotomy of earth and sky would be upward growth from Naomi's earthbound world. (The caring woman, bound by domestic ties, is also located in the earth and the house.) This growth occurs decisively in a series of images which transform the mother from a dead tree into a living forest in chapter 38—

Naomi's meditation after learning the fate of her mother in Japan.

In this chapter the emotional turbulence generated by Naomi's ambivalence towards the female ideal represented by Obasan and, especially, the memory of her mother, finds a climax and a resolution. In the case of her mother, this ambivalence is complicated by the mother's departure for Japan when Naomi was five years old and had been seduced by a neighbour. Any child might feel resentment at her mother's disappearance, but Naomi, burdened with secret guilt, might also imagine that her mother had rejected her because she had done something bad. Naomi's later discovery that her mother was alive in Japan after the war, along with the fact that the mother had never attempted to communicate with her, reinforces her sense of abandonment to the point where the mystery of the mother's fate becomes a persistent obsession. This ambivalence is concealed behind the image of the ideal mother of infancy, and Naomi's fixation on this image binds her to the traditional image of woman as represented by the mother and Obasan. The translation of her mother's letters from Japan enables Naomi to relate to her mother as an adult in a loving but also critical way, and thus she can affirm her allegiance to the "tender heart" while moving beyond the "silence" this ideal imposes on her in its traditional form. The account of the mother's fate provided by the letters enables Naomi to interpret her failure to communicate as a loving silence rather than the silence of rejection. At the same time as Naomi gains a new sense of relation to her mother, however, she also places the mother's silence in a critical perspective and thus distinguishes her own consciousness from her mother's traditional values.

This change in her sense of relation to her mother is accompanied by complex changes in a central image associated with her attitude towards her mother in early childhood. The warmth and security of Naomi's early relation to her mother and the communal world she represents are repeatedly symbolized by the image of the mother as a tree, beginning with the peach tree associated with the mother's telling of the story of Momotaro and the photo Obasan presents showing Naomi at the age of two or three clinging to her mother's leg; here Naomi sees the mother as a tree from which the child is growing as a branch, an extension of the mother both in body and consciousness: "Where she is rooted, I am rooted. . . . The shaft of her leg is the shaft of my body and I am her thoughts." Because of the disappearance of her mother and the disruption of her family life, however, Naomi's relation to her mother fails to develop as she grows older; the tree image also comes to represent her fixation on the ideal mother of childhood, by whom she now feels abandoned. After the mother's departure the tree becomes ambivalent: just before the internment Naomi becomes frightened of the peach tree, and in Slocan she has a nightmare in which the mother appears as a tree which deserts the child. Finally, the failure of the childhood image of the mother to give her strength is represented by the change of the living maternal tree of the photo into a dead tree on the prairie.

In the final paragraphs of chapter 38 Naomi re-emphasizes the image, derived from the photo, of mother and child as tree and branch, and then moves to an image of herself as a crippled child sitting beside a dead tree: "The tree is a dead tree in the middle of the prairies. I sit on its roots still as a stone." Her paralysis is linked to her inability to communicate with the childhood, "yasashi" image of the mother in the photo: "The child is forever unable to speak. . . . I beg that the woundedness may be healed and that the limbs may learn to dance. But you stay in a black and white photograph, smiling your yasashi smile." Then, with a sudden change of tone, Naomi addresses her mother as an adult, rejecting the code of silence for both of them—"we were lost together in our silences. Our wordlessness was our mutual destruction"—to finish with an image of a forest growing out of the graves of her family: "But the earth still stirs with dormant blooms. Love flows through the roots of the trees by our graves. . . . [W]e have come to the forest tonight . . . you turn to earth and form the forest floor." The conversion of a single tree into a forest suggests that she has found a new relationship to the outside world as well as to her mother, while the fact that this forest grows from graves suggests that she has accepted the permanent loss of relatives and community.

This sense of resolution is preceded by a violent image which combines the pain both of excessive attachment and separation. In a variant of the tree image, Naomi sometimes thinks of her mother as a maypole around which the child dances holding a ribbon attached to the pole—suggested by the streamers held both by the passengers on the ship which will take her mother to Japan and by the relatives on the dock. Towards the end of chapter 38 this image becomes the self-mutilating Sun Dance of the Sioux warriors, in which thongs attached to a pole were hooked into the chest muscles, then torn out as the initiate danced backwards: "Maypole Mother, I dance with a paper streamer in my hand. But the words of the May Day song are words of distress. The unknown is a hook that pierces the bone. Thongs hang down in the hot prairie air. Silence attends the long sun dance."

The pain of acknowledging physical separation from the mother frees Naomi to exist independently in the outside world, associated with the hostile emptiness of the prairie. As she imagines the mother as an adult, irreparably separated from her in a loving but mistaken silence, Naomi also experiences herself as an adult, freed from fixation on the ideal mother of childhood: "I am thinking that for a child there is no presence without flesh. But perhaps it is because I am no longer a child that I can know your presence though you are not here." By internalizing the family life of her childhood in a more mature way, Naomi can draw on the sense of self-worth that she found there, while moving beyond the limitations imposed by its language of silence. Thus the vanished mother becomes the focal point for an arrested, and finally completed, process of mourning for the whole communal world of her childhood.

The image of the forest, further developed in the next chapter, also indicates a new sense of identification with Canada. Naomi's first genuine sense of Canadian identity appears in a burst of anger in which she reproaches Canada as "a cold country": "Oh Canada, whether it is admitted or not, we come from you we come from you. From the same soil, the slugs and slime and bogs and twigs and roots." After recovering her past, she is able to end with a warmer image of trees growing around the graves of her lost relatives.

In her grandmother's description of the bombing of Nagasaki, Naomi finds the ultimate form of death inflicted from the sky and destruction of community—a much more visible example of racist atrocity than the hypocritical policies of the Canadian government. The grandmother's account of nuclear horror makes possible a release of inner rage which Naomi has never been able fully to acknowledge in relation to her own experience. In confronting the "catastrophes . . . possible in human affairs" and the fragmentation of time implied in the letter's long journey to reach her, Naomi enters the public world of injustice, genocide, and isolation which until now has been the exclusive domain of Aunt Emily. This enlarging of Naomi's vision prevents the final resolution from becoming sentimental—otherwise all too possible for a narrator of such "tender heart."

Whether or not Emily will be successful in her political project, the fact that Naomi has become able to acknowledge the validity of Emily's concerns indicates that Emily has succeeded in establishing a parental relation with her Sansei niece. In moving towards resolution, Naomi responds to two disturbing voices which represent different aspects of female strength—to Emily's polemic is added the "outpouring" of Grandma Kato, the most tough-minded of the traditional women, who breaks the code of silence to send her husband in Toronto "the burden of these words." Naomi's final sense of wholeness arises from her ability to reconcile Emily's Nisei activism with a traditional concept of woman inherited from the Issei, thus showing that the preceding generations can become a source of strength despite her isolation and the disruption of her community. It is on this sense of progressive change within continuity that the final affirmation of the novel depends.

The remarkable fusion of historical and psychological time in **Obasan** is facilitated by a clear distinction between the attitudes of the different generations towards the past, the public world, and the role of woman. Thus the history of the community is implicit in the various kinds of discourse with which the characters signify these attitudes. Uncle and Obasan are entirely oriented towards an idealized past, while Emily represents her generation's orientation towards a delayed future, only now she demands that the future acknowledge the unjust past which thwarted the aspirations of the Nisei. Uncle and Obasan represent conventional acceptance, Emily the revolt against tradition of the activists of her generation. If the Issei idealize their homeland, or family life in Vancouver before the internment, she is still looking for the ideal Canada which the Nisei longed to join. The image of the circling airplane suggests that since leaving Vancouver she has never found a new community. In her initial arguments with Aunt Emily, Naomi claims to have no interest in the past, but the images of the ideal mother with which her memories begin show that she is far more attached than Emily to the

past and its values. This can be an advantage as well as a vulnerability, because once she deals with her own past Naomi will be in a position to appreciate the strengths of both generations.

Although Naomi at first rejects Emily's angry discourse, we cannot fully understand the changing dynamic of Naomi's memory unless we realize that within the "sealed vault" guarded by the "cold icon" of a decorous silence lies a profound if wordless anger. Naomi's identification with the "yasashi" ideal of woman should not blind us to the bitter sense of injury which gradually rises in her narrative, reaching a climax with her permanent exile in Alberta. The gentle underground stream of the proem and the first chapter changes to a torrent of anger and grief: "I must . . . release the flood gates one by one."

Finally the "outpouring" of pain and implied anger in Grandma Kato's letter provides a public object for indignation, while the hideous physical injuries it describes correspond to Naomi's sense of an inner injury which has resulted in psychic crippling. Near the beginning of her narrative Naomi sees Emily as crusading to bring medicine to all injuries inflicted by injustice—"wounds seen and not seen." Actually, Naomi knows more than Emily about unseen wounds and the difficulty of healing them. Beginning with her stay in hospital in Slocan, Naomi increasingly represents her sense of psychic injury through grotesque imagery involving crippling, head injuries, and growths which must be cut away.

The universal destruction and maiming revealed in the letter provides an objective correlative to Naomi's repressed feelings—a graphic physical wounding which corresponds to her sense of inner injury. The wounds "not seen" may be almost as damaging as the wounds made horribly visible in the letter. Because of war and racism the mother suffers physical disfigurement in Japan, her daughter a more subtle kind of psychic disfigurement in Canada. The mother's feeling that disfigurement is a disgrace which renders her unfit for family life represents a conventional Japanese response to nuclear injuries, while Naomi's acknowledgement of her psychological injuries enables her to regain her family life in memory and to establish a strongly felt if angry identity as a Canadian. In her narrative she discovers a capacity for self-expression and communication with others which is necessary for psychic survival in a culturally fragmented world where the individual may be isolated and cut off from the past.

Naomi's narrative could be seen as a synthesis of two opposing kinds of discourse present in her situation as she begins to remember. As she ponders Emily's documents in the silence of Obasan's house, Naomi has already responded to the silent discourse implicit in the accumulation of carefully preserved objects which makes the house a filing cabinet of the family's past. Naomi praises her aunt as the characteristic "old woman" who preserves the past—"the bearer of keys to unknown doorways. . . . the possessor of life's infinite personal details"—but here the doorways remain unknown because Obasan refuses to supply any narrative which could link these objects to the present. Rather, she insists that all her objects be viewed in the timeless togetherness of a family photo album; in response to Naomi's interest in the family group-photo, Obasan says only, " 'Such a time there was once.' " When Naomi asks about some sheets of paper covered with Japanese writing (the grandmother's letters) Obasan deliberately suppresses narrative in favour of image when in reply she brings Naomi the photo of herself as a child clutching her mother's leg and insists, " 'Here is the best letter. This is the best time. These are the best memories.' " Meanwhile, Naomi's memories of the family past remain as depressing and incoherent as the spider webs and shredded blanket in Obasan's attic.

Emily's polemical view of the past, on the other hand, does not at first reveal to Naomi any concrete reason why, as she thinks early in the novel, "Crimes of history" should not "stay in history." Naomi and her two aunts represent three different ways of dealing with the past: Emily seeks to research historical fact and to publicize moral issues arising from it; Obasan preserves the past in objects but uses these only to reinforce a narrativeless ideal of family unity; making use of the material supplied by both aunts, Naomi, in her day in the silent house, relives the past in a narrative both poetic and factual, establishing a conscious relation to the past while freeing herself from the secret burden it imposed.

In response to Emily's exhortation to remember and the associations aroused by Obasan's file of objects, Naomi discovers a "living language" which can give a narrative to the family photographs, revealing the full depth of her psychic injury while animating the "infinite personal details" of family life still contained in Obasan's house. Through a loving disclosure of family life which ruthlessly violates all the taboos of silence, Naomi revives the living content of the silence with which her community endured injustice, thus finding a speech within silence. Naomi also resolves the conflict between her identification both with Emily and with the traditional "yasashi" concept of woman through a narrative in which sympathy becomes a mode of vision, including her understanding of Emily, yet which also expresses a deep anger, perhaps even deeper than is openly admitted.

In conclusion, I should like to review the history of Naomi's development and to consider some implications of her changing relation with Emily. Naomi begins with an apparent acceptance of her present world and a professed lack of interest in her past as a Japanese Canadian. In fact, however, she is ill at ease with herself in the present while, in her resistance to Emily, remaining loyal to the most conservative values of her former community. Her ideally communal childhood, repressed from conscious memory because of its contrast to later experience, continues to influence her identity, blocking acknowledgement of the pain and anger caused by her brutal separation from it. A period of intense recall enables Naomi to relive her past while retaining an adult perspective informed by Emily's documents and advice. While much of the past returns readily, the emotional impact of her most painful and ambivalent experiences finds expression only in symbolic terms; to complete her task she must confront a layer of grotesque images involving inner wounding, dismemberment, conflict between inner and outer reality, and be-

tween ideal togetherness and self-mutilating separation. The final transformation of these into images of a growing forest suggests a new sense of rootedness in that hostile outer world which Emily has forced her to acknowledge, but where Emily herself never seems to have found a landing place.

Since Naomi has experienced the full impact of the internment and dispersal in her formative years, she can render in personal detail a period which Emily—aside from her diary—presents in moral abstractions; thus Naomi reinforces Emily's argument by showing that the psychological consequences of this experience extend into the present. The depth and convincingness with which Naomi's inner conflicts are presented provide the basis for an intensely personal narrative which can assimilate the objective, historical elements presented by Emily. The novel emphasizes a fracture between inner and outer worlds as a central problem for Naomi and her community, but also suggests a resolution in the very effectiveness with which it combines historical and subjective reality.

The difference in discourse between Emily and Naomi also suggests a conflict between the literary and political consciousness. Naomi's awareness of the connotative value of

---

Robin Potter on *Obasan*:

On the surface *Obasan* is the story told by a woman about her childhood as a Japanese Canadian during World War II, a time when the Japanese living in Canada were singled out by the Canadian Government as a threat to National Defense and were subsequently, through a series of edicts, removed from the West Coast and sent to Japan, or dispersed throughout the British Columbia interior and eventually through the Prairies. Naomi Nakane tells of the forced fragmentation of her family and community, and in doing so discloses a quest for the M/mother and an understanding of herself, both accomplished through reunification, purification, and the spirit of survival.

Surprisingly, below the surface, this story is the tale of a totem, a tribe, and the sacrificial victims—and the dialectic is one of abjection. The tribal totem is the Canadian ethos, while the high priests are figured as the various levels of government, its (pseudo and authentic) representatives of the people, and the documents by which it perpetuates its power. The tribe in the novel's context is made up of the Canadian people/s, while the Japanese Canadians, during World War II and after, can be viewed as the sacrificial victims. The continued current of abjection is based on the mystery of the absent mother and the need for a strong father, needs that do not become satisfied. In the novel, the mother or matriarchal powers are suppressed so much that abjection surfaces in her place. The abject is prefigured in masculinist power structures; that is, those structures that form the foundation of law and order, such as religion, politics, and family/community.

Robin Potter, in her "Moral—in Whose Sense?: Joy Kogawa's Obasan *and Julia Kristeva's* Powers of Horror," *in* Studies in Canadian Literature, *1990.*

words, which makes possible the poetic aspects of the novel, also provides a part of the motivation for her resistance to Emily and the purely political world her discourse implies. Emily's rapid-fire, exhortatory and rather indiscriminate use of language suggests a lack of sensitivity to the subjective self: "she never stays still long enough to hear the sound of her own voice. . . . from the moment we met, I was caught in the rush-hour traffic jam of her non-stop conference talk." As she begins to appreciate Emily's values, however, Naomi moves towards a vision where the public and private life—political activism and poetic sensibility—are no longer irrelevant to each other. Naomi remains sceptical of the effectiveness of her aunt's activities, but in her painful sense of growing from Canadian soil she affirms Emily's assertion that " 'We are the country.' " (pp. 41-55)

> Mason Harris, "Broken Generations in 'Obasan'," in Canadian Literature, No. 127, Winter, 1990, pp. 41-57.

Sandra Martin   (review date March 1992)

[*In the following excerpt, Martin argues that Kogawa lacks the distance from the events described in* Itsuka *to translate them into fiction.*]

Nobody can lay greater claim to the literary territory of the Japanese internment during the Second World War than Joy Kogawa. Through her poetry, her sublime novel *Obasan,* her children's story *Naomi's Road,* and now *Itsuka,* Kogawa has written poignantly about how innocent and loyal Japanese Canadians were stripped of their homes and their possessions, interned, and dispersed.

In writing *Itsuka,* Kogawa is not so much writing a sequel as reclaiming themes and characters from *Obasan.* In her compulsion to bear witness to these shameful events once again, she covers a lot of familiar territory in the lives of Naomi Nakane, her militant aunt Emily, her aloof brother Stephen, and her loving aunt, Obasan. As well Kogawa introduces a slew of new characters as she records the poignant struggle to rebuild a sense of community and to pry an apology and financial redress from the Canadian government. I use the word "record" deliberately because Kogawa seems too close to the partisan squabbling that accompanies any such movement. She hasn't yet absorbed the facts and translated them into fiction. They jab and poke through the fabric of her story like kittens in a sack on the way to market.

Novels, even those incorporating real people and incidents, are not about events. They are about ideas and characters. It is only when the imagined world enhances the real world, gives it greater credibility and dimension, that a fiction writer can legitimately stake a claim to a literary territory. There isn't enough documentation in *Itsuka* for it to be a history; conversely, there is too much undigested detail to let Naomi and her soulmate Father Cedric breathe, let alone flourish.

> Sandra Martin, "Staking Out Literary Turf," in Quill and Quire, Vol. 58, No. 3, March, 1992, p. 57.

Janice Kulyk Keefer   (review date April 1992)

[*Keefer is a Canadian poet, novelist, short story writer, educator, and critic. In the following mixed review, she describes* Itsuka *as a political novel about contemporary Canadian society that addresses such issues as compensation for the victims of World War II internment camps and the politics of multiculturalism.*]

"We'll disappear if we don't care. We can't care if we don't know our stories," remarks a character in Joy Kogawa's new novel, *Itsuka* (the title translates as "Someday"). One of the stories that *Itsuka* tells continues the history of Naomi Nakane and her family, with whom Kogawa's first novel, *Obasan,* is centrally concerned. While *Obasan* ends with the breaking of the stone of silence that has virtually entombed Naomi as a child and a young woman, *Itsuka* opens with the middle-aged Naomi taking the first tentative steps towards freeing herself from a prison of emotional, physical, and spiritual homelessness. Having lived through the slow and painful dying of the aunt who raised her after her mother's disappearance, Naomi is commanded by her other aunt, the activist Emily, to leave the prairies for Toronto, where she goes to work for a multicultural journal run by the man who becomes her first lover, a maverick Anglican priest. With him, she becomes involved in the movement to win meaningful redress for victims of those wartime policies of internment and deportation whose traumatic consequences *Obasan* so poignantly evokes. The erotic and political plots of *Itsuka* are made to intertwine under the influence of something that can only be called mystical: a vision of love that survives and indeed transcends the death of individuals, and yet also becomes the moving force behind the kind of people-power politics that the novel so engagingly depicts.

For of all the stories offered us by *Itsuka,* it is the political, rather than the erotic, mystic, or familial, that compels this reader's attention. Naomi's involvement with Father Cedric seems to me a rather unconvincing substitute for what might have been at the heart of the novel—the failure of Naomi's relationship with her brother Stephen, and the crucial questions raised by his abdication from any involvement with family or community due to his absolute commitment to his art. I must admit to a certain disappointment, too, at the absence in *Itsuka* of the kind of poetically charged language and intensity of perception that give *Obasan* its extraordinary beauty and power.

Yet it would be wrong to fault *Itsuka* for not being *Obasan Revisited.* What Kogawa has done in her new novel is to move into a different kind of imaginative territory, exposing the politics of a multiculturalism that has in many ways abetted rather than eradicated the racism that she presents as an institutionalized aspect of Canadian life. Her account of the formation of the Japanese-Canadian redress movement and its bitter and protracted struggle against a succession of obstructive ministers of multiculturalism makes absorbing reading. So, too, does Kogawa's depiction of how the powers-that-be (including the supposedly arm's-length CBC) attempted to manipulate and coerce the redress movement, and of how officially sanctioned multiculturalism presses ethnic and racial minorities to stick to singing "pretty songs" instead of allowing them "access to power."

If **Obasan** helped to effect a transformation of the Canadian sense of self, a transition from the notion of this country as a bi- to a multicultural society, **Itsuka** forces us to confront the serious obstacles that prevent this society from becoming truly just, and its members equal. Though the novel stresses the power of love to "extinguish the night," it argues that action as well as words, political as well as aesthetic energies are needed in order to transform established ways of perceiving "the other," and to create a celebratory rather than punitive response to racial and ethnocultural difference. Kogawa's inclusion in her novel of the text of the government's formal apology to those whose lives were torn apart for "the public good," an apology containing the pledge that "such events will not happen again," takes on special significance at a time when Canadians are debating the conditions for our very survival as a nation. For no amount of insistence on the need for national unity should make us forget or silence the stories of any group of Canadians unjustly treated in their "home and native land." Only if we continue to remember and relate such stories can we approach that vital crossroads where, as Kogawa suggests, "the beginning of an altogether new story touches a turning point in the old." And as **Itsuka** shows, it is the storytellers who can help us hear "the breath of life" in a country where so much of what we should most value seems to be in danger of demise.

Janice Kulyk Keefer, "A Celebration of Difference," in Books in Canada, *Vol. XXI, No. 3, April, 1992, p. 35.*

FURTHER READING

Fujita, Gayle K. " 'To Attend the Sound of Stone': The Sensibility of Silence in *Obasan.*" *MELUS* 12, No. 3 (Fall 1985): 33-42.

Thematic analysis of *Obasan*.

Jones, Manina. "The Avenues of Speech and Silence: Telling Difference in Joy Kogawa's *Obasan.*" In *Theory between the Disciplines: Authority / Vision / Politics,* edited by Martin Kreiswirth and Mark A. Cheetham, pp. 213-29. Ann Arbor: University of Michigan Press, 1990.

Postmodern examination of the relationship between language, discourse, and event in *Obasan*. Classifying the novel as "historiographic metafiction," Jones maintains that Kogawa's focus on language and narrative structure "radically revises both the concept of 'documentary history,' which claims to reconstruct reliably the contents of the past . . . and 'documentary realism,' which aims to literally inform the past by writing it."

Lim, Shirley Geok-Lin. "Japanese American Women's Life Stories: Maternality in Monica Sone's *Nisei Daughter* and Joy Kogawa's *Obasan.*" *Feminist Studies* 16, No. 2 (Summer 1990): 288-312.

Examines mother-daughter relationships in *Nisei Daughter* and *Obasan* and contends that these works demonstrate the vitality of a female Asian-American "literary tradition that incorporates intertextuality, the thematics of internment, maternality, race, and gender."

Magnusson, A. Lynne. "Language and Longing in Joy Kogawa's *Obasan.*" *Canadian Literature,* No. 116 (Spring 1988): 58-66.

Argues that the protagonist's "individual drama is closely caught up in her linguistic anxiety, which comes to serve as a synecdoche for her estrangement—from others, from her cultural origins, from the absent mother who preoccupies her thoughts, from her past."

Merivale, P. "Framed Voices: The Polyphonic Elegies of Hébert and Kogawa." *Canadian Literature,* No. 116 (Spring 1988): 68-82.

Examines thematic and structural similarites between Anne Hébert's *Les fous de Bassan* and Kogawa's *Obasan,* which Merivale contends are elegies about the destruction of individuals and communities.

Additional coverage of Kogawa's life and career is contained in the following sources published by Gale Research: *Contemporary Authors,* **Vol. 101; and** *Contemporary Authors New Revision Series,* **Vol. 19.**

Dean R. Koontz

1945-

(Full name Dean Ray Koontz; also wrote under the pseudonyms David Axton, Brian Coffey, Deanna Dwyer, K. R. Dwyer, Leigh Nichols, Anthony North, Richard Paige, and Owen West) American novelist, short story writer, and nonfiction writer.

The following entry provides an overview of Koontz's career through 1992.

INTRODUCTION

Koontz is best known for novels in which he combines the popular literary genres of science fiction, horror, suspense, and romance. With his books frequently topping bestseller lists, he has won both popular readership and critical admiration for his finely drawn characters and fast-moving, tightly constructed plots. Critics consider Koontz's work distinctive for its optimistic display of confidence in the ability of individuals to overcome extreme obstacles and hardships. Several of his books have been adapted for film, including *Demon Seed, Shattered,* and *Watchers.*

Born in Everett, Pennsylvania, Koontz has described his childhood as "a nightmare" characterized chiefly by his father's violent behavior, alcoholism, and habitual unemployment. From an early age Koontz read and wrote fiction as an escape from his troubled home life. Encouraged by a high school teacher to major in English at Shippensburg State College, Koontz won an *Atlantic Monthly* creative writing award in 1966. While working as a high school English teacher, he published several science fiction novels. In 1972 Koontz began to experiment with other literary genres, although his work continued to feature narratives with a strong grounding in science and technology.

Critics observe that the most prevalent theme in Koontz's work is the conflict between reason and emotion. Usually his characters learn to reconcile detached analysis with intuitive feeling, especially when dealing with technology. In *Phantoms,* for example, the protagonists turn to myth and religion when logic fails to explain the mass deaths in a resort town. The source of the menace is a prehistoric being that recurs in folklore and ancient religious beliefs and uses modern technology in the form of computers, radio, and telephones against the town's citizens. That the characters in the novel finally use technology to defeat the "Ancient Enemy" indicates to commentators Koontz's fundamental faith in human resourcefulness. In *Darkfall* Koontz again presents religion and ritual as the foils of logic. For the protagonists to triumph they must believe in the potentially evil powers of voodoo and the ultimately superior powers of good. In *Watchers* Koontz explores the positive and negative potential of technology as represent-

ed by two genetically engineered beings: Einstein, an endearing golden retriever with human intelligence who prevails over the Outsider, a monstrous superbeing capable of horrific deeds.

Since moving from science fiction to cross-genre writing, Koontz has broadened his appeal and, according to critics, strengthened his storytelling. Bill Munster has suggested that Koontz's examination of "the tenuous nature of life and the tissue-thin barrier that separates us from sudden terror and tragedy" gives his work a resonance not often found in most popular fiction.

PRINCIPAL WORKS

Star Quest (novel) 1968
The Fall of the Dream Machine (novel) 1969
Anti-Man (novel) 1970
Beastchild (novella) 1970
The Dark Symphony (novel) 1970
Soft Come the Dragons (short stories) 1970

Chase [as K. R. Dwyer] (novel) 1972
A Darkness in My Soul (novel) 1972
The Flesh in the Furnace (novel) 1972
Warlock (novel) 1972
Demon Seed (novel) 1973
Hanging On (novel) 1973
The Haunted Earth (novel) 1973
Shattered [as K. R. Dwyer] (novel) 1973
A Werewolf Among Us (novel) 1973
After the Last Race (novel) 1974
Dragonfly [as K. R. Dwyer] (novel) 1975
Nightmare Journey (novel) 1975
The Wall of Masks [as Brian Coffey] (novel) 1975
Night Chills (novel) 1976
The Face of Fear [as Brian Coffey] (novel) 1977
The Vision (novel) 1977
The Key to Midnight [as Leigh Nichols] (novel) 1979
The Funhouse [as Owen West] (novelization of screen-play) 1980
Whispers (novel) 1980
The Eyes of Darkness [as Leigh Nichols] (novel) 1981
How to Write Best-Selling Fiction (nonfiction) 1981
The House of Thunder [as Leigh Nichols] (novel) 1982
Phantoms (novel) 1983
Darkfall (novel) 1984
Twilight [as Leigh Nichols] (novel) 1984
Twilight Eyes (novel) 1985
Strangers (novel) 1986
Shadowfires [as Leigh Nichols] (novel) 1987
Watchers (novel) 1987
Lightning (novel) 1988
Midnight (novel) 1989
The Bad Place (novel) 1990
Cold Fire (novel) 1991
Dragon Tears (novel) 1992
Hideaway (novel) 1992

CRITICISM

Joanna Russ (review date February 1971)

[*In the following excerpt, Russ unfavorably reviews* The Dark Symphony.]

[**The Dark Symphony**] is a silly, ritualistic adventure story of Rebellious Hero in Repressive Society. There is no pretense about the book; all is as economical, ridiculous, and flamboyant as can be. It will probably be morally corrupting to adolescents who take it seriously, but it is so stripped-down an example of its kind that I can't imagine anyone taking it seriously. There are as few scenes in the book as is compatible with the plot's moving at all: Hero in Arena (with background of Bad Society), Hero with Rebellious Mutants, Revolution, Hero Beating Up Best Friend, Hero and Heroine Escaping to New Land. It is

rather silly and lurid ("bloodlust in every cell") but it is unpretentious and quirky, and it has all the glomph of the stories we told ourselves when we were twelve. It also has a Women's Lib heroine, ta-rah! (well, sort of). There is one good idea: Manbats (known as bat-men to other writers). . . . [But] it's unabashed trash and will do to prop up a table leg.

> *Joanna Russ, in a review of "The Dark Symphony," in* The Magazine of Fantasy and Science Fiction, *Vol. 40, No. 2, February, 1971, p. 65.*

Carol Sherr Hand (review date March 1985)

[*In the following review, Hand gives a mixed appraisal of what she considers Koontz's use of formula writing in* Darkfall.]

Dean R. Koontz has *finally* given in and written a straight supernatural novel, without feeling obliged (as he did in the earlier **Whispers** and **Phantoms**) to end the book with a "logical explanation" for all the bizarre happenings. The result is an improvement over Koontz's earlier works.

Darkfall has many elements which are becoming "standard Koontz": a series of inexplicably gruesome murders (in **Darkfall,** all related to New York City's leading family of drug-dealers); a male-female pair of investigators (in **Darkfall,** both police detectives) leading to the inevitable involvement; the female of the pair, as always, is a tough-minded, gratifyingly competent, no-nonsense type—but with a heart!; two children (the male detective's) endangered by the evil stalking the city; and the evil itself—the same Ancient Ones, straight from the Gates of Hell, that appeared in **Phantoms.** Only their forms differ.

Koontz writes good, competent horror novels, each a good read, each better than the last. I am pleased that he has finally decided to "go straight" with the supernatural. I like his strong characterizations and careful psychological motivation. And yet—there is something missing. Perhaps I'm annoyed at the sameness, the tendency to write "formula horror." Perhaps I'm looking for a spark, an imaginative something that just isn't in Koontz's writing. But somehow, I don't quite feel the chilling terror that Koontz's characters feel. This is a good, but not a great, horror novel.

> *Carol Sherr Hand, "A Competent, Readable Horror Novel," in* Fantasy Review, *Vol. 8, No. 3, March, 1985, p. 27.*

Bill Collins (review date January-February 1987)

[*In the following excerpt from a review of* Strangers, *Collins criticizes what he considers the artificial and confusing plot of the novel.*]

I've never been hungry an hour after eating Chinese food, so in my experience the old saying to that effect is false. But it may be true of Koontz's latest novel, a Harold Robbins-Judith Krantz sized book at almost 700 pages: though **Strangers** lacks the sleaze common to those two writers, it shares with their work an essential artificiality that one overlooks in the reading, but which hits one like the proverbial post-chow mein hunger an hour after the book has been finished. (pp. 38-9)

[Much] of the plot's artificiality has to do with the way each of the main characters approaches the scene of the finale, the ironically-named Tranquility Motel in rural Nevada. . . . Whatever your favorite paranoid fantasy is, Koontz manages to suggest in the opening third of the book that it might be part of the cause of the inexplicable behavior that terrifies the novelist from California, the beautiful Boston surgeon, the lapsed priest who can work miracles, the Las Vegas divorcee and her moonstruck daughter, the embittered ex-Special Forces veteran turned master criminal. Is the source of their erratic behavior the supernatural, the CIA, aliens, terrorists, the Mob, or what?

By the time they all realize that their memories have been drained of one shared weekend's events . . . and get on with confronting the inimical forces arrayed against them, the reader has forgotten all the red herrings, the author had planted earlier. I can't deny that Koontz's episodic style, jumping from one protagonist to another like a crazed movie serial, keeps one's interest, or that many readers will probably stay up much later than they'd planned when they first opened the book to read a bit of it. But when it was all over, I felt I'd been manipulated— not in the straightforward, emotional-button-pushing manner of a Stephen King, but rather unfairly, as if the first 500 pages of *Strangers* had been written after the last 200 and details arbitrarily distributed among the leading characters to provide the maximum confusion of seemingly unrelated terrors. I also wonder whether the apocalyptic last chapter is really in keeping with the tone of the rest of the novel; it seemed rather like tacking the final scene of *Childhood's End* onto a Robert Ludlum thriller.

Strangers is good only for an evening when you want to disconnect your mind. (p. 39)

> Bill Collins, "The Suspense Novel as Oriental Food," in Fantasy Review, *Vol. 10, No. 1, January-February, 1987, pp. 38-9.*

Paul Wilner (review date 8 March 1987)

[*In the following excerpt, Wilner examines the social criticism and philosophy inherent in fantasy fiction, negatively reviewing* Watchers *based on this criteria.*]

[*Watchers*] is a yarn of recombinant DNA experiments on dogs at a government-sponsored research agency called Banodyne Laboratories. The laboratories sponsor something called the Francis Project, aimed, first, at endowing a certain golden retriever with human intelligence capable of spying on the Russians and, second, at creating "The Outsider," a hybrid canine bred to be a lone killer. The two are to be a sort of Good Dog, Bad Dog team.

But something goes wrong, dreadfully wrong, and both dogs escape into bucolic Southern California, where they are pursued by a variety of good guys, bad guys, local gendarmes, feds, Soviet counteragents and confused veterinarians. . . .

I won't reveal the ending of this veterinary epic. But it may be worth observing that the real purpose of fantasized terror is not the plot, per se, and certainly not the prose style with which the narrative unfolds. What accounts for its popularity is its philosophy. It works like a metaphysical Movie of the Week on the burning social, political and ethical questions of our time.

As one law-enforcement officer tells another in *Watchers*:

> Honest to God, Walt, when you see that animal in action, see what Weatherby created, it gives you enormous hope for this sorry species of ours. (. . .) I mean, if we can do these amazing things, if we can bring such a wonder into the world, then there's something of profound value in us no matter what the pessimists and doomsayers believe.

Just as the traditional mystery and tough guy novels have been subverted into morality plays, so the Gothics have become mystery plays, carrying with them the eerie subtext of fear about the unknown scientific future. That they are so often violent only underscores the immediacy of their concerns.

Having said that, one is forced to add that while such meta-societal musings may become serious literature in the hands of an Aldous Huxley or a Gore Vidal, the work of Dean R. Koontz falls considerably short of that mark.

Any book that persistently refers to its protagonist as "fur face" (Travis to "fur face": "You turned me around in one day. I swear, it's like you were sent to show me that life's mysterious, strange, and full of wonders") forfeits its right to escape without a snicker.

But in an extra-literary sense, the probable popularity of *Watchers* and its fictional kindred spirits indicates something disturbing about our fascination with military violence and with the violence of our own souls. And you don't have to be Einstein to figure out that this broader fascination betokens problems that can't be resolved through wish-fulfillment fiction.

> Paul Wilner, in a review of "Watchers," in Los Angeles Times Book Review, *March 8, 1987, p. 6.*

Stan Brooks (essay date 1988)

[*In the following excerpt, Brooks traces Koontz's development from a science fiction writer to a popular writer who employs aspects of various genres.*]

At the age of twenty, Dean Koontz won an *Atlantic Monthly* fiction award. The same year he sold his first short story, **"Soft Come the Dragons,"** to *Fantasy and Science Fiction.* Within the next eight years, Koontz would see two dozen short stories and twenty-two novels published—most in the science fiction genre. And with that accomplishment Koontz was justly awarded the title science fiction writer, which he wore around his neck like a set of dog tags.

At first, those dog tags fit rather comfortably. Koontz was a success. He was young. He was making a living—albeit an unspectacular one—from the symbiosis of his imagination and his typewriter. And during the early years, they were dog tags he wore with more than a little pride.

But something happened.

Koontz began to evolve as a writer. He wanted more. Science fiction was limiting his creative talents, limiting his ability to express the wide range of emotions the muse was whispering from within. Also the genre was scorned by critics as merely disposable fiction, and although his novels were successful as science fiction went, they faded quickly into oblivion. And it wasn't long before Koontz began to long for the respect, the immortality, and the financial rewards of the popular mainstream writer. It was then that he discovered those dog tags were made of lead, pulling him down in the literary river in which he was trying to advance.

> . . . I had already been typecast by publishers, editors, and critics. Editors are usually reluctant to buy a manuscript from an author who is writing outside of the genre in which he is an established name, for they are worried about confusing book buyers. Many people in the publishing industry underestimate the reading public's intelligence and catholicity. Anyway, after being stuck with the *Science Fiction Writer* label, I knew I faced an exhausting, protracted battle to be recognized as simply a writer, period.

He decided to completely break from science fiction. To cover his footsteps he bought back the rights to fifteen of the eighteen books he had published in the genre. *Demon Seed* was the last book Koontz published that could be considered purely science fiction, and ironically it was his most successful and the first to be produced by the motion picture industry.

Through perseverance and considerable talent, Dean R. Koontz has erased the science fiction writer label. His feet are well-soaked in the mainstream of literature and his name turns up with frequency on the best-seller lists. His writing crosses genres and is equally embraced by suspense, mystery and horror fiction readers. But was his break from science fiction really that complete? A look through some of those eighteen early novels just might help answer that question.

It seems that science fiction writers have always had a fascination with religion. Dean R. Koontz, far from being an exception, frequently chose themes built around the concept of religion.

> . . . I was searching for an understanding of humankind's purpose, our reason for being, our relationship to creation. How do we fit in? Are we the beloved creations of a God? The playthings of a God? Creatures of natural evolution who *invented* a God? Are there morals given in the universe as real—or realer—than the laws of physics? Or do we make our morality as we go?

Being a creator himself, Koontz built future worlds to include future theologies, where often man has become Godlike. Such is the case in *The Flesh in the Furnace,* where a race of spider-men, the Vonopoens, have learned the secret of the creation of life, which they sell to traveling merchants in the form of an easily transportable furnace. Their holy book, The Book of Wisdom, is brought to earth along with the teachings of their saints.

> The identity of God changes, as his children unseat him. Each generation, we come under the hand of a fledgling deity who has gained his power through fratricide. This explains why God is clumsy and why his wisdom has never equaled that of his creations: He never had a full lifetime in which to learn.
>
>   Saint Zenopau

> We can rejoice in our humanity, for there will come a day when God's creatures will have grown more powerful than he. Then we will rise up and dethrone him and his children, and the magic of life-death suspension will be ours. This is not a threat to the divine powers, merely a statement of ecological progression.
>
>   Saint Eclesian

> God is the mark. We are the con-men. One day we will pull the shuffle on him, and then history will really begin my brothers—and my sisters. Then history will begin with fury!
>
>   Saint Eclesian

The writings of Saint Zenopau and the Rogue Saint Eclesian lay a groundwork of philosophy for much of Koontz's science fiction. Man versus God. Man competing with God, trying through technology to attain the divine power; the power over life.

There would seem to be two avenues man could take in his quest for divinity: by conquering death, or unlocking the secret of creation. Both are explored by Koontz, but it is the second in which he seemed to have held the greatest fascination—a fascination that he would carry with him over the borders of horror and mainstream writing.

In his 1970 novel *Dark of the Woods,* Koontz describes a paradise world once ruled by peaceful winged-people, the Demosians. The Demosians developed an artificial womb, which enabled them to regenerate still-living cells from the recently deceased into new bodies.

They had discovered the divine power—artificial creation of life. And at the same time, the conquest of death.

This power, which brings mortal beings on a Godlike level, is found regularly in Koontz's science fiction. And a few times, Koontz has allowed man to surpass God.

In his novel *A Darkness in My Soul,* expanded from his short story of the same name, man has done just that. It is the story of Simeon Kelly, a product of the artificial wombs who has the ability to travel into the minds of others. The world is on the verge of a holocaustal war, and the means of preventing annihilation may lie within the vast subsconscious mind of Child, another product of the artificial wombs. But Child remains mute, withdrawn into a world he has created within the vast intellect of his mind. The government contracts Simeon to travel into Child's mind and retrieve any information that may save the world. There, Simeon finds a universe created by Child, a universe in which Child is master. God. He eventually learns that Child has reached the mind of God himself, along with a darker revelation—*God is insane.* For centuries man has wondered why a sane God would allow cataclysm after cataclysm to devastate his creation. And man answered that it was his divine test, a test of courage to see how man could cope, strengthen. But the fact was that God had merely gone insane. Insanity brought upon him by extreme loneliness. Simeon, in essence, kills both Child and God by bleeding their energy away and meshing it with his own psychic power. By killing God, Simeon became God.

> I felt no remorse.
>
> Does one feel remorse when one shoots down a maniac who is wielding a gun in a crowded department store?
>
> Man as God. I retained the mortal form and the mortal outlook, with the emotions and prejudices of men. I did not think that would be a weakness, but that it might actually make me a more benevolent and stable deity than the previous owner of my power had been. Man as God . . .

Simeon learns from God's mistake, and transmits half of his newfound powers to a female partner. Each with half the power of the previous God, they set off to rule the universe. For ten thousand years they roam the corners of existence learning of the world they inherited. Finally, they become bored and decide to let Earth know of their existence.

> And though we had ended the rivalries of religions, we went down to Earth to revive them. We brought forth temples and synagogues, churches and altars, and garish robes and bejeweled priests. We created hierarchies of worthless prelates and we spoke our words to the masses through the mouths of men of less value than most other men.

As Simeon and his partner become bored again they revive hatred and warfare, and soon the world is no different than it had been in previous centuries under previous rule. Man as God.

But if man can ultimately surpass the powers of God with his own creations, can't those creations ultimately surpass the powers of man? According to Dean Koontz, the answer is decidedly yes. In his earlier mentioned work, *The Flesh in the Furnace,* the puppets, minature creations of human life, become dissatisfied with their existence. They are tired of "performing" for their "God," the puppetmaster. They have the puppetmaster killed, and in time conquer the Earth. Eventually, they conquer other worlds as well. The Vonopoens use the furnace to create a loyal warrior race of creatures which then destroy the puppets. And so the cycle continues.

And what would the Vonopoen Rogue Saint Eclesian say about this . . .

> We Vonopoens have long prided ourselves on what we think of as our highest artform, our realistic miniature puppets. We make them in our own images and in the images of animals and other races, and we have them perform for us. Perhaps if we spent less time playing Gods in this respect and examined the universe more closely, we would discover that we are all only puppets ourselves, on a much greater scale. We have our scripts. There are repetitious cycles. And somewhere, I think, there are voices that laugh at us. Even at me.
>
>   Saint Eclesian

In other of Koontz's science fiction novels, God turns up as a major character.

In *Anti-Man,* God turns out to be an alien intelligence so vast that only a micromial part of him can inhabit our universe at one time. He visits the Earth in the form of an android, with the intention of passing on some of his powers to mankind.

In his comic, science fiction, supernatural, detective novel, *The Haunted Earth,* God turns out to be a rather pathetic character who is a regular at nightclubs, guests on TV talk shows (where he is humiliated), and admits to orgies in heaven.

As he and his writing matured, Koontz dropped the "what is God" struggle from his novels, but a strong sense of the spiritual has continued into his horror fiction.

> Well, after all these years of mulling over the subject, I have formed the belief that humankind evolved—as did the universe—under the guidance of some greater consciousness and that we have a purpose and a destiny that we do not yet understand but that we must gradually discover and pursue. I suspect that our destiny might be to become as gods ourselves, a theme that surely is obvious in some recent books like *Strangers* and *Watchers.*

Man cannot fashion life in his image from clay and divine breath. He doesn't have to; he's got recombinant DNA—the genetic blueprint of life etched indelibly within his own cells. And it is the blueprint for more than one of Koontz's later works, especially his Leigh Nichols suspense novels.

In *The Eyes of Darkness,* recombinant DNA research is carried out secretly by the military in an effort to create biological weapons. In *The House of Thunder,* the government is secretly funding the milestone project to create biological and other weapons. In *Shadowfires,* a scientist is able to defeat death through the rejuvination of his own cells by altering his DNA—and, oh yes, the government has agents after him. In *Watchers,* DNA research has produced the most advanced biological weapon yet: a monstrous killing machine brought to us courtesy of—the government. Now, it's obvious that these four novels have something in common, and what they have most in common is not the obvious, for they are each very different tales.

Horror.

To Dean R. Koontz, horror is achieved by placing the ultimate weapon in the hands of the ultimate madmen. Not to say that all government men are mad, but the government, particularly the military and intelligence agencies, provides a petri dish in which madness can thrive, and madmen can attain high seats of authority. They sometimes operate on group-think, where rationality can take a back seat to "the good of the mission."

Koontz understands this well. His protagonists are just as likely to do battle with a government agent as with a lizard-skinned monster. And that agent may be just as horrifying.

In the Leigh Nichols novel, *The Eyes of Darkness,* the government is trying to discover why a thirteen-year-old boy, accidentally infected with a deadly Soviet-engineered virus—Gorki 400—has survived. To enable them to study the boy—by re-infecting him with the virus—the government has its secret security agency, Network, fake his death in a staged accident. His mother and her lover discover that there has been a cover-up and set out to find him. The Network, lead by its ruthless leader, George Alexander, intends to stop the pair by killing them.

Alexander justifies the murder of innocent people, who just happen to get in the way of national security, as his patriotic duty. But more than that, it gives him a spiritual power.

> For as long as he could remember, he had been fascinated with death, with the mechanics and the meaning of it, and he had longed to know what it was like on the other side—without, of course, wanting to commit himself to a one-way journey there. He didn't want to die; he only wanted to know. Each time that he personally killed someone, he felt as though he were establishing another link to the world beyond this one; and he hoped, once he made enough of those linkages, that he would be rewarded with a vision from the other side. One day, maybe he would be standing in a graveyard, before the tombstone of one of his victims, and the person he killed would reach out to him from beyond and let him see, in some vivid clairvoyant fashion, exactly what death was like. And then he would know.

Alexander has the dark power to bring death, which means, in a way, that he has the power over life. In the warped interiors of his mind, this power makes him God-like. It is a delusion Koontz has placed in the minds of a few of Alexander's literary colleagues.

In *Watchers,* Vince Nasco is an American assassin working for the Soviet government. He is probably the most ruthless, cold-blooded character to slash his way through a Koontz novel. He's dangerous because he kills not for patriotic pride, not for money, but for immortality. He believes that a small portion of the life force of his victims is absorbed within him after each assassination. His dream is to murder a pregnant woman, so that he may absorb the virgin energy of an unborn life.

Such assassins played a less prominent role in his science fiction, but they made occassional appearances. And, as in his later fiction, some were government agents.

In his short story, **"The Psychedelic Children"** the futuristic American government—The Constitutional Tolerant Party—employs both android and human agents to eliminate the Hallucino-Children. These are the decendants of people who regularly used LSD in the 1960's and 70's, and have gained, through mutation, psychic powers deemed dangerous by the government.

In his 1969 novel, **The Fall of the Dream Machine,** Koontz brings us a world quite nearly ruled by the electronic media. There is no television. There is SHOW, experienced by seven hundred million subscribers daily. SHOW is a complete sensory experience. Subscribers do not simply watch actors playing roles; they *become* the actors. They see what the actors see, think the same thoughts, share the same tactile sensations. It has made media addicts of the world, and there is but one pusher, Alexander Cockley, the director of SHOW. He is an evil man who seeks to rule the world, a deadly man who enjoys ordering others to their deaths. And long before Freddy Kruger, of *Nightmare On Elm Street,* Alexander Cockley had razor sharp retractable steel blades in his fingers, which he used with deadly accuracy to persuade others to his way of thinking.

The horrors in these novels do not ascend from the depths of slimy swamps; they need not turn into bats or wolves, or boogey-eyed monsters. They are just men, controlled by other men, and they are scary as hell.

In comparing these evil men, often turned to evil deed from the group-think mentality, there is one major difference between those appearing in Koontz's science fiction and his later novels. In his horror and suspense books, these men are generally renegades. They may work for the government, but they are involved in agencies so classified and sub-classified that they no longer represent attitudes of the government at all—assuming of course that the government is ruled by sane men.

Therefore, once these men are beaten and exposed, the hope remains that others will not be able to abuse the power given them. At the end of the novel, we return to the free people we are meant to be, living in a free society. Throughout these books, there is always hope.

Not so in science fiction.

Generally, these books take place far enough into the future that the government has been unrecognizably restructured—or for that matter, the government might well be an alien one. Often, this governmental restructuring is secondary to some cataclysmic event, which forces society to give up the freedoms we take for granted. Evil men in these books are not renegades. They represent a world different from our own. They have different values, an alien code of ethics. The world has changed. And even if the protagonists manage to escape into the mountains and be free of the sadistic military leader of the "Earth Alliance," "World Federational Government" or whichever—the fact is that nothing has really changed in the end—the madness has not been beaten, merely temporarily outsmarted. The oppression continues. Many times, early in such futuristic novels, hope is lost.

Hope. Hopelessness.

Optimism. Pessimism.

These are perspectives that, more often than not, [differentiate] science fiction from horror and mainstream fiction. And they are perspectives that [differentiate] the Koontz of 1970 from the Koontz of today.

> My books are about the great value of the individual (if each of us has within him the destiny to be God, how could he be anything *but* valuable), about the love relationships between mates and friends and relatives. With this philosophy, I am of course a thorough-going optimist, a believer in people and in the future, and my optimism makes my fiction considerably different from that of nearly anyone else I can think of in the dark-suspense, dark-fantasy genres, where misanthropy of one degree or another colors the work of virtually every writer.

Certainly, one reason for the change from pessimism to optimism is the fact that his science fiction novels were written during a time of social upheaval. The war in Vietnam was seemingly endless. Political assassinations were a commonly reported event on the evening news. The climate was right for social rebellion. And the natural way for a young writer to join that rebellion was through the power of the pen. The oppressed people may have been alien and winged instead of black, assassinations may have been carried out by androids instead of men, but the themes were often merely a reflection of that decade of social turbulence.

Still.

It seems that science fiction lends itself well to a feeling of pessimism. Even if it's not the intent of the writer to project a gloomy atmosphere, it is often unavoidable. People are more comfortable in familiar surroundings. They relate better to characters that they are familiar with, can empathize with. It's just not easy for us to feel strongly about what becomes of an android or mutant. Even if they prevail, they're still going to be a damned android or mutant.

Koontz's work became more optimistic from the moment he left the science fiction genre. Although his earliest diversions were pure horror, some under his Owen West moniker, in which very horrible things happen to some nice people, a feeling of hope persisted throughout those novels.

In *The Funhouse,* we know that death lurks in the traveling carnival. We know that Amy Harper is the target of the horror that haunts the funhouse, that this horror has been patiently waiting for her since before her birth, waiting to avenge a wrong her mother had committed twenty five years before. And we know—we hope—that Amy will eventually enter that funhouse and confront the horror. But we also know that if she can prevail, if she can survive, she will have a bright future. Optimism. Hope. We care about Amy Harper. We've all known someone like her.

In one of Koontz's most terrifying books, *Darkfall,* the horror comes from the very depths of Hell. In this horror novel, Koontz has created a tale as grim as any you are likely to read. The atmosphere is bleak throughout, where we enter a world of organized crime, drug dealing, and

voodoo priests. An evil practioner of Vodun uses his black arts to conjure up a few creatures from Hell to act as invincible hit men, to aid him in taking over the drug trade from a Mafia family in New York. But he opens the gates of Hell too wide and what results is a murderous rampage. A rampage carried out by demons. And it is up to two city cops to stop it.

Sound hopeless enough? Not really.

It is hope that holds us to the novel. Hope that good will prevail, no matter how powerful the evil. Koontz is a master at raising those hopes and then unexpectedly dropping them into the depths from which his demons have risen.

> In St. Patrick's Cathedral, Rebecca took two steps toward the piles of now-ordinary earth that had, only a moment ago, been living creatures, but she stopped short when the scattered dirt trembled with a current of impossible perverse life. The stuff wasn't dead after all. The grains and clots and clumps of soils seemed to draw moisture from the air; the stuff became damp; the separate pieces in each loose pile began to quiver and strain and draw laboriously toward the others. This evilly enchanted earth was apparently trying to regain its previous forms, struggling to reconstitute the goblins. One small lump, lying apart from all the others, began to shape itself into a tiny, wickedly clawed foot.

> "Die, damnit," Rebecca said. "Die!"

Yet he holds us by that thread, that strong filament of optimism that if only the cops can discover the secret, if only the Voodoo priest can be outsmarted, the world will return to normal and the characters live happily ever after.

It is hope which keeps us imprisoned in the tale, but it is the tale, itself, which must first capture us. And as jailer, Koontz seems to have imprisoned a wider audience since leaving the science fiction genre. And it was his horror fiction which brought critical acclaim, and it was this genre which launched him into the mainstream of literature.

The horror genre gave Koontz the freedom he needed to exercise literary muscles left to atrophy in his science fiction.

In science fiction, it is often the *science* that takes up the writer's energy. In a sea of robotix and computer chips, alien warriors and post-holocaustal disease, characterization can be left to drift aimlessly. Plots may not be strong enough to hold up under the weight of futuristic technology, which may serve to stretch but also [attenuate] the imagination.

In horror fiction, on the other hand, we know, or are intimately involved in, the world in which the story is taking place. We therefore care about this world. We can relate more closely to the characters and the emotions they express, and more importantly, so does the author.

By shunting his creative energy from amazing the reader with a futuristic world of technology, Koontz has sharply honed his characterization skills. Most of his characters are ordinary people with ordinary careers catapulted into extraordinary situations. We can laugh with them, cry with them, shiver in fear with them, and even, sometimes, very much hate them, because we *know* them. And that's something that's difficult to say about an alien lizard man from Pluto, no matter how much work the author put into the character.

When a novel's characters are universally appealing, when the plot is strong and the action jam-packed, that novel will find a wide audience. And when there's a wide audience, the critics will notice. And while Koontz has not won all the critics over, he has certainly won their attention.

But has Koontz really left science fiction entirely?

> Yes, ideas from my science fiction have crept into my latter work, but not consciously. I never set out to take elements used in early SF novels and rework them in a mainstream context. I've too many new ideas to bother looking toward the past for inspiration.

It would seem that those eighteen early science fiction novels may have dropped a few seeds into Koontz's fertile imagination. As discussed earlier, the idea of life created outside the womb appeared repeatedly in his science fiction and has appeared in some of his horror-suspense novels as well. Subliminal suggestion, the theme of *Night Chills,* popped up in his science fiction: it was prominent in *Demon Seed* and *The Fall of the Dream Machine. The Vision, The Face of Fear,* and *The Mask* all have characters who possess psychic powers but so did the science fiction novels *A Darkness in My Soul* and *Time Thieves.*

Strangers has appeared on all the best-seller lists. It is an epic tale of cross-genre appeal. But science fiction—although not until late in the novel—plays a significant role in the plot's twist. Science fiction finds a place in the plots of *Watchers* and *Shadowfires.* But none of these novels could be considered in the science fiction genre. They cover a broad literary spectrum. The strength of the story lies within the characterization and plot and not with the technology. They are action novels, horror novels, suspense novels, romance novels . . . *mainstream novels.*

Dean Koontz does not write in a vacuum, and the fact is that you don't write eighteen science fiction novels and not like the genre, so it seems that he's not likely to abandon it completely. And while he may no longer be flying on his plastic, fantastic chemical, like any ex-addict, he had to go through a period of withdrawal and he's bound to have an occasional flashback or two. But Koontz has accomplished what he set out to—he's not a science fiction writer, not even a horror writer but simply a *successful* writer. (pp. 72-84)

> *Stan Brooks, "A Mutation of a Science Fiction Writer," in* Sudden Fear: The Horror and Dark Suspense Fiction of Dean R. Koontz, *edited by Bill Munster, Starmont House, Inc., 1988, pp. 72-85.*

Michael A. Morrison   (essay date 1988)

[*In the following excerpt, Morrison examines Koontz's use of monstrous characters and creatures to explore the nature of evil.*]

The zombie. The maniac. The demon. Gigantic wasps, crabs, spiders. Voodoo priests. Monsters all, such figures of evil leer out at us from the pages of countless horror tales and flicker across screens where numberless genre films unreel. These creatures embody one of the central preoccupations of horror fiction: the representation and delineation of evil. What is Evil? What is its source? Is Evil innate in man? Is it the Devil's doing? Or is it a cosmic, disembodied power, the incarnation of uncaring—or worse, inimical—gods that rule the universe? The monster vivifies these anxieties and looms large in tales of horror, fantasy, and science fiction.

As it does in mainstream thrillers such as the novels of Dean Koontz. In three successive novels—*Whispers* (1980), *Phantoms* (1983), and *Darkfall* (1984)—Koontz uses a familiar figure of the monstrous to posit three quite different views of the nature of Evil. And, particularly in the first two, he plays upon the expectations we readers of horror fiction bring to these novels, implicitly criticizing conventional monsters of the genre as inadequate avatars of Evil for the modern world. (p. 116)

At first, *Whispers* seems a simple genre novel of the psychopathic-madman-assaults-woman variety. Hilary Thomas, a beautiful, successful Hollywood screenwriter, becomes the object of the unwanted attentions of Bruno Frye, whom she thinks is merely a California wine merchant. Indeed, her only prior encounter with Frye was at his Napa Valley vineyard, which she visited while researching a screenplay. But at times Bruno plunges into madness, and, for reasons unknown, he comes after Hilary with a knife.

But gradually, *Whispers* emerges as more subtle and complex than it initially appears. In the guise of a thriller, Koontz's novel uses such traditional icons of horror fiction as the maniac, the zombie, and the demon to develop a surprisingly liberal notion of the nature and source of the evil, the mindless violence, that seems to define late twentieth-century America.

Describing Frye's first attack, Koontz paints a quintessential portrait of the maniac. Raging towards Hilary "like a demon leaping out of a crack in hell," Frye is an elemental image of the monstrous in man:

> His demeanor was that of a lunatic. His eyes flashed, not icy as they had been, but watery and hot, fevered. Sweat streamed down his face. His lips worked ceaselessly, even though he was not speaking; they writhed and twisted, pulled back over his teeth, then pushed out in a childish pout, forming a sneer, then a weird little smile, then a fierce scowl, then an expression for which there was no name.

Frye's attack is overtly sexual—his chosen weapon is, after all, a knife. But Hilary is not one to let a slavering madman rape and murder her without a fight. Arming herself with a pistol, she confronts her attacker. She shoots at him twice, first shattering his knife, then hitting him. Frye goes down.

At which point Koontz introduces (implicitly) the image of the zombie, the walking dead. His description of the aftermath of Frye's shooting prefigures what is to come.

> She sighed and lowered the pistol.
>
> Dead. He was dead.
>
> She had killed a man.
>
> Dreading the coming ordeal with police and reports, she edged around the outstretched arm and headed for the hall door.
>
> Suddenly, he was not dead any more.

Merely wounded, Frye comes at Hilary again. This first attack is a paradigm of his role in the rest of the novel: for the next 400 pages, neither we nor Koontz's characters are sure whether he is dead.

Hilary ends Frye's second assult by planting her .32 automatic securely on his scrotum and making the obvious threat. But the madman escapes. Sensing that she couldn't kill even him in cold blood, he just walks out.

Hilary Thomas and Bruno Frye, heroine and villain, comprise a study in parallels and contrasts. Both are adults living in the shadow of childhood. Both are victims of parental abuse, and both carry deep-seated neuroses as a consequence. Indeed, all the main figures of Koontz's novel reflect the constricting influences of childhood on adult life—the sins of the fathers and mothers. This theme is vivified even in the personalities of less neurotic characters, such as the novel's hero Tony Clemenza, the Los Angeles cop who becomes Hilary's companion, protector, and lover.

To Hilary, at the pinnacle of success in her chosen field, life seems a little unreal, a "fantasy, a marvelous fairytale." Bright, talented, and self-reliant, she is also deeply insecure: for her, "the world was a dangerous place, a shadowy cellar with nightmare creatures crouching in the dark corners." As events will show, she is not far wrong: in the world of **Whispers** violence and horror descend on innocents with the capriciousness of a tornado. It is the world of Hollywood, of California in the 80's, a world whose moral underpinnings are no more stable than its earthquake-ridden landscape.

Hilary's quiet paranoia stems from her childhood in Chicago: a nightmare of abuse at the hands of her violent, alcoholic father Earl and her uncaring mother Emma. She emerged from those years terrified of emotional commitment, emotionally hamstrung by hatred of her parents, and plagued by unconscious guilt over her father, whom she knifed to death in self-defense. So, to repress her memories and salve her psychic wounds, Hilary has become a recluse and workaholic. Her operant myth is that there exists a level of success that will truly free her, that will provide sufficient security for her to "cast out the demons—my parents, Chicago, all those bad memories." But it will be not her work but rather the "crouching nightmare" of Bruno Frye that enables her to conquer her fears and her past.

Yet, if Hilary is seriously neurotic, Bruno Frye is in never-

land. The Napa Valley vintner can pass for human: various characters perceive him as "an important and successful man" and "a leading figure in the community." But Koontz portrays him as a human monster. He is a great bull of a man, immensely powerful and awesomely voracious. Celebrating violence and sadism, consumed by blood lust and rage, Frye comes at us "like an elemental force."

But amidst the sound and fury of Frye's first attacks on Hilary, Koontz drops a clue that this man/monster is more than your garden variety psychopath. Horrifying nightmares and hallucinations plague Bruno—dreams of whispers:

> [The nightmare] would come to him now as it always did when he slept, as it had all his life, and he would wake with a scream caught in the back of his throat. As always, he would not be able to recall what the dream had been about. But upon waking, he would hear the whispers, the loud but unintelligible whispers, and he would feel something moving on his body, all over his face, trying to get into his mouth and nose, some horrible *thing*.

Horrible indeed. As we will learn, Bruno's dreams are the key to his psychosis, a fearsome remembrance of abuses past.

As Koontz leads us deeper into Bruno's dementia, he reveals the delusion that drives it: Frye believes that Hilary is his mother reincarnate. Indeed, it is Hilary's chance resemblance to Bruno's long-dead mother Katherine, which he happened to notice during her visit to his vineyard, that determines him to kill her. She is, in fact, the 24th woman to fall victim to this phantasm.

With the introduction of Frye's delusion, Koontz explicitly invokes another icon of the living dead: the vampire. Bruno believes *literally* that Hilary is one of "the living dead," that she is "his mother come back from the grave," and that only through ritual can he "cancel out her supernatural powers of regeneration." His rituals and their implements derive explicitly from the post-Bram Stoker vampire tale. (At one point, Koontz shows an attendant at the city morgue reading "a few chapters of a really good Stephen King novel about vampires on the loose in New England.") Frye carries in his gray Dodge van the accoutrements of the folkloric vampire killer (linen bags of garlic, wooden stakes, etc.), and his fantasies of Hilary's slaughter exude images from vampire fiction and film:

> Cut out her heart. Pound a wooden stake through it. Cut off her head. Fill her mouth with garlic. He also intended to take the head and the heart with him when he left the house; he would bury the pair of grisly trophies in separate and secret graves, in the hallowed ground of two different churchyards, and far away from wherever the body itself might be interred.

We know, of course, that Hilary is neither vampire nor Katherine reincarnate and are thus clued in from the start that Koontz is making unconventional use of genre symbols of evil—in **Whispers,** of the living dead. In addition to the imagined vampire, he will soon introduce a zombie that is not undead, and a schizophrenic (the maniac) that is far more complex than Jekyll and Hyde.

Following Frye's escape, the police appear. Detective Tony Clemenza and his partner Frank Howard interrupt their hunt for a pusher and rapist named Bobby "Angel" Valdez to look into Hilary's case. Faced with overwhelming evidence of Frye's innocence, they are skeptical—until Frye attacks again. This time, Hilary kills him.

As if to assuage any doubt that Frye is indisputably dead, Koontz takes us and Hilary to the morgue. The corpse has Frye's ID, but Hilary doesn't need to identify the distinctive carcass of her assailant. Yet, even in this scene, Koontz foreshadows what is to come, invoking an image from a hundred zombie and vampire movies. Looking at Frye's corpse, Hilary has "the insane feeling that any moment he would turn his head towards her and open his eyes." Then "another absurd but chilling thought struck her: 'What if [the corpse] sits up on the cart and throws the sheet off?' " Nothing of the sort happens, though, and Hilary leaves "thoroughly relieved and even delighted that [Frye] was dead."

We are now 150 pages into a 502-page book. Frye is dead. Hilary is safe. And we are wondering what the devil Koontz is up to. His several subplots—the stress applied to Tony's and Frank's partnership by Frank's cynicism and bitterness, the budding romance between Hilary and Tony, the search for Bobby Valdez—seem inadequate to sustain several hundred more pages. And as these subplots unfold, we watch the journey of the corpse of Bruno Frye through embalment and burial in short, strangely ominous scenes that give no clue that he is not well and truly defunct.

Our first hints that the creature may still be among us are subtle ones: Hilary receives voiceless telephone calls; Frye's coffin is violated by parties unknown; Joshua Rhinehart, the executor of the Frye estate, senses "an evil presence in the darkness, a thing crouching and waiting" as he leaves the funeral home where Bruno lies in state. Implanted like seeds in the latter chapters of Part I ("The Living and the Dead"), these incidents will bear fruit in Part II ("The Living and the Living Dead") when Bruno returns.

But just before this happens, Joshua Rhinehart suffers a dream. Dreams in Koontz's novels are fraught with meaning, and this one is no exception:

> In the nightmare, several dead men—all of them duplicates of Bruno Frye—had risen up from their caskets and from the porcelain and stainless steel embalming tables; [Joshua] had run into the night . . . but they had come after him, had searched the shadows for him, moving jerkily, calling his name in their flat, dead voices.

In this dream, which reads like an outtake from *Night of the Living Dead,* Koontz foreshadows Bruno's return and embeds clues as to his true nature.

But now, Frye is back. Like a primal force of nature, he again attacks Hilary. Confronted with what appears unarguably to be a "walking dead man," she is almost as trou-

bled by the implied subversion of reality as by the immediate threat:

> As she watched Bruno Frye coming through the archway, Hilary thought she must be losing her mind. The man was dead. *Dead!* She had stabbed him twice, had seen his blood. She had seen him in the morgue, too, cold and yellow-gray and lifeless. An autopsy had been performed. A death certificate had been signed. *Dead men don't walk.* Nevertheless, he was back from the grave . . .

Bruno's return, "pasty-faced, shaking violently, obviously on the edge of hysteria," propels us into Part II, where Koontz's thriller turns into a mystery.

This change in the narrative structure of *Whispers* occurs as Hilary, her policeman lover Tony, and the Frye's lawyer Joshua Rhinehart dig into the history of the Frye family. Impelled almost as much by curiosity as by their desire to protect Hilary, they probe back in time: first into the recent past of Frye's autopsy, embalming, and burial; then further back into his adult life and relationships; and ultimately, in an interview with Rita Yancy, the prostitute who was midwife at Bruno's birth, into the dark history of the family Frye. Their search for the truth of Bruno Frye—"Was the impossible possible? Could a dead man walk?"—plunges them (and us) into a bewildering maelstrom of modern evil.

As Part II unfolds, the traditional, simplistic evil figures of the maniac and the zombie give way to a complex psychological portrait of a tortured victim. From the beginning of their quest, Hilary, Tony, and Joshua have thought of Frye as "the most evil, vicious sort of monster," as "the Beast from Hell [that] walks among us in the clothes of a common man." But as the community of truth-seekers penetrates the web of lies and half-truths that enmeshes the figure of Bruno Frye, their (and our) identification of him as the provenance of evil becomes as murky as the swamp of dementia and perversion that is the Frye family history.

For Hilary, Tony, and Joshua have discovered a fundamental principle of the world of *Whispers:* that truth is as unstable as the fault-ridden earth beneath their feet. Piecing together clues, rumors, and speculation, they consider several solutions to the mystery of Bruno's return, only to have to jettison each. What deflects them from the truth is the unreliability of public myth, of "common knowledge," about Frye's past: he was an only child; Katherine adopted him; she had no natural children, etc. All these stories are found to be wrong. So, in the face of such unreliable knowledge, speculations abound: Frye wasn't really killed; Frye has, in fact, returned from the dead; Frye had a brother; Frye had hired a look-alike. Although none of these explanations proves correct either, each moves the figure of the monster farther from traditional generic embodiment of evil, and takes us closer to the ambiguous heart of evil in the novel. Like petals on a diseased flower, the layers of the Frye family history unfold to expose a legacy of madness and abuse. Finally, from the midwife at Bruno's birth, prostitute Rita Yancy, the searchers learn the answer: Bruno is neither zombie nor supernatural creature; rather, he is the pathetic victim of his psychotic mother Katherine. From Rita they also learn that Bruno had a twin.

In Katharine's story, as recounted by Yancy, Koontz introduces a third genre icon: the demon. Katherine's delusion, which she passed on to the son she bore, Bruno Frye, and to his twin brother, was that she had been "raped by a thing from hell, a green scaly thing with huge eyes and a forked tongue and long claws." Like the figure of Hilary-as-vampire in the mind of her son, Katherine's demon lover exists only in her mind. But it was a delusion she needed desperately, and to preserve it Katherine lived the pretense that she was raising but a single child, the son of a friend. To this end she "gave the boys just one name. She allowed only one of them to go out in public at one time. She forced them to live one life." Thus was born Bruno's dementia. In the psychic pressure cooker of his mother's madness—and under the threat of her truly monstrous punishment, which now haunts his dreams—Bruno and his brother came to believe her "demon fantasy," accepting at the deepest levels of their minds that they were but a single person: "two individuals with one personality, one self-awareness, one self-image."

Thus is the figure of the monster in *Whispers* transformed into a victim. In the pantheon of horror, Bruno Frye is a variant on the split personality, the Jekyll/Hyde symbol of human duality. To be sure, Bruno—each Bruno—is truly schizophrenic. Appearing normal in society, he harbors a hidden self, "the demon half of his personality," that rages to the surface in the (imagined) presence of Katherine's reincarnated spirit. Koontz's clever variation is that Frye's personality has undergone both fission and fusion; he *is* both himself and his brother. But now

> . . . himself was dead. . . . For forty years, he had posed as an ordinary man, and he had passed for normal with considerable success. But he could not do that any more. Half of him was dead. . . . Without himself to turn to, without his other self to give advice and offer suggestions, he did not have the resources to maintain the charade.

The grotesque figure of Bruno Frye—a meld of the motifs of the dual personality, the doppleganger, and the monstrous twin—ranks with Niles Perry in Thomas Tryon's *The Other* (1971) as one of the most original psychological aberrations in horror fiction. For the characters in the novel and for us Bruno remains monstrous and malignant, but not evil—at least not in a traditional sense.

Is, then, Katherine the progenitor of evil in the uncertain world of this novel? No sooner had the question occurred to Hilary and her compatriots than up from the swamp of the Frye family history bubbles yet another awful horror. It was Leo, the insanely egomaniacal, ruthlessly autocratic patriarch of the Fryes, who brutalized, sexually abused, and finally impregnated his daughter Katherine. This truth leaves the wretched figure of Bruno's mother, frantically trying to preserve her public image of "a saintly woman who took in a poor foundling," too pathetic and tragic a figure to serve as the wellspring of evil. The history of horror stops at Leo, but we are left uncertain as to the

nature and source of evil. Indeed, evil itself seems to have gotten lost in the rack of victims that is the family tree of Bruno Frye.

Bruno Frye, at once monster and victim, berserker and figure of pathos, reminds us of our own dual natures—of the beasts within us all—and of how childhood traumas and terrors can shape our dreams and waking lives. But Bruno also symbolizes the motiveless malignity that surrounds us. And the transformation of his iconographic function in Koontz's novel—from traditionally evil maniac to simplistically evil zombie to psychologically complex victim—suggests that the source of evil is neither supernatural agency nor individual, but rather society. This evolution of the figure of the monster inverts and revises the traditional genre motifs Koontz has invoked and emphasizes their inefficacy as symbols of evil for the modern world. With his next novel *Phantoms,* Koontz will use another collection of horror icons to propound a quite different view of evil. (pp. 117-25)

If *Whispers* begins like a psychological thriller with overtones of a slasher film, *Phantoms* opens like a tautly directed 50's monster movie. Home to the mountain ski resort of Snowfield come Dr. Jennifer Paige and her kid sister Lisa. It is late afternoon in early September, the off-season, and the alpine hamlet is quiet. Too quiet. A predatory stillness lies upon Snowfield. It is the silence of mass death: the town is now a necropolis.

At her home, Jennifer discovers the first body: her maid Hilda. The condition of the corpse—bloated, decomposition unnaturally arrested, every inch severely bruised—is inexplicable. And its face is locked in the rictus of a scream. Sudden death has struck the people of Snowfield. Hundreds are dead. As twilight blankets the decimated town, Jennifer and Lisa begin one of their many explorations of Snowfield, explorations that will lead them to a confrontation with a monster immeasurably old and incalculably evil, yet horrifyingly familiar.

Unlike *Whispers* and *Darkfall, Phantoms* is set in a pastoral locale: an isolated resort nestled in the Sierras. Snowfield is a serene, upscale community, a haven from "the rude world where violence and unkindness were disconcertingly common"—from the world of *Whispers.* But in even so secure a setting, horror can erupt from the very fabric of the environment. For in *Phantoms,* as in so many modern horror novels, "there's no safety anywhere."

Phantoms is the monster tale as police procedural. It is built around a series of investigations aimed at solving "the mystery of Snowfield": who (or what) killed the town. Jenny and Lisa—later joined by Sheriff Bryce Hammond and several deputies from nearby Santa Mira and, later still, by an Army research team—ceaselessly explore the decimated town, seeking survivors and answers. They are men and women of reason: systematic, scientific, rational. And much of *Phantoms* examines the responses of such people to the presence of unknown Evil, which has visited Snowfield in the form of the monster of the piece: the Ancient Enemy.

Like Hilary, Tony, and Joshua in *Whispers,* the investigators in *Phantoms* consider a series of more-or-less plausible explanations for the death of the town: plague, radiation, poison, toxic waste, a mutant strain of rabies, even—later, when when the siege of Snowfield has begun anew and more radical alternatives seem in order—invasion from outer space. None comes close to the truth.

For the truth is inaccessible by reason alone. In *Whispers,* truth could be uncovered beneath layers of unreliable public myth; in *Phantoms* more primal means are required. Jennifer Paige learns this early in the novel. She is in the home of friends, Tom and Karen Oxley. Tom and Karen have been slaughtered; their corpses are in the den. And Jennifer wants very badly to call for help, but she knows the phones to be dead. Then the Oxleys' phone rings. Answering it, Jennifer hears only silence, but she senses on the line a presence "unspeakably malevolent; perfectly, purely evil":

> She was well educated, a woman of reason and logic, not even mildly superstitious. Thus far, she had attempted to solve the mystery of Snowfield by applying the tools of logic and reason. But for the first time in her life, they had utterly failed her. Now deep in her mind, something . . . *shifted,* as if an enormously heavy iron cover were being slid off a dark pit in her subconscious . . . Virtually on the level of racial memory stored in the genes, she sensed what was happening in Snowfield. The knowledge was within her; however, it was so alien, so fundamentally illogical, that she resisted it, fighting hard to suppress the superstitious terror that boiled up within her.

And, later in the novel, when Sheriff Hammond converses with the creature (via a computer terminal), he feels the same awareness, a "primitive superstitious terror," and senses that he is "in the presence of something evil, ancient, and . . . familiar." Like Jenny, Bryce understands intuitively that reason alone cannot comprehend, let alone combat, the evil that has come to Snowfield. Consciously, the answers he seeks elude him, but

> . . . perhaps he did know. Deep down. Instinctively. If only he could reach inside himself, down past his civilized veneer which embodied so much skepticism, if he could reach into his racial memory, he might find the truth about the thing that had seized and slaughtered the people of Snowfield.

Linked to this failure of reason and logic as deductive tools is the impotence of technology and its appropriation by Evil. Once Sheriff Hammond has gotten a look at the graveyard that was Snowfield, he calls in an investigative research team, a well-equipped group of scientists and support troops from the Army Medical Corps led by General Galen Copperfield. These are the experts, the scientists. Remote and forbidding in their decontamination suits, wandering in and out of their mobile field laboratories, they are the ultimate symbols of rationality. To Jennifer they're "the cavalry" come to the rescue: "The specialists had arrived. Like most Americans, she had enormous faith in specialists, in technology, and in science. Soon they would understand what had killed Hilda and . . . all the others."

But they don't. Copperfield's technocrats are initially no more successful at solving the mystery of Snowfield than were Jenny and Bryce. Their investigations and analyses uncover many facts, but no answers. And their leader's intellectual rigidity leads only to terror and death. Ignoring Bryce's protestations, Copperfield insists on considering only possibilities that he and his team have been trained to handle: nerve gas, virus, poison, and the like. This attitude has infected his team of scientists, who "appeared determined to *force* the evidence to conform to their preconceived notions of what they would find in Snowfield." This narrowness of vision leads Copperfield to send one of his support troops into a walk-in meat locker and thus into the tender embrace of the monster.

Ultimately, however, the depredations of the monster force the surviving members of Copperfield's team to a new open-mindedness, and they are then able to use their scientific knowledge and man-made technology to defeat Evil. It is, in fact, one of Copperfield's scientists—a geneticist named Sara Yamaguchi—who discovers the Ancient Enemy's weakness: since it is a creature of living, carbon-based tissue, its "delicate chemical balance" can be destabilized by, of all things, a man-made, genetically engineered microorganism. That it is technology and not religion or magic that ultimately overcomes the threat, restoring an uncertain order, is consistent with the science-fictional underpinnings of *Phantoms.*

Technology, the symbol of reason in the modern world, is impotent unless informed by instinct. And it is controlled by the Beast. The Ancient Enemy uses the telephone to terrorize its prey, manipulates the public power supply of Snowfield, communicates with its intended victims via computer terminal, and seizes control of the suit-to-suit radios of Copperfield's crisis team. Over phone lines and radios, the beast sings of nature, of animals and humans in torment. And sometimes, it sings with the voice of a child:

> Although it was a child's voice, tender and fragile, it nevertheless contained . . . something that shouldn't be in a child's voice. A profound lack of innocence. Knowledge, perhaps. Yes. Too much knowledge of too many terrible things. Menace. Hatred. Scorn. It wasn't audible on the surface of the lilting song, but it was there beneath the surface, pulsing and dark and immeasurably disturbing.

This theme—that technology, being morally neutral, can be made the handmaiden of evil—recurs in many of Koontz's novels, notably in *Darkfall.*

By combining instinct and reason, the humans in Snowfield deduce part of the truth of the Ancient Enemy: the (decidedly non-human) monsters that seem to control the town are manifestations of but a single entity, a mimic, a shape-changer. Catching on fast, Jenny explains that it "can impersonate anyone or any animal that it's previously fed on" and "can assume the shape of anything it has absorbed *and* anything it can imagine." Able to control its own DNA, the monster manifests itself in a variety of guises, many of which are images drawn from the grade-B SF/horror films of the 50's: "an obscenely fat black spider the size of a pony," "an enormous hound," with sulphurous breath, a "crab the size of a car," a winged serpent, even the devil himself.

But the full story is told by an outsider, Dr. Timothy Flyte. Like Rita Yancy in *Whispers* (and many other figures in Koontz's novels), Flyte is the Outsider Who Knows. He knows precisely what is going on in Snowfield, for he has made the Ancient Enemy the focus of his life's work. By training an archeologist, by nature a visionary, Flyte had been ostracized by the academic community for writing a book in which he attributes the hundreds of unexplained mass disappearances that punctuate recorded history to "pre-historic creature[s]" like the one now feeding on Snowfield. Koontz depicts Flyte as an amiable eccentric, "a character right out of Dickens," but leaves no doubt that he is eminently qualified to answer questions that, for Jenny and Bryce, are of more than academic interest.

The Ancient Enemy is as appropriate a symbol of Evil as one could want. It is a creature of paradox: shapeless, it nonetheless embraces all shapes. A denizen of the underworld of storm drains and tunnels, caverns and watercourses, the monster, like the subconscious evil in the humans on which it feeds, moves beneath the surface and appears without warning in unpredictable forms. And, like evil, this protean creature is "by nature unspecific." Underground, it assumes its natural state: amorphous, undifferentiated protoplasm. But above ground, it can be anything: a dog, a human, a demon from the Christian or Lovecraftian mythos—even the Devil.

Koontz describes this creature from "the bowels of the earth" using metaphors of filth and slime. His account of its first appearance in its natural state, erupting from an open manhole on a street in Snowfield, is a blend of the excretory and the phallic. Rendered as always in Koontz's sledgehammer prose, it is positively orgasmic:

> Abruptly, something rose out of that hole, came from the storm drain below the street, rose and rose into the twilight, shuddering, smashing up into the air with tremendous power, a dark and pulsating mass, like a flood of sewage, except that it was not a fluid but a jellied substance that formed itself into a column almost as wide as the hole from which it continued to extrude itself in an obscene, rhythmic gush. It grew and grew: four feet high, six feet, eight. . . .

Oozing blistering digestive juices, this omnivorous, thoroughly malevolent "ameboid thing" of pseudopods and tentacles explodes out of the grounds and buildings of Snowfield like a Lovecraftian vision of cosmic evil. (At one point Koontz nods to Lovecraft, referring to the survivors as "in the middle of a Lovecraftian nightmare.") Late in the novel we learn that until it rose into the caverns beneath Snowtop Mountain to feed, the creature dwelled in the icy darkness of deep ocean trenches, hibernating, Cthulhu-like, in a "dreamlike state." Yet, the allusion to Lovecraft seems not entirely apt: as we soon learn, the nature of Evil in *Phantoms,* embodied in and symbolized by the Ancient Enemy, is quite different from that in the Lovecraftian cosmos. So why evoke Lovecraftian horror?

Misdirection. In structure, imagery, and atmosphere, *Phantoms* is filled with red herrings. These feints lead us to expect a particular kind of Evil, one familiar from the genre, to be at the heart of the novel—when in fact Koontz has something very different in mind. From its spooky beginning, in which all the inhabitants of an isolated town are discovered to have vanished (remember the opening of the 1957 film *The Beginning of the End?*), to its effects-filled finale, in which a band of survivors face a vast, amorphous monster (*The Blob*), *Phantoms* plays like a 50's monster movie. Its inexplicable horrific deaths, ominous silences, unseen presences, and preposterous monsters (a gigantic moth, a spider-thing, tentacles galore) evoke the stark, vivid images of the black-and-white grade-B horror film. This referential quality is reinforced by Koontz's style—he is one of the most cinematic of contemporary horror novelists—which encompasses the literary equivalents of everything from jump cuts to zooms.

Koontz doesn't miss a trick. The novel's effectively spooky atmospherics, which often soar to Lovecraftian heights of horror, its ramblings about ancient evil, and its many invocations of Christian symbols of evil, all seduce us genre-conscious readers into anticipating a familiar resolution: that the Ancient Enemy is either religious (the Devil), supernatural (a Lovecraftian monster) or preternatural (e.g., a giant crab). Just as Bruno Frye seems, for a time, to be back from the dead, the very model of a modern genre zombie, the monsters of Snowfield appear to be horrors, perhaps supernatural, perhaps not, unrelated to man—except insofar as they want to kill him.

Throughout the novel, Koontz adroitly manipulates the elements of Christian theology. During the siege of Snowfield, the Ancient Enemy mocks human faith, exploiting belief in the religious supernatural to demoralize or enslave its prey. Christian images abound. And explicit references to Christianity come thick and fast during the creature's dialogue-by-computer with Bryce Hammond. It has seized control of one of General Copperfield's terminals and is speaking, via flickering images on the screen, in tones that ridicule the tenets of human faith: "JESUS IS DEAD. GOD IS DEAD . . . I AM ALIVE." Asked its name, the creature's answer recalls a host of demons from Christian theology: "I AM HABORYM. I AM A MAN WITH THREE HEADS—ONE HUMAN, ONE CAT, ONE SERPENT . . . I AM RANTAN . . . I AM PALLANTRE . . . I AM AMLUTHIAS, ALFINA, EPYN, FUARD, BELIAL, OMGORMA, NEBIROS, BAAL, ELIGOR, AND MANY OTHERS . . . I AM ALL AND NONE. I AM NOTHING. I AM EVERYTHING." And later in the novel the monster assumes the form of the most potent icon of Christian evil in the mythos: Lucifer himself.

But it's all a set up. The Ancient Enemy is neither Christian devil nor Lovecraftian monster; it is a creature of the prehistoric world. Originally amorphous and (presumably) morally neutral, it learned Evil from the only truly evil creature in the cosmos of the novel. Timothy Flyte explains:

> It's real, a creature of flesh—although not flesh like ours. It's not a spirit or a devil. Yet . . . in

a way . . . I believe it *is* Satan. Because, you see, I believe it was this creature—or another like it, another monstrous survivor from the Mesozoic Era—that inspired the myth of Satan. In prehistoric times, men must have encountered one of these things, and some of them must have lived to tell about it. They naturally described their experiences in the terminology of myth and superstition. I suspect most of the demonic figures in the world's various religions are actually reports of these shape-changers, reports passed down through countless generations before they were at last committed to hieroglyphics, scrolls, and then print. They were reports of a very rare, very real, very dangerous beast . . . but described in the language of religious myth.

Thus does the religious sub-text of *Phantoms* subvert traditional genre notions of supernatural Evil. According to its premise, Evil originates not in Christian demonology nor in an uncaring Lovecraftian cosmos. The source is man. From "the knowledge and memories of those on whom it feeds," from minds devoid of empathy, compassion, or love, did the Ancient Enemy derive its cruel humor, its penchant for sadism and mockery, and its viciousness. Thus the Beast is but a template on which has been impressed the unmediated evil of man.

The "devil on a glass slide" in *Phantoms* also inverts the Christian notion of evil: that human wickedness is but a reflection of the existence of the Devil. Jenny articulates Koontz's theme:

> . . . maybe the only real devils are human beings, not all of us; not the species as a whole; just the ones who're twisted, the ones who somehow never acquire empathy or compassion. If the shape-changer *was* the Satan of mythology, perhaps the evil in human beings isn't a reflection of the Devil; perhaps the Devil is only a reflection of the savagery and brutality of our own kind. Maybe what we've done is . . . create the Devil in our own image.

Yet another explosion of religious references occurs when, near the end of the novel, the dying monster beats a "Mephistophelian retreat," returning to its underworld of dark caverns and dank tunnels. Eaten from within by man's genetically engineered microorganism, the Ancient Enemy dies a fitting death: a death by plague, a death of lesions, suppurating sores, and massive tissue decomposition—a cancerous death. Koontz narrates its fate in terms expressly mythic and religious:

> It crept deeper, deeper, across the underworld river that flowed in Stygian darkness, deeper still, farther down into the infernal regions of the earth, into the chambers of Orcus, Hades, Osiris, Erebus, Minos, Loki, Satan . . . It went deeper, down into jahanna, into Gehenna, into Sheol, Abbadon, into the Pit. Over the centuries it had eagerly assumed the role of Satan and other evil figures, which men had attributed to it, had amused itself by catering to their superstitions. Now, it was condemned to a fate consistent with the mythology it had helped create . . . It had been cast down. It had been damned. It would

dwell in darkness and despair for the rest of its life.

> (pp. 125-34)

[Unlike] *Whispers, Phantoms* posits that evil is a real and potent force that originates in man. But like its predecessor, this novel critiques traditional images of the monster from genre fiction, suggesting that B-movie monsters, Lovecraftian horrors, and Christian demons are inadequate representatives of evil for the modern world. They remain useful only as symbols or repositories of the evil that is the ultimate monster, man. In his next novel, *Darkfall*, the theme of religious evil reappears, in a radically different way, and shares center stage with a quite different monster. (p. 135)

In its opening chapters, *Darkfall* seems to be a variation on *Whispers* and *Phantoms,* another monster-tale-as-police-procedural. Dimly seen creatures—small, rat-like, with featureless, glowing eyes—stalk 11-year-old Penny Dawson as her father Jack, a New York City homicide detective, and his partner Rebecca Chandler investigate a quartet of bizarre drug-related murders. Some of the slayings occurred in locked rooms, and the victims were horribly mutilated: gazing at a corpse, Rebecca observes, "He looks . . . *chewed."*

But *Darkfall* differs from its predecessors in both structure and theme. In this, the third panel in Dean Koontz's triptych of terror, religious Evil comes into its own. And the villain of the piece, the charming Baba Lavelle, with his psychically-directed pack of vicious, verminous, predatory demons, is one of Koontz's most compelling.

Lavelle is a Haitian *Bocor*—a voodoo priest who uses black magic. Tall, dark, handsome, and immutably evil, he is aptly characterized (by a prostitute) as "one smart, creepy, badass dude." While investigating the murder of a drug dealer named Vince Vastagliano, Jack and Rebecca learn that Lavelle is trying to take over the New York City drug trade by using voodoo curses to kill off members of the ruling Carramazzas, a Mafia family who quite handily represent human evil in the novel. But these are merely rumors, and Rebecca isn't having any of it. She stridently insists that "[the killer] is just another psycho like all the psychos who're crawling out of the walls these days. There's nothing special or strange about him."

But more inexplicable murders and a surprise visit with Don Gennaro Carramazza, the reptilian patriarch of the family ("The old man looked . . . like a snake in a thousand dollar suit.") convince Rebecca that Lavelle is real. But on the subject of voodoo, she's adamant: "So he exists? That doesn't mean voodoo works!" Before long a close encounter with Lavelle's little horde of horrors removes these last lingering doubts.

Iconographically, Lavelle functions in *Darkfall* as the shaman; symbolically, he is the embodiment of supernatural, religious evil—which in the universe of this novel exists as an independent force. Although Lavelle has struck an alliance with supernatural powers, his demeanor belies his nature: "his long association with evil had not given him a bleak, mournful or even sour aspect; he was a happy man . . . [who] virtually radiated self confidence." With his noble face, elegant voice, and engaging laugh, Lavelle seems the very antithesis of villainy. But behind the charming smile, Evil lurks. Carver Hampton, a voodoo priest of white magic who counterbalances Lavelle in the novel, explains to Jack Dawson what he is up against:

> He's an extremely powerful *Bocor,* Lieutenant. Not an amateur. Not your average spellcaster. He has the power of darkness, the ultimate darkness of death, the darkness of Hell, the darkness of the Other Side . . . he is very probably mad, insane; . . . That is a most formidable combination: evil beyond measure, madness, and the power of a masterfully skilled *Bocor.*

Unlike Bruno Frye, the human monster of **Whispers,** Lavelle is no victim. He is simply evil. And, unlike the madness that infects Frye, Lavelle's insanity neither excuses nor explains his wickedness. It is psychopathy after the fact, icing on the cake of evil.

Baba Lavelle is right at home in New York City, which Koontz depicts as a cesspool of depravity where currents of evil course through slate-gray skies above blood-drenched streets:

> . . . in this great city he had discovered an enormous reservoir of the power on which he depended in order to do his work: the infinitely useful power of evil . . . here, where so many people were crammed into such a relatively small piece of land, here where a score or two of murders were committed every week, here where assaults and rapes and robberies and burglaries numbered in the tens of thousands—even hundreds of thousands—every year, here where there were an army of hustlers looking for an advantage, legions of con men searching for marks, psychos of every twisted sort, perverts, punks, wife-beaters, and thugs almost beyond counting—*this* was where the air was flooded with raw currents of evil that you could see and smell and feel.

Lavelle draws strength and succor from "vast, tenebrous rivers of evil energy" that surge above and through Manhattan. Koontz treats this metaphor almost literally: these psychic streams are "Ethereal rivers, yes. Of no substance. Yet the energy of which they were composed was real, lethal, the very stuff with which Lavelle could achieve virtually any result he wished." This depiction of Evil contrasts strikingly with that in **Whispers** or **Phantoms:** here Evil is real, "a cosmic power, beyond human comprehension." As **Darkfall** progresses, Koontz will adhere to this explicitly religious notion, introducing Good as an (equally cosmic) counterpoint to Evil and constructing a narrative that hurtles arrow-straight towards a classic confrontation between the two.

The imagistic pattern of the novel evolves from the classic identification of Evil with darkness, Good with light. Not surprisingly, Lavelle is a creature of darkness, "at home in shadows," for "darkness, after all, was a part of him." (The good shaman Carver Hampton is also a black man, but he is associated with light. When, late in the novel, an increasingly desperate Jack Dawson goes to Hampton's Harlem voodoo shop to plead for help, he finds every light in the place blazing.) Darkness not only cloaks the elusive Lavelle, it succors him, heals him, caresses and embraces him: "He suckled on it. Nothing else soothed as completely and as deeply as the darkness."

Lavelle is motivated by the simplest of reasons: he's out to avenge his brother Gregory, who was murdered by the Carramazza family. Actually, it is not so much the rending of filial bonds that has incensed Lavelle as the slight to his ego: "The murder of my brother is an insult to me," he rages at Jack. "It diminishes me. It mocks me. I cannot tolerate that. . . . Blood must flow. The floodgates of death must be opened. Oceans of pain must sweep them away, all who mocked me by touching my brother."

Lavelle's vendetta is a family affair: he directs his supernatural agents to slaughter the wife, daughter, grandchildren, and brother of Don Gennaro Carramazza. Indeed, the motive force of **Darkfall** and one of the novel's central thematic preoccupations is threat of fragmentation of the family. Every major character has suffered a loss that has fractured his family. Jack's wife Linda—Penny and Davey's mother—was killed in an automobile accident. While Rebecca was a child her father, then her mother were blown away by a junkie—which horror was followed by the lingering death by cancer of her grandfather. (Out of Rebecca's loss grew her unyielding hostility and inability to trust or love. She and Jack are well-matched adversaries; she's as callous and cold as he is sensitive and caring. They squabble constantly.)

The threat of fragmentation of the family also dominates the second half of the novel, in which police procedural gives way to chase thriller. Once Jack and Rebecca cease bickering and fall in love, the formation of a new family—Jack, Rebecca, and Penny and Davey—seems in the offing. But Lavelle is on to Jack and to scare him off uses the rituals of voodoo magic to direct the daemonic horde to kill his kids. (Lavelle's least endearing trait is the delight he takes in the slaughter of children. He can hardly wait to send his capering demons out after Penny and Davey, and displays a zest that is downright unseemly: "He didn't mind killing children. He looked forward to it. There was a special exhilaration in the murder of the very young. He licked his lips.")

From this point on, one chase follows another. Jack and Rebecca fight their way through a violent snow storm to save Jack's kids, whom he has ensconced in the apartment of his dippy sister-in-law Faye Jamison. Then, pursued by Lavelle's implacable, ravening devils, the incipient family escapes into the blizzard-lashed streets of New York. Finally, they split up. Rebecca and the kids seek refuge in St. Patrick's cathedral while Jack sets off for Lavelle's lair.

Although the battle for the family in **Darkfall** takes place in one of the most populous cities in the world, it is fought in isolation. During the first half of the novel, the first snowstorm of the season cranks up into a blizzard of epic proportions. Hammering the streets of Manhattan, the tempest isolates the beleaguered family. Snow transforms the cityscape, obscuring and hiding its familiar features and creating an undifferentiated landscape of white violence against which the innocent are pursued.

To carry out his schemes, Lavelle infests New York with a plague of vicious, predatory monsters. To describe these creatures, which vivify the omnipresence of Evil, Koontz uses an extravagant range of tropes from nature, particularly those of reptiles and vermin. In many respects, the horde is like the Ancient Enemy in *Phantoms.* Lavelle's demons are denizens of the underworld, of darkness: they creep through the walls of apartment buildings and ventilation systems of hotels, slither through subway tunnels and storm drains beneath city streets, and lurk in the shadowed corners of parking garages. They may erupt anywhere, without warning, to terrorize and butcher innocent and guilty alike. Like the shape-changer, the horde is comprised of many forms. And they arouse an intense instinctual response in their prey. Their first victim (in the novel), a drug dealer with "the imagination of a tree stump," senses what he cannot see: "[H]is subconscious knew what it was, and that was why he fled from it in a blind panic, as wide-eyed and spooked as a dumb animal reacting to a bolt of lightning."

For much of the novel, Koontz keeps the creatures off stage. Their victims see only a "vague impression of . . . something small, about the size of a large rat; sleek and streamlined and slithery like a rat." But though shadows enshroud the shape of the fiend, nothing can hide its merciless, glowing eyes. Aglow with hell-fire, these eyes are windows to barren souls:

> They appeared not to be eyes at all; they had no pupils or irises, no solid tissue that he could discern. They were just empty sockets in the creature's malformed skull, crude holes from which radiated a harsh, cold, brilliant light . . . the very worst aspect of those mad eyes [was] the death-cold, hate-hot, soul-withering feeling they imparted when you dared to meet them. Looking into the thing's eyes, Jack felt both physically and spiritually ill.

When Koontz finally describes the capering horde, in one of the most baroque renderings of Evil in modern horror fiction, he pulls out all the stops:

> Beyond the worm-thing, the security foyer was crawling with other, different devils, all of them small, but all of them so incredibly vicious and grotesque in appearance that Jack began to shake and felt his bowels turn to jelly. There were lizard-things in various sizes and shapes. Spider-things. Rat-things. Two of the man-form beasts, one of them with a tail, the other with a sort of cock's comb on its head and along its back. Dog-things. Crablike, feline, snakelike, beetle-form, scorpionlike, dragonish, clawed and fanged, spiked and spurred and sharply horned *things.* Perhaps twenty of them. No. More than twenty. At least thirty. They slithered and skittered across the mosaic-tile floor, and they crept tenaciously up the walls, their foul tongues darting and fluttering ceaselessly, teeth gnashing and grinding, eyes shining.

This is Evil diverse and varied, secretive and intelligent, implacable and twisted, omnipresent and, just maybe, unstoppable.

The depredations of the demon horde focus the first half of *Darkfall,* where, as in the first half of *Phantoms* and the latter part of *Whispers,* Koontz's heroes ceaselessly investigate and speculate, trying to solve the mystery of the Nature of the Beast. Ultimately, they learn from Carver Hampton that Lavelle's devils are spiritual beings risen from Hell that acquired their shapes from the earth.

Behind Lavelle and his "small assassins" is the "great, malevolent pantheon" of the gods of voodoo, the gods of *Congo* and *Petro.* This legion of malefic deities lends a religious dimension to *Darkfall* that was absent from its predecessors. And this expressly religious context supports the apocalyptic threat that comes to dominate the novel. By cracking open the Gates of Hell to release his demon horde, Lavelle has inadvertently raised the stakes. For just on the other side of the entryway that he now controls are "vast multitudes of monstrous creatures [that] will come forth to slaughter the innocent, the meek, the good, and the just. Only the wicked will survive, but they'll find themselves living in Hell on Earth." It is the ultimate threat: biblical Armageddon.

Koontz realizes the religious dimension of Evil through the motif of the voodoo ritual. Voodoo codifies many elements of religion-in-the-abstract: Gods good and evil, rules and rituals, moral imperatives and the consequences of ignoring them. As Carver Hampton explains to Jack, it is "a synthesis of many doctrines that usually war against one another—everything from Christianity and Judaism to sun-worship and pantheism." Voodoo thus functions in the novel as generic religion.

But the voodoo practiced by the priests of *Darkfall* is notable for what it omits: it is voodoo without zombies. The goals of most rituals of West Indian voodoo, as described in such (non-fiction) books as Hugh B. Cave's *Haiti: Highroad to Adventure* (1952), are the displacement of the soul followed by possession by a dark god, or the resuscitation of a corpse who is then enslaved. Such are the ends sought also by evil priests in genre novels by Cave and stories by Henry S. Whitehead, Robert Bloch, Carl Jacobi, and others. But Baba Lavelle uses rites and incantations not to possess his victims but to command the demon horde to slaughter them. He also uses voodoo rituals to solicit advice from his dark benefactors—via his radio. (pp. 135-42)

Lavelle's use of a radio to chat with the gods is but one instance of the appropriation of technology by evil in *Darkfall*—a motif that was present also in *Whispers* and *Phantoms.* In his rituals, Lavelle uses photographs of Penny and Davey, rather than the stereotypical voodoo dolls. And he uses the telephone to terrorize Carver and Jack. In one of the most effective scenes in the novel, he phones Jack, who at the time is wading through the snow outside Carver's shop in Harlem. Through hypnosis, Lavelle transports Jack to a place of dreams. The buildings and cars and streets around him "evaporate," replaced by a "creeping mist, a white-white mist that was like a movie theater screen splashed with brilliant light but with no image." In this scene, which prefigures the pursuit later in the novel of Jack, Rebecca, Penny, and Davey through the snow-clogged streets of Manhattan, the stark dialectic of *Darkfall* is clear: the universe is reduced to good (Jack) and evil (Lavelle on the phone).

In this simple dialectic, unmitigated Evil is opposed by un-alloyed Good, embodied in the characters of Carver Hampton and Jack Dawson. Like Evil, Good is a palpable (though ethereal) force with its own pantheon of gods, the *Rada* of voodoo myth. And Carver Hampton, the *Houngon* of white magic, is their priest. Through most of the novel, Hampton seems to serve the same function as did Rita Yancy in *Whispers* and Timothy Flyte in *Phantoms:* the authentic source of wisdom and truth. Thus he instructs Jack about the threat Lavelle represents and the "special power" Jack can command in his war with evil. But unlike Yancy and Flyte, Hampton is an active force for good. He leads Jack through the ritual of purification Jack must undergo and, in spite of his understandable reluctance to do battle with Lavelle, accompanies Jack to the *Bocor's* hideout.

Jack's "special power" is the most problematical aspect of the novel. Because he is "a man whose soul bears the stains of only the most minor sins," Jack is immune to supernatural Evil. In his brightly lit Harlem shop, Carver Hampton tries to explain to an understandably skeptical Dawson:

> A *Bocor* has no power whatsoever to harm a righteous man. The righteous are well-armored . . . By the manner in which you've led your life, you've earned immunity to the dark powers, immunity to the curses and charms and spells of sorcerers like Lavelle. You cannot be touched.

This moralistic, explicitly religious premise that underlies Koontz's mainstream horror thriller almost turns it into an ecclesiastical polemic.

In his war with evil, the righteous man possesses two tools: the rituals of magic and instincts. *Darkfall* is riddled with rituals; they are vital to the schemes of Baba Lavelle, who must adhere to the rites of his gods in order to control the Hell-born spawn he summons. But the rituals of man, the rites of reason, are portrayed as ineffectual. Indeed, *Darkfall*, like *Phantoms*, questions the efficacy of rationalism in the face of true Evil. The exponent of rationalism in the novel is Jack's partner, Rebecca Chandler. Like Galen Copperfield in *Phantoms*, Rebecca insists on sticking to procedure; she is perpetually arguing that Jack's effectiveness is mitigated by "an excessive degree of open-mindedness," especially insofar as the supernatural is concerned, and insisting that he follow standard investigative methods. But just as it is the racial memory prodding at Jennifer Paige and Bryce Hammond in Snowfield that clues them in to the nature of the Ancient Enemy, it is Jack's "hunches" that lead him to the truth. And to vanquish Lavelle, Jack must violate and then dispense with the rituals of police procedures.

In *Darkfall*, as in *Whispers* and *Phantoms*, rigid adherence to reason, logic, and rational procedures isn't merely unsuccessful; it's downright dangerous. (Nor is such a practice rational, a point made by the quotation from Francis Bacon with which Koontz opens the last Part of *Darkfall:* "There is superstition in avoiding superstition.") Reason remains a potent tool, but rationalism uninformed by instinct, flexibility of mind, and compassion is but an empty artifice, serving those who follow it only as a means of avoiding fear—until Evil shoves it down their throats. This critique of pure reason is a thematic cornerstone of Koontz's novels.

Still, the cosmos according to *Darkfall* is a far cry from that of *Whispers*, where the concept of evil all but vanishes in the complex of psychoses of the Frye family history, or that of *Phantoms*, where the source of evil is man's mind. These novels do not permit the unambiguous (and reassuring) moral alignment of *Darkfall*. Yet, in all three novels Good and Evil transcend human comprehension. Man is not *irrelevant* to the conflict between cosmic good and evil, as in the more pessimistic streams of contemporary horror. Evil simply exists, and only through faith, love, duty, and courage can man hope to defeat it. (pp. 142-44)

> *Michael A. Morrison, "The Three Faces of Evil: The Monsters of Whispers, Phantoms, and Darkfall," in* Sudden Fear: The Horror and Dark Suspense Fiction of Dean R. Koontz, *edited by Bill Munster, Starmont House, Inc., 1988, pp. 116-44.*

Koontz on why he does not consider himself a horror novelist:

Too many writers in the field are content to go for the jugular, give their readers a chill—and that's it. Boring. They don't seek to explore other emotions, the whole complex web of human thought and feeling, and as a result the genre has gotten a reputation of being stale, one-note fiction. I am just not pleased to have my work lumped with the majority of what bears the horror label these days, primarily because too much horror is strictly negativistic, misanthropic, and therefore drearily predictable. You can't find much hope, love, or optimism in current horror, but you can find all the nihilism you want, enough doom-saying and cynicism and pessimism—a sort of self-conscious "hipness" that is based on the juvenile notion that optimists are squares. You see, by accepting the label, I have to accept all of the associations that come with it, and damned if I'll do that.

Dean R. Koontz, in an interview from Sudden Fear: The Horror and Dark Suspense Fiction of Dean R. Koontz, *edited by Bill Munster, 1988.*

Elizabeth Massie   (essay date 1988)

[In the following excerpt, Massie assesses Koontz's ability to create realistic female protagonists.]

In four of Dean R. Koontz's novels, *Darkfall, The Vision, Whispers,* and *Night Chills,* female characters play important if not the major roles within the tales. It is, of course, not often that one runs across a novel in which all the characters are of one of the same sex, especially not in the genre of horror fiction. Therefore, if a writer would make a character of the opposite sex realistic, particularly if that character is to be a major one, one whose feelings and motives are revealed to and understood by the reader, the writer has a basic challenge to face. When a writer creates a male and female-populated world, he or she must accept the task of making a world through which any reader, man or woman, would enjoy traveling for the time it takes to read the novel. A world in which, regardless of the evils and challenges and horrors, and even injustices, the reader can identify with the characters, with a character, and thus come away feeling satisfied. (pp. 155-56)

Horror fiction has traditionally put more females in perilous roles than it has males. And the females have fared worse for it. This, of course, could be based on the fact that horror tends to gravitate to the fantastic, and fantasy has usually, until quite recently, presented helpless females rescued by heroic males. Tradition changes slowly, as do attitudes and beliefs. The women's movement has affected all people, from the butcher to the baker to the horror novelist. Sensitivity heightened, sense of equality fine-tuned, horror writers are beginning to bring female characters into their own.

Does Dean R. Koontz do justice to his female characters?

Rebecca Chandler of *Darkfall* is a strong, single homicide detective who can hold her own with the best of her coworkers. She questions suspects cooly and efficiently; she views horribly disfigured corpses with the eye of an interested but detached examiner. Her personality is contrasted with that of her partner, Jack Dawson, father of two, who is unable or unwilling to be so distanced. As the story opens, Rebecca and Jack are investigating the body of a mutilated drug dealer. This death is one of the first hints that supernatural interferences are at work. Rebecca, who scoffs at Jack's beliefs in a possible link to the supernatural, seems relatively unaffected by the horrible scene. "These are rat bites," she said, "and they've disguised the real wounds. We'll have to wait for the autopsy to learn the cause of death . . . Queasy, Jack turned away from the dead man. Rebecca continued to look."

At the beginning, Koontz introduces Rebecca with all her stoicism and occupational drive. And yet, the reader is immediately thrown a curve, perhaps to soften the opinion of this tough woman, perhaps to mystify the reader as Jack is subsequently mystified. The reader is not shown whether Rebecca's speech is meant facetiously or with a bit of true longing.

> She stopped in the doorway and shook her head. "You know what I wish sometimes?" He stared at her. She said, "Sometimes I wish I'd married Tiny Taylor. Right now, I'd be up there in Connecticut, snug in my all-electric kitchen, having coffee and Danish, the kids off to school for the day, the twice-a-week maid taking care of the housework, looking forward to lunch at the country club with the girls. . . ."

> "Why is she doing this to me?" he wondered.

> "She noticed that he was still half out of his coat, and she said, 'Didn't you hear me, Jack? We've got a call to answer.'

> "Yeah. I—"

"We've got two more stiffs."

The police officers in Rebecca's department are uncomfortable with her presence. Concerning the first investigation, an officer corrects himself in front of her. The officer said, "See, this Parker broad . . . uh, I mean, this Miss Parker. . . ." When alone, however, the male officers are not quite so charitable. "I don't see how you put up with her, Jack . . . She's a regular cold one . . . A real ball-buster! . . . a ball-*crusher* . . . Does she go in for whips and chains . . . Does she wear leather bras?" And the infamous "You're pussy-whipped, Jack." This tirade is very probably true-to-life, but it is difficult to know whether or not it is solely critical or at all light-hearted. The reader has a difficult time interpreting the discussion, until the end of the section where it is told that it is merely "good-natured abuse," and Jack rides it out easily. Jack, it seems, is infatuated with his attractive partner.

The reader discovers that Rebecca is not a passive victim of her coworker's resentment. She retaliates with coarse, yet refreshing, banter. "He's extraordinarily tense this morning," Blaine said. "Extraordinarily tense."

"From the way he's acting," Rebecca said, "I thought maybe it was his time of the month."

Although a cop with much experience and time in his profession, Jack still retains a romanticism, a chivalric if not sometimes moralistic view of women. His mental image of Rebecca is appealing, not gushy, making it easy for both male and female readers to appreciate her physical attributes. "Rebecca Chandler got out of the driver's side and slammed the door. Her long blond hair streamed behind her in the wind . . . Viking woman, Jack thought. Stoical. Resolute. And just look at that profile!"

"Her's was the noble, classic, feminine face that seafarers had once carved on the prows of their ships, ages ago, when such beauty was thought to have sufficient power to ward off the evils of the sea and the more vicious whims of fate."

When comparing Rebecca to a street-wise Shelly Parker, criminal Vince Vastagliano's girlfriend, Koontz moralizes a bit through Jack's eyes, discussing the qualities of women that men lust after and fantasize about as opposed to those men lust after, fantasize about, and marry. It distances the reader somewhat, not because of Jack's feelings, as these are true to his character, but because of the amount of space given these comparison thoughts. The space could cause a reader to feel Koontz is speaking here, not merely Jack musing.

As the challenges in *Darkfall* escalate, Rebecca's humaneness, her softer side, comes through. She is forced to become a true partner to Jack within the realms of their work and private lives. Happily, she never evolves . . . or regresses . . . to the hausfrau to which she alluded at the opening of the novel. Her evolution is of a stronger kind, rounding her out to be able to embrace tenderness while retaining her personal inner strength. As terror mounts, evil forces gain in power, and Rebecca gives herself slowly but completely to Jack.

In *Darkfall,* sex embodies a power of its own, both for

good and the evil. In the first of Jack's and Rebecca's successful physical encounters, Jack probes gently and persistently, drawing Rebecca out of her shell of caution. And Rebecca, in relinquishing some of that shell, acquires a new strength, that of acknowledging her vulnerability.

> "It hurt me, the way you were today," he said. "I thought you were disgusted with me, with yourself, for what we'd done."
>
> "No. Never."
>
> "I know that now, but here you are drawing away again, keeping me at arm's length. What's *wrong*?"
>
> She chewed on her thumb. Like a little girl.
>
> "Rebecca?"
>
> "I don't know how to say it. I don't know how to explain. I've never had to put it into words for anyone before."

But she goes on to tell of her childhood, and the horrible experience of seeing her father blown to bits in the family sandwich shop, and then having the same happen to her mother not much later. Jack, surprised and sympathetic, is patient and supportive. The two form a bond not only of partners, but of lovers in the truest sense. Sex has provided a vehicle of cleansing and awakening.

On the other hand, sex is linked vitally with the power of evil, though not in such a detailed way. Koontz has created in Baba Lavelle a character of purest evil; a spiritual, sensual, base individual who exploits and harnesses all human desires, drives and emotions. In an attempt to stop Jack from endangering Lavelle's pursuits, Lavelle decides to murder Jack's children. "He didn't mind killing children. He looked forward to it. There was a special exhilaration in the murder of the very young. He licked his lips . . . Lavelle stripped out of his clothes. Fondling his genitals, he recited a short prayer." Linking sex, murder, and children seals Lavelle as one of the most frightening, detestable individuals in recent horror fiction.

As the tale reaches its climax, the bond formed by Rebecca and Jack is beautifully illustrated. Separated from each other for the entirety of the final conflict, each character must draw on what is his own and what each is to the other in order to defeat Lavelle and his hoards of seemingly indestructible demons. Love, openness, and trust have made Rebecca and Jack equals; Koontz has led them to become victors together.

> The wind was barely blowing now, but to his surprise it brought a voice to him. Rebecca's voice. Unmistakable. And four words that he much wanted to hear: "I love you, Jack."
>
> He turned, bewildered.
>
> She was nowhere in sight, yet her voice seemed to have been at his ear.
>
> He said, "I love you, too," and he knew that, wherever she was, she had heard him as clearly as he had heard her.

In contrast to Rebecca Chandler, Mary Bergen in *The Vi-sion* is a dependent woman who openly admits her need for and her reliance on her husband, Max. As the story unfolds, it is clearly shown that except for her ability as a psychic, there is little in which she has confidence concerning herself. She suffers to share her talents with investigating officers; she gives herself to the point of exhaustion to save intended victims from a killer's grasp. ". . . She slumped against the door. She took several deep breaths. She was forced to relax periodically to regroup her energies if she were to maintain the psychic thread. For some clairvoyants, Barnes knew, the visions came without strain, virtually without effort; but apparently not for this one." But in spite of her self-sacrifice and insecurities, the reader, from the beginning, is not presented with a stereotypical "weak" horror female character. The entire first chapter, as a matter of fact, consists solely of a journey with Mary through a clairvoyant excursion to thwart a murder. The reader is given a large, impressive dose of Mary's inner strength before, in the following chapters, being shown her deep dependence on Max. Koontz has established her as sympathetic, not pathetic.

Characters in *The Vision* find Mary difficult to understand. The police officers with whom she works find her unusual, if not unnerving. Mary's psychiatrist, Dr. Cauvel, is fascinated with her perceptions. He tests her twice a week in exchange for free counselling, but the depths of her insight amaze and frighten him. Lou Pasternak, a family friend and a "student of the occult" is an openminded individual who cannot have any true insight into what powers are coming to the front as Mary is unwittingly driven into the psychic path of a new, unknown, and very brutal murderer. Likewise, Max, Mary's closest friend and lover, is very supportive yet is also confused and alarmed.

The reader is not given a paragraph-long description of Mary's physical features. Rather, she is described in smaller clips, much in the way her thought processes are presented in bits and pieces. "The perspiration of Mary Bergen's face was like the ceramic glaze on the plaster countenance of an altar saint. Her smooth skin gleamed in the green light from the instrument panel. Her dark eyes also shone, but they were unfocused." And later— "This woman was so lovely, charming, earnest, so convincing that perhaps she'd made a believer of him." Still later, Mary is focused more by comparing and contrasting her with her brother, Alan, and with Max. "[Alan] had black hair and blue eyes, like Mary. He was handsome, while Max was so rough-hewn that he barely avoided ugliness." In down-playing the details of his beautiful heroine, Koontz has made her more universal in appeal.

Similar to Shelly Parker of *Darkfall,* a minor female character in *The Vision,* Miss Harrington, is described in detail from a male's point of view. Her features, as shown, seem to come more directly from Koontz than from the minds of the police who have come to question her. She is not merely described, but is evaluated. "She was a petite blonde in her early forties. She had a lush figure, but she wasn't carrying any excess weight.

"Apparently, her primary occupation was taking good care of herself . . . . " The reader does not spend enough time with Miss Harrington to find out if she is much more than a picturesque creature with orange fingernails and taut body.

Mary, perhaps more so than other female protagonists in Koontz novels, grows as the story progresses. At the onset, she depends on Max for everything, from being her "hand-holder" during clairvoyant experiences to managing all of the couple's money. Alan, more correct than the reader would hope, after the reader finds out about the true character of Alan, says, "You didn't marry him because he was exciting, or because he was intelligent or mysterious or romantic. You married him because he was big, strong, and gruff. A perfect father image." Mary relies on Dr. Cauvel to help her keep her balance. "I'll always need your help" she tells him.

But psychiatry loses its credibility, Max's strength seems faint, when poltergeist-like occurrences drive Mary to believe that a spirit is at work against her, and that she is no longer merely a sensitive psychic recipient. Glass figurines attack her in Dr. Cauvel's office, coming to life only after Mary is near to seeing the face of the murderer. Mary is awakened from a dream of the killer when a pistol, floating freely in her bedroom, fires bullets toward the bed. Mary clings to Max, but it is as though fate is shaking her from his arms, throwing her into a pit from which she alone must save herself.

Sex between Mary and Max is scant yet timely. Max is the giver; Mary the receiver. And yet, with Mary's situation and insecurities, it is as it should be, and gives the reader a few moments of comfort. When it is discovered by Mary and the reader simultaneously what "wicka wicka wicka" means, and why Mary has been haunted by other past sensations, that are not, as she imagines, due to seeing her father die, the reader may well wonder if Mary might need to return to Cauvel for extensive therapy if she is ever to enjoy normal sex with Max again.

Surprisingly, Mary remains a frightened, somewhat impotent actor until a mere six pages from the end of the novel. It is as though she grovels at the bottom of the pit, watching as flashes of light spark within her reach and then fade. Finally, the lights converge into a beam, that beam being clear memory of the day in the Mitchell's cabin when she was six years old, and only then is she able to leap upward and free herself with the power of anger and hatred. She has been horrendously raped, debased as much as any woman can be, and yet she becomes, momentarily, Anyman-Anywoman, who has the inner force of dignity and justice. "She snapped. Abruptly, violently, her fear vanished . . . She despised him. Loathed him. All she wanted was a chance to hurt him . . . to get him down, tie him down, torture him, cut him, choke him. . . . " Her revenge is just and profound.

The epilogue promises a brighter future. Knowing Mary as the reader has come to, there is hope that this is a true promise. Mary is strong now. She is no longer "afraid of the dark." She is now in charge of herself and her destiny. Max seems grateful for the change. Hopefully, he will be able to adjust to her extensive growth.

Whispers presents an independent character by the name of Hilary Thomas. She is a single woman, a successful screenwriter who has moved from Chicago to a lovely mansion in Los Angeles. Unlike some other female protagonist counterparts, Hilary is a strong yet modest individual from the beginning of the tale. In spite of the fact that something from her past keeps her hesitant about forming relationships with others, men in particular, she is still a person of hope and faith, letting go of caution a little at a time to reap the benefits of a full life. Her creative sense of hope is obvious. "And now I'm living in that dream," she thought. "That make-believe place is real, and I own it." (pp. 157-64)

But then an insane man breaks into her home in an attempt to rape and then murder her. Hilary's cool head allows her to thwart his attempt, but after reporting the attack to the police, she is attacked in her home a second time. Her assailant, Bruno Frye, is determined to finish the job he had started. Hilary stops Frye again, killing him with a hidden knife. Hilary feels horrified by what has happened. She feels betrayed as well. ". . . Bruno Frye had taken that fragile dream by the throat and throttled it. . . . [He] sent her tumbling back where she came from, down into doubt and fear and suspicion, down into the awful safety of loneliness."

Tony Clemenza, one of the two police officers who takes Hilary's report, becomes interested in her immediately. He must endure the brazenly critical assumptions of his partner Frank, who trusts no woman since his wife stole his money and left him. But Tony believes Hilary, and Hilary, in spite of having been so badly shaken, agrees to go out with him. Obviously, Hilary is stronger than she realized, and the reader feels comfortable with that strength. It allows the story to take off flying. It allows the tale to spend the majority of its energy with the character Bruno Frye, which it is well advised to do. Having seen Hilary in action against Frye, the reader can know that, regardless of peril, Hilary will put up the good fight.

The description of Hilary, given through Tony's eyes, might well be a distraction from her other qualities. Not that beauty and brains can't exist simultaneously, and work well together, but a particular description may tint a reader's feelings toward Hilary. After seeing how beautiful she is, from her flawless complexion to the "perfect shape of her patrician nose" to her enormous eyes and thick raven hair, the reader is told that her face is balanced by "the almost obscene fullness of her lips." Female readers could easily be put off by this description. It seems sluttish. Male readers might be intrigued by the same sluttish connotations. Either way, it is a small statement with the ability to snag the reader. Hilary has to prove herself beyond this.

Lana Haverby is the minor female character that is, as happens in ***Darkfall*** and ***The Vision,*** used as a comparison, both mentally and physically, to Hilary Thomas. Tony is more of a moralizer than Jack Dawson. Interspersed with dialogue concerning a convict Tony is seeking, the description of Lana consists of three paragraphs. Again, statements or evaluations made here don't seem to do anything for the story line.

> Her legs were okay, but the rest of her was far from prime . . . Her gelatinous breast jiggled

and swayed alarmingly, in what she evidently thought was a wildly provocative display. She affected that ass-swinging, tippy-toe-walk that didn't look good on any coquette over twenty-one; she was forty, a grown woman unable to discover and explore the dignity and special beauty of her own age, trying to pass for a teenager, and she was pathetic.

Granted, a woman of Lana's type is certainly realistic. But the amount of space given Tony's observation, and the evaluation of her, makes a look at Lana seem like a mini-sermon. The reader might want to determine for himself/herself if Lana is pathetic.

Except for Hilary's repeated resistance to admit her love for Tony, there is an equalness between these two major characters. Their first date is exemplary, full of humorous, lively bantering as the two size each other up.

> [Tony said] "I've already lost my head over you."
>
> Hilary groaned.
>
> "Too saccharine?" he asked.
>
> "I need a bit of lemon after that one."
>
> "But you liked it."
>
> "Yes, I admit I did. I guess I'm a sucker for flattery."

After this first date Hilary, alone in her house, can't get Tony out of her mind. "Half an hour later, upstairs, in bed, Hilary's body ached with frustration. Her breasts were full and taut; she longed to feel his hands on them . . . She tossed and turned for maybe an hour before she finally got up and took a sedative." Another woman in Hilary's position would have most likely masturbated, hopefully to climax, or if not, at least with fingers pretending to be her lover, dreaming, wishing. Hilary, as independent as she is, seems like the type of woman who would have no problem with this. It could have been described without resorting to graphics. Would she have been too much like Lana with this approach to horniness? Would Tony-Koontz feel that this would make her less than perfect if she so indulged?

When Tony and Hilary finally consummate their relationship, and the experience continues for nearly four pages, the effect on the reader is sensuously staggering. The mutual respect along with the erotic quality of the prose creates a scene not soon forgotten. Particularly when Tony discovers a cruel scar along Hilary's side, traveling from her belly to back. He sees it not as distracting or ugly, but as something that emphasizes her beauty even more. He knows that she has, in some way, suffered painfully. He does not pity her, but is increasingly respectful. Hilary is embarrassed, but says nothing.

The bond between Tony and Hilary strengthens as the two, together, seek out the unexplained "revival" of Bruno Frye. Bruno, who apparently has come to life again, believes that his abusive, deceased mother is being repeatedly reincarnated as different women, and he must kill these women to save himself. The remainder of the novel con-sists of unraveling the mystery. Intermissions of uninhibited, enjoyable sex give brief respites from the horror. Hilary and Tony work now as a balanced unit. Hilary's courage and ability, shown the reader at the very beginning of the story, do not falter. The reader can count on Hilary and can therefore more completely become carried away with the evil, fascinating works of Bruno Frye.

Two female characters share limelight in *Night Chills.* Jenny Edison is a young and attractive woman who lives with her father and is a partner with him, running Edison's General Store in Black River, Maine. She has discovered that Black River is the haven she needs, a soul-soothing asylum from California and a soured, seven-year marriage to a self-centered musician. A year earlier, she met Paul Annendale, a widower, who vacations in the small town, bringing his two children to the country for hiking and camping. Jenny, as is her father, is a well-respected member of the Black River community. Before actually "meeting" Jenny, the reader is introduced to her through the memories and anticipations of Paul.

> Paul had met Jenny Edison just last year. . . .
> Catching sight of her—Paul had for a moment been unable to get his breath.

It happened that quickly between them. Not love at first sight. Something more fundamental than love. Something more basic that had to come first, before love could develop. . . . Jenny felt the attraction too, powerfully, immediately—but almost unwillingly.

The "something special" isn't strong enough to allow Jenny to trust romance again.

Rya Annendale, age eleven, is undoubtedly a precocious, worthy character. She is bright, observant, and sensitive. She has had a happy childhood, shadowed by the death of her mother, but enlightened by the love and support of her father. Rya does more than tolerate her younger brother; she reacts with mature concern when he is unhappy. She does more than watch the relationship between her father and Jenny, she encourages it. The reader is given a hopeful feeling that Rya will prove to be more than an average, minor, child character. Luckily, that hope is not left unsated.

Physically, Jenny is a beautiful, slender, dark-haired woman. She is described through the mental scrutiny of Paul as he rides with her to a tavern for their first date of the season.

> Her face—too beautiful to appear in *Vogue:* she would have made the other models in the magazine look like horses—was in repose. Her full lips were slightly parted as she sang softly with the music and this bit of animation, this parting of the lips had more sensual impact than a heavy-eyed, full-faced leer from Elizabeth Taylor.

Unlike the female protagonists in *Darkfall* and *Whispers,* Jenny is not morally judged or substantiated through the eyes of a man. And opposed to *Darkfall, The Vision,* and *Whispers,* Jenny is not contrasted by a male protagonist to a sexually blatant beauty of, as is hinted, less character. This is to Jenny's advantage. One female comes close, the waitress Alice to whom evil Ogden Salsbury compares his wife in the early years. But a comparison by Ogden doesn't affect the reader very much, as it is not he with whom the reader would likely identify. Therefore, the reader can be the judge of Alice, and more importantly, of Jenny.

Rya, pictured lovingly through the eyes of her father, is slim, blue-eyed, with long brown hair. And as a father would describe through the pride of parenthood, Rya is shown not so much physically as through her characterization, her appealing traits, her peculiar and lovable habits.

Jenny resists a serious relationship with the persistent Paul at first, but she admits she loves him. It is marriage she fears. However, in terms of sexual interest and drive, she is Paul's equal. Jenny can become sexually involved quickly, she can initiate it, and can joke about sex easily. (pp. 164-68)

Sex between Jenny and Paul exemplifies their affection for each other, but it clarifies Jenny's reluctance to commit herself to marriage's legalities. This reluctance remains throughout the novel, until crisis opens her eyes to life beyond the original pain of failed love.

The evil that confronts Jenny, Rya, Paul, and the residents of Black River originates in the brilliant, warped mind of scientist Ogden Salsbury. Ogden has developed a drug that makes people receptive, unconditionally so, to subliminal control. Although near genius, Ogden is an individual with twisted intentions, rooted in a nightmarish childhood. The nightmare consisted of the women in Ogden's life. His mother beat him mercilessly. His mother's lover raped him when he was eleven while his mother stood by and watched. Ogden was put into a foster home with all girls. According to Ogden's foster father, Mr. Barger, "The older girls knew what had happened to him. They used to tease him something fierce. He couldn't take it. He'd blow up everytime. . . . Of course that was what they wanted, so they just teased him some more.' " Mr. Barger, a stereotypical chauvinistic male, in trying to help Ogden deal with his dilemma, sealed in Ogden's soul a most hideous attitude concerning woman. Mr. Barger said, " 'I'd take him aside and talk to him—almost father to son. I used to tell him not to pay them any mind. I used to tell him that they were just women and that women were good for only two things. Fucking and cooking'." The impact of this on the reader is as sickening as Ogden's rape. Ogden's unbalanced psyche is irreparably damaged by ignorance.

Ogden sees his subliminal control as a means of regaining power he never had as a child or even as an adult. And, of course, much of the power he seeks consists of having women debase themselves for his sexual and temporary emotional gratification.

Rya is the first to witness the horrors of Ogden's subliminal powers. Bob Thorp, police chief and friend of the Edisons, kills Rya's brother Mark as Rya, at first undetected, watches from outside. Rya fights the disbelief of her father and Jenny, holding to her story regardless of the terror. Her bravery allows her to break back into the Thorp home

to find proof of the murder—a bucket of bloody rags hidden beneath the sink.

Both Jenny's and Rya's characters are changed, are deepened, through the course of the tale. Although the two of them fade from the forefront a bit as the conflict begins to escalate, they are pivotal in the climax. Jenny and Rya, hiding in a bell tower, trying to keep safe as Paul and Sam Edison face off Ogden Salsbury and his mind-controlled troops, are confronted by a partner of Ogden's, Ernst Klinger. With enviable courage, they stage their own turntable surprise attack, killing Klinger.

Fighting with Paul has eased Jenny's marital fears. Together, they launch a new future with Rya's blessings. Rya, although still somewhat stunned by all the terrors she has faced, is able to look ahead with hope. At the conclusion of the novel, the reader might begin to wonder what kind of adult heroine Rya would make. It is interesting to ponder, considering the strength already such an integral part of her.

Does Dean R. Koontz do justice to his female characters?

The females in *Darkfall, The Vision, Whispers,* and *Night Chills* are strong individuals in their own right. All different on certain levels, they are all masters of their own fates. They are intelligent characters. They are sexual equals to their partners. Although they are sometimes judged, fairly or not so fairly, by their male counterparts, they shine through, allowing the reader, after working through the perils with them, to make his/her own judgment calls.

It would be a curious thing to see Koontz write of a not-so-beautiful heroine; to have her as interesting and strong as his gorgeous protagonists. The fantasy aspect of horror need not always play on fantasy wishes. The male protagonists are not always attractive—Max, of *The Vision,* is a wonderful, appealing individual who is described as being very close to ugly.

Koontz on his female protagonists:

Many reviewers have gone out of the way to say how strong my women characters are and how sympathetically I portray a woman's viewpoint. I was writing strong, capable female leads in my books before it was fashionable for male writers to do so. In fact, it still isn't done much in the horror genre, where most of the women characters are either bitches or wimps or hapless victims. One of my consuming interests as a writer, one endless fascination, is the man-woman relationship. A great many of my books have the unfolding of such a relationship at the very core of them, the exploration of emotional bonds based on mutual respect and trust—see *Whispers* especially—and there's no way I could write about these things or be interested in writing about them if I was anti-woman.

Dean R. Koontz, in an interview from Sudden Fear: The Horror and Dark Suspense Fiction of Dean R. Koontz, *edited by Bill Munster, 1988.*

Dean R. Koontz treats his female characters, and his male characters, fairly. They are true to themselves. Male or female, their actions reveal a writer who does not guide his characters but follows their lead. The reader of Koontz novels is not betrayed. On the contrary. The reader is delighted. (pp. 168-70)

> *Elizabeth Massie, "Femmes Fatales? The Women Protagonists in Four Koontz Novels," in* Sudden Fear: The Horror and Dark Suspense Fiction of Dean R. Koontz, *edited by Bill Munster, Starmont House, Inc., 1988, pp. 155-70.*

Edward Bryant   (review date March 1990)

[*In the following excerpt from a review of* The Bad Place, *Bryant focuses on Koontz's ability to combine elements from different popular literary genres.*]

Dean R. Koontz successfully does what most editors warn their writers not to do. He crosses genre boundaries with impunity. The editorial argument is that booksellers don't know where to shelve science fiction-romances or horror-mysteries or gothic-western-nurse novels. Koontz solved the problem neatly. He simply does pretty much what he wants, and the novels are then categorized as "Dean Koontz books." Hey, it's great work if you can get it.

The Bad Place is a pretty fair example. Is it horror? Science fiction? Suspense? Murder mystery? The correct answer is (e) all the above. It's also a certified bestseller, as have been all the author's books for the past few years.

The author knows how to sink a narrative hook. The story opens with a guy who knows he's named Frank Pollard, but has no other memories, carrying a heavy bag along a night-time Orange Country street. Then something mysterious and deadly, clothed in bright blue light, attempts to kill him. Pollard finally escapes and discovers his bag is full of odd but valuable looking gems. In an effort to find out who he is and what's happened to him, Pollard goes to the husband-and-wife detective firm of Bobby and Julie Dakota.

The Dakotas do their best. They discover that Pollard regularly disappears. Instantly. Physically. Where does he go? And why doesn't he remember what happens when he vanishes? And how does he keep returning with riches?

The stakes rise as we meet Candy, a large and completely looney-tunes killer. How does he connect to Frank Pollard? And what about Candy's twin sisters, Violet and Verina, who have a telepathic communion with feral cats?

Things get more complicated rapidly. There are some very nice and affecting touches, such as Julie Dakota's brother Thomas, an adult Down's Syndrome sufferer who may hold a key to the escalating mysteries. It's his term for death, "the bad place," that gives the novel its title.

Telepathy and teleportation enter the equations. There's an alien ship on a distant world. There are medical oddities galore: a woman with complete sets of male and female equipment who becomes all the parents of her children; a man with four undescended testicles who is maddened with uncontrollable testosterone rage; bizarre mutants created by incest and natural hallucinogenics. Grotesquerie abounds.

Koontz is especially adept at creating interesting subsidiary characters. Julie's brother Thomas is wonderful. The Dakota's staff are good—we want to meet them more. The twin telepaths, Violet and Verbina, are intriguing.

The Southern California landscapes are quite adroitly handled. At any moment, the reader expects to see a billboard reading "See Orange County and Die." In *The Bad Place,* that seems a likely possibility. (pp. 67-8)

> *Edward Bryant, in a review of "The Bad Place," in* Locus, *Vol. 24, No. 3, March, 1990, pp. 67-8.*

John R. Carroll   (review date February-March 1991)

[*In the following excerpt, the reviewer praises Koontz's storyline, character development, and use of suspense in* Cold Fire.]

[*Cold Fire*] is not the book to take on an airplane flight. It includes a vivid description of an air disaster calculated to turn the most jaded frequent flyer's palms sweaty. What *Jaws* did for swimming, this book does for flying. And this occurs before things get really scary!

Reporter Holly Thorne witnesses an incredible rescue by a mysterious stranger to her town. His name is Jim Ironheart, she learns; but before she can schedule an interview, the man disappears.

Holly's research tells her that the same man has been methodically rescuing people across the country—having, it seems, a sixth sense in knowing when disasters will strike. Intrigued, Holly tracks him down and learns he has a psychic calling that impels him to rescue people moments before their certain death, a modern-day Superman without the funny costume. . . .

Koontz is in wonderful form as he rekindles every fear we had as kids. The story is compelling, and readers will not be able to second-guess the master storyteller's plot. The characters are very real while the situation is so bizarre that in lesser hands it would be laughable. Here, it is deadly serious.

The ending comes so swiftly that the reader will close the book reluctantly, wishing for a tad more denouement. (After all, we want a little breathing space with these characters, now that we've been with them through hell.) Koontz ties up the plot's loose ends and lets us off the roller coaster rather abruptly.

But that quibble is minor. *Cold Fire* remains a very spooky book that is lots of fun to read . . . as long as you have no plans to fly real soon.

> *John R. Carroll, in a review of "Cold Fire," in* West Coast Review of Books, *Vol. 16, No. 1, February-March, 1991, p. 24.*

Kirkus Reviews (review date 1 November 1992)

[*In the following excerpt, the reviewer praises* Dragon Tears.]

[**Dragon Tears** is an] electrifying terrorfest in which Koontz, inking his silkiest writing yet, takes on the serial-killer novel and makes it his own.

Koontz hooks us at once ("Tuesday was a fine California day, full of sunshine and promise, until Harry Lyon had to shoot someone at lunch") and never lets go. Harry is a cop, and the man he guns down—with help from Harry's partner, Connie Gulliver—is a crazy who disrupts the cops' restaurant-lunch by shooting the joint to bits. It's an exhilarating opener—and it's also a lovely red herring, because the crazy has no connection, other than as another symptom of the rot of modern life, with the killer that Harry and Connie take on later. He's Bryan Drackman, who fixates on the cops when he's drawn to the restaurant carnage. Bryan, like most serial killers, believes that he has godlike powers; but Bryan—and here's Koontz's ace—really does. Mutated in the womb by radiation and drugs, Bryan has grown into a sociopath who can conjure up any entity he wants—especially "Ticktock," a giant who stalks Harry, Connie, and several others, including a dog whose periodic narration ("Piece of paper. Candy wrapper. Smells good.") is so charming that you don't mind that Koontz used a similar dog-ploy in **Watchers** (1986). Ticktock warns Harry & Co. that they'll die at dawn—and it's only late into the night that they learn of Bryan's greatest power: the power to stop time, which unveils in a jaw-dropping set-piece in which the cops flee through a frozen world with Ticktock close behind.

Koontz gets a bit preachy about social decay—but his action never flags in this vise-tight tale. . . .

> *A review of "Dragon Tears," in* Kirkus Reviews, *Vol. LX, No. 21, November 1, 1992, p. 1327.*

FURTHER READING

Breque, Jean-Daniel. "A Second Opinion." *Science Fiction and Fantasy Book Review,* No. 4 (October 1983): 25-6.

> Negative review of Koontz's *Phantoms,* calling it "fit for the supermarket racks" and "horror completists only."

Bryant, Edward. Review of *Hideaway,* by Dean R. Koontz. *Locus* 28, No. 3 (March 1992): 62.

> Calls *Hideaway* "an admirable and thoroughly effective piece of entertainment."

Callender, Newgate. "Criminals At Large." *The New York Times Book Review* (12 January 1975): 18.

> Reviews *After the Last Race,* an early crime novel by Koontz, pointing out that although the plot is familiar, "Koontz is much more imaginative than most writers."

Gordon, James S. "Demonic Children." *The New York Times Book Review* (11 September 1977): 3, 52-3.

> Includes Koontz's *Demon Seed* in a critical discussion of representations of evil and possessed children in popular fiction of the 1970s, concluding that the trend revealed adults' underlying fear and resentment of children.

Hand, Jack. Review of *Phantoms,* by Dean R. Koontz. *Science Fiction and Fantasy Book Review,* No. 4 (October 1983): 25-6.

> "Heartily" recommends *Phantoms* as "straight" supernatural horror.

Lochte, Dick. "The Perils of Little Laura." *Los Angeles Times Book Review* (31 January 1988): 8.

> Reviews Koontz's *Lightning,* praising the first part of the novel for its "believable characters and situations," but faulting Koontz for allowing his characters to become static in the second half.

Munster, Bill, ed. *Sudden Fear: The Horror and Dark Suspense Fiction of Dean R. Koontz.* Mercer Island, Wash.: Starmont House, 1988, 182 p.

> Includes critical essays, an interview, and a complete chronology.

Whitmore, Tom. Review of *Midnight,* by Dean R. Koontz. *Locus* 22, No. 2 (February 1989): 21.

> Praises Koontz's plot and characters, but ultimately criticizes the novel for being "technophobic" in that it "perpetuates the horror tradition of conservatism."

Additional coverage of Koontz's life and career is contained in the following sources published by Gale Research: *Authors and Artists for Young Adults,* **Vol. 9;** *Bestsellers 89,* **No. 3 and** *Bestsellers 90,* **No. 2;** *Contemporary Authors,* **Vol. 108;** *Contemporary Authors New Revision Series,* **Vols. 19, 36; and** *Major 20th-Century Writers.*

Norman Maclean

1902-1990

(Full name Norman Fitzroy Maclean) American essayist, critic, novella and short story writer, and nonfiction writer.

The following entry provides an overview of Maclean's career.

INTRODUCTION

A professor of English literature, Maclean wrote his only works of fiction when he was in his early seventies. These were collected in *A River Runs Through It, and Other Stories,* which consists of three narratives centering on life in Montana in the first half of the twentieth century. The title story of this volume, an amalgam of fiction and autobiography, is considered a classic of modern American literature.

The son of an immigrant Scottish Presbyterian minister, Maclean was born in Clarinda, Iowa. In 1909 his family moved to Missoula, Montana, where Maclean spent the better part of his childhood learning to hunt and fish along the Big Blackfoot River. He was educated at home until the age of ten, when truant officers found him hunting and enrolled him in elementary school. Although both his parents encouraged the young Maclean's love of poetry, he often felt a conflict between the expectations of his affectionate mother and his disciplinarian father. Maclean later told an interviewer: "[My mother] and my father fought for my soul when I was young, my father wanting me to be a tough guy and my mother wanting me to be a flower girl. So I ended up being a tough flower girl." In 1924 he graduated from Dartmouth College and went on to teach literature at the University of Chicago, where he remained until his retirement in 1973. Three years later he published *A River Runs Through It, and Other Stories.* A posthumously published second book, *Young Men and Fire,* offers a painstakingly researched account of a devastating 1949 forest fire and exhibits Maclean's knowledge of and fascination with the American West. This work was unfinished when Maclean died in 1990.

Maclean's most acclaimed work, the novella *A River Runs Through It,* is a semi-fictionalized account of his experiences fly-fishing on the Big Blackfoot River in 1937. Critics have pointed out that the story, which was adapted for film in 1992, is also a tribute to Maclean's father and an elegy for his brother Paul, who was beaten to death in 1937 for reasons still unclear. Commentary on *A River Runs Through It* often focuses on the version of the American western myth that Maclean presents in this work. At the center is Paul, Maclean's charming but reckless younger brother who is a master fly-fisherman. Asking help from no one, even when he is in serious trouble, Paul is

the typical western hero who says little and dies valiantly. Maclean's narrative is also typical of American western fiction in giving little attention to women characters, who are treated as outsiders and threats to male solitude. Helen Lojek observed that reading *A River Runs Through It* "is . . . to enter a world shaped by an unexamined and probably unconscious masculinity." Critics almost unanimously praise the novella for its engaging prose style and its probing examination of the deepest implications of family ties.

For *Young Men and Fire,* Maclean researched the 1949 forest fire at Mann Gulch in Montana. First thought to be a routine brush fire, the blaze killed thirteen United States Forest Service fire fighters, or "smoke jumpers" as they are called. Having worked in the Forest Service from 1924 to 1926, Maclean became haunted by the incident and returned to the scene of the fire many times during his life. Critics praise Maclean's attempts not only to discover the actual causes of the deaths, which remain controversial, but also to tell the story in the manner of classical tragedy. The book ends with Maclean's personal meditation on mortality, graced with what James R. Kincaid has called the "redemptive quality" of Maclean's "heroic tragedy."

PRINCIPAL WORKS

A Manual for Instruction in Military Maps and Aerial Photographs [with Everett C. Olson] (nonfiction) 1943

"Episode, Scene, Speech, and Word: The Madness of Lear" (criticism) 1952; published in *Critics and Criticism: Ancient and Modern*

"From Action to Image: Theories of the Lyric in the Eighteenth Century" (criticism) 1952; published in *Critics and Criticism: Ancient and Modern*

A River Runs Through It, and Other Stories (short story and novellas) 1976

Norman Maclean (criticism, essays, and interviews) 1988

Young Men and Fire (nonfiction) 1992

CRITICISM

John Cawelti (review date 1 May 1976)

[*Cawelti has written several studies of American popular culture and genre fiction, including* The Six-Gun Mystique *(1971) and* Adventure, Mystery and Romance: Formula Stories as Art and Popular Culture *(1976). In the following review of* A River Runs Through It, and Other Stories, *Cawelti praises Maclean as an important writer of American western fiction.*]

Both the pulp Western with its heroics and the serious Western novel in its attempt at an epic statement of the confrontation between man and nature or between White and Indian are expressions of the myth of the West as otherness, as the expression of something unique to human experience and history which must be treated in an appropriately grand and distinctive fashion. The importance of this myth to American culture has been often indicated by scholars, most recently in Richard Slotkin's superb *Regeneration Through Violence.* Yet, there is also an important truth in discovering the universal constants of human experience which lie beneath that distinctive landscape of mythical action. This is the discovery that flashes through many of the most memorable writings about the West—it is there in Twain's *Roughing It,* in Stephen Crane's two great Western stories, "The Blue Hotel," and "The Bride Comes to Yellow Sky," in Andy Adams' *Log of a Cowboy,* in the best parts of Wister's *The Virginian,* in the stories of H. L. Davis, in Walter Van Tilburg Clark's *The Ox-Bow Incident,* in Thomas Berger's *Little Big Man* and, most recently, in Norman Maclean's *A River Runs Through It and Other Stories.*

Maclean's stories are semi-autobiographical and told in the form of reminiscences: an older man looks back on some central experiences of his youth: how he learned to fish and how fishing was entangled in his relations with his father and younger brother (*A River Runs Through It*); how he worked with a superhuman logger who turned out to be a pimp during the winter season ("**Logging and Pimping and 'Your Pal, Jim'** "); and how he became part of a Forest Service crew's summer-end ritual of "cleaning out the town" and learned something about life and art in the process (***USFS 1919: The Ranger, The Cook and a Hole in the Sky***). But the stories are conceived as fictions. Instead of being primarily attempts to remember and state the exact particulars of a past time and place, they use the particular to express, through the devices of art, some general truths about human nature and life. They are like memories which have been revolved in the mind throughout a lifetime until their hidden truths have been brought to the surface and revealed. Thus there is a wonderful interplay between the consciousness of the old man telling us the stories and the perspective of the boy of over half a century ago. We see not only what the boy thought or failed to think, but how he began to understand his life and something of what that boy, as a man in his 70s, has made of it since:

> I was young and I thought I was tough and I knew it was beautiful and I was a little bit crazy but I hadn't noticed it yet.

So begins ***USFS 1919,*** which becomes a wide-open Western anecdote about a comic-heroic trek across the Bitterroot Mountains, an encounter with a whore who cursed in iambic pentameter, and a climactic fight in a saloon over a crooked card game. The story even contains a Western-style hero, one Ranger Bill, who rides off into the sunset, as it were, at the end. Yet these Western elements are not deployed for the sake of creating an epic mythos or telling of high adventure but to explore what Maclean sees as one of the most profound human discoveries:

> I had as yet no notion that life every now and then becomes literature—not for long, of course, but long enough to be what we best remember, and often enough so that what we eventually come to mean by life are those moments when life, instead of going sideways, backwards, forward, or nowhere at all, lines out straight, tense and inevitable, with a complication, climax, and, given some luck, a purgation, as if life had been made and not happened.

These stories have that magical balance of the particular and the universal that good literature is all about and that so many attempts at Western fiction miss completely. Indeed, it would be more just to say that these are not Western fictions at all, but stories about life as it happened and was created by one man who lived through his formative years in western Montana and who has the gift of words and the shaping imagination to make it possible for us to share some of that experience. Maclean gives us the West in full measure. His stories are permeated with the monumental landscape of the "Big Sky Country" observed with a keen documentary eye as well as a sense of the awesome beauty of mountains and rivers. He writes brilliantly about work and sport. His pages describing logging, packing, mule-skinning, trail-cutting and fishing are full of precise images which convey as rich a sense of the spiritual form of these activities together that bear comparison with such classics as Adams' *Log of a Cowboy.* Humor of the tall-tale variety abounds, side by side with an extravagant comedy of manners detailing the peculiar social rituals of loggers, fishermen and other Western types. Yet underneath the richness of particular details, there runs a wise and compassionate understanding of life and art forged through a lifetime of experience and learning and embodied in a prose that is richly colloquial yet highly controlled and which sometimes rises to extraordinary eloquence. Perhaps nothing conveys the rich and deep sense of human life which runs through this book than the beautiful words which conclude the title story:

> Now nearly all those I loved and did not understand when I was young are dead, but I still reach out to them.
>
> Of course, now I am too old to be much of a fisherman, and now of course, I usually fish the big waters alone, although some friends think I shouldn't. Like many fly fishermen in western Montana where the summer days are almost Arctic in length, I often do not start fishing until the cool of the evening. Then in the Arctic half-light of the canyon, all existence fades to a being with my soul and memories and the sounds of the Big Blackfoot River and a four-count rhythm and the hope that a fish will rise.
>
> Eventually, all things merge into one, and a river runs through it. The river was cut by the world's great flood and runs over rocks from the basement of time. On some of the rocks are timeless raindrops. Under the rocks are the words, and some of the words are theirs.
>
> I am haunted by waters.
>
> (pp. 24-6)

> *John Cawelti, in a review of "A River Runs Through It, and Other Stories," in* The New Republic, *Vol. 174, No. 18, May 1, 1976, pp. 24-6.*

George Core   (review date Winter 1977)

[*In the following excerpt, Core discusses the autobiographical aspects of* A River Runs Through It, and Other Stories.]

In one of his stories [in *A River Runs Through It, and Other Stories*] Mr. Maclean remarks that "by the middle of that summer when I was seventeen I had yet to see myself become part of a story." He continues: "I had as yet no notion that life every now and then becomes literature—not for long, of course, but long enough to be what we best remember, and often enough so that what we eventually come to mean by life are those moments when life, instead of going sideways, backwards, forward, or nowhere at all, lines out straight, tense and inevitable, with a complication, climax, and, given some luck, a purgation, as if life had been made and not happened." This aside constitutes a persuasive definition of the form of Maclean's narratives—what he calls autobiographical fiction.

A River Runs Through It is an affecting account of the au-

thor's life as a fly fisherman and the way that life intersected with the lives of his brother, a reporter, and his father, a Presbyterian minister. Maclean incorporates strong dimensions of ritual (the rituals of nature and religion) into the story, and the rhythms of the natural world are embodied in the cadence of his prose. **"Logging and Pimping and 'Your Pal, Jim' "** is a brief recollection which is not nearly so good as either of the long stories which constitute the remainder of the book. *USFS 1919* is the better of the two so far as its fictive dimensions are concerned: the proportions and pace of *A River Runs Through It* are too much marked by the facts of life, too little shaped by art. In *USFS 1919* Maclean re-creates his experience as a logger in the U.S. Forest Service in 1919, experience which included the painful facts of cardsharping. The details of this rough masculine world—of working, hiking, fighting, and drinking—are as authentic as the sensitive descriptions of catching trout in a mountain stream. I leave this world regretfully, wondering how Norman Maclean could have given it up for the effeminate realm of academia. In his late years he has plumbed the waters of memory and has recovered a past that is as charged with light as it is with conviction. (pp. ii,iv)

> *George Core, "Wanton Life, Importunate Art," in* The Sewanee Review, *Vol. LXXXV, No. 1, Winter, 1977, pp. ii, iv, vi, viii, x.*

Walter Hesford   (essay date Winter 1980)

[*In the following essay, Hesford compares* A River Runs Through It *to the piscatory writings of Henry David Thoreau and Izaak Walton.*]

"In our family," writes Norman Maclean, "there was no clear line between religion and fly fishing." In *A River Runs Through It,* he is faithful to family tradition. As he pays tribute to the art of fishing, especially as practiced by his younger brother Paul, he fishes with words for the words of life that his father, a Presbyterian minister, heard beneath the river's current. In so doing, Maclean is also faithful to the tradition of piscatory prose as established by Izaak Walton's *The Compleat Angler.* It is a generous prose, one that reflects and fosters a love for its subject, one that will not be hurried as it circles toward the synthesis of contemplation and action, piety and practice, and beauty and power which, both Maclean and Walton suggest, is the hallmark of genuine art and genuine religion.

This is not to say that *A River Runs Through It* strives to imitate *The Compleat Angler* in either stance or substance. Indeed, Maclean's father warned his teen-age sons against its influence: "Izaak Walton is not a respectable writer. He was an Episcopalian and a bait fisherman." One suspects or hopes that this was intended to be humorous, though bait fishermen are consistently castigated in the story as unredeemably fallen mortals. Perhaps a more devastating criticism of Walton came from brother Paul, age thirteen or fourteen: "The bastard doesn't even know how to spell 'complete.' Besides, he has songs to sing to dairymaids." Norman, the future professor of English and writer, defends Walton: "Some of those songs are pretty good."

Paul, unimpressed, asks, "Whoever saw a dairymaid on the Big Blackfoot River?"

Clearly, western Montana, where the Big Blackfoot runs and where the Macleans grew up, sponsors a different aesthetic from Walton's seventeenth-century English countryside (though this countryside was torn by civil war, and not likely to give unmediated birth to piscatory pastorals). *A River Runs Through It* does not shy away from the rough realities that encompass the author and eventually overcome his brother. As "preacher's kids," they seemed to find it necessary to play rough, to adopt a tough, irreverent stance in order to achieve independent status, a stance still evident in the style of the mature author, but tempered with wit, generosity, and wisdom. Maclean's witty assertion that his father "told us about Christ's disciples being fishermen, and we were left to assume, as my brother and I did, that all first-class fishermen on the Sea of Galilee were fly-fishermen and that John, the favorite, was a dry-fly fisherman" would certainly have shocked Walton, who took devout pride in his holy precursors. The reader, however, should not be misled into taking lightly Maclean's discipleship. His irreverence ultimately does reverence to his brother, whose keeper he proves, and keeps alive the faith of his father. He is thus truly pious, and as seriously committed as Walton was to exploring the religious significance of his subject.

To give this significance a broader context, I would like to claim the privilege of all writers tracing piscatory themes and meander a bit. Maclean is not the first American to fish with words for the words of life. It seems worthwhile to look at the synthesis of contemplation and action worked out by an earlier American disciple in the brotherhood of anglers. It is a select brotherhood. Washington Irving, perhaps the first noted American writer to attempt to cast himself as a compleat angler, acknowledges his complete failure in his humorous essay, "The Angler," included in *The Sketch Book*. He can no more put Walton to use along the Hudson highlands than Maclean's brother can along the Blackfoot. After tangling himself up in the recommended gear, Irving abandons the art and treats himself and the reader to various recollections, culminating in a loving portrait of a Cheshire fisherman, a true follower of Walton. There is difficulty, it seems, in imagining such a man in an American setting. Ernest Hemingway's Nick Adams might, in the "Big Two-Hearted River" stories, fish with the requisite dedication, but his aims are solipsisticly therapeutic rather than spiritual, and Hemingway's prose is informed by a limiting, ritualistic intensity which militates against piscatory meditation.

Maclean's efforts, I think, may most fruitfully be compared with those of Henry David Thoreau, who combines the receptiveness of an Irving and the involvement of a Hemingway. Thoreau's first book, *A Week on the Concord and Merrimack Rivers*, is replete with a Waltonian catalogue of fish that inhabit Concord waters, and with portraits of anglers who inhabit Concord, the most complete of whom, fittingly, is an Englishman by birth. In *Walden*, Thoreau portrays himself as a complete angler who, obeying higher laws and an ascetic sensibility, finally transcends the practice altogether.

There are three strains in Thoreau's piscatory prose that also achieve significance in *A River Runs Through It*. The first is an antinomian strain. I am taking the liberties with this old heresy-tainted term usually taken by Americanists, and applying it to the celebration of the truth of the individual heart or consciousness as opposed to the laws of an established religion or society, to the cultivation of inner laws which may supplant the laws of the land. It comes as some surprise that there is even a hint of antinomianism in Walton, the conservative Anglican—though perhaps it shouldn't, when we remember that in his day the Puritans were establishing the law. Walton's true anglers love to be quiet and stay clear of noisy legal affairs. They also follow in the footsteps of the holy fishermen who preached *"freedom from the incumbrances of the Law, and a new way to everlasting life"* (emphasis Walton), who preached a gospel of religious and social deliverance. It may seem paradoxical that Walton schools his disciples in the tradition and discipline of his art, and at the same time suggests that their traditional predecessors spread freedom. The paradox may be resolved if one believes that the gospel liberates as it fulfills rather than violates the law, that freedom is discipline transfigured. This seems to be the unheretical belief of true anglers, including Thoreau and Maclean.

Thoreau compares with pleasure the free, natural life of the fisherman with the cramped "civil politic life" of a judge; the former, though, perhaps, a social outcast, is wiser, Thoreau implies, than the arbiter of social justice (*A Week*). The fishermen Thoreau honors are "wild men, who instinctively follow other fashions and trust other authorities than their townsmen . . ." (*Walden*). What authorities these wild men follow is not clear, but no doubt they are more conducive to their discipline and freedom than are the laws of the land—especially such as might attempt to regulate where and how they should conduct their business. Thoreau spoofs distant legislators who "regulate the number of hooks to be used" at Walden Pond, but "know nothing about the hook of hooks with which to angle for the pond itself, impaling the legislature for bait." Thoreau, one gathers, does know about such a hook. It is his art, with which he has caught forever Walden, and through which he has put to death the old law, establishing for himself and his readers a new law and gospel.

We might expect a romantic like Thoreau to be an antinomian, but we expect to find a taint of the heresy even less in a Presbyterian than in an Anglican. Yet when he gave his sons catechism lessons Sunday afternoons as prelude to a walk on the hills, the Rev. Maclean tried to arouse their hearts rather than their fears: "he never asked us more than the first question in the catechism, 'What is the chief end of man?' And we answered together so one of us could carry on if the other forgot, 'Man's chief end is to glorify God, and to enjoy him forever.' This always seemed to satisfy him, as indeed such a beautiful answer should have, and besides he was anxious to be on the hills where he could restore his soul and be filled to overflowing for the evening sermon."

Though he enjoyed himself in nature, the Rev. Maclean

did not believe that man could *naturally* achieve his chief end, either in religion or fly fishing. He held the orthodox position "that man by nature was a mess and had fallen from an original state of grace," a state not easily regained: "all good things," he felt, "—trout as well as eternal salvation—come by grace and grace comes by art and art does not come easy." Art meant "picking up God's rhythms" (for the fly fisherman, this was a "four-count rhythm between ten and two o'clock"). These rhythms enabled man "to regain power and beauty." The poor sinner and poor fisherman were likely "to attain power without recovering grace," and their performance was thus, according to the minister, lacking in the beautiful. "Unlike many Presbyterians," reports his son, "he often used the word 'beautiful'."

It is Maclean's brother Paul who comes to embody the beautiful. He may be a doomed sinner in the judgment of the world and in the judgment of his father's congregation, but in the eyes of both father and brother he seems redeemed by his beautiful fishing. Early on Paul decided that "he had two major purposes in life: to fish and not to work, or at least not allow work to interfere with fishing." When he became a reporter, writes his brother, "he had come close to realizing life's purposes, which did not conflict in his mind from those given in answer to the first question in *The Westminster Catechism*." Paul could enjoy God by perfecting his chosen art, even while, as a natural man, he entangled himself in affairs and in gambling debts. Within his art, he disciplines himself, lives by the rhythm preached by his father, makes himself worthy of grace.

After he is brutally beaten to death because, it appears, he failed to pay his debts, Paul's father and brother derive some ultimate solace from remembering him as a fisherman. When the father pushes Maclean for more information about Paul's death, the author replies,

> "I've said I've told you all I know. If you push me far enough, all I really know is that he was a fine fisherman."
>
> "You know more than that," my father said. "He was beautiful."
>
> "Yes," I said, "he was beautiful. He should have been—you taught him."
>
> My father looked at me for a long time—he just looked at me. So this was the last he and I ever said to each other about Paul's death.

Paul's beauty may not count much toward heaven in orthodox circles, but if it is informed with God's rhythm, if he has been pious in his art, he may be said to enjoy God forever. It seems the intention of his brother so to say.

A second strain common to the piscatory prose of Thoreau and Maclean reflects an involvement with the natural world befitting anglers. Both men try to synthesize the natural and the supernatural; both consider the possibilities of a natural religion. Walton in his quiet way also celebrates the natural kingdom, wherein "the goodness of the God of *Nature* is manifest" (emphasis Walton). He would not, of course, take nature for God, nor therein ground his

faith. His complete angler would be apt to carry his Bible with him to read in solitude by a stream whereas Thoreau's would be more likely to *substitute* his natural activity for Bible study. The Walton of the Concord River fishes as "a sort of solemn sacrament," without biblical sanction or benefit of clergy (*A Week*). (pp. 34-41)

Fishing has a part in Thoreau's own sustained sacrament at Walden, in his incorporation of the natural and the supernatural. He tells of dark nights in which his "thoughts wandered to vast and cosmogonal themes in other spheres" until a "faint jerk" on his line in the water linked him once more to the natural sphere. "It seemed," he concludes, "as if I might cast my line upward into the air, as well as downward into this element which was scarcely more dense. Thus I caught two fishes as it were with one hook." His whole life at Walden became one artful hook with which to catch experience, body and soul, to enjoy God forever right now, to attain a perfection in space and time that breaks the boundaries of space and time.

Maclean as well as Thoreau takes seriously Christ's command, "Be ye therefore perfect, even as your father which is in heaven is perfect" (Matt. 5:48). Like Thoreau, he looks to nature for perfection, seeks high moments of integration with a world "perfect and apart" from the messy affairs of men. He achieves identity with the river, feels, incorporates its past, future, and present. He experiences romantic "spots of time" in which "eternity is compressed into a moment," in which all time and space are now and here. One such spot concludes when a big fish he has been trying to land disappears or is transfigured into a bush. "Even Moses," asserts Maclean, "could not have trembled more when his bush blew up on him." His tone suggests that he thinks this episode more comic than romantic or sacramental, but by casting himself as a Montana Moses standing before the natural turned supernatural, Maclean wittily testifies to the religious dimensions of his life and art.

Maclean's aesthetic quest for perfection in nature, for a purely natural religion such as Thoreau sustained himself with, is tempered and qualified by two sets of circumstances, of realities. The realities of fishing often leave him with a tangled line and an empty hook, cutting short those spots of time that should have culminated in a big catch, and confirming the Presbyterian notion of the world of men as a mess. More importantly, the circumstances of human life, the realities, especially, of his brother's story, compel Maclean to look at perfection—and nature—more humanistically. In doing so, he explores the ultimate religious significance of his subject, a significance to be considered in the conclusion of this paper.

The third strain present in Thoreau's writing and *A River Runs Through It* is elegiac. The authors pay tribute to past or passing cultures and to loved ones they have lost. Walton also memorializes old friends, old habits, and an old faith. (Some of the "how to" content common to piscatory prose reflects, I think, the desire to honor and keep alive dying skills.) Thoreau's wild fishermen are a dying breed, remnants of less civilized, populated, and propertied times. Moreover, they remind him of his freer, more natural youth. In elegizing them, he, in a sense, elegizes himself. Maclean too honors scenes and skills dear to him as a young man. With rough tenderness, he describes a time when one could leave some locally brewed beer in the Blackfoot and some clothes on its shore without worrying about marauding hordes (of, needless to say, bait fishermen) from Great Falls, not to mention the West Coast. Montana is presented in this story as, paradoxically, violent and pastoral, rugged and innocent—all in all, a "beautiful world" if one could survive.

There is not much religious significance to this aspect of the elegiac strain, except in that it seeks to keep old ways and values vital, to keep the faith. The strain runs deeper, however. Thoreau's *A Week* is his elegy for his brother John, with whom he took his river journey, and who now, Thoreau assures himself, ascends "fairer rivers." The death of his brother was a shattering experience for Thoreau, complicated by guilt over not being open enough in his love for him in life, and not being able to rescue him from the grip of lockjaw. Thoreau works out his guilt in his writing, overcomes his doubts about the efficacy of love, and sustains through art his brother's life.

A River Runs Through It is an elegy for brother Paul. It tests the efficacy of brotherly love. Brotherly love is a tradition among anglers; Walton traces it back to the brotherhood of fishing disciples surrounding Jesus. Maclean centers his concern on a belief or instinct that preceeds the gospel, one which reflects a common situation: "I knew there were others like me who had brothers they did not understand but wanted to help. We are probably those referred to as 'our brothers' keepers,' possessed of one of the oldest and possibly one of the most futile and certainly one of the most haunting of instincts. It will not let us go." His concern as his brother's keeper will not let him go as he tries to enter the perfect world fishermen and other artists like to immerse themselves in. It eventually fosters a richer understanding of perfection and love, but it fails to keep his brother alive. It appears, indeed, to be one of the most futile of instincts.

Much of Maclean's story deals with his failure to help his brother, who drinks and gambles too much, always desperate, it seems, to prove himself, to stake himself. He won't accept money or advice; the best Maclean can do is go fishing with him, share in an art which Paul has perfected, in which his essential beauty is manifest. A fishing trip provides a "momentary stay against confusion, "but it does not settle his gambling debts or bring order out of the confusion of the world beyond the river. A subplot of the story, which has Maclean trying to help a brother-in-law, a prodigal son of Montana turned West Coast debauchee and bait fisherman, appears to reconfirm the failure of brotherly concern: all the brother-in-law gets out of the fishing expedition his sister (Maclean's wife) and mother hope will help him is a lot of whiskey and beer, a bad sunburn, and a whore. Believing Maclean to be in trouble with his wife and mother-in-law over the condition of their burnt-up and burnt-out baby, Paul becomes, in a change of roles, *his* brother's keeper. He organizes a family fishing trip. It is this trip, the last the brothers and their father take together, that, as recollected by Maclean, provides him and the reader with the assurance that brotherly love

does have its efficacy, that neither this nor any love is in the long run futile. This trip, furthermore, completes his and our religious education.

It would be helpful, I think, to set the lessons of this, the climactic scene of the story, in the context of the story's genesis. Maclean traces its beginnings to a hot afternoon on the river:

> As the heat mirages on the river in front of me danced with and through each other, I could feel patterns from my own life joining with them. It was here, while waiting for my brother, that I started this story, although, of course, at the time I did not know that stories of life are often more like rivers than books. But I knew a story had begun, perhaps long ago near the sound of water. And I sensed that ahead I would meet something that would never erode so there would be a sharp turn, deep circles, a deposit, and quietness.

Waiting for his brother, he senses the patterns and sounds of the river stimulating and shaping his responses and making available a model for his art. He might have found in Thoreau or elsewhere the conventional analogy between the course of a river and the course of a life, but he could not find in any book, nor did he yet know, the realities of life that do not lend themselves, any more that rivers do, to neat and happy aesthetic or philosophic formulations. Waiting for his brother, he does not have the human realities to work with. When his brother arrives, in love and in death, he does. In one sense, Paul's death is that "something that would never erode," thereby determining the shape of his life and the shape of his brother's story. In another sense, it is love that never erodes, that informs life with significance, that fosters any story worth telling.

Love does not depend on understanding. Father and son agree on this when, after Paul's death, they struggle to explain what happened: " 'Are you sure you have told me everything you know about his death?' he asked. I said, 'Everything.' 'It's not much, is it?' 'No,' I replied, 'but you can love completely without completely understanding.' 'That I have known and preached,' my father said." The father does not need to be educated in the gospel—that is his profession. In a later conversation which still reflects the presence of Paul, the father, however, prods his storytelling son toward an easier profession:

> "You like to tell true stories, don't you,?" he asked, and I answered, "Yes, I like to tell stories that are true."

> Then he asked, "After you have finished your true stories sometime, why don't you make up a story and the people to go with it?

> "Only then will you understand what happened and why.

> "It is those we live with and love and should know who elude us."

Maclean, however, follows his father's practice rather than his advice. He fishes with words for those real and

elusive people he has lived with and loved. The result is
A River Runs Through It.

The last family fishing trip is filled with complete acts of
love: Paul bringing the family together; Paul hugging his
mother, who loves best the son she understands least; Paul
rising early to make breakfast after a night on the town;
Paul suggesting that he and Maclean fish close together;
and Paul wading across the river to give his brother the
fly to catch the last fish his brother ever caught in his company. Maclean thinks of these as his finest fish, the fruit
of brotherly love. Through Paul, Maclean achieves a new
definition of "finest," a more humanistic understanding of
perfection which humanizes his art.

The author is satisfied with his day's catch. While waiting
for Paul to fish his limit, which he always does as if to fulfill the law, Maclean searches out his father, whom he
rightly suspects is finished fishing and reading the gospel.
When the preacher comments on the biblical passage he
has been pondering, a dispute ensues:

> "In the part I was reading, it says the Word was
> in the beginning, and that's right. I used to think
> water was first, but if you listen carefully you
> will hear that the words are underneath the
> water."
>
> "That's because you are a preacher first and then
> a fisherman," I told him. "If you ask Paul, he
> will tell you that the words are formed out of
> water."
>
> "No," my father said, "you are not listening
> carefully. The water runs over the words. Paul
> will tell you the same thing."

The father affirms the assertion of the first verse of John:
Logos, the Word—Reason, Spirit—precedes and informs
the material world, is its life, its rhythm, its significance.
He has come to believe in the primacy of meaning. We are
not told what meaning he discerns in the words underneath the water. That is left to our imagination and religion.

The young Maclean feels his father is biased because he
lives by words, and thinks Paul, a man of action, who lives
most fully when fishing the water, will support the liberal,
empiricist, naturalistic position he himself apparently
holds. The father thinks not. We never hear from Paul on
the subject; his last words in the story announce his not-to-
be-honored wish for three more years to perfect his ability
to think like a fish, to perfect an art which his father and
brother already see as perfectly beautiful. Why is the father sure that his younger, somewhat prodigal son shares
his faith? Perhaps the key is "carefully," a word the father
emphasizes through repetition. A man who carefully, religiously devotes himself to his natural sphere of action, as
Paul does when fishing, concludes, or knows without concluding, that within this sphere there is a rhythm, a rightness, a Word which comes to inform his art.

The conclusion of *A River Runs Through It* suggests this,
and suggests that Maclean has listened carefully for a long
time, heard the words, and been converted to the faith of
his father and brother:

Now nearly all those I loved and did not understand when I was young are dead, but I still
reach out to them.

Of course, now I am too old to be much of a fisherman, and now of course I usually fish the big
waters alone, although some friends think I
shouldn't. Like many fly fishermen in western
Montana where the summer days are almost
Arctic in length, I often do not start fishing until
the cool of the evening. Then in the Arctic half-
light of the canyon, all existence fades to a being
with my soul and memories and the sounds of
the Big Blackfoot River and a four-count
rhythm and the hope that a fish will rise.

Eventually, all things merge into one, and a river
runs through it. The river was cut by the world's
great flood and runs over rocks from the basement of time. On some of the rocks are timeless
raindrops. Under the rocks are the words, and
some of the words are theirs.

I am haunted by waters.

Maclean leaves us reaching and fishing, fishing and writing. He leaves us in hope and he leaves us haunted. He has
explored the basement of time and found timeless raindrops. As timeless as the raindrops are the words under
the rocks.

Whose words? There is some difficulty in catching the antecedent of "theirs." Logical antecedents are "rocks" and
"raindrops"; they make natural sense. It is, however,
human sense that Maclean has been making. I propose
leaping up two paragraphs to those he loves, to those he
has been trying to reach. Some of the words, I think, are
theirs. More especially, it is his father and brother to
whom he has been listening carefully. They offer him the
words of life. Not the Word, but the words. Like the wa-

Maclean on his early education:

My father did not allow me to start elementary school but
taught me himself. Most everything crucial that happened
to me since has been influenced by his teaching. He was a
very stern teacher, very harsh. He put me in a room across
from his, where he worked every morning on his sermons
while my mother ran the church. I'd study for forty-five
minutes and then I'd recite to him for fifteen. He might start
me off in the morning by telling me to write a theme on such
and such. All I got was writing and reading, nothing else.
So I would write this thing and three-quarters of an hour
later I would bring it in to him and he'd tear it apart and
say take it back and write it half the length. So I'd take it
back with tears in my eyes. It was rough, this kind of treatment, learning economy of style when kids my age were
learning their ABC's. So I'd give it back to him, and he'd
say, "O.K., now do it half as long again," so I'd take it back
and do it again and by that time it would be a quarter of
twelve, and he'd say, now throw it away.

Norman Maclean, in an interview from TriQuarterly,
Spring 1984.

ters that haunt Maclean, the Word assumes a multitude of forms, including human. Men and women contribute their own words, help bring the world into significance. The author, a sign broker by profession, is fundamentally humanistic, as is his art. Nevertheless, reaching out to loved ones and reaching out to readers, he follows a high religious calling: Maclean is a fisher of men. (pp. 41-45)

> *Walter Hesford, "Fishing for the Words of Life: Norman Maclean's 'A River Runs through It',"* in Rocky Mountain Review of Language and Literature, *Vol. 34, No. 1, Winter, 1980, pp. 34-45.*

Harold P. Simonson (essay date August 1982)

[*Simonson is an American critic, educator, and author who has written several books on American literature and history. In the following essay, Simonson examines the religious symbolism and imagery in* A River Runs Through It.]

"In our family, there was no clear line between religion and fly fishing." With this arresting opener, Norman Maclean begins his novella, ***A River Runs Through It*** (1976), the first work of original fiction ever published by the University of Chicago Press in its long history. It is also Maclean's own first work of fiction, written after his return to Montana following retirement as William Rainey Harper Professor of English at the University of Chicago. Remarkable in many ways, his novella deserves recognition as (I believe) a classic in western American literature. As for the analogy between religion and fly fishing, Maclean hooks it, plays and fights it, and finally lands it with masterful form. In short, the analogy works artistically. Moreover, the river (Montana's Big Blackfoot River) takes on intriguing dimensions, which I will argue include both symbolic and typological significance. For the author, his closing sentence says it all: "I am haunted by waters."

Christ's disciples were fishermen, those on the Sea of Galilee were *fly* fishermen, and Maclean's favorite, John, had to be a *dry-fly* fisherman. This was the logic Maclean as a boy learned from his father's Presbyterian sermons. Yet for all the sermons preached and heard, and all the hours the boy and his brother Paul studied *The Westminster Shorter Catechism*, what really restored their souls, including that of their clergyman father, was to be in the western Montana hills where trout rivers run deep and fast. Ernest Hemingway had said in "Big Two-Hearted River" that swamp fishing was a "tragic adventure"; for Maclean, fishing the Big Blackfoot River was a redemptive one, thanks not only to divine grace but to self-discipline. The theology is sound Calvinism: God does all, man does all.

As for human nature, theologically speaking, just try to use a fly rod for the first time and, says the author, "you will soon find it factually and theologically true that man by nature is a damned mess." Again, Calvin couldn't have said it better. Only the "redeemed" know how to use it. Until such time, a person "will always take a fly rod too far back, just as natural man always overswings with an ax or golf club and loses all his power somewhere in the air." Natural man does everything wrong; he has fallen from an original state of harmony. And he will continue to be a mess until through grace and discipline he learns to cast "Presbyterian-style." The great lesson the father taught his two sons was that "all good things—trout as well as eternal salvation—come by grace and grace comes by art and art does not come easy."

All this theological business isn't as heavy-handed as it sounds. Indeed, Maclean transforms it into characterization, metaphor, humor, and fine detail. He also transforms memories of his father and brother into Rembrandt portraiture edged in darkness and tragedy but also pervaded by a haunting presence, a prelapsarian truth associated with sacred origins, the divine *logos*. Maclean would have us see fishing as a rite, an entry into "oceanic" meanings and eternities compressed into moments, epiphanous "spots of time," the *mysterium tremendum*. Entering the river to fish its dangerous waters is to fish eternity, and to unite in love with those few persons who also obey the exacting code. No one obeyed the code more religiously than brother Paul who, when entering the river, made fishing into a world perfect and apart, a place where joy comes first in a perfect cast, then in a strike that makes the magic "wand" jump convulsively, and finally in a big rainbow trout in the basket—in all, a performance of mastery and art.

Narrator Maclean remembers his brother Paul as a master dry-fly fisherman, indeed as a true artist when holding a four-and-a-half ounce rod in his hand. But more, Paul was one for whom the river in its sacrality held answers to questions, and for whom fly fishing was the search for those answers. That, Paul said, was what fly fishing was, and "you can't catch fish if you don't dare go where they are." Paul dared, and he showed his brother and his Presbyterian father, both expert fishermen too, how to dare. On what was to be their last fishing trip together, before Paul's murder and the father's later death, all things seemed to come together—the river, the fishing, the father and two sons. Sinewing the union was love, and in the union the powerful Big Blackfoot River spoke to them.

It is truly a redemptive moment, caught and held secure in Maclean's memory and in his narrative art. I find it difficult to restrain my admiration; I find Maclean in this story equal to anything in Hemingway and a good deal more courageous, theologically.

In order for this assertion to sink in, I need to emphasize that Maclean's theology includes a doctrine of man. To reiterate, Maclean says that man is a "damned mess." Maclean's courage comes not in asserting this doctrine, which Hemingway and numberless other twentieth-century writers have had no trouble with, but in juxtaposing it with a doctrine of salvation. Without the juxtaposition, damnation is no less a bromide than is salvation. The courage comes in one's affirming a larger context of reality in which the juxtaposition both is and is not reconciled. To change the image, we might imagine a world where a river runs *through* it but is not *of* it. The test of courage is to embrace the paradox.

As for the messiness unto damnation, Maclean's story

does not equivocate. The world is a fallen one, people are liars and cheats, family entanglements ruin the most blessed vision. When the narrator's brother-in-law steps off the train at Wolf Creek, we see in Neal the genus, *phonus bolonus*, dressed in white flannels, a red-and-white-and-blue V-neck sweater over a red-and-white-and-blue turtleneck sweater, and elegant black-and-white shoes. At Black Jack's Bar his big talk with oldtimers and the town's whore, Old Rawhide, shows him in his true element. The family picnic the following day on the Elkhorn River shows him disgustingly out of it. He fishes not with flies but worms and gets nothing; he whimpers from his hangover and feigns sickness to avoid picnic chores. A genuine bastard, he doesn't deserve the solicitude he gets, and he wouldn't get it except for family loyalty. The two brothers know he doesn't even deserve Montana. Neal violates everything that is good, including the code of fishing. On a subsequent trip he violates a trust by stealing beer that the two brothers have left to cool in the river—and in *this*, the Big Blackfoot River. Even worse, he has brought not only a coffee can of worms for bait but also Old Rawhide, and has screwed his whore on a sand bar in the middle of "our family river." The brothers find the two asleep, naked and sunburned. On the cheeks of her ass they see the tattooed letters: LO / VE. The river sanctuary has been defiled; never again will the brothers throw a line here at this hole.

Close as narrator Maclean appears to be to his brother Paul, both reverencing the river whose secrets only the best dry-fly fishermen can hope to touch, a vast gulf nevertheless separates them. If they both find the river an oceanic enigma where answers lie hidden in watery shadows, the narrator finds his brother an enigma as well.

That Paul seeks answers in fishing leaves his brother wondering about the questions being asked. Somewhere deep in Paul's shadowy inner world is chaos that the four-count rhythm of casting has not disciplined, a hell that grace has not transformed. Yet Paul seeks no help either from brother or father. Only the visible things show—namely, that he drinks and gambles and fights too much, that gambling debts translate into enemies, that his job as reporter on a Helena newspaper confirms a world full of bastards, and, finally, that he wants no help, asks for none, expects none except what the hard-driving river can bring. Clearly, Paul lives in a world more profoundly fallen than that represented even by Neal's damned messiness. Confirmation of this fact comes in the manner of Paul's death: beaten by the butt of a revolver, nearly all the bones of his right hand (his fighting hand) broken, and his body dumped in an alley—this, the death of a dry-fly fisherman whose rod was a wand of magical power and beauty, and who, when inhabiting this river-world, embodied laughter and discipline and joy.

Wherein, then, is saving grace? In the water? In the words that the father reads in his Greek New Testament? In the Word, the *logos*, from the Fourth Gospel that the father seeks to interpret as the two of them, father and son, wait on the riverbank to watch Paul catch his final big fish? "In the part I was reading," the father explains, "it says the Word was in the beginning, and that's right. I used to

think water was first, but if you listen carefully you will hear that the words are underneath the water."

Now comes the crucial distinction.

"If you ask Paul," the son says, "he will tell you that the words are formed out of water."

"No," the father replied, "you are not listening carefully. The water runs over the words. Paul will tell you the same thing."

Of course, Paul never tells, and we suspect he never found out. Neither his brother nor his father knows the truth about him. Yet the distinction deserves close attention together with the images that Maclean allows to arise from his memory, images that come out of the past to bear new meanings, joining the past and the present in the image and the image bearing the truth.

Watery images bring forth fish seen sometimes as "oceanic," with their black spots resembling crustaceans. The river itself flows from origins shaped by the ice age, the rocks by more elemental forces emanating "almost from the basement of the world and time." The rain is the same as "the ancient rain spattering on mud before it became rock . . . nearly a billion years ago." Whereas in the sunny world where the river-voice is "like a chatterbox, doing its best to be friendly," in the dark shadows where the river "was deep and engaged in profundities" and where it circled back on itself now and then "to say things over to be sure it had understood itself"—in these primal depths the voice issues from a "subterranean river" where only the most courageous ever venture and where only *real* fishing takes place.

Through such imagery Maclean takes us to foundations antecedent to water. From these foundations the father in the narrative hears words—words beneath the water, words before the water. The distinction between words formed out of water and words formed out of foundations beneath the water is the distinction between mystical pantheism and the Christian *logos*. The distinction is between the *unity* of creator and creation on the one hand and their *separation* on the other. Again, the distinction is between the saving grace found in one's merging with nature, and that found in one's belonging to the God antecedent to nature, the God in nature but not of nature, immanent yet transcendent. And whatever the word spoken in the pantheistic unity, it is not the same as that spoken in the separateness, spoken in the *logos*, spoken from under and before the timeless rocks.

I am not suggesting that Maclean, the author, is involved in mere theological dialectic. What he is saying is not what comes from such abstractions but from memory and images, from time past when he and his father and brother were one in love if not in understanding. And now those he loved but did not understand are dead. "But," he adds, "I still reach out to them." Something of this love he still hears in the waters of the river and in the foundations beneath. Perhaps he hears the Word itself as did John of the Fourth Gospel. This is what the father must have heard too and what his brother Paul did not. Whether the words come from water or from the deeper foundations, they are words his memory translates into those of father and brother, words that spoke of love. In their words he has his epiphany, yes his redemption, and thus he can say, "I am haunted by waters."

I said earlier that Maclean's story is a classic, deserving a place in the pantheon of western American literature. Putting aside such matters as structure and tone, characterization, imagery, and a hundred other elements that subtly harmonize (whether the art be that of Maclean's fiction or his fishing), I find something else, something identifying the river as *symbol* and *type*.

As for symbol, all the age-old meanings associated with living waters—one immediately thinks of purification, fertility, and renewed life—are predicated upon a perceiving mind and a symbolic mode of perception. I'm concerned here more with the act of perception than with the object, more with the perceiver than the perceived or percept. In short, the perceiver as symbolist finds significance through the interaction of experience and imagination, whereas the perceiver as typologist finds significance through a sacred design that is prior to, and independent of, the self. The mode of perception makes all the difference, and in this analysis the two modes are radically different. Symbolism eventuates in a direct interpretation of life, whereas typology relates to history, prophecy, teleology. The symbol is created in the womb of the perceiver's imagination, whereas the type is revealed within the perceiver's faith. Again, the symbolist possesses a special quality enabling him to fuse object and meaning; the typologist possesses a special but different quality enabling him to see what has already been fused and now revealed but is separate from, and independent of, him. Finally, the symbolist enters the river, as it were, and is redeemed by the waters which his imagination transforms into purification and renewal. But the typologist enters what has already been transformed or, more accurately, what flows from a sacred design, purpose, or destiny, made visible through the regenerate eyes and ears of faith.

In Maclean's story the two modes of perception show the river as both symbol and type. When attention is upon Paul's marvelous artistry, validating the halo of spray often enclosing him, we see by means of the narrator's imagination not only a transformed fisherman but a river metamorphosed into a world apart. Fishing becomes a world apart, a world perfect, an imagined and sinless world fusing person with vision. For Paul, when he steadied himself and began to cast, "the whole world turned to water." The narrator shares in the imagined oneness of his brother's world.

But the narrator does not lose himself in it. He also hears his father's words bespeaking a separate design, revealed as the *logos* or Word that was in the beginning—before the river and before human imaginings. More than speech, this Word is divine action—creating, revealing, redeeming. That the father carries his Greek New Testament along with his fishing rod is a fact not lost upon the author as narrator. Through his father's faith the son reaches out to hear this other Word. No wonder he is haunted by waters.

In truth, the river runs through his mind and consciousness and language and life. But something also runs through the river itself, something that is in it but not of it, something more elemental than water. (pp. 149-55)

Harold P. Simonson, "Norman Maclean's Two-Hearted River," in Western American Literature, *Vol. XVII, No. 2, August, 1982, pp. 149-55.*

Mary Clearman Blew   (essay date 1988)

[*In the following essay, Blew analyzes Maclean's female characters in* A River Runs Through It, and Other Stories.]

Very early in the title novella of *A River Runs Through It,* Norman Maclean reveals, in a single scene, a glimpse of a woman so compelling that her image refuses to fade even though she hardly is mentioned again:

> His girl was sitting on the floor at his feet. . . . Looking down on her now I could see only the spread of her hair on her shoulders and the spread of her legs on the floor. Her hair did not glisten and I had never seen her legs when they were just things lying on a floor. Knowing that I was looking down on her, she struggled to get to her feet, but her long legs buckled and her stockings slipped down on her legs and she spread out on the floor again until the tops of her stockings and her garters showed.

So carefully does Maclean arrange this scene, indeed so carefully does he present *A River Runs Through It* as heightened memory, as *true,* that it is at once familiar and disturbing to recognize in his snapshot of the Northern Cheyenne girl drunk and degraded on the floor of the jail at the feet of Maclean's brother, Paul, not only a real girl as, apparently, recalled exactly by Maclean, but also one of the sensual and destructive Dark Women out of the mainstream of American fiction: Cooper's Cora or Judith; Hawthorne's Hester, Miriam, or Zenobia; Poe's Ligeia and Twain's Roxana. Indeed, Maclean's Northern Cheyenne girl shares so many of the characteristics of these fictional antecedents that the crucial ways in which she differs from them seem at first obscure.

To begin, she is endowed with a beauty like theirs, and particularly the beauty of her hair, which Maclean lingers over in language reminiscent of Hawthorne: "When her black hair glistened, she was one of my favorite women. . . . when her hair glistened . . . she was worth it." And she is dark in coloring, a trait which the earlier writers used as an emblem not only of a terrifying capacity for passion but also of a dark heritage which carries with it the threat, or "taint," as Cooper would have called it, of miscegenation. "Mo-nah-se-tah," Maclean nicknames her, a nickname he says she "took to" only after she learned its true significance as the name of the Cheyenne girl who was Custer's mistress and who was said to have borne his son.

Like other Dark Women, the Northern Cheyenne girl has a claim of her own to artistry: "She was one of the most beautiful dancers I have ever seen. She made her partner feel as if he were about to be left behind, or already had been. . . . She was as beautiful a dancer as [Paul] was a fly caster." Her claim to artistry is, in other words, as great as Paul's; she is, in this respect at least, an equal and fitting mate for Maclean's flawed brother whose genius haunts the novella.

Finally and pointedly, like the earlier Dark Women, she is dangerous. She is dangerous not only because she can stir passion and respond to it, or because she carries within her the old threat of the woman of a primitive race luring the white-skinned man away from civilization and its moral restraints, or even, on the most basic level, because of her relish for starting street fights or for drinking. Rather, she is a threat in a way Maclean establishes explicitly in the story of her Cheyenne great-grandmother, who helped cut the testicles off Custer's still living troopers, and implicitly in the one direct glimpse he allows of her, drunken and stinking in jail, her wonderful long legs reduced to "just things lying on a floor." The legs themselves are a further clue, as Leslie Fiedler has remarked of another degraded *anima,* "those improbable legs which America has bred onto the naturally short-legged female form to symbolize castrating power." By now it should be clear that the Northern Cheyenne girl's portrait is drawn from more than heightened memory. Indeed, after such a powerful evocation of the Dark Woman of American fiction, any reader might be excused for expecting to have found, here in the early pages of the novella, a potential solution to the disturbing question at its core; the question, that is, of Maclean's brother Paul. The Northern Cheyenne girl is, surely, Paul's Bad Angel. (Maclean himself has been saved from committing the worst of Paul's sins, from this point of view, by marrying a good Scotch-Irish girl.) On one level, the Northern Cheyenne girl is the bad girl, the bad influence, any son's mother's nightmare, who leads Paul on drinking bouts and gets him into fights. On another level, from this same point of view, she is a projection of Paul's worst impulses, his *anima,* the dark side of his heart in contrast to the side of him reflected in the sparkling waters of the trout rivers. Lending credence to this reading is the shame Paul shows when Maclean comes to get him and his girl out of jail: "his enlarged casting hand was over his face. . . . His overdeveloped right wrist held his right hand over his eyes so that in some drunken way he thought I could not see him."

One indication, however, that such a reading ultimately is unsatisfactory is the Northern Cheyenne girl's subsequent disappearance from the novella. She is allowed no space to develop either into temptress or projection of dark impulses, but rather is left as a kind of accoutrement of Paul's, taken up briefly and dropped. She is the kind of dangerous woman a man like Paul might squire around town as a token of his own toughness. Going out with an Indian in Montana of the nineteen-thirties, where Indians could not at that time legally live within the city limits of the state capitol, and where anti-miscegenation laws lingered into the nineteen-fifties, is a gesture as provocative as getting in the first punch in a street fight.

Another indication that the Northern Cheyenne girl is at the same time both more or less than the Dark Woman

of American fiction lies in the fact of Paul's shame itself. What, one finally has to ask, is he ashamed of ? Certainly not of his girl. Certainly not of punching the man who leaned out of a restaurant booth and yelled "Wahoo!" as they walked by. Certainly not of going out with an Indian even in, especially in, Montana in 1937. Maclean himself supports all these actions up to a point.

> The sergeant said, "The guy said to me, 'Jesus, all I meant is that it's funny to go out with an Indian. It was just a joke.' "
>
> I said to the sergeant, "it's not very funny," and the sergeant said, "No, not very funny, but it's going to cost your brother a lot of money and time to get out of it. What really isn't funny is that he's behind in the game at Hot Springs. Can't you help him straighten out?"

Paul, one concludes, is ashamed of himself in defeat. The tough Montana boy has bet on himself and lost; true, against impossibly high odds, but defeated all the same in the big stud poker game, in the restaurant fight, in the streets. Most humiliating of all, he has been exposed in defeat before the brother whose life is diverging so far from his.

The Northern Cheyenne girl, meanwhile, has followed a course curiously parallel to Paul's. The descendent of women who castrated Custer's troopers has been reduced to life in a camp next to a slaughterhouse and to the ultimate sordidness, described in sexually charged language like "the spread of her legs," of the jail floor. As tough a woman as Paul is a man, she has been pitted against the inexorable forces of a civilization that avenged Custer, wiped out the culture of the Northern Cheyennes along with the rest of the Indians in Montana, and eventually will pollute the beauty of the Big Blackfoot River. The odds against her as well as Paul have been impossibly high; the dancer has been overcome by the dance.

As for Maclean, he is ashamed of them both: "They smelled just like what they were," he says, "a couple of drunks whose stomachs had been injected with whatever it is the body makes when it feels cold and full of booze and knows something bad has happened and doesn't want tomorrow to come." He does not, however, assign extra blame to the Northern Cheyenne girl for leading the dance to the gutter; she and Paul may have reached the brink together, but they have each fallen on their own, and in fact Maclean gives the girl the final judgment of the episode (and her last words in the novella): "He should have killed the bastard," she says just before she passes out.

After her disappearance from the novella, the Northern Cheyenne girl is replaced in several respects by a character who corresponds more nearly than she to an American fictional type. A sizable portion of narrative and dramatic interest, along with the role of Bad Angel to a mother's son, is taken over by the whore of Wolf Creek, Old Rawhide.

Like the Northern Cheyenne girl, Old Rawhide is described as strong, aggressive, and attractive. Unlike her, she is white (an early indication that she is much more closely related to the blonde American bitches of Fitzgerald and Hemingway than to the Dark Woman of the older fictional tradition); and unlike her, she invades the exclusively male and sacred preserve of the trout rivers in a particularly blasphemous way. Perhaps because of the latter incursion, during which she violates the sacrament of fly fishing by bringing along a bait can, drinking all the beer, and seducing his brother-in-law on a sandbar in the middle of the Big Blackfoot River, Maclean denies her even the qualified respect he showed the Northern Cheyenne girl. His contempt for her is barely relieved by humor:

> About ten years before, at a Fourth of July celebration, she had been elected beauty queen of Wolf Creek. She had ridden bareback standing up through the 111 inhabitants, mostly male, who had lined one of Wolf Creek's two streets. Her skirts flew high, and she won the contest. But, since she didn't have what it takes to become a professional rider, she did the next best thing. However, she still wore the divided skirts of a western horsewoman of the day, although they must have been a handicap in her new profession.

Where Maclean gave his Dark Woman a certain integrity of her own and linked her, through her defeat, to the spiritual values associated with the trout rivers, he explicitly depicts Old Rawhide as corrupt. As anti-virgin, she has aligned herself with the social forces that have turned over the Big Blackfoot River from a private paradise to "dude ranches, the unselected inhabitants of Great Falls, and the Moorish invaders from California." If the Northern Cheyenne girl looks back to a violent but essentially innocent past, Old Rawhide looks ahead to a violent and banal future.

The image of woman as anti-virgin recurs in Maclean's fiction, always in association with male weakness. She is present in the whores of Hamilton in *USFS 1919: The Ranger, the Cook, and a Hole in the Sky*, against whose malignancy the young Norman invokes the protection of iambs, like a Celtic satirist's charms, and whose rapacity ultimately exposes the fraudulence of the card-shark cook. In **"Logging and Pimping, and 'Your Pal, Jim,'"** she appears as the "Southern" whores who personify the antagonist's limitations and with him create "a warm family circle of lies."

So it also is that, by aligning herself with Maclean's passive brother-in-law, who fishes with bait, that Old Rawhide is revealed as Bad Angel. Clearly the aggressor in the relationship with Neal, who early has learned the power of passivity in manipulating his mother and sister, Old Rawhide further unmans him with her strength. Although Neal already has been revealed as a poseur and a bad liar who tries to claim the wilderness values he cannot begin to comprehend or live up to, Old Rawhide humiliates him during the sandbar episode to the point that he virtually becomes catatonic.

First, by seducing Neal under the full glare of the sun on the river, Old Rawhide not only parodies the theme of love which dominates the novella, but also exposes Neal: literally, he is exposed to sunburn, and metaphorically, to the stripping away of his last claims to dignity. She degrades him with her promiscuity, propositioning Maclean and

Paul over his limp body. She shames him with her strength, helping him to wade through the swift current from sandbar to shore—"The man couldn't have made it without the strength in her legs," Maclean acknowledges. Finally, and without an inkling of its significance, she retrieves for him the red Hills Bros. coffee can that has become a kind of scarlet letter for bait fishermen and Neal's special badge of inadequacy. At the conclusion of the episode, Neal, lacking even the strength to pull up his pants by himself, is delivered over to his mother and sister in a state approaching the infantile.

It is Paul, however, and not Neal that Old Rawhide recognizes as her true adversary. In this respect she differs dramatically from Bad Angels in Maclean's other fiction. Unlike the whores of Hamilton, Old Rawhide refuses to snarl from the confines of the crib or to content herself with robbing a man already exposed as counterfeit. Nor, like the "Southern" whores, is she a faceless extension of a pimp. Old Rawhide, aggressive in her own context, pits her toughness against Paul's toughness, her banality against his artistry, the perversion she represents against his special ability to worship at the inmost shrine of the trout rivers. But it really is no contest; here, at least, the victory is Paul's. When he kicks her squarely in the source of her perversion, right between the LO and the VE tattooed on her buttocks, Maclean leaves no doubt about his own stance:

> Suddenly, I developed a passion to kick a woman in the ass. I was never aware of such a passion before, but now it overcame me. I jumped out of the car, and caught up to her, but she had been kicked in the ass before and by experts, so I missed her completely. Still, I felt better for the effort.

That Paul's triumph will be brief already has been foreshadowed. Neither does his rout of Old Rawhide answer the unresolved questions about Paul. Maclean's gloss suggests that, to Paul, defeating Old Rawhide is meaningless. "Much as he hated her, he really had no strong feeling about her. It was the bastard in the back seat without any underwear that he hated . . . [Neal] who was untouchable because of three Scotch women."

The three Scottish women are more formidable by far than either the Northern Cheyenne girl or Old Rawhide. Mother, sister, and sister-in-law to Neal; wife, mother-in-law, and sister-in-law to Maclean, they are presented consistently as a unified force, as a trinity. Neal, although under their protection, is terrified of them. "I don't want to see three women," he keeps whimpering during the drive home from the ill-fated fishing trip, and Maclean silently adds, "I didn't want to see three women either."

The Scottish women's strength is drawn from familiar sources. Never intruding upon the exclusively male territory of the trout rivers, they hold absolute sway over their traditional domestic and social preserves. They practice the healing arts—"the three of them were thought of as the medical center of Wolf Creek"—and preside over the complexities of familial ties and their Scottish and Presbyterian heritage. Theirs is the combined authority of blood, custom, and church.

These are not their only sources of strength. Elsewhere Maclean has painted the fate of a Presbyterian woman, "a big woman on a big horse," who becomes the object of the ferocious lumberjack of **"Logging and Pimping and 'Your Pal, Jim.'"** He seduces her to a chorus of ribaldry from the entire logging camp, humiliates her—"By late afternoon she rode back into camp. She never stopped. She was hurried and at a distance looked white and didn't have any huckleberries. She didn't even have her empty pail." Indeed, humiliation alone is not punishment enough; for her fall, Maclean disallows all sympathy:

> At first I felt kind of sorry for her because she was so well known in camp and was so much talked about, but she was riding "High, Wide, and Handsome." She was back in camp every Sunday. She always came with a gallon pail and she always left without it.

"Logging and Pimping and 'Your Pal, Jim,'" however, is a story of inadequacies masked by humor. The distance between it and the novella, like the difference between the Presbyterian woman's abandoned pail and the red coffee can Old Rawhide wades the Blackfoot River to retrieve, is the distance between weakness and strength. The three Scottish women of the novella draw strength from sources far beyond the conventional ones of the Presbyterian woman on the big horse.

One of these sources is their solidarity. Typifying regional western painting and narrative, where white women often are depicted as members of a group, where what they represent is emphasized over their individuality, the three Scottish women emerge separately only once, at a point crucial for Maclean, to speak in individual voices. Nor does Maclean render them separately visually, as he does Old Rawhide or the Northern Cheyenne girl, in one of his vivid snapshots of frozen action. As a trinity, however, the three Scottish women loom up from the depths of nightmare with a force worthy of the Northern Cheyenne girl's great-grandmother:

> The truck emerged out of the storm as if out of the pioneer past, looking like a covered wagon besieged by circling rain. . . .
>
> First it was the women who appeared and then the mattress, the women appearing first because two of them held carving knives and the other, my wife, held a long fork, all of which glittered in the semidarkness under the tarps. The women squatted on the floor of the box, and had been making sandwiches until they saw my head appear like a target on canvas. Then they pointed their cutlery at me.

It is a male glimpse into the female mysteries—one might almost say, into the coven. To understand its significance for Maclean and the answer it provides to the mystery of Paul, it is helpful to note how the three Scottish women have sapped Neal's strength, but also how they lend their own strength to Maclean.

Maclean points on several occasions to Neal's mother as the source of his inadequacy. The straw suitcase which belonged to his mother and which held all Neal took out of Montana and all he brought back, is one example; his mother cries at the sight of it. Another example is Neal's habit of manipulating women. Certainly in the coven scene in the back of the truck, Maclean is explicit:

> . . . it took some time for my eyes to get adjusted to my brother-in-law lying on the mattress. The light first picked up his brow, which was serene but pale, as mine would have been if my mother had spent her life in making me sandwiches and protecting me from reality.

The unmanning of Neal clearly began long before he met Old Rawhide. However, Maclean just as clearly regards the three Scottish women and the established culture they represent, not necessarily as foes of male freedom and potency, but rather as a rare source of love and courage for the man who is strong enough to receive it. Neal, weak in himself, is undone by their implacable love; but Maclean, face to face with each of them consecutively in the one scene where they emerge as individual women, is rewarded by their love. It is a scene unparalleled in the American fiction tradition from which *A River Runs Through It* springs. One could not imagine a Hemingway protagonist accepting these declarations of love, any more than one could discover a Nick Adams, say, walking out of the wilderness as the adolescent Maclean does in *USFS 1919: The Ranger, the Cook, and a Hole in the Sky,* and carrying with him like talismen the values of his father the Presbyterian minister and his mother the poet.

"I love you," says each of the three Scottish women to Maclean in turn, and "never lose touch with me," says his wife. "And we never have," Maclean notes, "although her death has come between us." Buoyed by these avowals of love, Maclean returns to his parents, his brother, and the Big Blackfoot River where, "on this wonderful afternoon when all things came together, it took me one cast, one fish, and some reluctantly accepted advice to attain perfection."

It is a perfection denied his brother, Paul, however unparalleled the artistry of his fly casting. "Just give me three more years," Paul asks, but he will not be given them. Early the following spring, Maclean must tell his parents that Paul has been beaten to death, all the bones in his casting hand broken, and his body dumped in an alley.

To the tragedy of Paul, Maclean offers no easy answers, although he and his parents search for understanding, and at one point his father even ventures, like an echo of Neal's family, "Do you think your mother helps him by buttering his rolls?" But if Neal's spineless acquiescence is not Paul's, neither is his the capacity of Maclean's to receive love. In a world split between male and female, Paul seems curiously unable to achieve wholeness. Whether his is original sin or flawed pride, he is unable to accept succor from any source outside himself.

For Maclean, on the other hand, drawing as he does from the powers of the trout rivers as well as those of blood and custom, the story is a fiction—that is, a story that is true, a way of understanding the truth. And it is a comedy—a healing, a reconciliation, a wholeness achieved through the love of trout rivers and the love of family, an integration completed by the Northern Cheyenne girl, Old Raw-hide, and the three Scottish women. (pp. 190-200)

> Mary Clearman Blew, "Mo-nah-se-tah, the Whore, and the Three Scottish Women," in Norman Maclean, edited by Ron McFarland and Hugh Nichols, Confluence Press, Inc., 1988, pp. 190-200.

Glen A. Love (essay date 1988)

[*Love is an American critic and educator. In the follow-ing excerpt, he discusses the connection between Maclean's literary criticism and* A River Runs Through It, and Other Stories.]

At some point during my first reading of *A River Runs Through It and Other Stories*—perhaps in the tale of Jim Grierson, the tough logger whose summer and winter lives seemed so incongruous—I can remember wondering how the two halves of the author's life cohered. A professor of English holding an endowed chair at a distinguished met-ropolitan university who wrote wonderful autobiographi-cal stories in his retirement years, and a boy and young man formed in the Montana mountains and woods, log-ging and working for the U. S. Forest Service and fly-fishing on the Big Blackfoot River with his brother and their Scottish Presbyterian minister father. I have read Norman Maclean's book with increasing pleasure several times since that first reading, and have introduced it to many of my students in American literature, and I have not lost my curiosity about this figure who so ably spans two different worlds.

At least two sets of literary contrasts are at work in what I have been describing: the contrasts between West and East, country and city, nature and civilization on the one hand, and those between youth and age, heart and head, energy and wisdom, naivete and tragic awareness on the other. These patterns of opposition are, of course, not un-familiar to readers. The *Bildungsroman* has characteristi-cally depicted the shock of experience upon impression-able and searching innocence; and the pastoral has for cen-turies recorded the progress of the youth from the prov-inces who comes to the metropolis but continues to mea-sure his life by the standards derived from the green world of his past. American readers may recognize a more indig-enous figure in Maclean's work. That is the peculiarly American type—born out of Melville, Whitman, Twain, Crane, London, Hemingway, Mailer, and countless oth-ers—of what has been called the sensitive roughneck, the young man who has been around, but whose perceptive and reflective qualities open his world to the interests of a larger audience. Still, even within these recognizable tra-ditions, Maclean's achievement seems compelling to me, partly because of the extent to which it stretches these pat-terns of contrast to their extremes. Here was a life a good deal more dramatically divided than could be described by the characteristic American stance of the tender tough guy, or by the comfortable oppositions of the English country gentleman, whose "All winter in the study, all summer in the field" balanced neatly as a golden mean. It is a unique and startling distance, among the lives of our writers, between gyppo logging and a University of Chica-go chair in literature.

Maclean's work gathers interest and complexity from an-other set of opposites, that is from the extremes of time which it encompasses. Not having begun to write stories until he was the age of seventy—surely another American literary record—and looking back to his early years, Maclean invests his fiction with a distinctive quality of wonder and sagacity, a memorable blend of youthful dreams, Montana horse-sense, and the varied reflections of his long life. Writing of this aspect of *A River Runs Through It,* John Cawelti thoughtfully notes that the sto-ries

> . . . are like memories which have been revolved in the mind throughout a lifetime until their hid-den truths have been brought to the surface and revealed. Thus there is a wonderful interplay be-tween the consciousness of the old man telling us the stories and the perspective of the boy of over half a century ago. We see not only what the boy thought or failed to think, but how he began to understand his life and something of what that boy, as a man in his 70's, has made of it since.

As in Cooper's Leatherstocking series, Maclean's charac-ter grows ever younger as the stories progress, but his youth at the end of the last story reflects not so much the sloughing off of age which D. H. Lawrence found in Natty Bumppo's youthful emergence, but rather a kind of distil-lation of the experience of both youth and age, and of the mutually enriching perspectives of each.

Faced with these kinds of contrasts, then, one may be tempted, as I have been, to find connections between the sage and the stripling, between the rapt stories of a western youth and the teller's life as a scholar and intellectu-al. . . . As he cites one purpose of his book in his intro-duction, that of letting his "children know what kind of people their parents are or think they are or hope they are," so it is inevitable that his appreciative readers will seek to extend that sort of awareness, thus enhancing the pleasure of what are now their stories as well. Then, too, as the author has included scholars among those for whom these stories are intended, he knows what to expect from these most burrowing of readers. Eventually, as he says, all things merge into one. And the river which runs through it may have its ideational as well as its physical and spiritual existence. How do the words and ideas of the author's intellectual life flow into his haunting waters?

In approaching some of the scholarly undercurrents of these stories one might begin by citing smaller and more discrete features of the prose, such as literary allusions. There seem to be relatively few of these, for a professor's book, but they're carefully patterned, moving, for exam-ple, in the first, title story, from the comic to the serious and philosophical. Early in the story we learn that Isaac Walton " 'is not a respectable writer. He was an Episcopa-lian and a bait fisherman.' " Thus cautions Maclean's fa-ther to his sons, while brother Paul privately confides to the narrator, after locating a copy of *The Compleat Angler,* that " 'the bastard doesn't even know how to spell "com-

Maclean's brother Paul.

plete.' ' " The narrator finds some of Walton's songs to dairymaids appealing, but cannot shake realist Paul's scornful opinion, " 'Whoever saw a dairymaid on the Big Blackfoot River?' " But this first story also has its tragic movement. As it progresses, the apparent and submerged references to Christian grace and salvation, to religious typology and symbolism and myth—perceptively explicated by critic Harold P. Simonson—come increasingly to our attention, deepening our sense of the three characters— the narrator, the father, and the doomed brother Paul— and of the relationships between them.

In the second story, logger Jim Grierson spends his winters pimping and "rereading Jack London, omitting the dog stories." In the last story, ***USFS 1919: The Ranger, the Cook, and a Hole in the Sky,*** the allusions are more frequent, including a quotation from Matthew Arnold which opens and closes the story, and to which I wish to return later. Elsewhere in this story reference is made to Dante's *Inferno,* to a prostitute who spoke blank verse, to the prize-winning sonnet which Maclean wrote as a high school student "On Milton's Blindness," or rather which his mother wrote with her right hand while he held her trembling left hand, to his further efforts at scanning Milton and Shakespeare under his mother's tutelage.

Pursuing the references to spoken rhythm in ***USFS 1919,*** it is worth noting that Maclean has written . . . of the importance of students' understanding the rhythm of poems, and of teaching to college students, including even graduate students often ignorant of such matters, the rhythms of such apparently simple ballads as "Lord Randal" (**"The Pure and the Good"**). Thus Maclean's interest in speech

rhythm in his stories may be credited to more than a naturally good ear, although his ear is very good indeed. Rhythms of various kinds underlie all of the book: the four-count rhythm of fly-casting, learned on a metronome, or to his father's clapping out a four-count rhythm with his hands, the rhythm of downward moving water in a mountain river, with its three-part pattern of rapids, deep pools, and shallowing tail-outs, before the pattern repeats itself. That rhythm, Maclean writes, reminds us that

> . . . stories of life are often more like rivers than books. But I knew a story had begun, perhaps long ago near the sound of water. And I sensed that ahead I would meet something that would never erode so there would be a sharp turn, deep circles, a deposit, and quietness.

There is the rhythm of geologic time, of the succession of stages in the earth's history which is described in the title story and in ***USFS 1919,*** where Blodgett Canyon's glacial record, written in stupendous mountain forms, seems to overwhelm the boy on his marathon hike, walking to the rhythm of " 'It's time to quit. It's time to quit.' " And again underlying this entire story there is the rhythm of the epic boyhood summer, ending with Quitting Time and Cleaning Out the Town. In the logging story, there is the rhythm of two-man crosscut sawing, the participants "lost in abstractions of motion and power. But when sawing isn't rhythmical, even for a short time, it becomes a kind of mental illness—maybe even something more deeply disturbing than that. It is as if your heart isn't working right."

Maclean shows a liking for rhythmic triads in two of his three story titles, "Logging and Pimping and 'Your Pal, Jim,' " and ***USFS 1919: The Ranger, the Cook, and a Hole in the Sky,*** triads which actually scan. And there are Maclean's beautiful parallel syntactic structures when the balanced and controlled effects of series consisting of two or three elements are spun out into hypnotic chains of four or five, with each element in the series held fixed and memorable by the polysyndeton of the repeated "ands": "Then in the Arctic half-light of the canyon, all existence fades to a being with my soul and memories and the sounds of the Big Blackfoot River and a four-count rhythm and the hope that a fish will rise." At their best, as in the Blodgett Canyon scene in ***USFS 1919*** and at the end of the title story where the Biblical allusions are echoed in Maclean's own verbal patterns, the author's rhythms of rock and river and the human presence and the grace or art are beautifully interrelated within a prose of sonorous power:

> Eventually, all things merge into one and a river runs through it. The river was cut by the world's great flood and runs over rocks from the basement of time. On some of the rocks are timeless raindrops. Under the rocks are the words, and some of the words are theirs.
>
> I am haunted by waters.

The literary scholar's interest in the profound differences between life and literature, between a mere record of events and a meaningful shaping of these events into art, informs both the title story and ***USFS 1919.*** "What I remember most about my life is its literature," Maclean has said in describing his own reaction and that of young readers to his book (**"The Pure and the Good"**). Writing of *King Lear* in an essay published 35 years ago, Maclean had noted this same distinction, and had similarly probed the sources of art's appeal:

> . . . the world that is each poem is bound together so that it binds the hearts of those who look upon it, of whom the poet is one. To look upon a poem, then, as distinct from looking upon much of the succession of life, is to be moved, and moved by emotions that, on the whole, attract us to it and are psychologically compatible
>   (**"Episode, Scene, Speech, and Word"**).

The wonder which accompanies the transformation of life into literature is a central theme of ***USFS 1919*** and Maclean sets forth its essence early in the story:

> I had as yet no notion that life every now and then becomes literature—not for long, of course, but long enough to be what we best remember, and often enough so that what we eventually come to mean by life are those moments when life, instead of going sideways, backwards, forward, or nowhere at all, lines out straight, tense and inevitable, with a complication, climax, and given some luck, a purgation, as if life had been made and not happened.

The allusion to Aristotle here brings us closer to Maclean's scholarly touchstones. Without making too much of the concept of the "Chicago school" of literary criticism, and recognizing the plurality of critical approaches of the University of Chicago English faculty during Maclean's years there, it is still worth noting that Maclean's book reveals a close adherence to what might be considered the Chicago group's Neo-Aristotelian precepts. Among those tenets which seem most relevant to an understanding of ***A River Runs Through It and Other Stories*** are the beliefs that poetry, written large as literature, is more philosophical than history, that poetry or art thus seeks and expresses inevitable wholes, and that criticism inquires into the various parts by which these wholes achieve unity. Further, that the criticism of literature, in R. S. Crane's words, ought "to play a more influential role in the culture and action of the contemporary world," and that criticism must be seen as part of the range of humane studies, whose ideal "is the fullest possible discovery, in every subject matter, of its varied humanistic aspects."

Two of Norman Maclean's essays are included by Crane in his important manifesto of the Chicago Neo-Aristotelians, *Critics and Criticism: Ancient and Modern*, published in 1952. One of the Maclean pieces, on *King Lear*, cited earlier, is closely Neo-Aristotelian in its part-whole treatment of the play. The other, a much longer and more wide-ranging essay, represents the field of Maclean's principal scholarship, the theory of lyric poetry between the Renaissance and the Romantic age. Within this full and rewarding essay, **"From Action to Image: Theories of the Lyric in the Eighteenth Century,"** may be found several important literary and aesthetic ideas which seem to me to inform the stories of *A River Runs Through It*.

"From Action to Image" describes and analyzes the effect upon the writers and critics of the late seventeenth and eighteenth centuries of the rediscovery of the ancient Greek philosopher-critic Dionysius Longinus' treatise, *On the Sublime*. To summarize Maclean's argument briefly, the reappearance of Longinus' essay had a major effect upon lyric poetry and literary theory in the late seventeenth and eighteenth centuries. Longinus brought the attention of contemporary scholars and writers to the qualities of literature which " 'transport' the reader out of his normal senses and invest literary works with immortality." Although he does not stress the sources of the sublime in the natural world (as do many of his followers), Longinus does cite the presence of sublime natural objects as evidence of a creator whose intentions for men are made clear in these natural features. Like Maclean's own minister father, whose favorite catechism—"Man's chief end is to glorify God, and to enjoy Him forever"—justifies his sense of joy in God's natural world, Longinus conveys the belief that the creator inspires us to search in the wonders of creation for the beauty which renders it delightful.

Later in the eighteenth century, under the influence of critics like Edmund Burke, a second term, beauty, is added to the sublime to account for the entire aesthetic experience. Natural objects were sublime or they were beautiful. The sublime—the massive, the elevated, the awesome in the natural world—moved the beholder toward emotional feelings of turbulence and transport. The beautiful aroused the opposite effects of love and pity and sympathy for one's fellow human beings, and of an emotional state of relaxation. The concept of the beautiful, for the eighteenth century, was the lesser of the two responses, and came to be associated, according to Maclean, with the lesser lyric poem. The higher part of the aesthetic response was accorded to the sublime, whose associations were with the more powerful emotions of fear and self-preservation, and which came to be identified with the higher lyric form, the Great Odes of the century.

In scholar Maclean's examination of how "this 'non-lyrical' age regarded the highest form of the lyric—the Great Ode—as one of [its] supreme expressions," we may find suggestive connections to artist Maclean's fictions. Writing in another non-lyrical age, Maclean also reaches toward sublimity, but in a contemporary laconic western American voice which must eschew not only the overt concept of sublimity—elevation, nobility, grandeur, solemnity, awe—but also the word itself and all its synonyms. Maclean nevertheless intimates the presence of sublimity in his stories through the lesser but more available concept of *beauty*.

The word "beautiful" rings like a ballad's refrain through the book, particularly in the title story and in ***USFS 1919***, those stories in which sublimity is felt as an unstated force. It is his father's word, we are told. "Unlike many Presbyterians, he often used the word 'beautiful.' " Something of an eighteenth-century figure himself, with his stylish casting, his gloved casting hand, and his metronomical regularities of religion and fly-fishing, the elder Maclean serves to revivify for the sake of the stories the eighteenth-century belief that the beauties of the earth "were God's manifestation of his attributes and the lesser glories of man." ("**From Action to Image**"). Maclean says of his father, "He was about the only man I knew who used the word 'beautiful' as a natural form of speech, and I guess I picked up the habit from hanging around him when I was little."

So the father's word becomes the son's, and in turn the scholar's and the writer's, each stage adding its own accretion of meaning. The Big Blackfoot where they fish is "a beautiful stretch of water." Making an ash-soft cast, dropping the fly softly to the water is like "becoming the author of something beautiful." The tragic brother Paul was "beautiful," both father and son concur. The memorable **USFS 1919** has this as its first sentence: "I was young and I thought I was tough and I knew it was beautiful and I was a little bit crazy but hadn't noticed it yet." Even unpacking horses who have been loaded by a master is

> . . . beautiful—one wet satin back after another without saddle or saddle sore. . . . Perhaps one has to know about keeping packs balanced on the backs of animals to think this beautiful, or to notice it at all, but to all those who work come moments of beauty unseen by the rest of the world.
>
> So, to a horseman who has to start looking for horses before daybreak, nothing is so beautiful in darkness as the sound of a bell mare.

The wonder and terror of life are in these stories: in the title story, Paul, swimming the turbulent and dangerous river with his rod in his right hand, reaching the rock in the middle, to which he clings precariously with his free left hand, then rising, streaming water, to begin his magnificent casting, the spray from which "enclosed him in a halo of himself." Later, Paul moving into the river canyon's subterranean shadows, presaging the early death which will claim him. The river and the rocks beneath it, with raindrops on them, and beneath the rocks the words. The enormous ages of the earth. Masses of time to match masses of space. While it will not do for the author to say it, the sublime is present in all of this. **USFS 1919** also stirs something of awe within us. As a fire lookout on a mountain top, the boy learns that it doesn't take much body or mind to be a lookout:

> It's mostly soul. It is surprising how much our souls are alike, at least in the presence of mountains. For all of us, mountains turn into images after a short time, and the images turn true. Gold-tossed waves change into the purple backs of monsters, and so forth. Always something out of the moving deep, and nearly always oceanic. Never a lake, never the sky.

Lines from Matthew Arnold's "The Buried Life" begin and end this story, and their summoning of "the hills where his life rose" reinforces, with Arnoldian high seriousness, the sublimity of great mountains, and of the oceanic, the moving deep to which that life flows, and of the hole in the sky which the boy turned man and writer must invest with meaning.

Willa Cather claimed early in the 1920's that the thing not present on the page might be the most powerful presence there, that stories could be stronger for what they did not overtly state. It was an idea that she proved again and again in her great understated works like *A Lost Lady, The Professor's House,* and *Death Comes for the Archbishop.* Young Ernest Hemingway was working along the same lines toward his "iceberg theory" that you could omit, if you knew that you omitted, and the omission would cause readers to feel more than they understood (*A Moveable Feast*). "The dignity of movement of an iceberg," he said, "is due to only one-eighth of it being above water" (*Death in the Afternoon*).

Something of that same dignity—perhaps only another name for sublimity—is present through our sense of its being withheld in stories like **USFS 1919** and **A River Runs Through It.** In their way, they may be seen as exemplifying the classical unification of fear and pity, the sublime and the beautiful, which exist side by side in Aristotle and Longinus, but which a later age had seen fit to separate. In Maclean's best stories, they come together again, as lyric and ode, under the appellation of the beautiful, but bearing the force of the sublime. (pp. 201-11)

> Glen A. Love, "On the Sublime and the Beautiful: Montana, Longinus, and Professor Norman Maclean," in Norman Maclean, edited by Ron McFarland and Hugh Nichols, Confluence Press, Inc., 1988, pp. 201-12.

Maclean on the Chicago literary scene in the 1930s:

We came in and Sherwood Anderson just stopped and froze and looked at Carl Sandburg. Sandburg is engaged in one of his monologues. Conversation was not possible with him. He was a monologist. So he's mooning along about Emerson, the first really great true American. And Sherwood listens for a while. Finally he stops Sandburg right in the middle of a sentence. He says, "Emerson was the first great Rotarian." Boom. The place just froze. There we stood, up on the platform like actors, with a stunned audience beneath us. Well, there was no more to the evening at all. Nobody could get anything started after that.

So, a couple of days later, I'm going in to Chicago and Ferdinand Schevill takes me down to Michigan City, and I got on the Yellow Peril. Who's sitting in the Yellow Peril but Sandburg. You know, with his snap-brim hat and his long thin cigar. So I go over and sit by him and he looks at me for a while and he doesn't say a word. Then he says, "That sorry . . . that son of a bitch!" he said. "What does he mean? What does he mean about Emerson being the first great Rotarian?" He pulled the brim of his hat down until it touched his cigar and never said another word to me all the way to Chicago. All was not quiet on the Chicago literary front in those days.

> Norman Maclean, in an interview from TriQuarterly, Spring 1984.

Helen Lojek   (essay date August 1990)

[*In the following essay, Lojek criticizes aspects of the*

"western American myth" apparent in A River Runs Through It.]

To read Norman Maclean's 1976 story *A River Runs Through It* is to enter a world in which tight, rhythmic prose (sentences flowing together like molecules of the Big Blackfoot River they describe) yields much comprehension of the joys and difficulties of family love. It is also, however, to enter a world shaped by an unexamined and probably unconscious masculinity. In large part, that masculinity is linked to elements of western American myth, and Maclean seems too much of a western insider to be fully aware of the limitations of that myth. To recognize the joys and beauties of *A River Runs Through It* without recognizing the restrictions of its masculine myth is to miss the complex, often ambiguous, ways in which the work continues patterns commonly found in writings about the American West.

There are, of course, several mythic American Wests: the frontier, the cattle range, the mining fields, to mention a few of the broadest categories. But heroes in fictional portrayals of all of these Wests have generally shared a cluster of personal characteristics. Tight-lipped, powerful, independent loners governed by a "code" of fair but assertive behavior, they are uncomfortable with the strictures and conventions of encroaching civilization. It is that category of western hero into which Maclean's brother Paul fits, and recognizing Maclean's recasting of elements of the western myth into a tale of fly fishing in Montana in the 1930s reveals continuities and connections between his story and a long literary tradition.

Maclean himself envisioned his tales as western. "I started reading western stories kind of to refresh myself on them before going very far with [my own stories]," he has said (Interview). And he has twitted publishers for their hesitancy about accepting his works. "Then, to add further to their literary handicaps, these stories turned out to be Western stories—as one publisher said in returning them, 'These stories have trees in them.' " (*River*).

Critics too have pointed to the work's regional nature. Harold Simonson calls it "a classic in western American literature." Wallace Stegner contrasts the popularity of Maclean's stories with the fact "they are about the West . . . they are about a *historical* West . . . and they contain some of the mythic feeling and machinery . . . made all too familiar by horse opera." And Kenneth Pierce fulminates about the "pigfuckers in the East" who refuse to render Maclean's "dazzling achievement" its due.

There are, of course, westerns and westerns. Or, as John Milton puts it, there are westerns and Westerns. The small *w* western "deals in stereotyped characters and stock patterns of action; it exploits the myths of the frontier, it depends upon a two-sided morality of good and evil. . . ." The upper case Western, on the other hand, "is of high literary quality . . . is sensitive to human behavior as well as to meaningful qualities of the land, is conscious of the relationship between the historical past and the present, is engaged in defining western man (in both senses of the term *western*). . . . " As a whole, I think, Maclean's tale

is in fact a Western. But it is not as unambiguously in that category as readers often assume, and a primary reason for its tenuous categorization is Maclean's perpetuation of aspects of western myth which allow him to slip into stereotyped characters and prevent him from fully exploring the relationship between past and present.

It is in his casting of Paul as a mythic western hero that Maclean's indebtedness to western myth is most clearly visible. At thirty-five and the "height of his power," Paul is noticeably superior to other Montanans (who are, of course, generally superior to the rest of us). Standing on the top of a cliff, putting "all his body and soul into a four-and-a-half-ounce magic totem pole," Paul casts his line rhythmically out over the water, making loops and circles designed to convince the fish that a hatch of flies is out.

> The mini-molecules of water left in the wake of his line made momentary loops of gossamer, disappearing so rapidly in the rising big-grained vapor that they had to be retained in memory to be visualized as loops. The spray emanating from him was finer-grained still and enclosed him in a halo of himself. The halo of himself was always there and always disappearing, as if he were candlelight flickering about three inches from himself. The images of himself and his line kept disappearing into the rising vapors of the river, which continually circled to the tops of the cliffs where, after becoming a wreath in the wind, they became rays of the sun.

To the strangers who pause to watch, says Maclean, Paul "must have looked something like a trick rope artist at a rodeo, doing everything except jumping in and out of his loops." These observers find Paul's physique and skill so awe-inspiring that they can only watch and murmur "Jesus."

The canyon where Paul is fishing is a worthy opponent for such a fisherman. It is where the Blackfoot "roars loudest," so powerful that even Meriwether Lewis skirted it, "no place for small fish or fishermen." Yet Paul swims it casually, in his clothes, with one hand holding his rod high and his fish basket hung on his shoulder. So sure are his instincts, in fact, that he does not even pause to study the river before plunging in.

If we postpone momentarily a consideration of why this mythic western hero has come to be fly fishing, there is no doubt that Paul is another in a long line of such heroes. The hero's superiority is immediately evident to the admiring observer—especially to the observer/narrator, a figure whose previous incarnations include an easterner in *The Virginian* and a child in *Shane*. Paul is almost godlike, ringed by a halo and holding a magic totem pole. And the patterns of his casts merge with the patterns of the vapor and the wind and the sun, creating a mystical unity of man and nature—a momentary unity also achieved by western heroes from Deerslayer to the Virginian to (later in this story) Norman Maclean himself.

Paul is also the sort of loner idealized by American literature in general and idolized in lower case westerns. He never marries, knows he will never leave Montana, seeks neither wealth nor status, and refuses all offers of help. He neither puts his problems into words nor acknowledges their severity. This insistence on reticent self-sufficiency ranges from a refusal to borrow flies to a refusal to accept a loan which might save his life, since his eventual murder apparently stems from unpaid gambling debts. At the same time that he refuses to accept aid, however, he renders it with unself-conscious generosity, swimming the river in order to lend flies to the brother from whom he refused to borrow them, and taking time off to go fishing when his brother needs that escape. The twin strands of Paul's character—his willingness to help those less capable plus his adherence to a credo of tight-lipped "toughing it out"—are lineal descendants of the western code perpetuated by authors from James Fenimore Cooper to Louis L'Amour.

Maclean never uses the word *code* to describe Paul's beliefs, but he hardly needs to. The credo is described with such precision, and its elements are so familiar, that we recognize it instantly for what it is—witness Wallace Stegner's constant use of *code* in discussing Maclean's work (which he links to the Montana of his own youth). Paul's firm code includes a determination never to be bested, and absolute fidelity to his word—having given it, he never "kicks" about keeping it. Most of all, however, Paul's code centers around the ritual of fly fishing, mandating that "real" fishermen be on time, despite pains of morning fatigue or hangover, and that they not steal each other's beer. Paul never drinks while fishing (beer is not "drink") but reaches for a bottle as soon as he is finished. And he reserves his greatest scorn for those who "fish" with worms—especially worms collected in a red Hills Brothers coffee can.

The westerner's desire to die with his boots on is reflected in the consolation which Norman and his father take in the fact that Paul, beaten to death in a back alley, has not died before breaking every bone in his right hand (his fishing hand) fighting back. And the westerner's favorite object of scorn, the tenderfoot who will never understand the code, is reincarnated in Neal, an offensive brother-in-law who, though born in Montana, has moved to California— which Paul describes as the migratory destination for failed fly fishermen—and returns wearing tennis sweaters. When Neal decides to go fishing he remembers the worms in the red can but forgets his rod. Because he is *not* in fact an easterner, but a failed westerner, there is no chance Montana can make a man of Neal. He has had his chance, and he has failed to learn the lessons the West has to teach. For such an individual there can be no salvation.

Maclean's recasting of the western myth into fly fishing terms affords opportunities for spiritual examination and growth, as commentators like Glen Love and Wendell Berry have pointed out. But it also involves him in more problematic aspects of the myth. Like every classic western hero before them, Maclean and his brother prefer a world without women, and the masculinity of the fly fishing domain is one of its prime attractions.

In Maclean's world women do not fish. That in itself is not a problem, given the right of individuals to select their own activities. But the implications of this masculine narrative are more far-reaching than may at first appear. Fly fishing is clearly the most desirable activity in this imperfect world, but it is an activity unavailable to women, who if they visit the river at all go there to pick huckleberries or to fix sandwiches for the men who fish. Before what turns out to be Maclean's last fishing trip with his father and brother, his mother (who has not been invited to accompany them) helps to locate the gear his father has not used in years. She knew, the narrator tells us, "nothing about fishing or fishing tackle, but she knew how to find things, even when she did not know what they looked like." His mother-in-law has an equally carefully defined role.

> She knew how to clean fish when the men forgot to, and she knew how to cook them, and, most important, she knew always to peer into the fisherman's basket and exclaim "My, my!" so she knew all that any woman of her time knew about fishing, although it is also true that she knew absolutely nothing about fishing.

The women in Maclean's family are bonded in a female community which nurses and supports and loves—but which knows nothing about the heroic, meditative activity of fishing. They, however, have sense enough not to try to participate in the true significance of fishing. A passing stranger is not so wise. Having impressed Maclean initially with her bulging "motherly breasts," she inquires whether he will stay to see Paul land his fish. Maclean's reply seems designed to emphasize her inability to comprehend the true significance of fishing.

> "No," I answered, "I'd rather remember the molecules."
>
> She obviously thought I was crazy, so I added, "I'll see his fish later." And to make any sense for her I had to add, "He's my brother."

The deliberate riddling, the implication that important sense is beyond this woman, and the fact that the young Norman's emotional and verbal distancing are addressed to her, not to her equally present (but more appropriately reticent) husband, reveal his protectiveness of fishing as an exclusively masculine preserve. And it is fishing which, properly undertaken, is most likely to yield genuine understanding.

So clearly linked are fishing and masculinity, in fact, that Maclean and his brother (like Huck and Deerslayer and Shane before them) are often fleeing the troubling world of women when they light out for the river. At the same time, of course, the brothers are motivated by awareness that "To women who do not fish, men who come home without their limit are failures in life"—an analysis oddly similar to the one which suggests that men go to war because women are watching. In either case, the story clearly presents what Simone de Beauvoir first identified as Woman as Other.

In describing this gender-divided world, Maclean the author often seems unaware of the implications. "We regarded [the Big Blackfoot] as a family river," he admits, obscuring the fact that only the male part of his family knew the river well. And "each one in our family considered himself the leading authority on how to fish the Blackfoot." The masculine pronoun *himself* is more than a grammatical convention here, since it accurately reflects the reality that no woman in his family presumed any authority about fishing. But Maclean's easy assumption that "each one in our family" is a *himself* is revealing.

Asserting that Maclean is generally unaware of the implications of such word choices is, of course, a tenuous proposition, one dependent on what is *not* included. What is not included in passages revealing the gender division of this world is the balance of voices Maclean achieves in much of the rest of the narrative, where younger and older selves are regularly juxtaposed so that the tale takes full advantage of the gain in perspective which comes with age. That faintly ironic tone about the foolishnesses of youth cannot be heard when Maclean is using elements of the western myth.

This absence of awareness in the narrative is illustrated if two similar passages from Maclean's other works are juxtaposed. First, a section from a 1978 speech **"Teaching and Story Telling."**

> In our family, men folk did not go around saying they loved each other. In our family, nature was a medium of our love, a carrier of it, an object of it, a cause of it. We loved each other because we loved the same sights and sounds and rivers, because we recognized, not only that we were part of it but that all of us in some ways were masters of it—swinging an axe, building our log cabins, leading ducks on the wing, noting Caddis flies hatching from the bottom of shallow water in early September, and just leaning on the oars at sunset. And we knew that nature was often the master of us, and we loved both nature and ourselves because of that. Any description of nature in this story has something to do about family love.

This passage is very close to the one quoted earlier from *River.* In it, *family* clearly means *male family. Men* don't say they love each other. Further, though some women may indeed have mastered nature, Maclean's mother—judging by everything he has ever written about her—never swung an axe, built a cabin, or fly fished. "Family love" is too broad a term for what Maclean is describing. "Fraternal love" would be closer.

Second, a snippet from a 1984 interview.

> My family . . . didn't talk much about how much we loved each other. Fishing is where we all opened our hearts, including my mother.
> ("Two Worlds")

In this second passage Maclean's phrasing hints at a greater degree of awareness about the gender-specific nature of his approach. In the interview's relatively full three-paragraph passage about "family love," every example refers to his relationship with his father or his brother. The phrase "including my mother" stands out awkwardly, an assertion unsupported by evidence, but a brief reminder (to us? to himself?) that Maclean knows that the twenty-five per cent of his immediate family represented by his mother should be included in a discussion of "family love."

The self-conscious inclusion of his mother in the passage is doubly odd because it contrasts with the entire body of Maclean's work: stories, essays and interviews all suggest that if his mother went on fishing trips at all, it was only to sit on the bank and make sandwiches. Perhaps her inclusion (however brief) in this discussion of fishing's more significant spiritual aspects indicates a heightened awareness on Maclean's part of the restrictive masculinity of his memories of fishing.

In any case, one thing is clear in *A River Runs Through It:* fishing is masculine. Fishing is also an indication of virility, and handling a rod well is important in more than one sense. Explaining why the tennis-appareled brother-in-law wants to go fishing, the character Norman observes: "he doesn't like to fish. He just likes to tell women he likes to fish. It does something for him and the women."

Neal may be eager to impress women, but the narrative as a whole indicates that women constantly threaten emasculation. Mary Clearman Blew has convincingly identified in Paul's Northern Cheyenne girl a descendant of "the sensual and destructive Dark Women out of the mainstream of American fiction." The Cheyenne girl is also, as Blew notes, a descendant of a great-grandmother who "helped cut the testicles off Custer's still living troops," and she clearly represents a danger to Paul—both in her own right and because she allows him to act on his own most self-destructive impulses. But "good" women as well as "bad" are a threat in this Montana world. Denied

Maclean's father, John Norman Maclean.

admittance to the covered truck bed which shelters the others from the rain, for example, Maclean (who had offended the women by failing to take adequate care of the brother-in-law) pokes his head through the sheltering canvas and sees the glitter of slashing cutlery: "When the women weren't using their hardware to make sandwiches . . . they were pointing it at me." The instruments of nurture are simultaneously instruments of threat, and although Maclean says he's worried about his *throat*, one wonders.

In one of the funniest episodes of the story, Neal manages to violate all elements of the fly fishing code. He forgets his rod, brings his worms, drinks whiskey, and steals beer. Worst of all, however, he brings a woman with him and conducts a minor orgy which leaves them lying on a sandbar, sunburned in embarrassing places. The woman, Old Rawhide, is a particularly unattractive version of the western whore, lacking any semblance of the mythic heart of gold (possession of which might have made her understand why she should not go fishing). Old Rawhide is in sharp opposition to the "virgin" family women who have sense enough to remain at home. But the heightened, tall-tale elements serve unintentionally to underscore what seems to be the real crime—the intrusion of *any* woman into this masculine idyll.

Neal's actions are described as a "violation" of the fishing ritual, and when Paul disposes of Old Rawhide by kicking her right between the LO and the VE tattooed on her buttocks, it is clear that he is disposing of more than one particular whore. That, no doubt, is why he does not kick Neal as well: the violation may have been masculine, but it is the woman who needs to be disposed of. The narrator suggests that Old Rawhide is a surrogate for Neal, who can't be touched because his sister (Norman's wife) and his mother (Norman's mother-in-law) have asked Norman to look out for him. That explanation leaves the basic situation unchanged. The fault is woman's—good women ask what they should not; bad women go where they should not; and even mythic heroes are hapless when the frontier gives way to Petticoat Junction.

The confrontation between Paul, laconic representative of the real West, and Old Rawhide, the whore whose presence threatens to rob fly fishing of its spiritual value, begins, Maclean informs us, at high noon, "Just as if the scene had been taken for a Western film." And one sign of Paul's heroic stature is his ability to deliver this dismissive kick in the ass, a feat which Norman, who tries it later, cannot manage. Old Rawhide's defeat, however, is not without ironies. The Maclean brothers have difficulty dislodging her from Neal's side, where she clings with a tenacious insistence that "I'm your woman. I'll take care of you." And it is Old Rawhide who helps the sunburned, drunken Neal back across the water from the sandbar to the shore, even though she is not in much better shape than he is. This sturdy individual, whose name indicates her toughness and durability, has partially assumed the role usually reserved for the heroic male protector. The Maclean brothers are not amused by the inverted relationship between Old Rawhide and Neal.

Popular western myth, with its simplistic distinction be-

tween good guys and bad guys and its innately virtuous hero, has always had parallels with the Calvinism so deeply ingrained in much of American life. Paul's vulnerability to sexual women—to the Indian woman who tempts him and to the white woman who challenges him—reminds us of another link between western mythology and Calvinism, for both distrust women, especially sexual women. Paul's Cheyenne girl and Old Rawhide do not *cause* his failure (at least not entirely) but his inability to deal with them signals a fatal weakness in his character and women in general threaten his world. The Emersonian responsiveness to the healing power of nature which is also part of western mythology is finally not enough to save Paul.

A disturbing aspect of Maclean's exclusion of women from the world of fly fishing and spiritual quest goes beyond its apparent denial of these opportunities to women. Ultimately the implication is that such heroic ventures are impossible for *either* sex in a heterosexual world. And so the preferences which show in Paul Maclean's life patterns and in Norman Maclean's language choices continue increasingly anachronistic patterns of disconnection between men and women.

Maclean's use of mythic western patterns may stem from his conception of story telling as a male activity—both teller and listeners are male. He originally told these stories to his children, for whom he set out to create "pictures of how *men and horses* did things in Western parts of the world" (emphasis added). But his first public presentation of autobiographical material, in the mid-1970s, was to an all male club, Stochastics (the Thinkers), who refer to the yearly meeting at which wives are allowed as their "heterosexual meeting." (*River*). Maclean has identified his storytelling models as the bunkhouse story in which "a lot happens" (**"Teaching"**) and the tale told next to a Forest Service campfire (**"Hidden Art"**). Western storytelling seems not in fact to have been an exclusively male activity, but the models Maclean cites are all masculine. In his Montana there are no Scheherazades and the EEOC has not yet encountered the bunkhouse or the USFS—and so his tales naturally take on overtones of male bonding or male rites of passage. The readings for the Stochastics and the regular appearance in *Esquire* of articles by and about Maclean seem natural extensions of the male storytelling models.

Ordinarily, the typical western hero Paul so clearly resembles duplicates the actions of his mythological folk hero precursors and battles the forces of evil to a standstill. But Paul is ignominiously defeated when he should have been righteously triumphant. This is a tale of Paradise Lost, and the nostalgic tone is unsurprising. "What a beautiful world it was once," when no one stole beer, and when "unselected inhabitants of Great Falls and the Moorish invaders from California" had not usurped the Blackfoot. Like Deerslayer and Jeremiah Johnson and the Brave Cowboy before them, the Macleans are forced to realize that their world is doomed by the very American spirit and culture which opened it originally. And that doom, as was the case in other losses of Paradise, is linked with the coming of women. What Walker Percy, in another context, has called the "nomadic, bachelor West" gives way to the "housed, married West." Fly fishing is where western masculinity makes its last stand.

From one point of view it seems odd to make of fly fishing an activity whose significance looms so monumentally. Does it really make sense for men casting into the waters of Montana's Blackfoot to envision themselves as rightful heirs of the skills and prerogatives of generations of western folk heroes? Is not the very notion of a code oddly diminished when it prohibits Hills Brothers cans and tennis sweaters but allows the "hero" to kick a woman and drop her off partially naked on the edge of town? Used in this context, the idea of a code too often seems foolish, a case of life imitating art and men attempting to assert significance for their actions by casting them in heroic modes. These questions remain not just unanswered, but also unexplored in Maclean's story. Similarly unexplored is the possibility that what really destroys Paul is not a corrupt world, but Paul's own unthinking adherence to an outmoded myth.

As Maclean presents it, Paul's experience matches that of Deerslayer and Jeremiah Johnson and Huck Finn in many ways. Not the least of those ways is that all these males find that the greatest dangers in life lie not in the power and vagaries of nature, which they can master, but in the ugliness of society which—if they do not flee it—will first corrupt and then destroy them. Paul, the master of the river, is mastered by the town. Drink, gambling, back alley brawling, and the attractions of a dark woman with beautiful legs join forces to corrupt his heroic status. He is an American Adam without a Virgin Land to which to flee— or so Maclean would have us believe.

There is, however, another possibility suggested by the evidence Maclean presents. Paul's difficulties may in fact be a result not just of the corruptions of civilization, but also of his own adherence to a credo which no longer matches his world. Paul refuses to accept help from his father and brother, or even to discuss his problems. He adheres to an ideal of self-sufficient male behavior, going it alone without admitting difficulties or accepting help (an ideal now frequently labeled "macho"). At one point Maclean begins to explore the implications of Paul's choice.

> [T]he Greeks . . . believed that not wanting any help might even get you killed. Then I suddenly remembered that my brother was almost always a winner and often because he didn't borrow flies. So I decided that the response we make to character on any given day depends largely on the response fish are making to character on the same day.

That, however, is as far as Maclean pushes his thinking on the subject, shifting "rapidly back to reality" and concentrating on his fishing.

There are considerable ironies in Maclean's failure to explore fully the possibilities that Paul's code may be his major problem. Maclean admires his brother (sometimes excessively), and his dominant tone in describing Paul is reverential. Yet Norman Maclean himself, the brother who is "saved," does not observe the rigidities of the code which shapes his brother's life. He marries, he actually talks to his father, he both asks for and accepts help when

he needs it. One of the story's most important moments comes when Norman, repenting the difficulties caused when he and Paul leave Neal to burn (literally and metaphorically) in the sun, is reconciled with the women in his family. One by one they come out of the sickroom and embrace Norman, each in her separate way letting him know that he is forgiven and that all is well between them. It is a scene involving mutual respect, love, and support which crosses gender barriers. It is also a scene in which it is impossible to imagine Paul.

In the 1930s the western myth of independent masculinity no longer matched, if it ever had, even Montana, last outpost of the "real West." Paul's adherence to a frontier pattern, in the absence of a new territory to escape to, seems the greatest tragedy of all. Had he been able to reach out to those who were reaching out to him, to accept their support and perhaps their help, he might not have been overwhelmed by his difficulties. But that is a possibility Norman Maclean considers only in his passing hint that fish are responding differently to character these days, and Paul's is a tragedy he never directly confronts. The contrast between Paul's experience and Norman's experience is not one Maclean analyzes. It speaks only between the lines of his tale.

In tracing the beginnings of his story to his feeling that the patterns of his life joined the patterns of the river, Maclean voices his understanding "that stories of life are often more like rivers than books." He goes on, however, to describe his sense that "ahead I would meet something that would never erode so there would be a sharp turn, deep circles, a deposit, and quietness." It is Paul's death which will never erode. And one reason that it will not erode— for writer or for reader—is that Maclean fails to analyze the inadequacy of the western myth as a pattern for his brother's life.

A River Runs Through It, then, perpetuates a worldview which has strict limitations. An insider, accepting the framework of the myth, Norman Maclean never steps outside his world long enough for significant analysis of its limitations. Making such a charge about a work I find deeply moving always leaves me with a nagging sense that I am being ungracious (and ungracious is the most gracious term male colleagues have used in protesting my analysis). But I believe these things need to be said. Like the loops of gossamer formed by Paul's fishing line, the loops of western myth, with its gender-divided world, are often difficult to see. And like those fishing-line loops, the myth's restrictions as well as its values have been retained in our memories and continue to shape American life and American literature. We need to recognize the restrictions as well as the values. (pp. 145-56)

> *Helen Lojek, "Casting Flies and Recasting Myths with Norman Maclean," in* Western American Literature, *Vol. XXV, No. 2, August, 1990, pp. 145-56.*

Christopher Lehmann-Haupt   (review date 10 August 1992)

[*Lehmann-Haupt is a Scottish-born American educator*

and chief book reviewer for The New York Times. *In the following review, he favorably assesses* Young Men and Fire.]

Norman Maclean's *Young Men and Fire* is a reconstruction of the catastrophic Mann Gulch forest fire, which blazed over some 4,500 acres in the mountains of western Montana on Aug. 5, 1949. The first question the story raises is, why did the author choose to write it as a factual report instead of imagining it as fiction?

After all, the best way to describe a forest fire would seem to be from inside it, and the best way to do that would be to imagine it, unless you happened to be right there in the middle of it, which Mr. Maclean was not. Moreover, he had proved his ability to make fiction out of fact, if one can judge from his previous book, a collection of three stories based on his rowdy Montana youth that he put together after retiring from his position as a professor of English at the University of Chicago in 1973. It was called *A River Runs Through It and Other Stories,* and the title piece, about fly-fishing and spiritual redemption, has achieved the fame of a minor classic since the book first appeared in 1976.

The answer to why Mr. Maclean wrote *Young Men and Fire* as nonfiction lies in the particular circumstances of the Mann Gulch fire. It produced a high percentage of casualties: of the 15 so-called smoke jumpers who parachuted into the mountains to fight it, only 3 survived. And it was one of the least understood, because what began as an apparently small, containable fire that had been ignited by a bolt of lightning, suddenly blew up into a deadly holocaust.

Of the three survivors, two were resourceful enough to outrace the flames and dive through a crevice in a rock formation near the ridge on the north side of the gulch. The third, the foreman of the crew, R. Wagner Dodge, judged that the rest of his men could not outrun the flames and so improvised an "escape fire" by igniting an unburned area of grass, waiting the few seconds it took to burn a bare patch, lying down in its ashes and ordering his men to join him. The men, thinking him crazy, chose to race for the ridge. They didn't make it. In the aftermath, though Dodge's actions were supported by a review board, there were many who believed that it was the escape fire that had burned some of the men instead of the main fire.

So when Mr. Maclean decided to confront the Mann Gulch fire, he faced several challenges that required him to write about it factually. First, he needed something to do. With his wife dead of esophageal cancer and his academic career ended now that he was past 70, he wanted to exercise his "homespun anti-shuffle-board philosophy of what to do when I was old enough to be scripturally dead." He wanted to answer certain practical questions so that future smoke jumpers could learn from the incident instead of being mystified by it: What had caused the fire to blow up? Why had the survivors escaped? Was Dodge wrong to have built his escape fire?

He also needed to exorcise some of his own ghosts. As a young man he had once been forced to outrace a forest fire. The experience had haunted him all his life. What made him different from the brave young men who had died? Finally, he needed to learn whatever details there might be that would elevate a catastrophe into the realm of tragedy. As he writes, "There must have been a good many reasons drawing me back to the job, and certainly one of them was that, the more accurately the race between fire and crew was analyzed, the more it took on the form of the plot of a tragedy emerging from concealed to complete inevitability."

As it turns out *Young Men and Fire* suffers little handicap from having been written as fact instead of fiction. Mr. Maclean gives us a taste of what is to come by describing a "terribly burned" deer he saw drinking insatiably from a stream shortly after the Mann Gulch fire, its eyes "red bulbs that illuminated long hairs around its eyelids." When the deer saw the author, it bounded off "euphorically," ran into a fallen log and died.

He evokes the hell of the conflagration with details of rolling rocks and exploding trees and tiny dust devils of flame that suddenly rise up into apocalyptic whirlwinds. He describes rescuers coming upon a smoke jumper named Joe Sylvia, who, like that deer, was "badly burned and euphorically happy." "Say, fellows," he greeted his rescuers cheerfully, "I don't think I'll be able to walk out of here." Within 12 hours his kidneys had given out and he was dead.

Remarkably, the drama of Mr. Maclean's report even heightens when, years after they occurred, he attempts to reconstruct the events of the fire. Summer after summer, for at least a dozen years, he went back and explored Mann Gulch. One afternoon he noticed the odd patterns in which the trunks of the dead trees were lying on the slopes beside the gulch. From these he and companions were able to deduce how the winds must have formed to create the mysterious blow-up. Returning with two of the three survivors he witnessed an intriguing drama involving their failing memories of the terrain.

Finally, the issues of *Young Men and Fire* boiled down to making computer models of the rate at which fires race over ground under various circumstances. The vital question was could Dodge's escape fire have saved the men had they obeyed him? Or might they have made it to the ridge had he not started it?

Here Mr. Maclean's narrative grows unduly deliberate and a little tedious. As his editors explain in an introductory note to the volume, he slowed down badly near the end of the project and was unable to finish it. But he did reach certain conclusions. The men who had failed to survive the Mann Gulch fire had not suffered "terrible" deaths. "It is something like drowning," a doctor told him. He ends his story surprisingly: "I have lived to get a better understanding of myself and those close to me, many of them now dead. Perhaps it is not odd, at the end of this tragedy where nothing much was left of the elite who came from the sky but courage struggling for oxygen, that I have often found myself thinking of my wife on her brave and lonely way to death."

And perhaps of himself. He would die in 1990, at the age of 87.

Christopher Lehmann-Haupt, "Exorcising Ghosts of Searing Flames," in The New York Times, *August 10, 1992, p. C18.*

James R. Kincaid (review date 16 August 1992)

[*Kincaid is an American critic and educator who has written extensively on nineteenth-century literature. In the following review, Kincaid discusses Maclean's use of tragic elements in* Young Men and Fire.]

On Aug. 5, 1949, at about 4:10 on the hottest afternoon ever recorded in the Montana mountains, 15 cocky Forest Service smoke jumpers were, one by one, patted on the left calf, the signal to walk into the sky and float downward to fight a fire in the rugged wilderness. They regarded the fire as routine, figured they would be home by the next morning. They were, you see, terribly young, most of them really boys and "not very big boys" at that. The Forest Service preferred very young men for stamina and agility, and, as Norman Maclean says in *Young Men & Fire,* it placed height and weight limits on recruits since big men "don't seem to be made to drop out of the sky."

Because the drop into Mann Gulch, a place that was about to become infamous in the history of firefighting, had been made from almost twice the usual height, the men's gear was scattered and it took them until 5 o'clock to gather it, eat a quick meal and start up the gulch and into the burning forest. Their leader, R. Wagner (Wag) Dodge, scouted the extent of the fire and took a lunch break before joining them at 5:20. Mann Gulch, up near where the Missouri River begins its long cruise down to the Mississippi, is a place where, as Maclean says, two totally different geological regions of the continent seem to come suddenly together, on the one side the Great Plains end and on the other the Rocky Mountains begin a precipitous rise. On the Rockies side the vegetation was a dense growth of towering pine, on the Plains side scatterings of lighter, mixed timber and a dense carpet of waist-high prairie grass climbing up the three-and-a-half-mile length of the gulch.

The fire had been started by lightning on the Rockies side among the trees and appeared relatively small to observers from the air and on the ground little more than an hour before. But there was a great updraft in the scorching gulch. When Dodge joined his crew, he did not like what he saw and got his men out of woods he regarded now as a "death trap" and over to the other, grassy side of the gulch. But the hot fire crossed the gulf too, in a leap, and, hitting the grass, began to move far more quickly. Seeing this, Dodge reversed direction and began to pull the men back up the hill with him.

And then the fire exploded, forming itself into whirls that created spinning fire funnels—a "blow-up" that soon made a solid front nearly 300 feet deep and 200 feet tall, a roaring 2,000-degree monster chasing the men up the mountain. It was now about 5:40. They had a 200-yard head start at most and it was a gulch with a 76 percent slope, so steep that Norman Maclean on a visit years later had to crawl and hold himself in place by clutching the grass. It was never a fair race. It was the race we run in nightmares.

They were now 16 strong, one Forest Service man on patrol having accidentally met them, "and he might as well have run into General Custer and the Seventh Cavalry on June 26, 1876," Maclean remarks. Headed for the top at a pace no one since has been able to duplicate in attempts at reconstruction, they found themselves blocked by an irregular ridge yards below the summit, the remains of a prehistoric ocean reef. Perhaps, but only perhaps, they were also blocked by a strategy hatched by their leader, Wag Dodge. Ahead of them he lit what he called an "escape fire," a fire in the embers of which he was able to lie face down and live while the main fire passed over him seconds later. It was that escape fire that made Mann Gulch a milestone in the history of forest firefighting and Maclean treats it as the elusive clue that can be explained, if ever, only at the very end of his search. Without giving too much away, it can be said that Dodge, knowing that the huge firestorm sweeping up behind with the speed of a tornado would kill his men by suffocation as it burned all the oxygen out of the air around it, also knew or guessed that if there was a space where there was no fuel to be added to the main fire, there might also be a thin layer of oxygen inches above the ground. So he quickly burned off a plot of grass and lay flat on the smoldering embers.

But, as Maclean points out, a firestorm not only blots out vision with sheets of flame and torrents of smoke; its approach is made known by a roar like that of a train barreling out of a tunnel. For whatever reason—perhaps they could not see or hear him—none of the men heeded Dodge's pleas to enter this redemptive fire with him, and 13 perished, never quite reaching the reef or caught from behind as they ran parallel to it searching for an opening. In the following week, Forest Service rangers placed a wooden cross at the spot where each body was found, and today concrete crosses with the names of the men in bronze still stand in those places. To give some notion of how rapidly the fire devoured the gulch, one need only remember that when it was first spotted, it covered barely 60 acres and it had not grown spectacularly by the time the smoke jumpers arrived; from the time it leaped the gulch after 5:20 until it swept over the top of the mountain just before 6 o'clock it had destroyed between seven and eight square miles.

The two smoke jumpers who survived along with Dodge, Robert Sallee and Walter Rumsey, managed to escape, though barely, by reaching Dodge's fire first and following its upper edge, using it as a buffer until they could find an opening in the reef. With the fire pounding their backs they squeezed through a crevice, whereupon Rumsey fell exhausted into a juniper bush and would have stayed there and died had not Sallee stopped and stared at him so coldly he was shamed into motion. The two, roommates at the jumpers' camp, then outscrambled the fire to the top of the mountain and stumbled luckily into a rockslide on the other side. There they dodged backward and forward as the inferno swept over the mountain and around them. Rumsey and Sallee were very young, Sallee at 17 actually a year younger than the minimum smoke jumper age, and this had been their first jump onto a fire. Though two other smoke jumpers lived a few hours until they died of their burns, the members of the group who were veterans were now mostly just scattered corpses on the other side of the reef. A watch belonging to one of the dead was found the next day, torn from the body and blown by the fire yards away, its hands frozen at 5:56.

Norman Maclean died before he could finish shaping this catastrophe into a tragedy, refusing to be a mere "historian" and taking on the more dangerous role of "storyteller," following "compassion wherever it leads him" and bearing witness to the horror and greatness of the dead. "They were young," he says, "and did not leave much behind them and need someone to remember them." They could not have found a storyteller with a better claim to represent their honor or to call for our attention.

Maclean, who as a fisherman explored the rivers near Mann Gulch for much of his life, taught English at the University of Chicago for 43 years before he retired in 1973. But a brief part of his university career must have given him special advantages in investigating the Mann Gulch fire and writing precisely and vividly about it: from 1943 to 1945 he headed the university's Institute of Military Studies and was co-author of a wartime text, *A Manual of Instruction in Military Maps and Aerial Photographs.* After his retirement, he had warmed up for *Young Men & Fire* by writing *A River Runs Through It and Other Stories* (1976), also set on the Missouri River, just one gulch downstream from the Mann Gulch fire. The earlier work seems, in comparison, protected and thin, Thoreau and soda: it's a nostalgic-paranoid celebration of fly-fishing set over against its enemies—those who use bait, steal the beer and bring women along with them.

There is a tiny strain of *Young Men & Fire* that is similar bicep-flexing: Maclean compares the smoke jumpers to Marines, Shriners, Knights of Columbus and other groups having "dim ties seemingly with religion," all of whom are striving, he says, to say to the cosmos "that they love the universe but are not intimidated by it." If this sort of juvenile-macho blather were continuous, we might regard the Mann Gulch catastrophe as simply a fraternity initiation gone wrong; but generally when Maclean moves upriver to the next ravine, he stands in a far sterner artistic world, one that has no room for cornball pastoral.

It is, however, a multilayered world, holding not simply or even mainly the Mann Gulch fire but Maclean's search to get at the truth of that fire, at the truth of his own artistry and his own mortality, at the truth of tragic form. By the time we are a third of the way through the book, the Mann Gulch fire has cooled and Maclean is trying to encircle a different kind of enemy. The major story now is his attempt to mold this tragedy and to confront his own life and approaching death. He does so by telling other and related stories, examining documents, conducting interviews, learning new science and new art, and returning obsessively to the site where the young men lost the race with the monster.

This last two-thirds of the book dramatizes its writing: "The only poem I had a chance of writing about the Mann Gulch fire was the truth about it." He tells of Harry Gisborne, a scientist who died of a heart attack on the slopes of Mann Gulch while investigating the fire in November 1949, and who learned just at the end that his theories didn't hold—a good way, Maclean says, to die, "excitedly finding we were wrong and excitedly waiting for tomorrow to come so we can start over."

The sense of being wrong haunts Maclean, and yet he hugs it, returning again and again to Mann Gulch not so much to win a brawl with truth as to pay his respects to her and hope for a few gifts. Even as he is crawling the fatally sheer slopes in 1978 with the two remaining survivors, and worrying over whether the crosses are accurately placed to mark the 13 deaths, Maclean is gathering death to himself, imagining what it must have been like to be so close to safety, so high on the hill and "not quite high enough."

Maclean is inside the fire in a way even the survivors are not. Walter Rumsey and Robert Sallee confidently locate on their return visit the opening in the crevice through which they escaped, wondering only that the juniper bush has disappeared. It is Maclean who later finds the actual, much narrower, slot they made it through, and the same juniper bush where one of them nearly rested to death.

He is always with the brave young dead—from the time of his first arrival on the spot a few days after the 1949 disaster. The editors of this volume open it with a story, written in the first person, that was found among Maclean's papers. They did not know how he intended to use it, but it makes a fine beginning. The narrator, like the author, had gone out there to fish and stayed to invest himself with this tragedy, soon finding the fire gossip of the local postmistress insufficient and moving in on Mann Gulch himself while it was still smoking. The fire never left Maclean, though he did not begin this book about it until 1976, when he was 74. He was forced to abandon the writing a few years before his death in 1990, in his 88th year, but he never quit trying to get a trench around this terrible blaze.

In his relentless circling of the fire and the story, Maclean is faithful above all to its mystery, to how much can never be known. The most spectacular mystery is still whether Dodge's fire, set as an escape, was, in fact, what devoured his crew or at least forced them away from their only exit through the ridge into a sideways and losing race with the main fire. But that debate is only part of a larger, uglier spectacle of charges and evasions. Almost immediately a public outcry against the Forest Service arose, led by the father of 19-year-old Henry Thol, whose cross is closest to the top of the ridge. Henry Thol Sr., himself a retired forest ranger, and representatives of three other dead jumpers filed eight damage suits charging negligence and denouncing every one of the major orders given to the jumpers as an "unpardonable error in woodsmanship." The Forest Service, Maclean argues, responded by coaching or bullying key witnesses into altering their official statements, by retouching and reshaping some official documents, by burying others and scattering more, and by apparently hiding seven or eight recovered watches so that the one released would seem to indicate the official time of death.

In his account, the aging investigator, Maclean, drives some distance to interview A. J. Cramer, a Forest Service investigator at the time of the fire, who by this time is retired and living on a beautiful Montana lake feeding geese. Maclean's questions so frighten the other old man that his distressed wife steps in to protect him, says he does not remember, has had an operation, "brain trouble." Graciously, Maclean leaves, and leaves behind him unsolved one of the small mysteries within the great mystery he is confronting.

He is concerned above all with honoring the dead and with finding himself through that honor, all of which he can do, he says, by being true to "my homespun anti-shuffle-board philosophy": "The nearest anyone can come to finding himself at any given age is to find a story that somehow tells him about himself." For Maclean, that story is clearly tragedy, a tragedy based on primal terrors looked full in the face, acknowledged, even joked with: "I felt another trip to Mann Gulch coming on." When Maclean reached the top of his ridge, the fire eating through him from behind, he turned and embraced it.

His version of tragedy is hard won, first because it drives so unswervingly to the center of horror: the awful sense of multiple traps. The airplane jumper, in his "equipment made by the lowest bidder," becomes "thinned out to the vanishing point of being only decisions once made that he can't do anything about ever after." Then we are trapped in the terror of being outside temperature ranges we can tolerate and, worst of all, in a chase where we are the game with the much-faster monster nipping at our heels, grabbing at our ankles as we try to draw them up, reaching out from under the bed. This monster will not go away; it will get us any second now.

Worse than primal terror is the possibility of meaninglessness, and Maclean's most courageous struggle is with literary forms. For the sake of these dead men and for his own sake, he cannot allow the deaths to be pointless, accidents that offer neither redemption nor purgation. Refusing to leave us in "moral bewilderment," he conducts a search "for the carefully measured grains of consolation needed to transform catastrophe into tragedy." This is a modern tragedy, he believes, not a classical drama of "a monumental individual crossing the sword of his will with the sword of destiny" but a collective tragedy, the "tragedy of a crew," a tragedy of "little details rather than big flaws," a tragedy, he concedes, of "screwups" rather than the errors of gods.

But is it any kind of tragedy? Maclean plays this drama of writing as fully before us as the drama of the fire, indeed he makes them the same. The fire threatens to obliterate all meaning: "viewing total conflagration is literally blinding." It threatens to reduce these gallant heroes to desperate animals caught running away in panic. Still, Maclean holds, "although young men died like squirrels in Mann Gulch, the Mann Gulch fire should not end there, smoke drifting away and leaving terror without consolation of explanation." Why should it not? Is it a thirst for truth that

drives Maclean through his heroic writing or a tragic resistance of his own to the possibility that there is no pattern, no tragedy, no story that can hold its form?

He does what great artists have always done: refuse to give up on the shapes they can find in or impress on their materials. And so he remains true to the power of his own language and his own heart. He does not lie. He finds in these young smoke jumpers the classic hubris, the heartbreaking panache, with which they tackled all fires, never realizing that their very facility in keeping all little fires little was unfitting them for dealing with a big fire. He brilliantly traces the small details, which, as in "Othello" or "Oedipus Rex," build to overwhelming force; he calls them "screwups," true, but they have the same dignity and terrifying force as Desdemona's handkerchief.

As in much sublime tragedy, a comic subplot drains off some of the absurdity that might otherwise corrupt the main story. Maclean tells of a movement against the Mann Gulch fire from the bottom, a squadron manned by drunks recruited from bar stools as volunteers, drunks who would rather have stayed "alive on a stool exposed to the possibility of being converted by the Salvation Army than be found dead on a fireline"—"like the rest of us," he says, "but perhaps more so."

Maybe the acid test of tragedy is its redemptive quality, and in this case, in at least a practical sense, the Mann Gulch terror was formed into a series of lessons, improvements, new training techniques that have kept the smoke jumpers free from that time of any deaths by fire. Finally, Maclean allows into his conception of tragedy so much uncertainty and mystery that perhaps it simply includes the absurd: "There's a lot of tragedy in the universe that has missing parts and comes to no conclusion, including probably the tragedy that awaits you and me."

This great book takes us to that ancient reef blocking us from the summit and then whirls and looks straight into the heart of the fire. It is that valiant honesty that allows it to stand against the fire and hold its own even as the flames advance over it.

At the end, as Maclean takes his beautifully hard prose toward death, he thinks not of himself or his victory over these recalcitrant materials, but of the young men and of his wife, who had died of cancer two decades earlier: "Perhaps it is not odd, at the end of this tragedy where nothing much was left of the elite who came from the sky but courage struggling for oxygen, that I have often found myself thinking of my wife on her brave and lonely way to death." Earlier he had remarked about the silly drunks, ennobled by their effort and their fire-tuned hearts: "One of the finest things men and women do is rescue men and women, even when they know they are rescuing the dead." Maclean has done that and more; his heroic tragedy may even rescue some of the living, some of us. (pp. 1, 27-8)

James R. Kincaid, "With the Brave Young Dead," in The New York Times Book Review, *August 16, 1992, pp. 1, 27-8.*

FURTHER READING

Foote, Timothy. "A New Film About Fly Fishing—and Much, Much More." *Smithsonian* 23 (September 1992): 121-2, 124-34.

> Traces Robert Redford's film adaptation of *A River Runs Through It* from the initial bargaining between Redford and Maclean to the final film version, giving a detailed comparison of the film and the novella.

Jackson, Donald Dale. "The Fire That Time." *Audubon* 94 (November-December 1992): 126, 128.

> Favorably reviews *Young Men and Fire*, calling it "sometimes poetic, often earthy, and full of asides that connect the fire to experiences we all share."

Kazin, Alfred. "Frontiers of True Feeling: Norman Maclean's Montana Classic." *Tribune Books* (6 August 1989): 1, 9.

> Reviews a republished edition of *A River Runs Through It*.

McFarland, Ron and Nichols, Hugh, eds. *Norman Maclean*. Lewiston, Idaho: Confluence Press, 1988, 226 p.

> Includes articles and lectures by Maclean, plus interviews and critical essays.

Morrow, Patrick D. Review of *A River Runs Through It, and Other Stories*, by Norman Maclean. *Western American Literature* 11, No. 4 (Winter 1977): 358-9.

> Favorable review of *A River Runs Through It, and Other Stories*, praising the collection's "intellectual substance and artistic skill."

Sale, Roger. "Bradley and Maclean." In his *On Not Being Good Enough: Writings of a Working Critic*, pp. 84-93. New York: Oxford UP, 1979.

> Reprints Sale's review of *A River Runs Through It, and Other Stories*, calling the short story "Logging and Pimping and 'Your Pal, Jim' " "inconsequential" and the novella *USFS 1919* "flawed," while reserving high praise for *A River Runs Through It*.

Additional coverage of Maclean's life and career is contained in the following source published by Gale Research: *Contemporary Authors,* Vols. 102, 132.

Bernard Malamud

The Assistant

Malamud was an American novelist and short story writer who lived from 1914 to 1986.

This entry presents criticism of his second novel, *The Assistant* (1957). For further information on Malamud's life and career, see *CLC* Volumes 1, 2, 3, 5, 8, 9, 11, 18, 27, and 44.

INTRODUCTION

The first of Malamud's novels to receive critical acclaim, *The Assistant* established his prominence among post-World War II American authors. It is in this work that Malamud first experimented with the theme of Jewishness, a prevalent motif in his subsequent novels and short stories. Centering on the relationship of a Jewish immigrant shopkeeper and his new employee, a directionless young Italian-American man, *The Assistant* has been praised for its depiction of moral forbearance as well as for the idiomatic language of its characters, who demonstrate, according to David R. Mesher, that "to accept one's Jewishness means, in *The Assistant,* to experience and understand the human condition."

Malamud was born in Brooklyn, New York, to Russian Jewish immigrants. Much of his youth was spent working in his parents' grocery store, and critics contend that these experiences are reflected in the setting of *The Assistant.* Malamud attended high school in Brooklyn and received his Bachelor's degree from the City College of New York in 1936. After graduation, he worked in a factory and as a clerk at the Census Bureau in Washington, D. C. Although he wrote in his spare time, Malamud did not begin writing seriously until the advent of World War II. Becoming increasingly aware of the horrors of the Holocaust, Malamud began questioning his religious identity and started reading about Jewish tradition and history. He explained: "I was concerned with what Jews stood for, with their getting down to the bare bones of things. I was concerned with their ethnicity—how Jews felt they had to live in order to go on living." In 1949, he began teaching at Oregon State University; he left this post in 1961 to teach creative writing at Bennington College in Vermont. He remained there until shortly before his death in 1986.

The Assistant, Malamud's second novel, relates the experiences of Morris Bober, the humble, elderly owner of a small, profitless Jewish market in an urban and predominantly Gentile neighborhood. Morris leads a difficult life, struggling to provide financially for his wife and their daughter Helen, who wishes to attend college. One night, Morris is robbed and beaten by a neighborhood thug and his accomplice, Frank Alpine. As recourse for his actions, Frank returns to the store and volunteers as the shopkeep-

er's assistant in order to clandestinely repay the stolen money. During the course of his employment, Frank engages Morris in discussions of theology, morality, and human existence, and is profoundly influenced by Morris's convictions. Frank also befriends Helen, and eventually falls in love with her, but his affection is debased when, immediately after saving her from an attacker, he rapes her. Both attempting to atone for the wrong he has done and reacting to Morris's strong moral influence, Frank begins the process of proselytization and, after Morris's unexpected death, completes his conversion to Judaism through ritual circumcision. At the conclusion of the novel, Frank assumes management of Morris's store.

Critical reaction to *The Assistant* has often focused on Malamud's use of symbolism, the theme of the doppelgänger or the "double," and Jewishness as a literary archetype. Citing Morris's altruistic attitude towards the neighborhood's poor and Frank's decision to repay the stolen money, critics have discussed Morris and Frank as symbolic representatives of goodness in human nature. Max F. Schulz has argued that the actions of the two men support the characterization of Morris as a "mythic hero renewing life for the community," and Frank as a "proletarian hero winning justice for society." Religious imagery in *The Assistant,* in the opinion of some critics, is used to introduce the theme of the double. Citing Frank's identification with St. Francis of Assisi, his namesake and acknowledged hero, and Morris's Christlike selflessness, commentators have observed that Frank's relationship to Morris mirrors St. Francis's celebrated emulation of Christ. Critics have also noted doubling in Frank's conversion to Morris's faith, adoption of his humane moral outlook, and assumption of his duties. For example, the final scene of the novel portrays Frank opening the shop early for a regular customer, directly duplicating Morris's actions at the beginning of the novel.

Many critics find Frank and Morris to be examples of the allegorical Everyman, an individual whose experiences are representative of those encountered by all humanity. Accordingly, the suffering and perseverance of Morris and the self-examination and metamorphosis of Frank are viewed as elements common to the personal growth of every individual. Stressing the universal significance of *The Assistant,* commentators have also asserted that Jewishness functions metaphorically in this work, transcending specific religious codes and ethnic traditions. Extrapolating from the behavior of the protagonists, David Daiches stated: "If all sensitive men are Jews, a man can be a Jew simply by being a sensitive man." Many critics additionally perceived Frank's conversion as a commitment to integrity and morality rather than as an assertion of Judaism over Christianity, Frank's original faith. Summarizing the result of Malamud's fusion of realistic portraiture and symbolic representation in *The Assistant,* Meyer Levin observed: "He has succeeded . . . in individualizing his people to a point where one feels able to continue conversation with them outside the book and yet he has kept for each of them a symbolic role, so that the tale has moral echoes, almost a runic quality; it is essentially a parable."

PRINCIPAL WORKS

The Natural (novel) 1952
The Assistant (novel) 1957
The Magic Barrel (short stories) 1958
A New Life (novel) 1961
Idiots First (short stories) 1963
The Fixer (novel) 1966
Pictures of Fidelman: An Exhibition (short stories) 1969
The Tenants (novel) 1971
Rembrandt's Hat (short stories) 1973
Dubin's Lives (novel) 1979
God's Grace (novel) 1982
The Stories of Bernard Malamud (short stories) 1983

CRITICISM

William Goyen   (review date 28 April 1957)

[*Goyen was an American novelist, short story writer, dramatist, scriptwriter, poet, and nonfiction writer. An esteemed author of mythopoeic fiction, he used lyrical prose and imagery to explore the depths of the imagination. In the following review, he praises Malamud's narrative voice in* The Assistant *as succinct and compelling.*]

Readers will remember Bernard Malamud's stories in *The New Yorker, Commentary, Harper's Bazaar* and *Partisan Review;* and his first novel, *The Natural,* which was highly praised as an imaginative work. Now his second novel, **The Assistant,** will bring more pleasure to his readers and reaffirm his talent as a writer about simple people struggling to make their lives better in a world of bad luck. The clarity and concreteness of his style, the warm humanity over his people, the tender wit that keeps them firm and compassionable, will delight many.

The Assistant is the story of Morris Bober, neighborhood grocer, his wife, Ida, and their daughter, Helen. Their life is hard and small, fraught with ill luck and disappointment. When Frank Alpine becomes Morris Bober's assistant, things take a turn for the better. Frank, whose reactions to Jews is ambivalent, falls in love with Helen Bober. He begins to steal from the store. There is this kind of dual-leveled, double-working meaning that begins to work through the story until, in the end, Frank himself becomes a Jew after Passover.

It is the lucidity of this story that makes it distinctive and that makes Mr. Malamud's vision shine simply throughout the stumblings and strugglings and heartbreaks of the Bobers. In Mr. Malamud's hands, Frank Alpine, the alien and the outsider, becomes a kind of redeemer. The speech of these people is marvelously true and adds another dimension to the story that is told. There is a kind of crystalline hardness over the tautly lyrical descriptions of people and scenes; there is never a literariness or any intrusion of philosophic values in Mr. Malamud's world.

All is kept simple, real, basic; there is the rightness that permeates this book. Yet around the simplicity of it there gathers and grows in the mind of the reader a sense of values and destinies and large truths—there is this mysterious accretion that contributes weight and size and beauty to **The Assistant.**

Mr. Malamud's people are memorable and real as rock, and there is not one gesture of sentimentality or theatrics to render them so. He knows his people and keeps them free with the kind of writer's control that one does not find often enough in the myriad novels about simple people.

> William Goyen, "A World of Bad Luck," in
> The New York Times Book Review, *April 28,*
> *1957, p. 4.*

Alfred Kazin   (review date July 1957)

[*A highly respected American literary critic, Kazin is*

best known for his essay collections The Inmost Leaf *(1955),* Contemporaries *(1962), and* On Native Grounds *(1942), a study of American prose writing since the era of William Dean Howells. In the following review, he criticizes* The Assistant *as lacking literary subtlety.*]

Bernard Malamud's second novel has been getting extremely friendly reviews, for he is a talented writer, has a particularly intense sympathy for his Jewish material, and—what doesn't always accompany sympathy—an utterly objective ear for the harsh and plaintive American Yiddish speech. But none of the reviews that I have seen has suggested that Malamud's seemingly modest and "warm" little tale about a Jewish grocer in Brooklyn and his Italian assistant is really a hymn to a symbolic Jew as he is confronted by a hostile, baffled, and finally envious Gentile. And it is because I think that Malamud's book tries for so much more, in symbol, than what he actually gives us as fiction that I find myself regretfully dissenting from the other reviews.

Like most second-generation American Jewish novelists, Malamud's problem is to form a creative synthesis out of the Yiddish world of his childhood and his natural sophistication and heretical training as a modern writer. As one can see in his highly surrealistic baseball novel, *The Natural,* and in his eery *Partisan Review* story of a Jewish marriage broker, **"The Magic Barrel,"** Malamud is naturally a fantasist of the ordinary, the commonplace, the average. He writes, a little, the way Chagall paints—except that the natural course of Malamud's imagination is to seek not the open and the lyrical but symbols of the highly involuted personal life of Jews. He loves what he himself calls "violins and candles" in the sky, old-clothes-men who masquerade something sinister yet unnamable; he has a natural sense for the humdrum transposed to the extreme, of the symbolic and the highly colored. He tends to the bizarre, the contorted, the verge of things that makes you shiver, not laugh. Although his dialogue in *The Assistant* is marvelously faithful to Yiddish-American, he makes you think not that Jews really talk this way but how violent, fear-fraught, always on the edge, Jewish talk can be. In the superb **"The Magic Barrel,"** Malamud really caught the accents of the hallucinated, the visionary, and the bizarre that belong to a people whose images are as much of the next world, and of other worlds, as they are of this one.

Now the trouble with *The Assistant,* from my point of view, is that Malamud's natural taste for abstraction, his gift for symbolic representation, has gone to make up a morality story which is essentially a glorification of the Jew as Jew. My objection is that his understandable allegiance to this theme has been made the overriding motive of the book despite the fact that Malamud's talent is inherently too subtle to serve what I would call an emotional motive. Malamud is an extremely sympathetic and feeling writer, and I don't mean to suggest that he is a surrealist pure; his hold on reality is too strong, and he is, as I admiringly feel about him, very "Jewish," very much of this world. But in **"The Magic Barrel"** his sympathy with suffering and his deliberately distorted perspective—that sense of "magic" which seems to me the strongest element

in his work—worked to represent things that could not be moralized; the character of the marriage broker was revealed entirely by technique, rendered exclusively by the use of incongruities rarely employed to describe Jewish life. The final effect was "strange" and true—there was nothing left over to paraphrase, to moralize.

In *The Assistant,* however, just the opposite is true. For what he is getting at in the life of the Jewish grocer, Morris Bober, is precisely what, after Bober's death, a rabbi—who never knew him—can say over his coffin:

"Yes, Morris Bober was to me a true Jew because he lived in the Jewish experience, which he remembered, and with the Jewish heart. Maybe not to our formal tradition . . . but he was true to the spirit of our life—to want for others that which he wants also for himself. . . . For such reasons he was a Jew. What more does our sweet God ask his poor people?"

Morris Bober is a Jew in exile, exiled even from most of his own formal traditions: in short, he is *the* Jew. But he opens his grocery at six each morning, groaning, in order to give a Polish woman a three-cent roll. When the Irish detective's bummer son, Ward Minogue, holds up Morris, Minogue curses him as a "Jew liar." When, in a fit of conscience, Frank Alpine, the other robber, forces himself on Morris as an "assistant," insists on working for spending money, he explains to Morris that "I always liked Jews." And watching Morris's miserable existence reveal itself all day long in the shabby little grocery, Frank reflects— "What kind of a man did you have to be to shut yourself up in an overgrown coffin and never once during the day, so help you, outside of going for your Jewish newspaper, poke your head out of the door for a snootful of air? The answer wasn't very hard to say—you had to be a Jew. They were born prisoners." When Frank, increasingly moved by Morris's virtuous and threadbare existence, decides to confess his part in the robbery, it turns out that originally it was *because* Morris was a Jew that Ward Minogue planned to rob him, "so Frank agreed to go with him."

But as for Morris Bober himself—"he was Morris Bober and could be nobody more fortunate. With that name you had no sure sense of property, as if it were in your blood and history not to possess, or if by some miracle to own something, to do so on the verge of loss." He is *the* Jew in everything and to everyone. His grocery is devouring him; his wife, Ida, who never gives him a moment's tenderness, but loves him harshly, cries bitterly when she sees her daughter kissing the *goy:* "Why do I cry? I cry for the world. I cry for my life that it went away wasted. I cry for you." His unmarried daughter, Helen, is twenty-three and getting anxious, but she will not compromise in her demand for love. So that into this Jewish circle, this archetype family, the dark outsider, Frank Alpine, the "assistant," comes as another symbol. And the whole story turns on the fact that he learns from Morris not, as the jacket delicately puts it, "the beauty of morality," but the beauty of the Jews. Morris recounts his life to the assistant during the many dull stretches in the store, tells him how he ran away from the Czar's conscription to America. When Frank asks Morris what it is to be a Jew and taunts him with not obeying the dietary laws, Morris answers him—"Nobody will tell me that I am not Jewish because I put in my mouth once in a while, when my tongue is dry, a piece of ham. But they will tell me, and I will believe them, if I forget the Law. This means to do what is right, to be honest, to be good. . . . For everybody should be the best, not only for you or me. We ain't animals. This is why we need the Law. This is what a Jew believes." Frank persists: "But tell me why it is that the Jews suffer so damn much, Morris? It seems to me that they like to suffer, don't they. . . . What do you suffer for, Morris?" "I suffer for you."

At the end of the story, Helen is raped by Ward Minogue, and Frank, after rescuing her, forgets himself and hysterically forces himself upon her, too: to which symbol Helen replies by naming it. She calls him "Dog—uncircumcised dog!" Frank can expiate his guilt only by taking Morris's place, after Morris dies from the effects of shoveling snow from in front of his store so that people can pass. The point of the novel is made at the end: Morris has been cheated by his fellow Jews as well as robbed and assaulted by Ward Minogue. But Frank himself becomes Morris Bober, sends Helen to N.Y.U., and on the last page, is circumcised and converted to Judaism. The point, as he says, is not merely that for the Jews "Suffering is like a piece of goods. I bet the Jews could make a suit of [it]. . . . " but: "The funny thing is that there are more of them [Jews] around than anybody knows about."

All these sentiments are unexceptionable, but the novel as constituted doesn't bear them out. The detail, while marvelously faithful, is always too clear in outline, the moral is too pointed, to convince me. And touching and utterly authentic as Morris is, there is a peculiarly unemphasized quality about him, as if Malamud were writing entirely from memory, were trying to get a beloved figure right rather than to create, with the needed sharp edges, the character demanded by the imagination. Bober himself remains too generalized a Jew, as Frank Alpine is too shadowy and unvisualized the Gentile, to make their symbolic relationship simply felt.

Where Malamud's very real talent comes through best in this book, it seems to me, is in figures of suffering—his natural element—who are not average but extreme figures. Malamud is the poet of the desperately clownish, not of the good who shall inherit the earth—and this unusual gift of his comes through in two wonderful little portraits of Jews. One is of Breitbart, a bankrupt, deserted by his wife, who took to peddling. "He bought electric bulbs at wholesale and carried two cartons of them slung, with clothesline rope, over his shoulder. Every day, in his crooked shoes, he walked miles, looking into stores and calling out in a mournful voice, 'Lights for sale.' " The other is of a professional arsonist, "a skinny man in an old hat and a dark overcoat down to his ankles. His nose was long, throat gaunt, and he wore a wisp of red beard on his bony chin." The "scarecrow" comes in saying "a gut shabos," though "shabos" is a day away and looking around the Bober grocery, remarks, "It smells here like an open grave." He wets his lips and whispers, "Insurinks you got—fire insurinks?" and taking out a piece of "celluloy,"

shows how he does his work. "Magic," he hoarsely announced. "No ashes. This is why we use celluloy, not paper, not rags." The word "magic" naturally occurs in Malamud's best work—or when he is at his best. And then, as befits a writer who has lived "in the Jewish experience," it serves to clarify and intensify our sense of what that experience really is. (pp. 89-92)

> Alfred Kazin, "Fantasist of the Ordinary," in Commentary, *Vol. 24, No. 1, July, 1957, pp. 89-92.*

Harvey Swados   (review date Winter 1958)

[*Swados was an American novelist and short story writer whose works primarily explore socialist themes and depict working-class individuals in an industrial society. In the following review, he asserts that* The Assistant *possesses a quality that ensures the novel's prominence in the spectrum of Jewish-American literature.*]

While Jews have had an honorable place on the American literary scene since the 19th Century, that place has for the most part been marginal. It would hardly be unfair to say that while their brothers were busily engaged in Americanizing themselves and making the giant stride from sweatshop and tenement to office and suburb, American Jewish writers achieved prominence primarily as either bestseller sentimentalists or genre painters of ghetto and immigrant life. They were never able, not even after World War I, to conquer the ramparts of high art in the world of fiction; there were no Jewish writers to rank with Dos Passos, Fitzgerald, Faulkner, Hemingway. Really it is only since World War II that the American Jew has battered his way (as all writers must batter their way in this country) into the front rank of serious American fiction.

But if this development has been belated, it has been extraordinarily rapid too. Already it is impossible to call the roll of outstanding imaginative novelists and short story writers in this country without including the younger Jewish talents who have come to the fore in the last decade. This unusual development (I omit mention of the parallel and more predictable success of Jewish commercial writers in the movies and television) can be seen as analagous to the sudden emergence of Jewish painters concurrently with the great sweep of School of Paris painting of the last seventy-five years. From Pissarro to Pascin, Soutine, Modigliani and Chagall, it is impossible to imagine what that great creative upsurge would have been like without the participation and indeed the imaginative leadership of the Jewish graphic artists newly freed from centuries of proscription of brush and palette.

So too I venture to suggest that one day it will be impossible to conceive of what course American literature would have taken in the Fifties and Sixties without the active leadership of those American Jewish creative figures who turned from their fathers' conquest of business America to the conquest of the demon of Art. One of the foremost among those figures will be Bernard Malamud, who has been too long neglected but who, after the publication of *The Assistant,* can be neglected no longer. Mr. Malamud has arrived, and from now on anyone who pretends to speak seriously, either here or abroad, of the American literary scene, will have to come to grips with his vision of the inner reality of American life.

We know of Bernard Malamud first as the creator of a number of remarkable short stories (in this reader's opinion the most powerful and passionate group of stories to come from the pen of a single writer in the last ten years), then as the author of an unusual and highly amusing, but not wholly successful, allegorical novel about a baseball hero, *The Natural.* Now Mr. Malamud has returned, in this new novel, to the milieu with which he has concerned himself almost exclusively in his short stories: the depression slum; and to the central figure: the small Jewish storekeeper.

Morris Bober owns a flyblown grocery in a rundown goyish neighborhood; he keeps open sixteen hours a day. Behind the store he has a partition in which he can heat coffee and wait with the *Forward* for the Poilisheh who comes for her three-cent roll at 6 A.M., for his Italian tenant who comes for sandwich meat at seven o'clock, and thereafter for his regulars. Above the store he has rooms, just enough space for himself, his nagging wife Ida, his disappointed daughter Helen, and the tender memory of his dead son Ephraim. Ida bulks hardly larger in her husband's life than their dead son, except when her nagging ambition punctures the thin and vulnerable envelope of his pride. It is Helen who embodies not only the female principle, but the striving of the Bobers not merely for a better life than the grocery store trap, but for the very best that life has to offer; Helen, who at twenty-three has quixotically turned down Nat Pearl because she dreams of something better than the middle-class security he can offer, who has missed her chance for day-school college, but still hopes to get her degree at night while she works for a Manhattan undergarment firm by day. It is not the least of Mr. Malamud's achievements that he breathes life into Helen Bober, who, with her yearning for culture and refinement, has been an easy figure of fun for so many Jewish highbrow writers (and commercial writers too), as a woman endowed with dignity and noble aspirations, worthy of our compassion and even our admiration.

This family, no single member of which is actually in communication with any other—they live in poverty-stricken physical proximity but otherwise as separated from one another as utter strangers—moves from crisis to crisis with the sickening predictability of a roller coaster ride or a man going to pot from drink. Morris gets sick; he is robbed and beaten by holdupniks; his already dwindling business is slashed past the point of bankruptcy with the opening of a modern delicatessen around the corner.

So far we are in a world which is familiar; if not familiar to us through our own life-experiences, then through our readings of earlier Yiddish or American Jewish writers who also treated of the desperate situation of the immigrant generation at the mercy of economic flux and bewildered by its entrapment. True, it has rarely been treated of so well before; Yiddish speech rhythms and inflections have seldom been incorporated into American prose with such subtle effectiveness; but still we remain in an area previously canvassed by others and if this were the total

of Mr. Malamud's explorations we might well wonder at his reasons for recrossing territory already posted and charted. But then a stranger enters the scene, a mysterious young Italian. With the entrance of this man, the one for whom the book has so rightly been titled, we move with Bernard Malamud into a new dimension, and we are lifted into a new realm of vision from which the lives of the Bobers take on a vaster and more complex symbolic shape. Now we begin to see that this is no mere breast-beating tale of poor Jews, although it is always that too. It is a saga of alienation and frustration, of man's yearning for brotherhood and his fear of communion.

Frank Alpine (*né* Alpino) is not a Lochinvar out of the West, but a bum out of the West, a homeless orphan who carries about with him only some remembered tales of the gentleness of St. Francis of Assisi and some recollections of Jewish kindness. These do not prevent him from stealing bread and milk from the grocer's doorstep when he is jobless and hungry, nor from shortchanging and rifling the till when later on Morris allows him to sleep in the cellar, nor from peering through the dumbwaiter shaft at Helen naked in her bath.

Gradually however Frank takes over in the store, first as an unpaid volunteer assistant, then as a paid clerk when business picks up and Morris, sick and unable to put in his sixteen hours, is desperately in need of what Frank can do for him. Rescued becomes rescuer, and in the course of this reversal of roles strange and wonderful and terrible things happen to Morris Bober, his daughter, and the assistant. I must refrain from taking the story any further because it is among other things a mystery story, in precisely the sense that *Crime and Punishment* and *The Brothers Karamazov* are mystery stories. It is one of Mr. Malamud's great strengths that he is a story teller and a believer in plot and I shall add only that the last chapter, searing and wrenching as it is, culminates in a final paragraph that in its boldness and shocking rightness rivals any other ending I have seen in contemporary fiction.

By now I hope I have made it amply clear that it is my firm opinion that *The Assistant* is one novel in a thousand, and that Bernard Malamud is one writer in a thousand. I am afraid that this book—although it is more profoundly affirmative than any of the yea-saying bestsellers of this age of acquiescence—is going to be criticized for its unrelieved air of gloom and doom (which will be, although true enough on the surface, a misreading of the amazing life of Frank Alpine) and for the same reasons may for a time go unread and unsold. This would be a pity, but the pity will be on those who deprive themselves of the opportunity for purgation and consequently of a deeper insight into the conditions of their own lives: for *The Assistant* will live. (pp. 149-51)

Harvey Swados, "The Emergence of An Artist," in Western Review, *Vol. 22, No. 2, Winter, 1958, pp. 149-51.*

Ihab Hassan   (essay date 1961)

[*Hassan is an Egyptian-born American critic and educator who has written several studies of twentieth-century*

*literature. In the following excerpt from an essay origi-
nally published in his 1961* Radical Innocence: Studies
in the Contemporary Novel, *he perceives in* The Assistant *an ironic inseparability of contradicting values and
experiences.*]

[Malamud's] first novel, **The Natural,** 1952, is a bizarre,
authentic, troubled work about a thirty-three-year-old
baseball player who suddenly emerges from painful oblivion into the crazy light of fame and big league corruption. The snappy slang of sport and gloomy language of the soul
are fused in an allegorical tale which probes deep into the
meaning of personal integrity but fails ultimately to make
itself comprehensible. His collection of short stories, **The
Magic Barrel,** 1958, includes some of his worst and best
fiction. The poorer pieces are usually set abroad; the best
deal with native Jewish material and have in common with
his second novel, **The Assistant,** 1957, a blazing poetic insight into the daily aches and indignities of man which add
up, somehow, to a kind of nobility, a form of aspiration.

The Assistant, presumably, is a love story, a domestic romance, a grocery store idyll of unwarranted poverty and
harsh spiritual deprivation. It is a tale of loneliness, of life-
long frustrations and delicate, budding hopes. It is a
"human" story albeit deeply ironic. For irony is indeed
the key to Malamud's attitude toward man, to his estimate
of him. The irony is not "dry," not scathing; it is best described by Earl Rovit when he says, "The affectionate insult and the wry self-depreciation are parts of the same
ironic vision which values one's self and mankind as both
less and more than they seem to be worth, at one and the
same time." This is the ambivalence of vision which qualifies, sometimes even undercuts, the affirmative power of
Malamud's fiction.

The world revealed by **The Assistant** is, materially speaking, bleak; morally, it glows with a faint, constant light.
Morris Bober and his wife, Ida, toil sixteen hours a day
in a grocery store, barely eking out a living. They are well
past middle age, and have given up their lives, their illusions, even the promise of a richer future which comes
with education for their single daughter, Helen. The store,
as we are told many times, is an open tomb. Twenty-one
years are spent in it, and in the end Bober dies of double
pneumonia, leaving his family penniless; he has to be buried in one of those huge anonymous cemeteries in Queens.
America! "He had hoped for much in America and got little. And because of him Helen and Ida had less. He had
defrauded them, he and the blood-sucking store." This is
what Bober thinks as one of two men who hold up his
store slugs him on the head, because he is a Jew, and Bober
falls to the ground without a cry. An appropriate ending
to his weary, profitless day. Others may have luck, like the
affluent Karp who owns a liquor store across the street,
or the Earls whose son, Nat, attends law school—and
takes Helen's virginity. But the Bobers live on stolidly,
honestly, in squalor and sickening destitution. They are,
like the grocery "assistant," Frank Alpine, victims of circumstance. What, then, gives these characters the measure of spiritual freedom they still possess?

The nature of the characters themselves holds the answer.
Morris Bober, to be sure, is another example of the *eiron,*

> It is obvious that if the world of *The
> Assistant* is not drained of values, it is
> nevertheless saturated with pain, flooded
> with contradictions. Its two major
> characters find their identity in
> humiliation, an extreme and quixotic sense
> of obligation.
>
> —*Ihab Hassan*

the humble man. He is more. He has endurance, the power
to accept suffering without yielding to the hebetude which
years of pain induce. He is acquainted with the tragic qualities of life—"The word suffer. *He* felt every schmerz"—
and he defines the Jew as a suffering man with a good
heart, one who reconciles himself to agony, not because
he wants to be agonized, as Frank suggests, but for the
sake of the Law—the Hebraic ideal of virtue. Yet this is
only one source of Bober's strength. His other source is
charity, which in his case becomes nearly quixotic. Bober,
though close to starvation himself, extends credit to his
poor customers. He wakes up every day before dawn so
that he may sell a three-cent roll to a Polish woman on her
way to work. He takes in Frank Alpine, feeds him, and
gives him an opportunity to redeem himself, though
Frank begins by stealing the grocer's bread and milk. Nor
can he bring himself, in the extremity of despair, to burn
down his property in order to collect insurance. Inured to
failure, Bober still strives to give suffering the dignity of
men who may trust one another in their common woe. But
Karp calls him a "schlimozel."

The central action of the novel, however, develops from
Bober's relation to Frank Alpine, and from the latter's relation to Helen. Frank, as the title suggests, is probably the
hero of the book. He, too, is an *eiron,* a collector of injustices—with a difference. The regeneration of Frank—his
literal and symbolic conversion to the Jewish faith—is the
true theme of the book. His regeneration, at best, is a
strange and mixed thing. When Frank first appears, he is
a wanderer, an anti-Semite, even a thief. Yet one of his
idols is St. Francis, and his hardened face conceals a hungry soul. "With me one wrong thing leads to another and
it ends in a trap. I want the moon so all I get is cheese,"
he tells Bober. The grocery store, which is Bober's grave,
becomes a cave or haven for Alpine. It also becomes the
dreary locus of his painful rebirth. Impelled by his gratitude to the grocer, and motivated by his guilt at having
robbed him, with the aid of tough Ward Minogue, Frank
puts all his energies into the store and ends by pumping
some of his own obstinate life into the dying business.
Meanwhile, he falls in love with Helen Bober.

From here on, ambiguities prevail. The racial prejudices
of Frank are matched by those of Ida Bober, and to some
extent, of her daughter Helen, against Gentiles. (The store
improves, it is suggested, precisely because Frank is not
a Jew.) Frank's gratitude to Morris does not prevent him
from continuing to steal petty cash from the register—

which he keeps account of and intends to return. Yet when Bober is incapacitated by sickness, Frank takes a night job, in addition to his grocery chores, and secretly puts his pay in the cash box. And his gnawing love for Helen, which she is slow to return, finally ends, ironically, with an act of near-rape as he rescues her from the clutches of Ward Minogue, only to force her himself, right there and then in the park, at the very moment in their relationship when she is at least ready to surrender herself freely to him. "Dog," she cries "—uncircumcised dog!" Guilt, gratitude, love—perhaps even the hope of a life he could glimpse but never attain—combined to sustain Frank Alpine, Bober's strange, saintly, pilfering assistant, in his impossible struggle against poverty, against hopelessness itself.

> He wanted her but the facts made a terrible construction. They were Jews and he was not. If he started going out with Helen her mother would throw a double fit and Morris another. And Helen made him feel, from the way she carried herself, even when she seemed most lonely, that she had plans for something big in her life—nobody like F. Alpine. He had nothing, a backbreaking past, had committed a crime against her old man, and in spite of his touchy conscience, was stealing from him too. How complicated could impossible get?

> He saw only one way of squeezing through the stone knot; start by shoveling out the load he was carrying around in his mind. . . .

> So the confession had to come first. . . . He felt he had known this, in some frightful way, a long time before he went into the store, before he had met Minogue, or even come east; that he had really known all his life he would sometime, through throat blistered with shame, his eyes in the dirt, have to tell some poor son of a bitch that he was the one who had hurt or betrayed him. This thought had lived in him with claws; or like a thirst he could never spit out, a repulsive need to get out of his system all that had happened—for whatever had happened had happened wrong; to clean it out of his self and bring in a little peace, a little order; to change the beginning, beginning with the past that always stupendously stank up the now—to change his life before the smell of it suffocated him.

Purgation in humility, rebirth through love—this is Frank's inchoate purpose, the reason for his willing acceptance of a backbreaking burden others—Minogue, Karp—find easy to reject. Yet it is in consonance with the character of the novel that purgation and rebirth both should appear ironic, awkward, and inconclusive. Frank tells Bober about his complicity in the robbery only to discover that the latter already knows. Bober catches his assistant rifling his till just when Frank had resolved never to steal again. And Frank's attempt to make a clean breast of it all to Helen merely serves to confirm her revulsion. His dogged and desperate love expresses itself in the form of a physical outrage. The Savior of the Bobers is, in a sense, their archenemy. (The symbolic inversion of this relation may be discovered in the burial scene in which Frank topples accidentally into Bober's open grave.) But

enemies suffer too, according to their conscience. Frank Alpine, it seems, can only expend the last vestige of his money, energy, or hope in agonized silence, a prey to the ironies which rip and twist his purpose. In the end, the value of confession is to the soul that makes it. And even love is a kind of realized solitude. Like Frank, Helen goes her lonely way, carrying the broken dreams of the Bobers to some distant and uncompromising end.

It is obvious that if the world of *The Assistant* is not drained of values, it is nevertheless saturated with pain, flooded with contradictions. Its two major characters find their identity in humiliation, an extreme and quixotic sense of obligation. They are not tragic heroes but merely heroes of irony. They retreat before the ultimate tragic ordeal: the fullness of tragic awareness itself. This is a fact the form of the novel supports.

Time, we know, leaves the characters suspended in the void which their failures create; the hints of regeneration are barely audible. Morris Bober dies in bankruptcy; Helen continues at her dreary job, dreaming of a better life; Frank slaves at the store, trying to provide for the Bobers, send Helen to college, and win back her love. The fate of each remains less than what it could be in heroic tragedy, less even than what it usually amounts to in realistic fiction. Thus, for instance, does Helen evaluate the life of her father: "People liked him, but who can admire a man passing his life in such a store? He buried himself in it; he didn't have the imagination to know what he was missing. He made himself a victim. He could, with a little more courage, have been more than he was." And thus does Frank reflect upon his incessant labors: " 'Jesus,' he said 'why am I killing myself so?' He gave himself many unhappy answers, the best being that while he was doing this he was doing nothing worse." Whatever awareness time brings to the characters, whatever qualified dignity it confers upon their failures, every act in the novel is whittled by irony, every motive is mixed with its opposite.

Because time cannot unravel the knotted relations of the characters—what could be more gnarled than the relation of Gentile to Jew, of savior, seducer, and thief to those upon whom he preys, those from whom he gains an identity—the point of view of *The Assistant* dissociates itself from the protagonists, veering toward one then the other in friendly detachment. The characters are simply there, and they criticize each other's behavior; the point of view encourages us to perceive how ludicrous pain can be, and how unhappy virtue. The subtle, incredible twists of the plot, the reversals and accidents which affect the fortunes of the Bobers, are finally envisioned in a moral as well as dramatic perspective which acknowledges no certainties except the fact of suffering. (It is appropriate that Morris Bober should be an unorthodox Jew, and that at his funeral the rabbi should say, "Yes, Morris Bober was to me a true Jew because he lived in the Jewish experience, and with the Jewish heart. . . . He suffered, he endured, but with hope.")

The achievement of Malamud's style, which survives his ironic play, lies in the author's capacity to convey both hope and agony in the rhythms of Yiddish speech.

"I think I will shovel the snow," he told Ida at lunch-time.

"Go better to sleep."

"It ain't nice for the customers."

"What customers—who needs them?"

"People can't walk in such high snow," he argued.

"Wait, tomorrow it will be melted."

"It's Sunday, it don't look so nice for the goyim that they go to church."

Her voice had an edge in it. "You want to catch pneumonia, Morris?"

"It's spring," he murmured.

There is a Hemingway cleanness in this dialogue, a kind of humility and courage, but also a softness Hemingway never strove to communicate.

Morris, however, does catch pneumonia and die. Nor can the poetry of the style persuade us to forget that the search of Frank Alpine for an identity ends, in the last, brief paragraph of the novel, with the ritual of circumcision. The act is one of self-purification, of initiation too, in Frank's case, but it is also an act of self-repudiation, if not, as some may be tempted to say, of symbolic castration. (pp. 6-10)

> *Ihab Hassan, "The Qualified Encounter," in* Bernard Malamud: Modern Critical Views, *edited by Harold Bloom, Chelsea House Publishers, 1986, pp. 5-10.*

Burns Singer on the prosaic subject matter of *The Assistant*:

[In *The Assistant* Bernard Malamud] has written a book of agonising sincerity. Most of the agony, however, comes from my sympathy for Mr. Malamud rather than from my pity for his characters. It *is* agonising to find that so much honesty, so much intelligence, such intense modesty and complete integrity do *not* produce a good book—that they produce only an honest, intelligent, modest, and well-integrated one. (I can think of a number of literary card-sharpers who do write good books.) Mr. Malamud tells the story of an orphaned Italian youth who, after having attacked a Jewish grocer, is struck by such remorse that the rest of his life is devoted to the Jew and his family; until finally he becomes a Jew himself. The fault is not sentimentality, though this resumé might give that impression. Lots of good books are sentimental. The fault is drabness. Mr. Malamud brings his characters to life, all right, but to such a life that both they and the reader would be better out of it. Yet it is an authentic life, though a very boring one.

Burns Singer, in "Fantasies and Sobrieties," Encounter, October 1957.

Norman Leer   (essay date Fall 1962)

[*Leer is an American educator and critic. In the excerpt below, he discusses the search for identity within society as depicted in* The Assistant.]

Malamud's novel, ***The Assistant,*** emphasizes the condition of alienation within social interaction, and the need to realize and be able to fulfill some obligation to others. It points out the need for a community of feeling by taking a storekeeper, Morris Bober, who represents the traditions of an older Jewish community, and subjecting him to the frustrations of the more competitive and fluid urban community. . . . The material conditions of the Depression hang heavily over the book, and poverty is the everyday fact of Morris Bober's life. Yet this is not a novel of organized protest, for society is seen largely through individual experience, and the solution suggested is in terms of character rather than program. Poverty is a symbol of a larger trap. The store is the only certainty in Morris's life, and it encloses him like a tomb:

> No, not for an age had he lived a whole day in the open. As a boy, always running in the muddy, rutted streets of the village, or across the fields, or bathing with the other boys in the river; but as a man, in America, he rarely saw the sky. In the early days when he drove a horse and wagon, yes, but not since his first store. In a store you were entombed.

Morris's business has always been "marginal," but he had usually managed to rise slightly with each new spasm of national prosperity. "Now, though he toiled the same hard hours, he was close to bankruptcy, his patience torn. . . . since the appearance of Schmitz across the street ten months ago, all times were bad." Such is the effect of competition. Morris's world is in a state of flux, the old stability broken by the opening of new stores and the coming and going of unsteady customers. "America," comments Malamud, "had become too complicated. One man counted for nothing. There were too many stores, depressions, anxieties."

In the midst of this hell, Morris Bober has a kind of identity. He is shown as a man of honesty, extreme to the point of running after a customer to return a nickel. He emerges, I think, from the European Jewish tradition of heroic poverty, the poor man who is so ethical that he appears as both victim and tragic hero. He is continually thwarted by the realities of poor health and destructive competition. Morris represents an ethic, an intensity of responsible feeling, that is almost anachronistic in modern society.

The novel is in part an attempt to recapture the grocer's heightened states of feeling. Consequently, the relationship between Morris and the "holdupnik," Frank Alpine, assumes a special significance. Frank is essentially the wanderer, the man who is without roots because he is both too naive and too experienced. His is a frustrated intensity, and he returns to Morris with a strong desire for stability and penitence. The two men are still able to find a partial solidarity in their poverty. To both, it is at once a curse and a kind of purposeful renunciation of the world. Frank has great admiration for Francis of Assisi, the saint who preached to the birds and gave away all his worldly possessions. Frank returns to the store, and insists on working without pay. To him, this is a means of attempting to find an anchor. Morris, at first not suspecting Frank's identity and later almost knowing, remains lenient and sympathetic. His first feeling is one of pity, mixed with a sense of the solidarity of poverty. The motif of Frank as an ironic Saint Francis is repeated throughout the book. Once Helen Bober, who has just refused an expensive present offered by Frank, sees him in the park, "squatting by one of the benches feeding the birds." Thus, "the assistant" is seen in part as a would-be hero; but he is also the indecisive boy, fighting impulses toward petty thefts and rubbing the pains left by Helen's rebuffs.

If a partial identity is gained through poverty, we also see that it is poverty, imposed by society, that smothers any possibilities of this identity becoming truly heroic. At the same time, Malamud introduces certain larger themes which indicate that the problem and solution are not fundamentally social, that the tomb of the store is a symbol of a larger death. Three themes in particular suggest an affinity with Joyce's *Ulysses:* the search for the father; the simultaneous search for a son by the father; and the decline of fertility. Morris Bober, we soon learn, is impelled to dream upon the spirit of his dead son. One night he cannot sleep. He decides to dress, "but there drifted into his mind, with ease and no sorrow, the form and image of his boy Ephraim, gone so long from him, and he fell deeply and calmly asleep." A variation on the father-son theme is provided by the relationship between Detective Minogue and his son Ward, Frank's accomplice in the holdup. "People felt sorry for the detective, for he was a strict man and they knew what it meant to him to have such a son." The decline of fertility, or the inability to love, is embodied in Helen Bober. A girl of intellectual ambitions, she resents her body for not forcing others into her view of herself:

> Virginity she thought she had parted with without sorrow, yet was surprised by torments of conscience, or was it disappointment at being valued under her expectations? Nat Pearl, handsome, cleft-chinned, gifted, ambitious, had wanted without too much trouble a lay and she, half in love, had obliged and regretted. Not the loving, but that it had taken her so long to realize how little he wanted. Not her, Helen Bober.

Love has proved for her a mockery, and it is partly from desire taunted by a fear of being mocked again, partly from a real inability to love, that she toys with Frank and rejects him. At first, he craves and magnifies Helen, and regards her as an ideal to which he can give himself. But she is afraid, mostly of herself; and one night Frank dreams that he is standing in the snow beneath her window. Helen has tossed him a white rose. As she let go the flower, "he saw the light of her room and even felt the warmth of it. Then when he looked again the window was shut tight, sealed with ice. Even as he dreamed, he knew it had never been open. There was no such window. He gazed down at his hand for the flower and before he could see it wasn't there, felt himself wake." But if his first reaction is idolatry, Frank soon surpasses Helen in his level of compassion. She has persuaded him to read Dostoevski;

and one day Frank ironically asks her what she has learned from the books if she cannot understand his own past. "The assistant" also has a compulsion to confess his part in the holdup to the grocer: "If Morris accepted his explanation and solemn apology, it would clear the rocks out of the road for his next move. . . . It wouldn't necessarily mean that Helen Bober would then and there fall for him—the opposite could happen—but if she *did,* he wouldn't feel bad about it." In Frank's return to the store after the crime, in his anxiety to stay and be discovered, we can see him as the son searching for a father. Significantly, he has been raised in an orphanage. But in his hope that confession will purify him enough to desire Helen, we see the painful need for love. All three of these thematic quests, the father-son searchings and the need for love, emphasize the author's awareness of isolated human beings, groping for some act that will relate them to each other. The focus of the book has by this point shifted almost completely to the individual, and this is underscored by the most individual type of imagery, that of the dream.

If the reality is one of isolation and futility, each of the major characters nonetheless attempts to relate to others, and to find a measure of heroism, a heroism found through the retention of identity, and often the will to suffer, within the heavy grotesqueness of the "tomb." Morris Bober in particular is an ironic and unsuccessful hero. He is the embodiment of fixed values in a state of flux. Frank asks once why he regards himself as a Jew, and Morris replies:

> Nobody will tell me that I am not Jewish because I put in my mouth once in a while, when my tongue is dry, a piece ham. But they will tell me, and I will believe them, if I forget the Law. This means to do what is right, to be honest, to be good. This means to other people. Our life is hard enough. Why should we hurt somebody else? For everybody should be the best, not only for you or me. We ain't animals. This is why we need the law. This is what a Jew believes.

The whole basis of the law is ethical fixity, and the irony of the novel lies in the fact that it is in part this very ethical impulse, the urge to seek an identity that transcends the emptiness, that makes Morris a victim. He is victimized not so much by poverty, as by the negligence of other individuals, even the few Jews in his neighborhood, to keep the law. And in this almost anarchistic context, the attempt to survive and still maintain the law becomes for Morris a physical day-to-day act. In the same sense, there is a sad triumph at the end of the novel when "the assistant," Frank, becomes a Jew through the tangible act of becoming circumcized, and seeks his redemption after Morris has died by accepting the storekeeper's life and his suffering. (pp. 72-5)

Morris Bober and his "assistant" are also struggling to find and maintain a strong personal response to moral values, but their world is made more inhibiting—and more definite—by economic poverty and struggle. Malamud envisions his society on two simultaneous levels—the hard struggle for naked survival, and the larger social reality in which moral values are suppressed beneath a drabness and evasion for which the bleak gray of the ghetto is only a

> **Frank is essentially the wanderer, the man who is without roots because he is both too naive and too experienced.**
>
> *—Norman Leer*

symbol. The first level can be seen in Morris' dogged attempt to survive and in Frank's involvement in the robbery. The second can be seen in the searching of Frank for a spiritual father, of Morris for a son, and in the final, half-ironic conversion through which the son assumes the suffering of the father. Because the world which Malamud creates has tangible economic lines, he is able to impart to the resistance of his characters a heroic quality, suggested by the Odyssean overtones. It is often a bitter heroism, but one in which the issues are fairly clear. . . . Both a part of and set apart from "mass society," they must . . . find roles to which their heroic dreams can apply. (p. 76)

> Norman Leer, "Three American Novels and Contemporary Society: A Search for Commitment," in Wisconsin Studies in Contemporary Literature, *Vol. III, No. 3, Fall, 1962, pp. 67-85.*

Walter Shear   (essay date Summer 1966)

[*In the excerpt below, Shear considers social and cultural influences acting upon the characters in* The Assistant.]

Although the novel as form is not always restricted to a concern with social milieu, certainly it is a type of literature that is often associated with social awareness. In a given society the writer has available classifications and stratifications which can provide some elements of a literary order and can give an indication, at least, of kinds and qualities of relationships between individuals. Culture, perhaps because of the ambiguity of the term itself, presents materials of a different order, even though it may, in appearance, seem spooned from the same pot. Pervaded with invisible, collective motivations, the novel of culture, as contrasted with the novel of manners, examines more minutely the ambiguities in the relationship between the individual and his values—and thus is both closer to its characters and at the same time attentive to an area beyond them.

Because of the diffused and dynamic society confronting it, the American novel has been inclined toward the broad area of culture rather than toward the national amalgam of behaviors available in its society. This tendency in American literature, a favorite of Eliot-inspired myth-seekers, has not only achieved academic respectability but has inevitably been subject to more and more analysis, one result of which has been to make contemporary novelists increasingly aware of their material, its limitations and possibilities. This is not to say that a critical trend has imposed literary methods on current novelists, but by cons-

tant reminder of what kind of novel has been written and will probably be written, literary analysis has contributed to the more sophisticated attitude the current novelist has towardf his fictional forms.

Perhaps no one better illustrates this kind of sophistication than Bernard Malamud, whose knowledge and manipulation of cultural and literary archetypes has frequently been commented on. Avoiding the analytical preoccupations of other American novelists, Malamud's treatment of his characters is flavored with sympathy, frustration, and exasperation. Knowing that he, as creator, is also contributor to their troubles, he cannot take their situations as seriously as they do. Often he seems to play with his role as "artist" by deliberately blurring the distinction between the archetype, which has universal significance, and the literary cliché, a mode which has exhausted its significance. The result of his peculiar relationship to the characters is that he becomes manipulator of the values they crucify themselves on and in order to remain true to both himself and his characters, two fictional modes—realistic and symbolic—so interact in his fiction as to comment upon each other simultaneously.

In **The Assistant** two cultures, the Jewish tradition and the American heritage (representing the wisdom of the old world and the practical knowledge of the new), collide and to some degree synthesize to provide a texture of social documentation which is manifested in a realistic aesthetic. However, the dichotomy is preserved and in fact given emphasis through an entirely different aesthetic presentation, one which tends to project the characters as types and treats their motivations, environments, and ideas as symbolic threads which link the narrative to the deeper level of personal significance from which the elements of human strength and weakness manage to emerge in the actions which both define and dramatize culture as a phenomenon.

Despite its more overt concern with a Jewish way of life, **The Assistant** deals basically with an implicit conflict between a heritage of ancient wisdom and traditional values and the American atmosphere of practicality and success, a conflict which not merely envelops the characters but— since they are not fully aware of its influence—exists as a constant source of confusion and bewilderment. For the characters these two systems of values become burdens, handicaps, imposers of demands which they cannot meet, most frequently because these demands pull them in opposite directions. Both these value worlds are embodied in all the characters, but the characters also exist in an ironic relationship to the worlds: all are in America, and all are basically secular, thus effectively removed from the traditional religious and social environment in which the old values flourished; in addition all of the major characters are the "have-nots" and blunderers in a country which sanctifies success and efficiency. Thus the characters in a most peculiar way are in the world but not completely in contact with it, a situation Malamud further emphasizes by omitting specific references to time.

On the other hand, the book presents the theme of alienation pushed to the point of an unphilosophic absurdity,

Despite its more overt concern with a Jewish way of life, *The Assistant* deals basically with an implicit conflict between a heritage of ancient wisdom and traditional values and the American atmosphere of practicality and success.

—Walter Shear

and this situation is reiterated in the relationship of the characters, most of whom regard each other with almost premeditated misunderstandings. There is, however, a common meeting ground on the personal level that becomes an important part of the theme: as Solotaroff states, "Malamud's Jews (and his Gentiles) are connected to each other not by religious and social ties but a common fate of error and ill luck and sorrow, of having lost much by their mistakes and recovered little by their virtues" [Theodore Solotaroff, "Bernard Malamud's Fiction: The Old Life; and the New," *Commentary* (1962)]. (pp. 367-69)

[The assistant, Frank Alpine, is a] young man, unencumbered by a past filled with family obligations, who is poor but ambitious, ready to start climbing to the top. In this respect he suggests the typical Horatio Alger hero, but Malamud complements and complicates this portrait with a related stereotype and, with some allusions to *Crime and Punishment* and Raskolnikov's great man theory, pushes Frank toward the journalistic and Hollywood underworld, toward the success dream of the gangster who may become a popular hero by gaining his own kind of fame and fortune.

In presenting such pieces of popular culture Malamud allows the characters to formulate their self-conceptions and speculate on their destinies as those destinies are popularly articulated. For example, Frank's vision of his criminal career is from a pseudo-romantic, sensational point of view with equal parts of the tabloids and Hollywood: "At crime he would change his luck, make adventure, live like a prince. He shivered with pleasure as he conceived robberies, assaults—murders if it had to be— each violent act helping to satisfy a craving that somebody suffer as his own fortune improved." Eventually, through the combination of misfortune, conscience, and the influence of a "good" woman, Frank is able to adjust his dreams to a more socially acceptable goal, that of a college education, and he proudly tells his girl, Helen, that he is going to make something of himself.

By juxtaposing such participations in national reveries with Frank's more real experiences, which reveal both incompetence and a deeper moral awareness, Malamud is able to criticize the more romantic tendencies in American culture and the willingness (frequently desperate) of many to prefer an imagined future to a personally unacceptable present.

This willingness to postpone life by a preoccupation with

abstract goals is made even more explicit in Malamud's treatment of Helen, a girl who is at once more practical and more idealistic than the confused Frank Alpine whose dreams are big but always dreams. Helen is the person who knows what she wants; she is very much aware of the importance of status and she reads—thereby coming in contact with the "higher things in life" and being intellectually cognizant of other levels of experience than the practical and materialistic.

But with her knowledge and experience (her loss of virginity and innocence is both a realistic and symbolic key to some of her practicality), she still remains determinedly a feminine Jay Gatsby, only slightly more mature. Certainly it is not an accident that some of her comments seem to be heavily colored by the Fitzgerald style: "When a person is young he's privileged with all kinds of possibilities. Wonderful things might happen, and when you get up in the morning you feel they will. That's what youth means, and that's what I've lost. I want a larger and better life. I want the return of my possibilities." "Her constant fear," Malamud informs us, "was that her life would not turn out as she had hoped. . . . she could not part with the substance of her dreams." Dreams, of course, have no substance. Eventually, with the assist of peculiar circumstances, she projects her fantasy into the man least able to bear the kind of ideals associated with success, Frank Alpine; and the dream-world turns to one version of a "practical" outlook, a woman's scorn; "She was filled with loathing at the fantasy she had created, of making him into what he couldn't be—educable, promising, kind and good, when he was no more than a bum." Thus one form of the American dream disintegrates again into the psychological tensions which Malamud seems to prefer, and the cultural tendencies of the characters are reduced to the level of personal relationships.

If we look at Morris Bober as a figure in the American success myth, we find a poor businessman, one who lacks the "get up and go" necessary "to reach the top." The business has not changed with the times—the sign which fell down ten years ago has never been replaced, and the customers are not an occasion for social amenities. Morris does not use the hard sell or the soft sell; he is simply there to serve the customers. (And in this regard Morris contrasts with Frank Alpine's later success as a salesman.) Yet Morris, who can be condemned by his family for failing to be at least the good provider and secure the better things in life for his daughter, strangely echoes an old legend about Abraham Lincoln; the rabbi in his funeral oration mentions that he ran two blocks to give back a nickel. Certainly Morris Bober *is* a part of American history, actually almost a stereotype of those many immigrants seeking to escape tyranny, famine, or persecution, who arrived in the New World with some hopes, some ambitions (at one time *he* had planned to be a pharmacist). To some degree he has not done badly; others have faced worse circumstances and have lived with more misery, but the images and dreams of success—even in his little neighborhood—are continual reminders that something has gone wrong, that Morris Bober, immigrant, has not lived or moved in harmony with the cultural dream. One might say that Morris does not move with the times (the new world constantly becoming newer); this, in fact, occurs to him: "America had become too complicated. One man counted for nothing. . . . What had he escaped to here?" However, his thoughts also accuse him: "He had the will of victim, no will to speak of." At this point he seems to be close to one of those truthful lies Malamud seems to relish—to live faithfully in the aura of the success dream one must believe; a defeatist attitude is fatal. At the end of a day of defeat Morris' unuttered words touch the heart of what sociologists might call the relationship between a man and his environment: "He went downstairs and had coffee at a dish-laden table in the Automat. America." As a final ironic twist of this half truth, Morris in his last thoughts accepts the American verdict upon him, "I gave away my life for nothing."

This is one version of *The Assistant,* but not the final word, for the old world has also figured deeply in the lives and actions of the characters, and in Malamud's treatment of its values, expressed chiefly in more traditional symbols and associations, tells us much more what matters about these people because it alone can explain these values in religious and ethical forms. Since the cultural backgrounds are not exclusive, since they do interact, the old not only explains the lives more fully than the immediate environment; it completes them.

While the characters spend much time thinking of the future and its more promising possibilities, they also at times examine themselves (never with complete insight), and they do want to *be* and *do* good. Thus they are capable of responding, if not morally at least with sympathy, to those around them. This tendency towards introspection and self-analysis is, in fact, what gives much comic and pathetic quality to the characterizations and what brings them closer to Malamud's own ethical perception; they know and think better than they are or can be for long. Malamud widens this discrepancy with what seem superficially to be ridiculous symbolic devices. Frank Alpine, the bungling petty criminal, is almost too heavy handedly associated with St. Francis. When he first appears, he just happens to open a magazine in Sam Pearl's counter and immediately recognizes St. Francis preaching to the birds; it is like a vision out of his childhood. St. Francis, Frank tells Sam, said "poverty was a queen and he loved her like she was a beautiful woman." In his comments here Frank expresses the major motives of his character: Like St. Francis he wants "a new view of things," to slough off the old life and put on garments of true worth. He will, in a stumbling way he has never dreamed, pursue both poverty and a woman; and poverty, love, and the woman will be completely intertwined. At first Frank's character, especially his past, seems to resemble the flitting birds more than St. Francis, but he comes very close to complete embodiment at times, most overtly in a scene in the park where Helen sees him feeding the birds and finally rising from the bench, "the pigeons fluttered up with him, a few landing on his arms and shoulders one perched on his fingers, pecking peanuts from his cupped palm." Yet this brief identification is shattered in the next sentence: "Another fat bird sat on his hat," and we return to reality.

Because he is almost a composite of fleshly weaknesses,

Frank Alpine can never really be Francis of Assisi, but he can struggle under the awareness of the image, approach it at times, turn from it and back again. His Catholic heritage, which for the most part is far in the background, seems to be at least indirectly a source of his pangs of conscience and his compulsion to confess everything to Morris. It is, however, this other compulsion, stealing—also the fruits of his childhood—that first involves Frank with Morris Bober, and this wrong becomes the thin but inseverable cord linking them simply as human beings. These ties of evil which Frank establishes with all the major characters are the strongest bonds Frank has with the human race, and it is only his conscience which forces him to live in terms of such simple elemental obligations and to attempt to correct what he cannot correct, what is already past. For all the unthinking harm he brings to others, he remains somewhat absurdly, "a man of stern morality," whose major problem is "to do good if he wanted." He thereby demonstrates the gap, which for Malamud seems permanent, between the will and the way.

Not simply an incompetent criminal and aspiring saint, Frank is also in love with Helen, the symbol and the person—a role which permits Malamud to explore the mixture and madness in traditional views of love. Frank is a lover with a vast range—from the sensuality of the peeping-tom and the sexual enthusiast to the idealism of a clumsy meeter of minds and unselfish giver of gifts and of himself. Throughout his relationship with Helen he attempts to formulate the proper kind of love, some combination of attitude and action that will be acceptable to both himself and his beloved, but the time and situation are never right. On the physical level his love suffers constant frustration by Helen's "ideals in sex"; from spying on her in the bathroom he progresses to an unsatisfactory meeting in his room and finally to a physical fulfillment in the rape-seduction scene in the park, a culmination on the physical level which is disastrous to the love itself. As the bearer of gifts and the intellectual companion, he also fails. Gifts, which for Helen seem tinged with responsibilities and involvement, are returned or thrown away; and his literary background and appreciation are too limited for the amorphous atmosphere of the intellect. Love in Frank's case is a matter of both receiving—on the physical level—and giving—in an idealistic sense; both difficulties seem to be reflected in a basically literary methodology, the search for an adequate correlative in actual terms which might allow the love relationship to flourish. As a key symbol for the entire relationship, Malamud uses the traditional rose, a token of his love which Frank carves out of wood, thus giving a form of beauty to natural material. As an emotionally charged object, however, "the flower reminded Helen of her unhappiness," and she drops it into the garbage can. But in Frank's day-dream at the end of the novel it reappears and changes into a real flower, specifically identified here with Helen and presented not by Frank Alpine, but by his idealized vision of himself, St. Francis.

Helen, as her name suggests, comes to represent the beauty and love all the major characters seek, but she herself is too practical to accept this as an accurate description of what she is at the moment. She is a Helen whose better judgment warns her away from the confusion between un-realized potentials and things as they are. Not wanting to exist merely as an object of love, she shies away from in-volvement even though she feels most acutely the loneli-ness which may be her fate. For her, love with Frank be-comes a resignation to fate, an accepting of the present with all its disappointments as a permanent condition, and therefore love turns to hatred—as she realizes, to divert hatred from herself. Ironically, the more she refuses to ac-quiesce to circumstances, the more abstract and symbolic she becomes to the others who feel they must be deeply immersed in ordinary life.

Both Morris and Ida seem to think of Helen more in terms of her future, and perhaps inevitably in terms of their fu-ture as well, than as an individual. As a man of deeper un-derstanding who is aware of a past involving more than simply his own disappointments and of a future which goes beyond his personal goals, Morris sees other people as having a value in themselves but also as a part of a broader fabric of life which incorporates, rather than tran-scends, the personal psychology of all individuals. Thus, while he is aware of the importance of success to his family obligation, his orientation is not toward the remedying of his failure but toward a form of duty and the acting out of a role, the basis for which he is only dimly aware of. His generosity is evidenced early in such acts as the giving of credit to the little girl whose mother is a drunk and who, Morris knows, will never pay.

He does this not with the conscious pride of doing a good deed—indeed, his conscious thoughts are that this is fool-ish, bad business—but with the half-awareness that he has done what, for his character, is the easiest course. Morris is the fool of goodness; he does good and helps others be-cause it is his nature, an integral part of the world-view he can only vaguely formulate. Basically, Morris is a prod-uct of Jewish thought, perhaps closely connected with the man whose name he echoes, Martin Buber, and this aspect of his character is so insisted upon that the reader is imme-diately aware of the importance of his comments on the Jew and the funeral message of the Rabbi which claims, perhaps on slim evidence, that Morris "was . . . a true Jew because he lived in the Jewish experience." In the dis-cussions between Morris and Frank on the Jewish experi-ence—and this must be interpreted as both historical and current experience—the characters shift from the contem-porary roles of storekeeper and assistant to their purer re-ligious selves, teacher and novitiate. The Jewish Law, Morris explains, "means to do what is right, to be honest, to be good. This means to other people." As Frank points out, these ideas are embodied in other religions, but he gets closer to the particular emphasis of Morris' view by asking about suffering. Do Jews merely suffer because they want to? "If you live, you suffer," Morris says, thereby giving voice to a point of view which sets him apart from the faith in success displayed by most of the people around him. Enlarging the proposition, Morris states that every-one suffers for everyone else. Thematically, such a state-ment can be illustrated by the lives of all the major charac-ters, who sacrifice themselves for others—with much re-sentment in most cases, since they do not possess Morris' vision. The statement is, however, hardly as convincing

out of context as it is an insight into the way Morris' ac-tions make religious sense and a vision of the lost path in which he walks.

As an outsider, rootless and moving, Frank Alpine is at first attracted by the stability of the store, unaware at the beginning that the Bober family regards it as a tomb from which they wish to escape into the American life. Once he starts to realize what it can really be, he struggles to make it a part of the thriving business community of America, gradually succumbing to its necessity to be what it is. In time he succeeds his teacher and accepts the philosophy of suffering and acquiescence, symbolically represented by his conversion to Judaism and his circumcision, the pain of which both "enraged and inspired him." In Malamud's manipulation of another old story, the wanderer has at last become a Jew.

On the other hand, the ideas about suffering and the will-ingness of Frank and Morris to accept such ideas can be accounted for by admitting that only in such a scheme of things could their lives make sense and have purpose. There is, however, imbedded in the novel an ultimate reli-gious perspective that carries the ideas even further than mere apprehensions of roles and duties. Just as Morris is entombed in the store, so all the souls of all the characters are imprisoned in external circumstance, in their culture, and in the very limitations of their senses and the physical demands of their bodies. Norman Leer mentions the social barrier as a symbol of alienation in this novel, but actually all the limitations of the characters serve to set them apart and contradict their best intentions toward one another. Malamud's conception of character is heavily influenced by the naturalistic view of human nature, but his idea of an escape from circumstances in love, and the awareness of the meaning of suffering goes back to an older tradition. The final meaning of such lives, if fiction can ever be final, is in the past, buried in old wisdom of which the characters have only a sketchy knowledge. Perhaps this tendency of Malamud to both give and withdraw his message is also reflected in Marcus Klein's view of his fiction: "The world does not come easily to Malamud, everything is on the verge of not being, and the process of his own holding on, rather than any moralizing he does, is indeed the excite-ment of his fiction, and its tension" [*After Alienation* (1964)].

Oddly enough, a minor character named Breitbart seems to summarize many of the cultural tensions in the novel. As a sufferer, both comic and grotesque, he is the typical victim appearing in sensational tabloid stories—his wife runs away with his brother, leaving him with "a drawerful of bills . . . and a not too bright five-year-old boy." On his back he lugs around a burden of light bulbs, suggesting many frames of reference from the spark of humanity or conscience to the modern world of progress. Perhaps all these meanings work in the same confused, half-comic, in-termittent light which pervades the entire novel. At any rate he appears in the final scene still trapped in his eco-nomic journeys, stops briefly for a cup of tea, and gives Frank a last word which may be both advice and descrip-tion, "Schwer." Moving between existence and nonexis-tence he has no definite role within either context of meaning and yet a possible place in each. His routine, like those of the other characters, is invested at different times with differing values.

Marcus Klein, paraphrasing some comments by Saul Bellow, writes, "The fat gods of the new materialism are all about us demanding our energies." One might say that in *The Assistant* the same situations exist in regard to meaning, and man, caught between the conflicting claims of cultural values, suffers not only because of his circumstances but because a fragmented abundance of world-views produces uncertainty about intentions, actions, and roles. If Malamud here seems to be on the side of older values, he refuses his characters willed preferences or convictions. They have faith enough to persevere but doubt enough to suspect themselves. (pp. 370-80)

> *Walter Shear, "Culture Conflict in 'The Assistant'," in* The Midwest Quarterly, *Vol. VII, No. 4, Summer, 1966, pp. 367-80.*

James M. Mellard   (essay date Fall 1967)

[*Mellard is an American critic and educator specializing in the study of modern fiction. In the following essay, he discusses the pastoral aspect of* The Assistant.]

Philip Roth has said that Bernard Malamud's Jews are "a metaphor to stand for certain human possibilities and certain human promises" and that "his people live in a timeless depression and a placeless Lower East Side." But instead of seeing this as an indication of Malamud's breadth and depth, Roth intends a rather sweeping condemnation because Malamud "does not—or has not yet—found the contemporary scene a proper or sufficient backdrop for his tales of heartlessness and heartache, of suffering and regeneration." It seems to me, however, that to make his characters less metaphorical and his settings more specific, Malamud would be forced to give up the major features of his special mode, the pastoral. Obviously invoking an entirely different set of novelistic assumptions, Roth, in looking for the specific, has denigrated the universal in Malamud's major fiction and has been unwilling to accept the fact that his Jewish characters stand for human types in much the same way as, say, Robert Frost's Yankee farmers and that his temporal and physical settings in the metropolis (usually) are as timeless and universal as Frost's agrarian New England "north of Boston."

To begin with, what are the pastoral elements of *The Assistant*? If we think of the pastoral at all, we normally associate it with shepherds and flocks, fields and streams and flowers. But by "pastoral" we mean here the pastoral *mode,* the pastoral manner, method, or power of acting, doing, or being; and this mode, according to William Empson, is no more than "putting the complex into the simple." In *The Assistant,* Malamud puts the complex into the simple in several ways. First, for his characters, in place of the conventional shepherds he uses simple lower-class and proletarian types, often Jewish, whose thoughts and language give Malamud an uncluttered, but highly lyrical style, and whose frustrations and privations mirror the basic human condition. A second and more important way in which Malamud implements the pastoral

mode is in the pervasive use of nature imagery. And this leads us to Malamud's most important method: nature imagery in *The Assistant* suggests that the narrative center of the novel lies in the pastoral vegetation myths, rituals, and ceremonies that celebrate the cycles of death and renewal in nature.

We might consider first the stylistic advantages Malamud gains by using the pastoral mode in *The Assistant.* There are, for modern fiction in general and Malamud's work in particular, virtually immeasurable advantages of language and thematic statement. Empson tells us, "The essential trick of the old pastoral . . . was to make simple people express strong feelings . . . in learned and fashionable language . . . " Although the language of *The Assistant* is not essentially learned, in terms of recent philosophical developments, particularly existentialism, it certainly is fashionable. Consider, for example, the kind of language and thought and emotion that go into the scene in which Frank Alpine and Morris Bober discuss Jewish law and Jewish suffering:

> "But tell me why is it that Jews suffer so damn much, Morris? It seems to me that they like to suffer, don't they?"
>
> Do you like to suffer? They suffer because they are Jews."
>
> "That's what I mean, they suffer more than they have to."
>
> "If you live, you suffer. Some people suffer more, but not because they want. But I think if a Jew don't suffer for the Law, he will suffer for nothing."
>
> "What do you suffer for, Morris?" Frank said.
>
> "I suffer for you," Morris said calmly.
>
> Frank laid his knife down on the table. His mouth ached. "What do you mean?"
>
> "I mean you suffer for me."

The language has the simplicity of a moral fable, but the thought and the emotional content have the depth and the ambiguity of modern poetry. Morris, called by critics an almost archetypal Jew, does suffer at the hands of the non-Jews; but Frank, the errant gentile, also suffers guilt and mental anguish because of Morris. And both the old man and the young are inevitably going to suffer from having been born into an absurd universe, as the existentialists tell us, in which the only meaningful values are those man can find or create for himself. Thus, here, we find a highly fashionable idiom combined with the "pastoral process of putting the complex into the simple," as Empson has it. And the advantages of this process are remarkable, for Malamud's characters think, dream, and say things that would be ridiculous in any other mode. Thus, Frank Alpine can express the theme of identity very clearly by saying, "I don't understand myself"; through Morris Bober, Malamud can summarize precisely the ironic themes of the novel: ". . . Morris saw the blow descend and felt sick of himself, of soured expectations, endless frustration, the years gone up in smoke . . . because of him Helen and Ida had less"; and, even more importantly, Helen Bober can say, "Life renews itself," and thus blandly capsulize the enormous truths of biology and the pastoral mode in one naive breath. Instead of denying her this insight, we eventually see that the entire thematic and narrative structure of *The Assistant* depends upon its truth.

There is little doubt about the basic simplicity of Malamud's characters in *The Assistant,* with its shopkeepers, laborers, and indigents, or his opening themes of frustration and privation, but not so frequently recognized is the way in which their attitudes toward nature express this simplicity while pushing the themes beyond the merely ironic. In the novel Malamud links the desires of the characters, and thus their needs, to the seasonal cycle, the cycle of life in nature. Consequently, in the first movement of the novel, most of the imagery has associations with an urban wasteland. In the beginning, before Frank Alpine appears, the vicissitudes of weather seem to express the Bober family's entrapment. Focusing on Morris Bober, the book opens with a "November street" that "was dark though night had ended," and a wind that, "to the grocer's surprise, already clawed." In a few moments, Morris "wished fleetingly that he could once more be out in the open, as when he was a boy—never in the house, but the sound of the blustery wind frightened him." Although Morris longs for the days of his youth when he was "always running in the muddy, rutted streets of the village, or across the fields, or bathing with the other boys in the river," he now feels only uneasiness when he pictures himself "without a roof over his head." Thus the winter wasteland of the barren New York City ghetto is an objectification of the Bobers' mental and physical plight: "He recalled the bad times he had lived through, but now times were worse than in the past; now they were impossible."

In the wintry desolation of the novel, even the young people whose ritualistic romance is to transform the wasteland are spiritually and emotionally snowbound. "Winter tormented Helen," we are told, and "she mourned the long age before spring and feared loneliness in winter." Thus when she is on Coney Island with Louis Karp, "gone from the sky was the umbrella of rosy light that glowed over the place in summertime" and, in an image reminiscent of Stephen Crane, "a few cold stars gleamed down. In the distance a dark Ferris wheel looked like a stopped clock," an image that suggests Helen's feeling that time has stopped, that the circuit of the seasons has hung up on winter. To the wintertime Helen, "December yielded nothing to spring." Even Frank, the slightly ambivalent force of renewal "lately come from the West, looking for a better opportunity," has his spells of *Weltschmerz.* Often "he stood at the window, thinking thoughts about his past, and wanting a new life. Would he ever get what he wanted?" But then looking out the window, Frank sees the Bobers' emblematic undergarments, "Morris's scarecrow union suits, Ida's hefty bloomers, modestly folded lengthwise, and her housedresses guarding her daughter's flowerlike panties and restless brassieres." As the season changes and winter gradually gives way to spring, it increasingly becomes clear that Frank's role is to replace the "scarecrow" father and to bring to fruition the "flowerlike" daughter if the human wasteland is to be revitalized along with nature.

As Malamud suggests the lacks and limitations of the characters in seasonal imagery, so he links the changes that occur in their lives to the seasonal cycle of changes. In the novel, this movement in the narrative is essentially an expression of the pastoral vegetation ritual of the aging father giving way to the son. Descended from romances of wastelands, dragon-killing heroes, aged kings, and beautiful daughters, this pattern in *The Assistant* is also closely associated with Oedipal-dream fantasies "in which the hero is not the old king's son-in-law but his son, and the rescued damsel the hero's mother" [Northrop Frye, *Anatomy of Criticism,* 1957]. Although these relationships are slightly "displaced" in *The Assistant,* it is clear enough that Frank Alpine is a symbolic and practical replacement for Bober's dead son, Ephraim, with whom Frank is often linked, as in Bober's dying dreams. And because of Frank's name, *Alpine,* his association with St. Francis, birds, a park and a lilac tree, the "son"-hero here becomes a kind of "god" of vegetation who both unifies and gives form to the two strands of the plot of the novel—the decline, death, and "resurrection" of Morris Bober and the conventional romantic relationship between Helen and Frank.

Malamud shows the replacement of the old storekeeper by Frank in its archetypal simplicity in the novel's first, ninth and tenth sections, in which Frank attacks Morris, Morris dies, and Frank takes over the store. But locally, in the intervening seven sections, strong pastoral associations also recur. The process of "atonement" . . . is introduced in the second section, for example, when Frank's and Morris's first official meeting becomes a symbolic communion, with Morris offering Frank a cup of coffee and a "seeded hard roll" that he "bit into hungrily," saying, "Jesus, this is good bread." It is also in this chapter that we learn that Frank's idol is St. Francis, who "took a fresh view of things." We learn, moreover, of Morris's real need for Frank: ". . . when he tried to lug the milk cases through the snow, he found it all but impossible. And there was no Frank Alpine to help him, for he had disappeared after washing the window," a window that happens to give Morris a fresh view of things too. Finally, at the end of this section, the nature of the coming change is foreshadowed in Ida's dream that "all the stock was gone, the shelves as barren as the picked bones of dead birds," Morris's fainting, and Frank's removing Morris's emblematic apron and taking over his job, saying, "I need the experience." In the section following, the quality of the change is further revealed, for Ida sees that under Frank's management "the store had improved," and now "people seemed less worried and irritable, less in competition for the little sunlight in the world." Furthermore, in section four, we learn that Morris is loath to go back to his old job: "Although he hadn't said so to Ida, the grocer, after his long layoff, was depressed at the prospect of having to take up his dreary existence in the store. He dreaded the deadweight of hours, mostly sad memories of his lost youth." Finally, in the remaining sections, the impediments to a more satisfactory relationship between surrogate son and father are removed; in five Morris discovers and condones Frank's petty thievery, in six Ida discovers and reveals to Morris Frank's courtship of Helen, and in eight Frank confesses to Morris about the original robbery and assault, about which Morris had already guessed the truth, and which brings about the completion of the "at-one-ment" with the father. After Morris's death, in section nine, and Frank's succession to the store, we recognize the full extent of the identification of Bober and Alpine in the very precise paralleling of the opening of the novel, focusing on the old man, and its closing, focusing on the younger man, who has begun even to *look* like Bober, as well as to imitate his actions and mannerisms.

No less closely allied to the pastoral vegetation myths of seasonal renewal is the romantic relationship of Helen Bober and Frank Alpine. Frank is even more important to Helen than to Morris, for he must only replace the aged grocer, but he has to bring a renewal of possibility, of hope, of life, even, to the daughter. Before Frank intrudes into Helen's life, she can insist that "life *has* to have some meaning," while, at the same time, she can only long for a "larger and better life" and the return of her "possibilities." Later, however, suddenly seeing that Frank has a "potential depth," she feels that "the future offered more in the way of realizable possibilities . . . if a person dared take a chance with it. The question was, did she?" For her, it is truly Frank who is her "man of possibilities," though the question, does she dare take a chance with him? is left only partially answered at the novel's conclusion.

Though Malamud leaves this question for the attentive reader, little doubt as to the true answer should remain if one is sufficiently aware of the sympathetic associations of Helen's and Frank's love affair and the rhythm of nature itself. We have seen that Helen "mourned the long age before spring and feared loneliness in winter" and that "Winter tormented" her, but at first she willfully ignores the force of life that can change her despair into hope and love. In a scene analogous to Frank's looking out at the Bober's wind-blown undergarments, Helen looks out a window at a view of desolation. "The remnants of last week's dirty snow. No single blade of green, or flower to light the eye or lift the heart. She felt as if she were made of knots and in desperation got on her coat, tied a yellow kerchief around her head and left the house again, not knowing which way to go. She wandered toward the leafless park." If the library is the Apollonian Helen's proper abode, the park is the Dionysian Frank's, so as Helen walks toward it she sees a man there feeding birds, in the image of St. Francis. Recognizing the man as Frank Alpine, Helen joins him and, as they sit hesitantly together on the park bench, "One of the pigeons began to chase another running in circles and landed on its back. Helen looked away but Frank idly watched the birds until they flew off." Emblematic of Helen's and Frank's contrasting attitudes toward sex and love and nature, this scene Malamud soon replaces by others in which even Helen begins to identify her warmer emotions with the climatic conditions.

If at first she resisted love—"fighting hesitancies, fears of a disastrous mistake"—she later embraces it healthily. Of Frank she thinks, "One day he seemed unknown, lurking at the far end of an unlit cellar; the next day he was standing in sunlight . . . "; and, as their relationship grows for her from one of head to one of heart, shifting in symbolic

locus from the library to the park, she kisses Frank and wonders, ". . . would it never come spring?" Then "one cold, starry night she led him through the trees in the park near where they usually sat, on to a broad meadow where on summer nights lovers lay in the grass." And from this symbolic setting, Frank and Helen soon go to an intimacy much more mature, described in some of the most lyrical language of the novel:

> She lay with closed eyes in his arms, feeling the warmth of the heater like a hand on her back. For a minute she half-dozed, then woke to his kisses. She lay motionless, a little tense, but when he stopped kissing her, relaxed. She listened to the quiet sound of the rain in the street, making it in her mind into spring rain, though spring was weeks away; and within the rain grew all sorts of flowers; and amid the spring flowers, in this flowering dark—a sweet spring night— she lay with him in the open under new stars and a cry rose to her throat. When he kissed her again, she responded with passion.

Though not for Frank, for Helen this moment represents the high point of their relationship as it is developed in the novel, for all that follows is her mother's discovery of their affair, Ward Minogue's attack, Frank's dramatic rescue and ritualistic assault, "on the winter earth," "under the trees" of "the star-dark field" in late February.

That this shall not be the end of Frank's and Helen's romance is implied in several ways. In the first place, Malamud tells us that she hates waste; yet as she waited for Frank in the park on the night of the rape, "she regretted the spring-like loveliness of the night; it had gone, in her hands, to waste." So, if Frank's assault upon her wintry flesh was premature, it was also both inevitable and, as she later understands herself, totally desirable, a knowledge that causes her to detest Frank and to feel an extreme guilt herself. And as she fights her conflicting impulses—"She wanted to be a virgin again and at the same time a mother"—she has a sexual dream that foreshadows the clearing of the way for love and marriage with Frank: "In the dream she had got up to leave the house in the middle of the night to escape Frank waiting on the stairs; but there he stood under the yellow lamp, fondling his lascivious cap." Recalling her imprecation, "uncircumcised dog," the "lascivious cap" represents perhaps the last impediment to Helen's love, but this is removed, finally, when "One day in April Frank went to the hospital and had himself circumcised."

What of the "hero," Frank Alpine, in these changes? Frank too undergoes a transformation, a transfiguration, one that is much more than his simply being circumcised and becoming a Jew. As he replaces Bober in the store and brings a renewed consciousness of life to Helen, Frank comes to an awareness of self, achieves a new identity, and begins a "new life." When Frank comes from the west, seeking to break out of the "trap" of his past, he is a typical *alazon,* a man who does not know who or what he is: "I've often tried to change the way things work out for me," he says, "but I don't know how, even when I think I do. I have in my heart to do more than I can remember," adding plaintively, "What I mean to say is that when I need it most something is missing in me, in me or account of me." And he sums up his plight: "I don't understand myself. I don't really know what I'm saying to you or why I am saying it," he tells Bober. But as Frank comes more and more to know the grocer and his daughter, so he comes more and more to understand himself. Early in their romance, Frank tells Helen, "My nature is to give and I couldn't change it even if I wanted." But stealing is not giving, so at this time Frank is at least trying to change his nature. But later he tells her, "I want you to know I am a very good guy in my heart. . . . Even when I am bad I am good," and soon he thinks, "I am not the same guy I once was." Although in the next few scenes Frank continues his moral oscillation, still taking money, pursuing his affair with Helen, and eventually assaulting her icy and, for the nonce, at least, impregnable fortress, he begins to see the value of suffering, as Morris does, and achieves an essentially selfless relationship to the old man, saying, when Ida asks him why he works so hard for nothing, "For Morris," though he wants to say, "for love." Beginning to read, moreover, of the history and achievements of the Jews, Frank comes to feel that a possible solution for his problem with Bober is confession of his part in the original holdup, though he "realized it was a wild chance that might doom rather than redeem him." Though Morris has already guessed, Frank does finally confess openly:

> "Even now I feel sick about what I am saying, but I'm telling it to you so you will know how much I suffered on account of what I did, and that I am very sorry you were hurt on your head—even though not by me. The thing you got to understand is I am not the same person I once was. I might look so to you, but if you could see what's been going on in my heart you would know I have changed."

And he has changed. After Morris Bober's death, he takes care of both Helen and Ida by working at a job at night as well as operating the store during the day. Once living only in the past, now he "lived in the future, to be forgiven." Finally, Malamud shows even Helen becoming aware of Frank's transfiguration. In a sudden epiphanic moment, Helen happens to see a thin, overworked, groggy Frank behind the counter of the store where he worked at night. "It came to her that he had changed. It's true, he's not the same man. . . . She had despised him for the evil he had done, without understanding the why or aftermath, or admitting there could be an end to the bad and a beginning of good."

Dreams in the novel often foreshadow events, suggest something of their importance, and even suggest the basic mythic patterns of the dual movements of the novel. But it is in Malamud's play upon the significance of the term *dance* that we recognize not the mythic but the *ritualistic* essence of the novel's major events. It is through ritual that man attempts to express his control over the natural world, or, if he cannot control nature, that he at least participates sympathetically in its movements. In *The Assistant,* when the movements of man and nature are in accord, Malamud suggests the unity through the image of the dance. For example, the love of Frank and Helen, so necessary for the renewal of human life in the novel, is

called, midway in the novel, a "dizzying dance," though Helen, at this point, "didn't want to" dance. Just as important to the novel as the young couple's love, the ritual of Frank's replacing Morris is also shown through the image of the dance. At Bober's funeral, Frank loses his balance and falls into the grave, where he "landed feet first on the coffin." Then, later, as Ida and Helen returned to the store from the funeral and ". . . toiled up the stairs they heard the dull cling of the register in the store and knew the grocer was the one who had danced on the grocer's coffin." Malamud suggests the successful completion of the two actions of the novel at the conclusion, where the images of the dance, a symbolic rose, St. Francis, Frank and Helen are all brought together in one of Alpine's daydreams:

> As he was reading he had this pleasant thought. He saw St. Francis come dancing out of the woods in his brown rags, a couple of scrawny birds flying around over his head. St. F. stopped in front of the grocery, and reaching into the garbage can, plucked the wooden rose out of it. He tossed it into the air and it turned into a real flower that he caught in his hand. With a bow he gave it to Helen, who had just come out of the house. "Little sister, here is your little sister the rose." From him she took it, although it was with the love and best wishes of Frank Alpine.

It is, I think, in these last images that the real significance of the pastoral rituals and mythic patterns in *The Assistant* lies. The ritual symbolizes a form of control over himself and his environment, and thus provides a way for man to make an art of *life,* a way for man to see and to create a meaningful form of his existence. We have discussed what Frank brings to Helen, but what has Helen brought to Frank? In part, at least, what Helen offers Frank is the discipline necessary for the dance of life. Thinking of Helen's word, *discipline,* Frank wonders why he is so moved by it, but then he supplies his own answer: it is connected to the idea of self-control and "with the idea of self control came the feeling of the beauty of it—the beauty of a person being able to do things the way he wanted to, to do good if he wanted. . . ." This, I think, is the heart of the difference between the dancing St. Francis, identified with the new Frank Alpine, and a Morris Bober "the victim in motion of whatever blew at his back" or an old Frank "blown around in any breath that blew." And this is why the wooden rose is so important to Frank, for, unlike the gift of a one-volume edition of Shakespeare, it provides the focal point for a ritualistic act that is undeniably creative rather than imitative. When, at the end of section seven, Frank is first shown carving, he produces "a bird flying" and "a rose starting to bloom." Wrapping the rose in store paper, Frank secretly gives it to Helen, but Helen, who now "lived in hatred of herself for having loved the clerk," throws it into a garbage can. But when St. Francis, in Frank's reverie, plucks the wooden rose out of the garbage can, it turns into a real rose, and Helen accepts it, we must feel, as Frank does, that at last he has succeeded not only with Helen but in gaining a measure of control over his fate, however savorless that fate might be to most of us. Through the ritual participation of man in nature's cycles, man has been able to unite eternal and temporal, desire and necessity, creativity and creation, art and life. And Frank Alpine, who tries everything from violence to theft to rise in the world and to find the way of plenitude, discovers the way of privation and the Heraclitean truth that "the way up and the way down are the same," for by falling into a grave of a store in the middle of New York City he loses himself and gains a life. (pp. 1-11)

> James M. Mellard, "Malamud's 'The Assistant': The City Novel as Pastoral," in Studies in Short Fiction, Vol. V, No. 1, Fall, 1967, pp. 1-11.

Arnold L. Goldsmith   (essay date Summer 1977)

[Goldsmith is an American educator and critic. In the essay below, he discusses nature imagery in The Assistant.]

In The Landscape of Nightmare, Jonathan Baumbach was one of the first critics to comment on Bernard Malamud's use of the changing seasons in **The Assistant** (1957) to provide "his timeless and placeless New York landscape with a kind of metaphysical climate. The novel starts in early November and ends in mid-April, symbolically covering the Fall, the Death, and the Redemption of Man. The seasons mirror the inner conditions of the central characters." Two years after The Landscape of Nightmare, James M. Mellard, following Baumbach's lead, published two thoughtful articles on Malamud's use of the pastoral mode, basing his argument on William Empson's belief that essentially, the pastoral mode can be defined as "putting the complex in the simple." According to Mellard [in "Malamud's The Assistant: The City Novel as Pastoral," Studies in Short Fiction (1967)], Malamud does this through 1) his use of lower-class, proletarian characters and 2) his "pervasive use of nature imagery." In **The Assistant,** the nature imagery "suggests that the narrative center of the novel lies in the pastoral vegetation myths, rituals, and ceremonies that celebrate the cycles of death and renewal in nature." Mellard sees Frank Alpine functioning as the mythical son-hero transforming the waste land: " . . . Frank's role is to replace the 'scarecrow' father and to bring to fruition the 'flower-like' daughter if the human wasteland is to be revitalized along with nature."

As interesting and illuminating as Mellard's argument is, it suffers from overemphasizing the myth approach to Malamud's second novel. Although this critical approach works brilliantly in analysis of **The Natural** (1952), it ultimately leads to a distortion of the tone of **The Assistant.** To see Frank as transforming the waste land is to magnify his limited ability and to find major change where there is only possibility of fulfillment. To emphasize Frank's role as ritual hero is to blur his movement from schlemiel to schlimazel. What Mellard overlooks is that the change of the seasons, the circular movement which leads to Frank's replacing Morris, also results in the new grocer's inheriting the old man's future. This is not to deny the important transformation of Frank's character from immoral drifter to moral benefactor, but despite the possibility of hope, there is the equal chance of failure. As Malamud

once wrote in an unpublished letter in response to a question about the ending of **"The Magic Barrel"**: "There's no proof Leo will be destroyed by Stella. Kaddish may express a hope as well as a mourning. I like the juxtaposition." The comparison is self-evident.

The myth approach to **The Assistant** has thrown considerable light on the thematic intent of Bernard Malamud, but a return to the text for a close study of the author's nature imagery and symbolism will contribute to a fuller understanding of his complex art. It will show that nature in this novel provides a major pattern of imagery which functions not only to supply a mythic substructure to universalize a contemporary story and to support theme and characterization, but also to reinforce mood, provide comic and ironic undertone, and to serve as a link between the world of dream and reality, fantasy and fact.

Metaphorically, there is no summer in the present existence of Malamud's characters—only what they dimly remember from their youth when things seemed to be better. The daily events in the lives of these people are reflected in the hard brown earth, leafless trees, bitter wind, yellow slush, and dark, cold rain. This correlation can best be seen in the hard life of Morris Bober, the sixty-year-old grocer whose life is a dismal story of repeated failure. When Morris, out of desperation, decides to ask for a cashier's job in a supermarket now owned by his former partner who once cheated him out of a promising business, Malamud writes that the weather, "though breezy, was not bad—it promised better, but he had little love for nature. It gave nothing to a Jew. The March wind hastened him along, prodding the shoulders. He felt weightless, unmanned, the victim in motion of whatever blew at his back." Though Morris may feel that nature is no friend or comfort to him, only another force contributing to his victimization, to Malamud, nature imagery and symbolism supply a motif which greatly enriches the texture of his story.

Malamud prepares his reader carefully for the drama that is about to unfold. The opening sentence of the novel announces that "The early November street was dark though night had ended, but the wind, to the grocer's surprise, already clawed." Wind imagery is associated mainly with Morris. In summarizing his life story for his new assistant, Morris tells how as an immigrant he was preparing to become a pharmacist by going to night school. One of his favorite poems, which he still remembers, began, " 'Come,' said the wind to the leaves one day, 'come over the meadows with me and play.' " It did not take Morris long to recognize the difference between the romantic sentimentality of the verse and the harshness of earning a living in America. Marriage made him impatient with the school and hastened his entrance into the world of business.

From the window of his store, Morris looks out at the street and remembers how, as a boy in Russia, he loved the outdoors: "No, not for an age had he lived a whole day in the open. As a boy, always running in the muddy, rutted streets of the village, or across the fields, or bathing with the other boys in the river; but as a man, in America, he rarely saw the sky. In the early days, when he drove a horse and wagon, yes, but not since the first store. In a store you were entombed." Now, "the sound of the blustery wind frightened him."

In late March, when Morris returns from the hospital after his inept attempt to commit suicide, his self-pity is interlaced with the pathetic fallacy. From his bedroom windows he watches winter's reluctance to surrender to spring:

> There was at least more light in the day; it burst through the bedroom windows. But a cold wind roared in the streets, giving him goose pimples in bed; and sometimes, after half a day of pure sunshine, the sky darkened and some rags of snow fell. He was filled with melancholy and spent hours dreaming of his boyhood. He remembered the green fields. Where a boy runs he never forgets. His father, his mother, his only sister whom he hadn't seen in years, gottenyu. The wailing wind cried to him. . . .

Both the self-pity and pathetic fallacy are seen again when Morris reflects on the irony of life. *His* grocery store is undamaged by the fire he tried to start; Karp's liquor store is accidentally burned to the ground by Ward Minogue, and the lucky owner collects the insurance. The day is overcast, "and there were snow flurries in the air. Winter still spits in my face, thought the weary grocer. He watched the fat wet flakes melt as they touched the ground. It's too warm for snow he thought, tomorrow will come April."

Morris thinks that his luck has finally improved as Karp accepts the inflated figure the old grocer asks for his store and apartments. Morris' rare happiness is once again identified with his boyhood in the Russian outdoors:

> The spring snow moved Morris profoundly. He watched it falling, seeing in it scenes of his childhood, remembering things he thought he had forgotten. All morning he watched the shifting snow. He thought of himself, a boy running in it, whooping at the blackbirds as they flew from the snowy trees; he felt an irresistible thirst to be out in the open.

At this point Malamud introduces the major ironic twist of the plot. Feeling the urge to shovel the snow for the gentiles who will be walking to church, ignoring Ida's warning that "It's winter," not spring, he waits until the evening before going outside. Clouds of snow are blowing through the streets. "To his surprise the wind wrapped him in an icy jacket, his apron flapping noisily. He had expected, the last of March, a milder night. The surprise lingered in his mind but the shoveling warmed him. He kept his back to Karp's burned hole, though with the black turned white it wasn't too hard to look at." Morris recalls the hard winters his first years in America, followed by a milder cycle. But now the harshness has returned and he is worn out from his exertion. Still he won't give in to Ida, who calls him to stop. " 'For twenty-two years,' he shouts to her, 'stinks in my nose this store. I wanted to smell in my lungs some fresh air.' " Morris' body, however, cannot take the shock, and that night the pneumonia sets in that kills him. The poor schlemiel-schlimazel cannot understand why nature has played such tricks on him: "So he had shoveled snow in the street, but did it have to snow in April? And if it did, did he have to get sick the minute he stepped out into the open air?"

Morris dies on April Fool's Day. Nature plays its last trick on him, an irony that he would have appreciated: "In the cemetery it was spring. The snow had melted on all but a few graves, the air was warm, fragrant." Here the voice is Malamud's—matter-of-fact, unemotional. The pathetic fallacy is conspicuously missing, the irony quietly effective.

One pattern of nature imagery subtly used by Malamud to add a quite different, almost surrealistic touch to the story of the grocer and his assistant involves the sea and marine life. Through his use of underwater images, Malamud suggests, sometimes comically, sometimes seriously, the dark, submerged quality of the life of the Bober family and their neighbors. A hint at this pattern of imagery can be found in the names of some of the characters—Karp, Pearl, Minogue, but more conclusive is the passage revealing Frank's thoughts after he is guilt-stricken over the rape of Helen. Taking advantage of the desperation of Ida because of Morris' illness, Frank, despite his having been fired by the grocer, moves back behind the counter. He is tortured by the sight of the grocer's daughter: "All this time he had snatched only glimpses of her, though his heart was heavy with all he hoped to say. He saw her through the plate glass window—she on the undersea side. Through the green glass she looked drowned, yet never, God help him, lovelier."

The image of drowning and the underseas quality of life in and around the store are also implied in passages describing Morris. Early in the novel, as he counts the day's receipts that come to only ten dollars, "He thought he had long ago touched bottom but now knew there was none." A few pages later, as he is numbed from the blow from Ward Minogue during the robbery, he thinks how little America has given him. He has defrauded Ida and Helen, "he and the bloodsucking store." Much later, when he cannot stand the dishonesty of trying to sell a worthless store to an unsuspecting immigrant buyer, Morris blurts out the truth that the store is run down, but that a young, energetic owner might be able to save it. Ida tries to prevent him from ruining the sale, "but Morris kept on talking till he was swimming in his sea of woes. . . . " And in a cliché purposely used by Malamud to characterize the uneducated assistant, Frank listens to Morris reminisce about his past and observes that the grocer had escaped out of the Russian army to America, but once in the store, "he was like a fish fried in deep fat."

Of the various marine or fish images seen in the characters' names, Nat Pearl's is the most ironic. This sexually aggressive law student falls far short of Helen's romantic dreams. Baumbach sees Nat as "the spiritual heir of his father, a good but materialistic man, whose livelihood comes from selling penny candy. That Helen's dream of a better life might be satisfied by marriage to Nat Pearl suggests the inadequacy of her aspirations." Nat, in short, is no Pearl.

The most interesting fish name in the novel is Karp. In the

first description of the liquor store owner, the fish image is clearly implied. Helen observes "paunchy Julius Karp, with bushy eyebrows and an ambitious mouth, blowing imaginary dust off a bottle as he slipped a deft fifth of something into a paper bag, while Louis, slightly popeyed son and heir, looking up from clipping to the quick of his poor fingernails, smiled aimiably upon a sale." The fat body, mouth puckered as it blows air, and the "popeyed" son—all suggest the fish analogy. More significant is Morris' dislike of this man, this fish which lives off the bottom of the lake, destroying the eggs and nests of more valuable fish. Morris, while convalescing, "discovered he disliked him more than he had imagined. He resented him as a crass and stupid person who had fallen through luck into flowing prosperity. His every good fortune spattered others with misfortune, as if there was just so much luck in the world and what Karp left over wasn't fit to eat." It is Karp who escapes from his store when the robbers drive around the block and then decide to rob Morris' instead. It is Karp who owns the empty store across the street from Morris' and breaks his word, renting it to another grocer. It is Karp whose store is destroyed by fire while Morris' attempt at arson fails. When Karp offers to buy Morris' store, "Morris couldn't believe his ears. He was filled with excitement and dread that somebody would tell him he had just dreamed a dream, or that Karp, fat fish, would turn into a fat bird and fly away screeching, 'Don't you believe me,' or in some heartbreaking way change his mind." Morris' skepticism foreshadows his disappointment, as another dream turns into another nightmare. Karp has a heart attack, survives, but is no longer interested in buying out Morris. The fat fish-fat bird will retire, living comfortably off the insurance money, leaving Morris to his doom.

In developing the character of Morris Bober's daughter, Helen, Malamud also makes extensive use of nature imagery. The barrenness of nature reflects the bleakness of her life. When she appears in the opening chapter, Helen gets off the subway two stops before her home and walks through the park "despite the sharp wind. . . . The leafless trees left her with unearned sadness. She mourned the long age before spring and feared loneliness in winter." Like her father, Helen spends hours "at the window, looking out at the back yards. The remnants of last week's dirty snow. No single blade of grass, or flowers to light the eye or lift the heart. She felt as if she were made of knots. . . . " Thus the grayness of fall and winter and especially the leafless trees become the objective epitome of Helen's existence.

Helen does not know what she really wants. A romantic dreamer, she is reading *Don Quixote* on the subway when the novel begins. Embarrassed by the presence of Nat Pearl, to whom she had lost her virginity the previous summer, she tries to hide "her thoughts behind the antics of a madman until memory overthrew him and she found herself ensnared in scenes of summer that she would gladly undo, although she loved the season; but how could you undo what you had done again in the fall, unwillingly willing?"

Helen sentimentally equates summer with romance, love,

friendship, and happiness. Nostalgically, she remembers her past as a youth, "spending every day of summer in a lively crowd of kids on the beach." Malamud writes that Helen's "summer face was gentler than her winter one. . . . " Early in the novel, Louis Karp takes her for a walk one dark windy night on the Coney Island boardwalk. As Helen gazes enviously at the large homes facing the ocean, she notices how deserted the Island is. Only an occasional hamburger stand or pinball concession is open. "Gone from the sky was the umbrella of rosy light that glowed over the place in summertime. A few cold stars gleamed down. In the distance a dark Ferris wheel looked like a stopped clock. They stood at the rail of the boardwalk, watching the black, restless sea." Helen longs for "the return of her possibilities," perhaps some vaguely realized dream of rosy lights, spinning Ferris wheels, and romantic attachment. Instead, she has to suffer the crude, animalistic advances of Louis Karp, who is bored by her philosophizing about her youth and complains of the cold: "Jesus, this wind, it flies up my pants. At least gimme another kiss." She removes his hands from her breasts and rejects his marriage proposal. The pathetic fallacy effectively expresses her mood as "She listened to the winddriven, sobbing surf," but Malamud deflates the romantic with the realistic as Louis replies, "Let's go get the hamburgers."

Repelled by Louis Karp, Helen wishes that Nat Pearl would call, but she is disappointed. Malamud continues his pattern of seasonal symbolism:

> December yielded nothing to spring. She awoke to each frozen, lonely day with dulled feeling. Then one Sunday afternoon winter leaned backward for an hour and she went walking. Suddenly she forgave everyone everything. A warmish breath of air was enough to inspire; she was again grateful for living. But the sun soon sank and it snowed pellets.

Here is a subtle foreshadowing of the affair she will soon have with Frank Alpine, her father's assistant.

As Helen's feelings for Frank slowly blossom, Malamud has the couple move from the prison-like confinement of the store to the openness of the local park. Their favorite trysting place is "in front of the lilac trees." It is in the park where they embrace for the first time. Helen is fascinated by the mysterious Italian, but he falls considerably short of her romantic ideal. Sickened by the drabness of her life, she cannot envision this man leading her out of her past. All of her dreams are summed up in her wondering, "Would it never come spring?" As the frequency of their meetings increases, they go from cold park bench to street corners. "When it rained or snowed, they stepped into doorways, or went home."

Because of the bad weather, the couple are forced to return indoors. At first Helen refuses to come to Frank's room, but seeing his disappointment, she relents, after two dreary days of cold rain. Allowing him only limited sexual play, Helen insists that he discipline his emotions until she is sure of her love for him. Lying on Frank's bed, Helen listens contentedly "to the quiet sound of the rain in the street, making it in her mind into spring rain, though spring was weeks away; and within the rain grew all sorts of flowers, in this flowery dark—a sweet spring night—she lay with him in the open under new stars and a cry rose in her throat." The romanticism of this passage is, of course, all in her imagination, and Malamud uses this misleading sentimentality to contrast vividly with the ironic plot development that follows.

Arranging their next meeting in the park because she has something nice to tell him, Helen rushes to Frank after an earlier date with Nat. Frank is sure that Helen is willing to sleep with him now. The bittersweet quality of Malamud's scene is hinted at when he describes the girl's mood: "The night's new beauty struck Helen with the anguish of loss as she hurried to the lamplit park a half-hour after midnight." Other young lovers sit embracing "in the dark under budding branches," but eventually they depart and Helen is left alone. Combining the ominous with the hopeful in the kind of ambiguity that Malamud loves in establishing mood and creating suspense, he describes the girl's emotions as follows: "She felt the stars clustered like a distant weight above her head. Utterly lonely, she regretted the spring-like loveliness of the night; it had gone, in her hands, to waste. She was tired of anticipation, of waiting for nothing."

It is at this point that the Malmudian irony is particularly effective. Ward Minogue attacks Helen in the park, ripping her clothes and banging her head against one of the trees. As she tries to fight off the rapist, Frank arrives just in time, like the hero he wishes he were, and drives the antagonist away. The couple kiss "under the dark trees," but Frank shows none of the discipline Helen had insisted on, drawing "her deeper into the dark, and from under the trees onto the star-dark field." As they sink "to their knees on the winter earth," Helen pleads with Frank to wait, but he cannot. With romantic love almost within his grasp, the schlemiel ruins his chances by completing the rape that Ward had started.

Three additional patterns of nature imagery closely identified with Helen Bober and Frank Alpine are moonlight, flowers, and birds. The way Malamud blends all three in *The Assistant* reveals a craftsmanship that depends more heavily on the imaginative than the mimetic. It is a technique that calls for the evocative, poetic, and legendary rather than the actual. It is his Chagall-like technique of Malamud's by which he transmutes the mundane into the bizarre that has led critics like Alfred Kazin to call him a "fantasist of the ordinary."

A good example of this hallmark of Malamud's in *The Assistant* can be found a few days after Christmas on a night with a full moon. Dressed in his new suit, Frank overtakes Helen on the way to the library and suggests they walk in the park. There he begins to tell her a beautiful story about his idol, St. Francis of Assisi. Thinking about the wife and family he could never have, Francis became despondent and was unable to fall asleep one winter night. He "got out of his straw bed and went outside of the church or monastery or wherever he was staying. The ground was all covered with snow. Out of it he made this snow woman, and he said, 'There, that's my wife.' Then he made two or three kids out of the snow. After, he kissed them all and went inside and laid down in the straw. He felt a whole lot better and fell asleep."

The moonlit park is a most appropriate setting for the telling of this story. This is the first time Helen and Frank have been alone together this long, and she is beginning to see a side of him of which she had been unaware. The sweet-sadness of the friar's story reflects her own mood after a drab day as secretary in an office. She senses that her father's strange assistant has something in common with her. When he sighs and she asks if anything is wrong, the following exchange takes place:

> "No, just something popped into my mind when I was looking at the moon. You know how your thoughts are."
>
> "Nature sets you thinking?"
>
> "I like scenery."
>
> "I walk a lot for that reason."
>
> "I like the sky at night, but you see more of it in the West. Out here the sky is too high, there are too many big buildings."

In this open setting, nature is more than mere scenery. Malamud uses it skillfully to create mood, develop character, and express theme. Frank is encouraged to tell Helen about a previous love of his which ended in a tragic automobile accident. The whole pattern of his sad, lonely life is revealed. For such people the sky is always too high, beyond their reach. As Helen ponders Frank's stories in bed that night, she realizes that "She had had her own moonlit memories to contend with." Unable to fall asleep, "she regretted she could not see the sky from her window in the wall, or look down into the street. Who was he making into a wife out of snowy moonlight?"

The most obvious identification of Frank with St. Francis occurs shortly after the above scene when a depressed and restless Helen walking in the park watches a man (actually Frank) "feeding the birds. Otherwise the island was deserted. When the man rose, the pigeons fluttered up with him, a few landing on his arms and shoulders, one perched on his fingers, pecking peanuts from his cupped palm. Another fat bird sat on his hat. The man clapped his hands when the peanuts were gone and the birds, beating their wings, scattered." This passage echoes one much earlier when Frank, hanging around Sam Pearl's store after robbing Morris, looks at pictures in a magazine and is excited to see one of St. Francis of Assisi, "standing barefooted on a sunny country road. His skinny, hairy arms were raised to a flock of birds that dipped over his head. In the background was a grove of leafy trees; and in the far distance a church in sunlight."

In preparing his readers for the growing relationship between Frank and Helen, Malamud also introduces bird images in his description of the grocer's daughter. The first is seen through the eyes of her doting father: "She looks like a little bird, Morris thought. Why should she be so lonely? Look how pretty she looks. Whoever saw such blue eyes?" The second bird image related to Helen is a cliché, as Frank longs for the grocer's daughter while he works in the store: "She was in her way a lone bird, which suited him fine, though why she would be with her looks he couldn't figure out." The most important of the three images is the comparison that Frank draws as he spies on Helen in the bathroom: "Her body was young, soft, lovely, the breasts like small birds in flight, her ass like a flower." Here Malamud brings together two of the main patterns of imagery associated with Helen and Frank—birds and flowers.

To throw some light on the complicated flower symbolism which follows, it is helpful at this point to summarize a popular legend about St. Francis even though Malamud does not explicitly refer to it in *The Assistant.* According to Nikos Kazantzakis, who gives his version of the story in his biography *Saint Francis of Assisi,* Sister Clare sent word to the sick Francis asking him to visit her and the other sisters at the convent of San Damiano. Francis tells the messenger, Father Silvester, that he will come "when the road from the Portiuncula to San Damiano's is covered with white flowers." Cynical Father Silvester takes this indirect answer to mean "never," but the more trusting Brother Leo, the narrator of the story, rushes outside to see whether God has performed a miracle. As he reaches the road this very cold morning, he is overjoyed to find the entire way, "hedges, stones, dirt . . . blanketed everywhere with white flowers, as far as the eye could see!" Pulling up a handful, he rushes back to the bedridden Francis and tells him what he has found. Thanking God for this miracle, Francis places the white flowers on his bloody eyelids and the wounds on his temples. Then he delivers a little sermon to his companions on the miracles of all nature: "Just look at the humblest leaf of a tree, just look at it in the light—what a miracle! The Crucifixion is painted on one side; you turn the leaf over on the other and what do you see—the Resurrection! It is not a leaf, my brothers, it is our hearts!" At this point Saint Francis gives Father Silvester the bloodied flowers to bring with his message to Sister Clare as a sign that God wants him to visit her. Father Silvester is to tell her that "When they touched the earth they became all covered with blood." Although Francis' knees buckle as he is taken outdoors, he is able to reach the road, where the flowers have now vanished: "it was as though they had been a layer of winter hoar frost melted by the rising sun." Francis calls their disappearance another miracle: "The flowers came down from heaven, delivered their message, and then returned. They did not want human feet to step on them."

Whether this particular story was known to Malamud is not important. It is characteristic of the many legends told about St. Francis, combining the fanciful with the ordinary in a manner that would have delighted Nathaniel Hawthorne, who also loved the twilight zone of the imagination. Perhaps, the storyteller hints, there never were any flowers. Perhaps the hoar frost excited the imagination of the friars who saw what they wanted to see. In either case, a pleasant, entertaining story is told, evolving a thoughtful moral. The juxtaposition of the white and the red, the beautiful and the painful, the real and the imaginary, instructs the reader in the need for faith, for a belief in miracles which can turn crucifixions into resurrections.

With this story in mind, with its patterns of flower-frost imagery, its theme of suffering and rebirth, its mixture of hope and skepticism, we can better understand Malamud's unusual use of rose symbolism which first appears in a strange dream Frank Alpine has in his troubled sleep after raping Helen:

> That night he dreamed he was standing in the snow outside her window. His feet were bare yet not cold. He had waited a long time in the falling snow, and some of it lay on his head and had all but frozen his face; but he waited longer until, moved by pity, she opened the window and flung something out. It floated down; he thought it was a piece of paper with writing on it but saw that it was a white flower, surprising to see in wintertime. Frank caught it in his hand. As she had tossed the flower out through the partly opened window he had glimpsed her fingers only, yet he saw the light of her room and even felt the warmth of it. Then when he looked again the window was shut tight, sealed with ice. Even as he dreamed, he knew it had never been open. There was no such window. He gazed down at his hand for the flower and before he could see it wasn't there, felt himself wake.

Through this dream Malamud is contrasting the romantic sentimentality of the St. Francis-Sister Clare legend with the harsh reality of the Frank-Helen affair. The spiritual relationship of the first couple is changed into the carnal relationship of the second. Frank Alpine is doomed to play the role of the schlemiel; for him, no flowers will miraculously appear in the snow.

Malamud extends this pattern of rose imagery in a fascinating way. One day, Frank finds a board in the basement of Morris' store and starts carving it to pass the time.

> To his surprise it turned into a bird flying. It was shaped off balance but with a certain beauty. He thought of offering it to Helen but it seemed too rough a thing—the first he ever made. So he tried his hand at something else. He set out to carve her a flower and it came out a rose starting to bloom. When it was done it was delicate in the way its petals were opening yet firm as a real flower.

Frank considers painting it red but leaves it unpainted, wraps it in store paper, prints Helen's name on the package, and leaves it taped to the mailbox. When Helen unwraps it, the wooden rose reminds her of her unhappiness. She throws the gift away, and "In the morning, as he aimed a pail of garbage into the can at the curb, Frank saw at the bottom of it his wooden flower."

The rose as a symbol of love is seen again at Morris' funeral. As Morris' coffin is lowered into the ground, "Helen tossed in a rose." A characteristic Malmudian irony follows: Frank Alpine leans forward to watch it land and falls into the grave. Poor Morris Bober cannot even be laid to rest in peace. This Chaplinesque humor, the mixture of the ludicrous with the pathetic, is Malamud's perfect touch to lighten the heavy-handed symbolism of the identification of Frank and Morris. The store-as-grave symbolism is now complete. Frank's future is sealed.

But Malamud makes one last extension of the rose-bird-St.

Francis pattern of imagery, ending his novel on that note of ambiguity which he loves so well. In a final imaginative flourish, he combines the ordinary with the fanciful, the serious with the comedic, and the depressing with the hopeful. Frank Alpine, exhausted from working two jobs to support Ida and Helen, suddenly has a remarkable rebirth. The internal warfare between his good and evil impulses abruptly ends, and he stops both his dishonesty in the store and his voyeurism. Helen has sensed the change that has taken place in her benefactor but rejects his generous suggestion that she transfer from evening college to day classes. Afraid of rejection if he asks her to renew their relationship, Frank turns to the Bible to calm his nerves:

> As he was reading he had this pleasant thought. He saw St. Francis come dancing out of the woods in his brown rags, a couple of scrawny birds flying around over his head. St. F. stopped in front of the grocery, and reaching into the garbage can, plucked the wooden rose out of it. He tossed it into the air and it turned into a real flower that he caught in his hand. With a bow he gave it to Helen, who had just come out of the house. "Little sister, here is your little sister the rose." From him she took it, although it was the love and best wishes of Frank Alpine.

Here Malamud has dipped once again into his magic barrel to provide hope for the frustrated grocer. If the Helen of his fantasy accepts the rose of love from St. Francis, perhaps she will eventually accept it from him. James Mellard prefers the happy ending to support his analysis of the vegetation myth underlying the novel. To him, Helen's accepting Frank's offering proves "that Frank's sterile lust has now become life-giving love" [James Mellard, "Malamud's Novels: Four Versions of the Pastoral," *Critique* 9 (1967)]. To Mellard, Frank's reverie shows that the grocer has at last "succeeded not only with Helen but in gaining a measure of control over his fate, however savorless that fate might be to most of us. Through the ritual participation of man in nature's cycles, man has been able to unite eternal and temporal, desire and necessity, creativity and creation, art and life" ["Malamud's *The Assistant*: The City as Pastoral"]. But with this partial truth Mellard misses the purposeful ambiguity that is so characteristic of Malamud's craftsmanship. True to his literary creed, Malamud ends his novel on a note of uncertainty. "It's part of life," he once wrote in the late sixties. "I want something the reader is uncertain about. It is the uncertainty that produces drama. Keep the reader surprised. That is enormously important to me." As the drama of Morris Bober and his assistant closes, the only certainty Malamud allows his reader is the pain of suffering. The Saint Francisis and Morris Bobers of this world have taught their disciples well. The test of man's humanity is to suffer for one's fellow man, be he Christian or Jew. As the novel ends, an exhausted, frustrated, but determined Frank Alpine, right after the Passover celebration of freedom from bondage, accepts the martyrdom of suffering as a sign of his redemption, and becomes a convert to Judaism. (pp. 211-22)

> Arnold L. Goldsmith, "Nature in Bernard Malamud's 'The Assistant'," in *Renascence*, Vol. XXIX, No. 4, Summer, 1977, pp. 211-23.

H. E. Francis on Frank's conversion in *The Assistant*:

[Frank's conversion] may be construed as Malamud's belief in the superiority of Judaism over Christianity, as some critics have implied. But the action points beyond that. By accepting Morris' faith, Frank fuses Judaism with Christianity. They complete each other since Frank's conversion is not an acceptance of understood doctrine, but of a practical faith which was the source of Morris' own capacity to endure life. Frank's conversion is important because he discovers—not alone, but through another human being—a law of conduct which might give meaning to the burden of suffering, to life. As he accepts faith, he paradoxically eradicates the barriers between theologies.

> *H. E. Francis, in "Bernard Malamud's Everyman," Midstream, Winter 1961.*

Moshe A. Moskowitz (essay date Fall 1979)

[*Moskowitz is an educator in the field of Hebraic Studies. In the essay below, he discusses Frank Alpine's role as a proselyte in* The Assistant.]

Although most critics would agree as to the artistic merit of **The Assistant,** there is some question as to whether the portrait of Frank Alpine is that of a true proselyte to Judaism. Particularly problematical are both the final intent and value of the circumcision at the end of the novel: is it indeed, as one critic put it, "the ritual confirmation of the completed act of psychic conversion"? [William Freedman, "From B. Malamud with Discipline and Love," *B. Malamud: A Collection of Critical Essays*, edited by Leslie A. Field and Joyce W. Field, 1975]. In the light of this questioning, Alpine's supposed regeneration via the *mohel* appears ironic and inconclusive.

Whatever else one may say about him, it would seem that at times Malamud's protagonist is genuinely touched by the concept of "Jewish suffering." He appears to give meaning to his own suffering through that of the Jews, and at the end of the novel he dons a "Jewish apron" and assumes the role of the suffering storekeeper, Morris Bober.

What remains doubtful, however, is whether Alpine's frustrations, his toiling day and night to support the storekeeper's widow and send his daughter to college, are in the true spirit of Jewish sufferings, trials, and history, or whether they represent a "fatal circle of guilt, recrimination, and failure" [Freedman]. Specifically, Alpine's shady background, his private thoughts and secretive actions, and his relationship with Helen, the daughter, make one wonder about the moral efficacy and spiritual durability of his conversion.

Although it seems at times that a certain strength of character emanates from him, in actuality Frank's nature is weak, impulsive, and compulsive. When the story opens, he is an accomplice in the holdup and robbery of Bober's grocery. It is true that he seeks expiation by working long hours in the store, yet he steals from the cash register while doing so. He also victimizes the perplexed Bober by stealing milk and rolls, and then pleads for sympathy and understanding when discovered. He saves the daughter from rape, yet forces himself upon her, and then is filled with remorse. While it might be suggested that Alpine's redemption comes only in part through his love for Helen, and that essentially he becomes a Jew because he, too, is the symbolic sufferer, the quality of his relationship with the girl casts doubt on the entire issue. To put it bluntly, Frank seems to "endure" so that he can get into bed with Helen:

> But he wouldn't try to push anything, for he had heard that these Jewish babes could be trouble-makers, and he was not looking for any of that now . . . besides, he didn't want to spoil any-thing before it got started. There were some dames you had to wait for—for them to come to you.

Though he regrets the holdup and returns to the scene of the crime to make amends, it is only after he notices Helen in the store window that he makes his move. Obsessed by her provocative gait and tiny breasts, he lurks in and around the store, waiting for her like a lone wolf for its prey. Jewishness is the furtherest thing from his mind: "He thought she didn't look Jewish, which was all to the good."

Furthermore, Frank Alpine's repentance is accompanied by an ambiguous brooding, and one suspects that without his hope of one day possessing the "Jewish babe," his atti-tude toward the Jews would remain mired in its anti-Semitic crassness:

> That's what they live for, Frank thought, to suf-fer. And the one that has got the biggest pain in the gut and can hold onto it the longest without running to the toilet is the best Jew. No wonder they got on his nerves.

It has been argued that the aforementioned negative senti-ments appear early in the novel; that Frank Alpine is hon-estly repentant; and that there is an ongoing growth and development of character. His leap into the grocer's grave at the end of the novel is thus viewed by some critics as the death of his old character, while his circumcision is perceived as a rebirth and initiation into the secrets of the tribe. Mythology, however, supports yet another view. As seen from this aspect, Alpine's circumcision signifies not only his bond with the Jews and their God, but it also sym-bolizes submission in the service of Eros. Put another way, the circumcision implies something other than resurrec-tion and redemption. It is the mark of Cain displaced below—the scar of the instinctual personality who has no intention of renouncing his desires but only of masking them by frequent displays of contrition.

It would also be a mistake to regard Frank's tramping about the states as an echo of the Wandering Jew, nor can his curling up in the womblike safety of the grocery store properly be regarded as a "homecoming." Frank Alpine does not truly seek the meaning of Judaism, nor does he ever evince anything but a passing interest in its tenets. That the spirit of his conversion is both questionable and superficial may be seen from a passage which occurs late

in the book, at a time when one would have thought that his regenesis as a Jew would have been more imminent:

> He read a book about the Jews, a short history. He had many times seen this book on one of the library shelves and had never taken it down, but one day he checked it out to satisfy his curiosity. He read the first part with interest, but after the Crusades and the Inquisition, when the Jews were having it tough, he had to force himself to keep reading. He skimmed the blood chapters but read slowly the ones about their civilization and accomplishments. He also read about the ghettos, where the half-starved, bearded prison-ers spent their lives trying to figure out why they were the Chosen People. He tried to figure out why but couldn't. He couldn't finish the book and brought it back to the library.
>
> (pp. 428-30)

Although much has been made of Frank Alpine's suffer-ings and passion, as has been indicated previously, it is pri-marily the latter which motivates him. It is to Malamud's credit as a writer that the reader nevertheless senses the palpability of Frank's distress. (p. 432)

> *Moshe A. Moskowitz, "Intermarriage and the Proselyte: A Jewish View," in* Judaism, *Vol. 28, No. 4, Fall, 1979, pp. 423-33.*

Iska Alter   (essay date 1981)

[*In the following excerpt from an essay originally pub-lished in 1981, Alter examines the nature of American materialism as presented in* The Assistant.]

In the explosion of Jewish-American fiction that has char-acterized this country's literary history since the Second World War, Bernard Malamud's work retains a certain singularity in both subject matter and form. Without the exuberant self-promotion of Norman Mailer, the black and bitter humor of Joseph Heller, the increasing self-absorption of Philip Roth, or, more significantly, the moral comedy of Saul Bellow, Malamud has continued to be a humanistic spokesman, albeit a frequently disappoint-ed one in recent years, for responsibility, compassion, and goodness in a world spinning out of control with frighten-ing speed. To embody his concerns as a Jew, an artist, and a moral man, Malamud has evolved a style that is unique-ly his. Its fusion of the fabulous and the factual, called "lyrical realism" by the Yiddish critic Mayer Shticker [in his "The Blossoming Epoch of Jewish-American Creativi-ty," translated by Sylvia Protter and Iska Alter in *The Forward* (1977)], is the fictive analogue to the Chasidic be-lief that the mystical connection to God is to be found not in ascetic isolation, but through man's participation in the ordinary activities and mundane events of daily existence.

Given Malamud's not-quite-fashionable content and his paradoxical technique, it should not be surprising that the critical response to his fiction has been varied, and some-times contradictory. On the one hand, he is condemned by Philip Roth for his distance from an actual, firmly pre-sented social environment; on the other, he is praised by Tony Tanner for this very same quality. Within this range of opposites, several distinct orientations are apparent.

For example, Alfred Kazin denigrates *The Natural* because it is rooted in fantasy, preferring those novels and short stories that seem to be a more naturalistic portrayal of the Jew's experiential reality, while Marcus Klein notes Malamud's variations on the accommodationist spirit that Klein perceives as the major force in post-World War II literature. Like Kazin, Klein is not entirely comfortable with what he believes to be Malamud's intense, parochial exoticism. But he recognizes that the characters in Malamud's fiction are driven "to be out of this world and in a more certainly felt reality. . . . And their adventure is precisely their frustration; the end of straining and the beginning of heroism, if achieved, is the beginning of acceptance. . . . His hero's heroism is his hero's loss" [*After Alienation* (1964)].

There are critics such as Leslie Fiedler, Stanley Edgar Hyman, and Earl Wasserman, who view Malamud only in his mythic context, counting as most worthy those works with an explicitly archetypal content, esteeming *The Natural,* in particular, for its lively sense of mythic play. Others belonging to this school are more interested in tracing the continuity of archetypal patterns from novel to novel. Of course, and with good reason, there are those who consider Malamud primarily as a Jewish-American writer mindful only of his use of Jewish motifs. Mayer Shticker has noted that with *The Assistant* Bernard Malamud "has brought into American literature . . . the emotional sensibility of the heart [*herzlekhayt*] that reminds us so strongly of the great masters of Jewish writing, Sholem Aleichem, Peretz, and David Bergelson." Robert Alter, however, believes that all but *The Fixer* are a vulgarization of that illustrious Yiddish tradition. For Josephine Zadovsky Knopp, the concept of *mentshlekhayt* is at the core of Malamud's work and is the source of its strength.

It would be foolish to deny or minimize the validity of much that the critics have observed and written about Bernard Malamud; yet there is one whole area of the author's fiction, his social criticism, that has been neglected, ignored, or even declared nonexistent. Indeed, the later novels, whose judgments about society are more pronounced, have usually been accorded less value than *The Assistant* or *The Magic Barrel.* But Malamud has, in fact, shown a constant awareness of the societies in which his fictions take place. He is not only interested in describing actual social structures, or the human interactions that sustain them; he is also concerned with defining and dramatizing the underlying forces which form the bases upon which a given community is built. This study will attempt to show that . . . Malamud has fictively presented the decline of the American dream into the nightmare of an entire civilization in decay, a surprising theme, perhaps, from an author supposedly unconcerned with the difficult realities of society and the problems of a disintegrating culture. (pp. 75-6)

Walter Shear has rightly perceived *The Assistant* to be a dramatization of the never-quite-resolved conflict between two cultures—the Jewish tradition of the Bobers, Pearls, and Karps and the American heritage, the wisdom of the old world versus the utilitarianism of the new ["Culture Conflict in *The Assistant,*" *The Midwest Quarterly* (1966)].

This analysis is true as far as it goes. But the encounter as presented in the novel is more subtly ironic. The Jewish tradition, as Malamud depicts it, may be morally admirable; but it is essentially heterodox and secular, divorced from its sources in orthodox Judaism and the European situation that conditioned it, and no longer appropriate in an open, liberal social system. Morris Bober may have brought with him his own entombment but without sufficient spiritual consolation to sustain him. And the American heritage, vital and promising as it may be, stands not only as a mockery of hopes betrayed, or as a series of poisoned expectations, but as a sardonic tribute to the hypocrisy that is also a part of the American dream. Karp succeeds in the financially approved way, but it is without joy and without love.

We begin with the only Jewish families who inhabit, resentfully, uncomfortably, an impoverished, decaying, non-Jewish neighborhood in New York—the Karps, the Pearls, the Bobers: "She [Ida Bober] had waked that morning resenting the grocer for having dragged her, so many years ago, out of a Jewish neighborhood into this. She missed to this day their old friends and landsleit—lost for parnusseh unrealized." Each represents, in some way, a facet of the Jewish experience in this *goldene medinah,* this golden land. While these families do have those aspirations common to American imagination, they are Jews who have, for the most part, been unable to enter the mainstream of middle-class life and acceptability. They are reminders of the immigrant past for whom the promise of *better* has not been kept. Fulfillment is for their children—Louis, Nat, and Helen. They are the generation who will belong. Although the patriarchs are entrepreneurs, self-employed businessmen—ironic exemplars of the classic American prescription for success—the isolated condition of these three Jewish families makes them vulnerable, susceptible to paralyzing memories of their ghetto history. Although these families are still anxious to participate in the flawed American dream, they are viewed by many of the Gentiles in the community as seeming embodiments of the anti-semite's stereotypical Jew, and therefore as legitimate targets for robbery and violence.

Julius Karp is the wealthy exception among the three families. At the end of Prohibition, good businessman that he was, Karp astutely (by society's valuation of such things) acquired the necessary license to transform cheap shoes into expensive bottles. The liquor store, not surprisingly, did well in so poor a neighborhood, and Karp flourished. But for Malamud, Karp's success had been bought at dehumanizing cost. After all, his wealth . . . is based on the exploitation of human frailty. "A business for drunken bums," says Morris Bober, the novel's moral voice, judging with disapproval and contempt. Karp, in an act that signifies the breaking of the human connections that have tied him to his fellow Jews, has also moved out of the neighborhood into "a big house on the Parkway . . . complete with two-car garage and Mercury," the middle-class American's vision of accomplishment. It is worth nothing here how often success, in this country, is measured by the geographical distance one has moved from his origins and roots—the further one goes, the more one has achieved. This fact has allowed Karp to become an absentee exploit-er, using the neighborhood for his own, as property, then leaving it to die from his poison, a singular example of the abdication of moral responsibility in favor of personal financial satisfaction.

But Julius Karp's deficiencies as a human being are more extensive. Having become the kind of success society values, he is now free to exercise the power conferred by money: the ability to transform human beings into commodities to be manipulated for gain. Because he has attained position, Julius Karp assumes also that he has been given wisdom. In this culture, the ability to acquire money attests to sagacity; therefore Karp is free to "run down the store and spout unwanted advice." After all, since Morris Bober is a poor man, a failure by anyone's estimation, what can he possibly know that is worth anything? And Karp, assuming that the world, as he knows, dances only to the tune of cash, even converts love into a business proposition with Helen Bober an object to be traded for financial security:

> Karp felt he could ease his son's way to Helen by making Morris a proposition he had had in the back of his head for almost a year. He would describe Louis' prospects after marriage in terms of cold cash and other advantages, and suggest that Morris speak to Helen on the subject of going with him seriously. If they went together a couple of months—Louis would give her an extravagant good time—and the combination worked out, it would benefit not only the daughter, but the grocer as well, for then Karp would take over Morris's sad gesheft and renovate and enlarge it into a self-service market with the latest fixtures and goods. . . . With himself as the silent partner giving practical advice, it would take a marvelous catastrophe to keep the grocer from earning a decent living. . . .

Finally, and perhaps most significantly, Karp betrays friendship, loyalty, and his own humanity for a mercenary reward by allowing into the neighborhood another grocery store to compete with the unfortunate Morris for business, since competition is the essence of the American way. Karp does this first at the beginning of the novel when, rejecting Morris's pleas, he sells the empty tailor shop to Schmitz: "Morris ran to Karp. 'What did you do to me?' The liquor dealer said with a one-shouldered shrug, 'You saw how long stayed empty the store. Who will pay my taxes? But don't worry,' he added, 'he'll sell more delicatessen but you'll sell more groceries. Wait, you'll see he'll bring you in customers.' " And he resells to Taast and Pederson, knowing full well that such competition will be destructive:

"What happened to Schmitz?"

"He has a bad blood disease and lays now in the hospital."

"Poor man," the grocer sighed. . . . "Will he give the store in auction?"

Karp was devastating, "What do you mean give in auction? It's a good store. He sold it Wednesday to two up-to-date Norwegian partners and they will open next week a modern fancy grocery and delicatessen. You will see where your business will go. . . . What could I do? I couldn't tell him to go in auction if he had a chance to sell."

That Karp chooses, in both instances, to sell to *goyim* is a further betrayal of Morris, who is portrayed as the essence of Jewishness.

Yet in Karp there exists a vague, ineffable, dissatisfaction, an unconscious recognition that perhaps his kind of achievement is incomplete, a suspicion that something is indeed more vital than dollars. For, like the crooked Charlie Sobeloff, Morris's former partner made rich at the expense of Bober's trusting innocence, Karp finds it necessary to have Morris's approval and acceptance: "For some reason that was not clear to him Karp liked Morris to like him. . . . " True wisdom makes itself known even to the most hardened.

As for the next generation, Louis Karp is the son of such a father. And it is hardly surprising that his ambitions are narrow, limited to those obtainable by purchase:

> "Louis," she [Helen Bober] said, watching a far-off light on the water, "what do you want out of your life?"
>
> He kept his arm around her. "The same thing I got—plus."
>
> "Plus what?"
>
> "Plus more, so my wife and family can have also."

However, in this version of America, unlike the landscape of *The Natural,* there is retribution for those who have made their pact with the American serpent, who have been seduced by the force and potency of economic materialism. Karp's liquor store, feeding on itself, is burnt to the ground by Ward Minogue, an ironic avenging angel. Karp himself has a heart attack, and he can no longer continue those activities that have given justification to his existence. And Louis, interested in immediate gain, goes to work as a salesman for a liquor concern, rather than rebuild his father's business. Perhaps punishment is possible because in *The Assistant* Malamud has chosen to portray a society of the helpless where there is only minimal power to be exercised. (pp. 81-4)

The Pearls are also foils for the values represented by Morris. Sam, in spite of his poor candy store, is an entrepreneurial success after a fashion, although not within the *legitimate* economic structure employed by Karp. While he "neglected the store . . . Sam's luck with the nags was exceptional and he had nicely supported Nat in college until the scholarships started rolling in." Like any good risk-taking capitalist, he spends his days brooding over the dope sheets in much the same way a broker studies stock quotations and Dow Jones averages—and to much the same end. And such an occupation requires a fierce dedication to the study of the main chance in order that every possible money-making opportunity be exploited. However, this commitment, according to Malamud, narrows one's encounters with the world and with humanity, a weakness that once again only Morris recognizes for what it is: "Morris took the *Forward* from the newsstand and dropped a nickel into the cigar box. Sam Pearl, working over a green racing sheet, gave him a wave of his hammy hand. They never bothered to talk. What did he know about race horses? And what did the other know of the tragic quality of life? Wisdom flew over his hard head."

More relevant for the novel's antipathy to America's driving materialism is the character of Nat Pearl, "magna cum laude, Columbia, now in his second year at law school," and, as Helen observes, a soon-to-be professional "with first-rate prospects, also rich friends he had never bothered to introduce her to." By virtue of his education, his job choice, and those values inherited from his father and the culture at large, Nat ultimately will become part of society's controlling machinery. That Nat has chosen the law is obviously significant, for, as a profession, it provides easy access to real wealth and power, temptation enough for anyone, let alone the son of immigrants: "Nat Pearl wanted to be 'somebody,' but to him this meant making money to lead the life of some of his well-to-do friends at law school." How unlike Morris, for whom the Law (always capitalized in Morris's usage) is seen as a mode of ethical behavior and right conduct.

It is important to understand how Nat's acceptance (and perhaps America's as well) of the law as a tool, simply a pragmatic device whose function is to wheedle, to manipulate, to justify, and to excuse wrong action, shapes his dealings with Helen Bober. First, however, it is necessary to acknowledge how much that relationship has been conditioned by the very fact of Nat's promise rather than his beliefs. This recognition is particularly fitting considering that America has always been the civilization symbolized by a commitment to a better future for all its inhabitants. Helen is acutely aware that the society's respect for Nat's possibilities has allowed her to act against her own personally developed moral sense: "Nat Pearl, handsome, cleft-chinned, gifted, ambitious, had wanted without too much trouble a lay and she, half in love, had obliged and regretted. Not the loving, but that it had taken her so long to realize how little he wanted." Nat, like Louis Karp, regards Helen as an object to be acquired and used. Louis offers money and fails. Nat, more sophisticated, knowing that he stands, in some way, for entry into that culture that has labelled the Bobers outsiders, offers possibilities and succeeds. But when Helen, recognizing the nature of her seduction, develops scruples, Nat does not hesitate to use a kind of legal chop-logic to defend his behavior and to demean her conscience—that is what being a lawyer means:

> "Helen, I honestly want to know how somebody's supposed to defend himself when he hasn't any idea what's in the indictment against him? What kind of crime have I committed? . . . "
>
> "I'm not a lawyer—I don't make indictments. . . . "
>
> "You're a funny kid," Nat was saying. "You've got some oldfashioned values about some things. I always told you punish yourself too much. Why should anybody have such a hot and heavy

conscience in these times? People are freer in the twentieth century. . . . What," Nat argued, "would peoples' lives be like if everybody regretted every beautiful minute of all that happened? Where's the poetry of living?"

When Helen finally rejects Nat and what he represents, she becomes for him only "You bitch." And Nat, because of an allegiance to a philosophy which turns people into things—a kind of transformational materialism endemic in American society—must suffer the loss of wisdom; hardly much of a loss, he would suspect, if it is to be defined by Morris Bober.

The Bobers are clearly failures, at least as society would judge them. They have neither money, nor power, nor the intense drive to belong that is characteristic of so many immigrants. And they lack that seemingly national trait, crucial if one is to succeed in America, the ability to create their own destiny. They do not control fate; it controls them. The Bobers are, in fact, frightened and disappointed in the country they have escaped to. They take no risks; they do not gamble (except on the grocery store—a losing proposition if there ever was one); they cannot hear opportunity's knock. And they are immobile, stationary, afraid to venture beyond the block. To a large degree, they are responsible for their entombment in that grave of a business, for their attitudes are unsuitable to achievement and accomplishment in American terms. Finally, Ida and Morris have, in the worst betrayal of the American dream, deprived their child of a future in this new golden land. Yet the Bobers, as a family, seem to represent a source of strength, goodness, wisdom, and morality unavailable to the rest of society, and perhaps unattainable if the price be social and economic failure.

Ida Bober, however, is considerably less willing to accept moral virtue if it is unaccompanied by sufficient financial rewards. In fact, Ida is obsessed by her need for monetary security to a degree that often dehumanizes her. She is suspicious of anyone who may attack what little position and self-respect she has acquired. She is therefore hostile to the newcomer Frank Alpine on two counts: as a stranger, he may steal money; and, as a non-Jew, he might steal a more valuable piece of property, a key to the future, her daughter. And because Ida is wise in the ways of the American world, her Cassandra-like prophecies of doom have much accuracy. Unlike Morris, she believes "a business is a business" even if the money is made at the expense of another's weakness. She clearly resents her husband's claims to superior moral sensitivity, "everybody is a stupe but not Morris Bober," especially if it means a loss in dollars. She nags if Morris trusts enough to give credit. Her measurement of human worth is material possessions. And significantly it is only Ida who respects and even admires Julius Karp for his foresight and his success, though it be to her husband's cost:

> "Why does he bring me buyers? Why didn't he keep out the German around the corner?"
>
> She sighed. "He tries to help you now because he feels sorry for you."
>
> "Who needs his sorrow?" Morris said. "Who needs him?"

"So why *you* didn't have the sense to make out of your grocery a wine and liquor store when came out the licenses?"

"Who had cash for stock?"

"So if you don't have, don't talk."

"A business for drunken bums."

"A business is a business. What Julius Karp takes in next door in a day we don't take in in two weeks."

Ida is perfectly capable, even anxious, to use the deceptive techniques of the good (in a monetary, if not a moral, sense) businessperson in order to cheat the naive refugee Podolsky if it means ridding herself of the millstone the store has become. That she might be imprisoning Podolsky, who had come to America for the mythical new life as Morris had so many years ago, is not her concern. Nor can she comprehend Frank's willingness to work for nothing in order to pay a symbolic debt to Morris and redeem his own soul.

But the most important factor, for Malamud, in Ida's adherence to this American version of reductive materialism is that it diminishes the value of love. Such an unpredictable emotion threatens the business of marriage, an arrangement, as perceived by Ida, to escape poverty, the only way that a woman can achieve status, wealth, and power. This view of matrimony is her only way of protecting and insuring what future Helen might have: " 'Helen,' she said, holding back her tears, 'the only thing I want for you is the best. Don't make my mistake. Don't make worse and spoil your whole life, with a poor man that he is only a grocery clerk which we don't know about him nothing. Marry somebody who can give you a better life, a nice professional boy with a college education. Don't mix up now with a stranger. Helen, I know what I'm talking. Believe me, I know.' "

Ida, therefore, measures potential husbands not by their inherent value as human beings, not by their ability to love, but by the money they have or might have: Nat Pearl will be "someday a rich lawyer"; even "the stupe" Louis Karp is acceptable since he can offer financial security. And any quality in Helen, particularly her intelligence— "Some people want their children to read more. I want you to read less."—that reduces her marketability is to be decried and condemned.

What has so embittered Ida is not simple nagging dissatisfaction but guilt, "her guilt that she had talked him into a grocery store when he was in the first year of evening high school, preparing, he had said, for pharmacy." She had settled for the immediate gratification of ownership and possession rather than wait for long-range possibilities, withheld fulfillment, and postponed satisfaction. It is only when Morris is dead (living he was a constant reminder of that guilt) and she no longer fears starving because of Frank's rent and Helen's salary and Rubin's job that she softens into humanity.

Helen Bober is a more complex character, a mass of American and old-country contradictions, whose perceptions, ambitions, and desires have been conditioned by the hard American materialism of her mother and the otherworldly, inappropriate wisdom of her father. Helen tends to see herself, as do Ida, the Karps, Nat Pearl, and even Frank Alpine initially, as merchandise upon whom a price has been set. Although she is concerned with abstract goals and impractical notions of morality, preoccupied with philosophy, an idealist believing in the something more beyond the material that gives life its meaning (symbolized by her addiction to literature), she nevertheless thinks of Helen Bober as a commodity to be judged by some sort of externally devised concept of worth. And that standard is a social one contingent on her lack of prospects, "as poor as her name sounded, with little promise of a better future." Therefore, in spite of her obvious intelligence, sensitivity, and capacity for love, she is constantly worried at being valued under her expectations, certain that she is worthless even to a man like Nat Pearl, whose ambitions she derides and suspects. As she says, she loves before she is loved, perhaps inviting the expected rejection because of her fear she is not worth the loving. Perhaps that is one of the reasons why Helen chooses Frank, so clearly less than she, an alien, a wanderer, a non-Jew, without position or stability.

As a true child of her parents, Helen romanticizes the power of education, placing her faith in it as the key to realizing her sense of potential, becoming American in the best sense of the word. She does not wish to use education simply to acquire a marketable skill, because such is not the true function of learning. To be educated according to Helen (and to Malamud, no doubt) is to possess wisdom and understanding of life. Helen desires education so that she may become a better person, hardly a useful talent, much less an appropriate one for the national economy. It is this deprivation that Helen feels most strongly, and Frank Alpine ultimately recognizes that it is the one gift he can offer that Helen cannot return.

At this point, we must examine Helen's curious ambivalence toward the act of gift-giving, a persistent motif throughout the novel. She is able to give *things*—her salary to her parents, for example—as an expression of her feelings, but she cannot, in the course of the novel, give her body because it is the concrete form taken by the self, the physical essence of the soul. To offer so precious a gift and to have it rejected or misvalued is to destroy the integrity of the person that is Helen Bober. Even Helen, in a subtle fashion, uses the external, the physical, the concrete, as a source and standard of individual worth. However, Helen is most reluctant to accept gifts for a number of reasons. First, to accept a gift is to acknowledge another's judgment on Helen-as-object, whose value is instantly visible by the quality of the gift: "Nat, at his best, had produced a half-dozen small pink roses," while Frank had given her an expensive scarf and a leather-bound copy of Shakespeare. Second, to accept a gift is to incur debt and obligation, is to become a human IOU, a particularly uncomfortable situation for the insecure. Says Helen, "for gifts you pay." And finally, to accept a gift is to put a price on love, to admit that affection can be bought for things, an idea that Helen instinctively knows to be false in spite of a culture that has made it a truth. Although Helen wants no part of Nat Pearl's materialism, admiring instead the intangible and impractical qualities of sensitivity, perception, and depth, and resents her treatment as a commodity, she nevertheless chooses to treat Frank Alpine as such a vehicle for the realization of a future.

Yet it is only when Helen realizes that gifts are merely an outward sign, an honest expression of true emotion, when she learns to take gracefully as well as to give generously, when she can thank Frank for his unselfish help, that Helen can become truly loving.

Because of the limitations placed on her needs and ambitions by economics and her own psychology, Frank, who has traveled, moved, *lived,* is transformed into the embodiment of her unfulfilled possibilities. Since she resents her loss—"The world has shrunk for me. . . . I want a larger and better life. I want the return of my possibilities"—she makes Frank the *tabula rasa* on which to write her dreams:

> And if she married Frank, her first job would be to help him realize his wish to be somebody. . . . Frank . . . was struggling to realize himself as a person, a more worthwhile ambition. Though Nat had an excellent formal education, Frank knew more about life and gave the impression of greater potential depth. She wanted him to become what he might, and conceived a plan to support him through college. Maybe she could even see him through a master's degree, once he knew what he wanted to do. She realized this would mean the end of her own vague plans for going to day college, but that was really lost long ago, and she thought she would at last accept the fact once Frank had got what she hadn't.

When she discovers that Frank is anything but a paragon, a mere man with considerably more than his share of human weaknesses (as thief and rapist), she hates him for being less than her fantasy of him, a deception using her body as a possession; and she hates herself for so radical a misjudgment and for once again being valued under her expectations. Helen can only accept her own flawed humanity when she recognizes the real humanity in Frank, acknowledging that he has in fact changed, that he has become that better person, not through a college education but through suffering. Hardly the American dream, Malamud believes, but it will do.

But it is in the creation of Morris Bober and his encounters with the world that Malamud offers his disapproval of aspects of the American dream: the expectations and promise defined, the defeats and loss explored. Morris's immigrant history may be seen as disappointment. First there is an escape from tyranny and persecution which was life in the old country. "They were poor and there were pogroms. So when he was about to be conscripted into the czar's army his father said, 'Run to America.'" Then comes a taste of freedom, the opening of possibilities. "After I came here I wanted to be a druggist. . . . I went for a year in night school. I took algebra, also German and English. 'Come,' said the wind to the leaves one day, 'come over the meadow with me and play.' This is a poem I learned. But I didn't have the patience to stay in night school, so when I met my wife I gave up my chances."

And finally, immobilizing entrapment in a dying economic venture, "He had escaped out of the Russian Army to the U.S.A., but once in a store he was like a fish fried in deep fat." Why then did a man who risked the wrath of the czar's sergeant fail when confronted with America's multiple opportunities? What spoiled the hope? And how could such a failure, with so many lost chances in a society that offered so many futures, become the moral center of *The Assistant*?

Josephine Zadovsky Knopp defines Morris's ethical beliefs as the concept of *mentshlekhkayt* which

> has as its fundamental premise the innocence of man, man free of the sins of the Fall. It recognizes that within man run opposing tendencies toward good and evil, and that within this context man is completely free to choose. It rests its ultimate faith in man's basic goodness and the implicit assumption that, in the final analysis, he will always choose what is morally and ethically right. It believes in action as the path toward moral redemption. . . . It is an ethic concerned with improving man's lot in this world. . . . To those who accept, perhaps even unconsciously, the ethical code of *mentshlekhkayt,* the concept of an "absurd" universe is foreign; to them the universe has a definite structure and meaning. . . . At least a part of this meaning resides in the code's implicit faith in the moral significance of man's action, . . . and that he has the obligation to apply this power in the cause of good.
>
> *Mentshlekhkayt* also encompasses the very strong sense of community that has traditionally been a feature of Jewish life. The paramount characteristic of this community feeling is the moral imperative of man's responsibility to his fellow man. . . .
>
> The code . . . is an order, a Law in a world of chaos and suffering, and thereby brings sanity and significance to life. [*The Trial of Judaism in Contemporary Jewish Writing*]

While this clearly describes elements of Morris's credo, Knopp does not appear to appreciate the irony of assigning such an ethical system to a man who inhabits a society that makes adherence to such values a sure sign of failure. Given American culture as it is portrayed in *The Assistant,* this admirable moral structure appears to be a source of passive endurance, rather than an active commitment for change.

It is in the creation of Morris Bober and his encounters with the world that Malamud offers his disapproval of aspects of the American dream: the expectations and promise defined, the defeats and loss explored.

—Iska Alter

Morris collapses into prisoner and victim because the national community that Morris has chosen as refuge and affirmation no longer uses or finds valuable the virtues of a truly good man. And while it is true that even Karp keeps returning to Morris for approval and spiritual sustenance, it does the liquor store owner no good, for he continues to denigrate, mock, and betray the values Morris subscribes to. In Morris's decline, embodied in his inability and unwillingness to adapt to an increasingly opportunistic culture, we witness the triumph of the dream as nightmare. The memories that haunt Morris throughout the novel are not, ironically, of an American paradise but of an Eastern European one: "No, not for an age had he lived a whole day in the open. As a boy, always running in the muddy, rutted streets of the village, or across the fields, or bathing with the other boys in the river; but as a man, in America, he rarely saw the sky. In the early days when he drove a horse and wagon, yes, but not since his first store. In a store you were entombed." The world of persecution has become a remembered Eden of open spaces, while America, the new land, is a closed box, a coffin.

In an environment where every penny is important and money an icon (notice how carefully Malamud accounts for the store's income before the robbery), Morris trusts and gives trust:

> "My mother says . . . can you trust her till tomorrow for a pound of butter, a loaf of rye bread and a small bottle of cider vinegar?"
>
> He knew the mother. "No more trust."
>
> The girl burst into tears.
>
> Morris gave her. . . . The total now came to $2.03, which he never hoped to see. But Ida would nag, . . . so he reduced the amount. . . . His peace—the little he lived with—was worth forty-two cents.

A Lincolnesque figure, his honesty is only the stuff of legends and eulogies, and about as relevant in this civilization: "Helen, his dear daughter, remembers from when she was a small girl that her father ran two blocks in the snow to give back to a poor Italian lady a nickel that she forgot on the counter." He is a man of responsibility in a culture of the irresponsible, who wakes early, morning after morning, to insure that the Poilisheh gets her three-cent roll.

In a society that elevates transcience and prizes mobility, Morris, especially after the death of his son and future, remains frozen and immobile, actually as well as metaphorically *going nowhere*. He does not cheat. He will not steal, even in a business situation where such behavior is not only commonplace and justified but also necessary to insure that magic word—profit.

> "It's easy to fool people," said Morris.
>
> "Why don't you try a couple of those tricks yourself, Morris? Your amount of profit is small."
>
> Morris looked at him in surprise. "Why should I steal from my customers? Do they steal from me?"

> "They would if they could."
>
> "When a man is honest he don't worry when he sleeps. This is more important than a nickel."

And in spite of his admiration for the greater efficiency and practicality of the modern, Morris is, not surprisingly, attached to the old ways. He teaches Frank the skills he possesses with a mixture of pride and embarrassment, remembering when it required real ability to be a grocer: "As if ashamed somebody could learn the business so easily, Morris explained to him how different it had been to be a grocer only a few years ago. In those days one was more of a macher, a craftsman. Who was ever called on nowadays to slice up a loaf of bread . . . or ladle out a quart of milk?" But since "the chain store kills the small man," of what significance are those abilities in a packaged culture valuing speed not technique, convenience not aptitude, and the plastic rather than the authentic: "Now is everything in containers, jars, or packages. Even hard cheeses that they cut them for hundreds of years by hand now come sliced up in cellophane packages. Nobody has to know anything any more."

As that traditional but impossible American paradigm—the small business where "at least you're your own boss"—Morris is a failure. Perhaps the ideal has become mendacious—"To be a boss of nothing." Certainly Ida and even Helen, trapped in a civilization that has divorced success from human worth, ethical conduct, and morality, condemn or minimize the quality of Morris's true achievement.

> I said Papa was honest but what was the good of such honesty if he couldn't exist in the world? . . . Poor Papa; being naturally honest, he didn't believe that others come by their dishonesty naturally. And he couldn't hold onto those things he had worked so hard to get. . . . He gave away, in a sense, more than he owned. . . . He knew, at least, what was good. . . . People liked him, but who can admire a man passing his life in such a store? He buried himself in it; he didn't have the imagination to know what he was missing. He made himself a victim. He could, with a little more courage, have been more than he was.

Morris's final judgment is also one of regret, loss, and disappointment: "He thought of his life with sadness. . . . His mood was one of regret. I gave away my life for nothing. It was the thunderous truth."

Ida, Helen, and Morris are to a limited degree correct in their assessment of Morris's accomplishments or lack of them. Unfortunately, the paradox (according to Malamud) is that, given the kind of man Morris Bober was, his future in America was inevitable. The essential characteristics that one must acknowledge and admire in him are those very characteristics that made financial success in the world impossible.

The America that has diminished and defeated Morris Bober accords respect, admiration, and power to the insensitive Karp who seizes the main chance at the expense of honor, loyalty, and friendship, and rewards with success and wealth the corrupt Charlie Sobeloff, "a cross-eyed but clever conniver" who cheated and defrauded the innocent and trusting Morris.

> Arriving at Soboloff's Self-Service Market, Morris . . . was amazed at its size. Charlie had tripled the original space. . . . The result was a huge market with a large number of stalls and shelved sections loaded with groceries. The supermarket was so crowded with people that to Morris . . . it looked like a department store. He felt a pang, thinking that part of this might now be his if he had taken care of what he had once owned. He would not envy Charlie Soboloff his dishonest wealth, but when he thought of what he could do for Helen with a little money his regret deepened that he had nothing.

As Morris joins that "silent knot of men who drifted along Sixth Avenue stopping at the employment agency doors to read impassively the list of jobs chalked up on the blackboard signs," he sees an America that has discarded the poor, the old, the sick, the uneducated, and has rendered them useless, unfit for participation in a society that popularly believes that "God loves the poor people but he helps the rich."

It is an America that has betrayed its symbolic promise and traditional ideals. For Morris, "America had become too complicated. One man counted for nothing. There were too many stores, depressions, anxieties. What had he escaped to here?" A good man can retain his soul only at the expense of a freedom too easily become opportunism, and an opportunism too easily become deceit, trickery, corruption.

Frank Alpine enters the story like a dingy American Lochinvar "lately come from the West, looking for a better opportunity." Like Helen, Frank is a divided personality, one who steals yet yearns for goodness, who wanders yet yearns for stability, who rapes yet yearns for love. He wants "money, nightclubs, babes," and at the same time wishes to be like St. Francis, for whom "poverty was a queen": "Every time I read about somebody like him I get a feeling inside of me I have to fight to keep from crying. He was born good, which is a talent if you have it." Frank is a man ensnared by the corruption of his culture, as well as by his own inner drives and compulsions; he is looking for a model to provide an alternative mode of being. Not finding St. Francis, he discovers the next best thing in contemporary America—Morris Bober—and becomes his surrogate son, and spiritual heir, giving up the opportunities of the world, the flesh, and the devil for the ascetic discipline of the imprisoning grocery store.

Frank is that not uncommon American phenomenon, the wanderer, the mover, the man without roots who leaves when things do not work out or disappears when responsibility weighs too heavily and commitments become too demanding. "I am too restless—six months in any one place is too much for me. Also I grab at everything too quick—too impatient. I don't do what I have to. . . . The result is I move into a place with nothing, and I move out with nothing." And like so many of his fellow citizens, he rationalizes this particularly American brand of irresponsibility as the testing of freedom, a trying of opportunities, the correct use of his country's promise. It is hardly surprising

that Helen, who longs for such motion and such possibilities, is seduced by Frank's words:

> "The way I figure, anything is possible. I always think about the different kinds of chances I have. This has stuck in my mind—don't get yourself trapped in one thing, because maybe you can do something else a whole lot better. That's why I guess I never settled down so far. I've been exploring conditions. I still have some very good ambitions which I would like to see come true. The first step to that, I know for sure now, is to get a good education. I didn't use to think like that, but the more I live the more I do."

An excellent statement of the national credo. That he may be using this pronouncement to seduce Helen does not obviate the fact that a portion of Frank's personality believes it.

Frank wants to be better than he is in both the financial and moral spheres of the American experience without perceiving that he cannot achieve both ambitions in the kind of driven, materialistic culture America has in fact become. He is particularly concerned with the acquisition of wealth, power, and importance; he is possessed by the sense that "he was meant for something a whole lot better—to do something big, different." Daniel Bell has indicated in his essay "Crime as an American Way of Life" that for a man with no skills, the American dream may be achieved through crime. Thus Frank thinks that:

> At crime he would change his luck, make adventure, live like a prince. He shivered with pleasure as he conceived robberies, assaults—murders if it had to be—each violent act helping to satisfy a craving that somebody suffer as his own fortune improved. He felt infinitely relieved, believing that if a person figured for himself something big, something different in his life, he had a better chance to get it than some poor jerk who couldn't think that high up.

Frank's dream is only partially influenced by its Dostoevskian counterparts. The Russian's protagonists are, in fact, concerned with the metaphysics of power while Frank wants the external accoutrements of success that can be acquired by crime.

But crime is taking, the way Frank takes from Morris by theft, from Helen by rape. It is simply another variant of the culture's dominating materialism that defines people as things for use, manipulation, exploitation, or expropriation. However, it is only when Frank can learn to give unselfishly, without hope for return or need of payment, that he can achieve moral success. And this education begins when he willingly attaches himself to the Bobers and to the enclosing confinement of the grocery store.

Initially Frank brings into the store the values of the American universe outside. Though improvements are made in the best sense of American business, Frank steals, exploits, uses. He robs Morris, defending his actions as the cause of the store's improvement. He (and Ida) are willing to make changes that the conservative Morris has resisted as a sign of integrity—the change from milk bottles to containers. He suggests, to Morris's horror, that they cheat customers. And perhaps most significantly, Frank is a salesman, a "supersalesman" one of the customers calls him, capable of utilizing all the manipulative techniques of salesmanship Morris disdains: "The customers seemed to like him. . . . He somehow drew in people she had never before seen in the neighborhood. . . . Frank tried things that Morris and she could never do, such as attempting to sell people more than they asked for, and usually he succeeded." Even the practical Ida wonders if she and Morris had been "really suited to the grocery business. They had never been salesmen."

We can clearly see that use of exploitation in Frank's treatment of Helen as well. Because he wants something from her and not Helen herself, he tells her what he senses she wants to hear. In fact, all of Frank's actions at the beginning of the novel are for an ulterior purpose, not for the doing of the actions themselves: either to alleviate guilt, or to seduce Helen, or to charm his way past Ida's suspicions. It is only when Frank ceases to act within the manipulative behavioral conventions approved by his society, when he can act unselfishly, with no thought of return or repayment, that the alterations he makes in both the store and his life are valuable and permanent.

But the reader is not meant to forget the ambiguous, uncomfortable price of Frank's commitments—isolation, entombment, and an emblematic castration. By enduring circumcision in order to become a Jew, that final echoing choice in *The Assistant,* Frank Alpine elects to assume what was Morris Bober's inevitable fate, moving out of the materialistic mainstream of his own culture, rejecting the values that had brought him to rob the grocer in the first place. For Malamud in this novel, to be a Jew is to be the moral man, a perpetual alien, an unacceptable phenomenon in a social system that defines success by the extent to which human beings have been devalued and transformed into exploitable toys, and calls the responsible, honest individual a failure. (pp. 84-96)

Malamud is no Rousseauistic idealist for whom individual and societal perfection are legitimate goals to be desired. Rather, the author believes that though a given society may be self-deceiving and exploitative, or an entire civilization corrupt and decaying, there can be no escape from or evasion of responsibility. These are a child's responses. Imperfect man living in an imperfect world must still attempt goodness, even if the results of his efforts are ambiguous, or incomplete, or futile. . . .

Frank Alpine, in *The Assistant,* makes the correct moral choice, only to become an imprisoned victim because he has learned goodness. In Malamud's America, the attempt to liberate others is to confine oneself. . . . (p. 96)

Iska Alter, "The Good Man's Dilemma: 'The Natural', 'The Assistant', and American Materialism," in Critical Essays on Bernard Malamud, edited by Joel Salzberg, G. K. Hall & Co., 1987, pp. 75-98.

M. Thomas Inge on Jewishness in *The Assistant:*

[For] Malamud, Jewishness is basically a metaphor for the tragic dimensions of everyman's life and for a code of personal morality that is less religious than metaphysical. The Jew's problems reveal the human condition, and his message tells of the necessity for accepting moral responsibility in this world. Discipline and suffering lead to enlightenment and ennoblement. *The Assistant,* therefore, fulfills easily the requirement for first-rate fiction in that it takes the Jewish immigrant experience and shapes out of it a novel with a message of universal relevance.

M. Thomas Inge, in "The Ethnic Experience and Aesthetics in Literature: Malamud's The Assistant *and Roth's* Call It Sleep," *The Journal of Ethnic Studies, Winter 1974.*

Regina Gorzkowska (essay date 1982)

[*In the following essay, Gorzkowska examines Slavic folklore motifs in* The Assistant.]

Bernard Malamud's quasi-symbolic, quasi-realistic "depression story," *The Assistant,* has generally been recognized as having the flavor of a folk tale. With its folk idiom and the *schlemiel-schlimazel* folk figures, it belongs to the tradition of the Yiddish comic tale, even though its humorous tone is lost and the idiom is exploited for poetic and, less obviously, ironic effects. To understand its folkloric elements, Malamud's novel has been connected either with the Hasidic storytelling tradition surviving in the neo-Hasidism of our day . . . or likened in its climate ("depth of feeling") to "great realistic masters of Yiddish literature" whose roots go back to folk tradition. . . . These are, however, tentative suggestions, rather than interpretations based on documented research. One can better appreciate the aura of genuine folk simplicity and mysteriousness preserved in Malamud's moral parable by comparing Malamud's "art novel" with the authentic folk "devil's apprenticeship" motif found in Slav folklore. Without claiming the Polish, Byelorussian, or Ukrainian popular tale to be the source of *The Assistant,* the convergence of the two may throw some light on Malamud's myth-forming imagination, which is a permanent topic in Malamud's criticism.

The devil's apprenticeship tale forces itself again and again upon Malamud's reader familiar with Slav folklore. Malamud's story about the remorseful robber who became his victim's helper strikes one as a realistic version of the folk story stripped of its supernatural and fanciful elements. The diverse and popular authentic folk tale is not obviously derived from a storyteller's individual imagination but is rather part of the collective lore. Striking upon the same motif, Malamud seems to have rejuvenated the archetypal pattern.

Reduced to its simplest core, the story of a devil in man's service is a variant of the Faustian theme or rather its reversal. Without glorifying man's rebelliousness and individualism, the Slav tale in its comic, heroic, and tragic elements, stresses his endurance and helplessness, and takes up the motif of eternal, cosmic pity as a self-correcting mechanism in a world governed by a folk sense of justice. The usual folk-tale story is as follows: A peasant who has reached the bottom of his misery is wronged by a minor devil (variously presented, from an imp to a primitive demonic force) who—according to the prevalent version—has stolen his last slice of bread which was to take him through a day's work. Hell itself having been moved to pity, the devil is punished for his senseless thievery and ordered by Lucifer to return to earth and serve the peasant until—the version followed by Malamud—the confession of his crime obtains for him the peasant's pardon. The devil manages to become employed by the pauper as a farm hand and is put to bone-breaking toil on his plot. A Slav Hercules, he accomplishes the tasks assigned to him due to his supernatural power (the motif of enslaving forces of nature is elaborated in various versions). Unwilling or unable to pay for his services, the cunning peasant conducts the ordinary farm business as sort of a competition between the devil and himself. A winner in every single competition, the protagonist has the servant do the whole job without having any share in his profit; the idea of the peasant having cheated the devil seems to have offered great satisfaction, considering the profusion of examples. However, the devil's damnation does not prove to be his partner's salvation. Despite the supernatural powers involved, the devil's assistance (note the moralistic tendency) proves futile and his contribution, the usual thing with the devil's wages, is questionable and brings little, if any, profit to the peasant who continues merely to eke out a meager living.

Condemned to serve the peasant, the devil relinquishes his original function of trying to ensnare and mold the man's soul. No longer a tempter, he remains as mischievous as ever, unable to resist his evil impulses, and is consequently thwarted in his hope of reconciliation. The living-in experiment with the devil does not prove to be an altogether happy idea. By renouncing his nature and adopting a peasant's guise, job, and customs, the devil tends to assimilate some of his host's personality, thus humanizing himself at his host's expense in place of corrupting him. Unlike in Far-Eastern folklore, this assimilation stops short of the appropriation of the other man's identity or the stealing of his soul. It nevertheless tends in that direction. In some endings, the devil-possessing man wastes away and recovers on his death-bed only after he unmasks the devil and sends him off. The particular symbiotic relationship between Frank and Morris in *The Assistant,* ending in the symbolic reincarnation of the one in the other, fits this vicious pattern suggested by the Slav tale.

The folk story has no final version or conclusive ending. It is in fact a loose, rambling narrative whose fragments and episodes can be freely rearranged or detached to cluster around other motifs, some fragments like the devil-peasant competitions, functioning as independent stories. In effect the devil's paradox remains largely unresolved which can hardly be said to be detrimental to the story told from the peasant's point of view: To be released from his bondage, the devil needs to secure the peasant's pardon through his good service to him. However, to be effective-

ly good, he needs to renounce his evil nature and this can only be done at the expense of the peasant through the absorption of his nature or humanization. By retaining his nature he can hope to bring no good; by turning good he does harm. There seems to be no hope of release for him. He is condemned for eternity to suffer and make the other suffer.

Following the basic plot-outlines of the folk story in his presumably independent narration, Malamud has also infused it with the spirit of compassion informing the folk original. Throughout the novel, Frank Alpine "lives in the future, to be forgiven," and he becomes a "changed man," achieving some balance between his tormented, guilt-ridden self and the imperfect world resisting his good actions by experiencing a sense of pity for himself in the world ("He felt pity on the world for harboring him"), echoing Morris's idea of reciprocity in suffering: "I suffer for you . . . You suffer for me." Frank's reentry into humanity and his conversion to Judaism through his complete identification with Morris is a psychological transposition of the soul-snatching motif, guilt and atonement being in both cases the beginning of the spiritual journey. Frank's transformation is detached from, though parallel to, Morris's decline in health and his death, which in Malamud's novel are merely circumstances offering an opening for Frank's sacrificial, self-forgetting work. An element of free will (Frank is aware that he has the option of leaving) enriches the psychological interpretation of the story but it also reduces its universal symbolism to the internal, microcosmic sphere. Some vestigial traces of "otherworldliness" in the characterization of Malamud's antihero may be noticed.

Never a Dostoevskian soul in torment, Frank Alpine is—in Saul Bellow's phrase—a "general poor human devil" whose fallen nature is but too obvious. He could hardly be taken for the personification of thorough-going evil. Even as a "holdupnick" he is a half-willing accomplice of the delinquent Ward Minoque. Envying St. Francis for being "born good, which is a talent if you have it," he hesitates between his good and bad impulses and drives. Neither is he endowed with the physical appearance which would be particularly evocative of the Prince of Darkness, though he has a broken nose, "haunting," "melancholy" eyes, and a dark beard "contrasting with the pallor of his face." [In a footnote the critic states: "By the way, Frank is an Italian and in Polish folklore an Italian—perhaps in memory of Queen Bona Sforza's courtiers—is one of the devil's possible incarnations."] To Morris he is at first "a stranger with the hungry eyes," "a 'goy' after all." Helen also remembers his "greedy eyes." He is separated, almost isolated, from humanity in many ways, being of uncertain origin and having an unstable and fragmentary past of poverty and crime; he is separated from the Bobers by a different ethnic and cultural background. Bereft of continuity and purpose, his life is made up of "lost chances," and conceived of by himself as a series of crises. Before meeting Morris Bober, "bearded, smelly, dragging himself through the seasons without a hope to go by," he let himself be "a bum," looking as though he were "half in his grave," sleeping in cellars and gutters, eating what "he scrounged out of garbage cans," conceiving his possibility for greatness in a criminal act. If Morris's "emporium", where his "bad luck" landed him, is close to the infernal regions, Frank lives in a pit, next door to the void. With a curious persistence he haunts Morris's premises trying by hook and by crook to be admitted.

In Morris's dreary, profitless grocery store which is the place of "soured expectations and endless frustrations," "a prison" and "a tomb" to its owner, Frank appears to be evoked by Morris's recollections of his dead child, mourned incessantly these several years. In this semi-dead place he fills the dead boy's place. Like the appearance of otherwordly visitants in folk tales, his first appearance in Morris's store is associated with a mask and a mirror, symbolic of the other side. He enters the store with the intention of robbing it masked with a white handkerchief over his face (a death mask) and, avoiding Morris's gaze, he exchanges his first glances with him through "a cracked mirror hung behind him on the wall above the sink." Later he repeatedly uses this particular cracked mirror to shave and, after an act of near-rape, he confesses to the mirror his disgust with himself: "Where have you ever been, he asked the other in the glass, except on the inside of the circle? What have you ever done but always the wrong thing?" He sees Helen for the first time in the store, "staring at her through the plate glass." Later he is observed through this glass by Bober who, seated in the barber shop across the street, observes him pilfering. He spies on Helen in her moment of despondency, disrobed in front of her mirror. Getting to know him better, Helen comments on his mirror-like personality: "You looked into mirrors and you saw mirrors and didn't know what was right or real or important." Besides his inscrutability and an inner incongruity and lack of moral standards, she senses his "appropriating" qualities: a mirror is reflecting what the onlooker brings to it. He is a shadow personality dependent for his existence on Morris and Helen.

A cup of water and circumcision seem to be other remnants of Malamud's magic gimmickry. Like his later window-washing, to serve a cup of water is an act of atonement and remuneration. But to drink from one cup is also a prefiguration of the affinity of Frank and Morris and their strong, almost uncanny communication. They share the same understanding of "the tragic quality of life." In his confession of dissatisfaction, Frank voices Morris's disappointment and defeats. "I am sixty," Morris admits to himself, "and he talks like me." Morris finds him replying to his unspoken suggestion: " 'Why don't he go home' Morris thought, 'I'm going,' Frank said." He even shares Morris's Jewish sense of humor. Similarly circumcision is a symbolic act of renewal, regeneration, and initiation. But the pain of circumcision is also the fairy-tale cost paid for humanization or crossing the border of reality, like a siren's metamorphosis into a human being in a Hans Christian Andersen tale.

Although bereft of the devil's magic powers and supernatural gifts, Alpine is perceived by the members of the Bober family without any obvious cause, as dangerous, hateful, and mischievous on his first appearance and they continue to be afraid of his "claim" on them. Different as their reaction is to the presence of the clerk they cannot afford, their first contact with him is colored with repulsion. Even Frank's protector, Morris, is not free from it. Having invited him to the store, he feels uncomfortable in his presence. He shifts his chair, "fearing to catch some illness." He harbors a not unfounded suspicion that Frank is hiding something from him, and discovers the guilt the other tries but is not able to communicate, all by himself. Neither Frank's sense of guilt nor racial and cultural differences are sufficient to account for the effect. The bigoted Ida's reaction is a deep distrust and open hostility to the Gentile's presence, which seems to her a violation of their family integrity and privacy. She is suspicious of some hidden malice and a threat to her daughter. She is continuously nagging Morris to dismiss the clerk because of a premonition that "a tragedy will happen." Helen is similarly uneasy about her father's young assistant, but she suppresses her aversion as a prejudiced response elicited by her mother's enmity to the non-Jew and a possible unwanted suitor.

When Helen becomes closer to Frank, she senses "something about him evasive hidden" which cannot be accounted for by his sense of guilt, but is rather a judgment on his "crisis" personality—his propensity to make a "wrong move."

> He sometimes appeared to be more than he was, sometimes less. His aspirations, she sensed, were somehow apart from the self he presented normally . . . There was more to him than his appearance. Still, he hid what he had and he hid what he hadn't. With one hand the magician showed his cards, with the other he turned them into smoke . . . She gradually got the feeling that he only pretended to be frank about himself, that in telling so much about his experiences, his trick was to hide the true self . . . he had done something—committed himself in a way she could not guess.

As Helen senses, Frank is not a "total person," exhibiting the same, stable and predictable characteristics, but an evasive character who at his best is "educable" and "promising" and at his worst "a bum," an unreliable, erratic personality. Apart from his lack of definite qualities accounting for his impressionability and adaptability, Frank's fatalism is part of his "infernal" characterization. He believes that there is a fatal pattern in his life which he is powerless to break and that his plans of attainment are repeatedly thwarted because of a single unguarded "wrong" step moving a close goal beyond his reach: "With me one wrong thing leads to another and it ends in a trap."

All in all, there is enough support in the text to interpret Frank as a strange visitant struggling to break to this side of existence, a ghostlike apparition haunting Morris's premises. Malamud is able to create mystery. The reasons given for Frank's self-sacrificing work in Morris's store, his insecurity, sense of guilt for taking part in robbery, and attraction to Helen, Morris's daughter, are all plausible but they do not seem to be exhaustive. They still leave a margin for mystery. Fatalism and superstition, which are generally integral parts of Malamud's folk world, go beyond mere "clever sociology" and are closer to folk imagination than suspected by Isaac Bashevis Singer who raised this charge of ethnographic, instead poetic, approach against much of Jewish-American writing. "Fortune" and "luck" are recurrent words, next in their frequency of use perhaps only to the adjectives "right" and "wrong," imparting to the story a moralistic simplicity. They characterize both the world of the Bobers and that of Frank who is constantly endeavoring to "change his life and luck." Morris is hesitant to part with the cellar-dweller who brought him "luck." Frank, on the other hand, is justifying his pinching from the cash register by a superstitious belief that it would conserve the grocer's "luck." Beyond those superstitions there lurks the stranger's mysterious personality.

Whatever its actual indebtedness to Slav folklore, Malamud's story evolves around two basic motives which it shares with the folk tale discussed: (1) guilt and pity, . . . : a crime committed against a person who is already badly disadvantaged, an awareness of guilt and groping for atonement, the wrongdoer's apprenticeship as a means of obtaining his pardon, and (2) a search for identity through the wrongdoer's identification with the wronged. The duality of the theme and the resultant duality in the function of the main protagonist is contained in the folk tale. Like his prototype, Frank Alpine is both a savior (bringing good) and an archenemy (bringing harm). In addition to preserving some "otherworldly" characteristics and attributes, Malamud maintained this double characterization which, in the original story, has the function of reconciling the natural and supernatural elements of the story.

The Slav folk story offers a clue for the separation of the two related motives and makes is possible to delineate Frank's groping toward confession and reconciliation from his identification with Morris and his eventual conversion to Judaism. It may be noted that, unlike the former, the "Judaization" is a completed process, independent of the other motif, since it does not imply Frank's acceptance by the Jewish community. Frank is not reconciled with Morris who "set his heart against his assistant." There is no fusion with the Bober family, no wedding bells, no parental blessing. He is not marrying into the new faith. His conversion is an outgrowth of the identification process, and his marriage to Helen may or may not follow.

The two motives—reparation and appropriation—are early separated in the delineation of the painful way in which Frank relates to Morris and later to Helen. It is realized that their relationship goes beyond the reality frame, ending as it does with his symbolic dybbuk-like "dance" on the grocer's coffin. The original impulse of atonement which brought him to the store in the first place (paralleled by Morris's charity) is never lost though it is undermined by the sinister concept of Frank's appropriation of Morris's position, place, ethics, Jewishness, store, and friends. In the closing scene Frank is presiding over Morris's usual morning routine in the store; he has completely absorbed the dead grocer's place.

The idea of his identification with Morris is presented in a succession of scenes. Frank is first admitted to the store and comes to live on the Jew's "hard bread" profiting by the grocer's illness. He saves the asphyxiated grocer in order to be able to go on saving him. He puts on the grocer's apron which was refused to him earlier when he offered his labor as an unpaid trainee.

> The Jew lay white and motionless on his couch. Frank *gently* (emphasis—R.G.) removed his apron. Draping the loop around his own head, he tied the tapes around him. 'I need the experience,' he muttered.

We see him wearing Morris's clothes which fitted him exactly after "Ida lengthened and pressed the cuffs"; we have him renounced by his accomplice as "a kike." His impulse of pilfering and stealing from the cash register is the way he appropriates the place for himself. Like his disorderly eating in the store, he needs it to appease his sense of insecurity. It gives him a measure of freedom and control in a place in which he is barely tolerated. The money that he gets this way will eventually return to the register. It is not so much the profit as the fact of staying in the store that matters to him most. Without intending or knowing it he buys his stay in the store by feeding into the register the money which was his part in the robbery. He actually cheats his way in. The sum in the register makes Ida feel that she cannot afford to close the store during her husband's absence. Later, by returning his illegal savings to the register Frank again helps to keep up appearances and create an illusion that the business is not as bad as it really is. Much of his help is really an illusion and his slaving dedication to Morris is, it becomes clear, a way of helping himself. The idea that his assistantship is linked to Morris's misfortunes becomes evident. Morris's pneumonia and death save Frank his place again and again. He breaks into the store to keep it open when Morris is hospitalized. Completely rejected by the bereaved family, he takes up another job to keep the business going for the widow. Although he is a benefactor, he is perceived as "a scheming presence downstairs."

His charity, grounded in the fragile hope of reconciliation, makes him the prisoner of the shop where he is shut up, much as Morris was before him, as "in an overgrown coffin." His "devil's fate" is not over until he is forgiven. Forgiving and hurting are the double ways of relating to Morris and Helen Bober: "People forgave people—who else? . . . Explaining was a way of getting close to somebody you had hurt; as if in hurting them you were giving a reason to love you."

The tortured sado-masochistic relationship of Malamud's *schlemiel-schlimazel* pair, which is a cultural trait of his world, becomes even more sophisticated when seen against the background of Slav folklore. Adapting the folk tale to his realistic framework, Malamud has preserved the spirit of his source. As the one who—to adopt Leslie Fiedler's phrase—put a "new signature" on the old myth, Malamud is an original cultivator of folk imagination. The author of *The Magic Barrel* emerges as an inheritor of his folk's cultural tradition next only to Singer in the imaginative use of his folk sources. (pp. 35-44)

> *Regina Gorzkowska, "The Poor Slav Devil of Malamud's 'The Assistant'," in* The Polish Review, *Vol. XXVII, Nos. 3-4, 1982, pp. 35-44.*

Jeffrey Helterman   (essay date 1985)

[*Helterman is an American educator and novelist. In the following excerpt, he studies Malamud's use of mythic and religious symbolism in* The Assistant.]

In *The Natural,* the characters are mythic at both levels: the literal story of the baseball season and the archetypal level of the Grail myth. Even though sometimes based on real people and no matter how fascinating or how sharply drawn, these are characters who never were. They are literary characters who have never dwelt beyond the covers of a book. This is not true of Malamud's second novel, *The Assistant* (1957), in which the novelist settles brilliantly into the mode that will inform most of his best fiction. The world of the grocery store is real, and its characters are flesh and blood. Malamud knows this world well. His father ran a grocery store not unlike Bober's, and Malamud's first published story in high school was an account of his own life "behind the counter."

The characters live and breathe the small lives of the most ordinary men, but what is extraordinary is that Malamud has also invested them with the mythic stature he had given his baseball players. This is partially because these characters have very carefully worked out mythic antecedents, but more because Malamud has made their every act meaningful. They are capable of deeds of courage and cowardice, hard-heartedness and compassion, worthy of the greatest of heroes.

> The world of the grocery store is real, and its characters are flesh and blood. Malamud knows this world well. His father ran a grocery store not unlike Bober's, and Malamud's first published story in high school was an account of his own life "behind the counter."
>
> —*Jeffrey Helterman*

In *The Assistant,* Malamud again retells medieval myth in a modern setting. This time, however, he counterpoints the Wasteland myth found in *The Natural* against the history of St. Francis of Assisi. Both medieval archetypes center around a pair of characters: Parzival and the Fisher King, Amfortas, in the first, and Francis and Christ in the second. The novel's principal characters, Frank Alpine and Morris Bober, find themselves in a set of antithetical relationships. Frank Alpine, a man who comes from San Francisco, whose favorite book is *The Little Flowers* (a medieval collection of vignettes of St. Francis), who is first seen feeding birds in the park (the saint loved birds so much he preached to them), will become St. Francis to Morris Bober's Christ. In this relationship, the morally weak Frank will learn from Bober's spiritual strength. In the Wasteland myth, however, Bober, is Amfortas, the maimed Fisher King who is waiting to be restored by Frank's Parzival. On this level, the despondent Bober will be cured by the energetic Frank.

St. Francis, the son of a wealthy cloth merchant, turned his back on his father's material possessions to enter the monastic life where he embraced poverty so completely that his followers were called Pauvres Frères ("impoverished brothers"). In giving up worldly wealth, he turned his back on the flesh and its pleasures, particularly, food and women. He was known for his fasts and would go off for weeks with a minimal amount of bread and water and return with half his supplies intact. In giving up the wealth of world, he was following literally Christ's admonition to "sell all you have and follow me." In all he did, Francis's aim was the imitation of Christ. His ultimate reward was the appearance of the stigmata, the five wounds of Christ, on his body. The stigmata signified that he had learned to suffer like Christ for mankind. In the novel, Morris is wounded in the robbery staged by Frank and the detective's son, Ward Minogue. This wound doubles as the Fisher King's wound and the original stigmata of Christ. Frank first appears to have stigmata when he scratches his hands with his nails in his frustrated desire for Helen, but the ultimate stigmata occur at the end of the novel when he is circumcised, making him a Jew like Bober.

When Frank first appears in Bober's grocery, he is filled with the same worldly appetites that Francis had to give up. Frank steals food, and even looks upon Bober's daughter Helen with "hungry eyes." Little by little, Frank learns to govern and then give up his appetites. This restraint is not a negative or limiting attitude, but is converted into a positive activity, feeding the poor, which he learns from the example of Bober. At the very beginning of the novel, Bober, standing under his No Trust (no credit) sign gives food on credit to a drunken woman he knows will never repay him. Later, Frank performs the same duty when he goes to collect a bad debt from Carl, the Swedish painter. Seeing the man's poverty, he forgives the debt just as Bober would do, though he still has much to learn about the extent of Bober's powers of forgiveness. Eventually, Frank feeds the hungry day and night by turning the grocery into an all-night restaurant and working in a diner by day to help pay Bober's bills. By this time, he, like the saint, has almost stopped eating entirely.

Frank also learns to restrain his sexual appetites. When St. Francis was wondering about his decision to become a friar, he built himself a snow woman and snow children and declared that they were all the family he needed because he was going to put the flesh behind him. Frank tells Helen this story, but she takes it in a self-centered way and begins to think of herself as an idealized snow woman whose chastity is her only valuable possession. After Frank forces himself upon Helen the night he rescues her from attempted rape, Helen wraps herself in the snow woman's mantle and looks on Frank with an icy face while Frank dreams of looking at her through a frozen window. From this stage of self-revulsion on his side and rejection on hers, Frank's love for Helen changes from appetitive lust to a love that is more responsibility than anything else.

As the maimed Fisher King in the Parzival legend, Morris Bober laments the fact that he cannot even feed his family, just as the king of the Wasteland cannot feed his people. Like Pop Fisher in *The Natural,* Morris attributes his failure to bad luck. Though his luck is bad, the real reason he fails is that he is too honest to take advantage of anyone. He continues to give credit to the poor and refuses to cheat his customers.

In his honesty and bad luck, Morris is contrasted with a neighboring shopkeeper, Julius Karp, a liquor store owner, who seems always to have good luck. Morris never realizes that most of Karp's luck is manufactured by his selfishness. In the robbery that opens the novel's action, Karp, who is afraid his liquor store is about to be robbed, goes to Bober to let him know he might want to use his telephone (Karp, the richer man, is too cheap to have a telephone) to call the police. The obligation to remain open in case Karp returns freezes Bober in the store, while Karp runs off and leaves Bober as the robbers' only victim.

Karp also keeps renting an empty storefront to rival grocers on Bober's block, even though he knows the neighborhood cannot support two groceries. Though Karp pleads financial hardship, he makes it clear he would leave the store empty if his son Louis married Helen. Only self-interest can make Karp charitable. The wonder of their relationship is that Karp appreciates Bober's virtue more than Bober does himself, and often finds ways to spend time with Bober, if only to be in the presence of such goodness. This contact with goodness does not, however, change Karp at all.

Bober, on the other hand, never takes advantage of anyone. When a poor immigrant is about to buy his wretched store, Bober cannot keep his mouth shut, and by telling him the truth about the store's meager earnings frightens off the potential buyer. Not only does Morris refuse to cheat the poor, he doesn't even feel jealous of the success of his expartner, Charlie Sobeloff, who has bilked him out of four thousand dollars and used the money to start a successful supermarket.

Morris's despair comes from the fact that he does not appreciate the value of his own virtue and charity. Though he despises the values of Karp, the worldly wise man, who makes his living selling brain-destroying alcohol rather than life-giving milk, Bober still measures his own success by Karp's standards, and seen on those terms, the little grocery is a wasteland as barren as Amfortas's.

The Wasteland can only be restored if a pure, but foolish, knight comes to the Grail feast where he must ask the right question. The question is different in different versions of the myth, but usually has to do with the nature of the king's wound or the meaning of the feast. In the legend, Parzival finds Amfortas, is too overwhelmed by decorum to ask the question, and is sent away after being told he has failed his quest forever. Parzival, too "foolish" to accept this judgment, finds the Fisher King again, asks the question, heals the Fisher King, takes his place, and the land is restored.

Frank makes much the same mistakes as Parzival. His mindless eating in the store is the same as Parzival's presence at the initial Grail feast. Frank does ask the questions, "What is a Jew?" and "Why do you suffer?" but he is not wise enough to understand the apparently simple answers, "a Jew is a good man" and "I suffer for you." Like Parzival, his intentions are good, but he is not ready to assume the place of the king and is thrown out when he makes a foolish mistake. Frank begins his virtuous life by putting back some of the money he has stolen from Morris. Morris catches Frank stealing Frank's own money, but doesn't realize it. He fires his assistant just at the moment that Frank has begun his reformation. This is the fate of men like Frank: every time he tries to do a good deed, it turns out wrong. He has yet to learn that the nature of the deed is more important than its result.

Frank's virtue, instead of easing Morris's despair, therefore, increases it, because Morris feels he has lost the "son" he thought he had found in Frank. At the same time, new rival grocers have driven Morris's business down to nothing, and he turns on the gas and "accidentally" forgets to light it. Frank rescues Morris and resumes his job while Morris recuperates. The gas-filled store becomes Morris's self-created gas chamber as he dreams the rival Norwegian grocers are speaking German. Between the apparent betrayal of Frank, his daughter's indiscretions with the assistant, and Karp's renting to the Norwegians, Morris becomes convinced of man's infinite inhumanity to man. Since he might as well have become a victim of the Nazis, he allows the gas to destroy his spirit, his breath of life.

Though Frank has saved his life, Bober has hardened his heart against him and refuses to let him stay, even after Frank confesses his part in the holdup. Bober already knew this, and it is not the original crime that makes him refuse the assistant. Bober wants Frank to stay, but is not yet Christlike enough to turn the other cheek. He had accepted the robbery that occurred when Frank was a stranger and desperate. He cannot accept the subsequent petty theft in the store (even though it is finished) because this time Frank had asked to be trusted. For Morris, the breakdown of trust is the breakdown of one man's responsibility for another.

When Frank finds out that Bober had known for a long time that he was one of the robbers, he begins to understand what Bober means by saying, "I suffer for you." In fact, Frank understands Bober better than Bober understands himself. By knowing about Frank's crimes without revealing them or using them for moral leverage, Bober has taken responsibility for Frank's life and suffers for him the way Christ suffered for mankind. Since Christ was crucified for our sins, the pain of his crucifixion is increased every time man sins. When Frank realizes this, he knows that he must take up Morris's burden in the store as Morris had taken up his burden of sin. In doing this, he learns what St. Francis had learned about taking up the burdens of Christ.

The two heroes continually counterpoint each other's successes and failures. Just when Frank understands the nature of his own temptations, Bober falls victim to temptation of another kind. Malamud injects one of his eerie otherworldly figures, a Satanic firesetter who offers Bober a way out of the store: a fire that will let him collect his insurance. The fire-starter seems more a primeval representation of Bober's despair than another person. For this reason it hardly matters that Bober's strong moral sense allows him to repel the man's temptation. He finally yields to his own despair and tries to start the fire himself using a photographic negative as a fuse. The burning negative symbolizes the absolute collapse of Bober's self-image. Once again Frank saves him, as he did from the gas and, at the beginning of the novel, when he collapsed carrying boxes in the snow. Though Morris still will not let him work in the store, Frank realizes that he is responsible for Morris and his family and knows that his only future is in the grocery. Morris's message, "I suffer for you," is beginning to be Frank's watchword as well.

Malamud marks the changes in his characters lives with elementary forces that take on the value of primitive ritual. Morris has to contend with ice and fire and then with fire and ice. A second fire after the one he tried to start seems to promise new hope. After watching his life go from one desperate moment to another, Morris suddenly thinks that his luck is beginning to change. A fire caused in a robbery attempt at Karp's liquor store burns down the Karp establishment, and the well-insured Karp begins negotiations to buy Bober's store so he can reopen his liquor business. For the first time, Bober sees hope for his family and in his high spirits goes out to shovel a late spring snow. The day, appropriately, is the day before April Fool's Day, and it is Bober who is the fool. The deceptive spring day is still wintry enough to give Bober a fatal case of pneumonia. Bober dies believing that his family will be provided for, but even this is a false hope. Karp suffers a heart attack, and since his lazy son doesn't want to keep up with the business, he never does buy Morris's store.

It would seem that Morris's life is a failure, but his funeral proves just the opposite. A favorite notion of Malamud's is one he borrows from Montaigne, "We should not judge of a man's happiness until after his death." To his wife and daughter, Morris's funeral seems to be a sham. His eulogy is delivered in extravagant terms by a rabbi who has never met him, but as Frank listens, he discovers that the rabbi is right: Bober's life has made a difference to all it touched.

Helen throws a rose into Morris's grave, and when Frank leans over to see what it is, he falls into the grave. Frank's rising from Morris's grave completes his symbolic rebirth and makes him into the new ruler of the Wasteland. His complete devotion to the store and his hard work make it, if not a wonderful success, at least a going concern.

Frank's "inheritance" of the grocery store turns him into the son Bober had long missed. Bober's own son, Ephraim had died of an unexplained ear infection, and with his death all of Bober's hopes beyond survival had also died. The Morris/Frank-father/son relationship is paralleled by three other pairs of fathers and sons. Each of the sons is "romantically" linked to Helen, and each corresponds to one of the four kinds of sons named in the Passover Seder, which is like the Grail story, a feast whose center is the asking of questions. The four sons are the wise son, the wicked son, the foolish son, and the son who wits not to ask. The wise son is Nat Pearl, who was Helen's lover at one time. Nat is the son who fulfills the immigrants' dream of surpassing his parents in wealth and wisdom and becoming fully assimilated in the new land. Nat is on his way to becoming a successful lawyer, though he manages to ignore the Law of his people to do it. The foolish son is Louis Karp, who is romancing Helen at the beginning of the story. He is the son who is too lazy to go into his father's successful business and will clearly do less well than his father without any compensating gain in morality. The wicked son is Ward Minogue, the son of a policeman. Minogue is Frank's partner in the robbery and the man who attempts to rape Helen in the park. Minogue tries to get Frank to return to his life of crime, and he represents what Frank might have become without the influence of Bober. Minogue is so outraged by Frank's decision to work in the grocery that he calls him a "kike" long before Frank even thinks about becoming a Jew. Ward is the son who disappoints his father in every way, so that when Morris discovers that it is Minogue who hit him on the head, his concern is not with revenge of any kind but rather with pity for the father. Frank, like Parzival, is the son who wits not to ask, though he finally overcomes this limitation and does ask the right questions. Frank eventually surpasses each of these sons and becomes more of a blessing to his "father" than they are. Unlike Louis Karp, he does take over his father's business, thereby leaving Bober's mark on society. He also learns the law as Pearl does, but it is the Jewish Law which Nat has forgotten. Frank even mimics Ward's defiance of his father, but only in refusing to listen when Morris warns him not to take over the store.

Frank's education in the grocery business is paralleled by the changes in his love for Bober's daughter, Helen. The romance of Frank and Helen finds two unsatisfied idealists yearning unhappily for each other. The two of them are idealistic both in what they want for themselves and in what they want in a beloved. Helen, stuck in her job at the Levenspiel bra factory, wants to be a college-educated person and is looking for a man with the same credentials. When she begins imagining herself in love with Frank, she dreams of a better-dressed, college-educated Frank with a smaller nose. To the end of the novel, she will not commit herself completely to Frank because she will not let go her dream of the ideal man, even the ideal Frank, coming along.

Frank also fosters a false self-image. Convinced he is a failure in life, he sees himself compensating by pursuing a glamorous life of crime, the kind of life projected in Hollywood gangster epics. This dream is dashed when his reward for his first "job" is half the take from Bober's grocery, half of fifteen dollars. Frank does have another ideal in mind, however, the St. Francis who had comforted him ever since his days in the orphanage. It is not until he establishes a proper relationship with both Helen and her father that he considers Francis a hero to be emulated.

Since both lovers are idealists who use the library as a trysting place, it is not surprising that their reading habits help define their idealism. Helen reads fiction, particularly epic tragedies of suffering like *Anna Karenina* and *Madame Bovary*. Helen would like to share the martyrdom of these heroines, but she fears the absolute commitment that destroys Anna and Emma. She tends toward self-dramatization, and her joyless life in the bra factory is boring, but hardly tragic. She crosses off the days on the calendar, not because they are finished, but because they are empty, and she believes they are empty because she is not living a life of epic emotional suffering.

Frank reads biographies of worldly successes like Napoleon and dreams of conquering the world like his heroes. The difference between Frank and Helen is that Frank is able to escape his idealism by living his life as it comes. He discovers that he does become a hero of sorts in emulating the worldly fool, St. Francis, and an even bigger fool, Morris Bober.

Frank's love for Helen also follows another medieval archetype. The medieval *Romance of the Rose* tells of a lover who receives one kiss from a rose and then spends the rest of the romance pursuing his unattainable love. This model is followed closely in the story that Frank tells Helen of his only love before her. Frank was in love with a carnival girl who died in an automobile accident after their affair had gone no farther than a single kiss. In this story, which foreshadows the romance of Frank and Helen, the carnival girl, though suggesting easy promiscuity, is a symbol pointing in the other direction. A carnival, like the Mardi Gras, originally marked the beginning of the Lenten season and in Latin meant "a farewell to the flesh." At first, Frank lusts after Helen, but his love soon idealizes her, first as a flower and then, more specifically, as a rose.

After forcing himself upon Helen, Frank tries to win her forgiveness by carving her a wooden bird and a wooden rose. She accepts only the rose, but when she finds out Frank's part in the robbery of her father's store, she throws the wooden rose in the trash. The rose becomes a symbol of Frank's death and rebirth when he falls into Bober's grave trying to see what Helen has thrown into it. When he recovers the rose, he feels the possibility of a new life and a new kind of love with Helen. At the end of the novel, Frank dreams that St. Francis has turned his wooden rose into a living one, suggesting his love for Helen has overcome its rigid idealism. Since it remains a rose, and a gift of the saint, Frank has perhaps turned his love into a higher ideal than the lustful romanticism of his first yearnings.

This spirit of transcendance illuminates both of the principals in Malamud's outwardly depressing tale. The store is many times called a prison, and Frank's wretched living quarters are seen as a cell. As Frank begins to take on the virtues of Bober, the cell becomes a place of monastic illumination. Each act of suffering for Bober and the rest of mankind strips away Frank's worldliness so that his act of becoming a Jew is, in St. Francis's terms, true *imitation Christi*. Frank, who entered the novel as an orphan, has found a father; he was a drifter and has found a home; he cared about nothing and has found a love. Ward Minogue's curse "you filthy kike" has become a blessing as he has learned to love all the wretched of the earth.

Though Frank and his goodness survive past the end of the novel, he could have achieved nothing except by imitating Morris. Bober's goodness is seen through his little acts of kindness as well as in his suffering for Frank. As

Frank, without Morris, could have ended up like Ward Minogue, so Morris could have ended up like two wretched Jews who wander through the novel, Breitbart, a light bulb salesman, and Marcus, a cancer-riddled paper bag peddler. They are men without hope, but Bober cares about them, and when he visits Breitbart, he leaves a present for his son, even though he has nothing himself. Morris's feeding by giving credit to the poor becomes a metaphor for taking care of mankind, and his little neighborhood seems to be a community of nations with its Swedes, Norwegians, Poles, Germans, Italians, Irish, and Jews. Though often his customers avoid his shop for cheaper prices somewhere else, they are all aware of him as the moral center of their universe and buy a little from him to assuage their guilt at choosing the world rather than its goodness. Such is the way of the world, but Malamud's humble heroes shine beyond it. (pp. 37-51)

> *Jeffrey Helterman, in his* Understanding Bernard Malamud, *University of South Carolina Press, 1985, 153 p.*

FURTHER READING

Bibliography

Salzberg, Joel. *Bernard Malamud: A Reference Guide.* Boston: G. K. Hall & Co., 1985, 211 p.
> Annotated and chronological list of writings about Malamud from 1952 to 1983.

Criticism

Baumbach, Jonathan. "The Economy of Love: The Novels of Bernard Malamud." *The Kenyon Review* XXV, No. 3 (Summer 1963): 438-57.
> Claims that in *The Assistant, A New Life,* and *The Natural* Malamud "has extended the tradition of the American romance-novel, has made the form into something uniquely and significantly his own."

Cohen, Sandy. "*The Assistant:* Ceremony of Innocence." In *Bernard Malamud and the Trial by Love,* pp. 37-55. Amsterdam: Rodopi N.V., 1974.
> Perceives several human relationships in *The Assistant* to be mutually beneficial and essential to the betterment of the characters involved.

Fiedler, Leslie A. "Malamud: The Commonplace as Absurd." In his *No! In Thunder: Essays on Myth and Literature,* pp. 101-10. Boston: Beacon Press, 1960.
> Asserts that Malamud's central theme in *The Assistant* is "the absurdity of existence in its most commonplace forms"—best evidenced, according to Fiedler, in the novel's unorthodox view of Judaism. This review was originally published in *The Reconstructionist,* 21 February 1958.

Gold, Herbert. "Dream to Be Good." *The Nation* 104, No. 16 (20 April 1957): 350.
> Concludes that *The Assistant* is "almost perfect as far as it goes."

Handy, W. J. "The Malamud Hero: A Quest for Existence." In *The Fiction of Bernard Malamud,* edited by Richard Astro and Jackson J. Benson, pp. 65-86. Corvallis: Oregon State University Press, 1977.

>Examines Malamud's vision of human existence as seen in several of his works, including *The Assistant.* Handy observes that Malamud presents existence as "characterized by struggle and suffering" and revolving around interpersonal relationships.

Hicks, Granville. "A Note on Literary Journalism, and Good Novels by Moore and Malamud." *The New Leader* XL, No. 17 (29 April 1957): 21-2.

>Regards *The Assistant* as "a somber, meticulous examination of the complexity of human motivation," and praises Malamud's insights on "the possibility of change in a human being."

Klein, Marcus. "Bernard Malamud: The Sadness of Goodness." In his *After Alienation: American Novels in Mid-Century,* pp. 247-93. Cleveland: World Publishing Company, 1962.

>Asserts that Malamud, as evidenced in *The Assistant* and several other works, creates characters whose behavior indicates a "compulsive urgency to be out of this world and in a more certainly felt reality—one often contained, it happens, in a special folklore."

Komizo, Yôko. "On Frank's Conversion in Malamud's *The Assistant.*" *Kyushu American Literature* 16 (May 1975): 47-9.

>Discusses the significance of Frank Alpine's conversion to Judaism, observing: "Frank . . . becomes a Jew when he suffers for others, not simply for himself."

Leer, Norman. "The Double Theme in Malamud's *Assistant:* Dostoevsky with Irony." *Mosaic* IV, No. 3 (Spring 1971): 89-102.

>Detailed comparison of Frank Alpine of *The Assistant* and Raskolnikov of Fyodor Dostoevsky's *Crime and Punishment.*

Levin, Meyer. "Growth in Brooklyn." *Saturday Review,* New York XL, No. 24 (15 June 1957): 21.

>Praises Malamud for taking, in *The Assistant,* "commonplace material" and producing "a sense of utterly fresh discovery of human qualities."

Mandel, Ruth B. "Bernard Malamud's *The Assistant* and *A New Life:* Ironic Affirmation." *Critique* VII, No. 2 (Winter 1964-65): 110-22.

>Asserts that Morris Bober in *The Assistant* discovers a personal ethic and is redeemed, but, ironically, "the state of grace is unaccompanied by paradise. Redemption is at once hopeful and hopeless."

Mellard, James J. "Malamud's Novels: Four Versions of Pastoral." *Critique* IX, No. 2 (1967): 5-19.

>Contends that Malamud's *The Assistant, The Natural, A New Life,* and *The Fixer* are pastoral works centered on "the pattern of vegetation rituals and myths."

Mesher, David R. "Malamud's Jewish Metaphors." *Judaism* 26, No. 1 (Winter 1977): 18-26.

>Considers the theme of Jewishness in several of Malamud's novels, including *The Assistant,* and states: "To accept one's Jewishness means, in *The Assistant,* to experience and understand the human condition."

Schulz, Max F. "Bernard Malamud's Mythic Proletarians." In his *Radical Sophistication: Studies in Contemporary Jewish-American Novelists,* pp. 56-68. Athens: Ohio University Press, 1969.

>Studies the construction of identity in several of Malamud's characters, including Frank Alpine of *The Assistant,* and concludes: "The Malamud protagonist functions simultaneously as mythic savior and as social scapegoat. His growth in conscience represents symbolically a victory for society and the forces of life."

Additional coverage of Malamud's life and career is contained in the following sources published by Gale Research: *Concise Dictionary of American Literary Biography, 1941-1968; Contemporary Authors,* Vols. 5-8, rev. ed., 118 [obituary]; *Contemporary Authors Bibliographical Series,* Vol. 1; *Contemporary Authors New Revision Series,* Vol. 28; *Contemporary Literary Criticism,* Vols. 1, 2, 3, 5, 8, 9, 11, 18, 27, 44; *Dictionary of Literary Biography,* Vols. 2, 28; *Dictionary of Literary Biography Yearbook* 1980, 1986; *Major 20th-Century Writers;* and *World Literature Criticism.*

Arthur Miller
The Crucible

Born in 1915, Miller is an American playwright, essayist, novelist, nonfiction writer, short story writer, scriptwriter, and autobiographer.

The following entry presents criticism on Miller's drama *The Crucible* (1953). For further information on Miller's life and career, see *CLC*, Volumes 1, 2, 6, 10, 15, 26, and 47.

INTRODUCTION

Winner of an Antoinette Perry (Tony) Award for best play, *The Crucible* is widely considered Miller's most controversial and best-known work since his highly acclaimed *Death of a Salesman.* Based upon the witch trials held in Salem, Massachusetts, in 1692, *The Crucible* uses characters based on historical personages to address the complex moral dilemmas of John Proctor, a man wrongly accused of practicing witchcraft. Through his depiction of the mass hysteria that propelled the witch-hunts, Miller examines the social and psychological aspects of group pressure and its effect on individual ethics, dignity, and beliefs.

The Crucible begins after the Reverend Parris discovers several teenage girls dancing nude in a forest after dark. To escape punishment, the girls accuse several townspeople of having possessed them and of initiating them into witchcraft. Abigail Williams, one of the girls, claims that she was under the spell of Elizabeth Proctor, who had employed her as a servant until she discovered that her husband and Abigail were having an affair. Several members of the community are subsequently accused, convicted of witchcraft, and threatened with a sentence of death unless they confess their involvement in demonism and name their co-conspirators.

Because she is pregnant, Elizabeth Proctor is not sentenced to hang; however, her husband's refusal to cooperate with the court and falsely confess his participation in witchcraft ultimately leads to his destruction. In an attempt to discredit Abigail as a witness, Proctor reveals his adultery to the court. Elizabeth denies the affair to save her husband's reputation, but Proctor refuses to retract his statement and denounces the self-serving corruption of all involved in the trials, declaring: "For them that quail to bring men out of ignorance, as I have quailed, and as you quail now when you know in all your black hearts that this be fraud—God damns our kind especially, and we will burn together!" Proctor then reconsiders his decision and signs a confession, but, though he still denies any knowledge of others consorting with the devil, his love for his wife convinces him to surrender his integrity for her. When he learns that his written testimony will be used to convict others, however, Proctor tears up the confession,

refusing to condone what he perceives as a perversion of justice. Proctor is ultimately hanged along with eighteen other victims by the hysterical mob.

When *The Crucible* was first staged, a number of critics maintained that Miller had failed in his characteristic attempt to merge the personal and the social. Several critics initially claimed that the play's characters are poorly developed, merely serving as mouthpieces for Miller's social commentary. Elizabeth Proctor, for example, is seen as a simplistic portrayal of a good and faithful wife, while John Proctor emerges as an admirable character, yet he lacks the depth and humanistic appeal of such tragic heroes as Shakespeare's Hamlet or Miller's Willy Loman from *Death of a Salesman.* A few commentators have observed that Miller may have taken excessive artistic license when creating the character of Abigail Williams. According to historical records Williams was a victim herself, a young child who became infected by a hysteria already rampant in her community. In *The Crucible* Abigail is depicted as a shrewd and sinister teenager and thus a difficult character for an audience to view as a victim of a corrupt society.

Soon after the play's first production, critics noted similarities between the events in *The Crucible* and the investigations headed by Senator Joseph McCarthy and his House Committee on Un-American Activities into an unsubstantiated communist conspiracy. *The Crucible,* commonly interpreted as a critique of these investigations, was initially judged stridently polemical in intent and execution, with some commentators questioning the validity of the parallels Miller established between the Salem witch-hunt and the congressional investigations. The relationship between the historical events depicted in the play and the events of the 1950s has continued to elicit debate among critics. In 1957, four years after the play's premiere, Miller testified before the House Committee; although he admitted that he had attended a meeting of communist writers, he denied ever having been a member of the Communist Party and refused to implicate anyone he had known. As a result, he was found guilty of contempt of Congress, a conviction that was later overturned. In an interview, Miller commented: "There was no response to McCarthyism, except for *The Crucible.* And when I was attacked, I was never defended. I think that's unforgivable. At the same time, I now recognize that this was one of the blackest periods in Russia. When you had Stalin around, the magnitude of the cruelty was unmatched. You've got to be either God or the Devil to figure this out."

One year after Miller's testimony, when the furor over communist activity in the United States had died down, *The Crucible* was revived off-Broadway. Freed from its immediate association with current events, the play was warmly received by critics and enjoyed a run of over six hundred performances. *The Crucible* is now considered to possess a more lasting and universal significance than had earlier been apparent. As Robert Martin asserted in 1977, *The Crucible* "has endured beyond the immediate events of its own time. If it was originally seen as a political allegory, it is presently seen by contemporary audiences almost entirely as a distinguished American play by an equally distinguished American playwright."

PRINCIPAL WORKS

The Man Who Had All the Luck (drama) 1944
Situation Normal (nonfiction) 1944
Focus (novel) 1945
Death of a Salesman: Certain Private Conversations in Two Acts and a Requiem (drama) 1949
An Enemy of the People [adaptation of Henrik Ibsen's play] (drama) 1950
The Crucible (drama) 1953
**A Memory of Two Mondays* (drama) 1955
**A View from the Bridge* [one-act version] (drama) 1955
A View from the Bridge [two-act version] (drama) 1956
The Misfits (screenplay) 1961
After the Fall (drama) 1964
Incident at Vichy (drama) 1964

I Don't Need You Any More (stories) 1967
The Price (drama) 1968
The Creation of the World and Other Business (drama) 1972
Up from Paradise [musical adaptation of *The Creation of the World*] (drama) 1974
The Archbishop's Ceiling (drama) 1977
The Theater Essays of Arthur Miller (essay) 1978
The American Clock [adaptation of Studs Terkel's nonfiction work *Hard Times*] (drama) 1980
†*Elegy for a Lady* (drama) 1982
†*Some Kind of Love Story* (drama) 1982
‡*Danger, Memory!* (drama) 1986
Timebends: A Life (autobiography) 1987

*These two works were first performed together in a single production.

†These two works were first performed together in a single production. *Elegy for a Lady* was published in the United States in 1982; *Some Kind of Love Story* was issued the following year. They were published together in Great Britain as *Two-Way Mirror* in 1984.

‡This work consists of two one-act plays: *I Can't Remember Anything* and *Clara.*

CRITICISM

Wolcott Gibbs   (review date 31 January 1953)

[*In the review excerpted below, Gibbs provides a positive assessment of* The Crucible.]

[In **The Crucible**], Arthur Miller has written, on its primary level, a play about the Salem witch trials in 1692. These, as you certainly know, were classic examples of mass hysteria, resulting in the hanging of a great many respectable men and women on charges of trafficking with the Devil; and they were convicted by people at least as respectable as themselves, largely on the evidence of four young girls who had been caught dancing in the moonlight and laid their dissolute behavior to the influence of Satan. On its secondary and contemporary level, of course, Mr. Miller's piece says that witch-hunting is still among the most popular of American pastimes, and that there is almost no charge too preposterous to be believed by even the most upright pillars of society. The parallel may seem a little strained at times, since the credulity and superstition of our New England ancestors clearly exceed our own powers of imagination, but the author has written with a compassion and felicity only slightly less than those he achieved in **Death of a Salesman. . . .** Altogether, I should say that **The Crucible** is one of the most impressive offerings of the season, and in spite of an occasional sacrifice of drama to polemics, it surely deserves your respectful attention.

The action focusses on John and Elizabeth Proctor, a farming couple, who are the victims of a former serving girl of theirs, who sets in motion the monstrous conspiracy that turns life in Salem into a nightmare of crazy lies and hallucinations and incredible perversions of justice. In addition to these three, the figures mainly involved are a deputy governor of Massachusetts, who represents a kind of implacable bureaucracy, and is fiercely jealous of his authority; two parsons, one unctuous and determined to exact the last possible life, the other a man who eventually rebels against the bloody work to which he is committed; a venomous village gossip; a judge who may well serve as a symbol of the bigotry of his time and presumably ours; and an elderly pair brave enough to resist the prevailing insanity. At the end, Proctor forfeits his neck by refusing to confess to the ludicrous accusations brought against him, and dies on the scaffold, along with eighteen fellow-victims of ignorance and militant theology. To the best of my recollection, Mr. Miller has stuck fairly close to the established facts. It is a powerful play, handsomely executed in every respect, and conceivably the most interesting one of the year. (p. 47)

> *Wolcott Gibbs, "The Devil to Pay," in* The New Yorker, *Vol. XXVIII, No. 50, January 31, 1953, pp. 47-9.*

Henry Hewes   (essay date 31 January 1953)

[*Hewes is an American critic and editor. In the following excerpt from a conversation with Miller, the playwright discusses his sources for* The Crucible *and explains why his works may be viewed as political and allegorical.*]

On the strength of two plays that sank deep into the heart of contemporary life, Arthur Miller has [like Tennessee Williams] risen to the unchallenged position of being one of this generation's two foremost American dramatists, and there is no reason to doubt that he will continue to write about everyday situations with equal truth, equal power, and equal success. But, being something of a non-conformist, Mr. Miller has [in *The Crucible*] chosen to turn away from the modern arena, where he is demonstrably at home, to try his hand at writing a historical play that involves some fairly remote events that happened during the Salem witchcraft trials of 1692.

Visited during a rehearsal break at the Martin Beck, the tall mantis-figured playwright seemed tired and watchful as he sat with his legs dangling over the orchestra seat in front of him. But serious and concerned as he was, he appeared surprisingly untroubled about the increase in complexity that goes with staging a twenty-two-character play set in another period, and putting into focus the tragedy of a whole society, not just the tragedy of an individual. "I've laid it out that way from the start," he said in a gently confident tone. "The first scene is purely an overture in which we emphasize the inability of these Puritans to cope with the strange sickness of the minister's little girl, and the resultant turn to accusations of witchcraft. The strict beliefs under which they all lived were doubly responsible. Their tenets were filled with witches and the devil, and they gave them an authority-weighted reason for something they found hard otherwise to explain. In addition, the circle of children who made the accusations had grievances against the Puritan women they named, because

these women had made their lives and the lives of their husbands cold and unpleasant. As Elizabeth Proctor, one of the accused wives, says:

> It needs a cold wife to prompt lechery. I counted myself so plain, so poorly-made, no honest love could come to me! Suspicion kissed you when I did; I never knew how I should say my love. It were a cold house I kept. . !

The thirty-seven-year-old writer maintains, however, that this remorseless, unbending ideology of the Puritans had constructive uses in settling this country, as proved by the fact that the Massachusetts colony succeeded against heavy odds, while the non-ideological Virginia Colony failed despite an easier climate. "But, by 1692, the usefulness of the ideology had passed and it had become an orthodoxy which had to destroy its opposition or be itself destroyed. The tragedy of *The Crucible* is the ever-lasting conflict between people so fanatically wedded to this orthodoxy that they could not cope with the evidence of their senses."

Also necessary to establish in the first scene is the atmosphere of seventeenth-century Salem. "I use words like 'poppet' instead of 'doll,' and grammatical syntax like 'he have' instead of 'he has.' This will remind the audience that *The Crucible* is taking place in another time, but won't make it too difficult to understand, which it might if I used all the old language with words like 'dafter' instead of 'daughter.' Also, I have varied some of the facts. Actually, the girls were reported as dancing in the woods and practising abominations. I have them dancing *naked* in the woods, which makes it easier for the audience to relate the Puritans' horror at such a thing to their own."

Mr. Miller has taken some other liberties with the historical facts, as he read them in the Salem courthouse and in a book written by Charles W. Upham in 1867. (Oddly enough, he is not familiar with Tennessee Williams's short story "The Yellow Bird," issued recently by Caedmon Records, which derives from the same incident.)

For instance, from Abigail Williams, whose actual age was between eleven and fourteen, plus the evidence that she tried to have Goody Proctor killed by incantations, he manufactured an eighteen-year-old wench who had seduced Goody Proctor's husband. Likewise there is no specific evidence that Proctor confessed and then recanted his confession as occurs in the play, although other accused persons did so. Says the author, "A playwright has no debt of literalness to history. Right now I couldn't tell you which details were taken from the records verbatim and which were invented. I think you can say that this play is as historically authentic as *Richard II*, which took place closer to Shakespeare's time than *The Crucible* did to ours."

After the overture of the first scene is over, the play more or less concentrates on the fate of one man, John Proctor. "Any play is the story of how the birds came home to roost," says Miller. "Proctor acts and has to face the consequences of his action. In so doing he discovers who he is. He is a good man. Willy Loman in *Death of a Salesman* went through the same process, but, because he had lost

Proctor's sense of personal inviolability and had yielded completely to every pressure, he never found out who he was. That's what Proctor means near the end of the play when he talks of his 'name.' He is really speaking about his identity, which he cannot surrender."

Another character who interests Miller is Reverend Hale, who initiates the witchcraft investigation. "Hale," he says, "is a man who permits a beloved ideology to overwhelm the evidence of his senses past the point when the evidence of his senses should have led him to question and revise his ideology. His tragic failure along with certain other honest leaders of that community was a lack of a sense of proportion."

While the dramatist is willing to talk about themes within his play, he doesn't pretend to know exactly what his play means. "I never know until at least a year after I've written it. A complex play can have many themes, but I don't sit down to write a play with a specific theme worked out in my mind. What I do have in my mind is a general sense of the quality I want it to have, much as you might try to present a picture of honesty or beauty by describing some honest or beautiful person you knew. Then I work on the script until it seems to have the aura of my original conception and at the same time I can see every moment of it as drama."

Although many people have seen Miller's previous plays as political or allegorical, the playwright is definite in his denial of any such simple intention. "I am not pressing an historical allegory here, and I have even eliminated certain striking similarities from *The Crucible* which may have started the audience to drawing such an allegory. For instance, the Salemites believed that the surrounding Indians, who had never been converted to Christianity, were in alliance with the witches, who were acting as a Fifth Column for them within the town. It was even thought that the outbreak of witchcraft was the last attack by the Devil, who was being pressed into the wilderness by the expanding colony. Some might have equated the Indians with Russians and the local witches with Communists. My intent and interest is wider and I think deeper than this. From my first acquaintance with the story I was struck hard by the breathtaking heroism of certain of the victims who displayed an almost frightening personal integrity. It seemed to me that the best part of this country was made of such stuff, and I had a strong desire to celebrate them and to raise them out of historic dust."

Mr. Miller believes the reason his plays are thought to be so political is that the complete vacuousness of so many of our contemporary plays makes works of any substance seem political by comparison.

He points out that Girardoux's *Madwoman of Chaillot* was a really radical play, but that because it was set in Paris people here did not take it as such. As far as he is concerned in his own plays, Miller prefers to consider the area of literature and the area of politics to be separate.

"Literature is a weapon, but not in the sense that Marxists, Fascists, and our own 'Americanists' believe. It is possible to read a royalist-Catholic writer and draw sustenance for a left-wing position from him; it is possible to draw a con-servative moral from an anti-conservative work. A work of art creates a complex world, and as the past hundred years have proved, the special 'truth' of one decade may turn out to be the reactionary falsehood of another. It is a poor weapon whose direction is so unstable as to serve one side at one moment and another side the next. The only sure and valid aim—speaking of art as a weapon—is the humanizing of man." (pp. 24-5)

Henry Hewes, "Arthur Miller & How He Went to the Devil," in The Saturday Review, *New York, Vol. XXXVI, No. 5, January 31, 1953, pp. 24-6.*

Miller on the language and style of *The Crucible*:

In *The Crucible,* we see the fate of the society from a religious, moral point of view; its merged sublime and political powers forcing the transmission of a man's conscience to others, and then of the man's final immortal need to take it back. In the area of morals and society it had to be a more explicit and "hard" play, hence its form. You know we adopt styles when we speak. When you're speaking to your mother you speak in a different tone of voice from when you're speaking to your class; you use different gestures when you speak to a friend and to the public; or to a policeman, or judge, or possibly a professor. So it's the kind of address that the play is going to make that also creates its form. The address in *The Crucible* was an insistence, hardly concealed in the play, that if the events we see in that play are not understood it can mean the end of social life—which is based primarily on a certain amount of shared trust. And when the government goes into the business of destroying trust, it goes into the business of destroying itself. So, saying this in *The Crucible,* what I believed at the time—the story of the Salem witch-hunt in 1692—was indeed saying it wanted that form. An aseptic form; it's less sensuous than *Salesman. The Crucible* is more pitiless, probably because power is at the bottom of it and because so much of the witch-hunt took place in a theocratic court. The witch-hunt was fundamentally a business of prosecutors and lawyers, witnesses, testimony. Literally the town of Salem did nothing anymore but attend court sessions in the church. It just about destroyed the town within the lifetime of those people.

Arthur Miller, in an interview with Matthew C. Roudane in Michigan Quarterly Review, *Summer, 1985.*

Freda Kirchwey (review date 7 February 1953)

[*Kirchwey was an American journalist, editor, and critic. In the following excerpt, she characterizes* The Crucible *as a complex parable of America's political situation in both 1692 and 1953 that is "self-contained, rather than contained by time or place."*]

Perhaps the proper way to judge Arthur Miller's play, *The Crucible,* would be to see it out of context—out of the pertinent, and thus painful, and thus perhaps distorting, setting of today. While watching it, I tried to do this, and now, writing about it after a lapse of days, I shall try again. But I shall not succeed except partially, and in my mind.

In literal fact, I cannot shed the sense of having experienced simultaneously the anguish and heroism of Salem's witch hunt and of today's. And since this is so I am driven to believe that the emotions of both tragic periods charged the lines with a power they would have missed had Mr. Miller visited the Salem Courthouse in a more tranquil time.

But if *The Crucible* is a drama of 1953, as well as of 1692, it does not follow that it is a simple parable. On the contrary, it is self-contained rather than contained by time or place. It is the terrible and tragic situation that provides the real setting; while the action develops a completely believable conflict between a handful of ordinary citizens and the epidemic madness which spreads from children—half-malicious, half-obsessed—to the top dignitaries of bench and church.

The situation is convincing to the last irrational detail. The conflict emerges in subtly differentiated forms and shadings. Mr. Miller is not afraid to point out how short a distance can separate spiteful lying from honest, screaming hysterics or stark courage at the foot of the gallows from the normal impulse to pay irrational authority the tribute of a lie in order to live.

Beginning slowly, with a prologue somewhat diffuse and confusing, the play gathers momentum and power with each act. The final scene, just before the hanging, is immensely moving, summarizing the theme of the play with an eloquence that carries the audience (carried this member of it, anyway) out of the theater in a mood of resolve rather than despair. (pp. 131-32)

> Freda Kirchwey, "The Crucible," in The Nation, *New York, Vol. 176, No. 6, February 7, 1953, pp. 131-32.*

Arthur Miller　(essay date 8 February 1953)

[*In the following essay, Miller recalls his impressions upon visiting Salem, Massachusetts, while conducting research for* The Crucible.]

The Crucible is taken from history. No character is in the play who did not take a similar role in Salem, 1692. The basic story is recorded, if briefly, in certain documents of the time. It will be a long time before I shall be able to shake Rebecca Nurse, John Proctor, Giles Corey and the others out of my mind. But there are strange, even weird memories that have connected themselves to this play, and these have to do with the present, and it has all got mixed up together.

I went to Salem for the first time early last spring. I already knew the story, and had thought about it for a long time. I had never been to Salem before and, driving alone up the brand new superhighway, I felt a shock at seeing the perfectly ordinary, steel sign reading, "Salem 3 mi." I confess it—some part of my mind had expected to see the old wooden village, not the railroad tracks, the factories, the trucks. These things were not real, suddenly, but intruders, as tourists are in the halls of Versailles. Underneath, in the earth, was the reality. I drove into the town.

I asked the courthouse clerk for the town records for 1692. A lawyer-looking man in an overcoat asked for 1941. A lady, who looked like she were planning to sue somebody, asked for 1913. The clerk handed over a volume to each of us and we sat at separate tables, the three of us, turning pages.

The lawyer began copying—possibly from a deed. The woman read perhaps a will—and got angrier. I looked into 1692. Here were wills, too, and deeds, and warrants sworn out, and the usual debris a town leaves behind it for the legal record.

And then . . . dialogue! Prosecutor Hathorne is examining Rebecca Nurse. The court is full of people weeping for the young girls who sit before them strangling because Rebecca's spirit is out tormenting them. And Hathorne says, "It is awful to see your eye dry when so many are wet." And Rebecca replies, "You do not know my heart. I never afflicted no child, never in my life. I am as clear as the child unborn."

They hanged her. She was in her seventies. They had hesitated to go and arrest her because of her high reputation; but they took her from her sickbed, they took her from her lovely house that stands in the countryside yet, and they hanged her by the neck over the long Salem Bay.

The lawyer in the overcoat was copying his deed; the lady was back at the counter, asking the clerk for 1912. Did they know what had happened here?

In the museum all is silent. An old man, looking like a retired professor, is reading a document. Two middle-aged couples come in from their automobile outside and ask to see the pins: The pins the spirits stuck the children with. The pins are in the courthouse, they are told. They look about at the books, the faded fragments of paper that once meant Proctor must hang tomorrow, paper that came through the farmhouse door in the hand of a friend who had a half-determined, half-ashamed look in his eyes.

The tourists pass the books, the exhibits and no hint of danger reaches them from the quaint relics. I have a desire to tell them the significance of those relics. It is the desire to write.

Day after day in the courthouse, until the evenings begin to arrive with forebodings in the night breeze. The locations of the old farmhouses are in my mind, their directions from the spot on which I stand; on Essex Street was a house, perhaps a few yards from here, where Reverend Parris lived and at night discussed with certain others who in the town was acting suspiciously, who might have shown signs of the Devil's touch. Salem was taken from the Hebrew, Sholom, meaning peace, but now in my mind and in the streets it is a dark word.

The stroll down Essex Street I remember, and the empty spaces between the parking meters, the dark storefronts—but further down a lighted store, and noise. I take a look. A candy store. A mob of girls and boys in their teens running in and out, ganging around on the vacant street; a jalopy pulls up with two wet-haired boys, and a whispered consultation with a girl on the running board; she runs into the store, comes out with a friend, and off they go into the night, the proud raccoon tail straightening from the radiator cap. And suddenly, from around a corner, two girls hopping with a broomstick between their legs, and a general laughter going up at the special joke. A broomstick. And riding it. And I remember the girls of Salem, the only Salem there ever was for me—the 1692 Salem—and how they purged their sins by embracing God and pointing out His enemies in the town.

And a feeling of love at seeing Rebecca Nurse's house on its gentle knoll; the house she lay in, ill, when they came, shuffling their feet, ashamed to have to ask her to come to court because the children said she had sent her spirit out.

And the great rock, standing mum over the Bay, the splintered precipice on which the gibbet was built. The highway traffic endlessly, mindlessly humming at its foot, but up here the barrenness, the clinkers of broken stones, and the vast view of the bay; here hung Rebecca, John Proctor, George Jacobs—people more real to me than the living can ever be. The sense of a terrible marvel again; that people could have such a belief in themselves and in the rightness of their consciences as to give their lives rather than say what they thought was false. Or, perhaps, they only feared Hell so much? Yet, Rebecca said, and it is written in the record, "I cannot belie myself." And she knew it would kill her. They knew who they were.

My friends return, the men of my own life—in the hotel taproom a circle of salesmen sitting around, waiting for bedtime. I listen. They are comparing the sizes of their television screens. Which one is the big-earner? Yep, that one. He says less, but they listen more when he says it. They are all wishing they were him. And all a little lost in the eyes, and nice fellas, so damned eager and men-among-men, and around the eyes ever so faintly lost; laughing a little more than they want to, listening longer than they want to, sorry without sorrow, laughing with less than joy, until up in the hotel room alone there is only one certainty—tomorrow will come. Another day, another chance to find out—who they are. How they got there. Where they're going.

The rock stands forever in Salem. They knew who they were. Nineteen.

Arthur Miller, "Journey to 'The Crucible'," in
The New York Times, *February 8, 1953, p. X3.*

Eric Bentley   (essay date 16 February 1953)

[*Bentley is an English-born American educator, critic, playwright, editor, and translator. In the following excerpt from his* The Dramatic Event: An American Chronicle, *originally published in 1954, he regards* The Crucible *as a play with a potential for greatness that is hampered by the "mentality of the unreconstructed liberal." This essay contains undated revisions to Bentley's 1953* New Republic *review of* The Crucible.]

The theatre is provincial. Few events on Broadway have any importance whatsoever except to that small section of the community—neither an élite nor a cross section—that sees Broadway plays. A play by an Arthur Miller or a Tennessee Williams is an exception. Such a play is not only better than the majority; it belongs in the mainstream of our culture. Such an author has something to say about America that is worth discussing. In *The Crucible,* Mr. Miller says something that *has* to be discussed. Nor am I limiting my interest to the intellectual sphere. One sits before this play with anything but intellectual detachment. At a moment when we are all being "investigated," or imagining that we shall be, it is vastly disturbing to see indignant images of investigation on the other side of the footlights. Why, one wonders, aren't there dozens of plays each season offering such a critical account of the state of the nation—critical and *engagé?* The appearance of one such play by an author, like Mr. Miller, who is neither an infant, a fool, or a swindler, is enough to bring tears to the eyes.

"Great stones they lay upon his chest until he plead aye or nay. They say he give them but two words. 'More weight,' he says, and died." Mr. Miller's material is magnificent for narrative, poetry, drama. The fact that we sense its magnificence suggests that either he or his actors have in part realized it, yet our moments of emotion only make us the more aware of half-hours of indifference or dissatisfaction. For this is a story not quite told, a drama not quite realized. Pygmalion has labored hard at his statue and it has not come to life. There is a terrible inertness about the play. The individual characters, like the individual lines, lack fluidity and grace. There is an O'Neill-like striving after a poetry and an eloquence which the author does not achieve. "From Aeschylus to Arthur Miller," say the textbooks. The world has made this author important before he has made himself great; perhaps the reversal of the natural order of things weighs heavily upon him. It would be all too easy, script in hand, to point to weak spots. The inadequacy of particular lines, and characters, is of less interest, however, than the mentality from which they come. It is the mentality of the unreconstructed liberal.

There has been some debate as to whether this story of seventeenth-century Salem "really" refers to our current "witch hunt" yet since no one is interested in anything *but* this reference, I pass on to the real point at issue, which is: the validity of the parallel. It is true in that people today are being persecuted on quite chimerical grounds. It is untrue in that communism is not, to put it mildly, merely a chimera. The word communism is used to cover, first, the politics of Marx, second, the politics of the Soviet Union, and, third, the activities of all liberals as they seem to illiberal illiterates. Since Mr. Miller's argument bears only on the third use of the word, its scope is limited. Indeed, the analogy between "red-baiting" and witch hunting can seem complete only to communists, for only to them is the menace of communism as fictitious as the menace of witches. The non-communist will look for certain reservations and provisos. In *The Crucible,* there are none.

To accuse Mr. Miller of communism would of course be to fall into the trap of over-simplification which he himself has set. For all I know he may hate the Soviet state with all the ardor of Eisenhower. What I am maintaining is that his view of life is dictated by assumptions which liberals have to unlearn and which many liberals have rather publicly unlearned. Chief among these assumptions is that of general innocence. In Hebrew mythology, innocence was lost at the very beginning of things; in liberal, especially American liberal, folklore, it has not been lost yet; Arthur Miller is the playwright of American liberal folklore. It is as if the merely negative, and legal, definition of innocence were extended to the rest of life: you are innocent until proved guilty, you are innocent if you "didn't do it." Writers have a sort of double innocence: not only can they create innocent characters, they can also write from the viewpoint of innocence—we can speak today not only of the "omniscient" author but of the "guiltless" one.

Such indeed is the viewpoint of the dramatist of indignation, like Miss Hellman or Mr. Miller. And it follows that their plays are melodrama—a conflict between the wholly guilty and the wholly innocent. For a long time liberals were afraid to criticize the mentality behind this melodrama because they feared association with the guilty ("harboring reactionary sympathies"). But, though a more enlightened view would enjoin association with the guilty in the admission of a common humanity, it does not ask us to underestimate the guilt or to refuse to see "who done it." The guilty men are as black with guilt as Mr. Miller says—what we must ask is whether the innocent are as white with innocence. The drama of indignation is melodramatic not so much because it paints its villains too black as because it paints its heroes too white. *Othello* is not a melodrama, because, though its villain is wholly evil, its hero is not wholly virtuous. *The Crucible* is a melodrama because, though the hero has weaknesses, he has no faults. His innocence is unreal because it is total. His author has equipped him with what we might call Superinnocence, for the crime he is accused of not only hasn't been committed by him, it isn't even a possibility: it is the fiction of traffic with the devil. It goes without saying that the hero has all the minor accoutrements of innocence too: he belongs to the right social class (yeoman farmer), does the right kind of work (manual), and, somewhat contrary to historical probability, has the right philosophy (a distinct leaning towards skeptical empiricism) . . .

The innocence of his author is known to us from life as well as art. [Director] Elia Kazan made a public confession of having been a communist and, while doing so, mentioned the names of several of his former comrades. Mr. Miller then brought out a play about an accused man who refuses to name comrades (who indeed dies rather than make a confession at all), and of course decided to end his collaboration with the director who did so much to make him famous. The play has been directed by Jed Harris.

I think there is as much drama in this bit of history as in any Salem witch hunt. The "guilty" director was rejected. An "innocent" one was chosen in his place. There are two stories in this. The first derives from the fact that the better fellow (assuming, for the purpose of argument, that Mr. Harris is the better fellow) is not always the better worker. The awkwardness I find in Mr. Miller's script is duplicated in Mr. Harris's directing. Mr. Kazan would have taken this script up like clay and re-molded it. He would have struck fire from the individual actor, and he would have brought one actor into much livelier relationship with another. . . . The second story is that of the interpenetration of good and evil. I am afraid that Mr. Miller needs a Kazan not merely at some superficial technical level. He needs not only the craftsmanship of a Kazan but also—his sense of guilt. Innocence is, for a mere human being, and especially for an artist, insufficient baggage. When we say that Mr. Kazan "added" to *Death of a Salesman,* we mean—if I am not saying more than I know—that he infused into this drama of social forces the pressure of what Freud called "the family romance," the pressure of guilt. *The Crucible* is *about* guilt yet nowhere in it is there any *sense* of guilt because the author and director have joined forces to dissociate themselves and their hero from evil. This is the theatre of two Dr. Jekylls. Mr. Miller and Mr. Kazan were Dr. Jekyll and Mr. Hyde. (pp. 62-5)

> Eric Bentley, "The Innocence of Arthur Miller," in his What is Theatre? Incorporating the Dramatic Event and Other Reviews: 1944-1967, *1968. Reprint by Limelight Editions, 1984, pp. 62-5.*

William H. Beyer   (essay date 21 March 1953)

[*In the following excerpt, Beyer faults Miller for placing greater emphasis on historical accuracy than on artistic originality in* The Crucible.]

The past several seasons our playwrights have been having quite a time exploring the annals of witchcraft. This season, Arthur Miller, who in the past decade has given us two memorable plays, *All my Sons* and *Death of a Salesman* offers *The Crucible* in which he is pamphleteering on behalf of today's political persecutions. The anti-Communist McCarthy drive was going full steam when he wrote *The Crucible,* and the overseas Communist anti-Semitism purge has been initiated since. The parallels today in the tensions created by totalitarian powers, actual and incipient, being apparent, Miller has shrewdly been content merely to indicate them, and so he corroborates our awareness of the paralysis of fear obsessing the authorities and intimidating our citizenry. Meanwhile, hysteria settles in, and its artificially generated recurrence establishes a native climate where the basic imbalance becomes the norm; license supersedes liberty, unbridled prejudice, intolerance, and bigotry gain control, and freedom's wings are clipped. Truly, now as then, the devil is in town. In *The Crucible* we witness the fiendish goings-on in 17th-century Salem, Massachusetts, with Miller's play chronicling the then prevailing witch-hunts.

The Crucible's opening scene is in the prayer-hushed bedroom of a coma-stricken, teen-age girl, a preacher's niece, who, it seems, is beyond medical help. Into the room stream her playmates in a frenzy, as they, like the dying girl, have been caught dancing naked in the moonlight—obviously witches' work. The girls, the preacher, his Negro servant, plus an assortment of equally frantic villagers who also pour hysterically into the room, are all variously involved in manifestations of witchcraft. These the authorities of Church and State calculatingly seize upon to insure their prestige, while cunning, vengeful citizens exploit the claim of witchcraft to further their own ends. Among the innumerable involvements posed is that of a farmer, Proctor, and his former serving-maid (the leading teen-ager in the moonlight episode) who have had an illicit love affair which his wife terminated. From here we go to Proctor's farmhouse and meet his loyal, though doubting, spouse. Confronted by the witch-hunters who bring contrived accusations against both the Proctors, they are arrested and taken to an examination in the meetinghouse, where he admits his lechery and his wife denies it. Both are imprisoned, tried, and found guilty, he to be executed. Given an opportunity to confess a lie and so go free, Proctor refuses to compromise and goes to his doom, along with other victims of the witch-hunt.

As indicated, at the play's opening we are catapulted into a plethora of witch-blamed catastrophes, and, though the stricken girl is apparently dying, we are inundated by frenetic explosions that confuse us as the violence and unrestrained alarms deafen us. After a brief interlude between Proctor and his wife at the farm, the group hysteria rises again, further blurring the details and deflecting our responses which are assailed again and again in the meetinghouse investigation with its thunderous accusations, recriminations, and hysteria. By the concluding scene, the parting of the Proctors, we are so bludgeoned that there is not a response left in us. As in life, the death of a friend moves one profoundly; the battle casualty lists, however, merely benumb one. So it is in our reactions to *The Crucible*'s mass hysteria, parallels in today's persecutions notwithstanding, for we come preconditioned to this catastrophe and accept the historical reaffirmation placidly. (p. 185)

The Crucible, according to Miller, is taken from the historical record and includes no character who did not play a similar role then. History, of course, is not art. Earlier, Miller had also stated that he did not know what the play was about—perhaps in a year he might know—contradictory statements which confound us. Pamphleteering as he is here, Miller certainly approached history knowing what it was about and also knowing what the contemporary score is. We found the play, like the historical record, not only clear, but obvious, which is self-evident under the circumstances since psychological parallels motivated *The Crucible.* We can only say, in contemplating Miller's quandary, that original plays, such as his two earlier successes, are obviously an act of total creation; being imaginatively persuasive they are emotionally provocative and have a complete artistic identity. A dramatization of the historical record, on the other hand, using historic characters, automatically robs the play of the suspense inherent in an original work, for one thing, and interests us primarily in the writer's technique of staging history—his theatrical "know-how" and ideological "know-why." The compulsion in the case of original plays that achieve an aesthetic entity is from a reaction to the ferment within the writer as he is stimulated by his life and times. In *The Crucible* the compulsion came from the outside, from history—it is explicit—a motivation that is inescapable here in the writing. . . . In *The Crucible,* Mil-

ler presents the bare anatomy of Salem's 17th-century hysteria and catastrophe pungently and in his characteristically trenchant, pithy dialogue, as in his earlier plays, but with ink for blood, hence the contrived melodrama. . . . Unfortunately, Miller has not digested his historic material to the point that the social and aesthetic values flow into a dramatic life-blood giving us pure tragedy which beats with the pulse of conviction. (pp. 185-86)

William H. Beyer, "The State of the Theatre: The Devil at Large," in School and Society, *Vol. 77, No. 1996, March 21, 1953, pp. 183-86.*

John and Alice Griffin   (essay date October 1953)

[*In the following excerpt, based on a conversation with the playwright, Miller explains his intention in writing* The Crucible.]

[*The Crucible*] has been described as a "powerful play," a "stirring melodrama," a "parable" and a work "chiefly concerned with what happened rather than why."

None of these interpretations, however, has been voiced by playwright Arthur Miller, who says that the idea of dramatizing the Salem witch trials had been in his mind for a considerable time, in fact, as far back as his student days at the University of Michigan in the thirties. "Salem," he explains, "is one of the few dramas in history with a beginning, a middle and an end. The drama is complete because the people saw the error of their ways quite soon after the tragedy occurred." He adds that he could not have written the play at any other time than the present.

The people of Salem appealed to Miller as characters for a drama because they were articulate. "I was dealing with people very conscious of an ideology, of what they stood for . . . the revolution they had lived through was still in their minds . . . they were special people and could voice the things that were buried deep in them. Today's writers describe man's helplessness and eventual defeat. In Salem you have the story of a defeat because these people were destroyed, and this makes it real to us today because we believe in defeat. But they understood at the same time what was happening to them. They knew why they struggled . . . they knew how to struggle . . . they did not die helplessly. The moral size of these people drew me . . . they didn't whimper.

"We should be tired by now of merely documenting the defeat of man. This play is a step toward an assertion of a positive kind of value in contemporary plays. Since 1920 American drama has been a steady, year-by-year documentation of the frustration of man. I do not believe in this . . . that is not our fate. It is not enough to tell what is happening; the newspapers do that. In our drama the man with convictions has in the past been a comic figure. I believe he fits in our drama more now, though, and I am trying to find a way, a form, a method of depicting people who do think."

In discussing the historical basis of the play, Miller revealed that the plot and characters, except for Proctor and his wife, are historically accurate. He went on to indicate that his hero Proctor is a man who fights against the loss of his identity, a loss which he believes would result if he joined the group.

"There is a certain pride operating in him," the author pointed out. "Proctor could not go to his death as easily as Rebecca Nurse does. He believed in paradise but didn't want to go there so quickly. Besides, if you confessed you were a witch, you confessed to being a fraud; you were someone who pretended to be decent but who really was a liar."

Illustrating how the playwright has to make concessions when the play goes into production, Miller mentioned that the first scene, as the play was originally written, took place in a forest, but this had to be altered because of the expense involved in building this set.

Later in the run, six months after the New York première, Miller was able to include a forest scene, printed here for the first time. This new production, completely restaged by the author, did away with all scenery, and had the action take place against drapes and a light-flooded cyclorama. Favoring the change, the critics praised the new scene as providing additional motivation for Abigail, and they found the new version more fluid, forceful and poetic. . . . Encouraged by the success of his initial attempt at directing, Miller has decided to direct his own plays in the future, as he is now convinced that he can achieve the dramatic effects he wants by working with the actors. (pp. 33-4)

The playwright was particularly interested in explaining whether *The Crucible* was intended to be more, or less realistic than his earlier *Death of a Salesman.* "In *Death of a Salesman,*" he said, "I tried to give people a sense of reality in depth. I could have done this by symbolic behavior, like impressionism, but felt that was an old technique. I tried to show the facade-like surface realism of life in realistic acting and at the same time melt this away and bring out the half-conscious, subconscious life and combine both of these with the social context in which the action was taking place. I had to have these two working against each other.

"In *The Crucible,* as I said before, the characters were special people who could give voice to the things that were inside them. There is great danger in pathos, which can destroy any tragedy if you let it go far enough. My weakness is that I can create pathos at will. It is one of the easiest things to do. I feel that Willy Loman lacks sufficient insight into this situation, which would have made him a greater, more significant figure. These people knew what was happening to them; they had insight in the sense that Hamlet has it. A point has to arrive where man sees what has happened to him. I think *The Crucible* is not more realistic but more theatrical than *Death of a Salesman.*"

A man who is always interested in cosmic themes, Miller appears much concerned with what he terms "diabolism"—the fear and hatred of opposites. "And when tensions exist," he explained, "this fear is organized. In Salem these people regarded themselves as holders of a light. If this light were extinguished, they believed, the world would end. When you have an ideology which feels itself

so pure, it implies an extreme view of the world. Because they are white, opposition is completely black."

Miller believes that the temptation toward diabolism has always existed in mankind and exists today. "We have come to a time when it seems there must be two sides, and we look back to the ideal state of being, when there was no conflict. Our idea is that conflict can be wiped out of the world.

"But until man arrives at a point where he realizes that conflict is the essence of life, he will end up by knocking himself out." (p. 34)

> *John Griffin and Alice Griffin, "Arthur Miller Discusses 'The Crucible'," in* Theatre Arts, *Vol. XXXVII, No. 10, October, 1953, pp. 33-4.*

George Jean Nathan   (essay date 1953)

[*An American critic, journalist, editor, and playwright, Nathan has been called the most learned and influential drama critic the United States has yet produced. During the early decades of the twentieth century, he was greatly responsible for shifting the emphasis of the American theater from light entertainment to serious drama and for introducing audiences and producers to the work of Eugene O'Neill, Henrik Ibsen, and Bernard Shaw, among others. In the following excerpt, he applauds Miller's artistic integrity, but faults him for undeveloped characters, structural flaws, and propagandism in* The Crucible.]

Though I am scarcely known as a congenital optimist, since in my old definition any such sugarteat is the kind of person who believes a housefly is looking for a way to get out, I can not entirely disbelieve that patience sometimes has its reward, even in the theatre. And so it has presently come about that, just as we all were more or less convinced that our American playwrights in the aggregate and with small exception had eyes only for the box-office, a man of some rather higher pride and ambition has made a reappearance on the cheapjack scene. His name, Arthur Miller, and his play, *The Crucible.* It was not, true, altogether a surprise, since though a pair of his earlier efforts, excursions into Ibsen, were critically questionable, even they indicated his independent resolve, and since his excellent *Death Of A Salesman,* that happily turned out to be box-office in spite of itself, indicated it even more. So it is that, while his newest play is very far beneath the merit of the last named and is in fact an out of hand dramatic performance, it provides us with the encouragement in respect to our theatre that we badly stand in need of. It may go down under critical gunnery, but its author's flag keeps flying, brightly.

Dealing with the historical Salem witch-hunts and witchcraft trials in the late years of the seventeenth century and wringing from them a lashing phillipic against superstition and ignorance and the bigotry that is their offspring, the play's chief fault is that its fire remains within it and does not communicate itself to its auditors. It has a powerful theme and its general direction . . . and some of its acting have an internal power as well but little energy comes out of it, as in the case of a powerhouse operating at full blast in a preliminary test and as yet with no outside connection. At one point in its second act when the group of girls in the grip of hysteria shriek a repetition of their witchcraft imaginings and overcome one of their hesitant number a touch of real drama quivers across the footlights. But the rest fore and aft, while dynamic in intention, boils only within itself and gives off little external steam.

The reasons are several. Miller has been remiss in developing character of any close approximation to recognizable warm humanity and has thus denied his audience any of the necessary sympathetic contact with his two central figures, the husband and wife victims of the witch-hunt. What he has contrived are simply a pair of spokesmen who serve as sounding-boards for his theme, which is volleyed against them and returned much like a damp tennis ball. They, and in particular the persecuted husband, do their full duty by the written speeches but the effect is of two obedient actors in passionate recitation rather than of two human characters that better playwriting might have made them. One listens to them with some interest but without that measure of conviction which would result were they less tape recordings and more flesh and blood. As they stand, they give the impression of figures out of mechanical old melodrama coldly intellectualized.

A second flaw in the writing . . . is a too great intensity in the early stages of the play which reduces the tension that should properly come later. The prologue, indeed, is so overwrought and conducted at so high a pitch that what follows, when the call is for emotional excitement and explosion, becomes fizzed out and flat, save alone for the one episode noted. . . . And thirdly there is the matter of contemporary parallels. Though Miller has been studiously careful not to finger-point and emphasize them and is to be critically endorsed in this respect, one nonetheless gets the feeling they are his primary concern and that the concern has here and there colored his treatment of his theme not to its advantage. There is consequently an underlying air of propaganda in the play that stubbornly permeates it for all the author's wish that it should not and, as with propaganda drama in the aggregate, the result is discommodious.

It is discommodious because what are unquestionably designed as parallels are not always rational parallels. It may be wholly true that what are currently referred to as political witch-hunts now and then proceed from mass hysteria and are grounded in fear, and also that they are sometimes cruel, irresponsibe and deplorable. But the author's hoped for parallel between the Salem of 1692 and conditions today bogs down when the consideration extends to religious superstition and ecclesiasticism. This may be drawing the line pretty fine, since there are other points well taken, but there is a considerable difference between persecution based on ignorant superstition and prosecution, however extremely and at times eccentrically conducted, in time of national peril. The general dramatic idea may be valid but particularized analysis devitalizes it. (pp. 105-07)

George Jean Nathan, "American Playwrights, Old and New," in his The Theatre in the Fifties, *Alfred A. Knopf, 1953, pp. 40-112.*

Robert Warshow   (essay date 1953)

[*In the following excerpt from an essay originally published in 1953, Warshow faults* The Crucible *as insubstantial and simplistic, and examines Miller's intent in light of both contemporary and historical American politics and philosophy.*]

One of the things that have been said of *The Crucible,* Arthur Miller's new play about the Salem witchcraft trials, is that we must not be misled by its obvious contemporary relevance: it is a drama of universal significance. This statement, which has usually a somewhat apologetic tone, seems to be made most often by those who do not fail to place great stress on the play's "timeliness." I believe it means something very different from what it appears to say, almost the contrary, in fact, and yet not quite the contrary either. It means: do not be misled by the play's historical theme into forgetting the main point, which is that "witch trials" are always with us, and especially today; but on the other hand do not hold Mr. Miller responsible either for the inadequacies of his presentation of the Salem trials or for the many undeniable and important differences between those trials and the "witch trials" that are going on now. It is quite true, nevertheless, that the play is, at least in one sense, of "universal significance." Only we must ask what this phrase has come to mean, and whether the quality it denotes is a virtue.

The Puritan tradition, the greatest and most persistent formulator of American simplifications, has itself always contained elements disturbingly resistant to ideological— or even simply rational—understanding. The great debate in American Calvinism over "good works" versus the total arbitrariness of the divine will was won, fortunately and no doubt inevitably, by those who held that an actively virtuous life must be at least the outward sign of "election." But this interpretation was entirely pragmatic; it was made only because it had to be made, because in the most literal sense one could not survive in a universe of absolute predestination. The central contradiction of Calvinism remained unresolved, and the awful confusions of the Puritan mind still embarrass our efforts to see the early history of New England as a clear stage in the progress of American enlightenment. Only Hawthorne among American writers has seriously tried to deal with these confusions as part of the "given" material of literature, taking the Puritans in their own terms as among the real possibilities of life, and the admiration we accord to his tense and brittle artistry is almost as distant as our admiration of the early New Englanders themselves; it is curious how rarely Hawthorne has been mentioned beside Melville and James even in recent explorations of the "anti-liberal" side of our literature.

The Salem witch trials represent how far the Puritans were ready to go in taking their doctrines seriously. Leaving aside the slavery question and what has flowed from it, those trials are perhaps the most disconcerting single episode in our history: the occurrence of the unthinkable on American soil, and in what our schools have rather successfully taught us to think of as the very "cradle of Americanism." Of Europe's witch trials, we have our opinion. But these witch trials are "ours"; where do they belong in the "tradition"?

For Americans, a problem of this sort demands to be resolved, and there have been two main ways of resolving it. The first is to regard the trials as a historical curiosity; a curiosity by definition requires no explanation. In this way the trials are placed among the "vagaries" of the Puritan mind and can even offer a kind of amusement, like the amusement we have surprisingly agreed to find in the so-called "rough justice" of the Western frontier in the last century. But the more usual and more deceptive way of dealing with the Salem trials has been to assimilate them to the history of progress in civil rights. This brings them into the world of politics, where, even if our minds are not always made up, at least we think we know what the issues are. Arthur Miller, I need hardly say, has adopted this latter view.

Inevitably, I suppose, we will find in history what we need to find. But in this particular "interpretation" of the facts there seems to be a special injustice. The Salem trials were not political and had nothing whatever to do with civil rights, unless it is a violation of civil rights to hang a murderer. Nor were the "witches" being "persecuted"—as the Puritans did persecute Quakers, for instance. The actual conduct of the trials, to be sure, was outrageous, but no more outrageous than the conduct of ordinary criminal trials in England at the time. In any case, it is a little absurd to make the whole matter rest on the question of fair trial: how can there be a "fair trial" for a crime which not only has not been committed, but is impossible? The Salem "witches" suffered something that may be worse than persecution: they were hanged because of a metaphysical error. And they chose to die—for all could have saved themselves by "confession"—not for a cause, not for "civil rights," not even to defeat the error that hanged them, but for their own credit on earth and in heaven: they would not say they were witches when they were not. They lived in a universe where each man was saved or damned by himself, and what happened to them was personal. Certainly their fate is not lacking in universal significance; it was a human fate. But its universality—if we must have the word—is of that true kind which begins and ends in a time and a place. One need not believe in witches, or even in God, to understand the events in Salem, but it is mere provinciality to ignore the fact that both those ideas had a reality for the people of Salem that they do not have for us.

The "universality" of Mr. Miller's play belongs neither to literature nor to history, but to that journalism of limp erudition which assumes that events are to be understood by referring them to categories, and which is therefore never at a loss for a comment. Just as in *Death of a Salesman* Mr. Miller sought to present "the American" by eliminating so far as possible the "non-essential" facts which might have made his protagonist a particular American, so in *The Crucible* he reveals at every turn his almost contemptuous lack of interest in the particularities—which is to say, the reality—of the Salem trials. The character and motives of all the actors in this drama are for him both simple and clear. The girls who raised the accusation of

witchcraft were merely trying to cover up their own misbehavior. The Reverend Samuel Parris found in the investigation of witchcraft a convenient means of consolidating his shaky position in a parish that was murmuring against his "undemocratic" conduct of the church. The Reverend John Hale, a conscientious and troubled minister who, given the premises, must have represented something like the best that Puritan New England had to offer, and whose agonies of doubt might have been expected to call forth the highest talents of a serious playwright, appears in *The Crucible* as a kind of idiotic "liberal" scoutmaster, at first cheerfully confident of his ability to cope with the Devil's wiles and in the last act babbling hysterically in an almost comic contrast to the assured dignity of the main characters. Deputy Governor Danforth, presented as the virtual embodiment of early New England, never becomes more than a pompous, unimaginative politician of the better sort.

As for the victims themselves, the most significant fact is Miller's choice of John Proctor for his leading character: Proctor can be seen as one of the more "modern" figures in the trials, hardheaded, skeptical, a voice of common sense (he thought the accusing girls could be cured of their "spells" by a sound whipping); also, according to Mr. Miller, no great churchgoer. It is all too easy to make Proctor into the "common man"—and then, of course, we know where we are: Proctor wavers a good deal, fails to understand what is happening, wants only to be left alone with his wife and his farm, considers making a false confession, but in the end goes to his death for reasons that he finds a little hard to define but that are clearly good reasons—mainly, it seems, he does not want to implicate others. You will never learn from this John Proctor that Salem was a religious community, quite as ready to hang a Quaker as a witch. The saintly Rebecca Nurse is also there, to be sure, sketched in rapidly in the background, a quiet figure whose mere presence—there is little more of her than that—reminds us how far the dramatist has fallen short.

Nor has Mr. Miller hesitated to alter the facts to fit his constricted field of vision. Abigail Williams, one of the chief accusers in the trials, was about eleven years old in 1692; Miller makes her a young woman of eighteen or nineteen and invents an adulterous relation between her and John Proctor in order to motivate her denunciation of John and his wife Elizabeth. The point is not that this falsifies the facts of Proctor's life (though one remembers uneasily that he himself was willing to be hanged rather than confess to what was not true), but that it destroys the play, offering an easy theatrical motive that even in theatrical terms explains nothing, and deliberately casting away the element of religious and psychological complexity which gives the Salem trials their dramatic interest in the first place. In a similar way, Miller risks the whole point of *Death of a Salesman* by making his plot turn on the irrelevant discovery of Willy Loman's adultery. And in both plays the fact of adultery itself is slighted: it is brought in not as a human problem, but as a mere theatrical device, like the dropping of a letter; one cannot take an interest in Willy Loman's philandering, or believe in Abigail Williams' passion despite the barnyard analogies with which the playwright tries to make it "elemental."

> The "universality" of *The Crucible* belongs neither to literature nor to history, but to that journalism of limp erudition which assumes that events are to be understood by referring them to categories, and which is therefore never at a loss for a comment.
>
> —*Robert Warshow*

Mr. Miller's steadfast, one might almost say selfless, refusal of complexity, the assured simplicity of his view of human behavior, may be the chief source of his ability to captivate the educated audience. He is an oddly depersonalized writer; one tries in vain to define his special quality, only to discover that it is perhaps not a quality at all, but something like a method, and even as a method strangely bare: his plays are as neatly put together and essentially as empty as that skeleton of a house which made *Death of a Salesman* so impressively confusing. He is the playwright of an audience that believes the frightening complexities of history and experience are to be met with a few ideas, and yet does not even possess these ideas any longer but can only point significantly at the place where they were last seen and where it is hoped they might still be found to exist. What this audience demands of its artists above all is an intelligent narrowness of mind and vision and a generalized tone of affirmation, offering not any particular insights or any particular truths, but simply the assurance that insight and truth as qualities, the things in themselves, reside somehow in the various signals by which the artist and the audience have learned to recognize each other. For indeed very little remains except this recognition; the marriage of the liberal theater and the liberal audience has been for some time a marriage in name only, held together by habit and mutual interest, partly by sentimental memory, most of all by the fear of loneliness and the outside world; and yet the movements of love are still kept up—for the sake of the children, perhaps.

The hero of this audience is Clifford Odets. Among those who shouted "Bravo!" at the end of *The Crucible*—an exclamation, awkward on American lips, that is reserved for cultural achievements of the greatest importance—there must surely have been some who had stood up to shout "Strike!" at the end of *Waiting for Lefty*. But it is hard to believe that a second Odets, if that were possible, or the old Odets restored to youth, would be greeted with such enthusiasm as Arthur Miller calls forth. Odets's talent was too rich—in my opinion the richest ever to appear in the American theater—and his poetry and invention were constantly more important than what he conceived himself to be saying. In those days it didn't matter: the "message" at the end of the third act was so much taken for granted that there was room for Odets's exuberance, and he himself was never forced to learn how much his talent was superior to his "affirmations" (if he had learned, perhaps the talent might have survived the "affirmations").

Arthur Miller is the dramatist of a later time, when the "message" isn't there at all, but it has been agreed to pretend that it is. This pretense can be maintained only by the most rigid control, for there is no telling what small element of dramatic *élan* or simple reality may destroy the delicate rapport of a theater and an audience that have not yet acknowledged they have no more to say to each other. Arthur Miller is Odets without the poetry. Worst of all, one feels sometimes that he has suppressed the poetry deliberately, making himself by choice the anonymous dramatist of a fossilized audience. In *Death of a Salesman,* certainly, there were moments when reality seemed to force its way momentarily to the surface. And even at *The Crucible*—though here it was not Miller's suppressed talent that broke through, but the suppressed facts of the outside world—the thread that tied the audience to its dramatist must have been now and then under some strain: surely there were some in the audience to notice uneasily that these witch trials, with their quality of ritual and their insistent need for "confessions," were much more like the trial that had just ended in Prague than like any trial that has lately taken place in the United States. So much the better, perhaps, for the play's "universal significance"; I don't suppose Mr. Miller would defend the Prague trial. And yet I cannot believe it was for this particular implication that anyone shouted "Bravo!"

For let us indeed not be misled. Mr. Miller has nothing to say about the Salem trials and makes only the flimsiest pretense that he has. *The Crucible* was written to say something about Alger Hiss and Owen Lattimore, Julius and Ethel Rosenberg, Senator McCarthy, the actors who have lost their jobs on radio and television, in short the whole complex that is spoken of, with a certain lowering of the voice, as the "present atmosphere." And yet not to say anything about that either, but only to suggest that a great deal might be said, oh an infinitely great deal, if it were not that—what? Well, perhaps if it were not that the "present atmosphere" itself makes such plain speaking impossible. As it is, there is nothing for it but to write plays of "universal significance"—and, after all, that's what a serious dramatist is supposed to do anyway.

What, then, *is* Mr. Miller trying to say to us? It's hard to tell. In *The Crucible* innocent people are accused and convicted of witchcraft on the most absurd testimony—in fact, the testimony of those who themselves have meddled in witchcraft and are therefore doubly to be distrusted. Decent citizens who sign petitions attesting to the good character of their accused friends and neighbors are thrown into prison as suspects. Anyone who tries to introduce into court the voice of reason is likely to be held in contempt. One of the accused refuses to plead and is pressed to death. No one is acquitted; the only way out for the accused is to make false confessions and themselves join the accusers. Seeing all this on the stage, we are free to reflect that something very like these trials has been going on in recent years in the United States. How much like? Mr. Miller does not say. But *very* like, allowing of course for some superficial differences: no one has been pressed to death in recent years, for instance. Still, people have lost their jobs for refusing to say under oath whether or not they are Communists. The essential pattern is the same, isn't it? And when we speak of "universal significance," we mean sticking to the essential pattern, don't we? Mr. Miller is under no obligation to tell us whether he thinks the trial of Alger Hiss, let us say, was a "witch trial"; he is writing about the Salem trials.

Or, again, the play reaches its climax with John and Elizabeth Proctor facing the problem of whether John should save himself from execution by making a false confession; he elects finally to accept death, for his tormentors will not be satisfied with his mere admission of guilt: he would be required to implicate others, thus betraying his innocent friends, and his confession would of course be used to justify the hanging of the other convicted witches in the face of growing community unrest. Now it is very hard to watch this scene without thinking of Julius and Ethel Rosenberg, who might also save their lives by confessing. Does Mr. Miller believe that the only confession possible for them would be a false one, implicating innocent people? Naturally, there is no way for him to let us know; perhaps he was not even thinking of the Rosenbergs at all. How can he be held responsible for what comes into my head while I watch his play? And if I think of the Rosenbergs and somebody else thinks of Alger Hiss, and still another thinks of the Prague trial, doesn't that simply prove all over again that the play has universal significance?

One remembers also, as John Proctor wrestles with his conscience, that a former close associate of Mr. Miller's decided some time ago, no doubt after serious and painful consideration, to tell the truth about his past membership in the Communist party, that he mentioned some others who had been in the party with him, and that he then became known in certain theatrical circles as an "informer" and a "rat." Is it possible that this is what Mr. Miller was thinking about when he came to write his last scene? And is he trying to tell us that no one who has been a member of the Communist party should admit it? Or that if he does admit it he should not implicate anyone else? Or that all such "confessions" may be assumed to be false? If he were trying to tell us any of these things, perhaps we might have some arguments to raise. But of course he isn't; he's only writing about the Salem trials, and who wants to maintain that John Proctor was guilty of witchcraft?

But if Mr. Miller isn't saying anything about the Salem trials, and can't be caught saying anything about anything else, what did the audience think he was saying? That too is hard to tell. A couple of the newspaper critics wrote about how timely the play was, and then took it back in the Sunday editions, putting a little more weight on the "universal significance"; but perhaps they didn't quite take it back as much as they seemed to want to: the final verdict appeared to be merely that *The Crucible* is not so great a play as *Death of a Salesman.* As for the rest of the audience, it was clear that they felt themselves to be participating in an event of great meaning: that is what is meant by "Bravo!" Does "Bravo!" mean anything else? I think it means: we agree with Arthur Miller; he has set forth brilliantly and courageously what has been weighing on all our minds; at last someone has had the courage to answer Senator McCarthy.

I don't believe this audience was likely to ask itself what it was agreeing to. Enough that someone had said something, anything, to dispel for a couple of hours that undefined but very real sense of frustration which oppresses these "liberals"—who believe in their innermost being that salvation comes from saying something, and who yet find themselves somehow without anything very relevant to say. They tell themselves, of course, that Senator McCarthy has made it "impossible" to speak; but one can hardly believe they are satisfied with this explanation. Where are the heroic voices that will refuse to be stilled?

Well, last season there was *The Male Animal,* a play written twelve or thirteen years ago about a college professor who gets in trouble for reading one of Vanzetti's letters to his English composition class. In the audience at that play one felt also the sense of communal excitement; it was a little like a secret meeting of early Christians—or even, one might say, witches—where everything had an extra dimension of meaning experienced only by the communicants. And this year there has been a revival of [Lillian Hellman's] *The Children's Hour,* a play of even more universal significance than *The Crucible* since it doesn't have anything to do with any trials but just shows how people can be hurt by having lies told about them. But these were old plays, the voices of an older generation. It remained for Arthur Miller to write a new play that really speaks out.

What does he say when he speaks out?

Never mind. He speaks out.

One question remains to be asked. If Mr. Miller was unable to write directly about what he apparently (one can only guess) feels to be going on in American life today, why did he choose the particular evasion of the Salem trials? After all, violations of civil rights have been not infrequent in our history, and the Salem trials have the disadvantage that they must be distorted in order to be fitted into the framework of civil rights in the first place. Why is it just the image of a "witch trial" or a "witch hunt" that best expresses the sense of oppression which weighs on Mr. Miller and those who feel—I do not say think—as he does?

The answer, I would suppose, is precisely that those accused of witchcraft did *not* die for a cause or an idea, that they represented nothing; they were totally innocent, accused of a crime that does not even exist, the arbitrary victims of a fantastic error. Sacco and Vanzetti, for instance, were able to interpret what was happening to them in a way that the Salem victims could not; they knew that they actually stood for certain ideas that were abhorrent to those who were sending them to death. But the men and women hanged in Salem were not upholding witchcraft against the true church; they were upholding their own personal integrity against an insanely mistaken community.

This offers us a revealing glimpse of the way the Communists and their fellow-travelers have come to regard themselves. The picture has a certain pathos. As it becomes increasingly difficult for any sane man of conscience to reconcile an adherence to the Communist party with any conceivable political principles, the Communist—who is still, let us remember, very much a man of conscience—must gradually divest his political allegiance of all actual content, until he stands bare to the now incomprehensible anger of his neighbors. What can they possibly have against him?—he knows quite well that he believes in nothing, certainly that he is no revolutionist; he is only a dissenter-in-general, a type of personality, a man frozen into an attitude.

From this comes the astonishing phenomenon of Communist innocence. It cannot be assumed that the guiltiest of Communist conspirators protesting his entire innocence may not have a certain belief in his own protest. If you say to a Communist that he is a Communist, he is likely to feel himself in the position of a man who has been accused on no evidence of a crime that he has actually committed. He knows that he happens to be a Communist. But he knows also that his opinions and behavior are only the opinions and behavior of a "liberal," a "dissenter." You are therefore accusing him of being a Communist because he is a liberal, because he is for peace and civil rights and everything good. By some fantastic accident, your accusation happens to be true, but it is *essentially* false.

Consider, for example, how the controversy over the Hiss case reduced itself almost immediately to a question of personality, the "good" Hiss against the "bad" Chambers, with the disturbing evidence of handwriting and typewriters and automobiles somehow beside the point. Alger Hiss, for those who believe him innocent, wears his innocence on his face and his body, in his "essence," whereas Chambers by his own tortured behavior reveals himself as one of the damned. Hiss's innocence, in fact, exists on a plane entirely out of contact with whatever he may have done. Perhaps most of those who take Hiss's "side" believe that he actually did transmit secret documents to Chambers. But they believe also that this act was somehow transmuted into innocence by the inherent virtue of Alger Hiss's being.

In a similar way, there has grown up around figures like Whittaker Chambers, Elizabeth Bentley, and Louis Budenz the falsest of all false issues: the "question" of the ex-Communist. We are asked to consider, not whether these people are telling the truth, or whether their understanding of Communism is correct, but whether in their "essence" as ex-Communists they are not irredeemably given over to falsehood and confusion. (It must be said that some ex-Communists have themselves helped to raise this absurd "question" by depicting Communism as something beyond both error and immorality—a form of utter perdition.)

Or, finally, consider that most mystical element in the Communist propaganda about the Rosenberg case: the claim that Julius and Ethel Rosenberg are being "persecuted" because they have "fought for peace." Since the Rosenbergs had abstained entirely from all political activity of any sort for a number of years before their arrest, it follows that the only thing they could have been doing which a Communist might interpret as "fighting for peace" must have been spying for the Soviet Union; but their being "persecuted" rests precisely on the claim that they are innocent of spying. The main element here, of course, is deliberate falsification. But it must be understood that for most partisans of the Rosenbergs such a falsification raises no problem; all lies and inconsistencies disappear in the enveloping cloud of the unspoken "essential" truth: the Rosenbergs are innocent *because* they are accused; they are innocent, one might say, by definition.

In however inchoate a fashion, those who sat thrilled in the dark theater watching **The Crucible** were celebrating a tradition and a community. No longer could they find any meaning in the cry of "Strike!" or "Revolt!" as they had done in their younger and more "primitive" age; let it be only "Bravo!"—a cry of celebration with no particular content. The important thing was that for a short time they could experience together the sense of their own being, their close community of right-mindedness in the orthodoxy of "dissent." Outside, there waited all kinds of agonizing and concrete problems: were the Rosenbergs actually guilty? was Stalin actually going to persecute the Jews? But in the theater they could know, immediately and confidently, their own innate and inalienable rightness.

The Salem trials are in fact more relevant than Arthur Miller can have suspected. For this community of "dissent," inexorably stripped of all principle and all specific belief, has retreated at last into a kind of extreme Calvinism of its own where political truth ceases to have any real connection with politics but becomes a property of the soul. Apart from all belief and all action, these people are "right" in themselves, and no longer need to prove themselves in the world of experience; the Revolution—or "liberalism," or "dissent"—has entered into them as the grace of God was once conceived to have entered into the "elect," and, like the grace of God, it is given irrevocably. Just as Alger Hiss bears witness to virtue even in his refusal to admit the very act wherein his "virtue" must reside if it resides anywhere, so these bear witness to "dissent" and "progress" in their mere existence.

For the Puritans themselves, the doctrine of absolute election was finally intolerable, and it cannot be believed that this new community of the elect finds its position comfortable. But it has yet to discover that its discomfort, like its "election," comes from within. (pp. 189-203)

> *Robert Warshow, "The Liberal Conscience in 'The Crucible',"* *in his* The Immediate Experience, *Doubleday & Company, Inc. 1962, pp. 189-203.*

Philip Hope-Wallace   (essay date 20 November 1954)

[*Hope-Wallace was an English journalist and drama critic. In the following excerpt, he faults* The Crucible *as excessively melodramatic.*]

We frivolous English like a leavening of humour in our drama no matter how solemn. The Americans, who have a glorious sense of humour themselves, still keep a liking for strong drama on the continental model—i.e. unrelieved by wit or humour of any kind. Neither Strindberg nor Wedekind get a hearing in England and if Mr Miller is puzzled by the relative unsuccess of his plays over here, he may be consoled to know that the fault is ours, not his.

All my Sons was *John Gabriel Borkman* with knobs on: **Death of a Salesman** which had 'em all weeping in New York was poorly esteemed here. Now **The Crucible,** much thought of elsewhere in the world, is left to the enterprise of the Bristol Old Vic who do it not very well but, by doing it at all, earn credit.

The play is made out of the terrible witch hunt in Salem, Mass, in 1692 when a coven of naughty girls tried to exculpate themselves by accusing others of witchcraft; and the Puritan judges taking up the cause with zeal strung up hundreds of innocent women. Mr. Miller works it down to particular cases of course: how a woman scorned tries to get an ex-lover back by accusing his wife of witchery. There are strong scenes, some very well written, in which these people are put in the familiar dilemma of characters in witch plays (or plays generally of moral indignation). Confess or be hanged; tell the truth and your husband will be lost; lie and, as it turns out, it is just the lie which condemns him. . . .

Arthur Miller of course is preaching a topical sermon—about McCarthyism; the impact of the play must have been great in New York. But there are plenty of other pogroms—nearer home. No, if it makes less impact than it should, it is because all witch hunt plays are the same in the long run; unless they are written by someone like Shaw. It was impossible in *this* trial scene, written in anger and self pity, not to recall Shaw's trial scene, so human, wise and balanced that it cleaves the heart. This was only melodramatically 'moving', like Meyerbeer's *The Huguenots.*

> *Philip Hope-Wallace, in a review of "The Crucible," in* Time & Tide, *Vol. 35, No. 47, November 20, 1954, p. 1544.*

Phillip Walker   (essay date Fall 1956)

[*In the following excerpt, Walker maintains that* The Crucible "*does not achieve full identity as either a personal tragedy or a political allegory but, rather, contains within itself the unfulfilled characteristics of both.*"]

Witch hunting as an American pastime is generally regarded as a legacy from the Puritans of Seventeenth Century New England. This attitude is justified in the popular mind by the notorious Salem witch hunt of 1692, which, beginning with the hysterical accusations of a group of young girls, ultimately resulted in the execution of twenty people as witches. Contrary to common belief, however, the Salem witchcraft hysteria was not primarily a violent expression of the repressive doctrines of the puritan sect and the bigotry of its adherents. It was, rather, an explosion resulting from the collision of several impersonal social forces among which puritanism was only a minor element. It was a tragedy in which there were no heroes or villains, in which the accused and the accusers were victimized with equal blamelessness.

The elements of conflict, however, in such a situation are too vast, too amorphous, to be either confined or defined

without some qualification within the rigidly prescribed limits of a play. It was necessary, therefore, that Arthur Miller, in using the historical incident as the basis of his play, **The Crucible,** narrow the conflict and, more important, define it in terms that could be effectively communicated in the theatre. This he did, offering his major character, John Proctor, as an embryonic philosophical liberal who was victimized by the witch hunt because of his more or less conscious opposition to Puritanism, whereas his historical counterpart, and most of the others accused of witchcraft in Seventeenth Century Salem, believed in Puritanism with an intensity equal to that of their accusers and judges. Proctor, furthermore, is burdened by the author with an intolerable conviction of guilt in relation to his wife, because of a marital infidelity, antecedent to the play's beginning, committed with the girl, Abigail Williams, who ultimately accuses him of witchcraft, and whose age, due to this dramatic embellishment, has been raised from eleven to seventeen years. Also, there is no historical evidence that the real John Proctor ever confessed to witchcraft. Finally, the accusers and judges of the play are motivated on the basis of conscious malevolence rather than, as in the actual event, an unthinking emotional paroxysm on the part of the afflicted girls and, on the part of the judges, an honest desire to carry through to a logical and just conclusion the dictates of their ideology and the laws of evidence. Thus, in the play, Abigail Williams, the leader of the accusing girls, is prompted primarily by her lust for John Proctor, hatred of his wife, and a general resentment toward the respectable people of the town, and Reverend Parris, the local pastor, and Deputy Governor Danforth, the Judge, by the desire for and the fear of losing personal prestige and power. These motivations, of course, might have been present in some of the historical figures of whom Miller's characters are the representation, but they were not, as in the play, of predominant importance.

Such departures from fact, undertaken as they are for the purpose of personifying conflict, are, of course, not only excusable, but are representative of sound dramaturgy. The only criticism that can be leveled justly in this regard is that Miller did not go far enough. In other words, the action of the play is not sufficiently reenforced by personal character motivation to establish Proctor's soul at the center of the conflict. At first glance, to be sure, the play seems to be a tragedy in the classic sense and the action primarily concerned with the personal problems of John Proctor. But further consideration leads one to a recognition of an apparent duality in the action between Proctor's personal tragedy and a political polemic in dramatic form, in which Proctor is nothing more than a hollow though major symbol in a dramatic allegory concerning McCarthyism.

The same confusion is present in the delineation of Deputy Governor Danforth. The potentialities as a tragic antagonist with which the author has attempted to invest this character, as well as those of the historical models from which that character has been drawn, are clearly apparent, but, in actual performance, the Deputy Governor emerges as pretty much of a cardboard villain, and once again the audience is placed in the dilemma, this one three horned, of determining whether Danforth is a tragic antagonist, a symbol of one aspect of McCarthyism, or simply a "ten-twent-thirt" villain.

The play, then, does not achieve full identity as either a personal tragedy or a political allegory but, rather, contains within itself the unfulfilled characteristics of both. That a play can achieve fulfillment as both an allegory and a tragedy is indisputable, but an essential fact to recognize is that the fulfillment of each cannot be simultaneous. Just as two objects cannot occupy the same space at the same moment, a play cannot at the same moment be received as both an allegory and a tragedy. Miller's more successful play, *The Death of a Salesman,* is a case in point. That this play may be accepted as both the personal tragedy of Willie Loman and a preachment against the falsity of some aspects of capitalist ideology is beyond question, but one can only contemplate the play as it fulfills each of these two functions from mutually exclusive vantage points, the first from that of empathic subjectivity as you watch Willie's travail from your seat in the darkened theatre, and the second from that of analytical objectivity as you rehash the play on your way home from the show. The trouble with *The Crucible* is that neither the tragic nor the allegorical aspects of the play are sufficiently developed to be mutually exclusive; neither is strong enough to exclude the other from one's consciousness. As a result, one is left hovering in the no-man's-land between allegory and tragedy, between objectivity and subjectivity, between thought and emotion, never sure whether a particular line is to be accepted on its own emotional terms or as a cryptic comment on the activities of Wisconsin's Junior Senator.

This confusion of function seems to mirror the author's own indecision concerning the import of his play. On one hand, Miller has repeatedly denied any allegorical intentions and has even excluded from *The Crucible* certain historical facts because of the symbolical inferences that might be drawn from them [Henry Hewes, *Saturday Review,* 31 January 1953] and, on the other hand, as a part of a lengthy interpolation into the text of the play's published edition, has drawn a parallel between the plot and contemporary political problems [Arthur Miller, *The Crucible,* 1953].

This confusion between allegory and tragedy cannot be resolved by the semantic trick of calling the play an allegorical tragedy or that of Mr. Miller in characterizing the play [in Hewes] as "the tragedy of a whole society." It only can be resolved by firmly establishing, through skillful staging, an empathic relationship between John Proctor and the audience of such strength and intensity that at no moment during the course of any performance will a connection be established between the Salem of 1692 and the Washington of 1954. The audience will have plenty of time and opportunity for that after the final curtain. (pp. 222-24)

> *Phillip Walker, "Arthur Miller's 'The Crucible': Tragedy or Allegory," in* Western Speech, *Vol. XX, No. 4, Fall, 1956, pp. 222-24.*

Arthur Miller   (essay date 1957)

[*In the following excerpt, Miller discusses his purpose in writing* The Crucible, *events that influenced its conception, and critical and public reaction to the play.*]

In the writing of *Death of a Salesman* I tried . . . to achieve a maximum power of effect. But when I saw the devastating force with which it struck its audiences, something within me was shocked and put off. I had thought of myself as rather an optimistic man. I looked at what I had wrought and was forced to wonder whether I knew myself at all if this play, which I had written half in laughter and joy, was as morose and as utterly sad as its audiences found it. Either I was much tougher than they, and could stare at calamity with fewer terrors, or I was harboring with myself another man who was only tangentially connected with what I would have called my rather bright viewpoint about mankind. As I watched and saw tears in the eyes of the audience I felt a certain embarrassment at having, as I thought then, convinced so many people that life was not worth living—for so the play was widely interpreted. I hasten to add now that I ought not have been embarrassed, and that I am convinced the play is not a document of pessimism, a philosophy in which I do not believe.

Nevertheless, the emotionalism with which the play was received helped to generate an opposite impulse and an altered dramatic aim. This ultimately took shape in *The Crucible,* but before it became quite so definite and formed into idea, it was taking hold of my thoughts in a purely dramatic and theatrical context. Perhaps I can indicate its basic elements by saying that *Salesman* moves with its arms open wide, sweeping into itself by means of a subjective process of thought-connection a multitude of observations, feelings, suggestions, and shadings much as the mind does in its ordinary daily functionings. Its author chose its path, of course, but, once chosen, that path could meander as it pleased through a world that was well recognized by the audience. From the theatrical viewpoint that play desired the audience to forget it was in a theater even as it broke the bounds, I believe, of a long convention of realism. Its expressionistic elements were consciously used as such, but since the approach to Willy Loman's characterization was consistently and rigorously subjective, the audience would not ever be aware—if I could help it—that they were witnessing the use of a technique which had until then created only coldness, objectivity, and a highly styled sort of play. I had willingly employed expressionism but always to create a subjective truth, and this play, which was so manifestly "written," seemed as though nobody had written it at all but that it had simply "happened." I had always been attracted and repelled by the brilliance of German expressionism after World War I, and one aim in *Salesman* was to employ its quite marvelous shorthand for humane, "felt" characterizations rather than for purposes of demonstration for which the Germans had used it.

These and other technical and theatrical considerations were a preparation for what turned out to be *The Crucible,* but "what was in the air" provided the actual locus of the tale. If the reception of *All My Sons* and *Death of a Salesman* had made the world a friendly place for me, events of the early fifties quickly turned that warmth into an illusion. It was not only the rise of "McCarthyism" that moved me, but something which seemed much more weird and mysterious. It was the fact that a political, objective, knowledgeable campaign from the far Right was capable of creating not only a terror, but a new subjective reality, a veritable mystique which was gradually assuming even a holy resonance. The wonder of it all struck me that so practical and picayune a cause, carried forward by such manifestly ridiculous men, should be capable of paralyzing thought itself, and worse, causing to billow up such persuasive clouds of "mysterious" feelings within people. It was as though the whole country had been born anew, without a memory even of certain elemental decencies which a year or two earlier no one would have imagined could be altered, let alone forgotten. Astounded, I watched men pass me by without a nod whom I had known rather well for years; and again, the astonishment was produced by my knowledge, which I could not give up, that the terror in these people was being knowingly planned and consciously engineered, and yet that all they knew was terror. That so interior and subjective an emotion could have been so manifestly created from without was a marvel to me. It underlies every word in *The Crucible.*

I wondered, at first, whether it must be that self-preservation and the need to hold on to opportunity, the thought of being exiled and "put out," was what the fear was feeding on, for there were people who had had only the remotest connections with the Left who were quite as terrified as those who had been closer. I knew of one man who had been summoned to the office of a network executive and, on explaining that he had had no Left connections at all, despite the then current attacks upon him, was told that this was precisely the trouble; "You have nothing to give them," he was told, meaning he had no confession to make, and so he was fired from his job and for more than a year could not recover the will to leave his house.

It seemed to me after a time that this, as well as other kinds of social compliance, is the result of the sense of guilt which individuals strive to conceal by complying. Generally it was a guilt, in this historic instance, resulting from their awareness that they were not as Rightist as people were supposed to be; that the tenor of public pronouncements was alien to them and that they must be somehow discoverable as enemies of the power overhead. There was a new religiosity in the air, not merely the kind expressed by the spurt in church construction and church attendance, but an official piety which my reading of American history could not reconcile with the free-wheeling iconoclasm of the country's past. I saw forming a kind of interior mechanism of confession and forgiveness of sins which until now had not been rightly categorized as sins. New sins were being created monthly. It was very odd how quickly these were accepted into the new orthodoxy, quite as though they had been there since the beginning of time. Above all, above all horrors, I saw accepted the notion that conscience was no longer a private matter but one of state administration. I saw men handing conscience to other men and thanking other men for the opportunity of doing so.

I wished for a way to write a play that would be sharp, that would lift out of the morass of subjectivism the squirming,

single, defined process which would show that the sin of public terror is that it divests man of conscience, of himself. It was a theme not unrelated to those that had invested the previous plays. In *The Crucible,* however, there was an attempt to move beyond the discovery and unveiling of the hero's guilt, a guilt that kills the personality. I had grown increasingly conscious of this theme in my past work, and aware too that it was no longer enough for me to build a play, as it were, upon the revelation of guilt, and to rely solely upon a fate which exacts payment from the culpable man. Now guilt appeared to me no longer the bedrock beneath which the probe could not penetrate. I saw it now as a betrayer, as possibly the most real of our illusions, but nevertheless a quality of mind capable of being overthrown.

I had known of the Salem witch hunt for many years before "McCarthyism" had arrived, and it had always remained an inexplicable darkness to me. When I looked into it now, however, it was with the contemporary situation at my back, particularly the mystery of the handing over or conscience which seemed to me the central and informing fact of the time. One finds, I suppose, what one seeks. I doubt I should ever have tempted agony by actually writing a play on the subject had I not come upon a single fact. It was that Abigail Williams, the prime mover of the Salem hysteria, so far as the hysterical children were concerned, had a short time earlier been the house servant of the Proctors and now was crying out Elizabeth Proctor as a witch; but more—it was clear from the record that with entirely uncharacteristic fastidiousness she was refusing to include John Proctor, Elizabeth's husband, in her accusations despite the urgings of the prosecutors. Why? I searched the records of the trials in the courthouse at Salem but in no other instance could I find such a careful avoidance of the implicating stutter, the murderous, ambivalent answer to the sharp questions of the prosecutors. Only here, in Proctor's case, was there so clear an attempt to differentiate between a wife's culpability and a husband's.

The testimony of Proctor himself is one of the least elaborate in the records, and Elizabeth is not one of the major cases either. There could have been numerous reasons for his having been ultimately apprehended and hanged which are nowhere to be found. After the play opened, several of his descendants wrote to me; and one of them believes that Proctor fell under suspicion because, according to family tradition, he had for years been an amateur inventor whose machines appeared to some people as devilish in their ingenuity, and—again according to tradition—he had had to conceal them and work on them privately long before the witch hunt had started, for fear of censure if not worse. The explanation does not account for everything, but it does fall in with his evidently liberated cast of mind as revealed in the record; he was one of the few who not only refused to admit consorting with evil spirits, but who persisted in calling the entire business a ruse and a fake. Most, if not all, of the other victims were of their time in conceding the existence of the immemorial plot by the Devil to take over the visible world, their only reservation being that they happened not to have taken part in it themselves.

It was the fact that Abigail, their former servant, was their accuser, and her apparent desire to convict Elizabeth and save John, that made the play conceivable for me.

As in any such mass phenomenon, the number of characters of vital, if not decisive, importance is so great as to make the dramatic problem excessively difficult. For a time it seemed best to approach the town impressionistically, and, by a mosaic of seemingly disconnected scenes, gradually to form a context of cause and effect. This I believe I might well have done had it not been that the central impulse for writing at all was not the social but the interior psychological question, which was the question of that guilt residing in Salem which the hysteria merely unleashed, but did not create. Consequently, the structure reflects that understanding, and it centers in John, Elizabeth, and Abigail.

In reading the record, which was taken down verbatim at the trial, I found one recurring note which had a growing effect upon my concept, not only of the phenomenon itself, but of our modern way of thinking about people, and especially of the treatment of evil in contemporary drama. Some critics have taken exception, for instance, to the unrelieved badness of the prosecution in my play. I understand how this is possible, and I plead no mitigation, but I was up against historical facts which were immutable. I do not think that either the record itself or the numerous commentaries upon it reveal any mitigation of the unrelieved, straightforward, and absolute dedication to evil displayed by the judges of these trials and the prosecutors. After days of study it became quite incredible how perfect they were in this respect. I recall, almost as in a dream, how Rebecca Nurse, a pious and universally respected woman of great age, was literally taken by force from her sickbed and ferociously cross-examined. No human weakness could be displayed without the prosecution's stabbing into it with greater fury. The most patent contradictions, almost laughable even in that day, were overridden with warnings not to repeat their mention. There was a sadism here that was breathtaking.

I believe that, from whatever cause, a dedication to evil, not mistaking it for good, but knowing it as evil and loving it as evil, is possible in human beings who appear agreeable and normal. I think now that one of the hidden weaknesses of our whole approach to dramatic psychology is our inability to face this fact—to conceive, in effect, of Iago.

—*Arthur Miller*

So much so, that I sought but could not at the time take hold of a concept of man which might really begin to account for such evil. For instance, it seems beyond doubt that members of the Putnam family consciously, coldly, and with malice aforethought conferred in private with some of the girls, and told them whom it was desirable to cry out upon next. There is and will always be in my mind the spectacle of the great minister, and ideological authority behind the prosecution, Cotton Mather, galloping up to the scaffold to beat back a crowd of villagers so moved by the towering dignity of the victims as to want to free them.

It was not difficult to foresee the objections to such absolute evil in men; we are committed, after all, to the belief that it does not and cannot exist. Had I this play to write now, however, I might proceed on an altered concept. I should say that my own—and the critics'—unbelief in this depth of evil is concomitant with our unbelief in good, too. I should now examine this fact of evil as such. Instead, I sought to make Danforth, for instance, perceptible as a human being by showing him somewhat put off by Mary Warren's turnabout at the height of the trials, which caused no little confusion. In my play, Danforth seems about to conceive of the truth, and surely there is a disposition in him at least to listen to arguments that go counter to the line of the prosecution. There is no such swerving in the record, and I think now, almost four years after the writing of it, that I was wrong in mitigating the evil of this man and the judges he represents. Instead, I would perfect his evil to its utmost and make an open issue, a thematic consideration of it in the play. I believe now, as I did not conceive then, that there are people dedicated to evil in the world; that without their perverse example we should not know the good. Evil is not a mistake but a fact in itself. I have never proceeded psychoanalytically in my thought, but neither have I been separated from that humane if not humanistic conception of man as being essentially innocent while the evil in him represents but a perversion of his frustrated love. I posit no metaphysical force of evil which totally posseses certain individuals, nor do I even deny that given infinite wisdom and patience and knowledge any human being can be saved from himself. I believe merely that, from whatever cause, a dedication to evil, not mistaking it for good, but knowing it as evil and loving it as evil, is possible in human beings who appear agreeable and normal. I think now that one of the hidden weaknesses of our whole approach to dramatic psychology is our inability to face this fact—to conceive, in effect, of Iago.

The Crucible is a "tough" play. My criticism of it now would be that it is not tough enough. I say this not merely out of deference to the record of these trials, but out of a consideration for drama. We are so intent upon getting sympathy for our characters that the consequences of evil are being muddied by sentimentality under the guise of a temperate weighing of causes. The tranquility of the bad man lies at the heart of not only moral philosophy but dramaturgy as well. But my central intention in this play was to one side of this idea, which was realized only as the play was in production. All I sought here was to take a step not only beyond the realization of guilt, but beyond the helpless victimization of the hero.

The society of Salem was "morally" vocal. People then avowed principles, sought to live by them and die by them.

Issues of faith, conduct, society, pervaded their private lives in a conscious way. They needed but to disapprove to act. I was drawn to this subject because the historical moment seemed to give me the poetic right to create people of higher self-awareness than the contemporary scene affords. I had explored the subjective world in *Salesman* and I wanted now to move closer to a conscious hero.

The decidedly mixed reception to the play was not easily traceable, but I believe there are causes for it which are of moment to more than this play alone. I believe that the very moral awareness of the play and its characters—which are historically correct—was repulsive to the audience. For a variety of reasons I think that the Anglo-Saxon audience cannot believe the reality of characters who live by principles and know very much about their own characters and situations, and who say what they know. Our drama, for this among other reasons, is condemned, so to speak, to the emotions of subjectivism, which, as they approach knowledge and self-awareness, become less and less actual and real to us. In retrospect I think that my course in *The Crucible* should have been toward greater self-awareness and not, as my critics have implied, toward an enlarged and more pervasive subjectivism. The realistic form and style of the play would then have had to give way. What new form might have evolved I cannot now say, but certainly the passion of knowing is as powerful as the passion of feeling alone, and the writing of the play broached the question of that new form for me.

The work of Bertolt Brecht inevitably rises up in any such quest. It seems to me that, while I cannot agree with his concept of the human situation, his solution of the problem of consciousness is admirably honest and theatrically powerful. One cannot watch his productions without knowing that he is at work not on the periphery of the contemporary dramatic problem, but directly upon its center—which is again the problem of consciousness.

The Crucible, then, opened up a new prospect, and, like every work when completed, it left behind it unfinished business. It made a new freedom possible, and it also threw a certain light upon the difference between the modern playwriting problem of meaning and that of the age preceding the secularization of society. It is impossible to study the trial record without feeling the immanence of a veritable pantheon of life values in whose name both prosecution and defense could speak. The testimony is thick with reference to Biblical examples, and even as religious belief did nothing to temper cruelty—and in fact might be shown to have made the cruel crueler—it often served to raise this swirling and ludicrous mysticism to a level of high moral debate; and it did this despite the fact that most of the participants were unlettered, simple folk. They lived and would die more in the shadow of the other world than in the light of this one (and it is no mean irony that the theocratic prosecution should seek out the most religious people for its victims).

The longer I dwelt on the whole spectacle, the more clear became the failure of the present age to find a universal moral sanction, and the power of realism's hold on our theater was an aspect of this vacuum. For it began to appear that our inability to break more than the surfaces of realism reflected our inability—playwrights and audiences—to agree upon the pantheon of forces and values which must lie behind the realistic surfaces of life. In this light, realism, as a style, could seem to be a defense against the assertion of meaning. How strange a conclusion this is when one realizes that the same style seventy years ago was the prime instrument of those who sought to illuminate meaning in the theater, who divested their plays of fancy talk and improbable locales and bizarre characters in order to bring "life" onto the stage. And I wondered then what was true. Was it that we had come to fear the hard glare of life on the stage and under the guise of an aesthetic surfeited with realism were merely expressing our flight from reality? Or was our condemned realism only the counterfeit of the original, whose most powerful single impetus was to deal with man as a social animal? Any form can be drained of its informing purpose, can be used to convey, like the Tudor façades of college dormitories, the now vanished dignity and necessity of a former age in order to lend specious justification for a present hollowness. Was it realism that stood in the way of meaning or was it the counterfeit of realism?

Increasingly over the past five years and more the poetic plays, so-called, some of them much admired by all sorts of critics, were surprisingly full of what in the university years ago was called "fine" writing. If one heard less of the creak of plot machinery there was more of the squeak of self-pity, the humming of the poetic poseur, the new romance of the arbitrary and the uncompleted. For one, I had seen enough of the "borrowings" of the set, the plot, the time-shifting methods, and the lighting of *Death of a Salesman* to have an intimate understanding of how a vessel could be emptied and still purveyed to the public as new wine. Was realism called futile now because it needed to illuminate an exact meaning behind it, a conviction that was no more with us? Confusion, the inability to describe one's sense of a thing, often issues in a genuine poetry of feeling, and feeling was now raised up as the highest good and the ultimate attainment in drama. I had known that kind of victory myself with *Salesman;* but was there not another realm even higher, where feeling took awareness more openly by the hand and both equally ruled and were illuminated? I had found a kind of self-awareness in the bloody book of Salem and had thought that since the natural, realistic surface of that society was one already immersed in the questions of meaning and the relations of men to God, to write a realistic play of that world was already to write in a style beyond contemporary realism. That more than one critic had found the play "cold" when I had never written more passionately was by this time an acceptable and inevitable detail of my fate, for, while it will never confess to it, our theater is trained—actors, directors, audience, and critics—to take to its heart anything that does not prick the mind and to suspect everything that does not supinely reassure. (pp. 38-47)

Arthur Miller, in an introduction to his Arthur Miller's Collected Plays, *The Viking Press, 1957, pp. 3-55.*

D. D. Raphael   (essay date 1960)

[*Raphael is an English educator, critic, editor, and translator. In the following excerpt, he asserts that* The Crucible *has "some claim to greatness" due to its universal theme of "the nature of human goodness and human evil."*]

Let me now mention a modern play which I think does have some claim to greatness, Arthur Miller's ***The Crucible.*** One hears it said that this was meant to be a propaganda play, castigating the 'witch-hunts' of the McCarthy era by pointing to parallels in the witch-hunt at Salem two and a half centuries before. There seems to be no doubt that Arthur Miller did have this purpose in mind, at least when he edited the play for publication, since several of the notes which interrupt the text explicitly indicate modern parallels. In the play itself, however, the genius of the dramatist swamps the motives of the propagandist. A person who saw this play and had not been told of its propagandist purpose would probably not think of modern witch-hunting specifically. Of course he would not be confined to the seventeenth-century scene either. He would see in the play something of universal import, as one sees in any play that touches greatness. He would see an exploration of the nature of human goodness and human evil, of how evil grows from things like envy and sexual frustration, *aided* by socially conditioned attitudes such as bigotry and superstition. He would see how the spread of this evil can bring calumny and death to innocent and even to saintly people. But he would also see how it can bring out, in a man who is no saint, goodness that might otherwise have remained merely potential.

Until we reach the end of the play, John Proctor is not a particularly good man. He can succumb to temptation as well as stand up for decency. His virtue is honesty. He is honest above all with himself. So when he is faced with the alternatives of death on a false charge and escaping death by a false confession, the decision is not clear cut for him, as it would be for the single-minded virtue of his wife, and as it is for the saintly character of Rebecca Nurse. He wrestles with his conscience, debating whether it would not be more dishonest for him to withhold the lie than to tell it. Up to now he has refused to 'confess' to sorcery, but he has no illusions about his reasons:

> Spite only keeps me silent. It is hard to give a lie to dogs.

If he now gives them the lie they want, it will not deceive anyone who is not already self-deceived. It would be more deceitful for him to play the martyr:

> I'd have you see some honesty in it. Let them that never lied die now to keep their souls. It is pretence for me, a vanity that will not blind God nor keep my children out of the wind. . . . I think it is honest, I think so; I am no saint. Let Rebecca go like a saint; for me it is fraud!

Yet in the end he tears up his confession, because he objects to his being used to incriminate others or to serve as an example of submission. So he joins Rebecca in martyrdom, but for a reason that is not false to his own humanistic code of conduct, and he can say of himself:

Now I do think I see some shred of goodness in John Proctor. Not enough to weave a banner with, but white enough to keep it from such dogs.

But the last word, and the truest estimate of what he has achieved, is spoken by his wife, when he has left the stage and she is urged to go and plead with him to accept the lie:

> He have his goodness now. God forbid I take it from him.

In this play we have an impressive example of moral philosophy *'in concreto'.* Where the philosopher will give an abstract definition of different types of virtue, here we have them shown in living examples. And we also have, what we do not often find in philosophy, an exploration of the complex relations between moral good and moral evil. All this comes out more prominently than any propagandist purpose of censuring witch-hunting, ancient or modern. If it were otherwise, ***The Crucible*** would not be, as I think it undoubtedly is, by far the best of Arthur Miller's plays. (pp. 103-05)

> *D. D. Raphael, "Philosophical Drama: The Dramatist as Philosopher," in his* The Paradox of Tragedy: The Mahlon Powell Lectures, 1959, *Indiana University Press, 1960, pp. 90-111.*

John Gassner   (essay date 1960)

[*Gassner was a Hungarian-born American journalist, editor, educator, and critic who broadly promoted the work of Miller and Tennessee Williams. In the following excerpt, he delineates Miller's intentions to combine history and poetry in* The Crucible, *a play he characterizes as an epic tragedy.*]

With the writing and production of ***The Crucible*** Miller moved in the directions that had already attracted him (he had written an unproduced poetic tragedy on the conquest of Mexico): history and tragedy. History was directly present in ***The Crucible,*** and tragedy was scaled higher than it had been in ***Death of a Salesman.*** His independent Colonial farmer, John Proctor, had more tragic stature than the superannuated traveling salesman, Willy Loman. The heroic death of Proctor, who chooses the gallows in preference to submission to unjust authority, is on an obviously higher level of tragic sacrifice than Willy's suicide.

We may surmise that Arthur Miller entertained poetic aspirations. Apparently he was following Maxwell Anderson's example in trying to write poetry in an historical drama before using it in a contemporary context (this came later in ***A View from the Bridge***). The poetry in ***The Crucible*** was a sort of prose-poetry rather than verse, and the seventeenth-century historical context in which it was employed justified a degree of formality and biblical austerity. Miller was not the man to hit upon poetic embellishments accidentally; his playwriting career appears to follow a planned progression from the well-made-play technique of ***All My Sons*** to the imaginative dramatic construction of ***Death of a Salesman*** and to the poetic historical writing of *The Crucible.* The author's various introductions to his plays make plain the deliberateness, the strong awareness of objectives, and the self-awareness that characterize his work in the theatre.

The Crucible, then, has importance in the career of a writer whose laudable ambition is to make contemporary American theatre aim high and who also wishes to express the tensions of his own time and place. Taking an exalted view of the theatre's responsibilities and of the artist's function in society as the guardian of its conscience, Miller wrote *The Crucible* in the midst of the McCarthy era. The author's motivation plainly included taking a public stand against authoritarian inquisitions and mass hysteria. These are pompous words perhaps. The play itself has a little too much pomp at times that better dramatic poetry might have transfigured, and too much stiffness that the author might have avoided had he dealt with his own times and been less conscious of period. But the sincerely maintained purpose behind the posture is clear, and it is one of Miller's distinctions that he was one of the very few writers of the period to speak out unequivocally for reason and justice. *The Crucible* will remain alive long after every carping criticism directed at its political implications has been forgotten. (Curiously these criticisms were not by benighted reactionaries but by enlightened intellectuals, and not in the popular press but in literary journals.)

There were some dramatic rewards available to a person of Miller's courage. The topical incitement to passion gave the author a strong impetus in the writing of the climactic scenes. These have since been rarely equalled in strength, and the excitement they provided proved distinctly serviceable when the play was given an off-Broadway revival in 1958, after McCarthyism had subsided as an issue. The later production proved that the play could hold its own without the support of topicality. That it stood up so well was due to the excitement of the action, to the author's underlying passion, and to the character drama and tragic pattern. All this does not mitigate a certain stiffness in the characterization, nor does it remove doubt as to the advisability of making the historical witchcraft trials hinge so much on the perversity of a passionate girl. But the fact remains that Miller built his play with exciting situations and characters rather than puppets.

The Crucible was momentous, if imperfect. I give my own reactions below as a specimen first reaction to the play and its reception. At the second night opening, during the 1952-53 season, the strong impression on the audience was almost the impact of an *event* rather than of just one more serious play. Even while aware of some creakiness in the work, I shared a feeling of grief and anger with others. Writing about the play several weeks later I had some doubts about the quality of the work. Yet I also wrote with some rage directed not only at the historical world of Salem, but at the evil and stupidity in men as well as at the frosty and what seemed to me at the time disingenuous reaction of various intelligent theatregoers:

> A history play by virtue of its subject, *The Crucible* is nonetheless a spiraling drama. Miller has once more demonstrated his ability to telescope dramatic material. In writing about the Salem

witchcraft trials he has avoided the danger of composing a sprawling chronicle. Moreover, he has made every effort to create a central tragic character in John Proctor, the independent farmer who faces one decision after another and, after some understandable hesitations, makes his choice. It would take too long to prove here the proficiency combined with insight into character that distinguishes *The Crucible.* . . .

(pp. 274-76)

How the contemporary higher criticism can tie itself up in knots when it is confronted by honest, forthright work is well shown in reviews of the play. As usual, the workaday New York newspaper reviewers come off better than the critics who write for recondite publications; the newspapermen report on what they see, whereas esoteric critics see only what they want to discuss. Regardless of Miller's original intentions or later explanations in the [Viking Press text], the play must be assessed simply as a play. If parallels between the past and the present appear, so much the worse for us or for humanity at large rather than for the playwright. If individual lines, such as the question whether the accuser is now always holy, are relevant and probably intentional on Miller's part, the fact remains that a play that holds audiences in its grip as *The Crucible* does, succeeds through the power of its overall dramaturgy rather than through its topical features.

If there are obvious weaknesses in the play they result mainly from the fact that Proctor and his wife are swamped by such a multiplicity of secondary characters that the personal drama of maintaining integrity in the face of compounded evil and folly is often dissipated. It is also unfortunate that the tragedy is started and brought to a climax—and therefore made melodramatic—by the willful action of a demoniacal girl, Abigail. Miller does not succeed in overcoming these defects. But he appears to be aware of them, and his awareness results in adjustments or corrections as the play proceeds. Both Proctor and his wife are made to grow in stature; at the end they are fully developed. . . . By the time the play ends, it is no longer the hit-or-miss chronicle of mass hysteria it tended to become earlier; it is a tragedy and its point is that men, no matter how erring, are capable of enduring everything for their sense of decency. This, too, is more apparent in the published text than it was in the stage production. Those who claim that *The Crucible* is inadequate as a revelation of what happened in Salem are quite correct. It is what transpired in the souls of John and Elizabeth Proctor that finally matters, and to that degree *The Crucible* is neither an exposé nor a merely contemporary protest, but a tragedy. (pp. 276-77)

Even if Miller did not succeed in drawing his epic material completely together, he created a powerful drama which overshadows current drama here or abroad. It may be sufficient to congratulate ourselves on the presence of Arthur Miller in our theatre. My major regret about this writer is that he is not enough of a poet. I doubt that any post-Shakespearian dramatist could have solved the problems inherent in Miller's material, but a true poet could have transcended them. He could have placed the play beyond time and locality and carried us into the center of tragic vision. A more poetic playwright could also have economized on those parts of the plot that are necessarily merely transitional and supplementary and therefore are relatively flat. (pp. 277-78)

> *John Gassner, "Affirmations?" in his* Theatre at the Crossroads: Plays and Playwrights of the Mid-Century American Stage, *Holt, Rinehart and Winston, 1960, pp. 274-312.*

Dennis Welland (essay date 1961)

[*Welland is an English educator and critic. In the following excerpt, he examines Miller's theme of civil and moral responsibility in* The Crucible *as well as Miller's revisions of his original text.*]

[The Salem witch-hunt of 1692] was an important subject ready to hand for an able dramatist to exploit, and Miller was the obvious man to tackle it. His background of Depression-engendered liberalism, his passionate belief in social responsibility, and his proven ability to handle themes of guilt and punishment, all qualified him for it. Indeed, he had almost inevitably been moving towards it for longer than he had realised. We hardly need his specific assurance that he "had known of the Salem witch hunt for many years before 'McCarthyism' had arrived"; more illuminating is his passing reference [in *Theatre Arts,* February 1953] to two of his earliest "desk-drawer" plays:

> . . . a play about two brothers caught on either side of radicalism in a university, then a play about a psychologist's dilemma in a prison where the sane were inexorably moving over to join the mad.

These sound like modern versions of two of the themes of *The Crucible,* . . . but I doubt whether a revision of either play would have been as effective a way of dramatising the problems of 1952 as *The Crucible.* [Joseph Wood Krutch's] objection that Salem does not present a sufficiently precise parallel, because "whereas witchcraft was pure delusion, subversion is a reality, no matter how unwisely or intemperately it may be combatted" [*American Drama since 1918,* 1957], ignores Miller's implication that, where evidence is only circumstantial, the dividing line between delusion and reality is so difficult to draw that the utmost caution is essential.

It also confuses the main issue of Miller's play which is much wider than this admits. He had been moving towards it in adapting *An Enemy of the People,* which had attracted him because it dealt with

> . . . the central theme of our social life today. Simply, it is the question of whether the democratic guarantees protecting political minorities ought to be set aside in time of crisis. More personally, it is the question of whether one's vision of the truth ought to be a source of guilt at a time when the mass of men condemn it as a dangerous and devilish lie. It is an enduring theme . . . because there never was, nor will there ever be, an organized society able to countenance calmly the individual who insists that he is right while the vast majority is absolutely wrong.

By treating this problem in a seventeenth- rather than in a twentieth-century context, Miller sacrifices the questionable advantage of extreme topicality for the greater gain of perspective. He is insisting on this as a perennial American problem, not merely a present-day one. The terms in which he defines his anxiety reminds us of this in yet another way:

> I saw accepted the notion that conscience was no longer a private matter but one of state administration. I saw men handing conscience to other men and thanking other men for the opportunity of doing so.

This is a modern restatement of Thoreau's central question in *On the Duty of Civil Disobedience:* "Must the citizen ever for a moment, or in the least degree, resign his conscience to the legislator?" (The frequent analogies adduced between Miller and Thoreau are intended to relate Miller to his predecessor in spirit only and not to imply direct influence.) It follows that, while fully accepting Miller's statement that he could not have written the play at any other time, I am disinclined to treat it narrowly as a tract against McCarthyism. Miller's own position on that issue is better discussed biographically, and the play itself is much more interesting than the sordid chapter of career-politics that occasioned it.

To begin with, it is of interest as an historical play, by which I mean something more than a mere costume-drama. [In his *Collected Plays*], Miller provides a note on its historical accuracy which indicates the care he has taken over it, and reference to Marion Starkey's account [*The Devil in Massachusetts,* 1949] or to the primary sources will quickly substantiate this. (As many as possible of the original documents bearing on the events and the trials were collated in a three-volume typescript in Essex County in 1938; that this was a Works Progress Administration project provides yet another instance of the influence—unexpected, belated, and indirect this time—of the Depression on Miller's work.) To document this would be tedious: sufficient, perhaps, to mention as an example the book written in 1697 by John Hale: *A Modest Inquiry into the Nature of Witchcraft.* There is an obvious identity between Miller's character in *The Crucible* and the man whose ambivalent attitude to the whole proceedings may be seen from the following extracts:

> I observed in the prosecution of these affairs, that there was in the Justices, Judges and others concerned, a conscientious endeavour to do the thing that was right.

Nevertheless, he is not easy in his own conscience, though what he questions is legal procedure rather than witchcraft itself:

> We may hence see ground to fear that there hath been a great deal of innocent blood shed in the Christian World, by proceeding upon unsafe principles, in condemning persons for Malefick Witchcraft.

There is a similar reservation in his recognition of the need for restitution to some (not, apparently, to all) of the victims:

I would humbly propose whether it be not expedient, that some what more should be publickly done than yet hath, for clearing the good name and reputation of some that have suffered upon this account.

Hale is prepared to admit that he and his colleagues may have made mistakes in an excess of zeal; he is still convinced that witchcraft may exist and that vigilance must be maintained:

Seeing we have been too hard against supposed Malefick Witchcraft, let us take heed we do not on the contrary become too favourable to divining Witchcraft [*sc.* fortune-telling.]

The note of uncertainty, of suspended judgment, that these quotations reveal is very close to the keynote of this play, which I find in the constant recurrence, on the lips of many different characters, of the phrase "I think." Much of the play could be summarised in Yeats's lines:

The best lack all conviction, while the worst Are full of passionate intensity.

It is not so much a story of two ideologies in conflict as a story of conscientious endeavour in an uncertain world. This emerges with particular force and clarity in Act II, in, for example, such exchanges as this, in which Elizabeth Proctor tells her husband what she has heard from Mary Warren:

ELIZABETH. The Deputy Governor promise hangin' if they'll not confess, John. The town's gone wild, I think. She speak of Abigail, and I thought she were a saint, to hear her. . . .

PROCTOR. Oh, it is a black mischief.
ELIZABETH. I think you must go to Salem, John. I think so. You must tell them it is a fraud.

Joe Keller had asked in vain for guidance: no one could give it to him. Willy Loman's bewilderment at Charley, who had never told his son what to do, is the bewilderment of the man who has confidently inculcated in his own sons a complete set of values that have turned out to be wrong (just as Ben's advice to Biff, "Never fight fair with a stranger, boy," is, in its context, implicitly criticised). In *The Crucible* the wiser characters do not presume to dictate anyone's duty to him, for that would be asking him to hand over his conscience. Moreover, they themselves are too perplexed by the conflicting implications of the issues to be dogmatic. Elizabeth's quietly-delivered suggestions here are the thoughts of a worried but honest mind spoken aloud for her husband's benefit, and he replies in the same key: "I'll think on it. . . . I think it is not easy to prove she's fraud, and the town gone so silly." Far from indicating a limited vocabulary, either of character or author, the repetition of this formula "I think" is in fact a very skilfully-managed way of suggesting the scruples, the misgivings, and the conscientious earnestness which are all that these people can bring against the diabolic impetus of the witch-hunt. It is significant that Miller chose to dramatise the story of John Proctor, the plain farmer, rather than the equally well-documented story of George Burrough, the minister, who was also accused of witchcraft and hanged for it. Miller's invention of Proctor's earlier

adultery with Abigail is not the outcome of a mercenary desire to add a spice of sensationalism to the play. It is a similar insistence on the human vulnerability of a man who is not a saint, not even an ordained minister fortified by a theological training, but just a decent man trying to understand and to translate into action the dictates of his conscience, trying to do, not what he *feels,* but what he *thinks,* is right.

There are more kinds of poetry, and more ways of attacking McCarthyism, than one. Anything more high-flown would be out of place in this play which insists so relentlessly on the precariousness of the foothold of goodness in a world swept by a wind of evil blowing at hurricane force.

—*Dennis Welland*

In this concern with conscience, and in other respects, too, *The Crucible* seems to be the most Shavian of Miller's plays. This is apparent in an immediate, but not superficial, respect when we notice how the printed text of this play is accompanied by a lengthy prefatory comment on the background, and by a postscript tracing the subsequent history of the characters; the dialogue of the opening scene, in particular, is also interrupted more than once for a Shavian elaboration on the theme, which is not in any sense a stage-direction. Miller had done something similar for a paperback edition of *Death of a Salesman* issued . . . in 1951, but in the *Collected Plays,* he reverts to the original text of this play. *The Crucible,* however, is a play for Puritans in [George Bernard Shaw's], as well as in the more historically literal, sense, and also has more in common with *St Joan* in particular than has been generally remarked. It is not just that each is a religious-historical play culminating in an impressive trial scene followed by martyrdom. In both the tension is further heightened by a dramatic *peripateia* in which the prisoner, having made a "confession" to escape death, suddenly realises the implications of it and recants by tearing the confession to pieces. The resemblance also extends to quite small incidents, as, for example, Proctor's conversation with his servant in Act II when he orders her to bed:

MARY WARREN. I'll not be ordered to bed no more, Mr. Proctor! I am eighteen and a woman, however single!

PROCTOR. Do you wish to sit up? Then sit up.
MARY WARREN. I wish to go to bed!

PROCTOR. [*in anger*] Good night, then!

In a similar way the Inquisitor, at Joan's trial, orders the English Chaplain, Stogumber, to sit down, and, when he refuses, replies, "If you will not sit, you must stand: that is all"; this is probably a more calculated move than Proctor's blunt directness, but it produces the same petulant compliance by the other person, for Stogumber immediately sits. It is of another aspect of Stogumber that we are reminded in the trial scene of *The Crucible* by the Reverend Parris, whose misplaced zeal makes him not only ridiculously quick to see insults to the dignity of the court in remarks that his betters are undisturbed by, but also makes him vindictive and severe in his questions to witnesses and in his fear lest any possible charge should be omitted.

Stogumber comes to mind yet again in Act IV, when Hale sees the consequences of his zeal. A more intelligent man than Stogumber, he is less abject, less hysterical, in his recognition of guilt, but his cry to Danforth—"There is blood on my head! Can you not see the blood on my head?"—is approaching hysteria; and his appeal to Elizabeth to persuade her husband to save his life by lying allows emotion to swamp principle: "Cleave to no faith when faith brings blood." Like Stogumber, he has needed to see the suffering of others before he can realise the implications of his own actions, and, like Stogumber, his immediate inclination is to swing to the other extreme. If we enquire why Miller does not humiliate Hale as Shaw humiliates the Chaplain, we are brought to the heart of both plays. To play Stogumber as a fool up to the burning of Joan and then to swing the audience's sympathy to him by his breakdown at the end of that scene is a temptation to any actor, but it blurs Shaw's point. Stogumber's collapse must be more grotesque than pathetic. This makes greater demands on the actor, but Warwick's attitude to him and the persistence of Stogumber's own chauvinistic narrowness are clear indications of Shaw's intentions, just as are the ineffectualness and silliness of Stogumber in the Epilogue. Stogumber's importance in the trial scene is far in excess of the comic relief that it is generally taken for: he is the bigot, the fanatic, and, above all, the self-deceiver who has allowed his principles to be overwhelmed by his passions. All the other members of the court, as Shaw emphasises in his Preface, were "far more self-disciplined and conscientious . . . than any English judge ever dreams of being in a political case in which his party and class prejudices are involved"; all of them act honestly, coolly, and in full accordance with their own convictions. Shaw's contempt is reserved for Stogumber, the one man who allows prejudice to blind him to his real moral beliefs.

Now Miller starts out from a wholly different premise, for which he claims the historical authority of his sources:

> I do not think that either the record itself or the numerous commentaries upon it reveal any mitigation of the unrelieved, straightforward, and absolute dedication to evil displayed by the judges of these trials and the prosecutors. After days of study it became quite incredible how perfect they were in this respect.

Hale, that is, like Stogumber, is the one exception, but in the opposite direction: he is the only one in whom there is any glimmer of hope, and as such he cannot be mocked as Stogumber is, though Miller's knowledge of human nature prevents him from sanctifying Hale's repentance. Danforth, Hathorne, and Parris are worse than Shaw's Chaplain: they are not only bigoted fanatics, but Miller sees them as positively evil (which Shaw never suggests Stogumber is), and he has said categorically that if he were

to re-write the play, he would accentuate this evil still more. He adds:

> I believe merely that, from whatever cause, a dedication to evil, not mistaking it for good, but knowing it as evil and loving it as evil, is possible in human beings who appear agreeable and normal. I think now that one of the hidden weaknesses of our whole approach to dramatic psychology is our inability to face this fact—to conceive, in effect, of Iago.

In American literature, probably more than in any other, there have always been influences at work to minimise the fact of evil. At the extreme there is the Emersonian Transcendentalism optimistically asserting that "Good is positive. Evil is merely privative, not absolute: it is like cold, which is the privation of heat," and "There is no pure lie, no pure malignity in nature. The entertainment of the proposition of depravity is the last profligacy and profanation." The Declaration of Independence may be said to have made evil an unAmerican activity, and although the buoyancy that American literature acquires from this heritage of optimism is often invigorating, yet it can be a limitation. Its writers have generally been quicker to recognise evils than to recognise evil. Part of the superiority of Melville and James over Hawthorne lies in their ability to conceive of evil where he thinks only in terms of sin, and Faulkner's superiority over many of his contemporaries is in part attributable to his awareness of evil where they see psychological maladjustment and environmental deprivation.

It is salutary, then, to find Miller enunciating this general belief in the need for literature to recognise evil, but it is a little disconcerting to find it in this specific context. The dedication to evil, of which he speaks, "not mistaking it for good, but *knowing it as evil* [my italics] and loving it as evil," may perhaps be imputed in this play—and we may disregard the sources in this discussion—to those characters who deliberately and cynically give false evidence, or incite others to do so, for their own personal gain or gratification. This means Thomas Putnam, with his greed for land, and Abigail, with her lust for Proctor. Putnam, however, is only a minor character, and Miller himself (as I shall shortly indicate) seems in two minds about the extent to which Abigail is evil or merely deluded. Evil can with much less certainty be imputed to the judges, who, hard and cruel as they may have been by our standards, and even culpably credulous, were trying, both in history and in the play, to judge in the light of evidence of an unprecedented nature. To make them more evil would be to destroy by distortion one of the virtues of the play in its present form. The very considerable dramatic power of *The Crucible* derives from its revelation of a mounting tide of evil gaining, in an entire society, an ascendancy quite disproportionate to the evil of any individual member of that society. What is so horrifying is to watch the testimony of honest men bouncing like an indiarubber ball off the high wall of disbelief that other men have built around themselves, not from ingrained evil, but from over-zealousness and a purblind confidence in their own judgment. What meaning has proof when men will believe only what they want to believe, and will interpret evidence only in the light of their own prejudice? To watch *The Crucible* is to be overwhelmed by the simple impotence of honest common sense against fanaticism that is getting out of control, and to be painfully reminded that there are situations in which sheer goodness ("mere unaided virtue," in Melville's phrase about Starbuck) is just not enough to counter such deviousness.

In this respect, too, it will remain a more important document of McCarthy's America than would a more partisan piece. The ugliness of that affair, which caused so much perplexed anxiety to friends of the United States, was not the megalomanic aspirations of a cynical demagogue, but the appalling ease with which his methods achieved results. So fast and so wide did the infection spread that it could only be visualised as a force of evil of which ordinary men and women were the unintentional agents and the unrecognising victims. In many ways its moral damage was more serious to those who accepted it than to those who fought against or were victimised by it, and this is what *The Crucible* so splendidly communicates. In the Introduction to the *Collected Plays,* Miller brings this out very movingly by his anecdotes of the investigations, and then obscures it by his retrospective attribution of a greater evil to the individual judges of Salem. *The Crucible,* of course, was written before Miller's own clash with the Congressional Committee, and is in that respect less biased, perhaps, than the later Introduction. The real moral of the play is the very Shavian one that in the life of a society evil is occasioned less by deliberate villainy than by the abnegation of personal responsibility. That is why Elizabeth quietly rejects as "the Devil's argument" Hale's impassioned plea:

> Beware, Goody Proctor—cleave to no faith when faith brings blood. It is a mistaken law that leads you to sacrifice. Life, woman, life is God's most precious gift; no principle, however glorious, may justify the taking of it.

Elizabeth, like St Joan, has learnt through suffering that "God's most precious gift" is not life at any price, but the life of spiritual freedom and moral integrity. Her simple reply to Hale substantiates a point I have already made: "I think that be the Devil's argument." She believes this, but she cannot prove it: "I cannot dispute with you, sir; I lack learning for it"; and again, as in *St Joan,* the learning of the scholars, the theologians, and the rulers is discredited, but not defeated, by the simple faith of a country woman.

The communication of this faith is Miller's best technical achievement in this play, for it depends very largely on his command of a new form of language specially adapted to the demands of his theme. Just as *St Joan* (to draw one final parallel) is the most poetic of Shaw's plays, so the language of *The Crucible* is heightened in exactly similar ways. However, where Shaw gives Joan a country dialect largely for anti-romantic and comic-realistic effect ("Where be Dauphin?" and "Thou art a rare noodle, Master"), the rustic-archaic speech of Miller's characters gives them such a natural eloquence and simple dignity that he does not need to abandon it as Shaw does in the more highly-charged situations but can (as my quotations will

have shown) use it to good purpose throughout. It is simple and unpretentious, relying mainly on the use of unusual forms of the verb and on "Mister" as a form of address that becomes unexpectedly successful in its suggestion of an unsophisticated kind of antagonistic formality. Far from finding its quaintness disturbing in the theatre, I have been impressed by its self-controlled candour even on the lips of English actors, and it contributes significantly to the keynote of the play, which I have defined as one of conscientious endeavour in an uncertain world. There is a forthrightness about *The Crucible* that is well supported by its language as well as by its structural simplicity. Miller has commented:

> I was drawn to this subject because the historical moment seemed to give me the poetic right to create people of higher self-awareness than the contemporary scene affords. I had explored the subjective world in *Salesman* and I wanted now to move closer to a conscious hero.

He has thus taken one step towards the greater faith in human nature that he defined in discussing *The Misfits,* and it is this that offsets and mitigates the power of darkness that dominates so much of the action.

It is not Proctor's heroism that matters so much as his consciousness:

> A point has to arrive where man sees what has happened to him. I think *The Crucible* is not more realistic but more theatrical than *Death of a Salesman.*

Thus Miller himself, in an interview in October 1953, in which he also spoke of himself as "trying to find a way, a form, a method of depicting people who do think." Six months after the play's New York opening Miller made some changes in the text, including the addition of a new scene, and critics are reported to have found the new version "more fluid, forceful and poetic." The changes mainly affected Proctor's part, making it more lyrical in Act II by the introduction of such lines as "Lilacs have a purple smell. Lilac is the smell of nightfall, I think." Similarly, in Act IV, his final speech to his wife had originally consisted simply of the exhortation "Give them no tear! Show a stony heart and sink them with it!"; the revision made him answer Hale (whom he had previously ignored) and expanded the speech as follows:

> HALE. Man, you will hang! You cannot!
>
> PROCTOR. [*his eyes full of tears*] I can. And there's your first marvel, that I can. You have made your magic now, for now I do think I see some shred of goodness in John Proctor. Not enough to weave a banner with, but white enough to keep it from such dogs. [*Elizabeth, in a burst of terror, rushes to him and weeps against his hand.*] Give them no tear! Tears pleasure them! Show honor now, show a stony heart and sink them with it!

It is not his heroism so much as his self-awareness that is increased by the change, just as his forthrightness had been emphasised by the introduction of the Cheever episode in Act III, as well as by minor additions elsewhere.

A less happy addition was a short scene in a wood, which was inserted before the trial scene. In it Proctor, on the eve of his wife's trial, meets Abigail to warn her of his intention to denounce her in court unless she abjures her denunciation of witches. Abigail, however, half-crazed with religious mania and with frustrated love for Proctor (of which she reminds him passionately) does not believe him:

> PROCTOR. . . . and you will never cry witchery again, or I will make you famous for the whore you are!
>
> ABIGAIL. [*she grabs him*] Never in this world! I know you, John—you are this moment singing secret Hallelujahs that your wife will hang!
>
> PROCTOR. [*throws her down*] You mad, you murderous bitch!
>
> ABIGAIL. . . . Fear naught. I will save you tomorrow. From yourself I will save you.

Obviously it is a powerful but quite superfluous scene, and Miller was wise to abandon it in subsequent editions. Its removal suggests, as I remarked earlier, that he is in two minds about Abigail, for in this scene her religiosity makes her more pathetically deluded than evil, so that the second thoughts which lead him to cut it out may be connected with the desire to accentuate the element of evil. In any case, the past relationship between Proctor and Abby has been clearly established in the first two Acts; Proctor's eyes have been opened to her true nature by the circumstances of his wife's arrest, after which he is hardly likely to seek a secret interview with her alone (if only for fear of being accused of interfering with a witness); and his disclosure of his intentions detracts from the dramatic power of the moment in Act III when he confesses his adultery. By the end of Act II, our attention has been effectively directed to Proctor, and the spotlight of the action is already narrowing into focus on his eventual clash with the court, so that we are becoming impatient of incidents that do not materially bear upon that. Thus this wood scene is an embarrassment, as is also the opening passage of Act IV, with Tituba and Sarah Good, which could easily be dispensed with as a distraction.

In general Miller is very skilful in his manipulation of his large cast. The characters are neatly differentiated and are all well utilised individually and corporately to develop the sense of a community. The only exception might be Francis Nurse, who is kept on the stage for a considerable part of Act II and even more of Act III with nothing to do; no exit is marked for him in Act II, though he obviously leaves with Corey, and no cue for his entrance is given in Act III, though he is in the room when Danforth orders it to be cleared. In the very earliest version of the play Miller seems to have reverted to the more extended manner of narration he was using before *All my Sons*: an opening scene set in a forest had to be abandoned because of the cost of building the set, but it is unlikely to have done much that is not better done in the final version by retrospective description. Something of the old realism still survives in some of the detailed settings and stage directions (at one point Danforth is even directed to blow his nose). Most interesting in this respect is Miller's preoccupation

with the source of light in each scene. In Act I the sun streams through the leaded panes of a narrow window; in Act III sunlight pours through two high windows; in Act IV moonlight seeps through the bars of another high window. This may not be readily translatable into a lighting plot, but it shows how Miller sees the mood of the play—darkness and gloom penetrated by the single shaft of light cast by conscientiously dogged goodness. The revised version of July 1953, staged under Miller's own direction, "did away with all scenery, and had the action take place against drapes and a light-flooded cyclorama." The starkness of such a production would well suit the starkness of the play's theme, for it is a play that hovers on the brink of nihilism in a nightmare of lost innocence. "If Rebecca Nurse be tainted, then nothing's left to stop the whole green world from burning." In simple phrases like this there is an eloquence of agony that makes this even more moving theatrically than *Death of a Salesman,* because there is no question of sentimentality. The Proctors' children, though mentioned, never appear. Our pity is demanded for an adult world run mad. When Proctor turns on Hale, the plain ordinariness of his language, lit by an unexpected simile, a rhetorical repetition, and an inversion of the normal order of two adjectives, is all that is needed to make it adequate to a situation that has already been brought almost unbearably close to us:

> Why do you never wonder if Parris be innocent, or Abigail? Is the accuser always holy now? Were they born this morning as clean as God's fingers? I'll tell you what's walking Salem—vengeance is walking Salem. We are what we always were in Salem, but now the little crazy children are jangling the keys of the kingdom, and common vengeance writes the law!

There are more kinds of poetry, and more ways of attacking McCarthyism, than one. Anything more high-flown would be out of place in this play which insists so relentlessly on the precariousness of the foothold of goodness in a world swept by a wind of evil blowing at hurricane force. (pp. 75-90)

Dennis Welland, in his Arthur Miller, *Oliver and Boyd Ltd., 1961, 124 p.*

James W. Douglass   (essay date Spring 1963)

[*Douglass is a Canadian educator and critic. In the following essay, he compares the seventeenth-century perspective on witches and witch-hunters to Miller's treatment of these subjects in* The Crucible.]

Although *The Crucible* achieved only a brief run on Broadway when it opened in New York in 1953 the play has since enjoyed a widespread success, including a filmed French version re-written by Jean-Paul Sartre and shown recently in the United States. According to Arthur Miller in a 1957 preface to his collected works, *The Crucible* "has been produced more often than any of the others, and more successfully the more time elapses from the headline 'McCarthyism' which it was supposed to be 'about.' " Its rate of production is especially striking when we note that

Mr. Miller was including *Death of a Salesman* among "the others."

The Crucible's current popularity is evidence that its treatment of the Salem witch trials appeals somehow to the modern playgoer's view of them. Our purpose here will be to determine the nature of Mr. Miller's treatment and its differences from the Salem viewpoint that it seeks to explain, and finally to compare the two viewpoints in an effort to arrive at their relative values. For the effort to be successful, we should reach a final understanding of what it means to be either a "witch" or a "witch-hunter" in two widely separated ages.

The Crucible's first act is, in a didactic sense, a genealogical explanation of the Salem trials: we are shown how the "witches" came into being; then, by our knowledge of their sources, we are equipped to understand the resulting drama among witches, witch-informers, and witch-hunters. According to Mr. Miller, the elements that will combine to produce a witch are: a strictly religious people who believed "that they held in their steady hands the candle that would light the world"; a self-interested and foolish ministry dedicated to a violent war on the Devil; a group of young girls discovering their power over a community which had scarcely been aware of their existence; and members of that community, symbolized by a vicious landholder, who see in their frenzied daughters the possibility for revenge and gain by the exposure of particular "witches." The one role necessary to complete the pattern, the role of the resulting "witch" as hero, Miller finds in the character of John Proctor, one of the nineteen Salemites hanged in 1692.

The source of Proctor's involvement in the accusations is his adultery with Abigail Williams. Refusing to believe that Proctor wishes a reconciliation with his wife, Abigail in her desire and hatred denounces Elizabeth Proctor as a witch. By a series of ironic developments in which Proctor tries to save Elizabeth, he is finally identified as a wizard and chooses to hang rather than save himself by a false confession.

For the readers who wish to distinguish drama from history, Mr. Miller has added a prefatory note to the play. He says, in effect, that the distinction is unnecessary. Although it is not history "in the sense in which the word is used by the academic historian," the play will convey to the reader "the essential nature of one of the strangest and most awful chapters in human history." The playwright does mention that he has introduced several variations into the action; he has followed the practice of fusing several characters into one; he has raised the age of Abigail Williams. What he does not mention is that by changing Abigail's age from eleven to seventeen years, he has made possible a dramatic structure that would have been clearly impossible given the original historical circumstances. The adulterous relationship between Abigail and Proctor which exerts a structural control over the entire play has no basis in fact. That it is the product of Mr. Miller's imagination is not in itself a fault, but in view of his claim to the "essential nature" of the trials, one would assume that he thought the psychological motives of hatred and desire intensified by this change made the meaning of Salem more transparent. The change makes dramatically apparent that the "crying-out" of the girls led by Abigail stems largely from her physical passion. David Levin in his recent article "Salem Witchcraft in Recent Fiction and Drama" (*New England Quarterly,* December 1955) writes, "One might fairly infer from the play itself that if Abigail had never lain with Proctor nobody would have been executed." Levin's statement is extreme, however. We have already pointed out that the girls' visions are as much a product of the community as an inspiration by Abigail. One could more fairly infer from the play that regardless of the adultery, Salem was destined for a witch-hunt. Abigail's motives were an immediate cause, and her new age makes plausible their more vicious character, but a number of sparks could have caused the final explosion in Salem. Mr. Miller makes clear the inevitability of the witch-hunt in his prologue:

> . . . social disorder in any age breeds such mystical suspicions, and when, as in Salem, wonders are brought forth from below the social surface, it is too much to expect people to hold back very long from laying on the victims with all the force of their frustrations.

Mr. Miller has made other changes of fact and emphasis in the story, none of which he evidently thinks alters its "essential nature." David Levin has noted the following discrepancies between fact and *The Crucible:* 1) In the play Deputy Governor Danforth declares the court in session in a waiting room in order to force a petitioner to implicate an innocent man or be held in contempt of court. The playwright's main source-book, Upham's *History of Witchcraft and Salem Village,* and the other records available contain no evidence of such a procedure. 2) Indictments and juries were a part of the original trials; they are absent from *The Crucible.* 3) Historically a three-month delay occurred between the first accusations and the first trial; dramatically the first "witch" is condemned to death eight days after the first accusation. 4) "Specter evidence" was a major issue in 1692 and a source of contention among intelligent ministers; it goes unmentioned in *The Crucible.* Reverend Hale, Mr. Miller's most sympathetic minister, is an absurdly confident witch-hunter in the first act and a broken man in the last, lacking the power to perceive the issues. 5) Finally, Mr. Miller ignores several historical factors that would have done much to alleviate and humanize his black portrayal of the court: after the first verdict a doubtful judge left the court; during a three weeks' recess the government sought procedural advice from the colony's leading ministers, who returned a paper which, Levin reports, "hit squarely on the very logical fallacies in the court's procedure which *The Crucible* so clearly reveals." Levin, in his 1960 study, *What Happened in Salem?* writes of the actual trial:

> From the very beginning the ministers cautioned the judges not to rely too heavily on spectral evidence, since the Devil could, they said, assume the shape of an innocent person while tormenting a victim. They saw, too, that by June 15 the list of alleged witches had grown almost too large to be credible. Yet the tales of confessors, which agree with each other in the few details

they gave, multiplied almost as rapidly as the number of accusations.

The people's panic and a bureaucratic confusion were important factors in the tragedy that followed.

The total effect of Mr. Miller's changes in fact (e.g., Abigail's new motives), his shifts in emphasis (e.g., the absence of an intelligent and conscientious minister), and his omission of mitigating procedures (e.g., the government's hesitation), is to evoke an atmosphere of almost unrelieved evil surrounding the condemned "witches," John and Elizabeth Proctor. Since Mr. Miller has eliminated and revised most of the confusing elements of history, we can see the "essential nature" of the situation clearly emerging.

Mr. Miller has obviously taken a kinder attitude toward the unconfessed "witches," and especially John Proctor, than he has toward the witch-hunters. Proctor is marked by characteristics that set him apart—dangerously in his neighbors' eyes, favorably in ours—from the rest of the community. "He had a sharp and biting way with hypocrites. . . . In Proctor's presence a fool felt his foolishness instantly—and a Proctor is always marked for calumny therefore." Proctor attends church less frequently than his neighbors and has avoided having his third son baptized because he is repelled by the minister's hypocrisy. An especially incriminating characteristic for a Salemite is the disbelief in witches on the part of him and his wife. Proctor's tendency to view things skeptically, although he shares many of his neighbors' beliefs, singles him out as the most "modern" figure in the drama.

The Crucible can be seen therefore in terms of two strongly opposed elements: a viciously crusading prosecution, gathering into its ranks those members of the accused who will admit the charges against them and cry-out against new "witches"; the steadfast "witches" who despite the threat of death refuse the compromise of a false confession. The "second" Reverend Hale, feeling the guilt of the previous witch-hunter, comes closest to bridging this dichotomy in characterization, but even he becomes a frantic, empty figure in his attempt to save Proctor by persuading him to sign a false confession. For the truth of the situation is that any compromise by Proctor would be an admission of guilt.

The comment made by *The Crucible* on the existence of witches is that their only mode of existence is in the mind of the accuser, at least until the accused has surrendered himself to that mind. When he does make the surrender, the accused consents to his being absorbed into the other's accusation, and with the loss of his own identity becomes truly the content of that accusation, a witch himself. The loss of personal integrity, of the individual's resistance to outside manipulations, makes him pliable to the demands of the witch-hunter. As an individual he becomes nothing more than an objective correlative, a spatially distinct form of the idea held securely in the accuser's consciousness. As long as he maintains the uniqueness of his own beliefs, making no surrender, the individual will be able to recognize himself. But if he surrenders those beliefs, or as Mr. Miller puts it, if he "hands over his conscience to another," he will become whatever that ruling consciousness wishes him to be, its now subservient witch.

Even if Proctor signed a confession while withholding his internal consent, he would still, in the context of *The Crucible,* become a witch. The "witch" by accusation only, would, by his act of signing and in spite of his inner reservations, admit in the very depths of his soul the truth of the court's charge. For what in the prosecution's terms is a witch but one who consorts with the Devil? And who in Mr. Miller's term is the Devil but the prosecution itself? By signing his name to a confession dictated by the court, John Proctor would in fact be signing the Book of the Devil, for Mr. Miller has made it clear that the real Devil in *The Crucible* is that same faction which nominally seeks the Devil's defeat.

In a drama filled with ironies, the biggest irony is that its author seems wholly unconscious of the fact that a Devil, even a Devil of his own creation, is actually present in *The Crucible.* Both in his play and in a long introduction to his *Collected Plays* published in 1957, Mr. Miller has given us a number of remarks on the problem of evil and the Devil. In a narrative portion of *The Crucible* available only to his reading audience, the playwright makes clear his own metaphysics of good and evil:

> Since 1692 a great but superficial change has wiped out God's beard and the Devil's horns, but the world is still gripped between two diametrically opposed absolutes. The concept of unity, in which positive and negative are attributes of the same force, in which good and evil are relative, ever-changing, and always joined to the same phenomenon—such a concept is still reserved to the physical sciences and to the few who have grasped the history of ideas. . . . when we see the steady and methodical inculcation into humanity of the idea of man's worthlessness—until redeemed—the necessity of the Devil may become evident as a weapon, a weapon designed and used time and time again in every age to whip men into a surrender to a particular church or church-state. . . . A political policy is equated with moral right, and opposition to it with diabolical malevolence.

The Devil is only an ideological weapon. Evil can never be absolute, but only relative, ever-changing. In a later essay the holder of these views defends himself against the critics who "have taken exception. . . . to the unrelieved badness of the prosecution in my play" by claiming:

> I was up against historical facts which were immutable. . . . I do not think that either the record itself or the numerous commentaries upon it reveal any mitigation of the unrelieved, straight-forward, and absolute dedication to evil displayed by the judges of these trials and the prosecutors. . . . I sought but could not at the time take hold of a concept of man which might really begin to account for such evil.

Although he rejects the idea of an "absolute" in referring to the forces of good and evil, and indeed blames an adherence to absolutes for the persecutions of history, Mr. Miller finds it necessary to return to the term in defending his own portrayal of the evil prosecution. By his larger frame of reference, these men are "absolutely dedicated" to a reality that is itself relative and ever-changing, existing in a kind of polarity with good. Such a reality does not seem to explain the violent depths of evil which Mr. Miller claims to have found in Salem, and which we find in *The Crucible.* The playwright himself is troubled in the above quotation by this disparity between his metaphysics and his drama. Nor does the explanation seem to lie in man alone, because Mr. Miller admits that he could take hold of no concept of man "which might really begin to account for such evil."

Whether or not we see a theology of absolutes as the only satisfying explanation for the evil shown in the prosecution, we can convict Mr. Miller on his own terms of including the Devil in his cast. The Devil, according to the playwright's view of history, arrives on the scene when "a political policy is equated with moral right, and opposition to it with diabolical malevolence." But if we reverse the usual sin of orthodoxy, which attributes diabolical malevolence to the government's opposition, and instead attribute diabolical malevolence to the government, how far have we traveled from the original "Devil-error"? We have only returned to the Devil in a different form. Unrelieved evil, regardless of whether we signify it by the term "absolute," is as much an attribute of the prosecution in Mr. Miller's eyes, as he would have us think it was an attribute of the accused in the prosecution's eyes. *The Crucible* tells us not that there were no witches in Salem, but that the witches were all members of the prosecution. Instead of a pin-pricked doll, the Devil had a gavel in his hand.

Mr. Miller has said in an interview which appeared in the Jan. 31, 1953 issue of *Saturday Review,* that "the tragedy of *The Crucible* is the everlasting conflict between people so fanatically wedded to this orthodoxy that they could not cope with the evidence of their senses." The "tragedy of Mr. Miller," if we are thus to term the faulty vision of an extremely gifted playwright, would seem to be that he was so firmly wedded to an a priori conception of Salem that he could not cope with the evidence of history. We have already shown how Mr. Miller overlooked or changed a number of circumstances which would have testified to conscience in the prosecution, tempering the vengeance that is its overriding characteristic in *The Crucible.* Even Cotton Mather, whom Miller has referred to as the "ideological authority behind the prosecution," wrote in a letter of counsel to one of the trial judges:

> And yet I must most humbly beg you that in the Management of the affair in your most worthy hands, you do not lay more stress upon pure Specter testimony than it will bear. When you are satisfied or have good plain legal evidence that the Demons which molest our poor neighbors, do indeed represent such & such people to the sufferers, though this be a presumption, yet I suppose you will not reckon it a conviction that the people so represented are witches to be immediately exterminated. It is very certain that the devils have sometimes represented the shapes of persons not only innocent, but also very virtuous.

Despite the nineteen hangings which in themselves argue vengeance as Salem's explanation, Mather's letter is one

indication that the Salem judges were probably more in doubt about the accused than Mr. Miller is in doubt about the accused's judges.

In reply to the critics who have said that *The Crucible* is about "McCarthyism," Mr. Miller has admitted that the impulse for writing the play arose from the "McCarthy atmosphere." On the other hand, he claims to have captured the "essential nature" of the Salem events. Mr. Miller thinks that the accusation, "witch," is native to no one age, but a recurring phenomenon that will arise when "wonders are brought forth from below the social surface" to sanctify the purges of a threatened orthodoxy. Without denying the elements of truth in this view or the value of Mr. Miller's concern for the individual conscience, we should nevertheless question his sweeping judgment on the effects of absolute moral values. Does the vengeance of the kind of witch-hunt portrayed in *The Crucible* necessarily follow from the nature of absolute values? Or is it not more likely that the very cry of "witch" is, when there is no witch, a perversion or a confusion of the values said to be threatened by witches? In the case of Salem, both elements, a perversion and a confusion, prompted the birth of witches. *The Crucible,* too, cries "witch," although it directs that cry at the prosecution, and implicitly at orthodoxy in general. The lapse of *The Crucible* into the evil it seeks to attack is evidence that concern for a value, whether it be the concern of an orthodox society or an individual playwright, must be founded on the final value of love to avoid giving birth to false witches. (pp. 145-51)

> *James W. Douglass, "Miller's 'The Crucible': Which Witch Is Which?" in* Renascence, *Vol. XV, No. 3, Spring, 1963, pp. 145-51.*

Henry Popkin　(essay date November 1964)

[*In the following essay, Popkin asserts that Miller's parallels between the McCarthy investigations and the Salem witch trials in* The Crucible *are flawed due to historical differences.*]

Although *The Crucible* is set in seventeenth-century America, Arthur Miller intended it as a comment on American life of his own time. For several years before the play opened in 1953, public investigations had been examining and interrogating radicals, former radicals, and possible former radicals, requiring witnesses to tell about others and not only about themselves. The House Committee to Investigate Un-American Activities evolved a memorable and much-quoted sentence: "Are you now, or have you ever been a member of the Communist Party?" Borrowing a phrase from a popular radio program, its interrogators called it "the $64 question."

Senator Joseph McCarthy built his international fame on his presumed knowledge of subversion in government and added a new word to our vocabulary—"McCarthyism," meaning ruinous accusation without any basis in evidence. A few months before *The Crucible* reached Broadway, McCarthy had helped to elect a President of the United States, and, two days before the premiere, that President was inaugurated. The elections had made McCarthy chairman of an important congressional subcommittee;

his power was greater than ever. The film and television industries gave every sign of being terrified by McCarthyism—but by the atmosphere that McCarthy created, more than by his own subcommittee. Show business found itself of more interest to the House Committee to Investigate Un-American Activities than to Senator McCarthy's subcommittee. Blacklists barred certain actors and writers from working in the popular media. Actors who refused to give testimony disappeared both from the large film screen and the small television screen, but "friendly witnesses" continued to work. On the other hand, the New York stage, since it was and still is a relatively chaotic enterprise, was comparatively unmanaged and untouched. Nevertheless, *The Crucible* was a bold as well as a timely play, written at a time when the congressional investigators had the power to do considerable damage. Senator McCarthy's personal authority wilted in the following year, but Miller was a somewhat unfriendly witness before a congressional committee in 1956. He described his own flirtation with Communism but refused to give the names of Communists he had known. He was ultimately absolved of the charge of contempt of the committee.

The Crucible dramatized the phrase that was popularly being used to describe the congressional hearings—"witch hunts." In the Salem witch trials, Miller chose an unmistakable parallel to current events. He has never permitted any doubt that the parallel was deliberate. In his introduction to his *Collected Plays* and in his interpretative remarks scattered through the text, he calls attention to the play's contemporary reference and invites comparisons between the two widely separated hearings.

The Salem witch trials are, equally, a historical event. In 1692, in Salem, Massachusetts, twenty people were found guilty of witchcraft and hanged; others who had been accused saved themselves by confessing to witchcraft and accusing others. As in the unhappy occurrences of the 1950's, naming others was taken to be a guarantee of sincerity and of a laudable desire to tell all. Also, the witchcraft scare was violent, alarming, and brief, like an epidemic and, again, like the Communist scare of the 1950's. It will be easy enough to discover and to expound still other parallels as we examine the play, but one preliminary difficulty needs to be stated: the parallel fails at one important point. There is such a thing as Communism; there is no such thing as witchcraft. This distinction indicates that the psychological state of the victims of the Salem trials is somewhat different from that of the victims of the investigations of the 1950's. Of course, people suffered equally in both centuries, and, while it may seem callous to weigh one anguish against another and to say that one man's suffering means more than another's, it is necessary to observe that the situation of our own time is more complex and therefore potentially more useful to the artist.

The distinction I am making is the same one that Aristotle made in our first treatise on literature, the *Poetics*. Aristotle writes that we are appalled by the suffering of the entirely blameless; such suffering, says Aristotle, is too disturbing to be a suitable subject for tragedy. Instead, we expect our tragic characters to exhibit some weakness, some sort of flaw. Scholars have disagreed for centuries as to the kind of flaw that Aristotle meant, but it is safe to say that the tragic hero is somehow imperfect and that his imperfection has some connection with his tragic catastrophe.

The unfortunate condemned innocents of Salem did nothing to bring on their ruin, nothing, at least, that had anything to do with the charge against them. Let me qualify that statement: it is conceivable that one aged eccentric or another actually thought she was in communication with the devil. That delusion is too special—not to say too lunatic—to be a very likely, interesting, or useful state of mind for a serious character. Miller seems to be of this opinion, since the only person in *The Crucible* who believes herself to be a witch is Tituba, who is not fully developed as a character and remains a minor figure. Furthermore, she confesses and is not executed; she need not suffer any pangs of conscience over her presumed witchcraft. If she thinks she has been a witch, she must also think she has atoned by confessing. The others, the true martyrs of Salem, had the consolation of knowing that they were innocent. Certainly, they were heroic in maintaining their innocence at a time when false confession was likely to save their lives. But to be heroic is not necessarily to be the complex, dramatic character who gives life to drama.

The events of the 1950's provided a more logical connection between character and fate. The American Communist Party existed, and, for a long time, its legality was unquestioned. It was perfectly possible and legal to join it—for any of a variety of reasons, both good and bad—for idealistic reasons, out of a desire for power, out of an instinctive interest in conspiracy, out of a general dissatisfaction with society, or even, as many later said, in order to offer effective opposition to Fascism. It was possible for many, like Miller himself, to have some association with Communism and Communists without joining the party. Great numbers of those accused in the 1950's came from the ranks of these party members and their non-member "fellow traveller" associates. Still others among the accused had no connection with the Communist Party; for the purposes of our comparison, they are exactly like the innocent victims of the Salem trials.

I have set up these elementary categories in order to demonstrate that the actor or director who was blacklisted and so lost his job in the 1950's was likely to have made some commitment in the 1930's that affected his subsequent fate. This was not necessarily so, but it was likely. He had not made a commitment to Satan, and few will now say that such a man deserved to be banished from his profession because of his past or present politics, but, in his case, we can say that character and fate roughly, very roughly, fit together, that there is a meaningful connection between what the man did and what later happened to him. Life is not always so logical, as the Salem trials tell us. The witchcraft trials in Salem were wild, unreasonable offenses against justice; they present intrinsic difficulties for any dramatist who wants to make an orderly drama out of them. Art tends to be neater and, superficially, more logical than the history of Salem. In contrast, the corresponding events of the 1950's have a cruel and inaccurate logic;

their injustice is, in a sense, logical, even though the logic is reprehensible.

If we were not able to point out that the historical parallel in *The Crucible* is imperfect, we might still justifiably object that the impact of a sudden and undeserved punishment upon entirely innocent people is a difficult subject for drama. Aristotle's criticism of the entirely blameless hero continues to be valid. In apparent recognition of this principle, Miller has constructed a new sort of guilt for his hero, John Proctor. In the play, Proctor has been unfaithful to his wife, and Miller goes out of his way to assure us directly that his infidelity violates his personal code of behavior. The girl whom he loved, jealous and resentful of being rejected, accuses Proctor's wife of witchcraft, and so Proctor, who has, in this peculiar fashion, caused his wife to be accused, has a special obligation to save her. In trying to save her, he is himself charged with witchcraft. So, he does suffer for his guilt—but for a different guilt, for adultery, not for witchcraft.

But it must be remembered that a play is not merely an exercise in ideas or even in characterization. It is a creation that moves forward in time, catching interest and creating suspense. While the historical context is useful to any preliminary understanding of a play, any full understanding and any proper evaluation must follow a close look at its plot. The plot presents to us an ebb and flow of argument and incident, an alternation of crises, turning, in *The Crucible,* about the issue of witchcraft.

The Crucible begins with a crisis, a moment of excitement that shows the false witnesses in full cry—one child on stage and another of whom we are told, both of them displaying the different but equally convincing symptoms of demonic possession. We note a number of fatuous adult responses to the children's behavior, and then the adults conveniently leave the stage to the children, who effectively clear up any mysteries by frankly discussing their deceitful actions. They incidentally, and very usefully, provide us with Abigail's special motive, her jealous hatred of Elizabeth Proctor. Directly upon this cue, John Proctor enters, and, perhaps a bit improbably revealing too many intimate secrets in the presence of a child feigning possession, he and Abigail tell us most of what we need to know about their love affair and its present consequences. In quick succession, then, we have seen the central disorder of the play, demonic possession, and the explanation for it; in the children's malice, we have also noted a particular form of malice that is to breed results to come—Abigail's jealousy. The main exposition has been effected, and the main lines of action are ready.

At once the skeptic, Proctor, clashes with Parris, the believer in witchcraft. The argument between the skeptical and the credulous, and the ensuing effort to convince the community dominate all of the play. Like other works by Miller, *The Crucible* has something of the quality of a trial, of a court case, even before the formal hearings begin. Throughout, the exponents of both views are arguing their cases, making their points, and, inadvertently, revealing their real motives. Proctor and Parris now engage in just such a dispute, showing us their own personal hostility and helpfully bringing in some additional exposition

concerning the land war, the rivalry over ministerial appointments, and the issue of Parris's salary. These are the real, underlying issues that motivate the men of Salem.

Once the local prejudices have been established, we have reached the appropriate moment for the arrival of the guileless outsider, the idealistic seeker of witches, John Hale. In theory, Hale is perfectly equipped to combat witchcraft, and he even enters carrying visible evidence of his qualifications, the heavy books that have enlightened him. In practice, he is as helpless as a child, much more helpless than the children of the play. He is totally unequipped, precisely because he is an outsider with a load of irrelevant academic knowledge, precisely because he has missed the informative conversations that just precede his entrance. He has pursued the wrong study; instead of demonology, he should have applied himself to economics, the psychopathology of children, and eavesdropping. Hale is the simple, eager man of good will, the human *tabula rasa* upon whom the experience of the play will write. His simplicity makes him the ideal audience for the wholesale charges of witchcraft that begin to be made as the curtain falls upon the first act. As we should expect, these charges proceed inevitably from the circumstances that the previous action has painstakingly interpreted.

After some preliminary exposition of the cool relationship between John Proctor and his wife, the second act provides, in order, Elizabeth Proctor's interrogation of her husband, the Proctors' joint interrogation of Mary Warren, and, finally, the real goal of the scene—Hale's examination of the Proctors. One incidental effect of this repeated use of courtroom technique is to show us that Elizabeth Proctor's justice to her husband is as lacking in mercy and understanding as the public justice of Salem. The crime of adultery that Elizabeth continues to probe and to worry over has already been adequately punished and repented for, but Elizabeth will never permit herself to forget it.

Following the troubled exchange between the Proctors comes the only courtroom procedure that brings out the truth, the Proctors' joint examination of Mary Warren. A suitable rigor on the part of the questioners and the threat of a whipping bring the whole truth out of her fast enough. Then Hale takes the initiative, less successfully. He is a sufficiently experienced investigator to hunt out a crime, but, without knowing it, he has found the wrong crime— adultery, not witchcraft. He causes Proctor to miss the seventh commandment and evidently takes that failure as a sign of the man's general impiety when it is really a sort of Freudian slip, an unwilling confession of his infidelity. In addition, Hale rightly sniffs out the general atmosphere of guilt and notes "some secret blasphemy that stinks to Heaven." He is responding to the chilly atmosphere that Elizabeth Proctor maintains and to the shame that it produces in John Proctor. His suspicion has an ironically appropriate result: it is Elizabeth herself who is the victim of her own heavy insistence on the reality of guilt. In a sense, Hale is right to arrest her. She is guilty of pharisaism, which is a more serious charge than witchcraft or adultery, and Miller gives the unmistakable impression that he considers pharisaism a very serious offense indeed. (Pharisiasm appears again and is again made to seem obnoxious in a later play of Miller's, *After the Fall,* where it is once more the trait of a wife whose husband has been unfaithful.)

The third act revolves about John Proctor's effort to save his wife; when the accusation is at last directed against him, the principal forward action of the play has come to an end. The charges of witchcraft have begun by hitting out blindly in all directions, but then, in accordance with the painstaking preparations that informed us of Abigail's jealousy of Elizabeth, the accusations fix upon Elizabeth. Proctor tries to reverse them by charging Abigail with adultery, but, in consequence, he is himself accused of witchcraft. Up to this time, slander has been spreading in all directions, attaching itself at random to one innocent victim after another, but now it finds its true and proper target. The real, the ultimate victim in this play is John Proctor, the one independent man, the one skeptic who sees through the witchcraft "craze" from the first. As if instinctively, in self-defense, the witchcraft epidemic has attacked its principal enemy. This is a climactic moment, a turning point in the play. New witches may continue to be named, but *The Crucible* now narrows its focus to John Proctor, caught in the trap, destroyed by his effort to save his wife, threatened by the irrationality that only he has comprehended.

The third act has an incidental function; it is climactic for Hale as well as for Proctor. Hale first appears as a zealous specialist; in the second act, he is shown going industriously about his work; in the third act, shaken by the obvious injustice of what he has brought to pass, he denounces the hearings. That is the crucial step for him, and, from that moment, his personal drama does not take any new direction, just as the general development of the play takes no distinctive new steps following these turning points for Proctor and Hale.

In addition, the third act is a carefully organized unit of argument and counterargument. Concerned to protect their authority, the judges promise a long period of safety for Elizabeth Proctor, and, when this stratagem fails, they start bullying the turncoat Mary Warren. Proctor counterattacks with the same low tactics that his enemies use— charging Abigail, the primary accuser, with the crimes that do her reputation the most damage; they are specifically anti-Puritan crimes, laughing during prayer and dancing. These are curious accusations from a skeptic, but he is learning, too late, to play his enemies' game. Abigail responds by attributing witchcraft to Mary Warren. This give-and-take continues when Proctor calls out "Whore! Whore!" After three acts of fencing, the real truth is out; the burden of establishing it rests with the one person whose truthfulness can be fully guaranteed—Elizabeth Proctor. All attention goes to her as she is asked the critical question. And, for once, in a moment of high excitement and suspense, this model of truthfulness lies because she values something more than the truth—her husband's good name.

The value Salem attributes to a good name has been indicated previously in the play; it becomes critically important in the last act. From the beginning, Salem has been presented as a community in which mutual evaluation is a generally popular activity. Prying, slander, and recrimination are unpleasant but persuasive testimonials to the value that attaches to a good name. Living in this environment and sharing its values, Elizabeth Proctor must value reputation even more than truth. This decision has disastrous results, for Mary Warren, facing serious punishment as a turncoat and possible witch, must defend herself by making a new charge—against the man who got her into this sorry mess, John Proctor. The path of the accusations has been circuitous, but Proctor is, in effect, being punished for his hostility to Salem's obsession with sin—in particular, his wife's obsession with adultery and the community's obsession with witchcraft. We may suspect a tacit hint that the two fixations are closely linked.

In the last act, public opinion has shifted: Andover is in revolt, even Parris is shaken, and more pressure is being applied to obtain confessions. Proctor can be saved only by a dishonest confession to witchcraft. Life is sufficiently dear for him to make the confession, but he will not let it become a public document. The issue is, once again, his good name. Previously preferred over truth, his good name is now preferred to life itself. This issue seems now to dominate the play, but, as we have observed, it has been prominent throughout, for accusations of witchcraft are harmful to the reputation as well as to the individual life. The citizens of Salem have been concerned with scoring points against one another, with establishing their own superior virtue and the depraved character of their enemies. To use the word "depraved" is to remind ourselves that this state of affairs is well suited to the Puritan theology, which held that divine election was the one balm for innate human depravity. Reputation served as an indispensable guide to the state of grace, for it was an outward sign of election. As a result, Proctor is not only expressing a characteristically modern concern for his good name, a concern equally important to the twentieth-century protagonist of Miller's next full-length play, *A View from the Bridge;* he is exhibiting a typically Puritan state of mind.

Proctor dies, then, for his good name; but to return to the troubling issue, his good name was not, in the most serious sense, threatened by the charges brought against him. His good name was, in fact, being threatened by his fear of death and by his knowledge of his own adultery, but it was shaken only in the most superficial way by the charge of witchcraft. Proctor is not merely innocent; he is *an* innocent, and his guilt as an adulterer is irrelevant, except insofar as it supplies Abigail with her motive for slandering his wife. We can see why Proctor's adultery had to be invented; surely it came into existence because Miller found himself compelled to acknowledge the Aristotelian idea that the blameless, unspotted hero is an inadequate protagonist for a serious play.

This problem may be further illuminated by reference to some of Miller's other works. In his first two Broadway successes, a relatively unsullied hero (played in each case by an actor named Arthur Kennedy) is present, but he does not have the leading role. The chief character in each of these plays, *All My Sons* and *Death of a Salesman,* is a guilty older man, who has lived by the wrong values. In this last respect at least, he resembles Hale of *The Cruci-*

ble, but he is more complex and more serious. Now, however, in **The Crucible,** the younger, unsullied hero (again played in the original production by Arthur Kennedy) moves into the foreground. Of course, Proctor is deeply conscious of his infidelity to his wife, but this fact does not affect his fundamental freedom from guilt; in a sense, he is unsullied, significantly less guilty than the sinful older men of the earlier plays. We are obviously expected to apply a modern "psychological" judgment to him and say that he was driven to adultery by a cold wife and by the irresistible attraction of the conscienceless girl who seduced him. Abigail is not made "a strikingly beautiful girl" (in the stage directions) for nothing. We must exonerate Proctor, just as we are required to exonerate a similar character in a later play by Miller, another man who stands between a cold, complaining wife and an irresistible child-woman—Quentin in **After the Fall** (Eddie Carbone in **A View from the Bridge** is another married man fascinated by a child-woman, but he is exonerated in another way: he is "sick.")

Miller expresses regret, in the Introduction to his **Collected Plays,** that he failed to make his villains sufficiently wicked; he thinks now that he should have represented them as being dedicated to evil for its own sake. I suspect that most students of **The Crucible** will feel that he has made them quite wicked enough. For one thing, he has established their depravity by inserting a number of clear references to the investigators and blacklisters of his own time. He has made Proctor ask, significantly: "Is the accuser always holy now?" To the automatic trustworthiness of accusers he has added the advantage of confession (always efficacious for former Communists), the necessity of naming the names of fellow-conspirators, the accusation of "an invisible crime" (witchcraft—or a crime of thought), the dangers threatening anyone who dares to defend the accused, the prejudice of the investigators, the absence of adequate legal defense for the accused, and the threat that those who protest will be charged with contempt of court. Most of these elements constitute what might be called a political case against the accusers and especially against the magistrates, Danforth and Hawthorne. Miller builds an economic case as well, suggesting that the original adult instigators of the witchcraft trials were moved by greed, particularly by a desire for the victims' lands. The whole case is stated only in Miller's accompanying notes, but much of it is given dramatic form.

The viciousness of the children, except for Abigail, is less abundantly explained. We are evidently to assume that when they make their false charges they are breaking out of the restrictive forms of proper, pious, Puritan behavior to demand the attention that every child requires. The same rebelliousness has led them to dance in the moonlight and to join in Tituba's incantations. The discovery of these harmless occupations has led then to their more destructive activity. Curiously, Miller chooses not to show us any good children—a category to which the Proctors' offspring surely belong. We hear of "Jonathan's trap" for rabbits, but these children are as absolutely banished from the stage as the protagonists' children in Shaw's **Candida.** Most modern dramatists are less self-conscious about presenting children than Shaw was, but Miller makes a simi-

lar omission in **After the Fall.** At a climactic moment, Quentin is confronted with his written statement that the only person in the world whom he has ever loved is his daughter, and yet this child is never seen in the play.

Over against the bad individual, the vengeful adults, and the lying children, Miller sets the basically sound community, in which the saintly Rebecca Nurse's benefactions are known even to the stranger Hale. At best, Salem is a bad, quarrelsome place; the good community is more warmly depicted in Miller's earlier plays, but even in Salem it exists, and it furnishes twenty honest souls who will not confess to witchcraft, even to save their lives. The underlying presence of the good community, however mis-ruled it may be, reminds us that Miller, even in face of his own evidence, professes to believe in the basic strength and justice of the social organism, in the possibility of good neighbors. If he criticizes society, he does so from within, as a participant and a believer in it.

The deliberately antique language surely reflects Miller's self-consciousness regarding his emphatically heroic hero and the extreme situation in which he finds himself. Issues are never made so clear, so black and white in any of Miller's other plays. And so, naturally, the statement of these issues must be colored, must be, to use Bertolt Brecht's term, "alienated" by quaint, unfamiliar ways of speech. Certainly, the peculiar speech of **The Crucible** is not a necessity, even in a play set in the seventeenth century. (Christopher Fry's fifteenth-century Englishmen in **The Lady's Not for Burning** speak a language closer to our own.) The purpose of the quirkish English of **The Crucible** is not only to give the impression of an antique time, although that is part of it; the purpose is to alienate us, to make us unfamiliar in this setting, to permit distance to lend its enchantment to this bare, simplistic confrontation of good and evil, and also to keep us from making too immediate, too naive an identification between these events and the parallel happenings of our own time. The issues are too simple, much more simple than the modern parallels. Language imposes a necessary complexity from without.

Any final comment must dwell upon **The Crucible** as a play of action and suspense. It falls short as a play of ideas, which is what it was originally intended to be. It falls short because the parallels do not fit and because Miller has had to adulterate—the pun is intentional—Proctor's all too obvious innocence to create a specious kind of guilt for him; he is easily exonerated of both crimes, the real one and the unreal one, so easily that no ideas issue from the crucible of this human destiny. And yet, **The Crucible** keeps our attention by furnishing exciting crises, each one proceeding logically from its predecessor, in the lives of people in whom we have been made to take an interest. That is a worthy intention, if it is a modest one, and it is suitably fulfilled. (pp. 139-46)

Henry Popkin, "Arthur Miller's 'The Crucible'," in College English, *Vol. 26, No. 2, November, 1964, pp. 139-46.*

Sheila Huftel (essay date 1965)

[*In the following excerpt, Huftel provides an overview of* The Crucible *and assesses critical response to the play.*]

Cry *witch!* The Salem witch-hunt marked a time when "long-held hatreds of neighbors could now be openly expressed, and vengeance taken, despite the Bible's charitable injunctions. Land-lust . . . could now be elevated to the arena of morality; one could cry witch against one's neighbor and feel perfectly justified in the bargain. Old scores could be settled on a plane of heavenly combat between Lucifer and the Lord."

Its climate of terror is the first we know of [*The Crucible*]. The slave Tituba's initial fright is followed by the Reverend Parris' fear—and the fear is of witchcraft. He has discovered some girls "dancing like heathen in the forest," and, shaken, he tells his niece Abigail (who led them) what he saw: "I saw Tituba . . . and I heard a screeching and gibberish coming from her mouth. She were swaying like a dumb beast over that fire!" In the shock of discovery a child has fallen sick, and the town leaps to cry witchcraft. Abigail, to escape whipping, embraces the excuse, and in the general hysteria vengeance breaks out.

Fear and guilt were in the air of Salem, heightened by the prim order of life. Children were regarded as young adults. "They never conceived that the children were anything but thankful for being permitted to walk straight, eyes slightly lowered, arms at the sides, and mouths shut until bidden to speak." Once this rigidity was broken the people found themselves prey to fantastic terrors never felt before. Ann Putnam, "a twisted soul of forty-five, a death-ridden woman, haunted by dreams," chillingly confesses to sending her young daughter Ruth to conjure up the dead and discover who murdered her brothers and sisters—all of whom had died at birth. Avidly the neighbors gather to inquire into Betty Parris' strange illness. "How high did she fly?" Complacently they assure one another that "the Devil's touch is heavier than sick." The fear in the Reverend Parris is greater than in all the rest. He will be hounded out of Salem for the witchcraft discovered in his house. He always feared for something, and now he fears his neighbors. It is as though a people suddenly turned savage. He expects to be turned out, and believes the people would be justified, since in his own eyes he is already tainted with the Devil.

The superstitions of the townspeople breed greater terror, and Abigail, quick to take advantage, warns her friends: "Let either of you breathe a word, or the edge of a word . . . and I will come to you in the black of some terrible night and I will bring a pointy reckoning that will shudder you. And you know I can do it; I saw the Indians smash my dear parents' heads on the pillow next to mine, and I have seen some reddish work done at night, and I can make you wish you had never seen the sun go down!" Abigail has been drinking blood, a charm to kill John Proctor's wife.

Abigail was a servant in the Proctors' house and loved John, until Elizabeth found them out and dismissed her. Now Abigail admits to him that Betty's sickness has nothing to do with witchcraft. Proctor is one of Miller's ten-feet-tall individualists, a farmer of unshakable integrity and dangerous directness. "I may speak my heart, I think." Putnam accuses him at once of being against Parris and against all authority. Proctor has no patience with Parris and complains that he preaches only hell-fire and forgets to mention God. He sees the man's weakness—a vacillation based on fear that makes it impossible for him to tell his parishioners they are wrong about witchcraft. Instead, he goes along with the mounting superstition and sends for Reverend Hale to discover whether or not there are witches in Salem. This opens the way for demonology to replace law.

For Hale, diabolism is a precise science that has nothing to do with superstition. But by the nature of his belief he could not be immune to the cry of "Spirits!" The shock of Abigail's attack on Tituba releases the hysteria and convinces Hale. Tituba is accused of conspiring with the Devil and a desperate bewilderment breaks upon her. She knows nothing but the terror, and understands nothing but that she will hang. Panic prompts a confession she does not know how to make. She gropes for a placating answer and out of this recounts promises made to her by the Devil: "You work for me, Tituba, and I make you free! I give you pretty dress to wear, and put you way high up in the air, and you gone fly back to Barbados!" It will not serve. Almost hypnotized, she gives names suggested by Putnam. Startlingly, Abigail joins Tituba's confession with her own and in an orgy of relief Betty feverishly joins in the random calling out of names. Blasted with ecstasy, the children cry out as if possessed, and the climate is created that makes witch-hunting possible.

Against this background Miller etches the Proctors' bleak relationship. Proctor describes Elizabeth as having an everlasting funeral marching round her heart. They live in isolation, while above them both tower the tremendous values by which they live.

In Salem a court has been set up to try and hang those accused of witchcraft, if they will not confess. Abigail has been elevated to sainthood. "Where she walks the crowd will part like the sea for Israel. And folks are brought before them, and if they scream and howl and fall to the floor—the person's clapped in jail for bewitchin' them." Proctor's servant, Mary Warren, returns with the news that the fourteen arrested have grown to thirty-nine, and that Goody Osburn will hang. Mary, a frightened, lonely girl, danced with the others and preens herself on being an official of the Court. Alarmed herself at its wonders, and alarming them, she explains how witchcraft is proved. "But then—then she sit there, denying and denying, and I feel a misty coldness climbin' up my back, and the skin on my skull begin to creep, and I feel a clamp around my neck and I cannot breathe air; and then—I hear a voice, a screamin' voice, and it were my voice—and all at once I remembered everything she done to me!"

Proctor is about to whip her when she yells that she saved Elizabeth's life that day. While Mary strives precariously for self-respect, Elizabeth realizes that Abigail wants her dead, and will cry out her name until she is taken.

The Reverend Hale interrupts this conflict. He has come

to test the Proctors' Christianity. Elizabeth cannot wait to convince him, but Proctor's guilt over Abigail makes him falter. Instead, he tells Hale of Abigail's confession that the children's sickness has nothing to do with witchcraft. Hale reminds him of confessions made to the Court. "And why not, if they must hang for denyin' it?" Those confessions prove nothing.

Intimations of Elizabeth's arrest that began with Mary Warren's outburst are taken further when Proctor's neighbors, Corey and Nurse, come with the news that Martha and Rebecca have been taken. Rebecca is charged with the supernatural murder of Goody Putnam's babies. If she is guilty, Hale insists, "then nothing is left to stop the whole green world from burning."

They come for Elizabeth. When, in spite of her proved innocence, she still leaves Hale questioning, Proctor can bear it no longer. "Why do you never wonder if Parris be innocent, or Abigail? Is the accuser always holy now? Were they born this morning as clean as God's fingers? I'll tell you what's walking Salem—vengeance is walking Salem . . . now the little crazy children are jangling the keys of the kingdom, and common vengeance writes the law!" But Elizabeth is taken and chained, while they watch, helpless.

Proctor insists that Mary testify in court and as her fear mounts so does his conviction. "Make your peace with it! Now Hell and Heaven grapple on our backs, and all our old pretense is ripped away—make your peace! Peace. It is a providence, and no great change; we are only what we always were, but naked now. Aye, naked! And the wind, God's icy wind, will blow!"

> **The Crucible counteracts etched characters with a text full to overflowing with passion. The play is written in a powerful, mounting prose, and the height and pitch of the dramatic scenes are found nowhere else in Miller's work.**
>
> —*Sheila Huftel*

On this surge of feeling, attention turns back to the Court. Here other charges are brought. Giles Corey insists that Putnam is killing his neighbors for their land. A man whose pigs die swears that Martha Corey is bewitching them. But primarily, Mary Warren tremblingly admits that she never saw spirits. Judge Danforth cannot believe it. "I have seen marvels in this Court. I have seen people choked before my eyes by spirits; I have seen them stuck by pins and slashed by daggers." He refuses to believe that people fear this Court; if they do there is only one explanation: "There is fear in the country because there is a moving plot to topple Christ in the country!"

Proctor insists that he has not come to overthrow the Court, but to save his wife. In that case, Danforth urges him to drop the charge; Elizabeth will not be hanged because she is pregnant. Proctor finds he cannot; Corey and Nurse are his friends, and their wives are also accused. Danforth agrees to hear Mary Warren. Falteringly she insists that she is with God now and is confronted with the other children and with Abigail's denial. To prove her story, Mary is ordered to faint at will, but lacking the hysteria she cannot. Doubt rises, and out of it the children create terror. They are about to cry out Mary Warren as a witch when Proctor checks them with the truth about Abigail: "A man will not cast away his good name. You surely know that . . . I have made a bell of my honor! I have rung the doom of my good name." Elizabeth is called to confirm his accusation; she lies to save his name.

Danforth believes her. Abigail cries out Mary Warren as a witch: Mary has assumed the shape of a bird and high on a beam she stretches her claws, about to swoop down on the children and tear their faces. Only Proctor and Hale do not share in this horror. The girls scream and Mary finds herself screaming with them. She goes wild and accuses Proctor of being the Devil's man. Danforth clamors for confession.

In the midst of these wild and whirling words that seem to presage a reeling universe, Proctor warns the Judge: "For them that quail to bring men out of ignorance, as I have quailed, and as you quail now when you know in all your black hearts that this be fraud—God damns our kind especially, and we will burn, we will burn together!" Reverend Hale quits the Court.

It is the morning of Proctor's execution. Meanwhile in Salem: "There are orphans wandering from house to house; abandoned cattle bellow on the highroads, the stink of rotting crops hangs everywhere, and no man knows when the harlots' cry will end his life." Abigail has stolen all Parris' savings and disappeared. Mr. Hale has come to urge those accused to confess, as if they die he counts himself their murderer. And still Danforth refuses to postpone the hangings. "While I speak God's law, I will not crack its voice with whimpering."

Elizabeth is fetched in the hope that she will persuade Proctor to confess. Hale tries to warn her by his own example. "The very crowns of holy law I brought, and what I touched with my bright confidence, it died; and where I turned the eye of my great faith, blood flowed up. Beware, Goody Proctor—cleave to no faith when faith brings blood." To her, this remains the Devil's argument.

Now this whole issue turns on the integrity of John Proctor, on his judgment or Danforth's. Elizabeth tells him how Giles Corey died. "Great stones they lay upon his chest until he plead Aye or Nay. They say he gave them but two words. 'More weight,' he says. And died." Proctor's guilt prompts him to confess, almost as a kind of expiation. He believes that it would be fraud for him to die like a saint and besmirch the honor of those that hang. It is as though his death has to be earned.

He looks to Elizabeth for absolution, but she reminds him that her forgiveness means nothing if he cannot forgive himself. All she can do is take her share of the guilt. "Do what you will. But let none be your judge. There be no higher judge under Heaven than Proctor is!" And there is no shedding of this particular responsibility. He decides to confess, but refuses to implicate others. "Then it is proved. Why must I say it? . . . I speak my own sins; I cannot judge another. I have no tongue for it."

But Proctor cannot turn so against himself. Painfully he recants because—"I have three children—how may I teach them to walk like men in the world, and I sold my friends? . . . Because it is my name! Because I cannot have another in my life! Because I lie and sign myself to lies! Because I am not worth the dust on the feet of them that hang! How may I live without my name? I have given you my soul; leave me my name!" In Miller, a man's name is his conscience, his immortal soul, and without it there is no person left.

Proctor recants, and in the wonder that he is capable of letting himself be hanged finds self-respect. Hale begs Elizabeth: "Be his helper!—What profit him to bleed? Shall the dust praise him? Shall the worms declare his truth? Go to him, take his shame away!" Indeed it is a longed-for absolution. But the fact remains that only Proctor can absolve Proctor. "And the drums rattle like bones in the morning air."

Given the plot of the Salem witch hunt, and knowing nothing of the history books, I suspect that one would try to trace it in *The Collected Works of Edgar Allan Poe.* But where Poe would have been content with the dramatic story of a witch-hunt—sanguinary forest orgies, charms of chicken blood, the marvelous murder of babies, a destructive yellow bird, crying out and confession, torture and hangings—for Arthur Miller, it is necessary to explain why these things take place and how, in fact, people come to believe in witches.

In a commentary written for the text Miller explores the background of his play and relates it to the present. He writes that no one can know what the people's lives were like, adding definitively: "They had no novelists—and would not have permitted anyone to read a novel if one were handy." Their hard life rather than their faith protected their morals, and their passion for minding each other's business created suspicions. Their lives were rigid, and with reason because—"To the best of their knowledge the American forest was the last place on earth that was not paying homage to God. . . . They believed, in short, that they held in their steady hands the candle that would light the world. We have inherited this belief, and it has helped and hurt us."

Since they believed they were living according to God's law, they saw in change a total disruption. The theocracy had been developed to keep the people together for their better protection materially and ideologically; but the time came when the imposed order outweighed the dangers. Miller sees the witch-hunt as "a perverse manifestation of the panic which set in among all classes when the balance began to turn toward greater individual freedom." The rest of the cause is in the temperament of the people: tightly reined, fear-driven, and deeply sin-conscious. But they had no means of absolution. The witch-hunt was an opportunity for mammoth public confession, by way of accusation. Miller points out: "Social disorder in any age breeds such mystical suspicions, and when, as in Salem, wonders are brought forth from below the social surface, it is too much to expect people to hold back very long from laying on the victims with all the force of their frustrations."

The scope of *The Crucible* is wide; a general illustration of a witch-hunt and an explanation of how and why they break out. To limit it to one particular twentieth-century witch-hunt is to wear blinkers. Miller's comment is for yesterday as well as for the day after tomorrow, and not merely the here-and-now of American politics. It is surely a kind of vanity to corner-off a section of a large work, identify with it, and claim that as the subject of the whole. It cannot be overlooked that *The Crucible* is applicable to any situation that allows the accuser to be always holy, as it also is to any conflict between the individual and authority. Timeless as *An Enemy of the People,* it symbolizes all forms of heresy-hunting, religious and political.

Miller himself covers the whole field by discussing contemporary diabolism alongside Hale's belief in the Devil. He writes of the necessity of the Devil: "A weapon designed and used time and time again in every age to whip men into a surrender to a particular church or church-state." He traces the Devil's progress, from Lucifer of the Spanish Inquisition to current politics. "A political policy is equated with moral right, and opposition to it with diabolical malevolence. Once such an equation is effectively made, society becomes a congerie of plots and counterplots, and the main role of government changes from that of the arbiter to that of the scourge of God."

In answer to the criticism, and much has been made of it, that witches are an impossibility whereas Communists are a fact, Miller writes that he has no doubt people were communing with the devil in Salem. He cites as evidence Tituba's confession and the behavior of the children who were known to have indulged in sorceries. It was, incidentally, a cardinal fault in Sartre's film of the play, *Les Sorciers de Salem,* that, not believing in witches himself, he allowed none of his characters to believe in them. This uncompromising twentieth-century attitude not only robbed the film of conviction, but of an important seventeenth-century viewpoint that should have been its concern.

It may be that I have a simple mind. But if a dramatist says his play deals with the Salem witch-hunt and goes to the length of writing about it, I am inclined to believe him. By implication the play would be about general witch-hunting and by inference about McCarthyism, which happened to be the current witch-hunt. I believe the play has been distorted by trying to link the two too closely. But some American critics found the link not close enough, and charged Miller with evasion. To ignore their objections would be evasive. I admit that their greater involvement would make them more sensitive to this aspect of the play; it might also lead them to a greater prejudice.

Legendary Arthur Millers range from Lincoln figure to Left-Wing Idol. He is the distinguished American dramatist of theatrical textbooks—from Aeschylus to Arthur Miller. He is the tough American dramatist of the gossip columnist in search of a caption. He is the man whom everybody knows—until you actually want to know something about him. Then suddenly nobody knows him very well. Ken Tynan once defined him as "someone you'd expect to find as a stonemason instead of a playwright." Alongside these, set some American critics' view of evader and fellow traveler. Conflicts surge around him and controversy crowds in.

Having read Eric Bentley, and been directed by him to Robert Warshow's article, "The Liberal Conscience in *The Crucible*," in *Commentary* (March, 1953)—"the best analysis of Mr. Miller yet written"—I assumed, overhastily, that American criticism of *The Crucible* had been political rather than dramatic. I was wrong. Of seven New York papers, three saw contemporary parallels, three did not, and one found the play just a melodrama. It is significant, perhaps, that all these critics but one mentioned parallels, whether they found them or not. At worst, this was a line on how Miller was regarded, what was expected of him, and what was uppermost in the critics' minds. By way of comparison, A. V. Cookman, critic of *The Times* (London) saw Miller's anger as being directed against human stupidity in general, and thought the play was provoked by contemporary happenings in the States.

To return to the *Commentary* article, couched in the vein of "Brutus is an honorable man," Robert Warshow found in Miller a steadfast, almost selfless refusal of complexity and an assured, simple view of human behavior. This, he believed, was Miller's trump card in captivating an educated audience. An audience which demanded of its artists—and in that case presumably found in Miller—"an intelligent narrowness of mind and vision and a generalized tone of affirmation, offering not any particular insights or any particular truths, but simply the assurance that insight and truth as qualities . . . reside somehow in the various signals by which the artist and the audience have learned to recognize each other." At this point I looked back at the title to check that we were, in fact, discussing the same playwright. Warshow admitted that Mr. Miller speaks out. He did not know what Mr. Miller is speaking out about, but he is speaking out!

In short, he was being evasive, and on this point political criticism of *The Crucible* turned. Arthur Miller said that he doubted whether he should ever have tempted agony by writing a play on the subject of the Salem witch-hunt, which he knew about for many years before McCarthyism. In his own terms, could he have walked away from it? If you believe he is evasive—yes. I think this view of the play as evasive could only be taken by those who expected Miller to hold to the party line. The fellow-traveler, or at best fellow-sympathizer, angle was taken further by Eric Bentley in *The Dramatic Event* and *What Is Theatre?*; in both books he is concerned with Miller's "evasion."

In *The Dramatic Event* (1954) there is a chapter provocatively entitled, "The Innocence of Arthur Miller." It begins with lavish praise; then, while applause still sounds, Bentley conjures Kafkaesque images and reminds us that Miller's mentality is that of the "unreconstructed liberal." *The Crucible* is interpreted politically; Bentley points out that "communism" is a word used to cover the politics of

Marx, the politics of the Soviet Union, and, finally, "the activities of all liberals as they seem to illiberal illiterates." The scope of Miller's argument was limited because it was concerned only with the third use. It was Bentley's argument that the analogy between red-baiting and witch-hunting was complete only to communists. "For only to them is the menace of communism as fictitious as the menace of witches. The non-communist will look for certain reservations and provisos. In *The Crucible* there are none."

It must not be thought that Bentley was actually accusing Miller of being a Communist. Perish the thought. "Arthur Miller is the playwright of American liberal folklore." But he was accusing him of assuming a general innocence and there was no doubt that this bothered him. What he seemed to want from Miller was a sense of guilt. He took up the theme again in *What Is Theatre?*, where he found that Miller stacked the cards; that his progressivism was too close to Communism, that *A View From the Bridge* should have been written by a poet, and wasn't, and that he did not recognize any synthesis in Miller. He claims that he could never know what a Miller play is about, and in this suspects a sinister device to mislead the audience. "Mr. Miller stands accused of no disingenuousness—except when he denies the possibility of his plays meaning what at the moment he wishes them not to mean. If *The Crucible* was set in the seventeenth century so that, on convenient occasions its twentieth-century reference could be denied, then its author *was* disingenuous." Would it be ingenuous of me to say that I cannot imagine Arthur Miller doing such a thing?

Some explanation of Bentley's opinion was necessary, and he gave it in the chapter (again provocatively titled) "The Missing Communist." Lenin said: "We must be able to . . . resort to various stratagems, artifices, illegal methods, to evasion and subterfuges. . . . " Bentley takes it up—"Or was Lenin really in favor of evasion, and did certain evasions multiply in geometric progression, until for millions of men, *Communist or not,* they became standard practice. I italicize *Communist or not* because the ultimate triumph of Leninism lies in the mystification of non-communists." The chapter was not about Miller, but he was mentioned in it.

I kept returning to the fact that Bentley never directly accused Miller of being a Communist. Instead, I found a cat's cradle of words that never seemed to chime exactly with the implication behind them. I was uncertain at this point who exactly was being evasive. It seemed a reflex with Bentley that whenever he wrote about Communism Miller's name happened to occur. Bentley's view of Miller seemed to be of someone who appeared to be innocent and was not. He suggested a dualism that I would take to be outside Miller's range: that while Miller was being dishonest, he had no doubt of his own integrity. There was nothing wrong with this—except its probability. Integrity is fundamental to Miller; all his plays turn on it, and he is too aware to fool himself in this fashion. This particular view of Bentley's is incredible; it is based on a kind of double negative reasoning—nothing is as it appears, and the only thing that is, is what is not. I was reminded of the dragon Proctor said he might have in his house but nobody had ever seen it.

Howard Fast, writing in the *Daily Worker,* found that *The Crucible* was about the Rosenbergs. I suspect that critics, as well as individuals, find what they seek and tend to line up a play's meaning with their particular problem or preoccupation. The fault looms large beside the ideal of an impartial critic, who is supposed to shed his prejudices with his coat. The difficulty of living up to the old ideal has called the ideal itself into question. It has been argued, and with truth, that dynamic critics were always thoroughly prejudiced—set Hazlitt beside Lamb, or Shaw beside Max Beerbohm. The argument runs that without opinion, prejudice, and preoccupation there is no person left watching the play. Just as the play was not created in a vacuum, it cannot be judged in one. The admission follows that a criticism of a play is a personal statement from a particular individual. For this reason, then, it is likely that the best judge of a play's meaning is the man who wrote it. He is the only person in the world who can know what he started with and what his intentions were.

The Crucible's reception was as contrary and two-headed as its criticism. On its first night, January 22, 1953, it took nineteen curtain calls, and was lightly picketed during its run.

In the general controversy roused by the play, audiences stopped short at the witch-hunt and McCarthyism and overlooked Miller's point. He explains in his Preface how the audience came to misunderstand him. Strong right-wing opinion on the first night inspired the initial confusion by making some people uneasy, afraid, and partisan. They were deflected from the play's inner theme—the handing over of conscience. Miller was concerned with the creation of terror in people, with fear cut off from reason. "The sin of public terror is that it divests man of conscience, of himself. . . . I saw accepted the notion that conscience was no longer a private matter but one of state administration. I saw men handing conscience to other men and thanking other men for the opportunity of doing so." Miller was seeing the witch-hunt from the inside and trying to increase awareness of why it had happened; what exactly prompted that terror that made the rest possible? The audience was looking at it from the outside, more eager to apply it generally to their lives than to understand the questions it raised.

"It was not only the rise of 'McCarthyism' that moved me," he wrote in his Preface, "but something which seemed much more weird and mysterious. It was the fact that a political, objective, knowledgeable campaign from the far Right was capable of creating not only a terror, but a new subjective reality, a veritable mystique which was gradually assuming even a holy resonance. . . . The terror in these people was being knowingly planned and consciously engineered, and yet . . . all they knew was terror. That so interior and subjective an emotion could have been so manifestly created from without was a marvel to me. It underlines every word in *The Crucible.*"

It seemed to Miller that, apart from self-preservation and fear of being exiled by society, social compliance is the result of a sense of guilt that people conceal by conforming. Believing guilt to be the mainspring of terror, *The Crucible* goes further than *All My Sons* and *Death of a Salesman,* which stop at its discovery. In *The Crucible* Miller suggests that it is possible to be aware beyond the point at which guilt begins. Proctor's guilt over Abigail did not blind him to the play-acting of the children and his own innocence of witchcraft. For Miller, guilt has changed from something impenetrable to "a betrayer, possibly the most real of our illusions, but nevertheless a quality of mind capable of being overthrown" [Preface to the *Collected Plays*].

The Salem witch-hunt was a subject ready-made for Miller's preoccupations in the early fifties. The handing over of conscience seemed to be the central fact of the time in Salem. In addition, the individual's abdication in favor of a higher authority was prompted by guilt rampant.

Miller discovered from the Court records that Abigail Williams, a child of eleven, sometime a servant in Proctor's house, cried out Elizabeth as a witch. Uncharacteristically, the child refused to incriminate John Proctor. He was a liberal-minded farmer, ahead of his time in that he insisted the trials were a fake. Miller writes in his Preface: "The central impulse for writing . . . was not the social but the interior psychological question, which was the question of that guilt residing in Salem which the hysteria merely unleashed, but did not create. . . . " Therefore, Miller says, "the structure reflects that understanding, and it centers on John, Elizabeth, and Abigail" [Preface to the *Collected Plays*].

Encouraged by the overpowering feeling of the time, part of the confusion over *The Crucible* arose through a general love of categories that opposed Miller's love of synthesis. Once again it proves that plays should not be categorized any more than people. Through the controversy his plays spark off the fact remains that that Miller is a straightforward, factual, and direct dramatist. If I have made him seem tortuous, the fault is mine and not his. A playwright lives by the amount of thought and feeling he can inspire, and traceless plays are like faceless people.

Taking up the running battle of *The Crucible,* it seems as though nothing about it escaped conflict. In spite of the play's success, its every aspect brings Miller squarely up against his critics and his audience. The play was to center on John, Elizabeth, and Abigail. Critics found the character-drawing abstract and accused Miller of replacing people by types, the easier to prove his thesis. Walter Kerr protested unassailably: "It is better to make a man than to make a point." This was cited as the play's main dramatic fault. But Miller was drawn to the people of Salem by their moral size and overwhelming values. Theirs was a society that believed it had found the right way to live and to die. Both prosecution and defense could speak in the name of colossal life values which "often served to raise this swirling and ludicrous mysticism to a level of high moral debate; and it did this despite the fact that most of the participants were unlettered, simple folk." These values are something our society has lost, and a search for them is inherent in all Miller's work.

But the reasons for the disappointment of critics and audience alike is altogether more personal, based on habit and conditioned expectation. Miller says: "The society of Salem was 'morally' vocal. People then avowed principles, sought to live by them and die by them. . . . I believe that the very moral awareness of the play and its characters—which are historically correct—was repulsive to the audience." Because of Miller's driving need to know *why*—his first and last question—the way people think is as important to him as the way they feel. It is this that dictates his move away from subjectivism to greater self-awareness in *The Crucible.* The flaw complained of in Willy Loman was corrected in John Proctor, and, for many reasons, prompted greater dissatisfaction. As Miller points out, audiences and critics alike are conditioned to subjectivism and for this reason found more common ground with Willy, regardless of the period of the play. The character was altogether more graspable to them. An audience will more readily accept a character governed by feeling, like Willy Loman, than one who cannot help thinking aloud, attracted to analysis, like John Proctor or Quentin. Their awareness seems to make them at once remote and detached. Audiences, for the present, tend to walk away from it, primarily because they are less interested in knowing *why* than is Arthur Miller.

Where Miller is interested in causes, the audience cares only for results. Rightly, Miller presupposes: "But certainly the passion of knowing is as powerful as the feeling alone." Only to find that there is nothing certain about it. His passion for awareness is not new. Shaw had it, so did Brecht. What *is* new is Miller's insistence that subjectivism's higher stage is not self-awareness, but a synthesis of feeling and awareness.

In *The Crucible* the synthesis Miller has in mind lies more in the play as a whole than in his characters. It is not achieved in a single character until Quentin in *After the Fall. The Crucible* counteracts etched characters with a text full to overflowing with passion. The play is written in a powerful, mounting prose, and the height and pitch of the dramatic scenes are found nowhere else in Miller's work. This particular balance held between play and character is necessary. Without it and with more subjective character-drawing the play could easily collapse into chaos. The second problem solved by this balance is that of "remoteness" in an aware character who, from the audience's point of view, thinks too much. Spare character-drawing is not new for Miller; with his minor characters he has always told you precisely what you need to know of them and nothing more. Here the technique extends from Giles and Rebecca to John and Elizabeth. But this leanness does not make the agony of John Proctor's outbursts any less real. A character does not become unreal because he speaks only those lines that will define him. To assume that he does is to confuse realism with naturalism. The width between the two is no more than a razor's edge, but the difference is basic. (pp. 124-43)

Sheila Huftel, in her Arthur Miller: The Burning Glass, *The Citadel Press, 1965, 256 p.*

Philip G. Hill   (essay date December 1967)

[*Hill is an American educator and critic. In the following essay, he responds to negative assessments of* The Crucible *and analyzes the play's structure.*]

The Crucible is too often spoken of as one of Arthur Miller's less successful plays. Its relative merits as compared with *Death of a Salesman* need not be argued here, but unquestionably the calumny that has been heaped upon it by well-meaning critics is little deserved—the play, however short it may fall of being *the* great American drama, is nevertheless a thoroughly successful, provocative, and stimulating theater piece. When competently performed, it can provide a deeply moving experience for the theatergoer.

The criticism of George Jean Nathan is perhaps typical. Nathan levels four principal charges at the play [in *The Theatre in the Fifties,* 1953], charges that in one form or another have been brought against it again and again by other critics. Nathan at least speaks from the advantageous position of having seen the play performed in New York, but too often it appears that wild charges are being flung at the play by critics who have never seen it staged—who have tried, perhaps inexpertly, to capture its full effectiveness from the printed page. This is a hazardous procedure at best, and in the case of *The Crucible* it has led to some gross distortions of what the play says and what it does. Let us examine each of Nathans' four charges and attempt to measure the validity of each.

In the first place, Nathan maintains that the power of the play is all "internal," that it is not communicated to an audience. If we take this criticism to imply that the action occurs within the mind and soul of the protagonist, then of course the statement that the play's power is internal is accurate, but that this in any sense damns the play is belied by the large number of plays throughout dramatic literature that have their action so centered and that are regarded as masterpieces. Most of the plays of Racine can be cited at once in support of this contention, together with selected plays of Euripides, Shakespeare, and Goethe, to name but a few. That *The Crucible* does not communicate this power to an audience is an allegation regarding which empirical evidence is lacking, but the long lines at the box offices of most theaters that have produced it since it "failed" on Broadway constitute, at least in part, a refutation of the charge. At one recent production of which the writer has first-hand knowledge, all previous attendance records were broken, and experienced theatergoers among the audience testified that they had enjoyed one of the rare and memorable theatrical experiences of their lives. This hardly describes a play that fails to communicate its power to the audience, whatever the quality of the production may have been.

The second charge brought by Nathan against *The Crucible,* and one that is almost universally pressed by those who are dissatisfied with the play, is that it suffers from poor character development. To this charge even the most vehement of its supporters must, in all justice, admit some truth. Elizabeth Proctor is a Puritan housewife, an honest woman, and a bit straight-laced; beyond this we know little of her. John Proctor is an upright and honest farmer confronted by a challenge to his honesty; more can and will be said of the struggles within his soul, but the fact remains that the multifaceted fascination of a Hamlet, an Oedipus, or even of a Willy Loman is indeed lacking. Danforth, on the other hand, is an all-too-recognizable human being: not at all the embodiment of all that is evil, but a conflicting mass of selfish motives and well-intentioned desires to maintain the status quo; not the devil incarnate, but a man convinced that a "good" end (maintaining the theocracy in colonial Massachusetts) can justify the most dubious means—in this case, the suborning of witnesses, the twisting of evidence, and the prostitution of justice. Reverend Hale, too, is a well developed and many-faceted character, a man who arrives upon the scene confident of his power to exorcise the Devil in whatever form he may appear, and who by the end of the play can challenge every value for which a hero ever died: "Life is God's most precious gift; no principle, however glorious, may justify the taking of it."

Still, it must be admitted that the principal power of *The Crucible* does not lie in its character development. The characters are entirely adequate for the purposes for which Miller designed them, and no immutable law requires that every play depend upon characterization for its success, but certainly there is some justice in suggesting that *The Crucible* exhibits only a moderate degree of character development.

Nathan's next point of criticism is one that was heard from many of the New York critics at the time of the play's original production, but that has ceased to have much potency since the McCarthy era has passed into history. It was loudly proclaimed in 1953 that *The Crucible* was essentially propagandistic, that it struck too hard at an isolated phenomenon, and that thus it was at best a play of the immediate times and not for all time. The thirteen years that have passed since this charge was leveled, and the continued success of the play both in this country and abroad in the interim, drain from the assertion all of the efficacy that it may once have appeared to have. From the short view inescapably adopted by critics themselves caught up in the hysteria of McCarthyism, the play may well have seemed to push too hard the obvious parallels between witch-hunting in the Salem of 1692 and "witch-hunting" in the Washington and New York of 1952. If so, then we have simply one more reason to be grateful for the passing of this era, for unquestionably the play no longer depends upon such parallels. A whole generation of theater-goers has grown up in these intervening years to whom the name McCarthy is one vaguely remembered from newspaper accounts of the last decade, and who nevertheless find in *The Crucible* a powerful indictment of bigotry, narrow-mindedness, hypocrisy, and violation of due process of law, from whatever source these evils may spring. Unquestionably, if the play were tied inextricably to its alleged connection with a political phenomenon now buried (a connection that Miller denied all along), it would even today not have a very meaningful effect upon its audiences. And yet it does.

The fourth charge against the play, and the one brought by the more serious and insightful of the critics dealing with *The Crucible,* is at the same time the most challenging of the four. For Nathan, together with a host of other critics, attacks the basic structure of the play itself, claiming that it "draws up its big guns" too early in the play, and that by the end of the courtroom scene there is nowhere to go but down. This charge, indeed, gets at the very heart of the matter, and if it can be sustained it largely negates further argument regarding any relative merits that the play might exhibit. I submit, however, that the charge cannot be sustained—that, indeed, the critics adopting such an approach reveal a faulty knowledge of the play's structure and an inaccurate reading of its meaning. Indeed, Miller appears to me to have done a masterful job of sustaining a central action that by its very nature is "internal" and thus not conducive to easy dramatic development, and of sustaining this central action straight through to its logical conclusion at the end of the play.

The term "central action" is being used here in what I take to be its Aristotelian sense: one central objective that provides the play's plot structure with a beginning, a middle, and an end; when the objective is attained, the play is over. This central action may be described in the case of *The Crucible* as "to find John Proctor's soul," where the term "soul" is understood to mean Proctor's integrity, his sense of self-respect, what he himself variously calls his "honesty" and (finally) his "name." Proctor lost his soul, in this sense of the term, when he committed the crime of lechery with Abigail, and thus as the play opens there is wanted only a significant triggering incident to start Proctor actively on the search that will lead ultimately to his death. That this search for Proctor's soul will lead through the vagaries of a witch-hunt, a travesty of justice, and a clear choice between death and life without honor is simply the given circumstance of the play—no more germane to defining its central action than is the fact that Oedipus' search for the killer of Laius will lead through horror and incest to self-immolation. Thinking in these terms, then, it is possible to trace the development of this central action in a straight-forward and rather elementary manner.

The structure of the play can conveniently be analyzed in terms of the familiar elements of the well-made play. The initial scenes involving Parris, Abigail, the Putnams, and the other girls serve quite satisfactorily the demands of simple exposition, and pave the way smoothly for the entrance of John Proctor. We learn quickly and yet naturally that a group of girls under Abby's leadership have conjured the Devil and that now at least two of them have experienced hysterical reactions that are being widely interpreted in terms of witchcraft. We also learn, upon Proctor's entrance, of the sexual attraction that still exists between him and Abby, and of the consummation of this attraction that has left John feeling that he has lost his soul. The inciting incident then occurs when Abby assures John that the girls' hysteria has "naught to do with witchcraft," a bit of knowledge that is very shortly to try John's honesty and lead him inevitably to his death.

The rising action of the play continues, then, through the arrival of Hale, Abby's denunciation of certain of the Puritan women (taking her cue from Tituba's success) in order to remove any taint of guilt from herself, and eventually, in the next scene, to the accusation of witchcraft being directed at Elizabeth Proctor. The significant point here, however, is that the rising action continues through the bulk of the courtroom scene, as horror piles upon horror, accusation upon accusation, and complication upon complication, until the action reaches not a climax but a *turning point* when Elizabeth, who purportedly cannot tell a lie, does lie in a misguided attempt to save her husband. This act on her part constitutes a turning point because, from that moment on, Proctor's doom is sealed; no device short of a totally unsatisfactory *deus ex machina* can save him from his inevitable fate. The *central action* of the play is not yet completed however; Proctor has not yet found his soul, and even moderately skillful playing of the play's final scene can demonstrate quite clearly that this struggle goes on right up to the moment at which Proctor rips up his confession and chooses death rather than dishonor. Thus, this prison scene does not, as some critics have charged, constitute some sort of extended denouement that cannot possibly live up in intensity to the excitement of the courtroom scene, but rather the scene is, in technical terms, the *falling action* of the play, moving inevitably from the turning point to the climax.

This structural significance of the prison scene may be observed in a careful reading of the play, but it is more readily apparent in a competent production. Thus, it is the business of the actor playing Proctor to convey to the audience the fact that signing the confession and then refusing to hand it over to Danforth is not, as has so often been charged, a delaying action and an anti-climactic complication on Miller's part, but rather a continuing and agonizing search on Proctor's part for his honesty—for the course of action that will be truest to his own honor and will recover for him his lost soul. In a dilemma for which there is no simple solution, Proctor first sees the efficacy of Hale's argument, that once life is gone there is no further or higher meaning. Feeling that his honesty has long since been compromised anyway, Proctor seriously feels a greater sense of dishonor is appearing to "go like a saint," as Rebecca and the others do, than in frankly facing up to his own dishonesty and saving his life. On the strength of this argument, he signs the confession. Yet, as Proctor stands there looking at his name on the paper (and here the way in which the actor works with this property becomes all-important), we have a visual, tangible stage metaphor for the struggle that is going on within him. Proctor, unable fully to express the significance of his own plight, cries out:

> Because it is my name! Because I cannot have another in my life! Because I lie and sign myself to lies! Because I am not worth the dust on the feet of them that hang! How may I live without my name? I have given you my soul; leave me my name!

The audience must see that this cry for his "name" is still the same search that has been at the heart of the entire play, and that here it has reached not some kind of anti-climax, but rather *the* climactic moment of the play.

But in stating outright that his confession is a lie (and this is the first moment at which he says so in so many words),

Proctor triggers in Danforth the one reaction that seals his own doom. For Danforth, however narrow-minded and bigoted he may be, does indeed believe in the fundamental fact of witchcraft, and he cannot allow a confession that is frankly and openly a lie:

> Is that document a lie? If it is a lie I will not accept it! What say you? I will not deal in lies, Mister! . . . You will give me your honest confession in my hand, or I cannot keep you from the rope. . . . What way do you go, Mister?

Thus stretched to the utmost on the rack of his dilemma, Proctor makes the decision that costs him his life but restores to him his soul: he tears up the confession. The denouement following this climactic moment consumes not a whole scene as has frequently been charged, but a mere twelve lines. Proctor is led out to die, and Elizabeth speaks the epitaph that once again, finally, sums up the central action and significance of the play: "He have his goodness now. God forbid I take it from him!"

Thus, a close structural view of *The Crucible* reveals that this fourth charge against it is also an unfair and inaccurate one. The play, however it may appear in the reading, does not, in performance, rise to a climax in the courtroom scene that cannot be equalled. Certainly the tension of the courtroom scene is great; certainly the prison scene, if poorly performed, could be a letdown. But in a competent performance the inevitable movement from the turning point toward a climax, technically called the "falling action" but certainly involving no falling interest or intensity, continues through the prison scene to that moment at which Proctor rips up his confession, after which a quick denouement brings us to a satisfactory, and at the same time stunning, conclusion.

The play is certainly not one of the great plays of all time. Still, it has been maligned unduly by a series of critics who apparently were either too close to their critical trees to see the theatrical forest or were relying on an inadequate understanding of the play's structure. That this structure is not immediately apparent to the reader, but rather must be brought out in performance, may suggest some degree of weakness in Miller's dramaturgy, but is certainly not a damning weakness in itself. Plays are, after all, written to be performed on a stage, and the ultimate test of their success is their effectiveness under production conditions. *The Crucible* stands up very well to this test. (pp. 312-17)

> *Philip G. Hill, " 'The Crucible': A Structural View," in* Modern Drama, *Vol. 10, No. 3, December, 1967, pp. 312-17.*

Donald Lyons   (review date January 1992)

[*In the following review, Lyons reaffirms initial negative criticism of* The Crucible, *characterizing the play as "a bad anti-Stalinist play" that fails to make what he perceives as a distinction between the fictitious nature of charges of witchcraft and the reality of communism.*]

[Miller's dramaturgy in *The Crucible*] is amazingly inept, blurring the contour of even the melodrama he wishes to create. The hero is guilty of adultery and must squirm with shame before his righteous, chilly wife; his partner in sin is the young woman who is leading the chorus of confessing and accusing witches and is apparently intending to have the hero's wife hanged for a witch. But she and a bunch of local maidens *have* been out dancing in the nude and making frog soup in the moonlight under the guidance of a voodoo priestess. So what's going on here anyway? Are the adultery and voodoo mere red (so to speak) herrings? It goes without saying (or rather would that it did) that the various Reverends and Judges and Governors who do the persecuting are venal or insane or both; but it does look, to judge from what we hear about, as if they're on to something. Hang the lot of them, I say. And then hang the hangers. . . . (p. 54)

[*The Crucible*] was, in 1953, Broadway's answer to McCarthyism, and its revival in 1991 doubtless intends a message for our day. About the inadequacy of the play to the issues of 1953, Robert Warshow in *Commentary* and Eric Bentley in *The New Republic* wrote definitively *in* 1953. Bentley, writing from the Left, saw the fundamental point:

> [T]he parallel . . . is true in that people today are being persecuted on quite chimerical grounds. It is untrue in that communism is not, to put it mildly, merely a chimera. . . . Indeed, the analogy between 'red-baiting' and witch hunting can seem complete only to communists, for only to them is the menace of communism as fictitious as the menace of witches. The noncommunist will look for certain reservations and provisos. In *The Crucible,* there are none.

(Bentley went on to make it clear he is referring not to Miller's unknown actual political allegiances but to his unexamined cultural assumptions.)

For all its faults in 1953, however, *The Crucible* does seem to make a new point in 1991. And it is not a point about Jesse Helms or Karen Finley or Robert Mapplethorpe. Rather, Arthur Miller, in gives the clue:

> There was no response to McCarthyism, except for *The Crucible.* And when I was attacked, I was never defended. I think that's unforgivable. At the same time, I now recognize that this was one of the blackest periods in Russia. When you had Stalin around, the magnitude of the cruelty was unmatched. You've got to be either God or the Devil to figure this out.

How much irony, how much tragic irony, is packed into that little word "now." What indeed does the cultural ambiance of *The Crucible* suggest today, with its show trials, signed confessions, conspiracies real and imagined, fanatical and irrational theology, murdering careerist bureaucracy, personal vendettas masquerading behind ideological correctitude, mass hangings, smuggling in of taboo music from abroad, joyless grimness of life, and so on? Salem in 1692? New York or Los Angeles in 1953? Or . . . Moscow and Prague and Budapest and Warsaw in 1953? Arthur Miller, by one of history's pranks, turns out to have written an objectively (as Marxists used to say) anti-Stalinist play. But it is a *bad* anti-Stalinist play. . . .

The matter of Salem, it is refreshing to recall, was treated by a great American artist, who wrote about it with an au-thority born of a deep knowledge of human history and the human heart. Nathaniel Hawthorne rejected persecutorial Calvinism as firmly as anyone, but saw its roots not in melodramatic villainy and heroism but in everyman's dreams and blood. "And when he had lived long, and was borne to his grave, a hoary corpse, followed by Faith, an aged woman, and children and grand-children, a goodly procession, besides neighbors, not a few, they carved no hopeful verse upon his tomb-stone; for his dying hour was gloom." Thus ends Hawthorne's "Young Goodman Brown," a small masterpiece about the terrible propinquity of Salem to the surrounding forest. Contrast Hawthorne's grim close with the smug and tinny exaltation of Miller's curtain: "He have his goodness now. God forbid I take it from him!" (p. 55)

> Donald Lyons, "Othertimes, Otherwheres," in The New Criterion, *Vol. X, No. 5, January, 1992, pp. 54-7.*

John Simon   (review date 6 January 1992)

[*An American writer and critic famous for his often acerbic theater reviews, Simon has served as a drama critic for* New York *magazine as well as a film critic for* Esquire *and* New Leader. *In the following excerpt, he faults the language of* The Crucible *as awkward and unrealistic and the characters as superficial and unconvincing.*]

The Crucible's problems are evident enough. Having proved himself bereft of a good ear for contemporary American speech in *Death of a Salesman,* Miller, in his next play, proceeded to prove an even greater lack of ear for Colonial American speech. I suppose it was only fitting, God having given him two ears to have no ear with. And there is certainly something to move you to tears upon hearing a 1692 Salem teenager say, "I only hope you will not speak so sarcastical to me no more," even if it's only a case of laughing till the tears well up. And please don't think this an isolated lapse (Puritanically speaking) from Grace; do you find "It were a grand sneeze" any better? But Miller has trouble even with basic grammar, as when the learned Reverend Hale proclaims, "God damns a liar less than he who . . . " etc.

Ah, well, what is language anyway? No more than a mere four fifths of a play. So what did Miller do with his remaining fifth? He constructed an elaborate parallel between the Salem witch-hunts and McCarthyism. For this, he was promptly accused of faulty analogy: Whereas there were no witches, Communists did exist. True, but unimportant; an analogy does not have to be total. If you say someone carries on like a bunny rabbit, it is not mandatory that the person have long ears.

The problem lies elsewhere: The numerous characters are too superficially and crudely conceived. Abigail Williams is too glaringly evil, and people who can't see through her are too perilously close to idiots. The noble (and quasi-autobiographical) John Proctor must—as everyone who has taken Playwriting 101 knows—have a tragic flaw. So Miller gives him lechery: He has had carnal knowledge of Abigail while his wife was sick. But where is Miller's artistic knowhow to make that carnal knowledge believable? Between Proctor and Abigail there is none of that love-hate that might make these ex-lovers, however mismatched and transient, complex and credible. Only Elizabeth Proctor, the wife, has some dimensionality, but even this Miller must spoil by having the tragedy hinge on a bit of dramatic irony that has DEVICE written all over it. The little white lie with which the upright Elizabeth tries to save her husband is precisely what dooms him. That little white lie has as much artistic depth as the black silk stockings that Willy Loman bestows on a hotel-room concubine, thereby sealing his family's doom.

Or take Proctor's recantation, which is both derivative (*Saint Joan*) and absurd: If a man is willing to sign a fake confession, he must expect it to be made public. You don't make Proctor either heroic or human by making him an ass. (p. 59)

> John Simon, *"Misses under the Mistletoe,"* in New York *Magazine, Vol. 25, No. 1, January 6, 1992, pp. 59-60.*

FURTHER READING

Bibliography

Hayashi, Tetsumaro. *An Index to Arthur Miller Criticism.* Rev. ed. Metuchen, N.J.: The Scarecrow Press, Inc., 1976, 151 p.
Comprehensive primary and secondary bibliography.

——. *Arthur Miller and Tennessee Williams: Research Opportunities and Dissertation Abstracts.* Jefferson, N.C.: McFarland & Company, Inc., 1983, 133 p.
Contains an extensive listing of dissertations on Miller's works and an essay citing aspects of Miller's works not yet represented in literary research.

Criticism

Atkinson, Brooks. Review of *The Crucible,* by Arthur Miller. *The New York Times* (2 July 1953): 20.
Review of a revised version of *The Crucible,* which Atkinson applauds as more humanistic and emotionally effective than the original.

Brown, John Mason. "Witch-Hunting." *Saturday Review,* New York XXXVI, No. 7 (14 February 1953): 41-2.
Faults Miller for being concerned more with ideas and contemporary parallels than with characters in *The Crucible,* but praises his choice of subject matter, commenting that the play "is about something that matters."

Duprey, Richard A. Review of *The Crucible,* by Arthur Miller. *The Catholic World* 193, No. 1158 (September 1961): 394-95.
Assesses *The Crucible* as "a perfectly valid human story written in an idiom of high dramatic intensity."

Ferres, John H., ed. *Twentieth Century Interpretations of 'The Crucible': A Collection of Critical Essays.* Englewood Cliffs, N.J.: Prentice-Hall, 1972, 122 p.
Compendium of commentary on *The Crucible* by such critics as John Gassner and Walter Kerr.

Funke, Lewis. Review of *The Crucible,* by Arthur Miller. *The New York Times* (12 March 1958): L36.
Asserts that *The Crucible* is so dramatically powerful that Miller's flaws in characterization are insignificant.

Hartley, Anthony. "Good Melodrama." *Spectator* 196, No. 6669 (20 April 1956): 547.
Praises the "solid tactile" poetic language of *The Crucible,* and characterizes the play as "effective and touching."

Miller, Arthur. *The Crucible: Text and Criticism.* Edited by Gerald Weales. New York: Viking Press, 1971, 484 p.
Combines Miller's original text with critical commentary.

Worsley, T. C. "A Play of Our Time." *The New Statesman and Nation* XLVIII, No. 1237 (20 November 1954): 642.
Acknowledges Miller's use of realistic, appropriate language and skillful structuring of climaxes and resolutions in *The Crucible,* but faults the playwright for presenting one-sided melodrama that detracts from the play's overall effectiveness.

Wyatt, Euphemia Van Rensselaer. Review of *The Crucible,* by Arthur Miller. *The Catholic World* CLXXVI, No. 1056 (March 1953): 465-66.
Recounts historical facts surrounding the Salem witch trials and outlines Miller's treatment of these in *The Crucible.*

Frank O'Hara

1926-1966

(Full name Francis Russell O'Hara) American poet, playwright, art critic, and essayist.

The following entry focuses on criticism on O'Hara published between 1977 and 1991. For further information on his life and career, see *CLC*, Volumes 2, 5, and 13.

INTRODUCTION

A member of the New York School of Poets, O'Hara applied the techniques of Abstract Expressionist painting and French Surrealism to his writing, constructing poems in which he often employed words as units of form and sound without meaning and juxtaposed seemingly random images and ideas. Often compared to Walt Whitman and William Carlos Williams, O'Hara drew on mundane details from urban life to create poetry characterized by immediacy and apparent superficiality. Although early critical reaction to O'Hara's poetry was mixed, his reputation has increased steadily since his death, and critics have noted his immense influence on subsequent poets.

Raised in Massachusetts, O'Hara entered Harvard in 1946 after serving two years in the U.S. Navy. He studied music at first, hoping to become a concert pianist, but later switched to English. While attending Harvard, he wrote his first poems and also met John Ashbery and Kenneth Koch, poets with whom he was later associated as a member of a literary circle known as the New York School of Poets. After graduating from Harvard, O'Hara studied for a year at the University of Michigan, earning a master's degree in English and creative writing and winning a Hopwood Award for a collection of poems and the verse play *Try! Try!* In the fall of 1951, O'Hara moved to New York City. Except for a two-year stint as an editorial associate for *Art News,* O'Hara worked for the Museum of Modern Art for the next fifteen years, rising from sales clerk to associate curator. He wrote reviews and articles for the museum and various journals during this time as well as poetry and plays. He published his first collection of verse, *A City Winter, and Other Poems,* in 1952. Like the other New York School poets, O'Hara established close personal ties with such Abstract Expressionist painters as Larry Rivers and Jackson Pollock. O'Hara died suddenly in 1966 from injuries sustained after being hit by a beach-buggy.

Most critics have focused on the importance O'Hara's poetry imputes to the present and the trivial. Described as spontaneous and nonreferential, O'Hara's poems create a collage of seemingly insignificant details from urban life. In explaining the apparent superficiality of his poetry, critics have argued that O'Hara's poems lack depth because he treats significant events in a trivial fashion and because

his images are fleeting and lack frames of reference. "The Day Lady Died," for instance, contrasts the mundane activities of an ordinary day with a few concluding lines concerning Billie Holiday and her death. "Personal Poem" lacks any periods or rests, suggesting that objects and ideas are events that should be immediately consumed and dropped; in "Essay on Style" O'Hara speculated on the elimination of logical connectives, including "as" and "but." Commentators argue that O'Hara's focus on everyday details reveals the significance inherent in all aspects of experience and suggests that the value of life is equivalent to the vitality with which it is experienced. O'Hara's focus on the present, as evidenced by his fast-paced style, has alsobeen interpreted as a warning against dwelling on the past, an explicit theme in *The General Returns from One Place to Another,* a play in which a caricature of General Douglas MacArthur attempts to recapture past glory.

Other critics have focused on O'Hara's presentation of self. Rarely the subject of his poems, O'Hara appears to be only an observer, as the title of the poem "A Step Away from Them" suggests. However, O'Hara fills his poems with personal details and private jokes intended for his circle of friends. He thus expresses both distance and intimacy, presenting the reader with an elusive and contradictory depiction of himself. Scholars have also observed O'Hara's interest in cultural images and myths. In his poem "On Seeing Larry Rivers' *Washington Crossing the Delaware* at the Museum of Modern Art," O'Hara mocks America's first president, George Washington, as well as the heroic myth associated with the general, depicting him as anxious, cold, and fearful. At the same time, however, he pays tribute to Washington and re-mythologizes the crossing by approaching an authentic rendering of the historical event and portraying Washington as a complex person engaged in a dangerous and difficult endeavor. Finally, critics have interpreted O'Hara's poetry as a reaction to literary history, particularly modernism. Responding to William Carlos Williams's "A Sort of Song," the poems "Today" and "Poetry" manifest O'Hara's concern with the preservation and revaluation of previous traditions. John Lowney has observed that O'Hara's reinterpretation of modernist poetics indicates an underlying tension of signification in O'Hara's poetry that "makes readers simultaneously attentive to significance in the seemingly insignificant and wary about attributing significance at all."

PRINCIPAL WORKS

Try! Try! (play) 1951
Change Your Bedding! (play) 1952
A City Winter, and Other Poems (poetry) 1952
The Houses at Fallen Hanging (play) 1956
Meditations in an Emergency (poetry) 1956
Jackson Pollock (criticism) 1959
Awake in Spain (play) 1960
Love's Labor: An Eclogue (play) 1960
Odes (poetry) 1960
Second Avenue (poetry) 1960
Featuring Frank O'Hara (poetry) 1964
The General Returns from One Place to Another (play) 1964
Lunch Poems (poetry) 1964
Love Poems (Tentative Title) (poetry) 1965
In Memory of My Feelings: A Selection of Poems (poetry) 1967
Two Pieces (poetry) 1969
Oranges (poetry) 1970
The Collected Poems of Frank O'Hara (poetry) 1971
Hymns of St. Bridget [with Bill Berkson] (poetry) 1974
The Selected Poems of Frank O'Hara (poetry) 1974
Art Chronicles, 1954-66 (criticism) 1975
Standing Still and Walking in New York (essays and criticism) 1975
Early Writing: 1946-1950 (poetry) 1977
Poems Retrieved: 1950-1966 (poetry) 1977
Selected Plays (plays) 1978

CRITICISM

Frank O'Hara   (essay date 1959)

[*In the following essay originally written in 1959, O'Hara proposes a literary approach termed Personism.*]

Everything is in the poems, but at the risk of sounding like the poor wealthy man's Allen Ginsberg I will write to you because I just heard that one of my fellow poets thinks that a poem of mine that can't be got at one reading is because I was confused too. Now, come on. I don't believe in god, so I don't have to make elaborately sounded structures. I hate Vachel Lindsay, always have, I don't even like rhythm, assonance, all that stuff. You just go on your nerve. If someone's chasing you down the street with a knife you just run, you don't turn around and shout, "Give it up! I was a track star for Mineola Prep."

That's for the writing poems part. As for their reception, suppose you're in love and someone's mistreating (*mal aimé*) you, you don't say, "Hey, you can't hurt me this way, I *care!*" you just let all the different bodies fall where they may, and they always do may after a few months. But that's not why you fell in love in the first place, just to hang onto life, so you have to take your chances and try to avoid being logical. Pain always produces logic, which is very bad for you.

I'm not saying that I don't have practically the most lofty ideas of anyone writing today, but what difference does that make? they're just ideas. The only good thing about it is that when I get lofty enough I've stopped thinking and that's when refreshment arrives.

But how can you really care if anybody gets it, or gets what it means, or if it improves them. Improves them for what? for death? Why hurry them along? Too many poets act like a middle-aged mother trying to get her kids to eat too much cooked meat, and potatoes with drippings (tears). I don't give a damn whether they eat or not. Forced feeding leads to excessive thinness (effete). Nobody should experience anything they don't need to, if they don't need poetry bully for them, I like the movies too. And after all, only Whitman and Crane and Williams, of the American poets, are better than the movies. As for measure and other technical apparatus, that's just common sense: if you're going to buy a pair of pants you want them to be tight enough so everyone will want to go to bed with you. There's nothing metaphysical about it. Unless, of course, you flatter yourself into thinking that what you're experiencing is "yearning."

Abstraction in poetry, which Allen recently commented on in *It is,* is intriguing. I think it appears mostly in the minute particulars where decision is necessary. Abstraction (in poetry, not in painting) involves personal removal by the poet. For instance, the decision involved in the choice between "the nostalgia of the infinite" and "the nostalgia *for* the infinite" defines an attitude towards degree of abstraction. The nostalgia *of* the infinite representing the greater degree of abstraction, removal, and negative capability (as in Keats and Mallarmé). Personism, a movement which I recently founded and which nobody yet knows about, interests me a great deal, being so totally opposed to this kind of abstract removal that it is verging on a true abstraction for the first time, really, in the history of poetry. Personism is to Wallace Stevens what *la poésie pure* was to Béranger. Personism has nothing to do with philosophy, it's all art. It does not have to do with personality or intimacy, far from it! But to give you a vague idea, one of its minimal aspects is to address itself to one person (other than the poet himself), thus evoking overtones of love without destroying love's life-giving vulgarity, and sustaining the poet's feelings towards the poem while preventing love from distracting him into feeling about the person. That's part of Personism. It was founded by me after lunch with LeRoi Jones on August 27, 1959, a day in which I was in love with someone (not Roi, by the way, a blond). I went back to work and wrote a poem for this person. While I was writing it I was realizing that if I wanted to I could use the telephone instead of writing the poem, and so Personism was born. It's a very exciting movement which will undoubtedly have lots of adherents. It puts the poem squarely between the poet and the person, Lucky Pierre style, and the poem is correspondingly gratified. The poem is at last between two persons instead of two pages. In all modesty, I confess that it may be the death of literature as we know it. While I have certain regrets, I am still glad I got there before Alain Robbe-Grillet did. Poetry being quicker and surer than prose, it is only just that poetry finish literature off. For a time people thought that Artaud was going to accomplish this, but actually, for all its magnificence, his polemical writings are not more outside literature than Bear Mountain is outside New York State. His relation is no more astounding than Dubuffet's to painting.

What can we expect of Personism? (This is getting good, isn't it?) Everything, but we won't get it. It is too new, too vital a movement to promise anything. But it, like Africa, is on the way. The recent propagandists for technique on the one hand, and for content on the other, had better watch out. (pp. 306-08)

Frank O'Hara, "Personism: A Manifesto," in Claims for Poetry, *edited by Donald Hall, The University of Michigan Press, 1982, pp. 306-08.*

Charles Altieri   (essay date 1979)

[*Altieri is an American educator and critic. In the following excerpt, he examines O'Hara's influence on later poets and asserts that value and renewal, according to O'Hara's poetry, are found in the details, familiar aspects, and prosaic elements of life.*]

Frank O'Hara's verse play, *Try, Try,* provides the most ready access to many characteristic qualities of his fictive world. On the surface, and the play is all surface, it appears merely a reminder of how far verse drama has slipped even from Eliot's not very successful attempts to bring dramatic verse to the world of contemporary cocktail parties. *Try, Try* presents two lovers, Violet and John, whose delightful provocations of each other are rudely interrupted by the return of Violet's husband, Jack, from the war. Jack, though, proves not much of an obstacle to their love. Asked by Violet to leave, he calmly accepts his fate, and the play ends with the lovers triumphantly in each other's arms. The play is farce, or better pop art, deliberately refusing Eliot's symbols and portentous psychological probings; the play, in fact, even refuses the conventional means for theatrical action in the love-triangle plot. There is no violence, no passionate confrontation, and no insight or recognition of any truths, profound or otherwise, by the characters—if such undifferentiated dramatic agents can be called characters.

Yet the play is both entertaining in itself and indicative of O'Hara's world view—precisely in the way O'Hara manipulates absolutely trivial and conventional materials. One realizes first of all that such materials are a comment on contemporary reality and on the materials that reality affords the artist. Traditionally, verse was called for in drama only when the materials were of the greatest importance, when the playwright wanted to project the nobility of his characters or have at his disposal linguistic and rhythmic means capable of rendering serious and complex materials. In *Try, Try,* on the other hand, verse is required because the material is so slight; only elaborate and witty language can interest one in such painfully insignificant and typical people and situations. Like many other pop artists, O'Hara is reminding his audience that this age has lost whatever it was that allowed people to think that certain materials were intrinsically significant and fit material for serious artistic exploration. The world no longer sustains or inspires powerful language. Yeats once said that modern tragedy was impossible because modern man, when deeply moved, did not indulge in emotional outbursts but stared quietly at the fireplace. Now, as Ionesco reminds us, even the man moved enough to stare at the fireplace seems somehow ridiculous. Powerful language is no longer a response to the intensity of experience but to

---

its poverty; man needs the artifice of witty and elaborate speech because without it he would have only the pressure of an absurd and oppressive reality. In one of his poems, O'Hara is eating a cheeseburger in Juliet's Corner when he fantasizes an association with Giulleta Massini, "e bell' attrice." In this situation, "e bell' attrice" is a contemporary version of Beatrice, now not a light leading one through the world to a transcendent informing principle but a goddess of illusion redeeming one only momentarily from the stereotyped trivia dominating contemporary life (cf. also **"Galanta"**).

As a poet, O'Hara explores facets of the pop aesthetic . . . In *Try, Try* the lover, John, does not win the girl from her husband, Jack, because of any inherent character traits. The men are almost exactly alike (as the names indicate), and if anyone were to have moral claims it would be the husband, who is also returning from service to his country. John wins simply because he has been living with the girl; wins, that is, because he has been present, there, while the husband was absent. Here is Violet's rejection of her husband: "I wish you'd / go away and stay away. All you've done is kept me / looking out windows, wondering what things were / really like. Get out!" The lover's seconding remarks are as philosophical as O'Hara will allow himself to be:

> You've got a claim on it, but I've got it
> These things don't happen temporarily . . .
>
> I suppose I'm the snake-in-the-grass but
> I can't say I'm sorry. Someone has to smile
> at her as she comes back from the bathroom.
> Do you think everything can stay the same,
> like a photograph? What for?

Presence then is a central value for O'Hara; but what kind of presence is it he affirms? First and foremost it is a demystified one stripped of the ontological vestments with which Bly and Olson endow it. For O'Hara the open road has lost its resident gods capable of mastering and directing the ego. There remains only the present as landscape without depth, satisfying only by contrast to the anxiety Violet felt when she tried to refer her condition to the needs and demands of an absent master. And if the present is without depth, whatever vital qualities it has depend entirely on the energies and capacities of the consciousness encountering it. Olson had opposed the dangerous tendencies toward passivity (the merger with the all that is death) in poetics like Bly's by insisting that man fulfills himself only in action. Yet this active creative self is always grounded in a cosmos at once lawful and itself continuously emergent or creative. With O'Hara, the self must be creative without such a ground; value depends entirely on the vitality with which one engages his experiences:

> You are of me, that's what
> and that's the meaning of fertility
> hard and moist and moaning

In **"Fantasy,"** the concluding poem in *Lunch Poems,* O'Hara tells his readers: "The main thing is to tell a story. / It is almost / very important," and he ends the fantasy with the playful reminder, "Never argue with the movies." Literally the lines refer to a movie, *Northern Pursuit,* which, because it is either in his memory or on television,

keeps intruding into his consciousness as he prepares medicine for Allen Ginsberg and converses with him. Seen, however, as figurative comments on the poetry of the entire volume, the lines become much more resonant. One notices first of all, in this poem titled **"Fantasy,"** the emphasis on story, an emphasis I take to be a way of summarizing the necessary and superficial creative intelligence celebrated in *Try, Try* and in the exuberance of *Lunch Poems.* The story is only "almost" very important both because the movie, *Northern Pursuit,* is a trite one, and, more significantly, because, given the centrality of stories or fictions, there are no acceptable structures of value to define genuine hierarchies of importance. And without terms that can distinguish the important from the trivial, there is a concomitant breakdown in one's sense of the necessary boundaries between fantasy and reality. Why privilege reality, even if one can distinguish it from fiction? Matters of truth then merge with matters of the creative imagination, and the imagination itself can no longer assume its noble form-creating role but tends instead to be conceived as story-maker whose major media is the B movie, the public equivalent of private daydreams. The movies, then, are at once emblem of contemporary views on the nature of reality (who hasn't seen his life as a B movie and himself as seedy director powerless to do more, with the budget and script he's been given?) and moral witness of our times. It is folly to argue with them for two reasons: one's arguments have no grounds not themselves as fictive and superficial as the movies, and (as the poem **"Ave Maria"** suggests) one stands to lose more than he would gain if he successfully argues with the movies. The movies at least engage one's imagination and enliven experience; most of the forms of argument used to refute movie truth are themselves analytic and sterile ways of returning one to the poverty of a present emptied of all vitality. [In a footnote Altieri states that "my own analysis of O'Hara, particularly the discussion of story, is based on a philosopher, Jacques Derrida, who tries to work out the epistemological and ethical implications of a postmodern reality without depth and impossible to interpret. I use the term *story* as literary embodiment of what Derrida calls 'free play,' in a world whose givenness is all one can have. And central in that givenness is one's own creative play among the phenomena one encounters. (Derrida insists far more than O'Hara on the strictly verbal qualities of this given reality.)"]

The way out of this emptiness is the story, but story in O'Hara requires careful definition since he is in no way a traditional narrative poet. Possible forms of story, of course, are fantasy and the witty artifice of *Try, Try,* forms O'Hara normally equates with pop art (see **"Poem"** on Lana Turner). But for O'Hara life provides fictions both more superficial and more interesting than pure fantasy or artifice. The poet keeps his story alive by a loving fidelity to the specific facts and qualities of his daily experience— seen for themselves and not as the building blocks of larger, more significant wholes traditionally called poems:

> I am mainly preoccupied with the world as I experience it, and at times when I would rather be dead the thought that I could never write another poem has so far stopped me. . . . What is

happening to me, allowing for lies and exaggerations which I try to avoid, goes into my poems. I don't think my experiences are clarified or made beautiful for myself or anyone else. . . .

It may be that poetry makes life's nebulous events tangible to me and restores their detail; or conversely, that poetry brings forth the intangible quality of incidents which are all too concrete and circumstantial.

It is in this context of life continually providing materials for the story that one must understand O'Hara's love affair with New York City (cf. **"Steps"**). For the city is a continual source of interesting and engaging details. Moreover, the city is a perfect metaphor for O'Hara's sense of the value in these details. Presence in the city is antithetical to presence in nature. City details, after all, have neither meaning, hierarchy, nor purpose not created absolutely by man. And more important, the city is committed to perpetual change; there are no enduring seasonal motifs or patterns of duration underlying and sustaining the multiplicity of city phenomena. They exist completely in the moment. And they exist superficially. In the city, as in O'Hara ontology, interesting and engaging details are continually becoming present. Yet not only do these momentary apparitions promise no underlying significance or meanings to be interpreted, they actually resist any attempt on one's part to know them better. City life offers a series of phenomena to notice, perhaps to play with in one's own psyche, but very rarely do these phenomena inspire or welcome any attempt to participate in their lives. O'Hara's analogue for the specific form of presence manifested by the city is his way of naming. His texture of proper names gives each person and detail an identity, but in no way do the names help the reader understand anything about what has been named. To know a lunch counter is called Juliet's Corner or a person O'Hara expects to meet is named Norman is a reminder for the reader that the specific details of another's life can appear only as momentary fragments, insisting through their particularity on his alienation from any inner reality they might possess.

What makes O'Hara so interesting a poet is his sense at once of the necessity for story, of its superficiality, and of the pain potentially lurking in every moment. The dialectic between presence and alienation found in his use of names is more strikingly evident in the larger rhythms of his work. Coexisting with O'Hara's evident joy in a kaleidoscopic rush of details and encounters are frequent perceptions of a lurking anxiety ready to seize him if the flow of events should give it a moment's foothold:

> I ducked out of sight behind the saw-mill
> nobody saw me because of the falls the gates the
>   sluice the tourist boats
>
> the children were trailing their fingers in the
>   water
> and the swans, regal and smarty, were nipping
>   their "little" fingers
>
> I heard one swan remark "That was a good nip
> though they are not as interesting as sausages"
>   and another

> reply "Nor as tasty as those peasants we got
>   away from the elephant that time"
>
> but I didn't really care for conversation that day
> I wanted to be alone
> which is why I went to the mill in the first place
> now I am alone and hate it
> I don't want to just make boards for the rest of
>   my life
> I'm distressed
> the water is very beautiful but you can't go into
>   it
> because of the gunk
> and the dog is always rolling over, I like dogs on
>   their "little" feet
> I think I may scamper off to Winnipeg to see
>   Raymond
> but what'll happen to the mill
> I see the cobwebs collecting already
> and later those other webs, those awful predato-
>   ry webs
> if I stay right here I will eventually get into the
>   newspapers
> like Robert Frost
> willow trees, willow trees they remind me of
>   Desdemona
> I'm so damned literary
> and at the same time the waters rushing past re-
>   mind me of nothing
>
> I'm so damned empty
> what is all this vessel shit anyway
> we are all rushing down the River Happy Times
> duckling poling bumping sinking and swimming
> and we arrive at the beach
> the chaff is sand
> alone as a tree bumping another tree in a storm
> that's not really being alone, is it, signed The
>   Saw

To be "alone" is also to be all one, but again, like city life, O'Hara has only the unity of mad process trying to make up in motion what it lacks in meaning. The self threatens always to dissipate into the surfaces it contemplates, to become merely a "skein of lust" unwinding in time. Yet one need only recognize the dangers to overcome them, to reaffirm his commitment and love of the processes he is engaged in: one must maintain, he says in his essay on Nakian, "a kind of despairing sensual delight" by achieving "a relation with physical truth that is both stoic and sybaritic." Notice how in the poem I have quoted, O'Hara never dwells on the problems but keeps turning instead to the details of the scene or his own fantasies of future possibilities. **"Naptha"** offers an even better example of a conclusion nicely capturing both the underlying sterility of his experience and the rich union of stoic and sybaritic roles he creates in response.

> how are you feeling in ancient September
> I am feeling like a truck on a wet highway
> how can you
> you were made in the image of god
> I was not
> I was made in the image of a sissy truck-driver
> and Jean Dubuffet painting his cows
> "with a likeness burst in the memory"
> apart from love (don't say it)
> I am ashamed of my century

for being so entertaining
but I have to smile

He "has" to smile—because he has no alternative, but also because his and his century's absurd situation are genuinely entertaining. O'Hara has to smile, not to laugh, and in that small difference one can realize the distance between his genuinely sybaritic stoicism and the less humane anguish of the black humorist.

Ontologically, O'Hara's demystified sense of process is very close to the tragic Lowell of *Notebook,* but there are two major differences. First there is O'Hara's exuberance; his awareness of lurking emptiness generates neither a constant sense of how forced pleasure is nor the limited context of personal experience that is all Lowell can trust. All O'Hara's poems are intensely personal, but they retain, even celebrate, the necessary public dimension and shared quality of the surfaces that constitute his story. The more important contrast lies in O'Hara's treatment of anxiety. For O'Hara the tragic themes so celebrated by the existentialist tradition are both ridiculous and dangerous. The tragic seems ridiculous because of its exalted and probably false sense of the heroic embattled ego—even if the ego is in the cathartic process of learning cosmic pity: "The strange career of a personality begins at five and ends / forty minutes later in a fog the rest is just a lot of stranded / ships honking their horns full of joy-seeking cadets in bloomers." The goal is not meeting or defying fate but "avoiding it," and tragic themes are dangerous because they encourage one to think he or she can turn on anxieties and successfully wrestle them to the ground. But people are more like Actaeon than Hercules, more prone to be devoured by anxiety than to conquer it in direct conflict.

"Adieu to Norman, Bon Jour to Joan and Jean-Paul" summarizes most of O'Hara's poetic strategies and makes evident the differences from Lowell:

It is 12:10 in New York and I am wondering
if I will finish this in time to meet Norman for
     lunch
ah lunch! I think I am going crazy
what with my terrible hangover and weekend
     coming up
at excitement-prone Kenneth Koch's
I wish I were staying in town and working on my
     poems
at Joan's studio for a new book by Grove Press
which they will probably not print
but it is good to be several floors up in the dead
     of night
wondering whether you are any good or not
and the only decision you can make is that you
     did it

yesterday I looked up the rue Frémicourt on a
     map
and was happy to find it like a bird
flying over Paris et ses environs
which unfortunately did not include Seine-et-
     Oise which I don't know
as well as a number of other things
and Allen is back talking about god a lot
and Peter is back not talking very much

and Joe has a cold and is not coming to Ken-
     neth's
although he is coming to lunch with Norman
I suspect he is making a distinction
well, who isn't

I wish I were reeling around Paris
instead of reeling around New York
I wish I weren't reeling at all
it is Spring the ice has melted the Ricard is being
     poured
we are all happy and young and toothless
it is the same as old age
the only thing to do is simply continue
is that simple
yes, it is simple because it is the only thing to do
can you do it
yes, you can because it is the only thing to do
blue light over the Bois de Boulogne it continues
the Seine continues
the Louvre stays open it continues it hardly
     closes at all
the Bar American continues to be French
de Gaulle continues to be Algerian as does
     Camus
Shirley Goldfarb continues to be Shirley Gold-
     farb
and Jane Hazan continues to be Jane Freilicher
     (I think!)
and Irving Sandler continues to be the balayeur
     des artistes
and so do I (sometimes I think I'm "in love"
     with painting)
and surely the Piscine Deligny continues to have
     water in it
and the Flore continues to have tables and news-
     papers and people under them
and surely we shall not continue to be unhappy
we shall be happy
but we shall continue to be ourselves everything
     continues to be possible

Rene Char, Pierre Reverdy, Samuel Beckett it is
     possible isn't it
I love Reverdy for saying yea, though I don't be-
     lieve it

Just as one has no grounds to measure adequately good and bad and so must look only at the qualities of his life as process, the poem can only counter the anxieties that continue to oppress by turning time and again to the details and possibilities to which one can keep saying yes, even if one does not believe them. O'Hara's characteristic strategies are clearest in the fourth stanza. In the initial line he tries to encounter his present sense of emptiness with an escape into fantasy and a possible future, but the escape does not work. By the third line he is returned to a dangerously static vision of himself as object (instead of as actor playing a creative role in process), one he escapes only by completely changing his vision and his theme to an awareness of the weather. And even here O'Hara is careful to avoid any illusion of depth. He swiftly metamorphoses spring's melting ice into the ice at cocktail parties so that none of spring's traditional symbolic overtones can emerge. For to admit spring as a symbolic entity is to remain on the symbolic generalized level of discourse where the problem of rootlessness is most pressing. While symbolic solutions might convince one for the moment he's overcome a philosophical problem, they also tempt his consciousness to continue operating on levels where further anxieties are inevitable. Symbolism perpetually promises qualities of experience that are not present and hence problematic.

While O'Hara reduces the present to sheer surface and the creative play of the individual consciousness, he also points to materials and attitudes that might constitute a genuine moral vision free of the systematic and abstract distortions of most philosophical attempts to define value.

—Charles Altieri

O'Hara himself is one whom other poets love for saying "yes" but do not actually believe. His influence and popularity are considerably greater than his achievement—a phenomenon attributable to many factors including his sheer entertainment value and the notoriety of his pathetic and unexpected death. But most of all I think his popularity stems from his sybaritic stoicism, or perhaps affirmative skepticism, and from his articulation of strategies, attitudes, and values that other poets find themselves momentarily sharing. In addition, many of O'Hara's strategies can be adapted to qualities of experience less camp and aggressively superficial. While O'Hara reduces the present to sheer surface and the creative play of the individual consciousness, he also points to materials and attitudes that might constitute a genuine moral vision free of the systematic and abstract distortions of most philosophical attempts to define value. (pp. 108-16)

Given the insistence on the open road and the denial of referential moral systems, it is impossible for the poet to affirm a morality stressing contents. The poet cannot recommend specific actions to be universally imitated, nor even propose very specific moral criteria individuals can use in defining their own rights and wrongs. All he can do is offer a set of moral attitudes. The poet illustrates and exemplifies modes of engaging whatever experiences a person might have, and his work becomes testament to the kind of effects these attitudes might bring about. This sense that poetry is moral through the attitudes it embodies permeates postmodern poetry, and O'Hara is an influential example of both a specific strategy and the general framework supporting such an emphasis: think, for example, of poets like Gary Snyder, Allen Ginsberg, [Robert] Bly, and W. S. Merwin who seek to embody modes of consciousness that one can or must inhabit to intuit moral truths; or consider others like John Logan, Bill Knott, David Ignatow, and John Ashbery (O'Hara's close friend whose ironic and disembodied voice suggests a mode of living almost exactly opposite O'Hara's, though the two share the same ontology) whose attitudes are more directly moral, more concerned with ways of acting in relation to suffering and to other people, than they are with leading readers to ontological truths. What all share, though, is a tendency to expand traditional lyric modes so that they become existential strategies. Lyric poetry has always had as its primary function the invention and testing of attitudes toward experience, and *persona* was a primary critical category for critics of the fifties. But within the tradition, attitude was always supplementary to the moral qualities of the experience itself. Thus critics and poets could conceive *persona* ironically and contemplate the gap between ideal modes of response suggested by the experience and the specific moral or intellectual failures of the specific voice in the poem. Contemporary poets cannot afford to be ironic about their *personae* because they cannot trust, either in the poem or in reality, that the experience itself provides norms for judging the response. Rather only the response itself—its appeal for the reader and the possibilities it offers for keeping him open to the reality of his own experiences—can be the measure of the poet's moral value.

O'Hara's specific attitude is also very influential—not only on those New York poets who continue in the pop-art tradition but on others more taken by his humility and affirmative skepticism. The qualities of skepticism and humility in fact often go hand in hand, for it is always tempting, if not always possible, to extend one's skepticism about external values to skepticism about the self. And O'Hara's poetry does just that: one so aware of the arbitrary creativity he requires to keep the present vital is not apt to take either himself, his poetry, or his world view as possible salvation for everyone. So O'Hara presents demystified views of both the reconciliation of opposites and the poetic image. The high Romantic doctrine of the form-creating imagination unifying and reconciling opposites promises a solution at once unlikely, without distorting experience, and undesirable. For what makes life interesting is precisely confusion, contradiction, and the constant presence of alternatives. O'Hara approaches [Charles] Olson's contention that only the multiplicity of the real can reconcile images, but he remains aware that this multiplicity will always seem contradictory to human consciousness. Yet like Donald Barthelme, his counterpart in prose fiction, O'Hara celebrates just this ironic reality of human experience. In a similar way, O'Hara presents a skeptical view of the poetic image: it is neither means for capturing the *Gott-natur* nor collocation of *topos, typos,* and *tropos.* Most often it is merely *topos,* the accurate and engaged description of interesting facets of experience, but when topology is not creative enough the poet self-consciously creates startling images and metaphors. O'Hara never allows himself, or his readers, to confuse will and perception or to mistake careful rhetorical construction for discovered ontological or psychological truth.

O'Hara's resultant universe may be superficial and impoverished, but it is also fun—and fun with a strong measure of truth. The second of O'Hara's **"2 Poems from the Ohara Monogatari,"** with its skeptical attitude toward created images and monistic world views, exemplifies both the truth and the fun:

After a long trip to a shrine
in wooden clogs so hard on the muscles
the tea is bitter and the breasts are hard
so much terrace for one evening

there is no longer no ocean
I don't see the ocean under my stilts
as I poke along

hands on ankles feet on wrists
naked in thought
like a whip made from sheerest stockings

the radio is on the cigarette is puffed upon
by the pleasures of rolling in a bog
some call the Milky Way
in far-fetched Occidental lands above the trees
where dwell the amusing skulls

The poem is never really meditative, but given its oriental setting and religious overtones the first two stanzas could be a slightly cranky version of modish Western poems about Eastern religion. Even the transformation of the wooden clogs into stilts need not yet suggest an equation between humble Eastern religions and Yeats' self-conscious creative poet on his stilts. It is only in the third stanza that the irony takes over and reminds one that religion, Eastern or Western, is a creature of the fictive imagination. At the moment when the meditative state seems realized ("naked in thought"), O'Hara introduces the metaphor of a whip made of sheer stockings. The metaphor is high camp, at once completely arbitrary and an ironic reminder of how out of tune urban Western man is with whatever natural and religious energies he hopes to experience in the setting. Finally, this intrusion of self-consciousness leads to the last stanza's presentation of the pain and death willfully overlooked in turning to Eastern monistic visions of cosmic unity—a unity mocked, one might add, by the obvious way the poet's mind cannot satisfactorily merge into the scene.

There is, however, another sense in which O'Hara's materials are at least as important as his attitudes to his influential position, not in their camp specifics but as indications of areas in human experience not often mined by poets. For O'Hara is quintessentially a poet of the domestic and the quotidian. Few poets, thank God, share his sense of what the domestic and quotidian entails, but the success of any domestic poetry encourages others to look freshly at the immediate experiences that matter to them and to ask poetically why they matter. As John Ashbery asks, "Have you begun to be in the context you feel?" Moreover, the philosophy I have extracted from O'Hara can be used to rediscover the moral content of domestic experience. For one need not believe in numinous forces in order to recognize specific values in all sorts of prereflective and prephilosophical forms of life—in one's choices, in commitments, and even in compromises and acceptances. If one can become aware of how important these energies, desires, and commitments are to one's enjoyment of life, one can realize how fully man in fact does live in a present charged with value contexts very difficult to define philosophically. In effect, O'Hara encourages readers to take Olson's admonitions about . . . man's necessity to recover the familiar without the ontological, cosmic, and epic perspectives Olson .cloaks them in. These grand ideas, as much of Olson's poetry unfortunately indicates, tend to lead one away from what they encourage one to recover. It is hard not to prefer the joyful, confident humility and honesty so fully witnessed in O'Hara's poetry.

Paul Carroll is the first critic I know to claim a really influential role for O'Hara in the poetry of the sixties. My argument complements and extends his, which deals primarily with the aesthetic aspects of the themes of domesticity and the process of continual creation. O'Hara's influence, he says, stems from three related factors in his work. He makes clear for poets how the dada and expressionist doctrines of creation can work for them, for his poems continually insist that they are not representations of reality but the enactment by the artist of certain attitudes and choices within that reality. Consequently there are no canonical or privileged subjects for poetry: "Anything, literally, can exist in a poem; and anything can exist in whatever way the poet chooses." O'Hara then shows how the poet need no longer feel committed to organic unity as a principle of poetic construction. His details need not be chosen because they enhance a specific lyric point or attitude; the objects chosen can embody the multiple facets of experience, only some of which might be essential to the lyric feeling. This antiorganicist aesthetic Carroll defines [in *The Poem in Its Skin* (1968)] as the aesthetic of the "impure poem."

The idea of the "impure poem" is both helpful and dangerous. It is helpful in so much as it calls one's attention to the materials and attitudes the contemporaries try to give poetic expression, but it oversimplifies the texture of relationships in the best poems using such materials. The organic poem need not be the single-minded evocation of simple emotions; "organic" simply means that all the aesthetic choices contribute to the complex effect of the poem. It is true that many of O'Hara's poems do not aim at single lyric effects but focus instead, like Duchamp's urinal and Warhol's Campbell's soup cans, on celebrating the powers of artistic choice and thus reminding one of the simple levels at which value experience continually takes place. But O'Hara's best lyrics employ details both as specific references to an impure, discontinuous texture of experience and as carefully related elements in a complex lyric feeling.

"The Day Lady Died" is Carroll's example of the archetypal impure poem; but that poem to me is one of the finest examples of the rich poetic possibilities in the domestic lyric. The poem not only captures the vitality of prereflective experience but arranges that experience so that it participates in and evokes for consciousness a complex, satisfying, and relatively traditional lyric emotion:

It is 12:20 in New York a Friday
three days after Bastille day, yes
it is 1959 and I go get a shoeshine
because I will get off the 4:19 in Easthampton
at 7:15 and then go straight to dinner
and I don't know the people who will feed me

I walk up the muggy street beginning to sun
and have a hamburger and a malted and buy
an ugly NEW WORLD WRITING to see what the
    poets

in Ghana are doing these days

> I go on to the bank
> and Miss Stillwagon (first name Linda I once
> heard)
> doesn't even look up my balance for once in her
> life
> and in the GOLDEN GRIFFIN I get a little Ver-
> laine
> for Patsy with drawings by Bonnard although I
> do
> think of Hesiod, trans. Richmond Lattimore or
> Brendan Behan's new play or Le Balcon or Les
> Negres
> of Genet, but I don't, I stick with Verlaine
> after practically going to sleep with quandari-
> ness
> and for Mike I just stroll into the PARK LANE
> Liquor Store and ask for a bottle of Strega and
> then I go back where I came from to 6th Avenue
> and the tobacconist in the Ziegfeld Theatre and
> casually ask for a carton of Gauloises and a car-
> ton
> of Picayunes, and a NEW YORK POST with her
> face on it
>
> and I am sweating a lot by now and thinking of
> leaning on the john door in the 5 SPOT
> while she whispered a song along the keyboard
> to Mal Waldron and everyone and I stopped
> breathing

One way of seeing how the poem is impure, Carroll suggests, is to recognize that twenty lines are devoted to the casual events of O'Hara's day and only four to the ostensive subject of the poem. He goes on, though, to offer two insights that help explain how the artist's apparently free creative selection of details really creates a single complex lyric emotion:

> I wonder how touching that beautiful final memory . . . would be if O'Hara had preceded it with emotional tributes and "props" customary in most traditional elegies. . . .
>
> In another sense, **"The Day Lady Died"** isn't about Billie Holliday at all. It is about the common but sobering feeling that life continues on its bumbling way despite the tragic death of an important artist or some loved one.

But it is not only the general configuration of details, the contrast between bumbling life and the suddenness of death, that unifies the poem. The actual particulars by which the poem captures the vitality of life at the same time constantly call attention to their own contingency and perpetual hovering on the brink of disconnection. O'Hara has plans for dinner but does not know the people who will feed him; he is divorced in space and attitude from the Ghana poets, in time and habit from the writers mentioned in the third stanza (one usually does not "go to sleep with quandariness"—one sleeps from boredom and the lack of choice—but O'Hara wants to suggest connections between multiplicity, lack of connections guiding choice, and forms of death); he encounters probably for the hundredth time a bank teller he has no communication with, yet who also disproves his expectations; and even the apparently most arbitrary item, the reference to Bastille

Day, has a curious appositeness in a poem so thoroughly about death, separation, and the fragility of established order. Moreover, the "and" rhetoric so pronounced in the poem further enhances one's sense of the tangential and problematic links between particulars: parataxis calls attention to the rush of time piling up details united only by sequential time alien to specifically human patterns of relationship. The rush of life then embodies also a process of continual death leading to the climactic stoppages of life and breath in the last four lines. But the initial twenty lines also allow the poet to find a meaning in Billie's death. Seeing in her art and his memories of it the experience of connection counters and helps mollify the pains of discontinuity. What he remembers about Billie is a moment of stasis that is at once death and very intense life—death because it so divorces him from the normal (and insignificant) activities of his daily life, and intense life for precisely the same reason since it has been that life which is really involvement in continual deaths. The moment he remembers is one of absolute communication when Billie controlled the entire audience and led them to a single ecstasy ("everyone and I stopped breathing"). And O'Hara's poem is itself an act like Billie Holiday's; the full elegiac effect depends on the reader's union with his memory. Like her singing, the poem also can claim at least for a moment to transcend the contingent multiplicities of daily experience and, through the poem's deliberate slowing in these last lines, allow a brief space where readers all stop that rushing breath always associated with process in O'Hara and realize how art and memory can console in the face of recurrent death.

O'Hara is not often so good: but neither are any other poets of the sixties. Nonetheless, Carroll is correct in insisting that **"The Day Lady Died"** is a crucial touchstone for postmodern poetry. The poem exemplifies how postmodern literature can thrive, though oppressed on the one side by philosophical nihilism and on the other by the oppressive burden of literary history always reminding poets of how little room there seems to be for meaningful originality. Literature can remain honest and "de-mystified," without succumbing to self-pitying nostalgia or refining away its content in the self-conscious acrobatics of what John Barth has called "the literature of exhaustion." Not only poetry, but even some of the basic values of civilized life can be discovered by pushing further than the past into the manifold particulars and the texture of domestic contemporary life. (pp. 116-22)

> *Charles Altieri, "Varieties of Immanentist Experience: Robert Bly, Charles Olson, and Frank O'Hara," in his* Enlarging the Temple: New Directions in American Poetry During the 1960s, *Bucknell University Press, 1979, pp. 78-127.*

Charles Molesworth   (essay date 1979)

[*Molesworth is an American educator, poet, and critic. In the following excerpt, he distinguishes four modes of expression in O'Hara's poetry, which Molesworth characterizes as distinct responses to trends in contemporary poetry and society.*]

Frank O'Hara's poems, as profuse in their inventiveness as they are pervasive in their influence, demand that we attempt to judge their place in American poetry. It is not only because these poems skirt the edges of such contiguous but opposed aesthetic qualities as artless simplicity and dazzling elaboration that they are hard to judge. These poems outline their own territory by operating with a high degree of consciousness about themselves as literature and simultaneously flaunting the notions of decorum and propriety. Just when they seem placed, or placeable, in some historical or theoretical classification, they are off again, saying that such classifications don't matter and that it's clearly wrongheaded of people to ask any poem to maintain an attitude long enough to be labelled. For all we can say about them, they yet remain chastely irreducible, as if they wanted nothing so much as to beggar commentary. But if read in bulk, the poems leave us with the peculiar sensation that we've been listening to a manic waif, someone for whom any audience becomes the most charitable therapy; for as soon as the poems stop talking, stop chatting, their speaker will fall dead. The chatter registers the *frisson*, the stimulation, but it also hints at the shiver of fear, the *gouffre*. Like all great improvisational artists, O'Hara thrives in the realm of nostalgia, in a looking back that can never for a moment become true regret. Like the Steinberg drawing of the hand holding the quill pen that has just created the profile of its own face, O'Hara's poetry startles, as does any utterance clearly self-begotten.

Self-begotten in more than one sense, for these are the most autobiographical poems we have; they make "confessional" poetry seem alexandrine or allegorical by comparison. The friends, the places, the objects, the very reverie: they are all his and all there for us to rummage through. Just by writing them down, just by taking note of them, O'Hara has won for his personal ephemerals another status. "Save him from the malevolent eyes of / spiders but do not throw him to the swans," he begs in **"Words to Frank O'Hara's Angel,"** wanting neither gothic terror nor fruity sublimation. This poem ends with a simple, a necessary plea: "Protect his tongue." His tongue assumes the duties of his soul, of course; it is the principle of his individuation. An ordinary biography of O'Hara would be a distraction from the poems. Yet, reading the poems in an autobiographical, chronological order, we're struck by an early despair, by the hint of a habit of mind that could have been crucial in the determination of the poetry's final texture. Frank O'Hara may well have despaired of ever escaping himself.

This early despair took the form of a fear of his own selfhood. Persistent emotional demands and the ability to be haunted by his own irremovable privacy characterize the fearful self, and it can be conquered only by turning over to the world of contingent actions all hope of finality. The solipsist must be conquered by the improvisor. Once the solipsist is conquered, it is as if O'Hara never allowed his own self to become the subject of the poetry. His self might be, almost always was, the *occasion* of the individual poems, but the poems' focus is rarely on that self as subject matter. His self is the great given of his poetry; it is what memory was for Wordsworth or moral excellence for Mil-

ton, that concern without which his poetry, the very idea of his poetry, would be unspeakable. Unlike Whitman, O'Hara never sings *of* his self; rather, his self is the instrument *on* which the poet sings. It is more than an instrument, though, for his various selves form an ensemble whose central organizing subject is always problematical, as in **"In Memory of My Feelings"**:

> I have lost what is always and every-
> where
> present, the scene of my selves, the occasion of
> these ruses,
> which I myself and singly must now kill
> and save the serpent in their midst.

There are several relatively early poems that record intimations of this despair, this many-selved situation that could be burdensome if it weren't possible to metamorphose this problem into the very means of escape from an even worse one. This is the end of **"Poem ('All the mirrors in the world')"**:

> I
> cannot face that fearful usage,
>
> and my eyes in, say, the glass
> of a public bar, become a
>
> depraved hunt for other re-
> flections. And what a blessed
>
> relief! when it is some
> disgusting sight, anything
>
> but the old shadowy bruising,
> anything but my private haunts.
> When I am fifty shall my
> face drift into those elongations
>
> of innocence and confront me?
> Oh rain, melt me! mirror, kill!

If this came later in his work, rather than in the Hopwood Award manuscript submitted at the University of Michigan in 1951, its tone might register as less sincerely grim. Here the problem is a self that is fixed yet longs to confront some chaos, some "disgusting thing," so that it might again become an Emersonian "transparent eyeball," some self with no private identity, nothing to contain or protect but the activity of its own indiscreet peering. But it must never look inward, nor must it see itself in the faces in the mirror. To do so would be to become a mere object in the world of objects, rather than the sustaining principle of the observed world. These poems are often personal in subject matter but seldom intimate in tone. Notions such as Laing's "ontological insecurity" might be applied here as well, since the speaking subject in O'Hara's poems often loses domination of himself to the surrounding objects. John Ashbery remarks that O'Hara would have been amazed to see his *Collected Poems* run to over five hundred pages, but surely the very dismemberment of O'Hara's consciousness has no rational limits, and once the dispersal of its contents starts there is no way to stop or even slow it.

Such dispersal reaches its characteristic limits in O'Hara's long poems, sustained flights of improvisational inclusiveness in which a Whitmanesque voice seems intent on driving through the detritus of a surreal world in order to celebrate and assume whatever it finds at hand. This is from **"Biotherm (for Bill Berkson)":**

                    extended vibrations
ziggurats ZIG I to IV stars of the Tigris-Euphrates basin
    leading ultimates such as kickapoo juice halvah Canton chinese
in thimbles
                paraded for gain, but yet a parade kiss me,
            Busby Berkeley, kiss me
you have ended the war simply by singing in your Irene Dunne foreskin
"Practically Yours"
            with June Vincent, Lionello Venturi, Caspar Citron
a Universal-International release produced by G. Mennen Williams
                directed by Florine Stettheimer
                continuity by the Third Reich
    after "hitting" the beach at Endzoay we drank up the liebfraumilch
        and pushed on to the Plata to the Pampas
        you didn't pick up the emeralds you god-damned fool you got
        no collarbone you got no dish no ears

O'Hara wrote a friend to say he was pleased he had kept this poem " 'open,' and so there are lots of possibilities, air and such." Seen in the light of avant-garde poetics, this poem is successful as an experiment—it is nothing if not open—but at the same time it is a failure as anything but a closed, nonreferential object. The allusion to Hemingway and the parody of his style aren't illuminated by the juxtaposed reference to Hollywood "gossip-fame"; rather, the poem is a tour de force only if we disregard all referential frameworks of meaning that it might momentarily generate. Like an "action painting," it might have begun as an attempt to register the energy that could accrue or discharge in any mind possessed of myriad contents in all their rigorous denial of hierarchy. But it ends as something else: a collocation, a collage that seldom rewards lingering attention or compels an energized response. Somehow the poem manages to bring the marvellous and the humdrum together, not so much as fragments of heterogeneous values jostling together, but as an aleatoric set of transcriptions, the recording of many merely different things. The things, of course, are not the objects referred to by the words but rather the words themselves, for language here is not employed to transmit information or express states of mind. In this poem, as in many of O'Hara's, the words possess an almost archeological status: they are the thrown up or thrown in phenomena of a particular sociocultural mix. Look, the words say, this is how we came out, this is how we were used *for the moment*. We may indeed have been used to point to something else, but whatever that is, or was, is surely gone now, and it couldn't have been ascertained or possessed in any case. "I hope the poem to *be* the subject, not just about it," O'Hara said. Here he has supplanted the fearful vacuum of a changeless, irreducible, yet contingent self with the screen of a jumbled, particularized, but impermeable language.

O'Hara may well have composed by lines, but it is more likely that the poems grew by phrases. The typography of the long poems isolates these phrases, or spurts of phrases, and it's hard to see any other architectonics at work. In the short lyrics this is also true, and the erratic syntax or arbitrary stanzaic patterns present no handicap to reading the lyrics, since we have to get the phrasing right on our own, regardless of line breaks or any traditional sense of poetic measure. Performance, that special quality of an individual self flashing forth in gestures and sudden turns, is crucial here and can be seen, dominant and offhand, in

such poems as **"Why I Am Not a Painter."** O'Hara talks about it most humorously in his manifesto, **"Personism":**

> I don't believe in god, so I don't have to make elaborately sounded structures. I hate Vachel Lindsay, always have; I don't even like rhythm, assonance, all that stuff. You just go on your nerve. If someone's chasing you down the street with a knife you just run, you don't turn around and shout, "Give it up! I was a track star for Mineola Prep."

It may help if you *were* a track star, even if it wouldn't help to announce it. This is supremely an American trait, this trust of activity over words, the sense that thought or cognition is a degraded form of motion. Going "on your nerve" requires something almost like a contempt for language, or at least an impatience with its discursive possibilities. This sensibility best registers itself in transcription, the literal recording of what is going on at the moment. Urban life, however, fragmented, skeptical, and alienated as it is, creates a feedback in the recording apparatus. It begins to skip, miss, and jump. The pieces of the pattern challenge the cohesiveness and ask only to be recorded as pieces. Performance and preservation become synonymous. "You had to be there," says the observer, for the gesture remains as unique as the moment of expression that allowed it to be witnessed. When words are asked to witness the unique, to become unduplicable, they may very well cling to a few neighboring words and then fall silent.

Many of O'Hara's short poems begin in one of the several modes and then continue in the same mode without development or variation; as such, the short poems present alternative (though similar) versions of the longer poems that surrealistically mix voices and levels of attention. These shorter poems manifest O'Hara's technical inventiveness as it shows forth both in challenging syntactical verve and, even more immediately, in the distinctive offhandedness so central to his sensibility. Take, for example, the openings of poems where this wit begins with such daring casualness. Here is what might be called the "personal madcap" mode:

> Diane calls me so I get up
> I wash my hair because
> I have a hash hangover then
> I noticed the marabunta have walked into the
>   kitchen!
> they are carrying a little banner
> which says "in search of lanolin"
> so that's how they found me!

The flat quotidian voice drops to the confessedly antiheroic only to raise the spectre of urban terror, till quickly we realize the terror exists only as the bizarre, salvaged from the realm of popular culture. The only thing to fear is that our momentary disorientation might make us discover how irrational the surfaces of life have been all along.

Then there's the more directly surrealist mode, where common objects perform fantastic maneuvers, where transformed memories and bizarre projections erupt in counterpoint against an almost relaxed, reflective structure:

> I watched an armory combing its bronze bricks
> and in the sky there were glistening rails of milk.
> Where had the swan gone, the one with the lame
>   back?
>   Now mounting the steps,
>   I enter my new home full
>   of grey radiators and glass
>   ashtrays full of wool.
> Against the winter I must get a samovar
> embroidered with basil leaves and Ukranian
>   mottos
> to the distant sound of wings, painfully anti-
>   wind

This mode, employed often by O'Hara's friends and imitators, from Kenneth Koch to Michael Benedikt, obviously satisfies a desire, felt by many modern poets, to include both armories and Ukranian mottoes in the poem if it is to maintain a level of interest commensurate with the world of objects. Owing much to use of collage and *objets trouvés* by modern painters and sculptors, this might be called the mode of "surreal serendipity." It resembles very strongly the "paranoiac-critical" method enunciated by Salvador Dali; in attributing occult and protean abilities to everyday objects, it has the same mixture of theatricalized terror and whimpering playfulness as do Dali's paintings. At the same time it spins off such delightful accidents as the notion of the wings of "anti-wind."

A third mode arises from O'Hara's fascinated interest in personality, especially as it is revealed in the lives of artists and the interrelationships of his own circle. This mode provides much of the tone that has caused many of O'Hara's followers to become known as the "gang-and-gossip" school. Here the quirkiness of human actions replaces the quirkiness of objects, and the quotidian finds itself suddenly redeemed by uniquenesses of temperament and gesture. The "Bill" in this typical opening is probably Bill Berkson:

> He allows as how some have copped out
> but others are always terrific, hmmmmmm?
> Then he goes out to buy a pair of jeans,
> moccasins and some holeless socks. It
> is very hot. He thinks with pleasure that
> his first name is the same as deKooning's.
> People even call him "Bill" too, and
> they often smile. He feels rather severe
> actually, about people smiling without a
> reason. He is naturally suspicious, but
> easily reassured, say by a pledge unto death.

The offhand approach to the extremism of a death pledge typifies the humor of this sort of poem, where endearing traits are simultaneously exaggerated and excused. This mode of praise must never be sentimental; even a sudden plunge into bathos or the absurdly inconsequential will be used to prevent any sentimental tone from developing. Camaraderie remains on guard against slack soppiness. This mode might be called "mock-ironic praise." (Provocative resemblances with mock-heroic satire suggest themselves. See especially Swift's "Description of a City Shower," a poem I imagine would have delighted O'Hara.) The attitudes of the speaker must shift as quickly as the facades

in a cityscape, and everything is both available and vanishing.

Related in part to each of the preceding modes, yet occurring often enough in its own distinctive way, the fourth mode concentrates on sentiment itself. Often seemingly surprised at his own ability (or should we say liability?) to experience sudden occurrences of ordinary or even banal emotions, O'Hara writes many poems where he confronts his own reserves of sentiment. This confrontation veers sharply and quickly, however, into the ambiguous. Such poems can often be either the most frustrating or the most intriguing of O'Hara's to read, and they often seem the most unstable, bearing most visibly the marks of conscious turns, labored leaps, and manifest evasions. Here is an opening, from **"Nocturne,"** where the first six lines promise something they never deliver:

> There's nothing worse
> than feeling bad and not
> being able to tell you.
> Not because you'd kill me
> or it would kill you, or
> we don't love each other.
> It's space. The sky is grey
> and clear, with pink and
> blue shadows under each cloud.
> A tiny airliner drops its
> specks over the U N Building.
> Everything sees through me,
> in the daytime I'm too hot
> and at night I freeze; I'm
> built the wrong way for the
> river and a mild gale would
> break every fiber in me. . . .

Traditionally, the poet finds counters in the landscape to measure his "inner weather," but that process visibly malfunctions here. (O'Hara's play with forms and formats reflects his inability to leave them alone; he was as much a tinkerer as an explorer.) The natural backdrop and the events that occur upon it have taken up the coloration of the poet's mood, even down to the quaint "tiny" that modifies "airliner," yet the poet refuses to maintain an attitude, either of constructive reflection or of purgative expressiveness. This sort of poem offers the illusion of development or variation, but the inconclusiveness recurs so constantly that after a while it's implicit in the very forthrightness with which such poems announce their mood. Characteristically direct at the opening, they always finish off with a zany nonsense (this poem concludes: "the Pepsi-Cola sign, / the seagulls and the noise."), signalling O'Hara's tacit admission that enough has been said or that words have to be put in their proper place. Their place, of course, is to be free wheeling through the consciousness, looking for random meanings, but mistrusting any discursive demands on their formal or syntactical possibilities. They are poems in the mode of "fitful sentiment." This mode presents the residue of that fear of selfhood mentioned earlier. John Ashbery says that O'Hara "talks about himself because it is he who happens to be writing the poem." But this is also why the poems are often evasive and fitful: O'Hara is as concerned to escape as he is to reveal himself.

> **Though his mastery of the low style in comport with the attitudes of high camp composes a significant portion of O'Hara's peculiar genius, I think his poetry reveals the stresses and offerings that arise out of larger, less easily named forces in contemporary poetry.**
>
> —*Charles Molesworth*

As was suggested above, these modes, though distinguishable, combine in varying degrees with one another and are often mixed in erratic ways in the longer poems. Each has close affinities with the others, yet they can be viewed separately as dominant influences on various poets who have chosen to emulate O'Hara's style. Anne Waldman, for example, often uses the "personal madcap" mode, mixing it with that of "fitful sentiment," while the other two occur much less frequently in her poetry. James Schuyler's poetry overflows with examples of "surreal serendipity" and "mock-ironic praise," but he never tosses off revelations and incidents just to reflect disorder and hence seldom indulges in "personal madcap." Bill Knott, on the other hand, alternates among all of the modes, using now one and then another in different books, changing styles (within a fairly narrow range) as the fashion dictates. Obviously, O'Hara's influence cannot be attributed simply to the fact that he developed certain stances or tones that would allow personal inventiveness to assimilate large hunks of mundane material. (These modes were employed concurrently by Ashbery and Koch, and all three men form the fountain of the influences that make up what is now all too tiringly, and resentfully by the poets themselves, known as the New York school.) Though his mastery of the low style in comport with the attitudes of high camp composes a significant portion of O'Hara's peculiar genius, I think his poetry reveals the stresses and offerings that arise out of larger, less easily named forces in contemporary poetry.

It could be argued, for example, that O'Hara's poetry, viewed in the context of the 1950s, formed a severe reaction against the "academic" poetry then in the ascendancy by mounting a challenging return to the true spirit of modernism. The breakthroughs of Eliot and especially of the earlier Williams (of *Kora in Hell,* say) had been allowed to calcify, so the argument runs, into the prettified ironic set pieces so beloved by anthologizers and New Critics. What was needed, or in any case what would be most interesting, was a reassimilation of the first energies of modernism bolstered by an infusion of the cosmopolitan, surrealist sensibility. Poetry would once again have a chance to get in touch with the crazily energized surfaces of modern life, but only by abandoning once and for all any lingering notions as to what constituted proper "poetic" subject matter. Something similar, but more polemical, can be presented as a further argument, namely, that the English and American traditions never really secured the attacking front of modernism. Eliot and his peers flirted with the more readily assimilated parts of the European avant-garde but withdrew when they realized what was really at stake. Stevens's hermeticism and Auden's conversion in the forties gave evidence that retrenchment was inevitable. What else might a young poet have done in 1950? It was only in the plastic arts that development seemed steadily exciting, that the forms had not set and the gestures had not stilled. Jackson Pollock and Willem de-Kooning and other abstract expressionists were the only American artists as interesting as the Continental giants of the early years of the century. You simply had to side-step the current literary scene in the States, a plunge not backward to recover something lost or fading, but a jig sideways to pick up the floating currents in other forms. The poetic idiom available to O'Hara was not so much depleted as simply irrelevant.

O'Hara's relations with his circle of painters and poets were the fruition, then, not only of a singular temperament but also of a larger national cultural need. Robert Creeley was listening to the improvisations of Charlie Parker, still digging out a native American idiom from the seemingly disreputable, chaotic cadences of a dispossessed class. Robert Bly was beginning to discover the European and South American surrealists; and voices from the San Francisco renaissance, such as Ginsberg and Snyder, were turning to Eastern mysticism and their own version of the beatified lunacy of William Blake. O'Hara's work was just one more of the freaky alternatives thrown out by the pressures of growing up absurd in the American society of the 1950s. Such a construction of literary history, however skeletal, may go a long way toward normalizing O'Hara's poetics, and allowing it to share the banner of innovation with others both qualifies and increases our appreciation of it. But I would hold out for a more radical formulation of its literary value, both intrinsic and extrinsic. For this formulation we must bear in mind several things, but perhaps most especially the course of O'Hara's influence on the second and third generations of poets to follow his lead. Hardly any young poet today has not written at least a dozen poems in one of the four modes outlined above, and I would argue that no poet born since 1920 has had more of an impact on American poets today than Frank O'Hara. His role in shaping the current idiom challenges overstatement.

His work, as we have seen, resonates more fully when seen in the context of the plastic arts than when seen in comparison to the work of his contemporaries who wrote poetry. This is because O'Hara wanted his poems to assume the status of things, and he was even willing to run the risk that they would sink to the level of commodities. His refusal to mark off clear aesthetic patterns in his work, his insistence that the poems bear all the marks of their occasional nature, and his deliberately nonpurified language reaffirm this commodity aspect of his poetry. In many important senses, O'Hara's poetry takes on the prospects of being the perfect expression of an industrialized world: it is the highest poetic product of commodity-market capitalism. In the two decades between the Second World War and O'Hara's death in 1966, American economics and society began to face, and some would say to resolve, the problems of capitalism at its highest stages of development and production. America did this with its own peculiar, but trend-setting, innovations, or set of innovatory social-engineering techniques: it created the consumer-oriented society. At its simplest level this can be seen as capitalism's enormous and pervasive effort, when faced with the prospect of shrinking industrial growth rates, to "manufacture" the one element that could sustain an expanding economy, namely, consumer demand. In order to do this, and in part as a result of attempting to overdo it, capitalism invaded areas of human activity it had previously left untouched, and their products were monetized and marketed. Activities usually regarded as nonutilitarian, or set apart as ludic and arbitrary escapes from the pressures of a market system, were transformed in both their productive and consumptive aspects. This happened most visibly in the plastic arts, where a pool of palpable objects lay ready for merchandising. Here is how Harold Rosenberg describes it [in the *New Yorker* (20 August 1973)]:

> In the reign of the market, the intellectual role of the artist, in which is embodied his social or philosophical motive for painting, is cancelled, and his public existence is restricted to the objects he has fabricated. . . . Today, art exists, but it lacks a reason for existing except as a medium of exchange, a species of money. Art as a commodity does not even exist for art's sake, since that implies existence for the sake of aesthetic pleasure.

Such socioaesthetic formulations are fairly commonplace, but they are seldom applied to contemporary poetry. Very few people would deny that this is what happened to modern painting in America, but I would extend the argument to include O'Hara's poetry as well, with certain important reservations. Unlike paintings, poetry has no market value (if we exclude the "market" of grants and awards), but its striving to remain autotelic and nonreferential raises the possibility that it can be considered as a kind of species of commodity. O'Hara's impulse to depersonalize his most intimate utterances, to see his poems as possessing their own status as objects, conflicts with his equally strong desire for spontaneity and freedom.

O'Hara's poetry, in seeking to reduce itself to the status of objects, wants above all to avoid what Susan Sontag calls the "curse of mediacy," that is, it will not serve as a reservoir of truth or value, created by an artist and offered to an audience in order to question, clarify, and reaffirm those values. O'Hara's poems point to nothing else; they are absolutely immediate. This flight from the referential uses of language has many modernist exemplars and many explanations; in novelists such as Joyce it is a final form of artistic heroism, an attempt to make the book suffice for the world, or even supplant it. In the fifties and early sixties, O'Hara was, I think, fascinated by this myth, the last viable myth of modernism. His poetry would be sufficient unto the day, in all its dailiness, mundane and fallen and inclusive. But it would also, as both a preliminary to and a result of its dailiness, not have to answer to anything but the poet and his own fantasies. If indeed the poems would take on a "currency" outside these strictures, they would do so by paying their own way, by being

taken up as the lingua franca and used by other poets in their commerce with the world of objects and words.

This aspect of O'Hara's work, of course, can be viewed under a different aegis. Some would call O'Hara a modern Whitman, the poet of the celebratory list, the praiser of the ordinary, the embracer of contradictions. We can agree with this view without denying or weakening the other view. As if overdetermined in a Freudian sense, O'Hara's poetic compulsions represent the confluence of several large movements; and this welter of possibilities that he both tosses up and mockingly refuses to choose among provides the richness his followers continue to tap. But central to O'Hara's poetics is the absence of any idealizing impulse, or any clash of opposing values; all is levelled into an ever more inclusive "yea," and the meretricious mixes easily with the meritorious. As Herbert Marcuse describes it, "works of alienation are themselves incorporated into this society and circulate as part and parcel of the equipment which adorns and psychoanalyzes the prevailing state of affairs. Thus they become commercials—they sell, comfort, or excite." It isn't simply that O'Hara's poems decline to oppose the current "state of affairs," rather it is that their particular mode of celebration leaves little room for any truly personal statement, any possible alternative vision. By using the language of fantasy in a flat, commonplace way and by projecting mundane reality onto a level occupied by the fabulous, O'Hara flattens his words into a scrap heap of nonsyntactical, nondiscursive fragments that can do little beyond record—or reify—a world of objects and objectified sensations. Again, Marcuse:

> For the expression of this other side [different from the established order], which is transcendence within the one world, the poetic language depends on the transcendental elements in ordinary language. However, the total mobilization of all media for the defense of the established reality has coordinated the means of expression to the point where communication of transcending contents becomes technically impossible. The spectre that has haunted the artistic consciousness since Mallarmé—the impossibility of speaking a non-reified language, of communicating the negative—has ceased to be a spectre. It has materialized. [*One-Dimensional Man*]

O'Hara was fitfully aware of this possibility, this sense that the fullest statements had all been said and, having been said, were now only capable of being fractured; but no countervailing statement, no alternative myth was comfortably possible. (See such poems as **"How to Get There"** and O'Hara's essay on Pasternak.) What has happened, I think, is that his imitators and followers have not possessed the same agonized tension between this desire for objectification and the need for spontaneity that O'Hara felt, therefore their poetry is increasingly threatened with inconsequentiality. The winners of the O'Hara Memorial Award published by Columbia University amply demonstrate this.

Finally, O'Hara's poetry reflects a needed vision and must be judged as work of a valuable consciousness because it is strung between two poles, each of which offers liberating possibilities and yet defeats them. These poles are the exaltation of sensibility and the celebration of a world of things. As the poems veer toward these polar extremes, their language faces its problematic limits: words reflect order, though sensibility is whimsical and chaotic; words are fleeting when things are stable and dense when things are evanescent. In his greatest poems, such as **"The Day Lady Died,"** the "personal madcap" mode vivifies the "mock-ironic praise," and the sense of "surreal serendipity" ("I buy / an ugly NEW WORLD WRITING to see what the poets / in Ghana are doing these days") never totally obliterates the "fitful sentiment." Such fortuitous combinations of the various modes are rare in his work, and even rarer in that of his followers.

Overloaded with gestures and attitudes as they are, O'Hara's poems are so fraught with their insistent personality that their status as objects never fully belies their existence in a special class. They reflect their humanness in a special way; they flaunt it and defy it at the same time. They flaunt it by their very availability (the "personal madcap"), heaving themselves forth, indiscriminately asking for recognition, yet careful to retain their idiosyncrasy. Personal and allusive, like an "in" joke, they say you can't know me fully unless you accept all the particularity of my context ("fitful sentiment"), yet simultaneously they promise that such intimate knowledge is worth more than any merely "objective" reality (the "mock-ironic praise"). You, too, can be in, they seem to say, and by accepting me fully in all my quirkiness, you will find that the value of your own quirkiness will become clear. Don't sell yourself cheap, the poems whistle irrepressibly,

> And
> before us from the foam appears
> the clear architecture
> of the nerves, whinnying and glistening
> in the fresh sun. Clean and silent.
> **("Early Mondrian")**

At the same time the poems defy their humanness by their levelling of all values. A sort of falling rate of idiosyncrasy sets in, and the poetry becomes nearly anonymous, like the scraps of printed matter in a Schwitters collage or the *disjecta membra* of a Cornell box (the "surreal serendipity"), floating between the ultimately arbitrary and the ultimately determined. A sharp dialectic of freedom and obsession energizes the poems; in spite of their desire to be objects, they retain numinous possibilities. For all their playfulness, the poems finally do affirm a set of values or, at least, by reflecting certain values in their high resplendence, allow affirmation without ever urging it. These values, of course, are insouciance and improvisation: though the poems want an objective structure, a clear architecture, they yet, inescapably it would seem, act out of a boundless trust of their own nerve. Hearing so many words and phrases that could apply to O'Hara's poetry—pragmatic; Adamic; individualistic; insane energies revolving around a calculated center; for sale and yet priceless—it should be no wonder if we settle for calling them, and judging them as, completely American. (pp. 85-97)

> *Charles Molesworth, " 'The Clear Architecture of the Nerves': The Poetry of Frank O'Hara,"*
> *in his* The Fierce Embrace: A Study of Contemporary American Poetry, *University of Missouri Press, 1979, pp. 85-97.*

Kenneth Koch and "Voice of America" (interview date 1980)

[An American poet, playwright, nonfiction writer, scriptwriter, novelist, and librettist, Koch was a personal friend of O'Hara and, along with O'Hara and John Ashbery, formed what became known as the New York School of Poets in the mid-1950s. Like the other New York School poets, Koch applied Abstract Expressionist painting techniques to his writing. In the following excerpt from an interview originally produced in 1980 for the "Voice of America" radio program, he discusses O'Hara's work habits, influences, and development as a poet.]

[*Voice of America*]: *Mr. Koch, we're always in danger of being perhaps gossipy when we ask one friend to talk about another. One surprising thing about Frank O'Hara, I found, was the smattering of published works during his lifetime, although he seemed to write like water flowing downhill.*

In the introduction to the book, The Collected Poems of Frank O'Hara, *John Ashbery said: "One of his most beautiful early poems, 'Memorial Day 1950,' exists only because I once copied it out in a letter to Kenneth Koch, and Kenneth kept the letter." Why was O'Hara so seemingly negligent about his work?*

[Koch]: I don't know. At the time Frank died, I had no idea how much he had written. When he died, I, Larry Rivers, and a few other friends went into his apartment and got all his manuscripts out. Then another poet and friend, Bill Berkson, and I went through all the manuscripts and catalogued them. I was astonished at the number of poems and at the quality of some of the poems that I had never seen. Frank kept them all in cardboard boxes. Every one was dated.

He didn't always write as easily as water flowing downhill, although I think he usually wrote rather quickly. On a number of the manuscript pages there are revisions—things crossed out and other things written in. They are often very radical revisions, in which lines and ideas are changed enormously. Some of his poems he worked on for days and even for weeks, for example, **"Second Avenue."** I remember that he and I were writing long poems at the same time: I was writing a poem called "When the Sun Tried to Go On" and Frank was writing **"Second Avenue."** We used to call each other up every day and read what we had written over the telephone. We inspired each other. Frank went on writing it for a long time.

Why didn't he publish a lot of work? For one thing, it wasn't easy for any of us to publish our work practically up to the time of Frank's death. Frank is a very famous poet now and his work has received the National Book Award. A lot of magazines have been eager to publish any poem of his. But we were all amassing quite a collection of rejection slips even into our 30s. So, first, it wasn't easy for him to publish his poems. Secondly, Frank had very, very high standards for his work although he knew it was good. I never knew how good he knew his poetry was until after his death when I read all his manuscripts; there were certain poems that I had not seen before, or there were certain poems that when I read them all together I saw that Frank had some idea, as a great poet would, that there was something in his work that was very good. But I remember having a talk with him when we were both in our middle 30s. I talked about so-and-so being great and someone else being great, and Frank said, "Listen. I think we can think about ourselves being great when we have done as much as Wallace Stevens or William Carlos Williams." I think he is as good as those poets, but I think it was hard to see it then when I hadn't seen all his work. And it was hard for him to see it because it is hard to see all one's own work. Then also he seemed to be always more interested in writing than publishing, in writing something new.

About the speed of his writing, he was terribly busy. Once he left his appointment book at my house, a little blue book, and I couldn't help looking at it. Almost every day for a month he had an appointment for lunch, dinner, cocktails, at night going to the theater, the opera, the ballet, and so on, or even sometimes an appointment for breakfast. This was along with working full-time at the Museum of Modern Art, where he not only had a job but sometimes had to write catalogues at home. And he spent a lot of time at painters' studios. Frank wrote a number of poems at his office at the museum on his lunch hour or when there would be a lull in the work for ten minutes. It was very often as though he were ready to write a poem, to be bursting with a poem, and whenever he had a moment, he would write it.

One extraordinary thing about Frank was that he could write with other people in the room. If he had an idea while people were there, he would just go and sit down and say, "Excuse me a minute." And he would write a poem. The strangest example of this I can remember was at a party in East Hampton. There were about 40 people in the room, and Frank sat down in the corner of the room with the typewriter and wrote a rather good poem. He did this without the slightest pretension. I tried to do that, too, but with no success.

If someone interrupted Frank when he was writing, he would put the interruption in the poem. If someone came up and said, "Frank, can I open the window?"—that phrase might get into the poem.

Another way Frank wrote was to music. He would turn on some music or be listening to music on the radio and write a poem inspired by the music. It was as though the poetry was all there in his head and some stimulus—music, something a friend said, or even just some free time—would start if off.

This seems contrary to many of the things I have read that said that painting was the springboard for much of his art. He got inspiration everywhere.

He seems to have been inspired by everything that was full of life, energy, excitement, and force. But, no, it wasn't just painting.

Let's go back to the beginning of Frank O'Hara's work, his early poems. How did he start writing poetry?

I don't know what made Frank decide to be a poet, and I don't know that anybody knows that about anybody. He began to write poetry when he was quite young. There are good poems by Frank from his late teens. Very early on, his work was very sophisticated and very good.

There is one which he wrote, I think, in his early 20s, that is about being a poet. The title is from Coleridge, **"Autobiographia Literaria."** It is characteristic of Frank's dash and humor to take the title of this momentous work and do something of his own with it. (pp. 201-03)

· · ·

It is very much like Frank in that it is very ironic about himself. He is making fun of the pretentious literary attitude that says, "Yes, I used to be very lonely and sad and nobody liked me, and now I'm a wonderful person." Yet, at the same time, it is clear that the irony is there because it is so exaggerated: hiding behind a tree and crying that he was an orphan, and then the exaggeration of calling himself the center of all beauty and asking everyone to marvel at this. At the same time, I believe it. I recognize the feelings. It seems to me to be lyrical and true at the same time it is funny.

"Today" is another early poem, which was also in that letter that John Ashbery sent to me in Paris in 1950. This poem is characteristic of Frank's early work in its energy, its excitement, its use of exclamations, more particularly perhaps in its love of ordinary but sort of dazzling words, and in its praise of plain, ordinary things as opposed to officially poetic things. (p. 204)

About the cross-influences of the New York poets: Did this environment, the city, mean a lot to you?

It meant a lot to me that we were all in the same place, wherever the place was. I don't think we would have been very happy in a smaller town, given our voracious appetites for culture, conversation, excitement, and other people. I don't know whether it was specifically New York; it is hard for me to say anything that would really be true about the city at that time. The important thing for me was that we were together in a city that could sustain us.

I suppose there are some general things that one shares in New York: that sort of dizzying anonymity, the feeling of freedom, the "availability of experience," as Marianne Moore says in a poem about New York, the feeling of excitement and nervousness. Frank liked New York an awful lot. He writes about it very directly, praises it, and is very excited by it. He writes more than John or I write about it certainly—about the experiences that we shared with one another. We were together a lot with Larry Rivers and Jane Freilicher, always in their studios and the studios of other painters. So we shared that whole painting scene. Whatever the painters gave us artistically, which was certainly something, I think we probably gave it back to them just as much. They also gave us their company and their social life. They usually had lofts as apartments and studios. They had openings, which were occasions for parties. They worked hard all day and so had some reason to be happy at night. They could actually make some money from their work and we couldn't. The other poets who were around that we knew of were, as I said in my poem "Fresh Air," always thinking about "the myth, the missus, and the midterms." They seemed to be sort of stuffy, precious, academic types, who were writing symbolically about things.

And you were the iconoclasts?

I don't know what the word means for me since I wasn't brought up to have any idols that I know of. So I don't know that I was destroying any idols. Frank certainly was not boring, if that's what you mean. Iconoclastic? I don't know. It seems to me that an iconoclast is someone who is really seriously oppressed by the official system in such a way that he has to rebel against it. Perhaps that's a revolutionary, not an iconoclast. An iconoclast may make the mistake of taking the ideas that are opposed to him too seriously and being overconcerned with destroying them, whereas maybe the best thing to do instead of destroying all the Fords is to build a good Chevrolet—which is what I think Frank did.

Was his poetry founded on a surrealistic or Dadaist approach?

No, it was not founded on surrealism or Dada. Frank read the French poets and knew them, but his poetry is not surrealistic. It seems to me the surrealist attitude—trusting the unconscious more than the conscious, doing automatic writing, saying whatever comes into your head, using accident in your poems, bringing in material from dreams—all those things that were programmatic for the surrealists (that is, you had to do them if you were going to be a card-carrying surrealist, so to speak), these characteristics have by now become a natural and almost instinctive part of the work of many poets writing in English. You can find them in poets who are not of the "New York School." But whereas a good deal of surrealist poetry tends to stay in this world of dreams and the unconscious and magic, Frank's poetry very clearly comes back to what would be considered ordinary reality. It always ends up back on the streets, back with the taxicabs, and most of all back with his emotional attachments in this life. I can demonstrate that point very clearly with a poem called **"Sleeping on the Wing."** (pp. 204-06)

It is a poem about going to sleep. Frank says in the beginning that maybe one goes to sleep to avoid a great sadness. Anyway he goes to sleep and has a dream about flying—a rather common kind of dream—and Frank in the poem finds himself way up high in the air, feeling very free and above everything. But then he thinks about something in his waking life, about a friend, that brings him back to consciousness and he wakes up. Although the poem uses certain kinds of very quick and perhaps seemingly nonrational verbal techniques that the surrealists either used or invented, it is not a surrealist poem at all because the whole idea of the poem is that you come back from that to something elsc. (p. 206)

. . .

Can you characterize the changes from those early poems,

"Today" and *"Autobiographical Literaria"*—*changes that were wrought on Frank O'Hara while he approached "Sleeping on the Wing"?*

Well, he got older and had more experiences. Frank experienced things strongly. He wrote this in 1955, at age 29. I don't really know how to account for the change in Frank's work. You can say that there was a general change in that the early poems seem almost sheer exuberance in trying out all kinds of different forms and styles. Later, after he had been in New York for a while, there are some poems about suffering, pain, and anger expressed in a direct, angry way. Then there are the poems that seem to express in a rather quiet, calm way a kind of wisdom that he seems to have gotten from both his exuberance and his suffering, but it never was a static wisdom. Frank was always changing and always moving. He was always writing about what was really there in his feelings, in front of him. He always used the words that he really spoke. He used words from books, of course, but there is always something very natural-seeming about his language. He put the names of friends in poems, the names of streets, the names of radio programs, anything, just because it was there. It was very radical of Frank, and it goes along with a whole tradition which has been very important in modern poetry beginning probably with Whitman, a tradition of using the spoken language and writing about ordinary things. Frank takes it even further than Wallace Stevens and William Carlos Williams did, I think. He doesn't at all turn things into literature, although what he writes is literature, of course.

As for the difference between his early and late poetry, well, his work is always about what is most immediate to him and his experience, but I think that when he went to Harvard and then to the University of Michigan as a graduate student, in those early days what seems to come out most strongly in the poems is what he was reading, his excitement about poetry, and then friends, and what was happening, too. What was important in the poems later on seemed increasingly to be his feelings, his relationships to people and the situations that he found himself in. So there is always terribly close attention being paid to what is really there, what's exciting, what's interesting, what's strong, what means something, but the subject changes. Towards the end of his life Frank wrote what I think are some of the most beautiful love poems of the century. One of those, called **"Poem,"** when I first read it, when I too was in my late 30s, I didn't understand very well. Now it seems to me to show a tremendous knowledge of love and relationships between people, and at the same time it is very quiet. It is an odd kind of love poem because it is not a poem written at the beginning of love or the end of love but in the middle. It's written apparently in the middle of a quarrel or is about that situation. (pp. 206-08)

. . .

We have seen that Frank O'Hara used natural language— it's quite evident in these poems—and he used the naturalness of his environment—it's also there. What was so special about Frank O'Hara?

Well, that is a hard question. What is special is the work

that he wrote. I find the language always exciting; I find the music of the poems exciting. In a lot of his poems he seems to be just talking, so that a naïve person might say, "But what's the subject?" He doesn't announce a subject. He's just talking with someone, talking with himself, talking with the reader, talking to a friend, and the subject is the feeling or the situation that has caused him to talk. That is a rather original way to organize a poem.

Sort of musing out loud?

I wouldn't say "musing" because musing suggests some sort of self-indulgent way of talking or thinking that is not going to end up as anything original. What original results have ever come from musing? No, Frank is musing in the midst of a hurricane. He called one of his books **Meditations in an Emergency.** The paradox is that he really is thinking all the time, but the situation he is in is more dramatic than those in which a person is usually able to think—at least to think so subtly and imaginatively.

I think it would be wrong to say that O'Hara's poetry is realistic; it's rather that he uses very real-seeming materials to make something extraordinary.

—Kenneth Koch

About the relation of art and life in his work, I think it would be wrong to say that his poetry is realistic; it's rather that he uses very real-seeming materials to make something extraordinary.

Frank O'Hara was very close to art. He worked in the Museum of Modern Art in New York City. What influence did this kind of exposure have?

He knew all about the painters that he dealt with at the museum before he was a curator there: he was involved in art the minute he came to New York so that it wasn't the job that gave him his familiarity with art. I guess he liked some aspects of his job at the Museum because he was very good at it. It took up an enormous amount of his time, but perhaps that was all right. Boris Pasternak in his autobiography *Safe Conduct* said something to the effect that life distracts us with things that seem necessary for us to do so that it (life) can get on with its real work. Obviously Frank's real work was writing poetry, and—I'm speculating—it's possible that it was good for Frank to have a job that kept him very busy, that those were conditions under which he wrote poetry well.

Pasternak was important to both you and Frank O'Hara. Frank wrote a critical essay on him.

Yes, I like that essay. It's a long one, called **"Zhivago and his Poems."** And I remember another thing about Frank and Pasternak. John Ashbery, Frank, and I all liked Pasternak's early poetry very much, which we read in translation, of course, and his early prose works like *Letters from*

Tula, Aeriel Ways, and *Safe Conduct.* He got the Noble Prize for *Dr. Zhivago,* and then the Russian government would not allow him to go to Stockholm. Frank and I were at a bar the night we got the news. I went home to go to bed, and at three in the morning Frank called on the phone, "Kenneth, we've got to do something." And I said, "What about?" "About Pasternak obviously. We've got to show him he has some support from us." We must have been 28 years old then, and Pasternak had surely never heard of us. Frank said, "We have to let him know that we stand behind him and that we appreciate his early work, too." I asked, "Well, what should we do?" "I think we should send him a cablegram." I said, "Do you think it will get through?" And Frank said, "It might, and I think we should send it." I said, "Do you think it will get him in trouble?" "No, I don't think so." So we composed a cablegram; it took us about a half hour to get the words right to say that we loved his work and that we liked the early stuff as well as *Dr. Zhivago.* And we sent it. And that's all we heard of it. I don't know that he got it. He certainly did not know who the people were who sent it to him or how to get in touch with us. But this was not at all arrogant on Frank's part. He felt that he and we all worked in the community of artists, and, of course, he was perfectly right. (pp. 208-10)

Kenneth Koch and "Voice of America," in an interview in American Writing Today, *edited by Richard Kostelanetz, The Whitston Publishing Company, 1991, pp. 201-11.*

James Breslin   (essay date November-December 1983)

[Breslin is an American educator and critic. In the following excerpt, which was originally published as an excerpt from his book From Modern to Contemporary: American Poetry, 1945-1965 *(1984), he analyzes the indeterminacy evident in O'Hara's poetic depiction of movement, the self, and the relationship between reality and representation.]*

> Grace / to be born and live as variously as possible

Frank O'Hara's indifference to collecting, publishing, and even preserving his poems is well known. "I think he was rather careless with his work," John Ashbery writes; "he had a tremendous energy and zest for it while he was working on it, and then seemed to rather lose interest once it was done" [Bill Berkson and Joe LeSeuer, eds., *Homage to Frank O'Hara*]. In fact, the achievement of O'Hara derives from his renunciation of poetic achievement. O'Hara did not seek to build a poetic career or to form a poetic style. In an interview he tells of an exchange between Max Ernst and Picasso, who asked Ernst to come out for a walk. Ernst refused "because I'm in search of a style": Picasso calmly walked on, declaring that "there is no style." O'Hara, then, did not follow his generation's pattern of adopting a period style which he then dismantled. O'Hara was never seduced by style in the first place; instead, he gives us a "multiplicity of styles" [Roland Barthes, *Writing Degree Zero*]. More concerned with the *activity* of creation than with fetishizing its *products,* O'Hara eluded the stability of any theoretical position, or any style. "To move is to love," he wrote, reversing the usual sense of love as a permanent commitment. His imagination remains uncommitted—mobile, protean, contradictory, and alive.

At a poetry reading held on Staten Island in the early sixties, O'Hara read a poem which he said he had written on the way over on the ferry. Robert Lowell, following O'Hara, sardonically apologized for *not* reading a poem he had written on the ferry. Lowell was no doubt annoyed by O'Hara's arrogant assurance that he could write a good poem so quickly and easily, but the anecdote also reveals a basic difference of poetic principle between the two men. Lowell had relinquished many of the traditional resources of poetry in *Life Studies,* but his poems remained serious acts designed both to include and to contain the movements of time and consciousness. Writing for O'Hara was a much more casual activity, taking place inside the flow of daily activities (like riding the ferry), many of the poems—the "lunch hour" poems, for instance—enacting sheer process: agile, shifting, unpredictable *movement.*

"A Step Away From Them"

It's my lunch hour, so I go
for a walk among the hum-colored
cabs. First, down the sidewalk
where laborers feed their dirty
glistening torsos sandwiches
and Coca-Cola, with yellow helmets
on. They protect them from falling
bricks, I guess. Then onto the
avenue where skirts are flipping
above heels and blow up over
grates. The sun is hot, but the
cabs stir up the air. I look
at bargains in wristwatches. There
are cats playing in sawdust.

          On
to Times Square, where the sign
blows smoke over my head, and higher
the waterfall pours lightly. A
Negro stands in a doorway with a
toothpick, languorously agitating.
A blonde chorus girl clicks; he
smiles and rubs his chin. Everything
suddenly honks: it is 12:40 of
a Thursday.

          Neon in daylight is a
great pleasure, as Edwin Denby would
write, as are light blubs in daylight.
I stop for a cheeseburger at JULIET's
corner. Giulietta Masina, wife of
Federico Fellini, *è bell' attrice.*
And chocolate malted. A lady in
foxes on such a day puts her poodle
in a cab.

          There are several Puerto
Ricans on the avenue today, which
makes it beautiful and warm. First
Bunny died, then John Latouche,
then Jackson Pollock. But is the
earth as full as life was full, of them?
And one has eaten and one walks,
past the magazines with nudes
and the posters for BULLFIGHT and

the Manhattan Storage Warehouse,
which they'll soon tear down. I
used to think they had the Armory
Show there.

          A glass of papaya juice
and back to work. My heart is in my
pocket, it is Poems by Pierre Reverdy.

"A Step Away from Them" charms us with its sense of artless immediacy, spontaneous energy and what O'Hara himself might call its "emotional verisimilitude." Mythical resonance, literary allusion, paradox, irony, hidden metaphoric systems, authorial distancing—in short, what Allen Ginsberg would call "the whole boatload of sensitive bullshit"—that provided the comfortable certainties of critical judgment in the fifties have all vanished. More than that, the absence of meter, rhyme, or any obvious alliteration or assonance leaves **"A Step Away from Them"** without many of the features that mark a piece of writing as a poem; in fact, the only such marker that remains, the breaking of the writing into lines of verse, is more apt to strike the reader as an arbitrary rather than a shaping act. All of this, plus the poem's way of proceeding by indiscriminate inclusion of mundane observations, suggests that the basic selecting, controlling, formalizing characteristics of art have been airily dispensed with.

The critic—"the assassin//of my orchards," as O'Hara once put it—may conclude that **"A Step Away from Them"** is not a bad poem but that it is no poem. Yet, O'Hara titled so many of his works "Poem" precisely because he was aware that many of his readers would deny them the status of poetry. But rather than closing the issue prematurely, we should explore the ways in which O'Hara has redefined the specifically poetic quality. "Picasso made me tough and quick," O'Hara writes in **"Memorial Day 1950,"** and he locates the poetic in a tough realism and an elusive mobility. Whereas normally in reading poetry we experience a tension between the urge to go on and the desire to linger over the parts and prolong our pleasure, in O'Hara the poem is *all* forward push. **"A Step Away from Them"** sits at the opposite end of the literary spectrum from the self-reflexive autonomous works of the Modernists: if the Modernists tried to spatialize lyric form, O'Hara radically temporalizes it.

> **"A Step Away from Them" represents time as an ongoing experience, purely physical and purely transitory.**
>
> **—James Breslin**

"A Step Away from Them" represents time as an ongoing experience, purely physical and purely transitory. During his lunch hour, O'Hara steps away from his fellow workers at the Museum of Modern Art and strolls out into the animate, shifting life of the city at noontime. He keeps moving, taking things in with the speed and precision of a movie camera; the poetic self seems a transparency—again, like a movie film—and experience is absorbed with a kind of evenly suspended attention that does not permit discrimination, emphasis, or even interpretation. O'Hara thus moves through a demystified and secular world of immediacy, from which all vertical, transcendent extensions of meaning have disappeared. Sensations are not "corridors" toward transcendent vision, as they are in James Wright; materiality is not given only in order to be chanted out of existence, as it is in Allen Ginsberg; the poem is no "temple," the poet no "priest," as they are in Denise Levertov. An O'Hara poem—unlike Oakland—is a there that is simply *there*. "After all / who does own anything?" he wryly asks in **"The Three-Penny Opera"**; physical objects in O'Hara do not invite, much less justify, any search for hidden meanings; they cannot be possessed (owned) by means of any frame of reference, sacred or secular. Objects in O'Hara lack depth and duration; they lack depth *because* they lack duration: they go by too quickly to yield meanings.

Of course, even in the relatively small body of criticism that has been written about O'Hara, the interpretative assassins, unwilling to revise their reading habits, have entered the orchards. In *Poems in Persons,* Norman Holland cites another of the lunch hour poems, **"The Day Lady Died,"** and confesses that he found the poem "irritating" because its details seemed "so random and inconsequential." "As for me," Holland writes, "I can only make sense of such a poem by trying to bring all its puzzling elements into some fairly tight relation." And so, rather than trying to discover the poetic motives behind the casual flow of detail in the poem, Holland instead chooses to allay his professional nervousness and reconfirm his belief in organic form—"by bringing a psychoanalytic concept to bear," specifically, the concept of orality. Where there was surface, Holland implies, let there be depths, preferably familiar depths. Once Holland or any other critic gets on a track like this he is not likely to be derailed and his critical engine runs smoothly across O'Hara's poetic orchards, if not converting snakes into penises, then converting the purchase of a pack of cigarettes into an oral fantasy.

Yet O'Hara's poems are filled with signals that such interpretative procedures are inappropriate to them. In his quick, forward-moving medium, observations are not held, weighed, ruminated over, fetishized; O'Hara does not even seem very involved with his objects—but a step away from them. As a result, both persons and objects—and ideas and feelings—become momentary events, experience consumed almost in the instant it is given. Sometimes the experience can be an unexpected sense of unity: "Everything / suddenly honks, it is 12:40 of / a Thursday," but the very precision with which O'Hara locates this moment of unity—12:40, in digits—reminds us of its ephemerality. [William Carlos] Williams is one of the few American poets who meant a lot to O'Hara, but if we contrast O'Hara with Williams we see how steadfastly O'Hara refused to eternalize his objects. Williams slows us down and concentrates our attention on both the object and the words representing it; his poems present isolated images arrested in an empty space. The object has been lifted out of the temporal flux and preserved in an "eternal

moment" [Webster Schott, ed., *Spring and All* in *Imaginations*]. But O'Hara's observations are not grasped and eternalized in this way; as he writes in **"Meditations in an Emergency,"** "my eyes are vague blue, like the sky, and change all the time; they are indiscriminate but fleeting." What is preserved in O'Hara is precisely this fleeting, ever-changing experience of temporal process itself.

To say all this is to say that it is not entirely true to argue that O'Hara replaces an aesthetic of "transcendence" with one of "presence." His lunch hour poems do create a wonderful sense of immediate experience; but they also represent immediacy as evanescent, fleeting, transitory. Sensations disappear almost as soon as they are presented. Objects and people thus remain alien to a poet who can never fully possess them. O'Hara, in other words, remains "a step away from them"; the poem's title in fact offers a double-edged statement that precisely defines the poet's relation toward experience. He's separate, different—the *observer* of all the others; yet his observations are detailed, close, and his own energy parallels the vital life he sees all around him: he's *just* a step away from them. He's both at home and alien, comfortable and anxious, in the city and, as **"A Step Away from Them"** shows, both of these contradictory feelings are necessary to O'Hara's sense of self. When he remarks that the "several Puerto / Ricans" make the street seem "beautiful and warm," he experiences the city as a pleasurable fullness, a feeling that passes almost instantly as O'Hara recalls loss and death: "First / Bunny died, then John Latouche, / then Jackson Pollock." With the next sentence, "But is the / earth as full as life was full, of them?" the flow of observations comes to a sudden halt. O'Hara pauses for self-conscious, reflective questioning; the reader is halted by the peculiar word order and by the need to spell out the ways in which the sentence plays with a cliché. Ordinarily we think of certain people as 'full of life,' but O'Hara turns the phrase around so that life was full with those now absent. Is the earth (where they are buried and decomposing) now full as life was once full with them? Is the earth, human life, now full as it used to be when they were alive—or is temporal experience one of loss and decline? The reader is brought to a heavy stop with the emphatically placed word "them"—which, in the poem's only self-reflexive gesture, takes us back to the title for another set of referents for its "them." Like everybody else, O'Hara is always just a step away from his lost friends, from his own mortality.

Conventionally, such thoughts of time and loss prompt the poet to adopt some eternal perspective from which they can be reconciled; in O'Hara, these weighty issues are simply dropped. O'Hara's mood does change; the ebullient, separate "I" becomes a melancholy, anonymous "one" who keeps moving but who seems merely to be going through the motions in a depressed, mechanical way—passing tawdry magazines and posters and a warehouse, once thought to be the scene of the heroic Armory Show, now about to be torn down. Temporality is felt to be destructive, not a fullness, and the poet seems passive and sad and empty. It's as if the thought of the mortality shared by all makes him just another anonymous figure in the city; he's lost his animating sense of difference.

But O'Hara's depression simply passes. The poem presents a rapid series of unconnected moments and any vestigial desire we may feel to spatialize the poem by viewing it as a conflict between feelings of presence and loss is thwarted by the way these issues are just dropped and by O'Hara's steadfast refusal to provide anything like a resolution at the end. In the final paragraph he drinks some papaya juice and cheerfully returns to work, with a book of poems he loves tucked away in his pocket. O'Hara's casualness, however, makes the poem not less but more moving—giving it an "emotional verisimilitude." O'Hara, then, is not the kind of writer who presses down on or even gently prods a subject until it yields its essence; another reason he called so many of his works "Poem" is that he didn't want them to have identifiable subjects. Instead, **"A Step Away from Them"** presents shifting, contradictory moods, tones, perspectives, selves without either gathering them together into a center or nailing them down with a resolution. As O'Hara said in **"Personism,"** "you just go on your nerve." The poetry that results offers plurality rather than unity, energy and movement rather than the comforts of a stabilizing form.

From Eliot to Ginsberg the modern city poem has been structured as a mythical purgatorial journey that strips away illusions and yields at least the possibility of transcendence. The differences between Eliot's aloof irony and Ginsberg's angry howl or between Eliot's sibylline Sanskrit revelations and Ginsberg's Blakean mysticism are profound; but both "The Waste Land" and "Howl" offer panoramic views of the modern city only in order to annihilate social and physical realities in a moment of hallucinatory vision. Frank O'Hara's lunch hour poems demythologize the poetry of the modern city—as we can see by looking at **"Personal Poem."**

> Now when I walk around at lunchtime
> I have only two charms in my pocket
> an old Roman coin Mike Kanemitsu gave me
> and a bolt-head that broke off a packing case
> when I was in Madrid the others never
> brought me too much luck though they did
> help keep me in New York against coercion
> but now I'm happy for a time and interested
>
> I walk through the luminous humidity
> passing the House of Seagram with its wet
> and its loungers and the construction to
> the left that closed the sidewalk if
> I ever get to be a construction worker
> I'd like to have a silver hat please
> and get to Moriarty's where I wait for
> LeRoi and hear who wants to be a mover and
> shaker the last five years my batting average
> is .016 that's that, and LeRoi comes in
> and tells me Miles Davis was clubbed 12
> times last night outside BIRDLAND by a cop
> a lady asks us for a nickel for a terrible
> disease but we don't give her one we
> don't like terrible diseases, then
> we go eat some fish and some ale it's
> cool but crowded we don't like Lionel Trilling
> we decide, we like Don Allen we don't like
> Henry James so much we like Herman Melville
> we don't want to be in the poet's walk in
> San Francisco even we just want to be rich

> and walk on girders in our silver hats
> I wonder if one person out of the 8,000,000 is
> thinking of me as I shake hands with LeRoi
> and buy a strap for my wristwatch and go
> back to work happy at the thought possibly so

Like **"A Step Away from Them," "Personal Poem"** creates an interplay of playful and serious tones in a quick, light movement. The poem begins with a paragraph of recollection in which the reader may be tempted to stop and to metaphorize the "old Roman coin" and the "bolt-head"—the one rare and the other plain—but he is not given enough clues to justify such a procedure. The charms simply affirm O'Hara's faith in chance and randomness rather than in control or coercion, and it would be a serious error to place them in "some fairly tight relation" with each other or with other details in the poem.

O'Hara is no poetic "mover and / shaker"; he just goes on his nerve and so does the poem. O'Hara did not like "elaborately sounded structures," he tells us in **"Personism";** in fact, he did not like elaborately articulated structures of any kind. "Pain always produces logic, which is very bad for you," he declares. Instead of intricate form or subtle argument, **"Personal Poem"** gives us a rapid catalogue of reflection, observation, conversation, fantasy. A catalogue presents material apparently without selection or hierarchy; it eliminates logical connections; and it *moves*—without containing any principle that would determine the end (goal or termination) of that movement. "Do you think we can ever / strike *as* and *but,* too, out of the language," O'Hara asks in **"Essay on Style";** "then we can attack *well* since it has no / application whatsoever neither as a state / of being or a rest for the mind no such / things available." In O'Hara's world of ongoing process *states* of being and rests for the mind are not available; that is why his speculation on the possibility of eliminating logical connectives from poetic language is at least half serious. That is why no periods (rests) are to be found in **"Personal Poem,"** which comes very close to a language of pure parataxis—of ongoingness. Nor is it the case that behind its discontinuous surface we can discover a hidden system of connections—the way we can in reading works as different as "The Waste Land" and *Spring and All.* O'Hara remains *inside* the flow of experience, not reaching nervously after some external perspective from which, safely, to view the modern city.

> **O'Hara works from a self that is mobile, shifting, multiple ("crowded with / windows"), contradictory, elusive, and incomplete.**
>
> —*James Breslin*

According to O'Hara, the trouble with Olson was his weakness for the "important utterance." The last thing that O'Hara wants to do with experience is to transmute it into conclusive statement: "no such / things available."

Abstract statements can be found in his poetry but ideas are to O'Hara what balls are to a juggler: the last thing you want to do is hang on to one. "We don't like Lionel Trilling"; "we don't like / Henry James so much"; "we don't want to be in the poet's walk in / San Francisco," but the childish insistence with which these attitudes are expressed makes them seem playful and theatrical rather than positions the speaker is deeply committed to—just as the fantasies in the poem ("we just want to be rich / and walk on girders in our silver hats") are mock fantasies rather than ones that O'Hara cherishes or is obsessed by. If the tone does become serious, he lightens it by making "terrible diseases" into a grammatical joke or by flippantly dismissing his concern about isolation ("possibly so"). At the same time **"Personal Poem"** is not merely flippant; it contains a continuous and realistic recognition of the pains and limits of urban life. There is an unspecified "coercion" that might have forced him out of New York (or did his charms keep him in New York up against coercion?), the low batting average in his love life, the beating of Miles Davis, the "terrible diseases," the "crowded" restaurant, the isolation and animosity of a large city and the feeling all through the poem of the pressure of time, the ephemerality of both pleasurable and painful experiences ("now I'm happy *for a time* and interested"). **"Personal Poem"** thus includes an awareness of the coercive and even violent realities of the city, but O'Hara does not respond with Ginsberg's outraged howl of protest. Ginsberg's dilemma is that he deifies coercion into "Moloch," a force so powerful and ubiquitous that it can only be eluded by soaring upward toward transcendence, permanence, and rest.

One of O'Hara's special qualities, then, is that while he does not long to control events, he is not controlled by them either. He dwells on his frustrations no more than he dwells on his satisfactions. If his "batting average / is .016," well, "that's that," and he goes on. The beating of Miles Davis—which Ginsberg would have made into an entire poem in lamentation for the martyred 'bop saint'—outrages O'Hara no more than did the rich lady putting her poodle into a cab in **"A Step Away from Them."** Social realities are not transformed into social issues; instead, they are simply presented—given equal weight and emphasis along with all the other items in the quick play of the poet's attention. At the end of the poem O'Hara wonders "if one person out of the 8,000,000 is / thinking of me"; it's an ironic speculation since he *is* shaking LeRoi Jones' hand at the time and he might assume that Jones has him in mind, but then of course O'Hara is not thinking of Jones so there's no reason to suppose that Jones is thinking of him. Isolation *is* a serious matter in the poem; it may be the cost of living (and writing) without connections; concern about it stays with O'Hara for a fairly long time, from shaking hands with Jones until he buys a strap for his watch. But in the *poem* the experience speeds by and O'Hara thus avoids self-pity; the tone, moreover, is lightened by the strap, a mundane and neutral object. **"Personal Poem"** thus does not close with epiphany, some moment of self-recognition; the serious mood merely dissolves as O'Hara playfully leaves the question to chance: "possible so."

"I was crowded with / windows," O'Hara exclaims in **"A Rant"**; or near the beginning of **"In Memory of My Feelings,"** he similarly writes, "my quietness has a number of naked selves." With their realistic precision and their swift, free, uncommitted movement, the lunch hour poems create the poetic self as a rapid, filmlike series of transparencies, open to experience, neutrally and indiscriminately taking it in, the self an "appropriate sense of space" in which things can remain themselves and poems become themselves. Such receptivity poses the dilemma of ending and entails real dangers. The self may be so open and sensitive to sensation that it may feel engulfed and glutted. "I know so much / about things, I accept / so much, it's like / vomiting," O'Hara complains in **"Spleen."** In fact, so fragile and unstable are the boundaries of the self that O'Hara lives just a step away from self-extinction; that is why the dangers of death and anonymity enter **"A Step Away from Them"** and **"Personal Poem."**

But by running these risks O'Hara created a poetic medium that seems freed from the violence of a formed style or personality. "Personism," he says, "does not have to do with personality or intimacy, far from it!" No confessional poet, O'Hara does not explore the unconscious depths in order slowly to construct a managing ego, the way Lowell does in *Life Studies;* nor does he plumb the unconscious looking for "deep images," the way Wright does in *The Branch Will Not Break.* Objects in the lunch hour poems lack metaphoric depth; the poems' speaker lacks psychic depth—as if he sensed the unconscious to be clogged with weighty obsessions, maddeningly repeated scenarios and themes, and so to descend to those depths would be to fix rather than to free the self. For the last hundred and eighty years poets have been pumping the well of the unconscious in order to explore new interior states and yet to claim a universal or shareable status for those private feelings. The only trouble with the unconscious, for O'Hara, is that it's a bore, a structure of repetition.

After all, who does own or even wants to own any thing—including a self? Rather than the self as the organized and organizing center, O'Hara works from a self that is mobile, shifting, multiple ("crowded with / windows"), contradictory, elusive, and incomplete. Always present and always open and exposed ("naked"), O'Hara is nevertheless continually disappearing over the next hill or, more accurately, around the corner of the next skyscraper. His protean movement reminds us of Whitman, whom O'Hara rated, along with Williams and Crane, as one of the three American poets who is "better than the movies." But Whitman's fluidity has the assurance of both an origin and an end in his transcendent "Me myself," an identity that persists outside of time and change. O'Hara has no such permanent center to start from or return to. Like many poets of the fifties, he repudiated the "impersonal ideal" or what he called in **"Personism"** the "abstract removal" of the poet. Instead, he gives us *Person*ism, or a "personal poem" that is spoken in a casual, intimate tone and filled with the quotidian details of his day. But although O'Hara went further than practically any of his contemporaries in stripping down the poem, he did not fall into his generation's trap of simply reversing an impersonal into a "naked" poetics. Personism, remember, does not have to do with personality or intimacy; the lunch hour poems offer no stable self for us to become intimate with.

The self in O'Hara is, then, at once transparent *and* opaque—perhaps his deepest contradiction. Like the color orange in **"Oranges,"** O'Hara exists both everywhere and nowhere in his poems. We see things through his eyes but we can never step back, surround, and frame him; he is "always bursting forth." If O'Hara is not the withdrawn artist of Modernism, he is not wholly present to himself or to us either. Many of the same features that make the poems seem so direct and immediate—absence of connections and depth—also estrange and conceal the speaker from us, just as his use of the names of his friends, as if they were just as familiar to us as to him ("First / Bunny died, then John Latouche"), creates a *tone* of intimacy while pressing upon us the *reality* of O'Hara's difference and distance from us. It is this sense of estrangement that makes these light, casual poems quietly unnerving and adds another voice to their rich, contradictory play of tones.

"The only way to be quiet / is to be quick," says O'Hara in **"Poetry,"** "so I scare / you clumsily, or surprise / you with a stab." Renouncing the prophetic voice of an Olson or Ginsberg, O'Hara approaches us in a quieter conversational tone. Yet this familiarity is assumed rather than actual, as his equation of intimacy with awkwardness and hostility reveals. O'Hara does wish he could exist on easy terms with his reader—"as if / I were used to you"; in fact, even this wish is exposed at the end of the poem as egoistic—"as if," O'Hara concludes, "you would never leave me / and were the inexorable / product of my own time." The clichéd language mocks this desire for a permanent fusion as a narcisistic fantasy, as if he wanted to get close only in order to take over. Yet poet and reader remain separate and O'Hara's efforts "to / deepen you by my quickness / and delight" only mobilize resistance in readers who cling to what's "logical and proven." Just as **"Poetry"** itself proceeds through quick turns of thought and witty reversals of "proven" truths, so O'Hara destablizes and complicates the relation between poet and reader; the gap between the two becomes a space in which familiarity, awkwardness, estrangement, delight, and hostility all coexist.

A similar gap divides the world from the poet, who can never fully possess ("own") his objects. Continually aware of this disparity between actuality and its representations, O'Hara offers both the most vivid instance *and* the most powerful critique of his generation's poetics of immediacy. In O'Hara—as in the poetry of Ashbery—an elusive immediacy always remains other, and if O'Hara's lunch hour poems strain toward a literal realism, their rapidity—they do move much faster than time actually does—suggests an uneasiness with reality, as if O'Hara kept moving because he was afraid to stop and get involved. To put it another way, O'Hara proposes no reality beyond and above time, but he is not comfortably at one with it either; he takes one short step back and away—*then* he starts moving. His separateness sometimes makes O'Hara anxious; sometimes it makes him playful; and sometimes it makes him both, as it does in **"On Seeing Larry Rivers'** *Washington Crossing the Delaware* **at the Museum of Modern Art."**

> Now that our hero has come back to us
> in his white pants and we know his nose
> trembling like a flag under fire,
> we see the calm cold river is supporting
> our forces, the beautiful history.
>
> To be more revolutionary than a nun
> is our desire, to be secular and intimate
> as, when sighting a redcoat, you smile
> and pull the trigger. Anxieties
> and animosities, flaming and feeding
>
> on theoretical considerations and
> the jealous spiritualities of the abstract,
> the robot? they're smoke, billows above
> the physical event. They have burned up.
> See how free we are! as a nation of persons.
>
> Dear father of our country, so alive
> you must have lied incessantly to be
> immediate, here are your bones crossed
> on my breast like a rusty flintlock,
> a pirate's flag, bravely specific
>
> and ever so light in the misty glare
> of a crossing by water in winter to a shore
> other than that the bridge reaches for.
> Don't shoot until, the white of freedom glinting
> on your gun barrel, you see the general fear.

Based on Emmanuel Leutze's "Washington Crossing the Delaware," Rivers' work managed simultaneously to mock the academicism of his source and to outrage the contemporary New York avant-garde. What made his painting a scandal was not his use of figuration—both De-Kooning and Pollock had already moved in that direction—Rivers' subject matter was not only recognizable; it was historical, patriotic, nostalgic, corny, pop—calendar art. As he later told O'Hara in an interview, "I was energetic and egomaniacal and what is even more important, cocky, and angry enough to want to do something no one in the New York art world could doubt was *disgusting, dead,* and *absurd.* So, what could be dopier than a painting dedicated to a national cliché—Washington Crossing the Delaware." Moreover, the research and the many sketches Rivers drew to prepare for the painting constituted an almost pedantic repudiation of Abstract Expressionist faith in spontaneity; his thin application of paint departed from their thick, painterly surface—just as his irony mocked their intense earnestness. Worst of all, Rivers rejected his predecessors' heroic conception, their sacralization, of the act of painting.

Rivers' work makes its double-edged comment by being, in O'Hara's phrase, "bravely specific." As Rivers goes on to say in the O'Hara interview, Leutze "thought crossing a river on a late December afternoon was just another excuse for a general to assume a heroic, slightly tragic pose. . . . What *I* saw in the crossing was quite different. I saw the moment as nerve-racking and uncomfortable. I couldn't picture anyone getting into a chilly river around Christmas time with anything resembling hand-on-chest heroics." Less illusionistic than Leutze's, Rivers' work is nevertheless more realistic, treating the father of our country with a mixture of mockery and tribute. This crossing *is* "nerve-racking and uncomfortable"; it is cold, as our hero's pink nose testifies, and it is disorderly, as the dispersion of the viewer's gaze *out* from the center to independent areas of interest (e.g., top and bottom left) testifies. Moreover, the cold white river, no mere background in Rivers' painting, becomes a threatening invasive force. Yet emerging out of the surrounding cold, disarray, blur (what O'Hara calls "the general fear") Washington struggles to achieve and does achieve presence, distinction, heroism. So Rivers does not merely parody Leutze and debunk heroism; he redefines it, locating the mythic in the real.

Like Rivers' painting, O'Hara's poem mixes mockery and tribute to create the complex image of a "revolutionary" hero. His fun with "pop" phrases from the "Star Spangled Banner" ("and ever so light in the misty glare") or from grade school histories ("Don't shoot until you see . . . ") were probably suggested by Rivers' play with Leutze's visual cliché and Rivers' use, while working on the painting, of illustrations from grade school history books; but in this poem at least O'Hara is less interested in adapting specific techniques from painting than he is in making his meditation on the Washington the occasion for formulating an aesthetic he shared with Rivers.

At first O'Hara's poem seems to pose a simplified antithesis between realistic and mythical versions of Washington, as if Rivers and O'Hara were somehow powerful enough to burn away all "theoretical considerations and / the jealous spiritualities of the abstract" to arrive at the authentic "physical event." Instead of the mythical "robot" of national folklore—noble, courageous, totally honest—they present an actual *person* who is cold, afraid ("his nose / trembling like a flag under fire"), a calm, cool, intimate killer, a secular but still abstracted idealist ("the white of freedom glinting / on your gun barrel") and an incessant liar. Mythologizing, which abstracts from and rigidifies what's "alive," O'Hara implies, is prompted by "anxieties and animosities"—"the general fear"; the alternative, he suggests, can be found in the "bravely specific" (and totally honest) works of Rivers and O'Hara, whose demythologizings create rather than allay anxiety—since intimacy and specificity become forms of violence when the audience clings to what's familiar, abstract, logical and "proven."

Rivers repudiates Abstract Expressionism; O'Hara repudiates the fifties' amalgam of Symbolist and New Critical principles. Both painter and poet move toward realism, the "bravely specific." Yet his oppositional stance did not force O'Hara into a simplified notion of poetic immediacy, and his poem on Rivers' Washington poses the antithesis between the real and the mythic, the immediate and the fictive, only in order to dissolve it by showing how the opposed terms are implicated with each other. In fact, neither poem nor painting is all that specific or realistic in manner; their textures are aptly described by O'Hara's phrase "misty glare"—indefinite and beautiful, clear and harsh. The "dear father of our country" is thus presented as both a frightened real person and as the mythical hero

in "white pants"; not the idealized "robot" of Leutze's work, "our hero has come back to us" as absurd, menacing, dear, duplicitous, scared and heroic. So O'Hara (like Rivers) does not so much *de-* as *re-*mythologize Washington; in fact, the poem playfully rejects the idea that we can shed all myths and abstractions to become, at last, free persons. "See how free we are! as a nation of persons," O'Hara sardonically exclaims. Hence, if O'Hara mocks the flight from "the physical event," he also criticizes the fantasy that we can be emancipated from "theoretical considerations" and "the abstract." Washington boldly repudiated the religious idealism and subservience of a "nun," but "to be more revolutionary than a nun" is not to be all *that* revolutionary, and Washington's desire to be secular and intimate is also quickly unmasked. He gets close in order, smiling, to kill, and he slays, ironically, to impose a new secular abstraction, "the white of freedom." Animosities and theoretical considerations persist—because of the "general fear" that stirs them.

But O'Hara is not a detached observer who is describing a condition from which he has exempted himself; he mocks his own revolutionary pretentions and he concedes his own experience (like that of Rivers' Washington) of the "general fear" in a way that makes the end of his ironic, sometimes flippant poem emotionally powerful. The poem's closing sentence begins with the reassurance of a "proven" heroic and verbal formula: "Don't shoot until. . . . " But O'Hara then interrupts the cliché with "the white of freedom glinting / on your gun barrel." The potential violence is ennobled by high purpose in "freedom," though "white" may suggest an unsullied beginning or a freedom that is all too abstract and pure, like Washington's impossibly white pants in the painting, and "glinting" makes ominous suggestions that are realized as O'Hara, turning the thought across the line break, uses the plain specificity of "gun barrel" to expose the realities behind the lofty abstraction, "freedom." At this point, ending the sentence with the expected cliché—"until you see the whites of their eyes"—would reassure the reader with its comforting familiarity and by providing a specific, locatable and intimate target for animosities. But like Rivers', O'Hara's work is dis-comforting, and so he does not resolve the poem's tensions by opting either for the dead formula or its mere debunking; instead, at the end, poet and reader are left, like Washington himself, within a "general fear" which *threatens* but *fails* to engulf and overwhelm us.

O'Hara and Rivers both combine improvisational energy, realism of detail, and a continual awareness of loss. O'Hara once remarked that Rivers' "fluctuation between figurative absence and abstract presence" played out "the drama of our lack." Rivers' paintings (like the Washington) are filled with human figures who are missing an eye, an arm, a leg; and "Washington Crossing the Delaware" is partly *about* the danger of being flooded by abstraction—losing distinct shape, color, substance. In his poem on the painting O'Hara too feels the threat of "theoretical considerations and / the jealous spiritualities of the abstract" obliterating "the physical event." The dispersed, transparent, mobile self of poems like **"A Step Away from Them"** exists at the edge of extinction and anonymity, while the people and things perceived, like ideas and feelings, vanish as quickly as they appear. Like Rivers', O'Hara's works assert a human presence always on the *verge* of disappearance; they play out the drama of our lack—and our substance.

Like Washington, O'Hara was "so alive" he "must have lied incessantly to be / immediate." One implication of the Washington poem is that a brave specificity is an assumed posture, that immediacy is a lie, an illusion, a poetic construction. "I really dislike dishonesty [more] than bad lines," O'Hara told an interviewer; but having ranked sincerity over literary values, O'Hara then reversed his grounds by declaring that dishonesty occurs when "someone is making themselves more elegant, more stupid, more appealing, more affectionate or more sincere than *the words will allow them to be*" (my emphasis). In short, honesty is a literary *effect,* a more or less persuasive illusion. Moreover, the very linguistic nature of poems marks them as constructs. Objects, persons, events all have a dynamic, elusive quality for O'Hara that converts writing into an activity which, as we have seen in **"Why I Am Not a Painter,"** can never finally enclose its objects. Poetic language is thus not magically incarnational for O'Hara, as it is for Levertov. Poetic works, even ones as close to ongoing process as O'Hara's lunch hour poems, are creations that are ultimately provisional, arbitrary, and artificial—literary.

As a result, the self in O'Hara's poetry—honest and duplicitous, transparent and opaque—becomes a fictional construct as well, even though it is not easy to pin down exactly *what* has been constructed. Confessional poetry often works by stripping away externally imposed, "false" selves in order to uncover an original, core self which, in a poet like Plath, turns out to be not her real but her idealized self: Ariel, the "fine, white flying myth." Such poetry, then, exploits a rhetoric of honesty and self-exposure in order to permit the writer to mythologize him or herself in ways that the ostensibly self-exploring poet remains blind to. O'Hara denounced the "emotional spilling over" he found in confessional verse; he attacked its excesses because he repudiated the model of consciousness that justified them. Rather than struggling to recover a lost core of identity, O'Hara creates a theatricalized self that is never completely disclosed in any of its "scenes." A title like **"My Heart"** leads us to expect revelation of the poet's inmost feelings. But O'Hara begins a little flippantly (and self-congratulatorily): "I'm not going to cry all the time / nor shall I laugh all the time, / I don't prefer one 'strain' to another." The poem continues to stress his elusive contradictoriness and concludes with what seems a simple affirmation of O'Hara's unguarded receptivity: "and my heart— / you can't plan on the heart, but / the better part of it, my poetry, is open." The heart is spontaneous, open to change, unpredictably alive, but this heart is not located in the flesh and blood Frank O'Hara but in his creations, "my poetry," where we encounter "the better part of it." That playfully ambiguous phrase may suggest that his poems contain the more acceptable part of himself or that they contain most but not all of him. Either way, a part of O'Hara remains outside of poems in which openness is an admitted act of contrivance and duplicity. "My final merit I refuse you," Whitman warned in "Song of My-

self"; like him, O'Hara cannot be contained even within the relatively gentle boundaries of his "open" literary creations, and in this self-absence we have O'Hara's final gesture of elusiveness. Perhaps more than any poet, O'Hara minimizes the difference between a poetic and an actual, interpersonal act of communication; "the poem is at last between two persons instead of two pages," he says in **"Personism."** O'Hara's conversational voice, along with his whole way of assuming our familiarity with his small circle of friends in New York, creates a very strong sense that the poems are spoken by an empirical individual, not the persona of the New Criticism. Yet the poet can no more present or even represent the real Frank O'Hara than he can the real George Washington; O'Hara, too, had to lie incessantly to be immediate.

"It is more important to affirm the least sincere," claimed the author of the seemingly artless and spontaneous lunch hour poems, suggesting that at least one of the two persons involved in a poetic transaction might be hard to locate. In fact, the oppositions between nature and artifice, authenticity and duplicity, provide O'Hara's most pervasive contradictions and many of his poems construct a world of display, disguise, and theatricality in which O'Hara exists with the same mixture of delight and uneasiness with which he speeds along the noontime sidewalks of New York. One place to locate O'Hara's fascination with illusion and appearance is in his film poems: **"The Three-Penny Opera," "An Image of Leda," "In the Movies," "To the Film Industry in Crisis," "Ave Maria,"** and the three elegies for James Dean. Unlike writing, movies present images directly; and it is this immediacy that makes the cinema "cruel / like a miracle"—like the swan's rape of Leda (**"An Image of Leda"**). Whereas we can step back and separate ourselves from a painting, this gap dissolves once the lights go out and the screen lights up at the movies: the medium floods the mind with images, giving film the invasive character of a sexual assault. As O'Hara portrays it in **"An Image of Leda,"** this violation is both resisted and desired, cruel and miraculous. Yet for all their sensual immediacy, films are finally no more (and no less) a "physical event" than a poem is; the cinema envelops us in the ravishing and miraculous presence—of an illusion, though the final paradox in **"An Image of Leda"** is that such an insubstantial "shadow" or "disguise" can give "real / pleasure."

In fact, a realm of illusion and disguise conveys the same instability and mobility that we found in the lunch hour poems, as we can see from O'Hara's poem on the movie of **"The Three-Penny Opera."** Polly Peachum and her friends are "free and fair"; Mack the Knife is a "splendid hero"—because they refuse to become passive sufferers in "the general fear." "After all / who does own any thing?": the question, as we've seen, alludes to the absence of human mastery and control in O'Hara's world. In its specific context, however, the question also gently mocks the self-justification of the lower-class thief: 'I'm not imposing my will on others because nobody really owns anything anyway.' But O'Hara shows how this defense circles back on its proponent; in **"The Three-Penny Opera"** objects possess an almost magical power to elude any would-be possessor, liberating thieves included. Polly's jewels "have price tags in case / they want to change / hands, and her pets" are not domesticated but "carnivorous. Even / the birds." Similarly, "Mackie's knife has a false / handle so it can express / its meaning as well as / his." It is not as if these objects took on the actively threatening powers of, say, Sylvia Plath's tulips; rather, our inability to make objects into mere extensions of our wills becomes at once scary and funny.

But what about Polly and Mackie themselves? Aren't these intriguing figures cinematic illusions rather than substantial presences? Or, to put the question a little differently, if O'Hara had been in Berlin in 1930, would he have found Polly and Mackie "ambling the streets like / Krazy Kat"? Of course, Krazy Kat, who may have been ambling the comic pages but hardly the streets of Berlin, collapses the distinction between reality and fiction that the question had begun by assuming. "You'd have seen all of us / masquerading"; rather than offering a fixed reference point that would permit us to discriminate between what's real and what's imaginary, reality itself is enigmatic, fictive, and theatrical. The actors in this play are all "chipper; but / not so well arranged"—like an O'Hara poem; they create a lively surface which it is easy to recognize as a contrivance, a role. Yet these charming surfaces and light-hearted disguises cannot finally be penetrated; as in the lunch hour poems, the self ("masquerading") becomes a construction with its depths concealed. It is now possible to understand more fully why Washington "must have lied incessantly to be / immediate": only by being tricky, slippery—by living variously—can anyone be *alive*.

"The Three-Penny Opera," moreover, makes it particularly clear that it is the very fact that people, objects are various and "free"—and thus, unconnected—that creates "the general fear," a feeling that O'Hara shares but is not dominated by. In the lunch hour poems this lack of connection permits a rapid, shifting mobility that has undertones of anxiety and even moments of melancholy. If the more ominous consequences of such gaps and discontinuities are stressed in "The Three-Penny Opera," O'Hara still crosses the sinister with the playful. "Those / were intricate days," he concludes of the Berlin of 1930; the precisely chosen "intricate" conveys his realistic awareness of, and his enjoyment of, the labyrinthine difficulties of an elusive reality.

"The Three-Penny Opera" also explicitly engages the issue of meaning. "Why, / when Mackie speaks we / only know / what he means / occasionally"—in part because he speaks German in the movie but more importantly because Mackie is such a liar that we can seldom be sure we know what he *really* means. "His sentence / is an image of the times"; both—sentence and times—are deceptive. Earlier in the poem O'Hara writes that "whenever our / splendid hero Mackie / Messer, what an honest / man! steals or kills, there / is meaning for you!" O'Hara here identifies fixed meaning with violence, as he does in "The Critic"; and by conflating "splendid hero" and "honest / man" with "steals or kills," O'Hara cracks open the fixed senses of these words: *his* sentence becomes an image of the times. O'Hara's use of contradictions to create a mo-

bility of meaning attains its most brilliant expression in his "In Memory of My Feelings."

"I don't prefer one 'strain' to another," says O'Hara. One of the important strains in O'Hara's writing is the surrealist, which he turned toward as one alternative to the mandarin orthodoxies of the postwar period. Rather than the Spanish and Latin American surrealists who intrigued Wright and Bly, O'Hara was stimulated by the earlier French group: Breton, Tzara, Péret, Desnos. No doubt he was fascinated by their annihilation of logic, their rapid, startling transformations, their blending of the ordinary and the hallucinatory, their clashing oppositions and wild disjunctions of image and tone. O'Hara's early experiments with surrealism—in "Oranges," "Easter," and "Second Avenue"—juxtapose the beautiful and the obscene, the natural and the mechanical, in ways that are more contrived than revelatory, as if bombastic French language games were a sufficient substitute for the current "academic parlor game." The linguistic difficulties posed by "In Memory of My Feelings," however, are generated by a complex emotional substance and a dazzling stylistic variety; surrealism, no longer for O'Hara merely the means to surprising effects, provides the adequate language for the dynamics of feeling and the problems of writing as they are experienced by a perpetually dislocated self. "In Memory of My Feelings" offers O'Hara's fullest exploration of the self, its relations to the world of material objects, its relations to a personal and cultural past, its love-hate relation to poetry. As such, the poem marks one of the major accomplishments of contemporary poetry.

At the start of its fifth and last section, O'Hara writes:

And now it is the serpent's turn.
I am not quite you, but almost, the opposite of visionary
You are coiled around the central figure,

                                                            the heart
that bubbles with red ghosts, since to move is to love
and the scrutiny of all things is syllogistic,
the startled eyes of the dikdik, the bush full of white flags
fleeing a hunter,
                    which is our democracy
                                                            but the prey
            is always fragile and like something, as a seashell can be
            a great Courbet, if it wishes. To bend the ear of the outer
            world.

Writing about a poem like this is like trying to write on water. Perhaps the best way to deal with this passage is not so much by trying to extract meaning from it—all too easy, as it turns out—but by trying to articulate the processes we follow as we read it. Our best position is thus a step away from it and from there we can see how reading the poem engages the reader with precisely those difficulties that the poet is writing "about." At the other end of the literary spectrum from the lunch hour poems, "In Memory of My Feelings" lacks any literal level, carrying to an extreme a tendency already apparent in poems like "Meditations in an Emergency" where all kinds of information that we would ordinarily get in such a poem— about the speaker, his lover, their breakup—have been omitted. Here, as we shall see, the absence of a literal level derives from O'Hara's inability, made clear at the end of the poem, to reach any originating cause or source for his feelings, his "selves." But the effect throughout the poem is to force the reader to understand all the poem's images as metaphoric, even those that are as realistic as objects in a painting by Courbet. Moreover, metaphoric levels multiply: the poem deals with the personal history of the poet, with western history (from the Arabs to the Greeks and Romans to the European aristocracy to the French Revolution, American democracy and World War II), with the history of poetry, with the nature of poetry (especially its relations to number, logic, resemblance), and with the activity of writing this poem. Presumably, there are other levels.

So the poem's images are contrifugal, metaphoric forces, proliferating meanings. But it's not as if these images were themselves stable points of departure; rather, they are constantly shifting in the poem's circling, self-revising movement where, it seems, anything can turn into anything else—"as a seashell can be / a great Courbet, if it wishes." One thing a reader tries to do is to isolate parts out of this slippery, moving mass—only to discover that the parts keep blending in with each other. When I originally turned to this passage, I wanted merely to talk about the phrase "red ghosts," but I quickly saw that to give its "full" sense I had to quote the entire sentence in which it appeared, and the following sentence, and the two preceding sentences; even stopping at that point is distorting and artificial, since "red ghosts" refers back to the closing lines of section 4 where O'Hara becomes an Indian standing on the beach watching the approach of Columbus, an Indian who quickly metamorphosizes into an ancient Hittite (mentioned earlier in section 4) who loves a horse in a "frieze." To love a horse on a frieze is, of course, the opposite of believing that "to move is to love." In a similar way, the last sentence in my quotation ("To bend the ear of the outer world")—along with the image of the serpent—receives a further twist of meaning from the next sentence: "when you turn your head / can you feel your heels, undulating? that's what it is / to be a serpent." In short, I discovered that units in the poem can only be distinguished by bringing to an artificial close the turning, transforming movement of the poem in process. So, in order to read at all we 'construct' parts—just as O'Hara has done in writing the poem, in order to write at all. But even this will not take us very far in domesticating the poem—because, again, of the way these "parts" generate multiple, sometimes contradictory meanings. The relatively simple phrase, "which is our democracy," momentarily isolated in a separate line, is syntactically ambiguous: "which" can refer either to "hunter" or "fleeing," so "democracy" becomes both hunter and hunted, like George Washington in the poem about the Larry Rivers painting. The serpent coiled around the heart may be embracing, it may be protective, it may be threatening to choke the heart; and the heart itself, proposed as "the central figure" in this poem about the poet's feelings, turns out to be multiple, consisting of many "red ghosts." And the "red ghosts" themselves? Like so many things in the poem, they contain many, opposing suggestions. They are wild, primitive, red, Indian-like, alive; they are ghosts, elusive memories from a dead personal / national past. "Red ghosts" both possess and lack substance, like feelings; they are quick and ephemeral yet haunting and timeless—like feelings.

One question that concerns O'Hara in this passage is whether by trying to 'capture' his fleeting emotions in language he is eternalizing or killing them. As soon as he imagines the heart as a kind of boiling cauldron bubbling with feelings, he turns to the language of logic and epigram to fix a truth about the mobility of love: "since to move is to love." But in the following line O'Hara, always a step ahead of us, turns around on his own propensity for freezing feelings into logical statements: "and the scrutiny of all things is syllogistic." As the passage goes on to suggest, the poet / logician may be a hunter with his feelings as his "prey." Earlier in the poem O'Hara had mocked the Greeks who "could speak / of time as a river and step across it into Persia, leaving the pain / at home to be converted into statuary," as he had mocked the Hittite in love with a horse in a "frieze." If **"The Critic"** externalizes the desire to fix objects with stable meanings, **"In Memory of My Feelings"** reveals the wish to control and master to be the poet's own, in fact to be integral with the activity of writing, the "trying desperately to *count* them [his feelings] as they die." Writing about his feelings makes O'Hara both the hunter and the hunted; but his self-conscious awareness of this dilemma creates the circling, metamorphic movement of his poem which, in turn, makes his poem the opposite of "statuary" or a "frieze."

A reader might feel more comfortable if he could grasp this dynamic, frustrating work and hold it still, if he could develop some distance and perspective that would allow him to create a text with stable parts in fixed relations. No such thing available. Instead, the reader is asked to 'open' himself and let the poem invade him the way the world constantly violates O'Hara's transparent self. Or, more accurately, the reader, too, becomes both hunter and hunted, alternately making O'Hara's "fragile" words and feelings his "prey" and becoming *their* "prey." The gratifications are those of process rather than product, movement rather than goal. In this poem, which combines self-reflexiveness and ongoing process in an even more radical way than did the **"Essay on Style,"** there is no terminus, no stable unity that we finally arive at. The refusal of ending in this poem can be characterized from yet another angle of approach. All of the poem's images are extensions of O'Hara; they reflect his feelings. Yet, his relation to these images is like his relation to the serpent: "I am not quite you, but almost." His images reflect O'Hara, but not quite: and this predicament has two important consequences. Objects and words cannot fully incarnate O'Hara any more than O'Hara can completely master words and objects and make them mere "prey." All three terms in this equation—world, poet, medium—remain independent from each other and in this way O'Hara acknowledges a realm of existential reality that remains resistant to himself and his poem. Yet all three terms remain intricately implicated with each other. Along with the kind of syllogistic scrutiny which strives to separate experience into fixed categories and relations, **"In Memory of My Feelings"** also offers resemblance, which reveals all the leaks in those fixed categories. At the very beginning of the poem, O'Hara writes that "my quietness has a man in it, he is transparent / and he carries me quietly, like a gondola, through the streets. / He has several likenesses, like stars and years, like numerals." With its third line, the poem's proliferation of resemblances begins: the man is like many things, not just gondolas; he is like stars, years, numerals; and he is also like them in having many—in fact, infinite—likenesses. Surrealism characteristically works by startling imagistic transformations; James Wright's version of surrealism, for example, offers the metamorphosis of the literal into the magical "deep" image. But O'Hara is the "opposite" of such a "visionary." **"In Memory of My Feelings"** offers not metaphoric transformations but likenesses—not identifications but resemblances. The poem, then, creates a dynamic field of proliferating resemblances among parts which, in turn, remain independent of each other; they are not pulled together into some full, spherelike form.

"Grace / to be born and live as variously as possible," O'Hara writes in section 4. The absence of any totalizing form allows him to explore the self fully, its insecurities, transparencies, defenses, evasions, yearnings, obsessions. He adopts, variously, a dazzling range of roles, styles, tones, "selves," in what becomes the most freewheeling and open-ended expression of his protean self. The mood of "quietness" with which the poem begins is abruptly shattered when O'Hara disperses himself into all the aspects of a scene at a race track:

> An elephant takes up his trumpet,
> money flutters from the windows of cries, silk
>   stretching its mirror
> across shoulder blades. A gun is "fired."
>
>   One of me rushes
> to window #13 and one of me raises his whip
>   and one of me
> flutters up from the center of the track amidst
>   the pink flamingoes,
> and underneath their hooves as they round the
>   last turn my lips
> are scarred and brown, brushed by tails masked
>   in dirt's lust,
> definition, open mouths gasping for the cries of
>   the bettors for the lungs
> of earth.
>   So many of my transparencies could not
>   resist the race!

Serpentlike, O'Hara keeps shedding and taking on new transparencies, new guises. "The conception / of the masque barely suggests the sordid identifications," he declares in section 4; neither the idealized, aristocratic masque nor the New Critical idea of the poem as mask can define the proliferations in the catalogue that follows:

> I am a Hittite in love with a horse. I don't know
>   what blood's
> in me I feel like an African prince I am a girl
>   walking downstairs
> in a red pleated dress with heels I am a champi-
>   on taking a fall
> I am a jockey with a sprained ass-hole I am the
>   light mist in which a face appears
> and it is another face of blonde I am a baboon
>   eating a banana
> I am a dictator looking at his wife I am a doctor
>   eating a child
> and the child's mother smiling I am a Chinaman
>   climbing a mountain

> I am a child smelling his father's underwear I am
>   an Indian
> sleeping on a scalp.

Yet, as these two passages suggest, O'Hara's ebullient mobility and his brave transparency make him feel vulnerable and helpless; they leave him either immersed in a frantic series of "sordid identifications" or close to a painful self-extinction. Other parts of O'Hara thus yearn for the stability of some "simple identification"; "one feels nostalgic/for mere ideas," he says, "and one of me has a sentimental longing for number" and the graceful assurances of the old order. In section 2 he tries to deal with familial losses and the threat of his own death in "an atmosphere of supreme lucidity" and philosophic detachment; in what becomes both an anticipation and a questioning of Lowell's poetic project in *Life Studies,* O'Hara wants to resolve feelings of loss by converting them into poetic "numbers." Elsewhere, O'Hara would like the protection of the "war hero" or the coercive power of the hunter; but these images of power and stability always dissolve and multiply in just the way the single man in O'Hara's "quietness" at the beginning of the poem almost immediately begins to proliferate. The cool "facade" in section 2 collapses into a rocketlike explosion of feeling and the desire to reify emotions collapses into "the trying desperately to count them as they die." The "war hero," no dependable model of a forceful, unified identity, has "many selves," as does the "meek subaltern" who replaces him; and the hunter in section 1 discovers that the serpent he wishes to kill turns into a Medusa, reversing the roles of victim and victimizer. Parts of O'Hara thus struggle for an ascendancy which always eludes them. O'Hara cannot conquer himself any more than we can conquer his poem; and for the same reasons.

> **"In Memory of My Feelings" shows what happens to the autobiographical poem when the writer can no longer find any vantage point from which to construct a sequential narrative or stable identity out of his experience.**
>
> **—James Breslin**

Given its dynamic, shifting, open character, how can O'Hara bring **"In Memory of My Feelings"** to an end? Here, offered with a self-conscious awareness of the arbitrariness in deciding where a poem's ending begins, are its closing lines:

>   And yet
> I have forgotten my loves, and chiefly that one, the cancerous
> statue which my body could no longer contain,
>
>   against my will
>   against my love
> become art,
>   I could not change it into history
> and so remember it,
>   and I have lost what is always and everywhere
> present, the scene of my selves, the occasion of these ruses,

which I myself and singly must now kill
and save the serpent in their midst.

Intimacy is experienced as invasive; a lover gets inside O'Hara like a "cancerous / statue"—a dead weight that has a poisonous life of its own. The poet struggles to exorcise his lover by turning him into "art," but he can't convert his experience into "history," the way Lowell does in *Life Studies,* and O'Hara's inability to detach himself from the past produces the poem's wild temporal dislocations, the past continually invading the present. **"In Memory of My Feelings"** contains a number of parodic journeys: ascending the mountains in section 1, crossing the desert in section 3, voyaging to the New World in section 4. Yet O'Hara always remains aware of the way the discoverer of a new "land," "so free," immediately changes into the conquistador, who tries to "stay" and "count" riches that elude him anyway. Throughout the poem, old orders are constantly crumbling—and *any* order instantaneously becomes an *old* order—but the rich new "land" of the present cannot be entirely separated from old patterns of thought and feeling. For this reason the poem abounds with old fictions—selves, images, plots—which were not invented by the poet yet have invaded him and his poem. It is this presentness of the past which explains why, in **"In Memory of My Feelings,"** ongoing process coexists with self-reflexiveness; O'Hara both moves on and repeats.

Feelings die quickly, yet they hang on like ghosts. As a result, O'Hara, in one of the many self-contradictory sentences in this passage, has "lost what *is* always and everywhere"; he has lost what he can no more grasp or lose than the past—namely, the present. The "real" literal present is thus a source or origin, "always and everywhere," which he can neither reach nor evade; it is like the poet's self which, as we have seen, is everywhere and nowhere "present" in his poems. Like the new "land" that turns out to be slippery territory, the present is experienced by O'Hara as a theatrical "scene" for the poet's many "selves," yet something substantial enough to be the occasion, the instigation, for his "ruses."

"In Memory of My Feelings" shows what happens to the autobiographical poem when the writer can no longer find any vantage point from which to construct a sequential narrative or stable identity out of his experience. The myth of psychoanalysis provided Lowell with an external perspective by means of which he could detach himself from himself, resolve the series of losses he records in "Life Studies," disengage himself from the past, strip away projections, and, in "Skunk Hour," enter the disintegrating but substantial ground of the present. No such things available for O'Hara, who always remains both inside and outside himself, his past, his feelings, his present, his poem. At the very end of **"In Memory of My Feelings"** O'Hara rises up in what looks like an heroic gesture aimed at striking through all the masks, penetrating to authenticity and pulling himself together at last. But the phrase "I myself and singly" splits the self in the very act of unifying it and the final line declares O'Hara's intent to "save" that slippery, invasive, poisonous, beautiful energy that keeps proliferating new transparencies, selves, guises—the energy that allows O'Hara to work inside all these old fictions and disguises and makes them *live* again. **"In Memory of**

My Feelings" ends by refusing closure. In its final turn, the poem affirms that turning, shifting power that is always and everywhere present in O'Hara's poetry. (pp. 7-16)

James Breslin, "The Contradictions of Frank O'Hara," in The American Poetry Review, Vol. 12, No. 6, November-December, 1983, pp. 7-16.

Mutlu Konuk Blasing   (essay date 1987)

[*Blasing is a Turkish-born American educator, translator, and critic. In the following excerpt, she explores the anagogic aspects of O'Hara's poetry, particularly in the poem "Biotherm."*]

> two parallel lines always meet
> except mentally
>
>   **"Poem V (F) W"**

"Great art," Frank O'Hara insists, "is seldom about art"—"except in baroque periods." Its insights may be so compelling and so pervasive that they can be applied to art as well, but its true subject is the "structure" of nature. In de Kooning's work, for example, "structures of classical severity" grant "insight into the structure of man's identification with nature and the play of forces which it involves." Similarly, "to think that late Mondrian is 'painting about painting' is a grievous error," and "when Keats wrote, 'Beauty is truth, truth beauty,'—it is a grievous error to think that he was writing about writing poetry"; instead, he was stating his "insight into the structure of human sensibility." O'Hara acknowledges another kind of art, however, "which *looks* to be about nature but is lacking in perceptions of it": "the real subject is not nature, but portraying nature, and while it may be very beautiful it is less grand to observe the structure of artistic effort as a metaphor for the structure of nature itself" [Frank O'Hara, **"Nature and New Painting,"** in *Standing Still and Walking in New York,* edited by Donald Allen]. To translate O'Hara's distinction into poetic terms, observing the structure of artistic creation as a metaphor for the structure of nature would make one a poet of analogies, but an anagogic poet—for whom "parallel lines always meet"—sees nature, human sensibility, and poetic form as isomorphic.

From Whitman's leaves, which identify humans and nature in the patterning drift of poetic language, to Pound's image or vortex, where energy creates pattern and emotion organizes form, the work of O'Hara's predecessors attests to the "implacable identifications of man with nature." Their vision of the identity of nature and human sensibility cannot be reduced to an insight into the structure of language, for the insight that is revealed in poetic language has also patterned the language of the poem itself. Such an insight exceeds the terms of language; as Pound claims, the imagist poem of the "super-position" of the outward or objective on the inward or subjective offers "freedom from time limits and space limits" ["A Retrospective," in *Literary Essays of Ezra Pound,* edited by T. S. Eliot].

A language that discloses and is informed by the structure

of nature and human sensibility does not subscribe to the codings of the ego, which include the dichotomies of subjective and objective, conscious and unconscious minds, space and time, foreground and background, past and future. According to O'Hara, too, "great art" transcends these distinctions in a coincidence or superimposition of total subjectivity and total objectivity. Consequently, he can insist on "a clearheaded, poetry-respecting objectivity" and, at the same time, allow that great art offers transcendence—in his words, "Well, great painting does make one feel like God." O'Hara attributes to Jackson Pollock the achievement of just such a total subjectivity/objectivity: "It is the physical reality of the artist and his activity of expressing it, united to the spiritual reality of the artist in a oneness which has no need for the mediation of metaphor or symbol" [*Art Chronicles, 1954-1966*]. The poetic analogue of this kind of art would be a writing more than writing and more than "style"—a writing that would identify nature and sensibility, the physical and the spiritual.

O'Hara's search for an anagogic writing for his time begins with a species of surrealism, a rejection of the mediating structures of figurative rhetoric, representation, and logical or grammatical progression. **"Second Avenue"** exemplifies this phase, about which O'Hara writes: "To put it very gently, I have a feeling that the philosophical reduction of reality to a dealable-with system so distorts life that one's 'reward' for this endeavor (a minor one, at that) is illness both from inside and outside." Although Pound could be more clinical about this "illness," O'Hara is referring to the same "economy," the same debased "currency," the same "disease." His concluding remarks about the poem suggest a possible cure: the "verbal elements," he writes, are "intended consciously to keep the surface of the poem high and dry, not wet, reflective and self-conscious." Yet, since a "high and dry" surface can signal a species of estheticism—promising "to destroy something but not us"—it does not make for the objectivity or transcendence of "great" art, and the question becomes how to deepen the surface so that the "nature" of language can keep pace with its "sensibility."

One way to give language such depth is to write in a measure that responds to "breath" or the physiology of writing. In an interview O'Hara remarks, "It seemed to me that the metrical, that the measure let us say, if you want to talk about it in Olson's poems or Ezra Pound's, comes from the breath of the person just as a stroke of paint comes from the wrist and hand and arm and shoulder and all that of the painter. So therefore the point is really more to establish one's own measure and breath in poetry, I think, than—this sounds wildly ambitious since I don't think I've done it but I think that great poets do do it—rather than fitting your ideas into an established order, syllabically and phonetically and so on." He adds that the painters inspired the poets in this project of trying to "be the work yourself." "Adherence to nature, indifference to conventions" guide O'Hara's emphasis on "breath" as a compositional force. The poet can do without the mediation of conventions if he can manage to reveal the passage or flow of energy that is the nature or structure of his medium. And O'Hara's description of Pollock's "spiritual

clarity" suggests that such a "state" is the poet's goal as well: "In this state all becomes clear. . . . This is not a mystical state, but the accumulation of decisions along the way."

In such a "strange ascent," it is technical engagement that opens up the "limitless space of air and light in which the spirit can act freely and with unpremeditated knowledge." The "light" of Whitman's "Crossing Brooklyn Ferry" and Pound's spectrum of lights—the "measureless seas and stars, / Iamblichus' light" in which the gods move; the sunlight/moonlight of the *ming* ideogram, which depicts the stillness at the center of natural time; and the final "little light, like a rushlight / to lead back to splendour"—are isomorphs of O'Hara's "light." At the end of **"Biotherm"**—which O'Hara believed he was able to keep " 'open' and so there are lots of possibilities, air and such"—a transcendent light shines through the elements into which the speaker dissolves:

> as I wave toward you freely
> the ego-ridden sea
> there is a light there that neither
> of us will obscure
> rubbing it all white
> saving ships from fucking up on the rocks
> on the infinite waves of skin smelly and crushed
>   and light and absorbed.

O'Hara's submergence in Whitman's and Pound's process, which takes him beyond surrealistic negativity and culminates in his identification with his poem in **"Biotherm,"** begins in **"In Memory of My Feelings,"** where he contrasts two kinds of memory and two kinds of poetry. The kind of art into which pain may be converted reifies forms and is exemplified by statuary. Such a conversion means forgetting one's temporality, "loves," and "feelings," and this choice of forgetfulness makes for the recorded history of Western art. It is what the "mountainous-minded Greeks" chose when they could "speak / of time as a river and step across it into Persia, leaving the pain / at home to be converted into statuary." The metaphoric elision of time and the formal conversion of pain into stone are versions of the same choice, O'Hara suggests, and adds, "I adore the Roman copies," extending the tradition through and beyond Rome to other examples of "supreme lucidity, / humanism, / the mere existence of emphasis," to end with the romantic apotheosis of a sublime "mountain-mindedness":

> At times, withdrawn,
> I rise into the cool skies
> And gaze on at the imponderable world with the
>   simple identification
> of my colleagues, the mountains. Manfred
>   climbs to my nape,
> speaks, but I do not hear him,
>   I'm too blue.

Peoples outside the Western humanist tradition—Hittites, American Indians before history, and the Arabs "racing into sands, converting themselves into / so many"—offer an alternative to such memorializing and forgetful art. "Sands," suggesting the erosion of mountains and statues, are not "cool"; nevertheless, the desert inhabitant remains protected:

> Rising,
> he wraps himself in the burnoose of memories
> 　against the heat of life.

At the conclusion of the poem, O'Hara calls such possession of one's temporality history; unlike art, history offers remembering. By history he means not a forgetful, codified, and "counted" history but the project of being in and of one's time.

In this project, Whitman remains O'Hara's guide, as his explosive catalogue of "sordid identifications" acknowledges. The spatial and temporal expansion of this section recalls the later sections of "Song of Myself," where Whitman traces the phylogeny of the systems of thought inscribed in the convolutions of his brain, as he had earlier traced the phylogeny inscribed in his physiology. Such a "repetition" on the poet's body, psyche, and tongue constitutes a "re-membering," a true "re-collecting" of spatial and temporal dispersal and variety; at the same time, however, it is destructive of the "ego," shattering the grid of space/time on which distinct lives are plotted, and dispersing the self into grains of sand, waves of light, leaves of grass. Yet O'Hara affirms that it is a

> 　　　　　　　　　　　　　　Grace
> to be born and live as variously as possible.

In the sequence of identifications that follows, O'Hara is "afoot" with his vision and travels through time and space, dissolving the categories of inside and outside. For O'Hara no less than for Whitman, the self is not a conceptualization of physiological, psychosexual, and psychosocial processes but a literal body, the stage on which such processes, dramas, and metamorphoses are played out. Thus O'Hara's series of identifications appears also to be triggered physiologically by alliteration, consonance, internal rhymes, and so on. While a series such as "I am a baboon eating a banana / I am a dictator looking at his wife I am a doctor eating a child / and the child's mother smiling I am a chinaman climbing a mountain" is open to psychological and sociological interpretation, the passage refuses to be reduced to an ulterior meaning. No such danger exists, because O'Hara's is a "deep" surface, which is itself the structure of the interpenetration of subject and object, mind and matter.

The "Grace" that precipitates O'Hara's catalogue is the fulcrum of the poem. Not unlike Whitman's "leaves," "Grace" is O'Hara's saving name, his Logos that redeems all the other proper names strewn through his pages and renders their dispersal a grace indeed. **"Second Avenue"** already hints at the transforming power of the word in a description of a Grace Hartigan painting:

> . . .Grace destroys
> the whirling faces in their dissonant gaiety
> 　where it's anxious,
> lifted nasally to the heavens which is a carrousel
> 　grinning
> and spasmodically obliterated with loaves of
> 　greasy white paint
> and this becomes like love to her, is what I desire
> and what you, to be able to throw something
> 　away without yawning

> "Oh Leaves of Grass! o Sylvette! oh Basket
> Weavers' Conference!"

The same name-word appears in **"Poem (Khrushchev is coming on the right day!)."** The turbulent, windy day, complete with atmospheric foreshadowings of an apocalypse or a second coming, is a day of "cool graced light" that miraculously "saves" or redeems the darkness of other names ("Purgatorio Merchado, Gerhard Schwartz") and other lives ("François Villon, his life, so dark"), if only in passing:

> and the light seems to be eternal
> and joy seems to be inexorable
> I am foolish enough always to find it in wind

—which is an unexpected and unmerited grace after all, what with still being "close to the fear of war and the stars which have disappeared." **"Poem"** also alludes to "Grace Hartigan's / painting *Sweden*," for in the superimposition of "Grace" and "grace"—of a proper name, a part of one's time and "loves," and the word that signifies divine love or transcendence of historical contingencies—lies the grace/Grace of an immanent Logos or light that can regather its temporal and spatial dispersal. And this one grace granted the poet is a pun, an accidental gift.

While **"In Memory"** retains both an autobiographical past and a narrative syntax, **"Biotherm"** aspires to forgo all such mediation and to *be* a poem of immanence. More academic than either long poem, **"Essay on Style"** outlines the difference between them, for it spells out the conditions of an "intimate" language. Here, O'Hara renounces subject matter and all other contingencies—mothers and their social-familial network, as well as the mediations of syntactic and grammatical connectives—that threaten to come between him and intimacy with his mother tongue. Likewise, "lettrism" is exposed in the metaphor it rides on—"treating / the typewriter as an intimate organ why not? / nothing else is (intimate)." Just as the poet will probably not eat alone for the rest of his life, however, he will probably continue to make use of *and, but, also,* and "NEVERTHELESS (thank you, Aristotle)." In **"Biotherm,"** O'Hara relinquishes as much as possible syntactic orders, subordinations, and hierarchies—all analogues of the social-familial relationships that repress the intimacy of the mother tongue—in order to sound a language intimate and intense, purified of "rhetoric." **"Biotherm"** engages the "serpent" of **"In Memory"** in action: shedding the orders of the self, all perspectives, calendars, histories, geographies, and even articulation itself, we uncover "the ardent lover of history . . . / tongue out."

O'Hara's last major poem, **"Biotherm"** can serve as a focal point for a study of his entire career, which in a sense is a countdown for this final explosion. The poem tests the limits of his conception of poetry as speech that informs the body of his work. From the beginning, the temporal line of speech is O'Hara's principle of organization, underlying his surface coherence. Yet his speech cannot be regarded as simply "chatter" or "conversation," which would reduce his poems to mere surface. O'Hara's description of Pollock's achievement—"The scale of the painting became that of the painter's body, not the image of a body"—provides a painterly analogue of his own deep surface. The "scale" of **"Biotherm"** is the poet's tongue, not a language that is the image of the tongue's activity. The tongue in all its functions is primary for O'Hara. It is the organ of speech, an erotogenic organ, and, as Webster's puts it, "an important organ in the ingestion of food." **"Biotherm"** is written in the impure language of the tongue performing all its functions, sometimes simultaneously; in these lines, for example, O'Hara speaks, drools over the words, and chews them up, all at once:

> no flesh to taste no flash to tusk
> no flood to flee no fleed to dlown flom the iceth
> loot

Still, the lines are consciously "poetry," complete with echoes of "The Rime of the Ancient Mariner." Although such impure speech appears in many other O'Hara poems, nowhere is the flow of words so torrential, so exhilarating and terrifying, as in **"Biotherm."** It is a *journal intime* that places us inside language as it is being spoken, and returns us to the root connection of "intimate" and "intestine" ("in time" of the body). The energy and excitement that charge the poem derive from an infantile wholeness predating the differentiation of the functions of the tongue. [In *Three Essays on the Theory of Sexuality*] Freud writes that sexual activity first "attaches itself to functions serving the purpose of self-preservation and does not become independent of them until later"; thus the erotogenic nature of the mouth grows out of the pleasurable sensation of "the warm flow of milk." It is this infantile mouth that speaks the fleshly speech of **"Biotherm."**

O'Hara's consumption of language—which is impersonal, synchronic or ahistorical, and grammatical—in speech that is of the flesh of his body determines not only the texture of the words but the organizing principle of **"Biotherm."** His method is not that of a dream if, following Freud, we define a dream as "a mutilated and altered transcript of certain rational psychical structures," to which it has a metonymic or metaphoric relationship [*Jokes and Their Relation to the Unconscious*]. **"Biotherm,"** however, cannot be resolved or translated back into a rational "metatext" of explainable sequences, for O'Hara constructs *his* sequences over the void of interpretation, the void that would connect the metatext to the text it would explain. For example, he writes:

> then too, the other day I was walking through
> a train
> with my suitcase and I overheard someone say
> "speaking of faggots"
> now isn't life difficult enough without that
> and why am I always carrying something
> well it was a shitty looking person anyway
> better a faggot than a farthead
> or as fathers have often said to friends of mine
> "better dead than a dope" "if I thought you were
> queer I'd kill you"
> you'd be right to, DAD, daddio, addled annie
> pad-lark (Brit. 19th C.)

The "analysis and synthesis of syllables"—the "syllabic chemistry" that Freud describes in *The Interpretation of Dreams*—is no more gratuitous here than in a dream. The alliteration ("faggot," "farthead," "fathers," "friends"), though it parodies the use of such a poetic device, still manages to be quite significant. Similarly, the sequence of words ending in verbal disintegration ("dead," "dope," "DAD, daddio, addled annie pad-lark") is a palpably significant sequence; yet any interpretation would be gratuitous. Either the sequence is related as a surface, or it is not related at all. For in the final two lines the chemistry of the words takes over and makes the words into things. When the tongue composes the line, the referentiality of the words appears all but irrelevant, and the very project of interpretation is challenged. The distinction between the surface and what hides behind it becomes untenable, for the surface is now a depth. The inner is turned inside out, giving us an intimate surface.

"Biotherm" is full of verbal improvisations that deepen its surface, for O'Hara's verbal play always has an emotional, psychic, and/or sexual undertow. Yet interpretation remains beside the point, since it is primarily the tongue that is playing with language. The various "translations" in the poem, for instance, are strictly lingual. *Vitalità nell' arte* is played into "vitality nellie arty," which, as O'Hara himself hints, is far from an insignificant phrase: "ho ho that's a joke pop." The passage playing with "balls" in two languages is another example of a kind of *Ursprache* of the tongue—a universal, physical human speech. Emphasizing the tongue as the poetic organ is one way of combating the alienation of language. At its inception, language seems to be distanced from its physical source. Edward Sapir tells how language is not a biological function, "for primary laryngeal patterns of behavior have had to be completely overhauled by the interference of lingual, labial, and nasal modifications before a 'speech organ' was ready for work. Perhaps it is because this 'speech organ' is a diffused and secondary network of physiological activities which do not correspond to the primary functions of the organs involved that language has been enabled to free itself from direct bodily expressiveness" [*Culture, Language, and Personality*]. This is the first kind of displacement or "difference" that O'Hara tries to undo by stressing the multifunctional nature of the tongue.

The intimate connection between words and food, between using language and eating in the infantile erotic/nourishing sense, provides O'Hara with a secular version of the "Word made flesh" and accounts for the overwhelmingly alimentary nature of his imagery, including his imagery about poetry. **"Biotherm"** contains a full range of images of questionable edibles, inedible edibles, and edible inedibles, for here O'Hara resists the merely edible just as he resists a transparently referential language that reduces words to currency:

> first you peel the potatoes
> then you marinate the peelies
> in campari all the while playing
> the Mephisto Waltz on your gram
> and wrap them in grape leaves
> and bake them in mush ouch
> that god damn oven delicacies
> the ditch is full of after dinner

And:

> oh god what joy
> you're here

       sob and at the
       most recent summit
       conference they
       are eating string
       beans butter
       smooth slurp
       pass me the filth
       and a coke pal
       oh thank you

And:

       perhaps
       marinated duck saddle with foot sauce and a
           tumbler of vodka

And even:

       (MENU)
       Déjeuner Bill Berkson
               30 August 1961
       Hors-d'oeuvre abstrait-expressionistes, améri-
           cain-styles, bord-durs, etc.
       Soupe Samedi Soir à la Strawberry-Blonde
       Poisson Pas de Dix au style Patricia
       Histoire de contrefilet, sauce Angelicus Fobb
       Le réunion des fins de thon à la boue
       Chapon ouvert brûlé à l'Hoban, sauce Fidelio
           Fobb
       Poèmes 1960–61 en salade
               Fromage de la Tour Dimanche 17 sep-
                   tembre
               Fruits de Jardins shakspériens
               Biscuits de l'*Inspiration* de Clarence
                   Brown

       Vin blanc supérior de Bunkie Hearst
       Vin rouge mélancholique de Boule de neige
       Champagne d'*Art News* éditeur diapré
       Café ivesianien "Plongez au fond du lac glacé"
                           Vodka-campari et TV

Food becomes a metaphor for everything one takes in and processes; from the most physical to the most spiritual, all things are converted into energy, body heat, "biotherm." The alimentary imagery, metaphors, and "sound effects" that turn words into food and food into words serve to re-define poetry as speech. This kind of speech is an activity of the whole person: it converts matter and motion; it re-cycles impressions, feelings, memories, emotions, hopes, loves, foods, drinks, poems, books, magazines, movies, languages. **"Biotherm"** is a "secular" microcosm of the *Cantos:* instead of Pound's patterning mind we have O'Hara's kind of patterning digestive system, and what we experience while reading it is the sense of the passage of time *through* the man writing it. Everything is in flux—ingested, processed, and voided by the poet's body. And if a poem is not the process of this passage, it is inert and alien—waste or excrement.

In **"Personism: A Manifesto,"** O'Hara takes credit for fin-ishing literature off and adds, "For a time people thought that Artaud was going to accomplish this, but actually, for all their magnificence, his polemical writings are not more outside literature than Bear Mountain is outside New York State." Of course, neither are O'Hara's poems, for whatever one writes is forever turning into "Art," always freezing into form on "one / after another filthy page of

poetry," and the problem remains that one cannot destroy literature except in literature. This is what Jacques Derri-da [in "La Parole Soufflée," in *Writing and Difference*] calls the "fatal complicity" of the destructive discourse, which must inhabit the structures it would destroy. O'Hara is trapped along with Artaud, and there is a basic affinity between them. Artaud promises an art of total presence—in Derrida's words, "an art which no longer yields works, an artist's existence which is no longer a route or an experience that gives access to something other than itself; Artaud promises the existence of a speech that is a body, of a body that is a theater, of a theater that is a text because it is no longer enslaved to a writing [i.e., a script] more ancient than itself, an ur-text or an ur-speech." For if one's speech is not the breath, if the body is not the text or the theater of life, then the excreted, frag-mentary, lifeless "work of art" is indeed "Pig-Shit," as Ar-taud calls it.

To conceive of writing as the physical activity of speech, as body chemistry and not its product (unless it be body heat or biotherm), has important implications for poetic forms. First of all, in Artaud's words, "when we speak the word 'life,' it must be understood we are not referring to life as we know it from its surface of fact, but that fragile, fluctuating center which forms never reach. And if there is still one hellish, truly accursed thing in our time, it is our artistic dallying with forms, instead of being like vic-tims burnt at the stake, signaling through the flames." The repeatable, "static" structures posited by forms are beside the point, since the center of life is elsewhere:

       The best thing in the world but I better be
       quick about it better be gone tomorrow
                   better be gone last night and
           next Thursday better be gone
                           better be
                               always

These lines open **"Biotherm"** and give fair warning that the poet is going to be "quick," because the present disap-pears as it occurs. In order to inhabit the fluctuating center of life, one has to keep up with time. Conventional formal devices, however, do not inhabit destructive real-time; they only represent it by abstracting it into a repeatable time. Thus, while William Carlos Williams may be "better than the movies," his "measure shmeasure" must be re-jected nonetheless, for measure surfaces the fragile, fluctu-ating center of life, the biological depth of words, by ab-stracting speech into a pattern. O'Hara attempts to de-stroy the concept of measure by undoing the word with "shmeasure"; yet such a gesture affirms his faith in word magic, which remains the basis of poetry.

O'Hara's parody of Williams—he has in mind the ending of Book Five of *Paterson*—continues:

       measure shmeasure know shknew
       unless the material rattle us around

The phrase "know shknew" suggests the second major formal implication of a poetic of speech. Seen as a physical activity, speech is total presence, and this conception of literature implies more than a rejection of narrative, syn-tactical, and metrical forms; it rejects signification altogether. Since words can be things only at zero-degree referentiality, signification can be achieved only at the cost of "presence"—only through the symbolic distancing of a word, which is "the murder of the thing" [Jacques Lacan, *The Language of the Self: The Function of Language in Psychoanalysis*]. Like grammar or meter, referential word use reduces language to a currency one can use and be used by. The analogue of O'Hara's emphasis on words as things is his transformation of monetary units, another currency, into color values ("the dime so red and the 100 dollar bill so orchid / the sickly fuchsia of a 1 the optimistic / orange of a 5 . . . / the magnificent yellow zinnia of a 10")—all so that when he adds two and two, he does not have to get four: "now this is not a tract against usury it's just putting two and two together / and getting five." The gibe at Pound reminds us that here, too, O'Hara's play is serious, for Pound and Williams are his acknowledged predecessors in this project. Williams also asks "for relief from 'meaning' " and admonishes:

> —never separate that stain
> of sense from the inert mass.   Never.
> Never that radiance
>
>   quartered apart,
> unapproached by symbols

Extracting "meaning" from the "mass" leaves behind dead matter or inert "lead," whether the husk of the signifier whose "soul" has been "stolen" by the signified, or the earth itself, which has become "an excrement of some sky" [William Carlos Williams, *Paterson*]. Pound attacks the same excremental, usurious "economy" of signification, which steals, absents, and defers life itself.

Again, however, O'Hara's attempt to undermine the currency of referential language is doomed to failure, since it must be carried out in referential language. He confronts once more the fatal complicity of destructive discourse in what it would demolish, and the desire for "presence" remains just that—a desire signifying a lack. Yet there is a way out, which is also a way in; and that way madness lies. Jacques Lacan defines psychotic language as a language of "regression"—of treating words like things: to the psychotic, "all the Symbolic is Real." As a result, his discourse is "composed of nothing but words, rather than of the Word"; it is "incomprehensible" discourse. If symbolic or referential word use is "sane," defines "sanity," and upholds the verbal arrangement called "reality," a confusion of the symbolic relationship between words and things represents a total derangement of reality, including a derangement of the words "world" and "I." But poets can work in this ground between word and thing. While the madman is caught in the "sliding" relationship between signifier and signified, a poet like O'Hara chooses to inhabit that slippery ground, asserting his freedom both from the convention of language as symbolic word use that cuts us off from things, and from the tyranny—the totalitarianism—of a world where signifier and signified are literally identical.

Madness and poetry meet in a writer like Artaud, for whom words are wholly body. Gilles Deleuze discusses Artaud in terms of the schizophrenic's experience of language and the body as all depth and no surface: "Freud

Front cover for Second Avenue.

emphasized this schizophrenic aptitude for perceiving the surface and the skin as if each were pierced by an infinite number of little holes. As a result, the entire body is nothing but depth." And "as there is no surface, interior and exterior, container and content no longer have precise limits; they plunge into universal depth," and language gets lost in "the vertigo of the bodies' depths and their alimentary, poisonous mixtures." Artaud's language, "articulating, insufflating, or palatalizing a word, causing it to blaze out so that it becomes the action of a partless body, rather than the passion of a fragmented organism," is a literary example of such language, in which the word is "still a sign, but one that merges with an action or passion of the body." In this state, the categories of both the signifier and the signified have disappeared, and " 'speaking' has collapsed onto 'eating,' and into all the imitations of a 'chewing mouth,' of a primitive oral depth" [Gilles Deleuze, "The Schizophrenic and Language"].

O'Hara's use of words in **"Biotherm"** springs from these depths and tests the limits of an anagogic rhetoric. Once again, the title is telling: the suntan lotion Biotherm with plankton—"practically the most health-giving substance ever rubbed into one's skin"—is food absorbed through the skin, which at the end of the poem becomes coextensive with the sea and swallows up the universe in a gaping innerness turned inside out. When the inside/outside dichotomy disappears, words lose their meaning. They may still retain a certain power of designation and signification, Deleuze argues, but this function is experienced as "empty," "indifferent," "false." **"Biotherm"** stands on this threshold, for the unavoidable residual referentiality of O'Hara's language becomes almost "irrelevant." Thus the "non-sense" of **"Biotherm"** is neither a metaphysical puzzle nor a mimicry of nonsense like Lewis Carroll's "Jabberwocky"; O'Hara's is the "non-sense" of the language we use—of referential language seen inside out. Thus the poet's resistance to meaning, referentiality, and an impersonal language that "steals" his breath-speech and alienates his life in the form of someone else's "message" renders him "mad" at the source.

"Poetry," written some ten years earlier, presents the same complex of ideas and suggests what might have set in motion the poetic that culminates/bottoms out in **"Biotherm"**:

> The only way to be quiet
> is to be quick, so I scare
> you clumsily, or surprise
> you with a stab. A praying
> mantis knows time more
> intimately than I and is
> more casual. Crickets use
> time for accompaniment to
> innocent fidgeting. A zebra
> races counterclockwise.
> All this I desire. To
> deepen you by my quickness
> and delight as if you
> were logical and proven,
> but still be quiet as if
> I were used to you; as if
> you would never leave me
> and were the inexorable
> product of my own time.

In nature, time is inseparable from essence, while the poet can only desire such presence. For the use of language places him in sequential time, so that he experiences his essence—which is time—as alien. Time is not an "accompaniment" to the "innocent fidgeting" of speech; time is the fatal fidgeting of speech, which can only yearn for the wholeness of the praying mantis, crickets, the zebra. All can race counterclockwise yet be of their "own time," for without speech their time is not sequential. The speech of poetry introduces the consciousness of an external time; this "mortal meaning," Lacan writes, "reveals in the Word a center exterior to Language." That center is time, and while O'Hara does not always write a nonsequential, nonreferential "speech," he is always conscious that the attempt to write as a mimesis of speech—the attempt to undercut an impersonal language—introduces another kind of absence, a nonbeing at our source. Thus O'Hara is always conscious of speaking **"A Step Away from Them,"** for he knows that the minute he begins to speak, he begins to thread his way to the dead. The darkness that backs the surface shimmer of a poem like **"A Step Away"** marks the essential O'Hara, whose dazzle of surfaces so

full of life's clutter and chatter is only so much "neon in daylight." (pp. 156-69)

Mutlu Konuk Blasing, "Frank O'Hara: The Speech of Poetry," in her American Poetry: The Rhetoric of Its Forms, *Yale University Press, 1987, pp. 156-69.*

Philip Auslander (essay date 1989)

[*In the following excerpt, Auslander examines several of O'Hara's plays, noting O'Hara's incorporation of Abstract Expressionist and proto-Pop Art painting styles into his writing.*]

> I want to be
> at least as alive as the vulgar
>
> **"My Heart"**

Frank O'Hara, museum curator and art critic, was also a prolific poet and playwright. Best known as a critic for his championing of the Abstract Expressionists (he wrote a monograph on Pollock and catalogue essays on Kline, Motherwell, and David Smith), O'Hara was also sympathetic to the second generation New York School artists. He collaborated with Grace Hartigan, Larry Rivers, Norman Bluhm, and others on projects combining poetry with visual art. He wrote favorably of Rivers, Rauschenberg, Claes Oldenburg, Jim Dine, and Red Grooms, but was less fond of Warhol and other artists who, in his estimation, "tend to make their art *out of* vulgar (in the sense of everyday) objects, images and emblems" rather than making such things "*into* art." This distinction is an important index to O'Hara's sensibility; his poems and plays have more in common with the work of Rivers and Rauschenberg than with that of Warhol. O'Hara's molding of his everyday experience into poetry produced a comprehensive record of his life; as he observes: "What is happening to me, allowing for lies and exaggeration which I try to avoid, goes into my poems" (**"Statement for *The New American Poetry*"**). Much the same can be said of O'Hara's plays, of which he wrote over twenty-three, mostly brief, examples in his lifetime. Many of the plays are occasional pieces, several coauthored with friends. *The Coronation Murder Mystery* by [John] Ashbery, O'Hara, and [Kenneth] Koch was written for James Schuyler on his birthday; *Flight 115* was composed by O'Hara and Bill Berkson while on an airliner, passing a typewriter back and forth between them. Others of O'Hara's plays are explicitly literary parodies, including an untitled *commedia dell' arte* scenario, and a mock pastoral entitled *Love's Labor: An Eclogue.* In this [essay], I focus on O'Hara's most fully realized dramatic works: his early Noh plays, the "combine" plays of 1952 and 1953, and his last play, written in 1961. These plays reflect O'Hara's awareness of the art of his day. His thematic preoccupation with the present moment relates to the gestural immediacy of Abstract Expressionism; his "combine" plays unite Abstract Expressionist compositional devices with an approach to imagery reminiscent of Robert Rauschenberg's, from whose work I have borrowed the adjective "combine." O'Hara's brand of irony and his approach to imagery in his last play, *The General Returns from One Place to Another,* bear comparison with Larry Rivers' work.

O'Hara's earliest dramatic experiments are the plays he called his Noh plays, produced in 1951 by the Poets' Theatre in Cambridge. It is likely that the inspiration for these plays came from a familiarity with W. B. Yeats's ritualistic dramas; O'Hara seems to have been interested initially in developing a contemporary poetic drama. Although O'Hara, like Yeats, wrote for a coterie theatre, his Noh plays reflect none of the elitism of Yeats's undertaking; in the best of his Noh plays, O'Hara scrutinizes the idea of modern ritual drama through the lens of mass culture, producing an ironic perspective closer to Pop Art than to Yeats.

O'Hara follows the outline of Noh drama very broadly. His Noh plays each have three characters who can be seen as the traditional Shite (protagonist), Waki (explainer), and Chorus of the Japanese theatre, though these functions overlap in O'Hara's characters in a way that they do not in traditional Noh drama. His plays conform to Ernest Fenollosa's observation that each Noh play "embodies some primary human relation or emotion" and examines it exhaustively [*"Noh" or Accomplishment* (1916)]. Each of O'Hara's plays deals with a single situation and a limited range of emotional response. In *Try, Try,* a soldier comes home from war to his disaffected wife; in *Change Your Bedding!,* a young man wants to marry a woman of whom his mother does not approve. An essential difference between O'Hara's plays and the Noh is that whereas the Noh is the province of "life . . . painted with the colours of memory" [*Arthur Waley, The No Plays of Japan* (1921)], O'Hara's plays focus on present action. As Arthur Waley indicates, the action of a Noh play is usually a reenactment of an event by the ghost of a participant for the spiritual edification of an observer, the Waki. Although O'Hara's plays contain lengthy passages in which characters recount their memories, they also offer a present conflict. This aspect of O'Hara's Noh reflects his commitment to the present. Marjorie Perloff observes [in *Frank O'Hara: Poet among Painters* (1977)]: "O'Hara loves the *motion* picture, *action* painting, and all forms of dance—art forms that capture the present rather than the past, the present in all its chaotic splendor." Whereas the traditional Noh emphasizes the importance of reexamining the past and learning from it, the theme of O'Hara's Noh plays is the danger of dwelling on the past.

The conflict in *Change Your Bedding!* is between Max and Lillian, his mother; Lillian's brother Alfred stands by as Chorus-cum-Waki. Allegorically, Alfred and Lillian represent Reason, while the woman Max loves stands for Passion. Alfred explains that he and Lillian need "to have reasons and a / guide" in life; Max seeks relief from their stultifying attitudes with a woman he describes as "a word / I hadn't yet pronounced / but had always longed for." Lillian and Alfred try to make Max feel guilty by enumerating the sacrifices his family has made for him. In this respect, the play anticipates O'Hara's well-known poem **"In Memory of My Feelings,"** whose second stanza begins:

> The dead hunting
> And the alive, ahunted.
>
> > My father, my uncle,
> my grand-uncle and the several aunts. My

grand-aunt dying for me, like a talisman, in the
> war,
> before I had ever gone to Borneo.

As Perloff notes, the poet believes he ought to feel remorse at the deaths of relatives who, his family insists, died that he might live, but he feels only indifference, or—in the case of the play—resentment. In the end, Alfred comes around to Max's way of thinking, warning Lillian that her "memories are / dreams of choked time, I / have watched their useless tangle contort itself till / your choices now obscure your very real disgust."

Change Your Bedding! is not altogether satisfactory as either poetry or drama. The symbolic and allegorical oppositions of Parent and Child, Passion and Reason, Present and Past, lend the play a measure of universality appropriate to the Noh format, but are overly facile. The play fails where **"In Memory of My Feelings"** succeeds because the subjective point of view O'Hara employs in both is more appropriate to the lyric than to the drama. In the poem, we can accept the speaker's vision of his dead relatives as an hyperbolic metaphor for his own feelings of detachment. When we see Max express similar sentiments in direct confrontation with his mother, the effect is artificial and forced. In the poem, the disparity between what the poet has been told he should feel and what he really does feel is an internal one; when this conflict is externalized and distributed amongst opposing characters, a universal emotional condition becomes a trite dramatic situation. But the biggest problem with the play is its earnest tone, the laboriousness of O'Hara's effort to write an archetypal play ritualistically evoking a rite of passage. In **"Autobiographia Literaria,"** a later poem about childhood (quoted here in full), O'Hara arrives at an archetypal expression by juxtaposing a child's sense of isolation with an adult's bemused retrospection:

> When I was a child
> I played by myself in a
> corner of the schoolyard
> all alone.
> I hated dolls and I
> hated games, animals were
> not friendly and birds
> flew away.
> If anyone was looking
> for me I hid behind a
> tree and cried out "I am
> an orphan."
> And here I am, the
> center of all beauty!
> Writing these poems!
> Imagine!

The poem is both ironic and jubilant, both celebrating and mocking the poet's self-image as "sensitive" child and adult artist. O'Hara makes it impossible to take the child-poet's rebellion too seriously; the enjambment seems to underline the child's petulance, isolating his most plaintive words in the last line of each of the first three stanzas. The adult poet is genuinely in awe of his own abilities, but does not permit us to be: his self-definition as "the / center of all beauty" is genially ironic. Using this kind of playful irony to cut away the potential for heavy-handedness from his theme, O'Hara communicates in **"Autobiographia**

Literaria" the pain and wonder of growing up that the solemnity of *Change Your Bedding!* states but does not convey.

In the first version of *Try, Try,* the O'Hara wit has more scope for play than in *Change Your Bedding!* The characters have the same first names as the actors who played them at Harvard: John (Ashbery), Violet (Lang), and Jack (Rogers). This identity of character and actor may have been intended to lend the proceedings an air of informal spontaneity; certainly, it must have contributed to the air of cliquishness of which John Simon complained. Violet, a bored housewife, awaits the return of her husband, Jack, from war; John, the chorus, keeps her company. Most of Violet's speeches are lamentations: she complains about her name, her loneliness, her lack of energy, her dread of Jack's return. John explains: "Jack created this emptiness / by his departure," An emptiness Violet has tried to fill by dancing with soldiers in clubs. When Jack returns, she finds that the emptiness remains.

At the level of diction, O'Hara succeeds in elevating his characters' expressiveness through metaphor. Violet says: "And after all these years of sorting / my feelings and piling them about / the kitchen, ready, classified and / clean, I don't know what I feel." The domestic metaphor conveys Violet's feeling of confinement and her sense of having examined her emotions over and over. The play's centerpiece, Jack's long description of his war experiences, compares favorably with much of O'Hara's poetry. Jack first describes himself as a wild Cossack ("I sat my mount prettily and hacked / babies and old women with a song / on my breath—I even let my eyebrows grow!"), then as Lief Ericson, defeated in a snowy waste, then as an admiral "bossing a bothersome / crew and pretending a good deal of confidence. . . . "

The effectiveness of Jack's long speech is due to this sequence of metaphors, which provides a graph of the character's changing feelings. He enters the war strong and defiant, but falls into despair. A state of relative equilibrium is represented by the admiral, who hides his lack of confidence but is genuinely elated "when suddenly there / was a hint of glory!" O'Hara's use of metaphoric identities in this speech is similar to a technique he employs in **"In Memory of My Feelings."** The first stanza of that poem presents the authorial voice's "several likenesses": "One of me rushes / to window #13 and one of me raises his whip and one of me / flutters up from the center of the track amidst the pink flamingoes. . . . " In both poem and speech, the multiplication and splitting of the speaker suggest that his emotions are confused and mutable.

In the last portion of his speech, Jack describes how the war ended for him:

> Finally a sniper in a tree
> on the edge of the Pacific's
> exciting waters—an oriental with
> lots of time for meditation—
> saw me clearly. At the right moment.
> It was time, you see, not
> topographical, like Achilles' heel.
> I was thinking of myself as heir
> to the Mississippi. My thoughts moved

> to De Soto—whose wouldn't? And
> that was when I was spotted, naked
> as the beach, caught within a few feet
> of safety.

The directness of the statements here shows that this is Jack, not the Cossack, Lief Ericson, or the admiral, speaking. The travelogue diction of "the Pacific's exciting waters," the image of the Oriental meditating in a tree, and the strange wandering of Jack's attention which caused him to be shot are bits of rueful, self-deprecatory humor indicative of the character's ability to distance himself from his own experience. The reference to De Soto is ambiguous, suggesting that Jack sees himself as an explorer rather than a conqueror, but also that he anticipates his own death (De Soto was buried at the mouth of the Mississippi River).

The poetry of *Try, Try* is framed by a strong element of parody in O'Hara's stagecraft. In a note, O'Hara offers a definition of Noh drama which stresses the ritualistic elements of Noh performance, such as the use of on-stage musicians and "symbolical decor." The decor for *Try, Try* consists of an ironing board, and a small table with an old-fashioned gramophone on it; the ironing board is the central physical image of the play. The on-stage musicians of the Noh have been replaced by the gramophone, on which John, acting as chorus, plays first a waltz, then dissonant music to underscore Jack's recounting of the horrors of war, then melancholy music when Jack and Violet resign themselves to unhappiness. The music, rather than heightening and abstracting the action, merely reinforces it in the manner of an unsophisticated film score. O'Hara also mocks the notion of hieratic stage action. Yeats's ritualistic "Plays for Dancers" begin and end with the folding and unfolding of a ritual cloth. The opening stage directions for *At the Hawk's Well* (1917) state: "The First Musician carries with him a folded cloth and goes to the centre of the stage towards the front and stands motionless, the folded cloth hanging from between his hands." *Try, Try* contains a very similar instruction: "Violet slumps over the ironing board, holding her arms out stiffly in front, and Jack ceremoniously removes his cap and jacket and hangs them over her clasped hands." O'Hara's direction may not be a direct parody of Yeats, though a Harvard audience could have been expected to catch the allusion, but it is clearly making light of the idea of ritualistic action in a contemporary dramatic context, while simultaneously reinforcing the image of Violet's stultifying domesticity by making of her a living coat rack. Apparently serious moments in the action of the play are often rendered comic by O'Hara's staging. Jack drapes Violet before launching into his long speech, during which she must support his clothing; when Jack and Violet first see one another, they "freeze into odd wooden positions staring at each other." John intervenes to explain: "In this moment of silence, the expected / lyricism begins." Here, John not only refers to the expectations of the reunited husband and wife, he announces (and thus undermines) the play's self-consciously "poetic" and "ritualistic" style.

Essentially, *Try, Try* is a soap opera disguised as poetic, ritual drama. O'Hara writes of the Noh that "The audience is supposed to know all the plays by heart." In a sense, though not the religious sense of Japanese Noh drama, O'Hara's audience did indeed know his play by heart—in 1951, the romantic problems of the returning veteran were acutely familiar to most Americans. The story O'Hara tells had already been the subject of countless movies, novels, and soap operas. The mythology of O'Hara's Noh is the mythology of mass culture, of cheap paperbacks and Hollywood movies, and the "ritual" aspect of his play, focused around the ironing board, is appropriately scaled to a soap-opera mentality. Like much proto-Pop art of the 1950s, *Try, Try* functions simultaneously on two levels of cultural reference. It is a skillful satire on the pretensions of high modernist experiments in poetic and ritual drama, while also being a domestic melodrama. Violet's ironing board is the locus at which the two levels intersect. Initially, it is a plausible dramatic symbol for the domesticity in which she finds herself trapped while waiting for Jack, and from which she escapes to the soldier's clubs. It refers as well to her own use of laundry as a metaphor for her examination of her own feelings. When Jack drapes Violet as she slumps over the ironing board, it becomes a parody of a ritual object. The domestic realism that is the convention of soap opera as a genre is incompatible with ritualistic or elevated stage action; hence the oddness and woodenness of the play's hieratic moments. Each level of cultural reference "frames" the other: the pretentiousness of modern poetic drama is underlined by the soap opera content of the play, while the vapidity of soap opera becomes all the more pronounced when it is forced into the mold of ritual drama. This framing opens up a broad spectrum of interpretive questions: Is O'Hara only mocking the pretensions of those who advocate a return to ritual and high seriousness in the theatre, or is he also attempting to elevate kitsch to the status of art? This question implies larger ones about the nature of American culture itself: Are we capable of producing a poetic drama such as Yeats sought to derive from Irish legend, or are our dominant myths, expressed as they are in mass and consumer culture, too shallow to support such a drama? Is O'Hara suggesting that the soap opera *is* our Noh, our ritual theatre, the drama we all know by heart? Like the visual art that would emerge from the New York School, O'Hara seems to want to have it all ways with *Try, Try,* to produce a play that is parody, soap opera, and ritual drama all at once, thus mirroring a culture that cannot seem to decide if its products ever really deserve to be called art.

The response of the audience at Harvard reflected the play's pregnant ambiguity. Daniel Ellsberg reported in ["The Playgoer" in] the *Harvard Crimson* [(1951)] that the audience "laughed loudly" at the play, especially at Violet Lang's "dryly satirical" performance, and granted the cast an extra curtain call. At the end of the evening, however, Thornton Wilder, then visiting Harvard, chided the audience for laughing at a serious work. In Ellsberg's opinion, "Mr. Wilder misjudged both the play and the audience's response. . . ."

The richness of the ambiguous irony that defines the tone of *Try, Try* is brought out by contrasting the original version with O'Hara's 1953 revision for an Artists' Theatre production. In the later version, he dispenses with the ritu-

alistic framework of the original; the play is no longer called a Noh drama. The two plays have in common their titles, the characters' names, and four passages: Jack's war speech, and three of Violet's. John is no longer the chorus, but a lover Violet has been living with in Jack's absence. The tone of the later play is set by John's caustic opening line, spoken as he and Violet listen to a record: "I like songs about hat-check girls, / elevators, bunions, syphillis, all the / old sentimental things." Violet and John "camp" and bicker with one another constantly, but when she must choose between lover and husband, she picks John.

O'Hara in fact stacks the deck against Jack in this later version. Our first encounter with him is through a letter he has written to Violet, which John reads. The letter is embarassingly personal and maudlin, but touching nevertheless:

> I cry at night sometimes with my prick tangled
> in the sheets—wishing it would go away and find
> you and leave me alone in my, in this lousy
> southern country where it's colder in the winter
> than it ever is in the cold countries. But all I do
> is bitch and what I mean is I love you.

John sneers at Jack's "funny style" of writing. Violet at first seems to defend Jack, but slips into a bout of repartee with John, after which they retire to make love. Jack enters to find his wife and her lover in their underwear; Violet's greeting is: "Oh Jack! My Jackson! / Why did you leave me? / Since you left I've had to sell the flute and the bathtub." This speech also appears in the earlier version of *Try, Try,* where it is a typical example of Violet's fraught manner of speaking. The more sophisticated, New York Violet, however, uses these words only as an arbitrary pose she adopts to avoid confronting Jack. Alan Feldman writes [in his *Frank O'Hara* (1979)] that the characters in the later play "avoid making their feelings explicit" by resorting to "witty and sometimes enigmatical metaphors." Feldman's generalization is inaccurate, for the characters make their feelings explicit enough when the need arises. Jack expresses his need for Violet; John does nothing to disguise his contempt for Jack; Violet barely hesitates in choosing between them. Feldman is correct, however, to observe that the characters sometimes hide behind their words. It is instantly clear that Jack, who wears his heart on his sleeve, does not stand a chance of winning Violet's love back from the urbane John.

The responses of the other characters to Jack's description of the war are also indicative of the differences between the two versions. In the first, John accuses Jack of dwelling on his own troubles without considering what Violet has been through; in the second, John makes snide comments during Jack's speech—"He *is* like his letters!"; "Do I wake or sleep?" (Inasmuch as Jack's "funny" style of writing somewhat resembles O'Hara's own, especially in its attenuated syntax, there may be an element of ironic self-parody here.) When Jack has finished, John shatters the mood by announcing: "I've got to take a terrific shit" and exiting. Violet responds to Jack by not responding: "Now don't say anything you don't mean. / Just go on with the news bulletin. We're all terribly interested in the outside world here." The play reiterates O'Hara's concern with the present tense in a line spoken by John to Jack: "Do you think everything can stay the same, / like a photograph? What for?" In the absence of the earlier version's Noh play framework, the characters and their interactions must be taken at face value. In the earlier version, the characters' two-dimensionality enables them to function simultaneously as soap opera characters and as characters in a contemporary poetic play; in the later version, they are simply stereotypes. The second *Try, Try* is an accomplished, small-scale comedy of manners in which style triumphs over sincerity (the similarity of the two men's names may suggest that it finally makes little difference which one Violet chooses), but it lacks the cultural resonance of the first version.

The first *Try, Try* is close to being a dramatic analogue for Hardcore Pop Art, in which the conventions of one mode of representation, fine art or poetic drama, clash with and thus "frame" the conventions of another mode of representation, advertising illustration or soap opera. In this respect, the play actually anticipates developments in the visual arts which would only begin to flower two years later. During his Surrealist-influenced "French Zen period," O'Hara adopted structures for his plays that make them more closely related to Abstract Expressionism and the proto-Pop art of Robert Rauschenberg than to Hardcore Pop. Whereas O'Hara's early plays employ a conventional dramatic narrative structure, the structures of these later texts are best understood by reference to concepts of pictorial composition adumbrated by the New York School artists.

O'Hara's plays are panoplies of heterodox elements, some recognizable, some invented, some purely abstract, reminiscent of Rauschenberg's "combine" paintings. The combine paintings are assemblages of objects and images brought together on canvas and unified through Rauschenberg's compositional skill. Rauschenberg often mixes high cultural images (for example, reproductions of old masters) with newspaper or magazine photographs, detritus, and personal items. The simultaneous presence of these several levels of reference imposes on the viewer the task of integrating them. An early critic of Rauschenberg's work, David Myers, remarks [in *School of New York: Some Younger Artists* (1959)] that he cannot help thinking of President Eisenhower, Gloria Vanderbilt, and dancer Merce Cunningham as cohabitants of the same social circle simply because he has seen all three represented in Rauschenberg's paintings. (The particular work he refers to is Rauschenberg's *Gloria* of 1956. . . .) Myers goes on to stress that this mental image "is, of course, my own contrivance, having little or nothing to do with Rauschenberg. . . . " O'Hara's "combine" plays bring together invented characters with historical figures and friends of the poet: Joan Crawford, Othello, Larry Rivers, and an animate Telephone share the same stage. The plays employ a broad range of diction and allude to such literary sources as Elizabethan drama and the pastoral. O'Hara examines the multiple interrelations of his elements; like the materials of Rauschenberg's combines, those elements are frequently loaded cultural images whose juxtaposition is provocative.

One of O'Hara's first combine plays is in the spirit of a Surrealist exercise. Act 1 of the brief *Mephisto* consists of a single, outlandish image: "One thousand eight orang-utangs in the corridor of the Hotel Surprise. They die noisily." The first scene of the second act is a speech by a Cloud, describing a woman who "lied like all the other spies." He is answered by a Multitude: "She is dammed [*sic*], that dancer, for her lack of energy and her understanding of arrivalism." In the second scene of the act, the Watercress Troubadour reminisces about an evening when he "asked my dancing partner to take / a tub with me but there weren't enough people there to make it worthwhile." Act 3 is a poem not assigned to any particular speaker.

Mephisto clearly is not stageable and is better thought of as a poem in dramatic form than as a play. The speeches are retrospective; they tell of disappointment and deception. The woman, "a vision of loveliness," lied to the Cloud; the Multitude punningly describes her treachery: "All the advertisements were wrong, I gave her to my son and she was not the moon." The first lines of the third act summarize the tone of the whole poem: "I tend to think that the brevity of the season is that white recall, / that paramour in the distance who is always dancing while she waits, / you know." *Mephisto* is a meditation on "that paramour in the distance," the event or person barely perceived or remembered, yet desired, that turns out to be disappointing. The play opens with an hilariously arbitrary image of death, and closes with a melancholy poem; as always, O'Hara suggests that dwelling on the past leads inevitably to unhappiness. Like *Try, Try, Mephisto* places theatrical images within a frame which parodies theatrical convention. The specific demand for one thousand *eight* orang-utangs, and the arbitrary designation of the Watercress Troubadour's speech as "Act 2, Scene A," a device that recalls Gertrude Stein's unpredictable act and scene divisions, make *Mephisto* a commentary on theatre and its arbitrary conventions.

What Century? and *Awake in Spain* are combine plays on a larger scale than *Mephisto,* involving large numbers of settings and characters (*What Century?* has thirteen characters, *Awake in Spain* eighty-five). Feldman remarks that "One of the themes of *Awake in Spain* seems to be change and discontinuity. . . . " Indeed, these are the central themes of both that play and *What Century?,* whose title seems to refer to a kind of question on a history quiz ("In what century did . . . ?"). *What Century?* contrasts the Old and New Worlds; *Awake in Spain* has to do with a deposed king whose elder son (named Frank) reinstates the monarchy, while his younger son plans to depose his brother. The play's political settings make them examinations of the mutability of power; the later play even ends with the appearance of Thomas Hardy, who intones: "O dynasties, incessantly tumbling!"

Awake in Spain is less provocative than *What Century?,* partly because it contains fewer culturally loaded images, partly because its narrative thread is more continuous, and partly because it has something of the tone of an inside joke. In the cast of characters are several of O'Hara's friends (Larry Rivers, Kenneth Koch); the text contains numerous in-jokes concerning the art world of the 1950s. The Grand Vizier of Spain, for example, exclaims that "*Art News* has promised to do a 'Zurbaran Paints a Picture' in the fall"; another character cries out: "It's another case of nature imitating Alfred Leslie!"

Whereas *What Century?* is best discussed in terms of O'Hara's use of cultural images, *Awake in Spain* responds to a formal analysis couched in terms derived from New York School painting. An important aspect of Abstract Expressionism was the impulse toward "all over" painting, decentralized compositions in which every part of the canvas is as active as every other. The related concept of "push and pull" taught by Hans Hofmann was highly influential. In visual terms, "push and pull" is the quality of some paintings that creates tension between the surface of the canvas and the illusion of depth: a third dimension is implied without violating the integrity of the two-dimensional surface. In a letter to Larry Rivers, O'Hara writes of wanting to invest his poems with "push and pull." In *Awake in Spain,* this quality is manifest in the shifting relationship of foreground to background, shifts often accomplished by association of images. A good example of such association occurs at the end of Part III. The ghost of the Grand Vizier appears and cannot understand what is taking place. He complains: "What's happening? Oh! I can't bear not to know what's happening!" and is answered by a telephone, which asks: "Excuse me! What number were you calling?" Up to this point, the telephone had not been a character in the play, but the association of a request for information and the telephone was clearly irresistible to O'Hara. In several instances, sequential associations of this kind lead the play away from its ostensible focus, as in a scene in Part II, Act I. The King and his son are plotting to retake the throne when a sheep stumbles onto the scene:

> SHEEP. Where am I? My nose is bleeding.
> STATUE. Go down, then.
> FUNICULAR. I'm like an angel, ain't I? Look everybody!

The Sheep's crisis necessitates the advice to move to lower ground, which in turn suggests the Funicular. Momentarily in the spotlight, the Funicular presents its own vision of itself. All of these incidents lead attention away from the expected content of the scene, the King's scheming, and redirect it to the story's background setting.

Shifts in relation between foreground and background are evident in the first part of the play which, until its last act, is entirely descriptive of a background. A Village Mayor, an American, a Flamenco Dancer, Joan Crawford, and a church steeple all have lines in Act I. Act III is given over to Larry Rivers' search for a picturesque cemetery. The Cemetery itself says: "Here I am, Larry" while a group of animals warns him not to fall into a brook; the Brook then complains of the animals' meddling. That these events have nothing to do with the plot becomes clear when the King and his court finally appear in Act IV; the plot as "figure" takes precedence over the background at this point. In the very next act, however, the background comes to the fore once again in the form of a pastoral scene. This shift of emphasis is underlined by the fact that

an important incident, the deposing of the King, takes place between acts. The shepherds are followed by twenty-one Demons, and it is not until each has had his say that the plot picks up where it left off. O'Hara's relentless personification of inanimate objects and landscape elements contributes to the effect of "push and pull": each thing on stage, no matter how incidental to the plot, speaks, for the plot is really just an armature on which to support the juxtapositions of imagery that constitute the play's real content. As in his "I do this, I do that poems," O'Hara's attention is distributed across his entire canvas—everything merits and receives attention, everything is given the opportunity to assert itself. The result is a play whose conventional plot seems constantly to be competing with other events rather than simply being the central focus one might expect.

The presence of popular cultural figures in *Awake in Spain* provides the audience with familiar reference points in O'Hara's fantastic kingdom. Like the juxtaposition of Eisenhower, Vanderbilt, and Cunningham in Rauschenberg's work, the juxtaposition of Joan Crawford, Marlene Dietrich, Larry Rivers, and Kenneth Koch makes the play at once personal and public, inclusive of hermetic in-jokes and broad cultural references. In some cases, the images seem already to have been filtered through O'Hara's sensibility: Crawford, for example, says only: "Ummmm, ummmm, ummmm" in the play, perhaps O'Hara's recollection of a scene in one of her films, or something he would have liked to have seen her say. As Myers remarks of Rauschenberg, any specific interpretation we make of these juxtapositions is bound to be our own contrivance, only partly dependent on O'Hara. O'Hara creates the occasion for meaning, but we must impose meaning upon his images.

Like *Mephisto, What Century?* exemplifies O'Hara's playful approach to stage conventions. His stage directions offer striking images which enhance the play as a text for reading, but contribute little to its stageworthiness ("Waves breaking like bees on the shelf of Armorica, while the scent of burning almond leaves fills the nippled sky"). Compositionally, the play is a series of tableaux: each brief act takes place in a different locale; Acts 2 and 3 each consist of a single speech; and the characters never speak to one another. The effect is of a series of images like those in Rauschenberg's paintings, connected by virtue of having been placed in the same context, but intrinsically unrelated. Each image stands alone and in relation to the others, a relation that is primarily cumulative rather than sequential, taking its place in a pictorial composition rather than a narrative.

The first act of *What Century?,* set in an unnamed Old World kingdom, burlesques seventeenth- and eighteenth-century dramas of love and intrigue at court. The King describes his exhaustion ("I am fatigued with being angry / my country's always hungry"); a Page discourses urbanely, if ribaldly, on his love affairs; the Queen rambles almost incoherently about her many obligations; and a Chamberlain complains of "those ratty pups, / the Crown Prince and his Crownier devious / and gullible step-brother, Connie." The second half of the play, comprising Acts 3 and 4, takes up American themes: Act 3 is a speech by Benjamin Franklin, Act 4 a scene set in turn-of-the-century New Orleans.

Thematically, O'Hara plays Old World refinement off against New World vitality. Exhausted by her royal activities ("Run, run. It's all I do"), the Queen yearns for the American west:

> . . . King
> Philip,
> the Indian bravest, blazed trails. What could be
>   dizzier
> than his famous Mohawk Romp, the motor
> cavalcade touring Drive-Ins and Auto-Camps
> and   Swing-Rendezvouses   and   Firemen's-
>   Ramps.

The excitement of the frontier, even in its most crassly commercialized forms, seems to offer more than the tired decadence of the home kingdom. Benjamin Franklin, too, finds himself trapped between worlds. Old and exhausted, he wants to "give up sentimentality and take down / my lovely French lace to hold my seat, term / after term, wrapped to the ears with eiderdown, / in fashionable America. But it's too late. . . ." Franklin, who stayed in Paris for its chic, its "beauty, / and onion soup and chocolate," cannot go home; his dedication to style has cost him dear: "what can you trade immaculate / urbanity for, when it has sinned, and owes, / and you can't pay a sou?" Both the Queen and Franklin, trapped in O'Hara's fanciful versions of the Old World, pine for America, its energy, its newly discovered fashionableness, but cannot have it.

Act 4 presents the America they pine for in a scene of "Creoles . . . smoking opium and complaining." Speaking in a harsh parody of the dialect spoken by Black characters in many Hollywood films, the Creoles themselves are parodies of the hard-working darkies of those same movies, working and singing against a background sporting a billboard reading "Swanee." After the Creoles offer an obscene choral postlude to the action of the first act, a "Handsome Cajun Cockteaser" emerges from the group to solo, singing of how he plans to go "to de citee to see whut ah be seen" and "enjoy my seff cuz date ahll, dat ahll [sic]." O'Hara's American landscape is vulgar and nihilistic, but direct and somehow energized. O'Hara is alert to the way mass culture works in America, the way Metacom, one of the least compromising of Native American chiefs, could have been domesticated as King Philip, star of some type of Wild West show, the way Creoles, Cajuns, and Blacks are lumped together and represented through the same dialect. At the same time, the Creoles' obscenity is a welcome relief after the Page's preciosity; even though the Cockteaser's ambition is presented in terms of a "country boy in the city" film cliché, he at least is looking forward, as opposed to the King, Queen, and Franklin, who seem able only to regret the past. O'Hara's America is garish, racist, obscene, self-seeking, but he recognizes that its surface razzle-dazzle, explicit in the song-and-dance form of the Creoles' scene, is also its driving force. Like Pop artists, O'Hara comes dangerously close here to glorifying the objects of his scrutiny, but each of his images is framed for critical examination by juxtaposition

with other images, causing the spectator to reflect on the sources of the images and the significance of those sources. In the last moment of the play, O'Hara deals a final, deadly blow to a nostalgia for Old World refinement which would condemn the American scene as merely vulgar. Cathedral Chimes express their "hopeless nostalgia for Paris," declaring: "May my tears / fall as / rust and stain the People."

In his last and longest play, *The General Returns from One Place to Another,* O'Hara returns to a less pictorial, more plot-centered dramaturgy. In a letter to John Ashbery dated February 1961, he writes:

> I have been writing in desultory fashion a little play called *The General's Return From One Place to Another* but am having quite a bit of trouble as to ending it. . . . I believe it was inspired by a wonderful production of Brecht's wonderful *In the Jungle of Cities* which the Living Theatre has in repertory now and my dislike for General MacArthur. . . .

O'Hara's play is an elaborate pun on MacArthur's famous proclamation "I shall return!" combining the flavors of both early Brecht and vintage Hollywood movies. The play is dedicated to Vincent Warren, to Taylor Meade (who played the title role in the 1964 production), and to Warner Brothers.

The strongest Brechtian element in *The General* is the main character's scramble for identity. "A general in search of a war," he begins the play almost nude, acquiring items of clothing as the action progresses so that when he dies at the end of the play, he does so as a fully uniformed and decorated officer. This symbolic use of clothing is a staple of Brecht's early work. In *Im Dickicht der Städte* (*In the Jungle of Cities*), Shlink robs Garga of his clothing, a symbolic skinning of Garga's identity. When Garga is prepared to take over Shlink's business, he asks for a new suit and is given an outfit identical to those of Shlink's henchmen. An even closer comparison is with Brecht's *Mann ist Mann* (*A Man's a Man*), in which part of the process of transforming the docker Galy Gay into the soldier Jeraiah Jip is to squeeze him into a uniform that is too small for him. For Brecht's characters, identity is a fragile thing dependent on appearances, and subject to expedience and the opinions of others. O'Hara's General too defines himself in terms of his image and of others' perception of himself. Commenting on world politics, he remarks: " 'Self-determination!' What an odd slogan. One might as well have a slogan reading 'Impossible!' "

The General's peacetime campaign consists in returning to the various locations in the South Pacific he first visited as a military leader, hoping to be greeted with open arms by the natives he once protected, and to be revered as a great man. Speaking to reporters in Singapore, he complains: "They don't recognize me: THEY DON'T EVEN SEE ME!" Losing his composure, he rambles on about Hollywood, explaining that Marion Davies would have been a bigger star than Norma Shearer had her image been properly managed. Received with indifference in some places and hostility in others, the General finally "returns" to Borneo, where he has never been before, to bask in his manufactured greatness. Greeted enthusiastically by natives who are completely unaware of his identity, he declares with satisfaction: "here they know who a person is. . . ." Feldman correctly interprets the General's desire to return to his former haunts as an attempt to deny the changes that come inevitably with the passage of time and, hence, to combat mortality. *The General* thus reiterates a major theme of O'Hara's work: his celebration of the present, and its obverse, his condemnation of the cult of the past.

The problem of identity as a dependent variable resonates through the play's most powerful image, the General philosophizing in a field of flowers:

> If it is true that the lily springs from the dung heap . . . then shouldn't we be offended by every place where beauty appears? Dung . . . animal dung, or the residue of our own human efforts? The question is vital. For if through our failures we can produce a beauty which has nothing to do with us, which is of a different nature from us, then that's pretty sinister. I mean, failure never produced a beautiful flower. . . .

This speech illustrates the General's way of thinking: if beauty can be a consequence of failure or waste, then it is a form of failure and must be destroyed; this is his rationale for military action. The General's inability to tolerate change, the growth of the lily from the dung heap, is echoed in his inability to accept that his function as military savior is neither relevant nor desirable in peacetime, and his failure to realize that he cannot expect to be perceived as he once was. Ironically, the General's rationalization of destruction turns against him. Because "Everything on the face of this earth stays around too long," things must be eradicated periodically. "The tragedy of architecture is: the only truly useful thing a building can do is let itself be bombed." Unconsciously, the General has defined his own situation—he has been around too long, is no longer needed. In this respect, he is somewhat analogous to Brecht's Shlink, whose symbiotically destructive relationship with Garga parallels the General's relationship to the flowers and buildings he at once admires and wants to eliminate. In Brecht's play, it is only after the symbiotic bond is broken by Shlink's death that Garga is able to go on with the business of living, a stronger man for having endured an apparently motiveless contest of wills. Perhaps O'Hara is implying that the world can get on with the business of living only after the flowers have triumphed over the General by rising from his burial mound, and beauty is allowed to spring up where it may, untrammeled. Ironically, the General's sojourn in the field earns him the admiration of Mrs. Forbes, an impoverished society woman, who becomes fixated on the delightfully paradoxical image of "The General in a field of flowers," and pursues him across Asia. She imposes her poetic image on the General as insistently as he subscribes to his own self-image; in the last scene, she walks with the General into another field, where he dies. Beauty triumphs over destruction, and the General's demise is brought about by one whose fixed way of thinking is not much different from his own.

O'Hara's concern with manufactured images and identities is underscored by the play's references to the greatest of American image-makers, Hollywood. *The General* is constructed cinematically in twenty-one very short scenes resembling movie takes, each set in a different location. O'Hara's set descriptions are reminiscent of seedy tropical adventure films: "A rather decrepit nightclub (native-style) on a small Pacific island. LUOA is singing 'Moon of Manakura' in her best Dorothy Lamour style"; "A neon sign blinking 'TOKYO NIGHTS' off and on." The characters too come from a Hollywood stock company: Luoa is a singing Matta Hari who turns out to be a Chinese spy; Mrs. Forbes is the kind of dazed society woman Margaret Dumont portrayed in Marx Brothers films. Their diction frequently echoes filmscript clichés, right down to the overly pregnant pauses: "One thing I'll say for the Japanese, the liquor's cheaper here"; "I guess . . . I was just running away . . . from life!"

If O'Hara's plays of 1952 and 1953 are comparable to Rauschenberg's paintings, *The General* is closer in spirit to Larry Rivers' work. In 1953, Rivers took on the United States' greatest national hero in his defiant *Washington Crossing the Delaware;* nearer the time O'Hara was writing *The General,* Rivers painted a series of pictures noting the death of the Civil War generation, including *The Next to Last Confederate Soldier* (1959), several versions of *The Last Civil War Veteran* (1959), and *Dying and Dead Veteran* (1961). Like *Washington Crossing the Delaware,* these works offer indistinct, painterly images of their subjects which are neither heroic nor pathetic, but detached and ironic. Rivers commented that *The Last Civil War Veteran* was a "non-hero who had become a hero by the simple fact of having outlived the others . . . and had managed to die on schedule to accomodate *Life* magazine which covered both the dying and death with appropriate journalistic ceremony." By photographing the dying man in full military regalia, *Life* created an entirely artificial heroic image with no necessary relation to the man's life, simply because he survived. Like O'Hara's General, who also dies in full uniform, the veteran becomes identical with his image only in death. As if to show how infinitely manipulable any reality becomes once it has been contextualized as image, Rivers takes the "reality" manufactured by *Life* as the sources of his own constructed image. By so doing, he defeats the purpose of *Life*'s original manipulation: the veteran becomes anonymous once again; the image of his death becomes yet another occasion for Rivers to display his paint-handling skill. O'Hara observes in a short essay on the painting that the veteran "is not the subject of this painting, but the occasion of its appearance" (*Standing Still*); the identity of the individual is submerged beneath Rivers' painterly schema as much as it was beneath *Life*'s glossy surface.

Clearly, O'Hara's meditation on the construction of identity through image in *The General* explores territory similar to Rivers' painting and employs similar strategies: both Rivers and O'Hara begin with heroic images manufactured for the benefit of the media and examine them critically, Rivers by blurring the veteran's countenance, O'Hara by making MacArthur's proclamation into a pun by taking it absolutely literally. In both cases, the remaking of the source image is in the interest of revealing it to have been a manufactured image in the first place.

O'Hara's point did not fall entirely on deaf ears: although the play was largely ignored by critics when produced in 1964, at least one writer objected to it on the grounds that it tastelessly satirized a great man known to be dying. But like Rivers' paintings and most Pop Art, the play is only apparently topical. It functions somewhat as a political cartoon—in addition to O'Hara's version of MacArthur, it features caricatures of General and Madame Chiang-Kai Shek, and Generalissimo Franco—and succeeds on this level for Perloff, who finds that O'Hara has "shrewd and funny things to say about East-West relations." But MacArthur is more the occasion for the play's appearance than its subject: like Rivers, O'Hara is primarily concerned with the images disseminated through our culture by Hollywood and the mass media, and the implications of that dissemination for our own sense of identity. The General is a victim of his own publicity; he has come to believe his own manufactured image. By evoking the conventions of Hollywood films in the play, O'Hara implicitly raises questions concerning the degree to which our perception and sense of identity are constructed by cultural imagery.

In O'Hara's writing for the theatre, one can see the same restless experimentation as in his poetry, the same effort to include the whole of his experience, from the personal and hermetic to the public and broadly cultural. His approach to drama ranges from the earnestness of his earliest effort to produce a contemporary poetic play to the more satirical and ironic tone of his later plays. The development of his plays parallels the development of New York School painting from the compositional strategies and abstraction of Abstract Expressionism to the juxtaposition and engagement of cultural images characteristic of the photo-Pop Art of Rauschenberg and Rivers. Throughout the ten years he wrote plays, O'Hara remained fundamentally committed to the Abstract Expressionist ethos of spontaneous personal expression; where he employs cultural images, it is always to make them "into art" by inserting them into his idiosyncratic dramatic structures. (pp. 49-73)

> *Philip Auslander, "Frank O'Hara," in his* The New York School Poets as Playwrights: O'Hara, Ashbery, Koch, Schuyler and the Visual Arts, *Peter Lang, 1989, pp. 49-75.*

John Lowney   (essay date Summer 1991)

[*In the following excerpt, Lowney relates signification in O'Hara's poetry to O'Hara's postmodernist concept of cultural and literary history.*]

> It's so
> original, hydrogenic, anthropomorphic, fiscal,
>   post-anti-esthetic,
>   bland, unpicturesque and
>   William CarlosWilliamsian!
> it's definitely not 19th Century, it's not even Partisan Review, it's new, it must be vanguard!
>   **("Poem Read at Joan Mitchell's")**
>   (p. 244)

"Poem Read at Joan Mitchell's" dramatizes a moment of emotional urgency: the fear of losing his close friendship

with Jane Freilicher informs O'Hara's subtle satire of the institution of marriage. Yet like so much of his poetry, this "occasional poem" self-consciously reflects on its own place in the "tradition of the new." The description of the marriage combines economic and aesthetic terms, situating this poetic act within the cultural politics of representing the "vanguard"; an "original" act, as the intensifier "so" implies, is original only insofar as it is mediated by definitions of the "new." The proper name describing this "original" marriage, "WilliamCarlosWilliamsian," epitomizes this recognition, for Williams's name represents a site of contention in the 1950s "poetry wars," not only for his literary reputation but for the meaning of American modernism. While Williams was variously invoked as a predecessor for the "new American poetry," the academic writing of him into the modernist canon was blunting the critical edge of his early "vanguard" poetics. This "WilliamCarlosWilliamsian" marriage marks both O'Hara's affiliation with Williams's poetics and the objectification of his name as the commodity, "vanguard" writer. The parodic tone of this gesture furthermore suggests O'Hara's critique of the masculinist, Americanist stance associated with Williams's postwar protégés. Whether in mock manifesto or mock epithalamion, such references to modern literary history—although seemingly offhand—challenge claims like Helen Vendler's influential overview of O'Hara that "the will *not* to impute significance has scarcely been stronger in lyric poetry" [*Part of Nature, Part of Us: Modern American Poets*]. Instead O'Hara's modulations of vanguardist rhetoric frequently foreground not only the politics of literary reputation but also his own position within conflicting constructions of modernism. In the following pages I will examine how the intertextual devices of parody, appropriation, and allusion operate in O'Hara's revision of modernism, especially of the modernist lyric, to show how his "post-anti-esthetic" poetics of the quotidian addresses the issue of cultural memory in postwar America.

The majority of O'Hara's academic readers have concurred with Vendler that his poetry levels the "significant" with the mundane, thus rejecting traditional modes of poetic transcendence. His best-known poems, the occasional poems he called his " 'I do this I do that' poems," are most frequently cited to exemplify his interest in the "ordinary incident" instead of the "important public" event [Marjorie Perloff, *Frank O'Hara: Poet among Painters*]. Vendler attributes O'Hara's refusal to "impute significance" to his effort "to make the personal the poetic," thus severing the personal from the ideological. Other critics have explained O'Hara's evasion of symbolist correspondences by demonstrating his radical transformation of lyric subjectivity. . . . I would like to concentrate on one question this leveling process raises, that of O'Hara's postmodernist representation of modern literary and cultural history. None of O'Hara's readers fully account for his intertextual evocations of the vanguardist stance whose critical edge he seeks to retain yet whose critical mode appears inadequate for addressing postwar American historical conditions. The tone of crisis so prevalent in O'Hara's poetry is informed by an acute sensitivity to the oppressive mechanisms that an ideology which represses difference can deploy. And this tone evokes the more general threat of nuclear annihilation, a threat which paradoxically levels distinctions between kinds of experience while heightening awareness of the ephemerality of the quotidian. O'Hara's poetry demonstrates that the progressivist faith in technology and technique that animates Williams's vanguardist dictum to "make it new" can no longer be asserted unproblematically.

If formulations of postmodernism tend to dispute how postmodernist texts reflect or subvert the social effects of postwar capitalism, they generally agree that postmodernist and modernist aesthetics can be differentiated by their positions toward the past. [In his foreword to *The Postmodern Condition: A Report on Knowledge* by Jean-François Lyotard] Frederic Jameson has argued that postmodernism's "commitment to surface and the *superficial*" signifies a retreat from the "protopolitical vocation and the terrorist stance of the older modernism." In distinguishing pastiche from parody, Jameson further argues that post-modernist art thematizes the failure of the modernist project ("Post-modernism and Consumer Society"). Given the eclipse of conditions for modernist stylistic innovation—that is, of individualism and of any linguistic norm with which to contrast styles—postmodernist imitation lacks any satirical impulse. Instead of parody, pastiche is thus the only possible mode for responding to the past: "All that is left is to imitate dead styles, to speak through the masks and through the voices of the styles in the imaginary museum. But this means that contemporary or postmodernist art is going to be about art itself in a new kind of way; even more, it means that one of its essential messages will involve the necessary failure of art and the aesthetic, the failure of the new, the imprisonment in the past." Jameson's formulation accurately describes the play of allusion and quotation on the textual surface of a writer like O'Hara. O'Hara's writing, however, represents less an "imprisonment in the past" than the recognition that history is accessible only through its representations. If O'Hara's multivalent texts suggest that style is not freely expressed but is written through cultural codes, they also reveal that history is not a given that is immediately accessible by allusion but rather must be always constructed. Furthermore, Jameson's totalizing formulation of postmodernism as a cultural dominant, following Ernest Mandel's socioeconomic periodization, obscures how postmodernist practices often retain the vanguardist oppositional impulse while rejecting the formalist notion of textual autonomy, as Andreas Huyssen and Linda Hutcheon have argued. Huyssen's analysis of postwar American cultural politics is especially germane for analyzing the poetry of the New York school. He underlines the importance of the reception and institutionalization of modernism—in the academy, as well as in the "burgeoning museum, gallery, concert, record and paperback culture"—for defining the adversarial stance of 1960s postmodernism: "It was this specific radicalism of the avant-garde, directed against the institutionalization of high art as a discourse of hegemony and a machinery of meaning, that recommended itself as a source of energy and inspiration to the American postmodernists of the 1960's. . . . The irony in all of this is that the first time the U.S. had something resembling an 'institution art' in the emphatic European sense, it was modernism itself, the kind of art

whose purpose had always been to resist institutionalization" [*After the Great Divide: Modernism, Mass Culture, Postmodernism*]. From his prominent position within "institution art," that is, within the New York art-publishing and museum world, O'Hara in his poetry actually invokes a dialogical relation between past traditions and the present more analogous to Charles Jencks's examples of postmodernist architecture and Hutcheon's examples of "historiographic metafiction" than to clearly politically marked postmodernist practices. Jencks argues that postmodernist architecture subverts modernist aestheticism through a process of "double coding," an interplay of modernist technique with allusion to popular traditions to communicate both with "experts" and a more general public audience. In O'Hara's case, if the "experts," literary critics and historians, concentrate primarily on the narrative surface of his poetry, it is because his process of double coding challenges this dichotomy of experts and public. Many of his most obscurely autobiographical texts also participate in the general project of rewriting modern literary history. While his poetry appeals to a general audience through its recognizable narrative structures, it challenges "experts" to become conversant with the details of his life, especially within the New York art world and the gay community, as well as with modern literary history. In stressing the moment and site of enunciation, and frequently the specific receiver as well as the sender of the poetic text, O'Hara subverts the expertise of literary critics while enhancing the value of "local" knowledge.

An early O'Hara poem which cogently, although obliquely, evokes the postwar crisis of historical memory that Jameson associates with the postmodern is **"Memorial Day 1950."** This "pastiche" of modernist styles critically interrogates the concept of the "vanguard," anticipating O'Hara's more specific, more explicit practice and explanation of intertextuality in his later lyric poetry and criticism. Marjorie Perloff cites this poem, written during O'Hara's final year at Harvard, as a breakthrough which adumbrates his later distinctive poetic achievement, the fusion of the surrealist "dialectic of polarized images" with Williams's colloquialism. Yet this poem not only replicates the vanguardist techniques of the artists it names, it enacts an interrogation of the subtexts relating modernism and modernity. From the poem's title—specifying a moment of reflection at the midpoint of the twentieth century—until its enigmatic yet apocalyptic conclusion, **"Memorial Day 1950"** fuses and confuses personal memory with codified historical memory, personal desire with textual knowledge, imagination with recollection. The title memorializes not only the moment of reflection but the moments reflected on, from the reflection on the war dead designated by the official holiday to the poet's reflection on his biological and literary "parents." In what seem like random associations between fractured literary fragments and recollections of childhood trauma, the poem explores the structures of feeling linking aesthetic vanguardism with military vanguardism. While mocking the self-aggrandizing posture of both the aesthetic manifesto and the bildungsroman, the poem conveys a version of modern literary history that acknowledges the rhetorical appeal of vanguardist utopianism while questioning the corresponding impulse to destroy past accomplishments.

In parodying modernist texts, it mocks its own destructive impulse. In leaving the poet's attitude toward his modernist predecessors ambivalent, **"Memorial Day 1950"** implicates its readers in a questioning of how aesthetic forms represent modes of interpreting history.

The semantic instability of **"Memorial Day 1950"** begins with its cryptic opening sentence:

> Picasso made me tough and quick, and the
>   world;
> just as in a minute plane trees are knocked down
> outside my window by a crew of creators.

The comma which separates "and the world" from the initial clause is especially puzzling, as it raises questions concerning both the production and the reception of complex artistic texts. What is the status of "made" in this clause? Do we locate the semantic stress on the act of making, the "made" text, or the audience "made . . . tough and quick" by the text? Did Picasso make "me . . . and the world," thus implying the poet's total identification with Picasso's made world? Or is he maintaining some distance from Picasso while affirming the effects of his painting? Such interpretive questions are specific to complex artistic texts, but they also foreground the interpreter's historical difference. To consider Picasso in 1950 calls into question the relation of cubist aesthetics to modern warfare posited by such commentaries as Gertrude Stein's: "I very well remember at the beginning of the war being with Picasso on the boulevard Raspail when the first camouflage truck passed. It was at night, we had heard of camouflage but we had not yet seen it and Picasso amazed looked at it and then cried out, yes it is we who made it, that is cubism" ["Picasso," in *Picasso: The Complete Writings*]. Furthermore, it is impossible to read "Picasso," perhaps *the* signifier for the international avant-garde, without acknowledging the diverse appropriations of his aesthetics and his name. As the poem's parody of Stein's syntax and diction suggests, the effect of Picasso's multiple technical revolutions on the poet's own development cannot be severed from the objectification of Picasso as a cultural icon. As the opening line of **"Memorial Day 1950"** dramatizes the semantic instability of vanguardist texts through its fractured syntax, the conclusion of this opening sentence, although an apparently straightforward statement, becomes more questionable in its equation of destruction and creation. The textualized trees, "in a minute plane" of the cubist surface, fuse with the "plane trees . . . outside my window." The mundane act of knocking down trees to "create" a new landscape, an act epitomizing bourgeois progressivism, evolves into the image of Picasso the ax wielder. In the understated tone of this first verse paragraph, the poem establishes a problematic affiliation of vanguardist manifesto rhetoric with the rhetoric of warfare: "to fight for the last ditch and heap / of rubbish" in response to Picasso asserts the value of the quotidian and the demotic for artistic texts, but only because the context of modern warfare animates our awareness of such value.

It could be argued that **"Memorial Day 1950"** is hardly surrealist at all, that the images of artistic production, warfare, and bourgeois family life follow an internal logic of violent rebellion that challenges the polarity of destruction and creation. The poem does not follow consistently logical rhetorical patterns, however. Its generative principle appears to arise from the exhaustion felt by the artist in the wake of the historical avant-garde, as the second verse paragraph implies:

> Through all that surgery I thought
> I had a lot to say, and named several last things
> Gertrude Stein hadn't had time for; but then
> the war was over, those things had survived
> and even when you're scared art is no dictionary.
> Max Ernst told us that.

This passage epitomizes the anxiety of the postmodernist poet that everything has been said, that formal innovation is no longer possible, and that the world wars have achieved the act of revolutionary destruction that vanguardist rhetoric called for. The postwar artist must then accept a role analogous to that of Alice B. Toklas, the "autobiographical" subject constructed by Stein, as the poet is "made" by Picasso. The remainder of the poem enacts this process of literary ventriloquism, as the names and words of Klee, Auden, Rimbaud, Pasternak, and Apollinaire, among others, comically reverberate through the fragments of battles the young poet has with his parents. In fusing vanguardist models of rebellion with the recollections of his own adolescent rebellion, O'Hara imparts an absurd sense of the quotidian to these artists whose earlier transformations of everyday life had earned them a monumental status by 1950. And in situating these fragmentary fusings of manifestos and family disputes in the bloodshed of modern warfare, O'Hara imparts an urgency to his poem's articulation of its own historical moment. **"Memorial Day 1950"** enacts a process of appropriation and distancing from O'Hara's modernist predecessors, as one of its buried narratives, the transformation of Picasso's "The Man with the Blue Guitar," epitomizes. At first the original "maker," Picasso is next invoked through his best-known commentary on wartime destruction: "Guernica hollered look out." Immediately following this, the poet figures himself as the artist in "tight blue pants," as he confronts his disapproving parents. His parents are then generalized as the "older people" who "entered / my cheap hotel room and broke / my guitar and my can / of blue paint." The figure made by Picasso has now become the maker, the man with the "can / of blue paint," as well as the made, the man with the guitar. This image reappears in the poem's conclusion:

> Guitar strings hold up pictures. I don't need
> a piano to sing, and naming things is only the in-
>   tention
> to make things.

In distancing himself from the maker of "The Man with the Blue Guitar," O'Hara does not reject the technical accomplishments of Picasso, not to mention Wallace Stevens; rather, he rejects the definition of art that limits the object to its exchange value as a commodity. In figuring his own poetic stance as an improvisational act of holding up pictures with guitar strings, O'Hara portrays the postmodernist representation of the past as a mode of bricolage. **"Memorial Day 1950"** is indeed a pastiche of vanguardist rhetoric, yet its parodic play on modes of rebellion underscores the complex historicity of any aesthetic, including (and especially) that of its own.

O'Hara's statements on the social functions of art are diffuse and sometimes contradictory, but his occasional writings on his contemporaries, in both the literary and visual arts, express a more complex consideration of the historical difference of the avant-garde in postwar American culture than is generally acknowledged. In differentiating between the European notion of vanguardism and its American counterpart in **"American Art and Non-American Art,"** O'Hara claims that European art treats the aesthetic and the political as equally important distinct categories, whereas American art combines the aesthetic with the political, thus resulting in its "metaphysical quality" (***Standing Still***). Yet this does not mean that art in America serves no social function. Citing Gregory Corso's poem "Bomb," he writes: "It is the character of the avant-garde to absorb and transform disparate qualities not normally associated with art, for the artist to take within him the violence and evil of his times and come out with something. . . . In this way society can bear and understand and finally appreciate the qualities of alien and even dangerous things." This description of the avant-garde's relation to "society" corresponds with O'Hara's understanding of how the vanguardist stance is internalized. In a 1965 interview with Edward Lucie-Smith, O'Hara generalizes that the avant-garde can no longer be defined by a political or socioeconomic condition of detachment or isolation, arguing that when artists such as Andy Warhol become celebrities, such a stance is absurd: "there's no reason to attack a culture that will allow it to happen, and even foster the impulse—and create it. Which is a *change,* you see, from the general idea of, that all avant-garde art has to be attacking the bourgeoisie" (***Standing Still***). As postwar American capitalism contains opposition to the extent that the marketplace even encourages it, the vanguardist impulse for innovation no longer plays such a viable critical role. What becomes most important, then, is how art positions itself within traditions of innovation and in doing so transforms our perception of past forms. O'Hara's monograph on Jackson Pollock is especially instructive for explaining this conception of intertextuality. (pp. 244-52)

Differentiating Pollock's "spirited revaluation" of modern painting from Arshile Gorky's more destructive mode of "assimilation," O'Hara writes that Pollock

> did not appropriate . . . what was beautiful, frenzied, ugly or candid in others, but enriched it and flung it back to their work, as if it were a reinterpretation for the benefit of all, a clarification and apotheosis which does not destroy the things seen, whether of nature or art, but preserves it in a pure regard. Very few things, it seems, were assimilated or absorbed by Pollock. They were left intact, and given back. Paint is paint, shells and wire are shells and wire, glass is glass, canvas is canvas. You do not find, in his work, a typewriter becoming a stomach, a sponge becoming a brain. [***Jackson Pollock***]

Although analogous to T. S. Eliot's familiar concept of intertextuality in "Tradition and the Individual Talent,"

O'Hara's explanation not only rejects the priority of a canonical tradition of high art but emphasizes the way artistic texts transform our perception of the world, or "nature," as well as our perception of previous texts. Pollock's painting retains the materials, techniques, and imagery of modern art, but they are transformed by his interpretation: the past takes on "reality for us outside his work, as a cultural by-product of his own achievement." With this emphasis on the historicity of formal innovation, the act of preservation O'Hara attributes to Pollock involves a nondestructive, nonadversarial attitude to the past that differs from the historical avant-garde as well as from Eliot's high modernism. Furthermore, Pollock's oeuvre exposes the limitations of reductive definitions of "tradition" or "the individual talent." In noting that artists who succeed in sustaining a "multiplicity of truths" in a multiplicity of styles are "met with the accusation of 'no coherent, unifying style,' rather than a celebration," O'Hara could be answering his own critics. His formulation of Pollock's intertextual "revaluation" of past traditions is especially appropriate for reinterpreting his relation to his modernist predecessors. I will now concentrate on one key example of O'Hara's "revaluation" of vanguardism, the example of his revision of Williams's objectivist poetics, to show how his appropriations of Williams's form, prosody, syntax, and diction play a role similar to Pollock's in accentuating the historical transmission of aesthetic forms. (pp. 253-54)

If we consider "A Sort of a Song," the introductory poem of *The Wedge,* as a sort of a summary of Williams's objectivist poetics, we can examine O'Hara's response in two significant instances, in **"Today"** and in **"Poetry."** Its title accentuating its historicity, O'Hara's poem **"Today"** answers the conclusion of "A Sort of a Song," Williams's demand for "No ideas / but in things," with a motley assortment of objects: "kangaroos, sequins, chocolate sodas" and "pearls, harmonicas, jujubes, aspirins." This "stuff they've always talked about" that "still makes a poem a surprise!" is hardly "what they've always talked about" in American poetry, hardly the "things" Williams refers to, and hardly the "stuff" which makes a poem a "small machine made of words." Yet what ultimately makes this short poem a surprise is its shift in tone as it concludes. The association of "these things" with "beachheads and biers" compels a reconsideration of their significance, as **"Today"** refers to the immediate postwar years. Rather than defamiliarizing the everyday, **"Today"** foregrounds the ephemerality of everyday "stuff," including everyday language, as objects seem to be linked as much by the sonorous sequence of names as by appeal to any readily apparent semantic codes. The poem affirms the "meaning" of "things" but does not impose a recognizable order on these things. The use of "stuff" to summarize these objects seems to flaunt a lack of specificity involved in quoting colloquial language. It raises the question of whether these objects are the "stuff" of which this poem is made or the "stuff" from which a poem may yet be made, engaging readers to question their role in producing the poem's meaning. The semantic range of "stuff" itself recalls the war, but its connotations of drugs, of other forms of contraband, and even of literary or journalistic copy call into question the rhetorical function of the poetic image. As if in direct response to "A Sort of a Song" ("through metaphor to reconcile / the people and the stones"), **"Today"** exerts no demonstrative control over readers' interpretations of the sequence of objects. Instead of Williams's "saxifrage," the poet's metaphor that "splits / the rocks," the "things" named are "strong as rocks." In relinquishing the will to power (to "reconcile," to "split"), **"Today"** affirms not "things" in themselves but the dialogue inherent in interpreting the codes that inform this surprising network of names, and that inform our conceptions of poetry's relation to the world of "today."

O'Hara answers "A Sort of a Song" even more explicitly in **"Poetry,"** as comparison of the poems' beginnings shows:

> Let the snake wait under
> his weed
> and the writing
> be of words, slow and quick, sharp
> to strike, quiet to wait,
> sleepless.
>
> (Williams)

> The only way to be quiet
> is to be quick, so I scare
> you clumsily, or surprise
> you with a stab.
>
> (O'Hara)

"Poetry" differs from "A Sort of a Song" most noticeably in its comic, self-deprecating tone. But more significantly, **"Poetry"** resembles a conversation in its address to an unidentified interlocutor, a "you" that gives this poem a sense of intimacy missing in Williams's more polemical mode. Accordingly, O'Hara replaces Williams's phallic figure of the "snake . . . under his weed" with the less aggressive, more enigmatic praying mantis, crickets, and zebra, images united by "time," the measured time of the poetic line figured in three diverse "natural" rhythms. But these "times" are also allusions to inevitable, unpredictable change, the historical "time" which makes such confident proposals as Williams's seem archaic to O'Hara. The conclusion of his poem reiterates this hypersensitivity to time and transformation. The return to the conversational mode of address is accompanied by the speaker's recognition of the fictionality, and perhaps even solipsism, of his projections. Williams's imperative mode of address is replaced with "all this I desire . . . as if you / were logical and proven, . . . as if / I were used to you; as if / you would never leave me." Yet the method of rejecting solipsism, of affirming a dialogical relation with the addressee, is adapted from Williams's characteristic use of enjambment, where the breaks of the short lines occur at surprising syntactic junctures. Thus to "deepen you by my quickness / and delight as if you" simultaneously suggests the speaker's production and reception of "delight." Similarly, with the line break in the concluding lines, "inexorable / product of my own time," the addressee/reader is simultaneously the "inexorable" and the "inexorable product" of the poet's time. In appropriating Williams's strategies of enjambment, O'Hara achieves a dramatic structure that engages readers to reflect on the desires informing their own sense of time and historical difference.

From the playful subversion of interpretive authority in **"Today"** to the more complex dramatization of historicity in **"Poetry,"** O'Hara's early parodies of "A Sort of a Song" exemplify the prominence of his "appropriation" of Williams's technique during the immediate postwar years. They also exemplify the significance of O'Hara's wartime experience for his ironic interpretation of the 1950s "poetry wars." In his "I do this I do that" poems, especially in "lunch poems" such as **"The Day Lady Died," "A Step Away from Them,"** or **"Personal Poem,"** O'Hara's postmodernist "revaluation" of modernist poetics more subtly confronts the philosophical and ideological subtexts of vanguardism. There is certainly minimal subordination of seemingly insignificant elements to greater patterns of meaning in these poems. Because they are narratives, the sequencing of events often overshadows any pattern of symbolic meaning. Although such poems resemble what Roland Barthes would call the classical "readerly" text in their apparently straightforward narrative structure, they continually submit the narrated events to questions concerning their ideological significance, concurring with Barthes's notion of structure in the "writerly" text: "structure is not a design, a schema, a diagram: everything signifies something" [*S/Z*]. The two polar hypotheses describing O'Hara's poetry—the "will *not* to impute significance" and "everything signifies something"—inform the process of "double coding" which compels readers continually to decide on what is significant while concurrently reflecting on the grounds for such decisions. Such tension makes readers simultaneously attentive to significance in the seemingly insignificant and wary about attributing significance at all. . . . (pp. 254-57)

> *John Lowney, "The 'Post-Anti-Esthetic' Poetics of Frank O'Hara," in* Contemporary Literature, *Vol. XXXII, No. 2, Summer, 1991, pp. 244-64.*

FURTHER READING

Bibliography

Smith, Alexander, Jr. *Frank O'Hara: A Comprehensive Bibliography.* New York: Garland Publishing, Inc., 1979, 323 p.
> Lists published works by and about O'Hara as well as the locations of manuscripts and other unpublished material relating to O'Hara.

Biography

Gooch, Brad. *City Poet: The Life and Times of Frank O'Hara.* New York: Knopf, 1993, 352 p.
> Biographical and critical discussion of O'Hara's life and career.

Criticism

Acocella, Joan. "Perfectly Frank." *The New Yorker* LXIX, No. 22 (19 July 1993): 71-8.
> Praises Brad Gooch's biographical study of O'Hara [see

citation above] as a "minutely researched book," but faults his handling of O'Hara's homosexual encounters. An overview of O'Hara's life and career is included.

Baker, Peter. "Style and Compassion in the Williams Tradition." In his *Modern Poetic Practice: Structure and Genesis,* pp. 177-212. New York: Peter Lang, 1986.

Examines the interconnections between style and compassion in the poetry of William Carlos Williams and Frank O'Hara.

Berthoff, Warner. "The Analogies of Lyric: Shelley, Yeats, Frank O'Hara." In his *Literature and the Continuances of Virtue,* pp. 223-73. Princeton, N.J.: Princeton University Press, 1986.

Analyzes the poetry of O'Hara in terms of "virtue," a property which Berthoff has proposed for determining literary value and meaning.

Blasing, Mutlu Konuk. "Frank O'Hara and the Poetics of Love." In her *The Art of Life: Studies in American Autobiographical Literature,* pp. 139-56. Austin: University of Texas Press, 1977.

Contends that O'Hara's poetry, like that of William Carlos Williams and Walt Whitman, is part of an American tradition of personal poetry in which the poet attempts to establish an "intercourse with the world."

Boone, Bruce. "Gay Language as Political Praxis: The Poetry of Frank O'Hara." *Social Text* 1 (Winter 1979): 59-92.

Maintains that O'Hara's poetic language, which Boone describes as sexually antagonistic and politically oppositional, "must be seen against the backdrop of the literary oppositional movements of the period" and "in the social context of gay community life."

Feldman, Alan. *Frank O'Hara.* Boston: Twayne Publishers, 1979, 172 p.

Focuses on theme, intention, and moral significance in O'Hara's poetry, which Feldman describes as a "blend of personal intensity and comic detachment" and as an illustration of "the way in which art . . . affirms life for its own sake."

Ferguson, Suzanne. "Crossing the Delaware with Larry Rivers and Frank O'Hara: The Post-modern Hero at the Battle of Signifiers." *Word & Image* 2, No. 1 (January-March 1986): 27-32.

Asserts that Rivers's painting, *Washington Crossing the Delaware* (1953), and O'Hara's poem about Rivers's painting, "are two representative post-modern works which demonstrate how their artists interpret, by imitation and distortion, the techniques earlier artists devised to glorify individuals or passages from history."

Finkelstein, Norman. "O'Hara, Ashbery, and the Loss of the Sublime." In his *The Utopian Moment in Contemporary American Poetry,* pp. 41-61. Lewisburg, Pa.: Bucknell University Press, 1988.

Maintains that "the loss of the sublime in O'Hara and Ashbery is contingent upon these poets' ambivalence toward the sublime itself. Because they have not altogether rejected the high idealism of the Romantic lyric (and in this regard they are less radical than the Objectivists), but forever doubt its power of assertion, theirs is a poetry built on vacillation and the play of extremes."

Gooder, R. D. "After the Deluge, Me: Some Reflections on the Poems of Frank O'Hara." *The Cambridge Quarterly* XIV, No. 1 (1985): 93-122.

Maintains that the poetry of O'Hara, unlike that of Walt Whitman, is unselfconscious and democratic.

Mariani, Paul. "Reading the Seismograph." *Denver Quarterly* 13, No. 1 (Spring 1978): 91-4.

Argues that Marjorie Perloff's *Frank O'Hara: Poet among Painters* "is an important book . . . because it has given us a reliable way of seeing and placing O'Hara" among post-World War II American poets.

Meyer, Thomas. "Glistening Torsos, Sandwiches, and Coca-Cola." *Parnassus* 6, No. 1 (Fall/Winter 1977): 241-57.

Reviews Marjorie Perloff's *Frank O'Hara: Poet among Painters* as well as O'Hara's *Early Writing* and *Poems Retrieved.*

Perloff, Marjorie. *Frank O'Hara: Poet among Painters.* New York: George Braziller, 1977, 234 p.

Influential critical study of O'Hara's poetry.

———. "'Alterable Noons': The 'Poèmes élastiques' of Blaise Cendrars and Frank O'Hara." *The Yearbook of English Studies* 15 (1985): 160-78.

Compares the poetry of Cendrars and O'Hara and proposes that "'postmodernism' in American poetry may be less the revolution its proponents claim it to be than an injection of French 'modernism' . . . into the native American stream that comes down to us from Emerson and Whitman."

Poirier, Richard. "The Scenes of the Self." *The New Republic* 209, No. 5 (2 August 1993): 33-9.

Mixed review of Brad Gooch's *City Poet: The Life and Times of Frank O'Hara;* includes a biographical and critical overview of O'Hara's life and work.

Additional coverage of O'Hara's life and career is contained in the following sources published by Gale Research: *Contemporary Authors,* **Vols. 9-12, 25-28, rev. eds.;** *Contemporary Authors New Revision Series,* **Vol. 33;** *Contemporary Literary Criticism,* **Vols. 2, 5, 13;** *Dictionary of Literary Biography,* **Vols. 5, 16; and** *Major 20th-Century Writers.*

Aleksandr Solzhenitsyn

1918-

(Full name Aleksandr Isayevich Solzhenitysn) Russian novelist, short story writer, poet, playwright, journalist, essayist, critic, nonfiction writer, and autobiographer.

The following entry provides recent criticism of Solzhenitsyn's works through *Rebuilding Russia: Reflections and Tentative Proposals* (1991). For further information on his life and career, see *CLC,* Volumes 1, 2, 4, 7, 9, 10, 18, 26, and 34.

INTRODUCTION

Best known for *Odin den' Ivana Denisovicha* (*One Day in the Life of Ivan Denisovich*) and *Arkhipelag GULag, 1918-1956: Op'bit khudozhestvennopo issledovaniia* (*The Gulag Archipelago, 1918-1956: An Experiment in Literary Investigation*), Solzhenitsyn confronts in his works the oppressive actions of the former Soviet Union as well as the political and moral problems of the West. Rejecting the precepts of Socialist Realism, he writes from a Christian perspective, depicting the suffering of innocent people in a world where good and evil vie for the human soul; in this he is thematically linked to such nineteenth-century Russian writers as Leo Tolstoy and Anton Chekhov. Although Soviet authorities frequently banned his works, Solzhenitsyn received the 1970 Nobel Prize for what the Nobel committee termed "the ethical force with which he has pursued the indispensable traditions of Russian literature."

Born in 1918 in Kislovodsk, Russia, Solzhenitsyn never knew his father, who died in a hunting accident before he was born. His mother, the daughter of a wealthy landowner, was denied sufficient employment by the Soviet government, forcing the family into poverty from 1924 to 1936. Solzhenitsyn harbored literary ambitions early in life, resolving before he was eighteen to write a major novel about the Bolshevik Revolution of 1918. After earning degrees in philology, mathematics, and physics, Solzhenitsyn began teaching physics in 1941. In 1945, while serving as the commander of a Soviet Army artillery battery, counter-intelligence agents discovered personal letters in which Solzhenitsyn had criticized Communist leader Josef Stalin. Found guilty of conspiring against the state, he was confined to numerous institutions over the course of a decade, including a labor camp at Ekibastuz, Kazakhstan, and Marfino Prison—a *sharashka,* or government-run prison and research institute. While in Moscow's Lubyanka prison, Solzhenitsyn began reading works by such authors as Yevgeny Zamyatin, a notable Soviet prose writer of the 1920s, and American novelist John Dos Passos, whose expressionist style later influenced Solzhenitsyn's own writing. During his imprisonment in Ekibastuz, Solzhenitsyn was diagnosed with intestinal cancer and underwent surgery. Due to bureaucratic incompetence, however, he did not receive radiation and hormone treatments until he was near death, but miraculously recovered from the disease. In 1953 he was released from prison and exiled to Kok-Terek in Central Asia. There he taught mathematics and physics in a secondary school and began writing poems, plays, and notes for a novel.

Freed from exile in 1956, Solzhenitsyn returned to central Russia where friends encouraged him to submit his writings to the Russian periodical *Novy Mir,* which published *One Day in the Life of Ivan Denisovich* in 1962. Appearing during a period of openness fostered by Soviet leader Nikita Khrushchev, the novel proved a considerable success. However, with the fall of Khrushchev and the rise of less tolerant regimes, Solzhenitsyn quickly fell from official favor and was closely monitored by security forces. When he was granted the Nobel Prize for Literature in 1970, he was unable to attend the awards ceremony because the Soviet government would not guarantee his reentry into Russia. The French publication of *The Gulag Archipelago* led to his arrest, and in 1974 he was expelled from his homeland and eventually settled in the United States.

Set in Stalinist Russia, *One Day in the Life of Ivan Deni-sovich* focuses on a simple prisoner who wants only to serve his sentence of hard labor with Christian integrity. In the novel Solzhenitsyn strove to avoid the aims of So-cialist Realism, which reflected the official directives of the state and so imposed thoughts and feelings on its readers. Instead he rendered his tale in an ironic, understated, el-liptical manner intended to elicit spontaneous feelings. Despite the book's popular success, most critics consider *V kruge pervom* (*The First Circle*) and *Rakovyĭ korpus* (*The Cancer Ward*) Solzhenitsyn's principal achieve-ments of the 1960s. Both works are set in institutions iso-lated from society, feature characters with diverse back-grounds and philosophies, and incorporate Solzhenitsyn's experiences as a prisoner and cancer patient. Although *The First Circle* is set in a prison, the novel begins as In-nokenty Volodin, an idealistic young diplomat, makes a telephone call to warn a family friend that the Soviet gov-ernment is trying to entrap him. Volodin's benevolence re-sults in his arrest and imprisonment in a *sharashka*. With *The First Circle* Solzhenitsyn countered Socialist Realism by relating his work to both Russian classics and Western culture, and by portraying Stalin as a monomaniac in the tradition of Fedor Dostoevski's Grand Inquisitor. In *The Cancer Ward* Solzhenitsyn uses disease as a metaphor for the political imprisonment and moral corruption of all as-pects of Russian society under the Soviet Regime.

The Gulag Archipelago, a detailed account of Stalinist re-pression that is widely considered Solzhenitsyn's most im-portant work of nonfiction, emphasizes the fact that arrest and torture were common practices in the Soviet Union. Solzhenitsyn approached the work in a scientific manner, creating a taxonomy of arrests and tortures and inviting readers to participate with him in categorizing forms of physical punishment. Solzhenitsyn also includes accounts of his arrest and confinement in different prisons and con-centration camps, as well as many personal narratives from other victims of arbitrary violence. In *The Gulag Ar-chipelago* Solzhenitsyn finds all Russians—including him-self—accountable for the evils of Stalinism. "We didn't love freedom enough," he writes. "We purely and simply deserved everything that happened afterward."

Avgust chetyrnadtsatogo (*August 1914*) is the first volume in *Krasnoe koleso: Povestvovanie v otmerennykh srokakh* (*The Red Wheel*), a series of novels intended as a panora-ma of modern Russia and a corrective to the Soviet re-gime's distortions of Russian history. *August 1914* centers on the World War I battle of Tannenberg as witnessed by Colonel Georgy Vorotyntsev, a graduate of a Russian mil-itary academy, and his friend Arseny Blagodaryov, an en-listed man. Vorotyntsev and Blagodaryov serve with a group of Russian soldiers who are surrounded by advanc-ing German troops yet succeed in breaking through enemy lines. In *August 1914* Solzhenitsyn employs the polyphonic style found in all his major works, incorporat-ing fictional, journalistic, cinematic, and historical writing techniques. In 1983 Solzhenitsyn published a revised ver-sion of *August 1914* that included three hundred pages of newly written material concerning Lenin's activities dur-ing World War I as well as the career of Pyotr Stolypin, the Russian Prime Minister assassinated in 1911 by anar-

chist Dmitry Bogrov. Critics responded negatively to the revised version, faulting Solzhenitsyn for his polemical thrust and for placing greater emphases on the dispensa-tion of historical information than on meaningful charac-terizations and literary quality. Many found *August 1914* disjointed and confusing, claiming that Solzhenitsyn's in-terpretations of historical events were distorted and inac-curate; others took issue with Solzhenitsyn's thesis that Stolypin's assassination had halted Russia's peaceful polit-ical development and made the Bolshevik Revolution pos-sible. In a review of the revised version of *August 1914,* Ir-ving Howe commented: "All is muddle, sloth, backward-ness, sly falsification. It is as if Mr. Solzhenitsyn were in-tent, though he probably is not, upon confirming the usual view of czarism's essential rottenness, or as if he were de-liberately following the judgments of Stendhal and Tol-stoy that warfare is inherently chaotic—though without the former's brilliance or the latter's penetration."

The second *Red Wheel* volume, *Oktyabr' shestnadtsatogo,* presents very little military action but emphasizes the war's effect on the home front. Among other plot lines, the book focuses on Vorotyntsev, a married man who falls in love with a female professor at Petrograd University. The 1986-87 publication of *March 1917,* for which no Russian edition exists, marked another major change in the em-phasis of *The Red Wheel*. In this volume, historical figures replace fictional characters as the narrative's focus shifts from World War I to the communist revolution. Solzheni-tsyn painstakingly details various historical events, de-scribing weather conditions as well as the actions, emo-tions, and physical appearances of the characters to allow readers to experience what happens when a society slowly but inexorably disintegrates.

In 1990 *Kak nam obustroit' Rossiiu?: posil'nye soobraz-heniia* (*Rebuilding Russia: Reflections and Tentative Pro-posals*), Solzhenitsyn's plan for the reorganization of Rus-sia after the fall of Communism, appeared in *Komsomol-skaya pravda,* the official newspaper of the Communist Youth League. Included in the article were Solzhenitsyn's recommendations for the social and political future of Russia and a largely negative historical portrait of Russia and the Russian people. In 1991 the English translation elicited strong disapproval from critics who claimed Sol-zhenitsyn's propositions were impractical and unrealistic. Tatyana Tolstaya observed: "If Solzhenitsyn took over the real Russia with its real population, uprisings, pogroms, and conflagrations would commence within a week. . . . The people in theory always diverge dramatically from the people in reality; and the horror of this truth is sooner or later discovered by everyone who pretends to the people's spiritual leadership, by everyone who knows how things should and should not be done."

In his fiction and nonfiction Solzhenitsyn continues to as-sert the strength of the human spirit and the responsibility of the writer. The task of the writer, he believes, is "to treat universal and eternal themes: the mysteries of the heart and conscience, the collision between life and death, the triumph over spiritual anguish." Critics generally agree that Solzhenitsyn's perceptive analysis of the human condition elevates his fiction above ordinary political writing and places him among Russia's greatest novelists. Many assert that from *One Day in the Life of Ivan Denisovich* to *Rebuilding Russia,* Solzhenitsyn's prevailing theme is the dissolution of an anachronistic, deeply divided society under the stress of exceptional circumstances, and the response of individuals to that dissolution.

PRINCIPAL WORKS

Odin den' Ivana Denisovicha (novel) 1962
 [*One Day in the Life of Ivan Denisovich,* 1963]
Dlia pol'zy dela (novel) 1963
 [*For the Good of the Cause,* 1964]
Sluchaĭ na stantsii Krechetovka [i] Matrenin dvor (novels) 1963
 [*We Never Make Mistakes,* 1963]
Sochineniia (selected works) 1966
Olen'i shalashovka (play) 1968
 [*The Love Girl and the Innocent,* 1969]
Rakovyĭ korpus (novel) 1968
 [*The Cancer Ward,* 1968]
Svecha na vetru (play) 1968
 [*Candle in the Wind,* 1973]
V kruge pervom (novel) 1968
 [*The First Circle,* 1968]
Avgust chetyrnadtsatogo (novel) 1971
 [*August 1914,* 1971; revised version published as *Krasnoe koleso: Povestvovanie v otmerennykh srokakh. Uzel I, Avgust chetyrnadtsatogo,* 1983 and republished as *August 1914,* 1989]
Stories and Prose Poems by Aleksandr Solzhenitsyn (short stories and poetry) 1971
Nobelevskaia lektsiia po literature 1970 goda (essay) 1972
 [*Nobel Lecture by Aleksandr Solzhenitsyn,* 1972]
Arkhipelag GULag, 1918-1956: Op'bit khudozhestvennopo issledovaniia (nonfiction) 1973-75
 [*The Gulag Archipelago, 1918-1956: An Experiment in Literary Investigation,* Vol. I, Parts 1 and 2, 1974; Vol. II, Parts 3 and 4, 1976; Vol. III, 1979]
Pis'mo vozhdiam Sovetskogo Soĭuza (essay) 1974
 [*Letter to Soviet Leaders,* 1974]
Prusskie nochi: pozma napisappaja v lagere v 1950 (poetry) 1974
 [*Prussian Nights: A Poem,* 1977]
Amerikanski rechi (essays) 1975
Bodalsia telenok s dubom (autobiography) 1975
 [*The Oak and the Calf,* 1975]
From under the Rubble [with others] (essays) 1975; also published as *From under the Ruins,* 1975
Détente: Prospects for Democracy and Dictatorship [with others] (essays) 1976
†*Lenin in Zurich* (novella) 1976
Warning to the West (essays) 1976
Victory Celebrations: A Comedy in Four Acts. Prisoners: A Tragedy (plays) 1983
Oktyabr' shestnadtsatogo (novel) 1984
March 1917 (novel) 1986-87

Kak nam obustroit' Rossiiu?: posil'nye soobrazheniia (essay) 1990
 [*Rebuilding Russia: Reflections and Tentative Proposals,* 1991]

*Part of the *Krasnoe koleso: povestvovanie v otmerennykh srokakh* (*The Red Wheel*) series.

†This work contains chapters omitted from the original version of *Avgust chetyrnadtsatogo.*

CRITICISM

Donald H. Roy   (essay date Winter 1981)

[*In the following essay, Roy analyzes Solzhenitsyn's writings to determine "the precise nature of [his] spirituality."*]

What is the heart of Solzhenitsyn's religious teaching? Given the nature of the published writings of Solzhenitsyn it would be unwise to search for some dogmatic pattern of beliefs that could be conveniently equated with Slavophilism or the Old Believer movement of the Russian Orthodox Church. Certainly Solzhenitsyn is to be connected, in some way, with these Russian traditions. But these influences have significance only after the fact of Solzhenitsyn's conversion in the depths of that whale, the Gulag. Solzhenitsyn does not intend to be a theologian or a simple apologist for a religious creed.

> So that the country and people do not suffocate, and so that they all have the chance to develop and enrich us with ideas, allow competition on an equal and honorable basis—not for power, but for the truth—between all ideological and moral currents, in particular between all religions: there will be nobody to persecute them if their tormentor, Marxism, is deprived of its state privileges. But allow competition honestly. . . .
>
> . . . the only church remaining was that church which, in accordance with the Scriptures, lay *within the heart.*

My argument will be that first and foremost Solzhenitsyn is an artist exploring the origins of religious consciousness from the dark depths of ignorance, indifference, skepticism and rejection. The coming-to-be of a spiritual awakening (given Solzhenitsyn's life experiences) is the heart of the matter under inquiry.

For Solzhenitsyn the artist's free exploration of religious consciousness has priority over political treatises and programs. The prison experience, which is so formative of Solzhenitsyn and his works, defines the arena for spiritual conversion. The Platonic Cave image, the crisis-trials and tribulations of the wandering, wayward soul, the dark night of the soul, **Darkness at Noon,** the wisdom that comes through unavoidable, personal suffering, all of these representative experiences should help us understand Solzhenitsyn's writings. Especially there is the remark in **One Day in the Life of Ivan Denisovich** which cuts to the core: "How could a man who is warm ever understand a man who is cold?" This problem of shared understanding is the test of any art. Art is a way of indirectly, yet potently, bringing to others the experience of a soul in the process of conversion. Not everyone should or can pass through the hell of suffering to reach the beyond. This is an additional reason why art is the only alternative for many. Further, art is self-verifying; lies simply cannot stand up against art. People readily see through deficient, sham art. True art has a unique way of touching the soul.

In Solzhenitsyn's Nobel Lecture the reasons are given for the priority of art over politics. In the process it is also shown how art is the mode for religious expression. The activity of artistic expression reveals some "mysterious inner light". But the question is, what is the source of this inspiration? There are two alternatives; there are two kinds of artists. Either man is the measure or God is the measure.

How does one choose between these two alternatives? Solzhenitsyn provides an outpouring of reflection on this dilemma. Starting from either premise, that man or God is the measure, draw out the consequences for human action. To assume man is the measure is to negate any possibility of a transcendent (transpolitical) standard as a guide for action. This could happen and it has happened, yet there is no basis for such religious escapism in Solzhenitsyn's writings, not when Solzhenitsyn takes on the burden of the story of millions who have entered the Gulag, not when Solzhenitsyn faces the terrible powers of destruction and evil in human hands.

To declare God as the center of one's existence (*amor Dei* not *amor sui*) is to see the world, i.e., creation, as founded on intelligible principles that no human being could originate, that no human being could master, that no human being could be at one with while still being mortal. There are many passages in Solzhenitsyn's writings descriptive of this breakthrough experience pointing beyond man-in-the-world.

REFLECTIONS

On the surface of a swift-flowing stream the reflections of things near or far are always indistinct; even if the water is clear and has no foam, reflections in the constant stream of ripples, the restless kaleidoscope of water, are still uncertain, vague, incomprehensible.

Only when the water has flowed down river after river and reaches a broad, calm estuary or comes to rest in some backwater or a small, still lake—only then can we see in its mirrorlike smoothness every leaf of a tree on the bank, every wisp of a cloud, and the deep blue expanse of the sky.

It is the same with our lives. If so far we have been unable to see clearly or to reflect the eternal lineaments of truth, is it not because we too are still moving towards some end—because we are still alive?

It towered so vast above petty human creation, so elemental in a man-made world, that even if all the men who had lived in all the past millennia had opened their arms as wide as they could and carried everything they had ever created or intended to create and piled it all up in massive heaps, they could never have raised a mountain ridge as fantastic as the Caucasus.

Not only is the human being puny without God. There is serious doubt that the conflict of "values", cultures, etc. could be resolved without "the more that human". Does not "man the measure" throw us back on our own inadequate resources, i.e., habits and conventions? Accordingly, whatever is, ought to be by its very dominating "is-ness". There is no surmounting that place "out there" where "ninety-nine weep and one laughs". There is no way to reconcile disputes by some higher appeal. There is no conscience informed by an other which one cannot call simply one's own. Is human reason on its own able to transcend human failings? God as the measure holds out the hope that the process of searching inquiry will reveal the universal, eternal, common scale, a hierarchy of dynamic being. How does a finite, subjective, particular human "know" this? According to Solzhenitsyn, you find your immortal soul; it is a discovery not a theologian's pontification, nor an ideologue's postulation. "Don't trust your brother; trust your own bad eye."

Formerly you never forgave anyone. You judged people without mercy. And you praised people with equal lack of moderation. And now an understanding mildness has become the basis of your uncategorical judgements. You have come to realize your own weakness—you can therefore understand the weakness of others. And be astonished at another's strength. . . .

Your soul, which formerly was dry now ripens from suffering. And even if you haven't come to love your neighbors in the Christian sense, you are at least learning to love those close to you.

Those close to you in spirit surround you in slavery. And how many of us come to realize: It is particularly in slavery that for the first time we have learned to recognize genuine friendship! . . .

Here is a rewarding and inexhaustible direction for your thoughts: Reconsider all your previous life. Remember everything you did that was bad and shameful and take thought—can't you possibly correct it now?

Yes, you have been imprisoned for nothing. You have nothing to repent of before the state and its laws.

But . . . before your own conscience? But . . . in relation to other individuals?

Within everyone's soul (whether a person is conscious of this or not) there is a longing for the eternal, or more precisely, Truth, Goodness and Beauty. Take for example the elderly Dr. Oreshchenkov in **Cancer Ward**:

He had to take frequent rests nowadays. His body demanded this chance to recoup its strength and with the same urgency his inner self demanded silent contemplation free of external sounds, conversations, thoughts of work, free of everything that made him a doctor. Particularly after the death of his wife, his inner consciousness had seemed to crave a pure transparency. It was just this sort of silent immobility, without planned or even floating thoughts, which gave him a sense of purity and fulfillment.

At such moments an image of the whole meaning of existence—his own during the long past and the short future ahead, that of his late wife, of his young granddaughter and of everyone in the world—came to his mind. The image he saw did not seem to be embodied in the work or activity which occupied them, which they believed was central to their lives, and by which they were known to others. The meaning of existence was to preserve unspoiled, undisturbed and undistorted the image of eternity with which each person is born.

Like a silver moon in a calm, still pond.

There is much in Solzhenitsyn that is Augustinian—the rejection of *amor sui* (for instance, when the artist chooses art only as a means of self-admiration); the life of excruciating turmoil and torment before the break-through conversion; the pursuit of the eternal and the rejection of transient pleasures; the emphasis on what the heart and conscience "know" that human reason alone cannot comprehend; and the recognition of goodness, beauty and order in God's creation. Through the artist's power of evoking self-discovery, "Beauty will save the world" as Dostoevsky stated.

Of the three transcendentals, Truth, Goodness and Beauty, Solzhenitsyn claims that Beauty can save Truth and Goodness. How can Solzhenitsyn say this when most of his own writing seems to be more in the spirit of exposing the Truth? What is there that is beautiful about the Gulag, the sharaska of the *First Circle,* the *Cancer Ward* or the battlegrounds of *August 1914* ? Even Solzhenitsyn's Nobel Lecture ends with the boldface utterance: "ONE WORD OF TRUTH OUTWEIGHS THE WORLD". Solzhenitsyn's controlled rage and righteous anger (eminently justifiable) are more truth-speaking than beautiful. Will not the Truth make the world beautiful and good?

Solzhenitsyn's rejoinder might be that only *after* passing through the dark valley of the shadow of death on the way to seeing the beauty of creation does a person have the will to speak the truth and pursue the good. It is all a matter of the order of experiences in this dia-phany (shining through) which is a conversion (turning around) of one's soul. In the chapter "The First Day of Creation . . . " in *Cancer Ward* Kostoglotov's release from the cancer ward (symbolic of the prison regimen in the Soviet Union) is carefully described:

> He walked onto the porch and stood still. He breathed in. It was young air, still and undisturbed. He looked out at the world—it was new and turning green. He raised his head. The sky unfolded, pink from the sun rising somewhere unseen. He raised his head higher. Spindleshaped, porous clouds, centuries of laborious

workmanship, stretched across the whole sky, but only for a few moments before dispersing, seen only by the few who happened to throw back their heads that minute, perhaps by Oleg Kostoglotov alone among the town's inhabitants.

> Through the lace, the cutout pattern, the froth and plumes of these clouds sailed the shining, intricate vessel of the old moon, still well visible.

> It was the morning of creation. The world had been created anew for one reason only, to be given back to Oleg. "Go out and live!" it seemed to say.

The rest of this chapter (especially Kostoglotov's visit to the zoo, the three letters he writes and the incident at the railroad station) demonstrates dawning truth and good will in Kostoglotov's heart following those moments of beauty and miracle.

Truth that Solzhenitsyn pursues in all his works centers on philosophic anthropology, the dimensions and tendencies of the human soul. Many of Solzhenitsyn's references to Russian proverbs develop this understanding of human nature. The good that Solzhenitsyn discovers is simply there in every human being: unpremeditated acts of kindness; forgiveness and understanding without rewards; exemplary acts that shine brilliantly so that others do not lose faith and hope in existence. Therefore, beauty as it pours into the open soul reveals what humans have yet to tarnish and converts fear and hatred into courage and good will. Most people will not readily recognize the good and the true, whereas beauty turns heads and energizes the will in the direction of right and loving action.

Besides this dawning experience of beauty, we must fasten on the prison experience itself in all of its suffering, despair, loneliness, torture and degradation to reexperience how the soul of a person *may* discover itself. Why is it said that the Gulag is a spiritual birthplace and homeland? Why is it that only a zek is certain to have an immortal soul?

Perhaps in modern times many people do not know what it means "to have a soul" as opposed to having a self. Self and ego have replaced the soul and, as a consequence, the reference is not the same. As Hume understood, the self or ego is that bundle of experiences that happens to you. In Marx's terms "Being determines consciousness". This is precisely what Solzhenitsyn rejects, given his prison experience. The discovery of one's soul is the discovery of one's own reflective consciousness otherwise known as that which is the fundamental source for our movement, i.e., free will and reflective consciousness, thought thinking itself. The soul is immortal because it cancels environmental and bodily limitations. The more-than-human, divine light within us defines us as unique beings. The soul cannot be taken away; you have grasped nothing if you attempt to dominate another's soul. A person can no longer be who he is without a soul.

The prison experience awakens the soul: "each of us is a center of the Universe, and that Universe is shattered when they hiss at you: *'You are under arrest.'*" Once you have been incarcerated, there is the upheaveal of one's former consciousness. The following occurs: Why Me? utter fear at the brink of death; readiness to save one's own skin by sacrificing anyone else, rationalizations of nastiness, disbelief in one's new existence, despair, and loss of self-respect. "And may you be judged by God, but not by people. . . . "

Arrest causes a transformation of life.

> From the moment you go to prison you must put your cozy past firmly behind you. At the very threshold, you must say to yourself: "My life is over, a little early to be sure, but there's nothing to be done about it. I shall never return to freedom. I am condemned to die—now or a little later. But later on, in truth, it will be even harder, and so the sooner the better. I no longer have any property whatsoever. For me those I love have died, and for them I have died. From today on, my body is useless and alien to me. Only my spirit and conscience remain precious and important to me."

> Confronted by such a prisoner, the interrogator will tremble.

> Only the man who has renounced everything can win that victory.

> But how can one turn one's body to stone?

This new-found (if found at all) superiority over material existence is a true coming alive, a liberation of the soul from the weight of corporeal existence. Your soul grows, and it is beyond the power of one's tormentors. In the presence of a friend (someone you can share experiences with) or foe (stool pigeons) some secret, internal, spiritual sensor relays the message that opens or closes one's heart. It is another miracle which Solzhenitsyn believes many people can experience. But they never develop this power as they live wholeheartedly in a technological, rationalistic age. They never will develop this in an anaesthetic society based on creature comfort.

The arrest, the interrogation, treatment as an object happening to occupy space, the destruction of time frame, being surrounded by alien beings, and isolation compel a person to revert to one's own resources. The security, safety, comfort and predictability of normal existence, the status quo, can no longer be taken for granted. A new space and a new time for the soul's activity is offered. Are you a hollow person? Can any person be an island? Will this emptiness of existence be filled? If you do begin to experience a growing sense of new-found wholenss, is it a product of the self's own achievement? Yet, is not the activity of the soul disanalogous to any production process involving the material world?

Spiritual growth and fullness become the antithesis to the omni-oppressive totalitarian regime. The activity of the soul is person-determining, free will, an experience of independence and otherness from the regime which assumes it will either master you or destroy you. Hence the rebellion begins.

Gleb Nerzhin (in the *First Circle*) and Oleg Kostoglotov

> Surrender to God involves a confession of guilt and acts of repentance. Solzhenitsyn expects this to happen on both the personal and the national levels . . . Repentance will lead to forgiveness, and this in turn will lead to personal restraint and personal reform. Unity in action with others will follow as a nation takes on these same moral and spiritual characteristics that individual persons have freely chosen.
>
> —*Donald H. Roy*

(in the *Cancer Ward*) best represent the period of skepsis through which the soul purges itself. (This, of course, is not to be confused with the Communist Party which attempts to purge the pages of human history to oblivion.) Be it in the slave labor camp or in the cancer ward the soul engages in dialectical argumentation in the Socratic not the Marxist-Leninist sense. Dialectic does not serve praxis as an *ex post facto* rationalization of the consequence of one's deeds or as the iron logic of power, force and terror marching through history. Dialectical argumentation permits free and open questioning and exploration of all viewpoints. Also, like Socrates and unlike Marx and Lenin, one is more frightened by one's own presumed intelligence than an other's errors or ignorance. Dialectical argumentation puts *theoria* (reflection and contemplation) before praxis in the sense that the reflective soul is the critical inquiring agency which judges deeds. In the end, a person is defined by choices made manifest in deeds. The soul is the resonating center in which the crisis of judgement and choice occur. Many of the characters of Solzhenitsyn's novels experience such a crisis of choice, or in their later years they painfully suffer or regret their previous, life-defining choices. All of the characters in the *First Circle* are defined by the tough choices that they have to make; some choices result in slavery, the loss of freedom to choose any longer.

Both Gleb and Oleg have to make life and death choices. Gleb's choice (but also for Sologdin, Gerasimovitch, Rubin and Ruska) involves complicity with a regime that persists in being an enemy to its people. Oleg's involves questionable cancer treatment that may or may not allow him to enjoy just a few years (even months) of joyful, blessed existence. But those are only the external choices; both Gleb and Oleg have made internal choices after a period of conflict and struggle with themselves. There are many idols in the world which provoke the temptation to sell your soul for the sake of easy creaturely happiness. Solzhenitsyn warns us not to pursue happiness if we hope to find it in the end; wisdom comes through suffering. The soul is strengthened through deprivation. Ivan Denisovich finds freedom by not having envy and greed for another's food and possession, by not rushing off to doctors at the first sign of pain, by being honest. This is the spiritual consciousness of strength, courage and independence transcending the environment one is in. There is spiritual strength in rejecting Marx's "being determines consciousness".

Yet a skeptical consciousness is only a means and not an end as Gleb discovers in his argument with Ruska.

> "I want to warn you, Ruska," Nerzhin replied very softly, leaning closer to his neighbor's ear. "No matter how clever and absolute the systems of skepticism or agnosticism or pessimism, you must understand that by their very nature they doom us to a loss of will. They can't really influence human behavior because people cannot stand still. And that means they can't renounce systems which affirm something which summon them to advance in some direction."
>
> "Even if it's into a swamp? Just to slog along?" Ruska asked angrily. . . .
>
> ". . . How did you put it: 'Whatever great minds think up, at the cost of great effort, eventually appears to still greater minds as something phantasmal'? Was that it?"
>
> "All right!" Nerzhin replied accusingly. "You're losing sight of everything solid, of every goal. One can certainly doubt, one is obliged to doubt. But isn't it also necessaray to love something?"

To have a goal, to love something—what will that be? You have to look deeper within yourself and you have to expand the horizon of your experiences through dialogue with others. Solzhenitsyn does not advocate one way for everyone. Spiritual experience by its very nature is as diverse as are people. For example, in the **First Circle** Agniya chooses religious faith because religious people are persecuted (the underdog phenomenon); the painter Kondrashev-Ivanov pursues an image of artistic perfection beyond his reach; Rubin gropes for some civil religion that would give some missing stimulus to the Marxist historical development process in the Soviet Union; even Stalin cannot free himself of his early seminary experiences. Other characters are rebelling on the borderline: Volodin and Clara cannot repress their conscience: Spiridon witnesses the wholesome peasant attitude towards life; Sologdin discovers that only in prison do you spiritually understand the role of good and evil in human life; and Gerasinovitch enacts the great refusal by refusing to benefit from the torment of others.

There are different spiritual experiences and various levels of attainment. This is the polyphonic novel at its best. There are many different, competing voices in the first circle of hell which symoblizes the highest attainment the human alone can attain. Solzhenitsyn partakes of all these voices as they undergo the spiritual quest which will or will not draw them from this first circle of hell.

In this context of searching skepticism there is the unforgettable prison conversation between Alyosha the Baptist (remember Alyosha in Dostoevsky's *Brothers Karamazov*) and Ivan Denisovich Shukhov.

> "Oh, we didn't pray for that, Ivan Denisovich," Alyosha said earnestly. Bible in hand, he drew

nearer to Shukhov till they lay face to face. "Of all earthly and mortal things Our Lord commanded us to pray only for our daily bread. 'Give us this day our daily bread.' " . . .

> Shukhov went on calmly smoking and watching his excited companion.
>
> "Alyosha," he said, withdrawing his arm and blowing smoke into his face. "I'm not against God, understand that. I do believe in God. But I don't believe in paradise or in hell. Why do you take us for fools and stuff us with your paradise and hell stories? That's what I don't like. . . .
>
> . . . "Well," he said conclusively, "however much you pray it doesn't shorten your stretch. You'll sit it out from beginning to end anyhow."
>
> "Oh, you mustn't pray for that either," said Alyosha, horrified. "Why do you want freedom? In freedom your last grain of faith will be choked with weeds. You should rejoice that you're in prison. Here you have time to think about your soul. As the Apostle Paul wrote: 'Why all these tears? Why are you trying to weaken my resolution? For my part I am ready not merely to be bound but even to die for the name of the Lord Jesus.' "

Alyosha was happy in prison; he had found peace. But can Solzhenitsyn himself find rest in the peace that passes understanding? Not yet; there is still a burden to bear here and now.

The decisive test of spiritual existence is the realization that you have only one life and one conscience. You are a unique being with the freedom to define your own existence. At the center of the **First Circle** is a long, pivotal passage which is a response to Gleb Nerzhen's search for a loving goal:

> Kondrashev-Ivanov rose to his full height. "Never! Never!" He looked upward, like a man being led to execution. "No camp must break a man's spirit."
>
> Nerzhin laughed coldly. "Perhaps it must not, but it does! You haven't been in camp yet, so don't judge. You don't know how they break us there. People go in, and when they come out—if they come out—they're unrecognizably different. Yes, its's well known: circumstances determine consciousness." . . .
>
> "No! . . . A human being," Kondrashev contginued, "possesses from his birth a certain essence, the nucleus, as it were, of this human being. His 'I'. And it is still uncertain which forms which: whether life forms the man or man, with his strong spirit, forms his life! Because—" Kondrashev-Ivanov suddenly lowered his voice and leaned toward Nerzhin, who was again sitting on the block—"because he has something to measure himself against, something he can look to. Because he has in him an image of perfection which in rare moments suddenly emerges before his spiritual gaze."

To recaptiulate: a hitherto lost, hidden bit of your soul awakens. You rebel against your former existence and your antagonist. These are the dark days of skepsis marked by provocative angry arguments with friend and foe. You begin to understand your soul to be an unexpected gift you know not from where. The image of perfection, the Holy Grail, the eternal quest, that your soul inherently longs for lays the basis for spiritual activity. Such perfection (the transcendentals, Beauty, Truth and Goodness) you have discovered not invented; they are not easily attainable; you are humbled like Kondrashev-Ivanov in their presence. Yet you now know that only they are the *telos* of your soul's activity and only they can fill your soul. This is the breakthrough experience of the soul fathoming "something more" than self, body and environment.

Now the prisoner's soul is prepared, which is to say willing and open, to share common experiences with others. There is nothing private and solipsistic about the soul's reflections on death, suffering, love, contrition, joy merely in the goal of existing, friendship, magnanimity, humility, and so on. In Solzhenitsyn's Nobel Lecture we learn that the activity of literary art will be the test of his powers in the questing communion with "something more".

With minute precision and at great length Solzhenitsyn has delineated the physical and psychological reactions of those incarcerated and condemned. The victims are brought to the threshold of life and death, of good and evil. The utter isolation and alienation of the person (do not expect the Church or your family and friends to speak a word or do a thing on his behalf) as well as the dehumanizing treatment of the person reduce the prisoner to a living nothingness. Why go on living?

Since we know that there are many who are incapable of surviving this kind of suffering, it is the mission of the Christian to bear the burden for others. "I came to understand that it was my duty to take upon my shoulders a share of their common burden—to bear it to the last man, until it crushed us." Solzhenitsyn's literary art is his way of bearing the burden of the fate of the Russian soul in the twentieth century. Marx too knew of that moment when human beings had nothing more to lose except their chains. Total revolution would throw off those chains once and for all. This is Marx's path of salvation—the final liberation. Solzhenitsyn offers the inversion of Marx's answer.

> "Why is it," Dyomka would ask Aunt Styofa, "that there's such rank injustice in fortune itself? There are people whose lives run smooth as silk from beginning to end, I know there are, while others' are a complete louse-up. And they say a man's life depends on himself. It doesn't depend on him a bit."
>
> "It depends on God," Said Aunt Styofa soothingly. "God sees everything. You should submit to him, Dyomusha."
>
> "Well, if it's from God it's even worse. If he can see everything, why does he load it all on one person? I think he ought to try to spread it about a bit. . . . "
>
> But there were no two ways about it—he had to submit. What else was there for him to do?

The spiritual conversion of one's soul (not the revolutionary transformation of despicable creation) results in a submission or surrender of self. This is most difficult to recommend and persuade. Solzhenitsyn has begun the effort in an essay **"Repentance and Self-Limitation in the Life of Nations"** and also in the final volume, *Gulag Archipelago Three.* Surrender to God involves a confession of guilt and acts of repentance. Solzhenitsyn expects this to happen on both the personal and the national levels. Once persons, a nation and nations of the world confess their sins, then there can be a redirection of energies towards those activities that acknowledge the self-limitations (*sophrosyne* not *hybrus*) inherent in human action as this involves other humans and the environment. Repentance will lead to forgiveness, and this in turn will lead to personal restraint and personal reform. Unity in action with others will follow as a nation takes on these same moral and spiritual characteristics that individual persons have freely chosen.

> . . . that the greatness of a people is to be sought not in the blare of trumpets—physical might is purchased at a spiritual price beyond our means—but in the level of its *inner* development, in its breadth of soul (fortunately one of nature's gifts to us), in unarmed moral steadfastness (in which the Czechs and Slovaks recently gave Europe a lesson, without however troubling its conscience more than briefly).

In conclusion, Solzhenitsyn rejects the modern persuasion of enlightened liberalism and Marxism. Both propose modernization programs founded on the secular belief in unlimited freedom and infinite progress in the name of man. This is the modern faith that Solzhenitsyn abandons in favor of Christian faith (albeit not specifically Catholic faith), since it is the Christian faith alone that is true to the dimensions of the human soul and God's creation. Thus aching souls will be healed. (pp. 305-18)

> *Donald H. Roy, "Solzhenitsyn's Religious Teaching," in* Faith and Reason, *Vol. VII, No. 4, Winter, 1981, pp. 305-19.*

David Matual   (essay date Fall 1982)

[In the following essay, Matual traces Solzhenitsyn's treatment of the "spiritual evolution" of characters in The Gulag Archipelago *to Dante's* Divine Comedy.]

That Alexander Solzhenitsyn is familiar with at least the imagery of Dante's *Divine Comedy* is evident from the title of his novel, *The First Circle.* In the second chapter, entitled "Dante's Idea," the character Rubin draws a parallel between the first circle of hell, where the pagan sages of antiquity are confined, and the *sharashka,* or special scientific installation, where arrested Soviet scientists are forced to devote their knowledge and skill to the advancement of the Soviet state. There are also hints of Dantean imagery, however few and subtle, in Solzhenitsyn's longest and most ambitious work, *The Gulag Archipelago.* In Part III, for example, before his account of the historical development of the correctional labor camps, the author calls upon I. L. Auerbach to be "our Virgil," i.e. to guide the reader through the maze of historical details about to be presented. It will be recalled, of course, that Virgil is Dante's guide through the nether regions in the *Comedy*. Moreover, the mythological "gates of the archipelago," which exist only in the imagination of the *zeks*, with their two signs reading "Do not be discouraged" for those entering and "Do not be too happy" for those leaving are inevitably reminiscent of the famous sign over Dante's inferno: "Lasciate ogni speranza voi ch'entrate."

While the occasional references to *The Divine Comedy* have no compelling hermeneutical value for **The Gulag Archipelago,** they point, nevertheless, to the possibility of a Dantean model for the proper ordering and understanding of the spiritual evolution which some of the *zeks* undergo. True, most of the men and women of the archipelago are static figures, fixed in this or that phase of the spiritual process. But others, like Dante, are made to pass through *inferno,* the site of torments, *purgatorio,* the place of cleansing and enlightenment, and *paradiso,* the realm of perfect knowledge and wisdom. The most notable and—for this study—the most interesting of these travelers is Solzhenitsyn himself, who, over the course of many years, proceeds from the unmitigated misery of the Soviet inferno, continues through the purgation of suffering, and ends at last in an exalted state of spiritual tranquility.

Each inhabitant of the archipelago, whether static or dynamic, is doomed to experience, if only for a short time, the horrors and anxieties of Solzhenitsyn's inferno. Though there is no fixed entrance to this twentieth-century hell (despite the myth of the "gates" with their portentous inscriptions), it affords easy access to everyone. Initiation into its terrors begins, as Solzhenitsyn demonstrates so powerfully in Part I, with the cataclysmic moment of arrest. But unlike Dante's Christian inferno, Solzhenitsyn's Stalinist hell does not presuppose the commission of serious sin or even the violation of man-made laws. Everyone without exception is subject to arrest, and it comes in the most varied ways and at the most implausible times. Once arrested, the anguished victim is then subjected to tortures, both physical and psychological, inflicted by interrogators during the inquest. After he has signed the obligatory confession of guilt, his agony assumes new forms—in prisons, transit stations, or forced labor camps. One of the most memorable passages in **The Gulag Archipelago** is devoted to the atrocities of the prison camps on the Solovetsky Islands, which Solzhenitsyn characterizes as the prototype of the entire archipelago, a cancer that metastasizes until it holds the entire nation in its power. During the first Five-Year Plan, it manifests itself in the building of the White Sea Canal and other construction projects with their ghastly tolls in human life. At the height of Stalin's terror the cancer becomes a vast network of labor camps (usually in the most inhospitable areas of the country), teeming with millions of prisoners tormented by NKVD demons. The atmosphere they breathe is polluted by falsehood and a never-ending stream of party propaganda, which Solzhenitsyn treats as one of the most onerous punishments imposed upon the condemned. They suffer too from subhuman living conditions: long hours of drudgery often in sub-zero temperatures; crowded barracks; inadequate clothing; malnutrition and disease. In addition to all these afflictions they must endure the company of venal informers and the depredations of rapacious thieves, who are given virtually free rein to do what they please to whomever they choose.

Yet Solzhenitsyn's inferno is much more than a place where suffering is caused by external forces which the *zeks* are powerless to resist. It is, to a certain extent, the creation of its own inhabitants. Through their hatred, mercilessness, and boundless selfishness they have poisoned their existence far more effectively than their demonic overseers. "The *zeks*," Solzhenitsyn remarks, "are not only an atheistic people, but nothing at all is sacred to them and they always ridicule or degrade everything exalted." The rules they live by are based on the deepest cynicism and the coldest calculation: mind your own business; leave me alone; trust no one; ask for nothing. If, as Dostoevsky claims in *The Brothers Karamazov,* hell is the inability to love, Solzhenitsyn has captured the essence of the experience. Moreover, he himself has known the horrors of arrest, investigation, prison, and camp; he too has felt the hatred and the gnawing desperation of the archipelago. So great are his tribulations in the inferno, that at the end of Part III, Chapter 6, he writes: "Lord, Lord. Under artillery shells and bombs I asked you to preserve my life. Now I ask you: send me death."

If, in Dante, hell, purgatory, and paradise are depicted as well defined *places,* in Solzhenitsyn they appear as states of mind or stages in the *zek*'s spiritual development. The

Solzhenitsyn wearing his Patriotic War medal after participating in the Soviet recapture of Orel in August 1943.

most decisive of these stages is the second. In purgatory sinners are cleansed of their offenses and prepared for the ultimate joy of heaven. The principal difference is that in Solzhenitsyn's version the emphasis is somewhat less on expiation and considerably more on intellectual growth and spiritual transformation.

On a purely intellectual level, Solzhenitsyn observes, the sensitive *zek,* as a result of accumulated experience, learns to perceive the world with an unprecedented clarity. This is especially true, he claims, at the transit stations, where prisoners gradually come to an understanding of what is happening to them, "to the people, and even to the world." One young man, experiencing the transforming power of his purgatory, writes to his girlfriend: "Here you listen to an inner voice, which, in a life of abundance and vanity, is drowned out by the roar outside." That same heightened consciousness enables a group of intellectuals, during their last hours on earth, to conduct seminars at which each shares with his fellow victims the knowledge he has acquired over a lifetime and which is destined soon to be lost forever.

Far more important than the intellect, however, is the spirit—specifically, the spirit considered in its purely religious dimensions. The intellectuals are noble in their unflagging devotion to knowledge and culture, but religious people are shown to possess a gift that transcends nobility and leads to the loftier spheres of paradise itself. There are many episodes scattered throughout *The Gulag Archipelago* in which Solzhenitsyn records his admiration for the numerous men and women whose Christian faith made them seem oblivious to the torments of the inferno. By contrast, the people who suffer most cruelly are those who lack a "stable nucleus," who "have not been enriched by any morality or any spiritual upbringing." Prisoners who are endowed with such a "spiritual nucleus" rise to an exalted state of being and present at the same time an impressive testimony to those still languishing in hell. Thus, Solzhenitsyn waxes eloquent as he describes the women in the camps who refused to wear number tags because they considered them to be the seal of Satan. Of the Lithuanian men and women who exchanged wedding vows over a wall which permanently separated them, Solzhenitsyn writes: "In this union with an unknown prisoner over a wall—and for Catholics the union was sacred and irreversible—I hear a choir of angels. It is like the disinterested contemplation of heavenly bodies. It is too lofty for an age of calculation and jumping jazz." Equally impressive to him is the story of a young girl named Zoia Leshcheva. At the age of ten, Zoia finds herself, in effect, an orphan; her parents, grandparents, and brothers have all been arrested and sent to camps throughout the USSR because of their religious faith. She is sent to an orphanage, where she adamantly refuses, despite the most persistent harassment, to remove the cross she always wears around her neck. She makes it clear that her cross as well as her convictions will be part of her until the moment of death.

Solzhenitsyn's own journey through purgatory begins rather modestly in Part II with a man named Boris Gammerov. The first step is taken during a conversation with him in which Solzhenitsyn dismisses as "bigotry" a prayer said by President Franklin Roosevelt and reprinted in many Soviet newspapers. Gammerov responds sharply to the remark: "Why don't you admit that a statesman can sincerely believe in God?" Astonished by such a reaction from a man born after the Revolution, Solzhenitsyn asks, "Do you believe in God?" Gammerov answers simply, "Of course." Solzhenitsyn is surprised not just by his reply and the confident tone in which it is made but by the sudden realization that his own opinions have been grafted on his mind by external pressures and that on the crucial questions of life and death he has no ideas that are truly his own.

In this state of intellectual insecurity and aroused curiosity he meets Anatolii Vasil'evish Silin, an erstwhile atheist who having experienced a conversion to Christianity while a prisoner in a German camp, is now a philosopher, theologian, and poet. Solzhenitsyn quotes a number of his verses, but one quatrain in particular goes to the heart of the question which troubles him most deeply at the earliest stages of his quest: the problem of evil, and especially the evil of the archipelago:

> Dukh Sovershenstva ottogo
> Nesovershenstvo dopuskaet—
> Stradan'e dush, chto bez nego
> Blazhenstva cenu ne poznaiut.

> The Spirit of Perfection
> Permits imperfection—
> The suffering of souls—because without it
> The value of bliss would not be known.

The dilemma of theodicy is even more effectively confronted by Boris Nikolaevich Kornfel'd, a Jewish convert to Christianity. Because it is not enough for Solzhenitsyn to know that his sufferings will enhance his appreciation of happiness, as Silin's quatrain implies, and because at this stage he is more interested in ultimate causes than in possible consequences, a remark made by Kornfel'd on the subject of evil makes a lasting impression on him: "You know, in general I've become convinced that no punishment in this earthly life comes to us undeserved. Apparently, it can come for something of which we are not truly guilty. But if we go over our lives and think them through carefully, we will always find a crime of ours for which the blow has now fallen upon us." Looking over his own life, Solzhenitsyn finds ample confirmation of Kornfel'd's contention. To deal with the difficulty of evil and guilt, he turns, as his friend has done, to religion. He begins to understand that the truth of religion is predicated upon its ability to combat evil in man. Revolutions, on the other hand, especially the Bolshevik Revolution, strive to eradicate "contemporary *carriers* of evil (and also in their haste the carriers of good)." Only religion (and for Solzhenitsyn that is the Christian religion) can effectively contend with the evil of the world and with the present evil of the Gulag archipelago. It is the path to the city of God, which is truth and salvation. Purely human contrivances designed to uproot the *expressions* of evil lead to the city of man, a realm of falsehood and destruction. In Part VI Solzhenitsyn tersely states his position: "The very deepest root of our life is the religious consciousness, and not party and ideological consciousness."

Solzhenitsyn's journey through purgatory has come to an end. He has observed and admired the strength of character typical of fervent believers: Orthodox priests and laymen, sectarians, Lithuanian Catholics, men, women, and children who lived only by faith and rejected Soviet rule as anathema. His conventional atheism has been softened by their courage and integrity and shaken by the quiet religious conviction of Boris Gammerov. Silin, the Christian poet, has introduced him to the Christian approach to the problem of external evil. Boris Kornfel'd has helped him to view that same evil as punishment, to connect punishment with guilt, and to associate guilt with that inner evil which runs through the heart of every man. Solzhenitsyn now realizes that parties and ideologies attempt to deal only with the outer manifestations of evil. Religion alone, he believes, is the antidote to man's misery and the key to his lasting and genuine happiness. He has come full circle. He no longer merely admires believers at a distance. He has become one of them.

As a result of his many observations and impressions Solzhenitsyn now finds himself far from the pangs of hell and the crucible of purgatory. He now lives in the empyrean, in a paradise founded on wisdom and bestowing an unearthly bliss. In Part IV he speaks of the spiritually salubrious effect of prison, and what he says on this subject can also be applied to his experience in the camps:

> That prison profoundly transforms a man has been well known for centuries. . . . In our country Dostoevsky is always mentioned. But what about Pisarev? What was left of his revolutionary spirit after the Peter-and-Paul Fortress? One can argue whether this is good for revolution, but these changes always tend to deepen the soul.

This "deepening of the soul" which is requisite for entrance into paradise proceeds in two directions. First, the man who has achieved wisdom understands, perhaps for the first time in his life, that earthly attachments are vain and ephemeral and that, as Solzhenitsyn succinctly puts it, "only he will win out who renounces everything." This means that the prisoner must divest himself of all possessions and obliterate from his heart whatever value he may ever have attached to them. Solzhenitsyn sees such material impoverishment as a common theme in the teachings of history's wisest men: " 'Have nothing.' This was taught to us by Buddha, Christ, the Stoics, and the Cynics. Why can't we greedy people get this simple lesson into our heads? Why can't we understand that we destroy our souls with property?" But there is still more to Solzhenitsyn's notion of renunciation. In addition to possessions one must give up one's family and friends. Any hope of seeing them again must be abandoned. The benefit which derives from such an unconditional abnegation and which constitutes at the same time a vital precondition of paradise itself is freedom. In Part IV he writes: "You cannot be deprived of family and property: you are already deprived of them. What does not exist even God will not take. That is basic freedom."

But freedom brings us only to the threshold of paradise. The very highest state of being, Solzhenitsyn's version of the Dantean contemplation of the Beatific Vision, is achieved by those who, in effect, shed their mortal crust and become pure spirits. As Tolstoy would say, they have learned to "live for the soul." Solzhenitsyn dramatically illustrates this transformation by contrasting those who have experienced it with those who are immune to its joys because they live "out in freedom." The scene is a railroad station. A prisoner about to be transferred eavesdrops on the conversations of the unarrested. One of them talks about problems with in-laws; another tells of a man who beats his wife; some complain about their neighbors while others discuss a new job in a new town. The prisoner is horrified by the vacuousness of all such chatter because only he has "the genuine measure of things in the universe." Solzhenitsyn pursues his theme in a remarkable rhetorical aside:

> Only you who are without flesh are truly, genuinely alive while all these people only mistakenly consider themselves to be living. And the abyss between you is unbridgeable. You cannot shout to them; you cannot cry over them; you cannot shake them by their shoulders. After all, you are spirit, you are a ghost, and they are material bodies.

In summary, the inhabitant of Solzhenitsyn's paradise has renounced family, friends, possessions, and all emotional attachments to them. Indeed, he has stripped himself of his very physical being and become, as Solzhenitsyn puts it, an "Interstellar Wanderer," whose body is fettered and abused but whose soul is subject to the whims of no one. He is now the possessor of the highest consciousness, the deepest wisdom, and the greatest happiness.

In a book so singlemindedly devoted to the subversion of the Soviet system it is paradoxical that the Gulag archipelago should emerge as a potential paradise as well as a veritable hell. Even more surprising is the fact that this vast realm of darkness proves to be more spiritually fruitful than the "free" expanses of the Soviet Union or Western Europe and the United States. In short, the profoundest evil somehow manages to become the highest good. Solzhenitsyn does not seem to notice his paradox. If he does, he does not dwell on its implications for the multitudinous, age-old theological disputations on the nature and causes of evil. He merely observes that in most cases the released prisoner who has first attained the most sublime level of consciousness has a better understanding of life than his fellow citizens, that he has a "new standard of things," and that he feels no despair or depression because he has been "spiritually born" in the camps and prisons. So great, in fact, is the difference between captivity and freedom that emotional adjustment is difficult and in some cases even impossible. One man, we are told, hanged himself on the very day he was to be released—apparently because he could not face an illusory life in freedom. Solzhenitsyn himself longs to cry out after only a few hours among the free: "I want to go home. I want to go to my archipelago." And in Part IV he utters the incredible words: "*Bless you, prison,* for being in my life." The Gulag archipelago remains, of course, an inferno for the vast majority of those who languish and toil there. But Solzhenitsyn clearly believes, in spite of its monstrosities, that for those who have risen from hell and wandered through purgatory it can become the occasion of the final and absolute spiritual triumph. (pp. 35-42)

David Matual, "The Gulag Archipelago: From Inferno to Paradise," in Studies in Twentieth Century Literature, *Vol. 7, No. 1, Fall, 1982, pp. 35-43.*

Thomas J. Napierkowski   (essay date Spring 1983)

[*In the following essay, Napierkowski asserts that negative critical responses to Solzhenitsyn's poem* Prussian Nights *"arise from a cultural bias and can be answered," maintaining that the poem must be placed within the context of Solzhenitsyn's imprisonment to be fully appreciated.*]

Critical responses to Aleksandr Solzhenitsyn's **Prussian Nights** have been predictable: for the most part, the poem has been denigrated and neglected. Carl Proffer, for example, writing in the *New York Times Book Review* [7 August 1977], has characterized the work as "a clumsy and disjointed 1400-line narrative which can be called poetry only because it is written in meter and rhyme. Sent to any publishing house or emigre Russian journal bearing any name but Solzhenitsyn's, it would be rejected unhesitatingly." In a similar vein, Suzanne Juhasz has suggested [in *Library Journal,* June 1977] that the "poem was probably more important for its author as an imaginative alternative to his prison environment than it is going to be for the general reader." And William J. Parente [in *Best Sellers,* August 1977] has implied that Solzhenitsyn is "too concerned with catechisis. . . ." Not all critics have been so severe with the poem; but the generally prevailing opinion [as stated by Patricia Blake in *Time,* 25 July 1977] seems to be that "**Prussian Nights** represents the young Solzhenitsyn, still a decade away from the fine tuned virtuosity of **One Day in the Life of Ivan Denisovich,** and remoter still from the prodigious sweep of **The Gulag Archipelago.**"

As students of fiction, most readers of Solzhenitsyn simply accept these charges. What they fail to realize is that these criticisms arise from a cultural bias and can be answered. Only in a broader and more appropriate context can **Prussian Nights** be fairly judged.

Most critics of **Prussian Nights** approach the poem with a limited and inadequate theory of poetry. Underlying most of their censure is the Romantic equation of poetry with the lyric: "the distillation of experience," "the precious record of moments of heightened perception." Implicit in this equation is the assumption that since moments of heightened perception are rare and brief, a slim volume of short pieces is the best assurance that a poet has experienced them. This attitude, much more common in the West than in the East, contrasts markedly with the pre-Romantic view that poetry differs only in form and style, not in kind, from other forms of discourse. Such a definition itself may not be totally satisfactory, but there can be no question that it is more traditional than the Romantic interpretation of poetry. In any case, poetry must be defined much more comprehensively than it is typically understood in the West if **Prussian Nights** is to be properly appreciated. Minimally we must acknowledge that the lyric, the prevailing poetic genre of the last two hundred years, is only one form of poem. Along these lines, it must also be stressed that in other milieux poetry, including the lyric, has been a public art; and, as such, its existence is conditioned by outer needs and pressures, not by inner ones.

Because of the West's preoccupation with the lyric, most critics admire poetry for its "economy of expression," "compression," "compactness," and "intensity." Syntax itself is often seen as something of a handicap. Different forms of poetry, on the other hand, characteristically produce their effects over longer stretches, the stanza or the verse paragraph. It is useful to note that the poetry of such greats as Chaucer and Dante is designed to operate over longer passages, not in single lines and phrases. Associated with this tendency are a relaxed kind of syntax and a wide use of free-running paratactic constructions. We must realize that intensity is one standard for poetry, but it is not the only one.

With particular regard to **Prussian Nights,** a corollary point is necessary. The unique demands and standards of orally composed poetry must be understood if Solzhenitsyn's poem is to be correctly judged. The identification of poetry with the lyric and the emphasis on intensity have resulted in hostility toward traditional metrical forms. Juhasz, for example, has complained that "the regularity of rhythm, coupled with a language that is for the most part literal, prosaic, and unconvincingly colloquial, make this [**Prussian Nights**], as poetry, rather unexceptional." **Prussian Nights** was composed in a concentration camp, where paper was scarce and punishment swift for prisoners caught writing. The ballad meter and rhyme pattern of the poem, useful as aids to memory, were dictated by the circumstances of composition. One might just as logically fault the regular stress patterns and alliteration of *Beowulf* as discredit **Prussian Nights** for its form.

Equally important is the fact that **Prussian Nights** is intended for oral delivery. Indeed, in 1969 Solzhenitsyn secretly made a recording of the poem which is now available in the West and which aids tremendously in assessing the success of the piece. The author delivers the poem in declamatory fashion, giving every line its special effect. In fact, Solzhenitsyn's recitation of **Prussian Nights**—which includes snatches of song, whispers, conversational asides, and other special effects—brings out dimensions which would normally be overlooked by audiences accustomed to the silent reading of poetry and makes apparent the dramatic nature of the poem. Thus, familiarity with the special nature and features of verse composed for oral delivery is essential. Amplification, repetition, diffuseness of sense, looseness of syntax, and regularity of meter are not only acceptable but desirable to a listening audience which has no opportunity to linger over close-packed lines. (How many literature professors have bluffed their way through poetry readings, pretending that they were enjoying themselves and understanding poems composed for written reception while surreptitiously glancing at their watches and fighting off yawns?) Listening audiences appreciate and demand precisely those qualities which lead modern "readers" to regard certain works as diffuse and verbose.

Finally, charges of dullness implicit in complaints about "interminable descriptions" and of "catechesis" require attention. While it may be true that there is no arguing about taste, it must be admitted that dullness is a subjective judgment. Homeric catalogs do not interest most modern readers, but they obviously fascinated the poet's original audience and served important functions within the poem. A reader's personal disinterest in a particular topic or section does not relieve him of the responsibility to investigate the purpose of that aspect of a composition. Only after a demonstration of irrelevance or detriment can the author be faulted. The usual meaning behind a charge of dullness, however, is a distaste for didacticism. This is especially true in the case of Solzhenitsyn whose lack of moral ambiguity has done more to tarnish his literary reputation than serious study or popular reaction. The simple fact is that serious literature has always functioned to endorse or attack values and ideas and that disagreement with a work's moral stance is not sufficient to dismiss that work as serious literature.

From this broader perspective a more accurate and fair evaluation of *Prussian Nights* is possible; and the simplest considerations with which to begin are technical. Although the poem is conventional in form and "metrically regular," it is neither monotonous nor singsong. Typically Solzhenitsyn maintains a ballad meter of trochaic tetrameters with alternating masculine and feminine rhymes, but he carefully includes numerous variations in meter and tempo for dramatic effect. In addition to correctness and variety, however, Solzhenitsyn has established an organic relationship, in the best poetic tradition, between the form and subject matter of his poem. The ballad meter and rhyme pattern contribute significantly to the poem's special handling of topics of soldiers and war, of looting, drinking, burning, murder, and rape.

Regarding other considerations, one must constantly bear in mind that *Prussian Nights* is fundamentally a narrative poem and must be judged as such. The work, of course, describes "the rampageous march of the Red Army across East Prussia to Berlin in the last months of the war" and chronicles the behavior of Russian soldiers which, after years of hardship and defeat, has been characterized as "excessive" even by Soviet military historians. The story, however, is more than a narrative of events in their time-sequence; the action has been shaped into a plot, an arrangement of incidents which emphasizes causality. Thus, the story is handled with considerable skill; but it is characterization which is Solzhenitsyn's greatest achievement in *Prussian Nights,* for the causality of the plot leads inexorably to a focus on character.

With rapid and brilliant strokes Solzhenitsyn creates a varitable portrait gallery of minor figures who make vividly concrete and personal the experiences which he is communicating. One woman refugee, for example, stands apart. "Blond and magnificent," she approaches the Russian soldiers as "proud and erect as ever." During the inspection of her possessions, however, looking "a little /

Askance at the Untermenschen there," she becomes "string-taut" and "flushed." Finally,

> Stooped to collect
> Her things, she turned
> —To understand!
> She screamed, down in the snow she fell,
> She froze up, curled in a ball,
> Like a little animal,
> Lying motionless and pale . . .

There is also a German baker who greets the Red Army with bread and salt, declaring, "Ich bin Dommunist, Genossen / Twelve years now I've waited for you." The man is stunned when he is detained for interrogation.

At their best, these portraits reveal a deft handling of irony and pathos. When Allenstein falls unexpectedly to the Russians, the German dispatcher at the railway station, under the surveillance of a General Service major, continues to send out the message, "Strecke frei," which brings trainloads of fleeing refugees into Russian hands. The relationship between the men is developed dramatically:

> the dispatcher, ever wearying,
> At the table slumped and wilting,
> Writes trains and routes into his ledger,
> Accepting carriages and trucks
> In sequences of ringing, blinking
> Lamp and signal and bell,
> Just as usual,
> Quite mechanical,
>
> Reliably, meticulously,
> Sending his fellow countrymen
> To a new life—hell or heaven,
> With the flat phrase "Stricke frei."

The major, on the other hand, at first "bitter" and "ominous," warms under the influence of drink. He reveals that he is a lecturer in literature at the Moscow IFLI Institute and that his special interest is "The Great Age—The Enlightenment! / The age of Bentham! Of Voltaire! / . . . the great eighteenth century / Proud only of Humanity." Indeed, the major turns "sensitive, subtle, kind":

> He speaks even of Germany
> With understanding, with sympathy.
> But on his broad, well-flung-back shoulder,
> The high proud epaulette remains,
> And—in a trance there the dispatcher
> Still goes on accepting trains.

Prussian Nights is, however, "more than a tale of brutality and historical document." It is the story of a troubled man overwhelmed by what is happening around and in him; and the portrait of the narrator is the triumph of the poem.

As the work begins, the narrator is caught up in the frenzy and jubilation of imminent victory but unable to quell a vague uneasiness: "But what starts / Up in us? Some strangeness hurts." With others he shares a sense of deprivation and of envy at German affluence which his colleagues in arms use to rationalize their looting, burning, and violence: "We won't let others lay their hands on / What we won with our own blood." "We could do with things like theirs. . . ." Although he has not taken part in the atrocities of the campaign, the narrator is haunted

> The contents of *Prussian Nights* are marked by passion, imagination, and an anguished concern for truth. Nothing less than the problem of evil and the question of individual conscience versus national morality challenge the reader. In this respect, the glimpse, which the poem provides, into the soul of the narrator makes the work a moving criticism of life.
>
> —*Thomas J. Napierkowski*

by a Sarasate theme which symbolically represents the temptation to join in the wanton destruction and sensuality of war. His desperate response to this temptation recurs regularly in the poem and acts as a refrain to the narrative: "And oh, what heart / Could well oppose?" Furthermore, the response is deliberately ambiguous. It refers to the narrator's resistance to the temptation and his attitude toward the behavior of others which he does not actively oppose. Indeed, the ambivalence of the narrator is reflected in his denial of any motives of revenge:

> Well, land industrious and proud,
> Blaze and smoke and flame away.
> Amid the violence of the crowd,
> In my heart no vengeance calls
> I'll not fire one stick of kindling,
> Yet I'll not quench your flaming halls.
> Untouched I'll leave you. I'll be off
> Like Pilate when he washed his hands.
> Between us, there is Samsonov,
> Between us many a cross there stands
> Of whitened Russian bones. For strange
> Feelings rule my soul tonight.

Despite his qualms, shame at earlier Russian defeats (Solzhenitsyn's father was killed in East Prussia in 1918) and the slogans of the Soviet High Command ("*Do not forget! Do not forgive! / Blood for blood!*") take their effect; and the narrator surrenders to the occasion:

> Russia advances a great power.
> Hail to the advance's thunder!
> Some schnapps would do me good, I feel.
> But what would cheer me even more—
> Is to go looking for some plunder.

But the narrator is no common looter; his booty is the stationery of a post office. As the supplies are carried to the truck, his conscience is pricked: "Should I really blush for shame." What follows is a dialectic of conscience in which the speaker argues that earlier deprivation and hardship which have hindered his creativity as a writer justify his actions, but acknowledges that "dressed up as an officer / In me a greedy pauper raves." Rationalization triumphs; and directing the removal of the supplies, the narrator dismisses objections:

> "That's to go . . . that too . . . that too!"
> Who should I blush in front of? Who?
> Anyone who points the finger

—Go live in the U.S.S.R.!

Other matters, however, are not so easily put aside. The narrator witnesses a gang of soldiers rape a girl whose only defense is the pathetic and unheeded plea "I'm not German! "I'm not German! / NO! I'm—Polish! I'm a Pole. . . . " His only response is the unconvincing refusal to become involved: "And, oh, what heart / Could well oppose?" Later a German infant is killed; the murderer's rationale is simple: " . . . he's a German! / He'll grow and put a helmet on. / Deal with him now. . . . / The order from Supreme Command / Is *Blood for Blood!* Give no quarter. . . . " This disorients the narrator who searches for excuses:

> We roll on and on over Europe
> As in a strange kaleidoscope.
> From lack of sleep and drunkenness
> We've turned daring, we've grown wings.
> Everything's mixed up, everything's
> Double—crossroads, signposts, faces,
> Explosions, meetings, wounds, and mines,
> Evil and good, fears and delights. . . .

Explanations and excuses notwithstanding, the complicity of the narrator in the crimes of his soldiers is illustrated by his conduct during the murder of the blond refugee. When the men inspecting the blond woman's possessions find the photograph of a Nazi soldier, the narrator finds nothing incriminating and, with a wave of his hand, rejects their concern: "What about it? Give it back to her." Still, when two of his men prepare to shoot the woman, he does not interfere until it is too late:

> She froze up, curled in a ball,
> Like a little animal,
> Lying motionless and pale . . .
> the firearms had not yet cracked.
> An instant passed. Another instant.
> I! Why had I waved my hand?
> My God!
> "Driver! Stop!
> Hey there, lads! . . . "
> The automatics.
> A burst of fire. Back to their trucks.
> . . . . .
> Get moving! Why did you pull up?

In his shame the narrator admits that this is not the first time he has allowed an innocent civilian to be killed, but he still refuses to acknowledge guilt:

> Once he took an old German to a wood
> And shot him there in cold blood.
> One word would have prevented that! . . .
> I was nearby . . . but in the heat
> Of battles, in the thick of hell,
> Who knows who's guilty? Who can tell?
> But from what distance can one judge? Is
> It easier after centuries?

Despite his feeble rationalization that "everyone behaves like that," the narrator continues to be tormented by the "worm of self-analysis"; and, once again, his only response is the familiar refrain: "And, oh, what heart / Could well oppose?"

The last section of **Prussian Nights** reports the narrator's rape (seduction is certainly not the proper word) of a German woman; and here, as elsewhere, his character is dramatically presented. Suddenly seized with the desire for a woman, the narrator nonchalantly inquires of his sergeant major whether there are women among the families allowed to remain within the estate walls. The sergeant replies that there are and, sensing his superior's hesitance, gladly arranges an opportunity "to check up on their looks" and to deliver the narrator's choice. In what follows the narrator is troubled by his surrender to this sudden appetite and his reliance on the sergeant major's services; but he consoles himself that "no one will know, we two alone. / No one else will ever know." The lack of passion and pleasure in the sexual encounter, however, forces a recognition by the narrator that his behavior in this matter has been "base"; and he is shattered by the plea of his victim: "Doch erschiessen Sic mich nicht" [Just don't shoot me!]. The poem ends with the narrator's response which suggests a new level of awareness: "Have no fear . . . For—oh!—already / Another's soul is on my soul. . . ."

Characterization is an acknowledged strength of the writings of Aleksandr Solzhenitsyn; but few of his characters surpass the narrator of *Prussian Nights.* This young military officer is a complex figure who has about him "the incalculability of life." Ranging in voice from the shout of the victor to the cry of the tormented, the narrator approaches, but does not accept within the text of the poem, the conclusion that personal morality transcends both nationality and ideology. This, however, like much else about the character, must be deduced by the reader; for Solzhenitsyn employs a dramatic method of characterization. Indeed, *Prussian Nights* is dramatic poetry at its best, making brilliant use of dialogue, monologue, individualized diction, tense situations, and emotional conflicts. If there is any problem at all with the narrator, it is that he, like the poet whose experiences are reflected in the poem, is somewhat larger than life and intimidates most readers who more successfully evade the "worm of self-analysis." But this is no artistic flaw; for Solzhenitsyn establishes a causality between the character and his actions. Furthermore, it should be noted that the circumstances of the narrator add a powerful lyric dimension to the poem; the anguished cry of self-incrimination is far too moving to allow any doubt about its validity.

The contents of *Prussian Nights* are marked by passion, imagination, and an anguished concern for truth. Nothing less than the problem of evil and the question of individual conscience versus national morality challenge the reader. In this respect, the glimpse, which the poem provides, into the soul of the narrator makes the work a moving criticism of life. The form of *Prussian Nights* is characterized by variety in uniformity, concreteness, and special use of language. As Alexander Schmemann has argued [in his "On Solzhenitsyn" in *Aleksandr Solzhenitsyn: Critical Essays and Documentary Materials,* ed. John B. Dunlop, et al.], "If the language of Solzhenitsyn is 'worse' than that of Bunin or Nabokov, it is because such is the living language of Russia. . . . Solzhenitsyn [has] *transformed* the Soviet language into his own, into the language of his art and his creative truth. This is linguistic [and poetic]

achievement. . . ." Finally, the effect of *Prussian Nights* is beauty—so long as one realizes, as Solzhenitsyn does, that beauty is inextricably one with truth and goodness. In short, *Prussian Nights* demonstrates to all but the most callous and effete that the genius of Aleksandr Solzhenitsyn crosses many genres. (pp. 59-69)

Thomas J. Napierkowski, " 'Prussian Nights' and American Critics," in Concerning Poetry, *Vol. 16, No. 1, Spring, 1983, pp. 59-69.*

Jeffrey Meyers   (essay date Spring 1983)

[*In the following essay, Meyers praises* Cancer Ward *as "the most complete and accurate fictional account of the nature of disease and its relation to love."*]

Modern European literature often concerns the abnormal and the pathological. Characterized by a macabre sensibility, an attraction to decay and nothingness, an obsession with physical corruption and death, it is defined by a mood of dissolution and disintegration, of paralyzing anxiety and metaphysical despair. Modern writers have inherited from the Romantic period the idea that the artist is ill, and that his illness gives him psychic knowledge and spiritual power. Thomas Mann—following Goethe's maxim: "The Classical I call the healthy, the Romantic the sick"—equates the latter with pathology [in "Dostoyevsky—in Moderation" in *The Short Novels of Dostoyevsky*]. He believes "Romanticism bears in its heart the germ of morbidity, as the rose bears the worm; its innermost character is seduction, seduction to death." In *Notes from Underground,* Dostoyevsky insists that "too great lucidity is a disease, a true, full-fledged disease" because this heightened consciousness forces one to see terrible truths about human existence. Rimbaud calls for a reasoned derangement of all the senses that would enable the tormented, sacrificial, even insane artist to become "the great invalid, the great criminal, the great accursed" and to plunge into unknown, "unheard of, unnameable" visions. And Nietzsche [in his *Ecce homo*] associates exuberance of the spirit with extreme pain and psychological malaise, and believes that artistic greatness is earned by physical suffering: "One pays dearly for immortality: one has to die several times while still alive."

In his great essay on "Goethe and Tolstoy" [in *Three Essays*] and his more cautious "Dostoyevsky—in Moderation," Mann places himself firmly in the Romantic tradition by a Nietzschean exaltation of the aesthetic aspects of "genius-bestowing disease." In the first essay he paradoxically claims that disease gives dignity to man because it brings out his spiritual qualities:

> Disease has two faces and a double relation to man and his human dignity. On the one hand it is hostile: by overstressing the physical, by throwing man back upon his body, it has a dehumanizing effect. On the other hand, it is possible to think and feel about illness as a highly dignified human phenomenon. . . . In disease, resides the dignity of man; and the genius of disease is more human than the genius of health.

In the second essay Mann quotes Nietzsche's dictum:

"Exceptional conditions make the artist . . . conditions that are profoundly related and interlaced with morbid phenomena; it seems impossible to be an artist and not be sick." He then connects Dostoyevsky's and Nietzsche's psychological insight and artistic genius with their diseases: epilepsy and syphilis. And he concludes with the Rimbaudian paradox that the health of humanity can be achieved only by the sacrificial sickness of its artists:

> Certain attainments of the soul and intellect are impossible without disease, without insanity, without spiritual crime, and the great invalids are crucified victims, sacrificed to humanity and its advancement, to the broadening of its feeling and knowledge—in short, to its more sublime health.

In Mann's own works, as Erich Kahler observes [in his *The Orbit of Thomas Mann*], the artist is portrayed as an outcast who renounces life in order to create art:

> culture and intellect are represented as decadence, love associated with decline; the artist is seen as a pariah from the start, iridescent with suspect hues, shading into the daemon, the invalid, the adventurer, the criminal; already he is stranded in the ironic situation of expressing a life he himself is unable to live.

And in Edmund Wilson's symbolic myth of "the wound and the bow" [in his book of the same title], the essential sickness of the artist is represented by the archer Philoctetes, who is degraded by a malodorous disease that renders him abhorrent to society, but "is also the master of a superhuman art which everybody has to respect and which the normal man finds he needs."

In her essay "On Being Ill" (1930) [in her *Collected Essays*], Virginia Woolf notes the importance of disease as a means of moral exploration and wonders why literature has not seriously concerned itself with this crucial area of human experience: "Considering how common illness is, how tremendous the spiritual change that it brings, how astonishing, when the lights of health go down, the undiscovered countries that are then disclosed . . . it becomes strange indeed that illness has not taken its place with love and battle and jealousy among the prime themes of literature." But in the last century writers (including a number of doctors: Anton Chekhov, William Carlos Williams, Gottfried Benn, Louis-Ferdinand Céline, Walker Percy) have increasingly turned to the kind of clinical literature which their predecessors tended to avoid. In the very greatest works—Tolstoy's *The Death of Ivan Ilych* (cancer), Gide's *The Immoralist* (tuberculosis), Mann's *Death in Venice* (cholera), *The Magic Mountain* (tuberculosis), *Doctor Faustus* (syphilis), *The Black Swan* (cancer), Camus's *The Plague* (bubonic plague), A. E. Ellis' *The Rack* (tuberculosis), and Solzhenitsyn's *Cancer Ward*—disease is both the literal subject of the novel and the symbol of moral, social, or political pathology.

Writers like Kafka, Lawrence, Mansfield, and Orwell, who died of tuberculosis, rarely wrote fiction about their own disease (though there are hints of it in the heroes of *Lady Chatterley's Lover* and *1984*) and confined their descriptions to personal letters. Solzhenitsyn—who suffered from cancer, endured the dreadful stages of dying, pondered the nature of life and death—writes directly about his own illness. But he was only able to transmute his illness into art *after* he was cured and had the strength to perceive his disease more objectively. In his novel cancer is horrible, suffering extreme, cure impossible.

Unlike Mann, who observed illness intellectually, Solzhenitsyn earned his insight through actual experience. He writes in the tradition of Russian realism, of Tolstoy and Chekhov, and resolutely renounces the Romantic attitude toward disease. He does not believe the artist is sick or that disease inspires creative genius, aesthetic insight, spiritual knowledge, or human dignity. And he certainly does not believe that the artist must stand outside society.

Cancer Ward (1968) rejects the spiritual self-destruction of *Notes from Underground,* in which the masochistic hero proclaims:

> "I'm a sick man . . . a mean man. There's nothing attractive about me. I think there is something wrong with my liver. . . . I'm fully aware that I can't spite the doctors by refusing their help. I know very well that I'm harming myself and no one else. But still, it's out of spite that I refuse to ask for the doctor's help. So my liver hurts? Good, let it hurt even more!"

It also rejects the physical disgust for the human body portrayed in Gottfried Benn's horrifying "Man and Woman Go Through the Cancer Ward" [in his *Primal Vision*]:

> The man:
> Here in this row are wombs that have decayed,
> and in this row are breasts that have decayed.
> Bed beside stinking bed. Hourly the sisters change.
>
> Come, quietly lift up this coverlet,
> Look, this great mass of fat and ugly humours
> was precious to a man once, and
> meant ecstasy and home.
>
> Come, now look at the scars upon this breast.
> Do you feel the rosary of small soft knots?
> Feel it, no fear. The flesh yields and is numb.
>
> Here's one who bleeds as though from thirty bodies.
> No one has so much blood.
> They had to cut
> a child from this one, from her cancerous womb.

The literary precursor of *Cancer Ward* is Chekhov's "Ward 6." In that bitter but compassionate story, the sane doctor is locked up in a mental ward by lunatics who symbolize the hopelessness and corruption of Russia. Solzhenitsyn follows Chekhov in his courageous confrontation of disease, his profound sympathy, his transformation of the clinical into the poetical, his concern with the moral aspects of illness, and his use of sickness to symbolize social pathology.

The facts established in David Burg and George Feifer's biography, *Solzhenitsyn* (1972), match (and are partly based on) Oleg Kostoglotov's autobiographical revelations in Chapter 6 of *Cancer Ward*. Solzhenitsyn was arrested by the KGB for criticizing Stalin in personal letters to a close friend, while fighting as an artillery officer in German territory in February 1945. He was sentenced to eight years of forced labor in a Siberian concentration camp, described in *One Day in the Life of Ivan Denisovich.* In Ekibastuz prison (southeast of Omsk) in February 1952, he was stricken by a fast-swelling intestinal cancer and was prepared for a prompt operation. But before it could be performed, the surgeon-prisoner was suddenly transferred to another camp.

The tumor was excised by a second surgeon, and a section of tissue—without his name or camp on it—was sent north to Omsk for laboratory analysis. The incision soon healed; and though still in pain, he returned to work carrying heavy boxes of liquid concrete. The medical report, which diagnosed the tumor as rapidly developing and acutely malignant cancer that needed immediate treatment, was eventually sent back to the camp. But the negligent officials did not bother to track down the anonymous prisoner-patient, and the diagnosis was not revealed to him. The operation retarded the tumor, the pain subsided, and he felt he had made an astonishing recovery.

Solzhenitsyn, forbidden to return to European Russia after his release from the prison camp, was sent to "perpetual exile" in remote Kazakhstan. In Berlik, in the fall of 1953, he was again stricken by cancer and frequently fainted from overpowering pain. Unable at first to get permission from the local police to enter a hospital, he traveled illegally into the nearby mountains to seek help from an old man who practiced folk medicine, and was temporarily kept alive by a root containing aconite. When he finally arrived at the hospital in Tashkent, Uzbekistan, in January 1954, the doctors gave him three weeks to live. On the frontier of death, deprived of the ability to eat and sleep, and poisoned by the tumor's toxin, he said: "I was practically a corpse. I came there expecting to die."

Solzhenitsyn was treated with x-rays and hormones, the pain disappeared, sleep and appetite eventually returned. Three months later he emerged from the hospital with renewed emotional strength and spiritual confidence. He still had to take powerful medicines, but said that the tumor no longer interfered with his life. It had changed its nature and forfeited its malignancy. In March 1954 he confessed: "I didn't dare admit even to myself that I was recovering. Even in fleeting dreams I measured the span that had been added to my life not in years, but months." That spring was the most painful and most lovely season of his life.

Solzhenitsyn's obsessive, even fanatical commitment to record the truth of his experiences, which became a paradigm for life in Stalinist Russia, was intensified by his sense of lost life and renunciation of love: in the army, prison, exile, and hospital. In his autobiographical *The Oak and the Calf* (1980), he explains:

> I had gone on writing—as a bricklayer, in over-crowded prison huts, in transit jails without so much as a pencil, when I was dying of cancer, in an exile's hovel after a double teaching shift. I had let nothing—dangers, hindrances, the need for rest—interrupt my writing. . . . I had made my years of exile miserable—years of furious longing for a woman—because I was afraid for my books, afraid that some Komsomol girl would betray me. After four years of war and eight years of imprisonment, my first three years as a free man were years of misery, repression and frustration.

When threatened by cancer, after surviving the war and prison, he feared "all that I had memorized in the camps ran the risk of extinction together with the head that held it. This was a dreadful moment in my life: to die on the threshold of freedom, to see all I had written, all that gave meaning to my life thus far, about to perish with me." *Cancer Ward,* whose subject (writes Solzhenitsyn) "is specifically and literally cancer, a subject avoided in literature, but nevertheless a reality as its victims know only too well from daily experience," is his tribute to human dignity and man's power of survival.

Cancer Ward is the most complete and accurate fictional account of the nature of disease and its relation to love. It describes the characteristics of cancer; the physical, psychological, and moral effects on the victim; the conditions of the hospital; the relations of patients and doctors; the terrifying treatments; the possibility of death. While discussing the concentration camps, Kostoglotov raises the central questions of the novel, and connects the pathological and political themes: "How much can one pay for life, and how much is too much?" He decides that "the betrayal or destruction of good and helpless people is too high a price, that our lives aren't worth it."

In the novel cancer, which in 1955 could never be completely cured, is a frightening disease that causes prolonged suffering. Its rapid but hidden growth, unseen and unsuspected, develops an inexorable will and "acquires rights of its own." It is usually not discovered until it has reached an advanced and often fatal state.

The spiritual wounds of the embittered patient are devastating. He attempts to fight self-pity with courage, and is grateful for any small comfort or brief remission—however temporary and deceptive. The treatment is not explained to the patient, who must face mockery, humiliation, and pain. The hard lump of tumor drags in the victim "like a fish on a hook" and isolates him from his past life. It diminishes the will, eliminates defenses, dignity, influence, status, reputation, and hope. It turns him inward toward his own sickness, so that Kostoglotov "learned how to be ill, he was a specialist in being ill, he was devoted to his illness."

The torture and inhuman conditions of the hospital, an antechamber to the tomb, intensify the mental and physical suffering. The smelly toilets and squalid wards reduce everyone to the common denominator of illness. The doctors—"assassins in white coats"—continually lie to the patients, who see through their falsehoods and resent their assumed omnipotence. They employ reckless and even savage treatments that are bound to be discredited in the future, take control of the patient's body, decide about his life and death.

Since "any damage to the body was justified if it saved life," the radical treatment of cancer—by surgery, radia-

Cancer Ward is the most complete and accurate fictional account of the nature of disease and its relation to love. It describes the characteristics of cancer; the physical, psychological, and moral effects on the victim; the conditions of the hospital; the relations of patients and doctors; the terrifying treatments; the possibility of death.

—*Jeffrey Meyers*

tion, and chemotherapy—is often worse than the disease. Dr. Dontsova contracts cancer from prolonged exposure to radium. Solzhenitsyn's description of the barbarous bombardment of x-rays, which pierces through the layers and organs of the body, streams into the walls and floors of the hospital, penetrates the soil and rocks of the earth, is a masterpiece of physiological and psychological insight:

> Through the square of skin that had been left clear on his stomach, through the layers of flesh and organs whose names their owner himself did not know, through the mass of the toadlike tumor, through the stomach and entrails, through the blood that flowed along his arteries and veins, through lymph and cells, through the spine and lesser bones and again through more layers of flesh, vessels and skin on his back, then through the hard wooden board of the couch, through the four-centimeter-thick floorboards, through the props, through the filling beneath the boards, down, down, until they disappeared into the very stone foundations of the building or into the earth, poured the harsh X-rays, the trembling vectors of electric and magnetic fields, unimaginable to the human mind, or else more comprehensible quanta that like shells out of guns pounded and riddled everything in their path.

Like x-rays, cancer strips the patient down to the essential core: behind Asya's "dressing gown there was nothing but her nightdress, her breasts and her soul." Only the passive Tartar can accept the heavy burden of truth. Death, "white and indifferent—a sheet, bodiless and void, walks toward him carefully, noiselessly, on slippered feet." Solzhenitsyn believes that "Modern man is helpless when confronted with death, [for] he has no weapon to meet it with"—no Christian faith or spiritual strength to oppose materialism. As Iris Murdoch observes in her perceptive, compassionate opening of *Nuns and Soldiers,* we defensively reject the dying so that we will not be too hurt by their loss. Death destroys our illusions about love and shows that it is ultimately selfish:

> We do not want to care too much for what we are losing. Surreptitiously we remove our sympathy, and prepare the dying one for death, diminish him, strip him of his last attractions. We

abandon the dying like a sick beast left under a hedge. Death is supposed to show us truth, but is its own place of illusion. It defeats love.

Kostoglotov's vital question about the price of life, symbolized by oxygen and blood, recurs in two of the greatest scenes of the novel, when he first establishes intimacy with the nurse Zoya and the doctor Vera. As Virginia Woolf observes: "Illness often takes on the disguise of love, and plays the same odd tricks." Kostoglotov, whose moral strength attracts these women, is assertive and masculine with Zoya, passive and feminine with Vera. He kisses the distracted Zoya while she inflates a tumescent oxygen balloon, which almost bursts. She then tells him that he has been deceived by the doctors and has been given hormone therapy (also used against cancer of the testes) that will make him impotent. And she strongly urges him to discontinue the treatment.

The question arises for the third time during the transfusion. As Kostoglotov becomes affectionate with Vera they abandon their patient-doctor roles and speak as equals, perhaps even lovers. She is "faithful" to and alone with him in the sunlit room; he sheds his suspicions, "gives himself to trust" and accepts the flow of a female's blood into his veins. By doing so, he forms a symbolic sexual

Solzhenitsyn during the first months of his imprisonment.

union with Vera and wants to kiss her (he later asks her to give him another transfusion: "I liked it then. I want more"): "The blood in the bottle had already dropped by more than half. It had once flowed in someone else's body, a body with its own personality, its own ideas, and now it was pouring into him, a reddish-brown stream of health."

But Kostoglotov protests that he is "paying too high a price" for his existence: "First my own life was taken from me [in prison], and now I am being deprived even of the right . . . to perpetuate myself. . . . If the only expectation I have is being consciously and artificially killed—then why bother to save [me]?" His question leads them to discuss some books written by the venerologist Dr. Friedland, and read by Kostoglotov and Vera in the 1930s. These works present a purely physiological and even statistical—rather than emotional and spiritual—view of sex and love. Their rejection of Dr. Friedland's materialism allows Kostoglotov to hope that he will be able to love a woman without sex or the possibility of procreation. He therefore accepts the advice of Vera, who (in contrast to Zoya) insists that he continue the hormone treatments in order to save his life.

A parallel scene and love affair (Kostoglotov mourns his lost virility, Asya her lost femininity) occurs between the young student Dyomka, who has cancer of the leg and is threatened with amputation, and the hedonistic and licentious schoolgirl, Asya. When Asya—crushed, trembling and tearful—reveals that the doctors must cut off her cancerous breast and asks (like Kostoglotov) "What have I to live for?," Dyomka ignores the dreadful consequences and offers to marry her. She then exposes her doomed breast and asks him to kiss it. Dyomka gratefully suckles the gently curving breast and becomes absorbed in its fiery aura: "He returned to its rosy glow again and again, softly kissing the breast. He did what her future child would never be able to do. No one came in, and so he kissed and kissed the marvel hanging over him. Today it was a marvel. Tomorrow it would be in the trash bin." Despite the bitter irony, Solzhenitsyn suggests, by merging the maternal and the sexual, that the spiritual *can* survive without the physical aspects of love, and reinforces the previous rejection of Dr. Friedland's materialistic view of love.

By the end of the novel Kostoglotov, who had experienced a brief sexual resurgence before he had been simultaneously saved and destroyed by the hormone therapy, is confronted with the reality of his condition. After his release from the hospital he is invited to spend the night with both Zoya ("life") and Vera ("faith"). He seeks out the brilliant flowering apricot tree which, like the splendid ballet *Sleeping Beauty,* symbolizes his personal resurrection and promising return to life. When he accidentally presses against an attractive young girl in the streetcar, he realizes that he has permanently lost his virility ("the libido remains, the libido but nothing else"). He is forced to accept the cruel fact that "his journey to see Vera would end as a torture and a deceit. It would mean his demanding more from her than he could ask from himself." He now understands that love must be both physical (as with Zoya) *and* spiritual (as with Vera), and refuses to sacrifice Vera's love

for his own well-being. His experiences in the cancer ward have made him unfit for life and led him to renounce love.

In *Illness as Metaphor,* Susan Sontag quite mistakenly insists that "*Cancer Ward* contains virtually no use of cancer as a metaphor—for Stalinism, or anything else." But the political allegory is both distinct and significant. As Solzhenitsyn says of his own characters: "Those were the words they used, but the looks they gave each other were keen and it was clear that they were really concerned with something quite different." The novel logically follows, in its consistent use of suggestive analogies, the inevitable mode of personal conversation, private correspondence and underground literature in the Soviet Union.

The hospital records five possible results for each category of medical treatment: "complete cure, improvement, no change, deterioration or death." These categories correspond to the five phases of Solzhenitsyn's life—youth, war, exile, prison and hospital—that are clearly reflected in the novel. Like Solzhenitsyn, Orwell draws a direct parallel between war and disease in his moving autobiographical essay, "How the Poor Die" [in his *Decline of the English Murder*]. "People talk about the horrors of war, but what weapon has man invented that even approaches in cruelty some of the commoner diseases? 'Natural' death, almost by definition, means something slow, smelly and painful."

In *Cancer Ward,* Solzhenitsyn draws on his military experience as a metaphor for both the invasion of the hostile disease and the victim's desperate battle against it. Solitary, destructive cells steal "through the darkness like landing craft"; spreading cancers tear "defenses to pieces like tanks"; victims are "wounded" and soon fall; survivors are heroes "from the hospital front line." Dr. Dontsova, who forces the skeptical Kostoglotov to accept his treatment, explains: "there was a battle, but he was defeated and he surrendered." The x-ray's "blind artillery cuts down its own men with the same pleasure as it does the enemy's." The tumor is driven back: "It's on the defensive."

Kostoglotov's years as a prisoner, like his experience as a soldier, are also analogous to his treatment in the confined and crowded hospital. The prison cell is like the cancer cell: "first I lived under guard, then I lived in pain." In prison he is torn from his family, banished from the world and put behind barbed wire. But that is no "easier to take than a tumor," which also denies him the rights of a free and healthy man. The patient-prisoner is powerless, watchful and suspicious. He is enclosed for an indefinite period of time, interrogated by doctors, and once again becomes "a grain of sand, just as [he] was in the camp." A confession of illness is like a confession of crime. In the hospital, "the rooms are full of bunks, complete with bedding, and on each bunk lies a little man terrified out of his wits."

A few men manage to survive the cancer ward just as they survived the camp. But Kostoglotov believes: "I probably won't be discharged till I'm crawling on all fours." When a deluded patient leaves the hospital, Kostoglotov is reminded of "those rare occasions when they saw off a prisoner who had been released. Was he to tell him that he'd be arrested again as soon as he set foot outside the gates?" Both camp and ward are places "where ninety-nine weep but [only] one laughs."

Kostoglotov is not the only one in this microcosmic society who has been in the camps. Just as the Tartars "had no difficulty in recognizing their own people in the clinic, [neither] did those who once lived in the shadow of barbed-wire." Lev Leonidovich has worked as a free doctor in the prison camps. The Tartar Ahmadjan, one of the very few patients who is ostensibly cured, has been a concentration camp guard. The brutal Podduyev, whose moral life is rather improbably transformed by studying Tolstoy's *What Men Live By,* has supervised convict labor. And the intelligent orderly Elizaveta Anatolyevna, who reads French novels, has been innocently imprisoned with her husband. The past of these characters tightens the links between prison and hospital. They draw Kostoglotov back—through memories, associations and conversations—to the world he is trying to escape.

The KGB man Rusanov, the one-dimensional villain of the novel, brings the prison world into the hospital by his practical support and ideological justification of Stalinism. He named his son after Beria; loves the People but cannot tolerate actual human beings; betrayed his friend Rodichev in order to get the other half of their communal apartment; carried out his "simple duty as a citizen" by dismissing and eliminating many others; and stoutly defends Stalin's purge trials, which he used to build his career at the expense of men like Kostoglotov: "In that excellent and honorable time, the years 1937 and 1938, the social atmosphere was noticeably cleansed and it became easier to breathe."

As cancer spreads secretly through his body, Rusanov's cynical, *arriviste* daughter Aviette announces that Stalin's cult of personality has come under attack. Moscow has initiated a massive review of legal proceedings ("It's like an epidemic"), and betrayers are now forced to confront their victims. Rusanov's fearful response is an attack on this painful process: "It's cruel to the exiles themselves. Some of them are dead—why disturb their ghosts? Why raise groundless hopes among their relatives and perhaps a desire for revenge? Again, what does rehabilitated actually mean? It can't mean the man was completely innocent! He must have done *something,* however trivial."

As the novel, and especially the part on Rusanov progresses, the allegorical implications of army and prison spread (like the disease) to include all of Stalinist Russia: "A man dies from a tumor, so how can a country survive with growths like labor camps and exiles?" In the hospital, as in totalitarian Russia, no one is allowed to speak the truth. Tumors are a "state secret." Despite the confessional mode of the novel, "when it came to ideology it was better to keep your trap shut." Official newspapers, distributed in the wards, are "written in fact in code," though skillful party functionaries soon learn to interpret them. Rusanov suspects the doctors of a plot to poison him; and doctors are actually put on trial in the hospital just as they were when Stalin accused them of plotting against him. Rusanov believes that public executions (like lethal x-rays) "would speedily bring complete health to our society."

Doctors, like KGB men, enjoy absolute authority over the lives of their dehumanized patients. They carry out "senseless, pointless instructions which they can't ignore on pain of losing their jobs." They "believe unquestioningly in their established methods and treatments." X-rays are used as indiscriminately as police arrests. Doctors do not know "what percentage of healthy cells [or innocent people] as compared to the diseased ones would be destroyed."

The remission of Kostoglotov's disease in the spring of 1955 coincides with the political thaw that began to take place two years after the death of Stalin. He expresses the feelings of the oppressed by publicly condemning Stalin's crimes in his argument with Shulubin. In contrast to Kostoglotov, Shulubin has sold out to political pressure, confessed "mistakes" he never made, been reduced from a professor in Moscow to a provincial librarian, participated in book burning—and has saved his life at the expense of his soul. During the purge trials, intelligent people like Shulubin, who wanted only to live, were forced to believe that "Millions of Russian soldiers . . . betrayed their country." Kostoglotov thinks "the traitors were those [like Rusanov] who wrote denunciations or stood up as witnesses." Even Lenin's widow Krupskaya failed to understand what was actually happening or lacked the courage to protest against these crimes. Other leaders preferred to die in mysterious circumstances or to commit suicide rather than confess to false crimes.

The thaw suggests the cure. The entire Supreme Court of the Soviet Union, which administered "justice" for a quarter of a century, is suddenly dismissed. Malenkov is relieved of his duties; Beria is overthrown, "falling with a tinny clang." Stalin is openly attacked. Rumors circulate that exiles are going to be released. And Kostoglotov is treated with extraordinary courtesy by the police Kommandant in Tashkent. The morally changed Podduyev expresses a major theme in the novel when he says that if the tumor (of Stalinism) is to be cured, "suddenly drain away, dry up and die by itself . . . I suppose for that you need to have . . . a clear conscience." Political change must reflect moral change in both the people and their leaders.

At the end of the novel Kostoglotov—who as a patient was treated as a zoological specimen—is released from the hospital, improved but impotent. Before deciding whether it might be possible to share his life with Vera—who feels eternally bound to the past by the promise to her dead lover just as he is bound to the army, prison and hospital—he visits a series of symbolic animals in the Tashkent zoo. He then decides to return to exile in Kazakhstan and to his humane friends, the Kadmins. Like Vera's friend Dr. Oreshchenkov, who also loves animals, they are the moral touchstones of the novel.

The first animal Kostoglotov sees is a dignified and reflective spiral-horned mountain goat, who stands on a steep precipice and represents "the sort of charcter a man [like Kostoglotov] needed to get through life." By contrast the squirrel, like the oppressed proletariat, revolves in his cage at a furious pace, its heart nearly bursting. It cannot understand that " 'It's all in vain!' No, there was clearly only one inevitable way out, the squirrel's death."

The Rhesus monkey (experiments on which led to the medical discovery of the Rh factor in human blood) stands for the third type of man: the helpless and tormented political prisoner. A crudely painted sign explains his empty cage: "The little monkey that used to live here was blinded because of the senseless cruelty of one of the visitors. An evil man threw tobacco into the Macaque Rhesus's eyes." Solzhenitsyn states in an Appendix to the novel that the perpetrator of this gratuitous cruelty—who is diametrically opposed to the views expressed in Tolstoy's *What Men Live By*—"is meant to represent Stalin specifically." Finally, Kostoglotov stares with hatred at a rapacious tiger with yellow eyes, whom he also associates (through his pre-Revolutionary place of exile) with Stalin.

The personal and political significance of this visit is intensified by its moral simplicity, by its characteristic combination of the obvious and the subtle. Solzhenitsyn argued, when attempting to justify the "progressive" aspects of his novel to the Secretariat of Soviet Writers in 1967, that his theme is ultimately affirmative: "life conquers death, the past is conquered by the future," and both "triumph over spiritual sorrow." But his fortunate cure, marriage and children, his courageous transformation of disease and death into great art, his "seed of hope on the very brink of the grave," must not blind us to his hero's tragic fate.

Kostoglotov's life shows that dictators, party officials, police, guards and prisoners are all trapped in the vast prison of Russia. There is no escape from cancer, despite periods of remission, just as there is no escape from the legacy of Stalinism, despite the apparent political thaw. Kostoglotov has been released by and destroyed by both prison and hospital. He survived his ordeal by cancer and is "free" to return to his place of exile. But he is no longer fit for sexual life, and must renounce love and the possibility of human happiness. *Cancer Ward* (like recent Russian history) is perhaps less life-affirming than Solzhenitsyn would have us believe, for it expresses a terrible truth: "The cells of the heart which nature built for joy die through disuse. The small place in the breast which is faith's cramped quarters remains untenanted for years and decays." (pp. 54-67)

> *Jeffrey Meyers, " 'Cancer Ward' and the Literature of Disease," in* Twentieth Century Literature, *Vol. 29, No. 1, Spring, 1983, pp. 54-68.*

Geoffrey A. Hosking   (review date 3 February 1984)

[*Hosking is a British educator and author of several works on Russian life and literature, including* Beyond Socialist Realism: Soviet Fiction Since 'Ivan Denisovich' *(1980). In the following review of Solzhenitsyn's revised novel* August 1914, *he praises the accuracy of Solzhenitsyn's depictions of historical figures but faults his blend of history and art as oversimplified.*]

Some books—a very few—have a history like a geological formation. Formed under tremendous pressure, they survive the metamorphoses of ages, changing and diversifying at each upheaval in the earth's crust. [*The Red Wheel: Fascicle 1, August 1914*] is one such. It was originally conceived, the author tells us, in Rostov-on-Don in 1937, and indeed some of the early chapters were written at that time. These then survived the years of war, arrest, imprisonment, exile, provincial isolation, sudden fame and political controversy to see the light as part of the novel *August 1914,* which Solzhenitsyn published with the YMCA Press in Paris in 1971. Now that novel has undergone further transformations, the result of Solzhenitsyn's exile to the West and the deeper research which this has made possible into the history of the Russian Revolution. Its thousand pages are, moreover, only the first *uzel* (fascicle) in a huge cycle of novels covering that revolution—a cycle which, if completed, is likely to make Sholokhov's ventures in the same field (also conceived not far from Rostov-on-Don) seem like mere miniatures.

The basic conception underlying the novel, however, has not undergone any changes. It has merely been filled out and clarified by Solzhenitsyn's historical research. In the first version of *August 1914* the milling engineer Arkhangorodsky predicted a great future for Russia, based on the economic development of the immense untapped resources of Siberia, as well as on the country's human potential. Russia's population, he calculated, would be 350 million by 1950. "That is", he added cautiously, "if we don't start disembowelling each other first."

Solzhenitsyn's concern is to explain why this great vision remained unrealized, why the country's economic growth took place in a lopsided and debilitating manner, why Siberia remained relatively undeveloped, and above all why Russians started disembowelling each other in great numbers. The roots of all this he sees in the revolution of 1917, and therefore in the events which led up to it. His narrative and historical method is to take the decisive turning-points and explain them from all sides. The result is the "fascicle", which he describes as a "dense, all-round exposition of the events of a brief time span".

In its new form, this particular "fascicle" centres on two such events, the murder of the prime minister, Stolypin, at the Kiev Opera House, on September 1, 1911, and the outbreak of the First World War. These two events, Solzhenitsyn evidently believes, broke off Russia's peaceful development and plunged her into the chaos which made the Bolshevik revolution possible. The war was utterly opposed to Russia's real interests, and the country should never have been drawn into it. That it was drawn in Solzhenitsyn attributes, on the evidence of his long new historical excursion (which nearly doubles the novel's original length), to the fact that the statesman who had Russia's real interests at heart, the man who had the strength and perspicacity to avoid false entanglements—namely Stolypin—was dead. Solzhenitsyn shows us the Emperor Nicholas II pacing up and down the room of his palace on the agonizing day in July 1914 when he is being urged, against his better judgment, to order general mobilization. He reflects bitterly on the incompetence and unreliability of all his ministers and generals. "He did not have a single firm, intelligent, outstanding individual who would take the responsibility and the decision-making on himself, and would say: 'no! this way and no other!' But there was such a man once—Stolypin! That's who he needed right here, right now—Stolypin!"

Solzhenitsyn therefore turns to a "dense, all-round exposition" of the events leading up to Stolypin's murder. His assassin was a police agent and somewhat questionable revolutionary, Dmitri Bogrov.

Bogrov is everything Solzhenitsyn despises. Privileged and rich, son of a successful barrister, and about to take up the same career, he is temporarily idle as young barristers are, but not penniless, as many have to be. Bogrov sticks to the narcissistic and destructive dreams of the terrorists of 1905–6, only unlike them he refuses to be bound hand and foot by political parties and their central committees. He believes that only a heroic and determined *individual* can defeat the system and reach the "central" targets, the ones that really matter.

That this man was admitted to the Kiev Opera House (where not only Stolypin but also the Emperor himself were among the spectators), with a revolver in his pocket, has always puzzled historians. His entrance pass was given to him by N. N. Kulyabko, head of the Kiev department of the Okhrana (the Tsar's security police), on the strength of Bogrov's story that he was going to keep an eye on a group of terrorists who were preparing an attempt on Stolypin's life. Solzhenitsyn maintains that Kulyabko was unaccustomed to having such an intelligent and socially distinguished secret agent on his books, and was simply flattered by Bogrov. Even more mysterious, though, is the fact that the issue of the pass was approved by P. G. Kurlov, Assistant Minister of the Interior, and head of the Empire's entire police network: he had come down from St Petersburg to oversee security during the festivities in Kiev. No one searched Bogrov when he entered the theatre, in spite of his avowed connections with revolutionaries, and no one tailed him; nor did anyone make an independent check on the story about the terrorist group.

These elementary oversights imply incompetence on such a mind-boggling scale that many historians (myself included) have felt inclined to hypothesize at least a degree of complicity on the part of Kurlov and Kulyabko in Stolypin's murder. Stolypin was known to distrust Kurlov, who in turn felt that Stolypin had blocked his career. Besides, Stolypin was by now very unpopular at court, especially among the senior advisers and officials, who felt displaced by the new constitutional system of government he was gradually making effective. Even the new legislative chambers, the Duma and the State Council, were not supporting Stolypin at the time, since he had recently treated them rather brusquely over a bill to introduce elective local government in the western provinces of the Empire. Perhaps Kurlov had grounds for believing that Stolypin's sudden death would not be too closely investigated. Certainly, in the event it was not: a senatorial inquiry produced material for charges of criminal negligence to be preferred against Kurlov and Kulyabko, but the Emperor, against the advice of Stolypin's successor, Kokovtsev, ordered that the case be dropped. As for Bogrov, he was secretly tried and executed with indecent haste, before the senators could question him.

Solzhenitsyn does not actually accuse Kurlov and Kulyabko of complicity in the crime. All he does maintain is that they were preoccupied with other matters more conducive to their personal advancement than guarding a premier who would probably soon have to resign anyway, and that they simply neglected to take basic precautions. To me this explanation does not quite hang together. Do security policemen have any tasks more urgent or more career-enhancing than protecting the monarch and the prime minister? But Solzhenitsyn advances his interpretation with his customary verbal panache and insight into the minds of people of widely differing backgrounds and persuasions. The explanation fits into his view—already clear in the first version of *August 1914*—of a modernizing, developing Russia being first held back and then ground down by two conflicting reactionary forces, the Black Hundreds and the Red Hundreds, as he calls them: idle high society from above, and the revolutionaries from below. Bogrov epitomizes both.

Stolypin, absent from the first version of the novel, has now become the hero of *August 1914.* An examination of his political career takes up the longest and most significant of the historical expositions filling out the body of the book. Solzhenitsyn sees Stolypin as the bearer of a renewed patriotic Russian consciousness, courageous in braving the assassin's bullet, determined in suppressing revolution, creative and far-sighted in his plans for reform. Taking the constitution which a nervous Witte (then prime minister) had hastily thrust on the Emperor at the height of the 1905 revolution, Stolypin set about actually trying to make it work, drawing the new legislative chambers into business-like activity instead of vapid speech-making, and fashioning them into a permanent part of the machinery of state. As Solzhenitsyn puts it, "he took the Duma more seriously than the Duma deputies themselves". He also intended to strengthen the local government assemblies—the zemstvos—and make them more responsive to local opinion by widening their franchise and removing some of the official tutelage which had hitherto impeded their freedom of action.

Most important of all Stolypin's reform projects was the dissolution of the traditional peasant land tenure, vested in the village commune, and its replacement by private peasant smallholdings. For Solzhenitsyn, the continuing dominance of the commune in the countryside was an example *par excellence* of the unholy symbiosis of reactionaries and revolutionaries. The reactionaries liked the commune because it guaranteed that peasants would stay put, pay their taxes and not become landless vagrants or "sturdy beggars", a threat to law and order. The revolutionaries liked it because its arrangements for periodic compulsory land redistribution and mutual social security constituted a kind of primitive socialism, and might enable the peasants to proceed to the real thing without going through the horrors of capitalism. Stolypin, however, felt that the peasants would never respect other people's property until they had full property rights of their own: they would continue to hanker after other people's land, and to burn manor houses till they got it.

> That was Stolypin's chief thought: that you can't create a law-abiding society without independent citizens—and that, in Russia, meant peasants. . . . The abstract right to freedom without the genuine freedom of the peasantry was mere "rouge on the corpse". Russia could not become a strong nation whilst its major social class had no stake in the system.

Altogether, Stolypin's political programme had some striking resemblances to the one Solzhenitsyn published in 1974, when he made known his *Letter to the Soviet Leaders*: both place great emphasis on private property, encouragement of industry, peasant resettlement in Siberia (which Stolypin promoted to good effect) and on peaceful Russian patriotism, avoiding all unnecessary international entanglements.

Historically speaking, Solzhenitsyn's admiration for Stolypin is well founded. There is no doubt, in my view, that Stolypin was the outstanding Russian statesman of the early twentieth century, and for precisely the reasons Solzhenitsyn puts forward. What is disturbing, however, about his historical exposition is a lack of nuance, the absence of any sense of the complexity of events: this distorts and flattens Solzhenitsyn's vision both as historian and as novelist. Take, for example, the assertion that Stolypin was determined to preserve Russia's new parliament and to consolidate its powers. I believe it to be correct on the whole, but there is no doubt that Stolypin himself undermined the Duma's authority by enacting a number of major reforms, including the cardinal act "On Withdrawal from the Commune", under emergency legislation, while the chambers were adjourned. A law which radically changes a centuries-old institution cannot be called "emergency legislation", as many members of the Duma indignantly pointed out. Solzhenitsyn argues that the agrarian reform was urgently needed, and that the Duma would debate it for years. Quite true: in other words, there was a genuine dilemma, and it distorts the complexity of historical trends to make out that there was a simple and obvious answer which could only be resisted by the ill-willed.

Or take the case of local government reform. Very little came of Stolypin's intentions in this area. But the reason was not purely, as Solzhenitsyn states, that the left-wing members of the Duma, the "freedom-loving defenders of the people", squashed them with the help of the reactionary right. On the contrary, those local government proposals which Stolypin actually brought before the Duma were passed by it. The difficulty lay elsewhere: with the independent landowners of central Russia, whose co-operation Stolypin was seeking for his agrarian programme. They feared that their influence in the new zemstvos would be diminished, as would indeed have been the case, since the new electoral law was more democratic—ie, less favourable to them—and their representatives, the Marshals of the Nobility, would no longer have the automatic right to select the chairmen of the assemblies. Because of opposition from these provincial nobles, Stolypin never even brought the reform of the upper-tier zemstvos

Solzhenitsyn wearing his number patches and prison garb from Ekibastuz, shortly after his release.

before the Duma. As for the bill to set up a lower-tier zemstvo, at the level of the *volost* (roughly equivalent to the former English rural district council), that was actually passed by the Duma, with some amendments, but rejected in the upper house, the State Council, where many provincial nobles voted against it. Their contribution was decisive to its defeat: those whom Solzhenitsyn normally calls "the spheres" (the court, the pre-1905 bureaucrats, the police officials) were not numerous enough in the State Council to sink it on their own.

Solzhenitsyn, in fact, does not give enough attention to the political and social forces which *supported* Stolypin, and which found difficulties with some elements of his programme. The image he projects is of Stolypin, almost alone as the bearer of progress and national honour, fighting a brave but unavailing battle. The whole account is melodramatic, concentrates too much on the assassination, and misses the complexities which constitute the true drama of history.

The same weakness vitiates Solzhenitsyn's achievement as a novelist. In *The First Circle* or *Cancer Ward,* he shows a gift for letting us see reality in the round, through the eyes of individuals of very different character and outlook. His language contributes to this three-dimensional effect, through its vivid epithets, its archaisms and neologisms, its personalized vocabulary, its subtle modulations of direct and indirect speech. In both novels it is clear enough what the author himself is trying to say, but he does not actually put a personal representative on stage to say it for him. Nerzhin's world-view is laid out in counterpoint with Rubin's, and the reader responds to the total effect.

Already in the first version of *August 1914* much of this "polyphony" had been lost in the author's evident readiness to intersperse his own spokesmen among the *dramatis personae*. Now the addition of a large historical section has made the problem worse. As though uncertain he is getting his point across, Solzhenitsyn has marked out parts of the new section in small type, and there he quite simply addresses the reader as historian or Olympian narrator, instructing him what to think. Here the language of subjectivity, which Solzhenitsyn has mastered so magnificently, is merely annoying. Significantly, to the techniques of first and third-person narration, which he has deployed elsewhere, he now occasionally adds that of *second-person* narration, a highly unusual mode (also employed in *The Gulag Archipelago*), whose aim appears to be to compel the reader linguistically to identify with the character then holding the stage. Some readers may feel inclined to resist the compulsion.

Nevertheless, *August 1914* contains, as it did before, many compelling and vivid pages, especially those on General Samsonov, the peasant Blagodaryov, and the staff officer Colonel Vorotyntsev, who between them personalize Russia's greatness and her tragedy. These pages, taken on their own, are among the finest things Solzhenitsyn has written. In the new version, too, he has added a graphic and, to my mind, very convincing portrait of Nicholas II. So there are many good things in this book. But as history and as art *August 1914* remains seriously flawed, and the addition of more history has highlighted the flaws of the art. (pp. 99-100)

> *Geoffrey A. Hosking, "The Plunge into Chaos," in The Times Literary Supplement, No. 4218, February 3, 1984, pp. 99-100.*

James George Jatras   (essay date Spring 1985)

[*In the following essay, Jatras disputes popularly held liberal assumptions about Solzhenitsyn's political beliefs by examining specific statements from his works.*]

Since he was exiled from his homeland over a decade ago, it has become increasingly clear that liberals, whatever they may regard as his merits as a writer, do not like Aleksandr Solzhenitsyn or what they represent to be his social and political views. What is not immediately clear is why they dislike him so intensely.

Liberalism, according to Webster's dictionary, is a philosophy which includes, among other principles, a belief in "the autonomy of the individual" and in "the protection of political and civil liberties." Now, certainly Solzhenitsyn is a conservative, and conservatives and liberals do

have significant differences which should not be underestimated. But I would like to think these differences would not, generally, include any basic disagreements about the rapacious nature of communist totalitarianism, unarguably the greatest single threat in today's world to the continued existence of "the autonomy of the individual" and "political and civil liberties." Liberals today, to the extent that they remain genuine liberals (and have not degenerated, as some conservatives claim they inevitably must, into collectivists), have every obligation to be actively anti-communist—as much, say, as genuine conservatives in the 1930s were obligated to be actively anti-Nazi and anti-fascist, as too many sadly were not. Solzhenitsyn is considered by many the world's foremost living anti-communist: others, Sakharov for example, have struggled valiantly against Soviet injustices, but it was Solzhenitsyn who for the first time forced us to admit to ourselves the reality of all the horrible things about the USSR that we had always known but preferred to overlook.

I have in mind here the desire to engage in *mythmaking* about the Soviet Union. For example, in the *New Republic* of February 26, 1936, Robert M. MacGregor praised "the speed, effectiveness, and accuracy" of work performed under the fraudulent Stakhanovite system, heralding the movement as pointing "to the possibility of wiping out the difference between manual and mental labor, one of the principal attributes, as Stalin interprets it, of actual communism." That Stakhanovism was in fact a cynical and brutal scheme to extort vastly increased work norms out of the shackled and impoverished Soviet worker seems to have been beyond MacGregor's knowledge or interest. Not only liberals believed in such myths. In his 1946 book *I Chose Freedom* the soon-to-defect Victor Kravchenko relates his excruciating inability to disabuse "some thoroughly anti-labor capitalists" of the notion that there prevailed in the USSR a hateful system in which "the workers ruled" and "everybody was equal."

Herein lies the value of Solzhenitsyn's art. The major difficulty with foreign perceptions of the Soviet Union is not that the facts have not been available but that our imagination was not up to admitting them to our consciousness. "The chief problem confronting the expert in Soviet affairs is not to keep his information up to date, as it is in other fields," wrote the French Sovietologist Alain Besançon in his 1978 book *The Soviet Syndrome,* a scant hundred pages well worth the reading. "His main difficulty lies in accepting as true what most people deem improbable, in believing the unbelievable." The facts, I emphasize, were there: nobody who has read S. P. Melgounov's 1926 book *The Red Terror in Russia* will find much shock value in Stalin's misdeeds. But it was Solzhenitsyn, through some artistic alchemy or fortuitous timing that cannot be entirely explained, who made the world admit as true what could not be true. Today it is commonly accepted that Soviet rule has cost Russia several tens of millions of lives, that the USSR is one vast prison peppered with concentration camps, that "real socialism" is a great engine of murder, torture, slavery. "The main result," wrote Robert Conquest in the *New Republic* in 1978, "has been that it is now no longer possible in any country with reasonably free publication for the Soviet system to find serious defenders. . . . The word *Gulag* has entered the language—every language." This was Solzhenitsyn's doing. It must be among the regime's greatest errors—perhaps a fatal one—that they did not kill him when they had the chance.

As we move through this perilous decade which, I suggest, could very well see the final resolution, one way or the other, of what Communists call "the international class struggle," I think we would do well to listen to what Solzhenitsyn has to say—not agree necessarily, but at least listen—for the sake of his tortured country and for the preservation of liberal values in what remains of the free world. It is not all just Gulag and the camps. Recently he has spoken, with insight and originality, on religion in the USSR and in today's world as a whole (the Templeton address, **"Men Have Forgotten God"**), on China (during a visit to Taiwan), and to the Japanese people (calling for a "genuine Japanese-Russo-Chinese friendship" in the Far East). But since his initial fanfare greeting in the West—and especially since his 1978 Harvard commencement address—Solzhenitsyn has all but disappeared from the major media, mostly, that is, from the liberal media. Today about the only place one can find his recent statements (such as the three noted above) is in *National Review.* To my knowledge, no other major periodicals—mostly liberal periodicals, or at least more liberal than *National Review*—have seen fit to give him more than passing coverage, usually not even that. There seems to be a common desire that he go away or at least just shut up. And the reason for this is not difficult to discern.

Mention Solzhenitsyn to just about any liberal. He is, you will hear (many times over), an "anti-democrat," an "authoritarian," a "theocrat," an unreconstructed "Russian imperialist," an extremist who borders on being a "fascist," as well as a "monarchist," and, of course, an "anti-Semite." Is it not enough—or, as some suggested after his 1978 Harvard commencement address, maybe too much—that we let him stay here? Why dignify the ravings of this scoundrel and ingrate by quoting him? (Ronald Reagan does in fact quote Solzhenitsyn in his speeches on occasion; so did Ambassador Kirkpatrick. Come to think of it, that's one more count against the three of them.)

There is, however, one public service that Solzhenitsyn performs that even his severest critics will probably concede, the utility of which must be appreciated: he is "Solzhenitsyn, Bogeyman of the Right." By associating people or institutions, however tangentially, with Solzhenitsyn, their credibility is instantly and effortlessly compromised. There are those for whom such a device is indispensable. For example, in a recent article in the *Washington Post,* Josef Joffe and Dimitri Simes sought to illustrate that "extremist" views run rampant at Radio Free Europe (RFE) and Radio Liberty (RL) by quoting an unnamed RL editorialist who, in introducing the speech given by Solzhenitsyn in Taiwan, called the author an "unofficial envoy of the Russian people to the Chinese island of freedom." Joffe and Simes note this characterization without comment, as if it were so patently absurd as to need no explanation.

From here others pick up the theme. Three liberal human rights organizations—Americas Watch, Helsinki Watch, and the Lawyers Committee for International Human Rights—in their subtly titled report *Failure: The Reagan Administration's Human Rights Policy for 1983* cite the *Post* article in support of their claims that RL lauds "Alexander Solzhenitsyn's diatribes against Western ideas of free expression" and that "broadcasters with anti-Western, monarchist, even fascist tendencies often monopolize the programming." See how easy it is. Just string the words together—Solzhenitsyn, anti-Western, monarchist, fascist.

And on it goes. In a report for the Senate Foreign Relations Committee by Minority Staff Director Geryld B. Christianson (submitted by Senators Percy and Pell), both the *Post* article and the concerns of Helsinki Watch are used to justify proposals to muzzle the radios, RL in particular. Christianson tosses around names from Russian history like Stolypin, Wrangel, and Vlasov in a manner designed to take advantage of the ignorance of readers unacquainted with the historical facts. (For example, he notes "favorable broadcasts" on Generals Alexeyev and Wrangel, who—and this apparently discredits them in Christianson's mind—"fought on the White Russian side in the Russian civil war." But the White armies represented every non-communist shade of political view in Russia, from monarchists on the Right to Social Revolutionaries on the Left, and included the democratic Center. In fact these political divisions—the only thing the Whites really agreed on was their opposition to the Communists—contributed to their eventual defeat. But what, in Christianson's mind, is objectionable *per se* about service with the Whites? Does he prefer the Reds?) Solzhenitsyn makes his obligatory appearance in the report. Airing of his Taiwan speech is characterized by Christianson as "the most egregious case" of RL's political bias. He calls Solzhenitsyn's views "clearly outrageous"—this, commenting on a speech where Solzhenitsyn's main point was that the Chinese and Russian peoples should free themselves from communism and should not allow the vicious regimes in Moscow and Peking to stir up hostility between them.

In short, the use of Solzhenitsyn's name and "well-known" political views is a handy cudgel for those desiring to smear Russian anti-communism and, it seems, anti-communism generally. Interestingly, however, his reputed views are usually simply characterized, often in the most extreme terms. Seldom are his opinions on anything exactly described and documented or his works quoted in detail.

There is a certain circularity here. Solzhenitsyn is damned for his supposedly reactionary views, but those who so portray him are loath to waste paper or ink letting him demonstrate just how reactionary he really is—or is not. One would think that giving him the opportunity to parade his "extremism" would be letting him have just so much rope with which to hang himself. In any case, it is an opportunity which his liberal critics have missed time and again. Consequently, I thought it might be useful to pick out those passages which give the sense of Solzhenitsyn's actual political orientation so that we can all see just what sort of reactionary he really is. For those who have taken the time to read him (and even among his fellow conservatives one rarely finds anybody who has managed to plow past the first half of *The Gulag Archipelago,* volume I) this may seem somewhat pedantic, but there may be some value in having the evidence in concentrated form.

It does not appear that there is anything in Solzhenitsyn's views which is specifically incompatible with democratic principles or with "the autonomy of the individual" and the protection of "civil and political liberties." In addition, many of the negative characterizations commonly attributed to him appear to be groundless.

—*James George Jatras*

To begin with, those who do have some familiarity with his writings are aware that Solzhenitsyn does not, strictly speaking, view his message as "political" but rather as moral. He believes that the essential matters for human beings and nations are not those relating to governmental structures but rather to choices between right and wrong, good and evil, truth and falsehood. As one of his characters in *August 1914* puts it, the differences that matter are not those between parties and nations but rather "the difference between decency and swinishness."

For instance, in his *Letter to the Soviet Leaders* (sent late in 1973) he states:

> This universal, obligatory force-feeding with lies is now the most agonizing aspect of existence in our country—worse than all our material miseries, worse than any lack of civil liberties.

Similarly, he believes that the way for his country to free itself from communism is for each person to refuse to participate in the lie (from the essay **"The Smatterers,"** which appears in the anthology *From Under the Rubble,* 1974):

> . . . in our country the daily lie is not the whim of corrupt natures but a mode of existence, a condition of the daily welfare of every man. In our country the lie has been incorporated into the state system as the vital link holding everything together, with billions of tiny fasteners, several dozen to each man.

> This is precisely why we find life so oppressive. But it is also precisely why we should find it natural to straighten up. When oppression is not accompanied by the lie, liberation demands political measures. But when the lie has fastened its claws on us, it is no longer a matter of politics! It is an invasion of man's moral world, and our straightening up and *refusing to lie* is also not political, but simply a retrieval of our human dignity. [Emphasis in original.]

To Solzhenitsyn the sphere of government is purely secondary (from the essay **"As Breathing and Consciousness Return,"** in *Rubble*):

> It would be more correct to say that in relation to the true ends of human beings here on earth . . . the state structure is of secondary significance. That this is so, Christ himself teaches us. "Render unto Caesar what is Caesar's"—not because every Caesar deserves it, but because Caesar's concern is not the most important thing in our lives.

Solzhenitsyn is often accused of advocating authoritarianism over democracy. However, since he does not see the state structure as a question of overriding importance, he has never, in any passage of which I am aware, stated a preference for any form of government (from **"The Mortal Danger,"** *Foreign Affairs,* Spring 1980):

> As concerns the theoretical question whether Russia should choose or reject authoritarianism in the future, I have no final opinion, and have not offered any.

Regarding practical considerations, he suggests that authoritarianism would be a realistic first step away from the current state of affairs (**"Breathing,"** in *Rubble*):

> If Russia for centuries was used to living under autocratic systems and suffered a total collapse under the democratic system which lasted eight months in 1917, perhaps—I am only asking, not making an assertion—perhaps we should recognize that the evolution of our country from one form of authoritarianism to another would be the most natural, the smoothest, the least painful path of development for it to follow? It may be objected that neither the path ahead, nor less still the new system at the end of it, can be seen. But for that matter we have never been shown any realistic path of transition from our present system to a democratic republic of the Western type. And the first-mentioned transition seems more feasible in that it requires a smaller expenditure of energy by the people.

He is concerned that Russia is not immediately prepared for democracy (from *Letter*):

> Here, in Russia, for sheer lack of practice, democracy survived for only eight months. . . . The emigré groups of Constitutional Democrats and Social Democrats still pride themselves on it to this very day and say that outside forces brought about its collapse. But in reality that democracy was *their* disgrace; they invoked it and promised it so arrogantly, and then created merely a chaotic caricature of democracy, because first of all they turned out to be ill-prepared for it themselves, and then Russia was worse prepared still. Over the last half-century Russia's preparedness for democracy, for a multi-party parliamentary system, could only have diminished. I am inclined to think that its sudden reintroduction now would merely be a melancholy repetition of 1917.

Aside from his discerning no realistic immediate path to a democracy of the Western type, Solzhenitsyn, who describes himself as an "opponent of all revolutions and all armed convulsions, including future ones" (*Letter*), assesses the "realistic" possibilities for change starting from the present rulers' obvious determination to retain at least their own personal power. This entire outlook was summed up in **"The Mortal Danger"**:

> But this letter was a genuine address to very real rulers possessed of immeasurable power, and it was plain that the very most one could hope for would be concessions on their side, certainly not capitulation: neither free general elections nor a complete (or even partial) change of leadership could be expected. The most I called for was a renunciation of communist ideology and of its most cruel consequences, so as to allow at least a little more breathing space for the national spirit, for throughout history only nationally-minded individuals have been able to make constructive contributions to society. And the only path down from the icy cliff of totalitarianism that I could propose was the slow and smooth descent via an authoritarian system. (If an unprepared people were to jump off that cliff directly into democracy, it would be crushed to an anarchical pulp.) This "authoritarianism" of mine also drew immediate fire in the Western press.

Solzhenitsyn's idea of a tolerable authoritarian structure includes a number of qualities which are usually considered prerequisites if not integral parts of a viable constitutional democracy. Again, his point of departure is "the lie" (from *Letter*):

> It is not authoritarianism itself that is intolerable, but the ideological lies that are daily foisted upon us. Not so much authoritarianism as arbitrariness and illegality, the sheer illegality of having a single overlord in each district, each province and each sphere, often ignorant and brutal, whose will alone decides all things. An authoritarian order does not necessarily mean that laws are unnecessary or that they exist only on paper, or that they should not reflect the notions and will of the population. Nor does it mean that the legislative, executive and judicial authorities are not independent, any of them, that they are in fact not authorities at all but utterly at the mercy of a telephone call from the only true, self-appointed authority. May I remind you that the *soviets,* which gave their name to our system and existed until July 6, 1918, were in no way dependent upon ideology: ideology or no ideology, they always envisaged the widest possible *consultation* with all working people. [Emphasis in original.]

Indeed, notwithstanding his views on the primacy of morality, the necessity of legality in place of arbitrariness is a recurring theme in Solzhenitsyn's writings. He suggests (in *Letter*) that the Soviet Constitution (superceded in 1977), which, in his view, "from 1936 . . . has not been observed for a single day," may not be entirely beyond hope but may present a basis for future improvements.

He also notes that authoritarian systems, though having

certain virtues ("stability, continuity, and immunity from political ague"), have "great dangers and defects":

> . . . the danger of dishonest authorities, upheld by violence, the danger of arbitrary decisions and the difficulty of correcting them, the danger of sliding into tyranny. (from **"Breathing,"** in *Rubble*)

He concludes that a sense of responsibility, "before God and their own conscience," is a necessary restraint on rulers:

> The autocrats of our own time are dangerous precisely because it is difficult to find higher values which would bind them.

In cleansing Russian society of the moral legacy of the Soviet period he says (in *The Gulag Archipelago,* volume I):

> We have to condemn publicly the very *idea* that some people have a right to repress others. [Emphasis in original.]

But as Solzhenitsyn states in **"The Mortal Danger"**: "My criticism of certain aspects of democracy is well known." However, his criticisms do not relate to the principle of democratic government but rather to what he sees as some difficulties of application:

> 1. *That the will of the people is not always served* when, for instance, governments rule in the minority or with only a slim majority and when great parts of the electorate are disillusioned to the point of not voting (**"Mortal Danger"**); "when a tiny party holds the balance between two big ones," "when superpowers are rocked by party struggles with no ethical basis." (**"Breathing,"** in *Rubble*)

> 2. *That democracies are often weak* against terrorists (**"Breathing,"** in *Rubble; Letter;* and **"Mortal Danger"**), "when unlimited freedom of discussion can wreck a country's resistance to some looming danger and lead to capitulation in wars not yet lost" (**"Breathing,"** in *Rubble*); and that democracies have an apparent "inability to prevent the growth of organized crime, or to check unrestrained profiteering at the expense of public morality." (**"Mortal Danger"**)

> 3. *That "the terrifying phenomenon of totalitarianism,* which has been born into our world perhaps four times, did not issue from authoritarian systems, but in each case from a weak democracy: the one created by the February Revolution in Russia, the Weimar and Italian republics, and Chiang Kai-shek's China. The majority of governments in human history have been authoritarian, but they have yet to give birth to a totalitarian regime." (**"Mortal Danger"**)

On top of his "authoritarianism," Solzhenitsyn has been accused of advocating a theocratic form of government. He denies the charge (from **"Mortal Danger"**):

> This is a flagrant misrepresentation; I have never said or written anything of the sort. The day-to-day activity of governing in no sense belongs to the sphere of religion. What I do believe is that the state should not persecute religion, and that,

furthermore, religion should make an appropriate contribution to the spiritual life of the nation. Such a situation obtains in Poland and Israel and no one condemns it; I cannot understand why the same thing should be forbidden to Russia—a land that has carried its faith through ten centuries and earned the right to it by sixty years of suffering and the blood of millions of laymen and tens of thousands of clergy.

In his *Letter* he states:

I myself see Christianity today as the only living spiritual force capable of undertaking the spiritual healing of Russia. But I request and propose no special privileges for it, simply that it should be treated fairly and not suppressed.

Nevertheless, Solzhenitsyn's strong commitment to religious and patriotic principles has prompted some critics to accuse him of seeking to revive the pre-1917 Russian imperial tradition. Indeed, it is safe to say that the supposed similarity between Solzhenitsyn's reputed Russian "imperialism" and Soviet expansionism has become bound up with the perennial question of whether Soviet policy is specifically Russian rather than communist. While an adequate examination of this subject is beyond the scope of this paper, it is reasonable to speculate whether Solzhenitsyn has simply been dragged into an effort to attribute the Soviet regime's demonstrable aggressiveness to some incorrigible Russian urge for conquest rather than to one of the idols of our age, socialism. In any event, in **"The Mortal Danger"** Solzhenitsyn summarizes the position he took in his *Letter* on Russia's role in the world:

In the sphere of foreign policy, my proposal foresaw the following consequences: We were not to "concern ourselves with the fortunes of other hemispheres," we were to "renounce unattainable and irrelevant missions of world domination," to "give up our Mediterranean aspirations," and to "abandon the financing of South American revolutionaries." Africa should be left in peace; Soviet troops should be withdrawn from Eastern Europe (so that these puppet regimes would be left to face their own people without the support of Soviet divisions); no peripheral nation should be forcibly kept within the bounds of our country; the youth of Russia should be liberated from universal, compulsory military service. As I wrote: "The demands of internal growth are incomparably more important to us, as a people, than the need for any external expansion of our power."

In his *Letter* he notes:

For the next half-century our only genuine military need will be to defend ourselves against China, and it would be better not to go to war with her at all. A well-established Northeast is also our best defense against China [Note: after jettisoning Marxist-Leninist ideology, Solzhenitsyn proposes that Russia shift her energies from promoting world revolution to internal development, primarily in Siberia and northeast Russia.] *No one else on earth* threatens us, and no one is going to attack us. [Emphasis in original.]

Among the epithets too commonly tossed around today is the word "fascist," and Solzhenitsyn, as have other conservatives, has on occasion been labeled as such. As to its applicability to him and his views, Solzhenitsyn seems to mention "fascism" (actually, Naziism) only once in *The Gulag Archipelago,* volume III, where he calls it a "quadruped" comparable to communism. It is noteworthy that in his observation that totalitarianism has come into being "four times" he apparently considers Italian Fascism and German National Socialism in a category with Marxism-Leninism and Maoism. It is worth mentioning that other notable Russians who share Solzhenitsyn's general perspective, including academician I. R. Shafarevich, the author of *The Socialist Phenomenon,* do not consider Fascism and National Socialism as "right-wing" or "conservative" movements (as they are generally regarded in the West) but rather as varieties of left-wing collectivist movements, types of socialism closely akin to communism.

Similarly, I could not find any direct reference to Solzhenitsyn's reputed preference for monarchy as opposed to republicanism. However, in his essay **"Repentance and Self-Limitation in the Life of Nations,"** in *From Under the Rubble,* he characterizes "the whole Petersburg period" in Russia as one of "external greatness, of imperial conceit." He considers that the Imperial Russian government managed "to preserve serfdom for a century or more after it had become unthinkable, keeping the greater part of our own people in a slavery which robbed them of all human dignity." He notes that in "what we may call the neo-Muscovite," *i. e.,* Soviet period, "the conceit of the preceding Petersburg period has become grosser and blinder."

In general, whatever idealization of a previous period of Russian monarchy which may exist seems to be directed toward pre-Petrine Muscovy, which, in his essay **"The Courage to See"** (*Foreign Affairs,* Fall 1980), he terms "the virtual antithesis" of St. Petersburg Russia.

As an illustration, in his view of pre-Petrine Russia Solzhenitsyn speaks favorably of the then-existing proto-parliamentary institution of the Zemskiy Sobor (Assembly of the Land), whose decisions, he says, "while not legally binding on the tsar" were "morally incontestable." The Zemskiy Sobor of 1612, which elected the first Romanov tsar and ended the "Time of Troubles," arranged, according to the historian S. V. Utechin, to meet regularly; at first its members were appointed by various nobility, clergy, and local assemblies, but later they were elected (by whom Utechin does not say). The Zemskiy Sobor as an institution was abolished by Peter the Great. Peter, the founder of Imperial Russia, is viewed negatively by Solzhenitsyn: in **"The Mortal Danger"** he says that "nationally-minded Russians" regard Peter as an "object of censure" and notes that in the popular folklore he was considered "an anti-Christ"; one of Solzhenitsyn's co-contributors to *From Under the Rubble,* the dissident historian Vadim Borisov, calls Peter "the first Russian Nihilist."

In addition to his putative sympathy for "fascism" and "monarchism," there is a common perception that there is something at least vaguely anti-Semitic about Solzhenitsyn. This is somewhat puzzling in that neither Jews nor issues specifically relating to Jews figure prominently in his works, which are mostly, as one might expect, on Russian themes. Such Jewish characters as do exist—for instance Rubin in **The First Circle** (the honest, idealistic Jewish Communist, patterned after Lev Kopelev); the fellow exile identified only as M———z in **The Gulag Archipelago,** volume III; and the "highly intelligent and respected" engineer Ilya Isakovich Arkhangorodsky from **August 1914**—are usually portrayed in a positive light.

It has been suggested that Solzhenitsyn, along with other (usually unidentified) members of what can be loosely described as the Russian patriotic or nationalist movement, "blames" the Revolution and its catastrophic consequences on the Jews, considering it something perpetrated on Russia by non-Russians in general, Jews in particular. However, to the extent that Solzhenitsyn concerns himself with ethnically non-Russian, including Jewish, contributors to the Revolution, his goal seems to be to demonstrate that communism is not an inherently Russian phenomenon—as it is often taken to be—but one which representatives of other peoples had a big part in shaping as well. Nonetheless, in **"Repentance and Self Limitation"** he accepts Russia's collective responsibility for the multimillion death toll of Soviet repression in that country:

> . . . *we, all of us,* Russia herself, were the necessary accomplices. [Emphasis in original.]

Later in the same essay he states:

> This article has not been written to minimize the guilt of the Russian people. Nor, however, to scrape all the guilt from mother earth and load it onto ourselves. True, we were not vaccinated against the plague. True, we lost our heads. True, we gave way, and then caved in altogether. All true. But we have not been the first and only begetters in all this time since the fifteenth century! [The reference to the fifteenth century represents Solzhenitsyn's view that modern totalitarianism is the logical culmination of philosophical trends beginning at that time.]

As Shafarevich, who also contributed to **Rubble,** puts it in his essay "Separation or Reconciliation? The Nationalities Question in the USSR":

> We have all had a hand in creating the problem that now confronts us: the Russian Nihilists, the Ukrainian "Borotbists," the Latvian riflemen and many others have each done their bit. How can we hope, separately, to disentangle the knot we all helped to tighten?

A theme related to the Jews/Revolution question is the extent to which Russian patriotism is inherently anti-Semitic. Michael Agursky, another of the contributors to **Rubble** and a self-described Jewish nationalist now resident in Israel, addressed this issue both generally and with regard to Solzhenitsyn personally in the article "Russian Isolationism and Communist Expansion" in the journal *Russia:*

> But no matter what the Russian roots of the revolution were like, not only anti-semites and monarchists have pointed to the mass Jewish participation in the revolution. . . .

But many Russian nationalists, including Solzhenitsyn himself, occupy a position in the question of the participation of Jewish revolutionaries in the Russian revolution which scarcely differs from that of Zionism, calling for Jews to refuse to participate in social movements in other countries and to devote themselves to the building of their own national home. Many Jews had a heavy presentiment of what the Trotskys, Zinovyevs and Sverdlovs would lead the Jews to in Russia.

Not without reason does Solzhenitsyn, who has been falsely accused of anti-semitism, relate sympathetically to Zionism and to the State of Israel, and he has spoken out on this problem many times. And for me this is much more important than his attitude towards the Jewish and non-Jewish revolutionaries and leaders of the Soviet state in its first period.

Notwithstanding his favorable attitude toward Israel and Zionism, Solzhenitsyn has been criticized for not being more concerned with the question of Jewish emigration:

> How can the problems of any major country be reduced to the issue of who is allowed to depart from it? (from **"Mortal Danger"**)

Solzhenitsyn's determination to view events from a specifically Russian perspective no doubt has an influence here; his concern, like charity, begins at home: *his* religion persecuted, *his* nation stagnating demographically. That is, he seems to have no objection to Jews' reasserting their Jewish identity, and he would certainly encourage them to do so. But his duty, as a Russian, is to be primarily concerned with Russia and Russians. He rejects the notion that Russian patriotism may be manipulated by the Soviet regime for evil purposes:

> But then the Soviet authorities also try to exploit the Jewish emigration from the U. S. S. R. in order to fan the flames of anti-Semitism, and not without success. ("See that? They're the only ones allowed to escape from this hell, and the West sends goods to pay for it!") Does it follow that we are entitled to advise Jews to forgo the quest for their spiritual and national origins? Of course not. Are we not all entitled to live our natural life on the earth and to strive toward our individual goals, without heed for what others may think or what the papers may write, and without worrying about the dark forces that may attempt to exploit those goals for their own ends? (from **"Mortal Danger"**)

Finally, it should not be ignored that the Soviet regime, trying to discredit Russian patriotism, has since the mid-1970s itself attempted to foster the notion that Solzhenitsyn is an anti-Semite. However, prior to this (in 1971–1973), they had attempted to give the impression that Solzhenitsyn was himself Jewish:

> There was a time when they happily made play with my patronymic, Isayevich. They would say, trying to seem casual: "Incidentally, his real name is Solzheni*tser* or Solzheni*tsker;* not, of course, that this is of any importance in our

country." (from the memoir *The Oak and The Calf*)

Later,

> . . . the *racial* line was again revived. Or more precisely, the Jewish line. A special major of state security named Blagovidov rushed off to check the personal files of all the "Isaakii's" in the archives of Moscow University for 1914 in the hope of proving that I was Jewish. . . .

> Alas, the racist researchers were thwarted: I turned out to be a Russian. (from *The Oak and The Calf*)

But by the time the Russian writer Vladimir Voinovich was called in for a "chat" with the KGB in mid-1975, the line had changed:

> From Marchenko we switch to Solzhenitsyn. In my letter to the Writers' Union I had called him a very great citizen. But they find he is not a very great citizen. He is a bad man and an anti-Semite (VV's note: "Previously he was counted a Jew.") to boot. And in general his ideas—orthodoxy, autocracy, national character—well, all doors are shut to these nowadays. [from "Incident at the Metropole (Facts Resembling a Detective Story)," in *Kontinent 2*]

In addition to the allegation of anti-Semitism—as if the KGB were in a position to call anyone anti-Semitic—it is interesting to note the references to "autocracy" and "national character," which are likewise absent from Solzhenitsyn's writings. One is tempted to wonder to what extent the attribution of certain views to Solzhenitsyn derives ultimately from KGB sources.

In conclusion, it does not appear that there is anything in Solzhenitsyn's views which is specifically incompatible with democratic principles or with "the autonomy of the individual" and the protection of "civil and political liberties." In addition, many of the negative characterizations commonly attributed to him appear to be groundless.

It is still to be explained, then, why his detractors, particularly liberal detractors, view him so negatively. No doubt Solzhenitsyn's indictment of the West's weakness is a discomfort to those who have devoted their professional lives to making it weak, an endeavor in which liberals have been at least as active as conservatives during these past thirty years of declining American power. Similarly, far too many liberals regard the idea of active resistance to communism as some sort of dangerous provocation, a threat to "peace."

However, there seems to be more to it. No one who has made an honest examination of Solzhenitsyn's works could find in them any indication of "fascism," "anti-Semitism," or the like. Rather, these characterizations have all the appearance of having been thrown up as diversions from what one suspects is the true reason liberals dislike Solzhenitsyn: the fact that the power of his vision and the values that embody it expose the hollowness of contemporary liberalism. Indeed, even Solzhenitsyn's attacks on communism are a source of discomfort, for most liberals know, or at least understand instinctively, that they

and the Communists ultimately worship at the altar of the same secular pantheon: Man, Progress, Reason, among other gods. They both seek to build the same earthly paradise; they differ only in their methodology. Solzhenitsyn's reminder that man and society cannot survive without God, that the twentieth century has become a slaughterhouse precisely because "men have forgotten God," is anathema to them. And because they are unable to refute him, they slander him.

And perhaps this should not come as a surprise. As the Romans said: *Veritas odium parit.* Truth purchaseth hatred. (pp. 143-52)

> *James George Jatras, "Solzhenitsyn and the Liberals," in* Modern Age, *Vol. 29, No. 2, Spring, 1985, pp. 143-52.*

Un-chol Shin   (essay date Fall 1985)

[*In the following essay, Shin traces Solzhenitsyn's treatment in* The First Circle *of the relationship between the human conscience and the threat of physical punishment for telling the truth in the former Soviet Union.*]

The Haunting Choice: to live with power, women, and money by concealing truth, or to be arrested and possibly to die in prison by revealing truth. Innokenty Volodin, state counselor second rank of Soviet Russia, is caught in this ethical dilemma at the beginning of Solzhenitsyn's *The First Circle.* He is a young diplomat who knows that in a few days he will be assigned to a new post in Paris. As an official working in the Ministry of Foreign Affairs, he also knows the government's secret plan to trap an innocent man, Dr. Dobroumov, who happens to be a family friend. Should he telephone his friend and expose this secret or not? This question has captivated him for several hours. It is a matter of conscience.

Having been brought up in the Soviet system and carefully shielded from so-called outcast books, Innokenty Volodin had believed until recently that pity and compassion were shameful emotions. In recent years, however, he had discovered that something was lacking in himself, and that "something" finally assumed a more precise identity a few days before while he was reading the diaries of his deceased mother. The diaries seemed to speak directly to him: "Pity is the first action of a good soul. . . . What is the most precious thing in the world? Not to participate in injustice. . . . You also have only one conscience. And just as you cannot recover a lost life, you cannot recover a wrecked conscience." This awareness of conscience makes Volodin realize that he cannot ignore the injustice of the trap intended for Dr. Dobroumov and that he should save the life of the innocent man despite the danger to his own life. Thus he comes to believe that one cannot "remain a human being" without conscience.

In the same novel readers find another character who holds Volodin's view on conscience: Gleb Nerzhin. Actually Nerzhin is the main character and is often identified with Solzhenitsyn himself. Toward the end of *The First Circle* Nerzhin defines his perceptions of conscience:

> I had no idea what good and evil were, and

whatever was allowed seemed fine to me. But the lower I sink into this inhumanly cruel world the more I respond to those who, even in such a world, speak to my conscience.

As their subsequent actions reveal, both Volodin and Nerzhin are willing to experience physical suffering in order to live according to their consciences. For both characters it is conscience that enables them to live as human beings. Solzhenitsyn does not define exactly what conscience is, nor does he even question where it originates. He is neither a philosopher nor a theologian. As a novelist he believes out of his own experience that "convictions based on conscience are as infallible as the internal rhythm of the heart." He thinks that conscience is a moral quality "inherent" in the human heart, a moral quality that must be awakened and polished, however. For those who take it seriously, conscience provides a tremendously strong inner force that asserts the meaning of life even in unendurable situations. On the other hand, unfortunately, conscience can be repressed or totally denied in the minds of those who never seriously acknowledge the meaning of human life. Until he read his mother's diaries, Volodin's conscience was dormant. Once awakened, though, it rebelled against injustice.

Solzhenitsyn with press photographers outside his house in Stapfer-strasse, Zurich, Spring 1974.

According to Solzhenitsyn, in *The First Circle* as well as in his other writings, conscience is a moral quality that basically works in an individual's mind and leads him to a sense of justice. When injustice is accompanied by overwhelming political power, so that an innocent man is arrested, what can make the man "stronger than the whole trap?" Solzhenitsyn's answer is this: only his "spirit and conscience remain precious and important" to him, and when "confronted by such a prisoner, the interrogator will tremble." How can a man who has lost nearly all things on earth, including his family and friends, make injustice tremble? Solzhenitsyn sees the answer in one's consciousness of spirit and of conscience. By placing conscience on the same level as spirit, Solzhenitsyn treats the moral quality of conscience as a spiritual quality that arms one to fight even the most severe injustice.

Conscience and injustice are integrated concepts in Solzhenitsyn. For example, in his *Letter to Three Students,* Solzhenitsyn explains their interdependence:

> There is nothing relative about justice, as there is nothing relative about conscience. Indeed justice is conscience, not a personal conscience but conscience of the whole of humanity. Those who clearly recognize the voice of their own conscience usually recognize also the voice of justice. I consider that in all questions, social or historical, justice will always suggest a way to act (or judge) which will not conflict with our conscience.

Examined carefully, this statement reveals conscience and justice as axiomatically absolute: conscience is related to the personal whereas justice is related to the social and "the whole of humanity." Thus, an individually conscientious man can be a socially just man without any internal conflicts. In Solzhenitsyn's philosophy there is no wall between the individual and society. Although he does not in this particular statement indicate a priority between them, his strong opposition to the collective value of Marxism obviously indicates his preference for the individual over society. Thus, consciousness of the individual conscience is a prerequisite to social justice, a view clearly demonstrated in Solzhenitsyn's sketches of individuals such as Shukhov in *One Day in the Life of Ivan Denisovich,* Matryona in *Matryona's House,* and Spiridon in *The First Circle.*

Another of Solzhenitsyn's tenets is that before individuals respond to their personal conscience, they first need to be conscious of it. Among the individuals portrayed in his novels and short stories, Solzhenitsyn depicts different degrees of awareness of conscience and of the individual responses to it. Unfortunately, in a Communist state like the Soviet Union individuals are not allowed to seek any personal meaning for their lives; and thus innate qualities such as conscience and spirit are intentionally (or rationally) denied. Therefore, the majority of the followers of communism try, or pretend, not to be conscious of conscience; and although some do gain such consciousness, they have either to deny it or to ignore it. Since conscience is innate, their denial of it is therefore tantamount to the denial of their inner lives. Can one be a human being without recognizing one's own inner life? Solzhenitsyn does not believe so. For instance, in *The First Circle* Kondrashev says, "A human being possesses from his birth a certain essence, the nucleus, as it were, of this human being. His 'I.' " As an inherent quality, conscience is for Solzhenitsyn this very "certain essence." When a person denies consciousness of this "essence," he is not a human being. He is no different from an animal. Thus Solzhenitsyn often compares Stalin's followers to dogs. The denial of this innately human quality is more conspicuous among rationally oriented intellectual Communists such as Rubin in *The First Circle* and Rusanov in *Cancer Ward.* Solzhenitsyn, however, finds evidence of unpolished conscience among peasants.

Solzhenitsyn's fiction, however, does not idealize peasants. He discovered personally during World War II that peasants, without intellectual guidelines, act instinctively for the most part according to the principle of self-preservation. And yet Solzhenitsyn is attracted to peasants for their simple lives in which they appear to have "retained and not perverted their human nature, as much of the intelligentsia has done."

Nerzhin's compassion for Spiridon in *The First Circle,* for example, is generated by his discovery of that essence of human nature in Spiridon. Nerzhin asks Spiridon:

> After all, life changes, doesn't it? I mean, if a person can't always be sure that he is right then how can he act? Is it conceivable that any human being on earth can really tell who is right and who is wrong? Who can be sure about this?

And to this philosophically relativistic question, Spiridon replies readily, "I will tell you: the wolf-hound is right and the cannibal is wrong." Nerzhin, who is "struck by the simplicity and force of the answer," now realizes that Spiridon's sense of right and wrong as a peasant is deeply based on that inherent quality of a human being—his conscience—not on an intellectually indoctrinated ideology. Spiridon is half-blind and cannot read. On June 15, 1970, in protesting the government policy on censorship, Solzhenitsyn warned:

> The lawless, the evildoers, must remember that there is a limit beyond which a man becomes a cannibal! It is short-sighted to think that one can live by constantly relying on force alone, constantly ignoring the protests of conscience.

Adherence to conscience by peasants is more vividly portrayed in Shukhov's life in *One Day in the Life of Ivan Denisovich.* With all the hardship and physical sufferings he has to endure every day under the freezing temperature of the labor camp, Shukhov never takes a bribe, and he willingly helps other prisoners. Similarly, the conscientious life of Matryona, a peasant, is impressively described in *Matryona's House.* No one can deny that these are righteous people. "Without them," Solzhenitsyn concludes at the end of *Matryona's House,* "no city can stand. Neither can the whole world." In other words, without people of conscience, no human society can stand, nor can the whole world of mankind stand.

A counterpart to his theme of conscience is Solzhenitsyn's personification of dishonesty and deceit. Compared with

Nerzhin's constant search for truth and Volodin's self-criticism in search of conscience, for instance, Stalin is portrayed in *The First Circle* as the epigone of the Grand Inquisitor. The seventy-year-old dictator thinks of himself as the greatest benefactor of humanity ever born. Doubting that Christ ever existed, he regards himself as the Omnipotent and the Immortal. Even at that age, he refuses to believe that he is getting old, not trusting the doctor's report. Believing that he is the only benevolent leader who can bring the Communist ideal of total happiness to all mankind, this character cannot die because he does not know "in whose care" he can leave humanity.

In describing Solzhenitsyn's portrait of Stalin, Vladislav Krasnov illustrates numerous satanic elements in this character, in many ways paralleling Dostoevsky's Grand Inquisitor: "Satan who spoke through the Grand Inquisitor in Dostoevsky's novel [*The Brothers Karamazov*] now appears to be speaking through Stalin." In fact, the deceptive nature of Satan as a great liar is found everywhere in Solzhenitsyn's descriptions of Stalin's self-concept, lifestyle, and relationships with his subordinates.

Stalin's self-concept is simply a self-deception. Denying that he is growing old and that he will die indicates his desire to deny reality. Even resigning himself to eventual death, he thinks that he will die as "the greatest of the Great, without equal in the history of the earth." He even fantasizes that people will build a monument to him on the peak of "Mount Kazbek and another on Mount Elbrus—so that his head would always be above the clouds."

> Suddenly he stopped.
>
> And up there? Higher? He had no equals, of course, but if there, up there. . . .

Aspiring to be man-god, Stalin subscribes to an absolute dogmatism which does not allow him to respect anyone else on earth. He has low respect for people who he believes cannot govern themselves, a point on which he disagrees with Lenin. He thinks that every cook is a cook and every housewife a housewife, so that their participation in meetings of the provincial executive committee is unthinkable. As for a cook, "Her job is to prepare dinner. As for governing people, that's high calling." He does not trust anyone. Solzhenitsyn summarizes his character with "Mistrust was his world view," and then describes him in more detail:

> He had not trusted his mother. And he has not trusted that God before whom he had bowed his head to the stone floor for eleven years of his youth. Later he did not trust his own fellow Party members, especially those who spoke well. He did not trust his fellow exiles. He did not trust the peasants to sow grain and reap harvest unless they were coerced and their work was regularly checked on. He did not trust workers to work unless production norms were set for them. He did not trust members of the intelligentsia not to commit sabotage. He did not trust soldiers and generals to fight without the threat of penalty regiments and machine guns in their rear. He did not trust his intimates. He did not trust his wives and mistresses. He did not trust

his children. And he always turned out to be right.

Stalin's disrespect for and mistrust of people and officials increase his suspicion about the motivations for their actions and thus intensify his use of terrorism in ruling them. General Abakumov, minister of State Security, knows this fact very well. In his meeting with Stalin at 2:30 in the morning he is afraid of telling the truth on the secret telephone project he now supervises under Stalin's order. One mistake means the end of Abakumov's life; and if asked about it, he has no choice but to tell a lie. As the head of State Security he knows better than anyone else that his government poses no obstacles to arresting and killing people. Thus, Abakumov resorts to lies and pretentions as the safest and most efficient way to survive personally and to get anything approved through Stalin's office. At one point, waiting to meet Stalin in the hallway, Abakumov asks Stalin's secretary what the leader's mood is. Even during his meeting with Stalin, he has a constant feeling of fear; and he knows that it is essential to respond immediately to his questions because Stalin interprets "any kind of hesitation as a confirmation of . . . evil thoughts."

Ironically but consistently, Abakumov's relations with his own subordinates are no different from Stalin's: he too is suspicious of his subordinates' answers. Demanding from them the completion date of the secret project, he says, "Don't lie. I don't like lies." There is no mutual trust among these Communist leaders at all.

According to Solzhenitsyn's description, trust is the last thing that concerns officials in the Soviet government. Submission of reports on time seems to be more important than reporting the truth, and the end result is always more important than the means. The government does not care how many innocent citizens are arrested to find one criminal. Even in the case of detecting the person who telephoned Dr. Dobroumov's house, the authorities arrest six or seven suspects. After they find that those suspects are the wrong ones, instead of releasing them, they still attempt "to pin the case on one of them." The concern of the authorities, then, is not to find the real criminal. Rather, their chief concern is their own promotions and winning of prizes, selfish goals pursued through lies and the arrest of innocent people. In fact, Solzhenitsyn calls the three subordinates of Abakumov "the troika of liars," a chapter title in *The First Circle;* and this chapter vividly describes the deceptive nature of the operation of the Soviet security system.

David M. Halperin, in his article "The Role of the Lie in *The First Circle*," [in *Alexandr Solzhenitsyn: Critical Essays and Documentary Essays,* ed. Dunlop, et al.], makes the following observation:

> In *The First Circle* Solzhenitsyn examines both the omnipresence of lying as a demonstrable feature of Soviet society and as a metaphysical, demonic device. By uniting these two aspects of the Lie, he has effectively forged his central metaphor—Hell; for it is from Stalin just as from the devil that lies emanate to poison a whole society.

Halperin's interpretation is so true that anyone reading *The First Circle* cannot avoid discovering how the lie can

be institutionalized as a political system. In the three volumes of *The Gulag Archipelago,* Solzhenitsyn untiringly discloses various functions of the lie in the Soviet government; *The First Circle* portrays just one case of several dozen included in that monumental work.

Since individual Soviet citizens do not have freedom to speak openly against government policies, Solzhenitsyn's fiction seems to depict the entire nation as a prison. Ironically, Nerzhin finds more freedom for exchanging opinions and thoughts in Mavrino, the special Soviet prison established after World War II to house scientist-prisoners so that the government might use their skills as well as their brains. At least in prison, in contrast with Soviet society at large, the prisoners are free to speak since they have already lost their freedom and need not be afraid of losing more. Most of them, like Nerzhin, are innocent prisoners, known as "zeks," arrested by Stalin for their conscientious actions. They know that what they read in books and newspapers and what they hear through communication media from the so-called free society outside Mavrino are lies and propaganda. Thus, in the gigantic system that protects the deceptive figure of the satanic Stalin and his policies, one can hardly distinguish between truth and lies. Solzhenitsyn reflected upon this fact in a 1975 speech to an American audience: "When so many lies have accumulated over the decades, we forget the radical and basic lie which is not on the leaves of the tree but at its very roots."

The imagery of lie is just as vivid, with two elements in particular symbolizing deception in *The First Circle:* the Mavrino buildings and the orange and blue van that carries the prisoners through the streets of Moscow. The buildings were once an old church and a seminary, and the government must have been afraid of revealing to the public that they are now being used as a prison. Family visits with the prisoners are not held at Mavrino; the prisoners are transported to other prisons for these visits. Even the van that moves the prisoners through the streets is symbolic of this deception. Written on its side are names of foods, advertisements prompting a French correspondent to write in his notebook:

> On the streets of Moscow one often sees vans filled with foodstuffs, very neat and hygienically impeccable. One can only conclude that the provisioning of the capital is excellent.

These symbols emphasize that in the materialistic sense of Marxism, human beings, like these prisoners, can be no more than mere meat since their spiritual element is not recognized. Solzhenitsyn challenges this ideology. To him a human being is a human being regardless of his status as long as he possesses "the essence," the innate quality with which he was born. He cannot be reduced to a thing or to an animal. For example, Nerzhin's skepticism about Stalin and the Soviet ideology is traceable back to his adolescence. He can accept neither the deterministic theory of communism nor the lies of Stalin. Even in prison, in spite of the prison officer's offer of his early release, Nerzhin refuses to cooperate with Stalin's subordinates in a project that would eventually harm innocent people. Contrary to the Communist dictum, he believes that circumstance should not dictate his consciousness. His consciousness is dictated by his own conscience. Because of his conscience Nerzhin is finally sent away to a northern labor camp. Symbolically, then, he is moved down to a lower hell, since Mavrino is the first circle of Dante's hell. Nevertheless, Nerzhin cannot give up his spirit and conscience because he would rather suffer in hell and die as a human being than live in a deceptive society and die as an animal.

Woven into the interdependent themes of conscience and the lie is Solzhenitsyn's complicated portrayal of suffering. Three levels of suffering are depicted in *The First Circle:* physical, psychological, and spiritual. Compared with his other major novels such as *One Day in the Life of Ivan Denisovich, Cancer Ward,* and *The Gulag Archipelago, The First Circle* has the least description of physical suffering. Prisoners in Mavrino, for example, no less than scientists in the general populace, are well fed and supplied with technical and professional journals appropriate for their work. Their fingers are not frozen, and they have meat at dinner. They live in the special first circle of Dante's hell. They are at Mavrino not for physical but primarily for mental work. Nerzhin's cutting wood in the chilly morning, in fact, is not forced labor but rather voluntary work to preserve his physical condition. In contrast, the most shuddering scenes of physical suffering in *The First Circle* occur when Volodin is arrested and interrogated at the Lubyanka Prison in Moscow. Still, physical suffering is the last significant category of suffering in this novel.

Nerzhin and his inmate friends, however, do experience significant psychological suffering. Separated from their families for several years and without much hope of being released in the near future, the majority of the prisoners are indifferent to one another as they struggle for daily survival. Among them some are opportunistically trying to gain more favorable treatment from the prison officials. Among the few who have not lost their psychological vivacity, there is one prisoner, Rubin, who still believes in the superiority of communism; he thinks that his imprisonment by Stalin must certainly be some mistake. Every year he pleads with the authorities for reconsideration. Gradually, however, through conversations with other inmates, he comes to realize the flaws of communism. Even though the flaws become clear in his mind, he is afraid of confronting his conscience and admitting them publicly. Another prisoner, Sologdin, stands in clear opposition to Rubin's view. He is a man of strong will, exceptional strength, and vitality. Sologdin even commits adultery with a female employee of the prison. He rejects Rubin's confidence in the philosophy of communism and takes the opposite view, which emphasizes self-centered individualism. Nevertheless, when he is offered an early release if he cooperates with the prison authorities, Sologdin deceives himself and accepts. Thus Solzhenitsyn dramatizes that preserving psychological integrity in prison life is very difficult.

Among the 281 inmates only a few overcome the psychological anguish and preserve their personal integrity. Gleb Nerzhin and the prison artist Kondrashev are two of them. How do they maintain their integrity? With their belief in the human spirit. The physical and psychological suffering of prison life forges their spirit rather than breaks it. Solzhenitsyn demonstrates in this novel that only spirit can overcome suffering. He believes that every human being needs to possess this spirit so that, even in this age of terrorism and violence, he can still live with dignity and with love for his fellow man.

Solzhenitsyn believes that the human spirit is forged through physical and psychological suffering, a process that can be understood only by understanding the spiritual meaning of any suffering. Solzhenitsyn's fiction relates the meaning of human suffering to the preservation of the human spirit, a concept closely related to the complementary themes of the conscience, acting against injustice, and the lie. The metaphysical meaning of human suffering must be understood in terms of the tension between conscience and lie in order to achieve a full appreciation of this novel.

The First Circle dramatizes the tension between conscience and lie prevalent not only in the Soviet Union but also in all other authoritarian nations. When political and social power is in the hands of liars who have the privilege of exercising violence and terrorism, the obvious victims are the innocent. And why do the innocent suffer? A perennial question in human history, it is a harsh paradox. Without the suffering of the innocent, however, very little in human history would be worthy of respect. In this novel the innocent suffer, and conscience is violated by terrorism. Volodin is arrested, and his interrogation is horrifying and hideous. Nerzhin, in his fifth year in prison, is sent to Siberia or an Arctic labor camp where he can hardly expect to survive. What is the meaning of these sufferings?

This fundamental question in Solzhenitsyn's writings is related to his belief that a man is not born merely to live. All animals are born to live, but what makes a human being different is that he chooses to live *humanly.* A human being is compelled to realize "how to live" as the ultimate concern. For prisoners, to "survive by whatever means" seems an instinctive order to themselves, and it is true that their desire to survive is more acute and desperate than that of anyone living in free society. And yet Solzhenitsyn asks: "Survive! At any price?" Survival should not be "at the price of someone else." Then, with deep passion, he concludes, "It is not the result that counts! It is not the result—but the spirit! Not *what*—but *how*." His message is clear: the idea valued only for its result is a lie.

In Solzhenitsyn's view, "the spirit" and "how" are identical. The spirit, like conscience, allows a man to be a reflective and critical being. With spirit man is autonomous. Thus, Solzhenitsyn's moral man cannot accept any deterministic ideology that attempts to break the spirit. Clearly this view poses a direct confrontation between the moral man and the totalitarian system of Soviet communism.

Under Stalin the intention of Soviet communism was to eliminate any individual critical of government policies. Human beings were simply tools working for goals set by Stalin and supported by the communist ideology. Whoever resisted being a tool in this system was arrested and imprisoned as a forced laborer. Solzhenitsyn himself was arrested, as was Nerzhin in *The First Circle.* Since violence and terrorism were part of the state system, a moral man within this system could not avoid suffering. This suffering was fundamentally and necessarily the human act of refusing to be a "thing."

In *The First Circle* Gleb Nerzhin obviously cannot accept the deterministic theory of communism. He is a skeptic, but not a pessimistic one. In his response to the young prisoner Ruska, Nerzhin says:

> "No matter how clever and absolute the systems of skepticism or agnosticism or pessimism, you must understand that by their very nature they doom us to a loss of will. They can't really influence human behavior because people cannot stand still. And that means they can't renounce systems which affirm something, which summon them to advance in some direction. . . . I personally believe that people seriously need skepticism. It's needed to split the rockheads. To choke fanatical voices. But skepticism can never provide firm ground under a man's feet. And perhaps, after all, we need firm ground."

In Nerzhin's mind it is clear that one needs, but must also go beyond, skepticism. Why? "Because people cannot stand still." As long as they live and have blood and feeling and the desire to live humanly, there have to be "systems which affirm something," a firm foundation, a firm ground on which a human being can stand. Ruska, as a young man, once had high hope; but that hope was overwhelmed by the winds of society. Circumstance now controls his consciousness until he is imprisoned and becomes a pessimistic skeptic. But Nerzhin advises Ruska not to lose hope, but to search for the meaning of life—advice implying that, without the ground of personal conscience, one can be blown away by the winds of social circumstances. To struggle against the winds causes suffering, but one cannot give up the ground because the ground gives meaning to one's life.

The symbolic meaning of human life and this "ground" of the conscientious spirit is vividly described in Kondrashev's painting "The Maimed Oak." Following his wife's visit, Nerzhin stops to see Kondrashev, the prison painter, at his studio. There Nerzhin finds a six-foot-high painting, disdained by the officials at Mavrino, but impressive to Nerzhin. He describes it with a sense of awe:

> It showed a solitary oak which grew with mysterious power on the naked face of a cliff, where a perilous trail wound upward along the crag. What hurricanes had blown here! How they had bent that oak! And the skies behind the tree and all around were eternally storm-swept. These skies could never have known the sun. This stubborn, angular tree with its clawing roots, with its branches broken and twisted, deformed by combat with the tireless winds trying to tear it from the cliff, refused to quit the battle and perilously clung to its place over the abyss.

In this painting, Nerzhin observes that the spirit of the maimed oak in refusing "to quit the battle" with "the tireless winds" is like a human being stubbornly refusing to lose the battle against the terrorism of the Soviet Union. This act of refusal, which characterizes the suffering of the stubborn and conscientious man, embodies the growth of a "mysterious power."

Solzhenitsyn's description of the painting emphasizes symbolically that the conscientious man, like the maimed oak, cannot lose the battle; and the mysterious power growing within him brings him dignity. For the one who suffers because of conscience, to win the battle is important. But more important is it to recognize that mysterious power that helps a man survive as a human being. Without this recognition one cannot survive humanly. The significance of suffering is found in a man's consciousness of that power—that power of spirit, conscience, and "the essence" forged from whatever suffering a man experiences.

For Solzhenitsyn suffering is an opportunity through which a man can test his spirit. When a man is imbued with that mysterious inner power that grows stronger as he refuses to compromise, he becomes too honest to lie even when it seems he should. When human beings stop lying, there will be no violence and terrorism in the world, the ideal world Solzhenitsyn dreams about. The author knows, however, that this world of individual and societal imperfections is far from realizing his ideal. Until mankind arrives at this insight wherein conscience overcomes the lie, suffering will be the inevitable path that the man of conscience must follow. In the thematic complexities of *The First Circle* Solzhenitsyn personifies his somber philosophy through vividly memorable characters and their perceptions of the world in which they struggle. To live humanly is a heavy burden that one cannot easily relinquish—for it is very difficult to be a human being—but to

---

János Rózsás relates memories of Solzhenitsyn during their internment at Ekhibastuz, Kazakhstan:

As I recall, Solzhenitsyn never talked about himself, his childhood or youth, and he did not even mention his earlier prison and camp experiences. Anyway, it was not customary in the camp to question others about their past, and particularly the circumstances of their sentence, if they themselves did not speak about it.

Solzhenitsyn was particularly reticent in this respect. Whatever I knew about his life I have learned from his works which have appeared in print, mainly *The Gulag Archipelago.* As regards his character and behaviour, there is no contradiction between the solzhenitsyn as he appears in the pages of his books and the solzhenitsyn I came to know. But I would never have thought that Solzhenitsyn, always so polite, helpful and smiling, had the resolution and prophetic vocation he displayed in later years.

Only once, on a single occasion did I notice the burning passion that animated him, when he recited a poem by Aleksandr Blok to me. Blood rose to his head, his eyes flashed, and the frail, thin man shook his fist.

János Rózsás, in his "In the Gulag with Solzhenitsyn,"
The New Hungarian Quarterly, *1990.*

grow into truth through suffering is the purest good attainable for the human conscience. (pp. 344-52)

Un-chol Shin, "Conscience, Lie and Suffering in Solzhenitsyn's 'The First Circle'," in Modern Age, Vol. 29, No. 4, Fall, 1985, pp. 344-52.

Nicholas Lee   (essay date 1986)

[In the following essay, Lee analyzes Solzhenitsyn's treatment of female characters in August 1914 as a paradoxical metaphor for stasis and change.]

Since *August 1914* resembles *War and Peace* in so many ways, comparisons between the female fictional characters in both novels have been inevitable. Those who find Solzhenitsyn's women no more than blurred copies of Tolstoy's fail to discern that Solzhenitsyn's historical narrative is different both in kind and in degree from its prototype, not only much bulkier, but also much more inherently complex. The greater number and variety of female fictional characters in the narrative, and the inclusion of women who actually played a part in Russian history, are pivotal manifestations of this complexity. Moreover, several female characters in the first version of *August 1914,* [*August chetyrnadisatogo* (1971); this will be cited in the text as A.; all translations are Lee's, from the original Russian.] have been developed more extensively in the revision that has appeared under the title *Krasnoe koleso* (*The Red Wheel*), which designates the whole cycle of novels centering around the October Revolution [*Krasnoe koleso: povestvovanie v otmerennykh srokakh. Uzel I, August chetyrnadisatogo,* 2 vols. (1983); this will be cited in the text as B I and B II. All translations are Lee's, from the original Russian.]. I am here concerned only with the fictional characters in both versions, since the first contains no women who figured in Russian history.

At the most basic level, the feminine spontaneously materializes in the male imagination as an incompletely differentiated magical projection of sexual desire. In this form a SHE figures in a dream that interrupts Colonel Vorotyntsev's brief sleep in the warm bed of a cottage in Prussia, during a respite from his efforts to save Russia's Second Army (A). The dream is lit from an unknown source that shows only what he needs to see—the partial vision of a female face with an expression on it, and breasts. This SHE he had never expected to find, whose unbidden appearance surprises him, has other logically contradictory, paradoxical features characteristic of dream figures. In *1914* B he experiences "sharp, sharp tenderness." SHE is the one he needs most, but is nothing more substantial than "the one who replaces all beautiful women, the whole female world." He recognizes HER instantly, though he has never seen HER in his life, and HER eyes and clothing have no color, yet he also feels their relationship is of long standing, its passion accepted by mutual consent. Without pronouncing a single audible word, they understand each other instantly.

Once awake, Vorotyntsev himself ponders the inconsistencies of his dream. In *1914* A it drowns them both in the joy of having found each other, yet later he wonders just who SHE might be, unaware that he had even been searching for anyone, and certain that he never indulged in sexual fantasies. What strikes him is not so much the fact that SHE has been "invented by a dream," but that the dream itself produces in him a vivid intensity of sensation he thought had died in him and did not feel in his waking hours.

The culmination of the dream is later interpreted as a sort of prophetic foreshadowing. At the outset of the war Vorotyntsev is already disenchanted after eight years of cloudless happiness with his wife Alina, and in the course of *October 1916* he embarks on a passionate affair with Ol'da Andozerskaya, the professor of medieval Western history at the Bestuzhev women's university in Petrograd, briefly glimpsed at the end of *August 1914.* During one of their amorous interludes he recounts his dream at the front to Andozerskaya and insists she is the SHE of his nocturnal vision. The end of the SHE dream sequence suggests changes in the way Solzhenitsyn has decided to treat Vorotyntsev's personal life as *Krasnoe koleso* has evolved over the years. In *1914* A the dream moves rapidly toward coitus, with only one delay. SHE hesitates to turn down the covers of the bed they are to share, and when he does so, under the pillow he finds Alina's nightdress, lacy and pink, the only colored object he observes. The sudden recollection that Alina exists and stands in their way is instantly set aside: "He sensed no hindrance: without any tenderness for this finely woven pink nightdress, without regret or hesitation, he took it out—and it was no longer in his hand, it had melted. And the bed was immediately ready. And there was nothing that got in the way any more." This version of the scene culminates with them clasped naked in each other's arms, inundated by the "boundless joy" of having found each other. When Vorotyntsev finds his wife's nightdress in *1914* B, however, "in bitter anguish he understood that for him and *her* there was no place, and he would lose her immediately. And in the last moments, with all the strength in his arms and legs he enfolded her tighter and tighter, inundated by love." The waking ruminations about the dream are the same in both versions, suggesting that whatever happens later between Vorotyntsev and Andozerskaya, he is little concerned with women at the outset of the Prussian campaign. The sensual lethargy that follows his dream he condemns as "the sinful weakness of the flesh," adding in *1914* A, "they compare it with death—and these sensations are close," while *1914* B has a briefer, somber "what is this—the way you feel just before death?"

As Vorotyntsev reviews his married life in his mind, he reveals how much of his attitude to the real woman who is his wife has been shaped by the same fantasy projection of himself that dominated in the dream about HER. Meeting Alina at a time in his life when he was ready to marry, he decided he wanted her as rapidly and categorically as he wanted the HER of his dream. The details of his courtship in *1914* A are meager: "from the first step he took toward her to kiss her hand, from the first word they spoke, he decided: here she is!—this is the one! There is no sense in measuring her against others, comparing, looking around—this is the only woman in the world for me, created especially for me." The text of *1914* B adds, "(he always knew instantly what he wanted and what was right)."

The version in *1914* B suggests psychological obstacles to marital stability that predate Alina in Vorotyntsev's life. He himself marvels at his rapid success in finding a wonderful wife despite his military preoccupations and ambitions: ". . . he should have been unlucky in marriage, like so many, but he had been lucky!" While still a student, he had been warned by General Levachev, the comanding officer at the Aleksandrovskii Military Academy, against marrying too early: ". . . in the advancement to top military positions there should be something monkish." These words confirm Vorotyntsev's childhood conviction that Duty is always more important than Love, and his adult practice of paying no attention to love.

Vorotyntsev agrees with General Levachev's advice in part because of unhappy childhood experiences. Aware that his parents were unhappily married, ". . . he sensed the drab joylessness and desperation of family life— perhaps in every family? Perhaps family life could develop in no other way?" Unable to console his mother, he avidly absorbs the mournful music she constantly plays on the piano and her teaching that a man should always treat a woman with chivalrous respect, using the excess of his strength to raise her above the cruelty of a world she lacks the power to overcome. Alina turns out to be suitable both physically and musically: slender and vivacious, she has just the sort of smile he expected to find in his future wife, and she plays the same Chopin piano mazurkas as his mother did. The parallel between wife and mother implies the possibility of a similar parallel between son and father with respect to marital happiness.

Vorotyntsev's disaffection with a marriage that has survived the strains of his higher education, lack of money, and an undesirable assignment to a remote outpost, occurs when he returns to Moscow in a high staff position. At a time when his work absorbs him more totally than ever before, she starts making demands of her own, which he realizes he is both unable and unwilling to satisfy. He knows she is right in accusing him of indifference to others, attacks of gloom, and self-absorption, but however justified her rebukes, they leave a bad aftertaste. He resigns himself fatalistically to the loss of the poetry in marriage that comes with the ebbing of desire, described a little more explicitly in *1914* A than in *1914* B: ". . . inevitably every love grows fibrous, every marriage grows tired. Evidently that was the way it had to be."

Alina appears once more later on, still a figment of her husband's imagination, as he prepares himself psychologically for the possibility of death in battle. At this moment of naked need he feels pity for her, gratitude for her self-sacrifice, and determination to be a better husband in the future. In *1914* A he thinks about her "unexpectedly, incoherently," experiences pity and regret, and looks forward to recovering the happiness of their earlier years together. In *1914* B pity over the way widowhood will affect her immediately gives way to resolutions based on the assumption he will survive, following the same illogic as his SHE dream.

Vorotyntsev does have a brief conversation with a real live woman, a nurse in a Prussian military hospital, but even it displays his tendency to draw the women he associates with into roles created for them by his imagination. He meets Tanya Belobragina while seeking fresh information about front-line action from recently admitted Russian patients. When one of them asks to be evacuated immediately from the hospital, Vorotyntsev tells Tanya to make sure the request is honored. His instructions are given with a peculiar play of expression and gesture noted in some detail by the authorial narrator: "—And,—although there was nothing frivolous in her face and she certainly didn't need to be threatened, for some reason he shook his finger at her, to his own surprise, and his lips smiled: 'Watch out, you won't get away from me. Where are you from?' " When she answers, he tells her, "I'll find you even there!" Their curious conversation ends when he nods abruptly and walks briskly off between the hospital beds.

Another officer who fantasizes about women amid the tension and danger of combat is Ensign Aleksandr Lenartovich. The opposite of Vorotyntsev ideologically, he is something like a badly smudged carbon copy psychologically. Both of them put women in second place after some other obsessive interest that feeds their ambition: for Vorotyntsev, glory in the tsar's army; for Lenartovich, glory in the Socialist Revolutionary Party. The desire for a woman as a reaction to escaping death in war, which prompted Vorotyntsev to marry, also seizes Sasha after he survives a dangerous skirmish with the Germans. Lenartovich feels a sudden pang of regret that his political preoccupations have distracted his attention from women, whom he here considers in general terms: "Absorbed by his Convictions and his Activity—how could he have passed women by in these years? After all, weren't they the most important reason we all stay alive?" He decides his intellectual attainments, political ambitions, even his individual life belong to a different order of being than the relationship between a man and a woman, though he knows such thoughts are "unworthy, base" for one in his position. The memory of having loved a woman, he realizes, would make it easier to die, and cannot even be erased by a bullet, since it has its own, abiding substance. Sasha's sexual hunger is a burning, open wound that is constantly being rubbed from some unexpected source. Like Vorotyntsev, he also briefly meets Tanya Belobragina. He does not even speak to her, but a fleeting glance at her statuesque, full-breasted figure suffices once more to flick his open wound on the raw.

The first one to open this wound is a girl he has met on a recent furlough, the best friend of his sister Veronika at the Bestuzhev university. As in the case of Alina, the male imagination defines the girl's contours. Alina is the faceless extension of a satisfied husband's ego, but "Yolya! Yolen'ka!—Yolochka!" is a projection of yearning in a young bachelor who has "failed to feel things through to the end" when with her, and suffers for this when without her. She appeals to him because she is as elusive as water: she is compared to the female figure with which the Scandinavians embellish the prows of ships, and to "the deceptively gentle swell that begins to rock and toss boats about when it reaches them." She is all undulating motion—

brows, head, neck, her whole slim body as she breaks into a comical trot when walking fast. Since her undulations also threaten to take him and his ambitions out to sea with her, he feels "this instant" that "he has to, he must, he can do nothing else but stop these undulations! Calm them, and only thus calm himself." His desire to possess her is a more or less unconscious desire to destroy what attracts him in her as a woman, the lack of stability and solidity he would despise in a man.

The next subjective view of Yolya comes from women instead of a man. They are Adaliya and Agnessa Lenartovich, who are bringing up Sasha and Veronika. In *1914* A Agnessa is their widowed mother, but in *1914* B the young people have lost both parents and been for some years under the care of a spinster Aunt Agnessa, still attractive at 42, and a slightly older sister, widowed Aunt Adaliya. With no party affiliation, Adaliya belongs "more or less on the meridian of populist socialism," while Agnessa oscillates between the stances of anarchist and maximalist. Agnessa has seen prison, Siberian exile, and amnesty, Adaliya nothing but a thirty-six-hour arrest, but their younger brother—Aleksandr in *1914* A, Anton in *1914* B—has been executed for terrorist activities, and the whole family lives and breathes the ideology of revolution. It is from this standpoint that they approach Veronika's best school friend. In *1914* A Veronika invents the nickname Likonya for her, to rhyme with her own nickname Veronya, and the girls have physical similarities, but *1914* B omits these details and concentrates on the ideological bias the aunts have against Yolya. For them she embodies everything they regard as wrong with a politically indifferent younger generation. They see in her the representative not merely of an alien class—her nickname comes from "the impossible merchant Elikonida"—but of an alien world. They notice the same physical features as Sasha, and others that catch their keen, disapproving eyes, such as the style of her clothes, the ribbons in her hair, and the way it falls to her shoulders, "as with a beauty of great experience." They pass off her enigmatic qualities as affectations and regard her as "doubly poisonous," in perverting both sister and brother: " . . . she had also bewitched Sasha, he devoured her with his eyes and immediately grew stupid, lost his proud independent look" with her.

As the authorial narrator recreates fruitless disputes between the women, trying to inculcate their revolutionary philosophy, and the girls, defending themselves as cultural revolutionaries, the aunts are characterized mainly by their words, Elikonida chiefly through comic physical details such as the pouting of childish lips, expressive glances, the furrowing of a diminutive brow, and the wrinkling of a little nose. The girls speak so nearly in unison that the speaker is not always identified when they rebut the polished rhetoric of the women with the clumsy clichés that express their own convictions. Yolya's voice can be distinguished from Veronika's only when she declaims symbolist poetry.

Yolya's inscrutability characterizes her in the scene where the authorial narrator shows her at the university with Andozerskaya, Veronika, and students like the ones Sasha knows, who "speak boldly, have opinions, and stand up for them." As the girls share their reactions to the new professor's personality and politics, Veronika spontaneously defends her from the majority who find her insufficiently revolutionary, but Yolya must be pressed to give any opinion. It finally comes with the usual undulations of brow, neck, and shoulders, and reveals a mind as hard to pin down as her body: "I liked her very much. Especially her voice. As if she were performing an aria. Such a complicated one that you can't make out the melody." As for the meaning of Andozerskaya's words, "I missed that."

The Veronika of *1914* B, less strikingly beautiful than her earlier prototype, is differentiated more clearly from Yolya in several scenes that show her alone during indoctrination sessions with her aunts, who are developed much more extensively in *1914* B than in *1914* A. At one point they stand on either side of her before the portrait of Uncle Anton (in *1914* B, Uncle Aleksandr in *1914* A) and try to inflame her with the views that caused his death and sustain their life. Her imperturbable temperament, which keeps her out of trouble with boys, also colors her approach to politics. The pity she feels for the suffering of oppressed and oppressors alike makes it impossible for her to grasp the arbitrary moral distinctions of socialism. She even goes so far as to offer her own version of Professor Varsonofiev's insistence on the primacy of personal morality: if terrorists resort to deception, even in pursuing noble aims, she asks, does that not destroy mutual trust, "and isn't it perhaps even more important than the liberation of the people?"

Veronika acts as a sort of pure fool with her aunts, her impartial innocence unmasking the dangerous inconsistencies in their views. The women serve several narrative purposes. As personally moral advocates of social immorality, they typify the politically active intelligentsia of their age. More specifically, they embody the contribution of women to the social revolutionary movement, discoursing at great length about the exploits of historical socialist heroines. In their argument about the true story of Stolypin's assassination, they introduce names and circumstances elaborated in much more detail later on by the author-historian.

Adaliya's and Agnessa's personalities and views converge and diverge in much the same way as Veronya's and Likonya's. Their temperamental affinities go deeper than their politics: "The sisters did not share the same party programs, but they were almost the same age, very close, very fond of each other . . . their enthusiasms, antipathies, praises, criticisms, hopes, and fears were almost always shared." When the differences in their views involve them in an argument, they both let food burn and water boil over on the stove. The authorial narrator, however, creates enough contrast between their physical and psychological attributes to enliven their long, verbose arguments on matters of principle.

Adaliya is thin, frail, gentle, self-controlled, maternal to her niece, sarcastic to her sister. Dressed in the faded grays and blacks of a nun, she is usually calm and mild, and with her sister even affectionately insinuating. She is characterized by gestures: mouth pursed in disapproval or doubt, which are also expressed by shaking her "smooth-haired, peaceable, aging" head. The thin fingers of her "not young" hands can express caustic self-confidence when clasped "into a knot that cannot be untied," sometimes she uses them to hug narrow thin shoulders, and when sufficiently aroused she throws them up just as if she were a simple housewife: " . . . she was unable to sustain a polemical style like Aunt Agnessa." When her idols are attacked her face "also" grows hard and fiery.

For Agnessa this is its customary expression. She is a stocky dragon of a woman. A cigarette is rarely out of her mouth; she chews its tip when she is not actually smoking, smoke surrounding her as if she were a volcano. She belches forth fiery words with a "passion of fire and smoke." There is a spark in the grayness of her flashing eyes. Her rebuttals flare suddenly like a match. In the ardor of dispute she turns into "a pinky-gray panther, pink blotches on her face and graying hair. Frightening. Then she clawed everybody, one after another, sparing nobody, fearing nobody." She glows pink as she strides around the room trailing smoke after her. A cloud of smoke envelops her as she recalls her youthful militancy. Tired of pacing about, she leans against a tiled stove, and the smoke surrounding her seems to be billowing from its cracks.

Sanya Lazhenitsyn is yet another male character who can neither include women in his plans nor exclude them from his thoughts. En route from his native Kuban village to volunteer for the army in Moscow, he gets out when the train stops at Mineral'nye Vody and on the platform unexpectedly runs into a former schoolmate, Varya. Her role has been somewhat altered and greatly expanded from *1914* A to *1914* B. In both versions she lacks the physical appeal Sanya finds in a dark-haired Kharkov girl who plays the guitar and sings love songs: in *1914* B her name is Lena, in *1914* A it is Lenochka, the love songs are Gypsy, and she is free and easy in some of her habits. In both versions Varya fails to dissuade Sanya from going to war by appeals to his populist and pacifist convictions, but *1914* B more insistently emphasizes several ironic polarities connected with their meeting. For both it underlines the gulf between their own experience and the picture of Russian life they have from school. Sanya realizes Tolstoyan pacifism has nothing to do with a Russia he wants to serve because he feels sorry for her, and Varya's arguments ("democratic and revolutionary" in *1914* B, simply "intelligentsia" in *1914* A) also fail to "throw a bridge across the dark abyss yawning before Russia." In *1914* A this moment of truth is only one more result of the constant inner labor that characterizes all Sanya's conscious life, but in *1914* B it is accompanied by much personal pain. Varya is plain—in *1914* A she has a large, bent, vulturelike nose and "an inborn cruelty of expression and sharpness of smile that were never completely smoothed over in her face and spoiled her appearance." In *1914* B she still has a broad mannish chin, sharp smile (also sharp features and words), and too long a nose, but her plainness is not emphasized beyond that. At their unexpected reunion, however, "there flared up the joyful excitement of the meeting that had scorched her, and she was downright pretty." In *1914* A they do not embrace, but in *1914* B they do, "for half a second," just long enough for him to be powerfully affected "not only by her lips, warmed as if

by the sun." In both versions Varya seeks a stabilizing influence in Sanya, and in *1914* B the tension felt by all in the early days of the war makes them both long to go back together to the places they know and love. Sanya's patriotism gives him the strength to resist this temptation, but there is no temptation to resist in *1914* A.

Varya, an orphan, meets Sanya as she returns from the university where Veronya and Likonya are her classmates to Pyatigorsk, to pay her last respects to the man who has financed her education. In *1914* A he is anonymous, but in *1914* B he has a name—Ivan Sergeevich Saratovkin; a social class—merchant; and a biography—a life of good works and success as a grocer. Varya has never met him, is "ashamed of his philanthropy," and thinks it is "dishonest to thank him: charity is a way of paying off a debt to society, they say," but she obeys when she is summoned to see him. She is unprepared for his kindness during his final hours. Though he has helped a score of girls beside her, he knows her name and circumstances, tactfully asks about her personal life, and gives her fateful advice: "God grant you, Varyusha, . . . that your education. Should work for the good. Both to you. And to others. The light of learning, you know, it's. Two-edged."

Varya's next lesson in not judging by appearances comes after she leaves the house of the fatherly reactionary and wanders about the city in search of an outlet for her sense of some boundless happiness waiting just around the corner for her. Passing a row of artisans' booths, she recognizes in a tinsmith a young anarchist she had met through older schoolmates several years before and not seen since. With his gray shirt, stiff black rubber apron, black hair, and stubble, Zhorzh looks as if he belongs in an underground cave. For Varya he embodies the romanticism of conspiracy and the need for warmth and affection she so acutely feels herself. In order to gain his confidence, she recites some of the anarchist slogans memory brings back to her. But just as "Sanya was a simpleton to the point of complexity," Zhorzh turns out to be far simpler than Varya imagines. Once he stops glowering hostilely at her, he summons her into the tiny dark enclosure at the back of his booth, for a purpose she fails to realize until "she felt on her shoulders the implacable pressure of his arms. Downward."

The episode ends with these words. Curiously, when Varya makes her only other appearance, in the scene with Andozerskaya, there is no mention of the Pyatigorsk experience, though in the chronology of the narrative it is very recent, and ought to have made a deep impression on a girl like Varya. Andozerskaya herself is the same in both versions: friendly to her students but flouting intelligentsia stereotypes in her elegant clothes, bearing, and coiffure. Just as nonconformist is her detached attitude to the present, based on her conviction that history is the study of sources rather than current events.

Another woman teacher is the mother of the young officer Vorotyntsev evacuated from the Prussian hospital, a socialist close to Adaliya Lenartovich in her views, the widowed head mistress of the best secondary school in Rostov, Aglaida Fedoseevna Kharitonova. An authoritarian matriarch, she also suffers the irony of fate through the rebellion of her children. Without consulting her, her daughter Zhenya leaves a Moscow teachers' college before her husband has finished engineering school, and less than nine months before becoming a mother. After briefly boycotting the young family, Kharitonova is persuaded to relent by Ksen'ya Tomchak, a close family friend and recent graduate of the school. While Zhenya is too liberal to suit her mother, Yarik is too conservative: she regards his decision to become an officer as a betrayal of both her socialist principles and her maternal authority. The authorial narrator begins with a biographical introduction of Kharitonova, complete with the story of the prodigal daughter, then shows the family with Ksen'ya, who visits them on her way back from her home in the Kuban to Moscow and one last term of advanced agronomy studies before her father says she must marry one of the neighboring landowners.

After a rapturous reunion with idyllically happy Zhenya and her family, Ksen'ya pays her respects to Kharitonova, worried at no news from Yarik in Prussia. The headmistress has kept her "obligatorily" erect carriage, her "habitual dry reticence," and imposing demeanor, but for the first time Ksen'ya notices her graying hair, wrinkled and sagging cheeks, and signs of apathetic preoccupation. During working hours, she is playing a card game in which she seeks the secret of her son's fate, lacking any other way to get in touch with the mysterious forces that control human destiny. As she shares her anxieties about Yarik, "the most simple tear" falls on the seven of hearts. Despite her closeness to the family, Ksen'ya has always been afraid of Kharitonova, but suddenly seeing in her "a mother, even more than a mother," she herself offers motherly affection and consolation.

Ksen'ya is never seen with her biological mother, Evdokiya Il'inichna, in the pages devoted to life on the large, wealthy Tomchak estate. The authorial narrator shows her acting out the role of a subservient peasant woman with her husband, Zakhar (Ferapontovich in *1914* A, Fedorovich in *1914* B), her only son, Roman, and his wife Irina. Irina observes the old woman's outer appearance, attitudes, and words: "excessive plumpness, accustomed calm," and a simplicity bordering on crudeness. She is benightedness incarnate, living as if she were poor when she is rich, deferring to men in everything, spoiling her son, and reproaching her daughter-in-law for not doing the same. Her feebleness, her illnesses, and her immutability all have symbolic dimensions. The only other peasant woman in the story is Kat'ka, the wife of Vorotyntsev's orderly at the front, who emerges idyllically embellished in his thoughts.

Irina has more light, shadow, breadth, and depth than any other female character. When with Ksen'ya she expresses her adherence to the ancient traditions of the Orthodox Church, her cultural Russophilism, her enlightened patriotism, and her distress at the lack of it in Roman and Ksen'ya, as in "all educated Russia." These moral and spiritual views explain her closeness to her father-in-law and her estrangement from her husband. Irina, alone among the female characters, has attributes that reach beyond the immediately functional: her love of the mysterious, the eclecticism of her religious imagination, her marksmanship, and her fantasies about a Natty Bumpo-like ideal man.

Ksen'ya is first glimpsed alone on a bright August morning, then in conversation with Roman when he comes to use the safe in her room. Overflowing with mental and physical life and health, loving and basically docile, she takes her many blessings for granted and longs to be different than she is. Her father's decision to make her marry threatens to destroy her hopes of becoming a dancer, but she lives so totally in the moment, physically and emotionally, that she cannot bring herself to worry about the future. She is all sturdy health, laughter, agility, generosity, and affection, uncomplicated and vivacious.

While in Rostov, Ksen'ya has dinner with the family of Sonya Arkhangorodskaya, a friend from Kharitonova's school. The guest of honor is a former anarchist who, like Sonya's father and Zhenya's husband, belongs to the number of politically conservative but intellectually innovative engineers transforming the face of Russia. Also at table is a family friend, a young SR named Naum Gal'erin. Most of the scene involves debate between the conservative engineers and the young radicals, Sonya and Naum, both endowed with abundant thick black hair, glittering eyes, and political ardor. They glance across the table at each other and their opponents as Naum challenges the guest and Sonya rebukes her father for taking part in a patriotic manifestation of Rostov Jews. In the meantime her mother, a frustrated actress who hates politics, fishes for compliments from her guest on her ambitiously conceived but imperfectly realized meal. At another place glumly sits Sonya's former governess, just engaged to a man about to be called up. In her corner Ksen'ya adds to the comic counterpoint by paying attention to her table manners, taking care to feign interest in the conversation without joining it, and thinking private thoughts about the personal happiness that inevitably awaits her.

The only woman actually to take part in the war is Tanya Belobragina. Volunteering after her fiancé jilts her, she shows unusual calm and devotion to duty in hopes she can die honorably at the front. She considers the pain of the men in her care a simple extension of her own pain. Hers is no less than theirs, because she knows the reasons for hers, while she attributes theirs to elemental forces beyond man's power to control. When she realizes the Russians are going to abandon the men in the hospital of the town from which they are retreating, she identifies a human agent in the suffering of her patients as well as of herself. In a defiant patriotic gesture, she sews to the inside of her slip the regimental flag brought in by one of her charges.

Ideologically, the women in Solzhenitsyn's narrative, like the men, can be divided into monarchist patriots and socialist nonpatriots. Psychologically, distinctions can be made between those willing and unwilling to change. At the far end of this scale, on the right, stand unthinking conservatives like Kat'ka Blagodareva, Evdokiya Il'inichna Tomchak, Zoya L'vovna Arkhangorodskaya, and her governess—politically inert women who either send their men submissively off to war or try to ignore it. Opposite them stand unquestioning radicals—the Lenartovich sisters, Sonya Arkhangorodskaya, Varya Matveeva—who pay no attention to anything that could change their preconceived ideas. Closer to the center on the right are Irina Tomchak and Ol'da Andozerskaya, conservatives by spiritual or intellectual conviction. In the same position on the left stand Veronika Lenartovich, Ksen'ya Tomchak, and Zhenya Filomanskaya, gentle but stubborn souls brought up in a socialist ambiance and loyal to it, but with natures that see beyond its narrow partisan antagonisms. At the next remove stand women whose suffering is an ironic reflex of their principles, with Alina Vorotyntseva on the monarchist right and Aglaida Kharitonova on the socialist left. At the center stand women whose individual feelings lead either to radical patriotic commitment, like Tanya Belobragina, or an equally militant apolitical stance, like Elikonida.

None of these women play a direct part in the political process during the course of the action. So far, they seem to be symbols of stasis that challenge stasis, and symbols of change that challenge change. Morally, they thus serve as a kind of pivotal collective metaphor. The unmarried women are the potential agents of change, embodiments of the future for which men fight. The married women are the forces for continuity, representing the past for which men fight. Whether or not they are connected with a specific male character, they engage both the imagination and the intellect, the scenes where they appear occupying a middle ground between the all-male war episodes and the chapters of historical analysis, giving warmth and relief, light and air to the otherwise almost overwhelmingly dense fabric of the narrative. (pp. 197-210)

> Nicholas Lee, "Manifestations of the Feminine in Solzhenitsyn's 'August 1914'," in Studies in Russian Literature in Honor of Vsevolod Setchkarev, edited by Julian W. Connolly and Sonia I. Ketchian, Slavica Publishers, Inc., 1986, pp. 197-211.

Irving Howe   (review date 2 July 1989)

[*Howe is a prolific American educator, editor, and critic whose works are collected in* Irving Howe: Selected Writings 1950-1990 *(1990). In the following review, he faults Solzhenitsyn for ignoring lyricism in order to assert "questionable theories" in* August 1914.]

What has happened to Aleksandr Solzhenitsyn? The novelist, now living in the United States, who sketched the gulag with such crisp exactitude in *One Day in the Life of Ivan Denisovich,* who grazed moral sublimity in his beautiful story **"Matryona's House"** and who created a vibrant exchange of Russian intellectual opinion in *The First Circle* has all but vanished. Replacing him is a shrill and splenetic polemicist who shatters his fictions in behalf of questionable theories, showers adversaries with sarcastic contempt and employs his talents to cudgel readers into submitting to his increasingly authoritarian views.

For at least 20 years Mr. Solzhenitsyn has been working on a vast cycle of novels called *The Red Wheel,* which he envisages as a panorama of modern Russia, but still more as a corrective to what he regards as the distortions of

Russian history by writers contaminated with liberal and radical ideas. *August 1914* appeared in an earlier version in 1972; now completely retranslated into serviceable English by H. T. Willetts, it is some 300 pages longer than the first version. The book forms the opening volume of *The Red Wheel,* which is structured as a series of what the author calls "knots," or renderings of crucial moments that have determined the course of Russian, perhaps all of modern, history.

This is a swollen and misshapen book, a good many of its pages laden with obscure historical detail in small print that, I can testify, causes strain on both eyes and nerves. Mr. Solzhenitsyn writes with the single-mindedness of a man possessed—prophecy being not the least risk of aging. He writes out of the conviction that he has the correct view—the only correct view?—of his country's tragic experience, and it becomes very hard, indeed impossible, to respond to *August 1914* in strictly literary terms. Mr. Solzhenitsyn himself would probably not want that; he is after "bigger" game.

Despite an occasional borrowing from modern literature, such as his use of the "newsreel" device in John Dos Passos' *U.S.A.,* Mr. Solzhenitsyn's novel begins in the customary manner of multilayered 19th-century fiction, with several vignettes of Russian figures and families shortly before World War I. We meet a wealthy merchant, Tomchak, and his daughter Ksenia. We meet an idealistic student, Sanya, who has a brief talk with the venerable Leo Tolstoy (a piquant incident that was, I think, richer in the 1972 version, which contained some Tolstoyan reflections on poetry that Mr. Solzhenitsyn has now cut).

Several strands of action are thus initiated, and readers familiar with the schema of the traditional novel will await the reappearance of these characters, juxtaposed in both amity and conflict. But that seldom happens in these 854 pages, and only at very long intervals. The characters glimpsed at the outset are suspended in limbo while Mr. Solzhenitsyn turns to what really concerns him: an exhaustive account of Russia's military disasters in 1914. By the time he troubles to get back to his fictional characters, mostly at the very end of this very long book, it has become hard even to recall who the characters are or why we should care about them—since Mr. Solzhenitsyn himself doesn't invest much emotional energy in them. The fictional portion of *August 1914* soon comes to seem merely dutiful, and largely without that desire to imagine other people that is the mark of the true novelist.

Mr. Solzhenitsyn has made a close study of czarism's military fiasco, for which he offers two plausible explanations: that Russia's haste in trying to help a beleaguered ally, France, led to throwing hundreds of thousands of ill-trained and poorly armed troops into battle, and that incompetence was rife among the higher officers of the Russian Army. Mediocrities favored by the byzantine court, the Russian generals proved "incapable of coordinating the movements of large bodies of men." One General Artamonov, for instance, might have made "a pretty good deacon," or "an excellent private soldier provided he had a strict NCO over him," but as a commander he is a total disaster.

All is muddle, sloth, backwardness, sly falsification. It is as if Mr. Solzhenitsyn were intent, though he probably is not, upon confirming the usual view of czarism's essential rottenness, or as if he were deliberately following the judgments of Stendhal and Tolstoy that warfare is inherently chaotic—though without the former's brilliance or the latter's penetration.

There are some good pages in the hundreds that sag under endless battle detail. Especially so are those about the historical General Samsonov, whom Mr. Solzhenitsyn models in part on Tolstoy's Kutuzov in *War and Peace,* but without Kutuzov's intuitive strategic grasp or mysterious good fortune. Also strong are some pages devoted to the fictional Colonel Vorotyntsev, an officer who travels from corps to corps as the witness of defeat and who comes, meanwhile, to serve as Mr. Solzhenitsyn's center of intelligence. Samsonov speaks for traditional patriarchal Russia, blunt and honest but quite lost in modern warfare (as Tolstoy's Kutuzov might also have been), while the nervously intelligent Vorotyntsev speaks as the modernizing voice that Mr. Solzhenitsyn apparently wishes had been commanding in 1914, loyal to czarism but impatient with the feeble Czar and his scraping court.

The pages devoted to battle on the eastern front—pages crammed with dull generals, obscure place names, confusing divisional maneuvers—soon become wearying. It is possible that some Russian readers, at least those leaning, in the days of glasnost, toward a chauvinist nostalgia, may be roused to excitement by the doings of Generals Zhilinsky and Martos, but it is hard to suppose anyone else will. Some fatal lack of proportion is at work here, an indulgence of authorial vanity and ideological obsession.

It will no doubt be said that in *War and Peace* Tolstoy also devoted many pages to battle. Yes, but Tolstoy was Tolstoy, the greatest master of prose narrative, we have ever had. Tolstoy was also generous enough to provision his novel with a rich and varied cast, taking the precaution to make most vivid precisely those characters with whose opinions he disagreed. By now Mr. Solzhenitsyn has become too impatient, too irritable for the novelist's job, and one readily surmises the reason: for a writer pulsing with prophetic urgency, mere literature dwindles in importance.

The new material in **August 1914** centers on historical events that took place several years before the war. Pyotr Arkadievich Stolypin, a shrewd politician, was Prime Minister of Russia from 1906 to 1911, when he was assassinated by Dmitri Bogrov, a shady figure who had successively been linked to revolutionary terrorists and the czarist secret police and who had perhaps become a double agent betraying both sides. In fairness, it should be said that Mr. Solzhenitsyn does try to get inside Bogrov to scrutinize his motives, but not with much success; for he cannot control his anger and disgust, and too often he descends to sarcasm, the lowest of rhetorical devices.

It is Mr. Solzhenitsyn's thesis that if Stolypin had been able to complete the reforms he had begun, Russia might have been spared the traumas of Bolshevism, but that a tacit alliance of reactionary officials and revolutionary in-

Solzhenitsyn with Heinrich Böll on the day of his expulsion from the Soviet Union, 14 January 1974.

surgents thwarted Stolypin's plans. He had proposed to grant the recently emancipated peasants legal right to small allotments of land and thereby to free them from their dependence on the mir, or agricultural commune. Had this happened, Mr. Solzhenitsyn argues, Russia might have become a modern society resting on an independent agrarian class.

Contemporary readers, especially non-Russians, need not hurry to form a judgment of this political speculation, though a touch of skepticism may be in order. A more balanced view of Stolypin—in 7, not 70, pages—appears in a book by the distinguished historian Leonard Schapiro, *Russian Studies.* Stolypin, Schapiro writes, was "a man who was both a repressive upholder of order and one who achieved reform by defiance of the constitution" granted by Czar Nicholas II in 1906. What seems decisive here is that after Stolypin's murder there was no significant leader or group of leaders in official Russia prepared to continue his work—the mental obscurantism of czarism was simply too thick.

Only when writing about Stolypin ("a figure of epic presence") does Mr. Solzhenitsyn relax into ease or rise to something like lyricism. This idealization of a bureaucrat who was hated by Russian democrats and leftists for his severe repressions after the 1905 revolution is not just a whim; it is the thought-out conclusion of the political outlook Mr. Solzhenitsyn has adopted in recent years, one that might be described as modernizing authoritarianism. "The secret ballot," he scoffs, "suited the Russian peasant as a saddle suits a cow"—and since peasants formed the bulk of the Russian population, democracy could have played little or no role. As for the rationale he offers, it is all too familiar: right and left authoritarians proclaim it everywhere, with the same haughty certitude.

Somewhat sprightlier than the long chapter on Stolypin is his 80-page historical excursus about Nicholas II, the last of Russia's hereditary autocrats. Though caustic at times about this royal dunce—some passages here recall Trotsky's more concise and elegant excoriation in his *History of the Russian Revolution*—Mr. Solzhenitsyn seems finally unable to come to a clear judgment about the Czar. At one point he writes that the Czar was a "weak but virtuous man," yet the overwhelming thrust of his own depiction is to show Nicholas as petty, selfish, mindless. When Stolypin lay dying in a hospital, the Czar did not even bother to visit his minister, apparently suspecting him of "liberalism." That hardly seems evidence of virtue, either weak or strong.

Mr. Solzhenitsyn winds up *August 1914* with one of his better scenes, in which Colonel Vorotyntsev reports to the Grand Duke, supreme commander of Russia's armies. The colonel's few honest words acknowledging defeat are scorned, the general staff clings to its deceptions, Russia is doomed.

What, I asked at the outset, has happened to Mr. Solzhenitsyn? The answer is that his zealotry has brought about a hardening of spirit, a loss in those humane feelings and imaginative outreachings that make us value a work of literature, regardless of the writer's political opinions. In *August 1914* Russian radicals are portrayed as rapists, murderers, "mad dogs"; and while, as polemicist, Mr. Solzhenitsyn has every right to attack them, as novelist he has a primary obligation to make them seem plausible versions of men and women. The Russian middle class, sneeringly referred to as "society," is shown to be preparing the way for Lenin by joining in irresponsible attacks on czarism.

A still deeper revelation of Mr. Solzhenitsyn's current state of mind is to be found in this sentence: "An aversion to Russia and the Russian people, and a belief that everyone in Russia was oppressed and that there was no freedom there, had been created by relentless Jewish propaganda" in America.

This is ugly stuff. Could Mr. Solzhenitsyn not have found it in his heart—it would have taken just two more lines—to mention that this "Jewish propaganda" was in response to the Kishinev pogrom of 1903 and a succession of pogroms two years later, during which czarist authorities either gave the killers a free hand or looked the other way? These pogroms "cost the Russian Jews about 1,000 dead [and] 7,000-8,000 wounded," we read in *The Russian Jew Under Tsars and Soviets* by Salo Baron (a scholarly work

that, in view of Mr. Solzhenitsyn's declared interest in history, he might do well to consult).

It is all very sad, this self-immolation of a once major writer who a quarter of a century ago, in *The First Circle* and *Cancer Ward,* won our admiration for his loveliness of feeling. The Russian critic M. M. Bakhtin once remarked that "for the prose artist the world is full of the words of other people." By now, for the prose artist Aleksandr Solzhenitsyn the world resounds with the words of only one person. (pp. 1, 17-18)

> Irving Howe, "The Great War and Russian Memory," in The New York Times Book Review, *July 2, 1989, pp. 1, 17-18.*

Aleksandr Solzhenitsyn with David Aikman   (interview date 24 July 1989)

[*In the following interview, Solzhenitsyn discusses his* Red Wheel *series, Russian politics and literature, and events that shaped his literary career.*]

[*Aikman*]: *The novel* **August 1914** *was first published in 1971 in Russian, and now the English translation of a completely new edition is just being published. Why did you feel it necessary to add some 300 pages to the original manuscript?*

[Solzhenitsyn]: The chapter on Lenin is the first addition. But the greater number of new chapters came from the fact that, with the years, I understood that the movement toward revolution and its causes could not be understood simply in terms of World War I, 1914. My initial conception was one that the majority of those in the West and East today share, namely that the main decisive event was the so-called October Revolution and its consequences. But it became clear to me gradually that the main and decisive event was not the October Revolution, and that it wasn't a revolution at all. What we mean by *revolution* is a massive spontaneous event, and there was nothing of the sort in October. The true revolution was the February Revolution. The October Revolution does not even deserve the name revolution. It was a coup d'état, and all through the 1920s the Bolsheviks themselves called it the "October coup." In the Soviet Union they consciously and artificially replaced the February Revolution with the October one.

Do you think, then, that the February Revolution was more of a break with Russian history than the October Revolution?

Yes, it was much more of a break. The February system—if you can call it that—never even got established before it already started to collapse. It was collapsing from week to week. The October coup only picked up the power that was lying on the ground and that belonged to no one.

Why did you decide to call the entire cycle of novels The Red Wheel, *and why do you refer to each different stage in the narrative as a "knot" [uzel in Russian]?*

We are not talking about the wheels of a car, after all. We are talking about a gigantic cosmic wheel, like a spiral galaxy, an enormous wheel that once it starts to turn—then everybody, including those who turn in it, becomes a helpless atom. A gigantic process that you can't stop once it has started. And I used the knots for the following reason: I started to deal with the period 1914-22. If I were to rewrite in detail about the period 1914-22, the volume would be too great, so I reached for episodes where I thought the course of events was being decided. These are the knots, the most decisive moments, where everything is rolled up and tied in a knot.

The one person in this novel whom you obviously admire greatly is [Russian Prime Minister Pyotr] Stolypin. How would you summarize his role in Russian history?

What is characteristic is that during the years he was active, conservative circles considered him the destroyer of Russia. And the Kadets [Constitutional Democrats], who considered themselves liberals but were in fact radicals in the European context, called him a conservative. Actually, he was a liberal. He thought that before creating civil society, we had to create the citizen, and therefore before giving the illiterate peasant all sorts of rights, you had to elevate him economically. This was a very constructive idea. Stolypin was, without doubt, the major political figure in Russian 20th century history. And when the revolution occurred, it was the free democratic regime of February 1917 that abolished all his reforms and went back to square one.

For 70 years, we have been destroying everything in our country, the life of the people, its biological, ecological, moral and economic basis. Naturally, people look to the past for some point of support, some constructive idea. Now people are looking here and there and finally coming across Stolypin's reforms and how he dealt with the peasantry.

How do you see Lenin in the whole complex of Russian culture?

Lenin had little in common with Russian culture. Of course, he graduated from a Russian gymnasium [high school]. He must have read Russian classics. But he was penetrated with the spirit of internationalism. He did not belong to any nation himself. He was "inter" national— between nations. During 1917, he showed himself to be in the extreme left wing of revolutionary democracy. Everything that happened in 1917 was guided by [proponents of] revolutionary democracy, but it all fell out of their hands. They were not sufficiently consistent, not sufficiently merciless, while he was merciless and consistent to the end, and in that sense his appearance in Russian history was inevitable.

The English philosopher Bertrand Russell, who was a self-professed atheist, met Lenin and said he thought Lenin was the most evil man he had ever met. Do you think Lenin was evil?

I never met Lenin, but I can confirm this. He was uncommonly evil.

What do you mean by evil?

The absence of any mercy, the absence of any humanity in his approach to the people, the masses, to anyone who did not follow him precisely. If anyone deviated the least little bit from him, like the Mensheviks, for example, he turned on them, he reviled them, he used every term of imprecation against them. He hated them. Even without using the word "evil" in a broad, metaphysical sense, you can still apply this word to Lenin in its everyday meaning.

I would propose the following definition: anti-Semitism is a prejudiced and unjust attitude toward the Jewish nation as a whole. If one accepts this definition, it becomes clear that . . . it would be impossible to have anti-Semitism in any genuinely artistic work. No real artist could be prejudiced and unjust toward any entire nation without destroying the artistic integrity of his entire work.

—Aleksandr Solzhenitsyn

Some critics have accused you of anti-Semitism on the basis of your depiction of the terrorist Bogrov in **August 1914,** *and one writer even used the words "a new* Protocols of the Learned Elders of Zion" *to describe the book. What is your response to these accusations?*

I described Bogrov in the most realistic way, with every detail of his life, his family, his ideology and his behavior. I recognized his brother's interpretation of him as the most correct and convincing. In no way did I belittle the heroic impulse that moved him. I think that the application of the term anti-Semitic to **August 1914** is an unscrupulous technique. I had earlier thought this was possible only in the Soviet Union. The book was not yet available because I had not released it, but people stated quite loudly that this was a disgusting, imperialist, revolting, loathsome book, etc. It wasn't possible to check what was being said, because people couldn't obtain the book.

But what is really at issue here? The word anti-Semitism is often used thoughtlessly and carelessly, and its actual meaning becomes soft and squishy. I would propose the following definition: anti-Semitism is a prejudiced and unjust attitude toward the Jewish nation as a whole. If one accepts this definition, it becomes clear that not only is there no anti-Semitism in **August 1914** but it would be impossible to have anti-Semitism in any genuinely artistic work. No real artist could be prejudiced and unjust toward any entire nation without destroying the artistic integrity of his entire work. A work of art is always multidimensional, is never made up of empty abstractions.

My novel has no generalizations about the Jewish nation in it. In writing a book one cannot always ask, How will this be interpreted? You have to think, What actually happened? My duty was to describe things as they happened.

Do you believe the completed Red Wheel *will be published some day in the Soviet Union?*

I have no doubt about that.

You have said your writings must return to the Soviet Union before you are willing to do so.

Yes. I worked 53 years on *The Red Wheel.* Everything I have thought, discovered and worked over in my mind has gone into it. If I had to return to the Soviet Union prior to *The Red Wheel,* I would be sort of mute. No one would know where I stood. I would have expressed nothing. Once people read it, then we can talk. The book has to be available at every bookstore in the U.S.S.R.

But more generally, my return does not depend only on me. The Soviet authorities have never yet rescinded the charge of treason that was lodged against me. There, I am considered subject to criminal sanctions for betraying my own country.

[Natalya Solzhenitsyn interjects:] The day before he was exiled, he was formally accused of treason. Nobody has ever changed this.

[Solzhenitsyn continues:] And then, instead of maybe shooting me, they exiled me.

You have said you are a writer in the 19th century Russian tradition. What do you mean by this?

It does not mean following precisely the genres and the artistic techniques of the period. Far from it. My material is entirely unusual and requires its own genres and its own technique. But it does mean maintaining the responsibility toward the reader, toward one's own country and toward oneself, which was found in Russian 19th century literature. They wrote very responsibly. They did not play games.

The American novelist Henry James once described Russian novels as "huge, loose, baggy monsters." Your own Red Wheel *epic will result in several thousand pages, many times larger in fact than* War and Peace. *Is there something about the Russian condition and Russian literature that asks for much greater length in the novel than is usual in other countries?*

Mine is indeed very large, I admit. There is an aphorism: He who forgets his own history is condemned to repeat it. If we don't know our own history, we will simply have to endure all the same mistakes, sacrifices and absurdities all over again. This book is not designed to be read through easily, for amusement, but to understand our history. And to understand our history, I feel that my readers definitely need this book.

So then, in your view, literature continues to have a very high, moral, philosophical and political purpose?

Yes, in Russia it's always been that way.

You have been compared with both Tolstoy and Dostoyevsky, both in scope of your subject matter and in your treatment of the psychology and ideas of your characters. What is your relationship to each of these two authors?

I have a very great feeling of respect and kinship to both of them, although in different ways. I am closer to Tolstoy in the form of the narrative, of the delivery of material, the

variety of characters and circumstances. But I am closer to Dostoyevsky in my understanding of the spiritual interpretation of history.

Did you feel a sense of destiny even when you were quite young, that you had something very important to write, to tell the world?

Apparently, there is some sort of intuition. We don't know where it comes from, but we have it. From the age of nine, I knew I was going to be a writer, although I didn't know what I was going to write about. Shortly after that, I was burned by the revolutionary theme, and so, starting in 1936, at age 18, I never had any hesitation about my theme, and there is nothing that could have deflected me from it. Sometimes you have a strange premonition. For instance, I started describing General Alexander Krýmov. Knowing almost nothing about him, I simply made a provisional sketch as I imagined him, and later I learned that I had described him almost as though I had seen him. It was astonishing how well I guessed him.

As a young man, at one point you were a convinced Communist, a member of the Komsomol. How did you come to change your ideas and become a Christian believer?

Let me make a correction. I was raised by my elders in the spirit of Christianity, and almost through my school years, up to 17 or 18, I was in opposition to Soviet education. I had to conceal this from others. But this force field of Marxism, as developed in the Soviet Union, has such an impact that it gets into the brain of the young man and little by little takes over. From age 17 or 18, I did change internally, and from that time, I became a Marxist, a Leninist, and believed in all these things. I lived that way up through the university and the war and up until prison, but in prison, I encountered a very broad variety of people. I saw that my convictions did not have a solid basis, could not stand up in dispute, and I had to renounce them. Then the question arose of going back to what I had learned as a child. It took more than a year or so. Other believers influenced me, but basically it was a return to what I had thought before. The fact that I was dying also shook me profoundly. At age 34 I was told I could not be saved, and then I returned to life. These kinds of upheavals always have an impact on a person's convictions.

Your ideas of both the Christian faith, in the form of Russian Orthodoxy, and of Russian nationalism have caused some critics to accuse you of being chauvinistic and xenophobic. Are you a Russian nationalist, and what does that mean to you?

It is quite extraordinary the extent to which I have been lied about. I will give you some of the accusations that are made about me: that I am an advocate of theocracy, that I want the state to be run by priests. But I have never written such a thing. Also, I am supposedly nostalgic for the Czars and want our modern Communist Russia to go back to czarism. Now, aside from the fact that only an imbecile thinks that one can bring back the past, nowhere have I written anything of the sort. Nowhere have I written that the monarchy is an ideal system. Everything comes from the fact that in the Soviet Union, Nicholas II was characterized as less than human, as a monkey, as the ultimate scoundrel, but I described him as a real person, as a human being. In other words, I deviated from the norm.

Some people distort things consciously, others just don't take the trouble to check their sources. It is remarkable, and it makes me ashamed of journalists. No one ever gives any quotes. The same is true for the charge that I am a nationalist. I am a patriot. I love my motherland. I want my country, which is sick, which for 70 years has been destroyed, and is on the very edge of death, I want it to come back to life. But this doesn't make me a nationalist. I don't want to limit anyone else. Every country has its own patriots who are concerned with its fate.

How do you account for the violent feelings about your views?

In Europe the response to me is very varied. But in the Soviet Union and the U.S., it's like an assembly line: all opinions about me are exactly the same. In the Soviet Union I can understand it. It is due to the Politburo. They push a button, and everybody speaks the way the Politburo orders. But in the U.S. fashion is very important. If the winds of fashion are blowing in one direction, everybody writes one way and with perfect unanimity. It is perfectly extraordinary.

Then there was the Harvard speech [in 1978], where I expressed my views about the weaknesses of the U.S., assuming that democracy is thirsty for criticism and likes it. Maybe democracy likes and wants criticism, but the press certainly does not. The press got very indignant, and from that point on, I became the personal enemy, as it were, of the American press because I had touched that sensitive spot. Some people said, "Why did our leaders take him into this country so uncritically? They shouldn't have taken him in."

I have to say this was especially saddening, because the main idea of the Harvard speech—"A World Split Apart"—which is very important for the U.S. and Western thought, is that the world is not monolinear, not made up of homogeneous parts that all follow the same course. The mistake of the West, and this is how I started my Harvard speech, is that everyone measures other civilizations by the degree to which they approximate Western civilization. If they do not approximate it, they are hopeless, dumb, reactionary and don't have to be taken into account. This viewpoint is dangerous.

Today there are events of enormous significance taking place both in the Soviet Union and throughout the whole Communist world. Why do you choose to be silent about these changes?

If I had started being silent at the onset of these changes, it might have been surprising. But I started in 1983, before there was even any suggestion of these changes. Was I going to interrupt my work and start acting as a political commentator? I didn't want to do that. I had to finish my work. I am over 70 years old, and age is pressing on me.

You have said the moral life of the West has declined during the past 300 years. What do you mean by that?

There is technical progress, but this is not the same thing as the progress of humanity as such. In every civilization this process is very complex. In Western civilizations—which used to be called Western-Christian but now might better be called Western-Pagan—along with the development of intellectual life and science, there has been a loss of the serious moral basis of society. During these 300 years of Western civilization, there has been a sweeping away of duties and an expansion of rights. But we have two lungs. You can't breathe with just one lung and not with the other. We must avail ourselves of rights and duties in equal measure. And if this is not established by the law, if the law does not oblige us to do that, then we have to control ourselves. When Western society was established, it was based on the idea that each individual limited his own behavior. Everyone understood what he could do and what he could not do. The law itself did not restrain people. Since then, the only thing we have been developing is rights, rights, rights, at the expense of duty.

More than anything else, your reputation in world literature is linked to your searing portrayal of Soviet labor camps. Did your experience of the camps provide you with a dimension of understanding of Soviet life that you could not have had without it?

Yes, because in those circumstances human nature becomes very much more visible. I was very lucky to have been in the camps—and especially to have survived. (pp. 57-60)

Aleksandr Solzhenitsyn and David Aikman, in an interview in Time, *New York, Vol. 134, No. 4, July 24, 1989, pp. 56-60.*

Alla Braithwaite   (essay date May 1990)

[*In the following essay, Braithwaite examines critical reaction to Solzhenitsyn's works and assesses the extent to which the author has contributed to political and social change in Russia.*]

In December 1988 Solzhenitsyn turned seventy. A feeling of great anticipation swept over Russia that the name of this great Russian writer and thinker would finally be officially vindicated; that his books would be freely published for all Russians to read; and that the government would gracefully apologise to him for past persecution, and would invite him back home. Countless petitions were signed and much lobbying went on. The official response was muted, hardly enthusiastic. These are the times of 'socialist pluralism', it is true, it was said, but Solzhenitsyn is hostile to any form of socialism, any socialist ideas. In other words: forget about his coming, it can never happen.

Yet the unthinkable did happen. The most influential official literary magazine *Novy Mir* ('New World') has just published in three instalments (Nos 8, 9, 10—1989) selected chapters from **The Gulag Archipelago.** What is more, the news is that the book is to be published in full by 'Sovetsky Pisatel' ('Soviet writer') publishers in the near future. Then came the news that Solzhenitsyn's Complete Works are in production, including the latest in his epic series of historical novels entitled *The Red Wheel,* of which **August 1914** is the first part.

It is truly the literary event of the year. Parts of lesser Solzhenitsyn works have been printed by minor publications in recent years, but Solzhenitsyn insisted that *Gulag* with its indictment of Stalinism and its prison camps be published before *Cancer Ward* and *The First Circle.*

It is said that President Gorbachev personally approved the publication of *The Gulag Archipelago.* It reaffirms *Novy Mir's* place as the sanctuary of liberal Russian thought at a time when thinking Russians are trying to decide where their hearts lie. When Moscow intellectuals first got hold of illicit copies of *Gulag* in the seventies, they were dumbstruck by the unprecedented meticulous piling of horror upon horror, but at the same time felt exhilarated by Solzhenitsyn's personal example of endurance and courage. This official publication also brought an unexpected reaction from the reading public, who found *Gulag* a spiritually uplifting work despite its gloomy and destructive subject-matter. Igor Vinogradov calls for a complete reappraisal of Solzhenitsyn, the writer and the man:

> *The Gulag Archipelago* shook the whole nation into realising the extent of the heroic deed performed by one man. But understanding of this man can be complete only when one understands his faith, which is at the heart of his vision of the world. For Solzhenitsyn is first and foremost a religious writer, a Christian writer who underlines the eternal moral issues, and rejects the temporal ones. . . . Solzhenitsyn is not only a great living Russian writer, he is also a teacher who appeals not only to your soul and conscience, but also to your moral responsibility and your behaviour.

These are indeed remarkable words, unthinkable in Russia only a few years ago. That Solzhenitsyn should be hailed as a prophet in his own country defies belief. 'Prophet' can be used to mean someone who has extraordinary insight into the nature of contemporary reality and has the courage to tell the truth as he or she sees it, even if many find it unpalatable. It can also suggest that the bearer of the title is not primarily an artist but something else (are Dostoyevsky and Tolstoy prophets or artists?). As Edward E. Ericson points out [in his *Solzhenitsyn: The Moral Vision*], 'although . . . much about him is indeed reminiscent of the style of the Old Testament prophets—it would be an egregious distortion of his life's work to use that term in order to dismiss or belittle his standing as a man of letters'.

It is very ironic that Solzhenitsyn never expected renewal or reform from within the Communist system. In his *Letter to the Soviet Leaders,* sent on September 5, 1973, less than six months before his exile from Russia, Solzhenitsyn said:

> . . . you will not allow power to slip out of your hands. That is why you will not willingly tolerate a two-party or multi-party parliamentary system in our country, you will not tolerate *real* elections, at which people might not vote you in. And on the basis of realism one must admit that this will be within your power for a long time to come. A long time—but not forever.

Yet the *Letter* is a remarkable testament especially in its predictions for Russia, most of which are fast coming true. In it he also called for:

1. The abandonment of Marxism as the official state philosophy (Russia is already halfway there).

2. Repudiation of revolutionary movements.

3. The end of support for client states throughout the world.

4. Agrarian reforms instead of the collective farm system.

5. Development of the Siberian Northeast, with careful protection of the environment.

6. The guarding of Russian economic resources for the future rather than selling them abroad.

7. As much disarmament as is possible in view of the Chinese threat.

8. Release of political prisoners, restoration of civil rights, and government by law.

9. Renewed emphasis on Orthodoxy and the family following the pre-revolutionary tradition.

10. Retention of some authoritarian aspects of the state when necessary.

Apparently Solzhenitsyn never received an acknowledgement that the Soviet leaders received his letter, let alone took his ideas seriously. In view of what has been happening in Russia today, we can only speculate on the effect this letter will have had in the long run.

Looking back it seems amazing that this letter should have been so misunderstood in the West. Newspaper articles about its publication ran under such headlines as 'A Russian Nationalist Looks to the Past' and 'Solzhenitsyn "contemptuous" of the US'. Anthony Astrachan, the author of the latter article, declared that 'the letter shows Solzhenitsyn to be a great Russian patriot, whose nationalism verges on chauvinism and racism though it falls into the abyss. . . . It reveals him as a passionate opponent of unbridled technological progress and a contemptuous critic of the West. . . . The letter is thus a reminder to outsiders that the courage to oppose Soviet tyranny from within does not make a dissenter a Western liberal'.

Other critics found Solzhenitsyn 'a fierce Russian nationalist who is contemptuous of the western democracies and sympathetic to authoritarian rule'. The irony of the situation is that this very lack of western liberalism and critical view of the West guaranteed the fact that today Solzhenitsyn's views are vigorously defended in Russia.

An interesting point was raised by James Schall, a Jesuit priest, that by focusing on Russia, Solzhenitsyn 'seems oblivious to the real needs of the rest of mankind.' Schall embraces the problem from the standpoint of international consciousness, which, in his opinion, is deficient where Solzhenitsyn is concerned. Schall came to a conclusion that, 'In this sense Marxism remains more Christian than Solzhenitsyn's vision, even though he is quite right in his analysis of its performance, its institutions and its procedures'. Schall may be right, but he does seem to miss the point that it is a long-standing vision among the Russian intelligentsia that Russia might teach the rest of the world important things. And in a perverse way such has been the case in the twentieth century: Marxism came to power first in the Soviet Union, and its allure had spread throughout the world. Not a few thinkers have perceived the Soviet Union as the future which works. Perhaps a vision of society will find its genesis in Russia. Perhaps only those who have had the dreadful experience of being under rubble will be able to point the way for mankind.

Malcolm Muggeridge [in his foreword to Ericcon's book] was one of the first in the West to point out the 'great merit of taking full account of the role of Christianity and of Solzhenitsyn's own Christian faith in all his thinking about life and the contemporary world.'

It is important to get straight what it is that Solzhenitsyn is saying. Edward E. Ericson calls Solzhenitsyn 'a man driven by a mission. He has a vision of life which permeates all his writing. . . . For Solzhenitsyn is ever the writer about the moral issues. . . . And it is his Christian vision of life and of the nature of man which always undergirds and provides the context for his moral judgements'.

It seems amazing that Solzhenitsyn made public his commitment to Christianity only in 1972, and since then his religious faith has been widely acknowledged. Yet his astonishing prayer to God dates a whole decade earlier:

> How easy it is for me to live with you, Lord!
> How easy for me to believe in you.
> When my spirit is lost, perplexed and cast down,
> When the sharpest can see no further than the
> 　night,
> And know not what on the morrow they must
> 　do
> You give me a sure certainty
> That you exist, that you are watching over me
> And will not permit the ways of righteousness
> 　to be closed to me.
> Here on the summit of earthly glory I look back
> 　astonished
> On the road which through depths of despair has
> 　led me here.
> To this point from which I can also reflect to
> 　men your radiance
> And all that I can still reflect—you shall grant
> 　to me
> And what I shall fail you shall grant to others.

It is not uncommon to dismiss Solzhenitsyn as old-fashioned, as someone who has nothing new to say to the twentieth century, as someone who wilfully ignores the spirit of the times. For example, in his art, as Dan Jacobson put it [in *Commentary*, May 1969], 'Solzhenitsyn takes for granted an absolutely direct and open connection between literature and morality, art and life. . . . In the West today such an assumption about the relationship between art and morality is distinctly unfashionable'. Solzhenitsyn is also in a minority within the cultural and intellectual elite, with its attachment to secular humanism which gives politics a kind of primacy as the category for understanding human problems and seeking their solution—here Solzhenitsyn stands largely opposed to them and relegates politics to a secondary status.

Dean Alexander Schmemann of St Vladimir's Theological School in the United States wrote in 1970, before Solzhenitsyn's going public, that he found in Solzhenitsyn 'a Christian writer', that is one who has 'a deep and all-embracing, although possibly unconscious perception of the world, man, and life, which, historically, was born and grew from Biblical and Christian revelation, and only from it'.

After reading an essay by Father Schmemann, Solzhenitsyn agreed,

> '. . . his article about me . . . was very valuable
> to me. It explained me to myself . . . It also for-
> mulated important traits of Christianity which
> I could not have formulated myself . . . '

Schmemann is concerned with the way Solzhenitsyn views the world. The triune intuition of creation, fall and redemption is the unexpressed presupposition of Solzhenitsyn's writing. This Russian orthodox priest aligns the writer not with Russian Orthodoxy in particular but with Christianity in general. He finds Solzhenitsyn's acceptance of the Christian doctrine of creation to be evident in his perception and acceptance of the original goodness of the world and life. Yet most of his stories are about suffering, ugliness, and evil. Schmemann urges that Solzhenitsyn views the 'mystery of evil from the Christian intuition of the fall as well as creation'. This means specifically that there is no evil in itself. Yet evil is not merely a negation; it is first and always a fall, one which was unnecessary in a world that was created 'very good'. Christ was not crucified by impersonal forces but by men. Evil is real because it is a personal choice. Christians cannot resign themselves to it stoically, even though it is not they who overcome it finally. This is Solzhenitsyn's strategy for survival, physical and spiritual.

Schmemann urges that Solzhenitsyn's intuition is also one of redemption. His faith is beyond despair. Because of God's reality, nothing is inevitably closed, condemned, or damned. Everything remains open.

Solzhenitsyn has taken his religious orientation from Russian Orthodoxy. Christianity has existed in Russia since the ninth century. The roots are in Byzantium rather than the Latin West, Constantinople and not Rome. Solzhenitsyn's loyalty is to a vital faith which is mediated through a tradition. Liturgy and sacraments are important in it as well as hierarchy and community. Yet he refuses sectarianism. He is concerned for the religious life of the entire nation. Solzhenitsyn's church is Catholic but not Roman Catholic. Its traditions antedate the Christianity of Rome itself.

The national experience reflects, and has a kind of parallel with, Solzhenitsyn's personal life. He states explicitly that his earlier pattern of thought and feeling underwent spiritual transformation in imprisonment. Rebirth began on the day of his arrest. Imprisonment is the most important thing that happened to him in his entire lifetime. Deprived of external freedom, he came to know truth through suffering. He was uplifted spiritually and came in touch with reality. Solzhenitsyn speaks of his first cell as his first love.

Only there did he begin to know his own inner life. The Hebrew-Christian warning against idolatry became meaningful: only God is absolute. To make any other reality ultimate is self-defeating. From this knowledge Solzhenitsyn's slavery to Marxism dissolved. Indeed, he was liberated from all ideology. Solzhenitsyn is emphatic that Christianity is not ideology. On the contrary, it is the destruction of ideology. Accepting the neighbour without class hatred, it makes possible communication with persons as persons. Ideology gives a distorted view of reality. Christianity, by contrast, is for Solzhenitsyn a living spiritual force with healing powers.

The Gulag Archipelago is not only a report, a record for history. Solzhenitsyn's mood is one of reflection about his data, but also of confession. There are important similarities with Augustine's *Confessions* in Solzhenitsyn's writings. Augustine's introspection is singularly powerful as he tells his sins to God, asking repentance. This kind of reflection is also present in passages of *The Gulag Archipelago.* Like Augustine, Solzhenitsyn makes apparently minor passing events a key to lasting religious insight. Augustine used the incident of his youth—a group of boys wantonly steal and destroy pears—as epitomising the sheer maliciousness of sin. Solzhenitsyn tells of the evil man who threw tobacco into the eyes of a monkey and blinded it; there is no real explanation apart from the fact of his wickedness. As in the case of Augustine, Solzhenitsyn introspects and examines his own motives intensely. He recalls how he refused to carry the pack of a German prisoner in need. The man, emaciated and exhausted, later met him and smiled. Solzhenitsyn takes this as a gesture of forgiveness. But the wrong remains and must not be forgotten. Solzhenitsyn will confess his sins to God. Like Augustine he recognises that wickedness is not simply an individual phenomenon. He confesses the sins of his people as well as the nation. Confession is salutary and necessary. There can be no healing without it. 'Only through repentance of a multitude of people can the air and soil of Russia be cleansed, so that a new, healthy national life can grow up'.

For Solzhenitsyn, man does not live simply in dependence on science and reason. All experience cannot be controlled simply or manipulated at will. Instead, he has a sense of destiny and providence. Haugh writes:

> Solzhenitsyn's vision of the source of art and value is ultimately rooted in his belief in the Absolute. In an unambiguous text from his Nobel Lecture, Solzhenitsyn states that the artist has not 'created this world, nor does he control it: *there can be no doubts about its foundations'.* For Solzhenitsyn the world is a created world. It is a world which might not have existed at all and hence it points beyond itself to its spiritual source. The world, for Solzhenitsyn, is necessary, dependent and participatory, deriving its value and meaning from the uncreated and eternal.

The first section of his Nobel lecture is the most important one, for in it Solzhenitsyn establishes the religious basis for his literary work. True art, he explains, is premised on two fundamental concepts: that truth is absolute, and that reality is objective. Both ideas grow organically from Solzhenitsyn's belief that there is a personal God who created and sustains the world. Art, then, is a gift from God, it entails the exercising of a God-given ability. Artists may misuse this gift, but 'Art is not profaned by our attempts, does not because of them lose touch with its source'.

In the same lecture Solzhenitsyn explains:

> So perhaps the old tri-unity of Truth, Goodness and Beauty is not simply the decorous and antiquated formula it seemed to us at the time of our self-confident materialistic youth. If the tops of these three trees do converge as the thinkers used to claim, and if the all too obvious and the overly straight sprouts of Truth and Goodness have been crushed, cut down, or not permitted to grow, then perhaps the whimsical, unpredictable and ever surprising shoots of Beauty will force their way through and soar up to *that very spot,* thereby fulfilling the task of all three.

This echoes Dostoyevsky's famous dictum that 'Beauty will save the world'.

Schmemann has pointed out how the Christian understanding of creation, the fall and redemption underlines Solzhenitsyn's writing; Solzhenitsyn himself has accepted this analysis. His profound grasp of the reality of evil is exemplified in the figure of a helpless monkey blinded by a wicked man who has thrown tobacco into its eyes. Solzhenitsyn has experienced the brute fact of wickedness throughout his own career, but he affirms Providence as well. Richard Haugh calls attention to the way in which Solzhenitsyn's conviction of the True, the Good, and the Beautiful helps to explain his own mission as a writer. God is authentically present in human creativity. In spite of all wickedness and suffering the divine is not absent from the world. Solzhenitsyn's moral sense led him back to God, not just as an idea but to the living God of history and personal experience.

Although Solzhenitsyn's novels are not religious novels in the proper sense, it is from them that we get a clear structure of his belief. He recalls the first impression made upon him by Christian worship as a youth even before he became conscious of anti-religious propaganda. As he grew up, the religious legacy of his family was almost fully overlaid by Marxist atheism. It was the experience of imprisonment which slowly changed the direction of his life. The basic problem of survival—life and death as well as evil—was raised with intensity. Yet even after he had been in confinement for more than a year, Solzhenitsyn reports, he still defended Communism. Its premises continued to be challenged by a wide variety of his fellow-prisoners—scientists, politicians, ex-Party members as well as priests. It was not their words but Solzhenitsyn's own moral sense, his conscience—the inescapable conviction of right and wrong—which caused him to turn increasingly to religion. Today he views his arrest as the beginning of his penance and conversion. He does not seem to have been a Christian at the time of his release. However, by the time of the publication of *One Day in the Life of Ivan Denisovich,* his first novel, he had come to explicit Christian belief.

For Solzhenitsyn, Christianity has been intrinsic to Russian culture for more than a thousand years. His native land and people cannot be saved without it. He is now a practising member of the Russian Orthodox community and shares its inclusive 'church-type' piety with sacraments and hierarchy. His Christian conviction came only through personal crisis and after long dialogue and reflection. Scepticism preceded faith. Solzhenitsyn came to recognise its value from the warning from an old Marxist, 'Doubt / question everything, *doubt / question everything*'. In time, he also concluded that scepticism does not provide a 'firm basis underfoot'. Spirit, and not matter, is primary; it can be corrupted in evil or redeemed by grace. For Solzhenitsyn evil is a corruption. Yet he is committed to the Eastern Orthodox view of free will. God does not pre-destine men to evil. The image of God continues in man in spite of his fallen condition. God's grace in creation remains and man can cooperate with it. Solzhenitsyn affirms the existence in tri-unity of Truth, Goodness and Beauty because he accepts the existence of the 'Absolute' or the 'perfect'. Where there is perfection, Truth and Goodness necessarily co-exist, the 'radiance' of which is Beauty.

N. C. Nielsen notes that Solzhenitsyn's 'protest is a genuinely contemporary one. Solzhenitsyn's conviction is that Stalin's atheism corrupted the political order. . . . Solzhenitsyn's *The Gulag Archipelago* saw the result of Solzhenitsyn's atheism as sixty-six million casualties for the new order in Russia alone. . . . In *Stories and Prose Poems,* Solzhenitsyn symbolizes Russia as a secret lake in a secret forest enslaved by an evil prince. The evil prince is Stalin, but this is not all that Solzhenitsyn is trying to say. The Revolution has failed in its promise to him and his fellow-prisoners. Rejection of its ideology is necessary to integrity. Solzhenitsyn does not believe that trust in God is only an opiate of the people as Marx declared. For him, personal Providence has become a living reality. His way to this knowledge was through the degradation and inhumanity of totalitarian imprisonment'.

Solzhenitsyn's protest is not unrelated to his religious faith. He will not deny that he trusts in God. He speaks of the impression which attendance at worship left on him as a child. In the camps he had witnessed the purity of life of believers.

In his imprisonment, Solzhenitsyn became more than ever conscious of an inner struggle for righteousness and selfhood. Both have their being from God. 'Is the end of life happiness?' he asked.

In order to clarify his views and make his sense of mission in life more explicit, Solzhenitsyn and some friends put together the eleven essays—three by Solzhenitsyn himself—which constitute *From Under the Rubble.* This manifesto heralds the proper direction of change. In his third essay Solzhenitsyn calls for a vanguard movement among the intelligentsia, something he calls 'a sacrificial elite'. He explains, 'And I am entirely in accord with those who want to see, who want to believe that they can already see the nucleus of an intelligentsia, which is our hope for spiritual renewal'. In *From Under the Rubble* Solzhenitsyn pleads with his fellow Russian intellectuals to resist the desiccat-

ed ideology of the state and to return to a humanism infused with Christian insight to place religion over politics:

> When oppression is not accompanied by the lie, liberation demands political measures. But when the lie has fastened its claws on us, it is no longer a matter of politics! It is an invasion of man's moral world, and our straightening up and *refusing to lie* is also not political, but simply a retrieval of our human dignity.

The only way to change is when inward development takes precedence: 'But this path is also the most moral: we shall be commencing this liberation with *our own souls.* Before we purify the country we shall have purified ourselves. And this is the only correct historical order . . . '

Grazzini said that 'the Russians have more than other people a shining audacity to make new beginnings'. They may detest the verbal ideologies, but they believe in the life of the heart. They mistrust rational mechanisms, because they have burnt their fingers on them, but they have a rich and vibrant imagination. The melancholy vein that runs through their nature does not diminish their keen interest in tomorrow. Not only Solzhenitsyn's work, but his personal example too, his combination of contemptuous pride and paternal understanding, warm their spirit and give them hope. He responds to the radical changes taking place in social life, and in individual life, by presenting to the consciousness of his readers the unavoidable questions, because they are the key questions of the age: whether man, if he is to keep the forces of nature and the new technologies under control, must not first and foremost preserve a sense of justice; whether civilisation is not to be measured by the respect it shows for the liberty of each and every individual; whether the inspiration of social life must not be a spirit of harmony between all created things.

It is with a sense of bewilderment that Russians learn of Solzhenitsyn's refusal to consider suggestions that he return to the Soviet Union from his chosen exile in Vermont, in the United States. But the hope remains. (pp. 179-84)

> *Alla Braithwaite, "Did Solzhenitsyn Change the World/Russia?" in* The Month, *Vol. 23, No. 5, May, 1990, pp. 179-85.*

Michael Scammell   (review date 16 November 1990)

[An American editor, critic, and biographer, Scammell is the author of Solzhenitsyn: A Biography *(1984). In the following review, he responds negatively to Solzhenitsyn's article first published in the Russian newspaper* Komsomolskaya pravda *in September 1990 and later translated in English as* Rebuilding Russia: Reflections and Tentative Proposals *(1991).]*

Alexander Solzhenitsyn's September [1990] homily on "How to Revitalize Russia" [published in English as *Rebuilding Russia: Reflections and Tentative Proposals* (1991), but first published in two Russian newspapers in September 1990], broke a silence on Gorbachev's *perestroika* and *glasnost* policies that had puzzled and intrigued the author's admirers. Did this silence (after repeated strident criticisms of Gorbachev's predecessors) in-

Solzhenitsyn at Harvard, June 1976.

dicate approval of the new man and his works? September's statement provided only a partial and ambiguous answer to that question. At no point did Solzhenitsyn condemn *perestroika* outright, although he did ridicule it for not moving fast or far enough. As for *glasnost,* he had nothing to say on the subject, although certain comments suggested that, if anything, he felt that the process had gone too far. In general, there was little in Solzhenitsyn's criticisms of the present system that does not appear daily in the Soviet press already (his article, for the record, appeared in the official organ of the Communist Youth League, *Komsomolskaya pravda*). Attention, therefore, is being directed at the other part of his article, namely his programme for Russia's future, which was clearly intended to influence the political debate now raging there and to stake out a personal position which may be a prelude to his own return.

Very early in Solzhenitsyn's career it became clear that, as a writer, he was addicted to the "big" questions in life, overtly patterning himself on classical Russian writers of the nineteenth century such as Tolstoy, Turgenev and Dostoevsky. Beginning in 1973, with the publication abroad of his *Letter to the Soviet Leaders* (he was still in the Soviet Union at the time), he also inaugurated a series

of public statements on the subject of Russia's social, political and spiritual health, with particular concern for her future development "after communism". His 1973 *Letter,* for example, was quickly followed by a volume he himself edited called *From under the Rubble,* and after his expulsion to the West in 1974, he produced numerous articles and speeches on similar themes and at regular intervals, as well as his big series of novels collectively known as *The Red Wheel,* about the First World War and the events leading up to the February and October revolutions in Russia. And then, about six years ago, for a variety of reasons he fell silent.

Of all the works mentioned above, the one which comes closest to his latest declaration in form and content is the *Letter to the Soviet Leaders,* and a comparison of the two documents reveals some interesting parallels and differences. The original *Letter* was divided into seven longish chapters. In Chapter One, "The West on Its Knees", Solzhenitsyn developed the thesis that the West was in a state of collapse as the result of a profound historical, psychological and moral crisis, whereas the Soviet Union was at the peak of a staggering series of successes. In Chapter Two he warned of an impending war with China, and exhorted the government to avoid such a conflict at all costs, since it would end in the ruination of the country. Chapter Three dealt with what Solzhenitsyn (basing himself on a Club of Rome report) called the impasse into which the whole of civilization had entered: "progress" was a myth; economic growth was unnecessary and ruinous; industrialization had polluted the world to the point where ecological disaster was imminent; and if humankind did not radically change its ways, it faced extinction "sometime between the years 2020 and 2070".

The West, according to Solzhenitsyn, might just avert catastrophe by virtue of its versatility and inventiveness. The Third World might also do so because it hadn't yet entered on the industrial path. But for Russia the danger was the greatest, because of its blind insistence on aping Western ways. On the other hand, its sheer backwardness gave it the opportunity to follow an alternative, "third" course, and in Chapters Four and Five of his *Letter,* Solzhenitsyn attempted to point the way. Russia should pull back not only from Eastern Europe, which he urged the Soviet leaders to renounce, along with all the trappings of empire, but from the world in general, and turn inward to nurture its unique material and spiritual riches on its own. For this he advocated that Russia transfer the centre of its development to the north-east of the country, adopt a policy of "small is beautiful". What the country needed was "an economy of non-gigantism . . . *new* towns of the *old* type". And he embellished his vision with eccentric details, such as: "we can perfectly well set up road barriers at all the entrances and admit horses and battery-powered electric motors, but not poisonous internal combustion engines. . . . "

Among the practical reforms Solzhenitsyn advocated were a reduction in the size of the armed forces, abolition of collective farms, the eradication of bribes, an upgrading of the school system, and improvements in the status of women. He proposed the abandonment of Marxism-Leninism as the State ideology, and he warned against the importation into Russia of Western-style democracy, because the country was not ready for it. "Should we not perhaps acknowledge", he wrote, "that for the foreseeable future . . . whether we like it or not, whether we intend it or not, Russia is nevertheless destined to have an authoritarian order?" Such an order would depend on building a strong moral foundation, which Solzhenitsyn maintained had existed for a thousand years in old Russia in the form of the Orthodox Church. It could be rebuilt once more, he argued, with the help of the Church. In the meantime, he allowed that political power should remain with the existing leaders, but recommended that the privileged status of the party be abolished, and that legislative power be transferred to the Soviets in preparation for more radical reforms to come.

The self-portrait of the writer that emerged from the *Letter* came as a shock to most people at the time. His personality up till then had been shrouded in secrecy and mystery, and attention had been concentrated on his magnificent duel with the repressive Soviet government. But now, instead of the presumed liberal democrat of the juicy blasts against censorship, party corruption, and human rights violations, there appeared an incurable romantic, a

Slavophile dreaming of a Russian golden age, a crusty conservative turning his back on the twentieth century.

Solzhenitsyn's claims for the spiritual superiority of the Russian people and his extreme conservatism undercut his authority with many readers at home; after he had arrived in the West, his new air of self-righteousness contributed to the alienation of much of his Western audience. Others, on the contrary, preferred to give him the benefit of the doubt, if only because they shared his unwavering hostility to the Soviet regime, and were conscious that there was nothing that regime desired more than to see one of its most persistent opponents discredited. However, during the past five years the regime itself has undergone a transformation, while Solzhenitsyn has kept his counsel, and legitimate questions were raised about how he viewed the changes and how they might fit into his vision of the future. People also began to wonder if the vision itself had changed, and if so, in which direction. Now, with his new statement, Solzhenitsyn has answered those questions.

> **Solzhenitsyn's deep love of his homeland and his moral authority are not in dispute, but as one liberal newspaper put it, 'as a political figure he has been eclipsed.'**
>
> **—Michael Scammell**

The latest document, "How to Revitalize Russia," [later published as ***Rebuilding Russia: Reflections and Tenative Proposals*** (1991)], is divided into two equal parts subtitled "The Near Future" and "Further Ahead", each of which is further divided into fourteen short sections. In part one, which is general and covers much of the same ground as *Letters of the Soviet Leaders,* there is naturally no mention of the decline of the West any more, of the triumph of the Soviet Union, or of the dangers of a war with China. Nor does Solzhenitzyn urge a national retreat to the Russian north-east, or stress the virtues of the Orthodox Church—indeed, he is surprisingly silent on the latter subject. However, he *can* point with satisfaction to the virtual abandonment of Marxism-Leninism as the State ideology, and to the Soviet retreat from empire, both of which he was urging (and was among the first to advocate) back in the early 1970s.

On this last matter, and in view of the virtual collapse not only of the Soviet empire, but also of the Soviet State itself, his thinking has developed considerably. He not only "accepts" the secession from the present union of the three Baltic republics, and Moldavia, but he insists on it: "We must declare it loudly, clearly, and without further delay." The only exception is Kazakhstan (where, incidentally, Solzhenitsyn lived in exile for three years after his release from the Gulag), which according to him should be divided in two, the northern portion going to Russia and the south declaring its independence (if it so wishes). The remaining state which would consist of the Russians, Byelorussians and Ukrainians, Solzhenitsyn proposes to call the "Russian Union". He is aware, of course, of secessionist tendencies in the Ukraine and Byelorussia too, but appeals to these peoples to remain with their Russian brothers, since they were all part of the original medieval Russian State known as Rus'. There is also a personal dimension to these sentiments: Solzhenitsyn's maternal grandfather was Ukrainian, and Solzhenitsyn grew up hearing the Ukrainian language at home. Outwardly, Solzhenitsyn seems prepared to make a concession even here: "Of course, if the Ukrainian people *really wishes* to separate itself, no one should dare to hold it back by force." But he accompanies this offer by a stipulation that in such an eventuality, referendums would have to be held in every settlement, district and region for the local populations to decide for themselves, a device that would effectively strangle secession at birth.

Similarly, he comes out unequivocally in favour of some forms of privatization, but the restrictions he proposes make many of them of very limited utility. On land, for example, he supports the right of farmers to possession of their plots for life, and even, grudgingly, their right to pass property on to their heirs. But the size of the landholdings must be strictly controlled (and kept small), there must be no agribusiness and above all no foreign ownership ("no latifundias"), while land must be granted only to those who will guarantee to cultivate it conscientiously (the implication is that land can also be taken away, but Solzhenitsyn doesn't spell this out very clearly). Similarly, private business should also be predominantly small-scale. There should be careful safeguards against concentrations of capital and strict controls over foreign investment, especially where raw materials are involved. Inviting foreign capital in to save Russia from its inefficiency is "a most dangerous idea. . . . We would be turned into a colony." Banks would also be necessary, but "they should not be allowed to turn into usurious growths and become the hidden masters of all our lives".

One of Solzhenitsyn's main concerns throughout his recommendations is to warn against "alien" Western influences. Western industrial practices not only lead to unnecessary waste and pollution, but have caused Western companies to jettison the "healthy concept of repairs". They also produce inflation, whereas Russia in the old days "lived for a century with the same prices". In the area of popular culture, Solzhenitsyn perceives the gravest dangers emanating from "American cultural imperialism": "The iron curtain did an excellent job of defending our country against everything good in the West . . . but the curtain didn't quite go all the way down, and allowed the liquid dung of a debauched and decadent 'pop mass culture' to ooze underneath, along with the most vulgar fashions and public displays—and our deprived youth greedily devoured this garbage." Not that Solzhenitsyn is any kinder to his countrymen, Soviet family life, inferior schooling, and barbaric surroundings. In a chapter entitled "But What Are We Ourselves Like?" Solzhenitsyn excoriates Russians for their complicity in the crimes of communism, and pillories the tribunes of *glasnost* and *perestroika* for their reluctance to repent, comparing them unfavourably with the West Germans after the Second

World War. In a final chapter, "Self-limitation", he points out that "human rights" bring in their train "human responsibilities", and recommends his countrymen to practise self-restraint as a condition of greater freedom.

Many of these themes have their counterparts in either *Letter to the Soviet Leaders* or Solzhenitsyn's essays, and Part One of "How to Revitalize Russia" [*Rebuilding Russia: Reflections and Tentative Proposals* (1991)] generally follows the form of the *Letter.* Part Two, however, has no parallel in the earlier declarations, although some of the arguments are familiar. Briefly it consists of a dense disquisition on the nature of democracy (with citations from Spengler, Montesquieu, Plato, Aristotle, Popper, Tocqueville, Mill, Pope John-Paul II, and Ronald Reagan), designed to show not only that representative democracy in all its known forms is a highly flawed kind of government and incapable of eradicating injustices, but also that it fails to reflect the true will of the people, and is therefore unsuitable for Russia. Solzhenitsyn examines, and rejects, in turn universal suffrage, the secret ballot, direct elections, proportional representation, first-past-the-post systems, or any form of majority rule, and above all any role in government for political parties, which, as he has demonstrated in the past, he hates with a rare intensity. " 'Party' means 'a part.' To divide ourselves into parties would be to split up into parts. To whom would a party, as a part of the people, be opposed? Obviously to the rest of the people who refuse to follow it."

Solzhenitsyn's ideal instead reflects the traditional Russian and Slavophile passion for consensus (in support of which Solzhenitsyn cites numerous Russian thinkers from the past). What Solzhenitsyn advocates and understands is "democracy on a small scale", and he takes as his models the traditional Russian village assembly (*mir*), American town meetings, and cantonal election gatherings in Switzerland. There everybody knows everybody else, voting is by an open show of hands, and elected representatives are responsible for their neighbours and peers. Taking these as his model, Solzhenitsyn recommends the building of democracy in Russia from the grass roots upwards, instead of from the top down. Thus the present "Soviets" or workers' and peasants' councils (themselves loosely modelled on the traditional *mir*) would be replaced with four tiers of Land Assemblies (the nineteenth-century Russian *Zemstvo*), which would exist on the village, district, town, and regional levels, and would elect delegates to a governing "All-*Zemstvo* Assembly". There would be a strong president with wide powers elected by popular vote, who could nevertheless be impeached by a three-quarters majority of the Assembly, or confirmed in office for an extra term by a two-thirds majority. Finally there would be a second chamber or Conciliary Council (*Duma*), vaguely resembling both the English House of Lords and the medieval Russian Synodal Councils that existed before Peter the Great.

The most surprising aspect of this second part of Solzhenitsyn's declaration is not so much the content as its sheer density and detail. As he openly acknowledges, he has been heavily influenced by his researches into pre-Revolutionary history for his novel series, *The Red Wheel,* and it clearly shows in the discrepancy between his impressionistic (and highly subjective) description of Western electoral practices and the more technical discussion of the role of *zemstvos, dumas,* and so on. The fact is that Solzhenitsyn is a patriarchal populist. He favours a strong, even authoritarian leader, and is passionately concerned about the fate of the "little people", but he loathes and detests the middle and professional classes, the "smatterers", as he calls them, and bypasses them in his blueprint for a power structure. Hence his support for small farms and small businesses, and hostility to anything larger; hence too his preference for informal, consensual politics and his hostility to parties.

His vision is quite clearly stuck in the nineteenth century, in an age without radio, television and a national press, let alone modern telecommunication systems and the rest of the paraphernalia that are transforming the world into a global village, a village from which Russia cannot possibly be excluded. Unfortunately, such myopia will almost certainly undermine his reputation, just as the sheer detail and circumstantiality of his proposals expose his ignorance. This is a pity. Solzhenitsyn's great authority and reputation have depended until now on his personal courage, his integrity as an artist, and his role as an upholder of moral and spiritual values. It is only toward the very end of Part One of his declaration that he strikes this authentic Solzhenitsynian note: "The source of a society's strength or weakness is its spiritual level, and only secondarily its level of industry. . . . Human freedom includes a voluntary self-restraint in favour of others. Our obligations must always exceed the freedom that is granted to us." There is more in this vein, but it comes very late in the argument, and is immediately swept aside by the detailed proposals in Part Two.

Had Solzhenitsyn stuck to what he knows and understands best, it is safe to say that the significance and impact of his words would have been greater. He could have acted (and might still act—it is not too late) as a moral force and beacon to his nation, reminding his fellow countrymen of the universal values underpinning all societies at all times, and drawing attention to the standards that need to be striven for, if not attained, even at the most difficult junctures in human history. Instead, he has gone even further than in 1973 with a detailed political and economic programme that is likely to be ignored, if not laughed out of court, because of its very eccentricity.

The first signs from Moscow are that this is what is likely to happen. It is true that Gorbachev, responding to questions in the Soviet parliament, felt obliged to comment on Solzhenitsyn's statement on the day after it appeared, and he acknowledged that Solzhenitsyn was "a great man". However, the author was "fully immersed in the past", and would do well to "stop roaming over this land with his scissors and plough"—a reference to Solzhenitsyn's plans for breaking up the Soviet Union. One could hardly expect the Soviet establishment to embrace Solzhenitsyn's views, of course, but the main opposition, represented by the "liberal" interregional group of deputies, was lukewarm as well, particularly with regard to Solzhenitsyn's

prescriptions for a "strong president", a subject that was actually being debated the day the statement appeared.

It seems that the part of Solzhenitsyn's plan that drew the most attention, and also the most support, in Moscow was his call for the break-up of the Soviet Union and the formation of a greater Russian, since it played into the current mood of Russian nationalism. Many had feared that because of his nationalistic fervour Solzhenitsyn would be espoused by members of the ultra-nationalist group Pamyat, but they have been silent so far, probably because they disapprove of his dismissal of empire and his critical comments on the present behaviour of the Orthodox church. On the other hand, a pro-reform group of Kazakhstani writers denounced the suggestion that Kazakstan be partitioned and accused Solzhenitsyn of Russian chauvinism.

Most of the available evidence suggests that the letter was a one-day wonder. In the early days of Solzhenitsyn's emigration, his ideological opponents derided him as a "Russian Ayatollah", thirsting to return to Russia as a new prophet and political leader. It seems increasingly unlikely that anything of the sort could happen, or that Solzhenitsyn would wish to head a political movement or to make government policy if he returns. He would certainly like to be consulted, but even that possibility seems remote. Valentin Rasputin, a prominent and respected writer whose nationalist views approximate to Solzhenitsyn's own, remarked after reading the statement that Solzhenitsyn had been away too long. Solzhenitsyn's deep love of his homeland and his moral authority are not in dispute, but as one liberal newspaper put it, "as a political figure he has been eclipsed". (pp. 1234, 1249)

Michael Scammell, "A Great Man Eclipsed,"
in The Times Literary Supplement, *No. 4572,*
November 16, 1990, pp. 1234, 1239.

Tatyana Tolstaya   (essay date 29 June 1992)

[*Tolstaya is a Russian short story writer, educator, and critic. In the following essay, she excoriates Solzhenitsyn for presumptuousness and hypocrisy in* Rebuilding Russia: Reflections and Tentative Proposals, *characterizing the work as, among other things, a mere imitation of Leninism lacking any concrete, realistic solutions to the problems faced by the Russian people.*]

As is well known, Aleksandr Solzhenitsyn supposes that there is a single truth, that the truth is one. The combined evidence of his work, especially his polemical articles, suggests also that he believes it is known to him alone. This sense of high exclusiveness became clear in 1974, immediately after his expulsion from the Soviet Union, when Russian émigrés, who would have gladly embraced this émigré by compulsion, ran into a hastily erected fence. It turned out that, in the mind of the involuntary émigré, they were all bad, since they had left Russia of their own will. (The horrible circumstances that forced them to flee, to save their lives and the lives of their families, were not taken into account.) But he, Solzhenitsyn, was good, since he had been expelled against his will.

Russian writers should not leave the motherland, they should stay home. Why? Because. Russian writers should not think about money. Russian writers should not criticize Russia (though they are obligated to curse the Soviet regime). Russian writers should not have their own opinions about other Russian writers (how dare Siniavsky love Pushkin so uncanonically, not the way the Leader and Teacher commands that he should?). It turned out, in short, that everyone should or should not do one thing or another, and that only Solzhenitsyn knew what precisely that thing was. Submit—or be condemned and excommunicated.

Russians learned a good lesson. For the umpteenth time they had raised up an idol, and for the umpteenth time, having barely settled on his pedestal, the idol began to kick, to bite, and to spit in their faces, and to demand the most terrible sacrifice: that they relinquish their free will, their liberty to reason and to feel, that they forsake, in other words, everything that constitutes individuality. The confusion and the dismay that this exposure of Solzhenitsyn caused among Russian émigrés actually benefited Russian thought and letters. The spat-upon matured from the experience; they left the Buddha behind to meditate on the far side of his fence, and they busied themselves with more productive matters than burning incense and offering flowers and honey to the little god.

Now, about the fence. As we know, on the mainland (as émigrés often refer to Russia) Solzhenitsyn's works were categorically forbidden. The émigrés that he shunned in their common exile were also forbidden. Thus, information about what was really going on between them in distant, inaccessible, legendary America didn't get through to Russia, or it arrived in distorted form. It was for this reason, and not only because of his extraordinary personal courage, that Solzhenitsyn gradually acquired the attributes of a quasi-mythological figure. Indeed, he was transformed into an archetype from Russian folklore, into one of those immortal, omnipotent, and often ornery old people who lives in a distant, inaccessible place, on an island or a glass mountain or an impenetrable forest, once-upon-a-time-in-a-far-off-kingdom. The famous writer came to be imagined rather like the ancient characters Koshei the Immortal or Grandfather Knowall or Baba Yaga, a powerful old crone who lives in the forest behind a pike fence decorated with human skulls.

The "immortality" of this man who had suffered from cancer, was miraculously cured, and was then transported by a supernatural power (by the KGB, and through the air) to the final point beyond the ocean, beyond the river of forgetfulness into a fairy-tale world, facilitated the formation of the myth. In Russia it was claimed that the fence around the Solzhenitsyn estate in the woods of Vermont was high and impenetrable, topped with barbed wire snares, like a labor camp. It was whispered that the gates were guarded by vicious German shepherds that didn't understand Russian or English, but only Old Slavonic (the sacred language of the Church); in mythological terms, that is, the dogs responded only to certain magical formulas.

The legend about the fence has persisted, with different variations, for fifteen years. I remember when it was born, and I have seen it take root and grow thick with outlandish details. Just recently Solzhenitsyn was visited by the director Stanislav Govorukhin, one of the few who have been allowed into the inner sanctum. And what was the very first thing that the visitor reported back to his listeners, who hunger for bedtime tales? That the fence was not what we had thought, that it was only an ordinary wire fence guarding the grounds from deer, that it was neither very tall nor very strong. (Now who asked him to go and destroy a myth?)

The immortal and irascible old wise men of Russian folklore rarely have direct dealings with anyone. The role of press spokesman or messenger is usually played by a quasi-magical woman, who is close to the old man but is kind and favorably disposed toward the people. It might be Vasilisa the Beautiful, captured by Koshei to be his wife and housekeeper, and to scratch his head at night; or the lass Chernavka, who serves Baba Yaga and scratches her heels before bedtime; or one of those nameless girls who warn mortal guests about the host's bad mood. Solzhenitsyn's wife plays this role: she delivers his manuscripts to the outside world and conveys his refusal (or, rarely, his agreement) to be interviewed. It is she who sometimes responds to Russian writers who have dared to request an audience, "Aleksandr Isaevich approves of your story, but you needn't come. He won't see visitors." Which brings to mind the skulls on Baba Yaga's fence. They were all that remained of the unfortunate travelers who tried to break into the enchanted enclave without the requisite passwords and skills, and without making use of the messenger's friendly assistance. They got what they deserved.

The consummation of the Solzhenitsyn myth is the half-joking conviction of Russian émigrés that the Solzhenitsyn in Vermont is not the "real" one, that there has been a switch, that the KGB sent a double and the "real" Solzhenitsyn rotted somewhere in the Gulag. In the eighteenth century, Russians spoke much the same way about Peter the Great, who traveled to the West and returned infected with Western ideas: that Russians should wear German clothes, shave their beards, and smoke tobacco, that Russian women should wear décolleté dresses and dance with men. It was whispered that Peter had been switched, and that the figure who returned to Russia was the Antichrist. In the Russian popular imagination, the West, where the sun goes down, is a bewitched location, denoting night, cold, death, the corridor to another world (which is why all those magical elders live in the West). The unseen line that divides "East" from "West" is a magic site where people are transformed. A transfiguration takes place, a turning inside out, a metamorphosis; werewolvery, werefolkery. (pp. 29-30)

The little book [*Rebuilding Russia: Reflections and Tentative Proposals*] by Solzhenitsyn that has recently appeared in English was published in Russian in two Soviet newspapers in September 1990. It appeared in the United States, in other words, after the revolution of August 1991, when the Soviet Union almost ceased to exist, when all the cracks and schisms, previously hidden under a deceptively smooth surface, suddenly emerged, tearing apart a huge power in all imaginable and unimaginable directions. The previous reality no longer exists, the old facts are obsolete, the logic of history, once unknown to all of us, now manifests itself before our very eyes, frightening peaceful citizens and awakening emotions that people never even suspected that they possessed.

In this sense Solzhenitsyn's book is completely outdated, though not by any fault of his own. Still, in another sense, in another dimension, in the mythological space in which the writer and his faithful audience dwell, this text is not in the least dated. Indeed, in its essence it can never become dated. For it is the stuff of myth, and in this myth, in this ideal world, a Great and Kind-Hearted Russia, populated by a Wise and Just People, endures. Evil Forces (communism, Soviet power) cast a temporary spell on the People and turn them from the path to the One and Only Truth, but these powers will be defeated by the Wisdom of the People.

Since this space is mythic, moreover, its size is not all that important. Thus, according to Solzhenitsyn in his book, a smaller Russia is better: in a smaller Russia, there will be fewer aliens. Time also is a secondary consideration, and therefore the writer speaks of prerevolutionary Russia as if it continues to exist, petrified and immobile, in some dreamtime. And, having established these fairy-tale parameters, it is only natural to furnish them with a fairy-tale Russian people; and this, in turn, requires the mythmaker personally to determine the criteria for belonging, the criteria of true Russianness, and hence to approve, to thunder, to command.

What is to be done with the former Soviet Union, which occupies one-sixth of our planet's land mass? Two hundred and eighty million people. More than 130 nationalities. Myriad religions, faiths, superstitions, sects. A babel of languages. The broadest spectrum of political views and passions. And everyone is wretched, everyone sees an enemy in his neighbor, everyone is running from someone or chasing others. The Soviet Union has collapsed, and yet it has not collapsed. The process continues. How much iniquity, blood, and injustice will we have to witness? The terrifying example of Yugoslavia stands before us. What is to be done?

I don't know. I am in no position to give any advice. I can only observe and ask more questions. Solzhenitsyn, by contrast, has the answers. "Should," "should," "should," "should," he hammers from the pages of his essay. Solzhenitsyn proposes his own formula for the collapse of the country, based not on real (and perhaps unsolvable) problems, but on a mythological paradigm in which Russia, surrounded by aliens, occupies the center. Solzhenitsyn is not stupid or ignorant; he cannot fail to understand that the conflicts of kindred peoples (Russians and Ukrainians, for example) are often more acrimonious than those of very different peoples. But reality doesn't have much place in his picture of the world. For him, Ukrainians are brothers, while Armenians, say, are not. His rigid and immutable design can only frighten and offend those who have other sympathies and other ties.

The English title of Solzhenitsyn's essay is ***Rebuilding Russia.*** That is imprecise. A more literal translation of the original would read: "How We [Should] Arrange Russia." The translator, Alexis Klimoff, has dropped that important "We," thereby dampening the author's clearly expressed desire to emphasize his membership in an exclusively Russian fellowship, and his intention to participate in the plans for rebuilding. In the original Russian, that "should" is implied rather than stated, but it is heard by every Russian ear. And "rebuilding" is also, really, an incorrect translation. Though the word "rebuilding" in fact conveys the idea of Solzhenitsyn's essay, Solzhenitsyn's own word craftily evades and flirts with the dictionary. For the word *obustroit* describes, more precisely, the process of turning a dwelling into a comfortable place: I'll put the wardrobe here, the bed there, the table over in the corner. I do not mean to be overly harsh toward the translator, for the task is titanic. One must translate Solzhenitsyn first into Russian, and then from Russian into English.

The Italian writer Tommaso Landolfi has a story about a man who learns Persian. Inspired by the divine harmonies of the language, he writes a marvelous poem. He is convinced that it is a work of genius, and seeks out the reaction of specialists. But it turns out that no one (other than his joker-teacher, who disappears) knows this "Persian" language. Such a Persian simply does not exist. The nasty prank torments the poet, since he cannot share the treasure that he possesses. He tries to translate his masterpiece into accessible Italian: no good, it's not right, it's merely a pale copy with little meaning and less poetry. The great beauty that has been revealed to him must remain unknown to others.

Solzhenitsyn is in a similar situation. Unlike the unfortunate poet, however, he himself invented this "Persian" language, which swaddles his speech and his mind in a thick shroud. In this particular text I counted more than 100 words that are not used in the Russian language, and my tally, I am certain, is not complete. It's not that these words are entirely incomprehensible: recognizable Russian linguistic roots show through each of them, the prefixes and the suffixes are more or less Russian, the nouns stand where nouns should, the verbs indicate action. A number of words, however, are transformed beyond recognition, so that as you read you have to stop and think, is this a verb? Imagine that your cat suddenly grew a cow's head. You might not object, but you would certainly pause to wonder if it will drink milk or produce it.

Solzhenitsyn may have invented some of these words. Others he clearly found in his favorite book, Vladimir Dahl's *Reasoned Dictionary of the Living Great-Russian Language* (1863-66). That lexicon is a marvelous collection of words that were and still are used in Russian, but as befits a dictionary, it is a storehouse, a treasury. It unites words in that imaginary, intellectual, theoretical space called language. No real individual speaks this language. Real individuals know only a part of it—otherwise we wouldn't need such collections of words.

Solzhenitsyn got his hands on Dahl relatively late—in 1946, when the future writer was about 30. It's obvious that he was bowled over by this Aladdin's cave of language, and he grabbed more gems than he was able to carry. I remember an interview Solzhenitsyn gave quite some time ago, in which he talked about how, with the help of his children, he was revising Dahl's dictionary with a view to determining which words Russians needed and which they did not. There is also a work that he recently compiled and published on the basis of that effort, the **Russian Dictionary of Linguistic Expansion,** a recommended list of words that are now little used or obsolete.

Again, these are wonderful words for a dictionary, but they are unthinkable as recommendations for the actual speech of real people; a joy for the historian, but incomprehensible to the contemporary ear; appropriate in rare contexts (a quotation of direct speech, a quarrel, a historical novel), but absolutely impossible in today's language, written or spoken. If medical instructions were to be written in the language of Beowulf, or judicial opinions in the language of Joyce, or road signs in cuneiform writing, if CNN's anchors appeared on the air in bathing suits and the president read a speech wrapped in a yashmak, then you might scream with frustration, even though you probably don't have anything against either Beowulf or bathing suits.

In Solzhenitsyn's little book, at least two lexical layers are clearly delineated. First, there is his "Persian," which includes verbs, adverbs, and nouns meaning "crazy," "doom," "to rob," "neglect," "blindness," "to spoil," "unfortunate," "bad," "very bad," and "horrible," and also "befriend" and "together." The meaning of a good half of these words can be reconstructed only by spotting their roots. This "Persian" vocabulary is rich, inexhaustible, and very expressive and, given the context, incredibly tasteless. And it is incorporated into a syntax that is equally unintelligible—not Russian literary syntax, but that of "popular" or "peasant" speech. This, of course, is no accident. Even if you ignore the meaning of what is said, and consider the style alone, it becomes quite clear that the writer is speaking to the "people," the "muzhik," the "peasant"—an imagined and generic peasant, to be sure. Addressing these archetypes in this archaic and obsolete language, Solzhenitsyn rails and curses. Others—notably foreigners, city-dwellers, and contemporaries—are not his intended interlocutors. Through his mythological fence Solzhenitsyn conjures a mythological Russia-dweller, and summons the spirit of the Russian land with spells and incantations. All are supposed to respond, mere mortals as well as the entire pantheon of our folklore: the talking steeds, wise ravens, all-powerful pikes, mice, hobgoblins, mermaids, and domestic spirits.

The second layer of Solzhenitsyn's language consists largely of political terminology: "parliament," "party," "democracy," "bureaucracy," "economy," "majority" and "minority," "monopoly," "voting," "procedure," "lawyer," "legislation," "proportional system," "information," "statistics," "national," and many other such words. The syntax in the section where these words dominate is normative, clear, easily mastered. This, too, is no coincidence. When you switch from magic to reality, you have to speak comprehensibly. There are no mermaids in parliament.

Solzhenitsyn's article is divided into two almost equal

parts, which consist, in turn, of fourteen short "chapters" each. In the first half of his book, the author speaks of the past and the present, and in the second half he gives his ideas regarding the future. I counted the frequency of "strange" words and locutions in both parts. In the first part there are 127 such expressions; in the second, 21. They are distributed among the fourteen chapters of each part in the following manner: in part one—12, 16, 11, 11, 6, 8, 12, 6, 7, 3, 8, 12, 11, 4. In part two—1, 1, 1, 1, 2, 2, 0, 5, 1, 5, 0, 0, 1, 1. This is surprising only at first glance. After all, it is in the first half of his text that Solzhenitsyn denounces, appeals, curses, and prophecies—and the apocalyptic mode, as is well known, requires inarticulateness, fervor, and hysteria. If a prophet runs about barefoot, his beard flailing in the wind and his trembling hands lifted heavenward, you listen to him. If the prophet is calm, polite, clean-shaven, and properly dressed, you won't give him the time of day.

It is impossible to expound a proposal for governmental organization in the tone of someone who has just been stung by a scorpion. Not that Solzhenitsyn is mad. Quite the contrary, he knows perfectly well where he is and what he is doing. Here's what he does. He identifies and juxtaposes two principles: "the people" and "the individual." According to Solzhenitsyn, the interests of the people are good, but the interests of the individual are bad. The people want to live a quiet, worthy, well-fed life; the individual wants to grab, to seize, to appropriate, to enjoy. Who are these greedy, disgusting creatures? Young people, the people of television and radio, speculators from the "shadow economy," bureaucrats, all political parties (by definition), the city of Moscow, the nomenklatura, 75 percent of "glasnost's troubadours," teachers, athletes, the military, the Communists, the KGB, the intelligentsia. The government is on the take, industry is "mindless and rapacious," the peasant estate has died out.

Taken individually, in short, everyone is no good. Perhaps this is true, but then how did all these scoundrels manage to constitute a good people? The answer is that "the people" is not "constituted of." According to Solzhenitsyn, "the people" is a living organism, not a "mere mechanical conglomeration of disparate individuals." This, of course, is the old, inevitable trick of totalitarian thinking: "the people" is posited as unified and whole in its multiplicity. It is a sphere, a swarm, an anthill, a beehive, a body. And a body should strive for perfection; everything in it should be smooth, sleek, and harmonious. Every organ should have its place and its function: the heart and brain are more important than the nails and the hair, and so on. If your eye tempts you, then tear it out and throw it away; cut off sickly members, curb those limbs that will not obey, and fortify your spirit with abstinence and prayer.

Having described quite colorfully the horrors and the consequences of communism, and sketched a broad (and in many respects accurate) picture of the country's desolation, Solzhenitsyn commands twelve (or eleven-and-a-half) republics to separate "unequivocally and irreversibly" from Russia proper, in the name of the people. He would leave only the Ukraine, Belorussia, and the Russian part of Kazakhstan in a "Russian Union." He similarly allows the more than 100 small nationalities and ethnic groups to remain part of Russia. "Should they wish to be with us, more the credit to them." And what should be done if one of the twelve "big" republics doesn't want to separate? "With the same resolve we—that is, those remaining—will then need to proclaim our separation from them." "We"—the three Slavic peoples—merge into a single whole and keep 100 smaller ethnic groups for ourselves, while banishing the twelve larger peoples utterly without regard to their desires. (There are chapters called "A word to the Great Russians," "A word to the Ukrainians and Belorussians," and "A word to the smaller nationalities and ethnic groups," but the rest are not found worthy of the patriarch's "words.")

Solzhenitsyn unconsciously and instinctively submerged himself in myth. But, as often happens with Russians, he overdid it. His drama . . . lies precisely in his Russian-ness: in the fact that he so completely and without any doubt identifies himself with Russia, being flesh of its flesh and blood of its blood.

—Tatyana Tolstaya

Solzhenitsyn knows perfectly well the horrors of such forced separation—what it means to cut across the lives of nations, cultures, families, and lands that are closely intertwined—but with biblical cruelty he divides people into "ours" and "not ours." To the Ukrainians, he cries:

> Brothers! We have no need of this cruel partition. The very idea comes from the darkening of minds brought on by the Communist years. Together we have born the suffering of the Soviet period, together we have tumbled into this pit, and together, too, we shall find our way out.

But he is short with "aliens": "panels of experts representing all concerned parties must begin deliberations" to figure out a separation plan. "This sorting process might well take several years."

On the one hand, brothers. On the other hand, commissions of experts. Who are these experts? About what are they expert? Where did they gain the experience that confers upon them such authority? Will this be something like the medieval councils of doctors, professors of phlegm and black bile, in velvet berets with quill pens, and saws near at hand for the necessary and justified amputations? Or will the commissions consist only of "brothers"? But can "brothers" really be relied upon, if, as Solzhenitsyn himself quite rightly says, we "have been hurled back to a state of semibarbarity," and "there is no guarantee whatever that the new leaders now coming to the fore will immediately prove to be farsighted and sober-minded," and "of all the possible freedoms, the one that will inevitably come to the fore will be the freedom to be unscrupulous," and

our souls have been "destroyed," and glasnost is defended by "tainted voices," and three of every four defenders of glasnost are unrepentant "toadies of Brezhnevism," and tens of thousands of intellectuals ("smatterers") have "festering moral sores," and our merchants are "sharks bred in the murky waters of the Soviet underground," and "our glasnost is bedecked, festooned with the same old plump and heavy clusters of lies," and so on?

Consider the chapter "Family and School," which is structured like the rest of them. First, the lamentations: woe is me, woe is us, alack and alas, all is lost! Then the advice on how to correct the situation: begin with children. But since the children have to be taught, begin with the teachers. But since the teachers also have to be taught, begin with the teachers of the teachers. Throw out all the textbooks. Rework everything. Change the university curriculum. But who, again, should do all this? The festering intelligentsia? The mendacious authorities? The wealthy sharks? And if, sharing Solzhenitsyn's horror of this vicious cycle of woe, I should attempt to do something by myself, without waiting for the proper help, well, what awaits me is the lash of control:

> In the near future we can probably also expect to see the appearance of tuition-charging private schools which will surpass the standards of the school system in particular subjects or in some other specific educational aspects. But such schools must not institute irresponsibly arbitrary curricula; they should be under the supervision and control of local educational authorities.

We have come full circle. We have arrived not at freedom, but at control. The unfortunate children, with whom the writer started, are abandoned and forgotten. They were only there for decoration, for rhetorical purposes, to attract attention.

Voting and elections, according to Solzhenitsyn's plan, are not necessary, since "the majority" cannot know what is better for the government and what is worse. In the Russian Union our lives are to be managed by a Sobornaya Duma, or Collective Council, which consists of representatives of the estates. (The writer clarifies that the estates are not the same thing as the trade unions: the unions fight for material welfare, "higher wages and other benefits," while the estates are based on a "common creative impulse," or, as the Russian has it literally, "spiritual co-creativity.") Moreover, these representatives—"the most worthy"—are to be appointed (without voting) by the method of "polling the wise men" (the model here is "the mountain people of the Caucasus") or some other equally enigmatic procedure. (But who will conduct the poll, one wonders? Who will determine the degree of wisdom? Of what does this wisdom consist? How will the disagreement of protesters, stupid people, and those armed to the teeth be resolved? Can the wise man be bought with money? Does he know human passions, weaknesses, fears?) Then, having received the highest authority, the Sobornaya Duma "will have the power to interdict any law or any action by a government institution or agency, and to mandate changes or corrections," for "moral principles must take priority over legal ones" and "any secret organization . . . will be subject to criminal prosecution for conspiracy against society."

If, at this point, the reader cannot dispel the feeling of déjà vu, he is right. The social organization that Solzhenitsyn proposes has already been attempted by somebody called Lenin. The similarities between Lenin and Solzhenitsyn are striking, and they make the differences seem inconsequential. Lenin had "soviets," Solzhenitsyn has "zemstvos," and both are forms of local "self-determination." According to Lenin, socialism is a matter of inventory and control; according to Solzhenitsyn, the future of Russia is a matter of inventory and control. For Lenin, there is the wisdom of the party. For Solzhenitsyn, there is the wisdom of the elders. For Lenin, the intelligentsia is "shit." For Solzhenitsyn, it is filth, pus, hypocrisy. (His polemical essay "Our Pluralists" is entirely directed against the intelligentsia, which he accuses of a diversity of opinion.)

Solzhenitsyn believes that "party rivalry distorts the national will." Lenin thought much the same and destroyed all parties save his own. Both, naturally, cite the will of the people, but neither will allow this people to vote and elect. Lenin detested Russian Orthodoxy and made atheism the government religion. Solzhenitsyn does the opposite, with the same fervor: atheism should be forbidden. Both hate the rule of law. Lenin called the rule of law "bourgeois," which for him was a synonym for "Western, democratic," and enough has been said of Solzhenitsyn's attitude toward the West. The fact that both of them say that "some things may be taken" from the West does not really change the situation. Both, in fact, took personal advantage of the most important things that the West has to offer: its freedoms of speech, the press, action, and movement. Both, living in the security of the West, worked out projects to deprive Russia's inhabitants of freedom, projects that prefer "opinions" to laws, that promote the "moral feeling" of the minority as the ruling power, that call for "democracy" without elections. The apogee of arbitrariness is Solzhenitsyn's statement that "power is a call to service and it cannot be the subject of interparty competition."

Russian readers, who are better acquainted with Lenin's works than they care to be (Lenin was required reading in school and university), immediately notice that even the title of Solzhenitsyn's work, "How We Should Arrange Russia," recalls the title of Lenin's "How We Should Reorganize Rabkrin" (the *rabkrin* were committees of inspection run by workers and peasants). Russia, in sum, has already been "arranged" once according to Solzhenitsyn's plan. And the wise men whose opinion was higher than the law found a cozy place for the writer: on a freezing bunk in the Gulag.

Human beings are awful, there's no denying it. My neighbor is especially awful. He behaves badly, looks strange, likes things that repulse me, and wants things I've already got my eye on; and worst of all, he dares to think the very same of me. History knows two opposite ways of handling such vile creatures. The first is to forbid everything. Fire (Sodom and Gomorrah), water (the Flood), wholesale deaths, inquisition, wars, witch hunts, the Gulag—it's all been tried, but without much apparent effect. Tell a

human being "No!" and you can bet that the moment you turn your back he'll be up to his old tricks.

The second way is to allow everything, to let people themselves work out laws, and to let those laws regulate the incessant flares and sparks of human caprice and need. Laws (like money, which reformers of humanity also hate) were not invented by wily scoundrels, as Solzhenitsyn and Lenin think. Laws are the result of the natural, collective efforts of humanity to establish a single measure on the path to some sort of justice in an imperfect world. For all their flawed approximateness, they have somehow saved humanity from arbitrariness, tyranny, and madness. It is perfectly true that everyone's moral sense differs, that everyone is piqued by different things, but that is precisely why any attempt to substitute "moral feelings" for law inevitably leads to the kind of situation in which, instead of getting a ticket for illegal parking, you and your entire city would be engulfed in fire and brimstone.

Invectives against human insatiability and calls for voluntary self-limitation, when they are not accompanied by specific indications of "how many seeds you must have before you can call them a bunch," may provoke alarm in the sensitive Russian. Can Solzhenitsyn himself have overstepped the mark? Might he, too, have become a shark? Worried, the simple soul scans the pages of Solzhenitsyn's books, of articles on him, of Michael Scammell's biography of him, in search of models to emulate. And one finds: fifty acres of land . . . two houses on the lot . . . twelve volumes of collected works . . . a second wife . . . three children . . . a son at Harvard, when he could have studied at a little Vermont college . . . a son playing piano and giving concert tours when he could have stayed home and beat humbly on a toy drum. Money? The author's income is not publicized, but as early as 1974 there is mention of $2 million to $3 million dollars . . . What a relief! The threshold of self-limitation established by the prophet of Vermont is clearly unattainable in actual Russian life. Russians may sleep soundly.

If someone in Russia were to take Solzhenitsyn's recommendations seriously and set about fulfilling them point by point, the country would collapse within a month. If Solzhenitsyn took over the real Russia with its real population, uprisings, pogroms, and conflagrations would commence within a week. The Russian people, of course, are no gift. Obedient but not acquiescent, submissive but willful, lazy but pliant—everyone wants to have a go at governing them, at deciding for them. Referring to the "Will of the People" (with capital letters, of course), Solzhenitsyn's pen frequently slips, and accidentally declares that no one knows what this will is or how it may be determined. On those occasions when he does detect traces of that will's free manifestation, however, he can find no kind words for it. Here's what the people have chosen to embrace from the West: the "continuous seepage of liquid manure—the self-indulgent and squalid 'popular mass culture,' the utterly vulgar fashions and the byproducts of immoderate publicity." But "popular," "mass," "vulgar," and "public" are all words that describe the people, and these, after all, are *its* music, *its* fashion, *its* byproducts, however revolting they might be or seem. The people in theory always diverge dramatically from the people in reality; and the horror of this truth is sooner or later discovered by everyone who pretends to the people's spiritual leadership, by everyone who knows how things should and should not be done.

Having settled in the most atypical state in the United States, built himself a fence, refused to allow mere mortals to enter (except for the few who agree to scratch his heels), Solzhenitsyn unconsciously and instinctively submerged himself in myth. But, as often happens with Russians, he overdid it. His drama, as I see it, lies precisely in his Russianness: in the fact that he so completely and without any doubt identifies himself with Russia, being flesh of its flesh and blood of its blood. And this proves that, although there is absolutely nothing Western about him, not the tiniest wrinkle, he is nonetheless only a part of Russia, and not Russia itself. For Russia is broader and more diverse, stranger and more contradictory, than any idea of it. It resists all theories about what makes it tick, confounds all the paths to its possible transformation. One can describe and explain Russia in a thousand ways, but as soon as the theorist and the dreamer lays down his pen, satisfied at last with his description, diabolical laughter will sound from the emptiness behind him, and the undried ink will evaporate, leaving not a trace on the white page. (pp. 31-6)

Tatyana Tolstaya, "The Grand Inquisitor," translated by Jamey Gambrell in The New Republic, *Vol. 206, No. 26, June 29, 1992, pp. 29-36.*

FURTHER READING

Bibliography

Fiene, Donald M. *Alexander Solzhenitsyn: An International Bibliography of Writings By and About Him, 1962-1973.* Ann Arbor, Mich.: Ardis, 1973, 158 p.

Catalogs Russian and English criticism on Solzhenitsyn's works through 1973.

Biography

Scammell, Michael. *Solzhenitsyn: A Biography.* New York: W. W. Norton & Company, 1984, 1051 p.

Comprehensive account of Solzhenitsyn's life and works through 1983.

Criticism

Bayley, John. "God and the Devil." *The New York Review of Books* XXXVI, No. 20 (21 December 1989): 11-13.

Review of the revised version of *August 1914* in which Bayley asserts that despite a certain dogmatism in the text, Solzhenitsyn remains a brilliant writer.

Six Later Reflections. Washington, D.C.: Ethics and Public Policy Center, 1980, 143 p.

Includes an English translation of Solzhenitsyn's 1976 Harvard address and collects several articles and essays on public and private reaction to the address.

Casillo, Robert. "Techne and Logos in Solzhenitsyn." *Soundings* LXX, Nos. 3-4 (Fall-Winter 1987): 519-37.

Outlines Solzhenitsyn's critique of technology in his works.

Confino, Michael. "Solzhenitsyn, the West, and the New Russian Nationalism." *Journal of Contemporary History* 26, Nos. 3-4 (September 1991): 611-36.

Examines Solzhenitsyn's politics and influence on Russian nationalist groups.

Diegel, Anna. "Human Rights and Literature: Solzhenitsyn and Pasternak." *Theoria* LXXV (May 1990): 77-85.

Traces the treatment of violations of human rights in the works of Solzhenitsyn and Boris Pasternak.

Dunlop, John B.; Haugh, Richard S.; and Klimoff, Alexis, eds. *Aleksandr Solzhenitsyn: Critical Essays and Documentary Materials.* Belmont, Mass.: Nordland Publishing Company, 1973, 569 p.

Collection of critical essays that includes a bibliography of works by and about Solzhenitsyn.

——. *Solzhenitsyn in Exile: Critical Essays and Documentary Materials.* Stanford, Calif.: Hoover Institution Press, 1985, 412 p.

A four-part collection of writings about Solzhenitsyn and his works which includes reactions to the author as a political figure in the United States and Europe from 1974 to 1985, criticism on his works during the same period, interviews with Solzhenitsyn, and a memoir by dissident novelist Lidiia Chukovskaia. Also contains a bibliography of criticism on Solzhenitsyn's works between 1973 and 1981.

Frankel, Edith Rogovin. "The Tvardovsky Controversy." *Soviet Studies* XXXIV, No. 4 (October 1982): 601-15.

Discusses the depiction of Aleksandr Tvardovsky, poet and editor of the journal *Novy Mir,* in Solzhenitsyn's works.

Halperin, David M. "Solzhenitsyn, Epicurus, and the Ethics of Stalinism." *Critical Inquiry* 7, No. 3 (Spring 1981): 475-97.

Illustrates how Solzhenitsyn uses Epicureanism as a metaphor for Stalinist ethics.

Kelley, Donald R. *The Solzhenitsyn-Sakharov Dialogue: Politics, Society, and the Future.* Westport, Conn.: Greenwood Press, 1982, 175 p.

Surveys the opinions of Solzhenitsyn and Andrei Sakharov on the subject of what type of social and political structure should replace Communism in Russia.

Krasnov, Vladislav. "The Social Vision of Aleksandr Solzhenitsyn." *Modern Age: A Quarterly Review* 28, Nos. 2-3 (Spring-Summer 1984): 215-21.

Examines *Letter to the Soviet Leaders* and several other essays to determine Solzhenitsyn's "social thinking as contrasted with that of his Western critics."

Leavis, Q. D. "Solzhenitsyn, the Creative Artist, and the Totalitarian State." *Modern Age: A Quarterly* 32, No. 4 (Fall 1989): 294-310.

Explores how writing within the oppressive climate of a totalitarian state affected the works of Solzhenitsyn and other artists.

Pontuso, James F. *Solzhenitsyn's Political Thought.* Charlottesville, Va.: University Press of Virginia, 1990, 272 p.

Outlines shifts in Solzhenitsyn's political views.

Rancour-Laferriere, Daniel. "The Deranged Birthday Boy: Solzhenitsyn's Portrait of Stalin in *The First Circle.*" *Mosaic: A Journal for the Interdisciplinary Study of Literature* XVIII, No. 3 (Summer 1985): 61-72.
Analyzes Solzhenitsyn's characterization of Stalin as mentally and emotionally disturbed in *The First Circle.*

——. "Solzhenitsyn and the Jews: A Psychoanalytic View." *Soviet Jewish Affairs* 15, No. 3 (November 1985): 30-54.
Illustrates through psychoanalytic investigation that there exists "an emotional ambivalence, a contradictory hate/love attitude at the heart of Solzhenitsyn's utterances about Jews."

Rózsás, János. "In the Gulag with Solzhenitsyn." *The New Hungarian Quarterly* XXXI, No. 117 (Spring 1990): 15-22.
Combines Rózsás' recollections of the time he spent at Eikhibastuz prison camp with Solzhenitsyn in the early 1950s with excerpts of his correspondence with Solzhenitsyn.

Siegel, Paul N. "The Political Implications of Solzhenitsyn's Novels." *Clio* 12, No. 3 (Spring 1983): 211-32.
Examines the often disparate political implications inherent in Solzhenitsyn's different works.

——. "Solzhenitsyn's Portrait of Lenin." *Clio* 14, No. 1 (Fall 1984): 1-13.

Assesses the historical accuracy of Solzhenitsyn's portrayal of Lenin in *Lenin in Zurich.*

Singer, Daniel. "Stalin's Grandchildren." *The Nation* 254, No. 6 (17 February 1992): 202-05.
Faults *Rebuilding Russia* as unrealistic.

Stent, Angela. "What is to be done?" *The Washington Post Book World* XXII, No. 7 (16 February 1992): 7.
Discusses *Rebuilding Russia,* characterizing Solzhenitsyn's suggestions for a modern Russian social and political structure as impractical and his interpretations of Russian history as arguable.

Tusa, John. "Interview with Alexander Solzhenitsyn." *The Listener* 109, No. 2810 (26 May 1983): 2-4.
Interview in which Solzhenitsyn discusses various events in world politics.

Venclova, Tomas. "War and Pieces." *The New Republic* 201, No. 9 (28 August 1989): 33-7.
Acknowledges Solzhenitsyn as a major literary talent but faults his ideological stance in *August 1914.*

Wilson, Raymond J., III. "Solzhenitsyn's *August 1914* and *Lenin in Zurich:* The Question of Historical Determinism." *Clio* 14, No. 1 (Fall 1984): 15-36.
Explores Solzhenitsyn's views on determinism as reflected in *August 1914* and *Lenin in Zurich.*

☐ Contemporary Literary Criticism

Indexes

Literary Criticism Series
Cumulative Author Index
Cumulative Nationality Index
Title Index, Volume 78

How to Use This Index

The main references

Calvino, Italo
1923-1985.....CLC 5, 8, 11, 22, 33, 39,
73; SSC 3

---

list all author entries in the following Gale Literary Criticism series:

CLC = Contemporary Literary Criticism
CLR = Children's Literature Review
CMLC = Classical and Medieval Literature Criticism
DC = Drama Criticism
LC = Literature Criticism from 1400 to 1800
NCLC = Nineteenth-Century Literature Criticism
PC = Poetry Criticism
SSC = Short Story Criticism
TCLC = Twentieth-Century Literary Criticism

The cross-references

See also CANR 23; CA 85-88;
obituary CA 116

---

list all author entries in the following Gale biographical and literary sources:

AAYA = Authors & Artists for Young Adults
AITN = Authors in the News
BLC = Black Literature Criticism
BW = Black Writers
CA = Contemporary Authors
CAAS = Contemporary Authors Autobiography Series
CABS = Contemporary Authors Bibliographical Series
CANR = Contemporary Authors New Revision Series
CAP = Contemporary Authors Permanent Series
CDALB = Concise Dictionary of American Literary Biography
CDBLB = Concise Dictionary of British Literary Biography
DLB = Dictionary of Literary Biography
DLBD = Dictionary of Literary Biography Documentary Series
DLBY = Dictionary of Literary Biography Yearbook
HW = Hispanic Writers
MAICYA = Major Authors and Illustrators for Children and Young Adults
MTCW = Major 20th-Century Writers
SAAS = Something about the Author Autobiography Series
SATA = Something about the Author
WLC = World Literature Criticism, 1500 to the Present
YABC = Yesterday's Authors of Books for Children

Antoninus, Brother
See Everson, William (Oliver)

Antonioni, Michelangelo 1912- ..... **CLC 20**
See also CA 73-76

Antschel, Paul 1920-1970. ..... **CLC 10, 19**
See also Celan, Paul
See also CA 85-88; CANR 33; MTCW

Anwar, Chairil 1922-1949 .... **TCLC 22**
See also CA 121

Apollinaire, Guillaume .. **TCLC 3, 8, 51; PC 7**
See also Kostrowitzki, Wilhelm Apollinaris
de

Appelfeld, Aharon 1932- .... **CLC 23, 47**
See also CA 112; 133

Apple, Max (Isaac) 1941-........ **CLC 9, 33**
See also CA 81-84; CANR 19; DLB 130

Appleman, Philip (Dean) 1926- ..... **CLC 51**
See also CA 13-16R; CANR 6, 29

Appleton, Lawrence
See Lovecraft, H(oward) P(hillips)

Apteryx
See Eliot, T(homas) S(tearns)

Apuleius, (Lucius Madaurensis)
125(?)-175(?) .... **CMLC 1**

Aquin, Hubert 1929-1977......... **CLC 15**
See also CA 105; DLB 53

Aragon, Louis 1897-1982....... **CLC 3, 22**
See also CA 69-72; 108; CANR 28;
DLB 72; MTCW

Arany, Janos 1817-1882........ **NCLC 34**

Arbuthnot, John 1667-1735......... **LC 1**
See also DLB 101

Archer, Herbert Winslow
See Mencken, H(enry) L(ouis)

Archer, Jeffrey (Howard) 1940- .... **CLC 28**
See also BEST 89:3; CA 77-80; CANR 22

Archer, Jules 1915- .... **CLC 12**
See also CA 9-12R; CANR 6; SAAS 5;
SATA 4

Archer, Lee
See Ellison, Harlan

Arden, John 1930- .... **CLC 6, 13, 15**
See also CA 13-16R; CAAS 4; CANR 31;
DLB 13; MTCW

Arenas, Reinaldo 1943-1990 .... **CLC 41**
See also CA 124; 128; 133; HW

Arendt, Hannah 1906-1975 .... **CLC 66**
See also CA 17-20R; 61-64; CANR 26;
MTCW

Aretino, Pietro 1492-1556 .... **LC 12**

Arguedas, Jose Maria
1911-1969 .... **CLC 10, 18**
See also CA 89-92; DLB 113; HW

Argueta, Manlio 1936-........... **CLC 31**
See also CA 131; HW

Ariosto, Ludovico 1474-1533........ **LC 6**

Aristides
See Epstein, Joseph

Aristophanes
450B.C.-385B.C....... **CMLC 4; DC 2**
See also DA

Arlt, Roberto (Godofredo Christophersen)
1900-1942 .... **TCLC 29**
See also CA 123; 131; HW

Armah, Ayi Kwei 1939-........ **CLC 5, 33**
See also BLC 1; BW; CA 61-64; CANR 21;
DLB 117; MTCW

Armatrading, Joan 1950-......... **CLC 17**
See also CA 114

Arnette, Robert
See Silverberg, Robert

Arnim, Achim von (Ludwig Joachim von
Arnim) 1781-1831 .... **NCLC 5**
See also DLB 90

Arnim, Bettina von 1785-1859.... **NCLC 38**
See also DLB 90

Arnold, Matthew
1822-1888 .... **NCLC 6, 29; PC 5**
See also CDBLB 1832-1890; DA; DLB 32,
57; WLC

Arnold, Thomas 1795-1842 ...... **NCLC 18**
See also DLB 55

Arnow, Harriette (Louisa) Simpson
1908-1986 .... **CLC 2, 7, 18**
See also CA 9-12R; 118; CANR 14; DLB 6;
MTCW; SATA 42, 47

Arp, Hans
See Arp, Jean

Arp, Jean 1887-1966............... **CLC 5**
See also CA 81-84; 25-28R

Arrabal
See Arrabal, Fernando

Arrabal, Fernando 1932- ... **CLC 2, 9, 18, 58**
See also CA 9-12R; CANR 15

Arrick, Fran.................... **CLC 30**

Artaud, Antonin 1896-1948 ..... **TCLC 3, 36**
See also CA 104

Arthur, Ruth M(abel) 1905-1979.... **CLC 12**
See also CA 9-12R; 85-88; CANR 4;
SATA 7, 26

Artsybashev, Mikhail (Petrovich)
1878-1927 .... **TCLC 31**

Arundel, Honor (Morfydd)
1919-1973 .... **CLC 17**
See also CA 21-22; 41-44R; CAP 2;
SATA 4, 24

Asch, Sholem 1880-1957 .... **TCLC 3**
See also CA 105

Ash, Shalom
See Asch, Sholem

Ashbery, John (Lawrence)
1927- ...... **CLC 2, 3, 4, 6, 9, 13, 15, 25,**
41, 77
See also CA 5-8R; CANR 9, 37; DLB 5;
DLBY 81; MTCW

Ashdown, Clifford
See Freeman, R(ichard) Austin

Ashe, Gordon
See Creasey, John

Ashton-Warner, Sylvia (Constance)
1908-1984 .... **CLC 19**
See also CA 69-72; 112; CANR 29; MTCW

Asimov, Isaac
1920-1992 ...... **CLC 1, 3, 9, 19, 26, 76**
See also BEST 90:2; CA 1-4R; 137;
CANR 2, 19, 36; CLR 12; DLB 8;
DLBY 92; MAICYA; MTCW; SATA 1,
26, 74

Astley, Thea (Beatrice May)
1925- .... **CLC 41**
See also CA 65-68; CANR 11

Aston, James
See White, T(erence) H(anbury)

Asturias, Miguel Angel
1899-1974 .... **CLC 3, 8, 13**
See also CA 25-28; 49-52; CANR 32;
CAP 2; DLB 113; HW; MTCW

Atares, Carlos Saura
See Saura (Atares), Carlos

Atheling, William
See Pound, Ezra (Weston Loomis)

Atheling, William, Jr.
See Blish, James (Benjamin)

Atherton, Gertrude (Franklin Horn)
1857-1948 .... **TCLC 2**
See also CA 104; DLB 9, 78

Atherton, Lucius
See Masters, Edgar Lee

Atkins, Jack
See Harris, Mark

Atticus
See Fleming, Ian (Lancaster)

Atwood, Margaret (Eleanor)
1939- ..... **CLC 2, 3, 4, 8, 13, 15, 25, 44;**
SSC 2
See also BEST 89:2; CA 49-52; CANR 3,
24, 33; DA; DLB 53; MTCW; SATA 50;
WLC

Aubigny, Pierre d'
See Mencken, H(enry) L(ouis)

Aubin, Penelope 1685-1731(?)........ **LC 9**
See also DLB 39

Auchincloss, Louis (Stanton)
1917- .... **CLC 4, 6, 9, 18, 45**
See also CA 1-4R; CANR 6, 29; DLB 2;
DLBY 80; MTCW

Auden, W(ystan) H(ugh)
1907-1973 ...... **CLC 1, 2, 3, 4, 6, 9, 11,**
14, 43; PC 1
See also CA 9-12R; 45-48; CANR 5;
CDBLB 1914-1945; DA; DLB 10, 20;
MTCW; WLC

Audiberti, Jacques 1900-1965 ...... **CLC 38**
See also CA 25-28R

Auel, Jean M(arie) 1936-.......... **CLC 31**
See also AAYA 7; BEST 90:4; CA 103;
CANR 21

Auerbach, Erich 1892-1957 .... **TCLC 43**
See also CA 118

Augier, Emile 1820-1889 .... **NCLC 31**

August, John
See De Voto, Bernard (Augustine)

Augustine, St. 354-430.......... **CMLC 6**

Aurelius
See Bourne, Randolph S(illiman)

Austen, Jane
    1775-1817 . . . . **NCLC 1, 13, 19, 33**
    See also CDBLB 1789-1832; DA; DLB 116;
    WLC

Auster, Paul 1947- . . . . **CLC 47**
    See also CA 69-72; CANR 23

Austin, Frank
    See Faust, Frederick (Schiller)

Austin, Mary (Hunter)
    1868-1934 . . . . **TCLC 25**
    See also CA 109; DLB 9, 78

Autran Dourado, Waldomiro
    See Dourado, (Waldomiro Freitas) Autran

Averroes 1126-1198 . . . . **CMLC 7**
    See also DLB 115

Avison, Margaret 1918- . . . . **CLC 2, 4**
    See also CA 17-20R; DLB 53; MTCW

Axton, David
    See Koontz, Dean R(ay)

Ayckbourn, Alan
    1939- . . . . **CLC 5, 8, 18, 33, 74**
    See also CA 21-24R; CANR 31; DLB 13;
    MTCW

Aydy, Catherine
    See Tennant, Emma (Christina)

Ayme, Marcel (Andre) 1902-1967 . . . **CLC 11**
    See also CA 89-92; CLR 25; DLB 72

Ayrton, Michael 1921-1975 . . . . **CLC 7**
    See also CA 5-8R; 61-64; CANR 9, 21

Azorin . . . . **CLC 11**
    See also Martinez Ruiz, Jose

Azuela, Mariano 1873-1952 . . . . **TCLC 3**
    See also CA 104; 131; HW; MTCW

Baastad, Babbis Friis
    See Friis-Baastad, Babbis Ellinor

Bab
    See Gilbert, W(illiam) S(chwenck)

Babbis, Eleanor
    See Friis-Baastad, Babbis Ellinor

Babel, Isaak (Emmanuilovich)
    1894-1941(?) . . . . **CLC 73**
    See also CA 104; TCLC 2, 13

Babits, Mihaly 1883-1941 . . . . **TCLC 14**
    See also CA 114

Babur 1483-1530 . . . . **LC 18**

Bacchelli, Riccardo 1891-1985 . . . . . **CLC 19**
    See also CA 29-32R; 117

Bach, Richard (David) 1936- . . . . **CLC 14**
    See also AITN 1; BEST 89:2; CA 9-12R;
    CANR 18; MTCW; SATA 13

Bachman, Richard
    See King, Stephen (Edwin)

Bachmann, Ingeborg 1926-1973 . . . . . **CLC 69**
    See also CA 93-96; 45-48; DLB 85

Bacon, Francis 1561-1626 . . . . **LC 18**
    See also CDBLB Before 1660

Bacovia, George . . . . **TCLC 24**
    See also Vasiliu, Gheorghe

Badanes, Jerome 1937- . . . . **CLC 59**

Bagehot, Walter 1826-1877 . . . . . . **NCLC 10**
    See also DLB 55

Bagnold, Enid 1889-1981 . . . . **CLC 25**
    See also CA 5-8R; 103; CANR 5, 40;
    DLB 13; MAICYA; SATA 1, 25

Bagrjana, Elisaveta
    See Belcheva, Elisaveta

Bagryana, Elisaveta
    See Belcheva, Elisaveta

Bailey, Paul 1937- . . . . **CLC 45**
    See also CA 21-24R; CANR 16; DLB 14

Baillie, Joanna 1762-1851 . . . . **NCLC 2**
    See also DLB 93

Bainbridge, Beryl (Margaret)
    1933- . . . . **CLC 4, 5, 8, 10, 14, 18, 22, 62**
    See also CA 21-24R; CANR 24; DLB 14;
    MTCW

Baker, Elliott 1922- . . . . **CLC 8**
    See also CA 45-48; CANR 2

Baker, Nicholson 1957- . . . . **CLC 61**
    See also CA 135

Baker, Ray Stannard 1870-1946 . . . **TCLC 47**
    See also CA 118

Baker, Russell (Wayne) 1925- . . . . . . **CLC 31**
    See also BEST 89:4; CA 57-60; CANR 11,
    41; MTCW

Bakshi, Ralph 1938(?)- . . . . **CLC 26**
    See also CA 112; 138

Bakunin, Mikhail (Alexandrovich)
    1814-1876 . . . . **NCLC 25**

Baldwin, James (Arthur)
    1924-1987 . . . . . . **CLC 1, 2, 3, 4, 5, 8, 13,**
            15, 17, 42, 50, 67; DC 1; SSC 10
    See also AAYA 4; BLC 1; BW; CA 1-4R;
    124; CABS 1; CANR 3, 24;
    CDALB 1941-1968; DA; DLB 2, 7, 33;
    DLBY 87; MTCW; SATA 9, 54; WLC

Ballard, J(ames) G(raham)
    1930- . . . . **CLC 3, 6, 14, 36; SSC 1**
    See also AAYA 3; CA 5-8R; CANR 15, 39;
    DLB 14; MTCW

Balmont, Konstantin (Dmitriyevich)
    1867-1943 . . . . **TCLC 11**
    See also CA 109

Balzac, Honore de
    1799-1850 . . . . **NCLC 5, 35; SSC 5**
    See also DA; DLB 119; WLC

Bambara, Toni Cade 1939- . . . . **CLC 19**
    See also AAYA 5; BLC 1; BW; CA 29-32R;
    CANR 24; DA; DLB 38; MTCW

Bamdad, A.
    See Shamlu, Ahmad

Banat, D. R.
    See Bradbury, Ray (Douglas)

Bancroft, Laura
    See Baum, L(yman) Frank

Banim, John 1798-1842 . . . . **NCLC 13**
    See also DLB 116

Banim, Michael 1796-1874 . . . . . . **NCLC 13**

Banks, Iain
    See Banks, Iain M(enzies)

Banks, Iain M(enzies) 1954- . . . . **CLC 34**
    See also CA 123; 128

Banks, Lynne Reid . . . . **CLC 23**
    See also Reid Banks, Lynne
    See also AAYA 6

Banks, Russell 1940- . . . . **CLC 37, 72**
    See also CA 65-68; CAAS 15; CANR 19;
    DLB 130

Banville, John 1945- . . . . **CLC 46**
    See also CA 117; 128; DLB 14

Banville, Theodore (Faullain) de
    1832-1891 . . . . **NCLC 9**

Baraka, Amiri
    1934- . . . **CLC 1, 2, 3, 5, 10, 14, 33; PC 4**
    See also Jones, LeRoi
    See also BLC 1; BW; CA 21-24R; CABS 3;
    CANR 27, 38; CDALB 1941-1968; DA;
    DLB 5, 7, 16, 38; DLBD 8; MTCW

Barbellion, W. N. P. . . . . **TCLC 24**
    See also Cummings, Bruce F(rederick)

Barbera, Jack 1945- . . . . **CLC 44**
    See also CA 110

Barbey d'Aurevilly, Jules Amedee
    1808-1889 . . . . **NCLC 1**
    See also DLB 119

Barbusse, Henri 1873-1935 . . . . **TCLC 5**
    See also CA 105; DLB 65

Barclay, Bill
    See Moorcock, Michael (John)

Barclay, William Ewert
    See Moorcock, Michael (John)

Barea, Arturo 1897-1957 . . . . **TCLC 14**
    See also CA 111

Barfoot, Joan 1946- . . . . **CLC 18**
    See also CA 105

Baring, Maurice 1874-1945 . . . . **TCLC 8**
    See also CA 105; DLB 34

Barker, Clive 1952- . . . . **CLC 52**
    See also AAYA 10; BEST 90:3; CA 121;
    129; MTCW

Barker, George Granville
    1913-1991 . . . . **CLC 8, 48**
    See also CA 9-12R; 135; CANR 7, 38;
    DLB 20; MTCW

Barker, Harley Granville
    See Granville-Barker, Harley
    See also DLB 10

Barker, Howard 1946- . . . . **CLC 37**
    See also CA 102; DLB 13

Barker, Pat 1943- . . . . **CLC 32**
    See also CA 117; 122

Barlow, Joel 1754-1812 . . . . **NCLC 23**
    See also DLB 37

Barnard, Mary (Ethel) 1909- . . . . **CLC 48**
    See also CA 21-22; CAP 2

Barnes, Djuna
    1892-1982 . . . **CLC 3, 4, 8, 11, 29; SSC 3**
    See also CA 9-12R; 107; CANR 16; DLB 4,
    9, 45; MTCW

Barnes, Julian 1946- . . . . **CLC 42**
    See also CA 102; CANR 19

Barnes, Peter 1931- . . . . **CLC 5, 56**
    See also CA 65-68; CAAS 12; CANR 33,
    34; DLB 13; MTCW

Baroja (y Nessi), Pio 1872-1956 . . . . **TCLC 8**
    See also CA 104

Baron, David
    See Pinter, Harold

Belloc, (Joseph) Hilaire (Pierre)
1870-1953 . . . . TCLC 7, 18
See also CA 106; DLB 19, 100; YABC 1

Belloc, Joseph Peter Rene Hilaire
See Belloc, (Joseph) Hilaire (Pierre)

Belloc, Joseph Pierre Hilaire
See Belloc, (Joseph) Hilaire (Pierre)

Belloc, M. A.
See Lowndes, Marie Adelaide (Belloc)

Bellow, Saul
1915- . . . . . . CLC 1, 2, 3, 6, 8, 10, 13, 15,
25, 33, 34, 63
See also AITN 2; BEST 89:3; CA 5-8R;
CABS 1; CANR 29; CDALB 1941-1968;
DA; DLB 2, 28; DLBD 3; DLBY 82;
MTCW; WLC

Belser, Reimond Karel Maria de
1929- . . . . CLC 14

Bely, Andrey . . . . TCLC 7
See also Bugayev, Boris Nikolayevich

Benary, Margot
See Benary-Isbert, Margot

Benary-Isbert, Margot   1889-1979 . . . CLC 12
See also CA 5-8R; 89-92; CANR 4;
CLR 12; MAICYA; SATA 2, 21

Benavente (y Martinez), Jacinto
1866-1954 . . . . TCLC 3
See also CA 106; 131; HW; MTCW

Benchley, Peter (Bradford)
1940- . . . . CLC 4, 8
See also AITN 2; CA 17-20R; CANR 12,
35; MTCW; SATA 3

Benchley, Robert (Charles)
1889-1945 . . . . TCLC 1
See also CA 105; DLB 11

Benedikt, Michael   1935- . . . . CLC 4, 14
See also CA 13-16R; CANR 7; DLB 5

Benet, Juan   1927- . . . . CLC 28

Benet, Stephen Vincent
1898-1943 . . . . TCLC 7; SSC 10
See also CA 104; DLB 4, 48, 102; YABC 1

Benet, William Rose   1886-1950 . . . TCLC 28
See also CA 118; DLB 45

Benford, Gregory (Albert)   1941- . . . . CLC 52
See also CA 69-72; CANR 12, 24;
DLBY 82

Bengtsson, Frans (Gunnar)
1894-1954 . . . . TCLC 48

Benjamin, David
See Slavitt, David R(ytman)

Benjamin, Lois
See Gould, Lois

Benjamin, Walter   1892-1940 . . . . . . TCLC 39

Benn, Gottfried   1886-1956 . . . . TCLC 3
See also CA 106; DLB 56

Bennett, Alan   1934- . . . . CLC 45, 77
See also CA 103; CANR 35; MTCW

Bennett, (Enoch) Arnold
1867-1931 . . . . TCLC 5, 20
See also CA 106; CDBLB 1890-1914;
DLB 10, 34, 98

Bennett, Elizabeth
See Mitchell, Margaret (Munnerlyn)

Bennett, George Harold   1930-
See Bennett, Hal
See also BW; CA 97-100

Bennett, Hal . . . . CLC 5
See also Bennett, George Harold
See also DLB 33

Bennett, Jay   1912- . . . . CLC 35
See also AAYA 10; CA 69-72; CANR 11;
SAAS 4; SATA 27, 41

Bennett, Louise (Simone)   1919- . . . . . CLC 28
See also BLC 1; DLB 117

Benson, E(dward) F(rederic)
1867-1940 . . . . TCLC 27
See also CA 114

Benson, Jackson J.   1930- . . . . CLC 34
See also CA 25-28R; DLB 111

Benson, Sally   1900-1972 . . . . CLC 17
See also CA 19-20; 37-40R; CAP 1;
SATA 1, 27, 35

Benson, Stella   1892-1933 . . . . TCLC 17
See also CA 117; DLB 36

Bentham, Jeremy   1748-1832 . . . . . NCLC 38
See also DLB 107

Bentley, E(dmund) C(lerihew)
1875-1956 . . . . TCLC 12
See also CA 108; DLB 70

Bentley, Eric (Russell)   1916- . . . . CLC 24
See also CA 5-8R; CANR 6

Beranger, Pierre Jean de
1780-1857 . . . . NCLC 34

Berger, Colonel
See Malraux, (Georges-)Andre

Berger, John (Peter)   1926- . . . . . . CLC 2, 19
See also CA 81-84; DLB 14

Berger, Melvin H.   1927- . . . . CLC 12
See also CA 5-8R; CANR 4; SAAS 2;
SATA 5

Berger, Thomas (Louis)
1924- . . . . . . CLC 3, 5, 8, 11, 18, 38
See also CA 1-4R; CANR 5, 28; DLB 2;
DLBY 80; MTCW

Bergman, (Ernst) Ingmar
1918- . . . . CLC 16, 72
See also CA 81-84; CANR 33

Bergson, Henri   1859-1941 . . . . TCLC 32

Bergstein, Eleanor   1938- . . . . CLC 4
See also CA 53-56; CANR 5

Berkoff, Steven   1937- . . . . CLC 56
See also CA 104

Bermant, Chaim (Icyk)   1929- . . . . . . CLC 40
See also CA 57-60; CANR 6, 31

Bern, Victoria
See Fisher, M(ary) F(rances) K(ennedy)

Bernanos, (Paul Louis) Georges
1888-1948 . . . . TCLC 3
See also CA 104; 130; DLB 72

Bernard, April   1956- . . . . CLC 59
See also CA 131

Bernhard, Thomas
1931-1989 . . . . CLC 3, 32, 61
See also CA 85-88; 127; CANR 32;
DLB 85, 124; MTCW

Berrigan, Daniel   1921- . . . . CLC 4
See also CA 33-36R; CAAS 1; CANR 11;
DLB 5

Berrigan, Edmund Joseph Michael, Jr.
1934-1983
See Berrigan, Ted
See also CA 61-64; 110; CANR 14

Berrigan, Ted . . . . CLC 37
See also Berrigan, Edmund Joseph Michael,
Jr.
See also DLB 5

Berry, Charles Edward Anderson   1931-
See Berry, Chuck
See also CA 115

Berry, Chuck . . . . CLC 17
See also Berry, Charles Edward Anderson

Berry, Jonas
See Ashbery, John (Lawrence)

Berry, Wendell (Erdman)
1934- . . . . CLC 4, 6, 8, 27, 46
See also AITN 1; CA 73-76; DLB 5, 6

Berryman, John
1914-1972 . . . . . . CLC 1, 2, 3, 4, 6, 8, 10,
13, 25, 62
See also CA 13-16; 33-36R; CABS 2;
CANR 35; CAP 1; CDALB 1941-1968;
DLB 48; MTCW

Bertolucci, Bernardo   1940- . . . . CLC 16
See also CA 106

Bertrand, Aloysius   1807-1841 . . . . NCLC 31

Bertran de Born   c. 1140-1215 . . . . . CMLC 5

Besant, Annie (Wood)   1847-1933 . . . TCLC 9
See also CA 105

Bessie, Alvah   1904-1985 . . . . CLC 23
See also CA 5-8R; 116; CANR 2; DLB 26

Bethlen, T. D.
See Silverberg, Robert

Beti, Mongo . . . . CLC 27
See also Biyidi, Alexandre
See also BLC 1

Betjeman, John
1906-1984 . . . . CLC 2, 6, 10, 34, 43
See also CA 9-12R; 112; CANR 33;
CDBLB 1945-1960; DLB 20; DLBY 84;
MTCW

Betti, Ugo   1892-1953 . . . . TCLC 5
See also CA 104

Betts, Doris (Waugh)   1932- . . . . CLC 3, 6, 28
See also CA 13-16R; CANR 9; DLBY 82

Bevan, Alistair
See Roberts, Keith (John Kingston)

Beynon, John
See Harris, John (Wyndham Parkes Lucas)
Beynon

Bialik, Chaim Nachman
1873-1934 . . . . TCLC 25

Bickerstaff, Isaac
See Swift, Jonathan

Bidart, Frank   1939- . . . . CLC 33
See also CA 140

Bienek, Horst   1930- . . . . CLC 7, 11
See also CA 73-76; DLB 75

Bridges, Robert (Seymour)
   1844-1930 .... **TCLC 1**
   See also CA 104; CDBLB 1890-1914;
   DLB 19, 98

Bridie, James.................... **TCLC 3**
   See also Mavor, Osborne Henry
   See also DLB 10

Brin, David   1950-................ **CLC 34**
   See also CA 102; CANR 24; SATA 65

Brink, Andre (Philippus)
   1935-..................... **CLC 18, 36**
   See also CA 104; CANR 39; MTCW

Brinsmead, H(esba) F(ay)   1922-.... **CLC 21**
   See also CA 21-24R; CANR 10; MAICYA;
   SAAS 5; SATA 18

Brittain, Vera (Mary)
   1893(?)-1970 .... **CLC 23**
   See also CA 13-16; 25-28R; CAP 1; MTCW

Broch, Hermann   1886-1951...... **TCLC 20**
   See also CA 117; DLB 85, 124

Brock, Rose
   See Hansen, Joseph

Brodkey, Harold   1930-........... **CLC 56**
   See also CA 111; DLB 130

Brodsky, Iosif Alexandrovich   1940-
   See Brodsky, Joseph
   See also AITN 1; CA 41-44R; CANR 37;
   MTCW

Brodsky, Joseph .... **CLC 4, 6, 13, 36, 50**
   See also Brodsky, Iosif Alexandrovich

Brodsky, Michael Mark   1948- ..... **CLC 19**
   See also CA 102; CANR 18, 41

Bromell, Henry   1947-............. **CLC 5**
   See also CA 53-56; CANR 9

Bromfield, Louis (Brucker)
   1896-1956 .... **TCLC 11**
   See also CA 107; DLB 4, 9, 86

Broner, E(sther) M(asserman)
   1930- .... **CLC 19**
   See also CA 17-20R; CANR 8, 25; DLB 28

Bronk, William   1918-............. **CLC 10**
   See also CA 89-92; CANR 23

Bronstein, Lev Davidovich
   See Trotsky, Leon

Bronte, Anne   1820-1849......... **NCLC 4**
   See also DLB 21

Bronte, Charlotte
   1816-1855 .... **NCLC 3, 8, 33**
   See also CDBLB 1832-1890; DA; DLB 21;
   WLC

Bronte, (Jane) Emily
   1818-1848 .... **NCLC 16, 35**
   See also CDBLB 1832-1890; DA; DLB 21,
   32; WLC

Brooke, Frances   1724-1789 .... **LC 6**
   See also DLB 39, 99

Brooke, Henry   1703(?)-1783 .... **LC 1**
   See also DLB 39

Brooke, Rupert (Chawner)
   1887-1915 .... **TCLC 2, 7**
   See also CA 104; 132; CDBLB 1914-1945;
   DA; DLB 19; MTCW; WLC

Brooke-Haven, P.
   See Wodehouse, P(elham) G(renville)

Brooke-Rose, Christine   1926-...... **CLC 40**
   See also CA 13-16R; DLB 14

Brookner, Anita   1928-...... **CLC 32, 34, 51**
   See also CA 114; 120; CANR 37; DLBY 87;
   MTCW

Brooks, Cleanth   1906- .... **CLC 24**
   See also CA 17-20R; CANR 33, 35;
   DLB 63; MTCW

Brooks, George
   See Baum, L(yman) Frank

Brooks, Gwendolyn
   1917- ...... **CLC 1, 2, 4, 5, 15, 49; PC 7**
   See also AITN 1; BLC 1; BW; CA 1-4R;
   CANR 1, 27; CDALB 1941-1968;
   CLR 27; DA; DLB 5, 76; MTCW;
   SATA 6; WLC

Brooks, Mel..................... **CLC 12**
   See also Kaminsky, Melvin
   See also DLB 26

Brooks, Peter   1938-............. **CLC 34**
   See also CA 45-48; CANR 1

Brooks, Van Wyck   1886-1963...... **CLC 29**
   See also CA 1-4R; CANR 6; DLB 45, 63,
   103

Brophy, Brigid (Antonia)
   1929-................... **CLC 6, 11, 29**
   See also CA 5-8R; CAAS 4; CANR 25;
   DLB 14; MTCW

Brosman, Catharine Savage   1934-.... **CLC 9**
   See also CA 61-64; CANR 21

Brother Antoninus
   See Everson, William (Oliver)

Broughton, T(homas) Alan   1936- ... **CLC 19**
   See also CA 45-48; CANR 2, 23

Broumas, Olga   1949-.......... **CLC 10, 73**
   See also CA 85-88; CANR 20

Brown, Charles Brockden
   1771-1810 .... **NCLC 22**
   See also CDALB 1640-1865; DLB 37, 59,
   73

Brown, Christy   1932-1981........ **CLC 63**
   See also CA 105; 104; DLB 14

Brown, Claude   1937- .... **CLC 30**
   See also AAYA 7; BLC 1; BW; CA 73-76

Brown, Dee (Alexander)   1908- .. **CLC 18, 47**
   See also CA 13-16R; CAAS 6; CANR 11;
   DLBY 80; MTCW; SATA 5

Brown, George
   See Wertmueller, Lina

Brown, George Douglas
   1869-1902 .... **TCLC 28**

Brown, George Mackay   1921-.... **CLC 5, 48**
   See also CA 21-24R; CAAS 6; CANR 12,
   37; DLB 14, 27; MTCW; SATA 35

Brown, (William) Larry   1951-...... **CLC 73**
   See also CA 130; 134

Brown, Moses
   See Barrett, William (Christopher)

Brown, Rita Mae   1944-........ **CLC 18, 43**
   See also CA 45-48; CANR 2, 11, 35;
   MTCW

Brown, Roderick (Langmere) Haig-
   See Haig-Brown, Roderick (Langmere)

Brown, Rosellen   1939-............ **CLC 32**
   See also CA 77-80; CAAS 10; CANR 14

Brown, Sterling Allen
   1901-1989 .... **CLC 1, 23, 59**
   See also BLC 1; BW; CA 85-88; 127;
   CANR 26; DLB 48, 51, 63; MTCW

Brown, Will
   See Ainsworth, William Harrison

Brown, William Wells
   1813-1884 .... **NCLC 2; DC 1**
   See also BLC 1; DLB 3, 50

Browne, (Clyde) Jackson   1948(?)-... **CLC 21**
   See also CA 120

Browning, Elizabeth Barrett
   1806-1861 .... **NCLC 1, 16; PC 6**
   See also CDBLB 1832-1890; DA; DLB 32;
   WLC

Browning, Robert
   1812-1889 .... **NCLC 19; PC 2**
   See also CDBLB 1832-1890; DA; DLB 32;
   YABC 1

Browning, Tod   1882-1962 .... **CLC 16**
   See also CA 117

Bruccoli, Matthew J(oseph)   1931- .. **CLC 34**
   See also CA 9-12R; CANR 7; DLB 103

Bruce, Lenny..................... **CLC 21**
   See also Schneider, Leonard Alfred

Bruin, John
   See Brutus, Dennis

Brulls, Christian
   See Simenon, Georges (Jacques Christian)

Brunner, John (Kilian Houston)
   1934-..................... **CLC 8, 10**
   See also CA 1-4R; CAAS 8; CANR 2, 37;
   MTCW

Brutus, Dennis   1924-............. **CLC 43**
   See also BLC 1; BW; CA 49-52; CAAS 14;
   CANR 2, 27; DLB 117

Bryan, C(ourtlandt) D(ixon) B(arnes)
   1936-..................... **CLC 29**
   See also CA 73-76; CANR 13

Bryan, Michael
   See Moore, Brian

Bryant, William Cullen
   1794-1878 .... **NCLC 6**
   See also CDALB 1640-1865; DA; DLB 3,
   43, 59

Bryusov, Valery Yakovlevich
   1873-1924 .... **TCLC 10**
   See also CA 107

Buchan, John   1875-1940 .... **TCLC 41**
   See also CA 108; DLB 34, 70; YABC 2

Buchanan, George   1506-1582 .... **LC 4**

Buchheim, Lothar-Guenther   1918-... **CLC 6**
   See also CA 85-88

Buchner, (Karl) Georg
   1813-1837 .... **NCLC 26**

Buchwald, Art(hur)   1925-.......... **CLC 33**
   See also AITN 1; CA 5-8R; CANR 21;
   MTCW; SATA 10

Buck, Pearl S(ydenstricker)
   1892-1973 .... **CLC 7, 11, 18**
   See also AITN 1; CA 1-4R; 41-44R;
   CANR 1, 34; DA; DLB 9, 102; MTCW;
   SATA 1, 25

Buckler, Ernest 1908-1984........ **CLC 13**
See also CA 11-12; 114; CAP 1; DLB 68;
SATA 47

Buckley, Vincent (Thomas)
1925-1988 .... **CLC 57**
See also CA 101

Buckley, William F(rank), Jr.
1925- .... **CLC 7, 18, 37**
See also AITN 1; CA 1-4R; CANR 1, 24;
DLBY 80; MTCW

Buechner, (Carl) Frederick
1926- .... **CLC 2, 4, 6, 9**
See also CA 13-16R; CANR 11, 39;
DLBY 80; MTCW

Buell, John (Edward) 1927-....... **CLC 10**
See also CA 1-4R; DLB 53

Buero Vallejo, Antonio 1916- ... **CLC 15, 46**
See also CA 106; CANR 24; HW; MTCW

Bufalino, Gesualdo 1920(?)-........ **CLC 74**

Bugayev, Boris Nikolayevich 1880-1934
See Bely, Andrey
See also CA 104

Bukowski, Charles 1920- .... **CLC 2, 5, 9, 41**
See also CA 17-20R; CANR 40; DLB 5,
130; MTCW

Bulgakov, Mikhail (Afanas'evich)
1891-1940 .... **TCLC 2, 16**
See also CA 105

Bullins, Ed 1935- .... **CLC 1, 5, 7**
See also BLC 1; BW; CA 49-52; CAAS 16;
CANR 24; DLB 7, 38; MTCW

Bulwer-Lytton, Edward (George Earle Lytton)
1803-1873 .... **NCLC 1**
See also DLB 21

Bunin, Ivan Alexeyevich
1870-1953 .... **TCLC 6; SSC 5**
See also CA 104

Bunting, Basil 1900-1985.... **CLC 10, 39, 47**
See also CA 53-56; 115; CANR 7; DLB 20

Bunuel, Luis 1900-1983........... **CLC 16**
See also CA 101; 110; CANR 32; HW

Bunyan, John 1628-1688 .... **LC 4**
See also CDBLB 1660-1789; DA; DLB 39;
WLC

Burford, Eleanor
See Hibbert, Eleanor Alice Burford

Burgess, Anthony
1917- ...... **CLC 1, 2, 4, 5, 8, 10, 13, 15,
22, 40, 62**
See also Wilson, John (Anthony) Burgess
See also AITN 1; CDBLB 1960 to Present;
DLB 14

Burke, Edmund 1729(?)-1797........ **LC 7**
See also DA; DLB 104; WLC

Burke, Kenneth (Duva) 1897- .... **CLC 2, 24**
See also CA 5-8R; CANR 39; DLB 45, 63;
MTCW

Burke, Leda
See Garnett, David

Burke, Ralph
See Silverberg, Robert

Burney, Fanny 1752-1840 .... **NCLC 12**
See also DLB 39

Burns, Robert 1759-1796 ...... **LC 3; PC 6**
See also CDBLB 1789-1832; DA; DLB 109;
WLC

Burns, Tex
See L'Amour, Louis (Dearborn)

Burnshaw, Stanley 1906- ..... **CLC 3, 13, 44**
See also CA 9-12R; DLB 48

Burr, Anne 1937- .... **CLC 6**
See also CA 25-28R

Burroughs, Edgar Rice
1875-1950 .... **TCLC 2, 32**
See also CA 104; 132; DLB 8; MTCW;
SATA 41

Burroughs, William S(eward)
1914- .... **CLC 1, 2, 5, 15, 22, 42, 75**
See also AITN 2; CA 9-12R; CANR 20;
DA; DLB 2, 8, 16; DLBY 81; MTCW;
WLC

Busch, Frederick 1941- ... **CLC 7, 10, 18, 47**
See also CA 33-36R; CAAS 1; DLB 6

Bush, Ronald 1946- .... **CLC 34**
See also CA 136

Bustos, F(rancisco)
See Borges, Jorge Luis

Bustos Domecq, H(onorio)
See Bioy Casares, Adolfo; Borges, Jorge
Luis

Butler, Octavia E(stelle) 1947- ..... **CLC 38**
See also BW; CA 73-76; CANR 12, 24, 38;
DLB 33; MTCW

Butler, Samuel 1612-1680 .... **LC 16**
See also DLB 101, 126

Butler, Samuel 1835-1902 ...... **TCLC 1, 33**
See also CA 104; CDBLB 1890-1914; DA;
DLB 18, 57; WLC

Butler, Walter C.
See Faust, Frederick (Schiller)

Butor, Michel (Marie Francois)
1926- .... **CLC 1, 3, 8, 11, 15**
See also CA 9-12R; CANR 33; DLB 83;
MTCW

Buzo, Alexander (John) 1944-...... **CLC 61**
See also CA 97-100; CANR 17, 39

Buzzati, Dino 1906-1972 .... **CLC 36**
See also CA 33-36R

Byars, Betsy (Cromer) 1928-....... **CLC 35**
See also CA 33-36R; CANR 18, 36; CLR 1,
16; DLB 52; MAICYA; MTCW; SAAS 1;
SATA 4, 46

Byatt, A(ntonia) S(usan Drabble)
1936- .... **CLC 19, 65**
See also CA 13-16R; CANR 13, 33;
DLB 14; MTCW

Byrne, David 1952-............... **CLC 26**
See also CA 127

Byrne, John Keyes 1926-.......... **CLC 19**
See also Leonard, Hugh
See also CA 102

Byron, George Gordon (Noel)
1788-1824 .... **NCLC 2, 12**
See also CDBLB 1789-1832; DA; DLB 96,
110; WLC

C.3.3.
See Wilde, Oscar (Fingal O'Flahertie Wills)

Caballero, Fernan 1796-1877..... **NCLC 10**

Cabell, James Branch 1879-1958 ... **TCLC 6**
See also CA 105; DLB 9, 78

Cable, George Washington
1844-1925 .... **TCLC 4; SSC 4**
See also CA 104; DLB 12, 74

Cabral de Melo Neto, Joao 1920-... **CLC 76**

Cabrera Infante, G(uillermo)
1929- .... **CLC 5, 25, 45**
See also CA 85-88; CANR 29; DLB 113;
HW; MTCW

Cade, Toni
See Bambara, Toni Cade

Cadmus
See Buchan, John

Caedmon fl. 658-680............. **CMLC 7**

Caeiro, Alberto
See Pessoa, Fernando (Antonio Nogueira)

Cage, John (Milton, Jr.) 1912-..... **CLC 41**
See also CA 13-16R; CANR 9

Cain, G.
See Cabrera Infante, G(uillermo)

Cain, Guillermo
See Cabrera Infante, G(uillermo)

Cain, James M(allahan)
1892-1977 .... **CLC 3, 11, 28**
See also AITN 1; CA 17-20R; 73-76;
CANR 8, 34; MTCW

Caine, Mark
See Raphael, Frederic (Michael)

Calderon de la Barca, Pedro
1600-1681 .... **LC 23; DC 3**

Caldwell, Erskine (Preston)
1903-1987 .... **CLC 1, 8, 14, 50, 60**
See also AITN 1; CA 1-4R; 121; CAAS 1;
CANR 2, 33; DLB 9, 86; MTCW

Caldwell, (Janet Miriam) Taylor (Holland)
1900-1985 .... **CLC 2, 28, 39**
See also CA 5-8R; 116; CANR 5

Calhoun, John Caldwell
1782-1850 .... **NCLC 15**
See also DLB 3

Calisher, Hortense 1911-.... **CLC 2, 4, 8, 38**
See also CA 1-4R; CANR 1, 22; DLB 2;
MTCW

Callaghan, Morley Edward
1903-1990 .... **CLC 3, 14, 41, 65**
See also CA 9-12R; 132; CANR 33;
DLB 68; MTCW

Calvino, Italo
1923-1985 ..... **CLC 5, 8, 11, 22, 33, 39,
73; SSC 3**
See also CA 85-88; 116; CANR 23; MTCW

Cameron, Carey 1952-............ **CLC 59**
See also CA 135

Cameron, Peter 1959-............. **CLC 44**
See also CA 125

Campana, Dino 1885-1932........ **TCLC 20**
See also CA 117; DLB 114

Campbell, John W(ood, Jr.)
1910-1971 .... **CLC 32**
See also CA 21-22; 29-32R; CANR 34;
CAP 2; DLB 8; MTCW

Cavanna, Betty .... **CLC 12**
See also Harrison, Elizabeth Cavanna
See also MAICYA; SAAS 4; SATA 1, 30

Caxton, William 1421(?)-1491(?) ..... **LC 17**

Cayrol, Jean 1911- .... **CLC 11**
See also CA 89-92; DLB 83

Cela, Camilo Jose 1916- ...... **CLC 4, 13, 59**
See also BEST 90:2; CA 21-24R; CAAS 10;
CANR 21, 32; DLBY 89; HW; MTCW

Celan, Paul .... **CLC 53**
See also Antschel, Paul
See also DLB 69

Celine, Louis-Ferdinand
.... **CLC 1, 3, 4, 7, 9, 15, 47**
See also Destouches, Louis-Ferdinand
See also DLB 72

Cellini, Benvenuto 1500-1571 .... **LC 7**

Cendrars, Blaise
See Sauser-Hall, Frederic

Cernuda (y Bidon), Luis
1902-1963 .... **CLC 54**
See also CA 131; 89-92; HW

Cervantes (Saavedra), Miguel de
1547-1616 .... **LC 6, 23; SSC 12**
See also DA; WLC

Cesaire, Aime (Fernand) 1913- .. **CLC 19, 32**
See also BLC 1; BW; CA 65-68; CANR 24;
MTCW

Chabon, Michael 1965(?)- .... **CLC 55**
See also CA 139

Chabrol, Claude 1930- .... **CLC 16**
See also CA 110

Challans, Mary 1905-1983
See Renault, Mary
See also CA 81-84; 111; SATA 23, 36

Challis, George
See Faust, Frederick (Schiller)

Chambers, Aidan 1934- .... **CLC 35**
See also CA 25-28R; CANR 12, 31;
MAICYA; SAAS 12; SATA 1, 69

Chambers, James 1948-
See Cliff, Jimmy
See also CA 124

Chambers, Jessie
See Lawrence, D(avid) H(erbert Richards)

Chambers, Robert W. 1865-1933... **TCLC 41**

Chandler, Raymond (Thornton)
1888-1959 .... **TCLC 1, 7**
See also CA 104; 129; CDALB 1929-1941;
DLBD 6; MTCW

Chang, Jung 1952- .... **CLC 71**

Channing, William Ellery
1780-1842 .... **NCLC 17**
See also DLB 1, 59

Chaplin, Charles Spencer
1889-1977 .... **CLC 16**
See also Chaplin, Charlie
See also CA 81-84; 73-76

Chaplin, Charlie
See Chaplin, Charles Spencer
See also DLB 44

Chapman, George 1559(?)-1634 ...... **LC 22**
See also DLB 62, 121

Chapman, Graham 1941-1989 ...... **CLC 21**
See also Monty Python
See also CA 116; 129; CANR 35

Chapman, John Jay 1862-1933 ..... **TCLC 7**
See also CA 104

Chapman, Walker
See Silverberg, Robert

Chappell, Fred (Davis) 1936-.... **CLC 40, 78**
See also CA 5-8R; CAAS 4; CANR 8, 33;
DLB 6, 105

Char, Rene(-Emile)
1907-1988 .... **CLC 9, 11, 14, 55**
See also CA 13-16R; 124; CANR 32;
MTCW

Charby, Jay
See Ellison, Harlan

Chardin, Pierre Teilhard de
See Teilhard de Chardin, (Marie Joseph)
Pierre

Charles I 1600-1649 .... **LC 13**

Charyn, Jerome 1937- .... **CLC 5, 8, 18**
See also CA 5-8R; CAAS 1; CANR 7;
DLBY 83; MTCW

Chase, Mary (Coyle) 1907-1981 ...... **DC 1**
See also CA 77-80; 105; SATA 17, 29

Chase, Mary Ellen 1887-1973 .... **CLC 2**
See also CA 13-16; 41-44R; CAP 1;
SATA 10

Chase, Nicholas
See Hyde, Anthony

Chateaubriand, Francois Rene de
1768-1848 .... **NCLC 3**
See also DLB 119

Chatterje, Sarat Chandra 1876-1936(?)
See Chatterji, Saratchandra
See also CA 109

Chatterji, Bankim Chandra
1838-1894 .... **NCLC 19**

Chatterji, Saratchandra .... **TCLC 13**
See also Chatterje, Sarat Chandra

Chatterton, Thomas 1752-1770 .... **LC 3**
See also DLB 109

Chatwin, (Charles) Bruce
1940-1989 .... **CLC 28, 57, 59**
See also AAYA 4; BEST 90:1; CA 85-88;
127

Chaucer, Daniel
See Ford, Ford Madox

Chaucer, Geoffrey 1340(?)-1400 ..... **LC 17**
See also CDBLB Before 1660; DA

Chaviaras, Strates 1935-
See Haviaras, Stratis
See also CA 105

Chayefsky, Paddy .... **CLC 23**
See also Chayefsky, Sidney
See also DLB 7, 44; DLBY 81

Chayefsky, Sidney 1923-1981
See Chayefsky, Paddy
See also CA 9-12R; 104; CANR 18

Chedid, Andree 1920- .... **CLC 47**

Cheever, John
1912-1982 ...... **CLC 3, 7, 8, 11, 15, 25,
64; SSC 1**
See also CA 5-8R; 106; CABS 1; CANR 5,
27; CDALB 1941-1968; DA; DLB 2, 102;
DLBY 80, 82; MTCW; WLC

Cheever, Susan 1943- .... **CLC 18, 48**
See also CA 103; CANR 27; DLBY 82

Chekhonte, Antosha
See Chekhov, Anton (Pavlovich)

Chekhov, Anton (Pavlovich)
1860-1904 ...... **TCLC 3, 10, 31; SSC 2**
See also CA 104; 124; DA; WLC

Chernyshevsky, Nikolay Gavrilovich
1828-1889 .... **NCLC 1**

Cherry, Carolyn Janice 1942-
See Cherryh, C. J.
See also CA 65-68; CANR 10

Cherryh, C. J. .... **CLC 35**
See also Cherry, Carolyn Janice
See also DLBY 80

Chesnutt, Charles W(addell)
1858-1932 .... **TCLC 5, 39; SSC 7**
See also BLC 1; BW; CA 106; 125; DLB 12,
50, 78; MTCW

Chester, Alfred 1929(?)-1971 .... **CLC 49**
See also CA 33-36R; DLB 130

Chesterton, G(ilbert) K(eith)
1874-1936 .... **TCLC 1, 6; SSC 1**
See also CA 104; 132; CDBLB 1914-1945;
DLB 10, 19, 34, 70, 98; MTCW;
SATA 27

Chiang Pin-chin 1904-1986
See Ding Ling
See also CA 118

Ch'ien Chung-shu 1910- .... **CLC 22**
See also CA 130; MTCW

Child, L. Maria
See Child, Lydia Maria

Child, Lydia Maria 1802-1880 .... **NCLC 6**
See also DLB 1, 74; SATA 67

Child, Mrs.
See Child, Lydia Maria

Child, Philip 1898-1978 .... **CLC 19, 68**
See also CA 13-14; CAP 1; SATA 47

Childress, Alice 1920- .... **CLC 12, 15**
See also AAYA 8; BLC 1; BW; CA 45-48;
CANR 3, 27; CLR 14; DLB 7, 38;
MAICYA; MTCW; SATA 7, 48

Chislett, (Margaret) Anne 1943- .... **CLC 34**

Chitty, Thomas Willes 1926- .... **CLC 11**
See also Hinde, Thomas
See also CA 5-8R

Chomette, Rene Lucien 1898-1981 .. **CLC 20**
See also Clair, Rene
See also CA 103

Chopin, Kate .... **TCLC 5, 14; SSC 8**
See also Chopin, Katherine
See also CDALB 1865-1917; DA; DLB 12,
78

Chopin, Katherine 1851-1904
See Chopin, Kate
See also CA 104; 122

Chretien de Troyes
c. 12th cent. - .... **CMLC 10**

Christie
  See Ichikawa, Kon

Christie, Agatha (Mary Clarissa)
  1890-1976 ..... **CLC 1, 6, 8, 12, 39, 48**
  See also AAYA 9; AITN 1, 2; CA 17-20R;
  61-64; CANR 10, 37; CDBLB 1914-1945;
  DLB 13, 77; MTCW; SATA 36

Christie, (Ann) Philippa
  See Pearce, Philippa
  See also CA 5-8R; CANR 4

Christine de Pizan   1365(?)-1431(?) .... **LC 9**

Chubb, Elmer
  See Masters, Edgar Lee

Chulkov, Mikhail Dmitrievich
  1743-1792 .... **LC 2**

Churchill, Caryl   1938- .... **CLC 31, 55**
  See also CA 102; CANR 22; DLB 13;
  MTCW

Churchill, Charles   1731-1764 .... **LC 3**
  See also DLB 109

Chute, Carolyn   1947- .... **CLC 39**
  See also CA 123

Ciardi, John (Anthony)
  1916-1986 .... **CLC 10, 40, 44**
  See also CA 5-8R; 118; CAAS 2; CANR 5,
  33; CLR 19; DLB 5; DLBY 86;
  MAICYA; MTCW; SATA 1, 46, 65

Cicero, Marcus Tullius
  106B.C.-43B.C. .... **CMLC 3**

Cimino, Michael   1943- .... **CLC 16**
  See also CA 105

Cioran, E(mil) M.   1911- .... **CLC 64**
  See also CA 25-28R

Cisneros, Sandra   1954- .... **CLC 69**
  See also AAYA 9; CA 131; DLB 122; HW

Clair, Rene .... **CLC 20**
  See also Chomette, Rene Lucien

Clampitt, Amy   1920- .... **CLC 32**
  See also CA 110; CANR 29; DLB 105

Clancy, Thomas L., Jr.   1947-
  See Clancy, Tom
  See also CA 125; 131; MTCW

Clancy, Tom .... **CLC 45**
  See also Clancy, Thomas L., Jr.
  See also AAYA 9; BEST 89:1, 90:1

Clare, John   1793-1864 .... **NCLC 9**
  See also DLB 55, 96

Clarin
  See Alas (y Urena), Leopoldo (Enrique
  Garcia)

Clark, (Robert) Brian   1932- .... **CLC 29**
  See also CA 41-44R

Clark, Eleanor   1913- .... **CLC 5, 19**
  See also CA 9-12R; CANR 41; DLB 6

Clark, J. P.
  See Clark, John Pepper
  See also DLB 117

Clark, John Pepper   1935- .... **CLC 38**
  See also Clark, J. P.
  See also BLC 1; BW; CA 65-68; CANR 16

Clark, M. R.
  See Clark, Mavis Thorpe

Clark, Mavis Thorpe   1909- .... **CLC 12**
  See also CA 57-60; CANR 8, 37; CLR 30;
  MAICYA; SAAS 5; SATA 8, 74

Clark, Walter Van Tilburg
  1909-1971 .... **CLC 28**
  See also CA 9-12R; 33-36R; DLB 9;
  SATA 8

Clarke, Arthur C(harles)
  1917- ..... **CLC 1, 4, 13, 18, 35; SSC 3**
  See also AAYA 4; CA 1-4R; CANR 2, 28;
  MAICYA; MTCW; SATA 13, 70

Clarke, Austin   1896-1974 .... **CLC 6, 9**
  See also CA 29-32; 49-52; CAP 2; DLB 10,
  20

Clarke, Austin C(hesterfield)
  1934- .... **CLC 8, 53**
  See also BLC 1; BW; CA 25-28R;
  CAAS 16; CANR 14, 32; DLB 53, 125

Clarke, Gillian   1937- .... **CLC 61**
  See also CA 106; DLB 40

Clarke, Marcus (Andrew Hislop)
  1846-1881 .... **NCLC 19**

Clarke, Shirley   1925- .... **CLC 16**

Clash, The .... **CLC 30**
  See also Headon, (Nicky) Topper; Jones,
  Mick; Simonon, Paul; Strummer, Joe

Claudel, Paul (Louis Charles Marie)
  1868-1955 .... **TCLC 2, 10**
  See also CA 104

Clavell, James (duMaresq)
  1925- .... **CLC 6, 25**
  See also CA 25-28R; CANR 26; MTCW

Cleaver, (Leroy) Eldridge   1935- .... **CLC 30**
  See also BLC 1; BW; CA 21-24R;
  CANR 16

Cleese, John (Marwood)   1939- ..... **CLC 21**
  See also Monty Python
  See also CA 112; 116; CANR 35; MTCW

Cleishbotham, Jebediah
  See Scott, Walter

Cleland, John   1710-1789 .... **LC 2**
  See also DLB 39

Clemens, Samuel Langhorne   1835-1910
  See Twain, Mark
  See also CA 104; 135; CDALB 1865-1917;
  DA; DLB 11, 12, 23, 64, 74; MAICYA;
  YABC 2

Cleophil
  See Congreve, William

Clerihew, E.
  See Bentley, E(dmund) C(lerihew)

Clerk, N. W.
  See Lewis, C(live) S(taples)

Cliff, Jimmy .... **CLC 21**
  See also Chambers, James

Clifton, (Thelma) Lucille
  1936- .... **CLC 19, 66**
  See also BLC 1; BW; CA 49-52; CANR 2,
  24; CLR 5; DLB 5, 41; MAICYA;
  MTCW; SATA 20, 69

Clinton, Dirk
  See Silverberg, Robert

Clough, Arthur Hugh   1819-1861 .. **NCLC 27**
  See also DLB 32

Clutha, Janet Paterson Frame   1924-
  See Frame, Janet
  See also CA 1-4R; CANR 2, 36; MTCW

Clyne, Terence
  See Blatty, William Peter

Cobalt, Martin
  See Mayne, William (James Carter)

Coburn, D(onald) L(ee)   1938- ...... **CLC 10**
  See also CA 89-92

Cocteau, Jean (Maurice Eugene Clement)
  1889-1963 .... **CLC 1, 8, 15, 16, 43**
  See also CA 25-28; CANR 40; CAP 2; DA;
  DLB 65; MTCW; WLC

Codrescu, Andrei   1946- .... **CLC 46**
  See also CA 33-36R; CANR 13, 34

Coe, Max
  See Bourne, Randolph S(illiman)

Coe, Tucker
  See Westlake, Donald E(dwin)

Coetzee, J(ohn) M(ichael)
  1940- .... **CLC 23, 33, 66**
  See also CA 77-80; CANR 41; MTCW

Coffey, Brian
  See Koontz, Dean R(ay)

Cohen, Arthur A(llen)
  1928-1986 .... **CLC 7, 31**
  See also CA 1-4R; 120; CANR 1, 17;
  DLB 28

Cohen, Leonard (Norman)
  1934- .... **CLC 3, 38**
  See also CA 21-24R; CANR 14; DLB 53;
  MTCW

Cohen, Matt   1942- .... **CLC 19**
  See also CA 61-64; CANR 40; DLB 53

Cohen-Solal, Annie   19(?)- .... **CLC 50**

Colegate, Isabel   1931- .... **CLC 36**
  See also CA 17-20R; CANR 8, 22; DLB 14;
  MTCW

Coleman, Emmett
  See Reed, Ishmael

Coleridge, Samuel Taylor
  1772-1834 .... **NCLC 9**
  See also CDBLB 1789-1832; DA; DLB 93,
  107; WLC

Coleridge, Sara   1802-1852 .... **NCLC 31**

Coles, Don   1928- .... **CLC 46**
  See also CA 115; CANR 38

Colette, (Sidonie-Gabrielle)
  1873-1954 ...... **TCLC 1, 5, 16; SSC 10**
  See also CA 104; 131; DLB 65; MTCW

Collett, (Jacobine) Camilla (Wergeland)
  1813-1895 .... **NCLC 22**

Collier, Christopher   1930- .... **CLC 30**
  See also CA 33-36R; CANR 13, 33;
  MAICYA; SATA 16, 70

Collier, James L(incoln)   1928- ..... **CLC 30**
  See also CA 9-12R; CANR 4, 33;
  MAICYA; SATA 8, 70

Collier, Jeremy   1650-1726 .... **LC 6**

Collins, Hunt
  See Hunter, Evan

Collins, Linda   1931- .... **CLC 44**
  See also CA 125

Collins, (William) Wilkie
    1824-1889 . . . . NCLC 1, 18
    See also CDBLB 1832-1890; DLB 18, 70

Collins, William 1721-1759 . . . . LC 4
    See also DLB 109

Colman, George
    See Glassco, John

Colt, Winchester Remington
    See Hubbard, L(afayette) Ron(ald)

Colter, Cyrus 1910- . . . . CLC 58
    See also BW; CA 65-68; CANR 10; DLB 33

Colton, James
    See Hansen, Joseph

Colum, Padraic 1881-1972 . . . . CLC 28
    See also CA 73-76; 33-36R; CANR 35;
    MAICYA; MTCW; SATA 15

Colvin, James
    See Moorcock, Michael (John)

Colwin, Laurie (E.)
    1944-1992 . . . . CLC 5, 13, 23
    See also CA 89-92; 139; CANR 20;
    DLBY 80; MTCW

Comfort, Alex(ander) 1920- . . . . CLC 7
    See also CA 1-4R; CANR 1

Comfort, Montgomery
    See Campbell, (John) Ramsey

Compton-Burnett, I(vy)
    1884(?)-1969 . . . . . . CLC 1, 3, 10, 15, 34
    See also CA 1-4R; 25-28R; CANR 4;
    DLB 36; MTCW

Comstock, Anthony 1844-1915 . . . . TCLC 13
    See also CA 110

Conan Doyle, Arthur
    See Doyle, Arthur Conan

Conde, Maryse . . . . CLC 52
    See also Boucolon, Maryse

Condon, Richard (Thomas)
    1915- . . . . CLC 4, 6, 8, 10, 45
    See also BEST 90:3; CA 1-4R; CAAS 1;
    CANR 2, 23; MTCW

Congreve, William
    1670-1729 . . . . LC 5, 21; DC 2
    See also CDBLB 1660-1789; DA; DLB 39,
    84; WLC

Connell, Evan S(helby), Jr.
    1924- . . . . CLC 4, 6, 45
    See also AAYA 7; CA 1-4R; CAAS 2;
    CANR 2, 39; DLB 2; DLBY 81; MTCW

Connelly, Marc(us Cook)
    1890-1980 . . . . CLC 7
    See also CA 85-88; 102; CANR 30; DLB 7;
    DLBY 80; SATA 25

Connor, Ralph . . . . TCLC 31
    See also Gordon, Charles William
    See also DLB 92

Conrad, Joseph
    1857-1924 . . . . TCLC 1, 6, 13, 25, 43;
                               SSC 9
    See also CA 104; 131; CDBLB 1890-1914;
    DA; DLB 10, 34, 98; MTCW; SATA 27;
    WLC

Conrad, Robert Arnold
    See Hart, Moss

Conroy, Pat 1945- . . . . CLC 30, 74
    See also AAYA 8; AITN 1; CA 85-88;
    CANR 24; DLB 6; MTCW

Constant (de Rebecque), (Henri) Benjamin
    1767-1830 . . . . NCLC 6
    See also DLB 119

Conybeare, Charles Augustus
    See Eliot, T(homas) S(tearns)

Cook, Michael 1933- . . . . CLC 58
    See also CA 93-96; DLB 53

Cook, Robin 1940- . . . . CLC 14
    See also BEST 90:2; CA 108; 111;
    CANR 41

Cook, Roy
    See Silverberg, Robert

Cooke, Elizabeth 1948- . . . . CLC 55
    See also CA 129

Cooke, John Esten 1830-1886 . . . . . NCLC 5
    See also DLB 3

Cooke, John Estes
    See Baum, L(yman) Frank

Cooke, M. E.
    See Creasey, John

Cooke, Margaret
    See Creasey, John

Cooney, Ray . . . . CLC 62

Cooper, Henry St. John
    See Creasey, John

Cooper, J. California . . . . CLC 56
    See also BW; CA 125

Cooper, James Fenimore
    1789-1851 . . . . NCLC 1, 27
    See also CDALB 1640-1865; DLB 3;
    SATA 19

Coover, Robert (Lowell)
    1932- . . . . CLC 3, 7, 15, 32, 46
    See also CA 45-48; CANR 3, 37; DLB 2;
    DLBY 81; MTCW

Copeland, Stewart (Armstrong)
    1952- . . . . CLC 26
    See also Police, The

Coppard, A(lfred) E(dgar)
    1878-1957 . . . . TCLC 5
    See also CA 114; YABC 1

Coppee, Francois 1842-1908 . . . . . . TCLC 25

Coppola, Francis Ford 1939- . . . . CLC 16
    See also CA 77-80; CANR 40; DLB 44

Corcoran, Barbara 1911- . . . . CLC 17
    See also CA 21-24R; CAAS 2; CANR 11,
    28; DLB 52; SATA 3

Cordelier, Maurice
    See Giraudoux, (Hippolyte) Jean

Corelli, Marie 1855-1924 . . . . TCLC 51
    See also Mackay, Mary
    See also DLB 34

Corman, Cid . . . . CLC 9
    See also Corman, Sidney
    See also CAAS 2; DLB 5

Corman, Sidney 1924-
    See Corman, Cid
    See also CA 85-88

Cormier, Robert (Edmund)
    1925- . . . . CLC 12, 30
    See also AAYA 3; CA 1-4R; CANR 5, 23;
    CDALB 1968-1988; CLR 12; DA;
    DLB 52; MAICYA; MTCW; SATA 10,
    45

Corn, Alfred 1943- . . . . CLC 33
    See also CA 104; DLB 120; DLBY 80

Cornwell, David (John Moore)
    1931- . . . . CLC 9, 15
    See also le Carre, John
    See also CA 5-8R; CANR 13, 33; MTCW

Corrigan, Kevin . . . . CLC 55

Corso, (Nunzio) Gregory 1930- . . . CLC 1, 11
    See also CA 5-8R; CANR 41; DLB 5,16;
    MTCW

Cortazar, Julio
    1914-1984 . . . . . . CLC 2, 3, 5, 10, 13, 15,
                        33, 34; SSC 7
    See also CA 21-24R; CANR 12, 32;
    DLB 113; HW; MTCW

Corwin, Cecil
    See Kornbluth, C(yril) M.

Cosic, Dobrica 1921- . . . . CLC 14
    See also CA 122; 138

Costain, Thomas B(ertram)
    1885-1965 . . . . CLC 30
    See also CA 5-8R; 25-28R; DLB 9

Costantini, Humberto
    1924(?)-1987 . . . . CLC 49
    See also CA 131; 122; HW

Costello, Elvis 1955- . . . . CLC 21

Cotter, Joseph S. Sr.
    See Cotter, Joseph Seamon Sr.

Cotter, Joseph Seamon Sr.
    1861-1949 . . . . TCLC 28
    See also BLC 1; BW; CA 124; DLB 50

Coulton, James
    See Hansen, Joseph

Couperus, Louis (Marie Anne)
    1863-1923 . . . . TCLC 15
    See also CA 115

Court, Wesli
    See Turco, Lewis (Putnam)

Courtenay, Bryce 1933- . . . . CLC 59
    See also CA 138

Courtney, Robert
    See Ellison, Harlan

Cousteau, Jacques-Yves 1910- . . . . . . CLC 30
    See also CA 65-68; CANR 15; MTCW;
    SATA 38

Coward, Noel (Peirce)
    1899-1973 . . . . CLC 1, 9, 29, 51
    See also AITN 1; CA 17-18; 41-44R;
    CANR 35; CAP 2; CDBLB 1914-1945;
    DLB 10; MTCW

Cowley, Malcolm 1898-1989 . . . . CLC 39
    See also CA 5-8R; 128; CANR 3; DLB 4,
    48; DLBY 81, 89; MTCW

Cowper, William 1731-1800 . . . . NCLC 8
    See also DLB 104, 109

Cox, William Trevor 1928- . . . CLC 9, 14, 71
    See also Trevor, William
    See also CA 9-12R; CANR 4, 37; DLB 14;
    MTCW

Cozzens, James Gould
1903-1978 .... **CLC 1, 4, 11**
See also CA 9-12R; 81-84; CANR 19;
CDALB 1941-1968; DLB 9; DLBD 2;
DLBY 84; MTCW

Crabbe, George 1754-1832...... **NCLC 26**
See also DLB 93

Craig, A. A.
See Anderson, Poul (William)

Craik, Dinah Maria (Mulock)
1826-1887 .... **NCLC 38**
See also DLB 35; MAICYA; SATA 34

Cram, Ralph Adams 1863-1942.... **TCLC 45**

Crane, (Harold) Hart
1899-1932 .... **TCLC 2, 5; PC 3**
See also CA 104; 127; CDALB 1917-1929;
DA; DLB 4, 48; MTCW; WLC

Crane, R(onald) S(almon)
1886-1967 .... **CLC 27**
See also CA 85-88; DLB 63

Crane, Stephen (Townley)
1871-1900 ..... **TCLC 11, 17, 32; SSC 7**
See also CA 109; 140; CDALB 1865-1917;
DA; DLB 12, 54, 78; WLC; YABC 2

Crase, Douglas 1944- .... **CLC 58**
See also CA 106

Craven, Margaret 1901-1980...... **CLC 17**
See also CA 103

Crawford, F(rancis) Marion
1854-1909 .... **TCLC 10**
See also CA 107; DLB 71

Crawford, Isabella Valancy
1850-1887 .... **NCLC 12**
See also DLB 92

Crayon, Geoffrey
See Irving, Washington

Creasey, John 1908-1973.......... **CLC 11**
See also CA 5-8R; 41-44R; CANR 8;
DLB 77; MTCW

Crebillon, Claude Prosper Jolyot de (fils)
1707-1777 .... **LC 1**

Credo
See Creasey, John

Creeley, Robert (White)
1926- ..... **CLC 1, 2, 4, 8, 11, 15, 36, 78**
See also CA 1-4R; CAAS 10; CANR 23;
DLB 5, 16; MTCW

Crews, Harry (Eugene)
1935- .... **CLC 6, 23, 49**
See also AITN 1; CA 25-28R; CANR 20;
DLB 6; MTCW

Crichton, (John) Michael
1942- .... **CLC 2, 6, 54**
See also AAYA 10; AITN 2; CA 25-28R;
CANR 13, 40; DLBY 81; MTCW;
SATA 9

Crispin, Edmund .... **CLC 22**
See also Montgomery, (Robert) Bruce
See also DLB 87

Cristofer, Michael 1945(?)- .... **CLC 28**
See also CA 110; DLB 7

Croce, Benedetto 1866-1952 ...... **TCLC 37**
See also CA 120

Crockett, David 1786-1836 .... **NCLC 8**
See also DLB 3, 11

Crockett, Davy
See Crockett, David

Croker, John Wilson 1780-1857 .. **NCLC 10**
See also DLB 110

Crommelynck, Fernand 1885-1970 .. **CLC 75**
See also CA 89-92

Cronin, A(rchibald) J(oseph)
1896-1981 .... **CLC 32**
See also CA 1-4R; 102; CANR 5; SATA 25,
47

Cross, Amanda
See Heilbrun, Carolyn G(old)

Crothers, Rachel 1878(?)-1958..... **TCLC 19**
See also CA 113; DLB 7

Croves, Hal
See Traven, B.

Crowfield, Christopher
See Stowe, Harriet (Elizabeth) Beecher

Crowley, Aleister.................. TCLC 7
See also Crowley, Edward Alexander

Crowley, Edward Alexander 1875-1947
See Crowley, Aleister
See also CA 104

Crowley, John 1942-............. **CLC 57**
See also CA 61-64; DLBY 82; SATA 65

Crud
See Crumb, R(obert)

Crumarums
See Crumb, R(obert)

Crumb, R(obert) 1943-........... **CLC 17**
See also CA 106

Crumbum
See Crumb, R(obert)

Crumski
See Crumb, R(obert)

Crum the Bum
See Crumb, R(obert)

Crunk
See Crumb, R(obert)

Crustt
See Crumb, R(obert)

Cryer, Gretchen (Kiger) 1935-...... **CLC 21**
See also CA 114; 123

Csath, Geza 1887-1919.......... **TCLC 13**
See also CA 111

Cudlip, David 1933-.............. **CLC 34**

Cullen, Countee 1903-1946 ..... **TCLC 4, 37**
See also BLC 1; BW; CA 108; 124;
CDALB 1917-1929; DA; DLB 4, 48, 51;
MTCW; SATA 18

Cum, R.
See Crumb, R(obert)

Cummings, Bruce F(rederick) 1889-1919
See Barbellion, W. N. P.
See also CA 123

Cummings, E(dward) E(stlin)
1894-1962 ...... **CLC 1, 3, 8, 12, 15, 68;**
                                      PC 5
See also CA 73-76; CANR 31;
CDALB 1929-1941; DA; DLB 4, 48;
MTCW; WLC 2

Cunha, Euclides (Rodrigues Pimenta) da
1866-1909 .... **TCLC 24**
See also CA 123

Cunningham, E. V.
See Fast, Howard (Melvin)

Cunningham, J(ames) V(incent)
1911-1985 .... **CLC 3, 31**
See also CA 1-4R; 115; CANR 1; DLB 5

Cunningham, Julia (Woolfolk)
1916- .... **CLC 12**
See also CA 9-12R; CANR 4, 19, 36;
MAICYA; SAAS 2; SATA 1, 26

Cunningham, Michael 1952- .... **CLC 34**
See also CA 136

Cunninghame Graham, R(obert) B(ontine)
1852-1936 .... **TCLC 19**
See also Graham, R(obert) B(ontine)
Cunninghame
See also CA 119; DLB 98

Currie, Ellen 19(?)-................ **CLC 44**

Curtin, Philip
See Lowndes, Marie Adelaide (Belloc)

Curtis, Price
See Ellison, Harlan

Cutrate, Joe
See Spiegelman, Art

Czaczkes, Shmuel Yosef
See Agnon, S(hmuel) Y(osef Halevi)

D. P.
See Wells, H(erbert) G(eorge)

Dabrowska, Maria (Szumska)
1889-1965 .... **CLC 15**
See also CA 106

Dabydeen, David 1955- .... **CLC 34**
See also BW; CA 125

Dacey, Philip 1939- .... **CLC 51**
See also CA 37-40R; CAAS 17; CANR 14,
32; DLB 105

Dagerman, Stig (Halvard)
1923-1954 .... **TCLC 17**
See also CA 117

Dahl, Roald 1916-1990........ **CLC 1, 6, 18**
See also CA 1-4R; 133; CANR 6, 32, 37;
CLR 1, 7; MAICYA; MTCW; SATA 1,
26, 73; SATA-Obit 65

Dahlberg, Edward 1900-1977... **CLC 1, 7, 14**
See also CA 9-12R; 69-72; CANR 31;
DLB 48; MTCW

Dale, Colin.................... TCLC 18
See also Lawrence, T(homas) E(dward)

Dale, George E.
See Asimov, Isaac

Daly, Elizabeth 1878-1967........ **CLC 52**
See also CA 23-24; 25-28R; CAP 2

Daly, Maureen 1921-............. **CLC 17**
See also AAYA 5; CANR 37; MAICYA;
SAAS 1; SATA 2

Daniels, Brett
See Adler, Renata

Dannay, Frederic 1905-1982....... **CLC 11**
See also Queen, Ellery
See also CA 1-4R; 107; CANR 1, 39;
MTCW

D'Annunzio, Gabriele
1863-1938 .... **TCLC 6, 40**
See also CA 104

Demijohn, Thom
See Disch, Thomas M(ichael)

de Montherlant, Henry (Milon)
See Montherlant, Henry (Milon) de

de Natale, Francine
See Malzberg, Barry N(athaniel)

Denby, Edwin (Orr) 1903-1983 ..... **CLC 48**
See also CA 138; 110

Denis, Julio
See Cortazar, Julio

Denmark, Harrison
See Zelazny, Roger (Joseph)

Dennis, John 1658-1734............ **LC 11**
See also DLB 101

Dennis, Nigel (Forbes) 1912-1989.... **CLC 8**
See also CA 25-28R; 129; DLB 13, 15;
MTCW

De Palma, Brian (Russell) 1940-.... **CLC 20**
See also CA 109

De Quincey, Thomas 1785-1859 ... **NCLC 4**
See also CDBLB 1789-1832; DLB 110

Deren, Eleanora 1908(?)-1961
See Deren, Maya
See also CA 111

Deren, Maya .... **CLC 16**
See also Deren, Eleanora

Derleth, August (William)
1909-1971 .... **CLC 31**
See also CA 1-4R; 29-32R; CANR 4;
DLB 9; SATA 5

de Routisie, Albert
See Aragon, Louis

Derrida, Jacques 1930-............ **CLC 24**
See also CA 124; 127

Derry Down Derry
See Lear, Edward

Dersonnes, Jacques
See Simenon, Georges (Jacques Christian)

Desai, Anita 1937- .... **CLC 19, 37**
See also CA 81-84; CANR 33; MTCW;
SATA 63

de Saint-Luc, Jean
See Glassco, John

de Saint Roman, Arnaud
See Aragon, Louis

Descartes, Rene 1596-1650 .... **LC 20**

De Sica, Vittorio 1901(?)-1974 ..... **CLC 20**
See also CA 117

Desnos, Robert 1900-1945........ **TCLC 22**
See also CA 121

Destouches, Louis-Ferdinand
1894-1961 .... **CLC 9, 15**
See also Celine, Louis-Ferdinand
See also CA 85-88; CANR 28; MTCW

Deutsch, Babette 1895-1982 .... **CLC 18**
See also CA 1-4R; 108; CANR 4; DLB 45;
SATA 1, 33

Devenant, William 1606-1649 .... **LC 13**

Devkota, Laxmiprasad
1909-1959 .... **TCLC 23**
See also CA 123

De Voto, Bernard (Augustine)
1897-1955 .... **TCLC 29**
See also CA 113; DLB 9

De Vries, Peter
1910- .... **CLC 1, 2, 3, 7, 10, 28, 46**
See also CA 17-20R; CANR 41; DLB 6;
DLBY 82; MTCW

Dexter, Martin
See Faust, Frederick (Schiller)

Dexter, Pete 1943-............ **CLC 34, 55**
See also BEST 89:2; CA 127; 131; MTCW

Diamano, Silmang
See Senghor, Leopold Sedar

Diamond, Neil 1941- .... **CLC 30**
See also CA 108

di Bassetto, Corno
See Shaw, George Bernard

Dick, Philip K(indred)
1928-1982 .... **CLC 10, 30, 72**
See also CA 49-52; 106; CANR 2, 16;
DLB 8; MTCW

Dickens, Charles (John Huffam)
1812-1870 .... **NCLC 3, 8, 18, 26**
See also CDBLB 1832-1890; DA; DLB 21,
55, 70; MAICYA; SATA 15

Dickey, James (Lafayette)
1923- .... **CLC 1, 2, 4, 7, 10, 15, 47**
See also AITN 1, 2; CA 9-12R; CABS 2;
CANR 10; CDALB 1968-1988; DLB 5;
DLBD 7; DLBY 82; MTCW

Dickey, William 1928-.......... **CLC 3, 28**
See also CA 9-12R; CANR 24; DLB 5

Dickinson, Charles 1951-.......... **CLC 49**
See also CA 128

Dickinson, Emily (Elizabeth)
1830-1886 .... **NCLC 21; PC 1**
See also CDALB 1865-1917; DA; DLB 1;
SATA 29; WLC

Dickinson, Peter (Malcolm)
1927- .... **CLC 12, 35**
See also AAYA 9; CA 41-44R; CANR 31;
CLR 29; DLB 87; MAICYA; SATA 5, 62

Dickson, Carr
See Carr, John Dickson

Dickson, Carter
See Carr, John Dickson

Didion, Joan 1934-..... **CLC 1, 3, 8, 14, 32**
See also AITN 1; CA 5-8R; CANR 14;
CDALB 1968-1988; DLB 2; DLBY 81,
86; MTCW

Dietrich, Robert
See Hunt, E(verette) Howard, Jr.

Dillard, Annie 1945-............ **CLC 9, 60**
See also AAYA 6; CA 49-52; CANR 3;
DLBY 80; MTCW; SATA 10

Dillard, R(ichard) H(enry) W(ilde)
1937- .... **CLC 5**
See also CA 21-24R; CAAS 7; CANR 10;
DLB 5

Dillon, Eilis 1920-................ **CLC 17**
See also CA 9-12R; CAAS 3; CANR 4, 38;
CLR 26; MAICYA; SATA 2, 74

Dimont, Penelope
See Mortimer, Penelope (Ruth)

Dinesen, Isak........... **CLC 10, 29; SSC 7**
See also Blixen, Karen (Christentze
Dinesen)

Ding Ling....................... **CLC 68**
See also Chiang Pin-chin

Disch, Thomas M(ichael) 1940-... **CLC 7, 36**
See also CA 21-24R; CAAS 4; CANR 17,
36; CLR 18; DLB 8; MAICYA; MTCW;
SAAS 15; SATA 54

Disch, Tom
See Disch, Thomas M(ichael)

d'Isly, Georges
See Simenon, Georges (Jacques Christian)

Disraeli, Benjamin 1804-1881 .. **NCLC 2, 39**
See also DLB 21, 55

Ditcum, Steve
See Crumb, R(obert)

Dixon, Paige
See Corcoran, Barbara

Dixon, Stephen 1936-............. **CLC 52**
See also CA 89-92; CANR 17, 40; DLB 130

Doblin, Alfred .... **TCLC 13**
See also Doeblin, Alfred

Dobrolyubov, Nikolai Alexandrovich
1836-1861 .... **NCLC 5**

Dobyns, Stephen 1941-............ **CLC 37**
See also CA 45-48; CANR 2, 18

Doctorow, E(dgar) L(aurence)
1931- ..... **CLC 6, 11, 15, 18, 37, 44, 65**
See also AITN 2; BEST 89:3; CA 45-48;
CANR 2, 33; CDALB 1968-1988; DLB 2,
28; DLBY 80; MTCW

Dodgson, Charles Lutwidge 1832-1898
See Carroll, Lewis
See also CLR 2; DA; MAICYA; YABC 2

Doeblin, Alfred 1878-1957........ **TCLC 13**
See also Doblin, Alfred
See also CA 110; DLB 66

Doerr, Harriet 1910- .... **CLC 34**
See also CA 117; 122

Domecq, H(onorio) Bustos
See Bioy Casares, Adolfo; Borges, Jorge
Luis

Domini, Rey
See Lorde, Audre (Geraldine)

Dominique
See Proust, (Valentin-Louis-George-Eugene-)
Marcel

Don, A
See Stephen, Leslie

Donaldson, Stephen R. 1947-....... **CLC 46**
See also CA 89-92; CANR 13

Donleavy, J(ames) P(atrick)
1926- .... **CLC 1, 4, 6, 10, 45**
See also AITN 2; CA 9-12R; CANR 24;
DLB 6; MTCW

Donne, John 1572-1631 .... **LC 10; PC 1**
See also CDBLB Before 1660; DA;
DLB 121; WLC

Donnell, David 1939(?)-........... **CLC 34**

Donoso (Yanez), Jose
1924-............. **CLC 4, 8, 11, 32**
See also CA 81-84; CANR 32; DLB 113;
HW; MTCW

Donovan, John 1928-1992 . . . . **CLC 35**
See also CA 97-100; 137; CLR 3;
MAICYA; SATA 29

Don Roberto
See Cunninghame Graham, R(obert)
B(ontine)

Doolittle, Hilda
1886-1961 . . . . . **CLC 3, 8, 14, 31, 34, 73;**
PC 5
See also H. D.
See also CA 97-100; CANR 35; DA;
DLB 4, 45; MTCW; WLC

Dorfman, Ariel 1942- . . . . **CLC 48, 77**
See also CA 124; 130; HW

Dorn, Edward (Merton) 1929- . . . **CLC 10, 18**
See also CA 93-96; DLB 5

Dorsan, Luc
See Simenon, Georges (Jacques Christian)

Dorsange, Jean
See Simenon, Georges (Jacques Christian)

Dos Passos, John (Roderigo)
1896-1970 . . . **CLC 1, 4, 8, 11, 15, 25, 34**
See also CA 1-4R; 29-32R; CANR 3;
CDALB 1929-1941; DA; DLB 4, 9;
DLBD 1; MTCW; WLC

Dossage, Jean
See Simenon, Georges (Jacques Christian)

Dostoevsky, Fedor Mikhailovich
1821-1881 . . . . **NCLC 2, 7, 21, 33; SSC 2**
See also DA; WLC

Doughty, Charles M(ontagu)
1843-1926 . . . . **TCLC 27**
See also CA 115; DLB 19, 57

Douglas, Ellen
See Haxton, Josephine Ayres

Douglas, Gavin 1475(?)-1522 . . . . **LC 20**

Douglas, Keith 1920-1944 . . . . **TCLC 40**
See also DLB 27

Douglas, Leonard
See Bradbury, Ray (Douglas)

Douglas, Michael
See Crichton, (John) Michael

Douglass, Frederick 1817(?)-1895 . . **NCLC 7**
See also BLC 1; CDALB 1640-1865; DA;
DLB 1, 43, 50, 79; SATA 29; WLC

Dourado, (Waldomiro Freitas) Autran
1926- . . . . **CLC 23, 60**
See also CA 25-28R; CANR 34

Dourado, Waldomiro Autran
See Dourado, (Waldomiro Freitas) Autran

Dove, Rita (Frances) 1952- . . . **CLC 50; PC 6**
See also BW; CA 109; CANR 27; DLB 120

Dowell, Coleman 1925-1985 . . . . **CLC 60**
See also CA 25-28R; 117; CANR 10;
DLB 130

Dowson, Ernest Christopher
1867-1900 . . . . **TCLC 4**
See also CA 105; DLB 19

Doyle, A. Conan
See Doyle, Arthur Conan

Doyle, Arthur Conan
1859-1930 . . . . **TCLC 7; SSC 12**
See also CA 104; 122; CDBLB 1890-1914;
DA; DLB 18, 70; MTCW; SATA 24;
WLC

Doyle, Conan 1859-1930
See Doyle, Arthur Conan

Doyle, John
See Graves, Robert (von Ranke)

Doyle, Sir A. Conan
See Doyle, Arthur Conan

Doyle, Sir Arthur Conan
See Doyle, Arthur Conan

Dr. A
See Asimov, Isaac; Silverstein, Alvin

Drabble, Margaret
1939- . . . . **CLC 2, 3, 5, 8, 10, 22, 53**
See also CA 13-16R; CANR 18, 35;
CDBLB 1960 to Present; DLB 14;
MTCW; SATA 48

Drapier, M. B.
See Swift, Jonathan

Drayham, James
See Mencken, H(enry) L(ouis)

Drayton, Michael 1563-1631 . . . . **LC 8**

Dreadstone, Carl
See Campbell, (John) Ramsey

Dreiser, Theodore (Herman Albert)
1871-1945 . . . . **TCLC 10, 18, 35**
See also CA 106; 132; CDALB 1865-1917;
DA; DLB 9, 12, 102; DLBD 1; MTCW;
WLC

Drexler, Rosalyn 1926- . . . . **CLC 2, 6**
See also CA 81-84

Dreyer, Carl Theodor 1889-1968 . . . . **CLC 16**
See also CA 116

Drieu la Rochelle, Pierre(-Eugene)
1893-1945 . . . . **TCLC 21**
See also CA 117; DLB 72

Drop Shot
See Cable, George Washington

Droste-Hulshoff, Annette Freiin von
1797-1848 . . . . **NCLC 3**

Drummond, Walter
See Silverberg, Robert

Drummond, William Henry
1854-1907 . . . . **TCLC 25**
See also DLB 92

Drummond de Andrade, Carlos
1902-1987 . . . . **CLC 18**
See also Andrade, Carlos Drummond de
See also CA 132; 123

Drury, Allen (Stuart) 1918- . . . . **CLC 37**
See also CA 57-60; CANR 18

Dryden, John 1631-1700 . . . . **LC 3, 21; DC 3**
See also CDBLB 1660-1789; DA; DLB 80,
101, 131; WLC

Duberman, Martin 1930- . . . . **CLC 8**
See also CA 1-4R; CANR 2

Dubie, Norman (Evans) 1945- . . . . . . **CLC 36**
See also CA 69-72; CANR 12; DLB 120

Du Bois, W(illiam) E(dward) B(urghardt)
1868-1963 . . . . **CLC 1, 2, 13, 64**
See also BLC 1; BW; CA 85-88; CANR 34;
CDALB 1865-1917; DA; DLB 47, 50, 91;
MTCW; SATA 42; WLC

Dubus, Andre 1936- . . . . **CLC 13, 36**
See also CA 21-24R; CANR 17; DLB 130

Duca Minimo
See D'Annunzio, Gabriele

Ducharme, Rejean 1941- . . . . **CLC 74**
See also DLB 60

Duclos, Charles Pinot 1704-1772 . . . . . **LC 1**

Dudek, Louis 1918- . . . . **CLC 11, 19**
See also CA 45-48; CAAS 14; CANR 1;
DLB 88

Duerrenmatt, Friedrich
1921-1990 . . . . . . **CLC 1, 4, 8, 11, 15, 43**
See also Durrenmatt, Friedrich
See also CA 17-20R; CANR 33; DLB 69,
124; MTCW

Duffy, Bruce (?)- . . . . **CLC 50**

Duffy, Maureen 1933- . . . . **CLC 37**
See also CA 25-28R; CANR 33; DLB 14;
MTCW

Dugan, Alan 1923- . . . . **CLC 2, 6**
See also CA 81-84; DLB 5

du Gard, Roger Martin
See Martin du Gard, Roger

Duhamel, Georges 1884-1966 . . . . **CLC 8**
See also CA 81-84; 25-28R; CANR 35;
DLB 65; MTCW

Dujardin, Edouard (Emile Louis)
1861-1949 . . . . **TCLC 13**
See also CA 109; DLB 123

Dumas, Alexandre (Davy de la Pailleterie)
1802-1870 . . . . **NCLC 11**
See also DA; DLB 119; SATA 18; WLC

Dumas, Alexandre
1824-1895 . . . . **NCLC 9; DC 1**

Dumas, Claudine
See Malzberg, Barry N(athaniel)

Dumas, Henry L. 1934-1968 . . . . . **CLC 6, 62**
See also BW; CA 85-88; DLB 41

du Maurier, Daphne
1907-1989 . . . . **CLC 6, 11, 59**
See also CA 5-8R; 128; CANR 6; MTCW;
SATA 27, 60

Dunbar, Paul Laurence
1872-1906 . . . . **TCLC 2, 12; PC 5; SSC 8**
See also BLC 1; BW; CA 104; 124;
CDALB 1865-1917; DA; DLB 50, 54, 78;
SATA 34; WLC

Dunbar, William 1460(?)-1530(?) . . . . **LC 20**

Duncan, Lois 1934- . . . . **CLC 26**
See also AAYA 4; CA 1-4R; CANR 2, 23,
36; CLR 29; MAICYA; SAAS 2;
SATA 1, 36

Duncan, Robert (Edward)
1919-1988 . . . . **CLC 1, 2, 4, 7, 15, 41, 55;**
PC 2
See also CA 9-12R; 124; CANR 28; DLB 5,
16; MTCW

Dunlap, William 1766-1839 . . . . **NCLC 2**
See also DLB 30, 37, 59

Dunn, Douglas (Eaglesham)
1942- . . . . **CLC 6, 40**
See also CA 45-48; CANR 2, 33; DLB 40;
MTCW

Dunn, Katherine (Karen) 1945- . . . . . **CLC 71**
See also CA 33-36R

Dunn, Stephen 1939- . . . . **CLC 36**
See also CA 33-36R; CANR 12; DLB 105

Dunne, Finley Peter 1867-1936.... **TCLC 28**
See also CA 108; DLB 11, 23

Dunne, John Gregory 1932-........ **CLC 28**
See also CA 25-28R; CANR 14; DLBY 80

Dunsany, Edward John Moreton Drax Plunkett 1878-1957
See Dunsany, Lord; Lord Dunsany
See also CA 104; DLB 10

Dunsany, Lord................... **TCLC 2**
See also Dunsany, Edward John Moreton
Drax Plunkett
See also DLB 77

du Perry, Jean
See Simenon, Georges (Jacques Christian)

Durang, Christopher (Ferdinand)
1949-.................... **CLC 27, 38**
See also CA 105

Duras, Marguerite
1914-...... **CLC 3, 6, 11, 20, 34, 40, 68**
See also CA 25-28R; DLB 83; MTCW

Durban, (Rosa) Pam 1947-........ **CLC 39**
See also CA 123

Durcan, Paul 1944-........... **CLC 43, 70**
See also CA 134

Durrell, Lawrence (George)
1912-1990 .... **CLC 1, 4, 6, 8, 13, 27, 41**
See also CA 9-12R; 132; CANR 40;
CDBLB 1945-1960; DLB 15, 27;
DLBY 90; MTCW

Durrenmatt, Friedrich
.... **CLC 1, 4, 8, 11, 15, 43**
See also Duerrenmatt, Friedrich
See also DLB 69, 124

Dutt, Toru 1856-1877.......... **NCLC 29**

Dwight, Timothy 1752-1817...... **NCLC 13**
See also DLB 37

Dworkin, Andrea 1946-........... **CLC 43**
See also CA 77-80; CANR 16, 39; MTCW

Dwyer, Deanna
See Koontz, Dean R(ay)

Dwyer, K. R.
See Koontz, Dean R(ay)

Dylan, Bob 1941-...... **CLC 3, 4, 6, 12, 77**
See also CA 41-44R; DLB 16

Eagleton, Terence (Francis) 1943-
See Eagleton, Terry
See also CA 57-60; CANR 7, 23; MTCW

Eagleton, Terry................... **CLC 63**
See also Eagleton, Terence (Francis)

Early, Jack
See Scoppettone, Sandra

East, Michael
See West, Morris L(anglo)

Eastaway, Edward
See Thomas, (Philip) Edward

Eastlake, William (Derry) 1917-..... **CLC 8**
See also CA 5-8R; CAAS 1; CANR 5;
DLB 6

Eberhart, Richard (Ghormley)
1904-.............. **CLC 3, 11, 19, 56**
See also CA 1-4R; CANR 2;
CDALB 1941-1968; DLB 48; MTCW

Eberstadt, Fernanda 1960-........ **CLC 39**
See also CA 136

Echegaray (y Eizaguirre), Jose (Maria Waldo)
1832-1916 .... **TCLC 4**
See also CA 104; CANR 32; HW; MTCW

Echeverria, (Jose) Esteban (Antonino)
1805-1851 .... **NCLC 18**

Echo
See Proust, (Valentin-Louis-George-Eugene-)
Marcel

Eckert, Allan W. 1931- .... **CLC 17**
See also CA 13-16R; CANR 14; SATA 27,
29

Eckhart, Meister 1260(?)-1328(?) .. **CMLC 9**
See also DLB 115

Eckmar, F. R.
See de Hartog, Jan

Eco, Umberto 1932-........... **CLC 28, 60**
See also BEST 90:1; CA 77-80; CANR 12,
33; MTCW

Eddison, E(ric) R(ucker)
1882-1945 .... **TCLC 15**
See also CA 109

Edel, (Joseph) Leon 1907-...... **CLC 29, 34**
See also CA 1-4R; CANR 1, 22; DLB 103

Eden, Emily 1797-1869 .... **NCLC 10**

Edgar, David 1948-.............. **CLC 42**
See also CA 57-60; CANR 12; DLB 13;
MTCW

Edgerton, Clyde (Carlyle) 1944- .... **CLC 39**
See also CA 118; 134

Edgeworth, Maria 1767-1849...... **NCLC 1**
See also DLB 116; SATA 21

Edmonds, Paul
See Kuttner, Henry

Edmonds, Walter D(umaux) 1903- .. **CLC 35**
See also CA 5-8R; CANR 2; DLB 9;
MAICYA; SAAS 4; SATA 1, 27

Edmondson, Wallace
See Ellison, Harlan

Edson, Russell................... **CLC 13**
See also CA 33-36R

Edwards, G(erald) B(asil)
1899-1976 .... **CLC 25**
See also CA 110

Edwards, Gus 1939-.............. **CLC 43**
See also CA 108

Edwards, Jonathan 1703-1758........ **LC 7**
See also DA; DLB 24

Efron, Marina Ivanovna Tsvetaeva
See Tsvetaeva (Efron), Marina (Ivanovna)

Ehle, John (Marsden, Jr.) 1925-.... **CLC 27**
See also CA 9-12R

Ehrenbourg, Ilya (Grigoryevich)
See Ehrenburg, Ilya (Grigoryevich)

Ehrenburg, Ilya (Grigoryevich)
1891-1967 .... **CLC 18, 34, 62**
See also CA 102; 25-28R

Ehrenburg, Ilyo (Grigoryevich)
See Ehrenburg, Ilya (Grigoryevich)

Eich, Guenter 1907-1972 .... **CLC 15**
See also CA 111; 93-96; DLB 69, 124

Eichendorff, Joseph Freiherr von
1788-1857 .... **NCLC 8**
See also DLB 90

Eigner, Larry..................... **CLC 9**
See also Eigner, Laurence (Joel)
See also DLB 5

Eigner, Laurence (Joel) 1927-
See Eigner, Larry
See also CA 9-12R; CANR 6

Eiseley, Loren Corey 1907-1977..... **CLC 7**
See also AAYA 5; CA 1-4R; 73-76;
CANR 6

Eisenstadt, Jill 1963-............. **CLC 50**
See also CA 140

Eisner, Simon
See Kornbluth, C(yril) M.

Ekeloef, (Bengt) Gunnar
1907-1968 .... **CLC 27**
See also Ekelof, (Bengt) Gunnar
See also CA 123; 25-28R

Ekelof, (Bengt) Gunnar............. **CLC 27**
See also Ekeloef, (Bengt) Gunnar

Ekwensi, C. O. D.
See Ekwensi, Cyprian (Odiatu Duaka)

Ekwensi, Cyprian (Odiatu Duaka)
1921-......................... **CLC 4**
See also BLC 1; BW; CA 29-32R;
CANR 18; DLB 117; MTCW; SATA 66

Elaine......................... **TCLC 18**
See also Leverson, Ada

El Crummo
See Crumb, R(obert)

Elia
See Lamb, Charles

Eliade, Mircea 1907-1986 .... **CLC 19**
See also CA 65-68; 119; CANR 30; MTCW

Eliot, A. D.
See Jewett, (Theodora) Sarah Orne

Eliot, Alice
See Jewett, (Theodora) Sarah Orne

Eliot, Dan
See Silverberg, Robert

Eliot, George
1819-1880 .... **NCLC 4, 13, 23, 41**
See also CDBLB 1832-1890; DA; DLB 21,
35, 55; WLC

Eliot, John 1604-1690 .... **LC 5**
See also DLB 24

Eliot, T(homas) S(tearns)
1888-1965 ..... **CLC 1, 2, 3, 6, 9, 10, 13,
15, 24, 34, 41, 55, 57; PC 5**
See also CA 5-8R; 25-28R; CANR 41;
CDALB 1929-1941; DA; DLB 7, 10, 45,
63; DLBY 88; MTCW; WLC 2

Elizabeth 1866-1941............. **TCLC 41**

Elkin, Stanley L(awrence)
1930- ... **CLC 4, 6, 9, 14, 27, 51; SSC 12**
See also CA 9-12R; CANR 8; DLB 2, 28;
DLBY 80; MTCW

Elledge, Scott.................... **CLC 34**

Elliott, Don
See Silverberg, Robert

Elliott, George P(aul) 1918-1980..... **CLC 2**
See also CA 1-4R; 97-100; CANR 2

Elliott, Janice 1931-.............. **CLC 47**
See also CA 13-16R; CANR 8, 29; DLB 14

Fante, John (Thomas) 1911-1983 ... **CLC 60**
See also CA 69-72; 109; CANR 23;
DLB 130; DLBY 83

Farah, Nuruddin 1945-............ **CLC 53**
See also BLC 2; CA 106; DLB 125

Fargue, Leon-Paul 1876(?)-1947 ... **TCLC 11**
See also CA 109

Farigoule, Louis
See Romains, Jules

Farina, Richard 1936(?)-1966 .... **CLC 9**
See also CA 81-84; 25-28R

Farley, Walter (Lorimer)
1915-1989 .... **CLC 17**
See also CA 17-20R; CANR 8, 29; DLB 22;
MAICYA; SATA 2, 43

Farmer, Philip Jose 1918-....... **CLC 1, 19**
See also CA 1-4R; CANR 4, 35; DLB 8;
MTCW

Farquhar, George 1677-1707........ **LC 21**
See also DLB 84

Farrell, J(ames) G(ordon)
1935-1979 .... **CLC 6**
See also CA 73-76; 89-92; CANR 36;
DLB 14; MTCW

Farrell, James T(homas)
1904-1979 .... **CLC 1, 4, 8, 11, 66**
See also CA 5-8R; 89-92; CANR 9; DLB 4,
9, 86; DLBD 2; MTCW

Farren, Richard J.
See Betjeman, John

Farren, Richard M.
See Betjeman, John

Fassbinder, Rainer Werner
1946-1982 .... **CLC 20**
See also CA 93-96; 106; CANR 31

Fast, Howard (Melvin) 1914- ...... **CLC 23**
See also CA 1-4R; CANR 1, 33; DLB 9;
SATA 7

Faulcon, Robert
See Holdstock, Robert P.

Faulkner, William (Cuthbert)
1897-1962 ..... **CLC 1, 3, 6, 8, 9, 11, 14,
18, 28, 52, 68; SSC 1**
See also AAYA 7; CA 81-84; CANR 33;
CDALB 1929-1941; DA; DLB 9, 11, 44,
102; DLBD 2; DLBY 86; MTCW; WLC

Fauset, Jessie Redmon
1884(?)-1961 .... **CLC 19, 54**
See also BLC 2; BW; CA 109; DLB 51

Faust, Frederick (Schiller)
1892-1944(?) .... **TCLC 49**
See also CA 108

Faust, Irvin 1924-................. **CLC 8**
See also CA 33-36R; CANR 28; DLB 2, 28;
DLBY 80

Fawkes, Guy
See Benchley, Robert (Charles)

Fearing, Kenneth (Flexner)
1902-1961 .... **CLC 51**
See also CA 93-96; DLB 9

Fecamps, Elise
See Creasey, John

Federman, Raymond 1928- ...... **CLC 6, 47**
See also CA 17-20R; CAAS 8; CANR 10;
DLBY 80

Federspiel, J(uerg) F. 1931-........ **CLC 42**

Feiffer, Jules (Ralph) 1929-.... **CLC 2, 8, 64**
See also AAYA 3; CA 17-20R; CANR 30;
DLB 7, 44; MTCW; SATA 8, 61

Feige, Hermann Albert Otto Maximilian
See Traven, B.

Fei-Kan, Li
See Li Fei-kan

Feinberg, David B. 1956-.......... **CLC 59**
See also CA 135

Feinstein, Elaine 1930-............ **CLC 36**
See also CA 69-72; CAAS 1; CANR 31;
DLB 14, 40; MTCW

Feldman, Irving (Mordecai) 1928-.... **CLC 7**
See also CA 1-4R; CANR 1

Fellini, Federico 1920-............ **CLC 16**
See also CA 65-68; CANR 33

Felsen, Henry Gregor 1916- .... **CLC 17**
See also CA 1-4R; CANR 1; SAAS 2;
SATA 1

Fenton, James Martin 1949-....... **CLC 32**
See also CA 102; DLB 40

Ferber, Edna 1887-1968........... **CLC 18**
See also AITN 1; CA 5-8R; 25-28R; DLB 9,
28, 86; MTCW; SATA 7

Ferguson, Helen
See Kavan, Anna

Ferguson, Samuel 1810-1886..... **NCLC 33**
See also DLB 32

Ferling, Lawrence
See Ferlinghetti, Lawrence (Monsanto)

Ferlinghetti, Lawrence (Monsanto)
1919(?)-........ **CLC 2, 6, 10, 27; PC 1**
See also CA 5-8R; CANR 3, 41;
CDALB 1941-1968; DLB 5, 16; MTCW

Fernandez, Vicente Garcia Huidobro
See Huidobro Fernandez, Vicente Garcia

Ferrer, Gabriel (Francisco Victor) Miro
See Miro (Ferrer), Gabriel (Francisco
Victor)

Ferrier, Susan (Edmonstone)
1782-1854 .... **NCLC 8**
See also DLB 116

Ferrigno, Robert 1948(?)-.......... **CLC 65**
See also CA 140

Feuchtwanger, Lion 1884-1958 ..... **TCLC 3**
See also CA 104; DLB 66

Feydeau, Georges (Leon Jules Marie)
1862-1921 .... **TCLC 22**
See also CA 113

Ficino, Marsilio 1433-1499 .... **LC 12**

Fiedler, Leslie A(aron)
1917- .... **CLC 4, 13, 24**
See also CA 9-12R; CANR 7; DLB 28, 67;
MTCW

Field, Andrew 1938-.............. **CLC 44**
See also CA 97-100; CANR 25

Field, Eugene 1850-1895 .... **NCLC 3**
See also DLB 23, 42; MAICYA; SATA 16

Field, Gans T.
See Wellman, Manly Wade

Field, Michael .... **TCLC 43**

Field, Peter
See Hobson, Laura Z(ametkin)

Fielding, Henry 1707-1754 .... **LC 1**
See also CDBLB 1660-1789; DA; DLB 39,
84, 101; WLC

Fielding, Sarah 1710-1768 .... **LC 1**
See also DLB 39

Fierstein, Harvey (Forbes) 1954- ... **CLC 33**
See also CA 123; 129

Figes, Eva 1932-................. **CLC 31**
See also CA 53-56; CANR 4; DLB 14

Finch, Robert (Duer Claydon)
1900-....................... **CLC 18**
See also CA 57-60; CANR 9, 24; DLB 88

Findley, Timothy 1930- .... **CLC 27**
See also CA 25-28R; CANR 12; DLB 53

Fink, William
See Mencken, H(enry) L(ouis)

Firbank, Louis 1942-
See Reed, Lou
See also CA 117

Firbank, (Arthur Annesley) Ronald
1886-1926 .... **TCLC 1**
See also CA 104; DLB 36

Fisher, M(ary) F(rances) K(ennedy)
1908-1992 .... **CLC 76**
See also CA 77-80; 138

Fisher, Roy 1930-................. **CLC 25**
See also CA 81-84; CAAS 10; CANR 16;
DLB 40

Fisher, Rudolph 1897-1934 .... **TCLC 11**
See also BLC 2; BW; CA 107; 124; DLB 51,
102

Fisher, Vardis (Alvero) 1895-1968.... **CLC 7**
See also CA 5-8R; 25-28R; DLB 9

Fiske, Tarleton
See Bloch, Robert (Albert)

Fitch, Clarke
See Sinclair, Upton (Beall)

Fitch, John IV
See Cormier, Robert (Edmund)

Fitgerald, Penelope 1916- .... **CLC 61**

Fitzgerald, Captain Hugh
See Baum, L(yman) Frank

FitzGerald, Edward 1809-1883 .... **NCLC 9**
See also DLB 32

Fitzgerald, F(rancis) Scott (Key)
1896-1940 .... **TCLC 1, 6, 14, 28; SSC 6**
See also AITN 1; CA 110; 123;
CDALB 1917-1929; DA; DLB 4, 9, 86;
DLBD 1; DLBY 81; MTCW; WLC

Fitzgerald, Penelope 1916-...... **CLC 19, 51**
See also CA 85-88; CAAS 10; DLB 14

Fitzgerald, Robert (Stuart)
1910-1985 .... **CLC 39**
See also CA 1-4R; 114; CANR 1; DLBY 80

FitzGerald, Robert D(avid)
1902-1987 .... **CLC 19**
See also CA 17-20R

Flanagan, Thomas (James Bonner)
1923-..................... **CLC 25, 52**
See also CA 108; DLBY 80; MTCW

Flaubert, Gustave
1821-1880 . . . . . NCLC 2, 10, 19; SSC 11
See also DA; DLB 119; WLC

Flecker, (Herman) James Elroy
1884-1915 . . . . TCLC 43
See also CA 109; DLB 10, 19

Fleming, Ian (Lancaster)
1908-1964 . . . . CLC 3, 30
See also CA 5-8R; CDBLB 1945-1960;
DLB 87; MTCW; SATA 9

Fleming, Thomas (James) 1927- . . . . CLC 37
See also CA 5-8R; CANR 10; SATA 8

Fletcher, John Gould 1886-1950 . . . TCLC 35
See also CA 107; DLB 4, 45

Fleur, Paul
See Pohl, Frederik

Flooglebuckle, Al
See Spiegelman, Art

Flying Officer X
See Bates, H(erbert) E(rnest)

Fo, Dario 1926- . . . . CLC 32
See also CA 116; 128; MTCW

Fogarty, Jonathan Titulescu Esq.
See Farrell, James T(homas)

Folke, Will
See Bloch, Robert (Albert)

Follett, Ken(neth Martin) 1949- . . . . CLC 18
See also AAYA 6; BEST 89:4; CA 81-84;
CANR 13, 33; DLB 87; DLBY 81;
MTCW

Fontane, Theodor 1819-1898 . . . . . NCLC 26
See also DLB 129

Foote, Horton 1916- . . . . CLC 51
See also CA 73-76; CANR 34; DLB 26

Foote, Shelby 1916- . . . . CLC 75
See also CA 5-8R; CANR 3; DLB 2, 17

Forbes, Esther 1891-1967 . . . . CLC 12
See also CA 13-14; 25-28R; CAP 1;
CLR 27; DLB 22; MAICYA; SATA 2

Forche, Carolyn (Louise) 1950- . . . . . CLC 25
See also CA 109; 117; DLB 5

Ford, Elbur
See Hibbert, Eleanor Alice Burford

Ford, Ford Madox
1873-1939 . . . . TCLC 1, 15, 39
See also CA 104; 132; CDBLB 1914-1945;
DLB 34, 98; MTCW

Ford, John 1895-1973 . . . . CLC 16
See also CA 45-48

Ford, Richard 1944- . . . . CLC 46
See also CA 69-72; CANR 11

Ford, Webster
See Masters, Edgar Lee

Foreman, Richard 1937- . . . . CLC 50
See also CA 65-68; CANR 32

Forester, C(ecil) S(cott)
1899-1966 . . . . CLC 35
See also CA 73-76; 25-28R; SATA 13

Forez
See Mauriac, Francois (Charles)

Forman, James Douglas 1932- . . . . . . CLC 21
See also CA 9-12R; CANR 4, 19;
MAICYA; SATA 8, 70

Fornes, Maria Irene 1930- . . . . . . CLC 39, 61
See also CA 25-28R; CANR 28; DLB 7;
HW; MTCW

Forrest, Leon 1937- . . . . CLC 4
See also BW; CA 89-92; CAAS 7;
CANR 25; DLB 33

Forster, E(dward) M(organ)
1879-1970 . . . . . CLC 1, 2, 3, 4, 9, 10, 13,
15, 22, 45, 77
See also AAYA 2; CA 13-14; 25-28R;
CAP 1; CDBLB 1914-1945; DA; DLB 34,
98; DLBD 10; MTCW; SATA 57; WLC

Forster, John 1812-1876 . . . . NCLC 11

Forsyth, Frederick 1938- . . . . . . CLC 2, 5, 36
See also BEST 89:4; CA 85-88; CANR 38;
DLB 87; MTCW

Forten, Charlotte L. . . . . TCLC 16
See also Grimke, Charlotte L(ottie) Forten
See also BLC 2; DLB 50

Foscolo, Ugo 1778-1827 . . . . NCLC 8

Fosse, Bob . . . . CLC 20
See also Fosse, Robert Louis

Fosse, Robert Louis 1927-1987
See Fosse, Bob
See also CA 110; 123

Foster, Stephen Collins
1826-1864 . . . . NCLC 26

Foucault, Michel
1926-1984 . . . . CLC 31, 34, 69
See also CA 105; 113; CANR 34; MTCW

Fouque, Friedrich (Heinrich Karl) de la Motte
1777-1843 . . . . NCLC 2
See also DLB 90

Fournier, Henri Alban 1886-1914
See Alain-Fournier
See also CA 104

Fournier, Pierre 1916- . . . . CLC 11
See also Gascar, Pierre
See also CA 89-92; CANR 16, 40

Fowles, John
1926- . . . . CLC 1, 2, 3, 4, 6, 9, 10, 15, 33
See also CA 5-8R; CANR 25; CDBLB 1960
to Present; DLB 14; MTCW; SATA 22

Fox, Paula 1923- . . . . CLC 2, 8
See also AAYA 3; CA 73-76; CANR 20,
36; CLR 1; DLB 52; MAICYA; MTCW;
SATA 17, 60

Fox, William Price (Jr.) 1926- . . . . . CLC 22
See also CA 17-20R; CANR 11; DLB 2;
DLBY 81

Foxe, John 1516(?)-1587 . . . . LC 14

Frame, Janet . . . . CLC 2, 3, 6, 22, 66
See also Clutha, Janet Paterson Frame

France, Anatole . . . . TCLC 9
See also Thibault, Jacques Anatole Francois
See also DLB 123

Francis, Claude 19(?)- . . . . CLC 50

Francis, Dick 1920- . . . . CLC 2, 22, 42
See also AAYA 5; BEST 89:3; CA 5-8R;
CANR 9; CDBLB 1960 to Present;
DLB 87; MTCW

Francis, Robert (Churchill)
1901-1987 . . . . CLC 15
See also CA 1-4R; 123; CANR 1

Frank, Anne(lies Marie)
1929-1945 . . . . TCLC 17
See also CA 113; 133; DA; MTCW;
SATA 42; WLC

Frank, Elizabeth 1945- . . . . CLC 39
See also CA 121; 126

Franklin, Benjamin
See Hasek, Jaroslav (Matej Frantisek)

Franklin, (Stella Maraia Sarah) Miles
1879-1954 . . . . TCLC 7
See also CA 104

Fraser, Antonia (Pakenham)
1932- . . . . CLC 32
See also CA 85-88; MTCW; SATA 32

Fraser, George MacDonald 1925- . . . . CLC 7
See also CA 45-48; CANR 2

Fraser, Sylvia 1935- . . . . CLC 64
See also CA 45-48; CANR 1, 16

Frayn, Michael 1933- . . . . . . CLC 3, 7, 31, 47
See also CA 5-8R; CANR 30; DLB 13, 14;
MTCW

Fraze, Candida (Merrill) 1945- . . . . . CLC 50
See also CA 126

Frazer, J(ames) G(eorge)
1854-1941 . . . . TCLC 32
See also CA 118

Frazer, Robert Caine
See Creasey, John

Frazer, Sir James George
See Frazer, J(ames) G(eorge)

Frazier, Ian 1951- . . . . CLC 46
See also CA 130

Frederic, Harold 1856-1898 . . . . . . NCLC 10
See also DLB 12, 23

Frederick, John
See Faust, Frederick (Schiller)

Frederick the Great 1712-1786 . . . . . . LC 14

Fredro, Aleksander 1793-1876 . . . . . NCLC 8

Freeling, Nicolas 1927- . . . . CLC 38
See also CA 49-52; CAAS 12; CANR 1, 17;
DLB 87

Freeman, Douglas Southall
1886-1953 . . . . TCLC 11
See also CA 109; DLB 17

Freeman, Judith 1946- . . . . CLC 55

Freeman, Mary Eleanor Wilkins
1852-1930 . . . . TCLC 9; SSC 1
See also CA 106; DLB 12, 78

Freeman, R(ichard) Austin
1862-1943 . . . . TCLC 21
See also CA 113; DLB 70

French, Marilyn 1929- . . . . . . CLC 10, 18, 60
See also CA 69-72; CANR 3, 31; MTCW

French, Paul
See Asimov, Isaac

Freneau, Philip Morin 1752-1832 . . NCLC 1
See also DLB 37, 43

Friedan, Betty (Naomi) 1921- . . . . . . CLC 74
See also CA 65-68; CANR 18; MTCW

Friedman, B(ernard) H(arper)
1926- . . . . CLC 7
See also CA 1-4R; CANR 3

Friedman, Bruce Jay 1930- .... **CLC 3, 5, 56**
See also CA 9-12R; CANR 25; DLB 2, 28

Friel, Brian 1929- .... **CLC 5, 42, 59**
See also CA 21-24R; CANR 33; DLB 13;
MTCW

Friis-Baastad, Babbis Ellinor
1921-1970 .... **CLC 12**
See also CA 17-20R; 134; SATA 7

Frisch, Max (Rudolf)
1911-1991 ..... **CLC 3, 9, 14, 18, 32, 44**
See also CA 85-88; 134; CANR 32;
DLB 69, 124; MTCW

Fromentin, Eugene (Samuel Auguste)
1820-1876 .... **NCLC 10**
See also DLB 123

Frost, Frederick
See Faust, Frederick (Schiller)

Frost, Robert (Lee)
1874-1963 .... **CLC 1, 3, 4, 9, 10, 13, 15,
26, 34, 44; PC 1**
See also CA 89-92; CANR 33;
CDALB 1917-1929; DA; DLB 54;
DLBD 7; MTCW; SATA 14; WLC

Froy, Herald
See Waterhouse, Keith (Spencer)

Fry, Christopher 1907- .... **CLC 2, 10, 14**
See also CA 17-20R; CANR 9, 30; DLB 13;
MTCW; SATA 66

Frye, (Herman) Northrop
1912-1991 .... **CLC 24, 70**
See also CA 5-8R; 133; CANR 8, 37;
DLB 67, 68; MTCW

Fuchs, Daniel 1909- .... **CLC 8, 22**
See also CA 81-84; CAAS 5; CANR 40;
DLB 9, 26, 28

Fuchs, Daniel 1934- .... **CLC 34**
See also CA 37-40R; CANR 14

Fuentes, Carlos
1928- ...... **CLC 3, 8, 10, 13, 22, 41, 60**
See also AAYA 4; AITN 2; CA 69-72;
CANR 10, 32; DA; DLB 113; HW;
MTCW; WLC

Fuentes, Gregorio Lopez y
See Lopez y Fuentes, Gregorio

Fugard, (Harold) Athol
1932- .... **CLC 5, 9, 14, 25, 40; DC 3**
See also CA 85-88; CANR 32; MTCW

Fugard, Sheila 1932- .... **CLC 48**
See also CA 125

Fuller, Charles (H., Jr.)
1939- .... **CLC 25; DC 1**
See also BLC 2; BW; CA 108; 112; DLB 38;
MTCW

Fuller, John (Leopold) 1937- .... **CLC 62**
See also CA 21-24R; CANR 9; DLB 40

Fuller, Margaret .... **NCLC 5**
See also Ossoli, Sarah Margaret (Fuller
marchesa d')

Fuller, Roy (Broadbent)
1912-1991 .... **CLC 4, 28**
See also CA 5-8R; 135; CAAS 10; DLB 15,
20

Fulton, Alice 1952- .... **CLC 52**
See also CA 116

Furphy, Joseph 1843-1912 .... **TCLC 25**

Fussell, Paul 1924- .... **CLC 74**
See also BEST 90:1; CA 17-20R; CANR 8,
21, 35; MTCW

Futabatei, Shimei 1864-1909 ...... **TCLC 44**

Futrelle, Jacques 1875-1912 ...... **TCLC 19**
See also CA 113

G. B. S.
See Shaw, George Bernard

Gaboriau, Emile 1835-1873 ...... **NCLC 14**

Gadda, Carlo Emilio 1893-1973 .... **CLC 11**
See also CA 89-92

Gaddis, William
1922- .... **CLC 1, 3, 6, 8, 10, 19, 43**
See also CA 17-20R; CANR 21; DLB 2;
MTCW

Gaines, Ernest J(ames)
1933- .... **CLC 3, 11, 18**
See also AITN 1; BLC 2; BW; CA 9-12R;
CANR 6, 24; CDALB 1968-1988; DLB 2,
33; DLBY 80; MTCW

Gaitskill, Mary 1954- .... **CLC 69**
See also CA 128

Galdos, Benito Perez
See Perez Galdos, Benito

Gale, Zona 1874-1938 .... **TCLC 7**
See also CA 105; DLB 9, 78

Galeano, Eduardo (Hughes) 1940- ... **CLC 72**
See also CA 29-32R; CANR 13, 32; HW

Galiano, Juan Valera y Alcala
See Valera y Alcala-Galiano, Juan

Gallagher, Tess 1943- .... **CLC 18, 63**
See also CA 106; DLB 120

Gallant, Mavis
1922- .... **CLC 7, 18, 38; SSC 5**
See also CA 69-72; CANR 29; DLB 53;
MTCW

Gallant, Roy A(rthur) 1924- .... **CLC 17**
See also CA 5-8R; CANR 4, 29; CLR 30;
MAICYA; SATA 4, 68

Gallico, Paul (William) 1897-1976 ... **CLC 2**
See also AITN 1; CA 5-8R; 69-72;
CANR 23; DLB 9; MAICYA; SATA 13

Gallup, Ralph
See Whitemore, Hugh (John)

Galsworthy, John 1867-1933 .... **TCLC 1, 45**
See also CA 104; CDBLB 1890-1914; DA;
DLB 10, 34, 98; WLC 2

Galt, John 1779-1839 .... **NCLC 1**
See also DLB 99, 116

Galvin, James 1951- .... **CLC 38**
See also CA 108; CANR 26

Gamboa, Federico 1864-1939 ...... **TCLC 36**

Gann, Ernest Kellogg 1910-1991 .... **CLC 23**
See also AITN 1; CA 1-4R; 136; CANR 1

Garcia, Christina 1959- .... **CLC 76**

Garcia Lorca, Federico
1898-1936 .. **TCLC 1, 7, 49; DC 2; PC 3**
See also CA 104; 131; DA; DLB 108; HW;
MTCW; WLC

Garcia Marquez, Gabriel (Jose)
1928- .... **CLC 2, 3, 8, 10, 15, 27, 47, 55;
SSC 8**
See also Marquez, Gabriel (Jose) Garcia
See also AAYA 3; BEST 89:1, 90:4;
CA 33-36R; CANR 10, 28; DA;
DLB 113; HW; MTCW; WLC

Gard, Janice
See Latham, Jean Lee

Gard, Roger Martin du
See Martin du Gard, Roger

Gardam, Jane 1928- .... **CLC 43**
See also CA 49-52; CANR 2, 18, 33;
CLR 12; DLB 14; MAICYA; MTCW;
SAAS 9; SATA 28, 39

Gardner, Herb .... **CLC 44**

Gardner, John (Champlin), Jr.
1933-1982 ..... **CLC 2, 3, 5, 7, 8, 10, 18,
28, 34; SSC 7**
See also AITN 1; CA 65-68; 107;
CANR 33; DLB 2; DLBY 82; MTCW;
SATA 31, 40

Gardner, John (Edmund) 1926- ..... **CLC 30**
See also CA 103; CANR 15, MTCW

Gardner, Noel
See Kuttner, Henry

Gardons, S. S.
See Snodgrass, W(illiam) D(e Witt)

Garfield, Leon 1921- .... **CLC 12**
See also AAYA 8; CA 17-20R; CANR 38,
41; CLR 21; MAICYA; SATA 1, 32

Garland, (Hannibal) Hamlin
1860-1940 .... **TCLC 3**
See also CA 104; DLB 12, 71, 78

Garneau, (Hector de) Saint-Denys
1912-1943 .... **TCLC 13**
See also CA 111; DLB 88

Garner, Alan 1934- .... **CLC 17**
See also CA 73-76; CANR 15; CLR 20;
MAICYA; MTCW; SATA 18, 69

Garner, Hugh 1913-1979 .... **CLC 13**
See also CA 69-72; CANR 31; DLB 68

Garnett, David 1892-1981 .... **CLC 3**
See also CA 5-8R; 103; CANR 17; DLB 34

Garos, Stephanie
See Katz, Steve

Garrett, George (Palmer)
1929- .... **CLC 3, 11, 51**
See also CA 1-4R; CAAS 5; CANR 1;
DLB 2, 5, 130; DLBY 83

Garrick, David 1717-1779 .... **LC 15**
See also DLB 84

Garrigue, Jean 1914-1972 .... **CLC 2, 8**
See also CA 5-8R; 37-40R; CANR 20

Garrison, Frederick
See Sinclair, Upton (Beall)

Garth, Will
See Hamilton, Edmond; Kuttner, Henry

Garvey, Marcus (Moziah, Jr.)
1887-1940 .... **TCLC 41**
See also BLC 2; BW; CA 120; 124

Gary, Romain .... **CLC 25**
See also Kacew, Romain
See also DLB 83

Gascar, Pierre . . . . CLC 11
See also Fournier, Pierre

Gascoyne, David (Emery) 1916- . . . . CLC 45
See also CA 65-68; CANR 10, 28; DLB 20;
MTCW

Gaskell, Elizabeth Cleghorn
1810-1865 . . . . NCLC 5
See also CDBLB 1832-1890; DLB 21

Gass, William H(oward)
1924- . . . CLC 1, 2, 8, 11, 15, 39; SSC 12
See also CA 17-20R; CANR 30; DLB 2;
MTCW

Gasset, Jose Ortega y
See Ortega y Gasset, Jose

Gautier, Theophile 1811-1872 . . . . . NCLC 1
See also DLB 119

Gawsworth, John
See Bates, H(erbert) E(rnest)

Gaye, Marvin (Penze) 1939-1984 . . . CLC 26
See also CA 112

Gebler, Carlo (Ernest) 1954- . . . . CLC 39
See also CA 119; 133

Gee, Maggie (Mary) 1948- . . . . CLC 57
See also CA 130

Gee, Maurice (Gough) 1931- . . . . CLC 29
See also CA 97-100; SATA 46

Gelbart, Larry (Simon) 1923- . . . CLC 21, 61
See also CA 73-76

Gelber, Jack 1932- . . . . CLC 1, 6, 14
See also CA 1-4R; CANR 2; DLB 7

Gellhorn, Martha Ellis 1908- . . . CLC 14, 60
See also CA 77-80; DLBY 82

Genet, Jean
1910-1986 . . . CLC 1, 2, 5, 10, 14, 44, 46
See also CA 13-16R; CANR 18; DLB 72;
DLBY 86; MTCW

Gent, Peter 1942- . . . . CLC 29
See also AITN 1; CA 89-92; DLBY 82

George, Jean Craighead 1919- . . . . . . CLC 35
See also AAYA 8; CA 5-8R; CANR 25;
CLR 1; DLB 52; MAICYA; SATA 2, 68

George, Stefan (Anton)
1868-1933 . . . . TCLC 2, 14
See also CA 104

Georges, Georges Martin
See Simenon, Georges (Jacques Christian)

Gerhardi, William Alexander
See Gerhardie, William Alexander

Gerhardie, William Alexander
1895-1977 . . . . CLC 5
See also CA 25-28R; 73-76; CANR 18;
DLB 36

Gerstler, Amy 1956- . . . . CLC 70

Gertler, T. . . . . CLC 34
See also CA 116; 121

Ghalib 1797-1869 . . . . NCLC 39

Ghelderode, Michel de
1898-1962 . . . . CLC 6, 11
See also CA 85-88; CANR 40

Ghiselin, Brewster 1903- . . . . CLC 23
See also CA 13-16R; CAAS 10; CANR 13

Ghose, Zulfikar 1935- . . . . CLC 42
See also CA 65-68

Ghosh, Amitav 1956- . . . . CLC 44

Giacosa, Giuseppe 1847-1906 . . . . . . TCLC 7
See also CA 104

Gibb, Lee
See Waterhouse, Keith (Spencer)

Gibbon, Lewis Grassic . . . . TCLC 4
See also Mitchell, James Leslie

Gibbons, Kaye 1960- . . . . CLC 50

Gibran, Kahlil 1883-1931. . . . . TCLC 1, 9
See also CA 104

Gibson, William 1914- . . . . CLC 23
See also CA 9-12R; CANR 9; DA; DLB 7;
SATA 66

Gibson, William (Ford) 1948- . . . CLC 39, 63
See also CA 126; 133

Gide, Andre (Paul Guillaume)
1869-1951 . . . . TCLC 5, 12, 36
See also CA 104; 124; DA; DLB 65;
MTCW; WLC

Gifford, Barry (Colby) 1946- . . . . CLC 34
See also CA 65-68; CANR 9, 30, 40

Gilbert, W(illiam) S(chwenck)
1836-1911 . . . . TCLC 3
See also CA 104; SATA 36

Gilbreth, Frank B., Jr. 1911- . . . . CLC 17
See also CA 9-12R; SATA 2

Gilchrist, Ellen 1935- . . . . CLC 34, 48
See also CA 113; 116; CANR 41; DLB 130;
MTCW

Giles, Molly 1942- . . . . CLC 39
See also CA 126

Gill, Patrick
See Creasey, John

Gilliam, Terry (Vance) 1940- . . . . CLC 21
See also Monty Python
See also CA 108; 113; CANR 35

Gillian, Jerry
See Gilliam, Terry (Vance)

Gilliatt, Penelope (Ann Douglass)
1932- . . . . CLC 2, 10, 13, 53
See also AITN 2; CA 13-16R; DLB 14

Gilman, Charlotte (Anna) Perkins (Stetson)
1860-1935 . . . . TCLC 9, 37
See also CA 106

Gilmour, David 1949- . . . . CLC 35
See also Pink Floyd
See also CA 138

Gilpin, William 1724-1804 . . . . NCLC 30

Gilray, J. D.
See Mencken, H(enry) L(ouis)

Gilroy, Frank D(aniel) 1925- . . . . CLC 2
See also CA 81-84; CANR 32; DLB 7

Ginsberg, Allen
1926- . . . . . . CLC 1, 2, 3, 4, 6, 13, 36, 69;
PC 4
See also AITN 1; CA 1-4R; CANR 2, 41;
CDALB 1941-1968; DA; DLB 5, 16;
MTCW; WLC 3

Ginzburg, Natalia
1916-1991 . . . . CLC 5, 11, 54, 70
See also CA 85-88; 135; CANR 33; MTCW

Giono, Jean 1895-1970. . . . . CLC 4, 11
See also CA 45-48; 29-32R; CANR 2, 35;
DLB 72; MTCW

Giovanni, Nikki 1943- . . . . . CLC 2, 4, 19, 64
See also AITN 1; BLC 2; BW; CA 29-32R;
CAAS 6; CANR 18, 41; CLR 6; DA;
DLB 5, 41; MAICYA; MTCW; SATA 24

Giovene, Andrea 1904- . . . . CLC 7
See also CA 85-88

Gippius, Zinaida (Nikolayevna) 1869-1945
See Hippius, Zinaida
See also CA 106

Giraudoux, (Hippolyte) Jean
1882-1944 . . . . TCLC 2, 7
See also CA 104; DLB 65

Gironella, Jose Maria 1917- . . . . CLC 11
See also CA 101

Gissing, George (Robert)
1857-1903 . . . . TCLC 3, 24, 47
See also CA 105; DLB 18

Giurlani, Aldo
See Palazzeschi, Aldo

Gladkov, Fyodor (Vasilyevich)
1883-1958 . . . . TCLC 27

Glanville, Brian (Lester) 1931- . . . . . . CLC 6
See also CA 5-8R; CAAS 9; CANR 3;
DLB 15; SATA 42

Glasgow, Ellen (Anderson Gholson)
1873(?)-1945 . . . . TCLC 2, 7
See also CA 104; DLB 9, 12

Glassco, John 1909-1981 . . . . CLC 9
See also CA 13-16R; 102; CANR 15;
DLB 68

Glasscock, Amnesia
See Steinbeck, John (Ernst)

Glasser, Ronald J. 1940(?)- . . . . CLC 37

Glassman, Joyce
See Johnson, Joyce

Glendinning, Victoria 1937- . . . . CLC 50
See also CA 120; 127

Glissant, Edouard 1928- . . . . CLC 10, 68

Gloag, Julian 1930- . . . . CLC 40
See also AITN 1; CA 65-68; CANR 10

Gluck, Louise (Elisabeth)
1943- . . . . CLC 7, 22, 44
See also Glueck, Louise
See also CA 33-36R; CANR 40; DLB 5

Glueck, Louise. . . . . CLC 7, 22
See also Gluck, Louise (Elisabeth)
See also DLB 5

Gobineau, Joseph Arthur (Comte) de
1816-1882 . . . . NCLC 17
See also DLB 123

Godard, Jean-Luc 1930- . . . . CLC 20
See also CA 93-96

Godden, (Margaret) Rumer 1907- . . . CLC 53
See also AAYA 6; CA 5-8R; CANR 4, 27,
36; CLR 20; MAICYA; SAAS 12;
SATA 3, 36

Godoy Alcayaga, Lucila 1889-1957
See Mistral, Gabriela
See also CA 104; 131; HW; MTCW

Godwin, Gail (Kathleen)
1937- . . . . CLC 5, 8, 22, 31, 69
See also CA 29-32R; CANR 15; DLB 6;
MTCW

Godwin, William   1756-1836......   **NCLC 14**
See also CDBLB 1789-1832; DLB 39, 104

Goethe, Johann Wolfgang von
1749-1832 .... **NCLC 4, 22, 34; PC 5**
See also DA; DLB 94; WLC 3

Gogarty, Oliver St. John
1878-1957 .... **TCLC 15**
See also CA 109; DLB 15, 19

Gogol, Nikolai (Vasilyevich)
1809-1852 ...... **NCLC 5, 15, 31; DC 1;**
SSC 4
See also DA; WLC

Gold, Herbert   1924-......   **CLC 4, 7, 14, 42**
See also CA 9-12R; CANR 17; DLB 2;
DLBY 81

Goldbarth, Albert   1948-........   **CLC 5, 38**
See also CA 53-56; CANR 6, 40; DLB 120

Goldberg, Anatol   1910-1982 ....   **CLC 34**
See also CA 131; 117

Goldemberg, Isaac   1945-..........   **CLC 52**
See also CA 69-72; CAAS 12; CANR 11,
32; HW

Golden Silver
See Storm, Hyemeyohsts

Golding, William (Gerald)
1911- ..... **CLC 1, 2, 3, 8, 10, 17, 27, 58**
See also AAYA 5; CA 5-8R; CANR 13, 33;
CDBLB 1945-1960; DA; DLB 15, 100;
MTCW; WLC

Goldman, Emma   1869-1940......   **TCLC 13**
See also CA 110

Goldman, Francisco   1955-........   **CLC 76**

Goldman, William (W.)   1931-....   **CLC 1, 48**
See also CA 9-12R; CANR 29; DLB 44

Goldmann, Lucien   1913-1970 ......   **CLC 24**
See also CA 25-28; CAP 2

Goldoni, Carlo   1707-1793 ....   **LC 4**

Goldsberry, Steven   1949-..........   **CLC 34**
See also CA 131

Goldsmith, Oliver   1728-1774........   **LC 2**
See also CDBLB 1660-1789; DA; DLB 39,
89, 104, 109; SATA 26; WLC

Goldsmith, Peter
See Priestley, J(ohn) B(oynton)

Gombrowicz, Witold
1904-1969 ....   **CLC 4, 7, 11, 49**
See also CA 19-20; 25-28R; CAP 2

Gomez de la Serna, Ramon
1888-1963 ....   **CLC 9**
See also CA 116; HW

Goncharov, Ivan Alexandrovich
1812-1891 ....   **NCLC 1**

Goncourt, Edmond (Louis Antoine Huot) de
1822-1896 ....   **NCLC 7**
See also DLB 123

Goncourt, Jules (Alfred Huot) de
1830-1870 ....   **NCLC 7**
See also DLB 123

Gontier, Fernande   19(?)- ....   **CLC 50**

Goodman, Paul   1911-1972....   **CLC 1, 2, 4, 7**
See also CA 19-20; 37-40R; CANR 34;
CAP 2; DLB 130; MTCW

Gordimer, Nadine
1923- .... **CLC 3, 5, 7, 10, 18, 33, 51, 70**
See also CA 5-8R; CANR 3, 28; DA;
MTCW

Gordon, Adam Lindsay
1833-1870 ....   **NCLC 21**

Gordon, Caroline
1895-1981 ....   **CLC 6, 13, 29**
See also CA 11-12; 103; CANR 36; CAP 1;
DLB 4, 9, 102; DLBY 81; MTCW

Gordon, Charles William   1860-1937
See Connor, Ralph
See also CA 109

Gordon, Mary (Catherine)
1949- ....   **CLC 13, 22**
See also CA 102; DLB 6; DLBY 81;
MTCW

Gordon, Sol   1923-.................   **CLC 26**
See also CA 53-56; CANR 4; SATA 11

Gordone, Charles   1925-........   **CLC 1, 4**
See also BW; CA 93-96; DLB 7; MTCW

Gorenko, Anna Andreevna
See Akhmatova, Anna

Gorky, Maxim...................   **TCLC 8**
See also Peshkov, Alexei Maximovich
See also WLC

Goryan, Sirak
See Saroyan, William

Gosse, Edmund (William)
1849-1928 ....   **TCLC 28**
See also CA 117; DLB 57

Gotlieb, Phyllis Fay (Bloom)
1926- ....   **CLC 18**
See also CA 13-16R; CANR 7; DLB 88

Gottesman, S. D.
See Kornbluth, C(yril) M.; Pohl, Frederik

Gottfried von Strassburg
fl. c. 1210- ....   **CMLC 10**

Gottschalk, Laura Riding
See Jackson, Laura (Riding)

Gould, Lois...................   **CLC 4, 10**
See also CA 77-80; CANR 29; MTCW

Gourmont, Remy de   1858-1915....   **TCLC 17**
See also CA 109

Govier, Katherine   1948-..........   **CLC 51**
See also CA 101; CANR 18, 40

Goyen, (Charles) William
1915-1983 ....   **CLC 5, 8, 14, 40**
See also AITN 2; CA 5-8R; 110; CANR 6;
DLB 2; DLBY 83

Goytisolo, Juan   1931- ....   **CLC 5, 10, 23**
See also CA 85-88; CANR 32; HW; MTCW

Gozzi, (Conte) Carlo   1720-1806 ..   **NCLC 23**

Grabbe, Christian Dietrich
1801-1836 ....   **NCLC 2**

Grace, Patricia   1937-.............   **CLC 56**

Gracian y Morales, Baltasar
1601-1658 ....   **LC 15**

Gracq, Julien..................   **CLC 11, 48**
See also Poirier, Louis
See also DLB 83

Grade, Chaim   1910-1982 ....   **CLC 10**
See also CA 93-96; 107

Graduate of Oxford, A
See Ruskin, John

Graham, John
See Phillips, David Graham

Graham, Jorie   1951-.............   **CLC 48**
See also CA 111; DLB 120

Graham, R(obert) B(ontine) Cunninghame
See Cunninghame Graham, R(obert)
B(ontine)
See also DLB 98

Graham, Robert
See Haldeman, Joe (William)

Graham, Tom
See Lewis, (Harry) Sinclair

Graham, W(illiam) S(ydney)
1918-1986 ....   **CLC 29**
See also CA 73-76; 118; DLB 20

Graham, Winston (Mawdsley)
1910- ....   **CLC 23**
See also CA 49-52; CANR 2, 22; DLB 77

Grant, Skeeter
See Spiegelman, Art

Granville-Barker, Harley
1877-1946 ....   **TCLC 2**
See also Barker, Harley Granville
See also CA 104

Grass, Guenter (Wilhelm)
1927- ..   **CLC 1, 2, 4, 6, 11, 15, 22, 32, 49**
See also CA 13-16R; CANR 20; DA;
DLB 75, 124; MTCW; WLC

Gratton, Thomas
See Hulme, T(homas) E(rnest)

Grau, Shirley Ann   1929-.........   **CLC 4, 9**
See also CA 89-92; CANR 22; DLB 2;
MTCW

Gravel, Fern
See Hall, James Norman

Graver, Elizabeth   1964-............   **CLC 70**
See also CA 135

Graves, Richard Perceval   1945- ....   **CLC 44**
See also CA 65-68; CANR 9, 26

Graves, Robert (von Ranke)
1895-1985 ......   **CLC 1, 2, 6, 11, 39, 44,**
45; PC 6
See also CA 5-8R; 117; CANR 5, 36;
CDBLB 1914-1945; DLB 20, 100;
DLBY 85; MTCW; SATA 45

Gray, Alasdair   1934- ....   **CLC 41**
See also CA 126; MTCW

Gray, Amlin   1946- ....   **CLC 29**
See also CA 138

Gray, Francine du Plessix   1930-....   **CLC 22**
See also BEST 90:3; CA 61-64; CAAS 2;
CANR 11, 33; MTCW

Gray, John (Henry)   1866-1934 ....   **TCLC 19**
See also CA 119

Gray, Simon (James Holliday)
1936- ....   **CLC 9, 14, 36**
See also AITN 1; CA 21-24R; CAAS 3;
CANR 32; DLB 13; MTCW

Gray, Spalding   1941- ....   **CLC 49**
See also CA 128

Gray, Thomas   1716-1771.......   **LC 4; PC 2**
See also CDBLB 1660-1789; DA; DLB 109;
WLC

Grayson, David
See Baker, Ray Stannard

Grayson, Richard (A.) 1951- .... **CLC 38**
See also CA 85-88; CANR 14, 31

Greeley, Andrew M(oran) 1928- .... **CLC 28**
See also CA 5-8R; CAAS 7; CANR 7;
MTCW

Green, Brian
See Card, Orson Scott

Green, Hannah .... **CLC 3**
See also CA 73-76

Green, Hannah
See Greenberg, Joanne (Goldenberg)

Green, Henry .... **CLC 2, 13**
See also Yorke, Henry Vincent
See also DLB 15

Green, Julian (Hartridge)
1900- .... **CLC 3, 11, 77**
See also CA 21-24R; CANR 33; DLB 4, 72;
MTCW

Green, Julien 1900-
See Green, Julian (Hartridge)

Green, Paul (Eliot) 1894-1981 ...... **CLC 25**
See also AITN 1; CA 5-8R; 103; CANR 3;
DLB 7, 9; DLBY 81

Greenberg, Ivan 1908-1973
See Rahv, Philip
See also CA 85-88

Greenberg, Joanne (Goldenberg)
1932- .... **CLC 7, 30**
See also CA 5-8R; CANR 14, 32; SATA 25

Greenberg, Richard 1959(?)- .... **CLC 57**
See also CA 138

Greene, Bette 1934- .... **CLC 30**
See also AAYA 7; CA 53-56; CANR 4;
CLR 2; MAICYA; SAAS 16; SATA 8

Greene, Gael .... **CLC 8**
See also CA 13-16R; CANR 10

Greene, Graham
1904-1991 .... **CLC 1, 3, 6, 9, 14, 18, 27,
37, 70, 72**
See also AITN 2; CA 13-16R; 133;
CANR 35; CDBLB 1945-1960; DA;
DLB 13, 15, 77, 100; DLBY 91; MTCW;
SATA 20; WLC

Greer, Richard
See Silverberg, Robert

Greer, Richard
See Silverberg, Robert

Gregor, Arthur 1923- .... **CLC 9**
See also CA 25-28R; CAAS 10; CANR 11;
SATA 36

Gregor, Lee
See Pohl, Frederik

Gregory, Isabella Augusta (Persse)
1852-1932 .... **TCLC 1**
See also CA 104; DLB 10

Gregory, J. Dennis
See Williams, John A(lfred)

Grendon, Stephen
See Derleth, August (William)

Grenville, Kate 1950- .... **CLC 61**
See also CA 118

Grenville, Pelham
See Wodehouse, P(elham) G(renville)

Greve, Felix Paul (Berthold Friedrich)
1879-1948
See Grove, Frederick Philip
See also CA 104

Grey, Zane 1872-1939 .... **TCLC 6**
See also CA 104; 132; DLB 9; MTCW

Grieg, (Johan) Nordahl (Brun)
1902-1943 .... **TCLC 10**
See also CA 107

Grieve, C(hristopher) M(urray)
1892-1978 .... **CLC 11, 19**
See also MacDiarmid, Hugh
See also CA 5-8R; 85-88; CANR 33;
MTCW

Griffin, Gerald 1803-1840 .... **NCLC 7**

Griffin, John Howard 1920-1980. ... **CLC 68**
See also AITN 1; CA 1-4R; 101; CANR 2

Griffin, Peter .... **CLC 39**

Griffiths, Trevor 1935- .... **CLC 13, 52**
See also CA 97-100; DLB 13

Grigson, Geoffrey (Edward Harvey)
1905-1985 .... **CLC 7, 39**
See also CA 25-28R; 118; CANR 20, 33;
DLB 27; MTCW

Grillparzer, Franz 1791-1872 ...... **NCLC 1**

Grimble, Reverend Charles James
See Eliot, T(homas) S(tearns)

Grimke, Charlotte L(ottie) Forten
1837(?)-1914
See Forten, Charlotte L.
See also BW; CA 117; 124

Grimm, Jacob Ludwig Karl
1785-1863 .... **NCLC 3**
See also DLB 90; MAICYA; SATA 22

Grimm, Wilhelm Karl 1786-1859 .. **NCLC 3**
See also DLB 90; MAICYA; SATA 22

Grimmelshausen, Johann Jakob Christoffel
von 1621-1676 .... **LC 6**

Grindel, Eugene 1895-1952
See Eluard, Paul
See also CA 104

Grossman, David 1954- .... **CLC 67**
See also CA 138

Grossman, Vasily (Semenovich)
1905-1964 .... **CLC 41**
See also CA 124; 130; MTCW

Grove, Frederick Philip .... **TCLC 4**
See also Greve, Felix Paul (Berthold
Friedrich)
See also DLB 92

Grubb
See Crumb, R(obert)

Grumbach, Doris (Isaac)
1918- .... **CLC 13, 22, 64**
See also CA 5-8R; CAAS 2; CANR 9

Grundtvig, Nicolai Frederik Severin
1783-1872 .... **NCLC 1**

Grunge
See Crumb, R(obert)

Grunwald, Lisa 1959- .... **CLC 44**
See also CA 120

Guare, John 1938- .... **CLC 8, 14, 29, 67**
See also CA 73-76; CANR 21; DLB 7;
MTCW

Gudjonsson, Halldor Kiljan 1902-
See Laxness, Halldor
See also CA 103

Guenter, Erich
See Eich, Guenter

Guest, Barbara 1920- .... **CLC 34**
See also CA 25-28R; CANR 11; DLB 5

Guest, Judith (Ann) 1936- .... **CLC 8, 30**
See also AAYA 7; CA 77-80; CANR 15;
MTCW

Guild, Nicholas M. 1944- .... **CLC 33**
See also CA 93-96

Guillemin, Jacques
See Sartre, Jean-Paul

Guillen, Jorge 1893-1984 .... **CLC 11**
See also CA 89-92; 112; DLB 108; HW

Guillen (y Batista), Nicolas (Cristobal)
1902-1989 .... **CLC 48**
See also BLC 2; BW; CA 116; 125; 129;
HW

Guillevic, (Eugene) 1907- .... **CLC 33**
See also CA 93-96

Guillois
See Desnos, Robert

Guiney, Louise Imogen
1861-1920 .... **TCLC 41**
See also DLB 54

Guiraldes, Ricardo (Guillermo)
1886-1927 .... **TCLC 39**
See also CA 131; HW; MTCW

Gunn, Bill .... **CLC 5**
See also Gunn, William Harrison
See also DLB 38

Gunn, Thom(son William)
1929- .... **CLC 3, 6, 18, 32**
See also CA 17-20R; CANR 9, 33;
CDBLB 1960 to Present; DLB 27;
MTCW

Gunn, William Harrison 1934(?)-1989
See Gunn, Bill
See also AITN 1; BW; CA 13-16R; 128;
CANR 12, 25

Gunnars, Kristjana 1948- .... **CLC 69**
See also CA 113; DLB 60

Gurganus, Allan 1947- .... **CLC 70**
See also BEST 90:1; CA 135

Gurney, A(lbert) R(amsdell), Jr.
1930- .... **CLC 32, 50, 54**
See also CA 77-80; CANR 32

Gurney, Ivor (Bertie) 1890-1937 ... **TCLC 33**

Gurney, Peter
See Gurney, A(lbert) R(amsdell), Jr.

Gustafson, Ralph (Barker) 1909- .... **CLC 36**
See also CA 21-24R; CANR 8; DLB 88

Gut, Gom
See Simenon, Georges (Jacques Christian)

Guthrie, A(lfred) B(ertram), Jr.
1901-1991 .... **CLC 23**
See also CA 57-60; 134; CANR 24; DLB 6;
SATA 62; SATA-Obit 67

Guthrie, Isobel
See Grieve, C(hristopher) M(urray)

Guthrie, Woodrow Wilson 1912-1967
See Guthrie, Woody
See also CA 113; 93-96

Guthrie, Woody.................. **CLC 35**
See also Guthrie, Woodrow Wilson

Guy, Rosa (Cuthbert) 1928-........ **CLC 26**
See also AAYA 4; BW; CA 17-20R;
CANR 14, 34; CLR 13; DLB 33;
MAICYA; SATA 14, 62

Gwendolyn
See Bennett, (Enoch) Arnold

H. D......... **CLC 3, 8, 14, 31, 34, 73; PC 5**
See also Doolittle, Hilda

Haavikko, Paavo Juhani
1931-.................... **CLC 18, 34**
See also CA 106

Habbema, Koos
See Heijermans, Herman

Hacker, Marilyn 1942- .... **CLC 5, 9, 23, 72**
See also CA 77-80; DLB 120

Haggard, H(enry) Rider
1856-1925 .... **TCLC 11**
See also CA 108; DLB 70; SATA 16

Haig, Fenil
See Ford, Ford Madox

Haig-Brown, Roderick (Langmere)
1908-1976 .... **CLC 21**
See also CA 5-8R; 69-72; CANR 4, 38;
CLR 31; DLB 88; MAICYA; SATA 12

Hailey, Arthur 1920- .... **CLC 5**
See also AITN 2; BEST 90:3; CA 1-4R;
CANR 2, 36; DLB 88; DLBY 82; MTCW

Hailey, Elizabeth Forsythe 1938-... **CLC 40**
See also CA 93-96; CAAS 1; CANR 15

Haines, John (Meade) 1924-....... **CLC 58**
See also CA 17-20R; CANR 13, 34; DLB 5

Haldeman, Joe (William) 1943-..... **CLC 61**
See also CA 53-56; CANR 6; DLB 8

Haley, Alex(ander Murray Palmer)
1921-1992 .... **CLC 8, 12, 76**
See also BLC 2; BW; CA 77-80; 136; DA;
DLB 38; MTCW

Haliburton, Thomas Chandler
1796-1865 .... **NCLC 15**
See also DLB 11, 99

Hall, Donald (Andrew, Jr.)
1928- .... **CLC 1, 13, 37, 59**
See also CA 5-8R; CAAS 7; CANR 2;
DLB 5; SATA 23

Hall, Frederic Sauser
See Sauser-Hall, Frederic

Hall, James
See Kuttner, Henry

Hall, James Norman 1887-1951 ... **TCLC 23**
See also CA 123; SATA 21

Hall, (Marguerite) Radclyffe
1886(?)-1943 .... **TCLC 12**
See also CA 110

Hall, Rodney 1935- .... **CLC 51**
See also CA 109

Halliday, Michael
See Creasey, John

Halpern, Daniel 1945-............ **CLC 14**
See also CA 33-36R

Hamburger, Michael (Peter Leopold)
1924-.................... **CLC 5, 14**
See also CA 5-8R; CAAS 4; CANR 2;
DLB 27

Hamill, Pete 1935-.............. **CLC 10**
See also CA 25-28R; CANR 18

Hamilton, Clive
See Lewis, C(live) S(taples)

Hamilton, Edmond 1904-1977...... **CLC 1**
See also CA 1-4R; CANR 3; DLB 8

Hamilton, Eugene (Jacob) Lee
See Lee-Hamilton, Eugene (Jacob)

Hamilton, Franklin
See Silverberg, Robert

Hamilton, Gail
See Corcoran, Barbara

Hamilton, Mollie
See Kaye, M(ary) M(argaret)

Hamilton, (Anthony Walter) Patrick
1904-1962 .... **CLC 51**
See also CA 113; DLB 10

Hamilton, Virginia 1936-.......... **CLC 26**
See also AAYA 2; BW; CA 25-28R;
CANR 20, 37; CLR 1, 11; DLB 33, 52;
MAICYA; MTCW; SATA 4, 56

Hammett, (Samuel) Dashiell
1894-1961 .... **CLC 3, 5, 10, 19, 47**
See also AITN 1; CA 81-84;
CDALB 1929-1941; DLBD 6; MTCW

Hammon, Jupiter 1711(?)-1800(?).. **NCLC 5**
See also BLC 2; DLB 31, 50

Hammond, Keith
See Kuttner, Henry

Hamner, Earl (Henry), Jr. 1923- ... **CLC 12**
See also AITN 2; CA 73-76; DLB 6

Hampton, Christopher (James)
1946-...................... **CLC 4**
See also CA 25-28R; DLB 13; MTCW

Hamsun, Knut............. **TCLC 2, 14, 49**
See also Pedersen, Knut

Handke, Peter 1942- .. **CLC 5, 8, 10, 15, 38**
See also CA 77-80; CANR 33; DLB 85,
124; MTCW

Hanley, James 1901-1985 ... **CLC 3, 5, 8, 13**
See also CA 73-76; 117; CANR 36; MTCW

Hannah, Barry 1942-.......... **CLC 23, 38**
See also CA 108; 110; DLB 6; MTCW

Hannon, Ezra
See Hunter, Evan

Hansberry, Lorraine (Vivian)
1930-1965 .... **CLC 17, 62; DC 2**
See also BLC 2; BW; CA 109; 25-28R;
CABS 3; CDALB 1941-1968; DA;
DLB 7, 38; MTCW

Hansen, Joseph 1923-............. **CLC 38**
See also CA 29-32R; CAAS 17; CANR 16

Hansen, Martin A. 1909-1955..... **TCLC 32**

Hanson, Kenneth O(stlin) 1922-.... **CLC 13**
See also CA 53-56; CANR 7

Hardwick, Elizabeth 1916- .... **CLC 13**
See also CA 5-8R; CANR 3, 32; DLB 6;
MTCW

Hardy, Thomas
1840-1928 ...... **TCLC 4, 10, 18, 32, 48;
SSC 2**
See also CA 104; 123; CDBLB 1890-1914;
DA; DLB 18, 19; MTCW; WLC

Hare, David 1947- .... **CLC 29, 58**
See also CA 97-100; CANR 39; DLB 13;
MTCW

Harford, Henry
See Hudson, W(illiam) H(enry)

Hargrave, Leonie
See Disch, Thomas M(ichael)

Harlan, Louis R(udolph) 1922-..... **CLC 34**
See also CA 21-24R; CANR 25

Harling, Robert 1951(?)- .... **CLC 53**

Harmon, William (Ruth) 1938-..... **CLC 38**
See also CA 33-36R; CANR 14, 32, 35;
SATA 65

Harper, F. E. W.
See Harper, Frances Ellen Watkins

Harper, Frances E. W.
See Harper, Frances Ellen Watkins

Harper, Frances E. Watkins
See Harper, Frances Ellen Watkins

Harper, Frances Ellen
See Harper, Frances Ellen Watkins

Harper, Frances Ellen Watkins
1825-1911 .... **TCLC 14**
See also BLC 2; BW; CA 111; 125; DLB 50

Harper, Michael S(teven) 1938- ... **CLC 7, 22**
See also BW; CA 33-36R; CANR 24;
DLB 41

Harper, Mrs. F. E. W.
See Harper, Frances Ellen Watkins

Harris, Christie (Lucy) Irwin
1907-.................... **CLC 12**
See also CA 5-8R; CANR 6; DLB 88;
MAICYA; SAAS 10; SATA 6, 74

Harris, Frank 1856(?)-1931....... **TCLC 24**
See also CA 109

Harris, George Washington
1814-1869 .... **NCLC 23**
See also DLB 3, 11

Harris, Joel Chandler 1848-1908 ... **TCLC 2**
See also CA 104; 137; DLB 11, 23, 42, 78,
91; MAICYA; YABC 1

Harris, John (Wyndham Parkes Lucas)
Beynon 1903-1969 .... **CLC 19**
See also CA 102; 89-92

Harris, MacDonald
See Heiney, Donald (William)

Harris, Mark 1922- .... **CLC 19**
See also CA 5-8R; CAAS 3; CANR 2;
DLB 2; DLBY 80

Harris, (Theodore) Wilson 1921-.... **CLC 25**
See also BW; CA 65-68; CAAS 16;
CANR 11, 27; DLB 117; MTCW

Harrison, Elizabeth Cavanna 1909-
See Cavanna, Betty
See also CA 9-12R; CANR 6, 27

Harrison, Harry (Max) 1925-...... **CLC 42**
See also CA 1-4R; CANR 5, 21; DLB 8;
SATA 4

Harrison, James (Thomas) 1937-
See Harrison, Jim
See also CA 13-16R; CANR 8

Harrison, Jim . . . . **CLC 6, 14, 33, 66**
See also Harrison, James (Thomas)
See also DLBY 82

Harrison, Kathryn 1961- . . . . **CLC 70**

Harrison, Tony 1937- . . . . **CLC 43**
See also CA 65-68; DLB 40; MTCW

Harriss, Will(ard Irvin) 1922- . . . . . . **CLC 34**
See also CA 111

Harson, Sley
See Ellison, Harlan

Hart, Ellis
See Ellison, Harlan

Hart, Josephine 1942(?)- . . . . **CLC 70**
See also CA 138

Hart, Moss 1904-1961 . . . . **CLC 66**
See also CA 109; 89-92; DLB 7

Harte, (Francis) Bret(t)
1836(?)-1902 . . . . **TCLC 1, 25; SSC 8**
See also CA 104; 140; CDALB 1865-1917;
DA; DLB 12, 64, 74, 79; SATA 26; WLC

Hartley, L(eslie) P(oles)
1895-1972 . . . . **CLC 2, 22**
See also CA 45-48; 37-40R; CANR 33;
DLB 15; MTCW

Hartman, Geoffrey H. 1929- . . . . **CLC 27**
See also CA 117; 125; DLB 67

Haruf, Kent 19(?)- . . . . **CLC 34**

Harwood, Ronald 1934- . . . . **CLC 32**
See also CA 1-4R; CANR 4; DLB 13

Hasek, Jaroslav (Matej Frantisek)
1883-1923 . . . . **TCLC 4**
See also CA 104; 129; MTCW

Hass, Robert 1941- . . . . **CLC 18, 39**
See also CA 111; CANR 30; DLB 105

Hastings, Hudson
See Kuttner, Henry

Hastings, Selina . . . . **CLC 44**

Hatteras, Amelia
See Mencken, H(enry) L(ouis)

Hatteras, Owen . . . . **TCLC 18**
See also Mencken, H(enry) L(ouis); Nathan,
George Jean

Hauptmann, Gerhart (Johann Robert)
1862-1946 . . . . **TCLC 4**
See also CA 104; DLB 66, 118

Havel, Vaclav 1936- . . . . **CLC 25, 58, 65**
See also CA 104; CANR 36; MTCW

Haviaras, Stratis . . . . **CLC 33**
See also Chaviaras, Strates

Hawes, Stephen 1475(?)-1523(?) . . . . . **LC 17**

Hawkes, John (Clendennin Burne, Jr.)
1925- . . . . . . **CLC 1, 2, 3, 4, 7, 9, 14, 15,
27, 49**
See also CA 1-4R; CANR 2; DLB 2, 7;
DLBY 80; MTCW

Hawking, S. W.
See Hawking, Stephen W(illiam)

Hawking, Stephen W(illiam)
1942- . . . . **CLC 63**
See also BEST 89:1; CA 126; 129

Hawthorne, Julian 1846-1934 . . . . . **TCLC 25**

Hawthorne, Nathaniel
1804-1864 . . . . **NCLC 39; SSC 3**
See also CDALB 1640-1865; DA; DLB 1,
74; WLC; YABC 2

Haxton, Josephine Ayres 1921- . . . . **CLC 73**
See also CA 115; CANR 41

Hayaseca y Eizaguirre, Jorge
See Echegaray (y Eizaguirre), Jose (Maria
Waldo)

Hayashi Fumiko 1904-1951 . . . . . . **TCLC 27**

Haycraft, Anna
See Ellis, Alice Thomas
See also CA 122

Hayden, Robert E(arl)
1913-1980 . . . . . . **CLC 5, 9, 14, 37; PC 6**
See also BLC 2; BW; CA 69-72; 97-100;
CABS 2; CANR 24; CDALB 1941-1968;
DA; DLB 5, 76; MTCW; SATA 19, 26

Hayford, J(oseph) E(phraim) Casely
See Casely-Hayford, J(oseph) E(phraim)

Hayman, Ronald 1932- . . . . **CLC 44**
See also CA 25-28R; CANR 18

Haywood, Eliza (Fowler)
1693(?)-1756 . . . . **LC 1**

Hazlitt, William 1778-1830 . . . . . . **NCLC 29**
See also DLB 110

Hazzard, Shirley 1931- . . . . **CLC 18**
See also CA 9-12R; CANR 4; DLBY 82;
MTCW

Head, Bessie 1937-1986 . . . . **CLC 25, 67**
See also BLC 2; BW; CA 29-32R; 119;
CANR 25; DLB 117; MTCW

Headon, (Nicky) Topper 1956(?)- . . . **CLC 30**
See also Clash, The

Heaney, Seamus (Justin)
1939- . . . . **CLC 5, 7, 14, 25, 37, 74**
See also CA 85-88; CANR 25;
CDBLB 1960 to Present; DLB 40;
MTCW

Hearn, (Patricio) Lafcadio (Tessima Carlos)
1850-1904 . . . . **TCLC 9**
See also CA 105; DLB 12, 78

Hearne, Vicki 1946- . . . . **CLC 56**
See also CA 139

Hearon, Shelby 1931- . . . . **CLC 63**
See also AITN 2; CA 25-28R; CANR 18

Heat-Moon, William Least . . . . **CLC 29**
See also Trogdon, William (Lewis)
See also AAYA 9

Hebert, Anne 1916- . . . . **CLC 4, 13, 29**
See also CA 85-88; DLB 68; MTCW

Hecht, Anthony (Evan)
1923- . . . . **CLC 8, 13, 19**
See also CA 9-12R; CANR 6; DLB 5

Hecht, Ben 1894-1964 . . . . **CLC 8**
See also CA 85-88; DLB 7, 9, 25, 26, 28, 86

Hedayat, Sadeq 1903-1951 . . . . **TCLC 21**
See also CA 120

Heidegger, Martin 1889-1976 . . . . . . **CLC 24**
See also CA 81-84; 65-68; CANR 34;
MTCW

Heidenstam, (Carl Gustaf) Verner von
1859-1940 . . . . **TCLC 5**
See also CA 104

Heifner, Jack 1946- . . . . **CLC 11**
See also CA 105

Heijermans, Herman 1864-1924 . . . **TCLC 24**
See also CA 123

Heilbrun, Carolyn G(old) 1926- . . . . . **CLC 25**
See also CA 45-48; CANR 1, 28

Heine, Heinrich 1797-1856 . . . . **NCLC 4**
See also DLB 90

Heinemann, Larry (Curtiss) 1944- . . **CLC 50**
See also CA 110; CANR 31; DLBD 9

Heiney, Donald (William) 1921- . . . . . **CLC 9**
See also CA 1-4R; CANR 3

Heinlein, Robert A(nson)
1907-1988 . . . . . . **CLC 1, 3, 8, 14, 26, 55**
See also CA 1-4R; 125; CANR 1, 20;
DLB 8; MAICYA; MTCW; SATA 9, 56,
69

Helforth, John
See Doolittle, Hilda

Hellenhofferu, Vojtech Kapristian z
See Hasek, Jaroslav (Matej Frantisek)

Heller, Joseph
1923- . . . . **CLC 1, 3, 5, 8, 11, 36, 63**
See also AITN 1; CA 5-8R; CABS 1;
CANR 8; DA; DLB 2, 28; DLBY 80;
MTCW; WLC

Hellman, Lillian (Florence)
1906-1984 . . . . . . **CLC 2, 4, 8, 14, 18, 34,
44, 52; DC 1**
See also AITN 1, 2; CA 13-16R; 112;
CANR 33; DLB 7; DLBY 84; MTCW

Helprin, Mark 1947- . . . . . **CLC 7, 10, 22, 32**
See also CA 81-84; DLBY 85; MTCW

Helyar, Jane Penelope Josephine 1933-
See Poole, Josephine
See also CA 21-24R; CANR 10, 26

Hemans, Felicia 1793-1835 . . . . . . **NCLC 29**
See also DLB 96

Hemingway, Ernest (Miller)
1899-1961 . . . . **CLC 1, 3, 6, 8, 10, 13, 19,
30, 34, 39, 41, 44, 50, 61; SSC 1**
See also CA 77-80;
CDALB 1917-1929; DA; DLB 4, 9, 102;
DLBD 1; DLBY 81, 87; MTCW; WLC

Hempel, Amy 1951- . . . . **CLC 39**
See also CA 118; 137

Henderson, F. C.
See Mencken, H(enry) L(ouis)

Henderson, Sylvia
See Ashton-Warner, Sylvia (Constance)

Henley, Beth . . . . **CLC 23**
See also Henley, Elizabeth Becker
See also CABS 3; DLBY 86

Henley, Elizabeth Becker 1952-
See Henley, Beth
See also CA 107; CANR 32; MTCW

Henley, William Ernest
1849-1903 . . . . **TCLC 8**
See also CA 105; DLB 19

Hennissart, Martha
See Lathen, Emma
See also CA 85-88

Henry, O. . . . . **TCLC 1, 19; SSC 5**
See also Porter, William Sydney
See also WLC

Henryson, Robert 1430(?)-1506(?). . . . **LC 20**

Henry VIII 1491-1547. . . . . **LC 10**

Henschke, Alfred
See Klabund

Hentoff, Nat(han Irving) 1925- . . . . . **CLC 26**
See also AAYA 4; CA 1-4R; CAAS 6;
CANR 5, 25; CLR 1; MAICYA;
SATA 27, 42, 69

Heppenstall, (John) Rayner
1911-1981 . . . . **CLC 10**
See also CA 1-4R; 103; CANR 29

Herbert, Frank (Patrick)
1920-1986 . . . . **CLC 12, 23, 35, 44**
See also CA 53-56; 118; CANR 5; DLB 8;
MTCW; SATA 9, 37, 47

Herbert, George 1593-1633 . . . . **PC 4**
See also CDBLB Before 1660; DLB 126

Herbert, Zbigniew 1924- . . . . **CLC 9, 43**
See also CA 89-92; CANR 36; MTCW

Herbst, Josephine (Frey)
1897-1969 . . . . **CLC 34**
See also CA 5-8R; 25-28R; DLB 9

Hergesheimer, Joseph
1880-1954 . . . . **TCLC 11**
See also CA 109; DLB 102, 9

Herlihy, James Leo 1927- . . . . **CLC 6**
See also CA 1-4R; CANR 2

Hermogenes fl. c. 175- . . . . **CMLC 6**

Hernandez, Jose 1834-1886 . . . . . . **NCLC 17**

Herrick, Robert 1591-1674 . . . . **LC 13**
See also DA; DLB 126

Herring, Guilles
See Somerville, Edith

Herriot, James 1916- . . . . **CLC 12**
See also Wight, James Alfred
See also AAYA 1; CANR 40

Herrmann, Dorothy 1941- . . . . **CLC 44**
See also CA 107

Herrmann, Taffy
See Herrmann, Dorothy

Hersey, John (Richard)
1914-1993 . . . . **CLC 1, 2, 7, 9, 40**
See also CA 17-20R; 140; CANR 33;
DLB 6; MTCW; SATA 25

Herzen, Aleksandr Ivanovich
1812-1870 . . . . **NCLC 10**

Herzl, Theodor 1860-1904 . . . . **TCLC 36**

Herzog, Werner 1942- . . . . **CLC 16**
See also CA 89-92

Hesiod c. 8th cent. B.C.- . . . . **CMLC 5**

Hesse, Hermann
1877-1962 . . . . **CLC 1, 2, 3, 6, 11, 17, 25,
69; SSC 9**
See also CA 17-18; CAP 2; DA; DLB 66;
MTCW; SATA 50; WLC

Hewes, Cady
See De Voto, Bernard (Augustine)

Heyen, William 1940- . . . . **CLC 13, 18**
See also CA 33-36R; CAAS 9; DLB 5

Heyerdahl, Thor 1914- . . . . **CLC 26**
See also CA 5-8R; CANR 5, 22; MTCW;
SATA 2, 52

Heym, Georg (Theodor Franz Arthur)
1887-1912 . . . . **TCLC 9**
See also CA 106

Heym, Stefan 1913- . . . . **CLC 41**
See also CA 9-12R; CANR 4; DLB 69

Heyse, Paul (Johann Ludwig von)
1830-1914 . . . . **TCLC 8**
See also CA 104; DLB 129

Hibbert, Eleanor Alice Burford
1906-1993 . . . . **CLC 7**
See also BEST 90:4; CA 17-20R; CANR 9,
28; SATA 2; SATA-Obit 74

Higgins, George V(incent)
1939- . . . . **CLC 4, 7, 10, 18**
See also CA 77-80; CAAS 5; CANR 17;
DLB 2; DLBY 81; MTCW

Higginson, Thomas Wentworth
1823-1911 . . . . **TCLC 36**
See also DLB 1, 64

Highet, Helen
See MacInnes, Helen (Clark)

Highsmith, (Mary) Patricia
1921- . . . . **CLC 2, 4, 14, 42**
See also CA 1-4R; CANR 1, 20; MTCW

Highwater, Jamake (Mamake)
1942(?)- . . . . **CLC 12**
See also AAYA 7; CA 65-68; CAAS 7;
CANR 10, 34; CLR 17; DLB 52;
DLBY 85; MAICYA; SATA 30, 32, 69

Hijuelos, Oscar 1951- . . . . **CLC 65**
See also BEST 90:1; CA 123; HW

Hikmet, Nazim 1902-1963 . . . . **CLC 40**
See also CA 93-96

Hildesheimer, Wolfgang
1916-1991 . . . . **CLC 49**
See also CA 101; 135; DLB 69, 124

Hill, Geoffrey (William)
1932- . . . . **CLC 5, 8, 18, 45**
See also CA 81-84; CANR 21;
CDBLB 1960 to Present; DLB 40;
MTCW

Hill, George Roy 1921- . . . . **CLC 26**
See also CA 110; 122

Hill, John
See Koontz, Dean R(ay)

Hill, Susan (Elizabeth) 1942- . . . . **CLC 4**
See also CA 33-36R; CANR 29; DLB 14;
MTCW

Hillerman, Tony 1925- . . . . **CLC 62**
See also AAYA 6; BEST 89:1; CA 29-32R;
CANR 21; SATA 6

Hillesum, Etty 1914-1943 . . . . **TCLC 49**
See also CA 137

Hilliard, Noel (Harvey) 1929- . . . . . . **CLC 15**
See also CA 9-12R; CANR 7

Hillis, Rick 1956- . . . . **CLC 66**
See also CA 134

Hilton, James 1900-1954 . . . . **TCLC 21**
See also CA 108; DLB 34, 77; SATA 34

Himes, Chester (Bomar)
1909-1984 . . . . **CLC 2, 4, 7, 18, 58**
See also BLC 2; BW; CA 25-28R; 114;
CANR 22; DLB 2, 76; MTCW

Hinde, Thomas . . . . **CLC 6, 11**
See also Chitty, Thomas Willes

Hindin, Nathan
See Bloch, Robert (Albert)

Hine, (William) Daryl 1936- . . . . **CLC 15**
See also CA 1-4R; CAAS 15; CANR 1, 20;
DLB 60

Hinkson, Katharine Tynan
See Tynan, Katharine

Hinton, S(usan) E(loise) 1950- . . . . . **CLC 30**
See also AAYA 2; CA 81-84; CANR 32;
CLR 3, 23; DA; MAICYA; MTCW;
SATA 19, 58

Hippius, Zinaida . . . . **TCLC 9**
See also Gippius, Zinaida (Nikolayevna)

Hiraoka, Kimitake 1925-1970
See Mishima, Yukio
See also CA 97-100; 29-32R; MTCW

Hirsch, Edward 1950- . . . . **CLC 31, 50**
See also CA 104; CANR 20; DLB 120

Hitchcock, Alfred (Joseph)
1899-1980 . . . . **CLC 16**
See also CA 97-100; SATA 24, 27

Hoagland, Edward 1932- . . . . **CLC 28**
See also CA 1-4R; CANR 2, 31; DLB 6;
SATA 51

Hoban, Russell (Conwell) 1925- . . **CLC 7, 25**
See also CA 5-8R; CANR 23, 37; CLR 3;
DLB 52; MAICYA; MTCW; SATA 1, 40

Hobbs, Perry
See Blackmur, R(ichard) P(almer)

Hobson, Laura Z(ametkin)
1900-1986 . . . . **CLC 7, 25**
See also CA 17-20R; 118; DLB 28;
SATA 52

Hochhuth, Rolf 1931- . . . . **CLC 4, 11, 18**
See also CA 5-8R; CANR 33; DLB 124;
MTCW

Hochman, Sandra 1936- . . . . **CLC 3, 8**
See also CA 5-8R; DLB 5

Hochwaelder, Fritz 1911-1986 . . . . . . **CLC 36**
See also Hochwalder, Fritz
See also CA 29-32R; 120; MTCW

Hochwalder, Fritz . . . . **CLC 36**
See also Hochwaelder, Fritz

Hocking, Mary (Eunice) 1921- . . . . . **CLC 13**
See also CA 101; CANR 18, 40

Hodgins, Jack 1938- . . . . **CLC 23**
See also CA 93-96; DLB 60

Hodgson, William Hope
1877(?)-1918 . . . . **TCLC 13**
See also CA 111; DLB 70

Hoffman, Alice 1952- . . . . **CLC 51**
See also CA 77-80; CANR 34; MTCW

Hoffman, Daniel (Gerard)
1923- . . . . **CLC 6, 13, 23**
See also CA 1-4R; CANR 4; DLB 5

Hoffman, Stanley 1944- . . . . **CLC 5**
See also CA 77-80

Hoffman, William M(oses) 1939- ... **CLC 40**
See also CA 57-60; CANR 11

Hoffmann, E(rnst) T(heodor) A(madeus)
1776-1822 .... **NCLC 2**
See also DLB 90; SATA 27

Hofmann, Gert 1931- .... **CLC 54**
See also CA 128

Hofmannsthal, Hugo von
1874-1929 .... **TCLC 11**
See also CA 106; DLB 81, 118

Hogan, Linda 1947- .... **CLC 73**
See also CA 120

Hogarth, Charles
See Creasey, John

Hogg, James 1770-1835 .... **NCLC 4**
See also DLB 93, 116

Holbach, Paul Henri Thiry Baron
1723-1789 .... **LC 14**

Holberg, Ludvig 1684-1754 .... **LC 6**

Holden, Ursula 1921- .... **CLC 18**
See also CA 101; CAAS 8; CANR 22

Holderlin, (Johann Christian) Friedrich
1770-1843 .... **NCLC 16; PC 4**

Holdstock, Robert
See Holdstock, Robert P.

Holdstock, Robert P. 1948- .... **CLC 39**
See also CA 131

Holland, Isabelle 1920- .... **CLC 21**
See also CA 21-24R; CANR 10, 25;
MAICYA; SATA 8, 70

Holland, Marcus
See Caldwell, (Janet Miriam) Taylor
(Holland)

Hollander, John 1929- ...... **CLC 2, 5, 8, 14**
See also CA 1-4R; CANR 1; DLB 5;
SATA 13

Hollander, Paul
See Silverberg, Robert

Holleran, Andrew 1943(?)- .... **CLC 38**

Hollinghurst, Alan 1954- .... **CLC 55**
See also CA 114

Hollis, Jim
See Summers, Hollis (Spurgeon, Jr.)

Holmes, John
See Souster, (Holmes) Raymond

Holmes, John Clellon 1926-1988.... **CLC 56**
See also CA 9-12R; 125; CANR 4; DLB 16

Holmes, Oliver Wendell
1809-1894 .... **NCLC 14**
See also CDALB 1640-1865; DLB 1;
SATA 34

Holmes, Raymond
See Souster, (Holmes) Raymond

Holt, Victoria
See Hibbert, Eleanor Alice Burford

Holub, Miroslav 1923- .... **CLC 4**
See also CA 21-24R; CANR 10

Homer c. 8th cent. B.C.- .... **CMLC 1**
See also DA

Honig, Edwin 1919- .... **CLC 33**
See also CA 5-8R; CAAS 8; CANR 4;
DLB 5

Hood, Hugh (John Blagdon)
1928- .... **CLC 15, 28**
See also CA 49-52; CAAS 17; CANR 1, 33;
DLB 53

Hood, Thomas 1799-1845........ **NCLC 16**
See also DLB 96

Hooker, (Peter) Jeremy 1941-...... **CLC 43**
See also CA 77-80; CANR 22; DLB 40

Hope, A(lec) D(erwent) 1907- .... **CLC 3, 51**
See also CA 21-24R; CANR 33; MTCW

Hope, Brian
See Creasey, John

Hope, Christopher (David Tully)
1944- .... **CLC 52**
See also CA 106; SATA 62

Hopkins, Gerard Manley
1844-1889 .... **NCLC 17**
See also CDBLB 1890-1914; DA; DLB 35,
57; WLC

Hopkins, John (Richard) 1931-...... **CLC 4**
See also CA 85-88

Hopkins, Pauline Elizabeth
1859-1930 .... **TCLC 28**
See also BLC 2; DLB 50

Hopley-Woolrich, Cornell George 1903-1968
See Woolrich, Cornell
See also CA 13-14; CAP 1

Horatio
See Proust, (Valentin-Louis-George-Eugene-)
Marcel

Horgan, Paul 1903- .... **CLC 9, 53**
See also CA 13-16R; CANR 9, 35;
DLB 102; DLBY 85; MTCW; SATA 13

Horn, Peter
See Kuttner, Henry

Hornem, Horace Esq.
See Byron, George Gordon (Noel)

Horovitz, Israel 1939- .... **CLC 56**
See also CA 33-36R; DLB 7

Horvath, Odon von
See Horvath, Oedoen von
See also DLB 85, 124

Horvath, Oedoen von 1901-1938... **TCLC 45**
See also Horvath, Odon von
See also CA 118

Horwitz, Julius 1920-1986........ **CLC 14**
See also CA 9-12R; 119; CANR 12

Hospital, Janette Turner 1942-..... **CLC 42**
See also CA 108

Hostos, E. M. de
See Hostos (y Bonilla), Eugenio Maria de

Hostos, Eugenio M. de
See Hostos (y Bonilla), Eugenio Maria de

Hostos, Eugenio Maria
See Hostos (y Bonilla), Eugenio Maria de

Hostos (y Bonilla), Eugenio Maria de
1839-1903 .... **TCLC 24**
See also CA 123; 131; HW

Houdini
See Lovecraft, H(oward) P(hillips)

Hougan, Carolyn 1943- .... **CLC 34**
See also CA 139

Household, Geoffrey (Edward West)
1900-1988 .... **CLC 11**
See also CA 77-80; 126; DLB 87; SATA 14,
59

Housman, A(lfred) E(dward)
1859-1936 .... **TCLC 1, 10; PC 2**
See also CA 104; 125; DA; DLB 19;
MTCW

Housman, Laurence 1865-1959 ..... **TCLC 7**
See also CA 106; DLB 10; SATA 25

Howard, Elizabeth Jane 1923- ... **CLC 7, 29**
See also CA 5-8R; CANR 8

Howard, Maureen 1930- ..... **CLC 5, 14, 46**
See also CA 53-56; CANR 31; DLBY 83;
MTCW

Howard, Richard 1929- ...... **CLC 7, 10, 47**
See also AITN 1; CA 85-88; CANR 25;
DLB 5

Howard, Robert Ervin 1906-1936... **TCLC 8**
See also CA 105

Howard, Warren F.
See Pohl, Frederik

Howe, Fanny 1940- .... **CLC 47**
See also CA 117; SATA 52

Howe, Julia Ward 1819-1910 ..... **TCLC 21**
See also CA 117; DLB 1

Howe, Susan 1937-............... **CLC 72**
See also DLB 120

Howe, Tina 1937-................. **CLC 48**
See also CA 109

Howell, James 1594(?)-1666 .... **LC 13**

Howells, W. D.
See Howells, William Dean

Howells, William D.
See Howells, William Dean

Howells, William Dean
1837-1920 .... **TCLC 41, 7, 17**
See also CA 104; 134; CDALB 1865-1917;
DLB 12, 64, 74, 79

Howes, Barbara 1914- .... **CLC 15**
See also CA 9-12R; CAAS 3; SATA 5

Hrabal, Bohumil 1914-........ **CLC 13, 67**
See also CA 106; CAAS 12

Hsun, Lu .... **TCLC 3**
See also Shu-Jen, Chou

Hubbard, L(afayette) Ron(ald)
1911-1986 .... **CLC 43**
See also CA 77-80; 118; CANR 22

Huch, Ricarda (Octavia)
1864-1947 .... **TCLC 13**
See also CA 111; DLB 66

Huddle, David 1942- .... **CLC 49**
See also CA 57-60; DLB 130

Hudson, Jeffrey
See Crichton, (John) Michael

Hudson, W(illiam) H(enry)
1841-1922 .... **TCLC 29**
See also CA 115; DLB 98; SATA 35

Hueffer, Ford Madox
See Ford, Ford Madox

Hughart, Barry 1934-............. **CLC 39**
See also CA 137

Hughes, Colin
See Creasey, John

Jackson, Sam
See Trumbo, Dalton

Jackson, Sara
See Wingrove, David (John)

Jackson, Shirley
1919-1965 .... **CLC 11, 60; SSC 9**
See also AAYA 9; CA 1-4R; 25-28R;
CANR 4; CDALB 1941-1968; DA;
DLB 6; SATA 2; WLC

Jacob, (Cyprien-)Max 1876-1944 ... **TCLC 6**
See also CA 104

Jacobs, Jim 1942-............... **CLC 12**
See also CA 97-100

Jacobs, W(illiam) W(ymark)
1863-1943 .... **TCLC 22**
See also CA 121

Jacobsen, Jens Peter 1847-1885 .. **NCLC 34**

Jacobsen, Josephine 1908-......... **CLC 48**
See also CA 33-36R; CANR 23

Jacobson, Dan 1929- .... **CLC 4, 14**
See also CA 1-4R; CANR 2, 25; DLB 14;
MTCW

Jacqueline
See Carpentier (y Valmont), Alejo

Jagger, Mick 1944-............... **CLC 17**

Jakes, John (William) 1932- .... **CLC 29**
See also BEST 89:4; CA 57-60; CANR 10;
DLBY 83; MTCW; SATA 62

James, Andrew
See Kirkup, James

James, C(yril) L(ionel) R(obert)
1901-1989 .... **CLC 33**
See also BW; CA 117; 125; 128; DLB 125;
MTCW

James, Daniel (Lewis) 1911-1988
See Santiago, Danny
See also CA 125

James, Dynely
See Mayne, William (James Carter)

James, Henry
1843-1916 ...... **TCLC 2, 11, 24, 40, 47;
SSC 8**
See also CA 104; 132; CDALB 1865-1917;
DA; DLB 12, 71, 74; MTCW; WLC

James, Montague (Rhodes)
1862-1936 .... **TCLC 6**
See also CA 104

James, P. D. .... **CLC 18, 46**
See also White, Phyllis Dorothy James
See also BEST 90:2; CDBLB 1960 to
Present; DLB 87

James, Philip
See Moorcock, Michael (John)

James, William 1842-1910..... **TCLC 15, 32**
See also CA 109

James I 1394-1437 .... **LC 20**

Jami, Nur al-Din 'Abd al-Rahman
1414-1492 .... **LC 9**

Jandl, Ernst 1925- .... **CLC 34**

Janowitz, Tama 1957- .... **CLC 43**
See also CA 106

Jarrell, Randall
1914-1965 .... **CLC 1, 2, 6, 9, 13, 49**
See also CA 5-8R; 25-28R; CABS 2;
CANR 6, 34; CDALB 1941-1968; CLR 6;
DLB 48, 52; MAICYA; MTCW; SATA 7

Jarry, Alfred 1873-1907....... **TCLC 2, 14**
See also CA 104

Jarvis, E. K.
See Bloch, Robert (Albert); Ellison, Harlan;
Silverberg, Robert

Jeake, Samuel, Jr.
See Aiken, Conrad (Potter)

Jean Paul 1763-1825 .... **NCLC 7**

Jeffers, (John) Robinson
1887-1962 .... **CLC 2, 3, 11, 15, 54**
See also CA 85-88; CANR 35;
CDALB 1917-1929; DA; DLB 45;
MTCW; WLC

Jefferson, Janet
See Mencken, H(enry) L(ouis)

Jefferson, Thomas 1743-1826 .... **NCLC 11**
See also CDALB 1640-1865; DLB 31

Jeffrey, Francis 1773-1850....... **NCLC 33**
See also DLB 107

Jelakowitch, Ivan
See Heijermans, Herman

Jellicoe, (Patricia) Ann 1927- ...... **CLC 27**
See also CA 85-88; DLB 13

Jen, Gish .... **CLC 70**
See also Jen, Lillian

Jen, Lillian 1956(?)-
See Jen, Gish
See also CA 135

Jenkins, (John) Robin 1912- .... **CLC 52**
See also CA 1-4R; CANR 1; DLB 14

Jennings, Elizabeth (Joan)
1926- .... **CLC 5, 14**
See also CA 61-64; CAAS 5; CANR 8, 39;
DLB 27; MTCW; SATA 66

Jennings, Waylon 1937-........... **CLC 21**

Jensen, Johannes V. 1873-1950.... **TCLC 41**

Jensen, Laura (Linnea) 1948- ...... **CLC 37**
See also CA 103

Jerome, Jerome K(lapka)
1859-1927 .... **TCLC 23**
See also CA 119; DLB 10, 34

Jerrold, Douglas William
1803-1857 .... **NCLC 2**

Jewett, (Theodora) Sarah Orne
1849-1909 .... **TCLC 1, 22; SSC 6**
See also CA 108; 127; DLB 12, 74;
SATA 15

Jewsbury, Geraldine (Endsor)
1812-1880 .... **NCLC 22**
See also DLB 21

Jhabvala, Ruth Prawer
1927- .... **CLC 4, 8, 29**
See also CA 1-4R; CANR 2, 29; MTCW

Jiles, Paulette 1943-........... **CLC 13, 58**
See also CA 101

Jimenez (Mantecon), Juan Ramon
1881-1958 .... **TCLC 4; PC 7**
See also CA 104; 131; HW; MTCW

Jimenez, Ramon
See Jimenez (Mantecon), Juan Ramon

Jimenez Mantecon, Juan
See Jimenez (Mantecon), Juan Ramon

Joel, Billy .... **CLC 26**
See also Joel, William Martin

Joel, William Martin 1949-
See Joel, Billy
See also CA 108

John of the Cross, St. 1542-1591 .... **LC 18**

Johnson, B(ryan) S(tanley William)
1933-1973 .... **CLC 6, 9**
See also CA 9-12R; 53-56; CANR 9;
DLB 14, 40

Johnson, Benj. F. of Boo
See Riley, James Whitcomb

Johnson, Benjamin F. of Boo
See Riley, James Whitcomb

Johnson, Charles (Richard)
1948- .... **CLC 7, 51, 65**
See also BLC 2; BW; CA 116; DLB 33

Johnson, Denis 1949-............. **CLC 52**
See also CA 117; 121; DLB 120

Johnson, Diane 1934-........ **CLC 5, 13, 48**
See also CA 41-44R; CANR 17, 40;
DLBY 80; MTCW

Johnson, Eyvind (Olof Verner)
1900-1976 .... **CLC 14**
See also CA 73-76; 69-72; CANR 34

Johnson, J. R.
See James, C(yril) L(ionel) R(obert)

Johnson, James Weldon
1871-1938 .... **TCLC 3, 19**
See also BLC 2; BW; CA 104; 125;
CDALB 1917-1929; DLB 51; MTCW;
SATA 31

Johnson, Joyce 1935-............. **CLC 58**
See also CA 125; 129

Johnson, Lionel (Pigot)
1867-1902 .... **TCLC 19**
See also CA 117; DLB 19

Johnson, Mel
See Malzberg, Barry N(athaniel)

Johnson, Pamela Hansford
1912-1981 .... **CLC 1, 7, 27**
See also CA 1-4R; 104; CANR 2, 28;
DLB 15; MTCW

Johnson, Samuel 1709-1784......... **LC 15**
See also CDBLB 1660-1789; DA; DLB 39,
95, 104; WLC

Johnson, Uwe
1934-1984 .... **CLC 5, 10, 15, 40**
See also CA 1-4R; 112; CANR 1, 39;
DLB 75; MTCW

Johnston, George (Benson) 1913- ... **CLC 51**
See also CA 1-4R; CANR 5, 20; DLB 88

Johnston, Jennifer 1930-........... **CLC 7**
See also CA 85-88; DLB 14

Jolley, (Monica) Elizabeth 1923- ... **CLC 46**
See also CA 127; CAAS 13

Jones, Arthur Llewellyn 1863-1947
See Machen, Arthur
See also CA 104

Jones, D(ouglas) G(ordon) 1929-.... **CLC 10**
See also CA 29-32R; CANR 13; DLB 53

Jones, David (Michael)
1895-1974 .... **CLC 2, 4, 7, 13, 42**
See also CA 9-12R; 53-56; CANR 28;
CDBLB 1945-1960; DLB 20, 100; MTCW

Jones, David Robert 1947-
See Bowie, David
See also CA 103

Jones, Diana Wynne 1934- .... **CLC 26**
See also CA 49-52; CANR 4, 26; CLR 23;
MAICYA; SAAS 7; SATA 9, 70

Jones, Edward P. 1951-.......... **CLC 76**

Jones, Gayl 1949-.............. **CLC 6, 9**
See also BLC 2; BW; CA 77-80; CANR 27;
DLB 33; MTCW

Jones, James 1921-1977.... **CLC 1, 3, 10, 39**
See also AITN 1, 2; CA 1-4R; 69-72;
CANR 6; DLB 2; MTCW

Jones, John J.
See Lovecraft, H(oward) P(hillips)

Jones, LeRoi .... **CLC 1, 2, 3, 5, 10, 14**
See also Baraka, Amiri

Jones, Louis B. .... **CLC 65**

Jones, Madison (Percy, Jr.) 1925- ... **CLC 4**
See also CA 13-16R; CAAS 11; CANR 7

Jones, Mervyn 1922- .... **CLC 10, 52**
See also CA 45-48; CAAS 5; CANR 1;
MTCW

Jones, Mick 1956(?)- .... **CLC 30**
See also Clash, The

Jones, Nettie (Pearl) 1941- .... **CLC 34**
See also CA 137

Jones, Preston 1936-1979 .... **CLC 10**
See also CA 73-76; 89-92; DLB 7

Jones, Robert F(rancis) 1934-....... **CLC 7**
See also CA 49-52; CANR 2

Jones, Rod 1953- .... **CLC 50**
See also CA 128

Jones, Terence Graham Parry
1942- .... **CLC 21**
See also Jones, Terry; Monty Python
See also CA 112; 116; CANR 35; SATA 51

Jones, Terry
See Jones, Terence Graham Parry
See also SATA 67

Jong, Erica 1942-.......... **CLC 4, 6, 8, 18**
See also AITN 1; BEST 90:2; CA 73-76;
CANR 26; DLB 2, 5, 28; MTCW

Jonson, Ben(jamin) 1572(?)-1637...... **LC 6**
See also CDBLB Before 1660; DA; DLB 62,
121; WLC

Jordan, June 1936-.......... **CLC 5, 11, 23**
See also AAYA 2; BW; CA 33-36R;
CANR 25; CLR 10; DLB 38; MAICYA;
MTCW; SATA 4

Jordan, Pat(rick M.) 1941- .... **CLC 37**
See also CA 33-36R

Jorgensen, Ivar
See Ellison, Harlan

Jorgenson, Ivar
See Silverberg, Robert

Josipovici, Gabriel 1940-........ **CLC 6, 43**
See also CA 37-40R; CAAS 8; DLB 14

Joubert, Joseph 1754-1824 .... **NCLC 9**

Jouve, Pierre Jean 1887-1976...... **CLC 47**
See also CA 65-68

Joyce, James (Augustine Aloysius)
1882-1941 .... **TCLC 3, 8, 16, 35; SSC 3**
See also CA 104; 126; CDBLB 1914-1945;
DA; DLB 10, 19, 36; MTCW; WLC

Jozsef, Attila 1905-1937.......... **TCLC 22**
See also CA 116

Juana Ines de la Cruz 1651(?)-1695 ... **LC 5**

Judd, Cyril
See Kornbluth, C(yril) M.; Pohl, Frederik

Julian of Norwich 1342(?)-1416(?) .... **LC 6**

Just, Ward (Swift) 1935- .... **CLC 4, 27**
See also CA 25-28R; CANR 32

Justice, Donald (Rodney) 1925- .. **CLC 6, 19**
See also CA 5-8R; CANR 26; DLBY 83

Juvenal c. 55-c. 127 .... **CMLC 8**

Juvenis
See Bourne, Randolph S(illiman)

Kacew, Romain 1914-1980
See Gary, Romain
See also CA 108; 102

Kadare, Ismail 1936- .... **CLC 52**

Kadohata, Cynthia................. **CLC 59**
See also CA 140

Kafka, Franz
1883-1924 .... **TCLC 2, 6, 13, 29, 47;**
SSC 5
See also CA 105; 126; DA; DLB 81;
MTCW; WLC

Kahn, Roger 1927-.............. **CLC 30**
See also CA 25-28R; SATA 37

Kain, Saul
See Sassoon, Siegfried (Lorraine)

Kaiser, Georg 1878-1945 .... **TCLC 9**
See also CA 106; DLB 124

Kaletski, Alexander 1946-......... **CLC 39**
See also CA 118

Kalidasa fl. c. 400- .... **CMLC 9**

Kallman, Chester (Simon)
1921-1975 .... **CLC 2**
See also CA 45-48; 53-56; CANR 3

Kaminsky, Melvin 1926-
See Brooks, Mel
See also CA 65-68; CANR 16

Kaminsky, Stuart M(elvin) 1934- ... **CLC 59**
See also CA 73-76; CANR 29

Kane, Paul
See Simon, Paul

Kane, Wilson
See Bloch, Robert (Albert)

Kanin, Garson 1912-.............. **CLC 22**
See also AITN 1; CA 5-8R; CANR 7;
DLB 7

Kaniuk, Yoram 1930-............. **CLC 19**
See also CA 134

Kant, Immanuel 1724-1804 ...... **NCLC 27**
See also DLB 94

Kantor, MacKinlay 1904-1977 ...... **CLC 7**
See also CA 61-64; 73-76; DLB 9, 102

Kaplan, David Michael 1946- ...... **CLC 50**

Kaplan, James 1951- .... **CLC 59**
See also CA 135

Karageorge, Michael
See Anderson, Poul (William)

Karamzin, Nikolai Mikhailovich
1766-1826 .... **NCLC 3**

Karapanou, Margarita 1946-....... **CLC 13**
See also CA 101

Karinthy, Frigyes 1887-1938...... **TCLC 47**

Karl, Frederick R(obert) 1927-..... **CLC 34**
See also CA 5-8R; CANR 3

Kastel, Warren
See Silverberg, Robert

Kataev, Evgeny Petrovich 1903-1942
See Petrov, Evgeny
See also CA 120

Kataphusin
See Ruskin, John

Katz, Steve 1935-................ **CLC 47**
See also CA 25-28R; CAAS 14; CANR 12;
DLBY 83

Kauffman, Janet 1945-............ **CLC 42**
See also CA 117; DLBY 86

Kaufman, Bob (Garnell)
1925-1986 .... **CLC 49**
See also BW; CA 41-44R; 118; CANR 22;
DLB 16, 41

Kaufman, George S. 1889-1961..... **CLC 38**
See also CA 108; 93-96; DLB 7

Kaufman, Sue .... **CLC 3, 8**
See also Barondess, Sue K(aufman)

Kavafis, Konstantinos Petrou 1863-1933
See Cavafy, C(onstantine) P(eter)
See also CA 104

Kavan, Anna 1901-1968......... **CLC 5, 13**
See also CA 5-8R; CANR 6; MTCW

Kavanagh, Dan
See Barnes, Julian

Kavanagh, Patrick (Joseph)
1904-1967 .... **CLC 22**
See also CA 123; 25-28R; DLB 15, 20;
MTCW

Kawabata, Yasunari
1899-1972 .... **CLC 2, 5, 9, 18**
See also CA 93-96; 33-36R

Kaye, M(ary) M(argaret) 1909-..... **CLC 28**
See also CA 89-92; CANR 24; MTCW;
SATA 62

Kaye, Mollie
See Kaye, M(ary) M(argaret)

Kaye-Smith, Sheila 1887-1956..... **TCLC 20**
See also CA 118; DLB 36

Kaymor, Patrice Maguilene
See Senghor, Leopold Sedar

Kazan, Elia 1909-.......... **CLC 6, 16, 63**
See also CA 21-24R; CANR 32

Kazantzakis, Nikos
1883(?)-1957 .... **TCLC 2, 5, 33**
See also CA 105; 132; MTCW

Kazin, Alfred 1915- .... **CLC 34, 38**
See also CA 1-4R; CAAS 7; CANR 1;
DLB 67

Keane, Mary Nesta (Skrine) 1904-
See Keane, Molly
See also CA 108; 114

Keane, Molly . . . . **CLC 31**
See also Keane, Mary Nesta (Skrine)

Keates, Jonathan 19(?)- . . . . **CLC 34**

Keaton, Buster 1895-1966 . . . . **CLC 20**

Keats, John 1795-1821 . . . . . . **NCLC 8; PC 1**
See also CDBLB 1789-1832; DA; DLB 96,
110; WLC

Keene, Donald 1922- . . . . **CLC 34**
See also CA 1-4R; CANR 5

Keillor, Garrison . . . . **CLC 40**
See also Keillor, Gary (Edward)
See also AAYA 2; BEST 89:3; DLBY 87;
SATA 58

Keillor, Gary (Edward) 1942-
See Keillor, Garrison
See also CA 111; 117; CANR 36; MTCW

Keith, Michael
See Hubbard, L(afayette) Ron(ald)

Kell, Joseph
See Wilson, John (Anthony) Burgess

Keller, Gottfried 1819-1890 . . . . **NCLC 2**
See also DLB 129

Kellerman, Jonathan 1949- . . . . **CLC 44**
See also BEST 90:1; CA 106; CANR 29

Kelley, William Melvin 1937- . . . . . . **CLC 22**
See also BW; CA 77-80; CANR 27; DLB 33

Kellogg, Marjorie 1922- . . . . **CLC 2**
See also CA 81-84

Kellow, Kathleen
See Hibbert, Eleanor Alice Burford

Kelly, M(ilton) T(erry) 1947- . . . . . . **CLC 55**
See also CA 97-100; CANR 19

Kelman, James 1946- . . . . **CLC 58**

Kemal, Yashar 1923- . . . . **CLC 14, 29**
See also CA 89-92

Kemble, Fanny 1809-1893 . . . . **NCLC 18**
See also DLB 32

Kemelman, Harry 1908- . . . . **CLC 2**
See also AITN 1; CA 9-12R; CANR 6;
DLB 28

Kempe, Margery 1373(?)-1440(?) . . . . . **LC 6**

Kempis, Thomas a 1380-1471 . . . . **LC 11**

Kendall, Henry 1839-1882 . . . . . . **NCLC 12**

Keneally, Thomas (Michael)
1935- . . . . . . **CLC 5, 8, 10, 14, 19, 27, 43**
See also CA 85-88; CANR 10; MTCW

Kennedy, Adrienne (Lita) 1931- . . . . **CLC 66**
See also BLC 2; BW; CA 103; CABS 3;
CANR 26; DLB 38

Kennedy, John Pendleton
1795-1870 . . . . **NCLC 2**
See also DLB 3

Kennedy, Joseph Charles 1929- . . . . . . **CLC 8**
See also Kennedy, X. J.
See also CA 1-4R; CANR 4, 30, 40;
SATA 14

Kennedy, William 1928- . . . **CLC 6, 28, 34, 53**
See also AAYA 1; CA 85-88; CANR 14,
31; DLBY 85; MTCW; SATA 57

Kennedy, X. J. . . . . **CLC 42**
See also Kennedy, Joseph Charles
See also CAAS 9; CLR 27; DLB 5

Kent, Kelvin
See Kuttner, Henry

Kenton, Maxwell
See Southern, Terry

Kenyon, Robert O.
See Kuttner, Henry

Kerouac, Jack . . . . . **CLC 1, 2, 3, 5, 14, 29, 61**
See also Kerouac, Jean-Louis Lebris de
See also CDALB 1941-1968; DLB 2, 16;
DLBD 3

Kerouac, Jean-Louis Lebris de 1922-1969
See Kerouac, Jack
See also AITN 1; CA 5-8R; 25-28R;
CANR 26; DA; MTCW; WLC

Kerr, Jean 1923- . . . . **CLC 22**
See also CA 5-8R; CANR 7

Kerr, M. E. . . . . **CLC 12, 35**
See also Meaker, Marijane (Agnes)
See also AAYA 2; CLR 29; SAAS 1

Kerr, Robert . . . . **CLC 55**

Kerrigan, (Thomas) Anthony
1918- . . . . **CLC 4, 6**
See also CA 49-52; CAAS 11; CANR 4

Kerry, Lois
See Duncan, Lois

Kesey, Ken (Elton)
1935- . . . . **CLC 1, 3, 6, 11, 46, 64**
See also CA 1-4R; CANR 22, 38;
CDALB 1968-1988; DA; DLB 2, 16;
MTCW; SATA 66; WLC

Kesselring, Joseph (Otto)
1902-1967 . . . . **CLC 45**

Kessler, Jascha (Frederick) 1929- . . . . **CLC 4**
See also CA 17-20R; CANR 8

Kettelkamp, Larry (Dale) 1933- . . . . **CLC 12**
See also CA 29-32R; CANR 16; SAAS 3;
SATA 2

Keyber, Conny
See Fielding, Henry

Khayyam, Omar 1048-1131 . . . . . . **CMLC 11**

Kherdian, David 1931- . . . . **CLC 6, 9**
See also CA 21-24R; CAAS 2; CANR 39;
CLR 24; MAICYA; SATA 16, 74

Khlebnikov, Velimir . . . . **TCLC 20**
See also Khlebnikov, Viktor Vladimirovich

Khlebnikov, Viktor Vladimirovich 1885-1922
See Khlebnikov, Velimir
See also CA 117

Khodasevich, Vladislav (Felitsianovich)
1886-1939 . . . . **TCLC 15**
See also CA 115

Kielland, Alexander Lange
1849-1906 . . . . **TCLC 5**
See also CA 104

Kiely, Benedict 1919- . . . . **CLC 23, 43**
See also CA 1-4R; CANR 2; DLB 15

Kienzle, William X(avier) 1928- . . . . **CLC 25**
See also CA 93-96; CAAS 1; CANR 9, 31;
MTCW

Kierkegaard, Soeren 1813-1855 . . . **NCLC 34**

Kierkegaard, Soren 1813-1855 . . . . **NCLC 34**

Killens, John Oliver 1916-1987 . . . . . **CLC 10**
See also BW; CA 77-80; 123; CAAS 2;
CANR 26; DLB 33

Killigrew, Anne 1660-1685 . . . . **LC 4**
See also DLB 131

Kim
See Simenon, Georges (Jacques Christian)

Kincaid, Jamaica 1949- . . . . **CLC 43, 68**
See also BLC 2; BW; CA 125

King, Francis (Henry) 1923- . . . . . **CLC 8, 53**
See also CA 1-4R; CANR 1, 33; DLB 15;
MTCW

King, Stephen (Edwin)
1947- . . . . **CLC 12, 26, 37, 61**
See also AAYA 1; BEST 90:1; CA 61-64;
CANR 1, 30; DLBY 80; MTCW;
SATA 9, 55

King, Steve
See King, Stephen (Edwin)

Kingman, Lee . . . . **CLC 17**
See also Natti, (Mary) Lee
See also SAAS 3; SATA 1, 67

Kingsley, Charles 1819-1875 . . . . . **NCLC 35**
See also DLB 21, 32; YABC 2

Kingsley, Sidney 1906- . . . . **CLC 44**
See also CA 85-88; DLB 7

Kingsolver, Barbara 1955- . . . . **CLC 55**
See also CA 129; 134

Kingston, Maxine (Ting Ting) Hong
1940- . . . . **CLC 12, 19, 58**
See also AAYA 8; CA 69-72; CANR 13,
38; DLBY 80; MTCW; SATA 53

Kinnell, Galway
1927- . . . . **CLC 1, 2, 3, 5, 13, 29**
See also CA 9-12R; CANR 10, 34; DLB 5;
DLBY 87; MTCW

Kinsella, Thomas 1928- . . . . **CLC 4, 19**
See also CA 17-20R; CANR 15; DLB 27;
MTCW

Kinsella, W(illiam) P(atrick)
1935- . . . . **CLC 27, 43**
See also AAYA 7; CA 97-100; CAAS 7;
CANR 21, 35; MTCW

Kipling, (Joseph) Rudyard
1865-1936 . . . . **TCLC 8, 17; PC 3; SSC 5**
See also CA 105; 120; CANR 33;
CDBLB 1890-1914; DA; DLB 19, 34;
MAICYA; MTCW; WLC; YABC 2

Kirkup, James 1918- . . . . **CLC 1**
See also CA 1-4R; CAAS 4; CANR 2;
DLB 27; SATA 12

Kirkwood, James 1930(?)-1989 . . . . . . **CLC 9**
See also AITN 2; CA 1-4R; 128; CANR 6,
40

Kis, Danilo 1935-1989 . . . . **CLC 57**
See also CA 109; 118; 129; MTCW

Kivi, Aleksis 1834-1872 . . . . **NCLC 30**

Kizer, Carolyn (Ashley) 1925-. . . **CLC 15, 39**
See also CA 65-68; CAAS 5; CANR 24;
DLB 5

Klabund 1890-1928 . . . . **TCLC 44**
See also DLB 66

Klappert, Peter 1942- . . . . **CLC 57**
See also CA 33-36R; DLB 5

Klein, A(braham) M(oses)
1909-1972 . . . . **CLC 19**
See also CA 101; 37-40R; DLB 68

Klein, Norma   1938-1989 . . . . **CLC 30**
See also AAYA 2; CA 41-44R; 128;
CANR 15, 37; CLR 2, 19; MAICYA;
SAAS 1; SATA 7, 57

Klein, T(heodore) E(ibon) D(onald)
1947- . . . . **CLC 34**
See also CA 119

Kleist, Heinrich von   1777-1811. . . . **NCLC 2**
See also DLB 90

Klima, Ivan   1931-. . . . . **CLC 56**
See also CA 25-28R; CANR 17

Klimentov, Andrei Platonovich   1899-1951
See Platonov, Andrei
See also CA 108

Klinger, Friedrich Maximilian von
1752-1831 . . . . **NCLC 1**
See also DLB 94

Klopstock, Friedrich Gottlieb
1724-1803 . . . . **NCLC 11**
See also DLB 97

Knebel, Fletcher   1911-1993. . . . . . . **CLC 14**
See also AITN 1; CA 1-4R; 140; CAAS 3;
CANR 1, 36; SATA 36

Knickerbocker, Diedrich
See Irving, Washington

Knight, Etheridge   1931-1991. . . . . . . **CLC 40**
See also BLC 2; BW; CA 21-24R; 133;
CANR 23; DLB 41

Knight, Sarah Kemble   1666-1727 . . . . . **LC 7**
See also DLB 24

Knowles, John   1926- . . . . . . **CLC 1, 4, 10, 26**
See also AAYA 10; CA 17-20R; CANR 40;
CDALB 1968-1988; DA; DLB 6; MTCW;
SATA 8

Knox, Calvin M.
See Silverberg, Robert

Knye, Cassandra
See Disch, Thomas M(ichael)

Koch, C(hristopher) J(ohn)   1932- . . . **CLC 42**
See also CA 127

Koch, Christopher
See Koch, C(hristopher) J(ohn)

Koch, Kenneth   1925- . . . . **CLC 5, 8, 44**
See also CA 1-4R; CANR 6, 36; DLB 5;
SATA 65

Kochanowski, Jan   1530-1584. . . . . . . **LC 10**

Kock, Charles Paul de
1794-1871 . . . . **NCLC 16**

Koda Shigeyuki   1867-1947
See Rohan, Koda
See also CA 121

Koestler, Arthur
1905-1983 . . . . **CLC 1, 3, 6, 8, 15, 33**
See also CA 1-4R; 109; CANR 1, 33;
CDBLB 1945-1960; DLBY 83; MTCW

Kogawa, Joy Nozomi   1935-. . . . . **CLC 78**
See also CA 101; CANR 19

Kohout, Pavel   1928-. . . . . **CLC 13**
See also CA 45-48; CANR 3

Koizumi, Yakumo
See Hearn, (Patricio) Lafcadio (Tessima
Carlos)

Kolmar, Gertrud   1894-1943. . . . . . . **TCLC 40**

Konrad, George
See Konrad, Gyoergy

Konrad, Gyoergy   1933- . . . . . . **CLC 4, 10, 73**
See also CA 85-88

Konwicki, Tadeusz   1926-. . . . . **CLC 8, 28, 54**
See also CA 101; CAAS 9; CANR 39;
MTCW

Koontz, Dean R(ay)   1945-. . . . . **CLC 78**
See also AAYA 9; BEST 89:3, 90:2;
CA 108; CANR 19, 36; MTCW

Kopit, Arthur (Lee)   1937- . . . . **CLC 1, 18, 33**
See also AITN 1; CA 81-84; CABS 3;
DLB 7; MTCW

Kops, Bernard   1926-. . . . . **CLC 4**
See also CA 5-8R; DLB 13

Kornbluth, C(yril) M.   1923-1958. . . . **TCLC 8**
See also CA 105; DLB 8

Korolenko, V. G.
See Korolenko, Vladimir Galaktionovich

Korolenko, Vladimir
See Korolenko, Vladimir Galaktionovich

Korolenko, Vladimir G.
See Korolenko, Vladimir Galaktionovich

Korolenko, Vladimir Galaktionovich
1853-1921 . . . . **TCLC 22**
See also CA 121

Kosinski, Jerzy (Nikodem)
1933-1991 . . . . **CLC 1, 2, 3, 6, 10, 15, 53, 70**
See also CA 17-20R; 134; CANR 9; DLB 2;
DLBY 82; MTCW

Kostelanetz, Richard (Cory)   1940- . . **CLC 28**
See also CA 13-16R; CAAS 8; CANR 38

Kostrowitzki, Wilhelm Apollinaris de
1880-1918
See Apollinaire, Guillaume
See also CA 104

Kotlowitz, Robert   1924-. . . . . **CLC 4**
See also CA 33-36R; CANR 36

Kotzebue, August (Friedrich Ferdinand) von
1761-1819 . . . . **NCLC 25**
See also DLB 94

Kotzwinkle, William   1938- . . . **CLC 5, 14, 35**
See also CA 45-48; CANR 3; CLR 6;
MAICYA; SATA 24, 70

Kozol, Jonathan   1936-. . . . . **CLC 17**
See also CA 61-64; CANR 16

Kozoll, Michael   1940(?)- . . . . **CLC 35**

Kramer, Kathryn   19(?)- . . . . **CLC 34**

Kramer, Larry   1935- . . . . **CLC 42**
See also CA 124; 126

Krasicki, Ignacy   1735-1801. . . . . . . **NCLC 8**

Krasinski, Zygmunt   1812-1859 . . . . **NCLC 4**

Kraus, Karl   1874-1936. . . . . **TCLC 5**
See also CA 104; DLB 118

Kreve (Mickevicius), Vincas
1882-1954 . . . . **TCLC 27**

Kristeva, Julia   1941- . . . . **CLC 77**

Kristofferson, Kris   1936-. . . . . **CLC 26**
See also CA 104

Krizanc, John   1956-. . . . . **CLC 57**

Krleza, Miroslav   1893-1981. . . . . **CLC 8**
See also CA 97-100; 105

Kroetsch, Robert   1927- . . . . . . **CLC 5, 23, 57**
See also CA 17-20R; CANR 8, 38; DLB 53;
MTCW

Kroetz, Franz
See Kroetz, Franz Xaver

Kroetz, Franz Xaver   1946- . . . . **CLC 41**
See also CA 130

Kroker, Arthur   1945-. . . . . **CLC 77**

Kropotkin, Peter (Aleksieevich)
1842-1921 . . . . **TCLC 36**
See also CA 119

Krotkov, Yuri   1917-. . . . . **CLC 19**
See also CA 102

Krumb
See Crumb, R(obert)

Krumgold, Joseph (Quincy)
1908-1980 . . . . **CLC 12**
See also CA 9-12R; 101; CANR 7;
MAICYA; SATA 1, 23, 48

Krumwitz
See Crumb, R(obert)

Krutch, Joseph Wood   1893-1970. . . . **CLC 24**
See also CA 1-4R; 25-28R; CANR 4;
DLB 63

Krutzch, Gus
See Eliot, T(homas) S(tearns)

Krylov, Ivan Andreevich
1768(?)-1844 . . . . **NCLC 1**

Kubin, Alfred   1877-1959 . . . . **TCLC 23**
See also CA 112; DLB 81

Kubrick, Stanley   1928-. . . . . **CLC 16**
See also CA 81-84; CANR 33; DLB 26

Kumin, Maxine (Winokur)
1925- . . . . **CLC 5, 13, 28**
See also AITN 2; CA 1-4R; CAAS 8;
CANR 1, 21; DLB 5; MTCW; SATA 12

Kundera, Milan
1929- . . . . **CLC 4, 9, 19, 32, 68**
See also AAYA 2; CA 85-88; CANR 19;
MTCW

Kunitz, Stanley (Jasspon)
1905- . . . . **CLC 6, 11, 14**
See also CA 41-44R; CANR 26; DLB 48;
MTCW

Kunze, Reiner   1933-. . . . . **CLC 10**
See also CA 93-96; DLB 75

Kuprin, Aleksandr Ivanovich
1870-1938 . . . . **TCLC 5**
See also CA 104

Kureishi, Hanif   1954(?)-. . . . . **CLC 64**
See also CA 139

Kurosawa, Akira   1910-. . . . . **CLC 16**
See also CA 101

Kuttner, Henry   1915-1958. . . . . **TCLC 10**
See also CA 107; DLB 8

Kuzma, Greg   1944-. . . . . **CLC 7**
See also CA 33-36R

Kuzmin, Mikhail   1872(?)-1936 . . . . **TCLC 40**

Kyd, Thomas 1558-1594...... **LC 22; DC 3**
See also DLB 62

Kyprianos, Iossif
See Samarakis, Antonis

La Bruyere, Jean de 1645-1696..... **LC 17**

Lacan, Jacques (Marie Emile)
1901-1981 .... **CLC 75**
See also CA 121; 104

Laclos, Pierre Ambroise Francois Choderlos
de 1741-1803 .... **NCLC 4**

Lacolere, Francois
See Aragon, Louis

La Colere, Francois
See Aragon, Louis

La Deshabilleuse
See Simenon, Georges (Jacques Christian)

Lady Gregory
See Gregory, Isabella Augusta (Persse)

Lady of Quality, A
See Bagnold, Enid

La Fayette, Marie (Madelaine Pioche de la
Vergne Comtes 1634-1693....... **LC 2**

Lafayette, Rene
See Hubbard, L(afayette) Ron(ald)

Laforgue, Jules 1860-1887........ **NCLC 5**

Lagerkvist, Paer (Fabian)
1891-1974 .... **CLC 7, 10, 13, 54**
See also Lagerkvist, Par
See also CA 85-88; 49-52; MTCW

Lagerkvist, Par
See Lagerkvist, Paer (Fabian)
See also SSC 12

Lagerloef, Selma (Ottiliana Lovisa)
1858-1940 .... **TCLC 4, 36**
See also Lagerlof, Selma (Ottiliana Lovisa)
See also CA 108; CLR 7; SATA 15

Lagerlof, Selma (Ottiliana Lovisa)
See Lagerloef, Selma (Ottiliana Lovisa)
See also CLR 7; SATA 15

La Guma, (Justin) Alex(ander)
1925-1985 .... **CLC 19**
See also BW; CA 49-52; 118; CANR 25;
DLB 117; MTCW

Laidlaw, A. K.
See Grieve, C(hristopher) M(urray)

Lainez, Manuel Mujica
See Mujica Lainez, Manuel
See also HW

Lamartine, Alphonse (Marie Louis Prat) de
1790-1869 .... **NCLC 11**

Lamb, Charles 1775-1834....... **NCLC 10**
See also CDBLB 1789-1832; DA; DLB 93,
107; SATA 17; WLC

Lamb, Lady Caroline 1785-1828.. **NCLC 38**
See also DLB 116

Lamming, George (William)
1927- .... **CLC 2, 4, 66**
See also BLC 2; BW; CA 85-88; CANR 26;
DLB 125; MTCW

L'Amour, Louis (Dearborn)
1908-1988 .... **CLC 25, 55**
See also AITN 2; BEST 89:2; CA 1-4R;
125; CANR 3, 25, 40; DLBY 80; MTCW

Lampedusa, Giuseppe (Tomasi) di ... **TCLC 13**
See also Tomasi di Lampedusa, Giuseppe

Lampman, Archibald 1861-1899 .. **NCLC 25**
See also DLB 92

Lancaster, Bruce 1896-1963....... **CLC 36**
See also CA 9-10; CAP 1; SATA 9

Landau, Mark Alexandrovich
See Aldanov, Mark (Alexandrovich)

Landau-Aldanov, Mark Alexandrovich
See Aldanov, Mark (Alexandrovich)

Landis, John 1950-.............. **CLC 26**
See also CA 112; 122

Landolfi, Tommaso 1908-1979... **CLC 11, 49**
See also CA 127; 117

Landon, Letitia Elizabeth
1802-1838 .... **NCLC 15**
See also DLB 96

Landor, Walter Savage
1775-1864 .... **NCLC 14**
See also DLB 93, 107

Landwirth, Heinz 1927-
See Lind, Jakov
See also CA 9-12R; CANR 7

Lane, Patrick 1939- .... **CLC 25**
See also CA 97-100; DLB 53

Lang, Andrew 1844-1912......... **TCLC 16**
See also CA 114; 137; DLB 98; MAICYA;
SATA 16

Lang, Fritz 1890-1976 .... **CLC 20**
See also CA 77-80; 69-72; CANR 30

Lange, John
See Crichton, (John) Michael

Langer, Elinor 1939- .... **CLC 34**
See also CA 121

Langland, William 1330(?)-1400(?) ... **LC 19**
See also DA

Langstaff, Launcelot
See Irving, Washington

Lanier, Sidney 1842-1881 .... **NCLC 6**
See also DLB 64; MAICYA; SATA 18

Lanyer, Aemilia 1569-1645 .... **LC 10**

Lao Tzu .... **CMLC 7**

Lapine, James (Elliot) 1949-....... **CLC 39**
See also CA 123; 130

Larbaud, Valery (Nicolas)
1881-1957 .... **TCLC 9**
See also CA 106

Lardner, Ring
See Lardner, Ring(gold) W(ilmer)

Lardner, Ring W., Jr.
See Lardner, Ring(gold) W(ilmer)

Lardner, Ring(gold) W(ilmer)
1885-1933 .... **TCLC 2, 14**
See also CA 104; 131; CDALB 1917-1929;
DLB 11, 25, 86; MTCW

Laredo, Betty
See Codrescu, Andrei

Larkin, Maia
See Wojciechowska, Maia (Teresa)

Larkin, Philip (Arthur)
1922-1985 .... **CLC 3, 5, 8, 9, 13, 18, 33,**
39, 64
See also CA 5-8R; 117; CANR 24;
CDBLB 1960 to Present; DLB 27;
MTCW

Larra (y Sanchez de Castro), Mariano Jose de
1809-1837 .... **NCLC 17**

Larsen, Eric 1941- .... **CLC 55**
See also CA 132

Larsen, Nella 1891-1964 .... **CLC 37**
See also BLC 2; BW; CA 125; DLB 51

Larson, Charles R(aymond) 1938-... **CLC 31**
See also CA 53-56; CANR 4

Latham, Jean Lee 1902-........... **CLC 12**
See also AITN 1; CA 5-8R; CANR 7;
MAICYA; SATA 2, 68

Latham, Mavis
See Clark, Mavis Thorpe

Lathen, Emma .... **CLC 2**
See also Hennissart, Martha; Latsis, Mary
J(ane)

Lathrop, Francis
See Leiber, Fritz (Reuter, Jr.)

Latsis, Mary J(ane)
See Lathen, Emma
See also CA 85-88

Lattimore, Richmond (Alexander)
1906-1984 .... **CLC 3**
See also CA 1-4R; 112; CANR 1

Laughlin, James 1914-............ **CLC 49**
See also CA 21-24R; CANR 9; DLB 48

Laurence, (Jean) Margaret (Wemyss)
1926-1987 .. **CLC 3, 6, 13, 50, 62; SSC 7**
See also CA 5-8R; 121; CANR 33; DLB 53;
MTCW; SATA 50

Laurent, Antoine 1952- .... **CLC 50**

Lauscher, Hermann
See Hesse, Hermann

Lautreamont, Comte de
1846-1870 .... **NCLC 12**

Laverty, Donald
See Blish, James (Benjamin)

Lavin, Mary 1912-...... **CLC 4, 18; SSC 4**
See also CA 9-12R; CANR 33; DLB 15;
MTCW

Lavond, Paul Dennis
See Kornbluth, C(yril) M.; Pohl, Frederik

Lawler, Raymond Evenor 1922- .... **CLC 58**
See also CA 103

Lawrence, D(avid) H(erbert Richards)
1885-1930 .... **TCLC 2, 9, 16, 33, 48;**
SSC 4
See also CA 104; 121; CDBLB 1914-1945;
DA; DLB 10, 19, 36, 98; MTCW; WLC

Lawrence, T(homas) E(dward)
1888-1935 .... **TCLC 18**
See also Dale, Colin
See also CA 115

Lawrence Of Arabia
See Lawrence, T(homas) E(dward)

Lawson, Henry (Archibald Hertzberg)
1867-1922 .... **TCLC 27**
See also CA 120

Lawton, Dennis
  See Faust, Frederick (Schiller)

Laxness, Halldor .... **CLC 25**
  See also Gudjonsson, Halldor Kiljan

Layamon   fl. c. 1200- .... **CMLC 10**

Laye, Camara   1928-1980 .... **CLC 4, 38**
  See also BLC 2; BW; CA 85-88; 97-100;
  CANR 25; MTCW

Layton, Irving (Peter)   1912- ..... **CLC 2, 15**
  See also CA 1-4R; CANR 2, 33; DLB 88;
  MTCW

Lazarus, Emma   1849-1887 .... **NCLC 8**

Lazarus, Felix
  See Cable, George Washington

Lazarus, Henry
  See Slavitt, David R(ytman)

Lea, Joan
  See Neufeld, John (Arthur)

Leacock, Stephen (Butler)
  1869-1944 .... **TCLC 2**
  See also CA 104; DLB 92

Lear, Edward   1812-1888 .... **NCLC 3**
  See also CLR 1; DLB 32; MAICYA;
  SATA 18

Lear, Norman (Milton)   1922- ...... **CLC 12**
  See also CA 73-76

Leavis, F(rank) R(aymond)
  1895-1978 .... **CLC 24**
  See also CA 21-24R; 77-80; MTCW

Leavitt, David   1961- .... **CLC 34**
  See also CA 116; 122; DLB 130

Leblanc, Maurice (Marie Emile)
  1864-1941 .... **TCLC 49**
  See also CA 110

Lebowitz, Fran(ces Ann)
  1951(?)- .... **CLC 11, 36**
  See also CA 81-84; CANR 14; MTCW

le Carre, John .... **CLC 3, 5, 9, 15, 28**
  See also Cornwell, David (John Moore)
  See also BEST 89:4; CDBLB 1960 to
  Present; DLB 87

Le Clezio, J(ean) M(arie) G(ustave)
  1940- .... **CLC 31**
  See also CA 116; 128; DLB 83

Leconte de Lisle, Charles-Marie-Rene
  1818-1894 .... **NCLC 29**

Le Coq, Monsieur
  See Simenon, Georges (Jacques Christian)

Leduc, Violette   1907-1972 .... **CLC 22**
  See also CA 13-14; 33-36R; CAP 1

Ledwidge, Francis   1887(?)-1917 ... **TCLC 23**
  See also CA 123; DLB 20

Lee, Andrea   1953- .... **CLC 36**
  See also BLC 2; BW; CA 125

Lee, Andrew
  See Auchincloss, Louis (Stanton)

Lee, Don L. .... **CLC 2**
  See also Madhubuti, Haki R.

Lee, George W(ashington)
  1894-1976 .... **CLC 52**
  See also BLC 2; BW; CA 125; DLB 51

Lee, (Nelle) Harper   1926- ...... **CLC 12, 60**
  See also CA 13-16R; CDALB 1941-1968;
  DA; DLB 6; MTCW; SATA 11; WLC

Lee, Julian
  See Latham, Jean Lee

Lee, Lawrence   1903- .... **CLC 34**
  See also CA 25-28R

Lee, Manfred B(ennington)
  1905-1971 .... **CLC 11**
  See also Queen, Ellery
  See also CA 1-4R; 29-32R; CANR 2

Lee, Stan   1922- .... **CLC 17**
  See also AAYA 5; CA 108; 111

Lee, Tanith   1947- .... **CLC 46**
  See also CA 37-40R; SATA 8

Lee, Vernon .... **TCLC 5**
  See also Paget, Violet
  See also DLB 57

Lee, William
  See Burroughs, William S(eward)

Lee, Willy
  See Burroughs, William S(eward)

Lee-Hamilton, Eugene (Jacob)
  1845-1907 .... **TCLC 22**
  See also CA 117

Leet, Judith   1935- .... **CLC 11**

Le Fanu, Joseph Sheridan
  1814-1873 .... **NCLC 9**
  See also DLB 21, 70

Leffland, Ella   1931- .... **CLC 19**
  See also CA 29-32R; CANR 35; DLBY 84;
  SATA 65

Leger, (Marie-Rene) Alexis Saint-Leger
  1887-1975 .... **CLC 11**
  See also Perse, St.-John
  See also CA 13-16R; 61-64; MTCW

Leger, Saintleger
  See Leger, (Marie-Rene) Alexis Saint-Leger

Le Guin, Ursula K(roeber)
  1929- .... **CLC 8, 13, 22, 45, 71; SSC 12**
  See also AAYA 9; AITN 1; CA 21-24R;
  CANR 9, 32; CDALB 1968-1988; CLR 3,
  28; DLB 8, 52; MAICYA; MTCW;
  SATA 4, 52

Lehmann, Rosamond (Nina)
  1901-1990 .... **CLC 5**
  See also CA 77-80; 131; CANR 8; DLB 15

Leiber, Fritz (Reuter, Jr.)
  1910-1992 .... **CLC 25**
  See also CA 45-48; 139; CANR 2, 40;
  DLB 8; MTCW; SATA 45;
  SATA-Obit 73

Leimbach, Martha   1963-
  See Leimbach, Marti
  See also CA 130

Leimbach, Marti .... **CLC 65**
  See also Leimbach, Martha

Leino, Eino .... **TCLC 24**
  See also Loennbohm, Armas Eino Leopold

Leiris, Michel (Julien)   1901-1990 ... **CLC 61**
  See also CA 119; 128; 132

Leithauser, Brad   1953- .... **CLC 27**
  See also CA 107; CANR 27; DLB 120

Lelchuk, Alan   1938- .... **CLC 5**
  See also CA 45-48; CANR 1

Lem, Stanislaw   1921- .... **CLC 8, 15, 40**
  See also CA 105; CAAS 1; CANR 32;
  MTCW

Lemann, Nancy   1956- .... **CLC 39**
  See also CA 118; 136

Lemonnier, (Antoine Louis) Camille
  1844-1913 .... **TCLC 22**
  See also CA 121

Lenau, Nikolaus   1802-1850 ...... **NCLC 16**

L'Engle, Madeleine (Camp Franklin)
  1918- .... **CLC 12**
  See also AAYA 1; AITN 2; CA 1-4R;
  CANR 3, 21, 39; CLR 1, 14; DLB 52;
  MAICYA; MTCW; SAAS 15; SATA 1,
  27

Lengyel, Jozsef   1896-1975 .... **CLC 7**
  See also CA 85-88; 57-60

Lennon, John (Ono)
  1940-1980 .... **CLC 12, 35**
  See also CA 102

Lennox, Charlotte Ramsay
  1729(?)-1804 .... **NCLC 23**
  See also DLB 39

Lentricchia, Frank (Jr.)   1940- ...... **CLC 34**
  See also CA 25-28R; CANR 19

Lenz, Siegfried   1926- .... **CLC 27**
  See also CA 89-92; DLB 75

Leonard, Elmore (John, Jr.)
  1925- .... **CLC 28, 34, 71**
  See also AITN 1; BEST 89:1, 90:4;
  CA 81-84; CANR 12, 28; MTCW

Leonard, Hugh
  See Byrne, John Keyes
  See also DLB 13

**Leopardi, (Conte) Giacomo (Talegardo
  Francesco di Sales Save**
  1798-1837 .... **NCLC 22**

Le Reveler
  See Artaud, Antonin

Lerman, Eleanor   1952- .... **CLC 9**
  See also CA 85-88

Lerman, Rhoda   1936- .... **CLC 56**
  See also CA 49-52

Lermontov, Mikhail Yuryevich
  1814-1841 .... **NCLC 5**

Leroux, Gaston   1868-1927 .... **TCLC 25**
  See also CA 108; 136; SATA 65

Lesage, Alain-Rene   1668-1747 .... **LC 2**

Leskov, Nikolai (Semyonovich)
  1831-1895 .... **NCLC 25**

Lessing, Doris (May)
  1919- ..... **CLC 1, 2, 3, 6, 10, 15, 22, 40;
  SSC 6**
  See also CA 9-12R; CAAS 14; CANR 33;
  CDBLB 1960 to Present; DA; DLB 15;
  DLBY 85; MTCW

Lessing, Gotthold Ephraim
  1729-1781 .... **LC 8**
  See also DLB 97

Lester, Richard   1932- .... **CLC 20**

Lever, Charles (James)
  1806-1872 .... **NCLC 23**
  See also DLB 21

Leverson, Ada   1865(?)-1936(?) .... **TCLC 18**
  See also Elaine
  See also CA 117

Levertov, Denise
1923- ...... **CLC 1, 2, 3, 5, 8, 15, 28, 66**
See also CA 1-4R; CANR 3, 29; DLB 5;
MTCW

Levi, Jonathan .... **CLC 76**

Levi, Peter (Chad Tigar) 1931- ..... **CLC 41**
See also CA 5-8R; CANR 34; DLB 40

Levi, Primo
1919-1987 .... **CLC 37, 50; SSC 12**
See also CA 13-16R; 122; CANR 12, 33;
MTCW

Levin, Ira 1929- .... **CLC 3, 6**
See also CA 21-24R; CANR 17; MTCW;
SATA 66

Levin, Meyer 1905-1981 .... **CLC 7**
See also AITN 1; CA 9-12R; 104;
CANR 15; DLB 9, 28; DLBY 81;
SATA 21, 27

Levine, Norman 1924- .... **CLC 54**
See also CA 73-76; CANR 14; DLB 88

Levine, Philip 1928-.. **CLC 2, 4, 5, 9, 14, 33**
See also CA 9-12R; CANR 9, 37; DLB 5

Levinson, Deirdre 1931-........... **CLC 49**
See also CA 73-76

Levi-Strauss, Claude 1908- .... **CLC 38**
See also CA 1-4R; CANR 6, 32; MTCW

Levitin, Sonia (Wolff) 1934- .... **CLC 17**
See also CA 29-32R; CANR 14, 32;
MAICYA; SAAS 2; SATA 4, 68

Levon, O. U.
See Kesey, Ken (Elton)

Lewes, George Henry
1817-1878 .... **NCLC 25**
See also DLB 55

Lewis, Alun 1915-1944............ **TCLC 3**
See also CA 104; DLB 20

Lewis, C. Day
See Day Lewis, C(ecil)

Lewis, C(live) S(taples)
1898-1963 .... **CLC 1, 3, 6, 14, 27**
See also AAYA 3; CA 81-84; CANR 33;
CDBLB 1945-1960; CLR 3, 27; DA;
DLB 15, 100; MAICYA; MTCW;
SATA 13; WLC

Lewis, Janet 1899- .... **CLC 41**
See also Winters, Janet Lewis
See also CA 9-12R; CANR 29; CAP 1;
DLBY 87

Lewis, Matthew Gregory
1775-1818 .... **NCLC 11**
See also DLB 39

Lewis, (Harry) Sinclair
1885-1951 .... **TCLC 4, 13, 23, 39**
See also CA 104; 133; CDALB 1917-1929;
DA; DLB 9, 102; DLBD 1; MTCW;
WLC

Lewis, (Percy) Wyndham
1884(?)-1957 .... **TCLC 2, 9**
See also CA 104; DLB 15

Lewisohn, Ludwig 1883-1955...... **TCLC 19**
See also CA 107; DLB 4, 9, 28, 102

Lezama Lima, Jose 1910-1976 ... **CLC 4, 10**
See also CA 77-80; DLB 113; HW

L'Heureux, John (Clarke) 1934-.... **CLC 52**
See also CA 13-16R; CANR 23

Liddell, C. H.
See Kuttner, Henry

Lie, Jonas (Lauritz Idemil)
1833-1908(?) .... **TCLC 5**
See also CA 115

Lieber, Joel 1937-1971............. **CLC 6**
See also CA 73-76; 29-32R

Lieber, Stanley Martin
See Lee, Stan

Lieberman, Laurence (James)
1935- .... **CLC 4, 36**
See also CA 17-20R; CANR 8, 36

Lieksman, Anders
See Haavikko, Paavo Juhani

Li Fei-kan 1904-................. **CLC 18**
See also CA 105

Lifton, Robert Jay 1926-......... **CLC 67**
See also CA 17-20R; CANR 27; SATA 66

Lightfoot, Gordon 1938-.......... **CLC 26**
See also CA 109

Ligotti, Thomas 1953- .... **CLC 44**
See also CA 123

Liliencron, (Friedrich Adolf Axel) Detlev von
1844-1909 .... **TCLC 18**
See also CA 117

Lima, Jose Lezama
See Lezama Lima, Jose

Lima Barreto, Afonso Henrique de
1881-1922 .... **TCLC 23**
See also CA 117

Limonov, Eduard.................. **CLC 67**

Lin, Frank
See Atherton, Gertrude (Franklin Horn)

Lincoln, Abraham 1809-1865..... **NCLC 18**

Lind, Jakov .... **CLC 1, 2, 4, 27**
See also Landwirth, Heinz
See also CAAS 4

Lindsay, David 1878-1945........ **TCLC 15**
See also CA 113

Lindsay, (Nicholas) Vachel
1879-1931 .... **TCLC 17**
See also CA 114; 135; CDALB 1865-1917;
DA; DLB 54; SATA 40; WLC

Linke-Poot
See Doeblin, Alfred

Linney, Romulus 1930- .... **CLC 51**
See also CA 1-4R; CANR 40

Linton, Eliza Lynn 1822-1898.... **NCLC 41**
See also DLB 18

Li Po 701-763................. **CMLC 2**

Lipsius, Justus 1547-1606 .... **LC 16**

Lipsyte, Robert (Michael) 1938-.... **CLC 21**
See also AAYA 7; CA 17-20R; CANR 8;
CLR 23; DA; MAICYA; SATA 5, 68

Lish, Gordon (Jay) 1934-......... **CLC 45**
See also CA 113; 117; DLB 130

Lispector, Clarice 1925-1977....... **CLC 43**
See also CA 139; 116; DLB 113

Littell, Robert 1935(?)- .... **CLC 42**
See also CA 109; 112

Littlewit, Humphrey Gent.
See Lovecraft, H(oward) P(hillips)

Litwos
See Sienkiewicz, Henryk (Adam Alexander
Pius)

Liu E 1857-1909............... **TCLC 15**
See also CA 115

Lively, Penelope (Margaret)
1933- .... **CLC 32, 50**
See also CA 41-44R; CANR 29; CLR 7;
DLB 14; MAICYA; MTCW; SATA 7, 60

Livesay, Dorothy (Kathleen)
1909- .... **CLC 4, 15**
See also AITN 2; CA 25-28R; CAAS 8;
CANR 36; DLB 68; MTCW

Livy c. 59B.C.-c. 17 .... **CMLC 11**

Lizardi, Jose Joaquin Fernandez de
1776-1827 .... **NCLC 30**

Llewellyn, Richard .... **CLC 7**
See also Llewellyn Lloyd, Richard Dafydd
Vivian
See also DLB 15

Llewellyn Lloyd, Richard Dafydd Vivian
1906-1983
See Llewellyn, Richard
See also CA 53-56; 111; CANR 7;
SATA 11, 37

Llosa, (Jorge) Mario (Pedro) Vargas
See Vargas Llosa, (Jorge) Mario (Pedro)

Lloyd Webber, Andrew 1948-
See Webber, Andrew Lloyd
See also AAYA 1; CA 116; SATA 56

Locke, Alain (Le Roy)
1886-1954 .... **TCLC 43**
See also BW; CA 106; 124; DLB 51

Locke, John 1632-1704 .... **LC 7**
See also DLB 101

Locke-Elliott, Sumner
See Elliott, Sumner Locke

Lockhart, John Gibson
1794-1854 .... **NCLC 6**
See also DLB 110, 116

Lodge, David (John) 1935-......... **CLC 36**
See also BEST 90:1; CA 17-20R; CANR 19;
DLB 14; MTCW

Loennbohm, Armas Eino Leopold 1878-1926
See Leino, Eino
See also CA 123

Loewinsohn, Ron(ald William)
1937- .... **CLC 52**
See also CA 25-28R

Logan, Jake
See Smith, Martin Cruz

Logan, John (Burton) 1923-1987..... **CLC 5**
See also CA 77-80; 124; DLB 5

Lo Kuan-chung 1330(?)-1400(?)...... **LC 12**

Lombard, Nap
See Johnson, Pamela Hansford

London, Jack........ **TCLC 9, 15, 39; SSC 4**
See also London, John Griffith
See also AITN 2; CDALB 1865-1917;
DLB 8, 12, 78; SATA 18; WLC

London, John Griffith 1876-1916
See London, Jack
See also CA 110; 119; DA; MAICYA;
MTCW

Long, Emmett
See Leonard, Elmore (John, Jr.)

Longbaugh, Harry
See Goldman, William (W.)

Longfellow, Henry Wadsworth
1807-1882 . . . . NCLC 2
See also CDALB 1640-1865; DA; DLB 1,
59; SATA 19

Longley, Michael 1939- . . . . CLC 29
See also CA 102; DLB 40

Longus fl. c. 2nd cent. - . . . . CMLC 7

Longway, A. Hugh
See Lang, Andrew

Lopate, Phillip 1943- . . . . CLC 29
See also CA 97-100; DLBY 80

Lopez Portillo (y Pacheco), Jose
1920- . . . . CLC 46
See also CA 129; HW

Lopez y Fuentes, Gregorio
1897(?)-1966 . . . . CLC 32
See also CA 131; HW

Lorca, Federico Garcia
See Garcia Lorca, Federico

Lord, Bette Bao 1938- . . . . CLC 23
See also BEST 90:3; CA 107; CANR 41;
SATA 58

Lord Auch
See Bataille, Georges

Lord Byron
See Byron, George Gordon (Noel)

Lord Dunsany . . . . TCLC 2
See also Dunsany, Edward John Moreton
Drax Plunkett

Lorde, Audre (Geraldine)
1934- . . . . CLC 18, 71
See also BLC 2; BW; CA 25-28R;
CANR 16, 26; DLB 41; MTCW

Lord Jeffrey
See Jeffrey, Francis

Lorenzo, Heberto Padilla
See Padilla (Lorenzo), Heberto

Loris
See Hofmannsthal, Hugo von

Loti, Pierre . . . . TCLC 11
See also Viaud, (Louis Marie) Julien
See also DLB 123

Louie, David Wong 1954- . . . . CLC 70
See also CA 139

Louis, Father M.
See Merton, Thomas

Lovecraft, H(oward) P(hillips)
1890-1937 . . . . TCLC 4, 22; SSC 3
See also CA 104; 133; MTCW

Lovelace, Earl 1935- . . . . CLC 51
See also CA 77-80; CANR 41; DLB 125;
MTCW

Lowell, Amy 1874-1925 . . . . TCLC 1, 8
See also CA 104; DLB 54

Lowell, James Russell 1819-1891 . . NCLC 2
See also CDALB 1640-1865; DLB 1, 11, 64,
79

Lowell, Robert (Traill Spence, Jr.)
1917-1977 . . . CLC 1, 2, 3, 4, 5, 8, 9, 11,
15, 37; PC 3
See also CA 9-12R; 73-76; CABS 2;
CANR 26; DA; DLB 5; MTCW; WLC

Lowndes, Marie Adelaide (Belloc)
1868-1947 . . . . TCLC 12
See also CA 107; DLB 70

Lowry, (Clarence) Malcolm
1909-1957 . . . . TCLC 6, 40
See also CA 105; 131; CDBLB 1945-1960;
DLB 15; MTCW

Lowry, Mina Gertrude 1882-1966
See Loy, Mina
See also CA 113

Loxsmith, John
See Brunner, John (Kilian Houston)

Loy, Mina . . . . CLC 28
See also Lowry, Mina Gertrude
See also DLB 4, 54

Loyson-Bridet
See Schwob, (Mayer Andre) Marcel

Lucas, Craig 1951- . . . . CLC 64
See also CA 137

Lucas, George 1944- . . . . CLC 16
See also AAYA 1; CA 77-80; CANR 30;
SATA 56

Lucas, Hans
See Godard, Jean-Luc

Lucas, Victoria
See Plath, Sylvia

Ludlam, Charles 1943-1987 . . . . . CLC 46, 50
See also CA 85-88; 122

Ludlum, Robert 1927- . . . . CLC 22, 43
See also AAYA 10; BEST 89:1, 90:3;
CA 33-36R; CANR 25, 41; DLBY 82;
MTCW

Ludwig, Ken . . . . CLC 60

Ludwig, Otto 1813-1865 . . . . NCLC 4
See also DLB 129

Lugones, Leopoldo 1874-1938 . . . . . TCLC 15
See also CA 116; 131; HW

Lu Hsun 1881-1936 . . . . TCLC 3

Lukacs, George . . . . CLC 24
See also Lukacs, Gyorgy (Szegeny von)

Lukacs, Gyorgy (Szegeny von) 1885-1971
See Lukacs, George
See also CA 101; 29-32R

Luke, Peter (Ambrose Cyprian)
1919- . . . . CLC 38
See also CA 81-84; DLB 13

Lunar, Dennis
See Mungo, Raymond

Lurie, Alison 1926- . . . . CLC 4, 5, 18, 39
See also CA 1-4R; CANR 2, 17; DLB 2;
MTCW; SATA 46

Lustig, Arnost 1926- . . . . CLC 56
See also AAYA 3; CA 69-72; SATA 56

Luther, Martin 1483-1546 . . . . LC 9

Luzi, Mario 1914- . . . . CLC 13
See also CA 61-64; CANR 9; DLB 128

Lynch, B. Suarez
See Bioy Casares, Adolfo; Borges, Jorge
Luis

Lynch, David (K.) 1946- . . . . CLC 66
See also CA 124; 129

Lynch, James
See Andreyev, Leonid (Nikolaevich)

Lynch Davis, B.
See Bioy Casares, Adolfo; Borges, Jorge
Luis

Lyndsay, Sir David 1490-1555 . . . . . . LC 20

Lynn, Kenneth S(chuyler) 1923- . . . . CLC 50
See also CA 1-4R; CANR 3, 27

Lynx
See West, Rebecca

Lyons, Marcus
See Blish, James (Benjamin)

Lyre, Pinchbeck
See Sassoon, Siegfried (Lorraine)

Lytle, Andrew (Nelson) 1902- . . . . . . CLC 22
See also CA 9-12R; DLB 6

Lyttelton, George 1709-1773 . . . . LC 10

Maas, Peter 1929- . . . . CLC 29
See also CA 93-96

Macaulay, Rose 1881-1958 . . . . . TCLC 7, 44
See also CA 104; DLB 36

MacBeth, George (Mann)
1932-1992 . . . . CLC 2, 5, 9
See also CA 25-28R; 136; DLB 40; MTCW;
SATA 4; SATA-Obit 70

MacCaig, Norman (Alexander)
1910- . . . . CLC 36
See also CA 9-12R; CANR 3, 34; DLB 27

MacCarthy, (Sir Charles Otto) Desmond
1877-1952 . . . . TCLC 36

MacDiarmid, Hugh . . . . . CLC 2, 4, 11, 19, 63
See also Grieve, C(hristopher) M(urray)
See also CDBLB 1945-1960; DLB 20

MacDonald, Anson
See Heinlein, Robert A(nson)

Macdonald, Cynthia 1928- . . . . . . CLC 13, 19
See also CA 49-52; CANR 4; DLB 105

MacDonald, George 1824-1905 . . . . . TCLC 9
See also CA 106; 137; DLB 18; MAICYA;
SATA 33

Macdonald, John
See Millar, Kenneth

MacDonald, John D(ann)
1916-1986 . . . . CLC 3, 27, 44
See also CA 1-4R; 121; CANR 1, 19;
DLB 8; DLBY 86; MTCW

Macdonald, John Ross
See Millar, Kenneth

Macdonald, Ross . . . . . CLC 1, 2, 3, 14, 34, 41
See also Millar, Kenneth
See also DLBD 6

MacDougal, John
See Blish, James (Benjamin)

MacEwen, Gwendolyn (Margaret)
1941-1987 . . . . CLC 13, 55
See also CA 9-12R; 124; CANR 7, 22;
DLB 53; SATA 50, 55

Machado (y Ruiz), Antonio
1875-1939 . . . . TCLC 3
See also CA 104; DLB 108

Machado de Assis, Joaquim Maria
 1839-1908 .... **TCLC 10**
 See also BLC 2; CA 107

Machen, Arthur .... **TCLC 4**
 See also Jones, Arthur Llewellyn
 See also DLB 36

Machiavelli, Niccolo 1469-1527 ...... **LC 8**
 See also DA

MacInnes, Colin 1914-1976 ...... **CLC 4, 23**
 See also CA 69-72; 65-68; CANR 21;
 DLB 14; MTCW

MacInnes, Helen (Clark)
 1907-1985 .... **CLC 27, 39**
 See also CA 1-4R; 117; CANR 1, 28;
 DLB 87; MTCW; SATA 22, 44

Mackay, Mary 1855-1924
 See Corelli, Marie
 See also CA 118

Mackenzie, Compton (Edward Montague)
 1883-1972 .... **CLC 18**
 See also CA 21-22; 37-40R; CAP 2;
 DLB 34, 100

Mackenzie, Henry 1745-1831 .... **NCLC 41**
 See also DLB 39

Mackintosh, Elizabeth 1896(?)-1952
 See Tey, Josephine
 See also CA 110

MacLaren, James
 See Grieve, C(hristopher) M(urray)

Mac Laverty, Bernard 1942- .... **CLC 31**
 See also CA 116; 118

MacLean, Alistair (Stuart)
 1922-1987 .... **CLC 3, 13, 50, 63**
 See also CA 57-60; 121; CANR 28; MTCW;
 SATA 23, 50

MacLeish, Archibald
 1892-1982 .... **CLC 3, 8, 14, 68**
 See also CA 9-12R; 106; CANR 33; DLB 4,
 7, 45; DLBY 82; MTCW

MacLennan, (John) Hugh
 1907- .... **CLC 2, 14**
 See also CA 5-8R; CANR 33; DLB 68;
 MTCW

MacLeod, Alistair 1936- .... **CLC 56**
 See also CA 123; DLB 60

MacNeice, (Frederick) Louis
 1907-1963 .... **CLC 1, 4, 10, 53**
 See also CA 85-88; DLB 10, 20; MTCW

MacNeill, Dand
 See Fraser, George MacDonald

Macpherson, (Jean) Jay 1931- ...... **CLC 14**
 See also CA 5-8R; DLB 53

MacShane, Frank 1927- .... **CLC 39**
 See also CA 9-12R; CANR 3, 33; DLB 111

Macumber, Mari
 See Sandoz, Mari(e Susette)

Madach, Imre 1823-1864 .... **NCLC 19**

Madden, (Jerry) David 1933- .... **CLC 5, 15**
 See also CA 1-4R; CAAS 3; CANR 4;
 DLB 6; MTCW

Maddern, Al(an)
 See Ellison, Harlan

Madhubuti, Haki R.
 1942- .... **CLC 6, 73; PC 5**
 See also Lee, Don L.
 See also BLC 2; BW; CA 73-76; CANR 24;
 DLB 5, 41; DLBD 8

Madow, Pauline (Reichberg) .... **CLC 1**
 See also CA 9-12R

Maepenn, Hugh
 See Kuttner, Henry

Maepenn, K. H.
 See Kuttner, Henry

Maeterlinck, Maurice 1862-1949 ... **TCLC 3**
 See also CA 104; 136; SATA 66

Maginn, William 1794-1842 ...... **NCLC 8**
 See also DLB 110

Mahapatra, Jayanta 1928- .... **CLC 33**
 See also CA 73-76; CAAS 9; CANR 15, 33

Mahfouz, Naguib (Abdel Aziz Al-Sabilgi)
 1911(?)-
 See Mahfuz, Najib
 See also BEST 89:2; CA 128; MTCW

Mahfuz, Najib .... **CLC 52, 55**
 See also Mahfouz, Naguib (Abdel Aziz
 Al-Sabilgi)
 See also DLBY 88

Mahon, Derek 1941- .... **CLC 27**
 See also CA 113; 128; DLB 40

Mailer, Norman
 1923- ...... **CLC 1, 2, 3, 4, 5, 8, 11, 14,**
           28, 39, 74
 See also AITN 2; CA 9-12R; CABS 1;
 CANR 28; CDALB 1968-1988; DA;
 DLB 2, 16, 28; DLBD 3; DLBY 80, 83;
 MTCW

Maillet, Antonine 1929- .... **CLC 54**
 See also CA 115; 120; DLB 60

Mais, Roger 1905-1955 .... **TCLC 8**
 See also BW; CA 105; 124; DLB 125;
 MTCW

Maitland, Sara (Louise) 1950- ...... **CLC 49**
 See also CA 69-72; CANR 13

Major, Clarence 1936- .... **CLC 3, 19, 48**
 See also BLC 2; BW; CA 21-24R; CAAS 6;
 CANR 13, 25; DLB 33

Major, Kevin (Gerald) 1949- .... **CLC 26**
 See also CA 97-100; CANR 21, 38;
 CLR 11; DLB 60; MAICYA; SATA 32

Maki, James
 See Ozu, Yasujiro

Malabaila, Damiano
 See Levi, Primo

Malamud, Bernard
 1914-1986 ..... **CLC 1, 2, 3, 5, 8, 9, 11,**
        18, 27, 44, 78
 See also CA 5-8R; 118; CABS 1; CANR 28;
 CDALB 1941-1968; DA; DLB 2, 28;
 DLBY 80, 86; MTCW; WLC

Malcolm, Dan
 See Silverberg, Robert

Malherbe, Francois de 1555-1628 ..... **LC 5**

Mallarme, Stephane
 1842-1898 .... **NCLC 4, 41; PC 4**

Mallet-Joris, Francoise 1930- ...... **CLC 11**
 See also CA 65-68; CANR 17; DLB 83

Malley, Ern
 See McAuley, James Phillip

Mallowan, Agatha Christie
 See Christie, Agatha (Mary Clarissa)

Maloff, Saul 1922- .... **CLC 5**
 See also CA 33-36R

Malone, Louis
 See MacNeice, (Frederick) Louis

Malone, Michael (Christopher)
 1942- .... **CLC 43**
 See also CA 77-80; CANR 14, 32

Malory, (Sir) Thomas
 1410(?)-1471(?) .... **LC 11**
 See also CDBLB Before 1660; DA;
 SATA 33, 59

Malouf, (George Joseph) David
 1934- .... **CLC 28**
 See also CA 124

Malraux, (Georges-)Andre
 1901-1976 ...... **CLC 1, 4, 9, 13, 15, 57**
 See also CA 21-22; 69-72; CANR 34;
 CAP 2; DLB 72; MTCW

Malzberg, Barry N(athaniel) 1939-... **CLC 7**
 See also CA 61-64; CAAS 4; CANR 16;
 DLB 8

Mamet, David (Alan)
 1947- .... **CLC 9, 15, 34, 46**
 See also AAYA 3; CA 81-84; CABS 3;
 CANR 15, 41; DLB 7; MTCW

Mamoulian, Rouben (Zachary)
 1897-1987 .... **CLC 16**
 See also CA 25-28R; 124

Mandelstam, Osip (Emilievich)
 1891(?)-1938(?) .... **TCLC 2, 6**
 See also CA 104

Mander, (Mary) Jane 1877-1949... **TCLC 31**

Mandiargues, Andre Pieyre de .... **CLC 41**
 See also Pieyre de Mandiargues, Andre
 See also DLB 83

Mandrake, Ethel Belle
 See Thurman, Wallace (Henry)

Mangan, James Clarence
 1803-1849 .... **NCLC 27**

Maniere, J.-E.
 See Giraudoux, (Hippolyte) Jean

Manley, (Mary) Delariviere
 1672(?)-1724 .... **LC 1**
 See also DLB 39, 80

Mann, Abel
 See Creasey, John

Mann, (Luiz) Heinrich 1871-1950... **TCLC 9**
 See also CA 106; DLB 66

Mann, (Paul) Thomas
 1875-1955 .... **TCLC 2, 8, 14, 21, 35, 44;**
              SSC 5
 See also CA 104; 128; DA; DLB 66;
 MTCW; WLC

Manning, David
 See Faust, Frederick (Schiller)

Manning, Frederic 1887(?)-1935 ... **TCLC 25**
 See also CA 124

Manning, Olivia 1915-1980 ...... **CLC 5, 19**
 See also CA 5-8R; 101; CANR 29; MTCW

Matute (Ausejo), Ana Maria
1925- .... CLC 11
See also CA 89-92; MTCW

Maugham, W. S.
See Maugham, W(illiam) Somerset

Maugham, W(illiam) Somerset
1874-1965 .... CLC 1, 11, 15, 67; SSC 8
See also CA 5-8R; 25-28R; CANR 40;
CDBLB 1914-1945; DA; DLB 10, 36, 77,
100; MTCW; SATA 54; WLC

Maugham, William Somerset
See Maugham, W(illiam) Somerset

Maupassant, (Henri Rene Albert) Guy de
1850-1893 .... NCLC 1; SSC 1
See also DA; DLB 123; WLC

Maurhut, Richard
See Traven, B.

Mauriac, Claude 1914- .... CLC 9
See also CA 89-92; DLB 83

Mauriac, Francois (Charles)
1885-1970 .... CLC 4, 9, 56
See also CA 25-28; CAP 2; DLB 65;
MTCW

Mavor, Osborne Henry 1888-1951
See Bridie, James
See also CA 104

Maxwell, William (Keepers, Jr.)
1908- .... CLC 19
See also CA 93-96; DLBY 80

May, Elaine 1932- .... CLC 16
See also CA 124; DLB 44

Mayakovski, Vladimir (Vladimirovich)
1893-1930 .... TCLC 4, 18
See also CA 104

Mayhew, Henry 1812-1887 ...... NCLC 31
See also DLB 18, 55

Maynard, Joyce 1953- .... CLC 23
See also CA 111; 129

Mayne, William (James Carter)
1928- .... CLC 12
See also CA 9-12R; CANR 37; CLR 25;
MAICYA; SAAS 11; SATA 6, 68

Mayo, Jim
See L'Amour, Louis (Dearborn)

Maysles, Albert 1926- .... CLC 16
See also CA 29-32R

Maysles, David 1932- .... CLC 16

Mazer, Norma Fox 1931- .... CLC 26
See also AAYA 5; CA 69-72; CANR 12,
32; CLR 23; MAICYA; SAAS 1;
SATA 24, 67

Mazzini, Guiseppe 1805-1872 .... NCLC 34

McAuley, James Phillip
1917-1976 .... CLC 45
See also CA 97-100

McBain, Ed
See Hunter, Evan

McBrien, William Augustine
1930- .... CLC 44
See also CA 107

McCaffrey, Anne (Inez) 1926- ...... CLC 17
See also AAYA 6; AITN 2; BEST 89:2;
CA 25-28R; CANR 15, 35; DLB 8;
MAICYA; MTCW; SAAS 11; SATA 8,
70

McCann, Arthur
See Campbell, John W(ood, Jr.)

McCann, Edson
See Pohl, Frederik

McCarthy, Cormac 1933- .... CLC 4, 57
See also CA 13-16R; CANR 10; DLB 6

McCarthy, Mary (Therese)
1912-1989 ... CLC 1, 3, 5, 14, 24, 39, 59
See also CA 5-8R; 129; CANR 16; DLB 2;
DLBY 81; MTCW

McCartney, (James) Paul
1942- .... CLC 12, 35

McCauley, Stephen 19(?)- .... CLC 50

McClure, Michael (Thomas)
1932- .... CLC 6, 10
See also CA 21-24R; CANR 17; DLB 16

McCorkle, Jill (Collins) 1958- ...... CLC 51
See also CA 121; DLBY 87

McCourt, James 1941- .... CLC 5
See also CA 57-60

McCoy, Horace (Stanley)
1897-1955 .... TCLC 28
See also CA 108; DLB 9

McCrae, John 1872-1918 .... TCLC 12
See also CA 109; DLB 92

McCreigh, James
See Pohl, Frederik

McCullers, (Lula) Carson (Smith)
1917-1967 .. CLC 1, 4, 10, 12, 48; SSC 9
See also CA 5-8R; 25-28R; CABS 1, 3;
CANR 18; CDALB 1941-1968; DA;
DLB 2, 7; MTCW; SATA 27; WLC

McCulloch, John Tyler
See Burroughs, Edgar Rice

McCullough, Colleen 1938(?)- ...... CLC 27
See also CA 81-84; CANR 17; MTCW

McElroy, Joseph 1930- .... CLC 5, 47
See also CA 17-20R

McEwan, Ian (Russell) 1948- ... CLC 13, 66
See also BEST 90:4; CA 61-64; CANR 14,
41; DLB 14; MTCW

McFadden, David 1940- .... CLC 48
See also CA 104; DLB 60

McFarland, Dennis 1950- .... CLC 65

McGahern, John 1934- .... CLC 5, 9, 48
See also CA 17-20R; CANR 29; DLB 14;
MTCW

McGinley, Patrick (Anthony)
1937- .... CLC 41
See also CA 120; 127

McGinley, Phyllis 1905-1978 ...... CLC 14
See also CA 9-12R; 77-80; CANR 19;
DLB 11, 48; SATA 2, 24, 44

McGinniss, Joe 1942- .... CLC 32
See also AITN 2; BEST 89:2; CA 25-28R;
CANR 26

McGivern, Maureen Daly
See Daly, Maureen

McGrath, Patrick 1950- .... CLC 55
See also CA 136

McGrath, Thomas (Matthew)
1916-1990 .... CLC 28, 59
See also CA 9-12R; 132; CANR 6, 33;
MTCW; SATA 41; SATA-Obit 66

McGuane, Thomas (Francis III)
1939- .... CLC 3, 7, 18, 45
See also AITN 2; CA 49-52; CANR 5, 24;
DLB 2; DLBY 80; MTCW

McGuckian, Medbh 1950- .... CLC 48
See also DLB 40

McHale, Tom 1942(?)-1982 .... CLC 3, 5
See also AITN 1; CA 77-80; 106

McIlvanney, William 1936- .... CLC 42
See also CA 25-28R; DLB 14

McIlwraith, Maureen Mollie Hunter
See Hunter, Mollie
See also SATA 2

McInerney, Jay 1955- .... CLC 34
See also CA 116; 123

McIntyre, Vonda N(eel) 1948- ..... CLC 18
See also CA 81-84; CANR 17, 34; MTCW

McKay, Claude .... TCLC 7, 41; PC 2
See also McKay, Festus Claudius
See also BLC 3; DLB 4, 45, 51, 117

McKay, Festus Claudius 1889-1948
See McKay, Claude
See also BW; CA 104; 124; DA; MTCW;
WLC

McKuen, Rod 1933- .... CLC 1, 3
See also AITN 1; CA 41-44R; CANR 40

McLoughlin, R. B.
See Mencken, H(enry) L(ouis)

McLuhan, (Herbert) Marshall
1911-1980 .... CLC 37
See also CA 9-12R; 102; CANR 12, 34;
DLB 88; MTCW

McMillan, Terry (L.) 1951- ..... CLC 50, 61
See also CA 140

McMurtry, Larry (Jeff)
1936- .... CLC 2, 3, 7, 11, 27, 44
See also AITN 2; BEST 89:2; CA 5-8R;
CANR 19; CDALB 1968-1988; DLB 2;
DLBY 80, 87; MTCW

McNally, Terrence 1939- ...... CLC 4, 7, 41
See also CA 45-48; CANR 2; DLB 7

McNamer, Deirdre 1950- .... CLC 70

McNeile, Herman Cyril 1888-1937
See Sapper
See also DLB 77

McPhee, John (Angus) 1931- ...... CLC 36
See also BEST 90:1; CA 65-68; CANR 20;
MTCW

McPherson, James Alan
1943- .... CLC 19, 77
See also BW; CA 25-28R; CAAS 17;
CANR 24; DLB 38; MTCW

McPherson, William (Alexander)
1933- .... CLC 34
See also CA 69-72; CANR 28

McSweeney, Kerry .... CLC 34

Mead, Margaret 1901-1978 .... CLC 37
See also AITN 1; CA 1-4R; 81-84;
CANR 4; MTCW; SATA 20

Meaker, Marijane (Agnes) 1927-
See Kerr, M. E.
See also CA 107; CANR 37; MAICYA;
MTCW; SATA 20, 61

Mitchell, James Leslie 1901-1935
See Gibbon, Lewis Grassic
See also CA 104; DLB 15

Mitchell, Joni 1943-.............. **CLC 12**
See also CA 112

Mitchell, Margaret (Munnerlyn)
1900-1949 .... **TCLC 11**
See also CA 109; 125; DLB 9; MTCW

Mitchell, Peggy
See Mitchell, Margaret (Munnerlyn)

Mitchell, S(ilas) Weir 1829-1914 .. **TCLC 36**

Mitchell, W(illiam) O(rmond)
1914- .... **CLC 25**
See also CA 77-80; CANR 15; DLB 88

Mitford, Mary Russell 1787-1855.. **NCLC 4**
See also DLB 110, 116

Mitford, Nancy 1904-1973........ **CLC 44**
See also CA 9-12R

Miyamoto, Yuriko 1899-1951 ..... **TCLC 37**

Mo, Timothy (Peter) 1950(?)-...... **CLC 46**
See also CA 117; MTCW

Modarressi, Taghi (M.) 1931-...... **CLC 44**
See also CA 121; 134

Modiano, Patrick (Jean) 1945-..... **CLC 18**
See also CA 85-88; CANR 17, 40; DLB 83

Moerck, Paal
See Roelvaag, O(le) E(dvart)

Mofolo, Thomas (Mokopu)
1875(?)-1948 .... **TCLC 22**
See also BLC 3; CA 121

Mohr, Nicholasa 1935-............ **CLC 12**
See also AAYA 8; CA 49-52; CANR 1, 32;
CLR 22; HW; SAAS 8; SATA 8

Mojtabai, A(nn) G(race)
1938- .... **CLC 5, 9, 15, 29**
See also CA 85-88

Moliere 1622-1673 .... **LC 10**
See also DA; WLC

Molin, Charles
See Mayne, William (James Carter)

Molnar, Ferenc 1878-1952........ **TCLC 20**
See also CA 109

Momaday, N(avarre) Scott
1934- .... **CLC 2, 19**
See also CA 25-28R; CANR 14, 34; DA;
MTCW; SATA 30, 48

Monroe, Harriet 1860-1936....... **TCLC 12**
See also CA 109; DLB 54, 91

Monroe, Lyle
See Heinlein, Robert A(nson)

Montagu, Elizabeth 1917- .... **NCLC 7**
See also CA 9-12R

Montagu, Mary (Pierrepont) Wortley
1689-1762 .... **LC 9**
See also DLB 95, 101

Montagu, W. H.
See Coleridge, Samuel Taylor

Montague, John (Patrick)
1929- .... **CLC 13, 46**
See also CA 9-12R; CANR 9; DLB 40;
MTCW

Montaigne, Michel (Eyquem) de
1533-1592 .... **LC 8**
See also DA; WLC

Montale, Eugenio 1896-1981... **CLC 7, 9, 18**
See also CA 17-20R; 104; CANR 30;
DLB 114; MTCW

Montesquieu, Charles-Louis de Secondat
1689-1755 .... **LC 7**

Montgomery, (Robert) Bruce 1921-1978
See Crispin, Edmund
See also CA 104

Montgomery, L(ucy) M(aud)
1874-1942 .... **TCLC 51**
See also CA 108; 137; CLR 8; DLB 92;
MAICYA; YABC 1

Montgomery, Marion H., Jr. 1925-.. **CLC 7**
See also AITN 1; CA 1-4R; CANR 3;
DLB 6

Montgomery, Max
See Davenport, Guy (Mattison, Jr.)

Montherlant, Henry (Milon) de
1896-1972 .... **CLC 8, 19**
See also CA 85-88; 37-40R; DLB 72;
MTCW

Monty Python .... **CLC 21**
See also Chapman, Graham; Cleese, John
(Marwood); Gilliam, Terry (Vance); Idle,
Eric; Jones, Terence Graham Parry; Palin,
Michael (Edward)
See also AAYA 7

Moodie, Susanna (Strickland)
1803-1885 .... **NCLC 14**
See also DLB 99

Mooney, Edward 1951- .... **CLC 25**
See also CA 130

Mooney, Ted
See Mooney, Edward

Moorcock, Michael (John)
1939- .... **CLC 5, 27, 58**
See also CA 45-48; CAAS 5; CANR 2, 17,
38; DLB 14; MTCW

Moore, Brian
1921-......... **CLC 1, 3, 5, 7, 8, 19, 32**
See also CA 1-4R; CANR 1, 25; MTCW

Moore, Edward
See Muir, Edwin

Moore, George Augustus
1852-1933 .... **TCLC 7**
See also CA 104; DLB 10, 18, 57

Moore, Lorrie .... **CLC 39, 45, 68**
See also Moore, Marie Lorena

Moore, Marianne (Craig)
1887-1972 .... **CLC 1, 2, 4, 8, 10, 13, 19,**
47; PC 4
See also CA 1-4R; 33-36R; CANR 3;
CDALB 1929-1941; DA; DLB 45;
DLBD 7; MTCW; SATA 20

Moore, Marie Lorena 1957-
See Moore, Lorrie
See also CA 116; CANR 39

Moore, Thomas 1779-1852....... **NCLC 6**
See also DLB 96

Morand, Paul 1888-1976.......... **CLC 41**
See also CA 69-72; DLB 65

Morante, Elsa 1918-1985........ **CLC 8, 47**
See also CA 85-88; 117; CANR 35; MTCW

Moravia, Alberto....... **CLC 2, 7, 11, 27, 46**
See also Pincherle, Alberto

More, Hannah 1745-1833 .... **NCLC 27**
See also DLB 107, 109, 116

More, Henry 1614-1687............. **LC 9**
See also DLB 126

More, Sir Thomas 1478-1535 .... **LC 10**

Moreas, Jean.................... **TCLC 18**
See also Papadiamantopoulos, Johannes

Morgan, Berry 1919-............. **CLC 6**
See also CA 49-52; DLB 6

Morgan, Claire
See Highsmith, (Mary) Patricia

Morgan, Edwin (George) 1920-..... **CLC 31**
See also CA 5-8R; CANR 3; DLB 27

Morgan, (George) Frederick
1922-...................... **CLC 23**
See also CA 17-20R; CANR 21

Morgan, Harriet
See Mencken, H(enry) L(ouis)

Morgan, Jane
See Cooper, James Fenimore

Morgan, Janet 1945- .... **CLC 39**
See also CA 65-68

Morgan, Lady 1776(?)-1859...... **NCLC 29**
See also DLB 116

Morgan, Robin 1941-............. **CLC 2**
See also CA 69-72; CANR 29; MTCW

Morgan, Scott
See Kuttner, Henry

Morgan, Seth 1949(?)-1990 .... **CLC 65**
See also CA 132

Morgenstern, Christian
1871-1914 .... **TCLC 8**
See also CA 105

Morgenstern, S.
See Goldman, William (W.)

Moricz, Zsigmond 1879-1942 ..... **TCLC 33**

Morike, Eduard (Friedrich)
1804-1875 .... **NCLC 10**

Mori Ogai .... **TCLC 14**
See also Mori Rintaro

Mori Rintaro 1862-1922
See Mori Ogai
See also CA 110

Moritz, Karl Philipp 1756-1793 ...... **LC 2**
See also DLB 94

Morland, Peter Henry
See Faust, Frederick (Schiller)

Morren, Theophil
See Hofmannsthal, Hugo von

Morris, Bill 1952-................ **CLC 76**

Morris, Julian
See West, Morris L(anglo)

Morris, Steveland Judkins 1950(?)-
See Wonder, Stevie
See also CA 111

Morris, William 1834-1896 .... **NCLC 4**
See also CDBLB 1832-1890; DLB 18, 35, 57

Morris, Wright 1910-... **CLC 1, 3, 7, 18, 37**
See also CA 9-12R; CANR 21; DLB 2;
DLBY 81; MTCW

Morrison, Chloe Anthony Wofford
See Morrison, Toni

Morrison, James Douglas 1943-1971
See Morrison, Jim
See also CA 73-76; CANR 40

Morrison, Jim . . . . **CLC 17**
See also Morrison, James Douglas

Morrison, Toni 1931- . . . . . **CLC 4, 10, 22, 55**
See also AAYA 1; BLC 3; BW; CA 29-32R;
CANR 27; CDALB 1968-1988; DA;
DLB 6, 33; DLBY 81; MTCW; SATA 57

Morrison, Van 1945- . . . . **CLC 21**
See also CA 116

Mortimer, John (Clifford)
1923- . . . . **CLC 28, 43**
See also CA 13-16R; CANR 21;
CDBLB 1960 to Present; DLB 13;
MTCW

Mortimer, Penelope (Ruth) 1918- . . . . **CLC 5**
See also CA 57-60

Morton, Anthony
See Creasey, John

Mosher, Howard Frank 1943- . . . . . . **CLC 62**
See also CA 139

Mosley, Nicholas 1923- . . . . **CLC 43, 70**
See also CA 69-72; CANR 41; DLB 14

Moss, Howard
1922-1987 . . . . **CLC 7, 14, 45, 50**
See also CA 1-4R; 123; CANR 1; DLB 5

Mossgiel, Rab
See Burns, Robert

Motion, Andrew 1952- . . . . **CLC 47**
See also DLB 40

Motley, Willard (Francis)
1912-1965 . . . . **CLC 18**
See also BW; CA 117; 106; DLB 76

Mott, Michael (Charles Alston)
1930- . . . . **CLC 15, 34**
See also CA 5-8R; CAAS 7; CANR 7, 29

Mowat, Farley (McGill) 1921- . . . . . **CLC 26**
See also AAYA 1; CA 1-4R; CANR 4, 24;
CLR 20; DLB 68; MAICYA; MTCW;
SATA 3, 55

Moyers, Bill 1934- . . . . **CLC 74**
See also AITN 2; CA 61-64; CANR 31

Mphahlele, Es'kia
See Mphahlele, Ezekiel
See also DLB 125

Mphahlele, Ezekiel 1919- . . . . **CLC 25**
See also Mphahlele, Es'kia
See also BLC 3; BW; CA 81-84; CANR 26

Mqhayi, S(amuel) E(dward) K(rune Loliwe)
1875-1945 . . . . **TCLC 25**
See also BLC 3

Mr. Martin
See Burroughs, William S(eward)

Mrozek, Slawomir 1930- . . . . **CLC 3, 13**
See also CA 13-16R; CAAS 10; CANR 29;
MTCW

Mrs. Belloc-Lowndes
See Lowndes, Marie Adelaide (Belloc)

Mtwa, Percy (?)- . . . . **CLC 47**

Mueller, Lisel 1924- . . . . **CLC 13, 51**
See also CA 93-96; DLB 105

Muir, Edwin 1887-1959 . . . . **TCLC 2**
See also CA 104; DLB 20, 100

Muir, John 1838-1914 . . . . **TCLC 28**

Mujica Lainez, Manuel
1910-1984 . . . . **CLC 31**
See also Lainez, Manuel Mujica
See also CA 81-84; 112; CANR 32; HW

Mukherjee, Bharati 1940- . . . . **CLC 53**
See also BEST 89:2; CA 107; DLB 60;
MTCW

Muldoon, Paul 1951- . . . . **CLC 32, 72**
See also CA 113; 129; DLB 40

Mulisch, Harry 1927- . . . . **CLC 42**
See also CA 9-12R; CANR 6, 26

Mull, Martin 1943- . . . . **CLC 17**
See also CA 105

Mulock, Dinah Maria
See Craik, Dinah Maria (Mulock)

Munford, Robert 1737(?)-1783 . . . . **LC 5**
See also DLB 31

Mungo, Raymond 1946- . . . . **CLC 72**
See also CA 49-52; CANR 2

Munro, Alice
1931- . . . . **CLC 6, 10, 19, 50; SSC 3**
See also AITN 2; CA 33-36R; CANR 33;
DLB 53; MTCW; SATA 29

Munro, H(ector) H(ugh) 1870-1916
See Saki
See also CA 104; 130; CDBLB 1890-1914;
DA; DLB 34; MTCW; WLC

Murasaki, Lady . . . . **CMLC 1**

Murdoch, (Jean) Iris
1919- . . . . . . **CLC 1, 2, 3, 4, 6, 8, 11, 15,
22, 31, 51**
See also CA 13-16R; CANR 8;
CDBLB 1960 to Present; DLB 14;
MTCW

Murphy, Richard 1927- . . . . **CLC 41**
See also CA 29-32R; DLB 40

Murphy, Sylvia 1937- . . . . **CLC 34**
See also CA 121

Murphy, Thomas (Bernard) 1935- . . . **CLC 51**
See also CA 101

Murray, Albert L. 1916- . . . . **CLC 73**
See also BW; CA 49-52; CANR 26; DLB 38

Murray, Les(lie) A(llan) 1938- . . . . . **CLC 40**
See also CA 21-24R; CANR 11, 27

Murry, J. Middleton
See Murry, John Middleton

Murry, John Middleton
1889-1957 . . . . **TCLC 16**
See also CA 118

Musgrave, Susan 1951- . . . . **CLC 13, 54**
See also CA 69-72

Musil, Robert (Edler von)
1880-1942 . . . . **TCLC 12**
See also CA 109; DLB 81, 124

Musset, (Louis Charles) Alfred de
1810-1857 . . . . **NCLC 7**

My Brother's Brother
See Chekhov, Anton (Pavlovich)

Myers, Walter Dean 1937- . . . . **CLC 35**
See also AAYA 4; BLC 3; BW; CA 33-36R;
CANR 20; CLR 4, 16; DLB 33;
MAICYA; SAAS 2; SATA 27, 41, 70, 71

Myers, Walter M.
See Myers, Walter Dean

Myles, Symon
See Follett, Ken(neth Martin)

Nabokov, Vladimir (Vladimirovich)
1899-1977 . . . . . **CLC 1, 2, 3, 6, 8, 11, 15,
23, 44, 46, 64; SSC 11**
See also CA 5-8R; 69-72; CANR 20;
CDALB 1941-1968; DA; DLB 2;
DLBD 3; DLBY 80, 91; MTCW; WLC

Nagai Kafu . . . . **TCLC 51**
See also Nagai Sokichi

Nagai Sokichi 1879-1959
See Nagai Kafu
See also CA 117

Nagy, Laszlo 1925-1978 . . . . **CLC 7**
See also CA 129; 112

Naipaul, Shiva(dhar Srinivasa)
1945-1985 . . . . **CLC 32, 39**
See also CA 110; 112; 116; CANR 33;
DLBY 85; MTCW

Naipaul, V(idiadhar) S(urajprasad)
1932- . . . . **CLC 4, 7, 9, 13, 18, 37**
See also CA 1-4R; CANR 1, 33;
CDBLB 1960 to Present; DLB 125;
DLBY 85; MTCW

Nakos, Lilika 1899(?)- . . . . **CLC 29**

Narayan, R(asipuram) K(rishnaswami)
1906- . . . . **CLC 7, 28, 47**
See also CA 81-84; CANR 33; MTCW;
SATA 62

Nash, (Frediric) Ogden 1902-1971 . . **CLC 23**
See also CA 13-14; 29-32R; CANR 34;
CAP 1; DLB 11; MAICYA; MTCW;
SATA 2, 46

Nathan, Daniel
See Dannay, Frederic

Nathan, George Jean 1882-1958 . . . **TCLC 18**
See also Hatteras, Owen
See also CA 114

Natsume, Kinnosuke 1867-1916
See Natsume, Soseki
See also CA 104

Natsume, Soseki . . . . **TCLC 2, 10**
See also Natsume, Kinnosuke

Natti, (Mary) Lee 1919-
See Kingman, Lee
See also CA 5-8R; CANR 2

Naylor, Gloria 1950- . . . . **CLC 28, 52**
See also AAYA 6; BLC 3; BW; CA 107;
CANR 27; DA; MTCW

Neihardt, John Gneisenau
1881-1973 . . . . **CLC 32**
See also CA 13-14; CAP 1; DLB 9, 54

Nekrasov, Nikolai Alekseevich
1821-1878 . . . . **NCLC 11**

Nelligan, Emile 1879-1941 . . . . **TCLC 14**
See also CA 114; DLB 92

Nelson, Willie 1933- . . . . **CLC 17**
See also CA 107

Nemerov, Howard (Stanley)
1920-1991 . . . . **CLC 2, 6, 9, 36**
See also CA 1-4R; 134; CABS 2; CANR 1,
27; DLB 6; DLBY 83; MTCW

O'Cathasaigh, Sean
See O'Casey, Sean

Ochs, Phil 1940-1976 . . . . **CLC 17**
See also CA 65-68

O'Connor, Edwin (Greene)
1918-1968 . . . . **CLC 14**
See also CA 93-96; 25-28R

O'Connor, (Mary) Flannery
1925-1964 . . . . **CLC 1, 2, 3, 6, 10, 13, 15,**
21, 66; SSC 1
See also AAYA 7; CA 1-4R; CANR 3, 41;
CDALB 1941-1968; DA; DLB 2;
DLBY 80; MTCW; WLC

O'Connor, Frank . . . . **CLC 23; SSC 5**
See also O'Donovan, Michael John

O'Dell, Scott 1898-1989 . . . . **CLC 30**
See also AAYA 3; CA 61-64; 129;
CANR 12, 30; CLR 1, 16; DLB 52;
MAICYA; SATA 12, 60

Odets, Clifford 1906-1963 . . . . . . **CLC 2, 28**
See also CA 85-88; DLB 7, 26; MTCW

O'Doherty, Brian 1934- . . . . **CLC 76**
See also CA 105

O'Donnell, K. M.
See Malzberg, Barry N(athaniel)

O'Donnell, Lawrence
See Kuttner, Henry

O'Donovan, Michael John
1903-1966 . . . . **CLC 14**
See also O'Connor, Frank
See also CA 93-96

Oe, Kenzaburo 1935- . . . . **CLC 10, 36**
See also CA 97-100; CANR 36; MTCW

O'Faolain, Julia 1932- . . . . **CLC 6, 19, 47**
See also CA 81-84; CAAS 2; CANR 12;
DLB 14; MTCW

O'Faolain, Sean
1900-1991 . . . . **CLC 1, 7, 14, 32, 70**
See also CA 61-64; 134; CANR 12;
DLB 15; MTCW

O'Flaherty, Liam
1896-1984 . . . . **CLC 5, 34; SSC 6**
See also CA 101; 113; CANR 35; DLB 36;
DLBY 84; MTCW

Ogilvy, Gavin
See Barrie, J(ames) M(atthew)

O'Grady, Standish James
1846-1928 . . . . **TCLC 5**
See also CA 104

O'Grady, Timothy 1951- . . . . **CLC 59**
See also CA 138

O'Hara, Frank
1926-1966 . . . . **CLC 2, 5, 13, 78**
See also CA 9-12R; 25-28R; CANR 33;
DLB 5, 16; MTCW

O'Hara, John (Henry)
1905-1970 . . . . **CLC 1, 2, 3, 6, 11, 42**
See also CA 5-8R; 25-28R; CANR 31;
CDALB 1929-1941; DLB 9, 86; DLBD 2;
MTCW

O Hehir, Diana 1922- . . . . **CLC 41**
See also CA 93-96

Okigbo, Christopher (Ifenayichukwu)
1932-1967 . . . . **CLC 25; PC 7**
See also BLC 3; BW; CA 77-80; DLB 125;
MTCW

Olds, Sharon 1942- . . . . **CLC 32, 39**
See also CA 101; CANR 18, 41; DLB 120

Oldstyle, Jonathan
See Irving, Washington

Olesha, Yuri (Karlovich)
1899-1960 . . . . **CLC 8**
See also CA 85-88

Oliphant, Margaret (Oliphant Wilson)
1828-1897 . . . . **NCLC 11**
See also DLB 18

Oliver, Mary 1935- . . . . **CLC 19, 34**
See also CA 21-24R; CANR 9; DLB 5

Olivier, Laurence (Kerr)
1907-1989 . . . . **CLC 20**
See also CA 111; 129

Olsen, Tillie 1913- . . . . . **CLC 4, 13; SSC 11**
See also CA 1-4R; CANR 1; DA; DLB 28;
DLBY 80; MTCW

Olson, Charles (John)
1910-1970 . . . . . **CLC 1, 2, 5, 6, 9, 11, 29**
See also CA 13-16; 25-28R; CABS 2;
CANR 35; CAP 1; DLB 5, 16; MTCW

Olson, Toby 1937- . . . . **CLC 28**
See also CA 65-68; CANR 9, 31

Olyesha, Yuri
See Olesha, Yuri (Karlovich)

Ondaatje, Michael
1943- . . . . **CLC 14, 29, 51, 76**
See also CA 77-80; DLB 60

Oneal, Elizabeth 1934-
See Oneal, Zibby
See also CA 106; CANR 28; MAICYA;
SATA 30

Oneal, Zibby . . . . **CLC 30**
See also Oneal, Elizabeth
See also AAYA 5; CLR 13

O'Neill, Eugene (Gladstone)
1888-1953 . . . . **TCLC 1, 6, 27, 49**
See also AITN 1; CA 110; 132;
CDALB 1929-1941; DA; DLB 7; MTCW;
WLC

Onetti, Juan Carlos 1909- . . . . **CLC 7, 10**
See also CA 85-88; CANR 32; DLB 113;
HW; MTCW

O Nuallain, Brian 1911-1966
See O'Brien, Flann
See also CA 21-22; 25-28R; CAP 2

Oppen, George 1908-1984 . . . . **CLC 7, 13, 34**
See also CA 13-16R; 113; CANR 8; DLB 5

Oppenheim, E(dward) Phillips
1866-1946 . . . . **TCLC 45**
See also CA 111; DLB 70

Orlovitz, Gil 1918-1973 . . . . **CLC 22**
See also CA 77-80; 45-48; DLB 2, 5

Orris
See Ingelow, Jean

Ortega y Gasset, Jose 1883-1955 . . . **TCLC 9**
See also CA 106; 130; HW; MTCW

Ortiz, Simon J(oseph) 1941- . . . . **CLC 45**
See also CA 134; DLB 120

Orton, Joe . . . . **CLC 4, 13, 43; DC 3**
See also Orton, John Kingsley
See also CDBLB 1960 to Present; DLB 13

Orton, John Kingsley 1933-1967
See Orton, Joe
See also CA 85-88; CANR 35; MTCW

Orwell, George . . . . **TCLC 2, 6, 15, 31, 51**
See also Blair, Eric (Arthur)
See also CDBLB 1945-1960; DLB 15, 98;
WLC

Osborne, David
See Silverberg, Robert

Osborne, George
See Silverberg, Robert

Osborne, John (James)
1929- . . . . **CLC 1, 2, 5, 11, 45**
See also CA 13-16R; CANR 21;
CDBLB 1945-1960; DA; DLB 13;
MTCW; WLC

Osborne, Lawrence 1958- . . . . **CLC 50**

Oshima, Nagisa 1932- . . . . **CLC 20**
Sec also CA 116; 121

Oskison, John M(ilton)
1874-1947 . . . . **TCLC 35**

Ossoli, Sarah Margaret (Fuller marchesa d')
1810-1850
See Fuller, Margaret
See also SATA 25

Ostrovsky, Alexander
1823-1886 . . . . **NCLC 30**

Otero, Blas de 1916- . . . . **CLC 11**
See also CA 89-92

Otto, Whitney 1955- . . . . **CLC 70**
See also CA 140

Ouida . . . . **TCLC 43**
See also De La Ramee, (Marie) Louise
See also DLB 18

Ousmane, Sembene 1923- . . . . **CLC 66**
See also BLC 3; BW; CA 117; 125; MTCW

Ovid 43B.C.-18th cent. (?) . . . **CMLC 7; PC 2**

Owen, Hugh
See Faust, Frederick (Schiller)

Owen, Wilfred 1893-1918 . . . . . . **TCLC 5, 27**
See also CA 104; CDBLB 1914-1945; DA;
DLB 20; WLC

Owens, Rochelle 1936- . . . . **CLC 8**
See also CA 17-20R; CAAS 2; CANR 39

Oz, Amos 1939- . . . **CLC 5, 8, 11, 27, 33, 54**
See also CA 53-56; CANR 27; MTCW

Ozick, Cynthia 1928- . . . . . . **CLC 3, 7, 28, 62**
See also BEST 90:1; CA 17-20R; CANR 23;
DLB 28; DLBY 82; MTCW

Ozu, Yasujiro 1903-1963 . . . . **CLC 16**
See also CA 112

Pacheco, C.
See Pessoa, Fernando (Antonio Nogueira)

Pa Chin
See Li Fei-kan

Pack, Robert 1929- . . . . **CLC 13**
See also CA 1-4R; CANR 3; DLB 5

Padgett, Lewis
See Kuttner, Henry

Padilla (Lorenzo), Heberto 1932- . . . **CLC 38**
See also AITN 1; CA 123; 131; HW

Percy, Walker
1916-1990 .... **CLC 2, 3, 6, 8, 14, 18, 47, 65**
See also CA 1-4R; 131; CANR 1, 23; DLB 2; DLBY 80, 90; MTCW

Perec, Georges 1936-1982 .... **CLC 56**
See also DLB 83

Pereda (y Sanchez de Porrua), Jose Maria de
1833-1906 .... **TCLC 16**
See also CA 117

Pereda y Porrua, Jose Maria de
See Pereda (y Sanchez de Porrua), Jose Maria de

Peregoy, George Weems
See Mencken, H(enry) L(ouis)

Perelman, S(idney) J(oseph)
1904-1979 ... **CLC 3, 5, 9, 15, 23, 44, 49**
See also AITN 1, 2; CA 73-76; 89-92; CANR 18, DLB 11, 44; MTCW

Peret, Benjamin 1899-1959 ...... **TCLC 20**
See also CA 117

Peretz, Isaac Loeb 1851(?)-1915 ... **TCLC 16**
See also CA 109

Peretz, Yitzkhok Leibush
See Peretz, Isaac Loeb

Perez Galdos, Benito 1843-1920 ... **TCLC 27**
See also CA 125; HW

Perrault, Charles 1628-1703 .... **LC 2**
See also MAICYA; SATA 25

Perry, Brighton
See Sherwood, Robert E(mmet)

Perse, St.-John .... **CLC 4, 11, 46**
See also Leger, (Marie-Rene) Alexis Saint-Leger

Perse, Saint-John
See Leger, (Marie-Rene) Alexis Saint-Leger

Peseenz, Tulio F.
See Lopez y Fuentes, Gregorio

Pesetsky, Bette 1932- .... **CLC 28**
See also CA 133; DLB 130

Peshkov, Alexei Maximovich 1868-1936
See Gorky, Maxim
See also CA 105; DA

Pessoa, Fernando (Antonio Nogueira)
1888-1935 .... **TCLC 27**
See also CA 125

Peterkin, Julia Mood 1880-1961 .... **CLC 31**
See also CA 102; DLB 9

Peters, Joan K. 1945- .... **CLC 39**

Peters, Robert L(ouis) 1924- .... **CLC 7**
See also CA 13-16R; CAAS 8; DLB 105

Petofi, Sandor 1823-1849 .... **NCLC 21**

Petrakis, Harry Mark 1923- ...... **CLC 3**
See also CA 9-12R; CANR 4, 30

Petrov, Evgeny .... **TCLC 21**
See also Kataev, Evgeny Petrovich

Petry, Ann (Lane) 1908- ...... **CLC 1, 7, 18**
See also BW; CA 5-8R; CAAS 6; CANR 4; CLR 12; DLB 76; MAICYA; MTCW; SATA 5

Petursson, Halligrimur 1614-1674 .... **LC 8**

Philipson, Morris H. 1926- .... **CLC 53**
See also CA 1-4R; CANR 4

Phillips, David Graham
1867-1911 .... **TCLC 44**
See also CA 108; DLB 9, 12

Phillips, Jack
See Sandburg, Carl (August)

Phillips, Jayne Anne 1952- ..... **CLC 15, 33**
See also CA 101; CANR 24; DLBY 80; MTCW

Phillips, Richard
See Dick, Philip K(indred)

Phillips, Robert (Schaeffer) 1938-... **CLC 28**
See also CA 17-20R; CAAS 13; CANR 8; DLB 105

Phillips, Ward
See Lovecraft, H(oward) P(hillips)

Piccolo, Lucio 1901-1969 .... **CLC 13**
See also CA 97-100; DLB 114

Pickthall, Marjorie L(owry) C(hristie)
1883-1922 .... **TCLC 21**
See also CA 107; DLB 92

Pico della Mirandola, Giovanni
1463-1494 .... **LC 15**

Piercy, Marge
1936- .... **CLC 3, 6, 14, 18, 27, 62**
See also CA 21-24R; CAAS 1; CANR 13; DLB 120; MTCW

Piers, Robert
See Anthony, Piers

Pieyre de Mandiargues, Andre 1909-1991
See Mandiargues, Andre Pieyre de
See also CA 103; 136; CANR 22

Pilnyak, Boris .... **TCLC 23**
See also Vogau, Boris Andreyevich

Pincherle, Alberto 1907-1990 ... **CLC 11, 18**
See also Moravia, Alberto
See also CA 25-28R; 132; CANR 33; MTCW

Pinckney, Darryl 1953- .... **CLC 76**

Pineda, Cecile 1942- .... **CLC 39**
See also CA 118

Pinero, Arthur Wing 1855-1934 ... **TCLC 32**
See also CA 110; DLB 10

Pinero, Miguel (Antonio Gomez)
1946-1988 .... **CLC 4, 55**
See also CA 61-64; 125; CANR 29; HW

Pinget, Robert 1919- .... **CLC 7, 13, 37**
See also CA 85-88; DLB 83

Pink Floyd .... **CLC 35**
See also Barrett, (Roger) Syd; Gilmour, David; Mason, Nick; Waters, Roger; Wright, Rick

Pinkney, Edward 1802-1828 ..... **NCLC 31**

Pinkwater, Daniel Manus 1941- .... **CLC 35**
See also Pinkwater, Manus
See also AAYA 1; CA 29-32R; CANR 12, 38; CLR 4; MAICYA; SAAS 3; SATA 46

Pinkwater, Manus
See Pinkwater, Daniel Manus
See also SATA 8

Pinsky, Robert 1940- .... **CLC 9, 19, 38**
See also CA 29-32R; CAAS 4; DLBY 82

Pinta, Harold
See Pinter, Harold

Pinter, Harold
1930- .. **CLC 1, 3, 6, 9, 11, 15, 27, 58, 73**
See also CA 5-8R; CANR 33; CDBLB 1960 to Present; DA; DLB 13; MTCW; WLC

Pirandello, Luigi 1867-1936 ..... **TCLC 4, 29**
See also CA 104; DA; WLC

Pirsig, Robert M(aynard)
1928- .... **CLC 4, 6, 73**
See also CA 53-56; MTCW; SATA 39

Pisarev, Dmitry Ivanovich
1840-1868 .... **NCLC 25**

Pix, Mary (Griffith) 1666-1709 ...... **LC 8**
See also DLB 80

Pixerecourt, Guilbert de
1773-1844 .... **NCLC 39**

Plaidy, Jean
See Hibbert, Eleanor Alice Burford

Plant, Robert 1948- .... **CLC 12**

Plante, David (Robert)
1940- .... **CLC 7, 23, 38**
See also CA 37-40R; CANR 12, 36; DLBY 83; MTCW

Plath, Sylvia
1932-1963 ..... **CLC 1, 2, 3, 5, 9, 11, 14, 17, 50, 51, 62; PC 1**
See also CA 19-20; CANR 34; CAP 2; CDALB 1941-1968; DA; DLB 5, 6; MTCW; WLC

Plato 428(?)B.C.-348(?)B.C....... **CMLC 8**
See also DA

Platonov, Andrei .... **TCLC 14**
See also Klimentov, Andrei Platonovich

Platt, Kin 1911- .... **CLC 26**
See also CA 17-20R; CANR 11; SATA 21

Plick et Plock
See Simenon, Georges (Jacques Christian)

Plimpton, George (Ames) 1927-..... **CLC 36**
See also AITN 1; CA 21-24R; CANR 32; MTCW; SATA 10

Plomer, William Charles Franklin
1903-1973 .... **CLC 4, 8**
See also CA 21-22; CANR 34; CAP 2; DLB 20; MTCW; SATA 24

Plowman, Piers
See Kavanagh, Patrick (Joseph)

Plum, J.
See Wodehouse, P(elham) G(renville)

Plumly, Stanley (Ross) 1939- ...... **CLC 33**
See also CA 108; 110; DLB 5

Poe, Edgar Allan
1809-1849 ... **NCLC 1, 16; PC 1; SSC 1**
See also CDALB 1640-1865; DA; DLB 3, 59, 73, 74; SATA 23; WLC

Poet of Titchfield Street, The
See Pound, Ezra (Weston Loomis)

Pohl, Frederik 1919- .... **CLC 18**
See also CA 61-64; CAAS 1; CANR 11, 37; DLB 8; MTCW; SATA 24

Poirier, Louis 1910-
See Gracq, Julien
See also CA 122; 126

Poitier, Sidney 1927- .... **CLC 26**
See also BW; CA 117

Polanski, Roman 1933- .... CLC 16
See also CA 77-80

Poliakoff, Stephen 1952- .... CLC 38
See also CA 106; DLB 13

Police, The...................... CLC 26
See also Copeland, Stewart (Armstrong);
Summers, Andrew James; Sumner,
Gordon Matthew

Pollitt, Katha 1949- .... CLC 28
See also CA 120; 122; MTCW

Pollock, Sharon 1936- .... CLC 50
See also DLB 60

Pomerance, Bernard 1940-........ CLC 13
See also CA 101

Ponge, Francis (Jean Gaston Alfred)
1899-1988 .... CLC 6, 18
See also CA 85-88; 126; CANR 40

Pontoppidan, Henrik 1857-1943 ... TCLC 29

Poole, Josephine .... CLC 17
See also Helyar, Jane Penelope Josephine
See also SAAS 2; SATA 5

Popa, Vasko 1922- .... CLC 19
See also CA 112

Pope, Alexander 1688-1744......... LC 3
See also CDBLB 1660-1789; DA; DLB 95,
101; WLC

Porter, Connie 1960- .... CLC 70

Porter, Gene(va Grace) Stratton
1863(?)-1924 .... TCLC 21
See also CA 112

Porter, Katherine Anne
1890-1980 ...... CLC 1, 3, 7, 10, 13, 15,
27; SSC 4
See also AITN 2; CA 1-4R; 101; CANR 1;
DA; DLB 4, 9, 102; DLBY 80; MTCW;
SATA 23, 39

Porter, Peter (Neville Frederick)
1929- .... CLC 5, 13, 33
See also CA 85-88; DLB 40

Porter, William Sydney 1862-1910
See Henry, O.
See also CA 104; 131; CDALB 1865-1917;
DA; DLB 12, 78, 79; MTCW; YABC 2

Portillo (y Pacheco), Jose Lopez
See Lopez Portillo (y Pacheco), Jose

Post, Melville Davisson
1869-1930 .... TCLC 39
See also CA 110

Potok, Chaim 1929- .... CLC 2, 7, 14, 26
See also AITN 1, 2; CA 17-20R; CANR 19,
35; DLB 28; MTCW; SATA 33

Potter, Beatrice
See Webb, (Martha) Beatrice (Potter)
See also MAICYA

Potter, Dennis (Christopher George)
1935- .... CLC 58
See also CA 107; CANR 33; MTCW

Pound, Ezra (Weston Loomis)
1885-1972 ...... CLC 1, 2, 3, 4, 5, 7, 10,
13, 18, 34, 48, 50; PC 4
See also CA 5-8R; 37-40R; CANR 40;
CDALB 1917-1929; DA; DLB 4, 45, 63;
MTCW; WLC

Povod, Reinaldo 1959-............ CLC 44
See also CA 136

Powell, Anthony (Dymoke)
1905- .... CLC 1, 3, 7, 9, 10, 31
See also CA 1-4R; CANR 1, 32;
CDBLB 1945-1960; DLB 15; MTCW

Powell, Dawn 1897-1965 .... CLC 66
See also CA 5-8R

Powell, Padgett 1952-............ CLC 34
See also CA 126

Powers, J(ames) F(arl)
1917- .... CLC 1, 4, 8, 57; SSC 4
See also CA 1-4R; CANR 2; DLB 130;
MTCW

Powers, John J(ames) 1945-
See Powers, John R.
See also CA 69-72

Powers, John R. .... CLC 66
See also Powers, John J(ames)

Pownall, David 1938-............. CLC 10
See also CA 89-92; DLB 14

Powys, John Cowper
1872-1963 .... CLC 7, 9, 15, 46
See also CA 85-88; DLB 15; MTCW

Powys, T(heodore) F(rancis)
1875-1953 .... TCLC 9
See also CA 106; DLB 36

Prager, Emily 1952-.............. CLC 56

Pratt, Edwin John 1883-1964 ...... CLC 19
See also CA 93-96; DLB 92

Premchand..................... TCLC 21
See also Srivastava, Dhanpat Rai

Preussler, Otfried 1923-........... CLC 17
See also CA 77-80; SATA 24

Prevert, Jacques (Henri Marie)
1900-1977 .... CLC 15
See also CA 77-80; 69-72; CANR 29;
MTCW; SATA 30

Prevost, Abbe (Antoine Francois)
1697-1763 .... LC 1

Price, (Edward) Reynolds
1933- .... CLC 3, 6, 13, 43, 50, 63
See also CA 1-4R; CANR 1, 37; DLB 2

Price, Richard 1949- .... CLC 6, 12
See also CA 49-52; CANR 3; DLBY 81

Prichard, Katharine Susannah
1883-1969 .... CLC 46
See also CA 11-12; CANR 33; CAP 1;
MTCW; SATA 66

Priestley, J(ohn) B(oynton)
1894-1984 .... CLC 2, 5, 9, 34
See also CA 9-12R; 113; CANR 33;
CDBLB 1914-1945; DLB 10, 34, 77, 100;
DLBY 84; MTCW

Prince 1958(?)-.................. CLC 35

Prince, F(rank) T(empleton) 1912- .. CLC 22
See also CA 101; DLB 20

Prince Kropotkin
See Kropotkin, Peter (Aleksieevich)

Prior, Matthew 1664-1721.......... LC 4
See also DLB 95

Pritchard, William H(arrison)
1932- .... CLC 34
See also CA 65-68; CANR 23; DLB 111

Pritchett, V(ictor) S(awdon)
1900- .... CLC 5, 13, 15, 41
See also CA 61-64; CANR 31; DLB 15;
MTCW

Private 19022
See Manning, Frederic

Probst, Mark 1925- .... CLC 59
See also CA 130

Prokosch, Frederic 1908-1989.... CLC 4, 48
See also CA 73-76; 128; DLB 48

Prophet, The
See Dreiser, Theodore (Herman Albert)

Prose, Francine 1947-............. CLC 45
See also CA 109; 112

Proudhon
See Cunha, Euclides (Rodrigues Pimenta) da

Proust, (Valentin-Louis-George-Eugene-)
Marcel 1871-1922 .... TCLC 7, 13, 33
See also CA 104; 120; DA; DLB 65;
MTCW; WLC

Prowler, Harley
See Masters, Edgar Lee

Prus, Boleslaw................... TCLC 48
See also Glowacki, Aleksander

Pryor, Richard (Franklin Lenox Thomas)
1940- .... CLC 26
See also CA 122

Przybyszewski, Stanislaw
1868-1927 .... TCLC 36
See also DLB 66

Pteleon
See Grieve, C(hristopher) M(urray)

Puckett, Lute
See Masters, Edgar Lee

Puig, Manuel
1932-1990 .... CLC 3, 5, 10, 28, 65
See also CA 45-48; CANR 2, 32; DLB 113;
HW; MTCW

Purdy, A(lfred) W(ellington)
1918- .... CLC 3, 6, 14, 50
See also Purdy, Al
See also CA 81-84

Purdy, Al
See Purdy, A(lfred) W(ellington)
See also CAAS 17; DLB 88

Purdy, James (Amos)
1923- .... CLC 2, 4, 10, 28, 52
See also CA 33-36R; CAAS 1; CANR 19;
DLB 2; MTCW

Pure, Simon
See Swinnerton, Frank Arthur

Pushkin, Alexander (Sergeyevich)
1799-1837 .... NCLC 3, 27
See also DA; SATA 61; WLC

P'u Sung-ling 1640-1715 .... LC 3

Putnam, Arthur Lee
See Alger, Horatio, Jr.

Puzo, Mario 1920-........ CLC 1, 2, 6, 36
See also CA 65-68; CANR 4; DLB 6;
MTCW

Pym, Barbara (Mary Crampton)
1913-1980 .... CLC 13, 19, 37
See also CA 13-14; 97-100; CANR 13, 34;
CAP 1; DLB 14; DLBY 87; MTCW

Pynchon, Thomas (Ruggles, Jr.)
1937- .. **CLC 2, 3, 6, 9, 11, 18, 33, 62, 72**
See also BEST 90:2; CA 17-20R; CANR 22;
DA; DLB 2; MTCW; WLC

Qian Zhongshu
See Ch'ien Chung-shu

Qroll
See Dagerman, Stig (Halvard)

Quarrington, Paul (Lewis) 1953-.... **CLC 65**
See also CA 129

Quasimodo, Salvatore 1901-1968 ... **CLC 10**
See also CA 13-16; 25-28R; CAP 1;
DLB 114; MTCW

Queen, Ellery................... **CLC 3, 11**
See also Dannay, Frederic; Davidson,
Avram; Lee, Manfred B(ennington);
Sturgeon, Theodore (Hamilton); Vance,
John Holbrook

Queen, Ellery, Jr.
See Dannay, Frederic; Lee, Manfred
B(ennington)

Queneau, Raymond
1903-1976 .... **CLC 2, 5, 10, 42**
See also CA 77-80; 69-72; CANR 32;
DLB 72; MTCW

Quevedo, Francisco de 1580-1645.... **LC 23**

Quin, Ann (Marie) 1936-1973 ...... **CLC 6**
See also CA 9-12R; 45-48; DLB 14

Quinn, Martin
See Smith, Martin Cruz

Quinn, Simon
See Smith, Martin Cruz

Quiroga, Horacio (Sylvestre)
1878-1937 .... **TCLC 20**
See also CA 117; 131; HW; MTCW

Quoirez, Francoise 1935-........... **CLC 9**
See also Sagan, Francoise
See also CA 49-52; CANR 6, 39; MTCW

Raabe, Wilhelm 1831-1910 .... **TCLC 45**
See also DLB 129

Rabe, David (William) 1940-... **CLC 4, 8, 33**
See also CA 85-88; CABS 3; DLB 7

Rabelais, Francois 1483-1553 .... **LC 5**
See also DA; WLC

Rabinovitch, Sholem 1859-1916
See Aleichem, Sholom
See also CA 104

Radcliffe, Ann (Ward) 1764-1823 .. **NCLC 6**
See also DLB 39

Radiguet, Raymond 1903-1923 .... **TCLC 29**
See also DLB 65

Radnoti, Miklos 1909-1944 .... **TCLC 16**
See also CA 118

Rado, James 1939-............... **CLC 17**
See also CA 105

Radvanyi, Netty 1900-1983
See Seghers, Anna
See also CA 85-88; 110

Raeburn, John (Hay) 1941-........ **CLC 34**
See also CA 57-60

Ragni, Gerome 1942-1991 .... **CLC 17**
See also CA 105; 134

Rahv, Philip.................... **CLC 24**
See also Greenberg, Ivan

Raine, Craig 1944-............... **CLC 32**
See also CA 108; CANR 29; DLB 40

Raine, Kathleen (Jessie) 1908- ... **CLC 7, 45**
See also CA 85-88; DLB 20; MTCW

Rainis, Janis 1865-1929......... **TCLC 29**

Rakosi, Carl.................... **CLC 47**
See also Rawley, Callman
See also CAAS 5

Raleigh, Richard
See Lovecraft, H(oward) P(hillips)

Rallentando, H. P.
See Sayers, Dorothy L(eigh)

Ramal, Walter
See de la Mare, Walter (John)

Ramon, Juan
See Jimenez (Mantecon), Juan Ramon

Ramos, Graciliano 1892-1953 ..... **TCLC 32**

Rampersad, Arnold 1941-.......... **CLC 44**
See also CA 127; 133; DLB 111

Rampling, Anne
See Rice, Anne

Ramuz, Charles-Ferdinand
1878-1947 .... **TCLC 33**

Rand, Ayn 1905-1982....... **CLC 3, 30, 44**
See also AAYA 10; CA 13-16R; 105;
CANR 27; DA; MTCW; WLC

Randall, Dudley (Felker) 1914-...... **CLC 1**
See also BLC 3; BW; CA 25-28R;
CANR 23; DLB 41

Randall, Robert
See Silverberg, Robert

Ranger, Ken
See Creasey, John

Ransom, John Crowe
1888-1974 .... **CLC 2, 4, 5, 11, 24**
See also CA 5-8R; 49-52; CANR 6, 34;
DLB 45, 63; MTCW

Rao, Raja 1909- .... **CLC 25, 56**
See also CA 73-76; MTCW

Raphael, Frederic (Michael)
1931- .... **CLC 2, 14**
See also CA 1-4R; CANR 1; DLB 14

Ratcliffe, James P.
See Mencken, H(enry) L(ouis)

Rathbone, Julian 1935- .... **CLC 41**
See also CA 101; CANR 34

Rattigan, Terence (Mervyn)
1911-1977 .... **CLC 7**
See also CA 85-88; 73-76;
CDBLB 1945-1960; DLB 13; MTCW

Ratushinskaya, Irina 1954-........ **CLC 54**
See also CA 129

Raven, Simon (Arthur Noel)
1927- .... **CLC 14**
See also CA 81-84

Rawley, Callman 1903-
See Rakosi, Carl
See also CA 21-24R; CANR 12, 32

Rawlings, Marjorie Kinnan
1896-1953 .... **TCLC 4**
See also CA 104; 137; DLB 9, 22, 102;
MAICYA; YABC 1

Ray, Satyajit 1921-1992....... **CLC 16, 76**
See also CA 114; 137

Read, Herbert Edward 1893-1968.... **CLC 4**
See also CA 85-88; 25-28R; DLB 20

Read, Piers Paul 1941- ...... **CLC 4, 10, 25**
See also CA 21-24R; CANR 38; DLB 14;
SATA 21

Reade, Charles 1814-1884 .... **NCLC 2**
See also DLB 21

Reade, Hamish
See Gray, Simon (James Holliday)

Reading, Peter 1946- .... **CLC 47**
See also CA 103; DLB 40

Reaney, James 1926- .... **CLC 13**
See also CA 41-44R; CAAS 15; DLB 68;
SATA 43

Rebreanu, Liviu 1885-1944 .... **TCLC 28**

Rechy, John (Francisco)
1934- .... **CLC 1, 7, 14, 18**
See also CA 5-8R; CAAS 4; CANR 6, 32;
DLB 122; DLBY 82; HW

Redcam, Tom 1870-1933 .... **TCLC 25**

Reddin, Keith.................... **CLC 67**

Redgrove, Peter (William)
1932- .... **CLC 6, 41**
See also CA 1-4R; CANR 3, 39; DLB 40

Redmon, Anne.................... **CLC 22**
See also Nightingale, Anne Redmon
See also DLBY 86

Reed, Eliot
See Ambler, Eric

Reed, Ishmael
1938- ...... **CLC 2, 3, 5, 6, 13, 32, 60**
See also BLC 3; BW; CA 21-24R;
CANR 25; DLB 2, 5, 33; DLBD 8;
MTCW

Reed, John (Silas) 1887-1920 ...... **TCLC 9**
See also CA 106

Reed, Lou.................... **CLC 21**
See also Firbank, Louis

Reeve, Clara 1729-1807......... **NCLC 19**
See also DLB 39

Reid, Christopher (John) 1949-..... **CLC 33**
See also CA 140; DLB 40

Reid, Desmond
See Moorcock, Michael (John)

Reid Banks, Lynne 1929-
See Banks, Lynne Reid
See also CA 1-4R; CANR 6, 22, 38;
CLR 24; MAICYA; SATA 22

Reilly, William K.
See Creasey, John

Reiner, Max
See Caldwell, (Janet Miriam) Taylor
(Holland)

Reis, Ricardo
See Pessoa, Fernando (Antonio Nogueira)

Remarque, Erich Maria
1898-1970 .... **CLC 21**
See also CA 77-80; 29-32R; DA; DLB 56;
MTCW

Remizov, A.
See Remizov, Aleksei (Mikhailovich)

Remizov, A. M.
See Remizov, Aleksei (Mikhailovich)

Remizov, Aleksei (Mikhailovich)
1877-1957 . . . . TCLC 27
See also CA 125; 133

Renan, Joseph Ernest
1823-1892 . . . . NCLC 26

Renard, Jules 1864-1910 . . . . TCLC 17
See also CA 117

Renault, Mary . . . . CLC 3, 11, 17
See also Challans, Mary
See also DLBY 83

Rendell, Ruth (Barbara) 1930- . . CLC 28, 48
See also Vine, Barbara
See also CA 109; CANR 32; DLB 87;
MTCW

Renoir, Jean 1894-1979 . . . . CLC 20
See also CA 129; 85-88

Resnais, Alain 1922- . . . . CLC 16

Reverdy, Pierre 1889-1960 . . . . CLC 53
See also CA 97-100; 89-92

Rexroth, Kenneth
1905-1982 . . . . . . CLC 1, 2, 6, 11, 22, 49
See also CA 5-8R; 107; CANR 14, 34;
CDALB 1941-1968; DLB 16, 48;
DLBY 82; MTCW

Reyes, Alfonso 1889-1959 . . . . TCLC 33
See also CA 131; HW

Reyes y Basoalto, Ricardo Eliecer Neftali
See Neruda, Pablo

Reymont, Wladyslaw (Stanislaw)
1868(?)-1925 . . . . TCLC 5
See also CA 104

Reynolds, Jonathan 1942- . . . . CLC 6, 38
See also CA 65-68; CANR 28

Reynolds, Joshua 1723-1792 . . . . LC 15
See also DLB 104

Reynolds, Michael Shane 1937- . . . . CLC 44
See also CA 65-68; CANR 9

Reznikoff, Charles 1894-1976 . . . . CLC 9
See also CA 33-36; 61-64; CAP 2; DLB 28,
45

Rezzori (d'Arezzo), Gregor von
1914- . . . . CLC 25
See also CA 122; 136

Rhine, Richard
See Silverstein, Alvin

R'hoone
See Balzac, Honore de

Rhys, Jean
1890(?)-1979 . . . . CLC 2, 4, 6, 14, 19, 51
See also CA 25-28R; 85-88; CANR 35;
CDBLB 1945-1960; DLB 36, 117; MTCW

Ribeiro, Darcy 1922- . . . . CLC 34
See also CA 33-36R

Ribeiro, Joao Ubaldo (Osorio Pimentel)
1941- . . . . CLC 10, 67
See also CA 81-84

Ribman, Ronald (Burt) 1932- . . . . CLC 7
See also CA 21-24R

Ricci, Nino 1959- . . . . CLC 70
See also CA 137

Rice, Anne 1941- . . . . CLC 41
See also AAYA 9; BEST 89:2; CA 65-68;
CANR 12, 36

Rice, Elmer (Leopold)
1892-1967 . . . . CLC 7, 49
See also CA 21-22; 25-28R; CAP 2; DLB 4,
7; MTCW

Rice, Tim 1944- . . . . CLC 21
See also CA 103

Rich, Adrienne (Cecile)
1929- . . . . CLC 3, 6, 7, 11, 18, 36, 73, 76;
PC 5
See also CA 9-12R; CANR 20; DLB 5, 67;
MTCW

Rich, Barbara
See Graves, Robert (von Ranke)

Rich, Robert
See Trumbo, Dalton

Richards, David Adams 1950- . . . . . . CLC 59
See also CA 93-96; DLB 53

Richards, I(vor) A(rmstrong)
1893-1979 . . . . CLC 14, 24
See also CA 41-44R; 89-92; CANR 34;
DLB 27

Richardson, Anne
See Roiphe, Anne Richardson

Richardson, Dorothy Miller
1873-1957 . . . . TCLC 3
See also CA 104; DLB 36

Richardson, Ethel Florence (Lindesay)
1870-1946
See Richardson, Henry Handel
See also CA 105

Richardson, Henry Handel . . . . TCLC 4
See also Richardson, Ethel Florence
(Lindesay)

Richardson, Samuel 1689-1761 . . . . LC 1
See also CDBLB 1660-1789; DA; DLB 39;
WLC

Richler, Mordecai
1931- . . . . CLC 3, 5, 9, 13, 18, 46, 70
See also AITN 1; CA 65-68; CANR 31;
CLR 17; DLB 53; MAICYA; MTCW;
SATA 27, 44

Richter, Conrad (Michael)
1890-1968 . . . . CLC 30
See also CA 5-8R; 25-28R; CANR 23;
DLB 9; MTCW; SATA 3

Riddell, J. H. 1832-1906 . . . . TCLC 40

Riding, Laura . . . . CLC 3, 7
See also Jackson, Laura (Riding)

Riefenstahl, Berta Helene Amalia 1902-
See Riefenstahl, Leni
See also CA 108

Riefenstahl, Leni . . . . CLC 16
See also Riefenstahl, Berta Helene Amalia

Riffe, Ernest
See Bergman, (Ernst) Ingmar

Riley, James Whitcomb
1849-1916 . . . . TCLC 51
See also CA 118; 137; MAICYA; SATA 17

Riley, Tex
See Creasey, John

Rilke, Rainer Maria
1875-1926 . . . . TCLC 1, 6, 19; PC 2
See also CA 104; 132; DLB 81; MTCW

Rimbaud, (Jean Nicolas) Arthur
1854-1891 . . . . NCLC 4, 35; PC 3
See also DA; WLC

Ringmaster, The
See Mencken, H(enry) L(ouis)

Ringwood, Gwen(dolyn Margaret) Pharis
1910-1984 . . . . CLC 48
See also CA 112; DLB 88

Rio, Michel 19(?)- . . . . CLC 43

Ritsos, Giannes
See Ritsos, Yannis

Ritsos, Yannis 1909-1990 . . . . . CLC 6, 13, 31
See also CA 77-80; 133; CANR 39; MTCW

Ritter, Erika 1948(?)- . . . . CLC 52

Rivera, Jose Eustasio 1889-1928 . . . TCLC 35
See also HW

Rivers, Conrad Kent 1933-1968 . . . . . . CLC 1
See also BW; CA 85-88; DLB 41

Rivers, Elfrida
See Bradley, Marion Zimmer

Riverside, John
See Heinlein, Robert A(nson)

Rizal, Jose 1861-1896 . . . . NCLC 27

Roa Bastos, Augusto (Antonio)
1917- . . . . CLC 45
See also CA 131; DLB 113; HW

Robbe-Grillet, Alain
1922- . . . . . . CLC 1, 2, 4, 6, 8, 10, 14, 43
See also CA 9-12R; CANR 33; DLB 83;
MTCW

Robbins, Harold 1916- . . . . CLC 5
See also CA 73-76; CANR 26; MTCW

Robbins, Thomas Eugene 1936-
See Robbins, Tom
See also CA 81-84; CANR 29; MTCW

Robbins, Tom . . . . CLC 9, 32, 64
See also Robbins, Thomas Eugene
See also BEST 90:3; DLBY 80

Robbins, Trina 1938- . . . . CLC 21
See also CA 128

Roberts, Charles G(eorge) D(ouglas)
1860-1943 . . . . TCLC 8
See also CA 105; DLB 92; SATA 29

Roberts, Kate 1891-1985 . . . . CLC 15
See also CA 107; 116

Roberts, Keith (John Kingston)
1935- . . . . CLC 14
See also CA 25-28R

Roberts, Kenneth (Lewis)
1885-1957 . . . . TCLC 23
See also CA 109; DLB 9

Roberts, Michele (B.) 1949- . . . . CLC 48
See also CA 115

Robertson, Ellis
See Ellison, Harlan; Silverberg, Robert

Robertson, Thomas William
1829-1871 . . . . NCLC 35

Robinson, Edwin Arlington
1869-1935 . . . . TCLC 5; PC 1
See also CA 104; 133; CDALB 1865-1917;
DA; DLB 54; MTCW

Robinson, Henry Crabb
1775-1867 . . . . NCLC 15
See also DLB 107

Robinson, Jill 1936- .... **CLC 10**
See also CA 102

Robinson, Kim Stanley 1952- ...... **CLC 34**
See also CA 126

Robinson, Lloyd
See Silverberg, Robert

Robinson, Marilynne 1944- .... **CLC 25**
See also CA 116

Robinson, Smokey................. **CLC 21**
See also Robinson, William, Jr.

Robinson, William, Jr. 1940-
See Robinson, Smokey
See also CA 116

Robison, Mary 1949- .... **CLC 42**
See also CA 113; 116; DLB 130

Roddenberry, Eugene Wesley 1921-1991
See Roddenberry, Gene
See also CA 110; 135; CANR 37; SATA 45

Roddenberry, Gene................. **CLC 17**
See also Roddenberry, Eugene Wesley
See also AAYA 5; SATA-Obit 69

Rodgers, Mary 1931- .... **CLC 12**
See also CA 49-52; CANR 8; CLR 20;
MAICYA; SATA 8

Rodgers, W(illiam) R(obert)
1909-1969 .... **CLC 7**
See also CA 85-88; DLB 20

Rodman, Eric
See Silverberg, Robert

Rodman, Howard 1920(?)-1985..... **CLC 65**
See also CA 118

Rodman, Maia
See Wojciechowska, Maia (Teresa)

Rodriguez, Claudio 1934-......... **CLC 10**

Roelvaag, O(le) E(dvart)
1876-1931 .... **TCLC 17**
See also CA 117; DLB 9

Roethke, Theodore (Huebner)
1908-1963 ...... **CLC 1, 3, 8, 11, 19, 46**
See also CA 81-84; CABS 2;
CDALB 1941-1968; DLB 5; MTCW

Rogers, Thomas Hunton 1927- ..... **CLC 57**
See also CA 89-92

Rogers, Will(iam Penn Adair)
1879-1935 .... **TCLC 8**
See also CA 105; DLB 11

Rogin, Gilbert 1929-............. **CLC 18**
See also CA 65-68; CANR 15

Rohan, Koda .... **TCLC 22**
See also Koda Shigeyuki

Rohmer, Eric.................... **CLC 16**
See also Scherer, Jean-Marie Maurice

Rohmer, Sax .... **TCLC 28**
See also Ward, Arthur Henry Sarsfield
See also DLB 70

Roiphe, Anne Richardson 1935- ... **CLC 3, 9**
See also CA 89-92; DLBY 80

Rojas, Fernando de 1465-1541 ...... **LC 23**

**Rolfe, Frederick (William Serafino Austin
Lewis Mary)** 1860-1913...... **TCLC 12**
See also CA 107; DLB 34

Rolland, Romain 1866-1944....... **TCLC 23**
See also CA 118; DLB 65

Rolvaag, O(le) E(dvart)
See Roelvaag, O(le) E(dvart)

Romain Arnaud, Saint
See Aragon, Louis

Romains, Jules 1885-1972.......... **CLC 7**
See also CA 85-88; CANR 34; DLB 65;
MTCW

Romero, Jose Ruben 1890-1952 ... **TCLC 14**
See also CA 114; 131; HW

Ronsard, Pierre de 1524-1585........ **LC 6**

Rooke, Leon 1934-............. **CLC 25, 34**
See also CA 25-28R; CANR 23

Roper, William 1498-1578.......... **LC 10**

Roquelaure, A. N.
See Rice, Anne

Rosa, Joao Guimaraes 1908-1967 ... **CLC 23**
See also CA 89-92; DLB 113

Rosen, Richard (Dean) 1949-....... **CLC 39**
See also CA 77-80

Rosenberg, Isaac 1890-1918...... **TCLC 12**
See also CA 107; DLB 20

Rosenblatt, Joe .... **CLC 15**
See also Rosenblatt, Joseph

Rosenblatt, Joseph 1933-
See Rosenblatt, Joe
See also CA 89-92

Rosenfeld, Samuel 1896-1963
See Tzara, Tristan
See also CA 89-92

Rosenthal, M(acha) L(ouis) 1917-... **CLC 28**
See also CA 1-4R; CAAS 6; CANR 4;
DLB 5; SATA 59

Ross, Barnaby
See Dannay, Frederic

Ross, Bernard L.
See Follett, Ken(neth Martin)

Ross, J. H.
See Lawrence, T(homas) E(dward)

Ross, Martin
See Martin, Violet Florence

Ross, (James) Sinclair 1908-....... **CLC 13**
See also CA 73-76; DLB 88

Rossetti, Christina (Georgina)
1830-1894 .... **NCLC 2; PC 7**
See also DA; DLB 35; MAICYA;
SATA 20; WLC

Rossetti, Dante Gabriel
1828-1882 .... **NCLC 4**
See also CDBLB 1832-1890; DA; DLB 35;
WLC

Rossner, Judith (Perelman)
1935- .... **CLC 6, 9, 29**
See also AITN 2; BEST 90:3; CA 17-20R;
CANR 18; DLB 6; MTCW

Rostand, Edmond (Eugene Alexis)
1868-1918 .... **TCLC 6, 37**
See also CA 104; 126; DA; MTCW

Roth, Henry 1906-........... **CLC 2, 6, 11**
See also CA 11-12; CANR 38; CAP 1;
DLB 28; MTCW

Roth, Joseph 1894-1939......... **TCLC 33**
See also DLB 85

Roth, Philip (Milton)
1933- ...... **CLC 1, 2, 3, 4, 6, 9, 15, 22,
31, 47, 66**
See also BEST 90:3; CA 1-4R; CANR 1, 22,
36; CDALB 1968-1988; DA; DLB 2, 28;
DLBY 82; MTCW; WLC

Rothenberg, Jerome 1931-....... **CLC 6, 57**
See also CA 45-48; CANR 1; DLB 5

Roumain, Jacques (Jean Baptiste)
1907-1944 .... **TCLC 19**
See also BLC 3; BW; CA 117; 125

Rourke, Constance (Mayfield)
1885-1941 .... **TCLC 12**
See also CA 107; YABC 1

Rousseau, Jean-Baptiste 1671-1741 ... **LC 9**

Rousseau, Jean-Jacques 1712-1778... **LC 14**
See also DA; WLC

Roussel, Raymond 1877-1933 ..... **TCLC 20**
See also CA 117

Rovit, Earl (Herbert) 1927-........ **CLC 7**
See also CA 5-8R; CANR 12

Rowe, Nicholas 1674-1718.......... **LC 8**
See also DLB 84

Rowley, Ames Dorrance
See Lovecraft, H(oward) P(hillips)

Rowson, Susanna Haswell
1762(?)-1824 .... **NCLC 5**
See also DLB 37

Roy, Gabrielle 1909-1983....... **CLC 10, 14**
See also CA 53-56; 110; CANR 5; DLB 68;
MTCW

Rozewicz, Tadeusz 1921-........ **CLC 9, 23**
See also CA 108; CANR 36; MTCW

Ruark, Gibbons 1941- .... **CLC 3**
See also CA 33-36R; CANR 14, 31;
DLB 120

Rubens, Bernice (Ruth) 1923-... **CLC 19, 31**
See also CA 25-28R; CANR 33; DLB 14;
MTCW

Rudkin, (James) David 1936- ...... **CLC 14**
See also CA 89-92; DLB 13

Rudnik, Raphael 1933-............. **CLC 7**
See also CA 29-32R

Ruffian, M.
See Hasek, Jaroslav (Matej Frantisek)

Ruiz, Jose Martinez............... **CLC 11**
See also Martinez Ruiz, Jose

Rukeyser, Muriel
1913-1980 .... **CLC 6, 10, 15, 27**
See also CA 5-8R; 93-96; CANR 26;
DLB 48; MTCW; SATA 22

Rule, Jane (Vance) 1931-......... **CLC 27**
See also CA 25-28R; CANR 12; DLB 60

Rulfo, Juan 1918-1986............. **CLC 8**
See also CA 85-88; 118; CANR 26;
DLB 113; HW; MTCW

Runeberg, Johan 1804-1877...... **NCLC 41**

Runyon, (Alfred) Damon
1884(?)-1946 .... **TCLC 10**
See also CA 107; DLB 11, 86

Rush, Norman 1933-............. **CLC 44**
See also CA 121; 126

Rushdie, (Ahmed) Salman
1947- . . . . **CLC 23, 31, 55**
See also BEST 89:3; CA 108; 111;
CANR 33; MTCW

Rushforth, Peter (Scott) 1945- . . . . . **CLC 19**
See also CA 101

Ruskin, John 1819-1900 . . . . **TCLC 20**
See also CA 114; 129; CDBLB 1832-1890;
DLB 55; SATA 24

Russ, Joanna 1937- . . . . **CLC 15**
See also CA 25-28R; CANR 11, 31; DLB 8;
MTCW

Russell, George William 1867-1935
See A. E.
See also CA 104; CDBLB 1890-1914

Russell, (Henry) Ken(neth Alfred)
1927- . . . . **CLC 16**
See also CA 105

Russell, Willy 1947- . . . . **CLC 60**

Rutherford, Mark . . . . **TCLC 25**
See also White, William Hale
See also DLB 18

Ruyslinck, Ward
See Belser, Reimond Karel Maria de

Ryan, Cornelius (John) 1920-1974 . . . **CLC 7**
See also CA 69-72; 53-56; CANR 38

Ryan, Michael 1946- . . . . **CLC 65**
See also CA 49-52; DLBY 82

Rybakov, Anatoli (Naumovich)
1911- . . . . **CLC 23, 53**
See also CA 126; 135

Ryder, Jonathan
See Ludlum, Robert

Ryga, George 1932-1987 . . . . **CLC 14**
See also CA 101; 124; DLB 60

S. S.
See Sassoon, Siegfried (Lorraine)

Saba, Umberto 1883-1957 . . . . **TCLC 33**
See also DLB 114

Sabatini, Rafael 1875-1950 . . . . **TCLC 47**

Sabato, Ernesto (R.) 1911- . . . . . . **CLC 10, 23**
See also CA 97-100; CANR 32; HW;
MTCW

Sacastru, Martin
See Bioy Casares, Adolfo

Sacher-Masoch, Leopold von
1836(?)-1895 . . . . **NCLC 31**

Sachs, Marilyn (Stickle) 1927- . . . . . **CLC 35**
See also AAYA 2; CA 17-20R; CANR 13;
CLR 2; MAICYA; SAAS 2; SATA 3, 68

Sachs, Nelly 1891-1970 . . . . **CLC 14**
See also CA 17-18; 25-28R; CAP 2

Sackler, Howard (Oliver)
1929-1982 . . . . **CLC 14**
See also CA 61-64; 108; CANR 30; DLB 7

Sacks, Oliver (Wolf) 1933- . . . . **CLC 67**
See also CA 53-56; CANR 28; MTCW

Sade, Donatien Alphonse Francois Comte
1740-1814 . . . . **NCLC 3**

Sadoff, Ira 1945- . . . . **CLC 9**
See also CA 53-56; CANR 5, 21; DLB 120

Saetone
See Camus, Albert

Safire, William 1929- . . . . **CLC 10**
See also CA 17-20R; CANR 31

Sagan, Carl (Edward) 1934- . . . . **CLC 30**
See also AAYA 2; CA 25-28R; CANR 11,
36; MTCW; SATA 58

Sagan, Francoise . . . . **CLC 3, 6, 9, 17, 36**
See also Quoirez, Francoise
See also DLB 83

Sahgal, Nayantara (Pandit) 1927- . . . **CLC 41**
See also CA 9-12R; CANR 11

Saint, H(arry) F. 1941- . . . . **CLC 50**
See also CA 127

St. Aubin de Teran, Lisa 1953-
See Teran, Lisa St. Aubin de
See also CA 118; 126

Sainte-Beuve, Charles Augustin
1804-1869 . . . . **NCLC 5**

**Saint-Exupery, Antoine (Jean Baptiste Marie
Roger) de** 1900-1944 . . . . **TCLC 2**
See also CA 108; 132; CLR 10; DLB 72;
MAICYA; MTCW; SATA 20; WLC

St. John, David
See Hunt, E(verette) Howard, Jr.

Saint-John Perse
See Leger, (Marie-Rene) Alexis Saint-Leger

Saintsbury, George (Edward Bateman)
1845-1933 . . . . **TCLC 31**
See also DLB 57

Sait Faik . . . . **TCLC 23**
See also Abasiyanik, Sait Faik

Saki . . . . **TCLC 3; SSC 12**
See also Munro, H(ector) H(ugh)

Salama, Hannu 1936- . . . . **CLC 18**

Salamanca, J(ack) R(ichard)
1922- . . . . **CLC 4, 15**
See also CA 25-28R

Sale, J. Kirkpatrick
See Sale, Kirkpatrick

Sale, Kirkpatrick 1937- . . . . **CLC 68**
See also CA 13-16R; CANR 10

Salinas (y Serrano), Pedro
1891(?)-1951 . . . . **TCLC 17**
See also CA 117

Salinger, J(erome) D(avid)
1919- . . . . **CLC 1, 3, 8, 12, 55, 56; SSC 2**
See also AAYA 2; CA 5-8R; CANR 39;
CDALB 1941-1968; CLR 18; DA;
DLB 2, 102; MAICYA; MTCW;
SATA 67; WLC

Salisbury, John
See Caute, David

Salter, James 1925- . . . . **CLC 7, 52, 59**
See also CA 73-76; DLB 130

Saltus, Edgar (Everton)
1855-1921 . . . . **TCLC 8**
See also CA 105

Saltykov, Mikhail Evgrafovich
1826-1889 . . . . **NCLC 16**

Samarakis, Antonis 1919- . . . . **CLC 5**
See also CA 25-28R; CAAS 16; CANR 36

Sanchez, Florencio 1875-1910 . . . . . **TCLC 37**
See also HW

Sanchez, Luis Rafael 1936- . . . . **CLC 23**
See also CA 128; HW

Sanchez, Sonia 1934- . . . . **CLC 5**
See also BLC 3; BW; CA 33-36R;
CANR 24; CLR 18; DLB 41; DLBD 8;
MAICYA; MTCW; SATA 22

Sand, George 1804-1876 . . . . **NCLC 2**
See also DA; DLB 119; WLC

Sandburg, Carl (August)
1878-1967 . . . **CLC 1, 4, 10, 15, 35; PC 2**
See also CA 5-8R; 25-28R; CANR 35;
CDALB 1865-1917; DA; DLB 17, 54;
MAICYA; MTCW; SATA 8; WLC

Sandburg, Charles
See Sandburg, Carl (August)

Sandburg, Charles A.
See Sandburg, Carl (August)

Sanders, (James) Ed(ward) 1939- . . . **CLC 53**
See also CA 13-16R; CANR 13; DLB 16

Sanders, Lawrence 1920- . . . . **CLC 41**
See also BEST 89:4; CA 81-84; CANR 33;
MTCW

Sanders, Noah
See Blount, Roy (Alton), Jr.

Sanders, Winston P.
See Anderson, Poul (William)

Sandoz, Mari(e Susette)
1896-1966 . . . . **CLC 28**
See also CA 1-4R; 25-28R; CANR 17;
DLB 9; MTCW; SATA 5

Saner, Reg(inald Anthony) 1931- . . . . **CLC 9**
See also CA 65-68

Sannazaro, Jacopo 1456(?)-1530 . . . . . . **LC 8**

Sansom, William 1912-1976 . . . . **CLC 2, 6**
See also CA 5-8R; 65-68; MTCW

Santayana, George 1863-1952 . . . . . **TCLC 40**
See also CA 115; DLB 54, 71

Santiago, Danny . . . . **CLC 33**
See also James, Daniel (Lewis); James,
Daniel (Lewis)
See also DLB 122

Santmyer, Helen Hooven
1895-1986 . . . . **CLC 33**
See also CA 1-4R; 118; CANR 15, 33;
DLBY 84; MTCW

Santos, Bienvenido N(uqui) 1911- . . . **CLC 22**
See also CA 101; CANR 19

Sapper . . . . **TCLC 44**
See also McNeile, Herman Cyril

Sappho fl. 6th cent. B.C.- . . . . **CMLC 3; PC 5**

Sarduy, Severo 1937- . . . . **CLC 6**
See also CA 89-92; DLB 113; HW

Sargeson, Frank 1903-1982 . . . . **CLC 31**
See also CA 25-28R; 106; CANR 38

Sarmiento, Felix Ruben Garcia 1867-1916
See Dario, Ruben
See also CA 104

Saroyan, William
1908-1981 . . . . . **CLC 1, 8, 10, 29, 34, 56**
See also CA 5-8R; 103; CANR 30; DA;
DLB 7, 9, 86; DLBY 81; MTCW;
SATA 23, 24; WLC

Sarraute, Nathalie
1900- . . . . **CLC 1, 2, 4, 8, 10, 31**
See also CA 9-12R; CANR 23; DLB 83;
MTCW

Sarton, (Eleanor) May
1912- .... **CLC 4, 14, 49**
See also CA 1-4R; CANR 1, 34; DLB 48;
DLBY 81; MTCW; SATA 36

Sartre, Jean-Paul
1905-1980 .... **CLC 1, 4, 7, 9, 13, 18, 24,
44, 50, 52; DC 3**
See also CA 9-12R; 97-100; CANR 21; DA;
DLB 72; MTCW; WLC

Sassoon, Siegfried (Lorraine)
1886-1967 .... **CLC 36**
See also CA 104; 25-28R; CANR 36;
DLB 20; MTCW

Satterfield, Charles
See Pohl, Frederik

Saul, John (W. III) 1942- .... **CLC 46**
See also AAYA 10; BEST 90:4; CA 81-84;
CANR 16, 40

Saunders, Caleb
See Heinlein, Robert A(nson)

Saura (Atares), Carlos 1932- .... **CLC 20**
See also CA 114; 131; HW

Sauser-Hall, Frederic 1887-1961.... **CLC 18**
See also CA 102; 93-96; CANR 36; MTCW

Saussure, Ferdinand de
1857-1913 .... **TCLC 49**

Savage, Catharine
See Brosman, Catharine Savage

Savage, Thomas 1915- .... **CLC 40**
See also CA 126; 132; CAAS 15

Savan, Glenn .... **CLC 50**

Saven, Glenn 19(?)- .... **CLC 50**

Sayers, Dorothy L(eigh)
1893-1957 .... **TCLC 2, 15**
See also CA 104; 119; CDBLB 1914-1945;
DLB 10, 36, 77, 100; MTCW

Sayers, Valerie 1952- .... **CLC 50**
See also CA 134

Sayles, John (Thomas)
1950- .... **CLC 7, 10, 14**
See also CA 57-60; CANR 41; DLB 44

Scammell, Michael .... **CLC 34**

Scannell, Vernon 1922- .... **CLC 49**
See also CA 5-8R; CANR 8, 24; DLB 27;
SATA 59

Scarlett, Susan
See Streatfeild, (Mary) Noel

Schaeffer, Susan Fromberg
1941- .... **CLC 6, 11, 22**
See also CA 49-52; CANR 18; DLB 28;
MTCW; SATA 22

Schary, Jill
See Robinson, Jill

Schell, Jonathan 1943- .... **CLC 35**
See also CA 73-76; CANR 12

Schelling, Friedrich Wilhelm Joseph von
1775-1854 .... **NCLC 30**
See also DLB 90

Scherer, Jean-Marie Maurice 1920-
See Rohmer, Eric
See also CA 110

Schevill, James (Erwin) 1920-....... **CLC 7**
See also CA 5-8R; CAAS 12

Schiller, Friedrich 1759-1805 .... **NCLC 39**
See also DLB 94

Schisgal, Murray (Joseph) 1926-..... **CLC 6**
See also CA 21-24R

Schlee, Ann 1934-................ **CLC 35**
See also CA 101; CANR 29; SATA 36, 44

Schlegel, August Wilhelm von
1767-1845 .... **NCLC 15**
See also DLB 94

Schlegel, Johann Elias (von)
1719(?)-1749 .... **LC 5**

Schmidt, Arno (Otto) 1914-1979.... **CLC 56**
See also CA 128; 109; DLB 69

Schmitz, Aron Hector 1861-1928
See Svevo, Italo
See also CA 104; 122; MTCW

Schnackenberg, Gjertrud 1953-..... **CLC 40**
See also CA 116; DLB 120

Schneider, Leonard Alfred 1925-1966
See Bruce, Lenny
See also CA 89-92

Schnitzler, Arthur 1862-1931 ...... **TCLC 4**
See also CA 104; DLB 81, 118

Schor, Sandra (M.) 1932(?)-1990 ... **CLC 65**
See also CA 132

Schorer, Mark 1908-1977 .... **CLC 9**
See also CA 5-8R; 73-76; CANR 7;
DLB 103

Schrader, Paul (Joseph) 1946-...... **CLC 26**
See also CA 37-40R; CANR 41; DLB 44

Schreiner, Olive (Emilie Albertina)
1855-1920 .... **TCLC 9**
See also CA 105; DLB 18

Schulberg, Budd (Wilson)
1914- .... **CLC 7, 48**
See also CA 25-28R; CANR 19; DLB 6, 26,
28; DLBY 81

Schulz, Bruno 1892-1942....... **TCLC 5, 51**
See also CA 115; 123

Schulz, Charles M(onroe) 1922- .... **CLC 12**
See also CA 9-12R; CANR 6; SATA 10

Schuyler, James Marcus
1923-1991 .... **CLC 5, 23**
See also CA 101; 134; DLB 5

Schwartz, Delmore (David)
1913-1966 .... **CLC 2, 4, 10, 45**
See also CA 17-18; 25-28R; CANR 35;
CAP 2; DLB 28, 48; MTCW

Schwartz, Ernst
See Ozu, Yasujiro

Schwartz, John Burnham 1965- .... **CLC 59**
See also CA 132

Schwartz, Lynne Sharon 1939-..... **CLC 31**
See also CA 103

Schwartz, Muriel A.
See Eliot, T(homas) S(tearns)

Schwarz-Bart, Andre 1928-....... **CLC 2, 4**
See also CA 89-92

Schwarz-Bart, Simone 1938-........ **CLC 7**
See also CA 97-100

Schwob, (Mayer Andre) Marcel
1867-1905 .... **TCLC 20**
See also CA 117; DLB 123

Sciascia, Leonardo
1921-1989 .... **CLC 8, 9, 41**
See also CA 85-88; 130; CANR 35; MTCW

Scoppettone, Sandra 1936-........ **CLC 26**
See also CA 5-8R; CANR 41; SATA 9

Scorsese, Martin 1942- .... **CLC 20**
See also CA 110; 114

Scotland, Jay
See Jakes, John (William)

Scott, Duncan Campbell
1862-1947 .... **TCLC 6**
See also CA 104; DLB 92

Scott, Evelyn 1893-1963.......... **CLC 43**
See also CA 104; 112; DLB 9, 48

Scott, F(rancis) R(eginald)
1899-1985 .... **CLC 22**
See also CA 101; 114; DLB 88

Scott, Frank
See Scott, F(rancis) R(eginald)

Scott, Joanna 1960- .... **CLC 50**
See also CA 126

Scott, Paul (Mark) 1920-1978.... **CLC 9, 60**
See also CA 81-84; 77-80; CANR 33;
DLB 14; MTCW

Scott, Walter 1771-1832......... **NCLC 15**
See also CDBLB 1789-1832; DA; DLB 93,
107, 116; WLC; YABC 2

Scribe, (Augustin) Eugene
1791-1861 .... **NCLC 16**

Scrum, R.
See Crumb, R(obert)

Scudery, Madeleine de 1607-1701..... **LC 2**

Scum
See Crumb, R(obert)

Scumbag, Little Bobby
See Crumb, R(obert)

Seabrook, John
See Hubbard, L(afayette) Ron(ald)

Sealy, I. Allan 1951- .... **CLC 55**

Search, Alexander
See Pessoa, Fernando (Antonio Nogueira)

Sebastian, Lee
See Silverberg, Robert

Sebastian Owl
See Thompson, Hunter S(tockton)

Sebestyen, Ouida 1924- .... **CLC 30**
See also AAYA 8; CA 107; CANR 40;
CLR 17; MAICYA; SAAS 10; SATA 39

Secundus, H. Scriblerus
See Fielding, Henry

Sedges, John
See Buck, Pearl S(ydenstricker)

Sedgwick, Catharine Maria
1789-1867 .... **NCLC 19**
See also DLB 1, 74

Seelye, John 1931-................ **CLC 7**

Seferiades, Giorgos Stylianou 1900-1971
See Seferis, George
See also CA 5-8R; 33-36R; CANR 5, 36;
MTCW

Seferis, George .... **CLC 5, 11**
See also Seferiades, Giorgos Stylianou

Segal, Erich (Wolf) 1937- .... **CLC 3, 10**
    See also BEST 89:1; CA 25-28R; CANR 20,
        36; DLBY 86; MTCW

Seger, Bob 1945-................. **CLC 35**

Seghers, Anna .... **CLC 7**
    See also Radvanyi, Netty
    See also DLB 69

Seidel, Frederick (Lewis) 1936-..... **CLC 18**
    See also CA 13-16R; CANR 8; DLBY 84

Seifert, Jaroslav 1901-1986..... **CLC 34, 44**
    See also CA 127; MTCW

Sei Shonagon c. 966-1017(?) ...... **CMLC 6**

Selby, Hubert, Jr. 1928- ..... **CLC 1, 2, 4, 8**
    See also CA 13-16R; CANR 33; DLB 2

Selzer, Richard 1928-............. **CLC 74**
    See also CA 65-68; CANR 14

Sembene, Ousmane
    See Ousmane, Sembene

Senancour, Etienne Pivert de
        1770-1846 .... **NCLC 16**
    See also DLB 119

Sender, Ramon (Jose) 1902-1982 .... **CLC 8**
    See also CA 5-8R; 105; CANR 8; HW;
        MTCW

Seneca, Lucius Annaeus
        4B.C.-65.................... **CMLC 6**

Senghor, Leopold Sedar 1906-...... **CLC 54**
    See also BLC 3; BW; CA 116; 125; MTCW

Serling, (Edward) Rod(man)
        1924-1975 .... **CLC 30**
    See also AITN 1; CA 65-68; 57-60; DLB 26

Serna, Ramon Gomez de la
    See Gomez de la Serna, Ramon

Serpieres
    See Guillevic, (Eugene)

Service, Robert
    See Service, Robert W(illiam)
    See also DLB 92

Service, Robert W(illiam)
        1874(?)-1958 .... **TCLC 15**
    See also Service, Robert
    See also CA 115; 140; DA; SATA 20; WLC

Seth, Vikram 1952-............... **CLC 43**
    See also CA 121; 127; DLB 120

Seton, Cynthia Propper
        1926-1982 .... **CLC 27**
    See also CA 5-8R; 108; CANR 7

Seton, Ernest (Evan) Thompson
        1860-1946 .... **TCLC 31**
    See also CA 109; DLB 92; SATA 18

Seton-Thompson, Ernest
    See Seton, Ernest (Evan) Thompson

Settle, Mary Lee 1918- .... **CLC 19, 61**
    See also CA 89-92; CAAS 1; DLB 6

Seuphor, Michel
    See Arp, Jean

Sevigne, Marie (de Rabutin-Chantal) Marquise
    de 1626-1696 .... **LC 11**

Sexton, Anne (Harvey)
        1928-1974 .... **CLC 2, 4, 6, 8, 10, 15, 53;**
                                               PC 2
    See also CA 1-4R; 53-56; CABS 2;
        CANR 3, 36; CDALB 1941-1968; DA;
        DLB 5; MTCW; SATA 10; WLC

Shaara, Michael (Joseph Jr.)
        1929-1988 .... **CLC 15**
    See also AITN 1; CA 102; DLBY 83

Shackleton, C. C.
    See Aldiss, Brian W(ilson)

Shacochis, Bob .... **CLC 39**
    See also Shacochis, Robert G.

Shacochis, Robert G. 1951-
    See Shacochis, Bob
    See also CA 119; 124

Shaffer, Anthony (Joshua) 1926-.... **CLC 19**
    See also CA 110; 116; DLB 13

Shaffer, Peter (Levin)
        1926- .... **CLC 5, 14, 18, 37, 60**
    See also CA 25-28R; CANR 25;
        CDBLB 1960 to Present; DLB 13;
        MTCW

Shakey, Bernard
    See Young, Neil

Shalamov, Varlam (Tikhonovich)
        1907(?)-1982 .... **CLC 18**
    See also CA 129; 105

Shamlu, Ahmad 1925- .... **CLC 10**

Shammas, Anton 1951-........... **CLC 55**

Shange, Ntozake
        1948- .... **CLC 8, 25, 38, 74; DC 3**
    See also AAYA 9; BLC 3; BW; CA 85-88;
        CABS 3; CANR 27; DLB 38; MTCW

Shanley, John Patrick 1950-....... **CLC 75**
    See also CA 128; 133

Shapcott, Thomas William 1935- ... **CLC 38**
    See also CA 69-72

Shapiro, Jane.................... **CLC 76**

Shapiro, Karl (Jay) 1913- .. **CLC 4, 8, 15, 53**
    See also CA 1-4R; CAAS 6; CANR 1, 36;
        DLB 48; MTCW

Sharp, William 1855-1905 .... **TCLC 39**

Sharpe, Thomas Ridley 1928-
    See Sharpe, Tom
    See also CA 114; 122

Sharpe, Tom..................... **CLC 36**
    See also Sharpe, Thomas Ridley
    See also DLB 14

Shaw, Bernard.................**TCLC 45**
    See also Shaw, George Bernard

Shaw, G. Bernard
    See Shaw, George Bernard

Shaw, George Bernard
        1856-1950 .... **TCLC 3, 9, 21**
    See also Shaw, Bernard
    See also CA 104; 128; CDBLB 1914-1945;
        DA; DLB 10, 57; MTCW; WLC

Shaw, Henry Wheeler
        1818-1885 .... **NCLC 15**
    See also DLB 11

Shaw, Irwin 1913-1984....... **CLC 7, 23, 34**
    See also AITN 1; CA 13-16R; 112;
        CANR 21; CDALB 1941-1968; DLB 6,
        102; DLBY 84; MTCW

Shaw, Robert 1927-1978 .... **CLC 5**
    See also AITN 1; CA 1-4R; 81-84;
        CANR 4; DLB 13, 14

Shaw, T. E.
    See Lawrence, T(homas) E(dward)

Shawn, Wallace 1943-........... **CLC 41**
    See also CA 112

Sheed, Wilfrid (John Joseph)
        1930- .... **CLC 2, 4, 10, 53**
    See also CA 65-68; CANR 30; DLB 6;
        MTCW

Sheldon, Alice Hastings Bradley
        1915(?)-1987
    See Tiptree, James, Jr.
    See also CA 108; 122; CANR 34; MTCW

Sheldon, John
    See Bloch, Robert (Albert)

Shelley, Mary Wollstonecraft (Godwin)
        1797-1851 .... **NCLC 14**
    See also CDBLB 1789-1832; DA; DLB 110,
        116; SATA 29; WLC

Shelley, Percy Bysshe
        1792-1822 .... **NCLC 18**
    See also CDBLB 1789-1832; DA; DLB 96,
        110; WLC

Shepard, Jim 1956-................ **CLC 36**
    See also CA 137

Shepard, Lucius 19(?)-............. **CLC 34**
    See also CA 128

Shepard, Sam
        1943- .... **CLC 4, 6, 17, 34, 41, 44**
    See also AAYA 1; CA 69-72; CABS 3;
        CANR 22; DLB 7; MTCW

Shepherd, Michael
    See Ludlum, Robert

Sherburne, Zoa (Morin) 1912-...... **CLC 30**
    See also CA 1-4R; CANR 3, 37; MAICYA;
        SATA 3

Sheridan, Frances 1724-1766........ **LC 7**
    See also DLB 39, 84

Sheridan, Richard Brinsley
        1751-1816 .... **NCLC 5; DC 1**
    See also CDBLB 1660-1789; DA; DLB 89;
        WLC

Sherman, Jonathan Marc.......... **CLC 55**

Sherman, Martin 1941(?)- .... **CLC 19**
    See also CA 116; 123

Sherwin, Judith Johnson 1936-... **CLC 7, 15**
    See also CA 25-28R; CANR 34

Sherwood, Robert E(mmet)
        1896-1955 .... **TCLC 3**
    See also CA 104; DLB 7, 26

Shiel, M(atthew) P(hipps)
        1865-1947 .... **TCLC 8**
    See also CA 106

Shiga, Naoya 1883-1971........... **CLC 33**
    See also CA 101; 33-36R

Shimazaki Haruki 1872-1943
    See Shimazaki Toson
    See also CA 105; 134

Shimazaki Toson .... **TCLC 5**
    See also Shimazaki Haruki

Sholokhov, Mikhail (Aleksandrovich)
        1905-1984 .... **CLC 7, 15**
    See also CA 101; 112; MTCW; SATA 36

Shone, Patric
    See Hanley, James

Shreve, Susan Richards 1939-...... **CLC 23**
    See also CA 49-52; CAAS 5; CANR 5, 38;
        MAICYA; SATA 41, 46

Shue, Larry 1946-1985........... **CLC 52**
See also CA 117

Shu-Jen, Chou 1881-1936
See Hsun, Lu
See also CA 104

Shulman, Alix Kates 1932- ...... **CLC 2, 10**
See also CA 29-32R; SATA 7

Shuster, Joe 1914- .... **CLC 21**

Shute, Nevil...................... **CLC 30**
See also Norway, Nevil Shute

Shuttle, Penelope (Diane) 1947- ..... **CLC 7**
See also CA 93-96; CANR 39; DLB 14, 40

Sidney, Mary 1561-1621 .... **LC 19**

Sidney, Sir Philip 1554-1586........ **LC 19**
See also CDBLB Before 1660; DA

Siegel, Jerome 1914- .... **CLC 21**
See also CA 116

Siegel, Jerry
See Siegel, Jerome

Sienkiewicz, Henryk (Adam Alexander Pius)
1846-1916 .... **TCLC 3**
See also CA 104; 134

Sierra, Gregorio Martinez
See Martinez Sierra, Gregorio

Sierra, Maria (de la O'LeJarraga) Martinez
See Martinez Sierra, Maria (de la
O'LeJarraga)

Sigal, Clancy 1926-................ **CLC 7**
See also CA 1-4R

Sigourney, Lydia Howard (Huntley)
1791-1865 .... **NCLC 21**
See also DLB 1, 42, 73

Siguenza y Gongora, Carlos de
1645-1700 .... **LC 8**

Sigurjonsson, Johann 1880-1919... **TCLC 27**

Sikelianos, Angelos 1884-1951 .... **TCLC 39**

Silkin, Jon 1930- .... **CLC 2, 6, 43**
See also CA 5-8R; CAAS 5; DLB 27

Silko, Leslie Marmon 1948- .... **CLC 23, 74**
See also CA 115; 122; DA

Sillanpaa, Frans Eemil 1888-1964... **CLC 19**
See also CA 129; 93-96; MTCW

Sillitoe, Alan
1928- .... **CLC 1, 3, 6, 10, 19, 57**
See also AITN 1; CA 9-12R; CAAS 2;
CANR 8, 26; CDBLB 1960 to Present;
DLB 14; MTCW; SATA 61

Silone, Ignazio 1900-1978 .... **CLC 4**
See also CA 25-28; 81-84; CANR 34;
CAP 2; MTCW

Silver, Joan Micklin 1935- .... **CLC 20**
See also CA 114; 121

Silver, Nicholas
See Faust, Frederick (Schiller)

Silverberg, Robert 1935- .... **CLC 7**
See also CA 1-4R; CAAS 3; CANR 1, 20,
36; DLB 8; MAICYA; MTCW; SATA 13

Silverstein, Alvin 1933-............ **CLC 17**
See also CA 49-52; CANR 2; CLR 25;
MAICYA; SATA 8, 69

Silverstein, Virginia B(arbara Opshelor)
1937- .... **CLC 17**
See also CA 49-52; CANR 2; CLR 25;
MAICYA; SATA 8, 69

Sim, Georges
See Simenon, Georges (Jacques Christian)

Simak, Clifford D(onald)
1904-1988 .... **CLC 1, 55**
See also CA 1-4R; 125; CANR 1, 35;
DLB 8; MTCW; SATA 56

Simenon, Georges (Jacques Christian)
1903-1989 .... **CLC 1, 2, 3, 8, 18, 47**
See also CA 85-88; 129; CANR 35;
DLB 72; DLBY 89; MTCW

Simic, Charles 1938-... **CLC 6, 9, 22, 49, 68**
See also CA 29-32R; CAAS 4; CANR 12,
33; DLB 105

Simmons, Charles (Paul) 1924- ..... **CLC 57**
See also CA 89-92

Simmons, Dan 1948-.............. **CLC 44**
See also CA 138

Simmons, James (Stewart Alexander)
1933- .... **CLC 43**
See also CA 105; DLB 40

Simms, William Gilmore
1806-1870 .... **NCLC 3**
See also DLB 3, 30, 59, 73

Simon, Carly 1945-.............. **CLC 26**
See also CA 105

Simon, Claude 1913-....... **CLC 4, 9, 15, 39**
See also CA 89-92; CANR 33; DLB 83;
MTCW

Simon, (Marvin) Neil
1927- .... **CLC 6, 11, 31, 39, 70**
See also AITN 1; CA 21-24R; CANR 26;
DLB 7; MTCW

Simon, Paul 1942(?)- .... **CLC 17**
See also CA 116

Simonon, Paul 1956(?)- .... **CLC 30**
See also Clash, The

Simpson, Harriette
See Arnow, Harriette (Louisa) Simpson

Simpson, Louis (Aston Marantz)
1923-................**CLC 4, 7, 9, 32**
See also CA 1-4R; CAAS 4; CANR 1;
DLB 5; MTCW

Simpson, Mona (Elizabeth) 1957-... **CLC 44**
See also CA 122; 135

Simpson, N(orman) F(rederick)
1919- .... **CLC 29**
See also CA 13-16R; DLB 13

Sinclair, Andrew (Annandale)
1935- .... **CLC 2, 14**
See also CA 9-12R; CAAS 5; CANR 14, 38;
DLB 14; MTCW

Sinclair, Emil
See Hesse, Hermann

Sinclair, Iain 1943-................ **CLC 76**
See also CA 132

Sinclair, Iain MacGregor
See Sinclair, Iain

Sinclair, Mary Amelia St. Clair 1865(?)-1946
See Sinclair, May
See also CA 104

Sinclair, May.................... **TCLC 3, 11**
See also Sinclair, Mary Amelia St. Clair
See also DLB 36

Sinclair, Upton (Beall)
1878-1968 .... **CLC 1, 11, 15, 63**
See also CA 5-8R; 25-28R; CANR 7;
CDALB 1929-1941; DA; DLB 9; MTCW;
SATA 9; WLC

Singer, Isaac
See Singer, Isaac Bashevis

Singer, Isaac Bashevis
1904-1991 .... **CLC 1, 3, 6, 9, 11, 15, 23,
38, 69; SSC 3**
See also AITN 1, 2; CA 1-4R; 134;
CANR 1, 39; CDALB 1941-1968; CLR 1;
DA; DLB 6, 28, 52; DLBY 91;
MAICYA; MTCW; SATA 3, 27;
SATA-Obit 68; WLC

Singer, Israel Joshua 1893-1944... **TCLC 33**

Singh, Khushwant 1915-........... **CLC 11**
See also CA 9-12R; CAAS 9; CANR 6

Sinjohn, John
See Galsworthy, John

Sinyavsky, Andrei (Donatevich)
1925- .... **CLC 8**
See also CA 85-88

Sirin, V.
See Nabokov, Vladimir (Vladimirovich)

Sissman, L(ouis) E(dward)
1928-1976 .... **CLC 9, 18**
See also CA 21-24R; 65-68; CANR 13;
DLB 5

Sisson, C(harles) H(ubert) 1914-..... **CLC 8**
See also CA 1-4R; CAAS 3; CANR 3;
DLB 27

Sitwell, Dame Edith
1887-1964 .... **CLC 2, 9, 67; PC 3**
See also CA 9-12R; CANR 35;
CDBLB 1945-1960; DLB 20; MTCW

Sjoewall, Maj 1935-.............. **CLC 7**
See also CA 65-68

Sjowall, Maj
See Sjoewall, Maj

Skelton, Robin 1925-............. **CLC 13**
See also AITN 2; CA 5-8R; CAAS 5;
CANR 28; DLB 27, 53

Skolimowski, Jerzy 1938-......... **CLC 20**
See also CA 128

Skram, Amalie (Bertha)
1847-1905 .... **TCLC 25**

Skvorecky, Josef (Vaclav)
1924- .... **CLC 15, 39, 69**
See also CA 61-64; CAAS 1; CANR 10, 34;
MTCW

Slade, Bernard................. **CLC 11, 46**
See also Newbound, Bernard Slade
See also CAAS 9; DLB 53

Slaughter, Carolyn 1946-.......... **CLC 56**
See also CA 85-88

Slaughter, Frank G(ill) 1908- ...... **CLC 29**
See also AITN 2; CA 5-8R; CANR 5

Slavitt, David R(ytman) 1935-.... **CLC 5, 14**
See also CA 21-24R; CAAS 3; CANR 41;
DLB 5, 6

Slesinger, Tess 1905-1945 . . . . TCLC 10
See also CA 107; DLB 102

Slessor, Kenneth 1901-1971 . . . . CLC 14
See also CA 102; 89-92

Slowacki, Juliusz 1809-1849 . . . . . NCLC 15

Smart, Christopher 1722-1771 . . . . LC 3
See also DLB 109

Smart, Elizabeth 1913-1986 . . . . CLC 54
See also CA 81-84; 118; DLB 88

Smiley, Jane (Graves) 1949- . . . . CLC 53, 76
See also CA 104; CANR 30

Smith, A(rthur) J(ames) M(arshall)
1902-1980 . . . . CLC 15
See also CA 1-4R; 102; CANR 4; DLB 88

Smith, Betty (Wehner) 1896-1972 . . . CLC 19
See also CA 5-8R; 33-36R; DLBY 82;
SATA 6

Smith, Charlotte (Turner)
1749-1806 . . . . NCLC 23
See also DLB 39, 109

Smith, Clark Ashton 1893-1961 . . . . CLC 43

Smith, Dave . . . . CLC 22, 42
See also Smith, David (Jeddie)
See also CAAS 7; DLB 5

Smith, David (Jeddie) 1942-
See Smith, Dave
See also CA 49-52; CANR 1

Smith, Florence Margaret
1902-1971 . . . . CLC 8
See also Smith, Stevie
See also CA 17-18; 29-32R; CANR 35;
CAP 2; MTCW

Smith, Iain Crichton 1928- . . . . CLC 64
See also CA 21-24R; DLB 40

Smith, John 1580(?)-1631 . . . . LC 9

Smith, Johnston
See Crane, Stephen (Townley)

Smith, Lee 1944- . . . . CLC 25, 73
See also CA 114; 119; DLBY 83

Smith, Martin
See Smith, Martin Cruz

Smith, Martin Cruz 1942- . . . . CLC 25
See also BEST 89:4; CA 85-88; CANR 6, 23

Smith, Mary-Ann Tirone 1944- . . . . . CLC 39
See also CA 118; 136

Smith, Patti 1946- . . . . CLC 12
See also CA 93-96

Smith, Pauline (Urmson)
1882-1959 . . . . TCLC 25

Smith, Rosamond
See Oates, Joyce Carol

Smith, Sheila Kaye
See Kaye-Smith, Sheila

Smith, Stevie . . . . CLC 3, 8, 25, 44
See also Smith, Florence Margaret
See also DLB 20

Smith, Wilbur A(ddison) 1933- . . . . . CLC 33
See also CA 13-16R; CANR 7; MTCW

Smith, William Jay 1918- . . . . CLC 6
See also CA 5-8R; DLB 5; MAICYA;
SATA 2, 68

Smith, Woodrow Wilson
See Kuttner, Henry

Smolenskin, Peretz 1842-1885 . . . . NCLC 30

Smollett, Tobias (George) 1721-1771 . . LC 2
See also CDBLB 1660-1789; DLB 39, 104

Snodgrass, W(illiam) D(e Witt)
1926- . . . . CLC 2, 6, 10, 18, 68
See also CA 1-4R; CANR 6, 36; DLB 5;
MTCW

Snow, C(harles) P(ercy)
1905-1980 . . . . CLC 1, 4, 6, 9, 13, 19
See also CA 5-8R; 101; CANR 28;
CDBLB 1945-1960; DLB 15, 77; MTCW

Snow, Frances Compton
See Adams, Henry (Brooks)

Snyder, Gary (Sherman)
1930- . . . . CLC 1, 2, 5, 9, 32
See also CA 17-20R; CANR 30; DLB 5, 16

Snyder, Zilpha Keatley 1927- . . . . . . CLC 17
See also CA 9-12R; CANR 38; CLR 31;
MAICYA; SAAS 2; SATA 1, 28

Soares, Bernardo
See Pessoa, Fernando (Antonio Nogueira)

Sobh, A.
See Shamlu, Ahmad

Sobol, Joshua . . . . CLC 60

Soderberg, Hjalmar 1869-1941 . . . . TCLC 39

Sodergran, Edith (Irene)
See Soedergran, Edith (Irene)

Soedergran, Edith (Irene)
1892-1923 . . . . TCLC 31

Softly, Edgar
See Lovecraft, H(oward) P(hillips)

Softly, Edward
See Lovecraft, H(oward) P(hillips)

Sokolov, Raymond 1941- . . . . CLC 7
See also CA 85-88

Solo, Jay
See Ellison, Harlan

Sologub, Fyodor . . . . TCLC 9
See also Teternikov, Fyodor Kuzmich

Solomons, Ikey Esquir
See Thackeray, William Makepeace

Solomos, Dionysios 1798-1857 . . . NCLC 15

Solwoska, Mara
See French, Marilyn

Solzhenitsyn, Aleksandr I(sayevich)
1918- . . . . . . CLC 1, 2, 4, 7, 9, 10, 18, 26,
34, 78
See also AITN 1; CA 69-72; CANR 40;
DA; MTCW; WLC

Somers, Jane
See Lessing, Doris (May)

Somerville, Edith 1858-1949 . . . . . . TCLC 51

Sommer, Scott 1951- . . . . CLC 25
See also CA 106

Sondheim, Stephen (Joshua)
1930- . . . . CLC 30, 39
See also CA 103

Sontag, Susan 1933- . . . CLC 1, 2, 10, 13, 31
See also CA 17-20R; CANR 25; DLB 2, 67;
MTCW

Sophocles
496(?)B.C.-406(?)B.C. . . . CMLC 2; DC 1
See also DA

Sorel, Julia
See Drexler, Rosalyn

Sorrentino, Gilbert
1929- . . . . CLC 3, 7, 14, 22, 40
See also CA 77-80; CANR 14, 33; DLB 5;
DLBY 80

Soto, Gary 1952- . . . . CLC 32
See also AAYA 10; CA 119; 125; DLB 82;
HW

Soupault, Philippe 1897-1990 . . . . . . CLC 68
See also CA 116; 131

Souster, (Holmes) Raymond
1921- . . . . CLC 5, 14
See also CA 13-16R; CAAS 14; CANR 13,
29; DLB 88; SATA 63

Southern, Terry 1926- . . . . CLC 7
See also CA 1-4R; CANR 1; DLB 2

Southey, Robert 1774-1843 . . . . NCLC 8
See also DLB 93, 107; SATA 54

Southworth, Emma Dorothy Eliza Nevitte
1819-1899 . . . . NCLC 26

Souza, Ernest
See Scott, Evelyn

Soyinka, Wole
1934- . . . . CLC 3, 5, 14, 36, 44; DC 2
See also BLC 3; BW 1; CA 13-16R;
CANR 27, 39; DA; DLB 125; MTCW;
WLC

Spackman, W(illiam) M(ode)
1905-1990 . . . . CLC 46
See also CA 81-84; 132

Spacks, Barry 1931- . . . . CLC 14
See also CA 29-32R; CANR 33; DLB 105

Spanidou, Irini 1946- . . . . CLC 44

Spark, Muriel (Sarah)
1918- . . . . CLC 2, 3, 5, 8, 13, 18, 40;
SSC 10
See also CA 5-8R; CANR 12, 36;
CDBLB 1945-1960; DLB 15; MTCW

Spaulding, Douglas
See Bradbury, Ray (Douglas)

Spaulding, Leonard
See Bradbury, Ray (Douglas)

Spence, J. A. D.
See Eliot, T(homas) S(tearns)

Spencer, Elizabeth 1921- . . . . CLC 22
See also CA 13-16R; CANR 32; DLB 6;
MTCW; SATA 14

Spencer, Leonard G.
See Silverberg, Robert

Spencer, Scott 1945- . . . . CLC 30
See also CA 113; DLBY 86

Spender, Stephen (Harold)
1909- . . . . CLC 1, 2, 5, 10, 41
See also CA 9-12R; CANR 31;
CDBLB 1945-1960; DLB 20; MTCW

Spengler, Oswald (Arnold Gottfried)
1880-1936 . . . . TCLC 25
See also CA 118

Spenser, Edmund 1552(?)-1599 . . . . LC 5
See also CDBLB Before 1660; DA; WLC

Spicer, Jack 1925-1965 . . . . . . CLC 8, 18, 72
See also CA 85-88; DLB 5, 16

Spiegelman, Art 1948- . . . . **CLC 76**
See also AAYA 10; CA 125; CANR 41

Spielberg, Peter 1929- . . . . **CLC 6**
See also CA 5-8R; CANR 4; DLBY 81

Spielberg, Steven 1947- . . . . **CLC 20**
See also AAYA 8; CA 77-80; CANR 32;
SATA 32

Spillane, Frank Morrison 1918-
See Spillane, Mickey
See also CA 25-28R; CANR 28; MTCW;
SATA 66

Spillane, Mickey . . . . **CLC 3, 13**
See also Spillane, Frank Morrison

Spinoza, Benedictus de 1632-1677 . . . . **LC 9**

Spinrad, Norman (Richard) 1940-. . . **CLC 46**
See also CA 37-40R; CANR 20; DLB 8

Spitteler, Carl (Friedrich Georg)
1845-1924 . . . . **TCLC 12**
See also CA 109; DLB 129

Spivack, Kathleen (Romola Drucker)
1938- . . . . **CLC 6**
See also CA 49-52

Spoto, Donald 1941-. . . . . **CLC 39**
See also CA 65-68; CANR 11

Springsteen, Bruce (F.) 1949- . . . . . . **CLC 17**
See also CA 111

Spurling, Hilary 1940-. . . . . **CLC 34**
See also CA 104; CANR 25

Squires, (James) Radcliffe
1917-1993 . . . . **CLC 51**
See also CA 1-4R; 140; CANR 6, 21

Srivastava, Dhanpat Rai 1880(?)-1936
See Premchand
See also CA 118

Stacy, Donald
See Pohl, Frederik

Stael, Germaine de
See Stael-Holstein, Anne Louise Germaine
Necker Baronn
See also DLB 119

**Stael-Holstein, Anne Louise Germaine Necker
Baronn** 1766-1817 . . . . **NCLC 3**
See also Stael, Germaine de

Stafford, Jean 1915-1979 . . . **CLC 4, 7, 19, 68**
See also CA 1-4R; 85-88; CANR 3; DLB 2;
MTCW; SATA 22

Stafford, William (Edgar)
1914- . . . . **CLC 4, 7, 29**
See also CA 5-8R; CAAS 3; CANR 5, 22;
DLB 5

Staines, Trevor
See Brunner, John (Kilian Houston)

Stairs, Gordon
See Austin, Mary (Hunter)

Stannard, Martin . . . . **CLC 44**

Stanton, Maura 1946- . . . . **CLC 9**
See also CA 89-92; CANR 15; DLB 120

Stanton, Schuyler
See Baum, L(yman) Frank

Stapledon, (William) Olaf
1886-1950 . . . . **TCLC 22**
See also CA 111; DLB 15

Starbuck, George (Edwin) 1931-. . . . **CLC 53**
See also CA 21-24R; CANR 23

Stark, Richard
See Westlake, Donald E(dwin)

Staunton, Schuyler
See Baum, L(yman) Frank

Stead, Christina (Ellen)
1902-1983 . . . . **CLC 2, 5, 8, 32**
See also CA 13-16R; 109; CANR 33, 40;
MTCW

Stead, William Thomas
1849-1912 . . . . **TCLC 48**

Steele, Richard 1672-1729 . . . . **LC 18**
See also CDBLB 1660-1789; DLB 84, 101

Steele, Timothy (Reid) 1948-. . . . . . **CLC 45**
See also CA 93-96; CANR 16; DLB 120

Steffens, (Joseph) Lincoln
1866-1936 . . . . **TCLC 20**
See also CA 117

Stegner, Wallace (Earle) 1909- . . . **CLC 9, 49**
See also AITN 1; BEST 90:3; CA 1-4R;
CAAS 9; CANR 1, 21; DLB 9; MTCW

Stein, Gertrude
1874-1946 . . . . **TCLC 1, 6, 28, 48**
See also CA 104; 132; CDALB 1917-1929;
DA; DLB 4, 54, 86; MTCW; WLC

Steinbeck, John (Ernst)
1902-1968 . . . . . . **CLC 1, 5, 9, 13, 21, 34,
45, 75; SSC 11**
See also CA 1-4R; 25-28R; CANR 1, 35;
CDALB 1929-1941; DA; DLB 7, 9;
DLBD 2; MTCW; SATA 9; WLC

Steinem, Gloria 1934-. . . . . **CLC 63**
See also CA 53-56; CANR 28; MTCW

Steiner, George 1929-. . . . . **CLC 24**
See also CA 73-76; CANR 31; DLB 67;
MTCW; SATA 62

Steiner, Rudolf 1861-1925 . . . . **TCLC 13**
See also CA 107

Stendhal 1783-1842. . . . . **NCLC 23**
See also DA; DLB 119; WLC

Stephen, Leslie 1832-1904 . . . . **TCLC 23**
See also CA 123; DLB 57

Stephen, Sir Leslie
See Stephen, Leslie

Stephen, Virginia
See Woolf, (Adeline) Virginia

Stephens, James 1882(?)-1950 . . . . . . **TCLC 4**
See also CA 104; DLB 19

Stephens, Reed
See Donaldson, Stephen R.

Steptoe, Lydia
See Barnes, Djuna

Sterchi, Beat 1949-. . . . . **CLC 65**

Sterling, Brett
See Bradbury, Ray (Douglas); Hamilton,
Edmond

Sterling, Bruce 1954-. . . . . **CLC 72**
See also CA 119

Sterling, George 1869-1926 . . . . **TCLC 20**
See also CA 117; DLB 54

Stern, Gerald 1925- . . . . **CLC 40**
See also CA 81-84; CANR 28; DLB 105

Stern, Richard (Gustave) 1928-. . . **CLC 4, 39**
See also CA 1-4R; CANR 1, 25; DLBY 87

Sternberg, Josef von 1894-1969 . . . . . **CLC 20**
See also CA 81-84

Sterne, Laurence 1713-1768. . . . . **LC 2**
See also CDBLB 1660-1789; DA; DLB 39;
WLC

Sternheim, (William Adolf) Carl
1878-1942 . . . . **TCLC 8**
See also CA 105; DLB 56, 118

Stevens, Mark 1951- . . . . **CLC 34**
See also CA 122

Stevens, Wallace
1879-1955 . . . . **TCLC 3, 12, 45; PC 6**
See also CA 104; 124; CDALB 1929-1941;
DA; DLB 54; MTCW; WLC

Stevenson, Anne (Katharine)
1933- . . . . **CLC 7, 33**
See also CA 17-20R; CAAS 9; CANR 9, 33;
DLB 40; MTCW

Stevenson, Robert Louis (Balfour)
1850-1894 . . . . **NCLC 5, 14; SSC 11**
See also CDBLB 1890-1914; CLR 10, 11;
DA; DLB 18, 57; MAICYA; WLC;
YABC 2

Stewart, J(ohn) I(nnes) M(ackintosh)
1906- . . . . **CLC 7, 14, 32**
See also CA 85-88; CAAS 3; MTCW

Stewart, Mary (Florence Elinor)
1916- . . . . **CLC 7, 35**
See also CA 1-4R; CANR 1; SATA 12

Stewart, Mary Rainbow
See Stewart, Mary (Florence Elinor)

Stifter, Adalbert 1805-1868 . . . . . . **NCLC 41**

Still, James 1906-. . . . . **CLC 49**
See also CA 65-68; CAAS 17; CANR 10,
26; DLB 9; SATA 29

Sting
See Sumner, Gordon Matthew

Stirling, Arthur
See Sinclair, Upton (Beall)

Stitt, Milan 1941-. . . . . **CLC 29**
See also CA 69-72

Stockton, Francis Richard 1834-1902
See Stockton, Frank R.
See also CA 108; 137; MAICYA; SATA 44

Stockton, Frank R. . . . . **TCLC 47**
See also Stockton, Francis Richard
See also DLB 42, 74; SATA 32

Stoddard, Charles
See Kuttner, Henry

Stoker, Abraham 1847-1912
See Stoker, Bram
See also CA 105; DA; SATA 29

Stoker, Bram . . . . **TCLC 8**
See also Stoker, Abraham
See also CDBLB 1890-1914; DLB 36, 70;
WLC

Stolz, Mary (Slattery) 1920-. . . . . . . **CLC 12**
See also AAYA 8; AITN 1; CA 5-8R;
CANR 13, 41; MAICYA; SAAS 3;
SATA 10, 70, 71

Stone, Irving 1903-1989. . . . . **CLC 7**
See also AITN 1; CA 1-4R; 129; CAAS 3;
CANR 1, 23; MTCW; SATA 3;
SATA-Obit 64

Stone, Oliver 1946-.............. CLC 73
See also CA 110

Stone, Robert (Anthony)
1937-................. CLC 5, 23, 42
See also CA 85-88; CANR 23; MTCW

Stone, Zachary
See Follett, Ken(neth Martin)

Stoppard, Tom
1937- ... CLC 1, 3, 4, 5, 8, 15, 29, 34, 63
See also CA 81-84; CANR 39;
CDBLB 1960 to Present; DA; DLB 13;
DLBY 85; MTCW; WLC

Storey, David (Malcolm)
1933-................. CLC 2, 4, 5, 8
See also CA 81-84; CANR 36; DLB 13, 14;
MTCW

Storm, Hyemeyohsts 1935-......... CLC 3
See also CA 81-84

Storm, (Hans) Theodor (Woldsen)
1817-1888 .... NCLC 1

Storni, Alfonsina 1892-1938 .... TCLC 5
See also CA 104; 131; HW

Stout, Rex (Todhunter) 1886-1975 ... CLC 3
See also AITN 2; CA 61-64

Stow, (Julian) Randolph 1935- .. CLC 23, 48
See also CA 13-16R; CANR 33; MTCW

Stowe, Harriet (Elizabeth) Beecher
1811-1896 .... NCLC 3
See also CDALB 1865-1917; DA; DLB 1,
12, 42, 74; MAICYA; WLC; YABC 1

Strachey, (Giles) Lytton
1880-1932 .... TCLC 12
See also CA 110; DLBD 10

Strand, Mark 1934- ...... CLC 6, 18, 41, 71
See also CA 21-24R; CANR 40; DLB 5;
SATA 41

Straub, Peter (Francis) 1943- ...... CLC 28
See also BEST 89:1; CA 85-88; CANR 28;
DLBY 84; MTCW

Strauss, Botho 1944- .... CLC 22
See also DLB 124

Streatfeild, (Mary) Noel
1895(?)-1986 .... CLC 21
See also CA 81-84; 120; CANR 31;
CLR 17; MAICYA; SATA 20, 48

Stribling, T(homas) S(igismund)
1881-1965 .... CLC 23
See also CA 107; DLB 9

Strindberg, (Johan) August
1849-1912 .... TCLC 1, 8, 21, 47
See also CA 104; 135; DA; WLC

Stringer, Arthur 1874-1950 .... TCLC 37
See also DLB 92

Stringer, David
See Roberts, Keith (John Kingston)

Strugatskii, Arkadii (Natanovich)
1925-1991 .... CLC 27
See also CA 106; 135

Strugatskii, Boris (Natanovich)
1933-...................... CLC 27
See also CA 106

Strummer, Joe 1953(?)-........... CLC 30
See also Clash, The

Stuart, Don A.
See Campbell, John W(ood, Jr.)

Stuart, Ian
See MacLean, Alistair (Stuart)

Stuart, Jesse (Hilton)
1906-1984 .... CLC 1, 8, 11, 14, 34
See also CA 5-8R; 112; CANR 31; DLB 9,
48, 102; DLBY 84; SATA 2, 36

Sturgeon, Theodore (Hamilton)
1918-1985 .... CLC 22, 39
See also Queen, Ellery
See also CA 81-84; 116; CANR 32; DLB 8;
DLBY 85; MTCW

Sturges, Preston 1898-1959 .... TCLC 48
See also CA 114; DLB 26

Styron, William
1925- .... CLC 1, 3, 5, 11, 15, 60
See also BEST 90:4; CA 5-8R; CANR 6, 33;
CDALB 1968-1988; DLB 2; DLBY 80;
MTCW

Suarez Lynch, B.
See Bioy Casares, Adolfo; Borges, Jorge
Luis

Suarez Lynch, B.
See Borges, Jorge Luis

Su Chien 1884-1918
See Su Man-shu
See also CA 123

Sudermann, Hermann 1857-1928 .. TCLC 15
See also CA 107; DLB 118

Sue, Eugene 1804-1857 .... NCLC 1
See also DLB 119

Sueskind, Patrick 1949-........... CLC 44

Sukenick, Ronald 1932-..... CLC 3, 4, 6, 48
See also CA 25-28R; CAAS 8; CANR 32;
DLBY 81

Suknaski, Andrew 1942- .... CLC 19
See also CA 101; DLB 53

Sullivan, Vernon
See Vian, Boris

Sully Prudhomme 1839-1907...... TCLC 31

Su Man-shu .... TCLC 24
See also Su Chien

Summerforest, Ivy B.
See Kirkup, James

Summers, Andrew James 1942-..... CLC 26
See also Police, The

Summers, Andy
See Summers, Andrew James

Summers, Hollis (Spurgeon, Jr.)
1916-....................... CLC 10
See also CA 5-8R; CANR 3; DLB 6

Summers, (Alphonsus Joseph-Mary Augustus)
Montague 1880-1948 .... TCLC 16
See also CA 118

Sumner, Gordon Matthew 1951-.... CLC 26
See also Police, The

Surtees, Robert Smith
1803-1864 .... NCLC 14
See also DLB 21

Susann, Jacqueline 1921-1974....... CLC 3
See also AITN 1; CA 65-68; 53-56; MTCW

Suskind, Patrick
See Sueskind, Patrick

Sutcliff, Rosemary 1920-1992 ...... CLC 26
See also AAYA 10; CA 5-8R; 139;
CANR 37; CLR 1; MAICYA; SATA 6,
44; SATA-Obit 73

Sutro, Alfred 1863-1933.......... TCLC 6
See also CA 105; DLB 10

Sutton, Henry
See Slavitt, David R(ytman)

Svevo, Italo .... TCLC 2, 35
See also Schmitz, Aron Hector

Swados, Elizabeth 1951- .... CLC 12
See also CA 97-100

Swados, Harvey 1920-1972 .... CLC 5
See also CA 5-8R; 37-40R; CANR 6;
DLB 2

Swan, Gladys 1934-............. CLC 69
See also CA 101; CANR 17, 39

Swarthout, Glendon (Fred)
1918-1992 .... CLC 35
See also CA 1-4R; 139; CANR 1; SATA 26

Sweet, Sarah C.
See Jewett, (Theodora) Sarah Orne

Swenson, May 1919-1989..... CLC 4, 14, 61
See also CA 5-8R; 130; CANR 36; DA;
DLB 5; MTCW; SATA 15

Swift, Augustus
See Lovecraft, H(oward) P(hillips)

Swift, Graham 1949- .... CLC 41
See also CA 117; 122

Swift, Jonathan 1667-1745.......... LC 1
See also CDBLB 1660-1789; DA; DLB 39,
95, 101; SATA 19; WLC

Swinburne, Algernon Charles
1837-1909 .... TCLC 8, 36
See also CA 105; 140; CDBLB 1832-1890;
DA; DLB 35, 57; WLC

Swinfen, Ann.................... CLC 34

Swinnerton, Frank Arthur
1884-1982 .... CLC 31
See also CA 108; DLB 34

Swithen, John
See King, Stephen (Edwin)

Sylvia
See Ashton-Warner, Sylvia (Constance)

Symmes, Robert Edward
See Duncan, Robert (Edward)

Symonds, John Addington
1840-1893 .... NCLC 34
See also DLB 57

Symons, Arthur 1865-1945 .... TCLC 11
See also CA 107; DLB 19, 57

Symons, Julian (Gustave)
1912-.................. CLC 2, 14, 32
See also CA 49-52; CAAS 3; CANR 3, 33;
DLB 87; DLBY 92; MTCW

Synge, (Edmund) J(ohn) M(illington)
1871-1909 .... TCLC 6, 37; DC 2
See also CA 104; CDBLB 1890-1914;
DLB 10, 19

Syruc, J.
See Milosz, Czeslaw

Szirtes, George 1948-............. CLC 46
See also CA 109; CANR 27

Tabori, George 1914- .... **CLC 19**
See also CA 49-52; CANR 4

Tagore, Rabindranath 1861-1941.... **TCLC 3**
See also CA 104; 120; MTCW

Taine, Hippolyte Adolphe
1828-1893 .... **NCLC 15**

Talese, Gay 1932-................ **CLC 37**
See also AITN 1; CA 1-4R; CANR 9;
MTCW

Tallent, Elizabeth (Ann) 1954- ..... **CLC 45**
See also CA 117; DLB 130

Tally, Ted 1952-................. **CLC 42**
See also CA 120; 124

Tamayo y Baus, Manuel
1829-1898 .... **NCLC 1**

Tammsaare, A(nton) H(ansen)
1878-1940 .... **TCLC 27**

Tan, Amy 1952- .... **CLC 59**
See also AAYA 9; BEST 89:3; CA 136

Tandem, Felix
See Spitteler, Carl (Friedrich Georg)

Tanizaki, Jun'ichiro
1886-1965 .... **CLC 8, 14, 28**
See also CA 93-96; 25-28R

Tanner, William
See Amis, Kingsley (William)

Tao Lao
See Storni, Alfonsina

Tarassoff, Lev
See Troyat, Henri

Tarbell, Ida M(inerva)
1857-1944 .... **TCLC 40**
See also CA 122; DLB 47

Tarkington, (Newton) Booth
1869-1946 .... **TCLC 9**
See also CA 110; DLB 9, 102; SATA 17

Tarkovsky, Andrei (Arsenyevich)
1932-1986 .... **CLC 75**
See also CA 127

Tartt, Donna 1964(?)-............. **CLC 76**

Tasso, Torquato 1544-1595 .... **LC 5**

Tate, (John Orley) Allen
1899-1979 .... **CLC 2, 4, 6, 9, 11, 14, 24**
See also CA 5-8R; 85-88; CANR 32;
DLB 4, 45, 63; MTCW

Tate, Ellalice
See Hibbert, Eleanor Alice Burford

Tate, James (Vincent) 1943- ... **CLC 2, 6, 25**
See also CA 21-24R; CANR 29; DLB 5

Tavel, Ronald 1940-................ **CLC 6**
See also CA 21-24R; CANR 33

Taylor, Cecil Philip 1929-1981 ..... **CLC 27**
See also CA 25-28R; 105

Taylor, Edward 1642(?)-1729........ **LC 11**
See also DA; DLB 24

Taylor, Eleanor Ross 1920-........ **CLC 5**
See also CA 81-84

Taylor, Elizabeth 1912-1975 ... **CLC 2, 4, 29**
See also CA 13-16R; CANR 9; MTCW;
SATA 13

Taylor, Henry (Splawn) 1942-...... **CLC 44**
See also CA 33-36R; CAAS 7; CANR 31;
DLB 5

Taylor, Kamala (Purnaiya) 1924-
See Markandaya, Kamala
See also CA 77-80

Taylor, Mildred D. .... **CLC 21**
See also AAYA 10; BW; CA 85-88;
CANR 25; CLR 9; DLB 52; MAICYA;
SAAS 5; SATA 15, 70

Taylor, Peter (Hillsman)
1917- ...... **CLC 1, 4, 18, 37, 44, 50, 71;**
SSC 10
See also CA 13-16R; CANR 9; DLBY 81;
MTCW

Taylor, Robert Lewis 1912-........ **CLC 14**
See also CA 1-4R; CANR 3; SATA 10

Tchekhov, Anton
See Chekhov, Anton (Pavlovich)

Teasdale, Sara 1884-1933......... **TCLC 4**
See also CA 104; DLB 45; SATA 32

Tegner, Esaias 1782-1846........ **NCLC 2**

Teilhard de Chardin, (Marie Joseph) Pierre
1881-1955 .... **TCLC 9**
See also CA 105

Temple, Ann
See Mortimer, Penelope (Ruth)

Tennant, Emma (Christina)
1937-................... **CLC 13, 52**
See also CA 65-68; CAAS 9; CANR 10, 38;
DLB 14

Tenneshaw, S. M.
See Silverberg, Robert

Tennyson, Alfred
1809-1892 .... **NCLC 30; PC 6**
See also CDBLB 1832-1890; DA; DLB 32;
WLC

Teran, Lisa St. Aubin de .... **CLC 36**
See also St. Aubin de Teran, Lisa

Teresa de Jesus, St. 1515-1582...... **LC 18**

Terkel, Louis 1912-
See Terkel, Studs
See also CA 57-60; CANR 18; MTCW

Terkel, Studs .... **CLC 38**
See also Terkel, Louis
See also AITN 1

Terry, C. V.
See Slaughter, Frank G(ill)

Terry, Megan 1932-............... **CLC 19**
See also CA 77-80; CABS 3; DLB 7

Tertz, Abram
See Sinyavsky, Andrei (Donatevich)

Tesich, Steve 1943(?)-.......... **CLC 40, 69**
See also CA 105; DLBY 83

Teternikov, Fyodor Kuzmich 1863-1927
See Sologub, Fyodor
See also CA 104

Tevis, Walter 1928-1984 .... **CLC 42**
See also CA 113

Tey, Josephine.................. **TCLC 14**
See also Mackintosh, Elizabeth
See also DLB 77

Thackeray, William Makepeace
1811-1863 .... **NCLC 5, 14, 22**
See also CDBLB 1832-1890; DA; DLB 21,
55; SATA 23; WLC

Thakura, Ravindranatha
See Tagore, Rabindranath

Tharoor, Shashi 1956- .... **CLC 70**

Thelwell, Michael Miles 1939- ..... **CLC 22**
See also CA 101

Theobald, Lewis, Jr.
See Lovecraft, H(oward) P(hillips)

The Prophet
See Dreiser, Theodore (Herman Albert)

Theroux, Alexander (Louis)
1939-..................... **CLC 2, 25**
See also CA 85-88; CANR 20

Theroux, Paul (Edward)
1941- .... **CLC 5, 8, 11, 15, 28, 46**
See also BEST 89:4; CA 33-36R; CANR 20;
DLB 2; MTCW; SATA 44

Thesen, Sharon 1946-............. **CLC 56**

Thevenin, Denis
See Duhamel, Georges

Thibault, Jacques Anatole Francois
1844-1924
See France, Anatole
See also CA 106; 127; MTCW

Thiele, Colin (Milton) 1920- .... **CLC 17**
See also CA 29-32R; CANR 12, 28;
CLR 27; MAICYA; SAAS 2; SATA 14,
72

Thomas, Audrey (Callahan)
1935-.................. **CLC 7, 13, 37**
See also AITN 2; CA 21-24R; CANR 36;
DLB 60; MTCW

Thomas, D(onald) M(ichael)
1935-.................. **CLC 13, 22, 31**
See also CA 61-64; CAAS 11; CANR 17;
CDBLB 1960 to Present; DLB 40;
MTCW

Thomas, Dylan (Marlais)
1914-1953 .... **TCLC 1, 8, 45; PC 2;**
SSC 3
See also CA 104; 120; CDBLB 1945-1960;
DA; DLB 13, 20; MTCW; SATA 60;
WLC

Thomas, (Philip) Edward
1878-1917 ....**TCLC 10**
See also CA 106; DLB 19

Thomas, Joyce Carol 1938-....... **CLC 35**
See also BW; CA 113; 116; CLR 19;
DLB 33; MAICYA; MTCW; SAAS 7;
SATA 40

Thomas, Lewis 1913-............. **CLC 35**
See also CA 85-88; CANR 38; MTCW

Thomas, Paul
See Mann, (Paul) Thomas

Thomas, Piri 1928-............... **CLC 17**
See also CA 73-76; HW

Thomas, R(onald) S(tuart)
1913-...............**CLC 6, 13, 48**
See also CA 89-92; CAAS 4; CANR 30;
CDBLB 1960 to Present; DLB 27;
MTCW

Thomas, Ross (Elmore) 1926-...... **CLC 39**
See also CA 33-36R; CANR 22

Thompson, Francis Clegg
See Mencken, H(enry) L(ouis)

Thompson, Francis Joseph
1859-1907 . . . . TCLC 4
See also CA 104; CDBLB 1890-1914;
DLB 19

Thompson, Hunter S(tockton)
1939- . . . . CLC 9, 17, 40
See also BEST 89:1; CA 17-20R; CANR 23;
MTCW

Thompson, Jim 1906-1977(?) . . . . . . CLC 69

Thompson, Judith . . . . CLC 39

Thomson, James 1700-1748 . . . . LC 16

Thomson, James 1834-1882 . . . . . NCLC 18

Thoreau, Henry David
1817-1862 . . . . NCLC 7, 21
See also CDALB 1640-1865; DA; DLB 1;
WLC

Thornton, Hall
See Silverberg, Robert

Thurber, James (Grover)
1894-1961 . . . . . . CLC 5, 11, 25; SSC 1
See also CA 73-76; CANR 17, 39;
CDALB 1929-1941; DA; DLB 4, 11, 22,
102; MAICYA; MTCW; SATA 13

Thurman, Wallace (Henry)
1902-1934 . . . . TCLC 6
See also BLC 3; BW; CA 104; 124; DLB 51

Ticheburn, Cheviot
See Ainsworth, William Harrison

Tieck, (Johann) Ludwig
1773-1853 . . . . NCLC 5
See also DLB 90

Tiger, Derry
See Ellison, Harlan

Tilghman, Christopher 1948(?)- . . . . . CLC 65

Tillinghast, Richard (Williford)
1940- . . . . CLC 29
See also CA 29-32R; CANR 26

Timrod, Henry 1828-1867 . . . . NCLC 25
See also DLB 3

Tindall, Gillian 1938- . . . . CLC 7
See also CA 21-24R; CANR 11

Tiptree, James, Jr. . . . . CLC 48, 50
See also Sheldon, Alice Hastings Bradley
See also DLB 8

Titmarsh, Michael Angelo
See Thackeray, William Makepeace

**Tocqueville, Alexis (Charles Henri Maurice
Clerel Comte)** 1805-1859 . . . . . NCLC 7

Tolkien, J(ohn) R(onald) R(euel)
1892-1973 . . . . . . CLC 1, 2, 3, 8, 12, 38
See also AAYA 10; AITN 1; CA 17-18;
45-48; CANR 36; CAP 2;
CDBLB 1914-1945; DA; DLB 15;
MAICYA; MTCW; SATA 2, 24, 32;
WLC

Toller, Ernst 1893-1939 . . . . TCLC 10
See also CA 107; DLB 124

Tolson, M. B.
See Tolson, Melvin B(eaunorus)

Tolson, Melvin B(eaunorus)
1898(?)-1966 . . . . CLC 36
See also BLC 3; BW; CA 124; 89-92;
DLB 48, 76

Tolstoi, Aleksei Nikolaevich
See Tolstoy, Alexey Nikolaevich

Tolstoy, Alexey Nikolaevich
1882-1945 . . . . TCLC 18
See also CA 107

Tolstoy, Count Leo
See Tolstoy, Leo (Nikolaevich)

Tolstoy, Leo (Nikolaevich)
1828-1910 . . . . . TCLC 4, 11, 17, 28, 44;
SSC 9
See also CA 104; 123; DA; SATA 26; WLC

Tomasi di Lampedusa, Giuseppe 1896-1957
See Lampedusa, Giuseppe (Tomasi) di
See also CA 111

Tomlin, Lily . . . . CLC 17
See also Tomlin, Mary Jean

Tomlin, Mary Jean 1939(?)-
See Tomlin, Lily
See also CA 117

Tomlinson, (Alfred) Charles
1927- . . . . CLC 2, 4, 6, 13, 45
See also CA 5-8R; CANR 33; DLB 40

Tonson, Jacob
See Bennett, (Enoch) Arnold

Toole, John Kennedy
1937-1969 . . . . CLC 19, 64
See also CA 104; DLBY 81

Toomer, Jean
1894-1967 . . . . . . CLC 1, 4, 13, 22; PC 7;
SSC 1
See also BLC 3; BW; CA 85-88;
CDALB 1917-1929; DLB 45, 51; MTCW

Torley, Luke
See Blish, James (Benjamin)

Tornimparte, Alessandra
See Ginzburg, Natalia

Torre, Raoul della
See Mencken, H(enry) L(ouis)

Torrey, E(dwin) Fuller 1937- . . . . CLC 34
See also CA 119

Torsvan, Ben Traven
See Traven, B.

Torsvan, Benno Traven
See Traven, B.

Torsvan, Berick Traven
See Traven, B.

Torsvan, Berwick Traven
See Traven, B.

Torsvan, Bruno Traven
See Traven, B.

Torsvan, Traven
See Traven, B.

Tournier, Michel (Edouard)
1924- . . . . CLC 6, 23, 36
See also CA 49-52; CANR 3, 36; DLB 83;
MTCW; SATA 23

Tournimparte, Alessandra
See Ginzburg, Natalia

Towers, Ivar
See Kornbluth, C(yril) M.

Townsend, Sue 1946- . . . . CLC 61
See also CA 119; 127; MTCW; SATA 48,
55

Townshend, Peter (Dennis Blandford)
1945- . . . . CLC 17, 42
See also CA 107

Tozzi, Federigo 1883-1920 . . . . TCLC 31

Traill, Catharine Parr
1802-1899 . . . . NCLC 31
See also DLB 99

Trakl, Georg 1887-1914 . . . . TCLC 5
See also CA 104

Transtroemer, Tomas (Goesta)
1931- . . . . CLC 52, 65
See also CA 117; 129; CAAS 17

Transtromer, Tomas Gosta
See Transtroemer, Tomas (Goesta)

Traven, B. (?)-1969 . . . . CLC 8, 11
See also CA 19-20; 25-28R; CAP 2; DLB 9,
56; MTCW

Treitel, Jonathan 1959- . . . . CLC 70

Tremain, Rose 1943- . . . . CLC 42
See also CA 97-100; DLB 14

Tremblay, Michel 1942- . . . . CLC 29
See also CA 116; 128; DLB 60; MTCW

Trevanian (a pseudonym) 1930(?)- . . . CLC 29
See also CA 108

Trevor, Glen
See Hilton, James

Trevor, William
1928- . . . . CLC 7, 9, 14, 25, 71
See also Cox, William Trevor
See also DLB 14

Trifonov, Yuri (Valentinovich)
1925-1981 . . . . CLC 45
See also CA 126; 103; MTCW

Trilling, Lionel 1905-1975 . . . . CLC 9, 11, 24
See also CA 9-12R; 61-64; CANR 10;
DLB 28, 63; MTCW

Trimball, W. H.
See Mencken, H(enry) L(ouis)

Tristan
See Gomez de la Serna, Ramon

Tristram
See Housman, A(lfred) E(dward)

Trogdon, William (Lewis) 1939-
See Heat-Moon, William Least
See also CA 115; 119

Trollope, Anthony 1815-1882 . . NCLC 6, 33
See also CDBLB 1832-1890; DA; DLB 21,
57; SATA 22; WLC

Trollope, Frances 1779-1863 . . . . . NCLC 30
See also DLB 21

Trotsky, Leon 1879-1940 . . . . TCLC 22
See also CA 118

Trotter (Cockburn), Catharine
1679-1749 . . . . LC 8
See also DLB 84

Trout, Kilgore
See Farmer, Philip Jose

Trow, George W. S. 1943- . . . . CLC 52
See also CA 126

Troyat, Henri 1911- . . . . CLC 23
See also CA 45-48; CANR 2, 33; MTCW

Trudeau, G(arretson) B(eekman) 1948-
See Trudeau, Garry B.
See also CA 81-84; CANR 31; SATA 35

Varda, Agnes 1928- .... CLC 16
See also CA 116; 122

Vargas Llosa, (Jorge) Mario (Pedro)
1936- .... CLC 3, 6, 9, 10, 15, 31, 42
See also CA 73-76; CANR 18, 32; DA;
HW; MTCW

Vasiliu, Gheorghe 1881-1957
See Bacovia, George
See also CA 123

Vassa, Gustavus
See Equiano, Olaudah

Vassilikos, Vassilis 1933-........ CLC 4, 8
See also CA 81-84

Vaughn, Stephanie................. CLC 62

Vazov, Ivan (Minchov)
1850-1921 .... TCLC 25
See also CA 121

Veblen, Thorstein (Bunde)
1857-1929 .... TCLC 31
See also CA 115

Vega, Lope de 1562-1635........... LC 23

Venison, Alfred
See Pound, Ezra (Weston Loomis)

Verdi, Marie de
See Mencken, H(enry) L(ouis)

Verdu, Matilde
See Cela, Camilo Jose

Verga, Giovanni (Carmelo)
1840-1922 .... TCLC 3
See also CA 104; 123

Vergil 70B.C.-19B.C. .... CMLC 9
See also DA

Verhaeren, Emile (Adolphe Gustave)
1855-1916 .... TCLC 12
See also CA 109

Verlaine, Paul (Marie)
1844-1896 .... NCLC 2; PC 2

Verne, Jules (Gabriel) 1828-1905 ... TCLC 6
See also CA 110; 131; DLB 123; MAICYA;
SATA 21

Very, Jones 1813-1880........... NCLC 9
See also DLB 1

Vesaas, Tarjei 1897-1970......... CLC 48
See also CA 29-32R

Vialis, Gaston
See Simenon, Georges (Jacques Christian)

Vian, Boris 1920-1959 .... TCLC 9
See also CA 106; DLB 72

Viaud, (Louis Marie) Julien 1850-1923
See Loti, Pierre
See also CA 107

Vicar, Henry
See Felsen, Henry Gregor

Vicker, Angus
See Felsen, Henry Gregor

Vidal, Gore
1925- ..... CLC 2, 4, 6, 8, 10, 22, 33, 72
See also AITN 1; BEST 90:2; CA 5-8R;
CANR 13; DLB 6; MTCW

Viereck, Peter (Robert Edwin)
1916- .... CLC 4
See also CA 1-4R; CANR 1; DLB 5

Vigny, Alfred (Victor) de
1797-1863 .... NCLC 7
See also DLB 119

Vilakazi, Benedict Wallet
1906-1947 .... TCLC 37

Villiers de l'Isle Adam, Jean Marie Mathias
Philippe Auguste Comte
1838-1889 .... NCLC 3
See also DLB 123

Vincent, Gabrielle a pseudonym...... CLC 13
See also CA 126; CLR 13; MAICYA;
SATA 61

Vinci, Leonardo da 1452-1519...... LC 12

Vine, Barbara .... CLC 50
See also Rendell, Ruth (Barbara)
See also BEST 90:4

Vinge, Joan D(ennison) 1948-...... CLC 30
See also CA 93-96; SATA 36

Violis, G.
See Simenon, Georges (Jacques Christian)

Visconti, Luchino 1906-1976...... CLC 16
See also CA 81-84; 65-68; CANR 39

Vittorini, Elio 1908-1966...... CLC 6, 9, 14
See also CA 133; 25-28R

Vizinczey, Stephen 1933-.......... CLC 40
See also CA 128

Vliet, R(ussell) G(ordon)
1929-1984 .... CLC 22
See also CA 37-40R; 112; CANR 18

Vogau, Boris Andreyevich 1894-1937(?)
See Pilnyak, Boris
See also CA 123

Vogel, Paula A(nne) 1951-........ CLC 76
See also CA 108

Voight, Ellen Bryant 1943-........ CLC 54
See also CA 69-72; CANR 11, 29; DLB 120

Voigt, Cynthia 1942- .... CLC 30
See also AAYA 3; CA 106; CANR 18, 37,
40; CLR 13; MAICYA; SATA 33, 48

Voinovich, Vladimir (Nikolaevich)
1932- .... CLC 10, 49
See also CA 81-84; CAAS 12; CANR 33;
MTCW

Voltaire 1694-1778........ LC 14; SSC 12
See also DA; WLC

von Daeniken, Erich 1935- .... CLC 30
See also von Daniken, Erich
See also AITN 1; CA 37-40R; CANR 17

von Daniken, Erich................ CLC 30
See also von Daeniken, Erich

von Heidenstam, (Carl Gustaf) Verner
See Heidenstam, (Carl Gustaf) Verner von

von Heyse, Paul (Johann Ludwig)
See Heyse, Paul (Johann Ludwig von)

von Hofmannsthal, Hugo
See Hofmannsthal, Hugo von

von Horvath, Odon
See Horvath, Oedoen von

von Horvath, Oedoen
See Horvath, Oedoen von

von Liliencron, (Friedrich Adolf Axel) Detlev
See Liliencron, (Friedrich Adolf Axel)
Detlev von

Vonnegut, Kurt, Jr.
1922- ...... CLC 1, 2, 3, 4, 5, 8, 12, 22,
40, 60; SSC 8
See also AAYA 6; AITN 1; BEST 90:4;
CA 1-4R; CANR 1, 25;
CDALB 1968-1988; DA; DLB 2, 8;
DLBD 3; DLBY 80; MTCW; WLC

Von Rachen, Kurt
See Hubbard, L(afayette) Ron(ald)

von Rezzori (d'Arezzo), Gregor
See Rezzori (d'Arezzo), Gregor von

von Sternberg, Josef
See Sternberg, Josef von

Vorster, Gordon 1924-............ CLC 34
See also CA 133

Vosce, Trudie
See Ozick, Cynthia

Voznesensky, Andrei (Andreievich)
1933-.................. CLC 1, 15, 57
See also CA 89-92; CANR 37; MTCW

Waddington, Miriam 1917-........ CLC 28
See also CA 21-24R; CANR 12, 30;
DLB 68

Wagman, Fredrica 1937-........... CLC 7
See also CA 97-100

Wagner, Richard 1813-1883....... NCLC 9
See also DLB 129

Wagner-Martin, Linda 1936-....... CLC 50

Wagoner, David (Russell)
1926-.................. CLC 3, 5, 15
See also CA 1-4R; CAAS 3; CANR 2;
DLB 5; SATA 14

Wah, Fred(erick James) 1939-...... CLC 44
See also CA 107; DLB 60

Wahloo, Per 1926-1975 .... CLC 7
See also CA 61-64

Wahloo, Peter
See Wahloo, Per

Wain, John (Barrington)
1925-.............. CLC 2, 11, 15, 46
See also CA 5-8R; CAAS 4; CANR 23;
CDBLB 1960 to Present; DLB 15, 27;
MTCW

Wajda, Andrzej 1926-............. CLC 16
See also CA 102

Wakefield, Dan 1932-.............. CLC 7
See also CA 21-24R; CAAS 7

Wakoski, Diane
1937-........... CLC 2, 4, 7, 9, 11, 40
See also CA 13-16R; CAAS 1; CANR 9;
DLB 5

Wakoski-Sherbell, Diane
See Wakoski, Diane

Walcott, Derek (Alton)
1930- .... CLC 2, 4, 9, 14, 25, 42, 67, 76
See also BLC 3; BW; CA 89-92; CANR 26;
DLB 117; DLBY 81; MTCW

Waldman, Anne 1945-.............. CLC 7
See also CA 37-40R; CAAS 17; CANR 34;
DLB 16

Waldo, E. Hunter
See Sturgeon, Theodore (Hamilton)

Waldo, Edward Hamilton
See Sturgeon, Theodore (Hamilton)

Walker, Alice (Malsenior)
1944- .... **CLC 5, 6, 9, 19, 27, 46, 58;**
SSC 5
See also AAYA 3; BEST 89:4; BLC 3; BW;
CA 37-40R; CANR 9, 27;
CDALB 1968-1988; DA; DLB 6, 33;
MTCW; SATA 31

Walker, David Harry 1911-1992.... **CLC 14**
See also CA 1-4R; 137; CANR 1; SATA 8;
SATA-Obit 71

Walker, Edward Joseph 1934-
See Walker, Ted
See also CA 21-24R; CANR 12, 28

Walker, George F. 1947- .... **CLC 44, 61**
See also CA 103; CANR 21; DLB 60

Walker, Joseph A. 1935- .... **CLC 19**
See also BW; CA 89-92; CANR 26; DLB 38

Walker, Margaret (Abigail)
1915- .... **CLC 1, 6**
See also BLC 3; BW; CA 73-76; CANR 26;
DLB 76; MTCW

Walker, Ted .... **CLC 13**
See also Walker, Edward Joseph
See also DLB 40

Wallace, David Foster 1962- .... **CLC 50**
See also CA 132

Wallace, Dexter
See Masters, Edgar Lee

Wallace, Irving 1916-1990 ...... **CLC 7, 13**
See also AITN 1; CA 1-4R; 132; CAAS 1;
CANR 1, 27; MTCW

Wallant, Edward Lewis
1926-1962 .... **CLC 5, 10**
See also CA 1-4R; CANR 22; DLB 2, 28;
MTCW

Walpole, Horace 1717-1797 .... **LC 2**
See also DLB 39, 104

Walpole, Hugh (Seymour)
1884-1941 .... **TCLC 5**
See also CA 104; DLB 34

Walser, Martin 1927- .... **CLC 27**
See also CA 57-60; CANR 8; DLB 75, 124

Walser, Robert 1878-1956 .... **TCLC 18**
See also CA 118; DLB 66

Walsh, Jill Paton .... **CLC 35**
See also Paton Walsh, Gillian
See also CLR 2; SAAS 3

Walter, William Christian
See Andersen, Hans Christian

Wambaugh, Joseph (Aloysius, Jr.)
1937- .... **CLC 3, 18**
See also AITN 1; BEST 89:3; CA 33-36R;
DLB 6; DLBY 83; MTCW

Ward, Arthur Henry Sarsfield 1883-1959
See Rohmer, Sax
See also CA 108

Ward, Douglas Turner 1930- .... **CLC 19**
See also BW; CA 81-84; CANR 27; DLB 7,
38

Ward, Peter
See Faust, Frederick (Schiller)

Warhol, Andy 1928(?)-1987 .... **CLC 20**
See also BEST 89:4; CA 89-92; 121;
CANR 34

Warner, Francis (Robert le Plastrier)
1937- .... **CLC 14**
See also CA 53-56; CANR 11

Warner, Marina 1946- .... **CLC 59**
See also CA 65-68; CANR 21

Warner, Rex (Ernest) 1905-1986.... **CLC 45**
See also CA 89-92; 119; DLB 15

Warner, Susan (Bogert)
1819-1885 .... **NCLC 31**
See also DLB 3, 42

Warner, Sylvia (Constance) Ashton
See Ashton-Warner, Sylvia (Constance)

Warner, Sylvia Townsend
1893-1978 .... **CLC 7, 19**
See also CA 61-64; 77-80; CANR 16;
DLB 34; MTCW

Warren, Mercy Otis 1728-1814... **NCLC 13**
See also DLB 31

Warren, Robert Penn
1905-1989 .... **CLC 1, 4, 6, 8, 10, 13, 18,**
39, 53, 59; SSC 4
See also AITN 1; CA 13-16R; 129;
CANR 10; CDALB 1968-1988; DA;
DLB 2, 48; DLBY 80, 89; MTCW;
SATA 46, 63; WLC

Warshofsky, Isaac
See Singer, Isaac Bashevis

Warton, Thomas 1728-1790 .... **LC 15**
See also DLB 104, 109

Waruk, Kona
See Harris, (Theodore) Wilson

Warung, Price 1855-1911 .... **TCLC 45**

Warwick, Jarvis
See Garner, Hugh

Washington, Alex
See Harris, Mark

Washington, Booker T(aliaferro)
1856-1915 .... **TCLC 10**
See also BLC 3; BW; CA 114; 125;
SATA 28

Wassermann, (Karl) Jakob
1873-1934 .... **TCLC 6**
See also CA 104; DLB 66

Wasserstein, Wendy 1950- ..... **CLC 32, 59**
See also CA 121; 129; CABS 3

Waterhouse, Keith (Spencer)
1929- .... **CLC 47**
See also CA 5-8R; CANR 38; DLB 13, 15;
MTCW

Waters, Roger 1944- .... **CLC 35**
See also Pink Floyd

Watkins, Frances Ellen
See Harper, Frances Ellen Watkins

Watkins, Gerrold
See Malzberg, Barry N(athaniel)

Watkins, Paul 1964- .... **CLC 55**
See also CA 132

Watkins, Vernon Phillips
1906-1967 .... **CLC 43**
See also CA 9-10; 25-28R; CAP 1; DLB 20

Watson, Irving S.
See Mencken, H(enry) L(ouis)

Watson, John H.
See Farmer, Philip Jose

Watson, Richard F.
See Silverberg, Robert

Waugh, Auberon (Alexander) 1939- ... **CLC 7**
See also CA 45-48; CANR 6, 22; DLB 14

Waugh, Evelyn (Arthur St. John)
1903-1966 ... **CLC 1, 3, 8, 13, 19, 27, 44**
See also CA 85-88; 25-28R; CANR 22;
CDBLB 1914-1945; DA; DLB 15;
MTCW; WLC

Waugh, Harriet 1944- .... **CLC 6**
See also CA 85-88; CANR 22

Ways, C. R.
See Blount, Roy (Alton), Jr.

Waystaff, Simon
See Swift, Jonathan

Webb, (Martha) Beatrice (Potter)
1858-1943 .... **TCLC 22**
See also Potter, Beatrice
See also CA 117

Webb, Charles (Richard) 1939- ...... **CLC 7**
See also CA 25-28R

Webb, James H(enry), Jr. 1946- .... **CLC 22**
See also CA 81-84

Webb, Mary (Gladys Meredith)
1881-1927 .... **TCLC 24**
See also CA 123; DLB 34

Webb, Mrs. Sidney
See Webb, (Martha) Beatrice (Potter)

Webb, Phyllis 1927- .... **CLC 18**
See also CA 104; CANR 23; DLB 53

Webb, Sidney (James)
1859-1947 .... **TCLC 22**
See also CA 117

Webber, Andrew Lloyd .... **CLC 21**
See also Lloyd Webber, Andrew

Weber, Lenora Mattingly
1895-1971 .... **CLC 12**
See also CA 19-20; 29-32R; CAP 1;
SATA 2, 26

Webster, John 1579(?)-1634(?) .... **DC 2**
See also CDBLB Before 1660; DA; DLB 58;
WLC

Webster, Noah 1758-1843 .... **NCLC 30**

Wedekind, (Benjamin) Frank(lin)
1864-1918 .... **TCLC 7**
See also CA 104; DLB 118

Weidman, Jerome 1913- .... **CLC 7**
See also AITN 2; CA 1-4R; CANR 1;
DLB 28

Weil, Simone (Adolphine)
1909-1943 .... **TCLC 23**
See also CA 117

Weinstein, Nathan
See West, Nathanael

Weinstein, Nathan von Wallenstein
See West, Nathanael

Weir, Peter (Lindsay) 1944- .... **CLC 20**
See also CA 113; 123

Weiss, Peter (Ulrich)
1916-1982 .... **CLC 3, 15, 51**
See also CA 45-48; 106; CANR 3; DLB 69,
124

Weiss, Theodore (Russell)
  1916- .... CLC 3, 8, 14
  See also CA 9-12R; CAAS 2; DLB 5

Welch, (Maurice) Denton
  1915-1948 .... TCLC 22
  See also CA 121

Welch, James 1940- .... CLC 6, 14, 52
  See also CA 85-88

Weldon, Fay
  1933(?)- ...... CLC 6, 9, 11, 19, 36, 59
  See also CA 21-24R; CANR 16;
  CDBLB 1960 to Present; DLB 14;
  MTCW

Wellek, Rene 1903- .... CLC 28
  See also CA 5-8R; CAAS 7; CANR 8;
  DLB 63

Weller, Michael 1942- .... CLC 10, 53
  See also CA 85-88

Weller, Paul 1958- .... CLC 26

Wellershoff, Dieter 1925- .... CLC 46
  See also CA 89-92; CANR 16, 37

Welles, (George) Orson
  1915-1985 .... CLC 20
  See also CA 93-96; 117

Wellman, Mac 1945- .... CLC 65

Wellman, Manly Wade 1903-1986 .. CLC 49
  See also CA 1-4R; 118; CANR 6, 16;
  SATA 6, 47

Wells, Carolyn 1869(?)-1942 ...... TCLC 35
  See also CA 113; DLB 11

Wells, H(erbert) G(eorge)
  1866-1946 ...... TCLC 6, 12, 19; SSC 6
  See also CA 110; 121; CDBLB 1914-1945;
  DA; DLB 34, 70; MTCW; SATA 20;
  WLC

Wells, Rosemary 1943-............ CLC 12
  See also CA 85-88; CLR 16; MAICYA;
  SAAS 1; SATA 18, 69

Welty, Eudora
  1909- .... CLC 1, 2, 5, 14, 22, 33; SSC 1
  See also CA 9-12R; CABS 1; CANR 32;
  CDALB 1941-1968; DA; DLB 2, 102;
  DLBY 87; MTCW; WLC

Wen I-to 1899-1946 .... TCLC 28

Wentworth, Robert
  See Hamilton, Edmond

Werfel, Franz (V.) 1890-1945 ...... TCLC 8
  See also CA 104; DLB 81, 124

Wergeland, Henrik Arnold
  1808-1845 .... NCLC 5

Wersba, Barbara 1932-............ CLC 30
  See also AAYA 2; CA 29-32R; CANR 16,
  38; CLR 3; DLB 52; MAICYA; SAAS 2;
  SATA 1, 58

Wertmueller, Lina 1928- .... CLC 16
  See also CA 97-100; CANR 39

Wescott, Glenway 1901-1987....... CLC 13
  See also CA 13-16R; 121; CANR 23;
  DLB 4, 9, 102

Wesker, Arnold 1932- .... CLC 3, 5, 42
  See also CA 1-4R; CAAS 7; CANR 1, 33;
  CDBLB 1960 to Present; DLB 13;
  MTCW

Wesley, Richard (Errol) 1945-....... CLC 7
  See also BW; CA 57-60; CANR 27; DLB 38

Wessel, Johan Herman 1742-1785 .... LC 7

West, Anthony (Panther)
  1914-1987 .... CLC 50
  See also CA 45-48; 124; CANR 3, 19;
  DLB 15

West, C. P.
  See Wodehouse, P(elham) G(renville)

West, (Mary) Jessamyn
  1902-1984 .... CLC 7, 17
  See also CA 9-12R; 112; CANR 27; DLB 6;
  DLBY 84; MTCW; SATA 37

West, Morris L(anglo) 1916-..... CLC 6, 33
  See also CA 5-8R; CANR 24; MTCW

West, Nathanael
  1903-1940 .... TCLC 1, 14, 44
  See also CA 104; 125; CDALB 1929-1941;
  DLB 4, 9, 28; MTCW

West, Owen
  See Koontz, Dean R(ay)

West, Paul 1930- .... CLC 7, 14
  See also CA 13-16R; CAAS 7; CANR 22;
  DLB 14

West, Rebecca 1892-1983 .. CLC 7, 9, 31, 50
  See also CA 5-8R; 109; CANR 19; DLB 36;
  DLBY 83; MTCW

Westall, Robert (Atkinson) 1929-.... CLC 17
  See also CA 69-72; CANR 18; CLR 13;
  MAICYA; SAAS 2; SATA 23, 69

Westlake, Donald E(dwin)
  1933- .... CLC 7, 33
  See also CA 17-20R; CAAS 13; CANR 16

Westmacott, Mary
  See Christie, Agatha (Mary Clarissa)

Weston, Allen
  See Norton, Andre

Wetcheek, J. L.
  See Feuchtwanger, Lion

Wetering, Janwillem van de
  See van de Wetering, Janwillem

Wetherell, Elizabeth
  See Warner, Susan (Bogert)

Whalen, Philip 1923- .... CLC 6, 29
  See also CA 9-12R; CANR 5, 39; DLB 16

Wharton, Edith (Newbold Jones)
  1862-1937 .... TCLC 3, 9, 27; SSC 6
  See also CA 104; 132; CDALB 1865-1917;
  DA; DLB 4, 9, 12, 78; MTCW; WLC

Wharton, James
  See Mencken, H(enry) L(ouis)

Wharton, William (a pseudonym)
  .... CLC 18, 37
  See also CA 93-96; DLBY 80

Wheatley (Peters), Phillis
  1754(?)-1784 .... LC 3; PC 3
  See also BLC 3; CDALB 1640-1865; DA;
  DLB 31, 50; WLC

Wheelock, John Hall 1886-1978.... CLC 14
  See also CA 13-16R; 77-80; CANR 14;
  DLB 45

White, E(lwyn) B(rooks)
  1899-1985 .... CLC 10, 34, 39
  See also AITN 2; CA 13-16R; 116;
  CANR 16, 37; CLR 1, 21; DLB 11, 22;
  MAICYA; MTCW; SATA 2, 29, 44

White, Edmund (Valentine III)
  1940- .... CLC 27
  See also AAYA 7; CA 45-48; CANR 3, 19,
  36; MTCW

White, Patrick (Victor Martindale)
  1912-1990 .. CLC 3, 4, 5, 7, 9, 18, 65, 69
  See also CA 81-84; 132; MTCW

White, Phyllis Dorothy James 1920-
  See James, P. D.
  See also CA 21-24R; CANR 17; MTCW

White, T(erence) H(anbury)
  1906-1964 .... CLC 30
  See also CA 73-76; CANR 37; MAICYA;
  SATA 12

White, Terence de Vere 1912-...... CLC 49
  See also CA 49-52; CANR 3

White, Walter F(rancis)
  1893-1955 .... TCLC 15
  See also White, Walter
  See also CA 115; 124; DLB 51

White, William Hale 1831-1913
  See Rutherford, Mark
  See also CA 121

Whitehead, E(dward) A(nthony)
  1933- .... CLC 5
  See also CA 65-68

Whitemore, Hugh (John) 1936-..... CLC 37
  See also CA 132

Whitman, Sarah Helen (Power)
  1803-1878 .... NCLC 19
  See also DLB 1

Whitman, Walt(er)
  1819-1892 .... NCLC 4, 31; PC 3
  See also CDALB 1640-1865; DA; DLB 3,
  64; SATA 20; WLC

Whitney, Phyllis A(yame) 1903-.... CLC 42
  See also AITN 2; BEST 90:3; CA 1-4R;
  CANR 3, 25, 38; MAICYA; SATA 1, 30

Whittemore, (Edward) Reed (Jr.)
  1919- .... CLC 4
  See also CA 9-12R; CAAS 8; CANR 4;
  DLB 5

Whittier, John Greenleaf
  1807-1892 .... NCLC 8
  See also CDALB 1640-1865; DLB 1

Whittlebot, Hernia
  See Coward, Noel (Peirce)

Wicker, Thomas Grey 1926-
  See Wicker, Tom
  See also CA 65-68; CANR 21

Wicker, Tom .... CLC 7
  See also Wicker, Thomas Grey

Wideman, John Edgar
  1941- .... CLC 5, 34, 36, 67
  See also BLC 3; BW; CA 85-88; CANR 14;
  DLB 33

Wiebe, Rudy (H.) 1934-...... CLC 6, 11, 14
  See also CA 37-40R; DLB 60

Wieland, Christoph Martin
  1733-1813 .... NCLC 17
  See also DLB 97

Wieners, John 1934-.............. CLC 7
  See also CA 13-16R; DLB 16

Wiesel, Elie(zer) 1928-..... **CLC 3, 5, 11, 37**
See also AAYA 7; AITN 1; CA 5-8R;
CAAS 4; CANR 8, 40; DA; DLB 83;
DLBY 87; MTCW; SATA 56

Wiggins, Marianne 1947-......... **CLC 57**
See also BEST 89:3; CA 130

Wight, James Alfred 1916-
See Herriot, James
See also CA 77-80; SATA 44, 55

Wilbur, Richard (Purdy)
1921-............ **CLC 3, 6, 9, 14, 53**
See also CA 1-4R; CABS 2; CANR 2, 29;
DA; DLB 5; MTCW; SATA 9

Wild, Peter 1940-................ **CLC 14**
See also CA 37-40R; DLB 5

Wilde, Oscar (Fingal O'Flahertie Wills)
1854(?)-1900 .... **TCLC 1, 8, 23, 41;
SSC 11**
See also CA 104; 119; CDBLB 1890-1914;
DA; DLB 10, 19, 34, 57; SATA 24; WLC

Wilder, Billy .... **CLC 20**
See also Wilder, Samuel
See also DLB 26

Wilder, Samuel 1906-
See Wilder, Billy
See also CA 89-92

Wilder, Thornton (Niven)
1897-1975 ...... **CLC 1, 5, 6, 10, 15, 35;
DC 1**
See also AITN 2; CA 13-16R; 61-64;
CANR 40; DA; DLB 4, 7, 9; MTCW;
WLC

Wilding, Michael 1942-........... **CLC 73**
See also CA 104; CANR 24

Wiley, Richard 1944-............. **CLC 44**
See also CA 121; 129

Wilhelm, Kate .... **CLC 7**
See also Wilhelm, Katie Gertrude
See also CAAS 5; DLB 8

Wilhelm, Katie Gertrude 1928-
See Wilhelm, Kate
See also CA 37-40R; CANR 17, 36; MTCW

Wilkins, Mary
See Freeman, Mary Eleanor Wilkins

Willard, Nancy 1936-........... **CLC 7, 37**
See also CA 89-92; CANR 10, 39; CLR 5;
DLB 5, 52; MAICYA; MTCW;
SATA 30, 37, 71

Williams, C(harles) K(enneth)
1936-................... **CLC 33, 56**
See also CA 37-40R; DLB 5

Williams, Charles
See Collier, James L(incoln)

Williams, Charles (Walter Stansby)
1886-1945 .... **TCLC 1, 11**
See also CA 104; DLB 100

Williams, (George) Emlyn
1905-1987 .... **CLC 15**
See also CA 104; 123; CANR 36; DLB 10,
77; MTCW

Williams, Hugo 1942-............. **CLC 42**
See also CA 17-20R; DLB 40

Williams, J. Walker
See Wodehouse, P(elham) G(renville)

Williams, John A(lfred) 1925-.... **CLC 5, 13**
See also BLC 3; BW; CA 53-56; CAAS 3;
CANR 6, 26; DLB 2, 33

Williams, Jonathan (Chamberlain)
1929-......................... **CLC 13**
See also CA 9-12R; CAAS 12; CANR 8;
DLB 5

Williams, Joy 1944-.............. **CLC 31**
See also CA 41-44R; CANR 22

Williams, Norman 1952-.......... **CLC 39**
See also CA 118

Williams, Tennessee
1911-1983 ..... **CLC 1, 2, 5, 7, 8, 11, 15,
19, 30, 39, 45, 71**
See also AITN 1, 2; CA 5-8R; 108;
CABS 3; CANR 31; CDALB 1941-1968;
DA; DLB 7; DLBD 4; DLBY 83;
MTCW; WLC

Williams, Thomas (Alonzo)
1926-1990 .... **CLC 14**
See also CA 1-4R; 132; CANR 2

Williams, William C.
See Williams, William Carlos

Williams, William Carlos
1883-1963 .... **CLC 1, 2, 5, 9, 13, 22, 42,
67; PC 7**
See also CA 89-92; CANR 34;
CDALB 1917-1929; DA; DLB 4, 16, 54,
86; MTCW

Williamson, David (Keith) 1942-.... **CLC 56**
See also CA 103; CANR 41

Williamson, Jack .... **CLC 29**
See also Williamson, John Stewart
See also CAAS 8; DLB 8

Williamson, John Stewart 1908-
See Williamson, Jack
See also CA 17-20R; CANR 23

Willie, Frederick
See Lovecraft, H(oward) P(hillips)

Willingham, Calder (Baynard, Jr.)
1922-....................... **CLC 5, 51**
See also CA 5-8R; CANR 3; DLB 2, 44;
MTCW

Willis, Charles
See Clarke, Arthur C(harles)

Willy
See Colette, (Sidonie-Gabrielle)

Willy, Colette
See Colette, (Sidonie-Gabrielle)

Wilson, A(ndrew) N(orman) 1950-.. **CLC 33**
See also CA 112; 122; DLB 14

Wilson, Angus (Frank Johnstone)
1913-1991 .... **CLC 2, 3, 5, 25, 34**
See also CA 5-8R; 134; CANR 21; DLB 15;
MTCW

Wilson, August
1945-........... **CLC 39, 50, 63; DC 2**
See also BLC 3; BW; CA 115; 122; DA;
MTCW

Wilson, Brian 1942-.............. **CLC 12**

Wilson, Colin 1931-............. **CLC 3, 14**
See also CA 1-4R; CAAS 5; CANR 1, 22,
33; DLB 14; MTCW

Wilson, Dirk
See Pohl, Frederik

Wilson, Edmund
1895-1972 .... **CLC 1, 2, 3, 8, 24**
See also CA 1-4R; 37-40R; CANR 1;
DLB 63; MTCW

Wilson, Ethel Davis (Bryant)
1888(?)-1980 .... **CLC 13**
See also CA 102; DLB 68; MTCW

Wilson, John 1785-1854.......... **NCLC 5**

Wilson, John (Anthony) Burgess
1917-................... **CLC 8, 10, 13**
See also Burgess, Anthony
See also CA 1-4R; CANR 2; MTCW

Wilson, Lanford 1937-....... **CLC 7, 14, 36**
See also CA 17-20R; CABS 3; DLB 7

Wilson, Robert M. 1944-......... **CLC 7, 9**
See also CA 49-52; CANR 2, 41; MTCW

Wilson, Robert McLiam 1964-..... **CLC 59**
See also CA 132

Wilson, Sloan 1920-.............. **CLC 32**
See also CA 1-4R; CANR 1

Wilson, Snoo 1948-.............. **CLC 33**
See also CA 69-72

Wilson, William S(mith) 1932-..... **CLC 49**
See also CA 81-84

Winchilsea, Anne (Kingsmill) Finch Counte
1661-1720 .... **LC 3**

Windham, Basil
See Wodehouse, P(elham) G(renville)

Wingrove, David (John) 1954-...... **CLC 68**
See also CA 133

Winters, Janet Lewis .... **CLC 41**
See also Lewis, Janet
See also DLBY 87

Winters, (Arthur) Yvor
1900-1968 .... **CLC 4, 8, 32**
See also CA 11-12; 25-28R; CAP 1;
DLB 48; MTCW

Winterson, Jeanette 1959-......... **CLC 64**
See also CA 136

Wiseman, Frederick 1930-........ **CLC 20**

Wister, Owen 1860-1938 .... **TCLC 21**
See also CA 108; DLB 9, 78; SATA 62

Witkacy
See Witkiewicz, Stanislaw Ignacy

Witkiewicz, Stanislaw Ignacy
1885-1939 .... **TCLC 8**
See also CA 105

Wittig, Monique 1935(?)-.......... **CLC 22**
See also CA 116; 135; DLB 83

Wittlin, Jozef 1896-1976 .... **CLC 25**
See also CA 49-52; 65-68; CANR 3

Wodehouse, P(elham) G(renville)
1881-1975 ... **CLC 1, 2, 5, 10, 22; SSC 2**
See also AITN 2; CA 45-48; 57-60;
CANR 3, 33; CDBLB 1914-1945;
DLB 34; MTCW; SATA 22

Woiwode, L.
See Woiwode, Larry (Alfred)

Woiwode, Larry (Alfred) 1941-... **CLC 6, 10**
See also CA 73-76; CANR 16; DLB 6

Wojciechowska, Maia (Teresa)
1927-....................... **CLC 26**
See also AAYA 8; CA 9-12R; CANR 4, 41;
CLR 1; MAICYA; SAAS 1; SATA 1, 28

Wolf, Christa 1929- .... CLC **14, 29, 58**
See also CA 85-88; DLB 75; MTCW

Wolfe, Gene (Rodman) 1931-....... CLC **25**
See also CA 57-60; CAAS 9; CANR 6, 32;
DLB 8

Wolfe, George C. 1954- .... CLC **49**

Wolfe, Thomas (Clayton)
1900-1938 .... TCLC **4, 13, 29**
See also CA 104; 132; CDALB 1929-1941;
DA; DLB 9, 102; DLBD 2; DLBY 85;
MTCW; WLC

Wolfe, Thomas Kennerly, Jr. 1930-
See Wolfe, Tom
See also CA 13-16R; CANR 9, 33; MTCW

Wolfe, Tom .... CLC **1, 2, 9, 15, 35, 51**
See also Wolfe, Thomas Kennerly, Jr.
See also AAYA 8; AITN 2; BEST 89:1

Wolff, Geoffrey (Ansell) 1937- ..... CLC **41**
See also CA 29-32R; CANR 29

Wolff, Sonia
See Levitin, Sonia (Wolff)

Wolff, Tobias (Jonathan Ansell)
1945- .... CLC **39, 64**
See also BEST 90:2; CA 114; 117; DLB 130

Wolfram von Eschenbach
c. 1170-c. 1220 .... CMLC **5**

Wolitzer, Hilma 1930-........... CLC **17**
See also CA 65-68; CANR 18, 40; SATA 31

Wollstonecraft, Mary 1759-1797..... LC **5**
See also CDBLB 1789-1832; DLB 39, 104

Wonder, Stevie .... CLC **12**
See also Morris, Steveland Judkins

Wong, Jade Snow 1922-.......... CLC **17**
See also CA 109

Woodcott, Keith
See Brunner, John (Kilian Houston)

Woodruff, Robert W.
See Mencken, H(enry) L(ouis)

Woolf, (Adeline) Virginia
1882-1941 .... TCLC **1, 5, 20, 43; SSC 7**
See also CA 104; 130; CDBLB 1914-1945;
DA; DLB 36, 100; DLBD 10; MTCW;
WLC

Woollcott, Alexander (Humphreys)
1887-1943 .... TCLC **5**
See also CA 105; DLB 29

Woolrich, Cornell 1903-1968....... CLC **77**
See also Hopley-Woolrich, Cornell George

Wordsworth, Dorothy
1771-1855 .... NCLC **25**
See also DLB 107

Wordsworth, William
1770-1850 .... NCLC **12, 38; PC 4**
See also CDBLB 1789-1832; DA; DLB 93,
107; WLC

Wouk, Herman 1915-......... CLC **1, 9, 38**
See also CA 5-8R; CANR 6, 33; DLBY 82;
MTCW

Wright, Charles (Penzel, Jr.)
1935- .... CLC **6, 13, 28**
See also CA 29-32R; CAAS 7; CANR 23,
36; DLBY 82; MTCW

Wright, Charles Stevenson 1932- ... CLC **49**
See also BLC 3; BW; CA 9-12R; CANR 26;
DLB 33

Wright, Jack R.
See Harris, Mark

Wright, James (Arlington)
1927-1980 .... CLC **3, 5, 10, 28**
See also AITN 2; CA 49-52; 97-100;
CANR 4, 34; DLB 5; MTCW

Wright, Judith (Arandell)
1915- .... CLC **11, 53**
See also CA 13-16R; CANR 31; MTCW;
SATA 14

Wright, L(aurali) R. 1939-......... CLC **44**
See also CA 138

Wright, Richard (Nathaniel)
1908-1960 .... CLC **1, 3, 4, 9, 14, 21, 48,
74; SSC 2**
See also AAYA 5; BLC 3; BW; CA 108;
CDALB 1929-1941; DA; DLB 76, 102;
DLBD 2; MTCW; WLC

Wright, Richard B(ruce) 1937- ...... CLC **6**
See also CA 85-88; DLB 53

Wright, Rick 1945-............... CLC **35**
See also Pink Floyd

Wright, Rowland
See Wells, Carolyn

Wright, Stephen 1946-............ CLC **33**

Wright, Willard Huntington 1888-1939
See Van Dine, S. S.
See also CA 115

Wright, William 1930-............ CLC **44**
See also CA 53-56; CANR 7, 23

Wu Ch'eng-en 1500(?)-1582(?)........ LC **7**

Wu Ching-tzu 1701-1754 .... LC **2**

Wurlitzer, Rudolph 1938(?)- ... CLC **2, 4, 15**
See also CA 85-88

Wycherley, William 1641-1715 .... LC **8, 21**
See also CDBLB 1660-1789; DLB 80

Wylie, Elinor (Morton Hoyt)
1885-1928 .... TCLC **8**
See also CA 105; DLB 9, 45

Wylie, Philip (Gordon) 1902-1971... CLC **43**
See also CA 21-22; 33-36R; CAP 2; DLB 9

Wyndham, John
See Harris, John (Wyndham Parkes Lucas)
Beynon

Wyss, Johann David Von
1743-1818 .... NCLC **10**
See also MAICYA; SATA 27, 29

Yakumo Koizumi
See Hearn, (Patricio) Lafcadio (Tessima
Carlos)

Yanez, Jose Donoso
See Donoso (Yanez), Jose

Yanovsky, Basile S.
See Yanovsky, V(assily) S(emenovich)

Yanovsky, V(assily) S(emenovich)
1906-1989 .... CLC **2, 18**
See also CA 97-100; 129

Yates, Richard 1926-1992 ..... CLC **7, 8, 23**
See also CA 5-8R; 139; CANR 10; DLB 2;
DLBY 81, 92

Yeats, W. B.
See Yeats, William Butler

Yeats, William Butler
1865-1939 .... TCLC **1, 11, 18, 31**
See also CA 104; 127; CDBLB 1890-1914;
DA; DLB 10, 19, 98; MTCW; WLC

Yehoshua, Abraham B. 1936- ... CLC **13, 31**
See also CA 33-36R

Yep, Laurence Michael 1948-...... CLC **35**
See also AAYA 5; CA 49-52; CANR 1;
CLR 3, 17; DLB 52; MAICYA; SATA 7,
69

Yerby, Frank G(arvin)
1916-1991 .... CLC **1, 7, 22**
See also BLC 3; BW; CA 9-12R; 136;
CANR 16; DLB 76; MTCW

Yesenin, Sergei Alexandrovich
See Esenin, Sergei (Alexandrovich)

Yevtushenko, Yevgeny (Alexandrovich)
1933- .... CLC **1, 3, 13, 26, 51**
See also CA 81-84; CANR 33; MTCW

Yezierska, Anzia 1885(?)-1970 ..... CLC **46**
See also CA 126; 89-92; DLB 28; MTCW

Yglesias, Helen 1915-........... CLC **7, 22**
See also CA 37-40R; CANR 15; MTCW

Yokomitsu Riichi 1898-1947 ...... TCLC **47**

Yonge, Charlotte (Mary)
1823-1901 .... TCLC **48**
See also CA 109; DLB 18; SATA 17

York, Jeremy
See Creasey, John

York, Simon
See Heinlein, Robert A(nson)

Yorke, Henry Vincent 1905-1974 ... CLC **13**
See also Green, Henry
See also CA 85-88; 49-52

Young, Al(bert James) 1939-....... CLC **19**
See also BLC 3; BW; CA 29-32R;
CANR 26; DLB 33

Young, Andrew (John) 1885-1971.... CLC **5**
See also CA 5-8R; CANR 7, 29

Young, Collier
See Bloch, Robert (Albert)

Young, Edward 1683-1765........... LC **3**
See also DLB 95

Young, Neil 1945-................ CLC **17**
See also CA 110

Yourcenar, Marguerite
1903-1987 .... CLC **19, 38, 50**
See also CA 69-72; CANR 23; DLB 72;
DLBY 88; MTCW

Yurick, Sol 1925-................ CLC **6**
See also CA 13-16R; CANR 25

Zamiatin, Yevgenii
See Zamyatin, Evgeny Ivanovich

Zamyatin, Evgeny Ivanovich
1884-1937 .... TCLC **8, 37**
See also CA 105

Zangwill, Israel 1864-1926........ TCLC **16**
See also CA 109; DLB 10

Zappa, Francis Vincent, Jr. 1940-
See Zappa, Frank
See also CA 108

Zappa, Frank.................... CLC **17**
See also Zappa, Francis Vincent, Jr.

Zaturenska, Marya   1902-1982.... **CLC 6, 11**
See also CA 13-16R; 105; CANR 22

Zelazny, Roger (Joseph)   1937- ..... **CLC 21**
See also AAYA 7; CA 21-24R; CANR 26;
DLB 8; MTCW; SATA 39, 57

Zhdanov, Andrei A(lexandrovich)
1896-1948 .... **TCLC 18**
See also CA 117

Zhukovsky, Vasily   1783-1852 .... **NCLC 35**

Ziegenhagen, Eric .... **CLC 55**

Zimmer, Jill Schary
See Robinson, Jill

Zimmerman, Robert
See Dylan, Bob

Zindel, Paul   1936- .... **CLC 6, 26**
See also AAYA 2; CA 73-76; CANR 31;
CLR 3; DA; DLB 7, 52; MAICYA;
MTCW; SATA 16, 58

Zinov'Ev, A. A.
See Zinoviev, Alexander (Aleksandrovich)

Zinoviev, Alexander (Aleksandrovich)
1922- .... **CLC 19**
See also CA 116; 133; CAAS 10

Zoilus
See Lovecraft, H(oward) P(hillips)

Zola, Emile (Edouard Charles Antoine)
1840-1902 .... **TCLC 1, 6, 21, 41**
See also CA 104; 138; DA; DLB 123; WLC

Zoline, Pamela   1941- .... **CLC 62**

Zorrilla y Moral, Jose   1817-1893 .. **NCLC 6**

Zoshchenko, Mikhail (Mikhailovich)
1895-1958 .... **TCLC 15**
See also CA 115

Zuckmayer, Carl   1896-1977....... **CLC 18**
See also CA 69-72; DLB 56, 124

Zuk, Georges
See Skelton, Robin

Zukofsky, Louis
1904-1978 .... **CLC 1, 2, 4, 7, 11, 18**
See also CA 9-12R; 77-80; CANR 39;
DLB 5; MTCW

Zweig, Paul   1935-1984........ **CLC 34, 42**
See also CA 85-88; 113

Zweig, Stefan   1881-1942 .... **TCLC 17**
See also CA 112; DLB 81, 118

CLC Cumulative Nationality Index

ALBANIAN
Kadare, Ismail **52**

ALGERIAN
Camus, Albert **1, 2, 4, 9, 11, 14, 32, 63, 69**
Cohen-Solal, Annie **50**

AMERICAN
Abbey, Edward **36, 59**
Abbott, Lee K., Jr. **48**
Abish, Walter **22**
Abrahams, Peter **4**
Abrams, M. H. **24**
Acker, Kathy **45**
Adams, Alice **6, 13, 46**
Addams, Charles **30**
Adler, C. S. **35**
Adler, Renata **8, 31**
Ai **4, 14, 69**
Aiken, Conrad **1, 3, 5, 10, 52**
Albee, Edward **1, 2, 3, 5, 9, 11, 13, 25, 53**
Alexander, Lloyd **35**
Algren, Nelson **4, 10, 33**
Allard, Janet **59**
Allen, Edward **59**
Allen, Woody **16, 52**
Alleyne, Carla D. **65**
Allison, Dorothy **78**
Alta **19**
Alter, Robert B. **34**
Alther, Lisa **7, 41**
Altman, Robert **16**
Ammons, A. R. **2, 3, 5, 8, 9, 25, 57**
Anaya, Rudolfo A. **23**
Anderson, Jon **9**
Anderson, Poul **15**
Anderson, Robert **23**
Angell, Roger **26**
Angelou, Maya **12, 35, 64, 77**

Anthony, Piers **35**
Apple, Max **9, 33**
Appleman, Philip **51**
Archer, Jules **12**
Arendt, Hannah **66**
Arnow, Harriette **2, 7, 18**
Arrick, Fran **30**
Ashbery, John **2, 3, 4, 6, 9, 13, 15, 25, 41, 77**
Asimov, Isaac **1, 3, 9, 19, 26, 76**
Auchincloss, Louis **4, 6, 9, 18, 45**
Auden, W. H. **1, 2, 3, 4, 6, 9, 11, 14, 43**
Auel, Jean M. **31**
Auster, Paul **47**
Bach, Richard **14**
Baker, Elliott **8**
Baker, Nicholson **61**
Baker, Russell **31**
Bakshi, Ralph **26**
Baldwin, James **1, 2, 3, 4, 5, 8, 13, 15, 17, 42, 50, 67**
Bambara, Toni Cade **19**
Bandanes, Jerome **59**
Banks, Russell **37, 72**
Baraka, Imamu Amiri **1, 2, 3, 5, 10, 14, 33**
Barbera, Jack **44**
Barnard, Mary **48**
Barnes, Djuna **3, 4, 8, 11, 29**
Barrett, William **27**
Barth, John **1, 2, 3, 5, 7, 9, 10, 14, 27, 51**
Barthelme, Donald **1, 2, 3, 5, 6, 8, 13, 23, 46, 59**
Barthelme, Frederick **36**
Barzun, Jacques **51**
Baumbach, Jonathan **6, 23**
Bausch, Richard **51**
Baxter, Charles **45, 78**
Beagle, Peter S. **7**
Beattie, Ann **8, 13, 18, 40, 63**

Becker, Walter **26**
Beecher, John **6**
Begiebing, Robert J. **70**
Behrman, S. N. **40**
Belitt, Ben **22**
Bell, Madison Smartt **41**
Bell, Marvin **8, 31**
Bellow, Saul **1, 2, 3, 6, 8, 10, 13, 15, 25, 33, 34, 63**
Benary-Isbert, Margot **12**
Benchley, Peter **4, 8**
Benedikt, Michael **4, 14**
Benford, Gregory **52**
Bennett, Hal **5**
Bennett, Jay **35**
Benson, Jackson J. **34**
Benson, Sally **17**
Bentley, Eric **24**
Berger, Melvin **12**
Berger, Thomas **3, 5, 8, 11, 18, 38**
Bergstein, Eleanor **4**
Bernard, April **59**
Berriault, Gina **54**
Berrigan, Daniel J. **4**
Berrigan, Ted **37**
Berry, Chuck **17**
Berry, Wendell **4, 6, 8, 27, 46**
Berryman, John **1, 2, 3, 4, 6, 8, 10, 13, 25, 62**
Bessie, Alvah **23**
Betts, Doris **3, 6, 28**
Bidart, Frank **33**
Birch, Allison **65**
Bishop, Elizabeth **1, 4, 9, 13, 15, 32**
Bishop, John **10**
Blackburn, Paul **9, 43**
Blackmur, R. P. **2, 24**
Blaise, Clark **29**
Blatty, William Peter **2**

Nationality Index

Nationality Index

CLC-78 Title Index